Dictionary of Classical Antiquities

Dictionary of

CLASSICAL
ANTIQUITIES

Mythology   Religion   Literature   Art

by OSKAR SEYFFERT

Revised and edited by
Henry Nettleship and J. E. Sandys

GLOUCESTER, MASS.

PETER SMITH

1978

A MERIDIAN BOOK
Published by The World Publishing Company
2231 West 110 Street, Cleveland 2, Ohio
First Meridian printing September 1956
Library of Congress Catalog Card Number: 56-10154
Printed in the United States of America   10MWP263
Reprinted, 1978, by
Peter Smith Publisher, Inc.

ISBN 0-8446-2910-3

PREFACE.

THE *Dictionary of Classical Antiquities*, which is here offered to the public, is founded on a work by Dr. Oskar Seyfferi, of Berlin, which has deservedly attained a wide circulation in Germany.[1] Dr. Seyffert is already known in England as one of the editors of a philological periodical, entitled the *Berliner Philologische Wochenschrift*, and as a distinguished Latin scholar, whose name is specially associated with the criticism of Plautus. The departments of classical learning included in his dictionary are the Mythology and Religion, the Literature and Art, and the constitutional and social Antiquities of Greece and Rome. Within the compass of a single volume it comprises all the subjects usually treated in a *Dictionary of Greek and Roman Antiquities*, while it also supplies information on matters of Mythology and Literature which has generally to be looked for in the pages of a *Classical Dictionary*. Besides separate articles on Greek and Roman divinities, and on the lives and works of the philosophers, the historians, the orators, the poets, and the artists of Greece and Rome, it gives a general and comprehensive view of such subjects as Greek and Roman Religion, Philosophy, History, Rhetoric, Literature, Architecture, Painting, Sculpture, Music, and the Drama. Similarly, in the department of Antiquities, besides separate treatment of subordinate details, it deals with important topics, such as the Boule and Ecclesia, the Comitia and the Senate, Commerce and War, the Houses, the Ships, the Temples, and the Theatres of the ancients.

The original text has been largely supplemented and corrected by Dr. Seyffert himself ; and the whole of the translation has been carefully revised and, in many cases, re-written or re-arranged by the editors. The larger part of the letter A (*Abacus* to *Astrology*) was translated by Mr. Stallybrass, owing to whose lamented death the remainder of the work was put into other hands. The succeeding articles, from *Astrology*

---

[1] *Lexikon der klassischen Alterthumskunde ; Kulturgeschichte der Griechen und Römer ; Mythologie und Religion, Litteratur, Kunst, und Alterthümer des Staats- und Privatlebens.* (Leipzig: Verlag des Bibliographischen Instituts, 1882.)

to *Herœa*, have been translated and prepared for the press by Professor Nettleship; the second part (*Hermœ* to *Zosimus*) has been translated under the supervision of Dr. Sandys; while the proof sheets of the whole have been repeatedly read by both editors. The additions inserted by the editors are generally distinguished by being placed within square brackets, or printed as notes at the foot of the page. Most of the notes and other additions bearing on Latin Literature, and a few bearing on Latin Antiquities, are due to Professor Nettleship; while Dr. Sandys has supplied references to classical authors and modern authorities wherever such references appeared either necessary or desirable. It is hoped that these additions may serve to increase the usefulness of the book. The references to Cicero and Pliny are by the shorter sections now in general use. The ancient authorities quoted include Aristotle's newly discovered *Constitution of Athens*, which has been cited under the head of the *Solonian Constitution* and other articles which have passed through the press since the publication of the *editio princeps*. In this and other respects every endeavour has been made to bring the articles up to date.

Dr. Sandys has written articles on the following archæological subjects, which were either omitted in the original work or appeared to deserve a fuller treatment than was there accorded them: *Mosaics*, *Pigments* (under *Painting*), *Cœlatura* (under *Toreutic Art*), and *Vases* (with 17 illustrations). He has also supplied brief notices of the Edict of *Diocletian*, the *Olympieum*, the artists *Mentor, Mys, Pauson*, and the younger *Polyclitus; Philo*, the architect, and three others of the same name who were not included in Dr. Seyffert's *Lexikon*. The short article on *Fulcra* is abridged from a valuable paper in the *Classical Review* by Mr. W. C. F. Anderson, Professor of Classics at Firth College, Sheffield; that on the Law of *Gortyn* has been kindly contributed by Mr. C. A. M. Pond, Fellow of St. John's College, Cambridge.

The number of the illustrations has been largely increased. These have been selected mainly from the following works: Schreiber's *Kultur-historischer Bilder-Atlas*, ed. 1888, and *Bilder-Atlas zur Ilias und Odyssee*, 1889, both published by Seemann of Leipzig; Baumeister's *Denkmäler des Klassischen Alterthums*, 1884–1888, by Oldenbourg of Munich; Guhl and Koner's *Life of the Greeks and Romans*, English edition (Chatto & Windus); and Perry's *Greek and Roman Sculpture* (Longmans, 1882). The publishers are also indebted to Messrs. George Bell & Sons for the additional illustrations in the article on *Gems*, and for the portraits of

Horace, Lucretius, Plato, and *Socrates,* selected from King's *Antique Gems and Rings* (1872) and Westropp's *Handbook of Archæology* (ed. 1878); to Messrs. Macmillan & Co. for Dr. Dörpfeld's *Plan of Olympia* and of the *Propylœa,* and for the engraving of a vase by Hieron (*Vases,* fig. 12). The two latter are from Miss Harrison's *Mythology and Monuments of Ancient Athens.* The Plan of the *Acropolis* is copied from the *Journal of Hellenic Studies* with the kind permission of the Council of the Hellenic Society. That of the Roman *Fora* is reproduced from Droysen's *Historischer Handatlas,* 1886. In the article on the *Olympian Games,* the metope on page 430 is a reduced copy from Overbeck's *Geschichte der Griechischen Plastik.* In that on *Vases,* figs. 3 and 5 are borrowed from the Catalogue of Pottery in the Jermyn Street Museum. The engraving of the Mænads (*Vases,* fig. 13) is reproduced by permission from Dr. Sandys' edition of the *Bacchæ* of Euripides published by the University· Press, Cambridge. All these additional illustrations (which are distinguished by an asterisk) have been selected by Dr. Sandys, who has indicated, so far as practicable, the original authority on which they rest, and, in the case of works of art, the collections in which they are to be found.

In stating the English equivalents for Greek money, the editors have adopted the estimate of Professor W. W. Goodwin, in his article *On the Value of the Attic Talent in Modern Money* published in the *Transactions of the American Philological Association,* 1885, xvi, pp. 117–119, according to which the intrinsic value of a drachma is approximately 8*d.,* and that of a talent £200. In the case of Roman money, they have followed Marquardt's *Handbuch der römischen Alterthümer* in reckoning 1,000 sesterces as equivalent to £10. [1]

For the convenience of students, as well as of general readers, the quantities of Greek and Latin words have been marked once, but once only, in every article in which they occur. The Latin spelling of Greek words has been generally adopted, but the Greek form has, in all cases where it appeared advisable, been added in brackets.

H. NETTLESHIP.
J. E. SANDYS.

March, 1891.

---

[1] See Preface to Third Edition of this Dictionary

PREFACE TO SECOND EDITION.

THE favourable reception that has been accorded to this work has enabled the publishers to issue a second edition at an exceptionally early date. The book has been revised by Dr. Sandys, and some minor inaccuracies have been removed. References to Aristotle's *Constitution of Athens*, which, in the former edition, could only be inserted in the last two hundred pages, have now been added in the first five hundred, wherever such addition seemed to be required. Lastly, an Index has been supplied, which, it is hoped, will make the work still further useful as a book of reference.

September, 1891.

PREFACE TO THIRD EDITION.

THE present edition has been further revised and corrected by Dr. Sandys. The articles in which the most considerable changes have been introduced are those on *Comitia*, *Music*, and *Theatre*. The article on *Comitia* has been revised in accordance with the views of Mommsen; that on *Music* takes account of Mr. Monro's recent work on the Modes of Ancient Music; and that on *Theatre* gives some additional details respecting the architectural theories of Dr. Dörpfeld.

In stating approximate English equivalents for Roman money, Dr. Sandys has thought it right to reconsider the choice made by the late Professor Nettleship between the alternative estimates given in Marquardt's *Handbuch*, vol. ii., p. 71. The sum of 1,000 sesterces is there reckoned as equivalent, under a gold standard, to 217·52 marks, or £10 17s. 6d.; and, under a silver standard, to 175·41 marks, or £8 15s. 6d. In the former editions the gold standard was adopted, and 1,000 sesterces taken as equivalent to £10; in the present, the silver standard has been preferred, and the equivalent is accordingly £8 15s. Under this estimate a Roman *denarius* is equivalent to 8½d., or very little more than a Greek *drachma*, which is here set at 8d.

It should be added that the Index here reprinted from the Second Edition is the work of the late Mr. H. D. Darbishire, Fellow of St. John's College, Cambridge.

December, 1894.

ABBREVIATIONS, ETC.

cp.	compare.	*ib.*	*ibidem.*
q.v.	*quod vide.*	⌣	indicates a short syllable.
l.c.	*locus* (or *liber*) *citatus.*	—	indicates a long syllable.

A

Abăcus (Gr. *ăbax, ăbăkĭŏn*). (1) A square plate, especially the stone slab that covers the capital of a column (*see* ARCHITECTURE, ORDERS OF, figs. 1 and 5). (2) A dice-board. (3) A mathematician's table strewn with fine sand, on which figures were drawn with a *stilus*. (4) A counting-board, on which sums were worked for private and public accounts. The reckoning was done with counters lying on the board (*calcŭlī*) or with beads sliding in vertical groovès. (On the sideboard called *Abacus, see* TABLES.)

Abolla. A thick woollen cloak, worn by Roman soldiers and philosophers.

Absyrtus. Son of king Æëtes, and brother of Medëa, who, in her flight with Jason the Argonaut, cut Absyrtus into pieces, and threw them one by one into the sea, so that her father, stopping to pick them up, might be delayed in his pursuit.

Academy (Gr. *Akădēmĭa*). A grove on the Cephissus near Athens, sacred to the hero Acădēmus, and containing a gymnasium. Here Plato, whose country-house was near, delivered his lectures; hence the school of philosophy founded by him received the name of "The Academy."

Acămās (Gr. *Akămas*). Son of Thēseus and Phædra, was brought up with his brother Demŏphoön by Elephēnor, king of Eubœa, and sent with Diomēdes as ambassador to Troy, to persuade Priam to send Helen back in peace. After the fall of Troy, in which he took a prominent part as one of the heroes concealed in the wooden horse, he with his brother recovered his father's sovereignty over Attica, and then led a colony from Athens to Cyprus, where he died. (*Comp.* DEMOPHOÖN, 2.)

Acarnān and **Amphŏtĕrus** (Gr. *Akarnan, Amphoterŏs*). Sons of Alcmæon and Callirrhŏë. Their mother, hearing of her husband's murder by Phēgeus and his sons, prays Zeus, who loves her, to let her boys grow up into men at once, so that they can avenge their father. This done, they slay the sons of Phegeus at Tĕgĕä and himself at Psŏphis, offer up at Delphi the Jewels of Harmŏnĭa, which they have thus acquired,

and then found a kingdom called after the elder of them Acarnānia. (*See* ALPHESIBŒA.)

Acastus (Gr. *Akastŏs*). Son of Pĕlĭas, king of Iōlcŏs, who joined the Argonautic expedition, though against his father's will, as a friend of Jason. At his father's death he celebrated funeral games which were the theme of ancient poets and artists, and in which Pēleus was represented as participating. He took part in the Calydonian boar-hunt. But his wife Astȳdămeia fell in love with Pēleus (*q.v.*), and this brought ruin on the wedded pair. His daughter was Lāŏdămeiă, renowned for her tender love to Prōtĕsĭlāŭs (*q.v.*).

Acca Lārentia. According to the common legend, wife of the herdsman Faustŭlus, and nurse to Rōmŭlus and Rĕmus; according to another, a favourite of Hercules, and wife to a rich Etruscan, Tarutius, whose possessions she bequeathed to Romulus or (according to another account) the Roman people. She is said to have had twelve sons, with whom she sacrificed once a year for the fertilizing of the Roman fields (*arva*), and who were thence named Arval Brothers (*fratres arvāles*). One of them having died, Romulus took his place, and founded the priesthood so called. (*See* ARVAL BROTHERS.) She at last disappeared on the spot where, afterwards, at the feast of Larentalia (Dec. 23), the flamen of Quirīnus and the pontiffs sacrificed to her while invoking Jupiter. All this, together with her name, meaning "mother of the Lares," shows that she was originally a goddess of the earth, to whose care men entrusted their seed-corn and their dead. (*See* LARES.) In particular she personified the city lands and their crops. Probably she is the Dea Dīa worshipped by the Arval Brothers.

Accensi. In the older constitution of the Roman army, the *accensi* were men taken from the lowest assessed class to fill gaps in the ranks of the heavy-armed soldiers. They followed the legion unarmed, simply in their clothes (*velātī*, or *accensi velāti*). In action they stood in the rear rank of the third line, ready to pick up the arms of the fallen and fill their places. They were also used as assistant workmen and as orderlies. This last employment may have caused the term *accensus* to be applied to the subordinate officer whom consuls and proconsuls, prætors and proprætors, and all officers of consular and prætorian rank had at their service in addition to lictors. In later times officers chose these attendants out of their own freedmen, sometimes to marshal their way when they had no lictors or had them marching behind, sometimes for miscellaneous duties. Thus the prætor's *accensus* had to cry the hours of the day, 3, 6, 9, and 12. Unlike the subordinate officers named appărĭtors, their term of office expired with that of their superior.

Accius, or **Attius** (*Lūcius*). A Roman poet, who was born 170 B.C. of a freedman and freedwoman, at Pisaurum in Umbria, and died about 90 B.C. He was the most prolific and, under the Republic, the most highly esteemed of tragic poets, especially for his lofty, impassioned style and powerful descriptions. His talents seem to have secured him a respectable position in Roman society, which he maintained with full consciousness of his merits. His poetical career can be traced through a period of thirty-six years, from B.C. 140, when he exhibited a drama under the same ædiles as the octogenarian Pacuvius, to B.C. 104. Of his tragedies, the titles and fragments of some fifty are preserved. Two of these treat of national subjects (*see* PRÆTEXTA), viz., the *Brutus* and the *Decius*. The former dealt with the expulsion of the Tarquins; the latter with the heroic death of Decius at Sentinum, B.C. 295. The rest, composed after Greek models, embrace almost all cycles of legend, especially the Trojan, which is treated in a great variety of aspects. Accius likewise handled questions of grammar, literary history, and antiquities in the Alexandrine manner and the fashion of his own time, and in many different metres. These works (the *Didascălĭca* in at least nine books; the *Pragmătĭca* on dramatic poetry and acting, etc.) have also perished.

Achæus. A Greek tragic poet of Eretria, born about 482 B.C., a contemporary of Sophocles, and especially famous in the line of satyric drama. He wrote about forty plays, of which only small fragments are preserved. Not being an Athenian, he only gained one victory.

Achĕlŏŭs. The god of the river of that name between Ætolia and Acarnania; eldest of the 3000 sons of Ocĕănus and Tēthys, and father of the Sirens by Stĕrŏpē, the daughter of Porthāōn. As a water-god he was capable of metamorphosis, appearing now as a bull, then as a snake, and again as a bull-faced man. In fighting with Hērăcles for the possession of Dēĭăneira, he lost one horn, but got it back in exchange for the horn of Amaltheia (*q.v.*). As the oldest and most venerable of river-gods, he was worshipped all over Greece and her colonies, especially Rhodes, Italy, and Sicily. The oracle of Dōdōna, in every answer which it gave, added an injunction to sacrifice to Achelous; and in religious usage his name stood for any stream or running water.

Achĕrōn. A river in the lower world. (*See* HADES, REALM OF.)

Achilles (Gr. *Achilleus*). (1) Son of Pēleus (king of the Myrmidons in Thessalian Phthia) by the Nereïd Thĕtis, grandson of Æacus, great-grandson of Zeus. In Homer he is duly brought up by his mother to man's estate, in close friendship with his older cousin Patroclus, the son of Menœtius, a half-brother of Æacus; is taught the arts of war and eloquence by Phœnix (*q.v.*) and that of healing by the centaur Chīrōn, his mother's grandfather. But later legends lend additional features to the story of his youth. To make her son immortal, Thetis anoints him with ambrosia by day, and holds him in the fire at night, to destroy whatever mortal element he has derived from his father, until Peleus, coming in one night, sees the boy baking in the fire, and makes an outcry; the goddess, aggrieved at seeing her plan thwarted, deserts husband and child, and goes home to the Nereïds. According to a later story she dipped the child in the river Styx, and thus made him invulnerable, all but the heel by which she held him. Then Peleus takes the motherless boy to Chiron on Mount Pēlĭŏn, who feeds him on the entrails of lions and boars, and the marrow of bears, and instructs him in all knightly and elegant arts. At the age of six the boy was so strong and swift that he slew wild boars and lions, and caught stags without net or hound. Again, as to his share in the expedition to Troy, the legends differ widely. In Homer, Achilles and Patroclus are at once ready to obey the call of Nestor and Odysseus, and their fathers willingly let them go, accompanied by the old man Phœnix. In later legend, Thetis, alarmed by the prophecy of Calchas that Troy cannot be taken without Achilles and foreseeing his fall in such a war, conducts the boy of nine to the island of Scýrŏs, where in female dress he grows up among the daughters of king Lýcŏmēdēs, and by one of them, Dēïdămeia, begets Neoptŏlĕmus (q.v.). But Calchas betrays his whereabouts, and Odysseus, in concert with Dĭŏmēdēs, unmasks the young hero. Disguised as a merchant, he spreads out female ornaments before the maidens, as well as a shield and spear; suddenly a trumpet sounds the call to battle, the maidens flee, but Achilles clutches at the arms, and declares himself eager to fight. At the first landing of the Greeks, on the Asian coast, he wounds Tēlĕphus (q.v.) ; at their second, on the Trojan shore, Cycnus (q.v.). Before Troy, Homer makes him the chief of Greek heroes, whom the favour of Hēra and Athēna and his own merit have placed above friend and foe. He is graced with all the attributes of a hero : in birth, beauty, swiftness, strength, and valour, he has not his peer; none can resist him, the very sight of him strikes terror into the foe. His anger may be furious, his grief immoderate ; but his nature is at bottom kind, affectionate, and generous, even to his enemies. Touching is his love for his parents, especially his mother, and his devotion to his friends. In the first nine years of the war he leads the Greeks on their many plundering excursions around Troy, and destroys eleven inland and twelve seacoast towns. The events of the tenth year, brought on by the deep grudge he bears Agamemnon for taking away Brisēïs (daughter of Brises), form the subject of Homer's Iliad. When he and his men withdraw from the fight, the Trojans press on irresistibly ; they have taken the camp of the Greeks, and are setting their ships on fire. In this extremity he lends Patroclus the arms his father (see PELEUS) had given him, and lets him lead the Myrmidons to battle. Patroclus drives the Trojans back, but falls by Hector's hand, and the arms are lost, though the corpse is recovered. Grief for his friend and thirst for vengeance at last overcome his grudge against Agamemnon. Furnished by Hephæstus, at the request of Thetis, with splendid new arms, including the shield of wondrous workmanship, he goes out against Hector, well knowing that he himself must fall soon after him. He makes frightful havoc among the enemy, till at last Hector is the only one that dares await him without the walls, and even he turns in terror at the sight of him. After

chasing him three times round the city, Achilles overtakes him, pierces him with his lance, trails his body behind his chariot to the camp, and there casts it for a prey to the birds and dogs. Then with the utmost pomp he lays the loved friend of his youth in the same grave-mound that is to hold his own ashes, and founds funeral games in his honour. The next night Priam comes secretly to his tent, and offers rich gifts to ransom Hector's body ; but Achilles, whom the broken-down old king reminds of his own father, gives it up without ransom, and grants eleven days' truce for the burying. After many valiant deeds (see TROJAN WAR), he is overtaken by the fate which he had himself chosen ; for the choice had been given him between an early death with undying fame and a long but inglorious life. Near the Scæan Gate he is struck by the shaft of Paris, guided by Apollo. According to a later legend he was wounded in the one vulnerable heel, and in the temple of Thymbræan Apollo, whither he had gone unarmed to be wedded to Priam's daughter Polyxĕna (q.v.). Greeks and Trojans fight furiously all day about his body, till Zeus sends down a storm to end the fight. Seventeen days and nights the Greeks, with Thetis and the sea-goddesses and Muses, bewail the dead ; then amid numerous sacrifices the body is burnt. Next morning the ashes, with those of Patroclus and of Nestor's son, Antĭlŏchus, whom Achilles had loved in the next degree, are placed in a golden pitcher, the work of Hephæstus, and gift of Dionȳsus, and deposited in the famed tumulus that crowns the promontory of Sigēum. The soul of Homer's Achilles dwells, like other souls, in the lower world, and is there seen by Odysseus together with the souls of his two friends. According to later poets Thetis snatched her son's body out of the burning pyre and carried it to the island of Leukē at the mouth of the Danube, where the transfigured hero lives on, sovereign of the Pontus and husband of Iphigeneia. Others place him in Elysium, with Mēdēa or Hĕlĕna to wife. Besides Leucē, where the mariners of Pontus and Greek colonists honoured him with offerings and games, he had many other places of worship ; the most venerable, however, was his tomb on the Hellespont, where he appeared to Homer in the full blaze of his armour, and struck the poet blind. In works of art Achilles was represented as similar to Ares, with magnificent physique, and hair bristling up like a mane. One of his most famous statues is that at Paris (from the Villa Borghese), though many take it for an Ares.

(2) *Tatïus*, a Greek mathematician of the 3rd century A.D. He wrote an introduction to the *Phænomena* of Arātus.

(3) *Achillēs of Alexandria*, about 450 A.D., probably a Christian; author of a Greek romance in eight books, the story of Cleitŏphōn of Tyre and Leucippē of Byzantium, two lovers who pass through a long train of adventures before they meet. As the whole story is put in the mouth of the hero, many scenes, being told at secondhand, lose in liveliness; and the flow of the narrative is checked by too many digressions, some interesting enough in themselves, by descriptions of places, natural

a son named Perseus. Then mother and child are put in a wooden box and thrown into the sea, but they drift to the island of Serīphus, and are kindly received. Perseus, having grown into a hero, sets out with his mother to seek Acrisius, who has fled from Argos for fear of the oracle coming true; he finds him at Larissa, in Thessaly, and kills him unawares with a discus.

Acro (*Hĕlĕnĭus*) A Roman grammarian of the end of the 2nd century A.D. He wrote commentaries (now lost) on Terence, Horace, and perhaps Persius. The collection of scholia bearing his name dates from the 7th century.

Acroliths. Statues whose uncovered extremities are made of stone, the covered

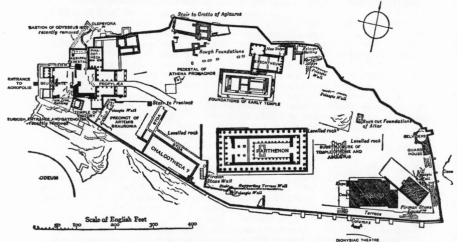

* PLAN OF THE ACROPOLIS IN 1889, INCLUDING RESULTS OF THE EXCAVATIONS BEGUN IN 1885.
(Reduced from plan by Messrs. Penrose and Schultz, *Journal of Hellenic Studies*, 1889, pl. viii.)

phenomena, works of art, feelings and passions, in which the author exhibits his vast reading. The style has considerable elegance, though often marred by an affectation of neatness and brevity. The novel continued to be popular until the fall of Byzantium.

Acontius (Gr. *Akontĭŏs*). See CYDIPPE.

Acrātisma (Gr. *Akrātisma*). See MEALS.

Acrisius (Gr. *Akrĭsĭŏs*). King of Argos, great-grandson of Dănäüs, son of Abas, and brother of Prœtus. An oracle having declared that a son of his daughter Dănäë would take his life, he shuts her up in a brazen tower; but Zeus falls into her lap in the shape of a shower of gold, and she bears

parts of another material, such as wood.

Acrŏpŏlis (Gr. *Akrŏpŏlĭs*). Properly = Upper Town. The Greek name for the citadel or stronghold of a town. The Acropolis of Athens was situated on a plateau of rock, about 200 feet in height, 1,000 in breadth from east to west, and 460 in length from north to south. It was originally called Cĕcrŏpĭa, after Cecrops, the ancestor of the Athenians, whose grave and shrine were shown on the spot. On the north side of the Acropolis was the Erechthĕum, the common seat of worship of the ancient gods of Athens, Athēnē Pŏlĭăs, Hephæstus, Poseidōn, and Erechtheus himself, who was said to have founded the sanctuary.

His house was possibly N.E. of the Erechtheum. Pisistrătus, like the ancient kings, had his residence on the Acropolis, and may have added the stylobate to the temple of Athene recently identified, S. of the Erechtheum. The walls of the fortress proper were destroyed in the Persian wars, 480 and 479 B.C., and restored by Cīmōn. But the wall surrounding the foot of the hill, called the Pĕlasgĭkŏn or Pĕlargĭkŏn, and supposed to be a relic of the oldest inhabitants, was left in ruins. Cimon also laid the foundation of a new temple of Athene on the south side of the hill. This temple was begun afresh and completed in the most splendid style by Pĕrĭclēs, and called the Parthĕnōn. (See PARTHENON.) Pericles at the same time adorned the approach to the west side of the Acropolis with the glorious Prŏpўlœa, and began to rebuild the Erechtheum in magnificent style. (See ERECHTHEUM, PROPYLÆA.) There were several other sanctuaries on the Acropolis, that, for instance, of Artĕmis Braurōnĭa, on the S.E. side of the Propylæa; the beautiful little temple of Athene Nīkē to the S.W.; and the Pandrŏsēum adjoining the temple of Erechtheus. There were many altars, that of Zeus Hypătŏs for example, and countless statues, among them that of Athene Prŏmăchŏs, with votive offerings. Among the numerous grottos in the rock, one on the north side was dedicated to Pan, another to Apollo.

Acta. The Latin term for official records of transactions, including Acta sĕnātŭs and Acta pŏpŭlī Rōmānī, both established by Cæsar in his first consulship, B.C. 59. (1) Acta senatus. Cæsar's law decreed that all transactions of the senate should be regularly written down and published, which had only been done hitherto in exceptional cases. The written reports were continued under the Empire, but Augustus put a stop to their publication. These documents were preserved among the state archives and in the public libraries, where they could only be inspected by permission of the city prefect. At first a temporary duty imposed on individual senators, the business of reporting grew into a separate office held in rotation, with the title of Ab actis senatus, and the officer holding it had a considerable staff of writers under him, called Actuārĭī. (2) The Acta (diurna) populi (Romani), or Acta publica, urbāna, urbis, diurna populi, or simply Acta or Diurna, were an official daily chronicle, which, in addition to official reports of

events in the imperial family, and state and city affairs, contained regulations by the magistrates, transactions and decrees of the senate, accidents, and family news communicated to the editors. They were publicly exhibited on a whitened board (album), which any one might read and copy; and there were men who made a business of multiplying and transmitting such news to the provinces. After a time the originals were placed among the state-archives for the benefit of those who wished to consult them.

Actæōn (Gr. Aktaiōn). Son of Aristæus by Autŏnŏē, the daughter of Cadmus of Thebes, was trained by Chīrōn into a finished huntsman. Having either seen Artĕmis (Diana) when bathing, or boasted his superiority in the chase, he was changed by her into a stag, and torn to pieces by his own hounds on Mount Cithæron. The hounds looked everywhere for their master, and would not be pacified till Chiron showed them an image of him. His statue was often set up on hills and rocks as a protection against the dangerous heat of the dog-days, of which probably the myth itself is but a symbol.

Actoridæ, Actoriones. See MOLIONES.

Actuārius. See ACTA.

Acusilāŭs. See LOGOGRAPHI.

Admētus. Son of Phĕres, king of Phĕræ in Thessaly, who took part in the Calydonian boar-hunt and the voyage of the Argo. Apollo served him for a time as a shepherd, either from love and as a reward for his piety, or to expiate a capital crime. When Admētus wooed Alcestis, the daughter of Pĕlĭas, and her father would only give her to one who should yoke lions and boars to a chariot, he fulfilled the task with Apollo's help; indeed, the god even prevailed on the Moirai to release him from death, provided that any one would volunteer to die for him. He is at length seized with a mortal sickness, and his aged parents refusing to give up the remnant of their days for him, Alcestis dies for her husband, but is sent back to the upper world by Persĕphŏnē, or, according to another story, is rescued out of the hands of Hades by Hēraclēs.

Adōnis. Sprung, according to the common legend, from the unnatural love of the Cyprian princess Myrrha (or Smyrna) for her father Cīnўras, who, on becoming aware of the crime, pursues her with a sword; but she, praying to the gods, is changed into a myrtle, out of whose bark springs the beautiful Adonis, the beloved of Aphrodītē. While yet a youth, he dies wounded by a boar in hunting; the goddess, inconsolable, makes the anemone grow out of his blood. As she will not give up her darling, and Persĕphŏnē has fallen in love with him, Zeus decrees that he shall pass half the year with one and half with the other goddess. Adonis (= lord) was properly a Syrian god of nature, a type of vegetation, which after a brief blossoming always dies again. The myth was embodied in a yearly Feast of Adonis held by women, which, starting from Byblos in Syria, the cradle of this worship, came by way of Cyprus to Asia Minor and Greece, then under the Ptolemies to Egypt, and in the imperial age to Rome. When the river Adonis by Byblos ran red with the soil washed down from Lebanon by the autumn rain, they said Adonis was slain by the boar in the mountains, and the water was dyed with his blood. Then the women set out to seek him, and having found a figure that they took to be his corpse, performed his funeral rites with lamentations as wild as the rejoicings that followed over his resurrection were licentious. The feast was held, in the East, with great magnificence. In Greece the celebration was much simpler, a leading feature being the little "Adonis-gardens," viz. pots holding all kinds of herbs that come out quickly and as quickly fade, which were finally thrown into the water. At the court of Alexandria a figure in costly apparel was displayed on a silver bier, and the next morning carried in procession by the women to the sea, and committed to the waves. In most places the feast was held in the hottest season.

Adoption. (1) At *Athens* adoption took place either in the adopter's lifetime or by will; or again, if a man died childless and intestate, the State interfered to bring into his house the man next entitled by the Attic law of inheritance as heir and adoptive son, so that the race and the religious rites peculiar to it might not die out. None but the independent citizen of respectable character could adopt, and he only while he was as yet without male heirs. If there were daughters, one of them was usually betrothed to the adopted son, and the rest portioned off with dowries. If after that a male heir was born, he and the adopted had equal rights.

(2) At *Rome* there were two kinds of adoption, both requiring the adopter to be a male and childless: *Arrogātio* and

Adoption proper. The former could only take place where the person to be adopted was independent (*sui juris*), and his adopter had no prospect of male offspring; at the instance of the pontifex, and after full proof of admissibility, it had to be sanctioned by the comitia curiata. Adoption proper applied to those still under paternal rule (*patria potestas*), the father selling his son by formal *mancipātio* (*q.v.*) to the adopter, who then, the paternal power being thus abolished, claimed the son before the court as his own, and the father allowed him to be adjudged to him. By either transaction the person adopted passed completely over into the family and rank of the adopter, and naturally took his name in full, but with the addition of a second *cognōmen* formed from his own former *nōmen gentīlĕ* by the suffix *-ānus, e.g.* Publius Cornelius Scipio Æmilĭ-anus (son of Lucius Æmilius Paullus). Women too could be adopted, but not arrogated; neither could they adopt. At the latter end of the Republic we find a testamentary Adoption in existence, which at first likewise produced a change of name, but not of status.

Adrasteia. *See* NEMESIS.

Adrastus. Grandson of Bias, son of Tălăus and Lysĭmăchē. In a quarrel between the three houses reigning in Argos, the Biantĭdæ, Mĕlampŏdĭdæ, and Prœtĭdæ, he is driven out by Amphiarāus, who also killed his father, flees to his mother's father, king Pŏlўbus of Sĭcўōn, and inherits his kingdom. But, reconciled to Amphiarāus, to whom he gives his sister Erĭphўlē, he returns and rules over Argos. During one stormy night a great scuffle is heard outside the palace: two fugitives, Polyneicĕs son of Œdĭpus of Thebes, and Tydeus son of Œneus of Călўdōn (one wrapped in a lion's hide, the other in a boar-skin), have sought refuge in the front-court, and are fighting for a night's lodging. Adrastus, coming forth, recognises the fulfilment of an oracle which had bidden him marry his daughters to a lion and a boar. He gives Argeia to Polyneices and Deïpўlē to Tydeus, promising to conduct those princes home and reinstate them in their rights. Thus began under his lead the far-famed and fatal expedition of the *Seven against Thebes* (*q.v.*). He alone escapes destruction by the help of his divine winged steed Areïōn. Ten years after, with the sons of the slain, the *Epĭgŏni* (*q.v.*), and his own son Ægiăleus, he again marches upon Thebes, takes and destroys the town, but loses his son, and dies of grief on his way home at Mĕgăra, where, as well as at Sĭcўon and Athens, he was worshipped as a hero.

Advŏcātus. At Rome, under the Republic, a competent friend who gave his advice in a law-suit and came into court in person, not to speak (the *patrōnus causœ* did that), but to support the cause by his presence. In the imperial age the term was applied to the counsel who pleaded in court in the presence of the parties, for doing which he was allowed, after the time of Claudius, to take a moderate fee.

Adýtŏn. In many Greek temples, a space set apart, sometimes underground, and only entered by the priest, a holy of holies. (*See* TEMPLE.)

Æa. The realm of the mythic Æētes; afterwards supposed to be Colchis on the Euxine.

Æăcus(Gr.*Aiăkŏs*). Ancestor of the heroic Æacidæ; son of Zeus by Ægīna, a daughter of the river-god Asōpus in Phlius, whom the king of gods, in the form of an eagle, carried off to the island named after her, where her son was born. As king of Ægīna he ruled the Myrmidons, whom Zeus at his request created out of ants (Gr. *myrmēkĕs*) to people his island, which, according to one story, was uninhabited, according to another, stricken with pestilence. Beloved by the gods for his piety, when a drought desolated Greece, his intercession obtained rain from Zeus; and the grateful Greeks built him in Ægina a temple enclosed by a marble wall. Pindar says he helped Poseidon and Apollo to rear the walls of Troy, erecting that very portion which was afterwards scaled by his son Tĕlămōn, and his grandson Neoptŏlĕmus. His justice caused him after death to be made a judge in the lower world. At Ægina and Athens he was worshipped as a demigod. His sons by Chiron's daughter Endeïs were Telamon and Peleus, the fathers of Ajax and Achilles; another son Phocus, by the Nēreïd Psămăthē, was slain by his half-brothers, for which their father banished them.

Ædīlēs. At Rome, two sets of magistrates, the Plebeian (*œdiles plēbis* or *plebeii*) and the Curule (*œdiles cŭrūles*). (1) The two *Plebeian Ædiles* were appointed B.C. 494 at the same time with the Tribuneship of the Plebs, as servants of the Tribunes, and at first probably nominated by them till 471, when, like them and under their presidency, they began to be elected by the whole body of the Plebs. They took their name from the temple (*œdes*) of the ple-

beian goddess Ceres, in which their official archives were kept. Beside the custody of the *plebi-scīta*, and afterwards of the *senatus-consulta*, it was their duty to make arrests at the bidding of the tribunes; to carry out the death-sentences which they passed, by hurling the criminal down from the Tarpeian rock; to look after the importation of corn; to watch the traffic in the markets; and to organize and superintend the Plebeian and Roman Games. Like the tribunes, they could only be chosen from the body of the Plebs, and wore no badge of office, not so much as the *toga prœtexta*, even after they became an authority independent of the tribunes. (2) The *Curule Ædiles*, from B.C. 366, were taken at first from the Patrician body alone, soon after from Patricians and Plebeians by turns, and lastly from either. Elected yearly in the comitia tribúta under the presidency of a consul, they were, from the first, officers of the whole people, though low in rank; they sat in the *sella curulis*, from which they took their name, and wore as insignia the *toga prœtexta*. As in rank, so in the extent of their powers they stood above the Plebeian Ædiles, being entitled to exercise civil jurisdiction in market business, where the latter could only impose a fine. The functions of the two were very much alike, comprising: (i) the superintendence of *trade* in the market, where they had to test weights and measures, and the quality of goods; to keep down the price of provisions, both by prohibitive measures, especially against regraters of corn, and by the purchase and liberal distribution of food (*cura annōnœ*); and, as regards the money-market, to prosecute those who transgressed the laws of usury; (ii) the care of the *streets and buildings* within the city and the circuit of a mile outside, by cleansing, paving, and improving the streets, or stirring up those who were bound to do it; by seeing that the street traffic was unimpeded; by keeping in repair the temples, public buildings, and works, such as sewers and aqueducts, and seeing that these latter and the fire-apparatus were in working order; (iii) a superintendence of *health and morals*, including the inspection of baths, taverns, and low houses, the putting down of all that endangered public order and decency, *e.g.* games of hazard, breaches of sumptuary laws, introduction of foreign religions, etc.; (iv) the exhibition of *Games* (of which the Roman and Megalensian devolved on the curule, the Plebeian on the plebeian ædiles), the supervision of festivities at the *feriæ Latinæ* and at games given by private men. The cost of the games given by themselves they defrayed partly out of a sum set apart by the State, but utterly inadequate to the large demands of later times ; partly out of the proceeds of fines which were also spent on public buildings, and partly out of their own resources. Thus the ædileship became an expensive luxury, and its enjoyment less and less accessible to men of moderate means. Ambitious men often spent incredible sums in getting up games, to win the people's favour with a view to higher honours, though the ædileship was not necessary as a stepping-stone to these. In Cicero's time the legal age for the curule ædileship was thirty-seven. From B.C. 366 their number was unchanged, till Cæsar in B.C. 44 added two more, the Plebeian *Ædiles Ceriáles*, to whom alone the *cura annonæ* and the management of the *ludi Ceriales* were entrusted. Under the Empire the office of ædile lost much in importance by some of its functions being handed over to separate officers, especially by the transference of its jurisdiction and its control of games to the prætors ; and it fell into such contempt, that even Augustus had to make a tenure of it, or the tribuneship, a condition of eligibility to the prætorship ; and succeeding emperors often had to fill it by compulsion. In the 3rd century A.D. it seems to have died out altogether.

Ædĭtŭus or Ædĭtŭmus. The overseer of a temple that had no priest of its own (*see* PRIESTS) ; also a major-domo. (*See* SLAVES.)

Aëdōn. Daughter of Pandărĕos, wife of the Theban king Zēthus, and mother of Itylus. Envious at her sister-in-law, Niŏbē, having six sons, she tries to kill the eldest, but by mistake kills her own. She is changed by Zeus into a nightingale, and for ever bewails her son. Later legend makes her the wife of an artificer Polytechnus at Cŏlŏphōn in Lydia ; she stirs the anger of Hera by boasting that she lives more happily with her husband than the goddess with Zeus. Hera sends Eris (= strife) to set on foot a wager between husband and wife, that whichever finishes first the piece of work they have in hand (he a chair, she a garment) shall make the other a present of a slave-girl. By Hera's help Aëdon wins, and Polytechnus in vexation fetches her sister, Chĕlīdŏnis, on a false pretext, from her father's house, and having reduced her to submission on the way, and bound her

to secrecy on pain of death, presents her to his wife unrecognised as a slave. One day Aëdon overhears her sister lamenting her lot at a fountain, and concerts with her to slay Itylus, cook him, and set him before his father to eat. On learning the truth, Polytechnus pursues the sister to her home ; but there the gods, to prevent more horrors, turn them all into birds, making Pandareos an osprey, his wife a kingfisher, Polytechnus a pelican, Chelidonis a swallow, and Aëdon a nightingale. (*Comp.* PROCNE.)

Æētēs. Son of Hēlios and the Ocean nymph Perseïs, brother of Circē and Pasĭphäë, king of Æa, father of Medēa and Absyrtus by the ocean nymph Idyia. (*See* ARGONAUTS and MEDEA.)

Ægeus. Son of Pandīōn (*q.v.* 2) and Pelia. Having with the help of his brothers Lycus, Pallas, and Nisus wrested Attica from the sons of his uncle Metiōn, who had driven out his father, he seized the sole sovereignty. Dethroned by his brother Pallas and his sons, he was rescued and restored by his son Thēseus (*q.v.*). Having slain Andrŏgĕōs, son of Minos (*q.v.*), he was conquered by that king, and compelled to send seven youths and seven maidens to Crete every nine years as victims to the Minotaur. When Theseus set out to free his country from this tribute, he agreed in case of success to exchange the black sail of his ship for a white ; but he forgot to do so, and Ægeus seeing the old sail on the returning vessel, gave up his son for lost, and threw himself into the sea, which is supposed to have been named after him the Ægēan. He had a *heröön* or shrine at Athens. Childless by his first two marriages, and ascribing the fact to the anger of Aphrŏdītē, he is said to have introduced her worship into Athens. (For his son Mēdus by Medēa, *see* both.)

Ægĭălē (Gr. *Ægĭaleia*). Daughter of Adrastus of Argos, wife of Diomēdes (*q.v.*).

Ægĭăleus. Son of Adrastus of Argos, and one of the Epĭgŏni (*q.v.*), who fell before Thebes.

Ægīna, a nymph, daughter of the river-god Asōpus, and, by Zeus, mother of Æăcus (*q.v.*).

Æginetan Sculptures. The marble pediments of Athena's temple at Ægīna, discovered in 1811, restored by Thorwaldsen, and preserved in the Glyptothek at Munich. Their great value consists in the full light they throw on the condition of Greek art, especially of the Æginetan school, in B.C. 480. (*Comp.* SCULPTURE.) Both groups

WEST PEDIMENT OF THE TEMPLE AT ÆGINA.

present, with lifelike accuracy and in strictly symmetrical distribution, combats of the Greeks before Troy, while Athēna in the centre, as protectress of the Greeks, retains the rigid attitude of the ancient religious statues. Of the figures, originally twenty-two in number, ten in the west pediment representing the contest for the body of Patroclus, are complete, while the eleventh is preserved in fragments; of those in the east pediment representing Hēraclēs and Tĕlămōn shielding the fallen Oïcles from Laŏmĕdōn, five remain and many fragments.

Ægis. The storm-cloud and thunder-cloud of Zeus, imagined in Homer as a shield forged by Hephæstus, blazing brightly and fringed with tassels of gold, in its centre the awe-inspiring Gorgon's head. When Zeus shakes the ægis, it thunders and lightens, and horror and perdition fall upon those against whom it is lifted. It is borne not only by Zeus "the Ægis-bearer," but by his daughter Athēna, and occasionally by Apollo. As the same word means a goat-skin, it was explained in later times as the skin of the goat which had suckled Zeus in his infancy. At the bidding of the oracle, he drew it over his thunder-shield in the contest with the Giants, and fastened on it the Gorgon's head. When the ægis became a standing attribute of Athena, it was represented as a skin either shaggy or scaly, with a fringe of snakes and the Gorgon's head in the middle, and either serving the goddess as a breastplate, or hanging behind to screen the back and shoulders, or fastened like a shield on the left arm.

Ægisthus. Son of Thyestes and his daughter Pelŏpia. At his birth he was exposed by his mother, and brought up by shepherds. His uncle Atreus, husband to Pelopia, finds him and brings him to Mycēnæ, thinking him to be his own son; but Ægisthus and his real father contrive to kill him and seize the sovereignty of Mycenæ. (*See*

ATREUS.) This position he loses again by his cousin Agamemnon's return from exile; but during that hero's absence at Troy he seduces his wife Clytæmnēstra, and with her help slays him treacherously on his return. In the eighth year after this deed comes young Orestes, and avenges his father's death by slaying Ægisthus.

Æglē. One of the Hesperides (*q.v.*).

Ægyptus. Son of Belus and twin-brother of Dănăüs (*q.v.*), who subdued the land of the Melampŏdĕs (Blackfeet), and named it after himself. Ignorant of the fate of his fifty sons, he comes to Argos and there dies of grief at their death; another account represents his only surviving son as reconciling him to his brother.

Æliānus. (1) *The Tactician*, a Greek writer on war, about 100 A.D., composed a work dedicated to Trajan on the Greek order of battle, with special reference to Macedonian tactics (*Taktĭkē Theōrĭa*), which is extant both in its original and in an enlarged form. The original used falsely to be attributed to Arrian.

(2) *Claudius Ælianus*, called *the Sophist*, a Roman of Præneste, who wrote in Greek, lived at Rome in the 2nd century A.D. as teacher of rhetoric. His surviving works are: (1) 20 insignificant *Peasants' Letters*, so called because attributed to Attic peasants; (2) *Variæ Historiæ* or miscellanies, in 14 books, some preserved only in extracts, and (3) *De Natūrā Animālium*. The two last-mentioned are copious and valuable collections of all kinds of curiosities in human and animal life, mostly taken from earlier writings now lost.

Æliānum Jus. *See* JURISPRUDENCE.

Ælius. (1) *Ælius Catus. See* JURISPRUDENCE.

(2) *Lucius Ælius Stīlo Prœconīnus*, a Roman grammarian born at Lanuvium, about 150 B.C., an *ĕquĕs*, and friend of the poet Lucilius, to whom he dedicated his first book of Satires: surnamed Stilo

(from *stilus*, pencil) because he wrote speeches for public men, and Præconinus because his father was a crier (*præco*). He was so strongly attached to the party of Optimātes, that in 100 B.C. he voluntarily accompanied Metellus Numidĭcus into exile. After his return he became the master of Varro and Cicero. Well versed in Greek and Latin literature, he applied himself chiefly to studying the oldest relics of his native tongue, commented on the Liturgies of the Salian priests and the Laws of the Twelve Tables, and earned the honour of having rescued the ancient Latin language from oblivion, and preserved some knowledge of it to posterity. Such scanty remnants of it as have come down to us in glossaries and the like seem to be taken chiefly from his writings, now all lost.

(3) and (4) *Ælius Lamprĭdius* and *Ælius Spartiānus*, Roman historians of the Empire. (*See* SCRIPTORES HIST. AUG.)

Æmilius Probus. *See* CORNELIUS NEPOS.

Æněas (Greek *Aineias*). (1) Son of Anchīses and Aphrodītē. Born on the mountains of Ida, he is brought up till his fifth year by his brother-in-law Alcăthŏus, or, according to another story, by the nymphs of Ida, and after his father's misfortune becomes ruler of Dardănŏs. Though near of kin to the royal house of Troy, he is in no hurry to help Priam till his own cattle are carried off by Achilles. Yet he is highly esteemed at Troy for his piety, prudence, and valour ; and gods come to his assistance in battle. Thus Aphrodītē and Apollo shield him when his life is threatened by Diomed, and Poseidon snatches him out of the combat with Achilles. But Priam does not love him, for he and his are destined hereafter to rule the Trojans. The story of his escape at the fall of Troy is told in several ways : one is, that he bravely cut his way through the enemy to the fastnesses of Ida ; another, that, like Antēnor, he was spared by the Greeks because he had always counselled peace and the surrender of Hělěna ; a third, that he made his escape in the general confusion. The older legend represents him as staying in the country, forming a new kingdom out of the wreck of the Teucrian people, and handing it down to his posterity. Indeed several townships on Ida always claimed him as their founder. The story of his emigrating, freely or under compulsion from the Greeks, and founding a new kingdom beyond seas, is clearly of post-Homeric date. In the earlier legend he is represented as settling not very far

from home; then they extended his wanderings to match those of Odysseus, always pushing the limit of his voyagings farther and farther west. The poet Stesĭchŏrus (about 600 B.C.) is, so far as we know, the first who brings him to Italy. Later, in face of the fast rising power of Rome, the Greeks conceived the notion that Æněas must have settled in Latium and become the 'ancestor of these Romans. This had become a settled conviction in their minds by the beginning of the 3rd century B.C., when Timæus, in the Roman interest, completed the Legend of Æneas, making room in it for Latian and Roman traditions ; and at Rome it was soon taken up and developed into a dogma of the state religion, representing the antagonism between Greece and Rome, the new Troy. From that time verse and prose endeavoured to bring the various places with which the name of Æneas was connected into historic and geographic harmony, now building on a bare resemblance of names, now following kindred fables and the holy places of Aphrodītē Aineias, a goddess of sea and seafaring, whose temples were generally found on the coasts. Thus by degrees the story took in the main the shape so familiar to us in Vergil's *Æneïd*. Æneas flees from the flames of Troy, bearing on his shoulders the stricken Anchises with the Penātes, leading his boy Ascănius and followed by his wife Creūsa (who is lost on the way), till he comes to Mount Ida. There he gathers the remnant of the Trojans in twenty ships, and sails by way of Thrace and Delos to Crete, imagining that to be the destination assigned him by Apollo. But driven thence by pestilence, and warned in a dream that Italy is his goal, he is first carried out of his course to Epīrus, and then makes his way to Sicily, where his father dies. He has just set out to cross to the mainland, when a hurricane raised by his enemy Juno casts him on the coast of Carthage. Here Juno and Venus have agreed that he shall marry Dido ; but at Jupiter's command he secretly quits Africa, and having touched at Sicily, Cumæ, and Caiēta (Gaëta), arrives, after seven years' wandering, at the Tiber's mouth. Latīnus, king of Latium, gives him leave to build a town, and betroths to him his daughter Lavīnia. Turnus, king of the Rutŭli, to whom she had been promised before, takes up arms in alliance with Mezentius of Cære ; in twenty days the war is ended by Æneas defeating both. According to another version (not Vergil's), he disappeared after the victory on the Numicius, and was worshipped as the god Jupiter Indĭges. The Roman version, in its earliest forms, as we see it in Nævius and Ennius, brought Æneas almost into contact with the founders of Rome, Romulus and Remus being regarded as children of his daughter Ilia by the god Mars. In later times, to fill up duly the space between the Fall of Troy and the Founding of Rome, the line of Alban kings, descended from Silvius, his son by Lavinia, was inserted between him and Romulus.

(2) *Æneas*, named "*the Tactician*," a Greek military author, wrote about 350 B.C. a book on the Art of War, of which only a small part on siege-operations, usually entitled *Poliorkētĭkŏn*, is preserved; it is clear in exposition, and contains much valuable historical information.

Æŏlus. (1) Grandson of Deucălĭon, son of Hellēn by the nymph Orseïs, brother of Dorus and Xuthus; king of Magnesia in Thessaly, and mythic ancestor of the Æolian race, his sons being founders of the Æolian settlements spread all over Greece. By his wife *Enărĕtē* he has seven sons: *Crētheus*, founder of Iolcus, and father, by Tyro, of Æson (Jason's father), of Phēres (founder of Phēræ in Thessaly, and father of Admētus and Lycurgus), and of Amythāon (father of Bias and Melampus); *Sĭsyphŭs*, founder of Ephўra (Corinth), father of Glaucus and grandfather of Bellĕrŏphōn; *Athămās*, king of Orchomenus, father of Phrixus and Hellē; *Salmōneus*, builder of Salmōnē in Elis, father of Tyro; *Deïŏn*, king of Phocis, father of Actor, Phўlucus, and Cēphălus; *Magnēs*, father of Dictys and Polydectes, who colonize the island of Serīphus (*see* PERSEUS); *Periēres*, king of Messenia, father of Aphareus and Leucippus. Also five daughters: *Canădē*, mother by Poseidon of Epopeus and Alōeus (*see* ALOADS); *Alcyŏnē* (*see* CEYX); *Peisĭdĭcē*; *Călўcē*, mother of Endўmion; and *Perĭmēdē*.

(2) In Homer a son of Hippŏtēs, and a favourite of the gods, whom Zeus has appointed keeper of the winds. On his Æolian island, floating in the far west, its steep cliff encircled by a brazen wall, he lives in unbroken bliss with his wife and his six sons and six daughters, whom he has wedded to one another. He hospitably entertains Odysseus, gives him the unfavourable winds shut up in a leathern bag, and a kindly breeze to waft him on

his voyage. But when the hero's comrades open the bag, the winds break out and blow him back to the Æolian Isle; then Æolus drives him from his door as one hateful to the gods. In the later legend he dwells on one of the Æolian isles to the north of Sicily, Lĭpăra or Strongўle, where, throned on a mountain, he holds the winds imprisoned in the hollow of the same; yet he does not seem to have received real worship. He was, moreover, brought into genealogical connection with Æolus of Thessaly, whose son Mimas begets Hippotes, and he (by Melanippē) a *second Æolus*, king of Æolis in Ætolia; this Æolus gives his daughter Arnē, the beloved of Poseidon, to a guest-friend from Metapontum in Lucania, where she has two sons by the god, the *third Æolus* and Bœōtus. These, adopted by the Metapontian, kill his wife Autŏlўtē and run away, Bœōtus returning with Arnē to his grandfather, and Æolus settling in the isles named after him, and founding the city of Lipara.

Æōra. Festival of the swing. *See* ICARIUS, 1.

Æquĭtās. At Rome, the personification of equity or fairness, as opposed to the justice that decides by the letter of the law. She was represented as a stately virgin with her left hand open, and often with a pair of scales.

Ærārii. By the constitution of Servius Tullius (*see* CENTURIA), the *Ærarii* were citizens not settled on land of their own, and therefore not included in any one of the property-classes founded on landownership. The term was also applied to those standing outside of the tribal union, who were excluded from the right of voting and from military service, and were bound to pay a poll-tax in proportion to their means. Citizens in the classes and tribes could be expelled from their tribe by the censors in punishment for any fault, and placed among the Ærarii. But when the latter were likewise admitted into the tribes (B.C. 308), being enrolled in the city tribes (B.C. 304), which were on that account less esteemed than the country ones, a penal transfer to the Ærarii consisted in expulsion from one's proper tribe and removal to one of the city tribes till at least the next census.

Ærārium. The state-treasury of Rome, into which flowed the revenues ordinary and extraordinary, and out of which the needful expenses were defrayed. It was kept in the basement of the temple of Saturn, under the charge of the quæstors. A special reserve fund was the *Ærarium sanctius*, in which the proceeds of receipts from the manumission-tax (one twentieth of the freed slave's value) were deposited in gold ingots. When Augustus divided the provinces into senatorial and imperatorial, there were *two* chief treasuries. The senatorial treasury, which was still kept in the temple of Saturn, was left under the control of the senate, but only as a matter of formal right. Practically it passed into the hands of the emperors, who also brought the management of the treasuries under their own eye by appointing, instead of the quæstors, two *præfecti ærarii* taken from those who had served as prætors. Besides, they diverted into their own *Fiscus* all the larger revenues, even those that legally belonged to the Ærarium. When in course of time the returns from all the provinces flowed into the imperial treasury, the senatorial Ærarium continued to exist as the city treasury. The *Ærārium militare* was a pension-fund founded by Augustus in A.D. 6, for disabled soldiers. Its management was entrusted to three *præfecti ærarii militaris*. It was maintained out of the interest on a considerable fund, and the proceeds of the heritage and sale duties.

Aëröpē. Daughter to Catreus of Crete (*q.v.*), who was given up by her father to Nauplius to be sold abroad. Married to Atreus (*q.v.*), she bore Agamemnon and Menelaüs, but was thrown into the sea by her husband for her adultery with his brother Thyestes.

Æsăcus. Son of Priam by Arisbē, who had learnt the art of interpreting dreams from his maternal grandfather Merops, and being consulted by his father as to Hĕcŭba's bad dreams before the birth of Paris, advised him to expose a child so clearly doomed to be the destruction of Troy. In despair at having caused the death of his wife Astĕrŏpē (or Hespĕria) he threw himself into the sea, and was changed into a bird, the diver.

Æschĭnēs. (1) *The Socratic*, son of a sausage-maker at Athens, lived in the most pinching poverty, but would not let it discourage him in his zeal for learning. Some

time after the death of Socrates, to whom he had clung with faithful affection, in B.C. 399, Æschines, probably to mend his fortunes, removed to Syracuse, and there found a patron in the younger Dionysius. On the

* ÆSCHINES THE ORATOR.
(Naples, National Museum.)

fall of that tyrant, he returned to Athens, and supported himself by writing speeches for public men. He composed Dialogues, which were prized for their faithful descriptions of Socrates, and the elegance of their style. Three pseudo-Platonic dialogues are conjecturally ascribed to him; *That Virtue can be Taught; Axiŏchus, or on Death,* and *Eryxias, or on Riches.* But it is doubtful whether they are really from his hand.

(2) *Æschines the Orator,* born at Athens B.C. 389, in a low station. As a youth, he assisted his father in keeping an elementary school, then acted as clerk to several inferior magistrates, was for a time an actor in third-rate parts, till an accident removed him from the stage, when he became secretary to the esteemed orators and statesmen Aristophon and Eubūlus, at whose recommendation he was twice elected to a government clerkship Having thus acquired a sound knowledge of the laws and of legal proceedings, and being gifted with considerable talent, fine elocution and a dignified manner, to which his experience on the stage had contributed, he now came forward as a public speaker, and soon became an important personage. As a member of the embassy sent to Philip of Macedon for the conclusion of peace, B.C. 347, he was won over by the king to second the plans which proved so fatal to Athens, and was therefore accused of high treason by Timarchus and Demosthenes in B.C. 345; but he managed to clear himself by a triumphant attack on the private life of Timarchus. In B.C. 342 Demosthenes, who hated him, the head of the Macedonian party, as bitterly as he was hated by him, renewed the charge in his oration *On the False Embassy.* Æschines, however, met it successfully by an equally brilliant speech bearing the same title. His unpatriotic conduct occasioned the war with Philip, which led to the overthrow of the Athenians and Thebans at Chæronēa, 338, and set the seal to the Macedonian supremacy over Greece. His own fall at last was brought on by his hatred of Demosthenes. Æschines had previously brought a charge of illegality against Ctēsĭphōn for proposing the distinction of a golden crown for Demosthenes. The charge was repeated B.C. 330, in a brilliant oration nominally directed *Against Ctesiphon,* but really aimed at his old rival. He was completely crushed by Demosthenes' great speech *On the Crown,* and being condemned to pay a fine of 1,000 drachmas, went into voluntary exile at Rhodes, where he is said to have opened a school of oratory. Thence he removed to Samos, and died B.C. 314. Beside the three orations named (*Against Timarchus, On the*

False Embassy, Against Ctesiphon), we have under his name a collection of twelve letters professing to be written from Rhodes, but really forged by a later hand. Among the orators of his time Æschines ranks next to Demosthenes. His orations are elaborated with the utmost care and reflexion, they have fulness, force, smoothness, and grace; but lack the terseness, the rhythm, and the moral inspiration of those of Demosthenes. They were spoken of in antiquity as the Three Graces.

Æschȳlŭs. The earliest of the three great tragic poets of Greece, son of Euphŏriōn. He was born at Eleusis, near Athens, B.C. 525, of an old and noble stock, fought at Marathon, Sălămis and Platææ, and in his 25th year appeared as a writer of tragedies and rival of Pratĭnas and Chœrĭlus, though he did not win his first victory till 488 B.C. About 476 he lived in Sicily, at the court of Hiero of Syracuse, and composed his *Ætnœans* for the consecration of the city of Ætna, founded by that king in the place of the ancient Cătăna. On his return to Athens he was beaten by the young Sophŏcles with his very first play, but vanquished him again the next year with the Tetralogy of which the *Seven against Thebes* formed a part. After the performance of his *Oresteia,* B.C. 459, he quitted home once more, perhaps in disgust at the growing power of the democracy; and after three years' residence at Gela in Sicily, was killed, says one story, by an eagle dropping a tortoise on his bare skull. The inhabitants of Gela buried his remains, and honoured them with a splendid monument. At a later time the Athenians, on the motion of the orator Lycurgus, placed a brazen statue of him, as well as of Sophocles and Eurĭpīdes, in the theatre; by a decree of the people a chorus was granted for every performance of his plays, and the garland of victory voted him as though he were still living among them. His tragedies, like those of the other two, were preserved in a special standard copy, to guard them against arbitrary alterations. His son Euphorion was also an esteemed tragic poet, so was his sister's son Phĭlŏcles and his descendants for several generations. (*See* TRAGEDY.) The number of Æschylus's plays is stated as 90, of which 82 are still known by title, but only 7 are preserved: (1) *The Persians,* performed in 473 B.C., was named from the chorus. Its subject was the same as that of Phrynichus' *Phœnissœ,* the defeat of Xerxes at Salamis, but was differently treated (2) *The Seven* *against Thebes*, part of a Tetralogy, embracing the cycle of Theban legend, of which *Laïus* and *Œdĭpūs* formed the first two pieces, and the satyric drama *Sphinx* the conclusion. (3) *The Suppliants*, the reception of Dănäus and his daughters at Argos, evidently part of another Tetralogy, and, to judge by the simple plot and its old-fashioned treatment, one of his earliest works. (4) *Promĕtheus Bound*, part of a Trilogy, the *Promĕtheia*, whose first and last pieces were probably *Prometheus the Fire-bringer* and *Prometheus Unbound*. Lastly, the *Oresteia*, the one Trilogy which has survived, consisting of the three tragedies, (5) *Agamemnon*, the murder of

* ÆSCHYLUS.
(Rome, Capitoline Museum.)

that hero on his return home ; (6) *The Choëphŏroe*, named from the chorus of captive Trojan women offering libations at Agamemnon's tomb, in which Orestes avenges himself on Ægisthus and Clytæmnēstra ; and (7) *The Eumĕnĭdĕs*, in which Orestes, pursued by the Furies, is acquitted by the Areŏpăgus at Athens. This Trilogy, composed B.C. 458, and probably the last work exhibited by Æschylus at Athens, gives us an idea of the whole artistic conception of the poet, and must be looked upon as one of the greatest works of art ever produced. The style is marked by sublimity and majesty, qualities partly attributable to the courageous and serious temper of the time, but chiefly the offspring of the

poet's individuality, which took delight in all that is great and grand, and loved to express itself in strong, sonorous words, an accumulation of epithets, and a profusion of bold metaphors and similes. His view of the universe reveals a profoundly philosophic mind, so that the ancients call him a Pythagorean ; at the same time he is penetrated by a heartfelt piety, which conceives of the gods as powers working in the interest of morality. However simple the plot of his plays, they display an art finished to the minutest detail. His Trilogies either embraced one complete cycle of myths, or united separate legends according to their moral or mythical affinity ; even the satyric dramas attached to the Tragedies stand in intimate connexion with them. Æschylus is the true creator of Tragedy, inasmuch as, by adding a second actor to the first, he originated the genuine dramatic dialogue, which he made the chief part of the play by gradually cutting down the lyrical or choral parts. Scenic apparatus he partly created and partly completed. He introduced masks for the players, and by gay and richly embroidered trailing garments, the high buskin, head-dresses, and other means, gave them a grand imposing aspect, above that of common men ; and he fitted up the stage with decorative painting and machinery. According to the custom of the time, he acted in his own plays, practised the chorus in their songs and dances, and himself invented new dance figures.

Æscŭlāpius. *See* ASCLEPIUS.

Æsŏn, son of Crētheus by Tyro (*see* ÆOLUS, 1), king of Iolcos in Thessaly, was deposed by his half-brother Pělĭas, and killed while his son Jason was away on the Argonautic Expedition. (*Comp.* ARGONAUTS.)

Æsŏpus (Gr. *Aisōpos*). The famous writer of fables, the first author who created an independent class of stories about animals, so that in a few generations his name and person had become typical of that entire class of literature. In course of time, thanks to his plain, popular manner, the story of his own life was enveloped in an almost inextricable tissue of tales and traditions, which represent him as an ugly hunchback and buffoon. In the Middle Ages these were woven into a kind of romance. A Phrygian by birth, and living in the time of the Seven Sages, about 600 B.C., he is said to have been at first a slave to several masters, till Iadmōn of Samos set him free. That he next lived at the court of Crœsus, and being sent by him on an embassy to Delphi, was murdered by the priests there, is pure fiction. Under his name were propagated in all parts of Greece, at first only by tradition in the mouth of the people, a multitude of prose tales teaching the lessons of life under the guise of fables about animals. We know how Socrates, during his last days in prison, was engaged in turning the fables of Æsop into verse. The first written collection appears to have been set on foot by Demetrius of Phalērum, B.C. 300. The collections of *Æsop's Fables* that have come down to us are, in part, late prose renderings of the version in choliambics by Babrius (*q.v.*), which still retain here and there a scrap of verse; partly products of the rhetorical schools, and therefore of very different periods and degrees of merit.

Æsymnētæ ("regulators," "judges"). A name given in some Greek cities to the ordinary magistrates and judicial functionaries. In earlier times the term was also applied to persons appointed for a definite term (or until the completion of their task) for putting an end, by legislation, to internal quarrels. Sometimes an *œsymnetēs* was voluntarily chosen by the community for life, and entrusted with supreme and unlimited power. The office of *œsymnetes* may to a certain extent be compared with the Roman dictatorship, though the latter was never conferred without a strict limitation of time.

Æthra, daughter of Pittheus, king of Trœzēn, mother of Thēseus by Ægeus or, according to another account, by Poseidon. While Homer merely mentions her as a servant of Helen at Troy, later legend adds that, when the Dioscūri took Aphidnæ and set free their sister whom Theseus had carried off, they conveyed Æthra to Sparta as a slave, whence she accompanied Helen to Troy; and that on the fall of that city, they brought her grandsons Acămas and Demŏphoön back to Athens.

Aëtiōn. A Greek painter in the latter half of the 4th century B.C., especially famed for his picture of Alexander the Great's wedding with the beautiful Roxāna, B.C. 328.

Aëtius (Gr. *Aëtiŏs*). Of Amĭda in Mesopotamia, a Greek physician of the 6th century A.D., who lived at Constantinople as imperial physician in ordinary. He was the author of a great miscellany on pathology and diagnosis in sixteen books.

Afrānius (*Lucius*). The chief master of the *Făbŭla Togāta*. (*See* COMEDY.) Flour-

ished B.C. 100. In his pictures of Roman life he took Menander for his model, and with great success. Cicero calls him witty and a master of language. To judge by the number of the titles of his comedies which have survived (more than forty, with scanty fragments), he was a prolific author; from them we gather that his subjects were mostly taken from family life. His plays kept possession of the stage longer than those of most comic poets, being still acted in Nero's time.

Agămēdēs. Son of Ergīnus of Orchŏmĕnus, and a hero of the building art, like his brother Trophōnius (*q.v.*).

Agamemnōn. The Atreïd, *i.e.* son of Atreus, and brother of Menelāus. Driven from Mycēnæ after the murder of Atreus (*q.v.*) by Thyestes, the two young princes fly to Sparta, where king Tyndareos gives them his daughters in marriage, Clytæmnēstra to Agamemnon, and Hĕlĕna to Menelaus. While the latter inherits his father-in-law's kingdom, Agămemnon not only drives his uncle out of Mycenæ, but so extends his dominions that in the war against Troy for the recovery of Helena the chief command is entrusted to him as the mightiest prince in Greece. He contributes one hundred ships manned with warriors, beside lending sixty to the Arcadians. (On the immolation of his daughter Iphigeneia at Aulis, *see* IPHIGENEIA.) In Homer he is one of the bravest fighters before Troy; yet, by arrogantly refusing to let Chryses, priest of Apollo, ransom his daughter Chrysēïs, who had fallen to Agamemnon as the prize of war, he brings a plague on the Grecian host, which he afterwards almost ruins by ruthlessly carrying off Brisēïs the prize of Achilles, who henceforth sits sulking in his tents, and refuses to fight. After the fall of Troy, Agamemnon comes home with his captive, the princess Cassandra; but at supper he and his comrades are murdered by his wife's lover Ægisthus, while the queen herself kills Cassandra. Such is Homer's account; the tragic poets make Clytæmnestra, in revenge of her daughter's immolation, throw a net over Agamemnon while bathing, and kill him with the help of Ægisthus. In Homer his children are Iphianassa, Chrysŏthĕmis, Laŏdĭcē, and Orestes; the later legend puts Iphigeneia and Electra in the place of Iphianassa and Laodice. Agamemnon was worshipped as a hero.

Agănippē, a spring sacred to the Muses on Mount Hĕlĭcon, near Thespiæ in Bœōtia, whose water imparted poetic inspiration. Also the nymph of the same, daughter of the river-god Permessus.

Agasĭas. A Greek artist of Ephesus, probably in the 1st century B.C. The *Borghese Gladiator* in the Louvre is from his hand. (*See* SCULPTURE.)

Agātharchĭdēs. A Greek grammarian of Cnidus, who lived at Alexandria in the 2nd century B.C. as tutor, and afterwards guardian, of a prince. He composed several historical works (one on the successors of Alexander), a well written performance, and a description of the Red Sea in five books. Of the former only a few fragments remain, of the last some considerable extracts from the first and fifth books.

Agātharchus. A Greek painter of Samos, the inventor of scene-painting. (*See* PAINTING.)

Agāthĭās. Of Myrīna in Asia Minor, a Greek poet and historian, born about 530 A.D., lived at Constantinople as a jurist, and died about 582. By his *Kyklos*, a collection of his own and contemporary poems, topically arranged in eight books, he helped to originate the Greek ANTHOLOGY (*q.v.*), which still contains 101 epigrams by him. In his last years he wrote, in a laboured florid style, a history of Justinian in five books, treating of the years A.D. 552–8 in continuation of Procopius.

Agāthŏdæmōn (= good dæmon). In Greek mythology a good spirit of the cornfields and vineyards, to whom libations of un-mixed wine were made at meals. In works of art he is represented as a youth, holding in one hand a horn of plenty and a bowl, in the other a poppy and ears of corn. (*Comp.* EVENTUS.)

Agāthŏn. A tragic poet of Athens, born B.C. 448, a friend of Eurīpĭdēs and Plato, universally celebrated for his beauty and refined culture. The banquet he gave in honour of his dramatic victory of B.C. 417 is immortalized in Plato's *Sympŏsĭŏn*. He was, together with Euripides, at the court of Archelāus, king of Macedonia, and probably died there about B.C. 402. He appears to have carried still further the rhetorical manner of Euripides, adopting entirely the views of the sophist Gorgias; and his namby-pamby style is ridiculed by Aristŏphǎnes. On the stage he introduced several innovations: he was the first to make the chorus a mere intermezzo, having nothing to do with the action, and in his tragedy of *Anthŏs* (= flower) he invented both characters and plot for himself, instead of resorting to old myths.

Agāvē (Gr. *Agaŭē*). Daughter of Cadmus and wife of Echīŏn. She, with other women, in a bacchanalian frenzy tore to pieces her own son Pentheus (*q.v.*).

Agdistis. *See* RHEA.

Ages. Since the time of Hesiod, the Greeks, and the Romans after them, generally assumed the existence of four ages.

(1) The age of gold, in which Krŏnŏs or Saturnus was king. During this period mankind enjoyed perpetual youth, joy, and peace

undisturbed, reaping in their fulness the fruits which the earth spontaneously brought forth. Death came upon them like a soft slumber; and after it they became good *dæmŏnĕs*, watching men like guardians in their deeds of justice and injustice, and hovering round them with gifts of wealth.

(2) The golden age was succeeded by that of silver. This was inferior to the golden both in physical and mental force. The people of the silver age remained for a hundred years in the condition of children, simple and weakly. Even if they attained maturity, their folly and arrogance prevented their living long. They continued to exist after death as spirits, living beneath the earth, but not immortal.

(3) Zeus then created the brazen age, so

named because in it all implements were made of brass.. The men, furnished with gigantic limbs and irresistible physical strength, destroyed each other by deeds of violence, and perished at their death.

(4) The iron age succeeded. This was the generation of work and laborious agriculture. Care and toil fill up the day and night; truth and modesty are departed; mischief alone survives, and there is nothing to arrest the progress of decay.

Agēla. In Crete, an association of youths for joint training; *Agelātēs*, the captain of an agela. (*See* EDUCATION, 1.)

Agēlādās. A Greek artist of the first half of the 5th century B.C., famed for his images of gods and Olympian victors, wrought in metal. His reputation was much enhanced by the fact that Phīdias, Myrōn, and Polyclītus were his pupils.

Agēma. The guard in the Macedonian army; in which the cavalry were a troop (*īlē*) formed of noblemen's sons who had grown up as pages in the royal service, while the infantry consisted of the *hypaspistæ* (*q.v.*), to whom the *argyraspĭdēs* (*q.v.*), were added later as heavy infantry.

Agēnōr. (1) Son of Poseidōn and Libya, king of Phœnicia, brother to Belus, and father of Cadmus and Eurōpa (*q.v.*).

(2) Son of Antēnor by Theāno, a priestess of Athēna, and one of the bravest heroes of Troy. In Homer he leads the Trojans in storming the Greek entrenchments, rescues Hector when thrown down by Ajax, and even enters the lists with Achilles, but is saved from imminent danger by Apollo. In the post-Homeric legend he dies by the hand of Neoptŏlĕmus.

Ager Publicus (= common land). The Latin name for the State domains, formed of territory taken from conquered states. The Romans made a practice, upon every new acquisition of land, of adding a part of it, usually a third, to the domain. So far as this land was under culture, portions of it were sometimes *assigned* to single citizens or newly-founded colonies in fee simple, sometimes *sold* by the quæstors on the condition that, though the purchaser might bequeath and alienate it, it still remained State property. In token of this it paid a substantial or merely nominal rent (*vectīgal*), and was called *ager prīvātus vectigālisque* or *quæstōrius.* The greater part was left to the old occupiers, yet not as free property, but as rent-paying land, and was called *ager publicus stipendiarius datus assignatus;* the rest remained under

State management, and was let by the censors. Of uncultivated districts, the State, by public proclamation, gave a provisional right of seisin, *occupātio*, with a view to cultivation, in consideration of a tithe of the corn raised and a fifth of the fruit, and reserving its right of resumption. Such seisin was called *possessio.* It could be bequeathed or otherwise alienated, yet never became private property, but remained a rent-paying and resumable property of the State. Though the Plebeians had as good a right to occupy lands won by their aid as the Patricians, yet in the early times of the Republic this right was exercised by the latter alone, partly because they had the greater command of means and men, and partly because by the right of the stronger they excluded the Plebeians from benefiting by the Ager Publicus. Against this usurpation the Plebeians waged a bitter and unbroken warfare, claiming not only a share in newly conquered lands, but a wholesale redistribution of existing *possessiōnes*, while the Patricians strained every nerve to maintain their vested interests, and managed to thwart the execution of all the enactments passed from time to time in favour of the Plebeians. Even the law of the tribune Gaius Licinius Stolo (B.C. 377), limiting *possessiones* to 500 *iūgĕra* (acres) per man, and ordering the distribution of the remainder, were from the first eluded by the *possessōrēs*, who now included both Patricians and well-to-do Plebeians. All possible means were employed, as pretended deeds of gift and other similar devices. The threatened extinction of the Italian peasantry by the great wars, and the rapid growth of huge estates (*latifundia*) worked by slaves, occasioned the law of Tiberius Gracchus (B.C. 133), retaining the Licinian limit of 500 acres, but allowing another 250 for each son, and granting compensation for lands resumed by the State. The land thus set free, and all the Ager Publicus that had been leased, except a few domains indispensable to the State, were to be divided among poor citizens, but on the condition that each allotment paid a quit-rent, and was not to be alienated. But again, the the resistance of the nobility practically reduced this law to a dead letter ; and the upshot of the whole agrarian movement stirred up by Tiberius and his brother Gaius Gracchus was, that the wealthy Romans were not only left undisturbed in their *possessiones*, but were released from paying rent. In the civil wars of Sulla the Ager Publicus in Italy, which had been nearly all used up in assignations, received so vast an increase by the extermination of whole townships, by proscriptions and confiscations, that even after all the soldiers had been provided for, there remained a portion undistributed. Under the Empire there was hardly any left in Italy; what there was, whether in Italy or in the provinces, came gradually under the control of the imperial exchequer.

Agēsander (Gr. *Agēsandrŏs*). A Greek artist of the school of Rhodes. The celebrated group of the Laŏcoön is the joint work of Agesander, Athēnodōrus, and Polydōrus. (*See* LAOCOON.)

Agger. In Roman siege-works, the mound or embankment raised against an enemy's walls. (*See* SIEGES.)

Aglāïa. One of the Graces. (*See* CHARITES.)

Agnātio. The Latin name for the relationship of real or adoptive descent from one father, which was necessarily expressed by identity of clan-name (*see* NAME, 2.) A brother and sister were *agnāti*, but her children were no longer *agnati* to his. At first *agnati* alone were entitled to inherit property or act as guardians; it was but gradually that the *cognāti* (*q.v.*) came to have a place by their side, till Justinian abolished the right of agnates, and brought that of cognates to complete recognition.

Agōn. The Greek name for a musical (=artistic) or gymnastic contest. The umpires who conducted them, and gave away the prizes, were called *Agōnŏthĕtæ*. (On those who officiated at scenic games in Athens, *see* DRAMA.) At Rome such contests, modelled on those of the Greeks, became frequent before the fall of the Republic; under the Empire they came round at periods of several years, like the great Grecian games. The most famous of all, which held its ground to the end of antiquity, was the *Agon Capitolīnus*, founded by Domitian in 86 A.D., and recurring every four years. He had an Odēum (*q.v.*) built for the musical performances, and a Stădiŏn for the athletic combats, both in the Campus Martius. Another great *Agon* was held in 248 A.D. in honour of the city having stood for a thousand years.

Agōnŏthĕtēs. *See* AGON.

Agōra (=assembly). The Greek name for the market-place, a consecrated open space, which in coast towns usually lay on the

seaside, in inland towns at the foot of the castle hill. As the centre of the city life, commercial, political, and religious, it was adorned with temples, statues, and public buildings, and planted with trees, especially planes. When newly built or rebuilt in late times, it was generally square, and surrounded by colonnades. In most towns it was the place for assemblies of the people.

Agŏracrĭtus. A Greek artist of Paros, who lived in the latter half of the 5th century B.C., and was a favourite pupil of Phĭdias. His noblest work was considered to be the statue of Nĕmĕsis, 40 feet in height, which some judges, on account of its excellence, took for a production of the elder artist. In any case it was said that Phidias had allowed the name of Agoracritus to be inscribed on several of his works.

Agŏrānŏmus (=market-master). In many Greek towns a magistrate somewhat resembling the Roman ædile. At Athens ten *agorănŏmi* were chosen by lot every year, five for the city, and five for the port of Piræus. They looked especially after the retail trade, gave strangers leave to engage in it, tested weights and measures, as well as the quality of goods, confiscating and destroying what was spoilt; they settled disputes between buyers and sellers on the spot, or, if a suit at law was necessary, presided over it [Aristotle's *Const. of Athens*, c. 51].

Agraulŏs. Daughter of Cecrops (*q.v.*).

Agriculture. (1) Agriculture was in *Greece* a leading industry, at least as early as Homer. The soil was stubborn, fertile plains being comparatively few, and mountains and rocky ground preponderating. But, favoured by a genial climate, agriculture was carried on almost everywhere with a zeal to which the wants of a dense population added their stimulus. That it was regarded as the very groundwork of social life is shown by the fact that its guardian goddess Dēmētēr (Lat. Cĕrĕs) presided also over wedlock and law. It was looked upon as the most legitimate way of earning a livelihood. It was carried to the highest pitch in the Peloponnēsus, where every scrap of cultivable soil was made to yield its crop, as may be seen to this day by the artificial terraces that scarp every mountain-slope. Much care was bestowed on irrigation. Scarcity of water was supplemented by artificial means; provision was made against irregular bursts of mountain torrents by embanking and regulating the natural outlets, while moist lands were channelled and stagnant waters drained. Water was distributed everywhere by ditches and canals, under the supervision of State officials; and laws of ancient date guarded against the unfair use of a water-course to a neighbour's damage.

The land was mainly cultivated by slaves and serfs, though field-labour was not deemed dishonourable to the freeman, except where law and custom forbade his engaging in any sort of handicraft, as at Sparta. In some countries, especially Arcadia, the old-world plan of every man tilling his field with his own hand remained in force to the latest times; and even eminent statesmen like Philopœmēn would not give it up. Four kinds of grain were chiefly grown: wheat, barley, and two kinds of spelt, to all of which the climate allowed two sowings in the year, beside millet, sesame, various leguminous plants, and several sorts of herbage for fodder. With no less diligence was Greek husbandry applied to gardening, especially to the cultivation of the vine. This, while steadily pursued on the mainland, was developed to an extraordinary extent in the islands, most of which, owing to their mountainous character, did not afford their inhabitants sufficient arable soil. In olive-culture no part of Greece competed with Attica, which also produced the best figs, the fruit most widely cultivated. Kitchen-gardening was practised on the largest scale in Bœotia. Considering the enormous consumption of flowers in wreaths, the rearing of them, especially of the rose, lily, narcissus, and violet, must have been a lucrative business, at least in the neighbourhood of great towns. Meadow-farming was of next to no importance, few districts having a soil adapted for it, and such meadows as there were being used for pasture rather than haymaking.

(2) In *Italy*. In Italy also the existence of the community was regarded as based upon agriculture. This is proved by the practice of marking the site of the future walls of a new town by a furrow drawn with the plough. At Rome especially, the body of irremovable peasantry long formed the core of the commonwealth. In political life the free peasant was the only factor held in account, and accordingly in war the object was to increase the number of free peasants by planting them out on as much of borderland as could be wrested from the enemy. In early times agriculture was thought the only respectable calling in which a Roman citizen could engage; and

manual labour on the land was held in unqualified esteem and as bringing no disgrace even upon persons in high place.

Husbandry was mainly directed to the raising of grain, the ordinary cereal being at first spelt, till, in the 5th century B.C., wheat began to take a place beside it. They also cultivated barley, millet, and leguminous plants, as well as turnips, greens, and herbs for fodder. On irrigation and drainage the Italians bestowed much pains. They had no lack of grass-lands, either for pasture or haymaking; and from an early time these were artificially watered. The cultivation of the vine and olive extended as that of grains declined (see below); so did the growth of orchard-fruit, which, under the late Republic and the early Empire, received a vast expansion both from the improvement of native kinds and the introduction and naturalization of many foreign fruits. In earlier times the prime favourite among fruit trees had been, as in Greece, the nutritious fig. Agriculture proper was ruined by the acquisition of the first extra-Italian possessions, Sicily and Sardinia; for the corn supplied by the provincials as tribute in kind began to be used, not only in provisioning the armies, but in feeding the urban population. (*See* ANNONA.) As the State, to humour the rabble of Rome, sold this corn at the lowest possible prices, sometimes even below its value, the growth of cereals ceased to be profitable; farmers kept it down to a minimum, and took to cattle-breeding or raising wine and oil. These branches of industry not only flourished in the face of competition, but with judicious management were highly remunerative. The death-blow was given to the Italian peasantry by the increasing employment of slaves and the absorption of small farms in large estates (*see* LATIFUNDIUM). On these, besides the growth of wine, oil, and fruit, the breeding of birds, game, and cattle was carried on, as well as woodcraft, and special industries, pottery, charcoal-burning, and others.

Farming implements, in addition to the plough (*q.v.*) usually drawn by oxen, which was much the same among Greeks and Romans, and always very imperfect, included a great variety of spades, hoes, and mattocks, and among Romans the harrow, the use of which among the Greeks is doubted. The season for sowing all cereals was usually autumn. At harvest the stalks were cut with the sickle about half-way down, and the rest left standing as stubble,

to be either burnt or utilized for manure.
The process of threshing (*q.v.*) was very
defective. (For ancient works on husbandry, *see* GEOPONICI.)

Agrimensōrēs. The Latin name for land-
surveyors, otherwise called *grōmătĭci*, from
grōma, their measuring instrument. This
consisted of two dioptric rods crossing each
other at right angles and fastened on an
iron stand so as to turn horizontally; on
the four arms stood four upright *dioptrœ*,
with threads stretched across the holes, and
in taking observations the threads of two
opposite *dioptrœ* had to cover each other.
The measuring was done on the same principle as the marking-out of a *templum* by
the Augurs (*q.v.*), viz. by drawing in the
centre of the piece of land two lines intersecting at right angles, one from north to
south (*cardo maxĭmus*), the other from
east to west (*dĕcŭmānus maximus*) ; the
further division of the ground was effected
by parallels to these lines (*lĭmĭtēs*). It
was not until the imperial period that land-
surveying became a separate profession.
Then surveyors were prepared in special
schools and appointed by the State, both
for quarter-master's duty in camp and for
measurements under Government; they
decided as judges in fixing boundaries,
and were consulted as specialists in disputes affecting land. Thus a literature
arose, half mathematical, half legal, the
remains of which extend over the first six
centuries A.D. The earliest of these *gro-
matici*, or writers on land-measurement, is
Frontīnus (*q.v.*), from whose work, written
from 81–96 A.D., and dealing more with the
legal side of the subject, extracts are preserved in the commentary of Aggēnus
Urbĭcus. Hygīnus, Balbus, and probably
Sĭcŭlus Flaccus, flourished in the time of
Trajan; later still, Nipsus, Innocentius, and
Aggenus.

Agrippa (*Marcus Vipsānius*). Born B.C.
63, died B.C. 12. He was the friend, son-in-
law, general, and minister of Augustus. He
was also a speaker and writer of some repute. Under his supervision was carried
out the great survey of the Roman empire
which Cæsar had begun in 44 B.C. With
the help of the materials thus obtained he
constructed a circular Map of the World.
About B.C. 7, Augustus had it engraved on a
large scale in marble, and set up for public
use in the colonnade built by Agrippa's
sister Polla (*portĭcus Pollœ*). It may be
regarded as the source and model of all
succeeding aids to geography, especially

the Itineraries (*q.v.*) and the Peutinger
Table. A book on the results of the survey, which Agrippa had begun writing,

* COIN OF AGRIPPA'S THIRD CONSULSHIP, B.C. 27.
(Berlin Museum.)
Obv. Head of Agrippa, wearing the *corona classica.*
Rev. Neptune with Dolphin and Trident.
S C=Senatus consulto.

was continued and published, by order of
Augustus, under the title of *Chōrogrăphia.*

Agyieus. A title of Apollo (*q.v.*) as god
of streets and highways.

Aiās (Lat. *Aiax*). (1) Son of the Locrian
king Oïleus, hence called the Locrian or
Lesser Aias in contrast to the Telamōnian.
In forty ships he led the Locrians to Troy,
where, notwithstanding his small stature
and light equipment, he distinguished himself beside his gigantic namesake, especially
in the battle by the ships and that over the
body of Patroclus. He was renowned for
hurling the spear, and as the swiftest
runner next to Achilles. On his voyage home,
to appease the anger of Athēna, he suffered
shipwreck on the Gyræan rocks off the
island of Mỹcŏnŏs or (according to another
story) on the southernmost point of Eubœa.
Poseidōn indeed rescued him on the rocks;
but when he boasted of having escaped
against the will of the gods, the sea-king
with his trident smote off the rock on which
he sat, and he sank in the waves. Later
accounts say that the goddess's anger fell
upon him because, at the taking of Troy,
when Cassandra had taken refuge at her
altar ànd embraced her image, he tore her
away by force, so that the statue fell.
Though Agamemnon took the maiden from
him, the Greeks left the outrage on the
goddess unpunished, and on their way home
she wreaked her wrath on the whole fleet.
He, like other heroes, was said to be still
living with Achilles in the island of Leucē.
The Locrians worshipped him as a hero,
and always left a vacant place for him in
the line of battle.

(2) Son of Tĕlămōn of Sălămis, and half-
brother of Teucer; called the Great Aias,
because he stood head and shoulders higher

than the other Greek heroes. He brings twelve ships to Troy, where he proves himself second only to Achilles in strength and bravery; and while that hero holds aloof from the fight, he is the mainstay of the Achæans, especially when the Trojans have taken their camp by storm and are pushing the battle to their ships. In the struggle over the corpse of Patroclus, he and his namesake the son of Oïleus cover Menelāüs and Merīŏnēs while they carry off their fallen comrade. When Thĕtis offered the arms and armour of Achilles as a prize for the worthiest, they were adjudged, not to Aias, but to his only competitor Odysseus. Trojan captives bore witness that the cunning of Odysseus had done them more harm than the valour of Achilles. Aias thereupon, according to the post-Homeric legend, killed himself in anger, a feeling he still cherished against Odysseus even in the lower world. The later legend relates that he was driven mad by the slight, mistook the flocks in the camp for his adversaries, and slaughtered them, and on coming to his senses again, felt so mortified that he fell on his sword, the gift of Hector after the duel between them. Out of his blood sprang the purple lily, on whose petals could be traced the first letters of his name, Ai, Ai. His monument stood on the Rhœtēan promontory, where he had encamped before Troy, and upon which the waves washed the coveted arms of Achilles after the shipwreck of Odysseus. As the national hero of Salamis, he had a temple and statue there, and a yearly festival, the Aianteia ; and he was worshipped at Athens, where the tribe Aiantis was named after him. He too was supposed to linger with Achilles in the island of Leucē. By Tecmēssa, daughter of the Phrygian king Teuthrās, whom he had captured in one of the raids from before Troy, he had a son Eurȳsăcēs, who is said to have removed from Salamis to Attica with his son or brother Philæus, and founded flourishing families, which produced many famous men, for instance Miltĭădēs, Cīmōn, Alcibĭădēs, and the historian Thucȳdĭdēs.

Aīdēs (Aïdōneus). See HADES.

Ajax. See AIAS.

Ala. The Latin name for (1) a wing in the line of battle. Till the extension of the citizenship to the Italian allies, the wings consisted of their contingents, viz. 10,000 foot and 1,800 horse to every consular army of two legions. Thus āla came to mean the allied contingent that composed a wing (see COHORT and LEGION). But it

meant more especially, in contrast to the cohorts that made up the infantry of the allies, the cavalry of the contingent, viz. on an average 300 men (5 turmæ, of 60 each). During the imperial period, when all the cavalry was raised in the provinces, the name of ala was given to a cavalry division of 500 or else 1,000 men, the one divided into 16, the other into 24 turmæ. The alæ were commanded by præfecti ĕquĭtum.

(2) A back room in a Roman house. See HOUSE.

Alabastrŏn. See VESSELS.

Alastŏr. The Greek term for an avenging dæmon, who dogs the footsteps of criminals, visiting the sins of fathers on their offspring.

Album. The Latin word for a board chalked or painted white, on which matters of public interest were notified in black writing. In this way were published the yearly records of the pontifex (see ANNALES), the edicts of prætors (q.v.), the roll of senators, the lists of jurors, etc.

Alcæus (Gr. Alkaĭŏs). A famous lyric poet of Mȳtĭlēnē in Lesbos, an elder contemporary of Sappho. Towards the end of the 7th century B.C., as the scion of a noble house, he headed the aristocratic party in their contests with the tyrants of his native town, Myrsĭlus, Melanchrūs, and others. Banished from home, he went on romantic expeditions as far as Egypt. When the tyrants were put down, and his former comrade, the wise Pittăcus, was called by the people to rule the State, he took up arms against him also as a tyrant in disguise; but attempting to force his return home, he fell into the power of his opponent, who generously forgave him. Of his further life nothing is known. His poems in the Æolic dialect, arranged in ten books by the Alexandrians, consisted of hymns, political songs (which formed the bulk of the collection), drinking songs, and love songs, of which we have but a few miserable fragments. In the opinion of the ancients, his poems were well constructed, while their tone tallied with the lofty passion and manly vigour of his character. The alcāïc strophe, so much used by his admirer and not unworthy imitator, Horace, is named after him. [For a relief representing Alcæus and Sappho, see SAPPHO.]

Alcămĕnēs (Gr. Alkămĕnēs). A Greek artist of Athens or Lemnos, and a pupil of Phĭdias, who flourished towards the end of the 5th century B.C. Following his master's ideal tendency, he devoted himself mainly to religious subjects, working like him in various materials, gold and ivory, bronze and marble. His statue of the winner in the Pentathlŏn was stamped as classic by the epithet of *Enkrīnŏmĕnos*, as the *Dŏrўphŏrŏs* of Polyclītus was by that of *Kānōn*. About 436 B.C. he was employed with Phidias in decorating the temple of Zeus at Olympia. The marble groups of the battle of Centaurs and Lăpīthæ in its western pediment are his work. Of these considerable remains have been brought to light by the recent German excavations. (*See* OLYMPIAN GAMES, fig. 2.)

Alcathŏüs (Gr. *Alkăthŏŏs*). The son of Pelops and Hippodameia. He slew the lion of Cithærŏn, which had torn to pieces Euippus, the son of Mĕgăreus. Thus he won the daughter of Megareus, Euæchma, and the sovereignty of Mĕgăra. With Apollo for his friend and helper, he rebuilt the city walls, and reared one of the two castles, Alcăthŏĕ, with temples to Artĕmis and Apollo. A singing stone in the castle was shown as the one on which the god laid down his lyre when at work. Alcathous' eldest son, Īschĕpŏlis, fell in the Calydonian hunt; the second, Callĭpŏlis, running in with the news to his father when sacrificing to Apollo, scattered the altar fire, and Alcathous struck him dead with a firebrand for the supposed sacrilege. By his daughters Automedūsa and Peribœa, the wives of Iphĭclēs and Tĕlămōn, he was grandfather to Iolāüs and Aias (Ajax).

Alcestis (Gr. *Alkēstis*). Daughter of Pĕliās, renowned for her tender love for her husband Admētus, and her voluntary death on his behalf. (*See* ADMETUS.)

Alcĭdămās (Gr. *Alkĭdămās*). A Greek rhetorician of Elæa in Æōlis, pupil and successor of Gorgias, a contemporary and opponent of Isocrătēs. Two declamations, bearing his name, have come down to us, one an imaginary indictment of Palamēdēs by Odysseus, the other a speech on the Sophists; but the latter only can with any probability be attributed to him. It is a cleverly written argument, intended to show that the culmination of rhetorical training consists in the power of speaking extempore on any subject from mere notes of the arrangement; nŏt the practice of carefully writing out speeches, and then learning them by heart for public delivery.

Alcīdes (Gr. *Alkīdēs*). A surname of Hērăclēs (*q.v.*).

Alcĭnŏüs (Gr. *Alkĭnŏŏs*). King of the Phæacians (*q.v.*), with whom Odysseus, and in later legend Jason and Medea, find shelter and aid. (*See* ODYSSEUS and ARGONAUTS.)

Alcĭphrŏn (Gr. *Alkĭphrŏn*). A Greek rhetorician of the 2nd century A.D., author of a collection of 118 fictitious Letters in three books, written in tolerably pure style and tasteful form, profess to be from sailors, peasants, parasites, and *hetæræ*. They are sketches of character, ingeniously conceived and carried out, which give us a vivid picture of the then state of culture, especially at Athens; the letters from *hetæræ* are particularly interesting, as their plots are taken from the New Attic Comedy, especially the lost plays of Menander.

Alcmæŏn (Gr. *Alkmaiōn*), of Argos. Son of Amphiaräüs (*q.v.*) and Eriphŷlē. As his father, in departing on the expedition of the Seven against Thebes, has bound him and his brother Amphĭlŏchus, then mere boys, to avenge him on their faithless mother, Alcmæon refuses to take part in the second expedition, that of the Epĭgŏni (*q.v.*), till he has first fulfilled that filial duty; nevertheless hiś mother, bribed by Thersander with the *garment of Harmŏnia*, persuades him to go. The real leader at the siege of Thebes, he slays the Theban king, Laŏdămās, and is the first to enter the conquered city. On returning home, he, at the bidding of the Delphian Apollo, avenges his father by slaying his mother, with, or according to some accounts, without, his brother's help; but immediately, like Orestēs, he is set upon by the Erīnўĕs, and wanders distracted, seeking purification and a new home. Phegeus, of the Arcadian Psŏphis, half purifies him of his guilt, and gives him his daughter Arsĭnŏĕ or Alphesibœa to wife, to whom he presents the *jewels of Harmonia*, which he has brought from Argos. But soon the crops fail in the land, and he falls into his distemper again, till, after many wanderings, he arrives at the mouth of the Achelŏüs, and there, in an island that has floated up, he finds the country promised by the god, which had not existed at the time of his dying mother's curse, and so he is completely cured. He marries Achelous' daughter, Callirrhŏĕ, by whom he has two sons, Acarnān and Amphŏtĕrus. Unable to withstand his wife's entreaties that she may have *Harmonia's necklace and robe*, he goes to Phēgeus in Arcadia, and begs those treasures of him, pretending that he will dedicate them at Delphi for the perfect healing of his madness. He obtains them; but Phegeus, on learning the truth, sets his sons to waylay him on his road, and rob him of his treasure and his life; and then Alcmæon's two sons avenge their father's death on these murderers. Alcmæon, like his father, received divine honours after death; he had a sanctuary at Thebes, and at Psophis a consecrated tomb.

Alcmān (Gr. *Alkmān*). The founder of Dorian lyric poetry, a Lydian of Sardēs. He came to Sparta in his youth as a slave, was set free, and seems even to have received the citizenship; he flourished in the latter half of the 7th century B.C. He abandoned the old nŏmic or dithyrambic poetry, written in hexameters, and composed in various metres Hymns, Pæans, Prosōdia, Parthĕnia, Scŏlia, and Erotics, the last of which he was supposed to have invented. His dialect was the Doric, softened by Epic and Æolic forms. Of his six books of poems a few fragments only are preserved; one, a rather long one, was found in Egypt.

Alcmēnē (Gr. *Alkmēnē*). Daughter of Electrȳŏn, wife of Amphĭtrȳŏn (*q.v.*), mother of Herăclēs by Zeus. On her connexion with Rhadamanthys, *see* RHADAMANTHYS. After her son's translation to the gods she fled from the face of Eurystheus to Athens, but went back to Thebes, and died there at a great age. She was worshipped at Thebes, and had an altar in the temple of Heracles at Athens.

Alcȳŏnē (Gr. *Alkȳŏnē*). (1) Daughter of Æŏlus, wife of Ceyx (*q.v.* 2).—(2) One of the Pleiades.

Alcȳŏneus (Gr. *Alkȳŏneus*). Son of Urănus and Gæa, the eldest and mightiest of the giants, who could not be overtaken by death in his own birthplace. Hence, in the war with the giants, Herăclēs had to drag him away from Pallēnē before he could kill him with his arrows. Legend also tells of a giant Alcyoneus who stole the oxen of Hēliŏs from the island of Erytheia, and as Heracles was crossing the Thracian isthmus of Pallene, crushed twelve of his wagons and twenty-five men with a huge piece of rock, which was shown on the spot. When he hurled it at Heracles himself, the hero struck it back with his club, and killed Alcyoneus with the same blow.

Aldobrandini Marriage. *See* PAINTING.

Alēctō. One of the Greek goddesses of vengeance. (*See* ERINYES.)

Alexander (Gr. *Alexandrŏs*). (1) *See* PARIS.

(2) *Alexander Ætōlus* (the Ætolian) of Pleurŏn in Ætolia, lived about 280 B.C. at Alexandria, being employed by Ptolemy in arranging the tragedies and satyric dramas in the Library. He was afterwards at the court of Antĭgŏnus Gonātās in Macedonia. As a writer of tragedies he was reckoned one of the so-called Pleiăd. He also tried his hand at short epics, at epigrams, elegies, and the like, of which some graceful fragments are preserved.

(3) A Greek rhetorician of the 2nd century A.D., son of the rhetorician Numēnĭus. He composed a work on figures of speech, of which one extract and a free Latin version by Aquĭla Rōmānus have survived.

(4) *Alexander of Aphrodīsias* in Caria, about 200 A.D., called *Exēgētēs* for his services in expounding the doctrine of Aristotle, wrote valuable commentaries on several Aristotelian treatises (especially the Metaphysics) as well as original works on Fate and Free-will, on the Soul, and others.

(5) *Alexander of Trallēs* in Lydia, a Greek physician, lived in the 6th century A.D. at Rome, and made a careful collection from older writers on therapeutics, in twelve books.

Alexandra. *See* CASSANDRA.

Alexandrian Period. *See* LITERATURE.

Alexĭkăkŏs (= warding off evil). An epithet of Apollo and Herăclēs.

Alexis. Alexis and Antĭphănēs were the most prolific and important writers of the Middle Attic Comedy. Alexis was born at Thurii, B.C. 392. He attained the age of 106, writing to the last, and is said to have died on the stage with the crown on his head. He was the reputed author of 245 plays, of which numerous extracts are still extant, showing considerable wit and elegance of language. He was uncle to the poet Menander.

Alimentāriī. The Latin name, during the imperial period, for children of needy but free-born parents, who, out of the interest of funds invested for the purpose, received monthly contributions to their support in goods or money up to a certain age (fixed in the case of boys at eighteen, in that of girls at fourteen). This scheme, the object of which was to encourage people to marry, and so to check the alarming decrease of the free population, was started by the Emperor Nerva (A.D. 96–98), and extended by Trajan to the whole of Italy. Succeeding emperors also, down to Alexander Sevērus (222–235), founded such bursaries; and private citizens in Italy and the provinces, as, for instance the younger Pliny, vied with them in their liberality.

Alōădæ or *Alōīdæ*. Sons of Poseidōn by Iphĭmĕdeia, the wife of Alōeus, son of Cănăcē (*see Æolos*, 1) and Poseidon; their names were *Ephialtēs* and *Otus*. They grew every year an ell in breadth and a fathom in length, so that in nine years' time they were thirty-six feet broad and fifty-four feet high. Their strength was such that they chained up the god Arēs and kept him in a brazen cask for thirteen months, till their stepmother Eribœa betrayed his whereabouts to Hermēs, who came by stealth and dragged his disabled brother out of durance. They threatened to storm heaven itself by piling Ossa on Olympus and Pēliŏn on Ossa, and would have done it, says Homer, had not Apollo slain them with his arrows ere their beards were grown. The later legend represents Ephialtes as in love with Hēra, and Otus with Artĕmis. Another myth represents Artemis as slaying them by craft in the island of Naxos. She runs between them in the form of a hind; they hurl their spears, and wound each other fatally. In the later legend they expiate their sins in the lower world by being bound with snakes to a pillar, back to back, while they are incessantly tormented by the screeching of an owl. On the other hand, they were worshipped as heroes in Naxos, and in the Bœotian Ascra were regarded as founders of the city and of the worship of the Muses on Mount Hĕlĭcōn.

Alōpē. Daughter of Cercўōn of Eleusis, and, by Poseidōn, mother of Hippothŏōn (*q.v.*); after whose birth her father was going to kill her, but the god changed her into a fountain.

Alphēus. See ARETHUSA.

Alphēsĭbœa (or *Arsĭnŏë*). Daughter of Phēgeus and first wife of Alcmæōn, whom, though unfaithful, she continued to love, and was angry with her brothers for killing him. Her brothers shut her up in a box, and brought her to Agapēnōr, king of Tĕgĕa, pretending that she had killed her husband. Here she came by her end, having compassed her brothers' death by the hand of Alcmæon's sons.

Altar. Originally a simple elevation above the ground, made of earth, field-stones, or turf; and such altars continued to be used in the country parts of Italy. But altars for constant use, especially in temple service, were, as a rule, of stone, though in exceptional cases they might be made of other materials. Thus, several in Greece

were built out of the ashes of burnt-offerings, as that of Zeus at Olympia. One at Delos was made of goats' horns. Their shape was very various, the four-cornered being the commonest, and the round less usual. A temple usually had two altars: the one used for bloodless offerings standing before the deity's image in the *cella*, and the other for burnt-offerings, opposite. the door in front of the temple. The latter was generally a high altar, standing on a platform which is cut into steps. Being an integral part of the whole set of buildings, its shape and size were regulated by their proportions. Some few of these high altars were of enormous dimensions; the one at Olympia had a platform measuring more than 125 feet round, while the altar itself, which was ascended by steps, was nearly 25 feet high. In Italy as well as Greece, beside the altars attached to temples, there was a vast number in streets and squares, in the courts of houses (*see* cut), in open fields, in sacred groves, and other precincts consecrated to the gods. Some altars, like some temples, were dedicated to more than one deity; we even hear of altars dedicated to all the gods. On altars to heroes, *see* HEROES.

*ROMAN DOMESTIC ALTAR (Berlin Museum.)

Althæa. Daughter of Thestius, wife of Œneus, king of Călўdōn, mother of Tydeus, Meleăger (*q.v.*), and Deïaneira.

Altis. The sacred grove near Olympia (*q.v.*), in which the Olympic Games were celebrated. (*See* OLYMPIA.)

Amalthēa (Gr. *Amaltheia*). A figure in Greek mythology. The name was sometimes applied to a *goat*, which suckled the newborn Zeus in Crete, while bees brought him honey, and which was therefore set among the stars by her nursling; sometimes to a *nymph* who was supposed to possess a miraculous horn, a symbol of plenty, and whose descent was variously given. According to one version she is the daughter of the Cretan king Melisseus, and brings up the infant god on the milk of a goat, while her sister Melissa (a bee) offers him honey. The horn of the goat is given to her by Zeus, with the promise that she shall always find in it whatever she wishes. From her the cornucopia passed into the possession of the river-god Achelöüs, who was glad to exchange it for his own horn, which Heracles had broken off. It is also an attribute of Dionȳsŭs, of Plutus, and other gods of earthly felicity.

Amazons (Gr. *Amăzŏnĕs;* = "breastless"). A mythical nation of women-warriors, whose headquarters are placed by early Greek legend in Themiscȳra, on the Thermōdōn, on the southern shore of the Euxine. In later accounts they also appear on the Caucasus and on the Don, where the nation called Saurŏmătæ was supposed to have sprung from their union with the Scythians. They suffered no men among them; the sons born of their intercourse with neighbouring nations they either killed or sent back to their fathers; the girls they brought up to be warriors, burning the right breast off for the better handling of the bow. Their chief deities were said to be Arēs and the Taurian Artĕmis. Even in Homer they are represented as making long marches into Asiatic territory; an army of them invading Lycia is cut to pieces by Bellĕrŏphōn; Priam, then in his youth, hastens to help the Phrygians against them. They gained a firm footing in Greek song and story through Arctīnus of Milētus, in whose poem their queen Penthesileia, daughter of Ares, as Priam's ally, presses hard on the Greeks, till she is slain by Achilles. After that they became a favourite subject with poets and artists, and a new crop of fable sprang up: Hērăclēs wars against them, to win the girdle of their queen, Hippŏlȳtē; Theseus carries off her sister Antĭŏpē, they in revenge burst into Attica, encamp on the Areopăgus of Athens, and are pacified by Antiope's mediation, or, according to an-

AMAZON AFTER POLYCLITUS.
(Berlin Museum.)

other version, beaten in a great battle. Grave-mounds supposed to cover the bones of Amazons were shown near Mĕgăra, and in Eubœa and Thessaly. In works of art the Amazons were represented as martial maids, though always with two breasts, and usually on horseback; sometimes in Scythian dress (a tight fur tunic, with a cloak of many folds over it, and a kind of Phrygian cap), sometimes in Grecian (a Dorian tunic tucked up and the right shoulder bare), armed with a half-moon shield, two-edged axe, spear, bow, and quiver, etc. The most famous statues of them in antiquity were those by Phīdias, Polyclītus, and Crēsĭlās, to one or other of which, as types, existing specimens are traceable. (*See* cut.) Among the surviving sculptures representing an Amazonian contest should be especially mentioned the reliefs from the frieze of Apollo's temple at Bassæ in Arcadia (in the British Museum, London).

Ambarvālia. The Italian festival of blessing the fields, which was kept at Rome on May 29th. The country people walked in solemn procession three times round their fields in the wake of the *su-ove-taur-īlia,* i.e. a hog, ram, and bull, which were sacrificed after a prayer originally addressed to Mars, afterwards usually to Cĕrēs and other deities of agriculture, that the fruits of the fields might thrive. *Comp.* ARVAL BROTHERS.

Ambĭtus (lit., a going round) meant at Rome the candidature for a public office, because going round among the citizens was originally the principal means of winning their favour. When unlawful means began to be used, and bribery in every form was organized into a system, the word came to mean obtaining of office by illegal means. To check the growing evil, laws were passed at an early period, and from time to time made more severe. The penalties, which ranged at different times from fines and inadmissibility to office to banishment for ten years and even for life, produced no lasting effect. At last a special standing criminal court was established for trying such cases, till under the Empire recourse was had to a radical change in the mode of election.

Ambrŏsia. Anything that confers or preserves immortality: (1) the food of the gods (as nectar was their drink), which doves, according to Homer, bring daily to Zeus from the far west: (2) the anointing oil of the gods, which preserves even dead men from decay: (3) the food of the gods' horses.

Amburbium. The Latin name for a solemn procession of the people, with the various orders of priesthood led by the pontifex three times round the boundaries of Rome. It was only resorted to at a time of great distress, and the animals destined to make atonement, *viz.* a hog, a ram, and a bull (the so called *suŏvetaurīlia*, see AMBARVALIA), were sacrificed with special prayers outside the city.

Ameipsiãs. A Greek poet of the old comedy, contemporary with Aristŏphănēs, whom he twice overcame. Of his plays only slight fragments remain.

Ammiãnus Marcellīnus. The last Roman historian of any importance, born at Antioch, in Syria, about 330 A.D., of noble Grecian descent. After receiving a careful education, he early entered military service, and fought under Julian against the Alemanni and Persians. In the evening of his days he retired to Rome, and about 390 began his Latin history of the emperors (*Rērum Gestārum Libri*), from Nerva, A.D. 96, to the death of Valens, in thirty-one books. Of these there only remain books xiv.-xxxi., including the period from 353 to 378 A.D., which he relates for the most part as an eye-witness. As his work may be regarded as a continuation of Tacĭtus, he seems, on the whole, to have taken that writer for his model. He resembles Tacitus in judgment, political acuteness, and love of truth. A heathen himself, he is nevertheless fair to the Christians. But he is far inferior in literary culture, though he loves to display his knowledge, especially in describing nations and countries. Latin was a foreign language to him; hence a crudeness and clumsiness of expression, which is made even more repellent by affectation, bombast, and bewildering ornamental imagery.

Ammon (or *Hammon;* Egyptian *Amun*, the hidden or veiled one). A god native to Libya and Upper Egypt. He was represented sometimes in the shape of a ram with enormous curving horns, sometimes in that of a ram-headed man, sometimes as a perfect man standing up or sitting on a throne. On his head was the royal emblems, with two high feathers standing up, the symbols of sovereignty over the upper and under worlds; in his hands were the sceptre and the sign of life. In works of art his figure is coloured blue. Beside him stands the goddess *Muth* (the "mother," the "queen of darkness," as the inscriptions call her), wearing the crown of Upper Egypt or the vulture-skin (*see* cut). His chief temple, with a far-famed oracle, stood in an oasis of the Libyan desert, twelve days' journey from Memphis. Between this oracle and that of Zeus at Dodōna a connexion is said to have existed from very ancient times, so that the Greeks early identified the Egyptian god with their own Zeus, as the Romans did afterwards with their Jupiter; and his worship found an entrance at several places in Greece, at Sparta, Thebes, and also Athens, whence festal embassies were regularly sent to the Libyan sanctuary (*see* THEORIA). When the oracle was consulted by visitors, the god's symbol, made of emerald and other stones, was carried round by women and girls, to the sound of hymns, on a golden ship hung round with votive cups of silver. His replies were given in tremulous shocks communicated to the bearers, which were interpreted by a priest.

AMMON AND MUTH.

Amor. The god of love. *See* EROS.

Ampēlius (*Lucius*). A Roman writer not earlier than the 2nd century A.D. He was the author of a notebook, *Liber Memoriãlis*, which contains a scanty collection of astronomical, geographical, and historical jottings. Paltry as the book is, a statement in its chapter on the wonders of the world has mainly led to the discovery (in 1878) of the magnificent sculptures of Pergămum, now at Berlin.

Amphĭărăüs, of Argos, the son of Oïclēs and Hypermnēstra, great-grandson of the seer, Mĕlampus. In Homer he is a favourite of Zeus and Apollo, alike distinguished as a seer and a hero, who takes part in the Calydonian boar-hunt, in the voyage of the

Argonauts, and the expedition of the Seven against Thebes. Reconciled to Adrastus after a quarrel, and wedded to his sister Eriphȳlē, he agrees that any future differences between them shall be settled by her. She, bribed by Polyneicēs with the fatal necklace of his ancestress Harmŏnia, insists on her husband joining the war against Thebes, though he foresees that it will end fatally for him, and in departing charges his youthful sons Alcmæon and Amphilŏchus (*q.v.*) to avenge his coming death. His wise warnings are unheeded by the other princes; his justice and prudence even bring him into open strife with the savage Tydeus; yet in the fatal closing contest he loyally avenges his death on the Theban Melanippus. In the flight, just as the spear of Periclȳmĕnus is descending on him, Zeus interposed to save the pious prophet and make him immortal by cleaving the earth open with his thunderbolt, and bidding it swallow up Amphiaraus, together with his trusty charioteer Batōn, like himself a descendant of Melampus. From that time forth Amphiaraus was worshipped in various places as an oracular god, especially at Orōpus on the frontier of Attica and Bœotia, where he had a temple and a famous oracle for the interpretation of dreams, and where games were celebrated in honour of him.

Amphidrŏmia. At Athens, a family festival, at which newborn infants received religious consecration. *See* EDUCATION.

Amphictyons (Gr. *Amphiktȳŏnĕs*). This Greek word meant literally "dwellers around," but in a special sense was applied to populations which at stated times met at the same sanctuary to keep a festival in common, and to transact common business. The most famous and extensive union of the kind was that called *par excellence* the *Amphictyonic League*, whose common sanctuaries were the temple of Pythian Apollo at Delphi, and the temple of Demētēr (Cĕrēs) at Anthēla, near Pȳlæ or Thermŏpȳlæ. After Pylæ the assembly was named the *Pylœan*, even when it met at Delphi, and the deputies of the league *pylăgŏræ*. The league was supposed to be very ancient, as old even as the name of Hellēnĕs; for its founder was said to be *Amphictyōn*, the son of Deucăliōn, and brother of Hellēn, the common ancestor of all Hellenes. It included twelve populations: Malians, Phthians, Æniānĕs or Œtœans, Dŏlŏpĕs, Magnetians, Perrhœbians, Thessalians, Locrians, Dorians, Phocians, Bœotians, and Ionians, together with the colonies of each. Though in later times their extent and power were very unequal, yet in point of law they all had equal rights. Beside protecting and preserving those two sanctuaries, and celebrating from the year 586 B.C. onwards, the Pythian Games, the league was bound to maintain certain principles of international right, which forbade them, for instance, ever to destroy utterly any city of the league, or to cut off its water, even in time of war. To the assemblies, which met every spring and autumn, each nation sent two *hieromnēmŏnĕs* (=wardens of holy things) and several *pylagoræ*. The latter took part in the debates, but only the former had the right of voting. When a nation included several states, these took by turns the privilege of sending deputies. But the stronger states, such as the Ionian Athens or the Dorian Sparta were probably allowed to take their turn oftener than the rest, or even to send to every assembly. When violations of the sanctuaries or of popular right took place, the assembly could inflict fines or even expulsion; and a state that would not submit to the punishment had a "holy war" declared against it. By such a war the Phocians were expelled B.C. 346, and their two votes given to the Macedonians; but the expulsion of the former was withdrawn because of the glorious part they took in defending the Delphian temple when threatened by the Gauls in 279 B.C., and at the same time the Ætolian community which had already made itself master of the sanctuary, was acknowledged as a new member of the league. In 191 B.C. the number of members amounted to seventeen, who nevertheless had only twenty-four votes, seven having two votes each, the rest only one. Under the Roman rule, the league continued to exist; but its action was now limited to the care of the Delphian temple. It was reorganized by Augustus, who incorporated the Malians, Magnetians, Ænianes, and Pythians with the Thessalians, and substituted for the extinct Dolopes the city of Nicŏpŏlis in Acarnania, which he had founded after the battle of Actium. The last notice we find of the league is in the 2nd century A.D.

Amphilŏchus. Son of Amphiaräus and Eriphȳlē, Alcmæon's brother. He was a seer, and according to some took part in the war of the Epĭgŏni and the murder of his mother. He was said to have founded the Amphilochian Argos (near Neokhori) in

Acarnania. Later legend represents him as taking part in the Trojan War, and on the fall of Troy going to Cilicia with Mopsus (q.v.), and there founding a famous oracle at Mallus. At last the two killed each other while fighting for the possession of it.

Amphīōn and Zēthus. The Bœotian Dioscūri, twin sons of Antĭŏpē (q.v.) by Zeus, though the later legend makes Zethus a son of Epōpeus. Exposed on Mount Cithærōn, they are found and brought up by a shepherd ; when grown up, they recognise their

* ZETHUS AND AMPHION.
(Rome, Spada Palace.)

mother, who has fled from imprisonment at Thebes, where she has been ill-treated by Dircē, the wife of Lycus who governs Thebes as guardian to Lāïus. They avenge their mother by tying her tormentress to the horns of a bull, which drags her to death. They then cast her corpse into a spring near Thebes, which takes from her the name of Dirce. Seizing the sovereignty by slaying Lycus, or, according to another account, having it given up to them by Lycus at the bidding of Hermēs, they

fortify Thebes with walls and towers, because (says Homer), despite their strength, they could no more inhabit the wide town without a wall to defend it. Zethus brings up the stones with his strong arm, while Amphion, a harper of more than mortal skill, fits them together by the music of his lyre. Zethus marries Thēbē, the daughter of Asōpus, or, according to another account, Aëdōn, daughter of Pandareos (q.v.); Amphion is the luckless husband of Niŏbē, and after seeing the ruin of his family, is said to have killed himself, and to have been been buried in one grave with his brother at Thebes. The punishment of Dirce is the subject of the marble group by Apollonius and Tauriscus, known as the *Farnese Bull* (now at Naples). (For cut, see DIRCE, and comp. SCULPTURE.)

[In the *Antiope* of Eurĭpĭdēs, and elsewhere, the two brothers were sharply contrasted with one another, Zethus being the rude and strong and active huntsman, Amphion the gentle and contemplative musician. This contrast is exemplified in works of art, especially in the fine relief in the Spada Palace. (*See* cut)].

Amphiprostȳlus. A temple with an open colonnade at each end. *See* TEMPLES.

Amphĭthălămŏs. A bedroom in a Greek dwelling-house. *See* HOUSE.

Amphitheātrŏn. A circular theatre, *i.e.* a building in which the space for spectators entirely surrounds that where the spectacle is exhibited. These buildings, designed for combats of gladiators and wild beasts (*venatiōnēs*), were first erected in Italy, but in Campania sooner than at Rome. The first known at Rome were temporary wooden structures, like that of Scribonius Curio, who in B.C. 50 made an amphitheatre out of two revolving theatres by joining them back to back, or that of Cæsar in 46. The first stone amphitheatre, erected by Statilius Taurus in B.C. 29, was burnt down in the fire of Nero, who then built a wooden one again. A second one of stone was begun by Vespasian, consecrated by Titus, A.D. 80, and finished by Domitian (all three of the Flavian gens). The ruins of this *Amphitheatrum Flavium*, which was 158 feet high, and accommodated 87,000 spectators, are the famous *Colossēum*. In the provinces too the large towns had their amphitheatres, of which the best preserved are those of Verona and Capua in Italy, Arles and Nîmes in France. Of this last our first two illustrations give the elevation and the ground-plan

An amphitheatre was usually an oval building, surrounding an *arēna* of like shape, which sometimes, as at Rome and Capua, was a plank floor resting on deep underground walls, the spaces underneath containing cages and machinery for transformations. The exterior was formed of several arcades, one above the other, the lowest one admitting to a corridor, which ran round the building, and out of which staircases led up to the various rows of seats. In the Colosseum this first arcade is adorned with Doric, the second with Ionic, the third with Corinthian "engaged" columns; the fourth is a wall decorated

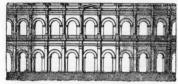

(1) THE AMPHITHEATRE AT NÎMES.
(External elevation.)

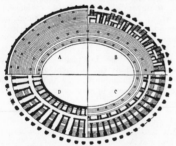

(2) THE AMPHITHEATRE AT NÎMES.
Ground plan in four quarters.
A. Bird's eye view of seats rising in tiers to highest part of external inclosure.
B. Plan of highest storey, exposed by removal of highest tiers of seats.
C. Plan of intermediate storey, exposed by removal of highest and intermediate tiers.
D. True ground plan, or plan of lowest storey.

with Corinthian pilasters, and pierced with windows (*see* ARCHITECTURE, figs. 8–10).

Immediately round the arena ran a high, massive wall, with vaults for the animals and for other purposes. On it rested the *pŏdium*, protected by its height and by special contrivances from the wild beasts when fighting ; here were the seats of honour, *e.g.* at Rome, those of the imperial family, the officers of state, and the Vestal Virgins. Above the *podium* rose the seats

of other spectators in concentric rows, the lowest ones being for senators and magistrates, the next for knights, and the rest for citizens. Women sat in the highest part of the building, under a colonnade, parts of which were portioned off for the common people. The whole space for seats could be sheltered from sun and rain by an awning supported on masts, which were let into corbels of stone that jutted out of the upper circumference. The arena could also be laid under water for the exhibition of sea-fights, the so-called *naumăchiæ* (*q.v.*).

Amphĭtrītē, daughter of Nereus and Doris, is the wife of Poseidŏn and queen of the sea. Poseidon saw her dancing with the Nereids on the island of Naxos, and carried her off. According to another account she fled from him to Atlas, when the god's dolphin spied her out and brought her to him. In Homer she is not yet called Poseidon's wife, but a sea-goddess, who beats the billows against the rocks, and has the creatures of the deep in her keeping. Her son is the sea-god Trītōn. She had no separate worship. She is often represented with a net confining her hair, with crabs' claws on the crown of her head, being carried by Tritons, or by dolphins and other marine animals, or drawn by them in a chariot of shells. As the Romans identified Poseidon with their Neptune, so they did Amphitrite with Salacia, a goddess of the salt waves.

Amphĭtrўŏn. Son of Alcæus, grandson of Perseus, and king of Tīryns. His father's brother, Elektrўŏn, king of Mycēnæ, had occasion to go out on a war of vengeance against Pterelāüs, king of the Taphians and Teleboans in Acarnania and the neighbouring isles, whose sons had carried off his cattle, and have slain his own sons, all but young Licymnius. He left Amphitryon in charge of his kingdom, and betrothed to him his daughter Alcmēnē. On his return Amphitryon killed him, in quarrel or by accident, and, driven away by another uncle, Sthĕnĕlus, fled with his betrothed and her brother Licymnius to Creŏn, king of Thebes, a brother of his mother Hippŏnŏmē, who purged him of blood-guilt, and promised, if he would first kill the Taumessian fox, to help him against Pterelaus ; for Alcmene would not wed him till her brethren were avenged. Having rendered the fox harmless with the help of Cĕphălus (*q.v.*) he marched, accompanied by Creon, Cephalus, and other heroes, against the

Teleboans, and conquered their country. Pterilaus' daughter Comætho had first killed her father by plucking out the golden hair, to whose continual possession was attached the boon of immortality bestowed on him by Poseidon. He slew the traitress, and, handing over the Taphian kingdom to Cephalus, he returned to Thebes and married Alcmene. She gave birth to twins; Iphicles by him, and Heracles by Zeus. At last he falls in the war with Ergīnus (*q.v.*), the Minyan king of Orchŏmĕnus.

Amphŏra, Lat. (Gr. *Amphŏreus*). A two-handled, big-bellied vessel, usually of clay, with a longish or shortish neck, and a mouth proportioned to the size, sometimes resting firmly on a foot, but often ending in a blunt point, so that in the store-room it had to lean against the wall, or be sunk in sand, and when brought out for use, to be put in a basket, wine-cooler, or hollow stand. (*See* VESSELS, fig. 2, *a* and *b*). It served to keep oil, honey, and more especially the wine drawn off from the big fermenting vats. It was fastened with a clay stopper, plastered over with pitch, loam, or gypsum, and had a ticket stating the kind, the year, and the quantity of the wine it contained. The Greek *amphoreus* was a large liquid measure, holding nearly 9 gallons (*see* METRETES), the Roman measure called *amphora* held 6 gallons and 7 pints.

Amphŏtĕrus. *See* ACARNAN.

Ampliātio. The Latin term for a delay of verdict pending the production of further evidence in a case not clear to the judges. *Comp.* COMPERENDINATIO.

Ampulla. *See* VESSELS.

Amўcus. Son of Poseidōn; a gigantic king of the Bebrycians on the Bithynian coast, who forced every stranger that landed there to box with him. When the Argonauts wished to draw water from a spring in his country, he forbade them, but was conquered and killed in a match with Polydeucēs (Pollux).

Amўmōnē. A daughter of Dănăus (*q.v.*), and mother of Nauplius by Poseidōn.

Anacrĕōn. A Greek lyric poet, born about 550 B.C. at Teos, an Ionian town of Asia, whose inhabitants, to escape the threatened yoke of Persia, migrated to Abdēra in Thrace B.C. 540. From Abdera Anacreon went to the tyrant Polycrătēs, of Samos, after whose death (B.C. 522) he removed to Athens on the invitation of Hipparchus, and lived there, till the fall of the Peisistrătīdæ, on friendly terms with his fellow

poet Simōnīdēs and Xanthippus, the father of Perīclēs. He is said to have died at Abdera, in his eighty-sixth year, choked by the stone of a dried grape. A statue of him stood in the Acrŏpŏlis at Athens in the guise of an aged minstrel inspired by the wine-god. For Anacreon was regarded as the type of a poet who, in spite of age, paid perpetual homage to wine and love. Love and wine and merry company formed the favourite subjects of his light, sweet, and graceful songs, which were cast in the metres of the Æolic poets, but composed in the Ionic dialect. Beside fragments of such songs and of elegies, we have also a number of epigrams that bear his name. His songs were largely imitated, and of such imitations we have under his name a collection of about sixty love-songs and drinking-songs of very various (partly much later) dates, and of different degrees of merit.

Anacrĭsis. In Attic law, the preliminary examination of the parties to a suit.

Anaxăgŏrăs. A Greek philosopher, of Clazomĕnæ in Asia Minor, born about 500 B.C. Sprung from a noble family, but wishing to devote himself entirely to science, he gave up his property to his kinsmen, and removed to Athens, where he lived in intimacy with the most distinguished men, above all with Perīclēs. Shortly before the outbreak of the Peloponnesian War he was charged by the political opponents of Pericles with impiety, *i.e.* with denying the gods recognised by the State; and though acquitted through his friend's influence, he felt compelled to emigrate to Lampsăcus, where he died soon after, aged 72. He not only had the honour of giving philosophy a home at Athens, where it went on flourishing for quite a thousand years, but he was the first philosopher who, by the side of the material principle, introduced a spiritual, which gives the other life and form. He laid down his doctrine in a work *On Nature* in the Ionic dialect, of which only fragments are preserved. Like Parmĕnīdēs, he denied the existence of birth or death; the two processes were rather to be described as a mingling and unmingling. The ultimate elements of combination are indivisible, imperishable *primordia* of infinite number, and differing in shape, colour, and taste, called by himself "seeds of things," and by later writers (from an expression of Aristotle) *hŏmœŏmĕrē*, *i.e.* particles of like kind with each other and with the whole that is made up of them. At first these lay mingled without order; but the divine spirit — simple, pure, passionless reason — set the unarranged matter into motion, and thereby created out of chaos an orderly world. This movement, proceeding from the centre, works on for ever, penetrating farther and farther the infinite mass. But the application of the spiritual principle was rather indicated than fully carried out by Anaxagoras; he himself commonly explains phenomena by physical causes, and only when he cannot find these, falls back on the action of divine reason.

Anaxandrĭdēs. A Greek poet of the Middle Comedy, a Rhodian, flourished in 376 B.C. He is stated to have been the first who made love affairs the subject of comedy. His plays were characterized by brightness and humour, but only fragments of them are preserved.

Anaxĭmander (Gr. -mandrŏs). A Greek philosopher of Milētus; born B.C. 611; a younger contemporary of Thalēs and Pherecȳdēs. He lived at the court of Polycrătēs of Samos, and died B.C. 547. In his philosophy the primal essence, which he was the first to call principle, was the immortal-imperishable, all-including infinite, a kind of chaos, out of which all things proceed, and into which they return. He composed, in the Ionic dialect, a brief and somewhat poetical treatise on his doctrine, which may be regarded as the earliest prose work on philosophy; but only a few sentences out of it are preserved. The advances he had made in physics and astronomy are evidenced by his invention of the sun-dial, his construction of a celestial globe, and his first attempt at a geographical map.

Anaxĭmĕnēs. (1) A Greek philosopher of Milētus, a younger contemporary and pupil of Anaximander, who died about 502 B.C. He supposed *air* to be the fundamental principle, out of which everything arose by rarefaction and condensation. This doctrine he expounded in a work, now lost, written in the Ionian dialect.

(2) A Greek sophist of Lampsăcus, a favourite of Philip of Măcĕdŏn and Alexander the Great. He composed orations and historical works, some treating of the actions of those two princes. Of these but little remains. On the other hand, he is the author of the *Rhetoric dedicated to Alexander*, the earliest extant work of this kind, which was once included among the works of Aristotle.

Anchīsēs. Son of Capys, of the royal house of Troy by both parents, ruler of Dardănus on Mount Ida. Aphrodītē loved him for his beauty, and bore him a son, Æneās. But having, in spite of her warnings, boasted of her favour, he is (according to various versions of the story) paralysed, killed; or struck blind by the lightning of Zeus. Vergil represents the disabled chief as borne out of burning Troy on his son's shoulders, and as sharing his wanderings over the sea, and aiding him with his counsel, till they reach Drĕpănum in Sicily, where he dies, and is buried on Mount Eryx.

Ancĭlĕ. The small oval sacred shield, curved inwards on either side, which was said to have fallen from heaven in the reign of Numa. There being a prophecy that the stability of Rome was bound up with it, Numa had eleven others made exactly like it by a cunning workman, *Mamurius Veturius*, so that the right one should not be stolen. The care of these arms, which were sacred to Mars was entrusted to the

* ANCILIA BORNE BY TWO SALII, WITH LEGEND IN ETRUSCAN CHARACTERS.

Above=Gk. ATKYAE, *ancile;* below=AAKE, *Alcæus*, the owner's name. (Gem in Florence.)

Salii (*q.v.*), who had to carry them through the city once a year with peculiar ceremonies. At the conclusion of their songs Mamurius himself was invoked, and on March 14th they held a special feast, the *Mamurālia*, at which they sacrificed to him, beating on a hide with staves, probably to imitate a smith's hammering. It is likely that the name Mamurius conceals that of the god Mars (or Mamers) himself.

Ancȳrānum Monumentum. The monument of Ancȳra (now Angora), a marble slab, of which the greater part is preserved. It belonged to the temple of Augustus at Ancyra, and contained the Latin text of a Greek translation of the report drawn up by that emperor himself on the actions of his reign (*Index Rērum a se Gestārum*). By the terms of his will this report, engraved in bronze, was set up in front of his mausoleum at Rome, and copies were made of it for other temples of Augustus in the provinces.

Andăbătæ. *See* GLADIATORS.

Andŏcĭdēs. The second in order of time in the roll of Attic orators. He was born B.C. 439, and belonged by birth to the aristocratic party, but fell out with it in 415, when he was involved in the famous trial for mutilating the statues of Hermēs, and, to save his own and his kinsmen's lives, betrayed his aristocratic accomplices. Having, in spite of the immunity promised him, fallen into partial *atīmia* (loss of civic rights), he left Athens, and carried on a profitable trade in Cyprus. After two fruitless attempts to recover his status at home, he was allowed at last, upon the fall of the Thirty and the amnesty of B.C. 403, to return to Athens, where he succeeded in repelling renewed attacks, and gaining an honourable position. Sent to Sparta in B.C. 390, during the Corinthian War, to negotiate peace, he brought back the draft of a treaty, for the ratification of which he vainly pleaded in a speech that is still extant. He is said to have been banished in consequence, and to have died in exile. Beside the above-mentioned oration, we have two delivered on his own behalf, one pleading for his recall from banishment, B.C. 410; another against the charge of unlawful participation in the mysteries, B.C. 399; a fourth, *Against Alcibiădēs*, is spurious. His oratory is plain and artless, and its expressions those of the popular language of the day.

Andrŏgĕōs. Son of Minos, king of Crete by Pasĭphăë. Visiting Athens at the first celebration of the Pana-thenæa, he won victories over all the champions, when king Ægeus, out of jealousy, sent him to fight the bull of Marathon, which killed him. According to another account he was slain in an ambush. Minos avenges his son by making the Athenians send seven youths and seven maidens every nine years as victims to his Minotaur, from which Theseus at last delivers them. Funeral games were held in the Cer|amīcus at Athens in honour of Androgeus under the name of Eurygyës.

Andrŏmăchē. The daughter of Eëtiōn, king of the Cilician Thebes, is one of the noblest female characters in Homer, distinguished alike by her ill-fortune and her true and tender love for her husband, Hec-

tor. Achilles, in taking her native town, kills her father and seven brothers; her mother, redeemed from captivity, is carried off by sickness; her husband falls by the hand of Achilles; and when Troy is taken she sees her one boy, Astyănax (or Scamander), hurled from the walls. She falls, as the prize of war, to Neoptŏlĕmus, the son of her greatest foe, who first carries her to Epīrus, then surrenders her to Hector's brother, Hĕlĕnus. After his death she returns to Asia with Pergămus, her son by Neoptolemus, and dies there.

Andrŏmĕda. Daughter of the Æthiopian

* ANDROMEDA AND PERSEUS.
(Rome, Capitoline Museum.)

king Cĕpheus (a son of Belus) by Cassiopeia. Cassiopeia had boasted of being fairer than the Nereïds, and Poseidōn to punish the profanity, sent a flood and a sea-monster. As the oracle of Ammon promised a riddance of the plague should Andromeda be thrown to the monster, Cepheus was compelled to chain his daughter to a rock on the shore. At this moment of distress Perseus appears, and rescues her, her father having promised her to him in marriage. At the wedding a violent quarrel arises between the king's brother, Phineus, to whom she had been betrothed before, and Perseus, who turns his rival into stone with the Gorgon's head. Andromeda follows Perseus to Argos, and becomes ancestress of the famous line of Perseïdæ. Athēna set her among the stars.

Andrōnītis. The men's apartments in a Greek house. See HOUSE.

Andrŏtīŏn. A Greek historian, an Athenian, and a pupil of Isocrates, who was accused of making an illegal proposal and went into banishment at Megara. (We have the speech composed by Demosthenes for one of the accusers.) At Megara he wrote a history of Attica (*see* ATTHIS) in at least 12 books, one of the best of that class of writings; but only fragments of it have survived.

Angdistis. See RHEA.

Anīus. Son of Apollo by Rhœo or Creüsa, whose father, Stăphÿlus of Naxos, a son of Dionÿsus and Ariadnē, committed her to the sea in a box. She was carried to Delos, and there gave birth to her son Anius. Apollo taught him divination, and made him his priest and king of Delos. His son Thasus, like Linus and Actæōn, was torn to pieces by dogs, after which no dogs were allowed in the island. His daughters by the nymph Dorippē, being descendants of Dionysus, had the gift of turning anything they pleased into wine, corn, or oil; but when Agamemnōn on his way to Troy wished to take them from their father by force, Dionysus changed them into doves.

Annalists. A series of writers on Roman history, older than those usually called the historians, beginning about 200 B.C., and covering about a century and a half. They related their country's story from its first beginnings down to their own times, treating the former briefly, the latter in full detail, and at first always in Greek, like FABIUS PICTOR and CINCIUS ALIMENTUS. With PORCIUS CATO (*q.v.*) commenced composition in Latin and a livelier interest in native history, which constantly stimulated new efforts to celebrate the deeds of their forefathers. Two main characteristics of these annalists are the free use they made of their predecessors, and an inclination to suppress unfavourable facts, which gradually grew into a habit of flattering the national vanity by exaggerations.

Works dealing in this manner with the whole of Roman history, or large sections of it, continued to be written in Cicero's time. The leading annalists of this class are: CASSIUS HEMINA, soon after Cato; CALPURNIUS PISO FRUGI, consul in B.C. 133; FANNIUS, consul in B.C. 122; GELLIUS, who wrote about the same time (ninety-seven books of *Annāles*); CLAUDIUS QUADRIGARIUS, a contemporary of Sulla, author of at least twenty-three books, from the Gallic conflagration to his own time; his younger contemporary VALERIUS ANTIAS (who treated all Roman history in seventy-five books); LICINIUS MACER, who died B.C. 66, author of the earlier history, in twenty-one books. Some few writers, on the other hand, confined themselves to the description of shorter periods: first, CÆLIUS ANTIPATER, about B.C. 120 (whose history of the Second Punic War in seven books, was noted for its accuracy); then SEMPRONIUS ASELLIO, about B.C. 100, who, in his account of events he had taken part in (*Rerum Gestarum Libri*, fourteen at least), was the first who, not content with barely relating facts, tried to explain the reasons of them; and CORNELIUS SISENNA, who lived 120–67 B.C. and wrote at least twenty-three books on the brief period between the Social War and Sulla's dictatorship. To these works, in which history has begun to assume the character of memoirs, we may add the autobiography of CORNELIUS SULLA the dictator (*Rērum Suārum Commentārii* in twenty-two books), which he wrote in self-justification at the end of his career. He died B.C. 78. All these works are lost, except scanty fragments; but the later Greek and Roman writers had made full use of them.

Annals (*Annāles*). Year-books. From early times a record of all important events at Rome had been kept in chronological order by the high priest (*pontĭfex maxĭmus*) for the time, who every year exhibited in his official residence a whited board (*album*), on which, after the names of the magistrates for the year, occurrences of all kinds—war, dearth, pestilence, prodigies—were set down briefly according to their dates. These *annales pontĭficum* or *annales maxĭmi* (supposed to be so called after the *pontĭfex maximus*), though destroyed at the burning of Rome by the Gauls, B.C. 389, were restored as far as possible, and continued till B.C. 130. Collected afterwards in eighty books, they were at once utilized and superseded by the so-called ANNALISTS (*q.v.*).

Anna Perenna. An ancient Italian goddess, about whose exact attributes the ancients themselves were not clear. She is probably the moon-goddess of the revolving year, who every month renews her youth, and was therefore regarded as a goddess who bestowed long life and all that contributes to it. About full moon on the Ides (fifteenth) of March (then the first month of the year), in a grove of fruit trees at the first milestone on the Flaminian Way, the Romans held a merry feast under the open sky, wishing each other as many years of life as they drank cups of wine. The learned men of the Augustan age identified Anna with Dido's sister, who, on the death of that queen, had fled from Carthage to Æneas in Italy, but, having excited Lavinia's jealousy, threw herself into the Numīcius, and became the nymph of that river.

Annōna. A Latin word meaning the year's produce, especially in wheat, the staple food of the city population; it was afterwards applied to the corn provided by the State to feed that population. As Italian agriculture decayed, and the city population steadily increased, the question of its maintenance became a constant care to the State, which, on the conquest of the first two provinces, Sicily and Sardinia, at once doomed them, especially the former, to the task of victualling the armies and feeding Rome, by imposing a tithe on corn, and forbidding its exportation to any country but Italy. The tenth paid as tribute, and other corn bought up by the State, was sold by the ædiles at a moderate price, usually on terms which prevented the treasury being a loser. Thus till the time of the Gracchi the *cura annonæ* was confined to the maintenance of a moderate price; but the corn law of Gaius Gracchus, B.C. 123, laid on the State the obligation to deliver to any Roman householder on demand $6\frac{1}{4}$ bushels of wheat a month at a fixed price, which even in cheap times was less than half the cost price; and Clodius in B.C. 58 went further, and made the delivery entirely gratuitous. By the year B.C. 46, the number of recipients had risen to 320,000, and the yearly outlay to a sum equivalent to £650,000. Cæsar then reduced the recipients to 150,000; but their number grew again, till Augustus cut it down to 200,000, whose names were inscribed on a bronze table, and who received their monthly portion on presentation of a ticket. This arrangement as a whole remained in force till about the end of the Empire, except that in the 3rd century bread was given instead of grain. And, side by side with these gratuitous doles, grain could always be bought for a moderate price at magazines filled with the supplies of the provinces, especially Egypt

and Africa, and with purchases made by the State. The expenses of the *annona* fell mainly on the imperial treasury, but partly on that of the senate. From Augustus' time the *cura annonæ* formed one of the highest imperial offices, its holder, the *præfectus annonæ*, having a large staff scattered over Rome and the whole empire. The *annona*, like so many other things, was personified by the Romans, and became a goddess of the importation of corn, whose attributes were a bushel, ears of wheat, and a horn of plenty.

Antæus. Son of Poseidōn and Gē (the earth); a huge giant in Libya, who grew stronger every time he touched his mother Earth. He forced all strangers to wrestle with him, and killed them when conquered, till Hērăclēs, on his journey to fetch the apples of the Hespĕrĭdĕs, lifted him off the ground, and held him aloft till he had killed him. His tomb was shown near Tingis in Mauretania.

Antæ. A *templum in antīs* was a temple in which the hall at either end was formed by prolongations of the side-walls (Lat. *antæ*), and a row of columns between the terminal pilasters of those prolongations. *See* TEMPLES, fig. 1.

Anteia (otherwise *Sthenobœa*). Wife of Prœtus of Tīryns; by slandering Bellĕrŏphŏn (*q.v.*), who had rejected her offers of love, she caused her husband to attempt his life.

Antēnōr. A Trojan of high rank, husband to Athena's priestess Thĕānō, the sister of Hecŭba. When Menelāüs and Odysseus, after the landing of the Greeks, came as envoys to Troy, demanding the surrender of Helen, he received them hospitably, protected them from Paris, and then as always advised peace. Because of this leaning to the Greeks, it was alleged in later times that he betrayed his native city by opening its gates to the enemy; in return for which his house, known by the panther's hide hung out of it, was spared, and he and his friends allowed to go free. One account was, that he sailed with Menelaus, was driven out of his course to Cyrēnē, and settled there, where his descendants the Antenŏrĭdæ were worshipped as heroes. Another, which became the accepted tradition, represented him as leading the Hĕnĕti, when driven out of Paphlagonia, by way of Thrace and Illyria, to the Adriatic, and thence to the mouth of the Padus (Po), where he founded Patavium (Padua), the city of the Vĕnĕti.

Antĕrōs. The god of requited love, brother of Erōs (*q.v.*).

Antesignāni. A Latin word denoting originally the soldiers fighting in front of the standards during a battle; afterwards a picked body in every legion, free of baggage, and intended to advance in front of the line of battle and seize important points, or to open the battle.

Antevorta. See CARMENTA.

Anthestēria. A feast at Athens held in honour of Dionȳsus. *Comp.* DIONYSIA (4).

Anthology (=garland of flowers). The Greek word *anthŏlŏgĭa* means a collection of short, especially epigrammatic poems, by various authors; we still possess one such collection dating from antiquity. Collections of inscriptions in verse had more than once been set on foot in early times for antiquarian purposes. The first regular anthology, entitled *Stĕphănŏs* (=wreath), was attempted by *Meleāger* of Gădăra in the 1st century B.C.; it contained, beside his own compositions, poems arranged according to their initial letters, by forty-six contemporary and older authors, including Archĭlŏchus, Alcæus, Sappho, Anacrĕŏn, Simōnĭdēs, etc., together with a prologue still extant. This collection was enriched, about 100 A.D., by *Phĭlippus* of Thessalonīca, with select epigrams by about thirteen later authors. Other collections were undertaken soon after by *Diogeniānus* of Heracleia and *Stratōn* of Sardis, and in the 6th century by *Agathĭās* of Myrīna, in whose *Kyklŏs* the poems are for the first time arranged according to subjects. Out of these collections, now all lost, *Constantīnus Cĕphălās* of Constantinople, in the 10th century, put together a new and comprehensive anthology, classified according to contents in fifteen sections. From this collection the monk *Maxĭmus Planūdēs*, in the 14th century, made an extract of seven books, which was the only one known till the year 1606. In that year the French scholar Saumaise (Salmasius) discovered in the Palatine Library at Heidelberg a complete manuscript of the anthology of Constantinus Cephalas with sundry additions. This MS., with all the other treasures of the library, was carried off to Rome in 1623, whence it was taken to Paris in 1793, and back to Heidelberg in 1816.

The epigrams of the Greek anthology, dating as they do from widely distant ages down to the Byzantine, and being the production of more than three hundred different authors, are of very various merit; but many of them are among the pearls of Greek poetry, and could hardly have survived unless enshrined in such a collection. Taken together with the rich store of epigrams found in inscriptions, the Anthology opens to us a view of the development of this branch of Greek literature such as we can scarcely obtain in the case of any other, besides affording valuable information on Hellenic language, history, and manners, at the most different periods.

Roman literature has no really ancient collection of so comprehensive a character, the so-called *Latin Anthology* having been gathered by modern scholars out of the material found scattered in various MSS. Among these, it is true, Saumaise's MS. of the 7th century, now in Paris, has a collection of about 380 poems, but these, with a few exceptions, are of very late authorship.

Antĭdŏsis (=exchange of properties). An arrangement peculiar to the Athenians, by which a citizen summoned to perform one of those services to the State named *leitourgĭæ* (*q.v.*), if he thought a richer than he had been passed over, could challenge him to exchange possessions, binding himself in that case to discharge the obligation. Each party could then have the other's property put in sequestration and his house sealed up; and within three days they handed in, before the proper authority and under oath, an inventory of their goods. If no amicable agreement was come to, and the judge's decision went against the plaintiff, he was bound to perform the public service; otherwise the defendant submitted either to the exchange or to the service.

Antĭgŏnē. (1) Daughter of Œdĭpūs and Iocasta, who accompanied her blind father into exile. After his death in Attica she returns to Thebes, and, in defiance of her uncle Crĕŏn's prohibition, performs the last honours to her brother Polyneicēs, fallen in single fight with Etĕoclēs, by strewing his body with dust. For this she is entombed alive in the family vault, and there hangs herself; and her betrothed, Hæmŏn, the son of Creon, stabs himself beside her corpse. Such is the version of Sophŏclēs. Another tradition represents Antigone and Argeïa, the widow of Polyneices, as secretly burning his body by night on the funeral pile of Eteocles. When seized by the guards, Creon hands her over to Hæmŏn for execution; but he hides her in a shepherd's hut, and lives with her in secret wedlock. Their son, grown up and engaging in some funeral games at Thebes, is recognised by a birthmark peculiar to the family. To escape

Creon's vengeance, Hæmon kills both Antigone and himself.

(2) Antigone, daughter of Eurȳtȋon and wife of Pēleus (*q.v.*), hanged herself for grief at the supposed infidelity of her husband.

Antĭgŏnŭs. A Greek writer of Carystus, about 240 B.C., author of a collection of all kinds of curiosities and fictions in natural history. The work is now extant only in a much abbreviated form, and is of no value but for its numerous quotations and fragments from lost writings.

Antigrăpheus. The name of a financial officer at Athens. *See* GRAMMATEUS.

Anticleia. Daughter of Autŏlȳcus, wife of Laërtēs, and mother of Odysseus (*q.v.*).

Antĭlŏchus. The son of Nestor, who accompanied his father to the Trojan War, and was distinguished among the younger heroes for beauty and bravery. Homer calls him a favourite of Zeus and Poseidōn. The dearest friend of Achilles next to Patroclus, he is chosen by the Greeks to break the news to him of his beloved companion's fall. When Memnōn attacks the aged Nestor, Antilochus throws himself in his way, and buys his father's safety with his life. He, like Patroclus, is avenged by Achilles, in whose grave-mound the ashes of both friends are laid; even in the lower world Odysseus beholds the three pacing the asphodel meadow, and in after times the inhabitants of Ilium offered to them jointly the sacrifices due to the dead on the foreland of Sigēum.

Antĭmăchus. A Greek poet and critic of Cŏlŏphōn, an elder contemporary of Plato, about 400 B.C. By his two principal works—the long mythical *epic* called *Thebaïs* and a cycle of *elegies* named after his loved and lost Lydē, and telling of famous lovers parted by death—he became the founder of learned poetry, precursor and prototype of the Alexandrians, who, on account of his learning, assigned him the next place to Homer amongst epic poets. In striving to impart strength and dignity to language by avoiding all that was common, his style became rigid and artificial, and naturally ran into bombast. But we possess only fragments of his works. As a scholar, he is remarkable for having set on foot a critical revision of the Homeric poems.

Antĭnŏüs. A beautiful youth of Claudiopŏlis in Bithynia, a favourite and travelling companion of the emperor Hadrian. He drowned himself in the Nile, probably from melancholy. The emperor honoured his memory by placing him among the heroes, erecting statues and temples, and founding yearly games in his honour, while the artists of every province vied in pourtraying him under various forms, human, heroic, and divine; *e.g.* as Dionȳsus, Hermēs, Apollo. Among the features common to the many surviving portraitures of Antinous are the full locks falling low down the forehead, the large, melancholy eyes, the full mouth, and the broad, swelling breast. Some of these portraits are among the finest works of ancient art, for instance, the colossal statue in the Vatican, and the half-length relief at the Villa Albani. (*See* cut.) There is also a fine bust in the Louvre.

MARBLE RELIEF OF ANTINOUS.
(Rome, Villa Albani.)

Antĭŏpē. (1) In Homer a daughter of the Bœotian river-god Asōpus, mother by Zeus of Amphīōn and Zēthus. In later legend her father is Nycteus of Hyria or Hysiæ. As he threatens to punish her for yielding to the approaches of Zeus under the form of a satyr, she flees to Epōpeus of Sĭcȳōn. This king her uncle Lycus kills by order of his brother Nycteus, now dead, and leads her back in chains. Arrived on Mount Cithærōn, she gives birth to twins, Amphion by Zeus, Zethus by Epopeus, whom Lycus leaves exposed upon the mountain. After being long imprisoned and ill-treated by Dircē, the wife of Lycus, she escapes to Cithærōn, and makes acquaintance with her sons, whom a shepherd has brought up. She makes them take a frightful vengeance upon Dirce (*see* AMPHION), for doing which Diŏnȳsus drives her mad, and she wanders. throught Greece, till Phŏcus, king of Phŏcis, heals and marries her.

(2) A' sister of Hippŏlȳtē, queen of the Amazons; who, according to one account, fall as a prize of war to Theseus for his share in Hērăclēs' campaign against the Amazons, according to another, was carried off by him and his friend Pirithŏüs. When the Amazons attacked Athens in return, she is variously represented as persuading them to peace, or falling in battle against them by the side of Theseus; or, again, as killed by Heracles, when she interrupted the marriage of her beloved Theseus with Phædra. Her son by Theseus was Hippolytus.

Antǐphănēs. The most prŏlific and important author, with Alexis, of the Attic Middle Comedy; he came of a family which had migrated from Larissa in Thessaly; was born B.C. 408, and died at the age of 74. He is said to have written 260 plays, of which over 200 are known to us by their titles and fragments, yet he won the prize only thirteen times. He is praised for dramatic ability, wit, and neatness of form.

Antǐphǐlus. A Greek painter born in Egypt in the latter half of the 4th century B.C., a contemporary and rival of Apellēs; he probably spent the last part of his life at the court of the first Ptolemy. The ancients praise the lightness and dexterity with which he handled subjects of high art, as well as scenes in daily life. Two of his pictures in the latter kind were especially famous, one of a boy blowing a fire, and another of women dressing wool. From his having painted a man named Gryllŏs (=pig) with playful allusions to the sitter's name, caricatures in general came to be called *grylloi.* [Pliny, *H. N.*, 35. 114, 138].

Antǐphōn. The earliest of the ten great Attic orators, born B.C. 480 at Rhamnūs in Attica, son of the sophist Sophǐlus, to whom he owed his training. He was the founder of political eloquence as an art, which he taught with great applause in his own school of rhetoric; and he was the first who wrote out speeches for others to deliver in court, though he afterwards published them under his own name. He also played an active part in the politics of his time as a leading member of the oligarchical party, and the real author of the deathblow which was dealt to democracy in 411 B.C. by the establishment of the Council of Four Hun-

dred. Then he went as ambassador to Sparta, to purchase peace at any price in the interest of the oligarchy. On the fall of the Four Hundred he was accused of high treason, and in spite of a masterly defence—the first speech he had ever made in public — was condemned to death B.C. 411. Of the sixty orations attributed to him, only fifteen are preserved, all on trials for murder; but only three of them are about real cases. The rest (named *tetralogies,* because every four are the first and second speeches of both plaintiff and defendant on the same subject) are mere exercises. Antiphon's speeches exhibit the art of oratory in its rudimentary stage as regards both substance and form.

Antisthĕnēs. A Greek philosopher of Athens, born about 440 B.C., but only a half citizen, because his mother was a Thracian. He was in his youth a pupil of Gorgias, and himself taught for a time as a sophist, till, towards middle life, he attached himself to Socrătēs, and became his bosom friend. After the death of Socrates in B.C. 399 he established a school in the gymnasium *Kȳnŏsargēs,* the only one open to persons of half-Athenian descent, whence his followers bore the name of Cȳnǐci (*Kȳnǐkoi*). He lived to the age of seventy. Like Socrates, he regarded virtue as necessary, indeed, alone sufficient for happiness, and to be a branch of knowledge that could⸤be taught, and that once acquired could not be lost, its essence consisting in freedom from wants by the avoidance of evil, *i.e.* of pleasure and desire. Its acquisition needs no dialectic argumentation, only Socratic strength. His pupils, especially the famous Diŏgĕnēs of Sinōpē, degraded his doctrine to cynicism by depreciating all knowledge and despising the current morality of the time. His philosophical and rhetorical works are lost, all but two slight declamations on the contest for the arms of Achilles, the *Aias* and *Odysseus;* and even their genuineness is disputed.

Antistius Lăbĕŏ (*Quintus*). A renowned jurist of Augustus' time, a man of wide scholarship and strict republican views, which lost him the emperor's favour. His writings on law amounted to 400 books, portions of which are preservad in the *Pandects* of Justinian's *Corpus Iuris.* Aiming at a progressive development of law, he became the founder of a school of lawyers named *Proculians* after his pupil *Semprōnius Prŏcŭlus. See* ATEIUS CAPITO.

Antōnīnus. (1) *Marcus Aurelius,* sur-

named *Philŏsŏphus*, born at Rome A.D. 121.
His real name was M. Annius Verus; at
the desire of the emperor Hadrian he was
adopted by his successor T. Aurelius Antoninus Pius, married his daughter Faus-
tīna, and became emperor in A.D. 161.
During his benevolent reign the empire had
to face dire distresses, famine, pestilence,
and constant wars with the Parthians in
the east, and the Marcomanni and other
Germans in the north, during which he
proved himself a prudent and active sovereign. In the midst of a new war with
the already vanquished Marcomanni he
died in A.D. 180, probably at Sirmium in
Pannonia. In his youth he was a pupil of
the orator Fronto, and loved him warmly
to the last, even after giving up rhetoric
and devoting himself to the Stoic philosophy. The gentleness and amiability of
his nature comes out both in his letters
to FRONTO (*q.v.*) and in his *Self-contem-
plations*, which are the moral reflections
of a Stoic in clumsy, over-concise, and
often obscure Greek.

(2) *Antōnīnus Lĭberālis*, a Greek grammarian of about 150 A.D., perhaps a freedman of Antoninus Pius; he wrote a collection, called *Metamorphōsēs*, of forty-one
myths dealing with transformations, most
of which is based on ancient authorities
now lost, and is therefore valuable as a
source of mythological knowledge.

Anûbis. An Egyptian
god, son of Osĭris, con-
ductor and watcher of
the dead, whose deeds he
and HORUS (*q.v.*) were
supposed to weigh in the
balance in presence of
their father Osiris. He
was represented with
the head of a jackal or
dog-ape. The worship of
Anubis was introduced
among the Greeks and
Romans (who represented
him in the form of a dog),
together with that of
Serāpis and Isis, espe-
cially in the time of the
emperors, as he was identified with Hermēs.

ANUBIS.

Apăgōgē. A technical term of Athenian
law, meaning the production of a criminal
taken in the act before the proper magistrate, who then took him into custody, or
made him find bail. The name was also
given to the document in which the accuser
stated the charge. But if the officer was con-

ducted to the spot where the accused was
staying, the process was called *ĕphēgēsis*.

Apăturĭă. The general feast of the PHRA-
TRIES (*q.v.*) held chiefly by Greeks of the
Ionian race. At Athens it lasted three days
in the month of Pyanepsiōn (Oct.–Nov.), and
was celebrated with sacrificial banquets.
On the third day the fathers brought their
children born since the last celebration
before the members (*phrātors*) assembled
at the headquarters of each *phrātria*, and
after declaring on oath their legitimate
birth, had their names inscribed on the roll
of *phratŏrĕs*. For every child enrolled a
sheep or goat was sacrificed, which went
to furnish the common feast. On the same
day the fathers made their children who
were at school give proofs of their progress,
especially by reciting passages from poets,
and those who distinguished themselves
were rewarded with prizes.

Apellēs. The greatest painter of antiquity, probably born at Cŏlŏphōn or in the
Island of Cŏs, who lived in the latter half
of the 4th century B.C. After studying at
Ephĕsus, and receiving theoretical instruction in his art from Pamphĭlus at Sĭcўōn,
he worked in different parts of the Greek
world, but especially in Macedonia, at the
court of Philip and that of Alexander, who
would let no other artist paint him. While
doing ready justice to the merits of contemporaries, especially Protŏgĕnēs, he could
not but recognise that no one surpassed himself in grace and balanced harmony. These
qualities, together with his wonderful skill
in drawing and his perfect and refined
mastery of colouring (however simple his
means), made his works the most perfect
productions of Greek painting. Among the
foremost were the *Alexander* with lightning
in his hand, painted for the temple of
Artĕmis at Ephesus, in which the fingers
appeared to stand out of the picture, and
the thunderbolt to project from the panel;
and the *Aphrodītē Anadyŏmĕnē* (=rising),
painted for the temple of Asclepius at Cos,
which Augustus brought to Rome and set
up in the temple of Cæsar, and which,
when the lower part was damaged, no
painter would attempt to restore. We owe
to Lucian a description of an allegorical
picture of *Slander* by this painter. [Pliny,
H. N., 35. 79–97.]

Aphrŏdītē (Lat. *Vĕnus*). The Greek goddess of love. Her attributes combine, with
Hellenic conceptions, a great many features
of Eastern, especially Phœnician, origin,
which the Greeks must have grafted on to

their native notions in very old times. This double nature appears immediately in the contradictory tales of her origin. To the oldest Greeks she was the daughter of Zeus and Diōnē (and is sometimes called that name herself); yet from a very early time she appears as *Aphro-gĕneia*, the "foam-born" (*see* URANUS), as *Anadyŏmĕnē*, "she who rises" out of the sea, and steps ashore on Cyprus, which had been colonized by Phœnicians time out of mind; even as far back as Homer she is *Kypris*, the Cyprian. The same transmarine and Eastern origin of her worship is evidenced by the legend of the isle of Cythēra, on which she was supposed to have first landed out of a sea-shell.

Again, the common conception of her as goddess of love limits her agency to the sphere of human life. But she is, at the same time, a power of nature, living and working in the three elements of air, earth, and water. As goddess of the shifting gale and changeful sky, she is *Aphrodite Urānia*, the "heavenly," and at many places in Greece and Asia her temples crowned the heights and headlands; witness the citadels of Thebes and Corinth, and Mount Eryx in Sicily. As goddess of storm and lightning, she was represented armed, as at Sparta and Cythera; and this perhaps explains why she was associated with Arē (Mars) both in worship and in legend, and worshipped as a goddess of victory.

The moral conception of Aphrodite Urania as goddess of the higher and purer love, especially wedded love and fruitfulness, as opposed to mere sensual lust, was but slowly developed in the course of ages.

As goddess of the *sea* and maritime traffic, especially of calm seas and prosperous voyages, she was widely worshipped by sailors and fishermen at ports and on sea-coasts, often as the goddess of calm, while Poseidon was the god of disturbance. Next, as regards the life of the *earth*, she is the goddess of gardens and groves, of Spring and its bounties, especially tender plants and flowers, as the rose and myrtle; hence,

*(1) CYPRIAN COIN OF CARACALLA

With the sacred cone, or symbol of Aphrodite, in a conventional representation of the temple at Paphos.

as the fruitful and bountiful, she was worshipped most of all at that season of the year in which her birth from the sea was celebrated at Paphos in Cyprus (*comp. cut*). But to this, her time of joyful action, is opposed a season of sorrow, when her creations wither and die: a sentiment expressed in her inconsolable grief for her beloved ADONIS (*q.v.*), the symbol of vegetation perishing in its prime.

In the life of gods and men, she shows her power as the golden, sweetly smiling goddess of beauty and love, which she knows how to kindle or to keep away. She outshines all the goddesses in grace and loveliness; in her girdle she wears united all the magic charms that can bewitch the wisest man and subdue the very gods. Her retinue consists of Erōs (Cupid), the Hours, the Graces, Peitho (persuasion), Pŏthŏs and Hīmĕrŏs (personifications of longing and yearning). By uniting the generations in the bond of love, she becomes a goddess of marriage and family life, and the consequent kinship of the whole community. As such she had formerly been worshipped at Athens under the name of *Pandēmŏs* (= all the people's), as being a goddess of the whole country. By a regulation of Solon, the name acquired a very different sense, branding her as goddess of prostitution; then it was that the new and higher meaning was imported into the word Urania. In later times, the worship of Aphrodite as the goddess of mere sensual love made rapid strides, and in particular districts assumed forms more and more immoral, in imitation of the services performed to love-goddesses in the East, especially at Corinth, where large bands of girls were consecrated as slaves to the service of the gods and the practice of prostitution. And later still, the worship of Astartē, the Syrian Aphrodite, performed by eunuchs, spread all over Greece.

In the Greek myths Aphrodite appears occasionally as the wife of Hephæstus. Her love adventures with Arēs are notorious. From these sprang Erōs and Antērōs, Harmonia, the wife of Cadmus, and Deimŏs and Phŏbŏs (fear and alarm), attendants on their father. By Anchīsēs she was the mother of Æneās. The head-quarters of her worship were Paphos, Amăthūs, and Idăliŏn (all in Cyprus), Cnidus in Dorian Asia Minor, Corinth, the island of Cythēra, and Eryx in Sicily. As mother of Harmonia, she was a guardian deity of Thebes. Among plants, the myrtle, the rose, and the apple were specially sacred to her as goddess of love; amongst animals, the ram, he-goat, hare, dove, sparrow, and other creatures of amorous nature (the ram and dove being widely-current symbols of great antiquity); as sea-goddess, the swan, mussels, and dolphin; as Urania, the tortoise.

In ancient art, in which Aphrodite is one of the favourite subjects, she is represented in a higher or lower aspect, according as the artist's aim was to exhibit Urania or the popular goddess of love. In the earlier works of art she usually appears clothed, but in later ones more or less undraped; either as rising from the sea or leaving the bath, or (as in later times) merely as an ideal of female beauty. In the course of time the divine element disappeared, and the presentation became more and more ordinary. While the older sculptures show

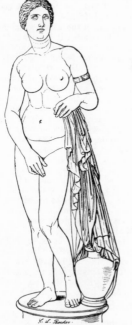

(2) REPLICA OF APHRODITE OF CNIDUS
BY PRAXITELES.
(Munich, Glyptothek.)

the sturdier forms, the taste of later times leans more and more to softer, weaker out-

lines. Most renowned in ancient times were the statue at Cnïdus by Praxĭtĕlēs (a copy

(3) APHRODITE OF MELOS.
(Paris, Louvre).

of which is now at Munich, *see* fig. 2), and the painting of Aphrodite Anadyomene by Apelles. Of original statues preserved to us, the most famous are the Aphrodite of Mēlos (*Milo, see* fig. 3) now at Paris, and that of Capua at Naples, both of which bring out the loftier aspect of the goddess, and the Medicean Venus at Florence, the work of a late Attic sculptor, Cleŏmĕnĕs, in the delicate forms of face and body that pleased a younger age.——On the identification of Aphrodite with the Roman goddess of love, *see* VENUS.

Aphthŏnius. A Greek rhetorician of Antioch, about 400 A.D., a pupil of Libanius, who wrote a schoolbook on the elements of rhetoric, the *Progymnasmătă*, or "First Steps in Style," much used in schools down to the 17th century. This book is really an adaptation of the chapter so named in Hermŏgĕnēs' *Rhetoric.* A collection of forty fables by Æsop also bears his name.

Apīcĭus (*Marcus Gāvius*). A glutton, who lived under Augustus and Tiberius. He borrowed the last name from an epicure of the republican age, and wrote a book upon cookery. He poisoned himself for fear of starving, though at the time of his death he was still worth £75,000. His name became a proverb, so that we find an *Apicius Cœlius*, author of a collection of recipes in ten books, *De Re Cūlīnāriā*, 3rd century A.D.

Apĭŏn. A Greek grammarian of the 1st century A.D., a pupil of Dĭdўmus, and president of the philological school at Alexandria. He also worked for a time at Rome under Tiberius and Claudius. A vain, boastful man, he travelled about the Greek cities, giving popular lectures on Homer. Of his many writings we have only fragments left. The glosses on Homer that bear his name are of later origin; on the other hand, the Homeric lexicon of the sophist Apollōnius is based on his genuine Homeric glosses. His bitter complaint, *Against the Jews*, addressed to Caligula at the instance of the Alexandrians, is best known from Josephus' noble reply to it.

Apodectæ (*apodektai* = receivers). The Athenian name for a board of ten magistrates yearly appointed by lot, who kept accounts of the moneys coming in to the State from various sources, took possession in the council's presence of the sums raised by the proper officers, and after cancelling the entries in their register, handed the money over to the several treasuries.

Apŏgrăphē (Gr.). An inventory, or register; also, in Attic law, a copy of a declaration made before a magistrate.

Apollō (Gr. *Apollōn*). Son of Zeus by Lēto (Lātōna), who, according to the legend most widely current, bore him and his twin-sister Artĕmis (Diāna) at the foot of Mount Cynthus in the island of Delos. Apollo appears originally as a god of *light*, both in its beneficent and its destructive effects; and of light in general, not of the sun only, for to the early Greeks the deity that brought daylight was Hēliŏs, with whom it was not till afterwards that Apollo was identified. While the meaning of his name Apollo is uncertain, his epithets of *Phœbus* and *Lўcius* clearly mark him as the bright, the life-giving, the former also meaning the pure, holy; for, as the god of pure light, he is the enemy of darkness, with all its unclean, uncouth, unhallowed brood. Again, not only the seventh day of the month, his birthday, but the first day of each month, *i.e.* of each new-born moon, was sacred to him, as it was to Janus, the Roman god of light; and according to the view that prevailed in many seats of his worship, he withdrew in winter time

either to sunny Lycia, or to the Hyperboreans who dwell in perpetual light in the utmost north, and returned in spring to dispel the powers of winter with his beams. When the fable relates that immediately after his birth, with the first shot from his bow he slew the dragon Pўthŏn (or Delphўnē), a hideous offspring of Gæa and guardian of the Delphian oracle, what seems to be denoted must be the spring-god's victory over winter, that filled the land with foul marsh and mist. As the god of light, his *festivals* are all in spring or summer, and many of them still plainly reveal in certain features his true and original attributes. Thus the *Delphĭnia*, held at Athens in April, commemorated the calming of the wintry sea after the equinoctial gales, and the consequent reopening of navigation. As this feast was in honour of the god of spring, so was the *Thargēlia*, held at Athens the next month, in honour of the god of summer. That the crops might ripen, he received firstfruits of them, and at the same time propitiatory gifts to induce him to avert the parching heat, so hurtful to fruits and men. About the time of the sun's greatest altitude (July and August), when the god displays his power, now for good and now for harm, the Athenians offered him *hecatombs*, whence the first month of their year was named *Hecatombæŏn*, and the Spartans held their *Hyacinthia* (*see* HYACINTHUS). In autumn, when the god was ripening the fruit of their gardens and plantations, and preparing for departure, they celebrated the *Pyanepsia* (*q.v.*), when they presented him with the firstfruits of harvest. Apollo gives the crops prosperity, and protection not only against summer heat, but against blight, mildew, and the vermin that prey upon them, such as field-mice and grasshoppers. Hence he was known by special titles in some parts of Asia. He was also a patron of flocks and pastures, and was worshipped in many districts under a variety of names referring to the breeding of cattle. In the story of Hermēs (*q.v.*) stealing his oxen, Apollo is himself the owner of a herd, which he gives up to his brother in exchange for the lyre invented by him. Other ancient legends speak of him as tending the flocks of Laŏmĕdŏn and Admētus, an act afterwards represented as a penalty for a fault. As a god of shepherds he makes love to the nymphs, to the fair Daphnē (*q.v.*), to Corōnis (*see* ASCLEPIUS), and to Cyrēnē, the mother of Aristæus, likewise a god of herds. Some forms of his worship and some versions of his story imply that Apollo, like his sister Artemis, was regarded as a protector of tender game and a slayer of rapacious beasts, especially of the wolf, the enemy of flocks, and himself a symbol of the god's power, that now sends mischief, and now averts it. Apollo promotes the health and well-being of man himself. As a god of prolific power, he was invoked at weddings; and as a nurse of tender manhood and trainer of manly youth, to him (as well as the fountain-nymphs) were consecrated the first offerings of the hair of the head. In *gymnăsĭa* and *palæstræ* he was worshipped equally with Hermes and Hērăclēs; for he gave power of endurance in boxing, with adroitness and fleetness of foot. As a warlike god and one helpful in fight, the Spartans paid him peculiar honours in their *Carneia* (*q.v.*), and in a measure the Athenians in their *Boëdrŏmia*. Another Athenian festival, the *Metageitnia*, glorified him as the author of neighbourly union. In many places, but above all at Athens, he was worshipped as *Agyieus*, the god of streets and highways, whose rude symbol, a conical post with a pointed ending, stood by streetdoors and in courtyards, to watch men's exit and entrance, to let in good and keep out evil, and was loaded by the inmates with gifts of honour, such as ribbons, wreaths of myrtle or bay, and the like. At sea, as well as on land, Apollo is a guide and guardian, and there, especially under the name *Delphĭnius*, taken from his friend and ally the dolphin, the symbol of the navigable sea. Under this character he was widely worshipped, for the most part with peculiar propitiatory rites, in seaports and on promontories, as that of Actium, and particularly at Athens, being also regarded as a leader of colonies. While he is *Alexicācus* (averter of ills) in the widest sense, he proves his power most especially in times of sickness; for, being god of the hot season, and himself the sender of most epidemics and the dreaded plague, sweeping man swiftly away with his unerring shafts, he can also lend the most effectual aid; so that he and his son Asclepius were revered as the chief gods of healing. As a saviour from epidemics mainly, but also from other evils, the *pæan* (*q.v.*) was sung in his honour.

In a higher sense also Apollo is a healer and saviour. From an early time a strong ethical tinge was given to his purely physical attributes, and the god of light became a god of mental and moral purity, and there-

fore of order, justice, and legality in human life. As such, he, on the one hand smites and spares not the insolent offender, Titўŏs for instance, the Aloīdæ, the overweening Nĭŏbē, and the Greeks before Troy ; but, on the other hand, to the guilt-laden soul, that turns to him in penitence and supplication, he grants purification from the stain of committed crime (which was regarded as a disease clouding the mind and crushing the heart), and so he heals the spirit, and readmits the outcast into civic life and religious fellowship. Of this he had himself set the pattern, when, after slaying the Delphian dragon, he fled from the land, did seven years' menial service to Admetus in atonement for the murder, and when the time of penance was past had himself purified in the sacred grove of baytrees by the Thessalian temple, and not till then did he return to Delphi and enter on his office as prophet of Zeus. Therefore he exacts from all a recognition of the atoning power of penance, in the teeth of the old law of vengeance for blood, which only bred new murders and new guilt. The atoning rites propagated by Apollo's worship, particularly from Delphi, contributed largely to the spread of milder maxims of law, affecting not only individuals, but whole towns and countries. Even without special prompting, the people felt from time to time the need of purification and expiation; hence certain expiatory rites had from of old been connected with his festivals.

As the god of light who pierces through all darkness, Apollo is the god of *divination*, which, however, has in his case a purely ethical significance; for he, as prophet and minister of his father Zeus, makes known his will to men, and helps to further his government in the world. He always declares the truth; but the limited mind of man cannot always grasp the meaning of his sayings. He is the patron of every kind of prophecy, but most especially of that which he imparts through human instruments, chiefly women, while in a state of ecstasy. Great as was the number of his oracles in Greece and Asia, all were eclipsed in fame and importance by that of Delphi (*q.v.*).

Apollo exercises an elevating and inspiring influence on the mind as god of *Music*, which, though not belonging to him alone any more than Atonement and Prophecy, was yet pre-eminently his province. In Homer he is represented only as a player on the lyre, while song is the province of the Muses ; but in course of time he grows to be the god, as they are the goddesses, of song and poetry, and is therefore *Musāgētēs* (Leader of the Muses) as well as master of the choric dance, which goes with music and song. And, as the friend of all that beautifies life, he is intimately associated with the Graces.

Standing in these manifold relations to nature and man, Apollo at all times held a prominent position in the religion of the Greeks; and as early as Homer his name is coupled with those of Zeus and Athena, as if between them the three possessed the sum total of divine power. His worship was diffused equally over all the regions in which Greeks were settled; but from remote antiquity he had been the chief god of the Dorians, who were also the first to raise him into a type of moral excellence. The two chief centres of his worship were the Island of Delos, his birthplace, where, at his magnificent temple standing by the sea, were held every five years the festive games called *Delia*, to which the Greek states sent solemn embassies; and Delphi, with its oracle and numerous festivals (*see* PYTHIA, THEOXENIA). Foremost among the seats of his worship in Asia was Pătăra in Lycia with a famous oracle.

To the *Romans* Apollo became known in the reign of their last king Tarquinius Superbus, the first Roman who consulted the Delphian oracle, and who also acquired the Sibylline Books (*q.v.*). By the influence of these writings the worship of Apollo soon became so naturalized among them, that in B.C. 431 they built a temple to him as god of healing, from which the expiatory processions (*see* SUPPLICATIONES) prescribed in the Sibylline books used to set out. In the *Lectisternia* (*q.v.*), first instituted in B.C. 399, Apollo occupies the foremost place. In 212 B.C., during the agony of the Second Punic War, the *Lūdi Apollĭnārēs* were, in obedience to an oracular response, established in honour of him. He was made one of the chief gods of Rome by Augustus, who believed himself to be under his peculiar protection, and ascribed the victory of Actium to his aid: hence he enlarged the old temple of Apollo on that promontory, and decorated it with a portion of the spoils. He also renewed the games held near it, previously every two years, afterwards every four, with gymnastic and artistic contests, and regattas on the sea; at Rome he reared a splendid new temple to him near his own house on the Palatine, and transferred

the *Ludi Sæcŭlārēs* (*q.v.*) to him and Diana.

The manifold symbols of Apollo correspond with the multitude of his *attributes*. The commonest is either the lyre or the bow, according as he was conceived as the god of song or as the far-hitting archer. The Delphian diviner, Pythian Apollo, is indicated by the Tripod, which was also the favourite offering at his altars. Among plants the bay, used for purposes of expiation, was early sacred to him (*see* DAPHNE). It was planted round his temples, and plaited into garlands of victory at the Pythian games. The palm-tree was also sacred to him, for it was under a palm-tree that he was born in Delos. Among animals, the wolf, the dolphin, the snow-white and musical swan, the hawk, raven, crow, and snake were under his special protection; the last four in connexion with his prophetic functions.

In ancient art he was represented as a long-haired but beardless youth, of tall yet muscular build, and handsome features. Images of him were as abundant as his worship was extensive: there was scarcely an artist of antiquity who did not try his

(1) THE BELVEDERE APOLLO.
(Rome, Vatican Museum.)

hand upon some incident in the story of Apollo. The ideal type of this god seems to have been fixed chiefly by Praxĭtĕlēs and Scopăs. The most famous statue preserved of him is the *Apollo Belvedere* in the Vatican (fig. 1), which represents him either as fighting with the Pythian dragon, or with his ægis frightening back the foes who threaten to storm his sanctuary. Other great works, as the *Apollo Musagetes* in the Vatican, probably from the hand of Scopas, show him as a *Citharœdus* in the long Ionian robe, or nude as in fig. 2. The *Apollo Sauroctŏnus* (lizard-killer), copied from a bronze statue by Praxiteles, is especially celebrated for its beauty. It represents a delicate youthful figure leaning against a tree, dart in hand, ready to stab a lizard that is crawling up the tree. It is preserved in bronze at the Villa Albani in Rome, and in marble at Paris.

(2) APOLLO, WITH LYRE AND GRIFFIN.
(Rome, Capitoline Museum.)

Apollŏdŏrus. (1) A Greek poet of the New Comedy, born at Carystus, between 300 and 260 B.C. He wrote forty-seven plays, and won five victories. From him Terence borrowed the plots of his *Phormio* and *Hĕcȳra*.

(2) A Greek grammarian and historian, of Athens, about 140 B.C., a pupil of Aristarchus and the Stoic Panætius. He was a most prolific writer on grammar, mythology, geography, and history. Some of his works were written in iambic *senārii, e.g.* a geography, and the *Chrŏnĭcă,* a condensed enumeration of the most important data in history and literature from the fall of Troy, which he places in B.C. 1183, down to his own time, undoubtedly the most important of ancient works on the subject. Besides fragments, we have under his name a book entitled *Bibliothēca,* a great storehouse of mythological material from the oldest theogonies down to Theseus, and, with all its faults of arrangement and treatment, a valuable aid to our knowledge of Greek mythology. Yet there are grounds for doubting whether it is from his hand at all, whether it is even an extract from his great work, *On the Gods,* in twenty-four books.

(3) A Greek painter of Athens, about 420 B.C., the first who graduated light and shade in his pictures, whence he received the name of *Sciagrăphus* (shadow-painter). This invention entitled him to be regarded as the founder of a new style, which aimed at producing illusion by pictorial means, and which was carried on further by his younger contemporary Zeuxis. [Pliny, *H.N.*, 35. 60].

(4) A Greek architect of Damascus, who lived for a time at Rome, where amongst other things he built Trajan's Forum and Trajan's Column. He was first banished and then put to death under Hadrian, A.D. 129, having incurred that emperor's anger by the freedom of his rebukes. We have a work by him on *Engines of War,* addressed to Hadrian.

Apollōnius, (1) *the Rhodian.* A Greek scholar and epic poet of the Alexandrian age, born at Alexandria about 260 B.C., a pupil of Callĭmăchus, wrote a long epic, *The Argonautĭca,* in four books, in which, departing from his master's taste for the learned and artificial, he aimed at all the simplicity of Homer. The party of Callimachus rejected the poem, and Apollonius retired in disgust to Rhodes, where his labours as a rhetorician, and his newly revised poem, won him hearty recognition and even admission to the citizenship. Hence his surname. Afterwards, returning to Alexandria, he recited his poem once more, and this time with universal applause, so that Ptolemy Epĭphănēs, in B.C. 196, appointed him to succeed Eratosthĕnēs as librarian. He probably died during the tenure of this office. His epic poem, which has survived, has a certain simplicity, though falling far short of the naturalness and beauty of Homer; its uniform mediocrity often makes it positively tedious, though it is constructed with great care, especially in its versification. By the Romans it was much prized, and more than once imitated, as by Varro of Atax and Valerius Flaccus. A valuable collection of *scholia* upon it testifies the esteem in which it was held by the learned of old.

(2) *Apollonius of Tralles.* A Greek sculptor of the school of Rhodes, and joint author with his countryman Tauriscus of the celebrated group of Dircē (*q.v.*). Among other artists of the name, the worthiest of mention is *Apollonius of Athens,* of the 1st century B.C. From his hand is the Herculēs, now only a torso, preserved in the Belvedere at Rome.

(3) *Apollonius of Perga* in Pamphylia. A Greek mathematician named " the Geometer," who lived at Pergămus and Alexandria in the 1st century B.C., and wrote a work on Conic Sections in eight books, of which we have only the first four in the original, the fifth, sixth, and seventh in an Arabic translation, and the eighth in extracts. The method he followed is that still in use.

(4) *Apollonius of Tyăna* in Cappadocia, the most celebrated of the Neo-Pythagoreans, lived about the middle of the 1st century A.D.; by a severely ascetic life on the supposed principles of Pythagŏrās, and by pretended miracles, he obtained such a hold on the multitude that he was worshipped as a god, and set up as a rival to Christ. The account of his life by the elder Philostrătus (*q.v.*) is more romance than history, and offers little to build upon. Having received his philosophical education, and lived in the temple of Asclēpius at Ægæ till his twentieth year, he divided his patrimony among the poor, and roamed all over the world; he was even said to have reached India and the sources of the Nile. Twice he lived at Rome; first under Nero till the expulsion of the philosophers, and again in Domitian's reign, when he had to answer a charge of conspiring against the emperor. Smuggled out of Rome during his trial, he continued his life as a wandering preacher of morals and worker of marvels for some years longer, and is said to have died at a great age, master of a school at Ephěsus. Of his alleged writings, eighty-five letters have alone survived.

(5) *Apollonius,* surnamed *Dyscŏlus* (= the surly). A Greek scholar, of Alexandria, where he had received his education, and where he ended his days a member of the Museum, after having laboured as a teacher at Rome under Antonīnus Pius, about 140 A.D. He is the father of Scientific Grammar, having been the first to reduce it to

systematic form. His extant works are the treatises on Pronouns, Adverbs, Conjunctions, and the Syntax of the parts of speech, in four books. He was followed especially by the Latin grammarians, above all by Priscian. His son Herodiānus accomplished even more than he did.

(6) *Apollonius the Sophist,* of Alexandria. His precise date A.D. is unknown. He was author of an extant Lexicon of Homeric Glosses, based on Apion's lost glossarial writings.

(7) *Apollonius, king of Tyre,* the hero of a Greek romance (now lost), composed in Asia Minor, in the 3rd century A.D., on the model of the *Ephesian History* of Xĕnŏphŏn (*q.v.* 2). We have a free Latin version made by a Christian, about the 6th century, probably in Italy, which was much read in the Middle Ages, and translated into Anglo-Saxon, English, French, Italian, Middle Greek and German, in prose and verse. Its materials are used in the pseudo-Shakspearian drama of *Pericles Prince of Tyre.*

Aporraxis. See BALL, GAMES OF.

Apŏthĕōsis (Lat. *Consecrātiŏ*). The act of placing a human being among the gods, of which the Greeks have an instance as early as Homer, but only in the single case of Leucŏthĕa. The oldest notion was that of a bodily removal; then arose the idea of the mortal element being purged away by fire, as in the case of Hērăclēs. There was a kind of deification which consisted in the decreeing of heroic honours to distinguished men after death, which was done from the time of the Peloponnesian War onwards, even in the case of living men (*see* HEROES). The successors of Alexander the Great, both the Seleucĭdæ and still more the Ptolemies, caused themselves to be worshipped as gods. Of the Romans, whose legend told of the translation of Ænēas and Rŏmŭlus into heaven, Cæsar was the first who claimed divine honours, if not by building temples to himself, yet by setting his statue among the gods in every sanctuary at Rome and in the empire, and by having a special flamen assigned to him. The belief in his divinity was confirmed by the comet that shone several months after his death, as long as his funeral games lasted; and under the triumvirate he was formally installed among the deities of Rome, as *Divus Iulius,* by a decree of the senate and people. His adopted son and successor Octavian persistently declined any offer of public worship, but he accepted the title of *Augustus* (the consecrated), and allowed his person to be adored in the provinces. On his death the senate decreed divine honours to him under the title of *Divus Augustus*, the erection of a temple, the founding of special games, and the establishment of a peculiar priesthood. After this, admission to the number of the *Divi*, as the deified emperors were called, becomes a prerogative of the imperial dignity. It is, however, left dependent on a resolution of the senate moved in honour of the deceased emperor by his successor. Hence it is not every emperor who obtains it, nor does consecration itself always lead to a permanent worship. Empresses too were often consecrated, first Augustus' wife Livia as *Diva Augusta*, and even other members of the imperial house.

The ceremony of Apotheosis used from the time of Augustus was the following. After the passing of the senate's decree a waxen image of the dead, whose body lay hidden below, was exhibited for seven days on an ivory bed of state in the palace, covered with gold-embroidered coverlets; then the bier was borne by knights and senators amidst a brilliant retinue down the Via Sacra to the ancient Forum, where the funeral oration was delivered, and thence to the Campus Martius, where it was deposited in the second of the four stories of a richly decorated funeral pile of pyramid shape. When the magistrates sacred and secular, the knights, lifeguard, and others concerned, had performed the last honours by processions and libations, the pile was set on fire, and as it burned up, an eagle soared from the topmost storey into the sky, a symbol of the ascending soul.

Apparitor. The general name in Latin for all public servants of the magistrates. They all had to be Roman citizens, and were paid a fixed salary out of the public treasury. Though nominated by the respective officers for a year at a time, they were usually re-appointed, so that practically their situations were secured for life, and they could even sell their places. The most important classes of these attendants were those of *scribæ, lictōrēs, viātōrēs* and *præcōnēs* (*q.v.*). These were divided into *decūriæ* of varying strength, which enjoyed corporate rights, and chose foremen from their own body. (*Comp.* ACCENSI.)

Appellātiō. The Latin term for an appeal to a magistrate to put his veto on the decision of an equal or inferior magistrate. Thus a consul could be appealed to against his colleague and all other magistrates except the tribunes, but a tribune both against his colleagues and all magistrates whatsoever. Another thing altogether was the *Provŏcātiō* (*q.v.*) under the Republic, an appeal from a magistrate's sentence to the People as supreme judge. During the imperial period the two processes run into one, for the emperor held united in his person both the supreme judicial function and the plenary power of all magistrates, particularly the tribunician veto, so that an appeal to him was at once an *appellatio* and a *provocatio*. This appeal, in our sense of the word, was only permitted in important cases; it had to be made within a short time after sentence was passed, and always addressed to the authority next in order, so that it only reached the emperor if no intermediate authority was competent. If the result was that the disputed verdict was neither quashed nor awarded, but confirmed, the appellant had to pay a fine. As the power of life and death rested with the emperor and senate alone, governors of provinces were bound to send up to Rome any citizen appealing on a capital charge.

Appiānus. A Greek historian, of Alexandria, who lived about the middle of the 2nd century A.D. At first he pursued the calling of an advocate at Rome; in later life, on the recommendation of his friend the rhetorician Fronto, he obtained from Antōnīnus Pius the post of an imperial procurator in Egypt. He wrote an extensive work on the development of the Roman Empire from the earliest times down to Trajan, consisting of a number of special histories of the several periods and the several lands and peoples till the time when they fell under the Roman dominion. Of the twenty-four books of which it originally consisted, only eleven are preserved complete beside the Preface: Spain (book 6), Hannibal (7), Carthage (8), Syria (11), Mithridates (12), the Roman Civil Wars (13–17) and Illyria (23), the rest being lost altogether, or only surviving in fragments. Appian's style is plain and bald, even to dryness, and his historical point of view is purely Roman. The book is a mere compilation, and disfigured by many oversights and blunders, especially in chronology; nevertheless the use made by the writer of lost authorities lends it considerable worth, and for the history of the Civil Wars it is positively invaluable.

Apsīnēs. A Greek rhetorician, of Gădăra, who taught at Athens in the first half of the 3rd century A.D., and wrote a valuable treatise on Rhetoric.

Apulēius (*Lucius*). Born about 130 A.D.

at Madaura in Numidia, of a wealthy and honourable family; the most original Latin writer of his time. Educated at Carthage, he went to Athens to study philosophy, especially that of Plato; then he travelled far and wide, everywhere obtaining initiation into the mysteries. For some time he lived in Rome as an advocate. After returning to Africa, he married a lady considerably older than himself, the mother of a friend, Æmilia Pudentilla, whereupon her kinsmen charged him with having won the rich widow's hand by magic, and of having contrived the death of her son: a charge to which he replied with much wit in his oration *De Măgiā* (earlier than A.D. 161). He afterwards settled down at Carthage, and thence made excursions through Africa, delivering orations or lectures. Of the rest of his life and the year of his death nothing is known. Beside the *Apologia* above-mentioned, and a few rhetorical and philosophic writings, another work, his chief one, also survives, which was composed at a ripe age, with hints borrowed from a book of Lucian's. This is a satirical and fantastic moral romance, *Metamorphōsĕōn libri XI* (*de Asĭno Aurĕo*), the adventures of one Lucius, who is transformed into an ass, and under that disguise has the amplest opportunities of observing, undetected, the preposterous doings of mankind. Then, enlightened by this experience, and with the enchantment taken off him by admission into the mysteries of Osiris, he becomes quite a new man. Of the many episodes interwoven into the story, the most interesting is the beautiful allegorical fairy tale of Cupid and Psychē, so much used by later poets and artists. Throughout the book Apuleius paints the moral and religious conditions of his time with much humour and in lifelike colours, though his language, while clever, is often affected, bombastic, and disfigured by obsolete and provincial phrases.

Aquælicium. The Roman name for a ceremony for bringing on rain. (*See* JUPITER.)

Aqueducts were not unfrequently constructed by the Greeks, who collected the spring-water of neighbouring hills, by channels cut through the rock, or by underground conduits of brick and stone work, into reservoirs, and thence distributed it by a network of rills. An admirable work of this kind is the tunnel, more than a mile in length, which was bored through the mountain now called Kastri, by the architect Eupalīnus of Mĕgăra, probably under

Polycrătēs (in the 6th century B.C.).—The *Roman* aqueducts are among the most magnificent structures of antiquity. Some of these were likewise constructed underground; others, latterly almost all, conveyed the water, often for long distances, in covered channels of brick or stone, over lofty arcades stretching straight through hill and valley. They started from a well-head (*căpŭt ăquārum*) and ended in a reservoir (*castellum*), out of which the water ran in Rome into three chambers, lying one above another, the lowest chamber sending it through leaden or clay pipes into the public fountains and basins, the middle one into the great bathing establishments, the uppermost into private houses. Private citizens paid a tax for the water they obtained from these public sources. Under the Republic the construction and repair of aqueducts devolved upon the censors, their management on the ædiles, but from the time of Augustus on a special *cūrātor aquarum* assisted by a large staff of pipe-masters, fountain-masters, inspectors, and others, taken partly from the number of the public slaves. The amount of water brought into Rome by its numerous aqueducts, the first of which, the *aqua Appia*, was projected B.C. 312, may be estimated from the fact that the four still in use—*aqua virgo* (now Acqua Vergine, built by Agrippa B.C. 20), *aqua Marcia* (now Acqua Pia, B.C. 144), *aqua Claudia* (now Acqua Felice, finished by Claudius A.D. 52), *aqua Traiana* (now Acqua Paola, constructed by Trajan A.D. 111)—are sufficient to supply all the houses and innumerable fountains of the present city in superfluity. Among the provincial aqueducts, one is specially well preserved, that known as Pont du Gard, near Nîmes, in the south of France (*see* cut on p. 48).

Arachnē (= spider). Daughter of the Lydian purple-dyer Idmōn, challenged Athēna, of whom she had learnt weaving, to a weaving match. When the offended goddess tore up Arachne's web, which represented the loves of the gods, Arachne hung herself, but Athena changed her into a spider.

Arātus. A Greek poet, of Soli in Cilicia, about 270 B.C., contemporary of Callĭmăchus and Theocrĭtus. At the request of the Macedonian king Antigŏnus Gonātās, at whose court he lived as physician, he wrote, without much knowledge of the subject, but guided by the works of Eudoxus and Theophrastus, an astronomical poem, *Phæ-nŏmĕna and Prognŏstĭca* (aspects of the sky and signs of weather). Without genuine

* THE PONT DU GARD. (*See p. 47*)

(Height of lowest row of arches above the water's edge, 65 ft.; second row above the lowest, 65 ft.; top row above second, 28 ft.; total, 158 ft.)

poetic inspiration, Aratus manages his intractable material with considerable tact, and dignified simplicity. The language, while not always free from stiffness, is choice, and the versification correct. The poem enjoyed a high repute with the general public, as well as with poets and specialists: thus the great astronomer Hipparchus wrote a commentary on it in four books. The Romans also took pleasure in reading and translating it, *e.g.* Cicero, Cæsar Germānĭcus, and Aviēnus.

Arbĭter. An umpire; especially a judge who decides according to equity, while a *iūdex* decides according to law.

Arcădius (Gr. *Arkădĭŏs*. A Greek grammarian of Antioch, who probably flourished in the 2nd century A.D. He was the author of a Doctrine of Accents in 20 books, an abstract of a work by the famous Herodian.

Arcăs (Gr. *Arkăs*). Son of Zeus by the nymph Callisto, and ancestor of the Arcadians, who was translated to the sky by Zeus as *Arctūrus* = Watcher of the Bear. (*See* CALLISTO.)

Archĕmŏrus (= leader in fate, *i.e.* the first to die). A surname given to Ŏpheltēs, the infant son of Lycurgus king of Nemĕa, who was killed by a snake during the march of the Seven against Thebes (*q.v.*). It was given him by the seer Amphiarāŭs, who foresaw the destruction awaiting himself and his confederates; and by it the child was invoked at the Nemean Games originally founded in memory of him.

Archestrătus, of Gela, in Sicily, flourished about 318 B.C., and composed the humorous didactic poem *Hēdўpătheia* (= good cheer), supposed to describe a gastronomic tour round the then known world, with playful echoes of Homer and the dogmatic philosophers. The numerous fragments display much talent and wit.

Archĭlŏchus. A Greek lyric poet, especially eminent as a writer of lampoons. Born at Paros, he was the son of Telēsĭclēs by a slave-woman, but was driven by poverty to go with a colony to Thasŏs B.C. 720 or 708. From Thasos he was soon driven by want and by the enmities which his unrestrained passion for invective had drawn upon him. He seems to have roamed restlessly from place to place, until, on his return to Paros, he was slain in fight by the Naxian Calōndās. Long afterwards, when this man visited the Delphian temple, the god is said to have driven him from his threshold as the slayer of a servant of the Muses, and refused to admit him till he had propitiated the soul of the poet

at his tomb: a story which expresses the high value set on his art by the ancients, who placed him on a level with Homer, Pindar and Sophŏclēs. For Archilochus had an extraordinary poetical genius, which enabled him to invent a large number of new metres, and to manipulate them with the ease of a master. He brought Iambic poetry, in particular, to artistic perfection. The many misfortunes of his stormy life had bred in his irritable nature a deeply-settled indignation, which, in poems perfect in form and alive with force and fury, vented itself in bitter mockery even of his friends, and in merciless, unpardonable abuse of his foes. Such was the effect of his lampoons, that Lycambēs, who had first promised and then refused him his daughter Neobūlē, hanged himself and his family in the despair engendered by the poet's furious attacks. Of his poems, which were written in the Old-Ionic dialect, and taken by Horace for his model in his Epodes, only a number of short fragments are preserved.

Archĭmēdēs. One of the greatest mathematicians and natural philosophers of antiquity, born B.C. 287 at Syracuse. He lived at the court of his kinsman, king Hĭĕrō, and was killed (B.C. 212) by a Roman soldier at the taking of the city which he had largely aided in defending with his engines. Of his inventions and discoveries we need only say, that he ascertained the ratio of the radius to the circumference, and that of the cylinder to the sphere, and the hydrostatic law that a body dipped in water loses as much weight as that of the water displaced by it; that he invented the pulley, the endless screw, and the kind of pump called the "screw of Archimedes"; and that he constructed the so-called "sphere," a sort of orrery showing the motions of the heavenly bodies. Of his works, written in the Doric dialect, the following are preserved: On the sphere and cylinder, On the measurement of the circle, On conoids and spheroids, On spiral lines, The psammītēs (or sand-reckoner, for the calculation of the earth's size in grains of sand), On the equilibrium of planes and their centres of gravity, and On floating bodies.

Architecture: (1) of the *Greeks*. Of the earliest efforts of the Greeks in architecture, we have evidence in the so-called *Cyclopean Walls* surrounding the castles of kings in the Heroic Age at Tīryns, Argos, Mycēnæ (fig. 1), and elsewhere. They are of enormous thickness, some being constructed of rude colossal blocks, whose gaps are filled up with smaller stones; while others are built of stones more or less carefully hewn, their

(1) WALL OF POLYGONAL STONES, MYCENÆ.

interstices exactly fitting into each other. Gradually they begin to show an approxi-

(2) THE LION-GATE, MYCENÆ.

mation to buildings with rectangular blocks. The gates let into these walls are closed at the top either by the courses of stone jutting over from each side till they touch, or by a long straight block laid over the two leaning side-posts. Of the latter kind is the famous *Lion-gate at Mycenæ*, so-called from the group of two lions standing with their forefeet on the broad pedestal of a pillar that tapers rapidly downwards, and remarkable as the oldest specimen of Greek sculpture. The sculpture is carved on a large triangular slab that fills an opening left in the wall to lighten the weight on the lintel (fig. 2).

Among the most striking relics of this primitive age are the so-called *Thēsauroi*, or treasuries (now regarded as tombs) of ancient dynasties the most considerable being the *Trea-*

sure-house of Atreus at Mycenæ. The usual form of these buildings is that of a circular chamber vaulted over by the horizontal courses approaching from all sides till they meet. Thus the vault is not a true arch (fig. 3). The interior seems originally to have been covered with metal plates, thus agreeing with Homer's descriptions of metal as a favourite ornament of princely houses. An open-air building preserved from that age is the supposed *Temple of Hēra* on Mount Ocha (now Hagios Elias) in Eubœa, a rectangle built of regular square blocks, with walls more than a yard thick, two small windows, and a door with leaning posts and a huge lintel in the southern side-wall. The sloping roof is of hewn flagstones resting on the thickness of the wall and overlapping each other; but the centre is left open as in the hypæthral temples of a later time.

From the simple shape of a rectangular house shut in by blank walls we gradually advance to finer and richer forms, formed especially by the introduction of columns detached from the wall and serving to support the roof and ceiling. Even in Homer we find columns in the palaces to support the halls that surround the courtyard, and the ceiling of the banqueting-room. The construction of columns (*see* ARCHITECTURE, ORDERS OF) received its artistic development first from the *Dorians* after their migration into the Peloponnēsus about 1000 B.C., next from the *Ionians*, and from each in a form suitable to their several characters. If the simple serious character of the Dorians speaks in the Doric Order, no less does the lighter, nimbler, and more

(3) * "TREASURE HOUSE" OF ATREUS, MYCENÆ.

A wall of entrance-passage (*dròmos*), 30 ft. long.   *B* entrance, 19½ ft. high.   *C* large chamber, 50 ft. high.   *D* entrance (9 ft. high) to small chamber.

showy genius of the Ionian race come out in the Order named after them. By about 650 B.C. the Ionic style was flourishing side by side with the Doric.

As it was in the construction of *Temples* (*q.v.*) that architecture had developed her favourite forms, all other public buildings borrowed their artistic character from the temple. The structure and furniture of private houses (*see* HOUSE), were, during the best days of Greece, kept down to the simplest forms. About 600 B.C., in the Greek islands and on the coast of Asia Minor, we come across the first architects known to us by name. It was then that *Rhœcus* and *Theodōrus* of Samos, cele-

period, in addition to many ruined temples in Sicily (especially at Selīnūs and Agrigentum), should be mentioned the Temple of Poseidōn at Pæstum (Poseidōnia) in South Italy, one of the best preserved and most beautiful relics of antiquity (figs. 4, 5). The patriotic fervour of the Persian Wars created a general expansion of Greek life, in which Architecture and the sister art of Sculpture were not slow to take a part. In these departments, as in the whole onward movement, a central position was taken by Athens, whose leading statesmen, Cīmōn and Perīclēs, lavished the great resources of the State at once in strengthening and beautifying the city. During this period arose a

(4) * EXTERIOR OF TEMPLE OF POSEIDON AT PÆSTUM (79 ft. × 195 ft.).

brated likewise as inventors of casting in bronze, built the great temple of Hēra in that island, while *Chersiphrōn* of Cnōsus in Crete, with his son *Metăgĕnēs*, began the temple of Artĕmis (Diana) at Ephĕsus, one of the seven wonders of the world, which was not finished till 120 years after. In Greece Proper a vast temple to Zeus was begun at Athens in the 6th century B.C. (*see* OLYMPIEUM), and two more at Delphi and Olympia, one by the Corinthian *Spinthărus*, the other by the Elean *Libōn*. Here, and in the Western colonies the Doric style still predominated everywhere. Among the chief remains of this

group of masterpieces that still astonish us in their ruins, some in the forms of a softened Doric, others in the Ionic style, which had now found its way into Attica, and was here fostered into nobler shapes. The Doric order is represented by the Temple of Theseus (fig. 6), the Propylæa built by *Mnēsĭclēs*, the Parthĕnōn, a joint production of *Ictīnus* and *Callicrătēs*; while the Erechthĕum is the most brilliant creation of the Ionic order in Attica. Of the influence of Attic Architecture on the rest of Greece we have proof, especially in the Temple of Apollo at Bassæ in South-Western Arcadia, built from the design of the above-mentioned Ictinus.

The progress of the Drama to its per-fection in this period led to a corresponding improvement in the *building of Theatres* (*q.v.*). A stone theatre was begun at Athens even before the Persian Wars; and the Odēum of Pericles served similar purposes. How soon the highest results were achieved in this department, when once the fundamental forms had thus been laid down in outline at Athens, is shown by the theatre at Epidaurus, a work of *Polyclītus*, unsurpassed, as the ancients testify, by any later theatres in harmony and beauty. Another was built at Syracuse, before B.C. 420. Nor is it only in the erection of single buildings that the great

increasingly fashionable. In the first half of the 4th century arose what the ancients considered the largest and grandest temple in the Peloponnesus, that of Athēna at Tĕgĕa, a work of the sculptor and architect *Scŏpās*. During the middle of the century, another of the "seven wonders," the splendid tomb of Mausōlus at Halicarnassus was constructed (*see* MAUSOLEUM). Many magnificent temples arose in that time. In Asia Minor, the temple at Ephesus, burnt down by Herostrătus, was rebuilt by Alexander's bold architect *Deinocrătēs*. In the islands the ruins of the temple of Athena at Priēnē, of Apollo at Milētus, of Dionȳsus at Teos, and others,

(5) * INTERIOR OF TEMPLE OF POSEIDON, PÆSTUM; *see* p. 51.

advance then made by architecture shows itself. In laying out new towns, or parts of towns, men began to proceed on artistic principles, an innovation due to the sophist *Hippodămus* of Milētus.

In the 4th century B.C., owing to the change wrought in the Greek mind by the Peloponnesian War, in place of the pure and even tone of the preceding period, a desire for effect became more and more general, both in architecture and sculpture. The sober Doric style fell into abeyance and gave way to the Ionic, by the side of which a new Order, the *Corinthian*, said to have been invented by the sculptor *Callimăchus*, with its more gorgeous decorations, became

even to this day offer a brilliant testimony to their former magnificence. Among Athenian buildings of that age the Monument of Lysicrătēs (*q.v.*) is conspicuous for its graceful elegance and elaborate development of the Corinthian style. In the succeeding age Greek architecture shows its finest achievements in the building of theatres, especially those of Asiatic towns, in the gorgeous palaces of newly-built royal capitals, and in general in the luxurious completeness of private buildings. As an important specimen of the last age of Attic architecture may also be mentioned the Tower of the Winds (*q.v.*) at Athens.

(2) *Architecture of the Etruscans and*

Romans. In architecture, as well as sculpture, the Romans were long under the influence of the *Etruscans*, who, though denied the gift of rising to the ideal, united wonderful activity and inventiveness with a passion for covering their buildings with rich ornamental carving. None of their temples have survived, for they built all the upper parts of wood; but many proofs of their activity in building remain, surviving from various ages, in the shape of *Tombs* and *Walls*. The latter clearly show how they progressed from piling up polygonal blocks in Cyclopean style to regular courses of squared stone. Here and there a building still shows that the Etruscans originally made vaultings by letting horizontal courses jut over, as in the ancient Greek *thēsauroi* above mentioned; on the other hand, some very old gateways, as at Volterra (fig. 7) and Perugia, exhibit the true *Arch* of wedge-shaped stones, the invention of which is probably due to Etruscan ingenuity, and from the introduction of which a new and magnificent development of architecture takes its rise. The most imposing monument of ancient Italian arch-building is to be seen in the sewers of Rome laid down in the 6th century B.C. (*See* CLOACA MAXIMA.)

When all other traces of Etruscan influence were being swept away at Rome by the intrusion of Greek forms of art, especially after the Conquest of Greece in the middle of the 2nd century B.C., the Roman architects kept alive in full vigour the Etruscan method of building the arch, which they developed and completed by the inventions of the *Cross-Arch* (or groined vault) and the *Dome*. With the Arch, which admits of a bolder and more varied management of spaces, the Romans combined, as a decorative element, the columns of the Greek Orders. Among these their growing love of pomp gave the preference more and more to the Corinthian, adding to it afterwards a still more gorgeous embellishment in what is called the *Roman* or *Composite* capital (*see* ARCHITECTURE, ORDERS OF). Another service rendered by the Romans was the introduction of building in brick (*see* POTTERY).

A more vigorous advance in Roman architecture dates from the opening of the 3rd century B.C., when they began making great military roads and aqueducts. In the first

(6) * "THESEUM" (46 ft. × 105 ft.); see p. 51.

half of the 2nd century they built, on Greek models, the first *Basīlĭca*, which, besides its practical utility served to embellish the Forum. Soon after the middle of the cen-

(7) * GATE OF VOLTERRA.
(After Canina.)

tury, appeared the first of their more ambitious temples in the Greek style. There is simple grandeur in the ruins of the *Tăbŭlārĭum*, or Record-Office, built B.C. 78

on the slope of the Capitol next the Forum. These are among the few remains of Roman republican architecture; but in the last decades of the Republic simplicity gradually disappeared, and men were eager to display aided by his son-in-law *Agrippa*, a man who understood building, not only completed his uncle's plans, but added many magnificent structures—the *Forum Augusti* with its Temple to *Mars Ultor*, the Theatre of Mar-

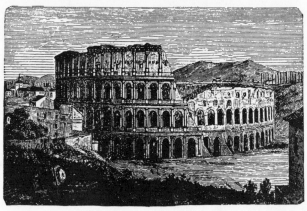

(8) * EXTERIOR OF COLOSSEUM; *see* p. 55.
(Cooke, *Views of the Coliseum*, pl. 13.)

a princely pomp in public and private buildings; witness the first stone theatre erected by Pompey as early as 55 B.C. Then all that went before was eclipsed by the vast works undertaken by *Cæsar*, the Theatre, cellus with its Portico of Octavia, the *Mausoleum*, and others. Augustus could fairly boast that "having found Rome a city of brick, he left it a city of marble." The grandest monument of that age, and one of the loftiest

(9) * INTERIOR OF COLOSSEUM; *see* p. 55.
(Cooke, *Views of the Coliseum*, pl. 4.)

Amphitheatre, Circus, *Basilica Iulia*, *Forum Cæsăris* with its Temple to Venus Genetrix. These were finished by *Augustus*, under whom Roman architecture seems to have reached its culminating point. Augustus, creations of Roman art in general, is the *Pantheon* (q.v.) built by Agrippa, adjacent to, but not connected with, his *Thermæ*, the first of the many works of that kind in Rome. A still more splendid aspect was imparted to the city by the rebuilding of the Old Town burnt down in Nero's fire, and by the "Golden House" of Nero, a gorgeous pile,

The progress made under the Flavian emperors is evidenced by *Vespasian's* Amphitheatre (q.v.) known as the *Colosseum* (figs.

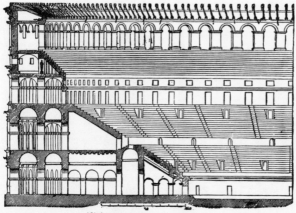

(10) * CROSS-SECTION OF COLOSSEUM.
(After Fontana and Hirt.)

the like of which was never seen before, but which was destroyed on the violent death of its creator. Of the luxurious grandeur of

(11) * ARCH OF TITUS.

private buildings we have ocular proof in the dwelling-houses of Pompeii, a paltry country-town in comparison with Rome.

8, 9, 10), the mightiest Roman ruin in the world, by the ruined *Thermæ*, or Baths, of *Titus*, and by his Triumphal Arch (q.v.), the oldest specimen extant in Rome of this class of monument, itself a creation of the Roman mind (fig. 11). But all previous buildings were surpassed in size and splendour when Trajan's architect Apollodōrus of Damascus raised the *Forum Trāiānum* with its huge *Basilica Ulpia* (fig. 12) and the still surviving Column of Trajan. No less extensive were the works of Hadrian, who, besides adorning Athens with many magnificent buildings, bequeathed to Rome a Temple of Venus and Roma, the most colossal of all Roman temples (fig. 13), and his own Mausoleum (q.v.), the core of which is preserved in the Castle of St. Angelo. While the works of the Antonines already show a gradual decline in architectural feeling, the Triumphal Arch of Severus ushers in the period of decay that set in with the 3rd century. In this closing period of Roman rule the buildings grow more and more gigantic, witness the Baths of Caracalla (fig. 14), those of Diocletian, with his palace at Salona (three miles from Spalatro) in Dalmatia, and the Basilica of Constantine breathing the last feeble gasp of ancient life. But outside of Rome and Italy, in every part of the enormous empire to its utmost barbarian borders,

(13) * SECTION OF TEMPLE OF VENUS AND ROMA; *see* p. 55.
(Restoration, after Canina.)

(14) * INTERIOR OF THERMÆ OF CARACALLA (RESTORED); *see* p. 55.

(12) * PLAN OF BASILICA ULPIA; *see* p. 55.
(After Canina.)

Scala   100 de Pele

bridges, numberless remains of roads and aqueducts and viaducts, ramparts and gateways, palaces, villas, market-places and judgment-halls, baths, theatres, amphitheatres and temples, attest the versatility, majesty, and solidity of Roman architecture, most of whose creations only the rudest shocks have hitherto been able to destroy.

Architecture, Orders of. In Greek architecture there were three orders of columns: the Doric, Ionic, and Corin-

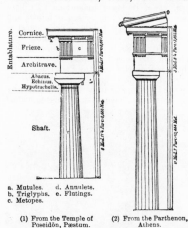

a. Mutules.   d. Annulets.
b. Triglyphs. e. Flutings.
c. Metopes.

(1) From the Temple of   (2) From the Parthenon,
   Poseidôn, Pæstum.   Athens.

DORIC ORDER.

thian. (I) *Doric*: Figures 1 and 2 give instances of the Doric style from the temple at Pæstum and the Parthênon at Athens. The Doric column consists of (*a*) of the shaft, which increases in diameter almost invisibly up to about one-quarter of its height, and diminishes slightly after that point. It has no base, but rests immediately on the stylobate. It is surrounded with semi-circular flutings, meeting each other at a sharp angle. These were chiselled with a cedarwood tool after the separate drums had been put together. (*b*) The capital (Lat. *capĭtŭlum*). This consists of three parts, (*a*) the *hypŏtrăchēlĭŏn*, or neck of the column, a continuation of the shaft, but separated by an indentation from the other drums. It is wider at the top than at the bottom, and is generally ornamented with several parallel and horizontal rings. (*b*) The *ĕchīnus*, a circular moulding or cushion, which widens greatly towards the top. (*c*) The *abax* or *ābăcus*, a square slab supporting the architrave or *epistȳlĭon*. The

height of the shaft is usually 5½ times, the distance between the columns 1½ times the diameter of the base of the column. The architrave is a quadrangular beam of stone, reaching from pillar to pillar. On this again rests the frieze, *zōphŏros*, so called from the metopes which are adorned with sculptures in relief. These metopes are square spaces between the triglyphs: the triglyphs are surfaces cut into three concave grooves, two whole grooves in the centre, and two half grooves at the sides. One is placed over each pillar, and one between each pair of pillars. The entablature is completed by a projecting cornice, a slab crowned with a simple heading-course, the lower surface of

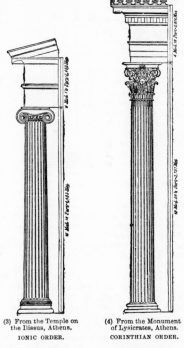

(3) From the Temple on   (4) From the Monument
   the Ilissus, Athens.   of Lysicrates, Athens.

IONIC ORDER.   CORINTHIAN ORDER.

which is ornamented with sloping corbels (Gk. *stăgŏnĕs*, Lat. *mŭtŭlī*).

(II) *Ionic Columns.* An instance is given in fig. 3 from the temple on the Ilissus at Athens. These are loftier than the Doric, their height being 8½–9½ times the diameter of the lower part. The enlargement of the lower part is also less than in the Doric columns, the distance between each column greater (two diameters), the flutings (generally 24 in number) deeper, and separated by small flat surfaces. The Ionic column has a base, consisting of a square slab (*plinthŏs*), and several cushion-like supports separated by grooves. The capital, again, is more artistically developed. The neck, instead of flutings, has five leaves worked in relief. The *echinus* is very small and ornamented with an egg pattern. Over it, instead of the *abacus*, is a four-cornered cushion ending before and behind in spiral volutes, supporting a narrow square slab, which is also adorned with an egg pattern. The architrave is divided into three bands, projecting one above the other, and upon it rises, in an uninterrupted surface, the frieze, adorned with reliefs continuously along its whole length. Finally, the cornice is composed of different parts.

(III) *The Corinthian column* (fig. 4, from the monument of Lysĭcrătēs, at Athens). The base and shaft are identical with the Ionic, but the capital takes the form of an open *cālix* formed of acanthus leaves. Above this is another set of leaves, from between which grow stalks with small leaves, rounded into the form of volutes. On this rests a small *ăbăcus* widening towards the top, and on this again the entablature, which is borrowed from the Ionic order. On the human figures employed instead of columns to support the entablature, *see* ATLAS, CANEPHORI, CARYATIDES.

The Romans adopted the Greek styles of column, but not always in their pure form. They were fondest of the Corinthian, which they laboured to enrich with new and often excessive ornamentation. For instance, they crowned the Corinthian capital with the Ionic, thus forming what is called the Roman or composite capital.

The style known as Tuscan is a degenerate form of the Doric. The Tuscan column has a smooth shaft, in height = 7 diameters of the lower part, and tapering up to three-quarters of its lower dimensions. Its base consists of two parts, a circular plinth, and a cushion of equal height. The capital is formed of three parts of equal height.

In other styles, too, the Romans sometimes adopted the smooth instead of the fluted shaft, as for instance in the Pantheon (fig. 5).

Single columns were sometimes erected by the Greeks, and in imitation of them by the Romans, as memorials to distinguished

Entablature. { Cornice. Frieze. Architrave. }

Capital.

Shaft.

Base.

a. Cyma recta.   g. Volutes.
b. Corona.   h. Astragal.
c. Modillions.   i. Torus.
d. Ovolo.   k. Trochilus.
e. Cymation.   l. Quadra.
f. Abacus.   m. Plinth.

(5) From the Pantheon, Rome.

CORINTHIAN ORDER.

(6) * COLUMN OF MARCUS AURELIUS.
(With its surroundings as restored by Canina, *Arch. Rom.* tav. 204.)

persons. A good example is the *Columna Rostrāta*, or column with its shaft adorned with the beaks of ships, in the Roman

Forum. This was set up in commemoration of the naval victory of Duīlĭus over the Carthaginians (261 B.C.). Among the columns which survive, the most magnificent is that of Trajan, erected in the Forum of Trajan 113 A.D. It rises on a quadrangular pediment to the height of 124 feet; its diameter below is about 10 feet, and a little less in the upper part. An interior spiral staircase of 185 steps leads to the summit. The shaft, formed of twenty-three drums of marble, is adorned with a series of reliefs, 3 feet 3 inches high and 200 feet long, in a series of twenty-two spirals. They represent scenes in Trajan's Dacian campaigns, and contain 2,500 human figures, with animals, engines, etc. On a cylindrical pedestal at the summit there once stood a gilded statue of the emperor, which, since the year 1587, has made way for a bronze figure of St. Peter. A similar column is that of Marcus Aurelius, 122 feet high, on the Piazza Colonna. Since 1589 the statue of St. Paul has been substituted for that of the emperor. The reliefs, in twenty spirals, represent events in the emperor's war with the Marcomanni.

Archĭthĕorĭa. One of the public services called *lĭturgĭæ* at Athens; it was the obligation to furnish forth the sacred embassies (*thĕorĭæ*) to the four great national festivals, also to Delphi and other holy places. (*See* LEITOURGIA.)

Archōn (=ruler), the Athenian name for the supreme authority established on the abolition of royalty. On the death of the last king, Codrus, B.C. 1068, the headship of the state for life was bestowed on his son Mĕdōn and his descendants under the title of Archon. In 752 B.C. their term of office was cut down to ten years, in 714 their exclusive privilege was abolished, and the right to hold the office thrown open to all the nobility, while its duration was diminished to one year; finally in B.C. 683 the power was divided among nine archons. By Solon's legislation, his wealthiest class, the *pentacŏsĭo-medimni*, became eligible to the office; and by Aristīdēs' arrangement after the Persian Wars it was thrown open to all the citizens, Cleisthĕnēs having previously, in the interests of the democracy, substituted the drawing of lots for election by vote. [*See* Note on p. 706.] The political power of the office, having steadily decreased with time, sank to nothing when democracy was established; its holders had no longer even the right to deliberate and originate motions, their action being limited to certain priestly and judicial functions, relics of their once regal power.

The titles and duties of the several Archons are as follows: (1) Their president, named emphatically *Archon*, or *Archon Epōnўmŏs*, because the civil year was named after him. He had charge of the Great *Dionўsia*, the *Thargēlia*, the embassies to festivals (*theorĭæ*), the nomination of *chŏrēgi;* also the position of guardian in chief, and the power to appoint guardians, the presidency in all suits about family rights (such as questions of divorce or inheritance), and in disputes among the *choregi*. ——(2) The *Archon Băsĭleus* (king), called so because on him devolved certain sacred rites inseparably connected with the name of king. He had the care of the Eleusinian Mysteries (and was obliged therefore to be an initiated person), of the *Lēnæa* and *Anthestēria*, of gymnastic contests, to which he appointed a superintendent, and of a number of antiquated sacrifices, some of which fell to the share of his wife, the *Basilissa* (queen); and lastly, the position of president in all suits touching religious law, including those trials for murder that came within the jurisdiction of the *Ephĕtæ* (*q.v.*).——(3) The *Archon Pŏlĕmarchŏs* (leader in war) was originally entrusted with the war-department, and, as late as the battle of Mărăthōn, had the right of voting with the ten generals, and the old royal privilege of commanding the right wing. Afterwards he only had charge of the state sacrifices offered to the gods of war and to the shade of Harmŏdius, the public funerals of those who fell in war and the annual feasts in honour of them; finally, the jurisdiction in all questions concerning the personal and family rights of resident aliens (*metœci*) and strangers. All this rested on the old assumption that foreigner meant enemy. Each of these three superior Archons had two assessors chosen by himself, but responsible. ——(4) The *Six Thesmŏthĕtæ* (literally lawgivers) administered justice in all cases not pertaining to the senior Archons or some other authority, revised the laws once a year, and superintended the apportioning of public offices by lot. The several Archons exercised their jurisdiction at different spots in the city; that of the Polemarch alone lay outside the walls. Duties common to all nine were: the yearly appointment by lot of the *Hēliastæ* (*q.v.*), the choice of umpires in the Panathenæa, the holding of elections of the generals and other military officers, jurisdiction in the case of officials suspended or deposed by the people, and latterly even in suits which had previously been subject to the *nautŏdĭcæ*. (*See* NAU-TODICÆ.) If they had discharged their office without blame, they entered the Areŏpăgus as members for life. The office of Archon lasted even under the Roman rule.

Archȳtas of Tarentum. Distinguished as a general, statesman and mathematician, a leading representative of the Pythagorean philosophy, who flourished about 400–365 B.C. (*See* PYTHAGORAS.)

Arctīnus (Gr. *Arktīnŏs*). A Greek epic poet. *See* EPOS.

Arëïthŏüs. King of Arnē in Bœotia, called the "club-swinger" because he fought with an iron mace. Irresistible in the open field, he was waylaid by king Lycurgus of Arcadia in a narrow pass where he could not swing his club, and killed. His son Menesthius fell by the hand of Paris, before Troy.

Arĕŏpăgus (Gr. *Areiŏs păgŏs*). An ancient criminal court at Athens, so named because it sat on Arēs' Hill beside the Acrŏpŏlis, where the god of war was said to have been tried for the murder of Halirrŏthius the son of Poseidōn. (*See* ARES.) Solon's legislation raised the Areopagus into one of the most powerful bodies by transferring to it the greater part of the jurisdiction of the Ephĕtæ (*q.v.*), as well as the supervision of the entire public administration, the conduct of magistrates, the transactions of the popular assembly, religion, laws, morals and discipline, and giving it power to call even private people to account for offensive behaviour. The "Court of Areopagus," as its full name ran, consisted of life-members (Areopagites), who supplemented their number by the addition of such archons as had discharged their duties without reproach. Not only their age, but their sacred character tended to increase the influence of the Areopagites. They were regarded as in a measure ministers of the *Erīnўĕs* or *Eumĕnĭdĕs* (Furies), who under the name of *Semnæ* (venerable) had their cave immediately beneath the Areopagus, and whose worship came under their care. The Areopagus proving too conservative for the headlong pace of the Athenian democracy, its general right of supervising the administration was taken from it by the law of Ephialtēs, in 462 B.C., and transferred to a new authority, the *Nŏmophўlăkĕs* (guardians of the laws); but it recovered this right on the fall of the Thirty. Its political powers seem never to have been clearly

defined; it often acted in the name of, and with full powers from, the people, which also accepted its decisions on all possible subjects. Under the Roman rule it was still regarded as the supreme authority. Then, as formerly, it exercised a most minute vigilance over foreigners.

Arēs (Lat. *Mars*). The Greek name for the god of war, son of Zeus by Hēra, whose quarrelsome temper Homer supposes to have passed over to her son so effectively that he delighted in nothing but battle and bloodshed. His insatiable thirst for blood makes him hateful to his father and all the gods, especially Athēna. His favourite haunt is the land of the wild and warlike Thracians. In form and equipment the ideal of warlike heroes, who are therefore called "Ares-like" and "darlings of Ares," he advances, according to Homer, now on foot, now in a chariot drawn by magnificent steeds, attended by his equally bloodthirsty sister *Eris* (strife), his sons *Deimŏs* and *Phŏbŏs* (fear and fright), and *Enȳō*, the goddess of battle and waster of cities (he himself being called *Enȳăliŏs*), rushing in blind rage through indiscriminate slaughter. Though fighting on the Trojan side, the bloodshed only is dear to his heart. But his unbridled strength and blind valour turn to his disadvantage, and always bring about his defeat in the presence of Athēna, the goddess of ordered battalions; he is also beaten by heroes fighting under her leadership, as by Hērăclēs in the contest with Cycnus, and by Diomēdēs before Troy. And this view of Ares as the bloodthirsty god of battles is in the main that of later times also. As early as Homer he is the friend and lover of Aphroditē, who has borne him Erōs and Antĕrōs, Deimos and Phobos, as well as Harmŏnia, wife of Cadmus the founder of Thebes, where both goddesses were worshipped as ancestral deities. He is not named so often as the gods of peace, but, as Ares or Enyalios, he was doubtless worshipped everywhere, notably in Sparta, in Arcadia and (as father of Œncmāüs) in Elis. At Sparta young dogs were sacrificed to him under the title of *Thērītās*. At Athens the ancient site of a high court of justice, the Arĕŏpăgus, was consecrated to him. There, in former days, the Olympian gods had sat in judgment on him and absolved him when he had slain Halirrhothius for offering violence to Alcippē, his daughter by Agraulus. His symbols were the spear and the burning torch. Before the introduction of trumpets, two priests of Ares, marching in front of the armies, hurled the torch at the foe as the signal of battle.

ARES.
(Rome, Villa Ludovisi.)

In works of art he was represented as a young and handsome man of strong sinewy frame, his hair in short curls, and a somewhat sombre look in his countenance; in the early style he is bearded and in armour, in the later beardless and with only the helmet on. He is often represented in company with Aphrodite and their boy Eros, who plays with his father's arms. One of the most famous statues extant is that in the Villa Ludovisi, which displays him in an easy resting attitude, with his arms laid aside, and Eros at his feet. (*See* cut.) On his identification with the Italian Mars, *see* MARS.

Arētæus. A Greek physician, born in Cappadocia, towards the end of the 2nd century A.D. He was the author of two valuable works (each in four books), written in the Ionic dialect, on the causes and symptoms of acute and chronic pains, and on their cure.

Arētē. Wife of Alcīnŏüs king of the Phæacians (*see* both), and protectress of Odysseus (*q.v.*).

Arēthūsa. (1) In Greece a frequent name of springs, especially of one in Elis, and one on the Island of Ortygia in the port of Syracuse, which was supposed to have a subterranean communication with the river Alphēus in Elis. The two fountains were associated by the following legend. As the nymph of Elis, tired with the chase, was bathing in the Alpheus, the river-god fell passionately in love with her; she fled from him to Ortygia, where Artĕmis hid her in the ground, and let her gush out of it in the form of a fountain; but Alpheus flowed on under the sea to Ortygia, and so united himself with his beloved one. The story is explained by the likeness of name in the fountains, by the circumstance that Artemis was worshipped both in Elis and Ortygia as *Alphecœa*, and by the fact that in some places the Alpheus actually does run underground.

(2) One of the *Hespĕrĭdĕs* (*q.v.*).

Argēï. The name of certain chapels at Rome, probably twenty-four in number, each of the four tribes of the city having six. To these chapels a procession was made on March 16 and 17, at which the wife of the Flamen Diālis walked with unkempt hair as a sign of mourning. On May 15 the Pontiffs, Vestal Virgins, Prætors, and all citizens who had a right to assist at sacrifices, marched to the wooden bridge over the Tiber (*Pons Sublĭcĭus*), and after sacrificing, threw into the river twenty-four men of straw, likewise named Argeï, which had probably been hung up in the chapels at the first procession, and were fetched away at the second. The sacrifice was regarded as expiatory, and the puppets as substitutes for former human victims. The meaning of the name was unknown to the ancients, and so was the deity to whom the sacrifice was offered.

Argentārĭi. *See* MONEY-CHANGERS.

Argentĕus. A Roman silver coin current from the end of the 3rd century A.D. and onwards. *See* COINAGE.

Argō. The ship of the Argonauts (*q.v.*), named after her builder Argos.

Argonauts. Those who sailed in the Argo with Jason, son of Æsōn and grandson of Crētheus (*see* ÆOLUS, 1), a generation before the Trojan war, to Æa, which in later times was understood to be Colchis, lying at the farthest end of the Black Sea. The object of the expedition was to fetch back the golden fleece of the ram on which Phrixus the son of Athămās (*q.v.*) had fled, from his father and his stepmother Inō, to the magician Æētēs, king of Æa.

Hospitably received by him, and married to his daughter Chalciŏpē, he had sacrificed the ram, and hung its fleece up in the grove of Arēs, where it was guarded by a sleepless dragon. The task of fetching it back was laid upon Jason by his uncle Pĕliās, son of Poseidōn and Tȳrō, who had deprived his half-brother Æson of the sovereignty of Iolcŏs in Thessaly. Æson, to protect his son from the plots of Pelias, had conveyed him secretly to the centaur Chīrōn on Mount Pēliŏn, who brought him up till he was twenty years of age. Then Jason came home, and without a shoe on his left foot, having lost it in wading through a mountain torrent, presented himself before Pelias, demanding his father's restoration to his sovereignty. The crafty Pelias, whom an oracle had warned against a one-shoed man, promised on his oath to do what he asked, if Jason would go instead of himself to fetch the golden fleece. This task the oracle had imposed upon himself, but he was too old to perform it. Another version of the story is, that Jason, after completing his education with Chīrōn, preferred to live in the country; that he came, with one shoe on, to a sacrifice that Pelias was offering to Poseidōn on the seashore; that Pelias asked him what he would do if he were king and had been forewarned of his death at the hand of a subject; and that, upon Jason answering that he would make him fetch the golden fleece, Pelias gave him the commission. Hera had put that answer in Jason's mouth, because she regarded him with favour, and wished to punish Pelias for having slain Sidērō in her temple. (*See* SALMONEUS.)

The vessel for the voyage, the fifty-oared *Argo*, is said to have been named after its builder *Argos*, a son of Phrixus, after his return to Orchŏmĕnus, the home of his fathers. The ship was built of the pines of Pelion under the direction of Athēna, like Hera, a protectress of Jason, who inserted in the prow a piece of the speaking oak of Dōdōna. The heroes who at Jason's call took part in the expedition, fifty all told according to the number of the oars, were originally, in the version to which the Minyan family gave currency, Minyans of Iolcos, Orchomenus, Pylos, and other places. Among them were Acastus the son of Pelias, a close friend of Jason, Admētus, Ergīnus, Euphēmus, Periclȳmĕnus, and Tiphys. But, as the story spread, all the Greek heroes that could have been living at the time were in-

cluded among the number of the Argonauts, *e.g.* Hērăclēs, Castor and Polydeucēs, Idās and Lynceus, Calāïs and Zētēs the sons of Borĕās, Peleus, Tydeus, Meleăger, Amphiarāüs, Orpheus, Mopsus and Idmōn the prophets of the expedition, and even the huntress Atalantē. Jason takes the command, and Tiphys manages the helm. Setting sail from Păgăsæ the port of Iolcos, the Argonauts make the Island of Lemnos, where only women dwell, and after some considerable stay there (*see* HYPSIPYLE) go past Samothrace and through the Hellespont to the island of Cyzĭcus, where they are hospitably received by Cyzĭcus, the king of the Doliŏnĕs, but attempting to proceed, are beaten back by a storm at night, and being taken by their late friends for pirates, are attacked, and have the ill-fortune to kill their young king. On the coast of Mysia they leave Heracles behind to look for Hylās (*q.v.*) who has been carried off by nymphs. On the Bithynian shore Polydeuces vanquishes the Bebrȳcian king Amȳcus (*q.v.*) in a boxing match. At Salmydēssus in Thrace the blind seer Phīneus, whom Calāïs and Zētēs had rid of the Harpies, his tormentors, instructs them with regard to the rest of their journey, and especially how to sail through the Symplēgădĕs, two floating rocks that clash together at the entrance to the Black Sea. By his advice Jason sends a dove before him, and as she has only her tail-feathers cut off by the colliding rocks, they venture on the feat of rowing the *Argo* through. By Hera's help, or, according to another account, that of Athena, they do what no man has done before; they pass through, the ship only losing her rudder. Skirting the southern shore of the Pontus, they meet with a friendly reception from Lycus, king of the Maryandīni, though here the seer Idmon is killed by a wild boar in hunting, and the helmsman Tiphys dies of a disease, whereupon Ancæus takes his place. Past the land of Amazons they come to the Island of Arētiăs, whence they scare away the Stymphalian birds (*see* HERACLES), and take on board the sons of Phrixus, who had been shipwrecked there on their way to Greece. At length they reach the mouth of the Phasis in the land of the Colchians. Upon Jason's demand, Æētēs promises to give up the golden fleece, on condition that Jason catches two brazen-hoofed, fire-breathing bulls, yokes them to a brazen plough, and ploughs with them the field of Ares, sows the furrows with dragons' teeth, and overcomes the mail-clad men that are to spring out of them. The hero has given up all hope of success, when Aphrodītē kindles in the breast of the king's daughter Mēdēa an irresistible love for the stranger. Medea gives him an ointment to protect him from the fiery breath of the bulls, as well as the strength to harness them, and advises him to throw a stone in among the earth-born giants, who will then kill each other. But when all this done, Æetes does not give up the fleece. Then Jason with the help of Medea, whom he promises to take home with him as his wife, throws the dragon that guards it into a sleep, takes it down, and escapes with Medea and his comrades. Æetes sends his son Absyrtus in pursuit, whom Jason kills by stratagem. Another story is, that Medea takes her little brother Absyrtus with her, cuts him to pieces, and throws the limbs one by one into the sea, that her father, while pursuing her, might be delayed in picking them up and laying them out.

As to the *Return* of the Argonauts the legends differ considerably. One of the oldest makes them sail up the Phasis into the river Oceănus, and over that to Libya, where they drag the ship twelve days' journey overland to Lake Trītōnis, and get home across the Mediterranean. Other accounts agree with this in substance, while others again mix up the older tradition with the adventures of Odysseus : the heroes sail up the Danube into the Adriatic, and are within hail of Corcȳra (Corfu), when a storm breaks out, and the piece of oak from Dōdōna foretells their ruin unless they have the murder of Absyrtus expiated by Circē. Then they sail up the Erĭdănus into the Rhone, and so into the Tyrrhenian sea to the island of Circe, who purifies them. They go past the island of the Sirens, against whose magic the songs of Orpheus protect them. All but Būtēs (*q.v.*) pass in safety between Scylla and Charybdis with the help of the gods, and reach the isle of the Phæacians, where Jason marries Medea to evade the sentence of their host Alcĭnŏüs, who, in his capacity as umpire, has given judgment that the *maid* Medea be delivered up to her Colchian pursuers. Already within sight of the Peloponnesus, a storm drives them into the Libyan Syrtes, whence they carry their ship, saved by divine assistance, to Lake Tritonis. Thence, guided by Trītōn (*see* EUPHEMUS) into the Mediterranean, they return by way of Crete to Iolcos.

During their absence Pelias has put to death Æson and his son Prŏmăchus, and Jason's mother has taken her own life. Medea sets to work to avenge them. Before the eyes of Pelias' daughters she cuts up an old he-goat, and by boiling it in a magic cauldron, restores it to life and youth. Promising in like manner to renew the youth of the aged Pelias, she induces them to kill their father, and then leaves them in the lurch. Driven away by Acastus, the son of the murdered king, Jason and Medea take refuge with Crĕōn king of Corinth. But, after ten years of happy wedlock, Jason resolves to marry Creon's daughter Crĕūsa or Glaucē. On this Medea kills the bride and her father by sending the unsuspecting maiden a poisoned robe and diadem as a bridal gift, murders her own two sons Mermĕrus and Pherēs in her faithless husband's sight, and escaping in a car drawn by serpents, sent by her grandfather Hēliŏs, makes her way to Ægeus king of Athens. (*See* MEDEA.) Jason is said to have come by his death through the Argo, which he had set up and consecrated on the Isthmus. One day, when he was lying down to rest under the ship, the stern fell off and killed him.

The legend of the Argonauts is extremely ancient ; even Homer speaks of it as universally known. We first find it treated in detail in Pindar ; then the Alexandrian poet Apollonius of Rhodes tried to harmonise the various versions, and was followed by the Latin poet Valerius Flaccus and the late Greek Pseudo-Orpheus.

Argus. (1) Son of Inăchus, Agēnōr or Arestōr ; or, according to another account, an earthborn giant, who had eyes all over his body, whence he was called Panoptēs, or all-seeing. Hēra set him to watch Iŏ (*q.v.*) when transformed into a cow ; but Hermēs, at Zeus' bidding, sent all his eyes to sleep by the magic of his wand and flute, and cut his head off with a sickle-shaped sword, whence his title *Argeiphontēs* was explained to mean " slayer of Argus." Hera set the eyes of her dead watchman in the tail of her sacred bird the peacock.

(2) Son of Phrixus and Chalcĭŏpē, the daughter of Æētēs. He is said to have come to Orchŏmĕnus, the home of his father, and to have built the Argo, which was named after him. According to another account he was shipwrecked with his brothers at the Island of Arētias on their way to Greece, and thence carried to Colchis by the Argonauts.

Argȳraspĭdēs (silver-shielded). In the later army of Alexander the Great, the remnant of the Macedonian heavy-armed infantry, who had crossed the Hellespont with the king, were formed into a corps of Guards in the heavy infantry of the line, and named from their shields being overlaid with Indian silver. After Alexander's death the corps was disbanded by Antĭgŏnus on account of its overweening pretensions.

Arĭadnē. The daughter of Mīnōs and Pasiphäë, who fell in love with Theseus when he came to Crete to kill the Minotaur, and gave him a clue of yarn, to help him to find his way back to the light of day after slaying the monster in the Labyrinth. She then fled away with him. Homer represents Ariadne as slain by Artĕmis in the Island of Dia, close to Crete, at the request of Dionȳsus. But the later legend shifts the scene to the Isle of Naxos, where the slumbering Ariadne is deserted by Theseus. Waking up, she is on the brink of despair, when Dionysus comes and raises her to the dignity of a god's wife. Zeus grants her immortality, and sets her bridal gift, a crown, among the stars. She received divine honours: at Naxos her festivals were held, now with dismal rites recalling her abandonment, now with bacchanalian revelry becoming the happy bride of Dionysus. At Athens in the autumn they held a joyous festival to her and Dionysus, which Theseus was supposed to have founded on his return from Crete. In Italy, where they identified Dionysus with their wine-god Līber, they also took Ariadne for the wine-goddess Lībĕra.

Arĭēs (Gr. *krĭŏs*). The *Battering-ram*, one of the most effective engines used by the ancients to make a breach in the walls of a besieged town. Originally it consisted of a strong pole, with iron-mounted head, brought up to the wall in earlier times by hand, in later times on wheels. In its final form it was constructed in the following manner. A stout beam, sometimes composed of several pieces, and measuring from 65 to 100 feet long or more, was hung by ropes on a strongly mounted horizontal beam, and swung backwards and forwards, so as to loosen the stones of the wall, and make it fall. As the engine stood close to

BATTERING RAM UNDER SHED.
TESTUDO ARIETINA.

the wall, the men working it were sheltered by a roofed shell of boards, called the ram-

tortoiseshell (*testūdo arĭētīna*), and resting on a framework that ran upon wheels. To protect the roof and sides of the shell against fire thrown from the walls, they were coated with raw or well soaked hides, or other similar contrivances. The loosened stones were picked out of the wall with a strong iron hook at the end of a pole, the wall-sickle (*falx mūrālis*) as it was called. Single holes were punched in the wall with the wall-borer (*tĕrĕbra*), a ram with a sharp point, which was pushed forward on rollers.

The besieged tried to knock the ram's head off by dropping heavy stones on it, or to catch it in a noose and turn the blow aside or upwards, or to deaden the force of its blows with sandbags and mats. If the town wished to secure indulgent treatment, it had to surrender before the ram touched the walls. (*See* SIEGES.)

Arīōn. A Greek poet and musician, of Methymna in Lesbŏs, who flourished about 625 B.C. In the course of a roving life he spent a considerable time at the court of Periander, tyrant of Corinth. Here he first gave the dithyramb (*q.v.*) an artistic form, and was therefore regarded as the inventor of that style in general. He is best known by the story of his rescue on the back of a dolphin. Returning from an artistic journey through Lower Italy and Sicily to his patron, he trusted himself to a crew of Corinthian sailors, who resolved to kill him on the open sea for the sake of his treasures. As a last favour he extorted the permission to sing his songs once more 'to the lyre, and then to throw himself into the sea. His strains drew a number of dolphins around him, one of which took him on its back, and carried him safe to land at the foot of the foreland of Tænărum. Thence he hastened to Corinth, and convicted the sailors, who were telling Periander they had left the minstrel safe at Tarentum. A bronze statue of a man on a dolphin, which stood on the top of Tænaron, was supposed to be his thankoffering to Poseidōn. [Herodotus, i 24.] A Thanksgiving Hymn to the god of the sea, preserved under his name, belongs to a later time.

Aristænĕtus. A Greek grammarian and rhetorician, of Nicæa in Bithynia, friend of Libanius, who praises him in the highest terms; he was killed in an earthquake at Nicomedia, A.D. 358. His name is erroneously attached to a collection, probably composed in the 5th or 6th century, of Erotic Epistles, feeble imitations of Alciphrōn, loose in tone and declamatory in style.

Aristæus. A beneficent deity worshipped in various parts of Greece, especially in Thessaly, Bœotia, the African colony of Cyrēnē, and the Islands of Ceos, Corcȳra, Sicily and Sardinia. He gives his blessing to herds, hunting, bee-keeping, wine, oil and every kind of husbandry. In particular he defends men, animals and plants from the destructive heat of the dog-days. According to the story most in vogue, he is the son of Apollo by the Thessalian nymph Cyrēnē, whom the god carried off to the country named after her. She is the daughter of Hypseus, and granddaughter (another story says daughter) of the river-god Pēnēus. After his birth Hermēs took Aristæus to the Hours and Gæa, the goddess of the earth, who brought him up and made him an immortal god. Sometimes he is called the son of Urănus (Heaven) and Gæa (Earth). In the Theban legend he and Autŏnŏë the daughter of Cadmus are represented as the parents of Actæon. He brought destruction upon the nymph Eurȳdĭcē, the beloved of Orpheus; for in fleeing from his persecutions she was killed by a snake. [Vergil, *Georg.* iv 315-558.]

Aristarchus. (1) A tragic poet of Tĕgĕa, a contemporary of Eurīpĭdēs; he is said to have lived more than a hundred years. Of his 70 dramas only two titles remain.

(2) A mathematician and astronomer of Samos, who lived and studied at Alexandria about 270 B.C., and with his pupil Hipparchus greatly advanced the science of astronomy. He was the first who maintained the earth's motion round the sun and on its own axis. We still possess a fragment of a treatise by him on the size of the sun and moon, and their distances from the earth.

(3) A scholar, born in Samothrace, and a pupil of Aristophănēs of Byzantium. He lived at Alexandria in the first half of the 2nd century B.C. as tutor to the royal princes, and keeper of the library. In the tyrannical reign of his pupil Ptolemy VII (Physcōn) he fled to Cyprus, and there died of dropsy about B.C. 153, aged 72. He is the most famous of the Alexandrian Critics, and devoted his attention mainly to the Greek poets, especially Homer, to whom he rendered essential service by his critical edition of the text, which remains in substance the groundwork of our present recension. This edition had notes on the margin, indicating the verses which Aristarchus thought spurious or doubtful, and anything else worthy of remark. The meaning of the notes, and the reasons for appending them, were explained in separate commentaries and excursuses, founded on a marvellously minute acquaintance with the language and contents of the Homeric poems, and the whole of Greek literature. He was the head of the school of *Aristarcheans*, who continued working on classical texts in his spirit till after the beginning of the Empire. Of his numerous grammatical and exegetical works only fragments remain. An idea of his Homeric studies, and of their character, can best be gathered from the Venetian *scholia* to the Iliad, which are largely founded on extracts from the Aristarcheans Dĭdȳmus and Aristonīcus.

Aristias. *See* PRATINAS.

Aristīdēs, (1) *of Thebes.* A celebrated Greek painter, the pupil of his father or brother Nicŏmăchus. He flourished about 350 B.C., and was distinguished for his mastery in the expression of the feelings. His most celebrated picture was that of a conquered city. Its central group represented a mother dying of a wound, and holding back her infant, who is creeping to her bosom, that it may not drink blood instead of milk. Notwithstanding the hardness of their colouring, his works commanded very high prices. Thus for one representing a scene in the Persian wars, containing 100 figures, he received 1,000 minæ (about £3,333). [Pliny, *N. H.* xxxv 98-100.]

(2) *Aristides of Miletus,* of the 1st or 2nd century B.C., was the author of a series of love-stories, called *Milēsĭăca,* from Milētus, the scene of the events. These, so far as we know, are the first examples of the prose romance. They were widely read in antiquity, especially among the Romans, for whose benefit they were translated into Latin by the historian Sisenna. Only a few fragments of them have survived.

(3) *Publius Ælius Aristides,* surnamed *Thĕŏdōrus,* was a Greek rhetorician, born at Hadriani in Bithynia A.D. 117 or 129. He was educated by the most celebrated rhetoricians of the time, Pŏlĕmōn of Pergămus, and Hērōdēs Attĭcus of Athens, and made long journeys through Asia, Egypt, Greece and Italy. On his return he was seized with an illness that lasted thirteen years, but which he never allowed to interrupt his studies. His rhetoric, in which he took Demosthĕnēs and Plato for his models, was immensely admired by his contemporaries; he also stood in high favour with the emperors, especially Marcus Aurelius,

who at his appeal caused Smyrna to be re-built after an earthquake in 178 A.D. The chief scenes of his activity were Athens and Smyrna, where he died about A.D. 190. Beside two treatises of rhetorical and technical import, we still possess fifty-five of his orations, which he took great pains to elaborate. They are characterized by depth and fulness of thought, and are written in powerful, concise, often difficult and obscure language. Some are eulogies on deities and cities (Rome, for instance, and Smyrna), others are declamations after ancient models, as the *Panathenäïcus* after Isocrătēs, and the speech against Leptĭnēs after Demosthenes. Others treat of historical subjects taken from the times of Greek independence. A peculiar interest attaches to the six Sacred Orations, so named because they treat of hints given by Asclepius on the cure of his illness, which he received in a state of somnambulism, and imparted aloud to his friends.

(4) *Aristides Quintiliānus*. A Greek musician, who lived probably in the 2nd century A.D., and composed an encyclopædia of music (*De Musĭcā*) in three books. The first gave a concise account of harmony, rhythm, and metre, the second dealt with the educating influence of music on the soul, and the third described, on Pythagorean principles, the doctrine of arithmetic intervals, and the harmony of the universe as resting on the same relations. Notwithstanding many defects, the work has the merit of being the completest of its kind which has come down to us from antiquity.

Aristippus. A Greek philosopher, a native of Cyrēnē, and a pupil of Socrates, after whose death in B.C. 399 he travelled about the Greek cities, imparting instruction for money. He was the founder of the Cyrenaic school, or the system of Hēdŏnism (from *hēdŏnē* = pleasure). His doctrine was, that as a basis for human knowledge the only things real and true are our sensations, not the external objects that produce them ; that the aim of life is what all living things strive after, pleasure ; and that virtue is only so far a good thing as it tends to the production of pleasure. The wise man shows his wisdom in governing his desires ; mental training, indeed, being the only thing which can qualify us for real enjoyment. In pleasure there is no difference of kind, only of degree and duration. Aristippus' writings seem to have disappeared early ; five letters in the Doric dialect, which have come down under his name, are undoubtedly spurious.

Aristŏbūlus. A Greek historian, who in his youth accompanied Alexander the Great on his campaigns. In his eighty-fifth year, when living at Cassandrēa in Thrace, he wrote a work upon Alexander, in which he recorded his careful observations on geography, ethnography, and natural science. The book is highly praised for its trustworthiness, but only fragments of it have reached us. He and Ptolemy were the chief authorities for Arrian's *Anăbăsis*.

Aristŏclēs. (1) A Greek artist, and like his brother Cănăchus, a sculptor in bronze at Sĭcўōn. He flourished about 480 B.C. ; and founded a school at Sicyon that lasted for a long time. (2) There was an Athenian sculptor of the same name and of the same period, author of a relief known as *The Athenian Hoplite*, one of our oldest monuments of Attic art. (*See* cut under HOPLITES).

Aristŏn. The second breakfast of the Greeks. (*See* MEALS.)

Aristŏphănēs. (1) *The comedian*, who lived at Athens, B.C. 444-388. His father Philippus is said to have been not a native Athenian, but a settler from Rhodes or Egypt, who afterwards acquired the citizenship. However this may be, the demagogue Clĕŏn, whose displeasure Aristophanes had incurred, tried to call in question his right to the citizenship. His first comedy came out in B.C. 427, but was not performed under his own name because of his youth ; and several more of his plays were brought on the stage by Callistrătus and Philōnĭdēs, till in 424 he brought out the *Knights* in his own person. Forty-four of his plays were known in antiquity, though four of them were considered doubtful. Of these we possess eleven, the only complete Greek comedies which have survived, besides the titles, and numerous fragments, of twenty-six others. The eleven are : (1) *The Acharnians*, which gained him the victory over Cratīnus and Eupŏlis B.C. 425, written during the great Peloponnesian war to induce the Athenians to make peace. (2) *The Knights* mentioned above, B.C. 424, also crowned with the first prize, and aimed directly against Cleon. (3) *The Clouds*, B.C. 423, his most famous and, in his own opinion, his most successful piece, though when played it only won the third prize. We have it only in a second, and apparently unfinished, edition. It is directed against the pernicious influence of the Sophists, as the representative of whom Sŏcrătēs is attacked. (4) *The Wasps*, brought out in B.C. 422 and, like the two following, rewarded with the second prize; it is a satire upon the Athenian passion for lawsuits. (5) *The Peace*, of the year B.C. 421, recommending the conclusion of peace. (6) *The Birds*, acted in B.C. 414, and exposing the romantic hopes built on the expedition to Sicily. This is unquestionably the happiest production of the poet's genius, and is marked by a careful reserve in the employment of dramatic resource. (7) *The Lysistrătē*, B.C. 411, a Women's Conspiracy to bring about peace ; the last of the strictly political plays. (8) *Thesmophŏriăzūsæ*, probably to be dated 410 B.C. It is written against Eurīpīdēs' dislike of women, for which the women who are celebrating the Thesmophŏrĭa drag him to justice. (9) *The Frogs*, which was acted in 405, and won the first prize. It is a piece sparkling with genius, on the Decay of Tragic Art, the blame of which is laid on Euripides, then recently deceased. (10) *Ecclēsiăzūsæ*, or The National Assembly of Women, B.C. 392. It is levelled against the vain attempts to restore the Athenian state by cut-and-dried constitutions. (11) *Plūtus*, or the God of Wealth. The blind god is restored to sight, and better times are brought about. This play was acted first in 408, then in 388 in a revised form suitable to the time, and dispensing with chorus and *parăbăsis*. This play marks the transition to the Middle Comedy.

In the opinion of the ancients Aristophanes holds a middle place between Cratinus and Eupolis, being neither so rough as the former nor so sweet as the latter, but combining the severity of the one with the grace of the other. What was thought of him in his own time is evident from Plato's *Symposium*, where he is numbered among the noblest of men; and an epigram attributed to that philosopher says that the Graces, looking for an enduring shrine, found it in the soul of Aristophanes. He unites understanding, feeling, and fancy in a degree possessed by few poets of antiquity. His keen glance penetrates the many evils of his time and their most hidden causes; his scorn for all that is base, and his patriotic spirit, burning to bring back the brave days of Marathon, urge him on, without respect of persons or regard for self, to drag the faults he sees into daylight, and lash them with stinging sarcasm; while his inexhaustible fancy invents ever new and original materials, which he manipulates

with perfect mastery of language and technical skill. If his jokes are often coarse and actually indecent, the fact must be imputed to the character of the Old Comedy and the licentiousness of the Dionysiac festival, during which the plays were acted. No literature has anything to compare with these comedies. Ancient scholars, recognising their great importance, bestowed infinite pains in commenting on them, and valuable relics of their writings are enshrined in the existing collections of *Scholia*.

(2) *Aristophanes the Grammarian* (or *Scholar*) of Byzantium, born about 260 B.C., went in his early youth to Alexandria, and was there a pupil of Zēnŏdŏtus and Callĭmăchus. On the death of Apollonius of Rhodes, Aristophanes, when past his sixtieth year, was appointed to be chief librarian, and died at the age of 77. His fame was eclipsed by that of his pupil Aristarchus, but he still passed for one of the ablest grammarians and critics of antiquity, distinguished by industry, learning and sound judgment. In addition to the Homeric poems, which formed his favourite study, and of which he was the first to attempt a really critical text, he devoted his labours to Hesiod, the lyric poets, especially Alcæus and Pindar, and the tragic and comic poets, Aristophanes and Menander in particular. The received Introductions to the plays of the Tragedians and Aristophanes are in their best parts derived from him. He was also the author of a large and much quoted work of a lexicographical character, considerable fragments of which still survive.

Aristotle (Greek *Aristŏtĕlēs*). One of the two greatest philosophers of antiquity, born B.C. 384 at Stageira, a Greek colony in Thrace. He was the son of Nicŏmăchus, who died while acting as physician in ordinary to Amyntas II at Pella in Macedonia. In B.C. 367, after the death of his parents and the completion of his seventeenth year, Aristotle betook himself to Athens, became a pupil of Plato, and remained twenty years, latterly working as a teacher of rhetoric. About his relations with Plato unfavourable rumours were current, which may have had their origin in his subsequent opposition to the Platonic doctrine of ideas. That he arrived pretty early at opposite opinions, and gave emphatic expression to them, is quite credible. This may have been the occasion of Plato's comparing him (so it is said) to a colt that kicks his mother; yet Plato is also said to have called him " the intellect " of his school, and " the reader," on account of his habit of incessant study. Comparing him with Xĕnŏcrătĕs, he remarked, that the one wanted a spur, the other a bridle. On the other hand, Aristotle, in one of his writings, combating his former master's theory of ideas, lays down the maxim that friendship, especially among philosophers, must not be allowed to violate the sanctity of truth; and in a fragment of an elegy he calls Plato the first man who showed in word and deed how a man is to become good and happy.

After Plato had handed over his school to his sister's son Speusippus, Aristotle quitted

*ARISTOTLE.
(Rome, Spada Palace.)

Athens, B.C. 347, and repaired to his friend Hermeiăs, despot of Atarneus in Mysia. When that prince had fallen a prey to Persian intrigues he withdrew, B.C. 345, with his wife Pythiăs, his friend's sister, to Mĭtўlēnē in Lesbos; and two years later accepted an invitation to Macedonia to be tutor to Alexander, then thirteen years old. He lived at the court eight years, though his tenure of office seems to have lasted barely half that time. Both Philip and his son esteemed him highly, and most liberally seconded his studies in natural science, for which he inherited his father's predilection. Alexander

continued till his death to respect and love him, though the affair of Callisthĕnĕs (q.v.) occasioned some coolness between them. When the king undertook his expedition in Asia, Aristotle betook himself once more to Athens, and taught for thirteen years in the Gymnăsĭum called the Lycĕum. In the mornings he conversed with his maturer pupils on the higher problems of philosophy, walking up and down the shady avenues, from which practice the school received the name of Peripatetics. In the evenings he delivered courses of lectures on philosophy and rhetoric to a larger audience. After Alexander's death, when all adherents of the Macedonian supremacy were persecuted at Athens, a certain Dēmŏphĭlus brought against him a charge of impiety, whereupon Aristotle, "to save the Athenians from sinning a second time against philosophy "—so he is reported to have said, alluding to the fate of Socrates —retired to Chalcis in Eubœa. There he died late in the summer of the next year, B.C. 322.

Of the very numerous writings of Aristotle, some were composed in a popular, others in a scientific form. A considerable number of the latter kind have come down to us, but of the former, which were written in the form of dialogues, only a few fragments. The strictly scientific works may be classed according to their contents, as they treat of Logic, Metaphysics, Natural Science or Ethics. (1) Those on LOGIC were comprehended by the later Aristotelians under the name of Orgănŏn ("instrument"), because they treat of Method, the instrument of research. They include the Categories, on the fundamental forms of ideas : the De Interpretătiŏne, on the doctrine of the judgment and on the proposition, important as an authority on philosophical terminology; the Analўtĭca Priŏra and Posteriŏra, each in two books, the former on the syllogism, the latter on demonstration, definition, and distribution; the Tŏpĭca in eight books, on dialectic inferences (those of probability); on Sophisms, the fallacies of sophists, and their solution.—(2) The METAPHYSICS as they were called by late writers, in fourteen books, consist of one connected treatise and several shorter essays on what Aristotle himself calls "first philosophy," the doctrine of Being in itself and the ultimate grounds of Being; a work left unfinished by Aristotle

and supplemented by foreign ingredients.—
(3) The works on NATURAL SCIENCE are
headed by the *Physics* in eight books, treating of the most general bases and relations
of nature as a whole. This is followed up
by four books on the *Heavens* or Universe,
two on *Beginning to be* and *Perishing*, and
the *Mĕtĕŏrŏlŏgĭca* in four books, on the phenomena of the air. A short treatise *On the
Cosmŏs* is spurious : that on the *Directions
and Names of Winds* is a fragment of a
larger work on the signs of storms ; and the
Problems (physical) is a collection gradually
formed out of Aristotelian extracts. Of
mathematical import are the *Mechanical
Problems* (on the lever and balance) and the
book about *Indivisible Lines*. Natural history is handled in the ten books of *Animal
History*, and in four books on the *Parts*,
five on the *Generation*, and one on the *mode
of Progression of Animals*. The work on
The Motion of Animals is probably spurious,
certainly so the one on *Plants* in two books.
Aristotle's treatise on this subject is lost.
Turning to Psychology, we have the three
books *On the Soul* and a number of smaller
treatises (on the *Senses* and the *Objects of
Perception ;* on *Memory and Recollection ;*
on *Sleep and Waking ;* on *Dreams ;* on
Divination by Sleep ; on the *Length and
Shortness of Life ;* on *Youth and Age, Life
and Death ;* on *Breathing ;* on *Sound and
Voice*, etc.; that on *Physiognomy* is probably spurious).—(4) Of the three general
works on ETHICS, the *Nicomachēan Ethics*
in ten books, the *Eudemian Ethics* in seven,
and the so-called *Magna Morălia* in two,
the first alone, addressed to his son Nĭcŏmăchus, and of marked excellence in matter
and manner, is by Aristotle himself. The
second is by his pupil Eudēmus of Rhodes,
and the third a mere abstract of the other
two, especially of the second. The essay on
Virtues and Vices is spurious. Closely connected with the *Ethics* is the *Politics* in
eight books, a masterly work in spite of
its incompleteness, treating of the aim and
elements of a State, the various forms of
Government, the ideal of a State and of Education. A valuable work on the *Constitution* of 158 states is lost, all but a few
fragments.[1] Of the two books on *Œcono-
mics* the first is spurious. Corresponding
partly with the *Logic*, and partly with the
Ethics, is the *Rhetoric* in three books,[2] and
the *Poetics*, a work of inestimable worth,

notwithstanding the ruinous condition in
which its text has come down to us. [The
Rhetoric is a masterly treatise on oratory,
regarded as an instrument for working
upon the various passions and feelings of
humanity.] Sundry other prose writings
are preserved under Aristotle's name, *e.g.*,
that on *Colours ;* the so-called *Mĭrăbĭlēs
Auscultātĭōnēs*, a collection of memoranda
on all sorts of strange phenomena and occurrences, mostly bearing on natural science ;
on *Melissus, Zēnō, and Gorgiās ;* six *Letters*,
which however are not regarded as genuine,
any more than the 63 epigrams out of a
supposed mythological miscellany entitled
Peplŏs. But we may safely assign to him
he beautiful *Scŏlĭŏn*, or impromptu song,
on his friend Hermeiās, which takes the
form of a Hymn to Virtue.

A story dating from antiquity informs us
that Aristotle bequeathed his own writings
and his very considerable library to his
pupil and successor in the office of teacher,
Theophrastus, who again made them over
to his pupil Nēleus, of Scēpsis in the Troad.
After his death his relations are said to
have buried them in a cellar, to guard them
against the mania for collecting books which
characterized the Pergamene princes. At
last they were unearthed by Apellĭcōn of
Tĕŏs, a rich bibliophile, who brought them to
Athens about 100 B.C., and tried to restore
them from the wretched state into which
they had fallen through the neglect of 130
years. Soon after, at the taking of Athens
by the Romans, they fell into Sulla's hands,
who brought them to Rome. Here the
grammarian Tyrannĭōn took copies of them,
and on this basis the Peripatetic Andronīcus of Rhodes prepared an edition
of Aristotle's works. This would indeed
partly account for the wretched condition in
which some of them are preserved. At the
same time it can be proved that the principal works were known during the 3rd
and 2nd centuries B.C., so that the story
affects only the author's original MSS.,
among which a number of works till then un-
published may have come to light. Though
the writings preserved form rather less than
half of the number which he actually wrote,
there is quite enough to show the univer-
sality of Aristotle's intellect, which sought
with equal ardour and acumen to explore
and subdue the entire domain of research.
He was the originator of many lines of study
unknown before him,—Logic, Grammar,
Rhetoric in its scientific aspect, Literary
Criticism, Natural History, Physiology,

---

[1] The *Constitution of Athens* has, however, been
recovered (ed. princeps, 1891).
[2] The *Rhetorica ad Alexandrum* is probably by
Anaxĭmĕnēs, *q.v.* 2.

Psychology; he was the first to attempt a History of Philosophy and of the forms of government then existing. His method, of which he must be considered the creator, is critical and empirical at once. In all cases he starts from facts, which he collects, sifts and groups as completely as he can, so as to get some general leading points of view, and with the help of these to arrive at a systematic arrangement of the subject, and a knowledge of its inmost being, its cause. For to him the Cause is the essential part of knowledge, and the philosophy that searches into ultimate causes for the mere sake of knowing is the best and freest science.

The form of Aristotle's works is by no means equal to their contents. Of the beautiful harmony between style and subject, that so charms us in Plato, there is not a trace in Aristotle; his manner of expression, though scientifically exact, lacks flavour, art, and elegance. But of exact scientific terminology he is the true founder. When the ancients celebrate the "golden stream" of his writing, the opinion can only refer to his lost popular works.

Aristotle's personality is one of those which have affected the history of the world. His writings, like those of Plato, were to the Christian centuries of antiquity a most stimulating incentive to scientific inquiry; in the Middle Ages they were for the Christian nations of the West and the Arabs the chief guide to philosophical method; and in the province of logic his authority remains unshaken to this day.

Aristoxĕnus. A Greek philosopher and musician, a native of Tarentum, and a pupil of Aristotle, lived about 330 B.C., and was a prolific writer on various subjects, but most particularly on Music. In contrast with the Pythagoreans, who referred everything to the relations of numbers, he regarded music as founded on the difference of tones as perceived by the ear. Of his *Elements of Harmony*, three books are preserved, but they are neither complete, nor in their original shape. Only a part of his *Elements of Rhythm* has survived.

Arms. *See* WEAPONS.

Army. (1) Greek. *See* WARFARE.
(2) Roman. *See* LEGION, DILECTUS, SACRAMENTUM, STIPENDIUM, CASTRA.

Arneïs. The festival of lambs. *See* LINOS.

Arnŏbĭus. An African, who won a high reputation as a master of rhetoric at Sicca in Numidia, in the reign of Diocletian. He was at first a heathen and an assailant of Christianity; but on becoming a Christian,

to prove the sincerity of his conversion, he wrote (about 295 A.D.) the extant work *Adversus Gentēs.* This is a superficial and rhetorical defence of Christianity and attack on Polytheism, but it is full of instruction with regard to the contemporary heathenism and its various worships.

Arrhĕphŏrĭă or *Errhephoria.* The Athenian term for a mystic festival in honour of Athēna as goddess of the fertilizing nightdew, held in the month of Scīrŏphŏrĭōn (June-July), in connection with the *Scirophoria.* It was named after the *Hersphŏroi* = dew-bearers, four maidens between seven and eleven years of age, who were chosen yearly from the houses of noble citizens, and had to spend several months at the temple of Athēna in the Acrŏpŏlis, and take part in its services. Two of them had the task of commencing the cloak or shawl which the women of Athens wove and presented to the goddess at the Panathenæa. The other two, on the night of the festival, received from the priestess of Athena certain coffers, with unknown contents, which they carried in procession on their heads to a natural grotto beside the temple of "Aphrodītē in the gardens," and delivering them there, received something equally mysterious in exchange, which they carried to the temple on the Acropolis. With this ceremony their office expired.

Arriānus *(Flāvius).* A Greek author, who wrote chiefly on philosophy and history, born at Nīcŏmēdēa in Bithynia towards the end of the 1st century A.D., and a pupil of the Stoic philosopher Epictētus. He lived under the emperors Hadrian, Antōnīnus Pius and Marcus Aurēlius, enjoying a high reputation for culture and ability, which procured him the citizenship of Rome and Athens, and high offices of state, such as the governorship of Cappadocia under Hadrian, A.D. 136, and the consulship under Antoninus. His last years were spent in his native town, where he filled the office of priest to Dēmētēr, and died at an advanced age. From the likeness of his character to that of the famous Athenian, he was nicknamed "Xĕnŏphōn Junior." Of his philosophical works we have still the first half (four books) of the *Discourses of Epictētus,* a leading authority for the tenets of that philosopher and the Stoical ethics; and the hand-book called the *Encheirĭdĭŏn of Epictetus,* a short manual of morality, which on account of its pithy and practical precepts became a great favourite with Pagans and Christians, had a commentary written on it by Simplicius in the 6th century, and after the revival of learning was long used as a schoolbook. Of his numerous historical writings we possess the chief one, the *Anăbăsis of Alexander* in seven books. This is a complete history of that conqueror from his accession to his death, drawn from the best sources, especially Ptolemy and Aristobūlus, and modelled on Xenophon, of whom we are reminded by the very title and the number of books, though it has none of Xenophon's charm. It is the best work on Alexander that has survived from antiquity. To this we should add the *Indĭca*, a short work on India, written in the Ionic dialect, and especially valuable for its abstract of Nearchus' report of his voyage from the mouth of the Indus to the Persian Gulf; also the description of another coasting voyage, the *Pĕrĭplŭs Ponti Euxīni*, and a trifling treatise on hunting, the *Cȳnĕgĕtĭcus*. A work on tactics wrongly ascribed to him is probably from the hand of Ælian the Tactician. Of his other Histories, *e.g.* of the Successors of Alexander, of Trajan's battles with the Parthians, of his own native country till its absorption in the Empire, and the campaign against the Alāni during his command in Cappadocia, we have only abstracts or fragments.

Arrŏgātĭō, one of the kinds of adoption known to the Romans. (For further information *see* ADOPTION.)

Arrows. *See* BOWS.

Arsĭnŏë. *See* ALPHESIBŒA.

Art. *See* ARCHITECTURE, ARCHITECTURE (ORDERS OF), PAINTING, and SCULPTURE; and comp. COINAGE and GEMS.

Artĕmĭdōrus, (1) *The Geographer*, of Ephĕsus, who travelled about 100 B.C. through the countries bordering on the Mediterranean and part of the Atlantic coast, and wrote a long work on his researches, the *Geographūmĕna* in eleven books, as well as an abstract of the same. Of both works, which were much consulted by later geographers, we have only fragments.

(2) *Artemidorus the Dream-Interpreter*, born at Ephesus at the beginning of the 2nd century A.D., surnamed "the Daldian" from his mother's birthplace, Daldis in Lydia, wrote a work on the Interpretation of Dreams, the *Oneirŏcrĭtĭca*, in four books. He had gathered his materials from the works of earlier authors, and by oral inquiries during his travels in Asia, Italy and Greece. The book is an acute exposition of the theory of interpreting dreams, and its practical application to examples systematically arranged according to the several stages of human life. An appendix, counted as a fifth book, gives a collection of dreams that have come true. For the light thrown on the mental condition of antiquity, especially in the 2nd century after Christ, and for many items of information on religious rites and myths relating to dreams, these writings are of value.

Artĕmis (Lat. *Diăna*). The virgin daughter of Zeus and Lētō (Lātōna), by the common account born a twin-sister of Apollo, and just before him, at Dēlŏs. The Ortȳgia (*see* ASTERIA) named in another tradition as her birthplace, was interpreted to mean Delos, though several other places where the worship of Artemis had long prevailed put forward pretensions to that name and its mythological renown, especially the well-known island of Ortygia off Syracuse. She, as well as her mother, was worshipped jointly with her brother at Delos, Delphi and all the most venerable spots where Apollo was honoured. She is armed, as he is, with bow and arrow, which, like him, and often together with him, she wields against monsters and giants; hence the *pœan* was chanted to her as well as to him. Like those of Apollo, the shafts of Artemis were regarded as the cause of sudden death, especially to maidens and wives. But she was also a beneficent and helpful deity. As Apollo is the luminous god of day, she with her torch is a goddess of light by night, and in course of time becomes identified with all possible goddesses of moon and night. (*See* SELENE, HECATE, BENDIS, BRITOMARTIS.) Her proper domain is that of Nature, with its hills and valleys, woods, meadows, rivers and fountains; there amid her nymphs, herself the fairest and tallest, she is a mighty huntress, sometimes chasing wild animals, sometimes dancing, playing, or bathing with her companions. Her favourite haunt was thought to be the mountains and forests of Arcadia, where, in many spots, she had sanctuaries, consecrated hunting-grounds, and sacred animals. To her, as goddess of the forest and the chase, all beasts of the woods and fields, in fact all game, were dear and sacred; but her favourite animal was held all over Greece to be the hind. From this sacred animal and the hunting of it, the month which the other Greeks called *Artemĭsĭōn* or *Artemisĭŏs* (March-April) was named by the Athenians *Elaphē-bŏlĭōn* (deer-shooting), and her festival as goddess of game and hunting, at which deer or cakes in the shape of deer were offered up, *Elaphēbŏlĭa*. As goddess of the chase, she had also some influence in war, and the Spartans before battle sought her favour by the gift of a she-goat. Miltiădēs too, before the battle of Mărăthōn, had vowed to her as many goats as there should be enemies fallen on the field ; but the number proving so great that the vow could not be kept, 500 goats were sacrificed at each anniversary of the victory in the month of Boëdrŏmĭōn. Again, she was much worshipped as a goddess of the *Moon*. At Amarynthus in Eubœa, the whole island kept holiday to her with processions and prize-fights. At Mŭnўchia in Attica, at full moon in the month of Munychiōn (April-May), large round loaves or cakes, decked all round with lights as a symbol of her own luminary, were borne in procession and presented to her ; and at the same time was solemnized the festival of the victory of Sălămīs in Cyprus, because on that occasion the goddess had shone in her full glory on the Greeks. An ancient shrine of the Moon-goddess at Braurōn in Attica was held in such veneration, that the *Braurōnĭa*, originally a merely local festival, was afterwards made a public ceremony, to which Athens itself sent deputies every five years, and a precinct was dedicated to "Artemis of Brauron" on the Acrŏpŏlis itself. (*See* plan of ACROPOLIS.) At this feast the girls between five and ten years of age, clad in saffron-coloured garments, were conducted by their mothers in procession to the goddess, and commended to her care. For Artemis is also a protectress of youth, especially those of her own sex. As such she patronized a Nurses' festival at Sparta in a temple outside the town, to which little boys were brought by their nurses ; while the Ionians at their *Apatūrĭa* presented her with the hair of boys. Almost everywhere young girls revered the virgin goddess as the guardian of their maiden years, and before marriage they offered up to her a lock of their hair, their girdle, and their maiden garment. She was also worshipped in many parts as the goddess of Good Repute, especially in youths and maidens, and was regarded as an enemy of all disorderly doings. With her attributes as the goddess of the moon, and as the promoter of healthy development, especially in the female frame, is connected the notion of her assisting in childbirth (*see* EILEITHYIA). In early times human sacrifices had been offered to Artemis. A relic of this was the yearly custom observed at Sparta, of flogging the boys till they bled, at the altar of a deity not unknown elsewhere, and named *Artemis Orthia* (the upright) probably from her stiff posture in the antiquated wooden image. At Sparta, as in other places, the ancient image was looked upon as the same which Iphigĕnĭa and Orestēs brought away from Tauris (the Crimea), viz., that of the *Tauric Artemis*, a Scythian deity who was identified with Artemis because of the human sacrifices common in her worship. The *Artemis of Ephesus*, too, so greatly honoured by all the Ionians of Asia [Acts xix 28] is no Greek divinity, but Asiatic. This is sufficiently shown by the fact that eunuchs were employed in her worship ; a practice quite foreign to Greek ideas. The Greek colonists identified her with their own Artemis, because she was goddess of the moon and a power of nature, present in mountains, woods and marshy places, nourishing life in plants, animals and men. But, unlike Artemis, she was not regarded as a

virgin, but as a mother and foster-mother, as is clearly shown by the multitude of breasts in the rude effigy. Her worship, frantic and fanatical after the manner of

Asia, was traced back to the Amazons. A number of other deities native to Asia was also worshipped by the Greeks under the name of Artemis.

Artemis appears in works of art as the ideal of austere maiden beauty, tall of stature, with bow and quiver on her shoulder, or torch in her hand, and generally leading or carrying a hind, or riding in a chariot drawn by hinds. Her commonest character is that of a huntress. In earlier times the figure is fuller and stronger, and the clothing more complete; in later works she is represented as more slender and lighter of foot, the hair loose, the dress girt up high, the feet protected by the Cretan shoe. The most celebrated of her existing statues is the *Diana of Versailles* (*see* cut). On the identification of Artemis with the Italian *Diana*, see DIANA.

Artillery. The machines used for sending large missiles to a great distance were

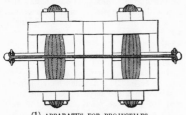

(1) APPARATUS FOR PROJECTILES.

supposed to have been invented in the East, and appear in Greece since 400 B.C. or thereabouts. They attained their highest perfection in the age of the Diădŏchi, and were adopted by the Romans after the Punic wars. There were two chief varieties, both imitations of the crossbow; but the elasticity of the bow is exchanged for elasticity in the twist of the cord. Consequently all pieces of heavy artillery were called by the Romans *tormenta*. The machine consisted of three parts: the stand, the groove for the shot, and the apparatus representing the bow. This consisted of a frame in three divisions, through the midmost of which passed the groove for the shot (fig. 1). In each of the lateral divisions was stretched, in a vertical direc-

tion, a set of strong elastic cords, made of the sinews of animals, or the long hair of animals or of women. These were stretched tight, and between each of them was fixed a straight unelastic arm of wood. The arms were joined by a cord, which was pulled back by a winch applied at the end of the groove. On letting this go, the arms, and with them the string and the object in front of it, were driven forward by the twisting of the vertical cords. The effectiveness of the engine thus depended on the power and *twist* of the cords, which may be said roughly to express its calibre. The engines were divided into two kinds. (1) *Catapultœ*, or scorpions (fig. 2). In these the groove for the shot was horizontal; and they projected missiles of length and thickness varying according to the calibre. (2) *Ballistœ* (fig. 3), which shot stones, beams, or balls up to 162 lbs. weight, at an angle of 50 degrees. The calibre of the *ballista* was at least three times as great as that of the catapult. The average range of the catapult was about 383 yards, that of the ballista from about 295 to 503 yards.

After Constantine we hear no more of catapults, but only of *ballistœ* and the *ŏnăger*. The *ballista* now shot arrows, and is described either as a huge cross-bow with an elastic bow of iron, or as virtually identical with the old catapult. The *onager*, also called *scorpio* (fig. 4) was a sling for

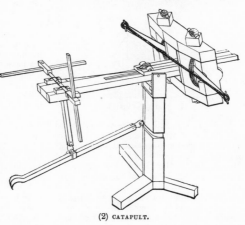

(2) CATAPULT.

stones. It consisted of a frame, in which was fastened a wooden arm with a sling at the end, standing upright when at rest, and furnished with two horizontal cords to pull it up and down. This was drawn back by a winch into a nearly horizontal position, and

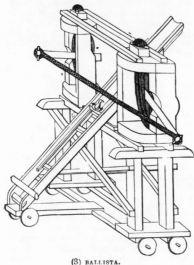

(3) BALLISTA.

then released. It started up, and meeting with a check-board fixed behind the engine, hurled the stones out of the sling. As a

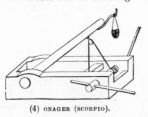

(4) ONAGER (SCORPIO).

rule, the heavy artillery was only employed in sieges; but artillery accompanied armies in the field for purposes of conquest or defence. The legions and the cohorts of the Prætorian Guard had their own artillery. And at the end of the 4th century every *centuria* in the legion had a *ballista* of the later kind drawn on wheels by mules (*carroballista*), and served by eleven men. Every cohort had an *onager*, carried on a cart drawn by two oxen.

Arusiānus Messius. A Latin grammarian who lived about 395 A.D., and made an alphabetical collection, for school use, of words that admit of various constructions, with examples from Vergil, Sallust, Terence and Cicero, under the title *Exempla Elocūtiōnum.*

Arval Brothers (*Frātrēs Arvālēs* = of the fields). The Latin name for a college of priests consisting of twelve life-members, who performed the worship of *Dĕa Dīa,* a goddess not otherwise mentioned, but probably identical with the old Roman goddess of cornfields, Acca Lārentia (*q.v.*), who also is said to have founded this fraternity. Our more accurate knowledge of it we owe to its annual reports inscribed on the marble tablets, ninety-six in number, which have been dug up (1570–1869) on the site of its meeting-place, a grove at the fifth milestone from Rome, and which extend from A.D. 14–241. About its condition under the Republic we have no information; but under the Empire its members were persons of the highest rank. The emperors themselves belonged to it, either as ordinary members, or, if the numbers were filled up, as extraordinary. The election was by co-optation on the motion of the president (*magister*), who himself, together with a *flāmen,* was elected for one year; their badge was a white fillet and a wreath of ears of corn. The Arvales held their chief festival on three days in May, on the 1st and 3rd in Rome, on the 2nd in the grove, with a highly complicated ceremonial, including a dance in the temple of the goddess, to which they sang the written text of a hymn so antiquated that its meaning could scarcely be understood. This *Arval Hymn,* in which the Lărēs and Mars are invoked, is one of the oldest monuments we possess of the Latin tongue. Amongst other duties of this priesthood should especially be mentioned the expiatory sacrifices in the grove. These had to be offered if any damage had been done to it through the breaking of a bough, the stroke of lightning, or other such causes; or again if any labour had been performed in it, though ever so necessary, especially if iron tools had been used. The Arval brothers had also to offer solemn vows on behalf of the Imperial House, both statedly on January 3rd, and on extraordinary occasions, and were bound to fulfil them.

As. In Latin, signifies any unit, which determines the value of fractional quantities in coins, weights and measures, or interest, inheritance and the like. The *as* was divided duodecimally into *unciæ.* The names of its parts are: *deunx* $\frac{11}{12}$, *dextans* $\frac{5}{6}$, *dodrans* $\frac{3}{4}$, *bes* $\frac{2}{3}$, *septunx* $\frac{7}{12}$, *semis* $\frac{1}{2}$, *quincunx* $\frac{5}{12}$, *triens* $\frac{1}{3}$, *quadrans* $\frac{1}{4}$, *sextans* $\frac{1}{6}$, *sescuncia* $\frac{1}{8}$, *uncia* $\frac{1}{12}$. In questions of inheritance, a sole heir was entitled *hērēs ex asse*, an heir to half the estate, *heres ex semisse*, and so on. As a coin, the copper *as* weighed a Roman pound (nominally 12, but practically only 10 *unciæ*), and was worth, previously to B.C. 269, nearly 6d. In the year 217 it was reduced to 1 *uncia*, and in later times to $\frac{1}{2}$ and $\frac{1}{4}$ *uncia*. In Cicero's time the *as* was = rather less than a halfpenny. *Comp.* COINAGE.

Ascănĭus. The son of Æneas and Crëūsa. According to the ordinary account, he accompanied his father to Italy, and, thirty years after the building of Lavīnium, founded Alba Longa, where, after his death, his stepbrother Silvius reigned. To him, by his name of *Iūlus*, the *gens Iūlia* traced its origin.

Asclēpĭădēs. A Greek poet, a native of Samos, and a younger contemporary of Theocrītus. He was the author of thirty-nine Epigrams, mostly erotic, in the Greek Anthology. The well-known Asclepiadean Metre was perhaps named after him.

Asclēpĭŏdŏtus. A Greek writer, pupil of the Stoic Pŏsīdōnius of Rhodes (who died B.C. 51). On the basis of his lectures Asclepiodotus seems to have written the military treatise preserved under his name on the Macedonian military system.

Asclēpĭus (Lat. *Æscŭlāpĭus*). The Greek god of Medicine, according to the common account a son of the healing god Apollo by Cŏrōnis, daughter of a Thessalian prince Phlĕgўās. Coronis was killed by Artĕmis for unfaithfulness, and her body was about to be burnt on the pyre, when Apollo snatched the boy out of the flames, and handed him over to the wise centaur Chīrōn, who instructed him in the cure of all diseases. According to the local legend of Epidaurus, Coronis, having accompanied her father on a campaign to the Peloponnēsus, is secretly delivered of the child, and exposes it on a mountain near that town, where it is nourished by a herd of goats. Such was the skill of Asclepius that he brought even dead men to life; so that Zeus, either for fear of his setting men altogether free from death, or at the complaint of Hādēs, killed him with his thunderbolt. Apollo in revenge slew all the Cyclōpĕs who forged the thunderbolts, as a punishment for which he had to serve Admētus for a time. In

Homer and Pindar, Asclepius is still but a hero, a cunning leech, and father of two heroes fighting before Troy, Măchāŏn and Pŏdăleirius. But he was afterwards universally worshipped as the god of healing, in groves, beside medicinal springs, and on mountains. The seats of his worship served also as places of cure, where patients left thank-offerings and votive tablets describing their complaint and the manner of its cure. Often the cure was effected by the

ASCLEPIUS.
(Paris, Louvre.)

dreams of the patients, who were required to sleep in the sacred building, in which there sometimes stood, as might be expected, a statue of Sleep or Dreaming. His worship extended all over Greece with its islands and colonies; his temples were especially numerous in the Peloponnēsus, the most famous being that of Epidaurus, where a great festival with processions and combats was held in his honour every five years. Next in estimation stood the temple at Pergămus, a colony from Epidaurus; that of Tricca in Thessaly enjoyed a reputation of long standing, and in the islands that of Cos, the birthplace of the physician Hippŏcrătēs.

At Rome, the worship of the deity there called *Æsculapius* was introduced by order of the Sibylline books, on occasion of the plague of 293 B.C., and the god was brought from Epidaurus in the shape of a snake. For in the form of a snake, the symbol of rejuvenescence and of prophecy, he was wont to reveal himself, and snakes were accordingly kept in his temples. He had a sanctuary and a much frequented sanatorium on the island in the Tiber. With him were worshipped his wife *Epĭŏnē* (= soother), his two sons mentioned above, and several daughters, especially *Hy̆gieia*, (*q.v.*); also *Telesphŏrŏs* (= fulness-bringer) the deity of Recovery, who was pictured as a boy. In later times Asclepius was often confounded with the Egyptian Serāpis. He is among the most favourite subjects of ancient art; at several places where he was worshipped he had statues of gold and ivory. He is commonly represented with a beard, and resembling Zeus, but with a milder aspect, sometimes with Telesphoros, in a thick veil, or little Hygieia, at his side; his usual attribute is a staff with a serpent coiled round it. The cock was sacrificed to him.

Ascŏnĭus Pĕdĭānus (*Quintus*), a Roman grammarian and historian, probably born at Patavium about the year 3 A.D. He lived latterly at Rome, where he enjoyed the favour of men in high place. During the reigns of Claudius and Nero, having carefully studied the literature of the Ciceronian age, and availing himself of state-papers then existing, he composed for the use of his own sons his valuable historical *Commentaries on Cicero's Orations*, of which only those on five orations (*In Pĭsōnem, Pro Scauro, Pro Mĭlōne, Pro Cornēlio, In tŏgā candĭdā*) are preserved, unfortunately in a very fragmentary condition. The commentaries on the Verrine Orations, which bear his name, belong probably to the 4th century A.D. They treat chiefly of grammatical points. No other works by Asconius have survived. He died, after twelve years' blindness, about 88 A.D.

Asellĭŏ (C. Sempronius). A Roman annalist. *See* ANNALISTS.

Asĭnius Pollĭŏ (Gaius). A celebrated Roman poet, orator, and historian. He was born B.C. 75, and made his first public appearance by bringing an impeachment in B.C. 54; in the Civil Wars he fought on Cæsar's side at Pharsālus and in Africa and Spain. After the murder of Cæsar he at first inclined to the Republicans, but in B.C. 43 joined Antony, and on the break-up of the Triumvirate obtained Gallia Transpadāna for his province. In the redistribution of lands there he saved the poet Vergil's paternal estate for him. After negotiating the Peace of Brundisium between Antony and Octavian, B.C. 41, he became consul in 40, conquered the Parthīni in Dalmatia in 39, and celebrated a triumph. He then retired from political life, and devoted himself to the advancement of learning. He served the cause of literature not only by his own writings, but by setting up the first public library at Rome, and by introducing the custom of reading new works aloud to a circle of experts, before publication. (*See* RECITATIO.) He was himself a stern critic of others, as we see by his strictures on Cicero, Sallust and Livy, though it was remarked that he was not always so severe upon himself. He was especially celebrated as an orator; yet his speeches, in spite of careful preparation, were devoid of elegance, and, as Quintilian remarks, might be supposed to have been written a century earlier than Cicero's. He wrote tragedies also, in which the same stiffness and dryness are complained of. And he composed a history of the Civil Wars in seventeen books, from the first Triumvirate to the battle of Philippi, which seems not to have been published in a complete form till after his death. Not one of his works has survived. [The history of Cæsar's African campaign, *Bellum Afrĭcum*, has recently been attributed to him, but on insufficient grounds.] He died 80 years old, A.D. 4.

Ascōlia. The second day of the rural *Dionysia* (*q.v.*).

Aspis. The Greek name for a long shield (For further information, *see* SHIELD.)

Assărācus, son of Trōs, and founder of the collateral line to which Anchīsēs and Ænēās belong in the royal house of Troy. (*Comp.* DARDANUS.)

Assignātio. The Latin term for the assignment of public lands to single citizens or to colonies. *See* COLONIES and AGER PUBLICUS.

Astĕria, daughter of the Titan Cœus and the Titanid Phœbē; sister of Lētō, and mother of Hĕcătē by Perses, son of the Titan Crius. She is said to have turned into an *ortyx* (= quail) and plunged into the sea to escape the love of Zeus. After her the Island of Delos was named *Astĕria*, and then *Ortỹgia*, till it received its ordinary name.

Astræa (= star-maiden), was daughter of Astræus and Eōs, or, according to another account, of Zeus and Thĕmis, and as such was identified with Dīkē. (*See* HOURS.) She lived among men in the golden age, and in the brazen age was the last of the gods to withdraw into the sky, where she shines as the constellation of the Virgin with her scales and starry crown.

Astræus (= star-man), son of the Titan Crius and Eurỹbīa, father by Eōs of the winds Argēstēs, Zĕphỹrus, Bŏrĕās and Nŏtus, as well as of Heōsphŏrus and the other stars. In the later legend he is also represented as father of Astræa.

Astrology and **Astronomy** were at first synonymous expressions among the ancients, both signifying " the science of the stars." But afterwards Astrology came to mean that part of the science which deals with the supposed influence of the stars on the destinies of men. Among the Greeks, Astronomy, the origin of which they themselves ascribed to the Assyrians, Babylonians and Egyptians, was for centuries the subject of philosophical speculation without a sufficient groundwork in observation, because mathematics and mechanics had not reached the requisite degree of perfection. The list of observing astronomers opens with *Eudoxus* of Cnĭdus in the first half of the 4th century, B.C., who assumed that the earth was spherical, and tried to explain the phenomena of the heavens by a complicated theory of concentric spheres. Aristotle too maintained and proved the spherical form of the earth, which he took to be the immovable centre of the universe. Astronomy was first raised into a real science after B.C. 300 at Rhodes and Alexandria, in the Museum of which town the first observatory was built, and *Aristyllus* and *Tĭmŏchărēs* determined the places of the fixed stars with comparative accuracy, though as yet with very rude apparatus. A great step in advance was taken by *Aristarchus* of Samos, who observed the summer solstice at Alexandria in B.C. 279, maintained the earth's rotation on her axis and revolution round the sun, and made an attempt, by no means contemptible, to ascertain the size and distance of the sun and moon. His successor *Erătosthĕnēs* also rendered essential service to the progress of the science; thus he came very near to determining the exact obliquity of the ecliptic. The true founder of scientific Astronomy, and the greatest independent observer of antiquity, was *Hipparchus* of Nicæa (in the 2nd century B.C.), who discovered the precession of the equinoxes, and determined the length of the solar year (at 365 days 5 hours 55′ 12″) as well as the time of the moon's revolution, and the magnitude and distances of the heavenly bodies. The last important astronomer of antiquity, and the greatest after Hipparchus, is *Claudius Ptŏlĕmœus* (in the 2nd century A.D.). In his chief work, commonly known by its Arabic name of *Almagest*, he digested the discoveries of his predecessors, especially Hipparchus, and his own, into a formal system, which passed current all through the Middle Ages. According to it the earth is a sphere resting motionless in the middle of the equally spherical universe, while the sun, moon, planets and fixed stars roll at various distances around her.

The Romans regarded Astronomy as an idle speculation, and gave little attention to it. When Cæsar reformed the Roman Calendar, he had to bring an astronomer from Alexandria, *Sōsĭgĕnēs*, to help him.

Astrology in the narrower sense of the word, meaning prediction on the faith of signs given by the stars, was an invention of the Chaldæans. All but unknown to the Greeks in their best days, it did not come into vogue until after the time of Alexander the Great. In Rome the professional astrologers were called *Chaldœi* or *Măthēmătĭcī*, the latter name referring to the astronomical calculations which they made. In the republican period they were known, but held in utter contempt. In 139 B.C. their unpopularity was so great that they were expelled from Rome and Italy. But in the turbulent times of the civil wars their reputation rose considerably, and still more under the Empire, when the most extensive demands were made upon their science. They were, indeed, repeatedly driven out of Italy and involved in trials for treason (*măiestās*); but this only enhanced the consideration in which they were held, the more so as they were frequently taken into counsel by the emperors and the members of the imperial family. In later times, all that the Chaldæans were forbidden to do was to consult the stars on questions referring to the emperor's life. This was a criminal offence. The Christian emperors (but none before them) issued

repeated prohibitions against all consultation of astrologers whatever.

In the practice of their art they used
calendars written on tablets, in which were
set down, for every day, the motion and
relative distances of the stars, whether
lucky or unlucky. With the help of
another set of tablets they proceeded to
make their calculations for every hour in
detail. They would, for instance, note the
hour of a person's birth, ascertaining the
relative position of the constellation dominant at the time. According to this they
determined the fortunes of the individual
who was born at the hour in question. In
the same way they ascertained the time
favourable to any given undertaking.
Among the lucky stars we may mention
Venus, Jupiter, and Luna; Saturn and Mars
were unlucky; Mercury was lucky or
unlucky according to the other circumstances of the case.

Astӯănax. Son of Hector and Andrŏmăchē. After the fall of Troy he was
thrown down from the wall by the Greeks,
because the prophet Calchās had pointed
him out as destined to become the avenger
of Troy.

Astӯdămās. A Greek tragedian, son of
Morsĭmus. (*See* PHILOCLES.) His first appearance was in 399 B.C., and he won the
prize fifteen times. He wrote 240 pieces,
but a few titles are all that remains of them.
His sons Astydamas and Phĭlŏclēs were
also tragic poets.

Astӯdămeia. Wife of Acastus of Iolcŏs.
Peleus had rejected her advances, and Asty-
dameia accordingly slandered him to Acastus, who made an attempt on the life of
Peleus, to her own destruction and that of
her husband. (*See* ACASTUS and PELEUS.)

Astӯnŏmi (Gr. *astŭnŏmoi*). The title
of ten functionaries at Athens, drawn annually by lot from the ten tribes, five for
the city and five for Piræus. They were
a kind of city police, responsible for keeping
the streets clean, for decency and quiet
among the public, and probably for the protection of buildings. They had such powers
of jurisdiction as were necessary to enforce
their authority. Flute-girls and female performers on the harp or cĭthăra were subject to
their control. [Arist., *Const. of Athens*, c. 50.]

Asӯlum. A Greek word meaning an
inviolable refuge for persons fleeing from
pursuit. Among the Greeks all holy shrines
were Asylums, and any pursuer who should
remove a suppliant by force was regarded as
a transgressor against the gods. The term

asylum was especially applied to such
shrines as secured to the suppliants absolute security within their limits, which were
often considerable. The priests and the
community in each case watched jealously
over this right. The sanctuary of Zeus
Lycæus in Arcadia, of Poseidōn in the
island of Calauria, and of Apollo in Delos,
are excellent examples of such asylums.
These sanctuaries were exceptionally numerous in Asia. In Rome there was an asylum
of great antiquity, said to have been founded
by Rŏmŭlus, in a grove of oaks on the
Capitoline Hill. (*See* VEIOVIS.) The erection
of buildings in its neighbourhood gradually
rendered it inaccessible. During the Roman
period the right of asylum attaching to
Greek sanctuaries was, at first, maintained
and even confirmed by Roman commanders.
But its abuse led to a considerable reduction of the number of asylums under
Tiberius. The right of asylum was now
confined to such shrines as could found their
claims upon ancient tradition. During the
imperial period, however, the custom arose
of making the statues of the emperors re-
fuges against momentary acts of violence.
Armies in the field used the eagles of the
legions for the same purpose.

Atălantē. A Greek heroine of the type
of Artĕmis. There were two slightly different versions of her story, one current in
Arcadia and the other in Bœōtia.

(1) *The Arcadian version.* Atalante,
daughter of Zeus and Clӯmĕnē, was exposed by her father, who had desired male
offspring only. She was suckled by a bear,
until she was found and brought up by a
party of hunters. Under their care she
grew up to be a huntress, keen, swift and
beautiful. She took part in the Calydonian
boar-hunt, was the first who struck the boar,
and received from Mĕlĕăger the head and
skin of the beast as the prize of victory. (*See*
MELEAGER.) She is also associated with
the voyage of the Argonauts. She turned a
deaf ear to the entreaties of her numerous
suitors; but at last she propitiated the
wrath of Aphrŏdītē by returning the faithful love of the beautiful Milänīon, who had
followed her persistently, and suffered and
struggled for her. Their son was Parthĕnŏpæus, one of the *Seven against Thebes*. (*See*
SEVEN AGAINST THEBES.)

(2) *The Bœotian version.* Atalante was
the daughter of Schœneus, son of Athămās,
and distinguished for beauty and swiftness
of foot. An oracle warns her against marriage, and she accordingly lives a lonely

life in the forest. She meets the addresses of her suitors by challenging them to race with her, overtaking them in the race and spearing them in the back. She is at length beaten by Hippŏmĕnēs, who during the race drops on the ground three golden apples given him by Aphrodite. Atalante stoops down to pick up the apples, and thus loses the race. Hippomenes forgets to render thanks to Aphrodite, and the goddess in anger causes the pair to wander into a sanctuary of Cўbĕlē, where they are changed into lions.

Atargatis. See DEA SYRIA.

Atē. According to Homer, the daughter of Zeus; according to Hesiod, of *Eris* or Strife. She personifies infatuation; the infatuation being generally held to imply guilt as its cause and evil as its consequence. At first she dwelt on Olympus; but after she had entrapped Zeus himself into his rash oath on the occasion of the birth of Hērăclēs (*see* HERACLES), he hurled her down to earth. Here she pursues her mission of evil, walking lightly over men's heads, but never touching the ground. Behind her go the *Lĭtai* ("Prayers"), the lame, wrinkled, squinting daughters of Zeus. The *Litai*, if called upon, heal the hurts inflicted by Ate; but they bring fresh evil upon the stubborn. In later times Ate is transformed into an avenger of unrighteousness, like *Dĭkē*, *Erīnŷs* and *Nĕmĕsis*.

Ateius Căpĭtō (*Gaius*). A Roman jurist of the age of Augustus and Tiberius, who was born about 30 B.C., and died about 22 A.D. Unlike his contemporary Antistius Lăbĕō (*q.v.*), he recommended himself to the ruling powers by his submissive attitude. He was rewarded by many tokens of distinction; among others, by the consulship, to which he was elected in 5 A.D., before attaining the legal age. As a jurist (again unlike Antistius) he represented the conservative tendency, and so became the founder of a special school called the *Sabĭniānī*, after his pupil Masŭrius Sabīnus.

Atellāna (i.e. *Atellāna fābŭla*. [A farce or comedy, which the ancients supposed was originally acted or invented at the Oscan town of Atella in Campania. Modern scholars incline to the opinion that it was a species of Latin drama representing scenes at Atella, or scenes of country-town life. Its characteristics were (1) that it was performed by free-born youths, not by professional actors; (2) that certain conventional characters, as *Buccō* ("Fatchaps"), *Dossennus* ("The Glutton"), *Pappus* ("The old

father"), *Maccus* ("The fool") always occurred in it; (3) that it contained puzzles to explain, either in the plot or in single lines.] The *Atellanœ* came into fashion at Rome as after-pieces (*exŏdia*) about the end of the 3rd century B.C., displacing the *sătŭrœ*. (*See* SATURA). Till the beginning of the last century of the Republic the *Atellana* was probably an improvisation; but, in the hands of Pompōnius of Bonōnia and Nŏvius, it was raised to the position of a regular comedy on the Greek model. From about the middle of the 1st century B.C., the *Atellana* went out of fashion in favour of the *mīmus*, but was revived, probably in the reign of Tiberius, by a certain Mummius. It lived on for some time under the Empire, till at last it became undistinguishable from the *mimus*.

Athămās. Son of Æŏlus, king of Thessaly, and Enărĕtē; brother of Crētheus, Sīsŷphus, and Salmōneus; king of the Mīnŷæ in the Bœotian Orchŏmĕnus. He was the husband of the cloud-goddess Nĕphĕlē, mother of Phrixus and Hellē, who left him on his union with a mortal, Inō the daughter of Cadmus. Nephele in anger visited the land with a drought, upon which Ino endeavoured, by means of a pretended oracle, to have her stepson Phrixus sacrificed on the altar of Zeus Laphystĭus. But Nephele conveyed the children away through the air on a golden-fleeced ram. During the passage Helle fell into the sea, which was afterwards, from her name, called the Hellespontus. But her brother arrived safely at the palace of Æētēs, king of Æa, who gave him his daughter Chalcĭŏpē in marriage. Afterwards Athamas was himself about to be sacrificed by his people to Zeus Laphystius; but he was saved by the appearance of Phrixus' son Cytissōrus, who brought the news that Phrixus was still alive. His escape, however, only brought down the wrath of the god upon his descendants. The first-born of his race was ever afterwards liable to be sacrificed to Zeus Laphystius, if he entered the council-chamber and did not get out of the way in time. Later on Athamas was visited with madness by Hēra, because Ino brought up her nephew Dionŷsus, the son of her sister Sĕmĕlē. In his frenzy he killed his son Learchus, and persecuted Ino, who with her other son Mĕlĭcertēs leaped into the sea. Here she became the sea-goddess Leucŏthĕa, and her son the sea-god Palæmōn. On recovering from his madness, Athamas was commanded by an oracle to settle in a place where he should be hospitably treated by wild beasts. In the part of Thessaly which was named, after him, the Athamanian plain, he came upon some wolves, who fled from him, and left him the sheep-bones on which they were feeding. He settled here, and wedded Themisto. (*See* THEMISTO.) The story is no doubt founded upon the old custom which the Minyæ had of offering the first-born of the race of Athamas to Zeus Laphystius, in case he failed to make good his escape as Phrixus did.

Athēnæus. (1) The engineer, a contemporary of Archĭmēdēs, who flourished about 210 B.C. He was the author of a work, still preserved, on engines of war.

(2) The Greek scholar, a native of Naucrătis in Egypt. He was educated at Alexandria, where he lived about 170–230 A.D. After this he lived at Rome, and there wrote his *Deipnosophistæ* (or "Doctors at Dinner"), in fifteen books. Of these the first, second, and part of the third, are only preserved in a selection made in the 11th century; the rest survive in a tolerably complete state. The work shows astonishing learning, and contains a number of notices of ancient life which would otherwise have been lost. The author gives us collections and extracts from more than 1,500 works (now mostly lost), by more than 700 writers. His book is thrown into the form of a conversation held in the year 228 A.D. at a dinner given by Larensius, a rich and accomplished Roman, and a descendant of the great antiquarian Varro. Among the guests are the most learned men of the time, including Galen the physician and Ulpian the jurist. The conversation ranges over numberless subjects connected with domestic and social life, manners and customs, trade, art, and science. Among the most valuable things in the book are the numerous passages from prose-writers and poets, especially from the masters of the Middle Comedy.

Athēnæum. The name of the first public educational institution at Rome, built by Hadrian about 135 A.D. The building was in the form of a theatre, and brilliantly fitted up. There rhetoricians and poets held their recitations, and salaried professors gave their lectures in the various branches of general liberal education, philosophy and rhetoric, as well as grammar and jurisprudence. This continued until late in the imperial age.

Athēnē or **Pallas Athene.** A Greek goddess, identified with the Roman Mĭnerva.

According to the story most generally current, she was the daughter of Zeus, who had swallowed his first wife Mētis ("Counsel"), the daughter of Ocĕănus, in fear that she would bring forth a son stronger than himself. Hēphæstus (or, according to another version, Promētheus) clave open the head of Zeus with an axe, on which Athene sprang forth in full armour, the goddess of eternal virginity. But her ancient epithet *Trĭtŏgĕneia* ("born of Trītōn," or the roaring flood) points to water (that is, to Oceanus) as the source of her being. Oceanus was, according to Homer, the origin of all things and of all deities. The worship of Athene, and the story of her birth, were accordingly connected with many brooks and lakes in various regions, especially in Bœotia, Thessalia, and Libya, to which the name *Triton* was attached.

From the first, Athene takes a very prominent place in the Greek popular religion. The Homeric hymns represent her as the favourite of her father, who refuses her nothing. When solemn oaths were to be taken, they joined her name with those of Zeus and Apollo, in a way which shows that the three deities represent the embodiment of all divine authority. With the exception of the two gods just mentioned, there is no other deity whose original character as a power of nature underwent so remarkable an ethical development. Both conceptions of Athene, the natural and the ethical, were intimately connected in the religion of Attica, whose capital, Athens, was named after Athene, and was the most important seat of her worship. Athene was originally the maiden daughter of the god of heaven; the clear, transparent æther, whose purity is always breaking forth in unveiled brilliancy through the clouds that surround it. As a deity of the sky she, with Zeus, is the mistress of thunder and lightning. Like Zeus, she carries the *ægis* with the Gorgon's head, the symbol of the tempest and its terrors. In many statues, accordingly, she is represented as hurling the thunder-bolt. But she also sends down, from sky to earth, light and warmth and fruitful dew, and with them prosperity to fields and plants. A whole series of fables and usages, belonging especially to the Athenian religion, represents her as the helper and protector of agriculture. The two deities Erechtheus and Erichthŏnius, honoured in Attica as powers of the fruitful soil, are her foster-children. She was worshipped with

Erechtheus in the temple named after him (the *Erechthēum*), the oldest sanctuary on the Athenian Acrŏpŏlis. The names of her earliest priestesses, the daughters of Cecrops, Aglaurus, Pandrŏsus, and Hersē, signify the bright air, the dew, and the rain, and are mere personifications of their qualities, of such value to the Athenian territory.

The sowing season was opened in Attica by three sacred services of ploughing. Of these, two were in honour of Athene as inventress of the plough, while the third took place in honour of Dēmētēr. It was Athene, also, who had taught men how to attach oxen to the yoke; above all, she had given them the olive-tree, the treasure of Attica. This tree she had made to grow out of the rock of the citadel, when disputing the possession of the land with Poseidōn. Several festivals, having reference to these functions of the goddess, were celebrated in Attica; the *Callyntērĭa* and *Plyntērĭa*, the *Scīrŏphŏrĭa*, the *Arrhēphŏrĭa* or *Hersĕphŏrĭa*, and the *Oschŏphŏrĭa*, which were common to Athene with Dionȳsus. (*See* DIONYSIA.) Even her chief feast, the *Panathēnœa*, was originally a harvest festival. It is significant that the presentation of the *pĕplŏs* or mantle, the chief offering at the celebration, took place in the sowing season. But afterwards more was made of the intellectual gifts bestowed by the goddess.

Athene was very generally regarded as the goddess of war; an idea which in ancient times was the prevailing one. It was connected with the fact that, like her father Zeus, she was supposed to be able to send storms and bad weather. In this capacity she appears in story as the true friend of all bold warriors, such as Perseus, Bellĕrŏphōn, Jāsōn, Hērāclēs, Dĭŏmēdēs, and Odysseus. But her courage is a wise courage, not a blind rashness like that of Arēs; and she is always represented, accordingly, as getting the better of him. In this connection she was honoured in Athenian worship mainly as a protector and defender; thus (to take a striking example) she was worshipped on the citadel of Athens under the name of *Prŏmăchŏs* ("champion," "protector.") But she was also a goddess of victory. As the personification of victory (*Athene Nīkē*) she had a second and especial temple on the Athenian Acropolis. (*See* Plan of ACROPOLIS.) And the great statues in the temples represented her, like Zeus, with Nike in her outstretched hand. The occupations of peace, however, formed the main sphere of her activity. Like all the other deities who were supposed to dispense the blessings of nature, she is the protectress of growing children; and as the goddess of the clear sky and of pure air, she bestows health and keeps off sickness. Further, she is (with Zeus) the patroness of the Athenian *Phrātrĭæ*, or unions of kinsfolk. At Athens and Sparta she protects the popular and deliberative assemblies; in many places, and especially at Athens, the whole state is under her care (*Athene Pŏlĭăs, Pŏlĭŭchus*). Elsewhere she presides over the larger unions of kindred peoples. The festival of Athene Itonia at Corōnēa was a confederate festival of all Bœotia. Under the title of *Panăchăïs* she was worshipped as the goddess of the Achæan League.

Speaking broadly, Athene represents human wit and cleverness, and presides over the whole moral and intellectual side of human life. From her are derived all the productions of wisdom and understanding, every art and science, whether of war or of peace. A crowd of discoveries, of the most various kinds, is ascribed to her. It has been already mentioned that she was credited with the invention of the plough and the yoke. She was often associated with Poseidon as the inventress of horse-taming and ship-building. In the Athenian story she teaches Erichthŏnius to fasten his horses to the chariot. In the Corinthian story she teaches Bellĕrŏphōn to subdue Pēgăsus. At Lindus in Rhodes she was worshipped as the goddess who helped Dănăüs to build the first fifty-oared ship. In the fable of the Argonauts it is she who instructs the builders of the first ship, the Argo. Even in Homer all the productions of women's art, as of spinning and weaving, are characterized as "works of Athene." Many a *Pallădĭŏn* or statue of Pallas bore a spindle and distaff in its left hand. As the mistress and protectress of arts and handiwork, she was worshipped at the *Chalkeia* (or Feast of Smiths) under the title of *Ergănē*. Under this name she is mentioned in several inscriptions found on the Acropolis. Her genius covers the field of music and dancing. She is inventor of the flute and the trumpet, as well as of the Pyrrhic war-dance, in which she was said to have been the earliest performer, at the celebration of the victory of the Gods over the Giants.

It was Phĭdias who finally fixed the typical representation of Athene in works of art. Among his numerous statues of her, three, the most celebrated, were set up on the acropolis of Athens. These were (1) The colossal statue of *Athene Parthĕnŏs*, wrought in ivory and gold, thirty feet in height (with the pedestal), and standing in the Parthĕnōn. (*See* PARTHENON.) The goddess was represented wearing a long robe falling down to the feet, and on her breast was the ægis with the Gorgon's head. A helmet was on her head; in one hand she bore a Victory, six feet in height,

ATHENE.
(From Velletri: Paris, Louvre.)

in the other a lance, which leaned against a shield adorned with scenes from the battles of the Amazons with the Giants. (2) The bronze statue of *Athene Promachos*, erected from the proceeds of the spoils taken at Mărăthōn, and standing between the Propylæa and the Erechthĕum. The proportions of this statue were so gigantic, that the gleaming point of the lance and the crest of the helmet were visible to seamen, on approaching the Piræus from Sūnium.

(3) The *Lemnian Pallas*, so named because it had been dedicated by the Athenian *Clĕrūchi* in Lemnos. The attractions of this statue won for it the name of "the Beautiful." Like the second, it was of bronze; as a representation of Athene as the goddess of peace, it was without a helmet.

Throughout the numerous and varying representations of her, Athene has an imposing stature, suggesting a masculine rather than a feminine form; an oval face, with a brow of great clearness and purity; thoughtful eyes, compressed lips, firm chin, and hair carelessly thrown back. (*See* cut.) Her ordinary attributes are the helmet, the ægis covering the breast or serving as a shield for the arm, the lance, the round shield with the Gorgon's head, the olive branch, and the owl. (On her identification with *Minerva, see* MINERVA.)

Athēnŏdōrus. A Greek sculptor, of the Rhodian school. He was associated with Agēsander and Pŏlȳdōrus in the production of the celebrated group of *Laocoon.* (*See* SCULPTURE.)

Athlētæ. This was the name given by the Greeks to the professional competitors for the prizes in gymnastic contests, such as boxing and the *pancrătĭŏn*, a combination of boxing with wrestling. The *athletæ* practised gymnastics as a means of livelihood, whereas in general Greek society it was regarded as a liberal art, useful for the harmonious development of the body, and as a training for military service. The professional athletes adopted a special regimen, which produced an exceptional development of bodily strength and muscle, but unfitted them for any other kind of life or pursuit. The profession of athlete was accordingly adopted mainly by men of low birth, and was more popular with the multitude than with persons of intelligence and education. Greek athletes did not make their appearance in Rome before 186 B.C. In the republican age they were not regarded with great favour; but under Augustus their contests became quite popular. No social stigma attached to them, as to actors and gladiators, and under the Empire they formed themselves into regular societies, each with its own president, travelling from place to place at the festivals, at which they would appear in pairs, arranged by lot, for a high remuneration. In 86 A.D. Domitian established a contest on the Capitol for musicians and athletes, to recur every four years; and erected a special race-course for the athletes on the *Campus Martius*. The Capitoline contest survived during the whole of antiquity.

Athlŏthĕtæ. The persons who arranged, and acted as umpires in, the various public games of Greece. They were also called *Agōnŏthĕtæ*, and at Olympia *Hellānŏdĭkæ*. (*See* also PANATHENÆA.)

Atilius Fortunātiānus. A Latin grammarian who flourished in the first half of the 4th century A.D., and was the author of a school manual of prosody.

Atīmĭa. This Greek word does not imply dishonour in the modern sense, but deprivation of civil rights, whether partial, complete, temporary, or perpetual. Partial *atimia* at Athens might consist, for instance, in depriving a citizen of the right to appear again as prosecutor, in case he had, in this capacity, failed to obtain a fifth part of the votes ; or of the right to propose a law again to the assembly, if he had been three times condemned for making illegal propositions. In cases of complete *atimia*, a person was excluded from taking part in any public proceeding whatever. He was forbidden access to the *ăgŏrā* and the public sanctuaries ; he was incapacitated from appearing in court as a prosecutor. In case of very serious offences the *atimia* might be followed by confiscation of property, and might even be extended to a man's children. *Atimia* might also be inflicted on debtors to the State, if the debt was not paid within the appointed time. It was then accompanied with a fine equivalent to the amount already owed. The payment of the debt brought the *atimia* to an end. But where it was inflicted for other offences, it was seldom removed, and then only after a vote of at least six thousand citizens.

In Sparta complete *atimia* was mostly inflicted on persons who had been guilty of cowardice in war. The offender was not only cut off from all civil rights, and from the common meals and exercises, but had to submit to every kind of insult. At the public festivals he had to take a low place. He was obliged to wear a patchwork cloak, to have his hair cut on one side ; to give way in the street to every one, even to young men ; no one would give him light for his fire, marry his daughter, or give him his daughter to wife. [Plutarch, *Agēsĭlāŭs* 30.] Bachelors were also subject to a kind of *atimia*. They were not allowed to be present at certain festivals, and had no claim to the marks of respect which the young, in other cases, were expected to show. The

full possession of civic rights and privileges was called *ĕpĭtĭmĭa*. (*See* INFAMIA.)

Atlās (the " bearer " or " endurer"). The son of the Titan Iăpĕtus and Clўmĕnē (or, according to another account, Asia), brother of Menœtius, Promētheus, and Epimētheus. In Homer [*Od.* i. 52] he is called " the thinker of mischief," who knows the depths of the whole sea, and has under his care the pillars which hold heaven and earth asunder. In Hesiod [*Theog.* 517] he stands at the western end of the earth, near where the Hespĕrĭdĕs dwell, holding the broad heaven on his head and unwearied hands. To this condition he is forced by Zeus, according to a later version as a punishment for the part which he took in the battle with the Titans. By the Ocean nymph Plēïŏnē he is father of the Plēïădĕs, by

* ATLAS (RESTORED).
(From the temple of Zeus at Agrigentum.)

Æthra of the Hyădĕs. In Homer the nymph Calypso is also his daughter, who dwells on the island Ogўgia, the navel of the sea. Later authors make him the father of the Hesperides, by Hesperis. It is to him that Amphitrītē flies when pursued by Poseidōn. As their knowledge of the West extended. the Greeks transferred the abode of Atlas to the African mountain of the same name. Local stories of a mountain which supported the heaven would, no doubt, encourage the identification. In later times Atlas was represented as a wealthy king, and owner of the garden of the Hesperides. Perseus, with his head of Medūsa, turned him into a rocky mountain for his inhospitality. In works of art he is represented as carrying the heaven; or (after the earth was discovered to be spherical), the terrestrial globe. Among the statues of Atlas the *Farnese*, in the Museum at Naples, is the best known. (*See also* OLYMPIC GAMES, fig. 3.)

In Greek architecture, the term *Atlantēs* was employed to denote the colossal male statues sometimes used in great buildings instead of columns to support an entablature or a projecting roof.

Atreus. Son of Pĕlops and Hippŏdămīa, grandson of Tantălus. (*See* PELOPS.) With the help of his brother Thyestēs he murdered his step-brother Chrȳsippus. To escape the wrath of their father, the pair of brothers took refuge with their brother-in-law Sthĕnĕlus, king of Mycēnæ, who gave them Media to live in. Eurystheus, the brother of their protector, was killed in battle with the Hēracleidæ. Atreus kept possession of the kingdom of Mycēnæ, which had been given him in charge by Eurystheus, and maintained it in virtue of possessing a golden lamb, which had been given him by Hermēs for the purpose of exciting discord in the house of Pelops and avenging the death of his son Myrtĭlus. Thyestēs debauched his brother's wife Aërŏpē, daughter of the king of Crete, and with her aid got possession of the golden lamb and the kingdom. But, as a sign that right and wrong had been confounded, Zeus turned the sun and the moon back in their course. Atreus accordingly recovered the kingdom and expelled Thyestēs. To revenge himself, Thyestēs sent Pleisthĕnēs, a son of Atreus whom he had brought up as his own, to Mycēnæ to murder Atreus. But Atreus slew Pleisthenes, not knowing that he was his son. Atreus replied by bringing back Thyestēs and his family from exile, and serving up to Thyestēs at table the limbs of his own sons. Thyestēs fled away; the land was visited with barrenness and famine. In obedience to an oracle, Atreus goes forth to seek him, but only finds his daughter Pelopīa, whom he takes to wife. Ægisthus, her son by her father Thyestes, who is destined to avenge him, Atreus adopts and rears as his own child. Thyestes is afterwards found by Agamemnōn and Menelāūs, who bring him to Mycēnæ. He is imprisoned, and Ægisthus ordered to murder him. By the sword which Ægisthus carries Thyestes recognises him as his son, and proposes to him to slay Atreus. Meanwhile Pelopīa, in horror at the discovery of her son's incestuous origin, drives the sword

into her own breast. Ægisthus takes the bloody sword to Atreus as a proof that he has executed his commission, and afterwards falls upon him with Thyestes, while he is engaged in making a thank-offering on the sea-shore. Thyestes and Ægisthus thereupon seize the government of Mycēnæ, and drive Agamemnon and Menelaus out of the country.

The older story knows nothing of these horrors. In Homer Pelops receives the sceptre from Zeus by the ministration of Hermes; he leaves it to Atreus, and Atreus to Thyestes, who hands it down to Agamemnon. Hesiod alludes to the wealth of the Pelŏpĭdæ, but is silent as to the rest.

Atrĭdæ (Gr. *Atrĕĭdœ, Atreidœ*). The sons of Atreus, Agamemnōn and Menelāūs.

Atrĭum. The original name for a Roman house, the interior of which consisted of a single chamber open at the front. Afterwards the term was applied to the large hall which extended along the whole breadth of the house, and was lighted by an opening in the roof. The *atrium* was entered by the floor of the house, and the other chambers were attached to it. (*See* HOUSE.) Other buildings, sacred or profane, possessing halls of this kind with dwelling-rooms attached, were known by the name of *ātria*, from the resemblance of their form to that of an ordinary house. The *Atrium Vestœ*, or abode of the Vestal Virgins, is an example of a consecrated *atrium*. The *Atrium Lībertātis* was secular. This was the official residence of the censor, and it was here that Asinius Pollio established the first public library known to have existed at Rome. Auction-rooms were also called *atria*, and halls of this description were often attached to temples, and used for the meetings and festivals of societies.

Atrŏpus. One of the three Fates. (*See* MŒRÆ.)

Atta (*T. Quinctius* [or *Quinticius*]). A Roman dramatic poet, author of *togātœ* (*see* COMEDY), who died B.C. 77, and was a contemporary of Afrănius. He was celebrated for his power of drawing character, especially in conversational scenes in which women were introduced. Of his comedies only twelve titles remain, with a few insignificant fragments.

Atthis. A chronicle of Attic history, in which special attention was paid to occurrences of political and religious significance. After the last half of the 4th century A.D., chronicles of this kind were composed by a number of writers (*Atthidŏgrăphi*), among whom Andrŏtiŏn and Philŏchŏrus (*q.v.*) deserve special mention. These writings were much quoted by the grammarians.

Attĭcus. (1) *T. Pompŏnius.* A Roman of an old and wealthy equestrian family, born 109 B.C. He received a good education in boyhood and youth, and went in the year 88 B.C. to Athens, where he lived until 65, devoting himself entirely to study, and much respected by the citizens for his generosity and cultivated refinement. In 65 he returned to Rome, to take possession of the inheritance left him by his uncle and adoptive father, Q. Cæcilius. He now became Q. Cæcilius Pomponiănus. From this time onward he lived on terms of intimacy with men like Cicero, Hortensius, and Cornēlius Nepos, who wrote a life of him which we still possess. He avoided public life and the strife of parties. This fact, in addition to his general amiability and good nature, enabled him during the civil wars to keep on the best of terms with the leaders of the conflicting parties, Cicero, Brutus, and Antonius. He died after a painful illness, of voluntary starvation, in the year 32 B.C.

Atticus was the author of several works, the most considerable of which was a history (*lĭber annālis*) dedicated to Cicero. This gave a short epitome of the bare events of Roman history down to B.C. 54, arranged according to the series of consuls and other magistrates, with contemporaneous notices. But his most important contribution to Latin literature was his edition of the letters which he had received from Cicero. He also did great service by setting his numerous slaves to work at copying the writings of his contemporaries.

(2) *Hērōdēs Atticus.* See HERODES.

Attis (or *Atys*). A mythical personage in the worship of the Phrygian goddess Cўbĕlē-Agdistis. The son of this goddess, so ran the story, had been mutilated by the gods in terror at his gigantic strength, and from his blood sprang the almond-tree. After eating its fruit, Nana, daughter of the river Sangarius, brought forth a boy, whom she exposed. He was brought up first among the wild goats of the forests, and afterwards by some shepherds, and grew up so beautiful that Agdistis fell in love with him. Wishing to wed the daughter of the king of Pessīnūs in Phrygia, he was driven to madness by the goddess. He then fled to the mountains, and destroyed his manhood at the foot of a pine-tree, which received his spirit, while

from his blood sprang violets to garland the tree. Agdistis besought Zeus that the body of her beloved one might know no corruption. Her prayer was heard ; a tomb to Attis was raised on Mount Dindўmus in the sanctuary of Cybele, the priests of which had to undergo emasculation for Attis' sake. A festival of several days was held in honour of Attis and Cybele in the beginning of spring. A pine-tree, felled in the forest, was covered with violets, and carried to the shrine of Cybele, as a symbol of the departed Attis. Then, amid tumultuous music, and rites of wildest sorrow, they sought and mourned for Attis on the mountains. On the third day he was found again, the image of the goddess was purified from the contagion of death, and a feast of joy was celebrated, as wild as had been the days of sorrow.

Attius. See ACCIUS.

Atys. See ATTIS.

Augē. Daughter of Alĕus of Tĕgĕa, and mother of Tēlĕphus by Hērăclēs.

Augeas or Augias. (Gr. *Augeiās* in verse, *Augĕas* in prose). Son of Hēliŏs, or, according to another account, of Phorbās, and Hermiŏnē. He was king of the Epeians in Elis, and one of the Argonauts. Besides his other possessions, for which Agamemnŏn and Trophōnius built him a treasure-house, he was the owner of an enormous flock of sheep and oxen, among which were twelve white bulls, consecrated to the Sun. When Hērăclēs, at the command of Eurystheus, came to cleanse his farmyard, Augeas promised him the tenth part of his flock. But, the task completed, he refused the reward, on the ground that the work had been done in the service of Eurystheus. Heracles replied by sending an army against him, which was defeated in the passes of Elis by Eurўtus and Cteătus, sons of Moliŏnē. But Heracles appeared on the scene, and slew the Moliŏnĭdæ, and with them their uncle Augeas and his sons. (*See* MOLIONIDÆ.)

Augŭrēs [not probably, from *avis*, a bird, but from a lost word, *aug-o*, to tell; so "declarers" or "tellers"]. A priestly *collēgium* at Rome, the establishment of which was traditionally ascribed to Romulus. Its members were in possession of the knowledge necessary to make the arrangements for taking the auspices, and for their interpretation when taken. Their assistance was called in on all those occasions on which the State had to assure itself, through auspices, of the approval of the gods. The *collegium* originally consisted of three Patricians, of whom the king was one. During the regal period the number was doubled; in B.C. 300 it was raised to nine (four Patricians and five Plebeians); and in the last century of the Republic, under Sulla, to fifteen, and finally by Julius Cæsar to sixteen, a number which continued unaltered under the Empire. It can be shown that the college of augurs continued to exist until the end of the 4th century A.D. The office was, on account of its political importance, much sought after, and only filled by persons of high birth and distinguished merit. It was held for life, an augur not being precluded from holding other temporal or spiritual dignities. Vacancies in the *collegium* were originally filled up by cooptation; but after 104 B.C. the office was elective, the tribes choosing one of the candidates previously nominated. An *augurium* had to be taken before the augur entered upon his duties. In all probability the augurs ranked according to seniority, and the senior augur presided over the business of the *collegium*.

* AUGUR WITH LITUUS.
(Bas-relief in Museum, Florence.)

The *insignia* of the office were the *trăbĕa*, a state dress with a purple border, and the *lĭtŭus*, a staff without knots and curved at the top.

The science of Roman augury was based chiefly on written tradition. This was contained partly in the *Libri Augŭrālēs*, the oldest manual of technical practice, partly in the *Commentārii Augurales*, a collection of answers given in certain cases to the enquiries of the senate. In ancient times the chief duty of the augurs was to observe, when commissioned by a magistrate to do so, the omens given by birds, and to mark out the *templum* or consecrated space within which the observation took place. The proceeding was as follows. Immediately after midnight, or at the dawn of the day on which the official act was to take place, the augur, in the presence of the magistrate, selected an elevated spot with as wide a view as was obtainable. Taking his station here, he drew with his staff

two straight lines cutting one another, the one from north to south, the other from east to west. Then to each of these straight lines he drew two parallel lines, thus forming a rectangular figure, which he consecrated according to a prescribed form of words. This space, as well as the space corresponding to it in the sky, was called a *templum*. At the point of intersection in the centre of the rectangle, was erected the *tabernācŭlum*. This was a square tent, with its entrance looking south. Here the augur sat down, asked the gods for a sign according to a prescribed formula, and waited for the answer. Complete quiet, a clear sky, and an absence of wind were necessary conditions of the observation. The least noise was sufficient to disturb it, unless indeed the noise was occasioned by omens of terror (*dĭræ*), supposing the augur to have observed them or to intend doing so. As he looked south, the augur had the east on his left, the west on his right. Accordingly, the Romans regarded signs on the left side as of prosperous omen, signs on the right side as unlucky; the east being deemed the region of light, the west that of darkness. The reverse was the case in ancient Greece, where the observer looked northwards. In his observation of birds, the augur did not confine himself to noticing their flight. The birds were distinguished as *ālĭtēs* and *oscĭnēs*. The *alites* included birds like eagles and vultures, which gave signs by their manner of flying. The *oscĭnēs* were birds which gave signs by their cry as well as their flight, such as ravens, owls, and crows. There were also birds which were held sacred to particular gods, and the mere appearance of which was an omen of good or evil. The augur's report was expressed in the words *avēs admittunt*, "the birds allow it"; or *ălĭo dĭē*, "on another day," *i.e.* "the augury is postponed." The magistrate was bound by this report. The science of augury included other kinds of auspices besides the observation of birds, a cumbrous process which had dropped out of use in the Ciceronian age. (*See* AUSPICIA.)

The augurs always continued in possession of important functions. In certain places in the city, for instance on the *arx*, and at the meeting place of the *comĭtĭa*, there were permanent posts of observation for taking the regular auspices. These places were put under the care of the augurs. Their boundaries might not be altered, nor the view which they commanded interfered with. The augurs had authority to prevent the erection of buildings which would do this. They had also the power of consecrating priests, as well as of inaugurating a part of the localities intended for religious purposes, and the places where public business was carried on. They were always present at the *comitia*, and were authorized, if the signs which they saw or which were reported to them justified the proceeding, to announce the fact and postpone the business. If the constitutional character of a public act was called in question, the college of augurs had the exclusive power of deciding whether there was a flaw (*vĭtium*) in it, or not. If there were, the act was necessarily annulled.

By the end of the republican period the augurs, and the whole business of the auspices, had ceased to be regarded as deserving serious attention.

Augustālēs. A religious association at Rome, formed for the maintenance of the worship paid to the deified Cæsars. (*See* MUNICIPIUM and SODALITAS.)

Augustīnus (*Aurēlius*). The greatest of the Latin Christian fathers. He was born 354 A.D. at Tagastē in Numidia. His father was a pagan, his mother, Mŏnĭca, a zealous Christian. After a wild life as a young man, he became professor of rhetoric in Tagaste, Carthage, Rome, and Milan, where he was converted to Christianity through the influence of Ambrose, and baptized in 387. He returned to Africa, and was ordained presbyter in 391, and bishop of Hippo in Numidia in 396. He died there in 430, after doing much good in the city during its siege by the Vandals. His literary activity was extraordinary. Four years before his death he reckons up the number of his works, exclusive of letters and sermons, as 93, making up 233 books. Among them are six books *De Musĭcā*, and essays on rhetoric, dialectic, and grammar. These productions, which testify to his interest in learning, were instalments of an encyclopædic work on the seven liberal arts, modelled upon the *Disciplīnæ* of Varro. Among his other writings two attracted especial notice on account of the extraordinary effect which they produced in after times. These are *The Confessions*, a history of his inner life in thirteen books, written in the form of a confession to the Almighty; and the *De Civitāte Dei*, a work in twenty-two books, demonstrating the providential action of God in the development of human history.

Augustus [" consecrated by augury "]. An honorary title given in the year 27 B.C. to Octaviānus, the founder of the Roman empire. It was not hereditary, but was taken by the succeeding emperors at the instance of the senate, a formality which was afterwards dispensed with. Thus it gradually became an official title. Properly speaking, it could only be assumed by the actual holder of the imperial dignity, not by his colleague. Marcus Aurelius was the first who broke through this rule. In 161 A.D. he conferred the entire imperial authority, with the title of Augustus, upon Lucius Vērus, after whose death he elevated his son Commŏdus to the same position. This arrangement had the advantage of dispensing with the necessity of a further recognition of the colleague by the senate and people after the death of the reigning emperor. It was frequently adopted, until, under Diocletian, it developed into the division of the empire into an eastern and western portion, each under its own Augustus.

The title of *Augustus* was reserved exclusively for the emperor ; but the corresponding feminine style of *Augusta* was assumed, as the highest of all honours, by the great ladies of the imperial house. The first of those who bore it was Livia, on whom her husband Octavianus conferred it by will. She was followed by Antonia, who received it from her grandson Calĭgŭla. The first lady who took it as consort of the reigning Cæsar was Agrippīna, the third wife of Claudius. After Domitian's time it became the rule to confer the title of *Augusta* not only on the consort of the reigning emperor, but on others among their near relations, especially their daughters. This was generally done upon some appropriate occasion, and never without the special consent of the Cæsar. In later times it was generally the senate who took the initiative in the matter.

Aulæum. *See* THEATRE.

Aulē. *See* HOUSE (Greek).

Aulŏs, Aulētĭkē, Aulŏdĭkē. *See* MUSIC.

Aurēliānus (*Cœlius*). A Latin writer on medicine, a native of Sicca in Numidia, who flourished in the 5th century A.D. He was the author of two works on Acute and Chronic Diseases, the first in three, the second in five books. These are translations, fairly literal, but abridged, of works by the Greek physician Soranus, who lived in the last half of the 2nd century A.D. Cælius also wrote a compendium of the whole science of medicine, in the form of a catechism (*Medicīnālēs Responsiōnēs*). Of this considerable fragments remain.

Aurelius, Marcus. *See* ANTONINUS.

Aurēlius Victor (*Sextus*). A Roman historian, born in Africa. He was probably governor of Pannonia under Julian in 361 A.D., and in 389 prefect of Rome. There is a history of the Cæsars from Julius to Constantine, written about 360 A.D., which bears his name. This appears, however, to be no more than an extract from a more comprehensive work. The same is the case with an *Epitŏmē*, continued down to the death of Theodosius. There is also a short but not altogether worthless book, entitled *De Vĭrīs Illustrĭbus Urbis Romæ*, which is attributed to Aurelius Victor. It begins with the Alban king Prŏcas, and comes down to Cleopatra. It is not by Aurelius Victor, nor again is a little book which has been attributed to him, called *Orīgo Gentis Romānæ*. This is full of forged quotations, and belongs to a much later period.

Aurēus. A Roman coin of the imperial period, originally weighing $\frac{1}{40}$ of a Roman pound, and worth from the time of Julius Cæsar to Nero, 25 *denārii*, or 100 *sestertii*; from 23 to 20 shillings. (*See* COINAGE.)

Aurīga. *See* CIRCENSIAN GAMES.

Aurōra. *See* EOS.

Aurum Corōnārium. *See* CORONA.

Ausōnius (*Dēcĭmus Magnus*). The most remarkable Latin poet of the 4th century A.D.; born about 310 at Burdīgăla (Bordeaux). He was son of the private physician of Valentinian I, and afterwards prefect of Illyria. Educated thoroughly in grammar, rhetoric, and law, he practised as an advocate in his native city, where he afterwards became professor of grammar and rhetoric. He was then invited by Valentinian to undertake the education of his son Gratian, who, after he had ascended the throne, conferred upon him the consulship and other distinctions. After the assassination of Gratian he retired to his estate near Burdigala, where he continued to reside, in full literary activity, till 390. He became a Christian, probably on accepting the office of tutor to the prince. Besides composing a turgid address of thanks to Gratian, delivered at Trèves, Ausonius wrote a series of poems, including verses in memory of deceased relatives (*Parentālia*), verses commemorating his colleagues (*Commemorātio Professōrum Burdigalensium*), *Epităphia*, *Eclŏgæ*, *Epistŭlæ*, *Epigrammăta*, and a number of miscellaneous pieces, one of which (*Mosella*) is the narrative of a tour from Bingen on the Rhine to Berncastel (*Tabernæ*) on the Moselle and then up the Moselle past Neumagen (*Nŏvĭŏmăgum*) to Trèves. Its subject has secured the poem some renown. Ausonius is not a real poet; but he tries to make up for lack of genius by dexterity in metre and the manipulation of words, and by ornaments of learning and rhetoric. The consequence is, that his style is generally neither simple nor natural.

Auspĭcĭa ("observations of birds"). In its proper sense the word means the watching of signs given by birds. But it was also applied to other signs, the observation of which was not intended to obtain answers about future events, but only to ascertain whether a particular proceeding was or was not acceptable to the deity concerned. It must be remembered that, according to Roman ideas, Jupiter gave men signs of his approval or disapproval in every undertaking; signs which qualified persons could read and understand. Any private individual was free to ask for, and to interpret, such signs for his own needs. But to ask for signs on behalf of the State was only allowed to the representatives of the community. The *auspicia publĭca pŏpŭli Rōmāni*, or system of public *auspicia*, were under the superintendence of the college of augurs. (*See* AUGUR.) This body alone possessed the traditional knowledge of the ceremonial, and held the key to the correct interpretation of the signs. The signs from heaven might be asked for, or they might present themselves unasked. They fell into five classes: (1) Signs given by birds (*signa ex ăvĭbus*). These, as the name *auspicia* shows, were originally the commonest sort, but had become obsolete as early as the 1st century B.C. (For the ceremonial connected with them, *see* AUGUR.) (2) Signs in the sky (*ex cælo*). The most important and decisive were thunder and lightning. Lightning was a favourable omen if it appeared to the left of the augur, and flashed to the right; unfavourable, if it flashed from right to left. (*See* AUGUR.) In certain cases, as, for example, that of the assembling of the *comĭtia*, a storm was taken as an absolute prohibition of the meeting. (3) Signs from the behaviour of chickens while eating. It was a good omen if the chicken rushed eagerly out of its cage at its food and dropped a bit out of its beak; an unfavourable omen if it was unwilling, or refused altogether, to leave its cage, or flew away, or declined its food. This clear and simple method of getting omens was generally adopted by armies in the field, the chickens being taken about in charge of a special functionary (*pullārius*). (4) Signs given by the cries or motion of animals, as reptiles and quadrupeds, in their course over a given piece of ground (*signa pedestria* or *ex quadrupĕdĭbus*). (5) Signs given by phenomena of terror (*signa ex dīrīs*). These might consist in disturbances of the act of

auspicātio, such as the falling of an object, a noise, a stumble, a slip in the recitation of the formula ; or a disturbance occurring in the course of public business, such as, for instance, an epileptic seizure taking place in the public assembly; an event which broke up the meeting.

The two last-mentioned classes of signs were generally not asked for, because the former were usually, the latter always, unlucky. If they made their appearance unasked, they could not be passed over, if the observer saw them or wished to see them. Every official was expected to take auspices on entering upon his office, and on every occasion of performing an official act. Thus the words *impĕrium* and *auspicium* were often virtually synonymous. The *auspicia* were further divided, according to the dignity of the magistrate, into *maxĭma* (" greatest ") and *minōra* (" less "). The greatest *auspicia* were those which were taken by the king, dictator, consuls, prætors, and censors ; the lesser were taken by ædiles and quæstors. If two magistrates, though *collēgæ* (colleagues) were of unequal

dignity—supposing, for instance, that a consul and prætor were in the same camp—-the higher officer alone had the right of taking the auspices. If the *collegæ* were equal, the auspices passed from one to the other at stated times. No public act, whether of peace or war (crossing a river, for instance, or fighting a battle), could be undertaken without auspices. They were specially necessary at the election of all officials, the entry upon all offices, at all *comitia*, and at the departure of a general for war. They had, further, to be taken on the actual day and at the actual place of the given undertaking.

The whole proceeding was so abused that in time it sank into a mere form. This remark applies even to the auspices taken from lightning, the most important sign of all. For the flash of lightning, which was in later times regularly supposed to appear when a magistrate entered upon office, was always (after the necessary formalities) set down as appearing on the left side. Moreover, the mere assertion of a magistrate who had the right of *auspicium* that he had taken observations on a particular day, and seen a flash of lightning, was constitutionally unassailable ; and was consequently often used to put off a meeting of the *comitia* fixed for the day in question. Augustus, it is true, tried to rehabilitate the *auspicia*, but their supposed religious foundation had been so thoroughly shaken, that they had lost all serious significance.

Autŏlўcus. Son of Hermēs and Chĭŏnē, or (according to another account) Philōnis, father of Anticleia, the mother of Odysseus. In Greek mythology he figured as the prince of thieves. From his father he inherited the gift of making himself and all his stolen goods invisible, or changing them so as to preclude the possibility of recognition. He was an accomplished wrestler, and was said to have given Hērăclēs instruction in the art.

Autŏmĕdŏn. Son of Diŏrēs; the comrade and charioteer of Achilles.

Auxĭlia (auxiliary troops). This name was given in the Roman army to the foreign troops serving with the legions, and to the contingents of Italian allies. In some cases, especially that of the slingers and archers, they were raised by free recruiting, in others by a levy in the provinces ; in others they were sent as contingents by kings or communities in alliance with Rome. Under the Empire the term *auxilia* was extended to all the corps stationed in the provinces and not included in the legions; as, for example, the divisions of veterans called *vexillārii*, and the cohorts called Italian, formed originally of free Italian volunteers. It was, however, employed especially of the corps levied in the provinces, which furnished the material not only of the whole cavalry of the Roman army, but of a number of infantry detachments (*cohortēs auxiliāriœ*). Of these, some were armed and trained in Roman fashion, others retained their national equipment. Consequently, a striking variety of troops might be observed in the provincial armies of Rome. (*See* ALA and COHORS.)

Auxo. One of the two *Chărĭtēs*, or Graces, worshipped at Athens. (*See* CHARITES.)

Aviānus. A Latin writer of fables. We have a collection of forty-two fables in elegiac metre, written by him, it may be conjectured, in the 4th century A.D. The work is dedicated to a certain Theodosius, with compliments on his acquaintance with Latin literature. He is perhaps to be identified with the well-known scholar Theodosius Macrŏbius. The dedication is in prose, and states that the author's models were Phædrus and Babrius. The book was largely used in schools, and consequently was much enlarged, paraphrased, and imitated in the Middle Ages. The result may be seen in the *Novus Avianus* of Alexander Neckam, written in the 13th century.

Aviēnus (*Rufius Festus*). A Latin poet, native of Volsinii in Etruria, pro-consul of Africa in 366 and of Achaia in 372 A.D. He was the author of a tasteful and scholarly translation, in hexameters, of the *Phœnŏmĕnă* of Arātus, and of the Geography of Dionysius Periēgētēs (*Descriptio Orbis Terrārum*); as well as of a piece called *Ora marĭtĭma*, or a description of the coasts of the Mediterranean, Black, and Caspian Seas. This was based on very ancient authorities, and written in iambics. Only a fragment of the first book remains, describing the Mediterranean coast from the Atlantic as far as Marseilles.

Axāmenta. The ancient hymns sung by the Sălii. (*See* SALII.)

B

Babrĭus (Greek). The compiler of a comprehensive collection of Æsop's fables in choliambic metre. The book is probably to be assigned to the beginning of the 3rd century A.D. Until 1844 nothing was known of Babrius but fragments and paraphrases, bearing the name of Æsōpus (*see* ÆSOPUS). But in that year a Greek, Minoides Minas, discovered 123 of the original fables in a monastery on Mount Athos. In 1857 he brought out 95 more, the genuineness of which is disputed. The style of Babrius is simple and pleasing, the tone fresh and lively.

Bacchānālia, Bacchus. *See* DIONYSUS.

Bacchȳlĭdēs. A Greek lyric poet who flourished in the middle of the 5th century B.C. He was a native of Iulis in the island of Ceos, the nephew and pupil of Simōnĭdēs, and a contemporary of Pindar. For a long time he lived with his uncle at the court of Hiĕro, tyrant of Syracuse. He also resided for a considerable time at Athens, where he won many victories in the dithyrambic contests. Later on his home was in the Peloponnese. It would appear that he attempted to rival the many-sided talent of his uncle, but fell behind him in sublimity and force. Only a few fragments of his poems remain. He attempted a great variety of styles : hymns, pæans, dithyrambs drinking-songs, love-songs, and epigrams.

Bakers and Baking. The original custom in Greece and Italy was to grind the corn and bake the necessary supplies at home ; a usage which maintained itself in large houses even after grinding and baking (for the two went together) had become a separate trade. Bakers first appear in Greece as a distinct class in the 5th century B.C. ; in Rome there is no sign of them till about B.C. 171. The millers or "pounders" (*pistōrēs*) at Rome were usually either freedmen or citizens of a low class ; but the position of the trade was improved by the care taken by the State to provide good and cheap bread of full weight. As early as the time of Augustus the State was served by a *collēgium* or guild of bakers, which was subsequently organized by Trajan. In his time it consisted of 100 members nominated by the emperor, with special privileges, and subordinate to the *prœfectus annōnœ* (*see* ANNONA). In the 3rd century A.D. the monthly distribution of bread was succeeded by a daily one. This naturally led to a considerable increase in the number of public bakeries. At the beginning of the 4th century A.D. there were 254, distributed through the fourteen *rĕ-*

glōnēs of Rome. Side by side with these there existed a number of private bakeries, which . made it their business to provide the finer sorts of bread, so numerous in antiquity.

Baking was carried on sometimes in furnaces (such as are found in Pompeii), sometimes in the *klĭbănŏs* or *krĭbănos* (Latin *clĭbănus*). This was a clay vessel with a lid on the top and small holes in the sides, wider at the bottom than at the top. To heat it they surrounded it with hot ashes. The ancients were unacquainted with rye, and made their bread mostly of wheat, with several varieties depending on the quality of the flour and the mode of preparation. The loaves were generally round, and divided into four parts, to facilitate breaking them.

Ball (*Games of*). Games of ball were among the commonest and most popular forms of exercise in antiquity, among the young and old alike. Playing went on in public places, such as the *Campus Martius* at Rome; and in *gymnăsia* and *thermœ* a room (*sphœristĕrium*, from the Greek *sphaira*, a ball) was set apart for the purpose, in which a professional attended to give instruction in the art (*sphairistĭkē*). During the imperial period country-houses often had a *sphœristerium* attached to them. The balls (Lat. *pĭlœ*) were made of hair, feathers, or fig-seeds, covered with leather or many-coloured cloth. The largest (as, for instance, the Roman *follis*) were filled with air. At this time there were five sorts of ball: the small, the middle-sized, the large, the very large, and the inflated ball. In throwing the little ball the rule was that the arm should not rise above the shoulder. There were games for one, two, three, or a larger number of players. In many of these several small balls were used at once. Two of the games with the little ball may be mentioned, called by the Greeks *Urănĭa* and *Aporraxis*. In the *urania* ("sky-high") the player threw the ball as high as possible, to be caught either by himself or his antagonist. In the *aporraxis* ("bounce-ball") the ball was thrown obliquely to the ground, and its several rebounds were scored up until another player caught it with the flat of his hand and threw it back. In another form of the game the point was to keep tossing the ball up, as long as possible, with the open hand. A very favourite game at Rome was the *trĭgōn* ("three-corner"), which required special dexterity with the left hand. The game of *episkўrŏs*, at first peculiar to Sparta, was played by a large number. It took its name from the line (*skўron*) which separated the two sides. On this line the player took his stand to throw the ball; another line, behind the players, marked the point beyond which you might not go back in catching it. If you failed to catch the ball when standing within this line, you lost the game. Another game played by a large number was the *harpastum* (Latin) or *phaininda* (Greek). In this the player made as though he were going to send the ball to a particular man on the other side, and then suddenly threw it in another direction. The *kōrўkŏs* was not so much a game as a trial of strength. The *kōrўkŏs* was a large leather bag filled with flour, sand, or fig-seeds. It hung from the ceiling so as to reach to about the middle of the player's body. His business was to keep the bag in increasingly violent motion, beating it back with breast and hands.

Ballista. *See* ARTILLERY.

Banks and Banking. Bankers were called by the Greeks *trăpezĭtœ*, because they sat at tables in the market-places, the centre of all business transactions. They acted as money-changers, exchanging for a commission heavy money or gold into smaller coin, and the moneys of different systems with each other. In commercial cities they would do a considerable trade in this way; the difference of standards and the uncertainty of the stamping of coins in Greece creating a great demand for their assistance. They also acted as money-lenders, both on a small and a large scale. Finally, they received money on deposit. People placed their money with them partly for safe custody, partly to facilitate the management of it. The depositors, according to their convenience, either drew out sums of money themselves, or commissioned their banker to make payments to a third person. In this line the business of the banks was considerable. If a citizen had a large sum of money circulating in business, he probably preferred to put it in a bank, and to hand over to the banker the business of making his payments. Strangers too found that the banks offered them such facilities that they were glad to make considerable use of them. The bankers kept strict accounts of all the monies in their charge. If a person were making a payment to another who was a depositor at the same bank, the banker would simply transfer the requisite sum from one account to the other. The bankers were generally well known from the public character of their occupation, and they naturally gained great experience in business. Consequently their advice and assistance were often asked for in the ordinary affairs of life. They would be called in to attest the conclusion of contracts, and would take charge of sums of money, the title to which was disputed, and of important documents. Business of this kind was generally in the hands of resident aliens. We hear, in isolated instances, of State-banks. But this business was carried on in the vast majority of cases by the great sanctuaries, such as those of Delphi, Delos, Ephesus, and Samos, which were much used as banks for loans and deposits, both by individuals and governments.

The *Romans* had, in some exceptional cases, State-banks under the superintendence of public officials. The *nummŭlārĭi* and *argentārĭi* occupied the same position among them as the *trapezitæ* among the Greeks. The *tabernæ argentāriæ*, or banks, were set up in the forum, especially about or under the three arched buildings called *Iānĭ*. The *nummularii* had a two-fold function. (1) They were officers of the mint, charged with assaying new coins, holding a bank (*mensa*) for putting new coins into circulation, taking old or foreign coinage into currency, and testing the genuineness of money on occasion of payments being made. (2) They carried on the business of exchange on their own account, at the same time acting as *argentarii*. In other words, they received money on deposit, put out capital at interest for their clients, got in outstanding debts, made payments, executed sales, especially auctions of property left to be disposed of by will, lent money or negotiated loans, and executed payments in foreign places by reference to bankers there. The *argentarii* and *nummularii* were alike subject to the superintendence of the state authorities. In Rome they were responsible to the *Præfectus Urbi*, in the provinces to the governors. They were legally bound to keep their books with strict accuracy. The books were of three kinds: (*a*) the *cōdex accepti et expensi*, or cash book, in which receipts and payments were entered, with the date, the person's name, and the occasion of the transaction; (*b*) the *lĭber rătĭōnum*, in which every client had a special page setting out his debit and credit account; and (*c*) the *adversārĭa*, or diary for the entry of business still in hand. In cases of dispute these books had to be pro-

duced for purposes of legal proof. The Roman bankers, like the Greek, usually managed payments from one client to another by alteration of the respective accounts.

Barbarians. *Barbărŏs* was originally the Greek epithet for a people speaking any language but Greek. It was not until after the Persian wars that the word began to carry with it associations of hatred and contempt, and to imply vulgarity and want of cultivation. The national feeling of the Greeks had then risen to such intensity, that they deemed themselves above all other peoples in gifts and culture, and looked down upon them with a sense of superiority.

The Romans were originally, like other non-Hellenic peoples, included by the Greeks under the name of *barbaroi*. But after the conquest of Greece, and the transference of Hellenic art and culture to Rome, the Romans took up the same position as the Greeks before them, and designated as barbarians all the nations who differed in language and manners from the Græco-Roman world.

Basil (Gr. *Băsĭleĭŏs*, Latin *Basilĭus*), surnamed the Great, of Cæsarēa in Cappadocia. He was born of a noble family in 329 A.D., was educated in rhetoric at Athens by Libanius and Himerius, and subsequently took up the profession of advocate. But it was not long before he dedicated himself to the service of the Church. He distinguished himself especially by his resistance to Arianism, and the measures he adopted for regulating the monastic system. He died, the bishop of his native city, in A.D. 379. Besides his writings on points of doctrine, we have an address by him to young men on the uses of Greek literature, the study of which he earnestly recommended, in opposition to the prejudices of many Christians. He has also left a collection of four hundred letters, which are models in their way. Among them are those addressed to Libanius, his pagan instructor.

Băsĭleus. The Greek word for king. On the *Archōn Basileus* see ARCHONTES. The name was also given to the toast-master in a drinking-bout. (*See* MEALS.)

Basilica (Gr. *basĭlĭkē* or "King's House"). A state-building, used by the Romans as a hall of justice and a public meeting-place. The earliest *basilica* built at Rome was called the *basilica Porcia*, after the famous M. Porcius Cato Censōrius, who built it in B.C. 184, probably on the model of the *Stŏa Basileĭŏs* ("royal colonnade") at Athens. It stood in the Forum near the Curia. The later basilicas usually bore the name of the persons who built them. Buildings of the same kind were constantly erected in the provinces to serve as halls of exchange or courts of justice. The form of the *basilica* was oblong; the interior was a hall, either without any divisions or divided by rows of pillars, with a main nave, and two or sometimes four side-aisles. Galleries for spectators were often added above. If the basilica was used as a

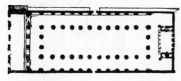

PLAN OF THE BASILICA, POMPEII.

hall of justice, a space, usually in the form of a large semicircular niche, and containing a tribunal, was set up at the end of the nave for the accommodation of the court. After the time of Constantine the Great, of whose great basilica, with its nave and two aisles, magnificent ruins still remain, many basilicas were turned into Christian churches, and many churches were built upon the same plan. (The annexed cut gives the plan of the basilica at Pompeii. *See* also ARCHITECTURE, fig. 11.)

Basterna. *See* LITTERS.

Baths. Warm baths were for a long time only used by the Greeks for exceptional purposes, to take them too often being regarded as a mark of effeminacy. It was only after the introduction of artificial bathing-places, public and private (*bălăneia*) that they came into fashion, especially before meals. Such baths were often attached to the *gymnăsia*. The Greeks, however, never attained, in this matter, to the luxury of the Romans under the Empire. To take a hot dry air-bath, in order to promote perspiration, followed by a cold bath, was a peculiar fashion of the Lacedæmonians. The ancient custom at Rome was to take a bath every week in the *lăvatrīna* or wash-house near the kitchen. But after the Second Punic War bathing establishments on the Greek model made their appearance, and the afternoon hour between two and three was given up to the bath, which, with gymnastics, came

to be one of the most important proceedings of the day. The public baths were under the superintendence of the ædiles. A small fee (*balneătĭcum*) was paid for their use: a *quadrans* (=about half a farthing) for men, and rather more for women. Children were admitted free. The baths were open from 2 p.m. till sunset; but outside the city precincts they were sometimes lighted up after nightfall. Under the Empire the baths became very luxurious. The splendour of the arrangements, especially in private houses, steadily increased, as did the number of public baths. 170 of these were added by Agrippa alone in his ædileship, and in the 4th century A.D. the number was reckoned at 952 in the city of Rome alone. From the time of Agrippa we find *thermæ* or hot baths, fitted up in the style of those attached to the Greek *gymnasia*, in use in Rome, Italy, and the provinces. No provincial town was without its baths; indeed they were found in many villages, as is proved by the remains scattered over the whole extent of the Roman empire.

The baths of later times consisted of at least three chambers, each with separate compartments for the two sexes. (1) The *tĕpĭdărium*, a room heated with warm air, intended to promote perspiration after undressing; (2) the *caldărium*, where the hot bath was taken in a tub (*sŏlium*) or basin (*piscīna*); (3) the *frīgĭdărium*, where the final cold bath was taken. After this the skin was scraped with a *strĭgĭlis*, rubbed down with a linen cloth, and anointed with oil. This took place either in the *tepidarium* or in special apartments, which were often provided in larger establishments, as were rooms for dressing and undressing. Round the basin ran a passage, with seats for the visitors. The Laconian or dry air-bath was a luxury sometimes, but not necessarily, provided. The heating was managed by means of a great furnace, placed between the men's and the women's baths. Immediately adjoining it were the *caldaria*, then came the *tepidaria* and the *frigidarium*. Over the furnace were fixed a cold-water, warm-water, and hot-water cistern, from which the water was conducted into the bath-rooms. The *caldaria* and *tepidaria* were warmed with hot air. The heat was conducted from the furnace into a hollow receptacle under the floor, about two feet in height (*suspensūra, hўpŏcaustum*), and thence by means of flues between the double walls.

The Romans were so fond of the bath that if the emperor or a rich citizen presented the people with a free bath for a day, a longer period, or in perpetuity, he won the credit of exceptional liberality. It was not uncommon for a person to leave a sum of money in his will for defraying the costs of bathing. Some towns applied their public funds for this purpose.

The accompanying cuts give the ground-plan of the hot baths at Pompeii, and of a private Roman bath found at Caerwent (*Venta Silurum*) in South Wales. (For a restoration of the *Baths of Caracalla*, see ARCHITECTURE, fig. 13.)

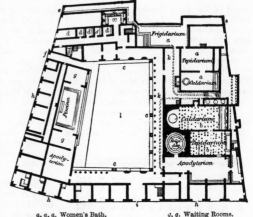

a, a, a. Women's Bath.	*g, g.* Waiting Rooms.
b, b. Men's Bath.	*h, h, h.* Shops.
c, c, c. Colonnade.	*i.* Chief Entrance.
d, d, d, d, d. Single Baths.	*k, k.* Heating Apparatus.
e, e. Entrance to Women's Bath.	*l.* Porticus.
f. Side Entrance.	

PLAN OF THE PUBLIC THERMÆ, POMPEII.

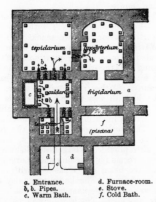

a. Entrance.	*d.* Furnace-room.
b, b. Pipes.	*e.* Stove.
c. Warm Bath.	*f.* Cold Bath.

ROMAN PRIVATE BATHS, CAERWENT (VENTA SILURUM, MONMOUTHSHIRE).

(O. Morgan, *Archæologia*, xxvi 2, p. 432, pl. 36.)

Batrăchŏmўŏmăchĭa. The Battle of the Frogs and the Mice. This was the title of an epic poem falsely bearing the name of Homer. It was a parody of the Iliad, and was probably written by Pigrēs. (*See* HOMER 1, end.)

Baucis. *See* PHILEMON 2.

Beds (Gk. *klīnē*, Lat. *lectus*). The Greek and Latin words were applied not only to beds in the proper sense of the

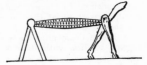

(1) Millingen, *Peintures d. Vases grecs*, pl. ix.

(2) Micali, *Monumenti Inediti*, tav. xxiii.

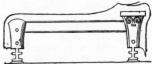

(3) Stackelberg, *Gräber d. Hellenen*, Taf. xxvi.

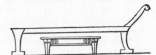

(4) Lenormant et De Witte, *Monum. céramogr.* II pl. xxxiii A.

BEDSTEADS, FROM GREEK VASES.

term, but to any kind of couch, as, for instance, to the sofas used at meals (*see* TRICLINIUM) or for reading and writing. The frame rested on four feet, and sometimes had no support at all, sometimes one for the head, sometimes one at each end for head and feet, sometimes one at the side. It was made of wood or bronze, and was usually richly adorned on the parts exposed to view. If of wood, these ornaments would consist of inlaid work of fine metal, ivory, tortoiseshell, amber, and rare coloured woods ; if of bronze, they would be sculptures in relief. The mattress (Gk. *knĕphallŏn, tyleiŏn,* Lat. *tŏrus, culcĭta*) was supported on girths stretched across the frame, and was stuffed with vegetable fibre, woollen flock, or feathers, and covered with linen, wool, or leather. Cushions were added to support the head or elbow (Gk. *proskĕphălaiŏn,* Lat. *pulvīnus* or *cervīcāl*). Coverings for the sleeper were spread over the mattrass, which in wealthy houses would be dyed purple, or adorned with patterns and embroidery. If the bed was high, it would have a footstool attached. At Pompeii couches have often been found built up in the niches of the sleeping apartments. (For various forms of Greek bedsteads, *see* the engravings.) *Cp.* FULCRA.

Bellĕrŏphŏn or **Bellĕrŏphontēs.** Son of Glaucus of Corinth (or according to another account, of Poseidōn), and grandson of Sīsўphus. His proper name is said to have been Hippŏnŏēs; the name Bellerophontes implies that he was the slayer of some now unknown monster. In later times his name was wrongly explained as the slayer of a certain Corinthian, Bellĕrŏs, on account of which he was supposed to have fled to Prœtus at Tīryns, or (as Homer has it) at Corinth. The wife of Prœtus, Anteia (or Sthĕnĕbœa), falls in love with the beautiful youth : he is deaf to her entreaties: she slanders him to her husband, who resolves on his destruction. He sends Bellerophon to Lycia, to his father-in-law Iobătēs, with a tablet in cypher, begging him to put the bearer to death. Iobates first commissions Bellerophon to destroy the fire-breathing monster Chimæra, a task which he executes with the help of his winged horse Pēgăsus (*see* PEGASUS). Thereupon, after a fierce battle, he conquers the Sŏlўmi and the Amazons, on his return slays an ambush of the boldest among the Lycians, and Iobates now recognises his divine origin, keeps him with him, and gives him the half of his kingdom,

and his daughter to wife. The children of this marriage are Isander, Hippolŏchus, the father of Glaucus and Laodamīa, and the mother of Sarpēdōn by Zeus. Afterwards Bellerophon was hated by all the gods, and wandered about alone, devouring his heart in sorrow. His son Isander was killed by Arēs in battle against the Solymi, while Laodamia was sacrificed to the wrath of Artĕmis. This is the Homeric version ; but, according to Pindar, Bellerophon's high for-

ANTEIA.   PRŒTUS.   BELLEROPHON.   PEGASUS.
* THE DEPARTURE OF BELLEROPHON.
(From a mural painting, Pompeii.)

tune made him so overweening that he wished to mount to heaven on Pegasus ; but Zeus drove the horse wild with a gadfly, and Bellerophon fell and came to a miserable end. He was honoured as a hero in Corinth, an enclosure being consecrated to him in the cypress grove of Craneion.

Bellōna. (1) The Roman goddess of war. An old Italian divinity, probably of Sabine origin. She was supposed to be wife or sister of Mars, and was identified with the Greek Enyō. Her temple, which was situated in the Campus Martius, outside the old *pōmērium,* was used for meetings of the senate when it was dealing with the ambassadors of foreign nations, or Roman generals who claimed a triumph on their return from war. It must be remembered that under such circumstances a general might not enter the city. The pillar of war (*Columna Bellīca*) stood hard by. It was from this, as representing the boundary of the enemy's territory, that the *Fētiālis* threw his lance on declaring war.

(2) Quite a different goddess is the Bellona whom the Roman government brought from Comana in Cappadocia towards the beginning of the 1st century B.C., during the Mithridatic war. This Bellona was worshipped in a different locality, and with a service conducted by Cappadocian priests and priestesses. These *Bellonārii* (such was their name) moved through the city in procession at the festivals of the goddess in black raiment, and shed their blood at the sacrifice, wounding themselves for the purpose in the arms and loins with a two-edged axe, and prophesying amid a wild noise of drums and trumpets.

* PRIEST OF BELLONA.
From a Roman sepulchral relief (Guigniant, *Nouv. Gall. Myth.*, p. 120, 368 *b*.)

Bēlus. Son of Libya, granddaughter of Io and Poseidōn. Father of Ægyptus, Dănăüs, Cēpheus, and Phīneus.

Bendis. A goddess of the moon among the Thracians. She was invested with power over heaven and earth, and identified by the Greeks with Artěmis, Hecătē, and Persěphŏnē. The worship of this goddess was introduced into Attica by Thracian aliens; and was so popular that in Plato's time it became a state ceremonial at Athens. A public festival was instituted called the *Bendideia*, at which there were torch-races and a solemn procession of Atheːnians and Thracians at the Piræus.

Bērōsus. A Greek writer, born in Bithynia, and a priest of Bēlus. He lived as early as the time of Alexander the Great, and about B.C. 280 wrote a work, dedicated to king Antiochus Sōtēr, on Babylonian history, in three books (*Babylōnĭca* or *Chaldăïca*). The work must have been of great value, as it was founded on ancient priestly chronicles preserved in the temple of Belus at Babylon. Its importance as an authority for the ancient history of Asia

is fully attested by the fragments that remain, in spite of their scanty number and disordered arrangement.

Bestiārii. *See* CIRCUS.

Biās. *See* ADRASTUS and MELAMPUS.

Bibliopōla. *See* BOOK-TRADE.

Bidentāl (*Roman*). A consecrated spot where lightning had passed into the ground. (*See* PUTEAL.)

Bidȳæ (*Spartan*). *See* EDUCATION.

Bīgæ. *See* CIRCUS, Games of.

Bikŏs (Greek.) *See* VESSELS.

Biōn. A Greek bucolic poet, who flourished in the second half of the 2nd century B.C. He lived mostly in Sicily, where he is said to have died by poison. Besides a number of minor poems from his hand, we have a long descriptive epic called *The Dirge of Adonis*. His style is more remarkable for grace than for power or simplicity.

Bŏēdrŏmia. A festival held at Athens in honour of Apollo *Bŏēdrŏmĭŏs*, the god who gave aid in battle. It was celebrated on the 6th day of the month Boēdrŏmĭōn, so named after the god (September–October). The origin of the festival was traced back in antiquity to the victory of Iōn over Eumolpus, or to that of Theseus over the Amazons. After 490 B.C. it was converted into a commemoration of the battle of Mărăthōn.

Bœotarchi. The highest officials of the Bœotian confederacy, two of whom were always chosen by Thebes, as the chief town in it, and one by each of the other towns. They held the post only for a year, but were capable of re-election in successive years. Their chief duties were to command the trːoops of the confederacy in time of war, and execute the decrees of its council.

Bŏēthĭus (*Anīcius Manlius Torquātus Severīnus*). Boethius was born in Rome, about 475 A.D., and belonged to the distinguished family of the Anicii, who had for some time been Christians. Having been left an orphan in his childhood, he was taken in his tenth year to Athens, where he remained eighteen years and acquired a stock of knowledge far beyond the average. After his return to Rome, he was held in high esteem among his contemporaries for his learning and eloquence. He attracted the attention of Theodŏric, who in 510 A.D. made him consul, and, in spite of his patriotic and independent attitude, gave him a prominent share in the government. The trial of the consul Albīnus, however, brought with it the ruin of Boethius. Albinus was accused of maintaining a secret understanding with the Byzantine court, and Boethius stood up boldly in his defence, declaring that if Albinus was guilty, so was he and the whole senate with him. Thus involved in the same charge, he was sentenced to death by the cowardly assembly whose cause he had represented. He was thrown into prison at Pavia, and executed in 525.

The most famous work of Boethius, his *Consolation of Philosophy*, was written in prison. It was much read in the Middle Ages, and translated into every possible language. The book is thrown partly into the form of a dialogue, in which the interlocutors are the author, and *Philosŏphia*, who appears to him to console him. As in the Menippean *sătŭra* (*see* SATURA), the narrative is relieved by the occasional insertion of musical verses in various metres. The consolatory arguments are strictly philosophical.

Boethius was at great pains to make Greek learning accessible to his contemporaries, by means of translations of, and commentaries upon, Greek books on philosophy, mathematics, rhetoric, and grammar. For this the following ages were much indebted to him. His writings, which were used as manuals throughout the Middle Ages, were the main storehouse of secular knowledge during that period. This is eminently true of his numerous philosophical works, and especially of his translations of Aristotle, which exercised immense influence upon the scholastic philosophy.

Bŏna Dĕa (" the good goddess "). An Italian deity, supposed to preside over the earth, and all the blessings which spring from it. She was also the patron goddess of chastity and fruitfulness in women. The names *Fauna, Maia,* and *Ops,* were originally no more than varying appellations given by the priests to the *Bona Dea.* She is represented in works of art with a sceptre in her left hand, a wreath of vine leaves on her head, and a jar of wine at her side. Near her image was a consecrated serpent; indeed a number of tame serpents were kept in her temple, which was situated in Rome on the slope of the Aventine. All kinds of healing plants were preserved in her sanctuary. She was regarded in Rome as an austere virgin goddess, whose temple men were forbidden to enter. She belonged, accordingly, to the circle of deities who were worshipped by the Vestal Virgins. The anniversary of the foundation of her temple was held on the 1st of May, when

prayers were offered up to her for the averting of earthquakes. Besides this, a secret festival was held to her on behalf of the public welfare, in the house of the officiating consul or prætor of the city, by matrons and the Vestal Virgins, on the night of May 3–4. The mistress of the house presided. No man was allowed to be present at this celebration, or even to hear the name of the goddess. After offering a sacrifice of sucking pigs, the women performed a dance, accompanied by stringed and wind instruments. Under the Empire the festival degenerated into a mystic performance of extravagant character.

Bŏnōrum emptĭō. The technical term in Roman jurisprudence for the seizure of goods. If a man sentenced to pay a certain sum did not perform his obligation within thirty days, the creditor obtained permission from the prætor to attach his goods. After a renewed respite of thirty days the sale followed by auction to the highest bidder, the intending purchaser bidding for the whole property, with its assets and liabilities. The former proprietor might intervene and promise payment at any time before the fall of the hammer. The property once knocked down to him, the buyer became the absolute owner. A person against whom these proceedings were taken incurred *infămia.*

Bŏnus Eventus. *See* EVENTUS.

Books and Book-trade. The Greeks were early familiar with the practice of multiplying copies of books by transcription, either to private order or for public sale. As far back as the 5th century B.C. the Athenians had a special place in their market-place for selling books, and it is clearly established that a regular book-fair existed at Athens by about 300 B.C. In Rome, towards the end of the republican age, the business of copying books and the book-trade in general developed on a large scale, and it became a fashionable thing to possess a library. The book-trade, in the proper sense of the term, owes its existence to Attĭcus, the well-known friend of Cicero. He kept a number of slaves skilled in shorthand and calligraphy (*librārii*), whom he set to copy a number of Cicero's writings, which he then disposed of at a considerable profit in Italy and Greece. His example was soon followed, especially as the interest in new literary productions, and the love of reading, greatly increased after the time of Augustus. To facilitate the appearance of a great number of copies at the same time, the

scribes were often set to write from dicta-
tion. Much use was made of the abbreviations (*nŏtæ*) invented by Tiro, the freedman
of Cicero. The binding was done, as well
as the writing, by the *librarii ;* and as the
brittle *papӯrus* was the usual material, the
book was generally made up in the form of
a roll (*see* WRITING MATERIALS). The
ends of the roll were strengthened with
thin strips of bone or wood, which were
either provided at top and bottom with a
knob (*umbilīcus*), or finished off in the
shape of a horn. Previously to this, the
upper and lower edges were carefully clip-
ped, smoothed with pumice-stone, and tinted
with black. To protect it from moths and
worms, the roll was dipped in cedar oil,
which gave it a yellowish tinge. The title
of the work (*titŭlus* or *index*) was written
in red on a strip of parchment attached to
the end of the roll. Expensive copies,
especially in the case of poems, had a gilt
umbilicus, as well as a parchment cover of
purple colour. The books were then exposed for sale in the bookseller's shops, and
sold at what appear, considering the circumstances, reasonable prices. The book-
sellers were called *librarii* or *bibliopōlæ ;*
their shops were situated in the most frequented parts of the city, and much used,
both as reading-rooms and *rendezvous* for
learned discussion. As a general rule there
was a good sale for books, especially such
as had won popularity before publication in
the public recitations (*see* RECITATIONS).
Books were also much bought in the provinces, whose inhabitants were anxious to
keep abreast with the intellectual life of
the capital. Even works which were little
thought of in Rome sometimes found an
easy sale in other parts of the empire. It
does not appear that the author received
any *honorarium* from the publisher.[1]

Bŏrĕās. In Greek mythology, the North
Wind, son of Astræa and Eōs, brother of
Zĕphӯrus, Eurus, and Nŏtus. His home
was in the Thracian Salmydĕssus, on the
Black Sea, whither he carried Orithyia
from the games on the Ilissus, when her
father, Erechtheus king of Athens, had refused her to him in marrage. Their children were Călăïs and Zētēs, the so-called
Borĕădæ, Cleopatra, the wife of Phīneus,
and Chiŏnē, the beloved of Poseidōn (*see*
EUMOLPUS). It was this relationship which
was referred to in the oracle given to the
Athenians, when the fleet of Xerxes was
approaching, that "they should call upon
their brother-in-law." Boreas answered their

prayer and sacrifice by destroying a part
of the enemy's fleet on the promontory of
Sepias; whereupon they built him an altar
on the banks of the Ilissus.

Boulē or **Būlē** ("Council"). The Council
instituted at Athens by Solon consisted of
400 members (*bouleutai*), 100 being taken
from each of the four Ionic tribes (*phӯlai*).
By Cleisthĕnēs the number was increased to
500, 50 being taken from each of the ten
newly constituted tribes, and chosen by lot;
whereas up to his time the councillors had
been elected from the number of candidates
who offered themselves for the position. In
306 B.C. two new tribes were added, and the
number of the council was accordingly increased to 600, at which figure it remained,
with some variations, down to the times of
the Roman empire. But in the 2nd century
A.D. it again fell to 500. In ancient times
no one was eligible as a councillor who did
not belong to one of the three wealthiest
classes; but after the time of Aristīdēs the
position was open to any free Athenian of
thirty years of age, and in possession of full
civic rights. In choosing councillors by lot,
two candidates were presented for each
vacancy. The same person might hold the
office several times, though not for two
years in succession. Every councillor had
to take a special oath, strictly formulated,
on entering the *Boulē.* At the meetings of
the Council its members wore myrtle crowns
as *insignia* of their office. They had the
further privilege of a place of honour at
the festivals, and were excused, during their
term of office, from military service. They
also received a payment of five obols (nearly
7*d.*) for every sitting they attended. Their
place of meeting was called the *bouleu-
tĕriŏn* ("council-chamber"); here they met
every day except on public holidays, each
member having his numbered seat. When
assembled, the Council was divided into ten
sections of 50 members each, each representing one of the tribes. These sections were
called *Prӯtăneis* ("Presidents"), and officiated in succession, as arranged at the beginning of each year, for 35–36 days, or in
leap-years for 38–39. This period was
called a *Prytaneia,* and during its continuance the *prytaneis* for the time being presided over the full sittings of the Council
and of the public assembly. At other times
they remained the whole day at their office
(*Thŏlŏs* or " dome ") near the council-chamber, where they usually dined at the expense of the State. A president (*Epistătēs*)
was chosen every day by lot from among the

[1] Cp. Marquardt, *Privatleben der Römer*, p. 829, ed. 1886.

prytaneis to act as chairman in the Council and the public assembly, to keep the keys of the fortress and the archives, and the seal of state. From 378 B.C. the presidency of the public assembly was committed to a special chairman, elected from among the nine *proëdroi* (" presidents "), who were chosen by lot by the *epistates* of the *prytaneis* from the remaining nine tribes at each sitting of the Council.

The first duty of the Council was to prepare all the measures which were to come before the public assembly, and to draw up a preliminary decree (*probouleuma*). Accordingly it was its business to receive the reports of the generals and of foreign ambassadors. Foreign affairs always stood first in the order of daily business. Besides this, the Council exercised a general superintendence over all public business, and especially over the financial administration. It gave the authority for the farming of the taxes, contracts for public works, sales of confiscated property, for adopting new lines of expenditure or modes of raising income, for arresting tax-gatherers and tax-farmers if they fell into arrear. The treasurers of the temples were also responsible to it. The cavalry and the navy were placed under its special supervision, and it had, in particular, to see that a certain number of new ships of war was built every year. It examined the qualifications of the newly elected archons. In many cases it acted as a court of justice, and had the power of inflicting fines up to the amount of 500 *drachmæ* (£16 13s. 4d.). But more serious cases it had to pass on to the *Hēliastai*, or to the public assembly (*see* HELIASTAI). The assembly would sometimes entrust the Council with absolute power to deal with cases which, strictly speaking, lay outside its jurisdiction. The decrees passed by the Council on matters affecting the public administration ceased to be binding on the expiration of its year of office, in case they were not adopted by its successors [Aristotle, *Const. of Athens*, 43–49].

The voting took place by show of hands (*cheirŏtŏnĭa*); voting pebbles and other devices being only used for judicial decisions. Private citizens could transact business with the Council only after previous application for an audience, generally made in writing. The official correspondence was transacted by three secretaries (called *grammăteis* or "writers") appointed from among the members, and assisted by a number of subordinate functionaries.

Boŭleutērĭŏn. *See* BOULE.

Bows. (Gr. *toxŏn*, Lat. *arcus*). Two kinds of bow were known to antiquity. One consisted of the two horns of a kind of antelope, or an arm of wood shaped like them, joined together by a bridge which served both as a hold for the hand and as a rest for the arrow. The string, made of plaited horse-hair or twisted ox-gut, was fastened to each end (fig. 1). The other, called the Scythian or Parthian bow, was made of a piece of elastic wood, the ends of which were tipped with metal, and bent slightly upwards to hold the string (fig. 2). The arrow (Gk. *oïstŏs*, or *toxeuma*, Lat. *sagitta*) was made of a stem of reed or

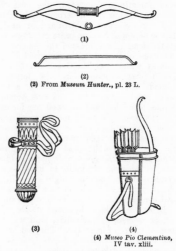

(1)

(2)
(2) From *Museum Hunter.*, pl. 23 L.

(3)

(4)
(4) *Museo Pio Clementino,* IV tav. xliii.

BOWS AND QUIVERS.

light wood, one end furnished with a three-cornered point, sometimes simple and sometimes barbed; the other end with feathers. A notch in the shaft served to place it on the string. The arrows (and sometimes the bow) were kept in a quiver (*phăretra*) made of leather, wood, or metal, fitted with a suspender, and sometimes open, sometimes having a lid. The quiver was worn either on the back, according to the Greek manner, or in Oriental fashion, on the left hip. The Cretans had the reputation of being the best archers among the Greeks. They generally served among the light-armed auxiliaries as a special corps. Mounted

bowmen were employed by the ancient
Athenians (see HIPPEIS); but it was not
until after the Punic wars that archers
formed a regular part of the Roman army.
They were then furnished by the allies, or
raised by recruiting, and were mostly taken
from Crete and the Balearic Islands.

Braurōnia. See ARTEMIS.

Brĭăreus. See HECATONCHEIROI.

Brisēïs. The favourite slave of Achilles.
Agamemnon took her from him, and thus
kindled the wrath of the hero, to the ruin
of the Greeks. (See TROJAN WAR.)

Britomartis ("sweet maid"). A Cretan
goddess, supposed to dispense happiness,
whose worship extended throughout the
islands and along the coasts of the Mediter
ranean. Like Artĕmis, with whom she
was sometimes identified, she was the
patroness of hunters, fishermen and sailors,
and also a goddess of birth and of health.
Her sphere was Nature, in its greatness and
its freedom. As goddess of the sea she bore
the name of Dictynna, the supposed deriva
tion of which from the Greek diktўŏn ("a
net") was explained by the following
legend. She was the daughter of a hun
tress, much beloved by Zeus and Artemis.
Mīnōs loved her, and followed her for nine
months over valley and mountain, through
forest and swamp, till he nearly overtook
her, when she leaped from a high rock into
the sea. She was saved by falling into
some nets, and Artemis made her a goddess.
She would seem originally to have been a
goddess of the moon, her flight symbolizing
the revolution of the moon round the earth,
and her leap into the sea its disappearance.

Brizo. A goddess localized in Dēlos, to
whom women, in particular, paid worship
as protectress of mariners. They set before
her eatables of various kinds (fish being
excluded) in little boats. She also presided
over an oracle, the answers of which were
given in dreams to people who consulted it
on matters relating to fishery and naviga
tion.

Brŏmĭus. See DIONYSUS.

Brontēs. See CYCLOPES.

Brutus (Marcus Junius). The well-known
friend of Cicero, and murderer of Cæsar.
He was born in 85 B.C., and died by his own
hand after the battle of Philippi, B.C. 42.
As an orator and a writer on philosophy
he held a prominent position among his con
temporaries. Two books of correspondence
between Brutus and Cicero have come down
to us, the authenticity of which is disputed.
There is also a collection of seventy letters

in Greek, purporting to represent correspon
dence between Brutus and the Greek cities

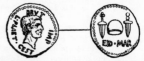

Obv., Head of Brutus: BRUTUS
IMPERATOR: L. PLÆTORIUS CES-
TIANUS (one of his partisans).   Rev., Cap of Liberty between two
daggers, EID. MAR.

* COIN OF BRUTUS, ISSUED IN ASIA MINOR, B.C. 44–42.

(Cohen, Méd. Cons., pl. xxiv. Junia 16.)

of Asia Minor ; but this is no more than the
patchwork of a rhetorician.

Bua, Buăgŏr. See EDU
CATION.

Būcĭna (properly "a
cow-horn") was the name
of a tin trumpet, shaped
like a serpent, and blown
by a trumpeter called
bucinātor. The bucina
gave the signal called
classĭcum, and also the
call for relieving guard
at night.

Bucolic (or pastoral)
Poetry. From very an
cient times it was the
habit of the Dorian shep
herds in Sicily to practise

* BUCINATOR.

From a mural
painting of gladia
tors (Gell and
Gandy, Pompeiana,
pl. 75).

a national style of song, the inventor of
which was supposed to be Daphnis, the hero
of shepherds (see DAPHNIS). The subject of
their song was partly the fate of this hero,
partly the simple experiences of shepherds'
life, especially their loves. There was a
good deal of the mimic element in these
poems, the shepherds contending with each
other in alternate verses, particularly at the
town and country festivals held in honour
of Artĕmis. Pastoral poems, relating the
story of Daphnis' love and of his tragic
end, had been written by the Sicilian poet
Stesichŏrus (about 600 B.C.). But it was
Theocrĭtus of Syracuse (about 270 B.C.) who
developed pastoral poetry into something
like an epic style, often with a strong
dramatic tinge. This was in the Alex
andrian period, when, as in all over-civilized
ages, men found pleasure and relief in the
contrasts afforded by the simple ways of
country life. Theocritus' sketches of rural
life, and indeed of the ways of the lower
orders in general, are true to nature and ex
quisitely finished. He called them eidyllia
or little pictures. Theocritus was unsur-

passed in his own style, which was cultivated after him by Biōn and Moschus.

The pastoral style was introduced into Latin poetry by Vergil, who, while closely imitating Theocritus, had the tact to perceive that the simple sketches of ancient rural life in Sicily given by his master would not be sufficient to satisfy the taste of his countrymen. Under the mask of shepherds, therefore, he introduced contemporary characters, thus winning attention by the expression of his personal feelings, and by covert allusions to events of the day. Two poems falsely attributed to him, the *Morētum* (" Salad ") and *Cōpa* (" Hostess "), are real idylls ; true and natural studies from low life. Vergil's allegorical style was revived in later times by Calpurnius in the age of Nero, and Nemesiānus at the end of the 3rd century A.D.

Būlē. *See* BOULĒ.

Bulla. A round or heart-shaped box containing an amulet, worn round the neck by free-born Roman children. The fashion was borrowed from the Etrurians. To wear a golden *bulla* was originally a privilege of the patricians, which was in later times extended to the *ĕquĭtēs*, and generally to rich and distinguished families. Leather *bullæ* were worn by the children of poor families and of freedmen. Boys ceased to wear the *bulla* when they assumed the *toga virīlis.* It was then dedicated to the *Lărēs*, and hung up over the hearth. Girls most probably left it off on marriage. It was sometimes put on by adults as a protection against the evil eye on special occasions, as, for instance, on that of a triumph. (*See* FASCINUM).

Būphŏnĭa. *See* DIIPOLIA.

Burial. (1) *Greek.* The Greeks regarded the burial of the dead as one of the most sacred duties. Its neglect involved an offence against the dead ; for, according to the popular belief, the soul obtained no rest in the realms of the dead, so long as the body remained unburied. It involved, further, an offence against the gods, both of the upper and the lower world. The unburied corpse was an offence to the eyes of the former, while the latter were deprived of their due. Any one finding an unburied corpse was expected at least to throw a handful of dust over it. If a general neglected to provide for the burial of the slain in war, he was deemed guilty of a capital offence. Burial of the dead was not refused even to the enemy, whether Greek or barbarian. It was a violation of

the laws of war to refuse to the conquered the truce necessary for this purpose ; and if the conquered were unable to fulfil the duty, the responsibility fell upon the conquerors. There were certain circumstances under which, according to Athenian law, children, during the lifetime of their fathers, were held free from all obligations to them ; but the obligation to give them burial after death was never cancelled.

The usages of the Athenians, and probably of the other Greeks, were as follows. The eyes of the dead having been closed, an *ŏbŏlŏs* was put in the mouth as passage-money for Charōn. The body was then washed and anointed by the women of the family, who proceeded to adorn it with fillets and garlands (commonly of ivy), to clothe it in white garments, and lay it out on a couch in the hall, with its face turned to the door. The kinsfolk and friends stood by, mourning ; but the laws of Solon forbade all exaggerated expressions of grief. Hired women were sometimes introduced, singing dirges to the accompaniment of the flute. Near the couch were placed painted earthenware vases containing the libations to be afterwards offered. Before the door was a vessel of water, intended for the purification of all who went out. This water might not be brought from another house in which a dead body lay. The corpse was laid out on the day following the death ; and on the next day before sunrise (lest the sun should be polluted by the sight) was carried out to the place of burial, attended by kinsmen and friends, who sometimes acted as bearers. This office, however, was usually performed by freedmen or hired assistants ; in the case of men of mark, it would be undertaken by young Athenian citizens. The procession was headed by men singing songs of mourning, or women playing the flute; then came the male mourners in garments of black or grey, and with hair cut short; and these were followed by the bier. Behind the bier followed a train of women, including all who were related to the dead as far as to the fifth degree. No other women might attend but those who were more than sixty years of age.

In the heroic age the bodies are always burnt, burial being unknown; but in later times burial and burning are found existing side by side, burial being preferred by the poor on the ground of expense. In case of burial, the body was placed in a coffin of wood, clay, or stone, or in a chamber in a

wall, or in a grave hollowed out in a rock.
If burning was resorted to, the corpse was
laid on a pyre, which, in the case of rich
families, was sometimes very large, splendid
and costly. It was kindled by the nearest
relative; the mourners threw into the flame
locks of hair, and objects of all kinds in
which the dead person had taken pleasure
during his life. When the fire was extinguished, the relations collected the ashes and
put them in an urn, which was set up in a
building constructed on a scale large enough
for whole families or clans. So, too, in case
of burial, the coffins which belonged to one
family or clan were laid together in a
common tomb. Near the urns and coffins
were placed a variety of vessels and other
objects which had been the property of the
dead. (Comp. fig. 1.)

The funeral was succeeded by a meal par-
taken of by the mourners in the house of
mourning. The virtues of the dead were

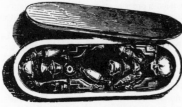

(1) * A CHILD'S COFFIN, ATTICA.
(Stackelberg, *Gräber der Hellenen*, Taf. vii.)

spoken of, and his faults passed over, to
speak evil of the dead being regarded as an
impiety. Then came the purification of the
house. On the third, ninth, and thirtieth
day after the funeral, libations of honey,
wine, oil, and milk or water, with other
offerings, were brought to the tomb. On
the ninth day, in particular, peculiar preparations of food were added. The outward
signs of mourning were laid aside at Athens
on the thirtieth, at Sparta as early as the
twelfth, day after the funeral. The kinsfolk
visited the graves at certain seasons of the
year, adorned them with garlands and
fillets, and brought offerings to them. This
was done more especially on the anniver-
saries of births and deaths, and at the
general festival of the dead (*Nĕkÿsia*) in
September. (Comp. fig. 2.)

After the time of Solon, a public burial
was sometimes given at Athens to men of
great mark. In time of war, too, the bones
of all the citizens who had fallen in the

campaigns of the year were sometimes
buried together at the public expense in the
outer Cĕramīcus, the most beautiful suburb
of the city. On these occasions a funeral

(2) * DECORATED GRAVE COLUMN.
From an Athenian vase (Stackelberg, l.c., Taf. xlv.)

oration was delivered by a speaker of mark,
chosen by the government. In later times
a memorial festival was observed, even in
time of peace, in honour of the dead thus
publicly buried. A special service was
held annually at Mărăthōn in memory of
the heroes who had fallen there, and been
buried on the spot in recognition of their
valour. (Comp. fig. 3.)

The ashes of persons who had died in a
foreign country were, if possible, brought
home and laid in a tomb. There were cases
in which this was impossible, or in which
the body could not be removed—if, for
instance, the deceased had been lost at sea.
Then a *kĕnotăphĭon*, or empty tomb, would
be erected to his memory. It was only to
very heinous offenders that a tomb in their
own country was refused. If a man's guilt
was proved after his death, his remains
were disinterred and sent across the frontier.

(3) * THE MOUND AT MARATHON.
(Dodwell's *Travels in Greece*, ii 160.)

As a rule—though there were exceptions,
as at Sparta—burial places were situated
outside the city, and in the neighbourhood
of the great roads. This was also the
favourite place for private tombs standing

on their own ground, apart from the common cemeteries. The body was generally buried with the feet turned towards the road. Monuments took the form of mounds, pilasters, columns, and flat grave-stones. We often find buildings in the style of temples, with very costly adornments, sculptures, and inscriptions in verse and prose. These inscriptions often give more than the name of the deceased, and contain notices of his life, sometimes with proverbs, sometimes with curses directed against any one violating the tomb and disturbing the rest of its occupants. The violation of a tomb, which was regarded with reverence as a consecrated spot, was a serious offence. One of the most aggravated forms of it was the intrusion into the family sepulchre of a body which had no right to be there.

(2) *Roman.* The worship of the dead among the Romans had, characteristically enough, a legal tinge, and formed a part of the pontifical law, which regulated the place and manner of the interment. The theory of the Romans, like that of the Greeks, was that there was an obligation to bury every dead body, except those of felons, suicides, and persons struck by lightning. Any one finding a corpse was expected at least to throw some earth upon it as a symbol of burial. The first duty of a man's survivors was to bury his body; if he died in a foreign country, the act had to be performed symbolically. If this duty was neglected, the offender incurred a taint of guilt from which he had to purify himself by an annually repeated atonement. After death the eyes and mouth were closed, the body bathed in hot water and then anointed, fully dressed, and adorned with the fitting *insignia* in case of the deceased having held high office. The corpse was then laid out on a state-bed in the *ātrium*, the feet turned towards the door. Near the bed were pans with burning odours, while in the *vestĭbŭlum* branches of pine and cypress were put up as signs of mourning. The custom of putting a coin in the mouth is not mentioned in literature before the imperial period; but the relics found in tombs show that it is much older. It was, however, only under the Empire that it became general.

In ancient times funerals took place after nightfall and by torchlight; and this was always the case with second burials, and if the deceased was a child, or a person of slender means. Hence the use of torches was never discontinued, even when the ceremony took place by day. It was held indispensable at every funeral, and became, in fact, the symbol of burial. The usual time at which funerals took place among the upper classes was the forenoon of the eighth day after death. In the laws of the Twelve Tables an attempt was made to check excess in funeral expenses, but with as little success as attended later enactments. If the funeral was one of unusual ceremony, the citizens were publicly invited by a herald to attend it. The arrangements were entrusted to a special functionary, who was assisted by lictors. The procession was headed by a band of wind instruments, the number of which was limited by the Twelve Tables to ten. In ancient times, and at least down to the Punic wars, these musicians were followed by professional female singers, chanting the praises of the dead (*see* NENIA). Then came a company of dancers and actors to amuse the spectators with their antics. Supposing the family was *honōrāta*, in other words, had it had one or more members who had held curule offices, and the consequent right of setting up masked statues of its forefathers in its house, the central point of the ceremony was the procession of ancestors. This consisted of persons dressed to represent the ancestors in their wax masks, their official robes, and other *insignia*. The indirect lines of relationship were represented as well as the direct. Each figure was mounted on a high carriage and preceded by lictors. The train included memorials of the deeds done by the deceased, torchbearers, and lictors with lowered *fascēs*.

The body followed, uncovered, on an elevated couch; sometimes in a coffin inside the bier. A wooden figure, clothed, and wearing the wax mask representing the dead, sat upright beside it in the attitude of life. The bearers were usually the sons, relations and friends of the deceased; in the case of emperors, they were senators and high officials. Behind the bier came the other mourners, men and women, the freedmen in mourning and without any ornaments. Arrived at the Forum, the bier was set down before the rostrum. The representatives of the ancestors sat down on wooden chairs; the rest arranged themselves in a circle round, while a son or kinsman ascended the rostrum and delivered a panegyric upon the dead. If the funeral was a public one, the orator was appointed by the senate. In the case of deceased ladies such speeches were not usual, until the last century of the Republic. After the speech, the procession moved on in the same order to the place of burial, which, according to the law of the Twelve Tables, must be situated outside the city. No one could be buried within the city but men of illustrious merit, as, for instance, generals who had won a triumph, and Vestal Virgins. By a special resolution of the popular assembly, these persons were allowed the honour of burial in the Forum. The tombs were in some cases situated on family estates, but the greater number formed a line extending from the gates of the city to some distance along the great roads, and especially the *Via Appia.* (Comp. fig. 4.)

Burial was, among the Romans, the oldest

mals. The followers threw in a variety of gifts as a last remembrance. The pyre was then kindled by the nearest kinsman and friends, who performed the office with averted faces. The ashes were extinguished with water or wine, and the procession, after saying a last farewell, returned home, while the nearest of kin collected the ashes in a cloth and buried the severed limb. After some days, the dry ashes were put by the nearest relations into an urn, which was deposited in deep silence in the sepulchral chamber, which they entered ungirt and bare-footed. After the burial or burning there was a funeral feast at the tomb. A sacrifice to the Lărēs purified the family and the house from the taint entailed by death. The mourning was ended on the

(4) ✻ THE STREET OF TOMBS AT POMPEII.
(Gell and Gandy, *Pompeiana*, pl. 3.)

form of disposing of the corpse. In certain families (*e.g.* the *gens Cornēlia*), it long continued the exclusive custom. Infant children, and poor people in general, were always buried. Even when the body was burnt, an old custom prescribed that a limb should be cut off and buried, otherwise the family was not regarded as having discharged its obligations. The body was laid in its tomb in full dress, and placed in a special sarcophagus. When the body was to be burnt, a pyre was erected on a specified place near the grave. The pyre was sometimes made in the form of an altar, and adorned in the costliest manner. The couch and the body were laid upon it, and with them anything which the deceased person had used or been fond of, sometimes one of his favourite ani-

ninth day after the burial by a sacrifice offered to the *Mānēs* of the dead, and a meal of eggs, lentils and salt, at which the mourning attire was laid aside. It was on this day that the games held in honour of the dead generally took place. (*See* MANES.)

Everything necessary for the funeral was provided by contract by the *lĭbĭtĭnārĭi* or officials of the temple of Lĭbĭtīna, at which a notification was made of all cases of death (*see* LIBITINA). There were public burial-places, but only for slaves and those who were too poor to buy burial-places for themselves. The bodies were thrown promiscuously into large common graves, called *pŭtĭcŭli*, or wells, on account of their depth. There was a burial place of this sort on the Esquiline, where the bodies of criminals were thrown to the dogs and birds, until Mæcēnās laid out his park there. Cheap and promiscuous burial was also provided by the so-called "dove-cots" or *columbāria*, a place in which could be purchased by persons of scanty means (*see* COLUMBARIUM). The graves of individuals and families were subterranean chambers, or buildings in the style of houses. Freedmen, and probably also clients and friends, were often buried with the family. The grave was regarded by the Romans and Greeks alike as the dwelling-place of the dead, and was accordingly decked out with every imaginable kind of domestic furniture. It is to this custom that we owe the preservation of so many remains of this sort. The monument often had a piece of land, with field and garden attached to it, surrounded by a wall, and intended to supply flowers, herbs, and other things necessary for the decoration of the tomb and maintenance of the attendants. Other buildings would often be attached, for burning the corpses, for holding the funeral feast, and for housing the freedmen who had the care of the spot. Inscriptions in verse and prose, giving information about the dead, would also be found there.

Būsīris. The son of Poseidōn and a daughter of Epăphus. The Greek mythology made him king of Egypt. The land was afflicted for nine years with a series of bad harvests, and a prophet named Phrăsius, of Cyprus, advised Busiris to sacrifice a stranger every year to Zeus. The king

made his counsellor his first victim. When Hēráclēs came to Egypt during his quest for the apples of the Hespĕrĭdĕs, he allowed himself to be bound and taken to the altar as a victim. Then he broke his bonds, and slew Busiris, with his sons and his whole following.

Būtēs. (1) A Thracian, the son of Bŏrĕās. His brother Lycurgus, whose life he had attempted, banished him, and he settled on the island of Strongȳlē or Naxos. Finding here no wives for himself and his companions, he carried off some women from Thessaly, while they were celebrating a sacrifice to Dionȳsus. One of these, Corōnis, whom he had forced to be his wife, prayed to Dionysus for vengeance. The god drove him mad, and he threw himself into a well.

(2) An Athenian hero, son of the Athenian Pandīōn and Zeuxippē. A tiller of the soil, and a neatherd, he was a priest of Athēnē the goddess of the stronghold, and of Poseidōn Erechtheus, and thus ancestor of the priestly caste of the Būtădæ and Etĕŏbūtădæ. He shared an altar in the Erechthēum with Poseidon and Hephæstus. The later story represented him as the son of Telĕōn and Zeuxippe, and as taking part in the expedition of the Argonauts.

(3) A Sicilian hero, identified in fable with the Athenian Butes. Butes the Argonaut was enticed by the song of the Sirens, and leaped into the sea, but was rescued and brought to Lilybæum in Sicily, by Aphrodītē, by whom he became the father of Eryx.

C

Căbīri (Gr. *Kabeiroi*). The name of certain deities, supposed to represent the beneficent powers of Nature, and worshipped in certain parts of Greece, in Bœotia, for instance, and in the islands of Imbros, Lemnos and Samothrace. Nothing certain is known of their real character, or the forms of their worship. The name is perhaps Phœnician, and, if so, means "the great or mighty ones." It would seem that they were originally imagined as possessing similar powers to those of the Telchīnĕs, Curĕtĕs, Corybantĕs and Dactȳli ; and that they were confused sometimes with the Dioscūri, sometimes with Dēmētēr and Hermēs, and sometimes (especially in Lemnos) with Hephæstus. Their worship was secret. The mysteries of the Cabiri of Samothrace stood in high consideration during the Mace-

donian and Roman periods, being regarded, indeed, as inferior only to the Eleusinian mysteries in sanctity. The initiated were supposed to have secured special protection against mishaps, especially by sea.

Cācus (a figure in Italian mythology). A fire-spitting giant, the son of Vulcan, who lived near the place where Rome was afterwards built. When Hercŭlēs came into the neighbourhood with the cattle of Gēryŏn, Cacus stole some of them while the hero was sleeping. He dragged them backwards into his cave under a spur of the Aventine, so that their footsteps gave no clue to the direction in which they had gone. He then closed the entrance to the cave with a rock, which ten pairs of oxen were unable to move. But the lowing of the cattle guided the hero, in his search, to the right track. He tore open the cave, and, after a fearful struggle, slew Cacus with his club. Upon this he built an altar on the spot to Jupiter, under the title of *Pater Inventor* ("the discoverer"), and sacrificed one of the cattle upon it. The inhabitants paid him every honour for freeing them of the monster, and Evander, who was instructed by his mother Carmentis in the lore of prophecy, saluted him as a god. Hercules is then said to have established his own religious service, and to have instructed two noble families, the *Potĭtii* and the *Pinārii*, in the usages to be observed at the sacrifice. This sacrifice was to be offered on the *Ara Maxĭma*, which he himself had built on the cattle market (*Forum Boārium*) where the cattle had been pastured.

Cadmus (Gr. *Kadmŏs*). (1) Son of Agēnōr king of Phœnicia, and of Tēlĕphassa. His sister Eurōpa being carried off by Zeus, Cadmus, with his brothers Phœnix and Cĭlix, was sent out with the command to look for her and not to return without her. In the course of his wanderings he came to Thrace. Here his mother, who had accompanied him so far, breathed her last; and Cadmus applied for counsel to the Delphic oracle. He was advised not to seek his sister any more, but to follow a cow which would meet him, and found a city on the spot where she should lie down. The cow met him in Phocis, and led him into Bœotia. He was intending to sacrifice the cǒw, and had sent his companions to a neighbouring spring to bring the necessary water, when they were all slain by a serpent, the offspring of Arēs and the Erīnys Tilphōsa, which guarded the spring. After a severe struggle, Cadmus destroyed the dragon, and, at the command of Athēnē, sowed its teeth over the neighbouring ground. A host of armed men sprung up, who immediately fought and slew each other, all except five. The survivors, who were called *Spartoi* (" sown "), helped Cadmus to build the Cadmēa, or the stronghold of what was afterwards Thebes, which bore his name. They were the ancestors of the Theban aristocracy; and one of them, Echīōn, or " the serpent's son," became the husband of Cadmus' daughter Agāvē. Cadmus did atonement to Arēs for eight years for the slaughter of the dragon. Then Zeus gave him to wife Harmŏnĭa, the daughter of Arēs and Aphrodītē, who bore him a son Polydōrus, and four daughters, Autonöē, Ino, Agāvē, and Sĕmĕlē. (*See* HARMONIA and SEMELE.) Crushed by the

terrible doom which weighed upon his home, he afterwards sought retirement among the Enchelei in Illyria, a country which he named after his son Illyrius, who was born there. He resigned the kingdom to Illyrius; and then he and his daughter Harmonia were changed into serpents, and carried by Zeus to Elysium.

Hermēs was worshipped in Samothrace as the ancestral god of the inhabitants under the name of Cadmus or Cadmĭlus (*Kadmĭlŏs*); and it is therefore natural to conjecture that the Theban Cadmus was originally an ancestral god of the Thebans, corresponding to the Samothracian deity. He was regarded as the inventor of agriculture, of working in bronze, and of civilization in general; and it is to be remarked at the same time that the oldest Greek poets know nothing of his migration from the East or from Egypt, or of the Phœnician origin of Thebes. When once the later story of his Phœnician descent had taken shape, his name was naturally connected with the introduction of the alphabet, for which the Greeks well knew that they were indebted to the Phœnicians.

(2) A Greek historian. *See* LOGOGRAPHI.

Cădūcĕus. *See* HERMES (conclusion).

Cădus. *See* VESSELS.

Cæcĭlius Stātius or **Statius Cæcilius.** A writer of Latin comedy. He was a Gaul, of the race of the Insubrians, who were settled in Upper Italy. He was brought to Rome, probably about 194 B.C., as a prisoner of war. He was set free by one of the Cæcilii, became very intimate with Ennius, and died not long after him, B.C. 166. It was long before he could obtain a footing on the stage; but, this once achieved, he won a considerable reputation, and was numbered among the masters of his craft. The influence of Ennius seems to have been apparent in the comparative care and regularity with which his pieces were constructed. Cicero, however, finds fault with his defective Latinity; and we must therefore infer that, being of Gaulish extraction, he never succeeded in fully mastering the niceties of colloquial Latin. The titles of some forty of his plays have survived; the contents he mostly borrowed from Menander.

Cælius. (1) *Cælius Antĭpăter;* see ANNALISTS.

(2) *Marcus Cœlius Rūfus*, a Roman orator, born 82 B.C. He was a man of great gifts, but dissolute life, as even his advocate Cicero was forced to admit in the speech which he made in his defence.

He belonged originally to the party of the *optimātēs;* but on the outbreak of the Civil War, attached himself to Cæsar; then, thinking himself slighted by the latter, he tried, during his prætorship, to stir up disorder in Rome. He was deprived of his office by the senate, fled from Rome, and, in the year 48 B.C., attempted to excite a rising in Lower Italy, in which he met with a violent death. According to Cicero, his strong point as an orator was his power of haranguing the people ; in the courts he shone mostly when on the side of the prosecution. His style was, if Cicero may be believed, brilliant, dignified, and witty. Several of his letters to Cicero are preserved in the eighth book of Cicero's *Epistŭlæ ad Familiārēs.* They constitute an important contribution to the history of the time.

Cæneus (Gr. *Kaineus*). The son of Elătus and Hippīa, one of the Lăpĭthæ of Gyrtōn in Thessaly. The story was that he was originally a girl named Cænis (*Kainis*), whom her lover Poseidōn changed, at her own request, into a man, and at the same time rendered her invulnerable. Cæneus took part in the Argonautic expedition and the Calydonian boar-hunt. At the marriage of Pīrithŏüs, the Centaurs, finding him invulnerable, crushed him to death with the trunks of trees, and he was afterwards changed into a bird. (*See* PIRITHOUS.)

Cæsar was for centuries the *cognōmen* of the ancient patrician family of the Iulii. From the dictator Gaius Iulius Cæsar it passed to his adopted son Octaviānus, the founder of the Roman empire, and was assumed by all the male members of the Julian dynasty, including the emperor. After this dynasty had died out, all the male members of the subsequent dynasties assumed it, to show that they belonged to the imperial house. But after the death of Hadrian in 138 A.D., the title of Cæsar was only assumed by the princes whom the emperors had named as their successors, or chosen to be their colleagues in the government.

Cæsar (*Gaius Iulius*). Julius Cæsar was born in 102 or 100 B.C., and was assassinated on March 15th, B.C. 44. He was famous no less as an orator and writer than as a general and statesman. Endowed with extraordinary natural gifts, he received a careful education under the superintendence of his mother Aurēlia. In B.C. 77 he came forward as the public accuser of Dolabella, and entered the lists against the

most celebrated advocates of the day, Cotta and Hortensius. From that time his fame was established as that of an advocate of the first rank.

The faculties of which he had given evidence he cultivated to their highest point under the tuition of the rhetorician Mŏlō in Rhodes, and attained such success,

* CÆSAR.
(Naples, Museum.)

that his contemporaries regarded him as an orator second only to Cicero. Indeed, Cicero himself fully recognizes his genius, awarding especial praise to the elegance and purity of his Latin. Cæsar, however, left but few speeches in a finished state, and these have not come down to us. A number of writings give evidence of the many-sidedness of his genius and literary activity, but these are also lost. There were poems, which never attained much reputation, including, besides boyish effusions, some verses on his journey to Spain in B.C. 46. A treatise on Latin accidence, dedicated to Cicero, and entitled *De Analŏgĭā*, was written during his march across the Alps to his army in Gaul. The *Anticatōnēs*, composed in his Spanish camp before the battle of Munda in B.C. 45, was a reply to Cicero's panegyric on Cato of Utĭca. A treatise on astronomy, *De Astrīs*, had probably some connection with the reform of the calendar introduced by him, as *Pontĭfex Maxĭmus*, in B.C. 45. His two great works have, however, survived. These are his *Commentārii de Bello Gallĭco*, 58–52 B.C., in seven books, and his *Commentarii de Bello Cīvīli*, 49–48 B.C., in three books. The former was written down rapidly, at the end of 52 and beginning of 51, in his winter quarters before Bibracte. The latter was probably composed in Spain after the conquest of the Pompeians in 45.

The history of the Gallic War was completed after Cæsar's death by Aulus Hirtius. This writer added an eighth book, which included the last rising of the Gauls in 51, and the events of the year 50 which preceded the Civil War. The book, as we now have it, is unfinished. There are three other anonymous books which continue the history of the Civil War. The *Bellum Alexandrīnum* (War in Alexandria) is perhaps from the hand of Hirtius. The *Bellum Afrĭcum* (War in Africa) is written in a pompous and affected style [and has recently been assigned, but without sufficient reason, to Asinius Pollio]. The *Bellum Hispānum* (Spanish War), is to be attributed to two different authors. Its style is rough, and shows that the writer was not an educated man.

Cæsius Bassus. A Latin poet, a friend of Persius the satirist, whose book he edited. He is said to have perished during the eruption of Vesuvius in 79 A.D. He had a high reputation in his day as a lyric poet, and is said to have composed a didactic poem on metre. There is a considerable fragment in prose on the same subject which bears the name of Cæsius Bassus, but this is perhaps from a prose version of the poetical treatise.

Călăis (Gr. *Kalaïs*) and *Zētēs*. The Bŏrĕădæ, or sons of Bŏrĕās and Orīthyia. They were both winged heroes, and took part in

the Argonautic expedition. Coming in the course of the enterprise to Salmydēssus, they set free Phīneus, the husband of their sister Cleopatra, from the Harpies, chasing them through the air on their wings (*see* PHINEUS). According to one story, they perished on this occasion; according to another, they were slain afterwards by Hērăclēs on the island of Tēnŏs, on their return from the funeral games of Pĕlĭās (*see* ACASTUS). This was in retribution for the counsel which they had given to the Argonauts on the coast of Mysia, to leave Heracles behind. Their graves and monuments were shown in Tenos. One of the pillars was said to move when the north wind blew.

Călămis (*Kălămis*). A Greek artist, who flourished at Athens about 470 B.C. He worked in marble and metal, as well as gold and ivory, and was master of sculpture in all its branches, from the chiselling of small silver vessels to the execution of colossal statues in bronze. His Apollo, at Apollōnia in Pontus, was 120 feet high. This statue was carried away to Rome by Lucullus, and set up on the Capitol. We hear of statues of the gods and heroic women from his hand, as well as of men on horseback and four-horsed chariots. His horses are said to have been unsurpassed. His female figures, if we may believe the ancient critics, were characterized by antique harshness and severity, but were relieved by a touch of grace and delicacy.

Călămus. *See* WRITING MATERIALS.

Calantĭca. *See* CLOTHING.

Călăthus (Gr. *Kălăthŏs*). *See* VESSELS.

Calcĕus. A shoe, part of the regular Roman dress, and usually worn in public. Each order, and every *gens*, had its particular kind of *calceus*. The patricians wore a *mullĕus* or *calceus patrĭcĭus*. This was a shoe of red leather with a high sole, like that of the *cothurnus*. The leather passed round the back of the heel, where it was furnished with small hooks, to which the straps were fastened. It was originally a part of the royal dress, and was afterwards worn by generals on the occasion of a triumph. In later times, with the rest of the triumphal costume, it became a part of the dress of the consuls. In the second rank came the *calceus senātŏrĭus*, or shoe worn by senators. This was black, and tied round the leg by four straps. In the case of patricians it was ornamented by a crescent-shaped clasp. The *calceus* of the *ĕquĭtēs*, and of ordinary citizens, was also black. The latter was called *pĕrō*; it rose as high as the ankle, and was fastened with a simple tie.

Calchas (*Kalchās*). Son of Thestōr of Mycēnæ. Calchas was the celebrated seer who accompanied the Greeks on their expedition against Troy. Homer calls him the best of soothsayers, who knew the past, the present, and the future. Before the fleet started from Aulis, Calchas predicted that the Trojan war would last ten years. His own death (so ran the prophecy) was to occur whenever he met a wiser seer than himself. After the Trojan war he came to the island of Claros, where, in the sacred precincts of Apollo, he fell in with the soothsayer Mopsus, who beat him in a match of guessing riddles. [*See* MOPSUS (2)]. Calchas died of grief, or, according to another story, took away his own life. A temple was erected to him in Apulia, where the votaries lay down to sleep on sheepskins, and received oracles in their sleep.

Caldārium. *See* BATHS.

Cǎlendæ (*Kalendæ*). *See* CALENDAR.

Calendar. (1) *Greek.* The Greek year consisted of twelve months, some "full"— *i.e.* of 30 days each—the others "hollow" or incomplete, of 29 days each. This made up a lunar year of 354 days, 11 days short of the solar year. To maintain some correspondence between the lunar and solar years, and to provide at least for the festivals of the seasons always occurring at the right time of year, the Athenians early resorted to the method of intercalation. A space of time was taken which included as many days as would exactly make up eight solar years, and could easily be distributed among the same number of lunar years. This space of time was called a "great year." Then in every 3rd, 6th, and 8th year a month of 29 or 30 days was inserted, so that the years in question consisted each of 383 or 384 days. This system was introduced at Athens by Solon. The period of eight years was sometimes called *ennǎĕtērĭs*, or a period of nine years, because it began again with every 9th year; some times *oktǎĕtērĭs*, or space of eight years. For this the astronomers, of whom Mĕtōn' in the Periclean age may be taken as a representative, substituted a more accurate system, which was afterwards adopted in Athens and other cities as a correction of the old calendar. This was the *ennĕakaidĕkǎĕtērĭs* of 19 years. The alternate "full" and "hollow" months were divided into three decades, consisting of 10 or 9 days each as the case might be. The days of the last decade were counted from more to less to correspond with the waning of the moon. Thus the 21st of the month was called the 10th of the waning moon, the 22nd the 9th, the 23rd the 8th, and so on. The reckoning of the year, with the order and names of the months, differed more or less in different states, the only common point being the names of the months, which were almost without exception taken from the chief festivals celebrated in them. The Athenians and the other Ionians began their year with the first new moon after the summer solstice, the Dorians with the autumnal equinox, the Bœotians and other Æolians with the winter solstice. The Attic months are as follows: 1. *Hĕkǎtombaiōn* (July–August); 2. *Mĕtǎgeitnĭōn* (August–September); 3. *Bŏēdrŏmĭōn* (September–October); 4. *Pўǎnepsĭōn* (October–November); 5. *Maimaktērĭōn* (November – December); 6. *Pŏseidĕōn* (December–January); 7. *Gǎmēlĭōn* (January–February); 8. *Anthestērĭōn* (February–March); 9. *Elǎphĕbŏlĭōn* (March–April); 10. *Mūnychĭōn* (April–May); 11. *Thargēlĭōn* (May–June); 12. *Skeirŏphŏrĭōn* (June–July). The intercalary month was a second *Poseideon* inserted in the middle of the year. The official system of numbering the years differed also very much in the various states. The years received their names from the magistrates, sometimes secular, sometimes spiritual. (*See* EPONYMUS.) Historical chronology was first computed according to Olympiads, beginning B.C. 776, by the historian Timæus in the 3rd century B.C.

(2) *The Roman year* was supposed to have consisted, under Rŏmŭlus, of 10 months, four full ones of 31 days (March, May, July and October), and six "hollow" of 30 days (April, June, August, September, November, December). But, as a space of 304 days makes up neither a solar nor a lunar year, it is difficult to understand the so-called "year of Romulus." King Numa was usually supposed to have introduced the year of 12 months by adding January and February at the end; for the Roman year, it must be remembered, began originally with March. On this system every month except February had an odd number of days : March 31, April 29, May 31, June 29, Quintīlis 31, Sextīlis 29, September 29, October 31, November 29, December 29, January 29, February 28. Numa is also credited with the attempt to square this

lunar year of 355 days with the solar year of 365 ; but how he did it is not certainly known. The *Decemvĭri* in 450 B.C. probably introduced the system of adjustment afterwards in use. According to this a cycle of four years was taken, in the second year of which an intercalary month (*mensis mercedōnĭus*) of 23 days was inserted between the 24th and 25th of February, and in the fourth year a month of 22 days between the 23rd and 24th February. Thus the period of 4 years amounted to 1465 days. But this gave the year an average of 366¼ days, or one day too many, so that a special rectification was necessary from time to time. This was probably carried out by the omission of an intercalary month. It was the business of the *Pontĭfĭcēs* to keep the calendar in order by regular intercalation ; but, partly from carelessness, partly from political motives, they made insertions and omissions so incorrectly as to bring the calendar into complete disorder, and destroy the correspondence between the months and the seasons. The mischief was finally remedied by Cæsar, with the assistance of the mathematician Sōsĭgĕnēs. To bring the calendar into correspondence with the seasons, the year 46 B.C. was lengthened so as to consist of 15 months, or 415 days, and the calendar known as the Julian was introduced on the 1st January, 45 B.C. This calendar is founded simply on the solar year, which is well known to be a discovery of the Egyptians. Cæsar fixed this year to 365¼ days, which is correct within a few minutes. After this the ordinary year consisted of 365 days, divided into 12 months, with the names still in use. Every fourth year had 366 days, a day being inserted at the end of February. The Julian calendar maintained its ground till 1582, when Pope Gregory XIII corrected the trifling error which still attached to it. The old names of the months were retained with two exceptions, that of Quintilis, which, in honour of Cæsar, was called *Iulius*, and that of Sextilis, which in 8 B.C. was called *Augustus* in honour of the emperor. The old divisions of the lunar month were also retained for convenience of dating. These were (*a*) the *Kălendœ*, marking the first appearance of the new moon ; (*b*) the *Nōnœ*, marking the first quarter ; (*c*) the *Idūs*, marking the full moon. *Kalendœ* means properly the day of summoning, from *calāre*, to summon. The *Pontifex* was bound to observe the first phase, and to make his announcement to the *Rex Sacrōrum*, who then summoned the people to the Capitol, in front of the *Curia Calābra*, so called from *calare*. Here he offered sacrifice, and announced that the first quarter would begin on the 5th or 7th day (inclusive) as the case might be. This day was called *Nonœ*, as (according to Roman calculation) the 9th day before the full moon, and fell in March, May, July and October on the 7th, in the other months on the 5th. The appearance of the full moon was called *Idus* (probably connected with the Etruscan word *iduāre*, to divide), because it divided the month in the middle. The days of the month were counted backwards, in the first half of the month from the Nones and Ides, in the last half from the Kalends of the following month. The Romans also had a week called *internundĭnum*, or the interval between two *nundĭnœ*. It consisted of eight days, and, like our weeks, could be divided between two months or two years. (For further details *see* FASTI.)

After the establishment of the Republic the Romans named their years after the consuls, a custom which was maintained down to the reign of Justinian (541 A.D.). After the time of Augustus it became the practice in literature to date events from the foundation of Rome, which took place according to Varro in 753, according to Cato in 751 B.C.

The Day. The Greeks reckoned the civil day from sunset to sunset, the Romans (like ourselves) from midnight to midnight. The natural day was reckoned by both as lasting from sunrise to sunset. The divisions of the day were for a long time made on no common principle. It was for military purposes that the Romans first hit on such a principle, dividing the night during service into four equal watches (*vĭgĭlĭœ*). Corresponding to this we find another division (probably calculated immediately for the courts of justice) into *māne* (sunrise to 9 or 10), forenoon (*ad mĕrīdĭem*), afternoon (*de meridie*) until 3 or 4, and evening (*suprēma*) from thence till sunset. After the introduction of sun-dials and water-clocks the day and night were divided each into 12 hours ; but the division was founded on the varying length of the day, so that each hour of the day was longer, and conversely each hour of the night shorter, in summer than in winter.

Cāliga. A boot with large nails in the sole, worn in ancient Italy by huntsmen, waggoners, and peasants, and, during the imperial period, by common soldiers.

Călix. *See* VESSELS.

Callicrătēs (Gr. *Kallikrătēs*). A Greek architect who, together with Ictīnus, built the Parthĕnōn (*q.v.*).

Callĭmăchus (Gr. *Kallĭmăchŏs*). (1) A Greek artist, who flourished in the second half of the 5th century B.C. He was the inventor of the Corinthian order of pillar, and the art of boring marble is also attributed to him, though perhaps he did no more than bring it to perfection. The ancient critics represent him as unwearied in polishing and perfecting his work; indeed, they allege that his productions lost something through their excessive refinement and purity. One of his celebrated works was the golden chandelier in the Erechthĕum at Athens.

(2) A Greek scholar and poet, the chief representative of the Alexandrian school. He was the son of Battus, and thus sprung from the noble family of the Battĭădæ. He at first gave his lectures in a suburb of Alexandria; but was afterwards summoned by Ptolemy Philadelphus to the Museum there, and in about 260 B.C. was made president of the library. He held this office till his death, which took place about 240 B.C. He did a great service to literature by sifting and cataloguing the numerous books collected at Alexandria. The results of his labours were published in his great work called *Pĭnăkĕs*, or "Tablets." This contained 120 books, and was a catalogue, arranged in chronological order, of the works contained in the library, with observations on their genuineness, and an indication of the first and last word in each book, and a note of its bulk. This work laid the foundation of a critical study of Greek literature. 800 works, partly in prose, partly in verse, were attributed altogether to Callimachus; but it is to be observed that he avoided, on principle, the composition of long poems, so as to be able to give more thought to the artistic elaboration of details. The essence of Callimachus' verse is art and learning, not poetic genius in the real sense. Indeed, some of his compositions had a directly learned object; the *Aĭtĭa*, or "Causes," for instance. This was a collection of elegiac poems in four books, treating, with great erudition, of the foundation of cities, the origin of religious ceremonies, and the like.

Through his writings, as well as through his oral instruction, Callimachus exercised an immense influence, not only on the course of learning, but on the poetical tendencies of the Alexandrian school. Among his pupils were the most celebrated *savants* of the time, Eratosthĕnēs, Aristŏphănēs of Byzantium, Apollōnius of Rhodes, and others. Of his writings only a very few have survived in a complete state: these are, six hymns, five of which are in epic and one in elegiac form, and sixty-four epigrams. The hymns, both in their language and their matter, attest the learned taste of their author. His elegy, entitled the *Coma Bĕrĕnīcēs*, or "Lock of Berenice," is imitated by Catullus in one of his remaining pieces. Ovid, in the twentieth of his *Herŏĭdēs*, as well as in his *Ibis*, took poems of Callimachus for his models. Indeed, the Romans generally set a very high value on his elegies, and liked to imitate them. Of his other works in prose and poetry—among the latter may be mentioned a very popular epic called *Hĕcălĕ*—only fragments have survived.

Callīnus (Gr. *Kallīnŏs*), the creator of the Greek political elegy, was a native of Ephesus, and flourished, probably, about 700 B.C., at the time when the kings of Lydia were harassing the Greek colonies of Asia Minor by constant wars. One elegy from his hand has survived, in which, in a simple and manly tone, he endeavours to kindle the degenerate youth of his fatherland to courage and patriotism.

Callĭŏpē (Gr. *Kallĭŏpē*). *See* MUSES.

Callirrhŏē (Gr. *Kallirrhŏē*). *See* ACARNAN and ALCMÆON.

Callisthĕnēs (Gr. *Kallisthĕnēs*). A Greek historian, born at Olynthus about 360 B.C. He was a relation of Aristotle, from whom he received instruction at the same time as Alexander the Great. He accompanied Alexander on his Asiatic campaign, and offended him by refusing to pay him servile homage after the Persian fashion, and by other daring exhibitions of independence. The consequence was that the king threw his friend into prison on the pretext that he was concerned in a conspiracy against his life. Callisthenes died in captivity in 328 B.C., in consequence, probably, of maltreatment. Of his historical writings, particularly those dealing with the exploits of Alexander, only fragments remain; but he was always ranked among the most famous historians. Indeed, his reputation as the companion of Alexander and the historian of his achievements maintained itself so well, that he was made responsible in literature for the romantic narrative of Alexander's life which grew up in the following centuries. This was translated into Latin towards the end of the 3rd century A.D. by Julius Valerius, and became the main authority for the mediæval adaptations of the myth of Alexander.

Callistō (Gr. *Kallistō*). A nymph, the daughter of the Arcadian Lycăŏn, and a companion of Artĕmis. She became, by Zeus, the mother of Arcăs, the ancestor of the Arcadians. She was turned into a bear, according to one account by the jealous Hēra, according to another by Zeus, who was anxious to protect her from Hera's wrath. In this shape she was slain by Artemis, and set among the constellations by Zeus under the title of the She-Bear. There was another story, according to which Callisto's son was intending to slay his transformed mother while hunting; upon which Zeus set him in the sky under the name of Arctūrus (*Arktourŏs*), the Watcher of the Bear, and his mother under the name of Arctus (*Arktŏs*), the She-Bear. As the stars bearing these names never set, Homer describes them as the only ones which have no share in the bath of the ocean. Later poets, accordingly, invented the further story that Tēthys, wishing to gratify Hera, refused to receive her former rival into her waters.

Callistrātus (Gr. *Kallistrātos*). A Greek rhetorician, who probably flourished in the 3rd century A.D. He was the author of descriptions of fourteen statues of celebrated artists, Scŏpās, for instance, Praxitĕlēs, and Lysippus, written after the manner of Philostrātus. His style is dry and affected, and he gives the reader no real insight into the qualities of the masterpieces which he attempts to describe.

Callyntērĭa (Gr. *Kallynterĭa*) and *Plyntērĭa* ("Feasts of Adorning and Cleansing"), were the names given to the two chief days of a service of atonement held at Athens from the 19th to the 25th of Thargēliōn (or May–June). The Erechthĕum, or sanctuary of Athēnē of the stronghold, was cleansed, the ancient wooden image of the goddess was unclothed, the garments washed and the image itself purified. These duties were performed, with mysterious rites, by the family of the Praxiegĭdæ, with the aid of certain women called Plyntrĭdĕs. The Plyntēria, or day on which the image was washed, was an unlucky day, on which no public business was transacted. The ceremonies would seem originally to have been intended to commemorate the season of the year and the ripening of the corn and fruit,

for which the votaries of the powerful goddess desired to secure her favour.

Calpis (Gr. *Kalpis*). See VESSELS.

Calpurnĭus. (1) *Calpurnius Pīsō Frūgī.* See ANNALISTS.

(2) *Titus Calpurnius Sĭcŭlus*, a Roman poet, who flourished in the middle of the 1st century A.D. At the beginning of Nero's reign he wrote seven *Eclŏgæ*, or bucolic poems, which are somewhat servile imitations of Theocrĭtus and Vergil. The language is declamatory, but the laws of metre are strictly observed. The poet was poor, and wished his writings to be brought under the notice of the young emperor, through the instrumentality of a personage high in favour at court. This individual appears under the name of Melibœus, and has sometimes been supposed to have been the philosopher Seneca, sometimes the Piso who was executed in 65 A.D. as the leader of a conspiracy against Nero. Calpurnius lavishes the most fulsome praises upon the emperor. Four of the *Eclŏgæ*, which were formerly attributed to Calpurnius, are now known to have been written by Nemesiānus, who not only imitates Calpurnius, but plagiarizes from him.

(3) *Calpurnius Flaccus*, a Latin rhetorician of uncertain date, under whose name fifty-one school-boy harangues, or rather extracts from them, have come down to us.

Călumnĭa (in old Latin *Kălumnĭa*). The Latin word for slander. It was technically applied to false accusations. The falsely accused person, if acquitted, had the right of accusing the prosecutor in his turn on the charge of *calumnia* before the same jury. In civil cases the penalty was a pecuniary fine; in criminal cases the *calumniātor* lost his right to appear again as a prosecutor, and in early times was branded on the forehead with a *K*.

Calydonian (Gr. *Kalydonian*) **Hunt.** See MELEAGER (1) and ŒNEUS.

Calypsō (Gr. *Kalypsō*). A nymph, the daughter of Atlas, who dwelt on the island of Ogȳgia, where she gave a friendly welcome to Odysseus, whom she kept with her for seven years. (*See* ODYSSEUS.)

Cămēnæ (Latin). The name of certain fountain nymphs, who presided over childbirth. They had also the gift of prophecy, and were identified by the Latin poets with the Greek Muses. (*See* MUSES.)

Cameos, and *The Gonzaga Cameo.* See GEMS.

Cămilli and **Camillæ.** The Latin name for the boys and girls who attended on the priests and priestesses during the performance of their religious functions. It was necessary that they should be born of free parents, and have both parents living. These attendants were especially attached to the *Flāmen Diālis*, and his wife the *Flamīnīca*, and also to the *Curiōnēs*.

The priests generally brought up their own children, by preference, for this service, to teach them their duties, and secure them a succession to the priestly office.

* CAMILLUS, WITH
ACERRA AND RICINIUM.
(Bartoli, *Admir.* 14.)

Campus Martius ("Field of Mars"). A plain lying to the north of Rome, outside the *Pōmērīum*, between the Tiber, the Quirinal and the Capitoline Hills. (*See* POMERIUM.) During the regal period it was part of the property of the Crown, and, after the expulsion of the kings, was dedicated to Mars. The northern part, on the banks of the Tiber, served as an exercise-ground for the Roman youth for athletics, riding, or military drill. The smaller part, next to the city, was used for the meetings of the *Comitia Centuriata*, and for holding the *lustrum*. In the midst of it stood an altar to Mars, which formed the centre of the ceremony of the *lustrum*, and of some other festivals held on the spot in honour of that deity. (*See* LUSTRUM.) Until the end of the republican age there was only one building on this part of the *Campus*, the *Villa Publīca*. This was the residence assigned to foreign ambassa-

* APOLLO AFTER CANACHUS.
(Bronze statuette in British Museum.)

dors and Roman generals on their return from war, to whom the senate granted audiences in the neighbouring temple of Bellona. But in B.C. 55 Pompeius erected in the Campus the first stone theatre built in Rome, with a great colonnade adjoining it. Here too Julius Cæsar commenced his marble *sæpta*, or inclosures for the *Comitia Centuriate*, with a great colonnade surrounding the *ŏvīlĕ*. (*See* COMITIA.) These were completed by Agrippa in 27 B.C. In B.C. 28, Octavianus Cæsar added the *Mausōlēum*, or hereditary burial-place of the Cæsars, and Agrippa the Pantheon and the first *Thermæ* or Baths. Under the succeeding emperors a number of buildings rose here; for instance, Domitian's Race-course (*Stădiŭm*) and *Odēum*. The rest of the *Campus* was left free for gymnastic and military exercises, the grounds being magnificently decorated with statues and colonnades. The altar survived until the last days of ancient Rome.

Cănăchus (Gr. *Kănăchŏs*). A Greek sculptor born in Sīcўōn about 480 B.C. He worked in bronze, in the combination of gold and ivory, and also in wood. His masterpiece was the colossal bronze statue of Apollo at Milētus, of which some idea may be still derived from ancient coins of that city. It seems to have been extremely antique in its character (*see* cut).

Candēlābrum. A lamp furnished with a point, on which a taper (*candēla*) was fixed. (*See* LIGHTING.) As the use of lamps became more common, the word *candelabrum* was transferred to the wooden or metal support, usually made up of a base, a tall thin shaft, and a disc (*discus*), on which the lamp was set up to illuminate a large room. There were other forms of *candelabra*, notably the *lampădārīum* or "lamp-bearer" (*see* cut, p. 114). This had no disc, but a number of arms, as many as the lamps it was intended to carry. Other *candelabra* had an apparatus for raising and lowering the lamps. The shaft was hollow, and contained a movable rod, supporting the disc or the arms, which could be fixed at any required height by bolts passed through it. Like lamps, *candelabra* were made in the greatest possible variety of forms, and ornamented in a number of different ways, especially by figures in relief. Besides the portable *candelabra* intended for common use, and set on a table or on the ground, there were large and heavy ones, shaped like pillars, and set up on fixed pedestals as ornaments for temples and palaces (*see* cut, p. 114).

Candĭdātus. The Latin term for a competitor for a public office. He was so called from the peculiar dress in which he usually showed himself to the people in the Forum. This was the *tŏga candĭda*, a new *toga* whitened with chalk. No one could appear as a *candidatus* unless his name had been given in to, and accepted by, the authorities presiding over the election.

Cănĕŏn (Gr. *Kănĕŏn*). *See* VESSELS.

Cănēphŏri (Gr. *Kănēphŏroi*), "basket-bearers." The title of certain maidens belonging to the first families at Athens, whose duty it was to carry baskets containing consecrated furniture, on their heads, at the solemn processions, particularly at the Panathenæa. The graceful attitude made

not simply recited, but sung or performed in melodrama with musical accompaniments.

Căpăneus (Gr. *Kăpăneus*). One of the *Seven against Thebes* who was struck by lightning during the assault upon the city. He was climbing the wall, and was boasting that not even the lightning of Zeus would scare him away. During the burning of his body on the funeral pyre, his wife Evadnē threw herself into the

‡ CANDELABRUM OF MARBLE.
(Naples Museum.)
From Gargiulo's *Raccolta*, tav. 40.

LAMPADARIA OF BRONZE. (*See* p. 113.)
(Naples Museum.)
(1) from Gargiulo's *Raccolta*, tav. 63.
(2) and (3) *Museo Borbonico*, VIII xxxi, and II xiii.

the figure of a *canephorŏs* a favourite one with sculptors. Such figures were often employed by architects as supports for the entablatures of temples. The Erechthēum on the Acropolis at Athens is an example. (*See* CARYATIDES.)

Canthărus. *See* VESSELS.

Cantĭcum. A technical term of the Roman stage. In the narrower sense, it denoted a melody or air composed in changing rhythms, the text to which was sung behind the stage to the accompaniment of a flute, while the actor expressed the meaning by pantomime. In Cicero's time, however, the *cantica* were sometimes performed by the actors. In a wider sense, the word might mean any part in a play which was

flames. His son was Sthĕnĕlus, the charioteer of Diomēdēs.

Căpēlĭum (Gr. *Kăpēleiŏn*). *See* INNS.

Căpella. *See* MARTIANUS CAPELLA.

Căper (*Flăvius*). A Latin scholar of some note, who flourished in the 2nd century A.D., and whose writings were frequently used and quoted by the later grammarians. Only two small treatises bearing his name have come down to us, the *De Orthŏgrăphĭā* ("On Orthography") and *De Verbīs Dubiīs* ("On Irregular Words"); but these are only meagre extracts from the original works.

Căpĭtĕ censi. *See* PROLETARII.

Căpĭtŏlīnus (*Iulius*). *See* HISTORIÆ AUGUSTÆ SCRIPTORES.

Căpĭtōlĭum. The southern summit of the Capitoline Hill at Rome, separated from the *arx* or northern summit by a saddle, on which were the *asȳlum* and the temple of Vēiŏvĭs. The Capitol was approached by a road mounting in several zig-zags from the Forum. On the highest point of the southern top was the temple of Jupiter Optĭmus Maxĭmus, begun by the Tarquins, but not finished till the first year of the Republic (509 B.C.). The temple was quadrangular and nearly square, with three rows of columns in front, six in each row, and four columns on each side. They were in the Doric, or rather the Tuscan, style. The interior was divided by parallel walls into three *cellæ* or chambers. The central chamber was dedicated to Jupiter, and contained a statue of the god in terra-cotta. The senate sometimes held its sittings here, particularly at the opening of the year, and on occasions when war was declared. The right-hand chamber was sacred to Minerva, the left-hand to Juno. The entablature was entirely constructed of wood; the pediment was of terra-cotta, as was the *quadrĭga* or four-horsed chariot, with the figure of the god, above. After the Third Punic War the entablature was gilded. In 83 B.C. the whole temple was burnt down to the vaults in which the Sibylline books and other consecrated objects were preserved. Sulla rebuilt the structure strictly on the lines of the old one, though with much greater splendour in detail; but the new temple was not consecrated till 69 B.C. A statue of Jupiter in gold and ivory, on the model of the Olympian Zeus, by Apollōnĭus, was substituted for the old image of terra-cotta. A hundred years later the building was again burnt down, in the civil war of Vitellius and Vespasian. Vespasian restored it, but the new structure was again destroyed by fire in 80 A.D. In 82 Domitian erected a new temple, a Corinthian *hexastȳlŏs*, which survived unhurt till the 5th century A.D. This was gradually destroyed, partly by the invading barbarians who plundered it, and partly in the dissensions of the Middle Ages. The Palazzo Caffarelli now stands upon its foundation.

Caprōtīna. A Roman epithet of Juno. A special feast, called the *Nōnæ Caprotinæ*, was celebrated in her honour on the Nones of Quintīlis, or 7th of July. In this celebration female slaves took a considerable part. The festival was connected with another, called *Poplĭfŭgĭum*, or the "Flight of the People," held on the 5th of July. Thus a historical basis was given to it, though the true origin of both festivals had been probably forgotten. After their defeat by the Gauls, the Romans were conquered and put to flight by a sudden attack of their neighbours, the Latins, who demanded the surrender of a large number of girls and widows. Thereupon, at the suggestion of a girl called Tutŭla (or Phĭlōtis), the female slaves disguised themselves as Roman ladies, went into the enemy's camp, and contrived to make the enemy drunk, while Tutŭla, climbing a wild fig-tree, gave the signal for the Romans to attack by holding up a torch. The *Poplĭfugia* were celebrated by a mimic flight. On the 7th July, the female slaves went in procession to the fig-tree, where they carried on all kinds of sports with the assembled multitude. Besides this, there was a sacrifice and a festal meal at the tree, and on the next day a thanksgiving, celebrated by the *pontĭficēs.*

Căpys (Gr. *Kăpys*). *See* DARDANUS and ANCHISES.

Carchēsĭum (Gr. *Karchēsĭŏn*). *See* VESSELS.

Cardĕa. The tutelary goddess of hinges, in other words, of family life, among the Romans. She was supposed to ward off all the noxious influences of evil spirits, especially of the *Strĭgæ*, who were believed to suck the blood of children by night. It is doubtful whether she is to be identified with the goddess Carna, who is said to have taken the larger organs of the body—heart, lungs and liver—under her especial protection. Carna had a shrine on the Cælian Hill, in Rome, and a festival on the 1st of June, at which they ate beans and bacon, and made offerings of them to the goddess.

Caristia. *See* MANES.

Carmenta or **Carmentis.** An ancient Italian goddess of prophecy, who protected women in child-birth. In Rome she had a priest attached to her, the *flämen Carmentālis*, and a shrine near the gate under the Capitol, named after her the *porta Carmentālis.* On this spot the Roman matrons celebrated in her honour the festival of the *Carmentalia*, the *flämen* and *pontĭfex* assisting. Two *Carmentēs*, called *Porrĭma* or *Antevorta*, and *Postvorta*, were worshipped as her sisters and attendants. These names were sometimes explained with reference to childbirth, sometimes as indicating the power of the goddess of fate to look into the past and future. In the legend of the foundation of Rome Carmenta appears as the prophetic mother, or wife, of the Arcadian stranger Evander.

Carna. *See* CARDEA.

Carnēa (Gr. *Karneia*). A festival celebrated in honour of Apollo Carnēus ("the
protector of flocks") as early as the time of
the immigration of the Dorians. In keeping
up the celebration, the Dorians characteristically gave it a warlike colour, by transforming their original pastoral deity into the
god of their fighting army. The *Carnēa*
lasted nine days, from the 7th to the 15th
of the month Carnēus (August–September).
The proceedings symbolized the life of
soldiers in camp. In every three *phrā-
triæ* or *ōbæ* nine places were set apart, on
which tents or booths were put up. In
these tents nine men had their meals in
common. All ordinary proceedings were
carried on at the word of command, giv⌐ɹ
out by a herald. One
part of the festival
recalled its originally
rural character. This
was a race, in which
one of the runners,
supposed to symbo-
lize the blessings of
harvest, started in
advance, uttering
prayers for the city.
The others, called
"vintage - runners,"
pursued him, and if
they overtook him, the
occurrence was taken
as a good omen, if they
failed, as a bad one.
After the twenty-sixth
Olympiad (676 B.C.) a
musical contest was
added, at which the
most celebrated artists
in all Greece were
accustomed to com-
pete. The first artist
who sang at this con-
test was Terpander.

CARYATID.
From the Erechtheum,
Athens (British Museum).

Carpentum. *See*
CHARIOTS.

Carpō. *See* HORÆ.

Carroballista. *See* ARTILLERY.

Carrūca. *See* CHARIOTS.

Caryātĭdĕs (Gr. *Karyātĭdēs*). A technical
term of Greek architecture. Caryatides
were female statues clothed in long drapery,
used instead of shafts, or columns, to support the entablature of a temple (*see* cut).
The name properly means "maidens of
Caryæ (*Karyai*)," a Spartan town on the
Arcadian frontier. Here it was the custom

for bands of girls to perform their country
dances at the yearly festivals of Artĕmis
Karyātis. In doing so they sometimes
assumed the attitude which suggested the
form adopted by the artists in the statues
mentioned above. (*See also* CANEPHORI.)

Cassandra (Gr. *Kassandra*). In Homer
Cassandra is the fairest of the daughters of
Priam and Hĕcŭba. For the promise of
her love, Apollo conferred upon her the
gift of prophecy; she broke her word, and
the god punished her by letting her retain
the gift, but depriving her of the power of
making her hearers believe her. Her utterances were therefore laughed to scorn as
the ravings of a mad woman. It was in
vain that, at the birth of Paris, she advised
that he should be put to death, and that,
when Helen came to Troy, she prophesied
the destruction of the city. When the city
was taken, she was dragged by Ajax the
son of Oïleus from the altar of Athēnē, at
which she had taken refuge; but Agamemnōn rescued her and took her as his slave
to Mycēnæ. Here she was slain by Clytæmnestra when Agamemnon was murdered.
She was worshipped with Apollo in several
places under the name of Alexandra.

Cassĭānus Bassus. *See* GEOPONICI.

Cassĭŏdōrus Sĕnātor (*Magnus Aurēlius*)
was born in Bruttium, about 480 A.D. He
belonged to an old Roman family which had,
particularly in the three preceding generations, distinguished itself in the public
service. His father stood in high favour
with Theŏdŏric, who had an equal regard
for his talented and highly educated son,
Cassiodorus Senator. On account of his
trustworthiness and ability as a statesman,
the younger Cassiodorus was appointed to
the highest offices by Theodoric and his
successors. He was consul A.D. 514, and
four times *præfectus*. For a period of
nearly forty years he enjoyed an active and
successful career in the public administration, notably as Theodoric's private secretary. After the fall of Vitĭgēs in 540,
Cassiodorus retired to the monastery of
Vivārium (Vivarese), which he had founded
on his estates in Bruttium. Here he passed
the rest of his life in religious exercises
and literary labour. He died about 575.

Among the works which he composed
during his career as a statesman, we have
a universal history called *Chrŏnĭca*, from
Adam down to the year when it was written. This consists mainly of a catalogue of
the Roman consuls, and is the longest of
all the lists which have come down to us.

Another work of his which has survived is the *Variæ* (*Epistŭlæ*) in twelve books. This is a collection of imperial rescripts, and has considerable historical importance. These rescripts he made out, partly in the name of Theodoric and his successors, partly in his own name as *præfectus*. The book likewise contains a collection of formularies for decrees of nomination. His Gothic history, in twelve books, is only preserved in extracts, and in the paraphrase of Jordanes.

The chief aim of his monastic life was a noble one. He hoped to make the monasteries an asylum of knowledge, in which the literature of classical antiquity and of the Christian age might be collected. The number of books was to be increased by copyists, and the clergy were to gain their necessary education by studying them. The libraries and schools of the monasteries in succeeding centuries were ultimately formed upon the model which he set up. Besides a number of theological writings, he composed, in about 544 A.D., a sort of Encyclopædia, in four books, for the instruction of his monks. This is the "Instructions in Sacred and Profane Literature" (*Institutiōnēs Divinārum et Sæculārium Litterārum*). The first part is an introduction to the study of theology, the second a sketch of the seven liberal arts. Finally, in his ninety-third year, he compiled a treatise *De Orthogrăphĭā* or on *Orthography*.

Cassĭŏpēa (Gr. *Kassĭŏpeia*). *See* ANDROMEDA.

Cassius. (1) *Cassius Hemīna*. *See* ANNALISTS. (2) *See* DIO CASSIUS.

Castălĭa (Gr. *Kastălĭa*). A nymph, the daughter of the river-god Achelöüs. Pursued by Apollo, she threw herself into a spring on Mount Parnassus, which took its name after her. The spring was consecrated to Apollo and the Muses, and it was in its water that the pilgrims to the neighbouring shrine of Delphi purified themselves.

The Roman poets indulged in the fiction that it conferred poetic inspiration.

Castor(Gr.*Kastōr*)& *Pollux*. *See* DIOSCURI.

Castră. A Roman camp, fortified with a rampart and ditch, outside of which a Roman army never spent a single night. It was marked out on a place selected by officers detached for the purpose, generally on the spur of a hill. The same plan was always observed, and the divisions indicated by coloured flags and lances, so that the divisions of the army, as they came in, could find their places at once. In the middle of the 2nd century B.C., according to the account of Polўbĭus [vi 27], the plan of

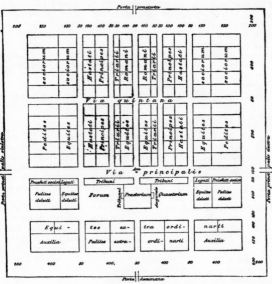

PLAN OF A ROMAN CAMP.

a camp for a consular army of two legions, with the proper contingent of Italian allies, and its auxiliary troops, was as follows (*see Plan*). The camp was square, its front being on the side furthest from the enemy. It had two main roads through it. (1) The *via princĭpālis*, 100 feet wide, which divided it into a front part amounting to about two-thirds of the whole, and a back part, turned toward the enemy. This road ended at two gates, the *porta princĭpalis dextra*, and the *porta princĭpalis sinistra*. (2) The *via prætŏrĭa*, which cut the *via princĭpalis* at right angles, and divided the whole length of the camp into two parts. This road was 50 feet in width, and ended in two gates, the *porta dĕcŭmāna* in front, and the *porta prœtōrĭa* on the side opening towards the enemy. In the front part were encamped the two legions, with their allied contingents. They lay in three double rows of tents on each side of the *via prœtoria*, which made a right angle with the *via principalis*. Its whole length was divided by roads 50 feet in width, while across it, from one lateral rampart to the other, ran the *via quintāna*. The front side of the rows of tents was turned towards the intervening roads. Starting from the *via prœtoria*, the first two lines of tents on each side contained the cavalry and infantry of one legion each, while the third row, lying nearest to the rampart, contained the cavalry and infantry of the allied contingents. In the hinder part of the camp, directly upon the *via principalis*, and on both sides of the *via prœtoria*, were the tents of the twelve military tribunes, opposite the four ranks of the legions. On both sides were the tents of the *prœfecti* of the allied contingents, placed in the same way opposite those of the troops under their command. Then followed the headquarters, or *prœtōrĭum*, a space 200 feet square, intersected by the *via prœtoria*. In this was the general's tent (*tabernācŭlum*); in front was the altar on which the general sacrificed, on the left the *augŭrāle* for taking the auspices, and on the right the *trĭbūnāl*. This was a bank of earth covered with turf, on which the general took his stand when addressing the troops, or administering justice. Right of the *prœtorium* was the *quœstōrĭum*, containing the quarters of the paymasters, and the train of artillery. On the left was the *forum*, a meeting place for the soldiers. Between these spaces and the lateral ramparts were the tents of the select troops who composed the body-guard of the general. Those of the cavalry had their front turned inwards, while those of the infantry were turned towards the wall. The tents of the picked allied troops occupied the hinder part of the camp, which was bounded by a cross road 100 feet in breadth. The tents of the cavalry looked inwards, those of the infantry towards the rampart. The auxiliary troops were posted at the two angles of this space. The rampart was divided from the tents by an open space 200 feet in width. This was specially intended to facilitate the march of the troops at their entrance and exit.

The construction of the fortifications always began before the general's tent was pitched. The legionaries constructed the rampart and ditch in front and rear, while the allies did the same on either side. The stakes required for the formation of an *abattis* on the outer side of the wall were carried by the soldiers themselves on the march The whole work was carried on under arms. The watches (*excŭbĭœ* and *vigĭlĭœ*) were kept with great strictness both by day and night. The *vigiliœ*, or night-watches, were relieved four times, the trumpet sounding on each occasion. The posts of each night-watch were inspected by four Roman *ĕquĭtēs*. The password for the night was given by the general. Each gate was guarded by outposts of infantry and cavalry, the light-armed troops (*vĕlĭtēs*) being also distributed as sentries along the ramparts. When the camp was to break up, three signals were given; at the first, the tents were taken down and packed up; at the second, they were put upon beasts of burden and in wagons, and at the third the army began its march.

After the time of Polybius the Roman military system underwent many changes, which involved alterations in the arrangements of the camp, but we have no trustworthy information on this subject in detail until the beginning of the 2nd century A.D. The treatise of one Hygīnus on castrametation gives the following statements as to the practice of his time. The ordinary form of a camp was that of a rectangle, the length of which was about a third part greater than the breadth. In former times the legions were posted inside the camp; but now, being regarded as the most trustworthy troops, they were encamped along the whole line of ramparts, the width of which was now limited to 60 feet. They were separated from the interior of the camp by a road 30 feet wide (*via sāgŭlāris*), running parallel to the line of ramparts. The interior was now divided, not into two, but into three main sections. The midmost of these lay between the *via principalis*, which was 60, and the *via quintana*, which was 40 feet wide. It was occupied by the *prœtorium* and the troops of the guard, and was called the wing of the *prœtorium* (*lātĕrā prœtorii*). The auxiliary troops were stationed in what was now the front part, or *prœtentūra*, between the *via principalis* and the *porta prœtoria*, and the rear, or *rĕtentūra*, between the *via quintana* and the *porta decumana*. The *via prœtoria*, which was also 60 feet wide, led only from the *prætorium* and the *forum* in front of it to the *porta prætoria*, as at this time the *quæstorium* was situated between the *porta decumana* and the *prætorium*. The general superintendence of the arrangements was, during the imperial period, in the hands of the *præfectus castrōrum*. (*See* PRÆFECTUS.)

Cătălĕptŏn [not *Catalecta*, but = Gr. *Katalepton* = "on a small scale"]. The title of a collection of short poems attributed in antiquity to Vergil. (*See* VERGIL.)

Cătăpulta. *See* ARTILLERY.

Căthĕdra (Gr. *Kathedra*). *See* CHAIRS.

Cătō (*Marcus Porcius*). The earliest important representative of Latin prose, and an ardent champion of Roman national feeling in life as in literature. He was born 234 B.C., at Tusculum, and passed his youth in a laborious life in the country. At the age of seventeen he entered the army, and fought with distinction in the Hannibalic war in Italy, Sicily and Africa. He was elected quæstor in 204, ædile in 199, and prætor in 198 B.C., when he administered the province of Sardinia. He attained the consulship in B.C. 195. As proconsul he was so successful in the measures he adopted for the subjugation of the province of Spain, that he was honoured with a triumph on his return. Four years later, in the capacity of *lēgātus*, he dealt the decisive stroke which gave the Romans the victory over the troops of king Antĭŏchus at Thermŏpȳlæ. In 184 he was elected censor, and administered his office with such strictness that he received the *cognōmen* of Censōrius. He was the enemy of all innovations, especially of the Greek influence which was making itself felt at Rome. Everything which he thought endangered the ancient Roman discipline, he met with unwearied opposition, regardless of any unpopularity he might incur. He is said to have been prosecuted forty-four times, and to have been always acquitted. The occasions on which he himself appeared as prosecutor were even more numerous.

Even in extreme old age he retained the vigour of his intellect, and was as active as before in politics and literature. He is said to have been an old man when he made his first acquaintance with Greek literature. He died 149 B.C., in his eighty-sixth year. [See Livy xxxix 40.]

Cato was the first writer who composed a history of Rome in Latin, and who published any considerable number of his own speeches. His chief work was the *Orīgĭnēs*, or seven books of Italian and Roman history. The title *Origines*, or "Early History," applied properly only to the first three books, which contained the story of the kings, and traced the rise of the various cities of Italy. But it was afterwards extended to the whole work, which included the history of Rome down to B.C. 151. In the narrative of his own achievements he inserted his own speeches. From early manhood he displayed great energy as an orator. More than 150 of his speeches were known to Cicero, who speaks with respect of his oratorical performances. The titles, and some fragments of eighty of his orations have survived.

In the form of maxims addressed to his son (*Præcepta ad Fīlium*) he drew a comprehensive sketch of everything which, in his opinion, was useful for a young man to know if he was to be a *vir bonus*. He also put together in verse some rules for every-day conduct (*Carmen De Mōrĭbus*). The only work of Cato which has come down to us in anything like completeness is his treatise on agriculture (*De Re Rustĭcā*), though even this we do not possess in its original shape. This was intended as a manual for the private use of one Manlius, and had reference to a particular estate belonging to him. One part is written systematically, the other is a miscellaneous collection of various rules. There is also a collection of 146 proverbs, each in a couple of hexameters, which bears the name of Cato. But this belongs to the later Empire, though it is probably not later than the end of the 4th century A.D. This little book was a well known manual all through the Middle Ages, and was widely circulated in translations.

Catreus (Gr. *Katreus*). In Greek mythology a king of Crete, the son of Mīnōs and of Pāsĭphāē. An oracle had prophesied that he would fall by the hand of one of his own children. He accordingly put his daughters, Aërŏpē and Clȳmĕnē, into the hands of Nauplius, who was to sell them into a foreign country; his son Althæmĕnēs, meanwhile, migrated to Rhodes with his sister Apēmŏsȳnē. His sister, who had been led astray by Hermēs, he killed with a blow of his foot, and slew his aged father, who had come to put into his hands the government of Crete, mistaking him for a pirate. Clymene became the wife of Nauplius, and the mother of Pălămēdēs and Œax. Aërŏpē married Atreus, and bore him two sons, Agamemnōn and Mĕnĕlāüs; but was finally thrown into the sea by her husband on account of her adultery with Thyestēs. (*See* ATREUS)

Cătullus (*Gāĭus Vălĕrĭus Catullus*). Perhaps the greatest of Roman lyric poets. He was born at Verona B.C. 87, and died about 54. He came to Rome while still young, and found himself in very good society there, being admitted to the circle of such men as Cicero, Hortensius, and Cornelius Nepos, and the poets Cinna and Calvus. He had an estate on the Lăcus Lārius (Lake of Como), and another at Tībur (Tivoli); but, if we may believe what he says about his debts and poverty, his pecuniary affairs must have been in bad order. In consequence of this he attached himself to the proprætor Gaius Memmius, on his going to Bithynia in the year 57. He gained nothing by doing so, and in the following spring returned home alone, visiting on the way the tomb of his brother, who was buried near Troy. Some of his most beautiful poems are inspired by his love for a lady whom he addresses as Lesbia, a passion which seems to have been the ruin of his life. She has been, with great probability, identified with the beautiful and gifted, but unprincipled sister of the notorious Clodius, and wife of Metellus Cĕler. Catullus was, in his eighteenth year, so overmastered by his passion for her, that he was unable, even after he had broken off all relations with her, and come to despise her, to disentangle himself.

In his intercourse with his numerous friends Catullus was bright and amiable, but unsparing in the ridicule he poured upon his enemies. He held aloof from public life, and from any active participation in politics, but none the less bitterly did he hate those whom he thought responsible for the internal decline of the Republic—themselves and all their creatures. On Cæsar, though his own father's guest, and on his dissolute favourite Mamurra, he makes violent attacks. But he is said to have apologized to Cæsar, who magnanimously forgave him.

Catullus' poems have not all survived. We still possess 116, which, with the exception of three, are included in a collection dedicated to Cornelius Nepos. The first half is taken up with minor pieces of various contents, and written in different lyric metres, especially the iambic. Then follows a series of longer poems, amongst them the wonderful lament of Attis, wonderful in spite of the repulsiveness of its subject; the epic narrative of the marriage of Peleus

and Thĕtis, and a paraphrase of Callimachus' best elegy, "The Lock of Bĕrĕnīcĕ." These are all in the Alexandrian manner. The remaining poems are short, and of different contents, but all written in elegiacs.

Catullus takes his place in the history of literature as the earliest classical metrist among the Romans. He is a complete master of all varieties of verse. More than this, he has the art of expressing every phase of feeling in the most natural and beautiful style; love, fortunate and unfortunate, sorrow for a departed brother, wanton sensuality, the tenderest friendship, the bitterest contempt, and the most burning hatred. Even his imitations of the Greek are not without an original stamp of their own.

Caupōna. *See* INNS.

Causĭa (Gr. *Kausĭa*). A flat, broad-brimmed felt hat, worn in Macedonia and by the Macedonian soldiers. When worn by persons high in society it was coloured purple ; the kings of Macedon surrounded it with the royal diadem, and thus the purple *causia* with the diadem continued to be the emblem of sovereignty in the kingdoms which arose from the empire of Alexander. The Macedonian hat was in later times adopted by fishermen and sailors at Rome, and in the imperial period was worn by the higher classes in the theatre as a protection against the sun.

Căvĕa. *See* THEATRE.

Cĕbēs (Gr. *Kĕbēs*). A Greek philosopher, the author of a school-book called *Pĭnax* or "The Picture," which was very popular, and was translated into Arabic. It is a dialogue upon an allegorical picture, representing the condition of the soul before its union with the body, and the nature of human life in general. The purport of the conversation is to prove that the foundations of happiness are development of the mind and the conscious practice of virtue. It is doubtful to which Cebes the book is to be referred, for there were two philosophers of the name. One was Cebes of Thebes, the disciple of Sōcrătēs, who wrote three philosophical dialogues, one of which bore the title *Pinax ;* the other was a Stoic of Cyzĭcus, who flourished in the 2nd century A.D.

Cĕcrops (Gr. *Kĕkrops*). One of the *aborigines* of Attica, and as such represented with a human body ending in a serpent (*see* cut). In the later story he was erroneously represented as having come to Attica from Saïs in Egypt. He was said to have been the first king of Attica, which was called after him Cecrŏpĭa. He divided the rude inhabitants into twelve communities, founded the stronghold of Athens, which was called Cecropia after him, and introduced the elements

* CECROPS.
(Vase painting at Palermo.)

of civilization, the laws of marriage and property, the earliest political arrangements, and the earliest religious services, notably those of Zeus and Athēnē.

When Poseidōn and Athene were contending for the possession of the land, Poseidon struck the rock of the acropolis with his trident, and water (or, according to another story, the horse) sprang forth; but Athene planted the first olive tree. Cecrops, on being called in to decide between them, gave judgment in favour of the goddess, as having conferred on the land the more serviceable gift.

Cecrops had four children by his wife Agraulŏs: a son Erўsichthōn, who died childless, and three daughters, Agraulŏs, Hersē, and Pandrŏsŏs. The names of the last two show them to be the deities of the fertilizing dew; and indeed the three were regarded as in the service of Athene, and as giving fruitfulness to the fields. Pandrosos was Athene's first priestess. She had a shrine of her own (*Pandrŏsēum*) in the temple of Erechtheus on the acropolis, and was invoked in times of drought with the two Attic *Horœ*, Thallō and Carpō (*see* ERECHTHEUM). In her templę stood the sacred olive which Athene had created.

Cēlænō (Gr. *Kĕlainō*). (1) *See* HARPIES. (2) *See* PLEIADES.

Cēlĕus (Gr. *Kĕlĕŏs*). A king of Eleusis, in whose home Dēmētēr, while seeking for her daughter, received an affectionate welcome and comfort while tending her newly-born son Dēmŏphŏōn. (*See* DEMETER and DEMOPHOON.)

Cella. *See* TEMPLE.

Celsus (*A. Cornēlius*). A Roman savant, eminent in several branches of knowledge, who flourished in the age of Tiberius, A.D. 14–37. He was the author of a great encyclopædic work called (it would seem) *Artĕs*, designed after the manner of Varro's *Disciplīnœ*. The work of Celsus included more than 20 books, treating of agriculture, medicine, philosophy, rhetoric, and the art of war. Of these all that remain are books 7–13, *De Mĕdĭcīnā*. This is the earliest and the most considerable work of the sort in the extant Roman literature. The material which the author has collected, partly from Greek sources, partly from his own experience, is treated in systematic order, and with a purity of style which won for Celsus the name of the Cicero of physicians.

Cēna. *See* MEALS.

Cēnācŭlum. *See* HOUSE.

Cĕnŏtăphĭum (Gr. *Kĕnŏtăphĭŏn*). *See* BURIAL.

Censōrēs (Roman). The officials whose duty it was (after 444 B.C.) to take the place of the consuls in superintending the five-yearly census. The office was one of the higher magistracies, and could only be held once by the same person. It was at first confined to the Patricians; in 351 B.C. it was thrown open to the Plebeians, and after 339 one of the censors was obliged by law to be a plebeian. On occasion of a *census*, the censors were elected soon after the accession to office of the new consuls, who presided over the assembly. They were usually chosen from the number of *consulārēs*, or persons who had been consuls. Accordingly the censorship was regarded, if not as the highest office of state, at least as the highest step in the ladder of promotion. The newly elected censors entered immediately, after due summons, upon their office. Its duration was fixed in 433 B.C. to eighteen months, but it could be extended for certain purposes. For the object of carrying out their proper duties, the census and the solemn purifications (*lustrum*) that concluded it, they had the power of summoning the people to the Campus Martius, where, since 434 B.C., they had an official residence in the *Villa Publĭca*. The tribunes had no right of *veto* as against their proceedings in taking the *census*; indeed, so far as this part of their duties was concerned, they were irresponsible, being bound only in conscience by the oath which they took on entering upon and laying down their office. Having no executive powers, they had no lictors, but only messengers (*viătōrēs*) and heralds (*præcōnēs*). Their insignia were the *sella curūlis* and a purple *toga*. The collegial character of the office was so pronounced, that if one censor died, the other abdicated. From the simple act of taking the *census* and putting up the new list of citizens, their functions were in course of time extended, so as to include a number of very important duties. Among these must be mentioned in particular a general superintendence of conduct (*rĕgĭmen mōrum*). In virtue of this they had the power of affixing a stigma on any citizen, regardless of his position, for any conceivable offence for which there was no legal punishment. Such offences were neglect of one's property, celibacy, dissolution of marriage, bad training or bad treatment of children, undue severity to slaves and clients, irregular life, abuse of power in office, impiety, perjury, and the like. The offender might be punished with degradation; that is, the censors could expel a man from the senate or *ordo equester*, or they could transfer him from a country tribe into one of the less respectable city tribes, and thus curtail his right of voting, or again they could expel him from the tribes altogether, and thus completely deprive him of the right of voting. This last penalty might be accompanied by a fine in the shape of additional taxation. The censors had also the power of issuing edicts against practices which threatened the simplicity of ancient Roman manners; for instance, against luxury. These edicts had not the force of law, but their transgression might be punished by the next censors. The effect of the censorial stigma and punishment lasted until the next *census*. The consent of both censors was required to ratify it, and it directly affected men only, not women. The censors exercised a special superintendence over the *ĕquĭtēs* and the senate. They had the *lectio senātūs*, or power of ejecting unworthy members and of passing over new candidates for the senatorial rank, as, for instance, those who had held curule offices. The *equites* had to pass singly, each leading his horse, before the censors in the forum, after the completion of the general census. An honourable dismissal was then given to the superan

nuated or the infirm; if an *equĕs* was now found, or had previously been found, unworthy of his order (as for neglecting to care for his horse), he was expelled from it. The vacant places were filled up from the number of such individuals as appeared from the general *census* to be suitable. There were certain other duties attached to the censorship, for the due performance of which they were responsible to the people, and subject to the authority of the senate and the veto of the tribunes. (1) The letting of the public domain lands and taxes to the highest bidder. (2) The acceptance of tenders from the lowest bidder for works to be paid for by the State. In both these cases the period was limited to five years. (3) Superintendence of the construction and maintenance of public buildings and grounds, temples, bridges, sewers, aqueducts, streets, monuments, and the like.

After 167 B.C. Roman citizens were freed from all taxation, and since the time of Marius the liability to military service was made general. The censorship was now a superfluous office, for its original object, the *census*, was hardly necessary. Sulla disliked the censors for their power of meddling in matters of private conduct, and accordingly in his constitution of 81 B.C. the office was, if not formally abolished, practically superseded. It was restored in 70 B.C. in the consulship of Pompey and Crassus, and continued to exist for a long time, till under the Empire it disappeared as a separate office. The emperor kept in his own hands the right of taking the census. He took over also the other functions of the censor, especially the supervision of morals, a proceeding in which he had Cæsar's example to support him. The care of public buildings, however, he committed to a special body.

Censŏrīnus. A Roman scholar of the 3rd century A.D. Besides some grammatical treatises now lost, he was the author of a short book, *De Dĭĕ Nātălī* ("On the Day of Birth"), in which he treats of the influence of the stars on the birth of men, of the various stages of life, and the different modes of reckoning time. In the course of the work he gives a number of valuable historical and chronological notices.

Census. After the establishment of the constitution of Servius Tullius the number of Roman citizens was ascertained every five years (though not always with perfect regularity) to determine their legal liability to the payment of taxes and to military service. This process was called *census*. The census was originally taken by the kings; after the expulsion of the kings by the consuls; after 444 B.C. by special officers called *censors* (*see* CENSORES). The censors took the auspices on the night preceding the census; on the next day their herald summoned the people to the Campus Martius, where they had an official residence in the *villa publica*. Each tribe appeared successively before them, and its citizens were summoned individually according to the existing register. Each had to state on oath his age, his own name, those of his father, his wife, his children, his abode, and the amount of his property. The facts were embodied in lists by the censors' assistants. The census of the provinces was sent in by the provincial governors. There was a special commission for numbering the armies outside the Italian frontier. The censors, in putting up the new lists, took into consideration not only a man's property but his moral conduct (*see* CENSORES, p. 122*a*). The census was concluded with the solemn ceremony of reviewing the newly constituted army (*lustrum*). (*See* LUSTRUM.) The republican census continued to exist under the early Empire, but the last *lustrum* was held by Vespasian and Titus in A.D. 74. The provincial census, introduced by Augustus and maintained during the whole imperial period, had nothing to do with the Roman census, being only a means of ascertaining the taxable capacities of the provinces.

Centauri (Gr. *Kentauroi*). Homer and the older mythology represent the Centaurs are a rude, wild race, fond of wine and women, dwelling in the mountains of Thessaly, especially on Pēlĭŏn and Œta. In Homer they are spoken of as shaggy animals, living in the mountains. It was, perhaps, not until the 5th century B.C. that they were represented in the double shape now familiar to us. Originally the Centaur was conceived as a being with the body of a man standing on a horse's legs; but in later times the human body was represented as rising up in the front of a horse's body and four legs (*see* cut). According to one version of the current legend they were the offspring of Nĕphĕlē and Ixīŏn; according to another, the son of this pair, Kentaurŏs, begat them upon mares (*see* IXION). The story of their contest with the Lăpĭthæ at the wedding of Pĭrĭthŏüs, born of their drunkenness and lust, is as early as Homer [Iliad i 268, Odyssey xxi 295 foll.] (*See* PIRITHOUS.) In Homer Nestor, and in the later story Thēseus, are represented as taking part in

it. It was a favourite subject with poets and artists. The Centaurs were driven from Pelion by Pirithous and the Lapithæ, and even the wise Chirōn was forced to gc

CENTAUR AND EROS.
(Paris, Louvre.)

with them (*see* CHIRON). Artists were always fond of treating the fabulous combats of the Centaurs and the heroes of old; but in later times the Centaurs appear in a different light. They form part of the following of Dionȳsus, moving peaceably in his festal train among satyrs, nymphs, and Bacchants, drawing the victorious car of the god and his queen Arĭadnē, playing on the lyre, and guided by gods of love. The forms of women and children were sometimes represented in the shape of Centaurs, and used in various ways by artists for their smaller pictures. For the *Centauro-Trītōnĕs* or *Ichthyŏcentaurī* (" Fish-Centaurs ") *see* TRITON.

Centō. Properly a patchwork garment. In its secondary meaning the word was applied to a poem composed of verses or parts of verses by well-known poets put together at pleasure, so as to make a new meaning. Homer and Vergil were chiefly used for the purpose. The Christians were fond of making religious poems in this way, hoping thus to give a nobler colouring to the pagan poetry. For instance, we have a Homeric *cento* of 2,343 verses on the Life of Christ, ascribed to Athēnaïs, who, under the title of Eudŏcĭa, was consort of the emperor Theodosius II. Another instance is a poem known as the *Christus pătĭens,* or "the suffering Christ," consisting of 2,610 verses from Eurīpĭdēs. Instances of Vergilian centos are the sacred history of Proba Faltōnĭa (towards the end of the 4th century A.D.), and a tragedy entitled *Mĕdĕa* by Hosidius Geta.

Centumvĭri ("*The hundred men*"). This was the title of the single jury for the trial of civil causes at Rome. In the republican age it consisted of 105 members, chosen from the tribes (three from each of the thirty-five). Under the Empire its number was increased to 180. It was divided into four sections (*consĭlĭa*), and exercised its jurisdiction in the name of the people, partly in sections, partly as a single *collēgium.* It had to deal with questions of property, and particularly with those of inheritance. In the later years of the Republic it was presided over by men of quæstorian rank; but from the time of Augustus by a commission of ten (*decem viri lĭtĭbŭs iudicandĭs*). The pleadings were oral, and the proceedings public. In earlier times they took place in the forum; under the Empire in a *basilica.* In the imperial age the centumviral courts were the only sphere in which an ambitious orator or lawyer could win distinction. The last mention of them is in 395 A.D. The peculiar symbol of the centumviral court was a *hasta* or spear (*see* HASTA).

Centŭrĭa ("a hundred"). In the Roman army of the regal period the *centuria* was a division of 100 cavalry soldiers. In the half-military constitution of Servius Tullius the word was applied to one of the 193 divisions into which the king divided the patrician and plebeian *pŏpŭlus* according to their property, with the view of allotting to each citizen his due share of civil rights and duties. Of the 193 *centuriæ* 18 consisted of cavalry soldiers (100 each) belonging to the richest class of citizens. The next 170, whose members were to serve as infantry, fell into five classes. The first 80 included those citizens whose property amounted to at least 100,000 *assēs.* The second, third, and fourth, containing each 20 centuries, represented a minimum property of 75,000, 50,000, and 25,000 *asses* respectively. The fifth, with 30 centuries, represented a minimum of 12,500, 11,000 or 10,000 *asses.* These 170 centuriæ were again divided into 85 centuries of *iūnĭōrēs,* or men from 18–45 years of age, who served in the field; and 85 of *sĕnĭōrēs,* citizens from 46 to 60 years

of age, who served on garrison duty in the city. Besides these there were 2 centuries of mechanics (*fabrum*), and 2 of musicians (*cornĭcĭnum,* and *tŭbĭcĭnum*).

The *centuriæ fabrum* were enrolled between the first and second class: the *centuriæ cornicinum* and *tubicinum* between the fourth and fifth. The 193d *centuria* consisted of citizens whose income fell below the minimum standard of the rest, and who were called *prōlĕtārii* or *căpĭtĕ censi.* These last had originally no function beyond that of voting at the assembly of the citizens in the *comĭtĭa centuriāta,* and were not liable to military service. But in later times the richer among them were admitted to serve in the army. A fresh division of *centuriæ* was made at every census. The military equipment of each citizen, and his position in battle array, was determined by the class to which his property entitled him to belong. (*See* LEGĬON.) On the political position of the different classes *see* COMITIA (2).

In military parlance *centuria* meant one of the 60 divisions of the legion, each of which was commanded by a *centurio.*

Centuriāta Comĭtĭa. *See* COMITIA (2).

Centŭrĭōnēs. The captains of the 60 centuries of the Roman legion. They carried a staff of vinewood as their badge of office. In the republican age they were appointed, on the application of the legion, by the military tribunes on the commission of the consuls. There were various degrees of rank among the centurions according as they belonged to the three divisions of the *trĭārii, princĭpēs,* and *hastāti,* and led the first or second *centuria* of one of the 30 *manĭpŭli.*

The centurion of the first *centuria* of a *manipulus* led his *manipulus* himself, and as *centurio prior* ranked above the leader of the second *centuria,* or *centurio postĕrĭor.* The highest rank belonged to the first *centurio* of the first *manipulus* of the triarii, the *prīmĭpīlus* or *prīmus pīlus,* who was admitted to the council of war. The method of promotion was as follows: The *centuriones* had to work first through the 30 lower *centuriæ* of the 30 *manipuli* of the *hastati, principes,* and *triarii,* and then through the 30 upper *centuriæ* up to the *primipilus.*

After the end of the Republic and under the Empire the legion was usually divided into 10 cohorts ranked one above the other, each cohort consisting of three *manipuli* or six *centuriæ.* The division into *prĭōrēs* and *posterĭōrēs,* and into *triarii, principes* and *hastati* still remained, but only for the centurions and within the cohort, which accordingly always included a *prior* and *posterior* of the three ranks in question. The method of promotion, which was perhaps not regularly fixed until the time of the standing armies of the Empire, seems to have been the old one, the centurions passing up by a lower stage through all 10 cohorts, and the higher stage always beginning in the tenth. The first centurion of each cohort probably led it, and was admitted to the council of war. The promotion usually ceased with the advancement to the rank of *primipilus*. If a centurion who had reached this point did not choose to retire, he was employed on special services, as commandant of a fortress for instance. Under the Empire, however, exceptional cases occurred of promotion to higher posts.

Cĕphălus (Gr. *Kĕphălŏs*). In Greek mythology the son of Hermēs and Hersē, the daughter of Cĕcrops king of Athens. According to another story he was son of Deïōn of Phōcis and Diŏmēdē, and migrated from Phocis to Thŏrĭcus in Attica. He was married to Prōcris, the daughter of Erechtheus, and lived with her in the closest affection. But while hunting one day in the mountains, he was carried away for his beauty by Eōs, the goddess of the dawn. To estrange his wife's heart from him, Eos sent him to her in the form of a stranger, who, by the offer of splendid presents, succeeded in making her waver in her fidelity. Cephalus revealed himself, and Procris, in shame, fled to Crete, where she lived with Artĕmis as a huntress. Artemis (or, according to another story, Mīnōs), gave her a dog as swift as the wind, and a spear that never missed its aim. On returning to Attica she met Cephalus hunting. He failed to recognise her, and offered his love if she would give him her dog and her spear. She then revealed herself, and, the balance of offence being thus redressed, the lovers were reconciled and returned to their old happy life together. But Procris at last fell a victim to her jealousy. When Cephalus went out hunting, he used often to call on *Aura*, or the breeze, to cool his heat. Procris was told of this, and, supposing *Aura* to be some nymph, hid herself in a thicket to watch him. Hearing a rustling near him, and thinking a wild beast was in the thicket, Cephalus took aim with the unerring spear which Procris had given him, and slew his wife. For this murder he was banished, and fled to Bœotia. Here he assisted Amphĭtrўōn in the chase

of the Taumessian fox; and both his dog and the hunted animal were turned to stone by Zeus. Subsequently he joined Amphitryon in his expedition against the Tēlĕbŏæ, and, according to one account, became sovereign of the Cephallenians. According to another he put an end to his life by leaping from the promontory of Leucātē, on which he had founded a temple to Apollo.

Cēpheus (Gr. *Kēpheus*). (1) The son of Bēlus, king of Æthiopia, husband of Cassiopēa and father of Andrŏmĕda. (*See* ANDROMEDA.)

(2) Son of Atĕus, king of Tĕgĕa and brother of Augē (*see* TELEPHUS). He fell with his twenty sons when fighting on the side of Hērăclēs against Hippŏcŏōn of Sparta.

Cēphĭsŏdŏtus (Gr. *Kēphĭsŏdŏtŏs*). A Greek artist, born at Athens, and connected with the family of Praxĭtĕlēs. He flourished towards the end of the 4th century B.C. The celebrated statue now in the Glyptothek at Munich, representing Eirēnē with the infant Plutus in her arms, is probably a copy of a work by Cephisodotus (*see* cut, under EIRENE). There was another Cephisodotus, a contemporary of his, and the son of Praxiteles, who was likewise in high repute as a sculptor.

Cēr (Gr. *Kēr*). In Greek mythology, a goddess of death, especially of violent death in battle. In Hesiod she is the daughter of Nyx (night), and sister of Mŏrŏs (the doom of death), Hypnŏs (sleep), and Dreams. The poets commonly speak of several Kērĕs, goddesses of different kinds of death. Homer and Hesiod represent them as clothed in garments stained by human blood, and dragging the dead and wounded about on the field of battle. Every man has his allotted Doom, which overtakes him at the appointed time. Achilles alone has two, with the power to choose freely between them. In later times the Keres are represented generally as powers of destruction, and as associated with the Erīnўĕs, goddesses of revenge and retribution.

Cerbĕrus (Gr. *Kerbĕrŏs*). In Greek mythology, the three-headed dog, with hair of snakes, son of Typhāon and Echidna, who watches the entrance of the lower world. He gives a friendly greeting to all who enter, but if any one attempts to go out, he seizes him and holds him fast. When Hērăclēs, at the command of Eurystheus, brought him from below to the upper world, the poisonous aconite sprang up from the foam of his mouth. (*See the cuts to the article* HADES.)

Cercis (Gr. *Kerkĭs*). *See* THEATRE.

Cercўŏn (Gr. *Kerkўŏn*). In Greek mythology the son of Poseidōn, and father of Alŏpē, who lived at Eleusis, and compelled all passers-by to wrestle with him. He was conquered and slain by the young Thēseus, who gave the kingdom of Eleusis to his grandson, Hippothŏōn. (*See* ALOPE, and THESEUS.)

Cĕrĕālĭa. *See* CERES.

Cĕrēs. An old Italian goddess of agriculture. The Ceres who was worshipped at Rome is, however, the same as the Greek Dēmētēr. Her *cultus* was introduced under the Italian name at the same time as that of Dionўsus and Persĕphŏnē, who in the same way received the Italian names of Līber and Lībĕra. It was in 496 B.C., on the occasion of a drought, that the Sibylline books ordered the introduction of the worship of the three deities. This worship was so decidedly Greek that the temple dedicated on a spur of the Aventine in 490 B.C., over the entrance to the Circus, was built in Greek style and by Greek artists; and the service of the goddess, founded on the Greek fable of Demeter and Persephone, was performed in the Greek tongue by Italian women of Greek extraction. The worshippers of the goddess were almost exclusively plebeian. Her temple was placed under the care of the plebeian ædiles who (as overseers of the corn market) had their official residence in or near it. The fines which they imposed went to the shrine of Ceres, so did the property of persons who had offended against them, or against the tribunes of the *plebs*. Just as the Patricians entertained each other with mutual hospitalities at the Megalesian games (April 4–10), so did the Plebeians at the *Cĕrĕālĭa*, or games introduced at the founding of the temple of Ceres. Those held in later times were given by the ædiles from the 12th–19th April, and another festival to Ceres, held in August, was established before the Second Punic War. This was celebrated by women in honour of the reunion of Ceres and Proserpīna. After fasting for nine days, the women, clothed in white, and adorned with crowns of ripe ears of corn, offered to the goddess the firstfruits of the harvest. After 191 B.C. a fast (*iēiūnĭum Cĕrĕris*) was introduced by command of the Sibylline books. This was originally observed every four years, but in later times was kept annually on the 4th of October. The native Italian worship of Ceres was probably maintained in its purest form in the country. Here the country offered Ceres a sow (*porca præcīdānĕa*) before the beginning of the harvest, and dedicated to her the first cuttings of the corn (*præmĕtĭum*). (*See* DEMETER.)

Cĕryx (Gr. *Kēryx*). The son of Pandrŏsŏs and Hermēs, and the ancestor of the Kērўcēs of Eleusis (*see* CERYX, 2). Hersē (or Ersē) was mother, by Hermes, of the beautiful Cĕphălus (*see* CEPHALUS). She had a special festival in her honour, the *Arrhĕphŏrĭa* (*see* ARREPHORIA). Agraulŏs, mother of Alcippē, by Arēs, was said in one story to have thrown herself down from the citadel during a war to save her country. It was, accordingly, in her precincts on the Acropolis that the young men of Athens, when they received their spears and shields, took their oath to defend their country to the death, invoking her name with those of the Chărĭtēs Auxō and Hēgĕmŏnē. According to another story, Athene entrusted Erichthŏnius to the keeping of the three sisters in a closed chest, with the command that they were not to open it. Agraulos and Herse disobeyed, went mad, and threw themselves down from the rocks of the citadel.

Cĕryx (Gr. *Kēryx*). (1) The Greek name for a herald. In the Homeric age the *keryx* is the official servant of the king, who manages his household, attends at his meals, assists at sacrifices, summons the assemblies and maintains order and tranquillity in them. He also acts as ambassador to the enemy, and, as such, his person is, both in ancient times and ever afterwards, inviolable. In historical times the herald, besides the part which he plays in the political transactions between different cities, appears in the service of the gods. He announces the sacred truce observed at the public festivals, commands silence at religious services, dictates the forms of prayer to the assembled community, and performs many services in temples where there is only a small staff of attendants, especially by assisting in the sacrifices. He has also a great deal to do in the service of the State. At Athens, in particular, one or more heralds were attached to the various officials and to the government boards. It was also the herald's business to summon the council and the public assembly, to recite the prayer before the commencement of business, to command silence, to call upon the speaker, to summon the parties in a lawsuit to attend the court, and to act in general as a public crier. As a rule, the heralds were taken from the poor, and the lower orders. At Athens they had a salary, and took their meals at the public expense, with the officials to whom they were attached. On the herald's staff (Gr. *kērykeiŏn*, Lat. *cădūcĕus*), see HERMES.

(2) In Greek mythology, the son of Hermes, the herald of the gods, by Agraulos the daughter of Cecrops, or (according to another story) of Eumolpus, and ancestor of the Eleusinian family of the Kērȳkĕs, one of whose members always performed the functions of a herald at the Eleusinian mysteries.

Cetra. The light shield of the Roman auxiliaries. (*See* SHIELD.)

Cēyx (Gr. *Kēyx*). In Greek mythology, (1) A king of Trāchis, the friend and nephew of Hērăclēs. (*See* HERACLES.)

(2) The son of Hĕŏsphŏrŏs or the Morning-Star, and the nymph Phĭlōnis ; the husband of Alkȳŏnē or Halkȳŏnē, daughter of the Thessalian Æŏlus. The pair were arrogant enough to style themselves Zeus and Hēra, and were accordingly changed respectively by Zeus into the birds of the same name, a diver and a kingfisher. Another story confused Ceyx with the king of Trachis, and dwelt on the tender love of the pair for each other. Ceyx is drowned at sea, and Alcyone finds his body cast up upon his native shore. The gods take pity on her grief, and change the husband and wife into kingfishers (*alcyŏnĕs*), whose affection for each other in the pairing season was proverbial. Zeus, or, according to another story, the wind-god Æŏlus (sometimes represented as the father of Alcyone), bids the winds rest for seven days before and after the shortest day, to allow the kingfishers to sit on their eggs by the sea. Hence the expression "halcyon days," applied to this season. Dædălĭŏn, the brother of Ceyx, was turned into a hawk, when he threw himself from a rock on Parnassus in grief at the death of his daughter Chĭŏnē.

Chalcūs (Gr. *Chalkous*). See COINAGE

Chaldæi. *See* ASTROLOGY.

Chăŏs. According to Hesiod, the yawning, unfathomable abyss which was the first of all existing things. From Chaos arose Gaia (Earth), Tartărus (Hell), and Erōs (Love). Chaos bore Erĕbus and Night; from their union sprang *Æthĕr* and *Hēmĕra* (Sky and Day). The conception of Chaos as the confused mass out of which, in the beginning, the separate forms of things arose, is erroneous, and belongs to a later period.

Chærēmŏn. A Greek tragedian, who flourished at Athens about 380 B.C. His style was smooth and picturesque, but his plays were artificial, and better adapted for reading than for performance. A few fragments of them remain, which show some imaginative power.

Chairs and **Seats.** Of these there was a great variety in the ancient world, some with, and some without, supports for the head and back. The latter sort (Gr. *diphrŏs*, Lat. *sella*) were mostly low, and

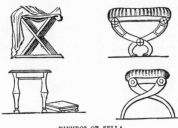

DIPHROS OR SELLA.
(From Greek Vases.)

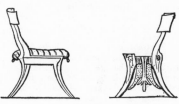

CHAIRS.
(From Greek Vases.)

THRONE.
(Zeus, Coin of Elis.)

were supported sometimes on four upright legs, sometimes on feet arranged and shaped like a sawing stool (*see* cuts). The seat being made of leather straps, the chair could, in the latter case, be folded up and carried by a servant. A chair of this kind, made of ivory, was one of the *insignia* of the curule magistrates at Rome (*see* SELLA CURULIS). The official chair of the Roman magistrates was always without a back. Stools without backs were also used by mechanics, soldiers, and boys at school. The backed chairs ordinarily in use much resembled our modern chairs. They generally had a sloping back, sometimes arched out in the centre (*see* cuts). Chairs of this form were made for women and invalids; and the *cathedra* or professor's chair was of the same description. The Greek *thrŏnŏs* and the Latin *sŏlium* were seats of honour. They were lofty, and had footstools accordingly; the back was high and straight, the legs were upright, and there were arms at the sides. The Roman *pater familias*, when giving his clients their morning audience, sat in a *solium*. Seats were not always stuffed, but cushions were put on them, and coverings on the backs. Chairs were made of metal and ivory, as well as of wood.

Chăres. (1) *Chares of Mĭtÿlēnē*. A Greek historian, court-marshal of Alexander the Great. He was the author of a comprehensive work, containing at least ten books, upon the life, chiefly the domestic life, of this monarch. This history had the reputation of being trustworthy and interesting. Only a few fragments of it remain.

(2) *Chares of Lindŏs in Rhodes*. A Greek artist, a pupil of Lysippus. In 278 B.C. he produced the largest statue known in antiquity, the colossal image of the sun, 280 feet high, placed at the entrance of the harbour of Rhodes, and generally known as the Colossus of Rhodes. This was destroyed by an earthquake as early as 222 B.C. The thumbs were thicker than the average span of a man's hand, the fingers larger than many ordinary statues.

Chariots. (1) *Greek*. The racing chariots in use at the public games require especial mention. These preserved the form of the war-chariots of the heroic age, made to carry the warrior and his charioteer (*see* cut). They were also used at Rome in the games of the circus and in festal processions. The chariot had two low wheels, usually with four spokes each. On these rested the car (*see* cut), elliptically shaped in front, protected by a board rising to the knees of the driver in front, and sloping off to the rear, where the chariot was open. In the triumphal chariot of the Romans this board was breast high. At the end of the pole was fastened the yoke. This consisted either of a simple arched piece of wood, or of two rings connected

by a cross-beam, and was fixed on the necks of the two horses or mules which were next to the pole. Sometimes a third and fourth horse were attached by means of a rope passing from the neckband to a rail forming the top of the front board. It was indeed the universal custom in antiquity to make the two principal horses draw by the yoke. It was only the extra horses that drew by traces, and this always at the side of the others, never in front of them. Carriages in ordinary use sometimes had two, sometimes four wheels. They were used mostly for carrying burdens. Only women, as a rule, travelled in carriages; men usually either walked or rode, thinking it affectation to drive except in case of old age or illness. It was, however, customary at Athens and elsewhere for a bride to be

WAR-CHARIOT.
(Vase painting.)

drawn to the house of the bridegroom in a carriage drawn by mules or oxen, sitting between the bridegroom and his friend.

(2) *Rome*. Among the Romans we find a great variety of carriages in use, for transport, travelling and state occasions. This variety is apparent in the number of different names, which cannot however always be referred with certainty to the forms of carriage presented in works of art. The various kinds of travelling-carriages must have been borrowed from abroad, as is proved by their names. The *reda*, for instance, came from Gaul. This was a four-wheeled travelling carriage for family and baggage, or for company. The *cĭsĭum* and *essēdum* were light two-wheeled conveyances. The *essedum* was probably a Gaulish war-chariot, as the *covinnus* was a British war-chariot. The four-wheeled *pilentum* came also from Gaul. It was drawn by

mules and generally used by the servants and suite. The *pilentum* and *covinnus* were used on state occasions. These were both covered carriages, the *pilenta* having four wheels, the *covinnus* two. The *covinnus* often mentioned in the literature of the empire had four wheels, and resembled a *reda*. We must also mention the *thensa*, a chariot adorned with gold and ivory, in which the images of the gods and deified emperors, lying upon a cushion on a frame or a litter, were borne to the circus through the streets and the Forum at the Circensian games. The use of carriages for travelling purposes was allowed in Roman society, but there was very little driving in Rome itself. Married ladies were from very old times permitted the use of *carpenta* in the city, and to drive in *pilenta* to sacrifices and games. The privilege was said to have been granted them in acknowledgment of their contributions to the ransom of the city after it was burnt by the Gauls, B.C. 390. In 45 B.C. Cæsar finally restricted their privilege to the public sacrifices to which the Vestal Virgins, the married ladies, and the *flamens* also drove in *pilenta*.

Men were strictly forbidden to drive in the city, except in two cases. A general at his triumph wås borne to the circus in a gilded chariot drawn by four horses and in the procession which preceded the games of the circus, the magistrates rode in chariots drawn by two horses. Six horses were sometimes allowed to the emperor. Throughout the cities of the empire driving in the streets was generally forbidden in the first two centuries after Christ. At length, in the 3rd century, the use of a carriage was allowed as a privilege to the senators and high imperial officials, who rode in *carrūcæ* plated with silver. In later times private citizens were permitted to drive in these coaches. Wagons (the general name of which was *plaustra*) were, with certain exceptions, forbidden by a law of Cæsar to ply between sunrise and the tenth hour (4 in the afternoon), in view of the immense traffic in the streets. Some wagons had two, some four wheels. They were generally drawn by oxen, asses, or mules. If they were meant to carry very heavy loads, the wheels would be made of one piece and without spokes.

Chărisius (*Flāvĭus Sōsĭpăter*). A writer on Latin grammar, who flourished towards the end of the 4th century A.D. His *Ars Grammătĭca*, a work in five books, imperfectly preserved, is a compilation, made without much intelligence, from the works of older scholars. Its value is derived from the numerous quotations it preserves from the older Latin literature.

Chărĭtĕs or **Graces**. Goddesses of grace, and of everything which lends charm and beauty to nature and human life. According to Hesiod they are the offspring of Zeus and the daughter of Ocĕănus and Eurynŏmē. Their names are Euphrŏsynē (joy), Thălīa (bloom), and Aglāïa (brilliance). Aglaia is the youngest, and the wife of Hephæstus. For the inspiration of the Graces was deemed as necessary to the plastic arts, as to music, poetry, science, eloquence, beauty, and enjoyment of life. Accordingly the Graces are intimate with the Muses, with whom they live together on Olympia. They are associated, too, with Apollo, Athēnē, Hermēs, and Peithō, but especially with Erōs, Aphrodītē, and Dionysus. Bright and blithe-hearted, they were also called the daughters of the Sun and of Ægle ("Sheen"). They were worshipped in conjunction with Aphrodite and Dionysus at Orchŏmĕnus in Bœotia, where their shrine was accounted the oldest in the place, and where their most ancient images were found in the shape of stones said to have fallen from heaven. It was here that the feast of the *Charitēsia* was held in their honour, with musical contests. At Sparta, as at Athens, two Charites only were worshipped, Clēta (*Kleta*) or Sound, and Phaënna or Light; at Athens their names were Auxō (Increase), and Hēgĕmŏnē (Queen). It was by these goddesses, and by Agraulŏs, daughter of Cecrops, that the Athenian youths, on receiving their spear and shield, swore faith to their country. The Charites were represented in the form of beautiful maidens, the three being generally linked hand in hand. In the older representations they are clothed; in the later they are loosely clad or entirely undraped.

Chărĭtōn, of Aphrodīsĭăs in Phrygia. The assumed name of the author of a Greek romance in eight books, on the fortunes of Chærĕās and Callirrhŏë. He was a Christian, probably of the 4th century A.D. His treatment of the story is simple, but full of life and movement; the narrative is easy and flowing, the language on the whole natural and unadorned.

Chărōn. (1) In Greek mythology, the son of Erĕbus and the Styx; the dark and grisly old man in a black sailor's cloak, who ferries the souls of the dead across the river of the lower world for the fare of an *ŏbŏlŏs*.

The coin was put into the mouth of the dead for this purpose. (*See* FUTURE LIFE.)

(2) A Greek historian. (*See* LOGOGRAPHI.)

Charybdis. See SCYLLA.

Cheiromantïa. See MANTIKE.

Cheirotönïa. A show of hands. The usual method of voting in Greek popular assemblies, whether at political meetings or elections. In elections, the *cheirotonia* was contrasted with the drawing of lots, which was usual since the time of Cleisthênês in the case of many offices.

Chelïdönis. See AËDON.

Chïliarchus. The leader of a division of 1,000 men. (*See* PHALANX.)

Chïmæra. A fire-breathing monster of Lycia, destroyed by Bellëröphön. According to Homer the Chimæra was of divine origin. In front it was a lion, behind it was a serpent, and in the middle a goat, and was brought up by Amisodarus as a plague for many men. Hesiod calls her the daughter of Typhâon and Echidna, and by Orthös the mother of the Sphinx and the Nemean lion. He describes her as large, swift-footed, strong, with the heads of a lion, and goat, and a serpent. In numerous works of art, as in statues, and the coins of Corinth, Sïcÿön, and other cities, the Chimæra is generally represented as a lion, with a goat's head in the middle of its back, and tail ending in a snake's head. The bronze Chimæra of Arretium, now in Florence, is a very celebrated work of art. Even in antiquity the Chimæra was regarded as a symbol of the volcanic character of the Lycian soil.

Chïönê. (1) Daughter of Börëäs and Oreithyia, mother of Eumolpus by Poseidön. (*See* EUMOLPUS.)

(2) Daughter of Dædälïön, mother of Philammön by Apollo, and of Autölÿcus by Hermês. She was slain by Artëmis for venturing to compare her own beauty with that of the goddess. (*See* DÆDALION.)

Chïrön. A Centaur, son of Crönus and the Ocean nymph Phïlÿra. By the Naiad nymph Chariclö he was father of Endeïs, wife of Æacus, the mother of Pêleus and Tëlämön, and grandmother of Achilles and Ajax. He is represented in the fable as wise and just, while the other Centaurs are wild and uncivilized. He is the master and instructor of the most celebrated heroes of Greek story, as Actæön, Jäsön, Castor, Polydeucês, Achilles, and Asclêpius, to whom he teaches the art of healing. Driven by the Läpïthæ from his former dwelling-place, a cave at the top of Pêlïön, he took up his abode on

the promontory of Mälëa in Lacönïa. Here he was wounded accidentally with a poisoned arrow by his friend Hëräclês, who was pursuing the flying Centaurs (*see* PHOLUS). To escape from the dreadful pain of the wound, he renounced his immortality in favour of Promêtheus, and was set by Zeus among the stars as the constellation *Archer*.

Chïtön. The undershirt worn by the Greeks, corresponding to the Roman *tünïca*. Two kinds were commonly distinguished, the short Doric *chiton* of wool (fig. 1) and

(1) SOLDIER IN A
DORIC CHITON.
(Bas-relief from Müller's
Denkm. I. taf. xxix.)

(2) DOUBLE CHITON.
(Bronze statuette from Herculaneum, in Naples Museum.)

the long Ionic tunic of linen, which was worn at Athens down to the time of Pericles. The *chiton* consisted of an oblong piece of cloth, wrapped round the body. One arm was passed through a hole in the closed side, while the two corners were joined together by a clasp on the shoulder. The garment, which thus hung down open on one side, was fastened together at both corners, or sometimes sewn together below the hips. At the waist it was confined by a belt. In course of time short sleeves were added to the arm-holes. Sleeves reaching to the wrist were by the Greeks regarded as effeminate; but they were worn by the Phrygians and Medians, and often appear on monuments as part of the dress of Orientals. The *chiton* worn on both shoulders was distinctive of free men. Workmen, sailors and slaves wore a *chiton* with one armhole only for the left arm, while the right arm and right breast were left uncovered. This was called the *exōmĭs*. Country folk wore a *chiton* of skins. The *chiton* worn by Doric ladies was a long garment like a chemise, slit upwards on both sides from the hips and held together by clasps at the shoulders. In the case of young girls it was fastened up so high that it hardly reached the knees. For the rest of Greece the usual dress of a lady was the Ionian *chiton*, long, broad, reaching to the feet in many folds, and only drawn up a short distance by the girdle. From this long ladies' *chiton* was developed the double *chiton*, a very long and broad piece of cloth, folded together round the body, and fastened with clasps at the shoulders. It was folded double round the breast and back, and was open or fastened with clasps on the right side, and fell simply down to the feet. Sometimes the open side was sewn together from the girdle to the lower edge. For the garments worn over the *chiton see* HIMATION, CHLAMYS, and TRI-BON.

Chlămỹs. An outer garment introduced at Athens from Thessaly and Macedonia. It consisted of an oblong piece of woollen cloth thrown over the left shoulder, the open ends being fastened with clasps on the right shoulder. The *chlamys* was worn by *ĕphēbĭ ;* it was also the uniform of general officers, like the *palū-dāmentum*, as it was called in later times among the Romans. It commonly served as an overcoat for travelling, hunting, and military service. (*See* cut.)

CHLAMYS.
(Statue of Phocion,
Vatican, Rome.)

Chlŏrĭs. (1) The personification of the spring season, and goddess of flowers, the wife of Zĕphỹrus, mother of Carpŏs ("Fruit"). She was identified by the Romans with Flora. (*See* FLORA.)

(2) Daughter of Amphīŏn of Orchŏmĕnus, wife of Nēleus, mother of Nestor and Periclỹmĕnus. (*See* PERICLYMENUS.)

Chœrĭlus. (1) An Athenian dramatist, one of the oldest Attic tragedians, who appeared as a writer as early as 520 B.C. He was a rival of Pratīnas, Phrỹnĭchus and Æschylus. His favourite line seems to have been the satyric drama, in which he was long a popular writer.

(2) A Greek epic poet, born in Samos about 470 B.C., a friend of Herodotus, and afterwards of the Spartan Lysander. He lived first at Athens and afterwards at the court of King Archĕlāŭs of Macedonia, where he was treated with great consideration, and died about 400 B.C. He was the first epic poet who, feeling that the old mythology was exhausted, ventured to treat a historical subject of immediate interest, the Persian wars, in an epic entitled *Persēïs*. According to one account the poem was read in the schools with Homer. The few fragments that remain show that it did not lack talent and merit; but little regard was paid to it by posterity.

(3) *Chœrĭlus of Iāsŏs in Caria.* This Chœrilus was also an epic poet, who accompanied Alexander the Great. Alexander promised him a gold piece for every good verse he wrote in celebration of his achievements, but declared that he would rather be the Thersītēs of Homer than the Achilles of Chœrilus.

Chŏes. *See* DIONYSIA.

Chŏrus. The word *chŏrŏs* in Greek meant a number of persons who performed songs and dances at religious festivals. When the drama at Athens was developed from the dithyrambic choruses, the chorus was retained as the chief element in the Dionysiac festival. (*See* TRAGEDY.) With the old dramatists the choral songs and dances much preponderated over the action proper. As the form of the drama developed, the sphere of the chorus was gradually limited, so that it took the comparatively subordinate position which it occupies in the extant tragedies and comedies. The function of the chorus represented by its leader was to act as an ideal public, more or less connected with the *drāmātis persōnæ*. It might consist of old men and women or of maidens. It took an interest in the occurrences of the drama, watched the action with quiet sympathy, and sometimes interfered, if not to act, at least to advise, comfort, exhort, or give warning. At the critical points of the action, as we should say in the *entr'actes*, it performed long lyrical pieces with suitable action of dance and gesture. In the better times of the drama these songs stood in close connexion with the action; but even in Eurīpĭdēs this connexion is sometimes loose, and with the later tragedians, after the time of Agăthōn, the choral performance sank to a mere *intermezzo*. The style of the chorus was distinguished from that of the dialogue partly by its complex lyrical form, partly by its language, in which it adopted a mixture of Attic and Doric forms. The proper place of the chorus was on the *orchĕstra*, on different parts of which, after a solemn march, it remained until the end of the piece drawn up, while standing, in a square. During the action it seldom left the orchestra to re-appear, and it was quite exceptional for it to appear on the stage. As the performance went on the chorus would change its place on the orchestra; as the piece required it would divide into semi-choruses and perform a variety of artistic movements and dances. The name of *Emmeleia* was given to the tragic dance, which, though not lacking animation, had a solemn and measured character. The comedy had its burlesque and often indecent performance called *Cordax*; the satyric drama its *Sicinnis*, representing the wanton movements of satyrs. The songs of the choruses, too, had their special names. The first ode performed by the entire body was called *părŏdŏs*; the pieces intervening between the parts of the play, *stăsĭma*; the songs of mourning, in which the chorus took part with the actors, *commoi*. The number of the members (*choreutai*) was, in tragedies, originally twelve, and after Sophocles fifteen. This was probably the number allowed in the satyric drama; the chorus in the Old Comedy numbered twenty-four.

The business of getting the members of the chorus together, paying them, maintaining them during the time of practice, and generally equipping them for performance, was regarded as a *Līturgia*, or public service, and devolved on a wealthy private citizen called a *Chŏrēgus*, to whom it was a matter of considerable trouble and expense. We know from individual instances that the cost of tragic chorus might run up to 30 minæ (about £100), of a comic chorus to 16 minæ (about £53). If victorious, the *Chŏrēgus* received a crown and a finely wrought tripod. This he either dedicated, with an inscription, to some deity as a memorial of his triumph, or set up on a marble structure built for the purpose in the form of a temple, in a street named the Street of Tripods, from the number of these monuments which were erected there. One of these memorials, put up by a certain

Lysicrătēs in 335 B.C., still remains. (*See* LYSICRATES.) After the Peloponnesian war the prosperity of Athens declined so much that it was often difficult to find a sufficient number of *choregi* to supply the festivals. The State therefore had to take the business upon itself. But many choruses came to an end altogether. This was the case with the comic chorus in the later years of Aristophanes; and the poets of the Middle and New Comedy accordingly dropped the chorus. This explains the fact that there is no chorus in the Roman comedy, which is an imitation of the New Comedy of the Greeks. In their tragedies, however, imitated from Greek originals, the Romans retained the chorus, which, as the Roman theatre had no *orchestra*, was placed on the stage, and as a rule performed between the acts, but sometimes during the performance as well.

Chŏrēgus, Chŏreutæ. *See* CHORUS.

Chŏrizontĕs. *See* HOMER.

Chrēsmŏlŏgi. *See* MANTIKE.

Chrysăōr. Son of Poseidōn and Mĕdūsa, brother of Pēgăsus, and father of the three-headed giant Gēryŏn and Echidna by the Ocean-Nymph Callirrhŏë.

Chrȳsēĭs. The daughter of Chrȳsēs, priest of Apollo at Chrȳsē. She was carried away by the Greeks at the conquest of her native city, and allotted to Agamemnōn. Agamemnon having refused the father's proffered ransom, Apollo visited the Greek camp with pestilence until Agamemnon gave her back without payment. (*See* TROJAN WAR.)

Chrȳsippus. (1) Son of Pĕlops and the Nymph Axiŏchē, murdered by his step-brothers Atreus and Thyestēs, who were consequently banished by Pelops.

(2) A Greek philosopher of Tarsus or Soli in Cilicia (about 282–206 B.C.). At Athens he was a pupil of the Stoic Cleanthēs, and his successor in the chair of the Stoa. Owing to the thorough way in which he developed the system, he is almost entitled to be called the second founder of the Stoic school; and, indeed, there was a saying "Had there been no Chrysippus, there had been no Stoa." The author of more than 705 books, he was one of the most prolific writers of antiquity, but his style was marred by great prolixity and carelessness. Only a few fragments of his writings survive.

Chthŏnĭa. (1) Daughter of Erechtheus of Athens, who was sacrificed by her father to gain the victory over the men of Eleusis. (*See* ERECHTHEUS.)

(2) An epithet of Dēmētēr (*q. v.*).

Chthŏnian Gods (from *Chthōn*, the earth). The deities who rule under the earth or who are connected with the lower world, as Hādēs, Plūtō, Persĕphŏnē, Dēmētēr, Dionȳsus, Hĕcătē, and Hermēs.

Chytroi (Feast of Pots) the third day of the Anthestēria. (*See* DIONYSIA.)

Cĭcĕro. (1) *Marcus Tullius Cicero.* The celebrated Roman orator, born at Arpīnum, January 3rd, 106 B.C. He was son of Marcus Tullius Cicero and Helvia, his family being of equestrian rank, but not yet ennobled by office. With his brother Quintus he received his education in Rome, where he soon had an opportunity of hearing and admiring the two most celebrated orators of the day, Crassus and Antonius. He took the *tŏga vĭrīlis* in 90 B.C., and, while practising rhetorical exercises, devoted himself with ardour to the study of law. In 89 he served on his first campaign in the Marsian War. After this he began his studies in philosophy, mainly under the guidance of the Academic philosopher, Philo of Larissa. The presence of the Rhodian rhetorician Molo in Rome, and afterwards the instruction in dialectic given him by the Stoic Diŏdŏtus, gave him the opportunity he desired for furthering his training as an orator. Having thus carefully prepared himself for his future vocation during the period of the civil disturbances, he started on his career as an orator under Sulla's dictatorship. He began with civil or private cases. One of his earliest speeches, the *Pro Quinctio,* still survives. This oration [in which he defends his client on the question of his conduct in a partnership] he delivered in 81 B.C., in his 26th year. In the following year he first appeared in a *causa publĭca,* and not on the side of the prosecution, the usual course for beginners, but on that of the defence. His client was Sextus Roscius of Amĕria, accused of murdering his own father. This speech laid the foundation of Cicero's fame, and not only because it was successful. People admired the intrepidity with which Cicero stood up against Chrysŏgŏnus, the favourite of the omnipotent dictator.

In the following year, for the sake of his delicate health, Cicero started on a two years' tour in Greece and Asia, taking every opportunity of finishing his education as a philosopher and orator. For philosophy he had recourse to the most celebrated professors at Athens: for rhetoric he went to Rhodes, to his former instructor, Molo. In B.C. 77 he returned to Rome, his health restored, and

his intellect matured. In this year he married Terentia. His career as an advocate he pursued with such success that he was unanimously elected quæstor in 76 B.C. He was stationed at Lilybæum, in Sicily, and administered his office unimpeachably. After his return he entered the senate, and developed an extraordinary activity as a speaker. In consequence he was elected to the curule ædileship in 70 B.C. It was in

* CICERO (*Madrid*).

M · CICERO · AN · LXIIII.

this year that the Sicilians, remembering the conscientiousness and unselfishness he had displayed in his quæstorship, begged him to lead the prosecution against Verrēs. For three years this man had, in the most infamous manner, ill-treated and plundered the province. Cicero had to contend with all kinds of hindrances thrown in his way by the aristocratic friends of Verres. By the *Dīvīnātio in Cæcilium* he had to make good his claims to prosecute against those of Cæcilius Niger. The defence was led by the most famous orator of the day, Hortensius. But Cicero managed to collect such a mass of evidence, and to marshal it with such ability, that after the *actio prima*, or first hearing, Verres found it advisable to retire into voluntary exile. The unused material Cicero worked up into an *actio secunda* in five speeches. The whole proceeding made him so popular that, spoiled as the multitude was, no one complained of his economical expenditure on the games during his ædileship. He was unanimously elected prætor in 67 B.C. In this office he made his first political speech in 66, successfully defending the proposal of the tribune Manilius to give Pompeius the command in the Mithridatic war, with unprecedented and almost absolute power.

In 64 B.C. he came forward as candidate for the consulship, and was successful, in spite of the efforts of his enemies. He owed his success to the support of the nobility, who had hitherto regarded him, as a *homo novus*, with disfavour, but had come to recognise him as a champion of the party of order. He obtained the office, as he had the rest, *suo anno*, that is in the first year in which his candidature was legally possible. The danger with which Catiline's agitation was threatening the State, determined Cicero to offer a vigorous opposition to everything likely to disturb public order. With this view he delivered three speeches, in which he frustrated the agrarian proposals of the tribune Servilius Rullus. He also led the defence of the aged Rabīrius, whom the leaders of the democratic party, to excite the people against the senate, had prosecuted for the murder of Saturnīnus thirty-six years before. To avoid the danger and excitement of a fresh consular election for 62, he undertook the defence of the *consul designātus* L. Murēna, on the charge of bribery; and this, although the accusers of Murena numbered among them Cicero's best friends, and, indeed, rested their case upon the very law by which Cicero had himself proposed to increase the penalties for bribery. The conspiracy of Catiline gave Cicero an opportunity of displaying in the most brilliant light his acuteness, his energy, his patriotism, and even his power as an orator. He discovered the conspiracy, and helped largely to suppress it by the execution of the chief conspirators, who had remained behind in Rome.

Cicero's consulship marks the climax of his career. He received, it is true, the honourable title of *pater patriæ*; but, a few weeks later, he had a clear warning of what he had to expect from the opposite party in the way of reward for his services. When laying down his office he was about to make a speech, giving an account of his administration. The tribune Metellus Nepos interrupted him, and insisted on his confining himself to the oath usual on the occasion. In the following year he had opportunities for displaying his eloquence in the defence of P. Cornelius Sulla and the poet Archias. But he was often attacked, and had, in particular, to meet a new danger in the hostility of Clodius Pulcher, whose mortal hatred only too soon hit upon a chance of sating itself. Cicero would not accede to the plans of Cæsar, Pompey and Crassus, but offered them a strenuous resistance. He deceived himself as to his own political importance, and refused to quit the city except under compulsion. The triumvirs accordingly abandoned him to the vengeance of Clodius. Clodius was elected tribune of the *plebs* in 58 B.C., and at once proposed that any person should be made an outlaw, who should have put Roman citizens to death without trial. Cicero met the charge by retiring into voluntary exile early in April, 58. He went to Thessalonīca and Macedonia, where he found a safe retreat at the house of the quæstor Plancius. The sentence was, however, pronounced against him; his house on the Palatine was burnt down, his country houses plundered and destroyed, and even his family maltreated. It is true that, as early as the next year, he was recalled with every mark of distinction, and welcomed in triumph by the people on his entrance into Rome at the beginning of September. But his political activity was crippled by the power of the triumvirs. His fear of Clodius forced him to comply with their commands as a means of keeping in their good graces. But all this only stimulated him to show greater energy as an orator. His chief efforts were put forth in defending his friends, when prosecuted by political antagonists, as, for instance, Publius Sestius in 56 B.C., Gnæus Plancius in 54, Titus Annius Milo in 52. His defence of the latter, accused of the murder of Clodius, was unsuccessful. It was at this period that he began to apply himself to literature.

In 53 B.C. he was elected augur; from July, 51, to July, 50, he administered the province of Cilicia as proconsul. In this capacity, his clemency, uprightness and unselfishness won for him the greatest respect. For his conduct in a campaign against the robber tribes of Mount Amānus he was honoured by the title of *Imperātor*, a public thanksgiving, and the prospect of a triumph.

He landed in Italy towards the end of November, B.C. 50, and found that a breach between Pompey and Cæsar was inevitable. The civil war broke out in the next year, and, after long hesitation, Cicero finally decided for Pompey, and followed him to Greece. But after the battle of Pharsālus, in which ill-health prevented him from taking a part, he deserted his friends, and crossed to Brundisium. Here he had to wait a whole year before Cæsar pardoned him, and gave him leave to return to Rome. Cæsar treated him with distinction and kindness, but Cicero kept aloof from public life. Nothing short of the calls of friendship could induce him to appear in the courts, as he did for Marcellus, Ligārius, and Deiotārus. The calamities of his country; his separation from his wife Terentia, in 46 B.C., after a married life of thirty-three years; his hasty union with the young and wealthy Publilia, so soon to be dissolved; the unhappy marriage and death of his favourite daughter Tullia; all this was a heavy affliction for him. He found some consolation in studying philosophy, and applying himself with energy to literary work.

The murder of Cæsar on March 15th, 44 B.C., roused him from his retirement, though he had taken no actual part in the deed. His patriotism excited him once more to take an active part in public life, and his first aim was to effect a reconciliation of parties. He succeeded so far as to secure the passing of a general amnesty. But it was not long before the intrigues and the hostility of the Cæsarian party forced him again to leave Rome. He was on his way to Greece, when, at the end of August, he was recalled, by false rumours, to the Capitol. In a moment of deep irritation against Antōnius, he delivered, on the 2nd of September, the first of his fourteen Philippic orations, so called after those of Demosthenes. The second Philippic was never spoken, but published as a pamphlet; the last was delivered on the 21st April, B.C. 43. On the retirement of Antonius from Rome, Cicero found himself again playing a promi-

nent part in politics. All the efforts of his party to bring about a restoration of the ancient republican freedom centred in him. But, when Octaviānus disappointed the hopes which he had excited, and attached himself to Antonius and Lĕpĭdus in the second triumvirate, Cicero, now the chief man in the senate, was declared an outlaw. Intending to fly to Macedonia, as he had done fifteen years before, he was overtaken by his pursuers near Caiēta, and put to death on September 7th, 43 B.C., shortly before he had completed his sixty-fourth year. His head and right hand were exposed on the *rostra* by Antonius.

The literary labours of Cicero signalize an important advance in the development of Latin literature. It is not only that he is to be regarded as the creator of classical Latin prose. He was also the first writer who broke ground, to any great extent, in fields of literature which, before him, had remained almost untouched. He had insight enough to perceive that his vocation lay in the career of an orator. His industry, throughout his whole life, was untiring; he was never blinded by success; to educate himself, and perfect himself in his art, was the object which he never lost sight of. His speeches, accordingly, give brilliant testimony to his combination of genius with industry. Besides the fifty-seven speeches which survive in a more or less complete shape, and the most important of which have been mentioned above, we have about twenty fragments of others, and the titles of thirty-five more. Cicero was justified in boasting that no orator had written so many speeches, and in such different styles, as himself [*Orator*, c. 29, 30]. These orations were partly political, partly forensic; the latter being mostly on the side of the defence. Cicero was also the author of panegyrics, as that, for instance, upon Cato. With few exceptions, as the second *actio* against Verres, the *Pro Mĭlōne*, and the panegyrics, they were actually delivered, and published afterwards. Extending over thirty-eight years, they give an excellent idea of Cicero's steady progress in the mastery of his art. They are of unequal merit, but everywhere one feels the touch of the born and cultivated orator. A wealth of ideas and of wit, ready acuteness, the power of making an obscure subject clear and a dry subject interesting, mastery of pathos, a tendency to luxuriance of language, generally tempered by good taste to the right measure, an unsurpassed tact in the use of Latin idiom and expression, a wonderful feeling for the rhythm and structure of prose writing: these are Cicero's characteristics. With all the faults which his contemporaries and later critics had to find with his speeches, Cicero never lost his position as the most classical representative of Latin oratory, and he was judged the equal, or nearly the equal, of Demosthenes.

The knowledge which he had acquired in his practice as a speaker he turned to account in his writings on Rhetoric. In these he set forth the technical rules of the Greek writers, applying to them the results of his own experience, and his sense of the requirements of Latin oratory. Besides the two books entitled *Rhetŏrĭca* or *De Inventĭōne*, a boyish essay devoid of all originality, the most important of his works on this subject are: (1) The *De Orātōre*, a treatise in three books, written 55 B.C. This work, the form and contents of which are alike striking, is written in the style of a dialogue. Its subject is the training necessary for an orator, the proper handling of his theme, the right style, and manner of delivery. (2) The *Brutus*, or *Dē Clārīs Orātōrĭbus*, written in B.C. 46; a history of Latin oratory from the earliest period down to Cicero's own time. (3) The *Orātor*, a sketch of the ideal orator, written in the same year as the *Brutus*.

Cicero also devoted a large number of books to Greek philosophy, a subject which he was concerned to render accessible to his countrymen. His writings in this line lack depth and thoroughness; but it must be said at the same time that he has the great merit of being the first Latin writer who treated these questions with taste and in an intelligible form, and who created a philosophical language in Latin. The framework which he adopts is usually that of the Aristotelian dialogue, though he does not always consistently adhere to it. It was not until after his fiftieth year that he began to write on philosophy, and in the years B.C. 45 and 44, when almost entirely excluded from politics, he developed an extraordinary activity in this direction. The following philosophical works survive, either in whole or in part: (1) Fragments, amounting to about one-third of the work, of the six books, *De Re Publĭcā*, written B.C. 54-51. (2) Three books of an unfinished treatise, *De Lēgĭbus*, written about 52. (3) *Părădoxa Stŏĭcōrum*, a short treatment of six Stoical texts, B.C. 46. (4) Five

books on the greatest good and the greatest evil (*De Fīnĭbus Bŏnōrum et Mălōrum*), B.C. 45. This is the best of his philosophical works. (5) The second book of the first edition, and the first book of the second edition, of the *Acădēmĭca*, B.C. 45. (6) The five books of the Tusculan Disputations, B.C. 44. In the same year appeared (7) the *De Nātūrā Dĕōrum*, in three, and (8) the *De Dīvīnātĭōnĕ*, in two books. (9) A fragment on the Stoical doctrine of Fate. (10) The *Cato Maior*, or *De Sĕnectūtĕ*. (11) *Lælĭus*, or *De Amīcĭtĭā*. (12) *De Offĭcĭīs*, or *On Ethics*, in three books. Besides these, a whole series of philosophical and other prose writings by Cicero are known to us only in fragments, or by their titles.

The multifarious nature of Cicero's occupation as a statesman and an orator did not hinder him from keeping up a voluminous correspondence, from which 864 letters (including 90 addressed to Cicero) are preserved in four collections. These letters form an inexhaustible store of information, bearing upon Cicero's own life as well as upon contemporary history in all its aspects. We have (1) The *Epistŭlæ ad Fāmĭlĭārēs*, in sixteen books, B.C. 63-43; (2) The *Epistŭlæ ad Attĭcum*, in sixteen books, B.C. 68-43; (3) Three books of letters to his brother Quintus; (4) Two books of correspondence between Cicero and Brutus after the death of Cæsar, the genuineness of which is [rightly] disputed.

Cicero also made some attempts to write poetry, in his youth for practice, in his later life mainly from vanity. His youthful effort was a translation of Arātus, of which some fragments remain. After 63 B.C. he celebrated his own consulship in three books of verses. [He is a considerable metrist, but not a real poet.]

(2) *Quintus Tullius Cicero*, the younger brother of Marcus, was born in B.C. 102. He was prætor in 62, and *lēgātus* to Cæsar in Gaul and Britain from 54-52 B.C. In the civil war he took the side of Pompey, but was pardoned by Cæsar. In 43 he was made an outlaw, at the same time as his brother, and in 42 was murdered in Rome. Like Marcus, he was a gifted man, and not unknown in literature, especially as a writer of history and poetry. In 54 B.C., for example, when engaged in the Gallic campaign, he wrote four tragedies in sixteen days, probably after Greek models. We have four letters of his, besides a short paper addressed to his brother in 64 B.C.,

on the line to be taken in canvassing for the consulship.

Cincius Alimentus. *See* ANNALISTS.

Cinctus Gābīnus. *See* TOGA.

Cinȳrās (*Kinȳrās*). Supposed, in the Greek mythology, to have been king of Cyprus, the oldest priest of Aphrŏdītē in Paphos, the founder of that city, and the ancestor of the priestly family of the *Cinyradæ*. His wealth and long life, bestowed upon him by Aphrodite, were proverbial; and from Apollo, who was said to be his father, he received the gift of song. He was accounted the founder of the ancient hymns sung at the services of the Paphian Aphrodite and of Adōnis. Consequently he was reckoned among the oldest singers and musicians, his name, indeed, being Phœnician, derived from *kinnor*, a harp. The story added that he was the father of Adōnis by his own daughter Myrrha, and that, when made aware of the sin, he took away his own life.

Cippus. The Latin name for a sepulchral monument. The form of the *cippus* was sometimes that of a pedestal with several divisions, supporting an upright cone, either

* CIPPUS WITH PHALERÆ.
(Olten: *Ann. d'Inst.* 1860 tav. E, 4.)

pointed at the end, or entirely cylindrical; sometimes that of a cube with several projections on its surface. (*See* cut here, and also under SIGNUM.)

Circē (*Kirkē*) (a figure in Greek mythology). A celebrated magician, daughter of the Sun (*Hĕlĭŏs*) and the Ocean nymph Persēïs, sister of Æētēs and Pāsïphäē. She dwelt on the island of Ææa. For her meeting with Odysseus and the son she bore him, Tĕlĕgŏnus, *see* ODYSSEUS.

Circus, Games of (*Lūdī Circensēs*). The name of *Circus* was given at Rome *par excellence* to the *Circus Maxĭmus*. This

was a recreation ground laid out by king Tarquĭnĭus Priscus in the valley between the Palatine and Aventine hills, south of the Capitol. Its centre was marked by the altar of Consus. A second circus, called the *Circus Flāmĭnĭus*, was built by the censor C. Flaminius on the Campus Martius in 220 B.C. Several more were built during the imperial period, some of which can still be recognised in their ruined state. Such

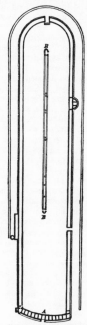

A, Carceres; B B, Metæ.
(1) PLAN OF CIRCUS OF MAXENTIUS.
(On the *Via Appia,* near Rome.)

is the Circus of Maxentius, erroneously called *Circo di Caracalla* (fig. 1). Similar racecourses existed in many other cities of the empire, *e.g.*, that still remaining amid the ruins of the town of Bovillæ. The length of the *Circus Maximus*, as enlarged by Cæsar, was some 1,800 feet, its breadth some 350. The seats, which rose in a series of terraces, rested on a substructure consisting of three stories of arched vaults. The lower seats were of stone, the upper of wood. Round the outside of the circus ran a building, containing booths and seats, as well as the entrances to the seats, the number of which amounted, in Cæsar's time, to 150,000, and in the 4th century, after the building had been repeatedly enlarged, to 385,000. The *pŏdĭum*, or lowest row of seats running immediately above the race-course, was protected from the wild animals by a railing and a trench (*eurīpus*) ten feet in width and depth. This trench was, however, filled up at the command of Nero. The end of the circus, at which were the gate of entrance and the partitions in which the chariots stood, was flanked by two towers (*oppĭda*) occupied by bands of music. Between these was the *loggia* of the presiding magistrate. The opposite end of the building was semicircular, and had a gate called the *porta triumphālĭs*, which seems to have been used only on extraordinary occasions. The senators and *ĕquĭtēs* had separate places allotted them, as in the theatre. The seats assigned to the common people were divided according to tribes, and the sexes were not separated. The eight or twelve openings (*carcĕrēs*) from which the chariots issued lay, as we have already mentioned, at both sides of the entrance, and were closed with bars. They were arranged in slanting lines, so that the distance from the *carceres* to the starting-point was equalized for all. The starting-point was marked by three conical pillars (*mētæ*), standing on a substructure. Three other similar *metæ*, corresponding to them, stood at the other or semicircular end of the circus. Between the two points where the *metæ* stood was built a low wall (*spīna*), extending through the whole length of the course. On this there used to stand the mast of a ship, which, after Augustus' time, gave place to an obelisk. The *spina* was adorned with pillars, little shrines, and statues of the gods, especially of Victory. A second and loftier obelisk was added by Constantine. The obelisk of Augustus now stands in the *Piazza del Popolo*, that of Constantine on the square in front of the Lateran. There was also an elevated substructure, supporting seven sculptured dolphins spouting water, and a pedestal with seven egg-shaped objects upon it, the use of which will be explained below.

The games were generally opened by a solemn procession from the Capitol through the forum to the circus, and through the whole length of the circus round the *spina*. At the head of the procession came the giver of the games, sitting on a car of triumph in triumphal costume. He was followed by the images of the gods borne on litters or carriages, and escorted by the *collēgia* and priestly corporations. In the imperial age the procession included the images of the deceased emperors and empresses, to whom divine honours were paid. The procession moved through the entrance, while the crowd rose up, cheered, and clapped their hands. The president dropped a white handkerchief into the arena, and the race began. Four, sometimes as many as six, chariots drove out from behind the barriers at the right hand of the *spina*. Then they rushed along the *spina* as far as the further posts, rounded these, and drove back down the left side to the starting-posts. They made the circuit seven times, and finally drove off the course through the barriers on the left of the *spina*. Seven circuits constituted one heat, or *missus*. A chalk line was drawn across the ground near the entrance, and the victory was adjudged to the driver who first crossed it. During the republican period the number of *missūs* or heats amounted to ten or twelve, and after the time of Calīgŭla to twenty-four, taking up the whole day.

To keep the spectators constantly informed how many of the seven heats had been run, one of the egg-shaped signals, mentioned above, was taken down after each heat, and probably also one of the dolphins was turned round. The chariots had two wheels, were very small and light, and were open behind. The team usually consisted either of two (*bīgæ*) or of four horses (*quadrīgæ*). In the latter case the two middle horses only were yoked together. The driver (*aurīga* or *ăgĭtātor*, fig. 2) stood in his chariot, dressed in a sleeveless tunic strapped round the upper part of his body, a helmet-shaped cap on his head, a whip in his hand, and a knife with a semi-circular blade in his girdle, to cut the reins with in case of need, for the reins were usually attached to his girdle. The main danger lay in turning round the pillars. To come into collision with them was fatal, not only to the driver himself, but to the driver immediately behind him. The chariots, and probably also the tunics and equipments of the drivers, were decked with the colours of the different *factions*, as they were called. Of these there were originally only two, the White and the Red. At the beginning of the imperial period we hear of two more, the Green and the Blue. Two more, Gold and Purple, were introduced by

Domitian, but probably dropped out of use after his death. Towards the end of the 3rd century A.D. the White faction joined with the Green, and the Red with the Blue. Accordingly in the late Roman and Byzantine period we generally hear only of Blue and Green. It was the party feeling thus engendered which was the mainspring of the passionate interest, often amounting almost to madness, which the people took in the games of the circus.

(2) * VICTORIOUS AURIGA.
(*Sala della biga*, Vatican.)

The necessary attendants, the horses, and the general equipment of the games were provided, at the cost of the giver, by special companies, with one or more directors at their head. These companies were distinguished by adopting the different colours of the factions. The drivers were mostly slaves, or persons of low position. The calling was looked down upon; but at the same time a driver of exceptional skill would be extraordinarily popular. The victors, besides their palms and crowns, often received considerable sums of money; and thus it would often happen that a driver would rise to the position of a contractor, or become director of a company of contractors. Numerous monuments survive to commemorate their victories. Sometimes, indeed, a celebrated horse would have a monument put up to him.

A contest of riders, each with two horses, was often added to the chariot-races. These riders were called *dēsultōrēs*, because they jumped from one horse to another while going at full gallop. The circus was also used for boxing-matches, wrestling-matches, and foot-racing; but during the imperial period separate buildings were usually appropriated to these amusements. Gladiatorial contests, and wild-beast hunts, were originally held in the circus, even after the building of the amphitheatre.

Besides these games, the circus was sometimes used for military reviews. The cavalry manoeuvres, for instance, of the six divisions of the knights (*ludi sēvĭrālēs*), with their six leaders (*sēvĭri*), and an imperial prince as *princeps iuventūtis* at their head, would occasionally be held there. Under the emperors of the Julian dynasty a favourite pastime was the *Troia* or *ludus Troiœ*. This consisted in a number of manoeuvres performed by boys belonging to senatorial and other respectable families. They rode on horseback in light armour in separate divisions, and were practised for the purpose by special trainers.

Cīris. *See* NISUS.

Cĭsĭum. *See* CHARIOTS.

Cĭthăra (*Kĭthăra*). A stringed instrument, invented (so the fable ran) by Apollo. The *cithara* was played on occasions of ceremony, such as public games and processions: the *lўra*, a smaller instrument

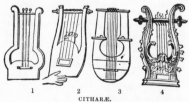

CITHARÆ.
(1), (2) and (4) *Museo Borbonico*, XIII xl, X vi, XII xxiv.
(3) *Welcker, Denkm.* III 31.,

and easier to hold, was more commonly used in ordinary life. The *cithara* consisted of a sounding board, which extended into two arms or side-pieces. The sounding-board, made of thin pieces of wood, plates of metal, or ivory, was generally of a quadrangular, but sometimes of an oval shape; and was deeply vaulted at the back. The arms, which were broad were hollow, like the sounding-board. As the instrument was rather heavy, and the player had to stand while performing on it, it was generally provided with straps for supporting it, so as to leave the player's hands free. The *phorminx*, generally regarded as an attribute of Apollo, seems to have been a special variety of the *cithara*. It is generally spoken of as "shrill-toned." Different forms of the *cithara* are given in the engraving. (For further details, and for the manner of playing on the *cithara*, see LYRA.)

Civĭtās. The technical Latin word for the right of citizenship. This was originally possessed, at Rome, by the patricians only. The plebeians were not admitted to share it at all until the time of Servius Tullius, and not to full civic rights until B.C. 337. In its fullest comprehension the *civitas* included: (1) the *iūs suffrāgĭi*, or right of voting for magistrates; (2) the *ius hŏnōrum*, or right of being elected to a magistracy; (3) the *ius prŏvŏcātĭōnis* or right of appeal to the people, and in later times to the emperor, against the sentences passed by magistrates affecting life or property; (4) the *ius cōnūbĭi*, or right to contract a legal marriage; (5) the *ius commercĭi*, or right to hold property in the Roman community. The *civitas* was obtained either by birth from Roman parents, or by manumission (*see* MANUMISSIO), or by presentation. The right of presentation belonged originally to the kings, afterwards to the popular assemblies, and particularly to the *cŏmĭtĭa trĭbūta*, and last of all to the emperors. The *civitas* could be lost by *dēmĭnūtĭō căpĭtĭs* (*see* DEMINUTIO CAPITIS). The *aerārĭi*, so called, had an imperfect *civitas*, without the *ius suffragii* and *ius honorum*. Outside the circle of the *civitas* stood the slaves and the foreigners or *pĕrĕgrīnī* (*see* PEREGRINI). The latter included: (1) strangers who stood in no international relations with Rome; (2) the allies, or *sŏcĭi*, among whom the *Lătīnī* held a privileged place (*see* LATINI); (3) the *dēdĭtīcĭi*, or those who belonged to nations conquered in war.

Though the Roman citizenship was conferred upon all the free inhabitants of the empire in 212 A.D. by the emperor Caracalla, the grades of it were not all equalized, nor was it until the time of Justinian that

civitas and *libertas* became convertible terms.

Classĭārĭi or *classĭcī* (from *classis*, a fleet). The crews of the Roman fleet. In the republican age the rowers (*rēmĭgēs*) were slaves, and the sailors (*nautæ*) were partly contributed by the allies (*sŏcĭi nāvālēs*), partly levied from among the Roman citizens of the lowest orders, the citizens of the maritime colonies, and the freedmen. Under the Empire the fleets were manned by freedmen and foreigners, who could not obtain the citizenship until after twenty-six years' service. In the general military system, the navy stood lowest in respect of pay and position. No promotion to higher posts was open to its officers, as those were monopolized by the army. In later times, a division of the marines stationed at Misēnum and Ravenna was appointed to garrison duty in Rome. This division was also used in time of war in repairing the roads for the armies. In Rome the marines were employed, among other things, in stretching the awnings over the theatre.

Classĭcum. The signal given by the *būcĭna* or horn for the meeting of the *cŏmĭtĭa centŭrĭāta* at Rome, and for the meeting of the soldiers in camp, especially before they marched out to battle.

Claudĭānus (*Claudius*). A Latin poet, born at Alexandria in the second half of the 4th century A.D. In 395 A.D. he came to Rome. Here he won the favour of the powerful Vandal Stĭlĭchō, and on the proposal of the senate was honoured with a statue by the emperors Arcādĭus and Hŏnōrĭus. The inscription on this statue is still in existence (Mommsen, *Inscriptiones Regni Neapolitani*, No. 6794). His patron Stilicho fell in 408, and Claudian, apparently, did not survive him. We have express evidence that the poet was not a Christian. He was familiar with Greek and Latin literature, and had considerable poetical gifts, including a mastery both of language and metre. These gifts raise him far above the crowd of the later Latin poets, although the effect of his writing is marred by tasteless rhetorical ornament and exaggerated flattery of great men. His political poems, in spite of their laudatory colouring, have considerable historical value. Most of them are written in praise of Honorius and of Stilicho, for whom he had a veneration as sincere as was his hatred of Rufīnus and Eutrŏpĭus. Against the latter he launched a number of invectives. Besides the *Raptus Prōserpĭnæ*, or *Rape of Proserpine*, an unfinished epic in which his descriptive power is most brilliantly displayed, his most important poems are (1) *De III, IV, VI, Consŭlātū Honorii ;* (2) *De Nuptĭīs Honorii Fescennīna ;* (3) *Epĭthālămĭum de Nuptiis Honorii et Mariœ ;* (4) *De Bello Gildŏnĭco ;* (5) *De Consulatu Stilichōnis ;* (6) *De Bello Pollentīno ;* (7) *Laus Sērēnœ*, Serena being Stilicho's wife. He also wrote epistles in verse, a series of minor pieces, narrative and descriptive, and a *Gĭgantŏmăchĭa*, of which a fragment has been preserved.

Claudius Quadrīgārĭus. *See* ANNALISTS.

Clĕanthēs (Gr. *Klĕanthēs*). A Greek philosopher, native of Assŏs in Asia Minor. He was originally a boxer, and while attending at Athens the lectures of Zēnō, the founder of the Stoic philosophy, he got a livelihood at night by carrying water. He was Zeno's disciple for nineteen years, and in 260 B.C. succeeded him as head of the Stoic school. He died in his eighty-first year by voluntary starvation. A beautiful hymn to Zeus is the only one of his writings that has come down to us.

Clēmens (*Tĭtus Flāvĭus*) A Greek ecclesiastical writer, born at Alexandria about 150 A.D. Originally a heathen, he gained, in the course of long travels, a wide knowledge of philosophy. Finding no satisfaction in it, he became a Christian, and about 190 A.D. was ordained priest in Alexandria, and chosen to preside over a school of catechumens there. The persecution under Septĭmĭus Sĕvērus having compelled him to take flight, he founded a school in Jerusalem, and came afterwards to Antioch. He died in 218 A.D. His writings contributing as they do to our knowledge of ancient philosophy, have an important place, not only in Christian, but also in profane literature. This is especially true of the eight books called *Strŏmătă ;* a title which properly means "many coloured carpets," or writings of miscellaneous contents.

Cleŏmĕnēs (*Klĕŏmĕnēs*). An Athenian sculptor, who probably flourished in the Augustan age. The celebrated Venus di Medici, now at Florence, is his work. [He is described on the pedestal as son of Apollodōrus. The *Germănĭcus* of the Louvre was the work of his son, who bore the same name.]

Clĕŏpātra (*Klĕŏpātra*) (in Greek mythology). (1) Daughter of Bŏrĕās and Orīthȳia, and wife of Phīneus. (*Sec* PHINEUS.)
(2) Daughter of Idās, and wife of Mĕlĕāger. (*See* MELEAGER.)

Clepsȳdra (*Klepsydra*). A water-clock, or earthenware vessel filled with a certain measure of water, and having a hole in the bottom of a size to ensure the water running away within a definite space of time. Such water-clocks were used in the Athenian law courts, to mark the time allotted to the speakers. They were first introduced in Rome in 159 B.C., and used in the courts there in the same way. In the field they were used to mark the night-watches. The invention of the best kind of water-clock was attributed to Plato. In this the hours were marked by the height of the water flowing regularly into a vessel. This was done in one of two ways. (1) A dial was placed above the vessel, the hand of which was connected by a wire with a cork floating on the top of the water. (2) The vessel was transparent, and had vertical lines drawn upon it, indicating certain typical days in the four seasons or in the twelve months. These lines were divided into twelve sections, corresponding to the position which the water was experimentally found to take at each of the twelve hours of night or day on each of these typical days. It must be remembered that the ancients always divided the night and day into twelve equal hours each, which involved a variation in the length of the hours corresponding to the varying length of the day and night.

Clērūchĭa (Gr. *Klērouchĭa*). A kind of Greek colony, which differed from the ordinary colonial settlement in the fact that the settlers remained in close connection with their mother-city. The Athenian *cleruchiœ* are the only ones of which we have any detailed knowledge. A conquered territory was divided into lots of land, which were assigned to the poorer citizens as *clērūchi*, or "holders of lots." The original inhabitants would be differently treated according to circumstances. In many cases they were compelled to emigrate ; sometimes the men were killed, and the women and children enslaved ; but ordinarily the old inhabitants would become the tenants of the settlers, and take, generally, a less privileged position. The settlers formed a separate community, elected their own officials, and managed their local affairs ; but they continued to be Athenian citizens, with all the rights and duties of their position. They remained under the authority of Athens, and had to repair to the Athenian courts for justice in all important matters.

Clībănŭs (Gr. *Klĭbănŏs*). *See* BAKERS.

Clientes. This was the name for such inhabitants of Rome as had lost, or given up, the citizenship of their own cities, and had settled in Roman territory. Here, having no legal rights, they were compelled, in order to secure their personal freedom, to seek the protection of some Roman citizen, a term which, in ancient times, could only mean a patrician. The relation thus set on foot was called *clientela*, and was inherited by the descendants of both parties. Accordingly the client entered into the family of his patron (*patronus*), took his gentile name, and was admitted to take part in the family sacrifices. The patron made over to him a piece of land as a means of support, protected him from violence, represented him at law, and buried him after his death. The client, on his part, accompanied his patron abroad and on military service, gave his advice in legal and domestic matters, and made a contribution from his property if his patron were endowing a daughter, or had to be ransomed in war, or to pay a fine. The relation between patron and client is also illustrated by the fact that neither party could bring an action against the other in a court of law, or bear witness against him, or vote against him, or appear against him as advocate. A man's duty to his client was more binding than his duty to his blood relations; and any violation of it was regarded as a capital offence.

When Servius Tullius extended the rights of citizenship to the clients as well as to the plebeians, the bond between patron and client still continued in force, although it gradually relaxed with the course of time. At the end of the republic age, the *status* of client, in the proper sense of the word, had ceased to exist. Under the Empire the *clientela* was a mere external relation between the rich and the poor, the great and the obscure. It involved no moral obligation on either side, but was based merely on the vanity of the one party, and the necessity of the other. It was no unusual thing to find people who had no settled means of subsistence trying, by flattery and servile behaviour, to win the favour of the great. Even philosophers and poets, like Statius and Martial, are found in this position. The client performs certain services, calls on his patron in the morning, accompanies him on public occasions, and is in turn invited to his table, receives presents from him, and (if he can get it) a settled provision. Instead of inviting their numerous clients, the rich would often present them with a small sum of money called *sportula*. The relation was entirely a free one, and could be dissolved at pleasure by either party.

In the republican age whole communities, and even provinces, when they had submitted to the Roman yoke, would sometimes become clients of a single *patronus*. In this case the *patronus* would usually be the conquering general. Marcellus, for instance, the conqueror of Syracuse, and his descendants, were patrons of Sicily. The practical advantages which were secured to a foreign community by this permanent representation at Rome are obvious. Accordingly we find that, under the Empire, even cities which stood to Rome in no relation of dependence, such as colonies and *municipia*, sometimes selected a *patronus*. The *patronus* was, in such cases, always chosen from among the senators or *equites*.

Cline (Gr. *Kline*). *See* MEALS.

Clio (Gr. *Kleio*). *See* MUSES.

Clipeus. *See* SHIELD.

Clitarchus (Gr. *Kleitarchos*). A Greek historian, son of the historian Dinon. He flourished about 300 B.C., and was the author of a great work, in at least twelve books, upon Alexander the Great. He was notoriously untrustworthy, and inclined to believe in the marvellous; his style was turgid and highly rhetorical; but his narrative was so interesting that he was the most popular of all the writers on Alexander. The Romans were very fond of his book, which was indeed the main authority for the narratives of Diodorus, Trogus Pompeius, and Curtius. A number of fragments of it still survive.

Clitus (*Kleitos*) (in Greek mythology). Son of Mantius, and grandson of Melampus: loved and carried off by Eos. *See* EOS.

Cloaca. A vaulted subterranean channel for carrying off drainage of every kind. As early as the 6th century B.C. Rome had an extensive system of sewers for draining the marshy ground lying between the hills of the city. By this the sewage was carried into a main drain (*Cloaca Maxima*) which emptied itself into the Tiber. Part of this sewer, in length quite 1,020 feet, is still in existence, and after a lapse of 2,500 years, goes on fulfilling its original purpose. The sewer, which is nearly twenty feet wide, is covered by a vaulted roof of massive squares of tufa, in which an arch of travertine is inserted at intervals of 12 feet 2 inches. The original height was 10 feet 8 inches, but has been reduced to 6 feet

6 inches by the accumulation of filth and rubbish. The drainage system of Rome was considerably extended, especially by Agrippa in the Augustan age.

The duty of keeping the sewers of Rome in repair fell originally to the censors. During the imperial age it was transferred to a special board, the *cūrātōrēs cloacārum*. Citizens who wished to establish a connexion between their property and the city drains had to pay a special tax to the State, called *cloacārium*.

Clocks were known to the ancients only under the form of sun-dials (*see* GNOMON) and water-clocks (*see* CLEPSYDRA).

Clothing. The dresses of the Greeks and Romans consisted of under garments or shirts, and upper garments or mantles. The Greek *chĭtōn* and the Latin *tŭnĭca*, common to both men and women, belong to the first class; so does the *stŏla* of the Roman matron, worn over the *tunica*. The *hĭmă-tĭŏn* was an upper garment, worn in Greece both by men and women. The Greek *chlămўs* and *trĭbōn* and *pĕplŏs* were upper garments, the *chlamys* and *tribon* confined to men, and the *peplos* to women. The upper dress worn in public life by a Roman citizen was the *tŏgă*; the *palla* was peculiar to married ladies. There were other dresses of the same kind commonly in use among the Romans, for instance the *lăcerna*, *lœna*, *pœnŭla*, and *synthĕsis:* the *săgum* and *pălūdāmentum* were confined to military service. (See, for further details, the articles on the words in question.) Trousers (Latin *brācœ*, Greek *anaxŭrĭdĕs*) were only known as worn by the Orientals and by the barbarians of the North. Among the Romans no one wore them but the soldiers stationed in the northern districts. In works of art, accordingly, trousers and the long-sleeved *chiton* are an indication of barbarian costume. The custom of wrapping up the calf and thigh as a protection against the cold was deemed excusable in sickly and elderly people, but was thought effeminate in others. The wool of the sheep was at all times the staple material for cloth stuffs. Linen, though known to the Greeks of the Homeric age, was worn chiefly by the Ionians, and less so by the inhabitants of Greece Proper. Among the Romans, the use of linen was mostly confined to the girdle, though common among the Italian tribes. Both sexes wore a linen girdle (*sublĭgăcŭlum*) and women a linen breastband. Women were the first to exchange wool for linen, and this during the re-

publican age. Linen garments for men do not appear until later, when the fine Egyptian and Spanish linen-stuffs became a special article of luxury. The *toga* was always made of wool. Cotton-stuffs, too, were known to the ancients, as well as the *sērĭca*, a material made wholly or partly of silk; but these were not commonly used until the imperial times (*see* WEAVING). Country folk in Greece, and especially shepherds, clothe themselves in the skins of animals. Pelisses, apparently, did not come into fashion until the Empire.

The colour of dresses among the Greeks and Romans was mostly, but by no means exclusively, white. For practical reasons the working classes used to wear stuffs of dark colour, either natural or artificial. Dark clothes were worn among the upper classes in Rome only in time of mourning, or by a person accused before the courts of law. Coloured dresses were put on by men in Greece mainly on festal occasions, and by the Romans not at all. Gay-coloured materials were at all times worn by Greek ladies, and often, too, by Roman ladies as early as the 1st century B.C. Strong colours do not appear to have been liked by the ancients. They were familiar with stripes, plaids, and other patterns, as well as with ornaments of needlework and all kinds of embroidery. With regard to the fitting of dresses, it should be observed that it was mostly the custom to weave them according to measure, and there was therefore no necessity, as in modern times, for artistic cutting. The art of sewing was quite subordinate, and confined mostly to stitching leaves together for garlands; though sleeved garments, no doubt, required rather more care. Hence the fact that there was no such thing in antiquity as a separate tailoring trade. The necessary sewing was done by the ladies of the house, or by their slaves, and sometimes by the fullers, whose business it was to measure the pieces of cloth, to sell ready-made garments, and to clean clothes. (*See* FULLERS.)

Shoes. The Greeks usually went barefoot, except when out of the house; but they did not think it necessary to wear shoes, even in the street. On entering a house, whether one's own or not, it was customary to uncover the feet. The simplest form of covering for the feet was a sole fastened by straps (*hŭpŏdĕma*.) This is to be distinguished from the sandal (*sandălŏn*, *sandālĭŏn*), which was worn originally by men and afterwards by women.

This was a more complicated set of straps, reaching as far as over the ankle, where they were fastened. They sometimes had leather added at the sides and heel, so as to resemble a shoe. Close shoes of various kinds, fastened over the foot, were also worn by men and women. There were, besides, several kinds of boots, among which may be mentioned the *endrŏmĭs* and *cŏthurnus* (*see* ENDROMIS, COTHURNUS).

Among the Romans, men and women when at home, and generally in private life, wore a sandal (*sŏlĕa*), which was only taken off at meals; but a respectable Roman would hardly show himself barefooted out of doors. With the *toga* went the shoe called *calcĕus*, of which there were differents kinds, varying according to rank (*see* CALCEUS). Ladies usually, when out of doors, wore shoes of white or coloured leather, which formed an important part of their toilette, especially under the Empire, when the sexes rivalled each other in the splendour of their shoes, the men appearing in white and red leather, the emperor and great personages wearing shoes adorned with gold and even with jewels. Among the Romans generally, a great variety of shoes was in use, many of them borrowed from other countries (*see* CREPIDA, SOCCUS). Wooden shoes (*sculpŏnĕæ*) were worn by slaves and peasants. For the military boot in use under the Empire, *see* CALIGA.

Coverings for the head. The upper classes in Greece and Italy generally went bareheaded. It was only when long in the open air, as on journeys, or while hunting, or in the theatre, that they used the caps and hats worn by artisans, country folk, and fishermen (*see* PETASUS, PILLEUS, CAUSIA). In Rome, for protection against sun and storm, they adopted from the northern countries the *cŭcullus* or *cucullĭŏ*, a hood fastened to the *pænŭla* or *lacerna*. The head was often protected, in the case both of men and women, by drawing the top of the garment over the head. Besides kerchiefs and caps, women also wore veils, which in some cases, as at Thebes (and as now in the East), covered the face as far as the eyes. Roman ladies would seldom appear in the street uncovered. A common covering was the *ricĭnĭum*, which also served as a wrapper. This was, in later times, only worn at religious ceremonials. It was a square cloth fastened to the head, which ladies folded round them, throwing it over the left arm and left shoulder. For

protection against the sun ladies carried umbrellas (Gr. *skiadeĭŏn*, Lat. *umbrācŭlum*, *umbella*), or made their servants carry them. Fans (Gr. *rhīpŏs*, Lat. *flăbellum*) were likewise in common use. These were made of gaily-painted bits of wood, and the feathers of peacocks or other birds, and were generally in the shape of leaves.

Ornaments. Rings were in fashion both among men and women. The only other metal ornaments which men would have any opportunity for wearing in ordinary life were the clasps or brooches (*fibŭlæ*) used for fastening dresses or girdles. These were of bronze, silver, or gold, and often adorned with costly jewels. Besides rings and clasps, women wore needles in their hair, and ear-rings, necklaces, and bracelets on their wrists and arms, sometimes even on their ankles. The trinkets that have been preserved from antiquity exhibit the greatest conceivable variety of form. One of the commonest forms for a bracelet is that of a snake, surrounding the arm once, or in several spirals. An equal variety is observable in the ornamentations of pearls, precious stones, and the like.

Clōthō (Gr. *Klōthō*). *See* MŒRÆ.

Clўmĕnē (Gr. *Klўmĕnē*) (in Greek mythology). (1) Daughter of Catreus, wife of Nauplĭus, and mother of Pălămēdēs. (*See* NAUPLIUS.)

(2) Daughter of Ocĕănus, and mother of Phăĕthōn by Hēliŏs. (*See* PHAETHON.)

Clўtæmnēstra (Gr. *Klўtaimnēstra*; more correctly *Klўtaimēstra*). Daughter of Tyndărĕus, and wife of Agămemnōn. With the aid of her lover, Ægisthus, she murdered her husband, and was, in turn, put to death by her son, Orestēs. (*See* AGAMEMNON, ÆGISTHUS, and ORESTES.)

Clўtĭa (*Klytĭa*). In Greek mythology an ocean nymph, beloved by the Sun-god, who deserted her. She was changed into the heliotrope, a flower which is supposed always to turn its head in the direction of the sun's movement.

Cŏcălus (*Kŏkălos*). In Greek mythology, the king of Camĭcus in Sicily, who gave Dædălus a friendly welcome when flying from the pursuit of Mīnōs. Cocalus (or his daughters, according to another account) suffocated Minos in a hot bath.

Cock-fighting. *See* VENATIONES. at end.

Cŏcўtus (Gr. *Kŏkўtŏs*). *See* HADES, REALM OF.

Cŏemptĭō. Properly "a joint taking," so "a joint purchase." One of the three forms of marriage among the Romans. It was so called from the fiction of a purchase supposed to take place on the occasion. In the presence of five witnesses and a *libripens*, or holder of the balance, the bridegroom struck the balance with a bronze coin, which he handed to the father or guardian of the bride. At the same time he asked her whether she would be his wife, and she, in turn, asked him whether he would be her husband.

Cōgnātiō. The Latin word for relationship. *Cognatio* included relationship on both the father's and mother's side, while *āgnātiō* implied relationship on the father's side only (*see* AGNATIO). *Agnatio* involved legal duties and rights, while *cognatio*, originally at least, brought with it only moral obligations. *Cognātī* to the sixth degree had the right of kissing each other (*iūs oscŭlī*), and also the right of refusing to appear as witnesses against each other in a court of law. On the other hand, *cognati* were forbidden by custom, at least in the earlier times, to intermarry, or to appear in court against each other as accusers. When a man died, his *cognati* were expected to put on mourning for him. In course of time the *cognati* gradually acquired the rights proper to *agnati*. But natural relationship did not win full recognition until the time of Justinian, by whose legislation the rights of *agnati* were abolished.

Cōgnōmĕn. *See* NAMES.

Cŏhors. A division of the Roman army. In the republican age the word was specially applied to the divisions contributed by the Italian allies. Down to 89 B.C., when the Italians obtained the Roman citizenship, they were bound to supply an infantry contingent to each of the two consular armies, which consisted of two legions apiece. This contingent numbered in all 10,000 infantry, divided into: (*a*) 20 *cohortēs* of 420 men each, called *cohortes ālārēs*, because, in time of battle, they formed the wings (*ālæ*) of the two combined legions; (*b*) four *cohortes extraordĭnārĭæ*, or select cohorts of 400 men each.

From about the beginning of the 1st century B.C., the Roman legion, averaging 4,000 men, was also divided into ten *cohortes*, each containing three *mănĭpŭlī* or six *centŭrĭæ*. In the imperial times, the auxiliary troops assigned to the legions stationed in the provinces were also divided into cohorts (*cohortes auxĭlĭārĭæ*). These cohorts contained either 500 men (=5 cen-

turiæ), or 1,000 men (=10 *centuriæ*). They consisted either entirely of infantry, or partly of cavalry (380 infantry + 120 cavalry, 760 infantry + 240 cavalry). For the commanders of these cohorts, *see* PRÆFECTUS. The troops stationed in Rome were also numbered according to *cohortes*. (1) The *cohortes prætōrĭæ*, originally nine, but afterwards ten in number, which formed the imperial body-guard. Each cohort consisted of 1,000 men, including infantry and cavalry (*see* PRÆTORIANI). The institution of a body-guard was due to Augustus, and was a development of the *cohors prætoria*, or body-guard of the republican generals. Its title shows that it was as old as the time when the consuls bore the name of *prætōrēs*. This *cohors prætoria* was originally formed exclusively of cavalry, mainly of equestrian rank. But towards the end of the republican age, when every independent commander had his own *cohors prætoria*, it was made up partly of infantry, who were mainly veterans, partly of picked cavalry of the allies, and partly of Roman *ĕquĭtēs*, who usually served their *tīrōcĭnĭum*, or first year, in this way. (2) Three and in later times four, *cohortes urbānæ*, consisting each of 1,000 men, were placed under the command of the *præfectus urbi*. They had separate barracks, but ranked below the body-guard, and above the legionaries. (3) Seven *cohortes vĭgĭlum*, of 1,000 men each, were under the command of the *præfectus vigilum*. These formed the night police and fire-brigade, and were distributed throughout the city, one to every two of the fourteen *rĕgĭōnēs*.

Coinage. (1) *Greek.* As late as the Homeric age, cattle, especially oxen, served as a medium of exchange, as well as a standard of price [*Il.* xi 211, xxi 385]. We find, however, that the metals were put to the same use, their value being decided by their weight as determined by a balance. The weight, as well as the balance, was called *tălantŏn*. [It is probable that the gold *talanton* of Homer weighed two *drachmæ*, and was equivalent in value to an ox; *see* Ridgeway, in *Journal Hell. Studies* viii 133.] The idea of giving the metal used in exchange a form corresponding to its requirements is no doubt an early one. The date of the introduction of a coinage in the proper sense, with an official stamp to denote its value and obviate the necessity of weighing the metal, cannot now be determined. But as early as the 6th century B.C. we find a highly developed and artistic system of coining money in existence. The various Greek standards of value were all developed—in several gradations, it is true—from the gold and silver standard of Asia Minor. It was not until a later time that the standard of the Persian gold money was in some cities transferred to the silver coinage. The proportion of gold to silver was commonly reckoned among the Greeks as 10:1, so that a gold piece weighing 2 *drachmæ* was = 20 silver *drachmæ*. But in commerce the proportion assumed was 12:1, and this was the average generally observed in the Roman empire. The measure of weight most commonly current was the *talent*, which contained 60 *minæ*. Like the talent, the *mina* was not a real coin, but a standard of measurement. The unit of coinage was the *drachma*, 100 drachmas being reckoned to the *mina*. The drachma, again, contained 6 obols. In ancient times the commonly accepted standard was that of Ægīna. The coins of the island of Ægina were stamped on one side with the figure of a tortoise, on the other side

(1) DIDRACHMON OF ÆGINA.
(B.C. 700–550.)

with a roughly executed incuse square. The largest silver coin was the *statēr* or *didrachmŏn* (fig. 1), (=about 2s. 2d., the Æginētan drachma being =1s. 1d.). Solon abolished this standard in Attica, and introduced a lighter drachma equal to about 8d. The Attic talent (=6,000 *drachmæ*) was thus worth about £200, the mina about £3 6s. 8d. The silver coins of Attica bore on the front the head of Pallas, and on the

Archaic head of Athene.   Owl.

(2) TETRADRACHMON OF ATHENS.
(Time of Persian wars.)

reverse the figure of an owl. The principal coin was the *tetradrachmŏn* or 4 *drachmæ*

(fig. 2), the largest (which was only issued occasionally) the *děkadrachmŏn* or 10 *drachmæ*. The *dĭdrachmŏn* (2 *drachmæ*) was in like manner issued rarely. The *trĭŏbŏlŏn* (3 obols), the *ŏbŏlŏs*, and the *hēmĭŏbŏlĭŏn* (½ obol) were small silver coins; the *tĕtartēmŏrĭŏn* (¼ obol) the smallest of all. The Greek states always adopted a silver currency, gold being rarely issued. The largest gold piece was the *dĭdrachmŏn* or golden *statēr* (=20 silver *drachmæ*). Besides this we find drachmas, triobols, obols, half-obols, quarter-obols, and even eighth obols in gold. The gold money most commonly current in Greece was, down to the Macedonian age, the royal Persian coin

(3) DARIC.

called *Dăreikŏs*, or Daric (fig. 3). It was stamped on one side with a crowned archer, on the other with an oblong incuse. This corresponded with the gold *stater* of Attica and of the cities of Asia Minor. Among these should be especially mentioned the *stater* of Cyzĭcus or the *Cyzicēnus* =28 silver *drachmæ*. The earliest copper coin issued at Athens was the *Chalkūs* =⅛ of a silver obol (440 B.C.). In the time of Alexander the Great the silver coinage stopped at the

Head of Apollo.   Victorious *biga*.
(4) GOLD STATER OF PHILIP II OF MACEDON.

triobolos, and it therefore became necessary to represent the smaller fractions in copper. The silver money of Attica was in very general use, but the Attic standard was not adopted in Greece Proper. It spread westward, however, in quite early times. In the greater part of Sicily, and in Tarentum and Etruria, the coinage was from the first regulated in accordance with the Attic standard. But the wide diffusion of this standard was mainly due to the action of Philip II of Macedon and Alexander the Great. The former adopted it when introducing his gold coinage (*Philippus*, fig. 4) the latter for his silver money (fig. 5). For even after Alexander's death this standard held its ground in the kingdoms of the

Head of Heracles.   Zeus.

(5) TETRADRACHMON OF ALEXANDER THE GREAT.

Macedonian empire, except in Egypt, where the Ptolemies maintained the old coinage of the country. Macedonian influence extended the Attic currency into many other states, *e.g.* Epirus, the coasts of the Black Sea, and even Parthia. The largest Greek gold coin is the 20-*stater* piece of the Græco-Bactrian king Eucrătĭdēs, now preserved in Paris; the largest silver coins are the 10-*drachma* pieces of Athens, Syracuse (fig. 6) and Alexander the Great.

Hellenic coins are important as giving a grand and complete idea of the development of plastic art among the Greeks. In the Greek cities of Italy and Sicily, in particular, the art of stamping coins had attained considerable importance as early as the 5th century B.C., and in the 4th century with its life-like characterisa-

(2) *Roman.* As in Greece, so in Rome, oxen and sheep were originally the medium of exchange. The oldest pecuniary fines were exacted in cattle, and the Latin word for money, *pĕcūnĭa*, is derived from *pĕcŭs*. In later times unwrought copper (*æs rŭdĕ*) given in pieces according to weight, took the place of oxen. Bars of cast copper marked on both sides with some figure (as of an ox, pig, or fowl) are said to have been introduced by king Servius Tullius, when he took in hand the regulation of weights and measures. The first demonstrable example of a coin is from the age of the decemvirs (about 450 B.C.). The unit of coinage was the *as* of cast copper, carrying the nominal weight of the Roman pound (*libra* = 12 *unciæ, see* fig. 7). The *as* (*æs*

Female Head (Persephone or Arethusa).   Quadriga and armour (prizes of victory).

(6) DECADRACHMON OF SYRACUSE.
(about 400 B.C.)

grăvĕ) bore the image of Janus: the coins representing its fractions were all stamped on the reverse side with the figure of a

Head of Janus.   Prow of Ship.

(7) ROMAN AS OF CAST COPPER.

tions, and with the rich variety and noble perfection of its forms, it reached the highest degree of finish.

ship's prow. These were, *sēmis*, with the head of Jupiter = $\frac{1}{2}$ *as* or 6 *unciae ; triens* with the head of Minerva, $\frac{1}{3}$ of an *as* =

unciæ; quadrans, with the head of Hercŭlēs, ¼ *as* = 3 *unciæ; sextans*, with the head
of Mercury, ⅙ *as* = 2 *unciæ; uncia*, with the
head of *Roma*, 1/12 *as*. As in the course of
time the copper money became lighter, the
smaller fractional coins were first struck,
and afterwards all the fractions. This
copper currency was calculated exclusively
for the home trade, so that it was easily
allowed to suffer a continuous depreciation,
at first to 4, then to 2, after 217 B.C. to 1
ounce, after B.C. 89 to ½ an ounce, and under
the Empire even to ¼ an ounce. In 269
B.C. a silver currency was introduced, and
a mint for it set up on the Capitoline Hill
in the temple of Juno Mŏnēta. The silver
fractional coins struck according to the
Athenian and Sicilian standard were the
dēnārĭus, somewhat higher in value than the

Roma.   Castor and Pollux.

(8) DENARIUS.

(9) DENARIUS OF JULIUS CÆSAR.

Attic drachma (about 9½*d.*, figs. 8 and 9) =
10 *assēs* of 4 ounces; the *quīnārĭus* = 5
assēs ; and the *sestertĭus* = 2½ *assēs*. These
coins were denoted by the marks X. V. and
II. S. (or 2½) respectively (fig. 10). They all

Roma.   Castor and Pollux.
(10) SESTERTIUS.

bore, on the upper side, the head of the goddess Roma with her winged helmet, and on
the reverse the two Dioscūri on horseback.
In later times Diana Victoria in her two-
horse chariot, and Jupiter in his four-horse
chariot, successively took the place of the
Dioscuri. From the middle of the 1st
century there was no fixed device for the
reverse side. The *sestertius* was the equivalent of the old heavy *as*, which although

long disused, survived as the standard of
reckoning. Payments were generally made
in *denarii*, but the account made up in
sestertii, whence the word *nummus* (coin)
was applied *par excellence* to the *sestertius*.
   The reduction of the copper *as* to 1 *uncia*
in 217 B.C. degraded the copper money to
the position of small coin, and a silver
currency drove out the copper. The
denarius sank at the same time to the value
of about 8½*d.*, which it maintained till the
time of Nero. The *denarius* was reckoned
as = 15 asses, the *quinarius* as 8, and the
sestertius (about 2*d.*) = 4. At about the
same period a temporary effort was made
to introduce gold coinage. This movement
was not taken up again till towards the
end of the Republic, when Cæsar struck a
large number of gold coins (*aurĕus*) equal
in weight to 1/40 of the Roman pound, and
in value 25 denarii or 100 sestertii (nearly
23 shillings). No regular coinage was
carried on in the time of the Republic, but
the necessary money was minted as occasion
required. This was done in Rome at the
commission of the senate under the superintendence of certain officials entrusted with
the duty. A permanent board of three
persons (*trēs vĭri mŏnētālēs*) was at last
appointed for the purpose. In the provinces
money was coined by the Roman generals
and governors. From the time of Augustus
the emperor retained the exclusive privilege
of coining gold and silver money, the
copper coinage being left to the senate.
The standard of the imperial coinage was
the *aureus* of Cæsar, the weight of which
sank (with many variations) lower and
lower as time went on, till in 312 A.D. Constantine fixed it at 1/72 of a lb. (= between

(11) AUREUS OF MARCUS AURELIUS.

12 and 13 shillings, fig. 11). The *aureus*
was now called *sŏlĭdus*, and was stamped
at first with the Latin mark LXXII, afterwards with the Greek OB (= 72). It continued in use until the fall of the Byzantine
empire. Of the silver coins of the Republic
the *denarius* and *quinarius* alone held
their ground under the Empire, the rest
being stamped in copper. The *denarius*
retained the value fixed 217 B.C. (about 8½*d.*)

until the time of Nero, under whom it fell in weight and purity till its value was only sixpence. During the 2nd century it sank to $3\frac{1}{2}d.$, below the half of its former value, and the silver coinage was consequently changed into small money. Diocletian was the first to restore some order to the currency. After 292 A.D. he issued a coin (*argentĕus*) of pure silver, and equal in weight to the Neronian *denarius*. The *argenteus* maintained its ground till 360 A.D., when it made way for a new system of silver coinage on the standard of the gold *solidus*. The copper coins bore the mark S.C. (*Senātūs Consulto*), because issued by the senate. Under the Empire the following small coins were minted; the *sestertius* =4 *asses*; *dupondiŭs* =2 *asses*, both of brass; the *semis* ($=\frac{1}{2}$ an *as*), and the *quadrans* $=\frac{1}{4}$ *as*, both of copper. These last were the smallest change. The *quadrans* went out of use as early as Trajan, at the beginning of the 2nd century A.D., the *dupondius*, *as*, and *semis*, in the middle, and the *sestertius* in the last half of the 3rd century, when Diocletian issued two new copper coins, one of which was called *denarius*.

Cŏlacrētæ (Gr. *Kōlakrētai*). A financial board at Athens, whose duty it was to administer the fund accruing from the fines taken in the courts of justice. It was this fund from which the cost of the public meals in the Prÿtănēum, and the salary of the Hēlïastæ, was defrayed. The name properly means "collectors of hams," and probably points to the fact that the hams of the victims sacrificed on certain occasions were given to the *Colacretæ* as contributions to the meals in question.

Collēgĭum. The general term in Latin for an association. The word was applied in a different sense to express the mutual relation of such magistrates as were *collēgæ*. Besides the *collegia* of the great priesthoods, and of the magistrates' attendants (*see* APPARITORES), there were numerous associations, which, although not united by any specifically religious objects, had a religious centre in the worship of some deity or other. Such were the numerous *collegia* of artisans (*ŏpĭfĭcum* or *artĭfĭcum*), and the societies existing among the poor for providing funerals, which first appear under the Empire. The political clubs (*collegia sŏdālĭcĭa*) were associated in the worship of the Lărēs Compĭtālēs, and were, indeed, properly speaking, *collegia compĭtālĭcĭa*, or "societies of the cross-ways." The religious

societies were, in some instances, established by the State for the performance of certain public religious services (*see* SODALITAS), in other cases they were formed by private individuals, who made it their business to keep up the shrines of particular deities (often foreign deities) at their own expense.

Collūthus (Gr. *Kollūthŏs*). A Greek poet, native of Lycŏpŏlis, in Upper Egypt, who flourished at the beginning of the 6th century A.D. He wrote an unimportant epic poem in 385 verses, on the rape of Helen, in which he followed the cyclic poets.

Cŏlōnī ("cultivators"). During the later imperial age the *coloni* were serfs, who, on payment of a certain rent, cultivated a piece of land, belonging to their masters, for their own profit. They were so far free that they could not be sold, could contract legal marriages, and could own property. But they were absolutely bound to the estate, and if this was sold, passed with the rest of what was upon it to the new owner. The *coloni* were probably the descendants of barbarians, who were settled in the provinces for agricultural purposes.

Colonies. (1) *Greek.* In Greece, colonies were sometimes founded by vanquished peoples, who left their homes to escape subjection at the hand of a detested enemy; sometimes as a sequel to civil disorders; sometimes to get rid of surplus population, and thereby to avoid internal convulsions. But in most cases the object was to establish and facilitate relations of trade with foreign countries. If a Greek city was sending out a colony, an oracle (before all others that of Delphi) was almost invariably consulted. Sometimes certain classes of citizens were called upon to take part in the enterprises; sometimes one son was chosen by lot from every house where there were several sons; and strangers expressing a desire to join were admitted. A person of distinction was selected to guide the emigrants and make the necessary arrangements. It was usual to honour these founders of colonies, after their death, as heroes. Some of the sacred fire was taken from the public hearth in the *Prÿtănĕiŏn*, and the fire on the public hearth of the new city was kindled thereat. And, just as each individual had his private shrines, so the new community maintained the worship of its chief domestic deities, the colony sending embassies and votive gifts to their principal festivals.

The relation between colony and mother-

city was viewed as one of mutual affection.
Any differences that arose were made up,
if possible, by peaceful means, war being
deemed excusable only in cases of extreme
necessity. The charter of foundation contained general provisions for the arrangement of the affairs of the colony, and also
some special enactments. The constitution
of the mother-city was usually adopted by
the colony, but the new city remained politically independent. If the colony sent out
a fresh colony on its own account, the
mother-city was generally consulted, or was
at least requested to furnish a leader. The
Clērŭchī formed a special class of Greek
colonists (*see* CLERUCHI). The trade factories set up in foreign countries (in Egypt,
for instance) were somewhat different from
the ordinary colonies, the members retaining the right of domicile in their own
fatherland.

(2) *Roman.* It was an old custom in
Italy to send out colonies for the purpose of
securing new conquests. The Romans, accordingly, having no standing army, used
to plant bodies of their own citizens in
conquered towns as a kind of garrison.
These bodies would consist partly of Roman
citizens, usually to the number of three
hundred, partly of members of the Latin
confederacy, in larger numbers. The third
part of the conquered territory was handed
over to the settlers. The *coloniæ
cīvĭum Rōmānōrum* (colonies of
Roman citizens) were specially intended to secure the two sea-coasts
of Italy, and were hence called
coloniæ marĭtĭmæ. The *coloniæ
Latīnæ,* of which there was a far
greater number, served the same
purpose for the mainland.

The duty of leading the colonists
and founding the settlement was
entrusted to a commission usually
consisting of three members, and
elected by the people. These men
continued to stand in the relation
of patrons (*patrōnī*) to the colony
after its foundation. The colonists
entered the conquered city in military array, preceded by banners, and
the foundation was celebrated with
special solemnities. The *coloniæ*
were free from taxes, and had their
own constitution, a copy of the Roman, electing from their own body
their senate and other officers of state. To
this constitution the original inhabitants
had to submit. The *coloniæ civium Ro-*

manorum retained the Roman citizenship,
and were free from military service, their
position as out-posts being regarded as an
equivalent. The members of the *coloniæ
Latīnæ* served among the *socii,* and possessed the so-called *ius Latinum* (*see*
LATINI). This secured to them the right of
acquiring property (*commercium*) and settlement in Rome, and, under certain conditions,
the power of becoming Roman citizens;
though in course of time these rights underwent many limitations.

From the time of the Gracchi the colonies
lost their military character. Colonization
came to be regarded as a means of providing
for the poorest class of the Roman populace.
After the time of Sulla it was adopted as a
way of granting land to veteran soldiers.
The right of founding colonies was taken
away from the people by Cæsar, and passed
into the hands of the emperors, who used it
(mainly in the provinces) for the exclusive
purpose of establishing military settlements,
partly with the old idea of securing conquered territory. It was only in exceptional cases that the provincial colonies
enjoyed the immunity from taxation which
was granted to those in Italy.

Cŏlossēum. *See* AMPHITHEATRE.

Cŏlossus of Rhodes. *See* CHARES.

Cŏlumbărĭŭm. Properly a dove-cote. The
word was metaphorically applied to a sub-

COLUMBARIUM OF THE FREEDMEN OF OCTAVIA.
(Near the *Porta Latina,* Rome.)

terranean vault provided with rows of small
niches, lying one above the other, and intended for the reception of the urns contain-

ing the ashes of the dead. These large burial places were built by rich people whose freedmen were too numerous to be interred in the family burial-place. They were also erected by the Cæsars for their slaves and freedmen. Several of these still exist, for instance, that of Livia, the consort of Augustus, who built one for her freedmen on the Appian road. Common burial-places, in which a niche could be bespoken beforehand, were sometimes constructed by private individuals on speculation for people who were too poor to have a grave of their own. *Columbaria* were usually built by religious or mercantile societies, or by burial clubs for their own members. In such cases the members contributed a single capital payment and yearly subscriptions, which gave them the right to a decent burial and a niche in the vault. The names of the dead were inscribed on marble tablets over each niche. (*See* cut.)

Cŏlŭmella (*Lūcĭus Iūnĭus Mŏdĕrātus*). A Latin writer on agriculture. He was a native of Gādēs, in Spain, and a contemporary of his countryman, the philosopher Sĕnĕca. He was the author of a thorough and exhaustive work on agriculture (*De Re Rustĭcā*), which he founded partly upon a study of all previous works on the subject, partly on his own experience, gathered in Spain, Italy, and Asia. The work was written about 60 A.D., and consists of twelve books, arranged as follows : I–II, on crops and pastures; III–V, on trees and vine-yards; VI–IX, on cattle, birds, fishes, and bees; X, on horticulture; XI–XII, on the duties and occupations of the farmer. The tenth book is written in polished hexameters, as a supplement to Vergil's fourth Georgic. This Columella did at the request of Publĭus Silvīnus, to whom the whole work is dedicated. Besides this, his great work, Columella had previously written a shorter treatise, of which the second book, on trees (*De Arbŏrĭbŭs*), still survives. Columella's exposition is clear and easy, and his language (if we pass over the rhetorical ornaments added after the fashion of his time) correct. The tenth book, though written in verse, has, it must be said, little poetical merit.

Cŏlumna Rostrāta. *See* ARCHITECTURE, ORDERS OF.

Comæthō (Gr. *Komaithō*). In Greek mythology, the daughter of Ptĕrĕlāüs, king of the Tēlĕbŏī. Her father had a golden lock in his hair, given him by Pŏseidōn, and conferring immortality. Of this he was deprived by his daughter, who was

slain for her treachery by Amphĭtrўōn, the enemy of her race. (*See* AMPHITRYON.)

Comedy. (1) *Greek*. The Greek comedy, like the Greek tragedy and satyric drama, had its origin in the festivals of Dĭŏnýsus. As its name, *kōmōdĭa*, or the song of the *kōmŏs*, implies, it arose from the unrestrained singing and jesting common in the *komos*, or merry procession of Dionysus. According to the tradition, it was the Doric inhabitants of Mĕgăra, well known for their love of fun, who first worked up these jokes into a kind of farce. The inhabitants of Megara accordingly boasted that they were the founders of Greek comedy. From Megara, it was supposed, the popular farce found its way to the other Dorian communities, and one Sūsărĭōn was said to have transplanted it to the Attic deme of Icăria about 580 B.C. No further information is in existence as to the nature of the Megarian or Dorian popular comedy. The local Doric farce was developed into literary form in Sicily by Epicharmus of Cōs (about 540–450 B.C.). This writer gave a comic treatment not only to mythology, but to subjects taken from real life. The contemporary of Epicharmus, Phormus or Phormis, and his pupil Dīnŏlŏchus, may also be named as representatives of the Dorian comedy.

The beginnings of the Attic comedy, like those of the Attic tragedy, are associated with the deme of Icaria, known to have been the chief seat of the worship of Dĭŏnýsus in Attica. Not only Thespis, the father of tragedy, but also Chĭŏnīdēs and Magnēs (about 550 B.C.), who, if the story may be trusted, first gave a more artistic form to the Megarian comedy introduced by Susarion, were natives of Icaria. Comedy did not become, in the proper sense, a part of literature until it had found welcome and consideration at Athens in the time of the Persian wars; until its form had been moulded on the finished outlines of tragedy ; and until, finally, it had received from the State the same recognition as tragedy. The Old Comedy, as it was called, had its origin in personal abuse. It was Crătēs who first gave it its peculiar political character, and his younger contemporary Crătīnus who turned it mainly or exclusively in this direction. The masters of the Old Comedy are usually held to be Cratinus and his younger contemporaries, Eupŏlis and Aristophănēs. It attained its youth in the time of Pĕrĭclēs and the Peloponnesian war ; the period when the Athenian democracy had reached its highest development. These three masters had many rivals, who fell, however, on the whole beneath their level, among others Phĕrĕcrătēs, Hermippus, Tĕlĕclīdēs, Phrȳnĭchus, Ameipsiās, Plato and Theopompus.

A good idea of the characteristics of the Old Comedy may be formed from the eleven surviving plays of Aristophanes.* The Greek tragedy has a meaning for all time; but the Old Comedy, the most brilliant and striking production of all Athenian literature, has its roots in Athenian life, and addressed the Athenian public only.

Dealing from the very first with the grotesque and absurd side of things, it was the scourge of all vice, folly, and weakness. The social life of Athens, so restless, and yet so open, offered an inexhaustible store of material; and the comedian was always sure of a witty, laughter-loving public, on whom no allusion was lost. The first aim of the Athenian comedy was, no doubt, to make men laugh, but this was not all. Beneath it there lay a serious and patriotic motive. The poet, who was secured by the license of the stage, wished to bring to light and turn to ridicule the abuses and degeneracy of his time. The Attic comedians are all admirers of the good old times, and, accordingly, the declared enemies of the social innovations which were beginning to make their way, the signs in many cases, no doubt, of approaching decline. It was not, however, the actual phenomena of life which were sketched in the Old Comedy. The latter is really a grotesque and fantastic caricature; the colours are laid on thick, and propriety, as we moderns understand it, is thrown to the winds. These plays abound in coarseness and obscenity of the broadest kind, the natural survival of the rude license allowed at the Dionysiac festival. The choice and treatment of the subjects show the same tendency to the grotesque and fantastic. Fancy and caprice revel at their will, unchecked by any regard either for the laws of poetical probability or for adequacy of occasion. The action is generally quite simple, sketched out in a few broad strokes, and carried out in a motley series of loosely connected scenes. The language is always choice and fine, never leaving the forms of the purest Atticism. The metres admit a greater freedom and movement than those of the tragedy.

* Only eleven have come down to us complete: the rest are in fragments.

A comedy, like a tragedy, consisted of the dramatic dialogue, written mostly in iambic sēnării, and the lyrical chorus. The division of the dialogue into prŏlŏgŏs, ĕpeisŏdĭŏn, and exŏdŏs, and of the chorus into părŏdŏs and stăsĭma, are the same as in tragedy (see TRAGEDY). But, while the tragic chorus consisted of fifteen singers, there were twenty-four in the comic. A peculiarity of the comic chorus is the părăbăsis, a series of lines entirely unconnected with the plot, in which the poet, through the mouth of the chorus, addresses the public directly about his own concerns, or upon burning questions of the day (see PARABASIS). Like the tragedies, the comedies were performed at the great festivals of Dionysus, the Dionysia and Lēnæa. On each occasion five poets competed for the prize, each with one play.

For a short time, but a short time only, a limitation had been put upon the absolute freedom with which the poets of the Old Comedy lashed the shortcomings of the government and its chief men. The downfall of the democracy, however, deprived them of this liberty. The disastrous issue of the Peloponnesian war had, moreover, ruined the Athenian finances, and made it necessary to give up the expensive chorus, and with it the parabasis. Thus deprived of the means of existence, the Old Comedy was doomed to extinction. In its place came what was called the Middle Comedy, from about 400–338 B.C. This was a modification of the Old Comedy, with a character corresponding to the altered circumstance of the time. The Middle Comedy was in no sense political; it avoided all open attack on individuals, and confined itself to treating the typical faults and weaknesses of mankind. Its main line was burlesque and parody, of which the objects were the tragedies and the mythology in general. It was also severe upon the lives of the philosophers. It dealt in typical characters, such as bullies, parasites, and courtesans. The writers of the Middle Comedy were very prolific, more than eight hundred of their plays having survived as late as the 2nd century A.D. The most celebrated of them were Antiphănēs of Athens and Alexis of Thurii; next to these came Eubūlus, and Anaxandrĭdās of Rhodes.

A new departure is signalized by the dramas of what is called the New Comedy. In these, as in the modern society drama, life was represented in its minutest details. The New Comedy offered a play regularly constructed like that of tragedy, characterized by fine humour, and but seldom touching on public life. The language was that of ordinary society, and the plot was worked out in a connected form from the beginning to the *dénouement*. The chief art of the poets of the New Comedy lay in the development of the plot and the faithful portraiture of character. The stock subjects are illicit love affairs; for honest women lived in retirement, and stories of honourable love, therefore, were practically excluded from the stage. The ordinary characters are young men in love, fathers of the good-natured or the scolding type, cunning slaves, panders, parasites, and bragging officers. Besides the dialogue proper, we find traces of parts written in lyric metres for the higher style of singing. These were, in all probability, like the dialogue, performed by the actors.

The fate of the New resembles that of the Middle Comedy, only a few fragments of its numerous pieces having survived. Of some of them, however, we have Latin adaptations by Plautus and Terence. Its greatest master was Menander, besides whom should be mentioned Dīphĭlus, Phĭlēmōn, Philippĭdēs, Posīdippus, and Apollŏdōrus of Carystus. The New Comedy flourished from 330 B.C. till far into the 3rd century A.D.

In about 300 B.C. the old Dorian farce was revived in a literary form in Southern Italy by Rhinthōn, the creator of the *Hĭlărŏtrăgœdia*. The *Hilarotragœdia* was for the most part a parody of the tragic stories.

(2) *Roman.* Like the Greeks, the Italian people had their popular dramatic pieces; the *versūs Fescennīni*, for instance, which were at first associated with the mimic drama, first introduced in 390 B.C. from Etruria in consequence of a plague, to appease the wrath of heaven (*see* FESCENNINI VERSUS). From this combination sprang the *sătŭra*, a performance consisting of flute-playing, mimic dance, songs, and dialogue. The *Atellāna* (*q.v.*) was a second species of popular Italian comedy, distinguished from others by having certain fixed or stock characters. The creator of the regular Italian comedy and tragedy was a Greek named Livius Andronīcus, about 240 B.C. Like the Italian tragedy, the Italian comedy was, in form and contents, an imitation, executed with more or less freedom, of the Greek. It was the New Greek Comedy which the Romans took as

their model. This comedy, which represents scenes from Greek life, was called *palliāta*, after the Greek *pallium*, or cloak. The dramatic *satura*, and the *Atellana*, which afterwards supplanted the *satura* as a concluding farce, continued to exist side by side. The Latin comedy was brought to perfection by Plautus and Terence, the only Roman dramatists from whose hands we still possess complete plays. We should also mention Nævius and Ennius (both of whom wrote tragedies as well as comedies), Cæcilius, and Turpilius, with whom, towards the end of the 3nd century B.C., this style of composition died out.

About the middle of the 2nd century B.C. a new kind of comedy, the *tŏgāta*, (from *tŏga*) made its appearance. The form of it was still Greek, but the life and the characters Italian. The *togata* was represented by Titinius, Atta, and Afrānius, who was accounted the master in this kind of writing. At the beginning of the 1st century B.C. the *Atellana* assumed an artistic form in the hands of Pompōnius and Nŏvius; and some fifty years later the *mimus*, also an old form of popular farce, was similarly handled by Laberius and Publilius Sȳrus. The *mimus* drove all the other varieties of comedy from the field, and held its ground until late in the imperial period.

The Roman comedy, like its model, the New Comedy of the Greeks, had no chorus, the intervals being filled up by performances on the flute. The play consisted, like the Roman tragedy, partly of passages of spoken dialogue in iambic trimeters, partly of musical scenes called *cantĭca*. (*See* CANTICUM.)

Cŏmissātĭō. See MEALS.

Cŏmĭtĭa. The popular assemblies of the Romans, summoned and presided over by a *măgistrātŭs*. In the *comitia* the Roman people appeared as distributed into its political sections, for the purpose of deciding, in the exercise of its sovereign rights, upon the business brought before it by the presiding magistrate. The *comitia* must be distinguished from the *contĭōnēs*. The *contiones* were also summoned and presided over by a magistrate, but they did not assemble in their divisions, and they had nothing to do but to receive the communications of the magistrate. In all its assemblies at Rome, the people remained standing. The original place of meeting was the *cŏmĭtĭum*, a part of the forum. There were three kinds of *comitia*, viz.:

(1) The *Comitia Cūriāta*. This was the assembly of the patricians in their thirty *cūriæ*, who, until the change of the constitution under Servius Tullius, constituted the whole *pŏpŭlus Rōmānus*. During the regal period they were summoned by the *rex* or *interrex*, who brought before them questions to be decided Aye or No. The voting was taken first in each *curia* by heads, and then according to *curiæ*, in an order determined by lot. The business within the competence of this assembly was : (*a*) to elect a king proposed by the *interrex ;* (*b*) to confer upon the king the *impĕrĭum*, by virtue of the *lex cūriāta de imperio ;* (*c*) to decide on declarations of war, appeals, *arrŏgātĭōnēs* (*see* ADOPTION), and the reception of foreign families into the body of the patricians. The Servian constitution transferred the right of declaring aggressive war, and the right of deciding appeals, to the *Comitia Centŭrĭātă*, which, from this time onward, represented the people, now composed of both patricians and plebeians. After the establishment of the Republic, the *Comitia Curiata* retained the right (*a*) of conferring, on the proposal of the senate, the *imperium* on the magistrates elected by the *Comitia Centuriata*, and on the dictator elected by the consuls ; (*b*) of confirming, likewise on the proposal of the senate, the alterations in the constitution decided upon by the *Comitia Centuriata*, and *Trĭbūta*.

The extinction of the political difference between Patricians and Plebeians destroyed the political position of the *Comitia Curiata*, and the mere shadow of their rights survived. The assembly itself became an unreality, so much so that, in the end, the presence of the thirty *lictōrēs cūrĭātĭ*, and three augurs, was sufficient to enable legal resolutions to be passed (*see* LICTORS). But the *Comitia Curiata* retained the powers affecting the reception of a non-patrician into the patrician order, and the powers affecting the proceeding of *arrŏgātĭō*, especially in cases where the transition of a patrician into a plebeian family was concerned. Evidence of the exercise of these functions on their part may be traced down the imperial period.

The *Comitia Cālāta* were also an assembly of the patrician *curiæ*. They were so called because publicly summoned (*calāre*). The *pontĭfĭcēs* presided, and the functions of the assembly were : (*a*) to inaugurate the *flāmĭnēs*, the *rex sacrōrum*, and indeed the king himself during the regal period. (*b*) The *dētestātĭō sacrōrum*, previous to an act of *arrogatio*. This was the formal release of a person passing by adoption into another family from the *sacra* of his former family (*see* ADOPTION). (*c*) The ratification of wills twice a year ; but this applies only to an early period. (*d*) The announcement of the calendar of festivals on the first day of every month.

(2) *Comitia Centuriata*. The assembly of the whole people, patrician as well as plebeian, arranged according to the *centuriæ* established by Servius Tullius. The original founder of the *comitia centuriata* transferred to them certain political rights which had previously been exercised by the *comitia curiata*. It was not, however, until the foundation of the Republic, when the sovereign power in the state was transferred to the body of citizens, that they attained their real political importance. They then became the assembly in which the people, collectively, expressed its will. The right of summoning the *comitia centuriata* originally belonged to the king. During the republican period it belonged, in its full extent, to the consuls and the dictator alone. The other magistrates possessed it only within certain limits. The *interrex*, for instance, could, in case of there being no consuls, summon the *comitia centuriata* to hold an election, but he could summon them for this purpose only. The censors could call them together only for the holding of the *census* and the *lustrum ;* the prætors, it may be conjectured, only in the case of capital trials. In all other instances the consent of the consuls, or their authorisation, was indispensable.

The duties of the *comitia centuriata* during the republican period were as follows : (*a*) To elect the higher magistrates, consuls, censors, and prætors. (*b*) To give judgment in all the capital trials in which appeal to the people was permitted from the sentence of the magistrate sitting in judgment. This popular jurisdiction was gradually limited to political trials, common offences being dealt with by the ordinary commissions. And in the later republican age the judicial assemblies of the *comitia centuriata* became, in general, rarer, especially after the formation of special standing commissions (*quæstĭōnēs perpĕtŭæ*) for the trial of a number of offences regarded as political. (*c*) To decide on declaring a war of aggression ; this on the proposal of the consuls, with the approval of the senate. (*d*) To pass laws proposed by the higher magistrates, with the approval of the senate. This right lost much of its value after 287 B.C., when the legislative powers of the *comitia tributa* were made equal to those of the *comitia centuriata*. After this time the legislative activity of the latter assembly gradually diminished.

The *comitia centuriata* were originally a military assembly, and the citizens accordingly, in ancient times, attended them in arms. On the night before the meeting, the magistrate summoning the assembly took the auspices on the place of meeting, the *Campus Martius.* If the auspices were favourable, signals were given, before daybreak, from the walls and the citadel by the blowing of horns, summoning the citizens to a *contĭō.* The presiding magistrate offered a sacrifice, and repeated a solemn prayer, and the assembly proceeded to consider the business which required its decision. Private individuals were not allowed to speak, except with the consent of the presiding magistrate. At his command the armed people divided themselves into their *centurĭæ,* and marched in this order to the *Campus Martius,* preceded by banners, and headed by the cavalry. Arrived at the *Campus,* they proceeded to the voting, the president having again put the proposal to the people in the form of a question ("Do you wish?" "Do you command?") While the voting was going on, a red flag stood on the *Jānĭcŭlum.* The *ĕquĭtēs,* who in ancient times used to begin the battles in war, opened the voting, and their eighteen centuries were therefore called *præ̆rŏgātīvæ.* The result of their vote was immediately published, and, being taken as an omen for the voters who were to follow, was usually decisive. Then came the 175 centuries, 170 of which composed the five *classēs* of infantry in their order. Each *centuria* counted as casting one vote; this vote was decided by a previous voting within the *centuria,* which was at first open, but in later times was taken by ballot. If the 18 centuries of *equites,* and the 80 centuries of the first class, with whom went the two centuries of mechanics (*centurĭæ fabrum*), were unanimous, the question was decided, as there would be a majority of 100 centuries to 93. If not, the voting went on until one side secured the votes of at least 97 centuries. The lower *classes* only voted in the rare cases where the votes of the higher *classes* were not united. The proceedings concluded with a formal announcement of the result on the part of the presiding magistrate, and the dismissal of the host. If no result was arrived at by sunset, or if unfavourable omens appeared during the proceedings, or while the voting was going on, the assembly was adjourned until the next convenient occasion.

This form of voting gave the wealthier citizens a decided advantage over the poorer, and lent an aristocratic character to the *comitia centuriata.* In the 3rd century B.C. a change was introduced in the interest of the lower *classes.* Each of the thirty-five *trĭbūs,* or districts, into which the Roman territory was divided, included ten *centurĭæ,* five of *iūnĭŏrēs* and five of *sĕnĭŏrēs.* (For the five *classes,* see CENTURIA.) Thus each of the five *classes* included 70 *centurĭæ,* making 350 *centurĭæ* in all. To this number add the eighteen *centurĭæ equitum,* and the five *centurĭæ* not included in the propertied classes; namely, two of *fabri* (mechanics), two of *tŭbĭcĭnēs* (musicians), and one of *prōlĕtārĭī* and *lĭberti* (the very poor and the freedmen), and the whole number of *centurĭæ* amounts to 373. The *centurĭæ,* it must be remembered, had by this time quite lost their military character. Under this arrangement the 88 votes of the *equites* and the first *classis* were confronted with the 285 votes of the rest. Besides this, the right of voting first was taken from the *equites* and given to the *centuria præ̆rogativa* chosen by lot from the first *classis.* The voting, it is true, was still taken in the order of the *classes,* but the *classes* were seldom unanimous as in former times; for the interests of the *trĭbūs,* which were represented in each *classis* by two *centurĭæ* respectively, were generally divergent, and the centuries voted in the sense of their tribe. The consequence was that it was often necessary — indeed, perhaps that it became the rule, at least at elections—to take the votes of all the *classes.*[1]

In old times the military arrangement was sufficient to secure the maintenance of order. But, after its disappearance, the *classes* were separated, and the *centurĭæ* kept apart by wooden barriers (*sæpta*), from which the *centurĭæ* passed over bridges into an open inner space called *ŏvĭlĕ* (sheep-fold). On the position of the *comitia centuriata* during the imperial age, see below.

(3) *Comitia Trĭbūta.* This was the collective assembly of the people arranged according to the local distribution of tribes (*see* TRIBUS). It must be distinguished from the *concĭlĭum plēbis,* which was an

---

[1] See, however, Cic. *pro Plancio,* 49, *nemo umquam prior eam* (sc. *centuriam prærogativam*) *tulerit quin renunciatus sit consul.*

assembly of the tribes under the presidency of plebeian magistrates, *i.e.*, the *trĭbūni* and the *œdĭlēs plēbeii*. As these magistrates had no right to summon patricians, the resolutions passed by a *concilium plebis* were (strictly speaking) only *plēbĭ scīta*. It was a *lex centuriata* of some earlier date than 462 B.C. that probably first made these resolutions binding on all the citizens, provided they received the approval of the senate. This approval was rendered unnecessary by the *lex* Hortensia of 287 B.C., and from that date onward the *concilia plebis* became the principal organ of legislation. The method of voting resembled that in the *comitia curiata*, and the regular place of meeting was the *Comitium*. No auspices were taken. From 471 B.C. the *concilia plebis* elected the *tribuni* and the *œdiles plebeii*. Among the other functions of the *concilia plebis* were the following:

(*a*) To give judicial decisions in all suits instituted by the tribunes and ædiles of the *plebs*, for offences against the *plebs* or its representatives. In later times these suits were mostly instituted on the ground of bad or illegal administration. The tribunes and ædiles had, in these cases, the power of inflicting pecuniary fines ranging up to a large amount. (*b*) To pass resolutions on proposals made by the tribunes of the *plebs* and the higher magistrates on foreign and domestic affairs, on the conclusion of peace, for instance, or the making of treaties. Their power was almost unlimited, and the more important because, strictly speaking, it was only the higher magistrates who required the authorization of the senate. Nor had the senate more than the right of quashing a measure passed without due formalities.

The *comitia tributa*, as distinguished from the *concilia plebis*, were presided over by the consuls, the prætors, and (in judicial cases) the curule ædiles. Until the latter years of the Republic, the assembly usually met upon the Capitol, and afterwards on the *Campus Martius*. The functions of the *comitia tributa*, gradually acquired, were as follows: (*a*) The election of all the lower magistrates, ordinary (as the *tribuni plebis*, *tribuni mĭlĭtum*, *œdĭlēs plebis*, *œdiles cŭrūlēs*) and extraordinary, under the presidency partly of the tribunes, partly of the consuls or prætors. (*b*) The nomination of the *pontĭfex maxĭmus*, and of the co-opted members of the religious *collēgĭa* of the *pontĭfĭcēs*, *augŭrēs*, and *decemvĭrī sacrōrum*. This nomination was carried out by a

committee of seventeen tribes chosen by lot. (*c*) The fines judicially inflicted by the *concilia plebis* required in all graver cases the sanction of the tribes.

The *comitia tributa* were summoned at least seventeen days before the meeting, by the simple proclamation of a herald. As in the case of the *comitia centuriata*, business could neither be begun nor continued in the face of adverse auspices. Like the *comitia centuriata* too, the tribal assembly met at daybreak, and could not sit beyond sunset. If summoned by the tribunes, the *comitia tributa* could only meet in the city, or within the radius of a mile from it. The usual place of assembly was the Forum or the *comitium (q.v.)*. If summoned by other authorities, the assembly met outside the city, most commonly in the *Campus Martius*. The proceedings opened with a prayer, unaccompanied by sacrifice. The business in hand was then discussed in a *contio* (*see* above, p. 155 *a*); and the proposal having been read out, the meeting was requested to arrange itself according to its thirty-five tribes in the *sœpta* or wooden fences. Lots were drawn to decide which tribe should vote first. The tribe on which this duty fell was called *princĭpĭum*. The result of this first vote was proclaimed, and the other tribes then proceeded to vote simultaneously, not successively. The votes given by each tribe were then announced in an order determined by lot. Finally, the general result of the voting was made known.

The proposer of a measure was bound to put his proposal into due form, and publish it beforehand. When a measure came to the vote, it was accepted or rejected as a whole. It became law when the presiding magistrate announced that it had been accepted.

The character of the *comitia* had begun to decline even in the later period of the Republic. Even the citizens of Rome took but little part in them, and this is still more true of the population of Italy, who had received the Roman citizenship in 89 B.C. The *comitia tributa*, in particular, sank gradually into a mere gathering of the city mob, strengthened on all sides by the influx of corrupt elements. The results of the voting came more and more to represent not the public interest, but the effects of direct or indirect corruption. Under the Empire the *comitia centuriata* and *tributa* continued to exist, in a shadowy form, it is true, down to the 3rd century A.D. Julius Cæsar had deprived them of the right of deciding on war and peace. Under Augustus they lost the power of jurisdiction, and, practically, the power of legislation. The imperial measures were indeed laid before the *comitia tributa* for ratification, but this was all; and under the successors of Augustus even this proceeding became rarer. Since the time of Vespasian the emperors, at their accession, received their legislative and other powers from the *comitia tributa;* but this, like the rest, was a mere formality. The power of election was that which, in appearance at least, survived longest. Augustus, like Julius Cæsar, allowed the *comitia centuriata* to confirm the nomination of two candidates for the consulship. He also left to the *comitia centuriata* and *tributa* the power of free election to half the other magistracies; the other half being filled by nominees of his own. Tiberius transferred the last remnant of free elective power to the senate, whose proposals, originating under imperial influence, were laid before the *comitia* for ratification. The formalities, the auspices, prayer, sacrifice, and proclamation, were now the important thing, and the measures proposed were carried, not by regular voting, but by acclamation.

Cŏmĭtĭum. The name of a small space in Rome, bounded on the north by the senate-house (*see* Curia), and on the south by the *rostra* (*see* Rostra). Down to the 2nd century B.C. it was used for the meetings the assemblies and of the courts of law. After the removal of the *rostra* it became part of the Forum. *See* Plan under Forum, No. 18.

Commerce. *Greece.* In the Homeric poems the Greeks are not represented as a people with a spontaneous inclination to commerce. Indeed, the position of the oldest Greek cities, far away from the sea, sufficiently shows that their founders can have had no idea of *trade* as a means of getting wealth. Greek navigation in ancient times was almost exclusively subservient to war and piracy, to which, for a long time, no stigma was attached in public opinion. And the trade carried on with Greece by the Asiatics, especially the Phœnicians, who then ruled the Greek seas, can hardly have been very active. The Greeks, having no agricultural or industrial produce to offer, could not have tempted many foreigners to deal with them. But in the centuries succeeding the Homeric age, the commerce of Greece was revolutionized.

The islands, especially Ægīna and Eubœa, were foremost in commercial undertakings; the only continental town which was at all successful in this way being Corinth, which was favoured by its incomparable position. It was the foundation of the Hellenic colonies in Asia Minor that first occasioned the free development of Greek trade. The exertions of the Ionians were mainly instrumental in creating two things indispensable to its success, namely, commercial activity, excited by contact with the ancient industries of the East, and a maritime power in the proper sense, which made it possible to oust the Phœnicians from the naval supremacy which they had so long maintained. This new commercial activity necessitated a larger use of the precious metals, and the establishment of a gold and silver coinage, which the Ionians were the first among the Greeks to adopt. This proved a powerful stimulus to the development of commerce, or rather it was the very condition of its existence. Milētus took the first place among the trading colonies. The influence of these cities upon their mother country was so strong that even the Dorians gradually lost their national and characteristic dislike of trade and commerce, and threw themselves actively into their pursuit. Down to the 6th century B.C., Greek commerce had extended itself to the coasts of the Mediterranean and the inland seas connected with it, especially towards the East. It was not until a later time that Athens joined the circle of commercial cities. Even in Solon's time the Athenians had lived mainly by agriculture and cattle-breeding, and it was only with the growth of the democratic constitution that their commercial intercourse with the other cities became at all considerable. The Persian wars, and her position as head of the naval confederacy, raised Athens to the position of the first maritime power in Greece. Under the administration of Pĕrĭclēs she became the centre of all Hellenic activity, not only in art and science, but in trade. It was only Corinth and Corcȳra whose western trade enabled them to maintain a prominent position by the side of Athens. The Greeks of Asia Minor completely lost their commercial position after their conquest by the Persians. The naval supremacy of Athens, and with it its commerce, was completely annihilated by the Peloponnesian war. It

was a long time before the Athenians succeeded in breaking down the maritime
power of Sparta which that war had established. Having done so, they recovered, but
only for a short time, a position of prominence not at all equal to their former
supremacy by sea. The victory of the
Macedonian power entirely destroyed the
political and commercial importance of
Athens, whose trade now fell behind that
of other cities. The place of Athens, as
the first maritime and commercial power,
was taken by the city of Rhodes, founded
in 408 B.C. By the second half of the 4th
century B.C. the trade of Rhodes had extended itself over the whole known world,
and its maritime law was universally observed until a much later period. After
the destruction of Corinth in the middle of
the 2nd century B.C. the island of Dēlŏs
enjoyed a brief but brilliant period of prosperity. Among the commercial cities of the
Græco-Macedonian empire, Alexandria in
Egypt took the first place, and rose indeed
to be the centre of European and Eastern
trade. It was mainly through Alexandria
that intercourse was kept up between
Greece and the Eastern countries opened up
by the campaigns of Alexander the Great.

One of the most important routes followed
by Grecian traffic was that leading to the
Black Sea, the coasts of which were fringed
with Greek colonies. Besides Byzantium
and Sinōpē, the chief commercial centres
in this region were Olbia, Pantĭcăpæum,
Phănăgŏria, and Phāsis, from which trade-
routes penetrated far into the barbarian
countries of the interior. Other main
routes led by Chios and Lesbos to the
coasts of Asia Minor and by the Cyclădĕs
to that part of the Asiatic coast where lay
the great cities of Samos, Ephesus, and
Miletus. Hence they continued to Egypt
and Cȳrēnē, by Rhodes and Cyprus and the
coast of Phœnicia. But in travelling to
these parts from the Peloponnesus, they
generally sailed by way of Crete, which had
been long celebrated for its maritime enterprise. Round the promontory of Mălĕa, the
southernmost point of the Peloponnese, and
by Corcyra, they sailed northwards to the
coasts of the Adriatic, or westward to Italy
and Sicily. Regular traffic beyond Sicily
was rendered impossible by the jealousy of
the Carthaginians and Etruscans, who were
masters of the commerce in this region, and
whose place was afterwards taken there by
the Romans. A considerable land-traffic
was carried on by the colonies with bar-

barians of the interior. But in Greece
Proper the mountainous nature of the
country and the absence of navigable rivers
were unfavourable to communication by
land, and the land-traffic accordingly was
entirely thrown into the shade by the maritime trade. The only opportunity for commerce by land on a large scale was afforded
by the great national festivals, which
brought together great crowds of people
from every part of Greece, and secured
them a safe conduct (see EKECHEIRIA).
In this way these festivals exactly corresponded to our trade fairs.

The exports of Greece consisted mainly
in wine, oil, and manufactured goods, especially pottery and metal wares. The imports included the necessaries of life, of
which Greece itself, with its dense population, artificially increased by slavery, did
not produce a sufficient quantity. The
staple was wheat, which was imported in
large quantities from the coasts of the
Black Sea, Egypt, and Sicily. Next came
wood for houses and for ships, and raw
materials of all kind for manufacture. The
foreign manufactures imported were mostly
objects of luxury. Finally we should mention the large number of imported slaves.

Comparing the circumstances of the ancient Greek maritime commerce with those
of modern trade, we may observe that the
ancients were much hampered by having
no commission agencies and no system of
exchange. The proprietor of the cargo
sailed with it, or sent a representative with
full powers. No transaction was carried
on without payment in ready money, which
was often rendered difficult by the existence of different systems of coinage. With
uncivilized tribes, notably those on the
Black Sea, a system of barter long maintained itself. As no goods could be bought
without cash payments, and men of property generally preferred to lend out their
capital to borrowers at high interest, a system of bottomry was extensively developed
in Greek maritime trade. The creditor
usually took care in lending the capital
necessary for loading the ship, to secure
a lien on the ship, or the cargo, or both.
With this he undertook the risks of the
business, charging interest at a very high
rate, generally 20 to 30 per cent. The written contract contained other specifications
as to the ship and the rate of interest, for
the breach of which certain customary
penalties were fixed. These had reference
to the destination of the ship, and, gener-

ally speaking, to the route and the time to be occupied, to the character and value of the wares, and to the repayment of the loan; the latter to determine whether it should be made on the ship's arriving at its destination, or on its return home. In the first case the creditor would often sail with the ship, if he had no representative on the spot or at the port for which she was bound.

At Athens, and no doubt in other cities, the interests of the creditor were protected by a strict code of laws. Fraudulent appropriation of a deposit was punishable with death; dilatoriness in payment with imprisonment. The creditor was allowed to seize not only the security, but the whole property of the debtor. In other respects Athenian legislation secured several advantages to traders. Commercial cases only came before the law courts in winter, when navigation was impossible, and they had to be decided within a month. In ordinary cases of debt the creditor could only seize on the debtor's property; but in commercial cases he was liable to be imprisoned if condemned to payment. In other matters aliens had to be represented in court by a citizen; in commercial cases they could appear in person. It was the duty of the Thesmŏthĕtæ to see to the preparation of these cases. The trial was carried on and the verdict given by a special tribunal, the Nautŏdĭcæ (see NAUTODICÆ). Merchants could easily obtain the considerable privilege of exemption from military service, though they were not legally entitled to it.

In general it may be said that the Greek states, in consideration of the importance of trade, went very far in providing for its interests. They did their best to secure its safety and independence by force of arms, and concluded treaties with the same end in view. This is especially true of those agreements which regulated the legal relations of the citizens of the two states in their intercourse with each other, and prescribed the forms to be observed by the citizens of one state when bringing suits against those of another. The institution of proxĕni, corresponding to that of the modern consuls, was of immense benefit to the trading community. The Greek governments did a great deal in the way of constructing harbours, warehouses, and buildings for exchange in the neighbourhood of the harbours. The superintendence of the harbour traffic, like that of the market traffic, was entrusted to special govern-

ment officials; in Athens, for instance, to the ten overseers of the Empŏrium (see AGORANOMI). The Athenians had also a special board, called mĕtrŏnŏmi, to see that the weights and measures were correct. It was only in exceptional cases that the freedom of trade was interfered with by monopolies, nor was it usual to lay prohibitions upon imports. Prohibitions of exportation were, however, much commoner. In many states, as e.g. in Macedonia, it was forbidden to export building materials, especially wood for ship-building; and no grain might be exported from Attica. Again, no Athenian merchant was permitted to carry corn to any harbour but that of Athens; no citizen or resident alien could lend money on the security of ships carrying corn to any place but Athens. Even foreigners who came with corn into the harbour of Athens were compelled to deposit two-thirds of it for sale there. To prevent excessive profits being realized in the corn trade, it was made a capital offence for any private citizen to buy up more than 50 bushels at a time, or sell it at a profit of more than an ŏbŏlŏs a bushel. The corn trade was under the superintendence of a board called sītŏphȳlăkēs. In the prevailing activity of commerce, the tolls on exports and imports were a plentiful source of revenue to the Greek government.

In Greek society petty trading was thought a vulgar and sordid pursuit, and was left to the poorer citizens and resident aliens. In Athens the class of resident aliens included a great number of the larger dealers; for the wealthier and more respectable citizens liked lending their capital to others engaged in trade better than engaging in trade themselves.

Italy. In Italy an active commerce was early carried on at sea by the Etruscans, the other Italian peoples taking only a passive part in it. But Rome, from a very early time, became the commercial centre of Middle Italy. It was situated on a river deep enough to admit large vessels, the upper course and tributaries of which were also navigable. Its position was much improved by the harbour at the colony of Ostĭa, said to have been constructed under king Ancus Martius. So long as the Etruscans and Carthaginians and (as in later times) the Greek cities of Southern Italy and Sicily, like Tarentum and Syracuse, ruled the sea, the maritime power and commerce of Rome were restricted within very narrow limits. Even as late as the middle of the 4th century B.C. the traffic of Rome was confined to Sardinia, Sicily and Africa. But, with the extension of the Roman power, Roman commerce assumed wider dimensions. At the end of the republican period Roman ships were on every sea, and there was a flourishing interior trade in Italy and all the provinces. Wherever there was a navigable river it was used for communication with the happiest results. After the second Punic War, Rome gradually acquired the character of a great commercial city, where the products of the whole world, natural and industrial, found a market. The most considerable import was corn, and this at all periods of Roman history (*see* ANNONA). The chief exports of Italy were wine and oil, to which we must add, after the development of Italian industry, manufactured goods. The trading harbour of Rome was Pŭtĕŏli (Pozzuoli), on the Bay of Naples, while Ostia was used mainly by corn-ships. Petty dealing was regarded unfavourably by the Romans as by the Greeks; but trade on a large scale was thought quite respectable, though in older times members of the senate were not allowed to engage in it. Most of the larger undertakings at Rome were in the hands of joint-stock companies (*see* PUBLICANI), the existence of which made it possible for small capitalists to share in the profits and risks of commerce. It was indeed an old maxim of business men at Rome that it was better to have small shares in a number of speculations than to speculate independently. The corn trade, in particular, was in the hands of these companies. The government allowed them to transport corn from Sardinia, Sicily, Spain, Africa, and Egypt to Rome ; whole fleets of vessels, constructed for the purpose, being appointed to this service. Foreign trade was subjected to a number of restrictions. The exportation of certain products was absolutely prohibited ; for instance, iron, whether unwrought or manufactured, arms, coin, salt, and gold ; and duties were levied on all imports. There were also numerous restrictions on trade in the interior, as each province formed a unit of taxation, in which toll had to be paid on entering or leaving it. Among the state monopolies, the most important was that of salt.

Commercium. A legal relation existing between two Italian states, according to which the citizens of each had the same right of acquiring property, especially landed property, in the territory of the other.

Commercium also included the powers of inheriting legacies and contracting obligations.

Compĕrendĭnātĭo. [The Latin name for the postponement of a trial for a definite time by consent of both parties, each being bound to appear. To be distinguished from *amplĭātĭo*, which seems to have meant an indefinite postponement, in consequence of uncertainty on the part of the jury.]

Compĭtālĭă. *See* LARES.

Complŭvĭŭm. *See* HOUSE.

Concordĭa. The Latin personification of concord or harmony, especially among Roman citizens. Shrines were repeatedly erected to *Concordia* during the republican period after the cessation of civil dissensions. The earliest was dedicated by Camillus in 367 B.C. The goddess Concordia was also invoked, together with Jānŭs, Sălūs, and Pax, at the family festival of the *Caristĭa*, on the 30th March, and, with Venus and Fortūna, by married women on the 1st of April (*see* MANES). During the imperial period *Concordia Augusta* was worshipped as the protectress of harmony, especially of matrimonial agreement, in the emperor's household.

Confarrĕātĭo. *See* MARRIAGE, 2.

Congĭārĭum. The Latin word for a present of oil and wine, given to the people in addition to the regular distribution of corn by magistrates and candidates for office (*see* ANNONA). The custom began in republican times. Under the Empire the word was further applied to the presents of oil, wine, and salt, and later of ready money, which the emperor made regularly to the people on certain festive occasions, as on his accession and on his birthday. (*See* DONATIVUM.)

Consĕcrātĭo. The act of the Roman *pontĭfĭcēs*, in virtue of which a thing was proclaimed as *săcer*, *i.e.* belonging to, or forfeited to, the gods. (On the rite of *consecratio* associated with the solemn dedication of a sanctuary, *see* DEDICATIO ; on *consecratio* as the apotheosis of the emperor, *see* APOTHEOSIS.) In case of certain offences, sentence of *consecratio căpĭtĭs et bŏnōrum* was pronounced upon the offender, whose person and property were then made over as a sacrifice to some deity. A married man who sold his wife was devoted to the gods below ; a son who beat his father, to the household gods ; one who removed his neighbour's landmark to Termĭnus ; a *patrōnus* who betrayed his client, or a client who betrayed his *patronus*, to Jupiter ;

one who stole corn in the ear, to Ceres. To kill a *hŏmŏ săcer* was not accounted as murder, but as the fulfilment of the divine vengeance.

Consĭlĭum. The Latin word for a council, or body of advisers. Such councils were called in, according to ancient custom, by the presiding magistrate in civil and criminal cases. Even in the family tribunals, which decided cases affecting the members of the *gens*, a *consilium* of kinsfolk was thought necessary. The custom was that the presiding judge bound himself by the decision of his freely chosen *consilium*, but took the responsibility himself. The expression *consilium* was afterwards transferred to the regular juries of the courts which decided civil and criminal cases (*see* CENTUMVIRI, JUDICES). The emperors, too, made a practice of inviting a *consilium* of friends to assist them in their judicial decisions. After the time of Hadrian, the members of the imperial *consilium* appear as regularly appointed and salaried officers, the *Consiliārĭī Augustī*. These were generally, though not exclusively, selected from the body of professional jurists. After the 4th century A.D. the word *consistŏrĭum* was substituted for *consilium ;* meaning, originally, the council-chamber in the imperial palace.

Consŭālĭă. *See* CONSUS.

Consŭlēs (originally called *Prætōrēs*). The Roman consuls were the magistrates to whom the supreme authority was transferred from the kings, after the expulsion of the latter in 510 B.C. The consuls gave their name to the year. They were elected by the *comĭtĭa centŭrĭāta*, and, down to B.C. 366, from the Patricians only. The legal age at which a man might be elected was, in the time of Cicero, forty-three. The time of entering on the office varied in the early periods : in 222 B.C. it was fixed to March 15th, in 153 to the 1st of January. The accession of the new consuls was attended with the performance of certain ceremonies, among which may be mentioned a procession of the consuls to the Capitol, with the senate, *ĕquĭtēs*, and other citizens of position, as escort; an offering of white bulls to Jupiter, and the utterance of solemn vows.

The consuls were the representatives of the royal authority, and consequently all other magistrates were bound to obey them, with the exception of the tribunes of the *plebs* and the dictator. During a dictatorship their powers fell into abeyance. In the city their authority was limited by the right of appeal to the people, and the *veto* of the tribunes. But in the army, and over their subordinates, they had full power of life and death. Some of their original functions passed from them in course of time. Thus in 444 B.C. the business of the census was made over to the Censors; in 366 the civil jurisdiction within the city, so far as it included the right of performing the acts of adoption, emancipation, and liberation of slaves, was transferred to the prætors. In the field, however, having the criminal jurisdiction in their hands, they had also the right of deciding in civil cases affecting the soldiers. In the general administration of public business the consuls, although formally recognised as the supreme authority, gradually became, in practice, dependent upon the senate and the *comitia*, as they had only the power of preparing the resolutions proposed, and carrying them out if accepted. Within the city, their powers were virtually confined to summoning the senate and *comitia*, and presiding over their meetings. They also nominated the dictators, and conducted the elections and legislation in the *comitia*, and the levies of soldiers. After the office of dictator fell into abeyance, the power of the consuls was, in cases of great danger, increased to dictatorial authority by a special decree of the senate.

An essential characteristic of the consular office was that it was *collegial* ; and therefore, if one consul died, another (called *consul suffectus*) was immediately elected. This *consul suffectus* had absolutely the same authority as his colleague, but he had to lay down his office with him at the end of the year for which the two had been originally elected.

The power of the two consuls being equal, the business was divided between them. In the administration of the city they changed duties every month, the senior taking the initiative. With regard to their *insignia*, namely, the *tŏga prætexta, sella cŭrūlis*, and twelve lictors, the original arrangement was that the lictors walked in front of the officiating consul, while the other was only attended by an *accensus*. In later times the custom was for the lictors to walk before the officiating consul, and behind the other.

In the field, each consul commanded two legions with their allied troops ; if they were in the same locality, the command changed from day to day. The question of the administration of the provinces they either settled by consent, or left it to be decided by lot. With the extension of the empire the consuls became unable to undertake the whole burden of warfare, and the prætors were called in to assist. The provinces were then divided into consular and prætorian; the business of assignment being left to the senate, which, after the year 122, was bound to make it before the elections. In the last century B.C. a law of Sulla deprived the consuls of an essential element of their authority, the military *impĕrium ;* for it enacted that the consuls should spend their year of office in Rome, and only repair to the provinces and assume the *imperium* after its conclusion.

In the civil wars the consular office completely lost its old position, and though it continued to exist under the Empire, it became, practically, no more than an empty title. The emperors, who often held the office themselves, and sometimes, like Cæsar, for several years in succession, had the right of nominating the candidates, and therefore, in practice, had the election in their own hands. It became usual to nominate several pairs of consuls for one year, so as to confer the distinction on as many persons as possible. In such cases, the consuls who came in on January 1st, after whom the year was named, were called *consules ordĭnārĭi,* the *consules suffecti* counting as *mĭnōrēs.* Until the middle of the 1st century A.D., it was a special distinction to hold the consulship for a whole year; but after that no cases of this tenure occur. In time the *insignia,* or *ornāmenta consulārĭa,* or honorary distinctions of the office, were given, in certain degrees, even to men who had not been consuls at all. The chief duties of the consuls now were to preside in the senate, and conduct the criminal trials in which it had to give judgment. But, besides this, certain functions of civil jurisdiction were in their hands; notably the liberation of slaves, the provision for the costly games which occurred during their term of office, the festal celebrations in honour of the emperor, and the like. After the seat of empire was transferred to Constantinople, the consulate was, towards the end of the 4th century, divided between the two capital cities. The consulate of the western capital came to an end in 534 A.D., that of the eastern in 541. From that time the Emperor of the East bore the title of *consul perpĕtŭus.*

Consus. An ancient Italian god, probably a god of the earth or of crops. His altar on the Circus Maxĭmus at Rome was covered with earth, apparently as a sign of the deity's activity in the bosom of the earth. Three times in the year only was it uncovered, on the occasion of sacrifices or festivities. The festival of Consus, the *Consŭālĭa,* was held twice a year; on the 21st August, after the harvest, and the 15th December, after the sowing was ended. Its establishment was attributed to Rŏmŭlus, and it was at the first celebration that the rape of the Sabine women was supposed to have taken place. At this festival the sacrifice was superintended by the Flāmĭnēs of Quĭrīnus with the Vestal Virgins, and was followed by a chariot race in the circus, under the direction of the *pontĭfĭcēs.* The horses and mules, their heads crowned with flowers, had their share in the holiday. In consequence of these games the god Consus was afterwards identified with Pŏseidōn Hippĭŏs, or Neptūnus Equester.

Contĭō. The Latin name for any assembly summoned and presided over by a magistrate. A *contio* differed from the *comĭtĭa* in the following points : (1) The people were not divided into centuries or tribes. (2) The people did not vote, but were only there to receive communications made by the presiding magistrate or some other official or private individual, whom he allowed to address the meeting. All magistrates had the right of summoning *contĭōnēs,* but the tribunes took precedence of all others, and a higher magistrate took precedence of a lower. *Contiones* were usually summoned by public heralds (*præcōnēs*) and generally met in the Forum. The *comitia* were immediately preceded by a *contio,* that the people might be prepared for the questions to come before them. If the *comitia* were to exercise judicial functions, it was a fixed rule that three *contiones* must be held previously for the purpose of investigation.

Contŭbernĭum. A Latin word properly meaning tent companionship, or companionship in military service. The word signified (1) the relation of young Roman nobles to the general officer to whom they had voluntarily attached themselves for the sake of military training, and in whose company they took their meals in the tent. It meant (2) the marriage of slaves, which was not legally accounted marriage, though under the Empire it was considered, as a rule, indissoluble if contracted by members of the same household. (3) The marriage between free persons and slaves, which was not considered legal.

Contŭmācia. The Latin term for disobedience to the commands of a magistrate or judge, especially absence from a trial without sufficient excuse. If the accuser were absent, he was considered as dropping his charge (*see* TERGIVERSATIO), which he was not allowed to renew. The absence of the accused was taken as an admission of guilt. In a civil trial the consequence was immediate condemnation; and the like was the case in criminal trials if the accused failed to appear at the appointed time, or on the last day of the trial. If the accused saw that his condemnation was certain, it was quite common for him to retire, and in capital cases to go into voluntary exile; a proceeding which in no way influenced the further course of the proceedings.

Cōnŭbĭum (Latin). The contracting of a *matrĭmōnĭum iustum*, or valid marriage, with all its legal consequences. As such a marriage could only take place between persons of equal status, the Patricians and Plebeians had each for a long time a separate *conubium*, until 445 B.C., when the two orders were equalised in this respect.

Convīvĭum. *See* MEALS.

Coöptātĭō (Latin). The election of a new member by the members of a corporation to supply a vacant place. Among corporations which filled their vacancies in this way may be mentioned the college of Pontĭfĭcēs and Augurs. The election was preceded by the nomination of a proper candidate by one of the members, and followed by his inauguration.

Cordax (*Kordax*). The licentious dance of the ancient Greek comedy. To perform it off the stage was regarded as a sign of intoxication or profligacy.

Cŏrē (*Kŏrē*). *See* PERSEPHONE.

Cŏrinna (*Kŏrinna*). A Greek lyric poetess, born at Tanagra in Bœotia, and surnamed Myia, or "the Fly." She flourished about 510 B.C. She was the instructress of Pindar, and is said to have beaten him five times in musical contests. Only a few fragments of her poems, of which there were five books, remain. They were written in the Bœotian dialect, and treated subjects of local mythology, as, for instance, the tale of the "Seven against Thebes."

Cŏrippus (*Flāvĭus Crescōnĭus*). An African scholar, who in the second half of the 6th century A.D. composed two historical epics, one in seven books, in

celebration of the Libyan war of Johannēs Patrĭcĭus (*Iōhannĭs, sīvĕ de bellĭs Lĭbўcĭs*), and the other on the exploits of Justinus (565–578), in four books (*De Laudĭbus Iustīnĭ*). The last is in the worst manner of Byzantine flattery, but is written in a flowing style and in imitation of good models, such as Vergil and Claudian.

Cornēlĭus. (1) *Cornelius Nĕpōs*. A Roman historian, a native of Upper Italy, who lived between 94 and 24 B.C. He was a contemporary of Cicero, Atticus, and Catullus, with whom he lived in friendly intercourse at Rome. The most comprehensive of his many writings was a collection of biographies of celebrated men (*De Vĭrĭs Illustrĭbus*) in at least sixteen books. This was dedicated to Atticus, and must therefore have been published before B.C. 32, the year of his death. The biographies were arranged in departments, and in each department the Greek and Roman celebrities were treated separately. Thus the still surviving book upon distinguished foreign generals (*De Excellentĭbus Dŭcĭbus Extĕrārum Gentĭum*) is followed by one on Roman generals, while a book devoted to the Greek historians had one on the Roman historians corresponding to it, from which the lives of the elder Cato and of Atticus are preserved. The lives of celebrated generals were in former times (in consequence of an ancient error in the MSS.) erroneously ascribed to a certain Æmĭlĭŭs Prŏbus of the 4th century A.D. Nepos' manner is easy and pleasant, but suffers from many weaknesses of matter and form. A superficial use of his authorities has led him into many errors, and the style is not seldom careless and incorrect.

(2) *Gaius Cornelius Gallus*. A Latin poet, born 69 B.C. in the Gaulish town of Fŏrum Iŭlĭi. Though of low birth, he was promoted by Octavian to the *ordo equester* in the year 30 B.C., and made governor (*prœfectus*) of the new province of Egypt, in consideration of his great services in the war against Antōnius. Through his cruelty and presumption he drew upon himself the displeasure of his former patron; in consequence of which he committed suicide in 26 B.C. He was one of the oldest friends of Vergil, who dedicated to him his tenth Eclogue, as well as an episode at the end of the fourth Georgic, which he, after Gallus' fall, suppressed at the wish of Augustus. The Romans regarded him as the founder of the Latin elegy. He wrote four books of elegies to his mistress, the actress Cўthēris (or Lўcōris, as he called her). They are in

the obscure and learned style of the Alexandrian poet Euphŏrīŏn. His poems are lost, but a collection of erotic myths made for his use by the Greek Parthĕnĭŏs has survived. [A few lines in Vergil's tenth Eclogue were borrowed from Gallus.]

Cornĭcĕn. A horn-blower in the Roman army, who gave the signal for attack, on an ox or bison-horn (*cornu*) set in silver.

Cornīfĭcĭus. The supposed author of an anonymous treatise on rhetoric in four books, dedicated to a certain Herennius (*Rhĕtŏrĭca ad Hĕrennĭum.*) This is the oldest Latin treatise of the sort that we possess. It was written in the time of Sulla, about 85 B.C., by a partisan of the Marian faction, who, though not a professed rhetorician, was an educated man, as is shown by his accomplishments and his correct style. Though

philosophical works one remains, an essay on the Nature of the Gods, written in Greek. This is perhaps only an extract from a larger work. Cassĭŏdōrus (*q. v.*) has preserved part of a grammatical treatise by Cornutus, entitled *De Orthŏgrăphĭā* ("On Orthography").

Cŏrollārĭum (Latin). A present consisting of a garland of gold or silver leaves, given to successful actors and performers in addition to other *honoraria*. It thus became a term for any free gift whatever.

Cŏrōna (Latin). A crown; among the Romans the highest distinction awarded for service in war. The most coveted were the *corona trĭumphālĭs* (fig. 1) or laurel crown of a general in triumph; and the *corona obsĭdĭōnālĭs* (fig. 2), presented to a general by the army which he had saved

(1) Corona triumphalis.　　　(2) Corona obsidionalis.　　　(3) Corona civica.

(4) Corona muralis.　　　(5) Corona vallaris.　　　(6) Corona navalis.

he followed Greek models, he endeavours to treat his subject from a Roman or national point of view, and therefore gives Latin equivalents for the Greek technical terms. His examples, too, he takes from older Roman writings, or makes them himself. Cicero, who passed for the author in late antiquity, used the same Greek original in his *De Inventĭōnĕ.*

Cornūtŭs (*Lucius Annœus*). A native of Leptĭs, in Africa. A professor of the Stoic philosophy, who lived in Rome in the middle of the 1st century A.D. He was a friend of the poets Lucan and Persius, especially of the latter, whose posthumous satires he prepared for publication. He was banished by Nero, in A.D. 68, for his uprightness and courage. He was the author of works on rhetoric, grammar and philosophy. Of his

from a siege, or from a shameful capitulation. This was woven of grass growing on the spot, and called *corona grāmĭnĕa*. The *corona myrtĕa*, or *ŏvālĭs*, was the crown of bay worn by the general who celebrated the lesser triumph (*ŏvātĭŏ*).

The *corona cīvĭca* (fig. 3) was of oak leaves, and was awarded for saving a citizen's life in battle. This secured for its possessor certain privileges, as freedom from taxes for himself, his father and paternal grandfather. The golden *corona mūrālĭs* (fig. 4), with embattled ornaments, was given for the storming of a wall; the *corona castrensis* or *vallārĭs* (fig. 5), also of gold, and ornamented in imitation of palisades, to the soldier who first climbed the wall of an enemy's camp; the *corona nāvālĭs* (fig. 6), with ornaments representing the beak of a ship, to the man who first boarded a ship. Under the Empire the garland of bay was reserved exclusively for the emperor, and thus came to be regarded as a crown.

The rayed crown, the *insignĕ* of the deified emperors, was not worn by the emperors of the 1st and 2nd century A.D. Golden crowns were originally the free offerings of provincials and allies to victorious generals for the celebration of their triumphs. But from this custom there arose, even in republican times, the habit of compelling a contribution of money (*aurum cŏrōnārĭum*) to the governor of the province. During the imperial age this contribution was on exceptional occasions offered as a present to the emperors, but it was often also made compulsory.

Among the Greeks a crown (*stĕphănŏs*) was often an emblem of office. At Athens, for instance, a crown of bay was worn by the archons in office, the senators (*bouleutai*), and the orators while speaking. It was also the emblem of victory at the games, and a token of distinction for citizens of merit (*see* THEATRE). Such crowns of honour were made originally of olive branches, but later of gold. The honour of a crown could be conferred by the people or the senate, or by corporations and foreign states. The latter would often present a crown to the whole commonwealth. If the people or senate presented the crown, the presentation took place in the great assembly, or in the senate house, but not in the theatre, except by special decree.

Since crowns played a considerable part as ornaments at religious rites and as well at festivals and banquets, the trade of crown-making (mostly in women's hands) was naturally extensive. The art of making what were called winter crowns of dry flowers was also understood. Artificial flowers, made of thin strips of painted wood, were also used.

Cŏrōnis (*Kŏrōnĭs*). *See* ASCLEPIUS.

Corpŭs Iūris Cīvīlis. The name of the great collection of authorities on Roman law, made by the lawyer Tribōniānus, of Sidĕ in Pamphylia, at the instance of the Eastern Emperor Justinian (527–565 A.D.). To this collection we owe the preservation of the treasures of the ancient jurisprudence, which must certainly otherwise have been lost. The *Corpus Iūris* consists of four parts:

(1) *Cōdex Iustīnĭānĕus*, called *rĕpĕtītæ prælectĭōnĭs*, as being the revised edition of a code now lost, but which had appeared in 529. This was published in 534, and contains in twelve books the imperial law (*iŭs princĭpālĕ*), or the *constĭtūtĭōnēs* of the emperors since Hadrian.

(2) *Pandectæ*, or *Dīgesta.* The law of the jurists (*ius vĕtus*). These, published A.D. 533, are extracts from the works of thirty-nine ancient jurists, arranged in fifty books, according to subjects.

(3) *Instĭtūtĭōnēs.* A handbook of jurisprudence, founded mostly upon Gaius, and published in the same year.

(4) *Novellæ* (*constitutiones*), or supplementary ordinances of Justinian, mostly in Greek. These are preserved only in private collections of various compass, one of which, the *Authentĭcum* or *Lĭber Authenticōrum*, was recognised as the authorized text, and gives the Greek rescripts in a Latin version.

Cŏrybantēs (*Kŏrўbantĕs*). The mythical attendants of the Phrygian goddess Rhea Cўbĕlē, who were supposed to accompany the goddess with wild dances and intoxicating music, while she wandered by torchlight over the forest-clad mountains. The name was further given in Phrygia to the eunuch priests of the goddess. (*See* RHEA.)

Cŏrўcus (Gr. *Kŏrўkŏs*). *See* BALL, GAMES OF.

Cosmi (*Kosmoi*). *See* GERUSIA.

Cŏthurnus, or more correctly *Coturnus* (Gr. *Kothornŏs*). A Greek name for a high shoe or buskin with several soles. It covered the whole foot, and rose as high as the middle of the leg. It was made so as to fit either foot, and was generally fastened in front with red straps. The cothurnus was properly a hunting boot, but Æschўlus made it part of the costume of his tragic actors to give them a stature above the average. At the same time the hair was dressed high in order to maintain the proportion of the figure. The cothurnus was also used in the Roman tragedy. (*See* SOCCUS.)

Cottăbus (*Kottăbŏs*). A Greek game very popular at drinking bouts. The player lay on the couch, and in that position tried to throw a few drops of wine in as high a curve as possible, at a mark, without spilling any of the wine. The mark was called *kottăbeĭŏn*, and was a bronze goblet or saucer, and it was a point to make a noise when hitting it. On the *kottabeion* was fastened a little image or a bust of Hermēs, which was called Manēs, and which the player had to hit first with the wine. The wine was supposed to make a sound both in hitting the figure and in falling afterwards into the saucer. This of course greatly increased the difficulty of the game.

There was another form of the game in which the point was to make the wine hit the saucer while swimming in a large vessel of water, and sink it. The game was played in a round chamber made for the purpose. The form of the room was circular, to give every player an equal chance of hitting the mark, which was placed in the centre. The victor generally received a prize agreed upon beforehand. The players also used the game to discover

Cŏtўs (Gr. *Kŏtyttō*). A Thracian goddess, originally, it would seem, connected with Rhea Cўbělē. Her worship was diffused over Greece and Italy, and was especially popular in Athens and Corinth. The licentious orgies associated with it, called *Cotyttĭa*, gave it a bad name.

Crăter. *See* VESSELS.

Crătēs (*Krătēs*). (1) A Greek comedian, who lived at Athens about 470 B.C. He was regarded as the founder of the Attic Comedy in the proper sense of the term, as his pieces were not, like those of his pre-

* COTTABUS.
(Vase from Corneto; *Annali d Inst.* 1876 *tav.* M.)

their chances of success in love. They uttered the name of their beloved while throwing the wine. A successful throw gave a good omen, an unsuccessful one a bad omen. A good player leaned upon his left elbow, remained quite quiet, and only used his right hand to throw with. The game came originally from Sicily, but became popular through the whole of Greece, and specially at Athens, where to play well was a mark of good breeding. It did not go out of fashion till the 4th century after Christ. [The cut represents one of the several methods of playing the game.]

decessors, mere lampoons on individuals, but presented subjects of a more general character. Only a few fragments of his plays have come down to us.

(2) *Crates of Mallŏs in Cilicia.* A Greek scholar, and adherent of the Stoic philosophy. He founded a school of interpretation at Pergămŏn. His principles were in direct opposition to those of Aristarchus; not only did he take an essentially different view of the Homeric text, but he favoured the allegorical method of exposition, to which the Stoics were so partial, and which was so disliked by the school of Aristarchus.

His chief work was a comprehensive commentary, critical and exegetical, on Homer. In 167 B.C. he was sent by king Attălus on an embassy to Rome. Here he broke his leg, and was thus forced to make a long stay. He used his enforced leisure in giving lectures, which gave the first impulse to the study of philology and literary criticism among the Romans. Only a few fragments of his works have survived.

Cratīnus (*Krătīnŏs*) was, with Eupŏlĭs and Aristŏphănēs, a chief representative of the Old Comedy at Athens. He was born in 520 B.C., and died in 423, thus flourishing in the age of Pĕrĭclēs, who was the special object of his attacks. He wrote twenty-one pieces, and gained the prize nine times. The last occasion on which he was victor was shortly before his death, and the defeated comedy was *The Clouds* of Aristophanes. Cratinus' play was the *Pўtĭnē* or "Wineflask," in which the poet courted the ridicule of the public by confessing himself a hard drinker. His wit was brilliant, but more caustic than humorous. He may be regarded as the founder of political comedy. Only the titles and a few fragments of his plays have survived.

Crĕōn (*Krĕōn*). (1) King of Corinth, and father of Glaucē: see ARGONAUTS (conclusion).

(2) Son of Mĕnœceus, great-grandson of Pentheus, brother of Iŏcastē, and father of Hæmon and Menœceus (*see* articles under these names). He governed Thebes after Laĭus' death until the coming of Œdĭpūs; and again after the fall of Etĕoclēs until the latter's son, Laŏdămās, came of age. (*See* ANTIGONE.)

(3) *See* AMPHITRYON and HERACLES.

Crĕpĭda (Greek *krēpĭs*). A kind of sandal, borrowed by the Romans from the Greeks, and used originally by the Roman soldiers. It had a thick sole, was of the same shape for each foot, and had low leather sides with straps for fastening.

*PERICLES (AFTER CRESILAS).
(British Museum).

Crĕsĭlās (*Krĕsĭlās*), a Greek artist, born at Cydōnĭa in Crete, who flourished at Athens in the second half of the 5th century B.C. Among his chief works may be mentioned: (1) a statue of Pĕrĭclēs, probably the original of the extant portrait-statues of the great statesman; (2) a statue of a man mortally wounded, in which the struggle between death and life was vividly portrayed; (3) the *Wounded Amazon* of Ephesus, a work in which he had to compete with Phīdĭās and Pŏlyclītus. This is generally supposed to be the original of one of the several types of *Wounded Amazons* which have survived. Cresilas seems to have followed the tradition of Mўrōn.

Crĕtheus (*Krētheus*). In Greek mythology, the son of Æŏlus and Enarĕtē, the founder of Iolcŏs, and by Tyrō father of Æsōn, Phĕrēs, and Amythāōn. (*See* ÆOLUS 1, and NELEUS.)

Crĕūsa (*Krĕousa*). (1) *See* ÆNEAS. (2) *See* GLAUCE. (3) *See* ION 1.

Crĭtĭās (*Krĭtĭās*). An Athenian, a disciple of Sōcrătēs and Gorgĭās of Lĕontīnī. He was one of the most accomplished men of his time, and was distinguished as a poet and an orator. But he is best known as the chief of the Thirty Tyrants, in defence of whose cause against the Liberators he fell in 403 B.C. He was the author of several tragedies. Some fragments of his poems have survived, the largest being from his political elegies. He seems to have had the gift of expression, but to have written in a harsh style of composition.

Crŏnus (*Krŏnŏs*). In Greek mythology, the youngest son of Urănus and Gæa, who mutilated and overthrew his father, and, with the assistance of his kinsfolk the Titans, made himself sovereign of the world. He took his sister Rhea to wife, and became by her father of Hestĭa, Dēmētēr, Hēra, Hādēs, Pŏseidōn, and Zeus. But his mother prophesied that one of his children would overthrow him He accordingly swallowed them all except Zeus, whom Rhea saved by a stratagem. Zeus, when grown up, obtained the assistance of the Ocean-nymph Thĕtis in making Cronus disgorge his children, and then, with the help of his kinsfolk, overpowered Cronus and the Titans. According to one version of the fable, Cronus was imprisoned in Tartărus with the Titans; according to another, he was reconciled with Zeus, and reigned with Rhădămanthys on the Islands of the Blessed. Cronus seems originally to have been a god of the harvest; whence it happens that in many parts of Greece the harvest month was called Crŏnĭōn. His name being easily confused with that of Chrŏnŏs ("Time"), he was afterwards erroneously regarded as the god of time. In works of art he was represented as an old man with a mantle drawn over the back of his head, and holding a sickle in his hand. The Romans identified him with Sāturnus, their god of sowing (see SATURNUS).

Crypteia (*Krypteia*). A kind of police maintained at Sparta, with the principal object of watching the Helots. The service was manned by young Spartans appointed annually for the purpose by the Ephors, and their duty was to put dangerous or apparently dangerous Helots out of the way without more ado. A later and erroneous idea represented the Crypteia as a murderous chase of the Helots, annually conducted by the Spartan youth.

Ctĕātŭs (*Ktĕātŏs*). See MOLIONIDÆ.

Ctēsĭās (*Ktēsĭas*). A Greek historian, born in Cnĭdus in Caria, and a contemporary of Xĕnŏphōn. He belonged to the family of the Asclēpĭădæ at Cnidus. In 416 B.C. he came to the Persian court, and became private physician to King Artaxerxēs Mnēmōn. In this capacity he accompanied the king on his expedition against his brother Cyrus, and cured him of the wound which he received in the battle of Cunaxa, B.C. 401. In 399 he returned to his native city, and worked up the valuable material which he had collected during his residence in Persia. partly from his own observation, and partly from his study of the royal archives, into a History of Persia (*Persĭca*) in twenty-three books. The work was written in the Ionic dialect. The first six books treated the history of Assyria, the remaining ones that of Persia, from the earliest times to events within his own experience. Ctesias' work was much used by the ancient historians, though he was censured as untrustworthy and indifferent to truth; a charge which may be due to the fact that he followed Persian authorities, and thus often differed, to the disadvantage of the Greeks, from the version of facts current among his countrymen. Only fragments and extracts of the book survive. The same is true of his *Indĭca*, or notices of the observations which he had made in Persia on the geography and productions of India.

Cŭbĭcŭlārĭus (Latin). A chamberlain. *See* SLAVES.

Cŭbĭcŭlum (Latin). A bed-chamber. *See* HOUSE.

Cŭcullus (Latin). A hood. *See* CLOTHING.

Cŭnĕus. See THEATRE.

Cŭpīdō ("Desire"). The Latin personification of Erōs, or the god of Love.

Cūra. The Latin term for the superintendence of a special department of business, such as the distribution of corn (*annōna*), making of roads, regulation of watercourses, aqueducts and the like. The officers entrusted with these special duties were termed *cūrātōrēs*. In the republican age they were *extra ordĭnem*. In the civil law *cura* denotes the guardianship of a madman (*fŭrĭōsus*) or a spendthrift (*prōdĭgus*). The *cūrātŏr* who managed his property and represented him at law was originally the next *āgnātus*, but afterwards he was always appointed by the authorities. Since 200 B.C. it was also customary to appoint *curatores* for young persons under twenty-five, under certain conditions, to protect them against being overreached in legal proceedings. From the time of Marcus Aurēlĭus, who made the legality of certain transactions dependent on the co-operation of a *curator*, the *cura mĭnōrum* became a standing institution.

Cūrētĕs (*Kourētĕs*). In Cretan mythology the Curetes were demi-gods armed with weapons of brass, to whom the new-born child Zeus was committed by his mother Rhea for protection against the wiles of Crŏnus. They drowned the cries of the child by striking their spears against their shields. They gave their name to the priests of the Cretan goddess Rhea and of the Idæan Zeus, who performed noisy wardances at the festivals of those deities.

Cūrĭa (Latin). The name of the thirty divisions into which the three *trĭbūs* of the Roman patricians were divided for political and religious objects. Every *curia* contained a number of *gentēs*, supposed to be exactly ten, and a president, *cūrĭō*, whose duty it was to look after its secular and religious business. At the head of all the *curiæ* stood the *Curio Maxĭmus*, who was charged with the notification of the common festivals *Fordĭcĭdĭa* and *Fornācālĭa* (*see* these words). The separate *curiones* were chosen by their respective curiæ, and the *Curio Maximus* was elected by the people in special *comĭtĭa* out of the number of *curiones*. For its special sacrifices every *curia* had its place of meeting, bearing the same name, with a hearth and dining-hall where the members met to feast and sacrifice. The plebeians seem to have been admitted to the sacrifices, which were offered on behalf of the whole people, and were paid for at the expense of the state (*see* further, COMITIA CURIATA). The term *curia* was also applied to certain houses intended for holding meetings, as, for instance, the official residence of the Salii on the Palatine, and especially the senate-house, *Curia Hostilia*, built by king Hostilius on the *cŏmĭtĭum*, and burnt down 52 B.C. In its place Faustus Sulla, the son of the Dictator, erected the *Curia Cornēlia*. Cæsar interrupted the progress of this work to set up the *Curia Iūlia* in its place. Then the senate met in the *Curia Pompēi*, in the entrance-hall of Pompey's theatre, where Cæsar was murdered. The *Curia Iulia* was not begun till 44 B.C., shortly before Cæsar's death, and was consecrated in 29 by Augustus. (*See* plan of Roman *Fora*, under FORUM.)

Cūrĭō. *See* CURIA.

Cŭrŏtrŏphŏs (Gr. *Kourŏtrŏphŏs*); "nurse of children." The title of several Greek goddesses, for instance Gæa, who were regarded as protectresses of youth.

Curtius Rūfus (*Quintus*). A Roman historian, who probably lived and practised as a rhetorician about the middle of the 1st century A.D., and wrote a history of Alexander the Great, in ten books, in the reign of Claudius (A.D. 44–54). The first two books are lost, and the fifth mutilated at the end, the sixth at the beginning. He seems to aim more at rhetorical effect than at historical accuracy. In the use of his authorities he is uncritical, as he follows untrustworthy writers like Clītarchus, knowing them to be untrustworthy. His work contains many errors in geography and chronology, and his accounts of the battles show that he had no military knowledge. But he understands the art of interesting his readers by a pleasant narrative and lifelike drawing, and there is a certain charm in the numerous speeches which he has inserted in his text, in spite of their strong rhetorical colouring. His language reminds us of Livy. It is curious that he is never mentioned in antiquity.

Cy̆ăthus (*Kyăthŏs*). *See* VESSELS.

Cybēbē, Cybēlē. *See* RHEA.

Cyclic Poets. *See* EPOS.

Cyclōpĕs (*Kyklōpĕs*). In Greek mythology, the round-eyed ones. According to Hesiod the Cyclopes are the gigantic sons of Urănus and Gæa, named Argos, Stĕrŏpēs, and Brontēs. For the rest, they resemble the gods, except that they have only a single eye in their forehead. Their father threw them into Tartărus, and they

assisted Crŏnus to the sovereignty. Cronus, however, put them again in prison, where they remained until Zeus set them free. For this they gave him the thunder, and forged him the lightning. Apollo slew them when Zeus struck his son Asclēpĭus by lightning.

In Homer the Cyclopes, like the giants and the Phæacians, are the kinsfolk of the gods; but in other respects they have nothing in common with the Cyclopes of Hesiod but their gigantic size and strength. They live a pastoral life in the far West, without knowledge of agriculture, law, morals, or social order. Each dwells separately with his family in caverns at the mountain tops, without troubling himself about the gods, to whom, indeed, the Cyclopes deem themselves easily superior in strength. The Phæacians used to live in their neighbourhood, but were driven by their violent dealing to emigrate. The figure of Pŏly̆phēmus, well known from his encounter with Odysseus, gives a typical notion of their rudeness and savagery. (*See* also GALATEA). The Homeric Cyclopes were in a later age localized in Sicily, and came to be identified with the Cyclopes of Hesiod. They were imagined as assistants of Hephæstus, and as helping him to forge lightnings for Zeus and arms for heroes in the bowels of Ætna or on the Æolian islands. A third variety of Cyclopes were the giants with arms to their belly as well as to their shoulders, whom Prœtus was supposed to have brought from Lycia to Argos. It was they who were supposed to have built the so-called Cyclopean walls at Mycēnæ and Tīryns (*see* ARCHITECTURE). In works of art the Cyclopes are represented as giants with one eye in their forehead, though there is generally an indication of a pair of eyes in the usual place.

Cycnus (*Kyknŏs*) or "Swan." (1) The son of Arēs and Pĕlŏpĭa, who threw himself in the way of Hĕrăclēs in Trāchis, when the hero was on his way to Cēyx. According to another story Heracles was sent against Cycnus by Apollo, because he lay in wait for the processions on their road to Delphi. In the contest between them, as described by Hesiod in his *Shield of Heracles*, Ares stood at the side of his son, while Heracles was supported by Athēnē and his faithful Iŏlāūs. Heracles slew Cycnus, and even wounded Ares, when the latter attempted to avenge the fall of his son. Cycnus was buried with all due honours by his father-in-law Ceyx, but Apollo destroyed the tomb by an inundation of the river Anaurus. There was a son of Ares and Pȳrēnē who bore the same name, and he too was said to have fallen in combat against Heracles. Ares attempted to avenge his son, when Zeus, by a flash of lightning, separated his angry children. After his death, said the story, Cycnus was changed by his father into a swan.

(2) The son of Pŏseidōn and Călȳcē. He was exposed by his mother on the sea-shore and found by some fishermen, who named him Cycnus because they saw a swan flying round him. He was invulnerable, and of gigantic strength and stature; his head (or, according to another account, his whole body) was as white as snow. He became king of Cŏlōnæ in the Troad, and was twice married. A slanderous utterance of his second wife stung him to fury against the children of his first wife, whom he threw into the sea in a chest. They were cast up alive on the island of Tĕnĕdŏs, where Tĕnēs was king. At a later time Cycnus repented of his deed, sought for his son, and marched with him to the aid of the Trojans against the Greeks. They prevented the Greeks from landing; but both were at last slain by Achilles, who strangled the invulnerable Cycnus with his own helmet strap. He was changed by Poseidon into a swan.

Cўdippē (*Kydippē*). The heroine of a very popular Greek love-story, which was treated by Callĭmăchus in a poem now unfortunately lost. The later Greek prose romances were founded upon this version. Cydippe was the daughter of a well-born Athenian. It happened that she and Acontĭus, a youth from the island of Cĕos, who was in love with her, had come at the same time to a festival of Artĕmis at Dēlos.

Cydippe was sitting in the temple of Artemis, when Acontius threw at her feet an apple, on which was written, "I swear by the sanctuary of Artemis that I will wed Acontius." Cydippe took up the apple and read the words aloud, then threw it from her, and took no notice of Acontius and his addresses. After this her father wished on several occasions to give her in marriage, but she always fell ill before the wedding. The father consulted the Delphic oracle, which revealed to him that the illness of his daughter was due to the wrath of Artemis, by whose shrine she had sworn and broken her oath. He accordingly gave her to Acontius to wife.

Cymbĭum (*Kymbĭŏn*). *See* VESSELS.

Cynics. *See* ANTISTHENES.

Cўnŏphontĭs (*Kynŏphontĭs*). *See* LINUS.

Cypriānus. (1) *Thascus Cœcĭlĭus.* A Latin ecclesiastical writer, born in Africa at the beginning of the 3rd century, of a respectable pagan family. Originally a teacher of rhetoric, he was converted and made Bishop of Carthage in 248 A.D. He was beheaded during the persecution under Valerian, in 257. In his numerous writings and exhortations he not only imitates Tertullian (whom he acknowledges as his master), but makes great use of his works. Besides these we have a large collection of his letters addressed to individuals and to churches.

[(2) *Cyprian of Toulon.* A bishop of Toulon, who lived during the last quarter of the 5th and first half of the 6th centuries A.D. He was in all probability the author of a metrical Latin Heptateuch, edited piecemeal by Morel, Martene, and Pitra ; critically reviewed by J. E. B. Mayor, Cambridge, 1889.]

Cȳrēnē (*Kyrēnē*). *See* ARISTÆUS.

Cȳzĭcus (*Kyzĭkŏs*). *See* ARGONAUTS.

D

Dædăla (" wooden images "). A peculiar festival held by the Bœotians in honour of Hēra. The goddess had, according to the story, once quarrelled with Zeus, and hidden herself on Mount Cĭthærōn. Her husband then spread the report that he was going to marry another wife, and had an image of oak-wood decked out in bridal attire and carried over Cithæron on a chariot with a numerous train amid the singing of marriage hymns. Hera, in her jealousy, threw herself upon her supposed rival, but, on dis-

covering the trick, reconciled herself with laughter to Zeus, took her seat on the chariot, and founded the festival in memory of the incident. The feast was celebrated every seven years by the Platæans alone, and called the little Dædala. But every sixtieth year all the cities of the Bœotian federation kept it as the great Dædala. At the little Dædala, guided by the note of a bird, they fixed on a tree in a grove of oaks, and cut a figure out of it, which they dressed in bridal attire and took, as in marriage procession, to the top of Cithæron. Here they offered a goat to Zeus and a cow to Hera, and burnt the image with the offering. At the great Dædala the images made at the little Dædala were distributed by lot among the cities of the Bœotian confederacy, and the same proceedings were then repeated.

Dædălĭŏn. Brother of Cēyx (*see* CEYX), threw himself down from a rock on Parnassus for grief at the death of his daughter Chĭŏnē, and was turned by the gods into a hawk.

Dædălus (*i.e.* "cunning artificer"). The mythical Greek representative of all handiwork, especially of Attic and Cretan art. As such he was worshipped by the artists' guilds, especially in Attica. He was said to be the son of the Athenian Mētĭŏn, son of Eupălămus (the ready-handed) and grandson of Erechtheus. He was supposed to have been the first artist who represented the human figure with open eyes, and feet and arms in motion. Besides being an excellent architect, he was said to have invented many implements, the axe for instance, the awl, and the bevel. His nephew and pupil (son of his sister Perdix) appeared likely to surpass him in readiness and originality. The invention of the saw, which he copied from the chinbone of a snake, of the potter's wheel, of the turning lathe, and of other things of the kind, was attributed to him. Dædalus was so jealous of him that he threw him from the Acrŏpŏlis; and being detected in the act of burying the body, was condemned by the Areopagus, and fled to Crete to king Mīnōs. Here, among other things, he made the labyrinth at Gnōsus for the Mīnōtaur. He and his son Icărus were themselves confined in it, because he had given Ariadnē the clue with which she guided Theseus through the maze. But the father and son succeeded in escaping, and fled over the sea upon wings of wax feathers made by Dædalus. Icarus, however, approached too near to the sun, so that the wax melted, and he fell into the sea and was drowned. The sea was called after him the Icarian, and the island on which his body was thrown up and buried by Hēraclēs, was called Icaria. Dædalus came to Camīcus

in Sicily, to king Cŏcălus, whose daughter loved him for his art, and slew Minos who came in pursuit of him. He was supposed to have died in Sicily, where buildings attributed to him were shown in many places, as also in Sardinia, Egypt and Italy, particularly at Cumæ. In Greece a number of ancient wooden images were supposed to be his work, in particular a statue of Heracles at Thebes, which Dædalus was said to have made in gratitude for the burial of Icarus.

Dactỹli (*Daktỹloi*). *See* IDÆAN DACTYLI.

Dădŭchus (Gr. *Daidouchŏs*). *See* ELEUSINIA.

* DÆDALUS AND ICARUS.
(Rome, Villa Albani.)

Damastēs. A monster living at Eleusis, in Attica, also called Procrustēs, or the Stretcher. His custom was to lay his guests upon his bed, and if they were too short for it, to rack them to death, if too long, to cut off as much of their limbs as would make them short enough. He was slain by Theseus.

Dæmōn (Gr. *Daimōn*). Originally a term applied to deity in general, manifested in its active relation to human life, without special reference to any single divine personality. But as early as Hesiod the *dœmŏnĕs* appear as subordinates or servants of the higher gods. He gives the name specially to the spirits of the past age of gold, who are appointed to watch over men and guard them. In later times, too, the *dœmŏnes* were regarded as beings intermediate between the gods and mankind, forming as it were the retinue of the gods, representing their powers in activity, and entrusted with the fulfilment of their various functions. This was the relation, to take an instance, which the Satyrs and Sĭlēnī bore to Dĭŏnȳsus. But the popular belief varied with regard to many of these deities. Erōs, *e.g.*, was by many expressly designated a dæmon, while by others he was worshipped as a powerful and independent deity. Another kind of *dœmones* are those who were attached to individual men, attending them, like the Roman *genius*, from their birth onwards through their whole life. In later times two *dœmones*, a good and bad, were sometimes assumed for every one. This belief was, however, not universal, the prevalent idea being that good and bad alike proceeded at different times from the *dœmon* of each individual; and that one person had a powerful and benevolent, another a weak and malevolent *dœmŏn*. *Agăthŏ-dœmon* (good *dœmon*) was the name of the good spirit of rural prosperity and of vineyards.

Dănăē. The daughter of Acrĭsĭus of Argos, who was shut up in a brazen tower by her father in consequence of an oracle which predicted that death would come to him from his daughter's son. Nevertheless, she bore to Zeus a son, Perseus, the god having visited her in the form of a shower of gold. She was then shut up with her son in a chest and thrown into the sea. Driven by the waves on to the island of Sĕrīphŏs, she was kindly received by a fisherman named Dictys. His brother, Pŏlȳdectĕs, the king of the island, wished to force her to marry him, but her son Perseus delivered her from him, and took her back to Greece. (*See* Perseus.)

Dănăī. Properly the name of the inhabitants of Argos, from their old king Dănăŏs, afterwards applied to the Greeks in general, especially the besiegers of Troy.

Dănăĭdĕs. The fifty daughters of Dănăus. *See* Danaus.

Dănăus. The son of Bēlus, king of Egypt, and Anchirrhŏĕ, and twin brother of Ægyptus. Ægyptus and his fifty sons drove Danaus and his fifty daughters from their home in the Egyptian Chemnis through Rhodes to Argos, the home of his ancestress Iō (*see* Io). Here he took over the kingdom from Pelasgus or Gĕlănōr, and after him the Achæans of Argos bore the name of Danai. Danaus built the acropolis of Larissa and the temple of the Lycian Apollo, and taught the inhabitants of the waterless territory how to dig wells. His daughters also conferred benefits on the land by finding springs, especially Amȳmŏnē, the beloved of Pŏseidōn, who, for love of her, created the inexhaustible fountain of Lerna. For this they were worshipped in Argos. The sons of Ægyptus at length appeared and forced Danaus to give them his daughters in marriage. At their father's command they stabbed their husbands at night, and buried their heads in the valley of Lerna. One only, Hypermnēstra, disregarding her father's threats, spared her beloved Lynceus, and helped him to escape. Danaus accordingly set on foot a fighting match, and bestowed his remaining daughter on the victor. Afterwards, though against his will, he gave Lynceus his daughter and his kingdom. According to another story, Lynceus conquered his wife and throne for himself, and took vengeance for his brothers by killing Danaus and his daughters. The Danaĭdĕs (or daughters of Danaus) atoned for their bloody deed in the regions below by being condemned to pour water for ever into a vessel with holes in its bottom. This fable is generally explained by the hypothesis that the Danaides were nymphs of the springs and rivers of the land of Argos, which are filled to overflowing in the wet season, but dry up in summer. The tombstone of Danaus stood in the market at Argos. He was also worshipped in Rhodes as the founder of the temple of Athēnē in Lindŏs, and as the builder of the first fifty-oared ship, in which he fled from Egypt. The story of Danaus and his daughters is treated by Æschȳlus in his *Supplĭcĕs*. Lynceus and Hypermnestra had also a common shrine in Argos; their son was Abās, father of Acrĭsĭus and Prœtus. The son of Amymone and Poseidon was Nauplĭus, founder of Nauplia, and father of Pălămēdĕs, Œax, and Nausĭmĕdōn.

Dancing (Gr. *orchēsĭs*, Lat. *saltātĭŏ*). As early as the Homeric age we find dancing an object of artistic cultivation among the Greeks. The sons and daughters of princes and nobles do not disdain to join in it, whether in religious festivals or at social gatherings. The Greek *orchēstĭkē*, or art of dancing, differed much from the modern. Its aim was to ennoble bodily strength and activity with grace and beauty. Joined with music and poetry, dancing among the Greeks embodied the very spirit of the art of music, mainly because the imitative element predominated in it. For its main aim was to make gesture represent feeling, passion and action; and consequently the Greek dance was an exercise not only for the feet, but for the arms, hands and the whole body. The art at first observed the limits of a noble simplicity, but was perfected, as time went on, in many directions. At the same time it inevitably tended to become more artificial. As in athletics, so in imitative dancing, mechanical execution was largely developed. This was to a great extent displayed in exhibitions of scenes from the mythology, which formed a favourite entertainment at banquets. On the other hand, a prejudice arose against dancing on the part of any one but professionals. For a grown-up person to perform a dance, even at social entertainments, was regarded as an impropriety. The religious performances, especially, as bound up with the worship of Apollo and Dĭonȳsus, consisted mainly in choral dances, whose movement varied according to the character of the god and of the festival. Sometimes it was a solemn march round the altar, sometimes a livelier measure, in which there was a strong dash of imitation. This was especially the case at the festivals of Dionysus. It was from these, as is well known, that the Greek drama was developed, and accordingly the dances formed a part of all dramas, varying according to the character of the piece (*see* CHORUS). Indeed, there was an infinite variety in the forms of the Greek dance. Not only had almost every country district its own, but foreign ones were in course of time adopted.

It must be noticed that in Greek society grown-up men and women were not allowed to dance together, but there were some dances which were performed together by the youth of both sexes. Among these was the *Hormŏs*, or chain-dance, performed by youths and maidens, holding their hands in a changing line, the youths moving in warlike measure, the girls with grace and softness. Another was the *Gĕrănŏs*, or Crane. This dance was peculiar to Dēlŏs, and was said to have been first performed by Thēseus after his deliverance from the Labyrinth, with the boys and girls whom he had rescued. Its elaborate complications were supposed to represent the mazes of the Labyrinth. At Sparta dances were practised, as a means of bodily training, by boys and girls. Among them two may be particularly mentioned : the *Căryātĭs*, performed in honour of Artemis of Căryæ, by the richest and noblest Spartan maidens; and the dances of boys, youths and men, at the festival of the *Gymnŏpædĭa*, consisting in an imitation of various gymnastic exercises (*see* CARYATIDES).

Among the Greek country dances was the *Epĭlēnĭŏs*, or dance of the wine-press, which imitated the actions of gathering and pressing the grape. There were also warlike dances, which were specially popular with the Dorians, and, like others, were partly connected with religious worship. One of the most celebrated of these was the *Pyrrhĭchē* (*see* PYRRHIC DANCE).

Roman. Dancing never played such a part in the national life of the Romans as it did in that of the Greeks. It is true that the ancient Roman worship included dances of the priests (*see* SALII), and that the lower orders in the country were fond of dancing on festive occasions. But respectable Romans regarded it as inconsistent with their dignity. After the second Punic War, as Greek habits made their way into Italy, it became the fashion for young men and girls of the upper class to take lessons in dancing and singing. But dancing was never adopted in Rome as a necessary and effective instrument of education, nor was there any time when public dancing was allowed in society. Performances by professional artists, however (the longer the better), were a favourite entertainment, especially during the imperial period, when the art of mimic dancing attained an astonishing degree of perfection.

Daphnē. A nymph, daughter of the Thessalian river-god Pēneius, or according to another story, the Arcadian Lādōn, was beloved both by Apollo and by Leucippus, the son of Œnŏmäus. The latter followed her in a woman's dress, but was discovered and killed by the nymphs at the instance of his rival. Pursued again by Apollo, the chaste maiden was, at her own entreaty, changed into a bay tree, the tree consecrated to Apollo.

Daphnis. A hero of the Sicilian shepherds, son of Hermēs and of a nymph. A beautiful child, he was exposed by his mother in a grove of bay trees, brought up by nymphs and Pan, and taught by Pan to play the shepherd's flute. He had plighted his troth to a nymph, but breaking his word, he was punished by her with blindness, or (according to another story) turned into a stone. According to another fable, Aphrŏdītē inflicted upon him a hopeless and fatal passion for a woman, because he had despised the love of a girl whom she had wished him to wed. Hermes took him up to heaven and created a fountain at the spot where he was taken. At this fountain the Sicilians offered yearly sacrifices. Daphnis was regarded as the inventor of bucolic poetry, and his fate was a favourite subject with bucolic poets. [See Theocritus, Idyll i.]

Dardănus. Son of Zeus and the Pleiad Electra, the father of the regal house of Troy. He left Arcadia, his mother's home, and went to the island of Samothrace. Here he set up the worship of the great gods, whose shrines, with the *Pallădĭum*, his first wife Chrȳsē had received as a gift from Athēnē at her marriage. Samothrace having been visited by a great flood, Dardanus sailed away with his shrines to Phrygia, where King Teucer gave him his daughter Bateia to wife, and land enough on Mount Ida to found the town of Dardănĭa. His son by Bateia was Erichthŏnĭus, whom Homer describes as the wealthiest of mortals, and the possessor of horses of the noblest breed and most splendid training. The son of Erichthonius was Trōs, father of Ilŏs, Assărăcus and Gănȳmēdēs. From Ilos, the founder of Ilĭŏn or Troy, was descended Lāŏmĕdōn, father of Priam. From Assaracus sprang Căpȳs, father of Anchīsēs, and grandfather of Æneas. Another story made Dardanus the native prince who welcomed Teucer on his arrival from Crete (see TEUCER).

Daricus (Gr. *Dareikŏs*). A gold Persian coin, bearing the stamp of a crowned archer, current in Greece down to the Macedonian period. It was equal in value to the Attic gold *stătēr*, *i.e.* according to the present value of gold, 24 shillings. [See COINAGE, fig. 3.]

Dărēs of Phrygia. In Homer the priest of Hēphæstus in Troy, supposed to have been the author of a pre-Homeric Iliad. It is doubtful whether there ever was any Greek work bearing this title, but a Latin piece of the 5th century A.D. (*Darētis Phrȳgĭi De Excĭdĭŏ Troiæ Histŏrĭa*), bearing a supposed dedication by Cornelius Nepos to Sallust, professes to be a translation of one. This absurd production, and the work of Dictys, was the chief source

followed by the mediæval poets in their stories of the Trojan war (see DICTYS).

Dĕa Dĭa. A Roman goddess, probably identical with Acca Lārentĭa, the ancient Roman goddess of the country. Her worship was provided for by the priestly *collēgĭum* of the *Frātrēs Arvālēs.*

Death (Gr. *Thănătŏs*). In the Homeric poems Death is called the twin brother of Sleep. In Hesiod he is born of Night without a father, with *Kēr* (the goddess of mortal destiny), *Mŏrŏs* (the fatal stroke of death), *Hypnŏs*, (sleep) and the Dreams. Hesiod represents Death, the hard-hearted one, hated by the immortal gods, as dwelling with his brother Sleep in the darkness of the West, whither the sun never penetrates either at his rising or his setting. On the chest of Cypsĕlus at Olympĭa is a representation of Night, holding in each hand a sleeping boy; the one in the right hand being white, and symbolizing Sleep; the other in the left hand, black, and symbolizing Death. Euripides introduces Death on the stage in his *Alcestis*. He has a black garment and black wings, and a knife to cut off a lock of hair as an offering to the gods below. In works of art he appears as a beautiful boy or youth, sometimes with, sometimes without, wings, and often with his brother Sleep. He is usually in slumber, and holds a torch, either lowered, or reversed and extinguished.

Dĕcemvĭrī (Latin). A *collēgĭum* of ten officers or commissioners. Such were the commissioners named for making a comprehensive code of laws in 451 B.C., *Dĕcemvĭrī Lēgĭbŭs Scrĭbundīs.* The *Decemviri Sacrīs Făcĭundīs* were a standing *collēgium* of priests appointed to read and expound the Sibylline books. The *Decemviri Lītĭbŭs Iūdĭcandīs* were also a standing *collegium* of *iūdĭcēs* appointed for certain trials. Commissions of ten (*decemviri agrīs dīvĭdundīs* and *cŏlŏnĭīs dēdūcendīs*) were frequently, though not always, appointed for assignations of public land and the foundation of colonies.

Dĕcŭma. A tithe. This name was applied by the Romans to the tribute in kind, which Sicily, and at one time Asia Minor had to pay out of the yearly produce of wheat, wine, oil and legumes, instead of the *stĭpendĭum* usual in other provinces. It was a burden on the land, called after it *ăger dĕcŭmānus*, and was exacted from the persons occupying at the time. Every year the number of cultivators, of acres under cultivation, and the produce of the harvest, was ascertained, and the right of exacting the *decuma* of the whole territory of a city sold to the highest bidder. In the case of Sicily this took place at Syracuse; in the case of Asia, in Rome. The purchaser of the *decuma* bound himself to deliver a certain quantity of corn in Rome; if the harvest were good, he found his advantage in the surplus. Such farmers of the *decumæ* were called *dĕcŭmānĭ* (*see* PUBLICANUS). If the amount delivered were insufficient for the needs of the city, a second amount could be exacted by decree of the senate or people, which was paid for by the State (*see* ANNONA).

Dĕcŭrĭa (Latin). Originally a division consisting of ten persons, as, for example, the three subdivisions of the *turma* of cavalry. Afterwards the word was applied to any division of a large whole, whether the number ten was implied or not. The *iūdĭcēs* for instance, and most *collĕgĭa* were divided into *decuriæ* (*see* APPARITOR).

Dĕcŭrĭō (1) The president of a *decuria*, or the cavalry officers bearing the name (*see* TURMA). (2) The members of the senate in municipal towns were also called *decuriōnēs* (*see* MUNICIPIUM).

Dēdĭcātĭō (Latin). The consecration of a public sanctury. The *pontĭfĭcēs* had to draw up the deed of foundation. When they had signified that they deemed the act permissible, and the consent of the people (in later times of the emperor) had been obtained, the rite was performed in the presence of the whole *collĕgĭum pontĭfĭcum*. The Pontifex Maxĭmus, whose head was veiled, and with him the representative of the people, took hold of the doorpost with one hand, the former dictating, and the latter repeating after him, the formula of dedication. The people was represented usually by one of the two consuls, or a person, or a commission (generally of two persons) elected by the people on the recommendation of the senate. One of the persons forming the commission was generally the man who had vowed the dedication. The day on which the shrine was dedicated was regarded as the day of its foundation, and was inscribed in the calendar as a festival.

Dēīănīra. Daughter of Œneus king of Cǎlȳdōn, and Althæa. She was the wife of Hĕrăclēs, whose death was brought about by her jealousy (*see* HERACLES).

Dēīdămīa. Daughter of Lȳcŏmēdēs, king of Scȳrŏs, and mother of Nĕoptŏlĕmus by Achilles.

Deimŏs and **Phŏbŏs.** *See* ARES, and comp. PALLOR and PAVOR.

Dēīphŏbus. Son of Priam and Hĕcŭba, and one of the chief Trojan heroes, next to Hector, after whose death he was the leader of the Trojan army. It was he and Paris who were said to have slain Achilles. In the later story he is the husband of Helen, after Paris' death, and is betrayed by her to Mĕnĕlāus on the taking of Troy. According to Homer's account he was surprised by Odysseus and Menelaus in his own house, and overcome only after a hard struggle.

Dēlĭa. The festival of Apollo held every five years at the island of Dēlŏs, and visited by ceremonial embassies from all the Greek cities.

Delphĭca Mensa. *See* TABLES.

Delphīnĭa. A festival held at Athens in honour of Apollo as the god of spring. The *Delphīnĭŏn* was a sanctuary of the Delphian Apollo at Athens. (*See* EPHETÆ.)

Delphic Oracle. A very ancient seat of prophecy at Delphi, originally called Pȳthō, and situated on the south-western spur of Parnassus in a valley of Phōcĭs. In historical times the oracle appears in possession of Apollo; but the original possessor, according to the story, was Gaia (the Earth). Then it was shared by her with Pŏseidōn, who gave up his part in it to Apollo in exchange for the island of Calauria, Thĕmis, the daughter and successor of Gaia, having already given Apollo her share. According to the Homeric hymn to the Pythian Apollo, the god took forcible possession of the oracle soon after his birth, slaying with his earliest bow-shot the serpent Pytho, the son of Gaia, who guarded the spot. To atone for his murder, Apollo was forced to fly and spend eight years in menial service before he could return forgiven. A festival, the *Septĕrĭa*, was held every year, at which the whole story was represented: the slaying of the serpent, and the flight, atonement, and return of the god. Apollo was represented by a boy, both of whose parents were living. The dragon was symbolically slain, and his house, decked out in costly fashion, was burnt. Then the boy's followers hastily dispersed, and the boy was taken in procession to Tempē, along the road formerly followed by the god. Here he was purified and brought back by the same road, accompanied by a chorus of maidens singing songs of joy. The oracle proper was a cleft in the ground in the innermost sanctuary, from which arose cold vapours, which had the power of inducing ecstasy. Over the cleft stood a lofty gilded tripod of wood. On this was a circular slab, upon which the seat of the prophetess was placed. The prophetess, called Pythia, was a maiden of honourable birth; in earlier times a young girl, but in a later age a woman of over fifty, still wearing a girl's dress, in memory of the earlier custom. In the prosperous times of the oracle two Pythias acted alternately, with a third to assist them. In the earliest times the Pythia ascended the tripod only once a year, on the birthday of Apollo, the seventh of the Delphian spring month Bysĭŏs. But in later years she prophesied every day, if the day itself and the sacrifices were not unfavourable. These sacrifices were offered by the supplicants, adorned with laurel crowns and fillets of wool. Having prepared herself by washing and purification, the Pythia entered the sanctuary, with gold ornaments in her hair, and flowing robes upon her; she drank of the water of the fountain Cassōtĭs, which flowed into the shrine, tasted the fruit of the old bay tree standing in the chamber, and took her seat. No one was present but a priest, called the *Prŏphētēs*, who explained the words she uttered in her ecstasy, and put them into metrical form, generally hexameters. In later times the votaries were contented with answers in prose. The responses were often obscure and enigmatical, and couched in ambiguous and metaphorical expressions, which themselves needed explanation. The order in which the applicants approached the oracle was determined by lot, but certain cities, as Sparta, had the right of priority.

The reputation of the oracle stood very high throughout Greece until the time of the Persian wars, especially among the Dorian tribes, and among them pre-eminently the Spartans, who had stood from of old in intimate relation with it. On all important occasions, as the sending out of colonies, the framing of internal legislation or religious ordinances, the god of Delphi was consulted, and that not only by Greeks but by foreigners, especially the people of Asia and Italy. After the Persian wars the influence of the oracle declined, partly in consequence of the growth of unbelief, partly from the mistrust excited by the partiality and venality of the priesthood. But it never fell completely into discredit, and from time to time its position rose again. In the first half of the 2nd century A.D. it had a revival, the result of the newly awakened interest in the old religion. It was abolished at the end of the 4th century A.D. by Theodosius the Great. The oldest stone temple of Apollo was attributed to the mythical architects, Trophōnĭus and Agămēdēs. It was burnt down in 548 B.C., when the Alcmæōnĭdæ, at that time in exile from Athens, undertook to rebuild it for the sum of 300 talents, partly taken from the treasure of the temple, and partly contributed by all countries inhabited by Greeks and standing in connexion with the oracle. They put the restoration into the hands of the Corinthian architect Spinthărus, and carried it out in a more splendid style than was originally agreed upon, building the front of Parian marble instead of limestone. The groups of sculpture in the pediments represented, on the eastern side, Apollo with Artĕmis, Lētō, and the Muses; on the western side, Dĭonȳsus with the Thyĭădĕs and the setting sun; for Dionysus was worshipped here in winter during the imagined absence of Apollo. These were all the work of Praxĭās and Androsthĕnēs, and were finished about 430 B.C. The temple was, on account of its vast extent, a hypæthral building; that is, there was no roof over the space occupied by the temple proper. The architecture of the exterior was Doric, of the interior Ionic, as may still be observed in the surviving ruins. On the walls of the entrance-hall were short texts written in gold, attributed to the Seven Wise Men. One of these was the celebrated "Know Thyself." In the temple proper stood the golden statue of Apollo, and in front of it the sacrificial hearth with the eternal fire. Near this was a globe of marble covered with fillets, the *Omphălŏs*, or centre of the earth. In earlier times two eagles stood at its side, representing the two eagles which fable said had been sent out by Zeus at the same moment from the eastern and western ends of the world. These eagles were carried off in the Phocian war, and their place filled by two eagles in mosaic on the floor. Behind this space was the inner shrine, lying lower, in the form of a cavern over the cleft in the earth. Within the spacious precincts (*pĕrĭbŏlŏs*) stood a great number of chapels, statues, votive offerings and treasure-houses of the various Greek states, in which they deposited their gifts to the sanctuary, especially the tithes of the booty taken in war. Here, too, was the council chamber of the Delphians. Before the entrance to the temple was the great altar for burnt-offerings, and the golden tripod, dedicated by the Greeks after the battle of Platæa, on a pedestal of brass, representing a snake in three coils. [The greater part of this pedestal now stands in the Hippodrome, or Atmeidan, at Constantinople.] Besides the treasures accumulated in the course of time, the temple had considerable property in land, with a population consisting mainly of slaves (*hĭĕrŏdouloi*), bound to pay contributions and to render service to the sanctuary. The management of the property was in the hands of priests chosen from the noble Delphian families, at their head the five *Hŏsĭoi* or consecrated ones. Since the first spoliation of the temple by the Phocians in 355 B.C., it was several times plundered on a grand scale. Nero, for instance, is said to have carried off 500 bronze statues. Yet some 3,000 statues were to be seen there in the time of the elder Pliny. [*See* an article on the Delphic temple by Professor Middleton, *Journal of Hellenic Studies*, ix 282–322.]

Dēmarchŏs. *See* DEMOS.

Dēmētēr (in Greek mythology). Daughter of Crŏnus and Rhea. Her name signifies

DEMETER AND PERSEPHONE CONSECRATING
TRIPTOLEMUS (?)
(Relief found at Eleusis, 1859.)

Mother Earth, the meaning being that she was goddess of agriculture and the civilization based upon it. Her children are, by

Iăsĭōn, a son Plūtus, the god of riches, and by her brother Zeus, a daughter Persĕphŏnē. Round Demeter and this daughter centre her worship and the fables respecting her. Hādēs carries off Persephone, and Demeter wanders nine days over the

DEMETER OF CNIDUS.
(British Museum.)

earth seeking her, till on the tenth day she learns the truth from the all-seeing sun. She is wrath with Zeus for permitting the act of violence, and she visits Olympus and wanders about among men in the form of an old woman under the name of Dēō or the Seeker, till at length, at Eleusis, in Attica, she is kindly received at the house of king Cĕlĕus, and finds comfort in tending his newly born son Dēmŏphŏōn. Surprised by his mother in the act of trying to make the child immortal by putting it in the fire, she reveals her deity, and causes a temple to be built to her, in which she gives herself up to her grief. In her wrath she makes the earth barren, so that mankind are threatened with destruction by famine, as she does not allow the fruit of the earth to spring up again until her daughter is allowed to spend two-thirds of the year with her. On her return to Olympus she leaves the gift of corn, of agriculture, and of her holy mysteries with her host, as a token of grateful recollection. She sends Triptŏlĕmus the Eleusinian round the world on her chariot, drawn by serpents, to diffuse the knowledge of agriculture and other blessings accompanying it, the settlement of fixed places of abode, civil order, and wedlock. Thus Demeter was worshipped as the goddess of agriculture and foundress of law, order, and especially of marriage, in all places where Greeks dwelt, her daughter being usually associated with her. (*See* THESMOPHORIA.) The most ancient seat of her worship was Athens and Eleusis, where the Rharian

DEMETER.
(Mural painting from Pompeii.)

plain was solemnly ploughed every year in memory of the first sowing of wheat. She was also much worshipped in Sicily, which from its fertility was accounted one of her favourite places of abode (*see* ELEUSINIA). As the goddess of fertility, Demeter was in many regions associated with Pŏseidōn, the god of fertilizing water. This was particularly the case in Arcadia, where Pŏseidon was regarded as the father of Persephone. She was also joined with Dionŷsus, the god of wine, and, as mother of Persephone and goddess of the earth, to which not only the seed, but the dead are committed, she is connected with the lower world under the name of Chthŏnĭa. In

later times she was often confused with Gaia and Rhea, or Cȳbĕlē. Besides fruit and honeycombs, the cow and the sow were offered to her, both as emblems of productivity. Her attributes are poppies and ears of corn (also a symbol of fruitfulness), a basket of fruit and a little pig. Other emblems had a mystic significance, as the torch and the serpent, as living in the earth, and as symbolizing a renewal of life by shedding its skin. The Romans identified her with their own Cĕrēs.

Dēmētrius Phălērēūs (of Phalērum, on the coast S.W. of Athens). He was born about 345 B.C., was a pupil of Theophrastus, and an adherent of the Peripatetic school. He was distinguished as a statesman, orator and scholar. His reputation induced Cassander to put him at the head of the Athenian state in 317 B.C. For ten years he administered its affairs, and so thoroughly won the affection of his fellow-citizens that they erected numerous statues to him, as many as 360, according to the accounts. On the approach of Demetrius Poliorcētēs in 307 B.C., he was deposed, and through the efforts of his opponents condemned to death by the fickle populace. On this he fled to Egypt, to the court of Ptolemy the First, who received him kindly and availed himself of his counsel. Thus Demetrius is credited with having suggested the foundation of the celebrated Alexandrian library. But Ptolemy withdrew his favour from him and banished him to Upper Egypt, where he died in 283 B.C. from the bite of a venomous snake. He was very active as a writer, and his stay in Egypt gave him plenty of leisure to indulge his taste; but only a few fragments of his works have survived. An essay *On Rhetorical Expression*, formerly attributed to him, was in reality from the hand of a Demetrius who lived in the 1st century A.D. As an orator Demetrius is said to have been attractive rather than powerful. He was supposed to have been the first speaker who gave rhetorical expression an artificial character, and also the first who introduced into the rhetorical schools the habit of practising speaking upon fictitious themes, juristic or political.

Dēminūtiō căpĭtis (diminution of civil rights and legal capacity). This was the term by which the Romans denoted degradation into an inferior civil condition, through the loss of the rights of freedom, citizenship or family. The extreme form of it, *deminutio capitis maxĭma*, was entailed by the loss of freedom, which involved the loss of all other rights. This would occur if a Roman citizen were taken prisoner in war, or given up to the enemy for having violated the sanctity of an ambassador, or concluding a treaty not approved of by the people. Or again if he was sold into slavery, whether by the State for refusing military service, or declining to state the amount of his property at the census, or by his creditors for debt. If a prisoner of war returned home, or if the enemy refused to accept him when given up to them, his former civil rights were restored. The intermediate stage, *deminutio capitis mědĭa* or *mĭnor*, consisted in loss of civil rights consequent on becoming citizen of another state, or on a decree of exile confirmed by the people, or (in imperial times) on deportation. Restoration of the civil status was possible if the foreign citizenship were given up, or if the decree of exile were cancelled. The lowest grade (*deminutio capitis mĭnĭma*) was the loss of hitherto existing family rights by emancipation (which involved leaving the family), adoption, or (in the case of a girl) by marriage.

Dēmĭurgī (*Dēmĭourgoi*, workers for the people). A general term among the Greeks for tradesmen, among whom they included artists and physicians. In old times they formed, at Athens, the third order, the other two being the *Eupătrĭdœ* and *Geōmŏrī* (*see* these names). In some states *demiurgi* was the name of the public officials; in the Achæan League, for instance, the ten *demiurgi* were among the highest officers of the confederacy.

Dēmŏcrătĭa (*Dēmokrătĭa*, sovereignty of the people). The Greek term for the form of constitution in which all citizens had the right of taking part in the government. This right was not always absolutely equal. Sometimes classes were formed on a property qualification, and civil rights conferred accordingly (*see* TIMOCRATIA); but no class in this case was absolutely excluded from a share in the government, and it was possible to rise from one class to another. Sometimes provision was made by law to prevent any person taking part in the administration but such as had proved their worth and capacity. In the absence of such limitations the democracy, as Plato in his *Republic* and Aristotle in his *Politics* observed, soon degenerated into a mob-government (*ōchlocrătĭa*), or developed into a despotism.

Dēmŏcrĭtus (*Dēmŏkrĭtŏs*). A Greek philosopher born at Abdēra in Thrace about 460 B.C. His father, who had entertained king Xerxës during his expedition against Greece, left him a very considerable property, which he spent in making long journeys into Egypt and Asia. On his return he held aloof from all public business, and devoted himself entirely to his studies. He was more than a hundred years old at his death, and left behind him a number of works on ethics, physics, astronomy, mathematics, art, and literature, written in an attractive and animated manner. We have the titles of some of his writings; but only scanty fragments remain. Democritus was the most learned Greek before Aristotle. In the history of philosophy he has a special importance, as the real founder of what is called the Atomic Theory, or the doctrine that the universe was formed out of atoms. It is true that his master Leucippus had already started the same idea. According to this theory there are in the universe two fundamental principles, the Full and the Void. The Full is formed by the atoms, which are primitive bodies of like quality but different form, innumerable, indivisible, indestructible. Falling for ever through the infinite void, the large and heavier atoms overtake and strike upon the smaller ones, and the oblique and circular motions thence arising are the beginning of the formation of the world. The difference of things arises from the fact that atoms differ in number, size, form and arrangement. The soul consists of smooth round atoms resembling those of fire; these are the nimblest, and in their motion, penetrating the whole body, produce the phenomena of life. The impressions on the senses arise from the effect produced in our senses by the fine atoms which detach themselves from the surface of things. Change is in all cases nothing but the union or separation of atoms.

The ethics of Democritus are based on the theory of happiness, and by happiness he means the serenity of the mind, undisturbed by fear or by anything else. The control of the appetites, attainable by temperance and self-culture, is the necessary condition of this. To do good for its own sake, without the influence of fear or hope, is the only thing which secures inward contentment. The system of Epĭcūrus is, of all other ancient systems, the most closely connected with that of Democritus.

Dēmŏphŏōn. (1) Son of Cĕlĕus of Eleusis and Mĕtănīra. He was tended in infancy by Dēmētēr, when, in her search for Persĕphŏnē, she came to Eleusis in the form of an old woman. Demeter found comfort in the care of the child, and wished to confer immortality on him by anointing him with ambrosia and holding him at night over the fire. The interference of the mother, however, prevented the fulfilment of her design (*see* DEMETER). Triptŏlĕmus in some versions takes the place of Demophoon (*see* TRIPTOLEMUS).

(2) Son of Thēseus and Phædra. With his brother Acămās he was committed by Theseus to Elĕphēnōr, prince of the Abantĕs in Eubœa. This was at the time when Theseus, on his return from the lower regions, found Menestheus in possession of the sovereignty of Attica, and was anxious to emigrate to Scȳrŏs. In the post-Homeric story Demophoon and Acamas march to Troy with their protector Elephenor. After the conquest of the city they liberate their grandmother Æthra, and take possession again of their father's kingdom, as Menestheus, who in Homer is the chief of the Athenians before Troy, had fallen there (*see* ÆTHRA). When Dĭŏmēdēs was thrown upon the coast of Attica on his return from Troy, and began to plunder it in ignorance of where he was, Demophoon took the Palladium from him. Subsequently he protected the children of Hēraclēs against the persecutions of Eurystheus, and killed the latter in battle. On his return from Troy he had betrothed himself to Phyllis, daughter of the king of Thrace. On the day appointed for the marriage he did not appear, and Phyllis hanged herself and was changed into a tree.

Dēmŏs. A Greek word meaning: (1) the people, either in contrast with a despot or the nobility, or as the depository of supreme power. (2) a district or region. Thus in the Athenian state the *demes* were the hundred administrative districts formed by Clīsthĕnĕs, of which ten were contained in each of the ten tribes or *phȳlæ*. The *demes* were named after the small towns and hamlets, and sometimes from distinguished families living there and owning property at the time of the division. In course of time the number of the *demes* increased through extension and division, so that in the age of Augustus it amounted to 174. According to the original arrangement all persons who belonged to a *deme* lived in its precincts. The descendants belonged to the same *demes* as their ancestors, even though they neither lived

nor owned property there. To pass from one *deme* to another was only possible by adoption. To own property in a strange *deme* it was necessary to pay a special tax to it. As every citizen was obliged to belong to a *deme*, the complete official description of him included the name of his *deme* as well as of his father. Every *deme* had certain common religious rites, presided over by special priests. The *dēmŏtœ*, or members of a *deme*, had also a common property, a common chest for receiving the rents and taxes, common officers with a *demarchus* at their head, and common meetings for the discussion of common interests, elections, and so forth. At these meetings the names of the young citizens of eighteen years old were written in the registers of the *deme*, and after two years were enrolled in the lists of persons qualified to take part in the meetings. It was also at these assemblies that the regular revision of the lists of Athenian citizens took place.

Dēmosthĕnēs. The greatest orator of antiquity, born in 384 B.C., in the Attic *deme* Pæānĭa. His father, who bore the same name, was the wealthy owner of a manufactory of arms. He died before his son was seven years old, and the young Demosthenes grew up under the tender care of his mother. The boy's ambition was excited by the brilliant successes of the orator Callistrătus, and he was eager at the same time to bring to justice his dishonest guardians for the wrong done to him and his sisters. He therefore devoted himself to the study of oratory under the special instruction of Isæus. The influence of this master is very evident in his speeches delivered in 364 against one of his guardians, Aphŏbus, with his brother-in-law Onētŏr. Demosthenes won his case, but did not succeed in getting either from Aphobus or from his other guardians any adequate compensation for the loss of nearly thirteen talents (some £2,600) which he had sustained. To support himself and his relations, he took up the lucrative business of writing speeches for others, as well as appearing in person as an advocate in the courts. His two first attempts at addressing the assembled people were, partly owing to the unwieldiness of his style, partly from a faulty delivery, complete failures. But Demosthenes, so far from being daunted, made superhuman efforts to overcome the defects entailed by a weak chest and a stammering tongue, and to perfect himself in the art of delivery. In this he was aided by the sympathy and experience of several friends, especially the actor Sătўrŭs. Thus prepared, he appeared again in public in 355 B.C. with his celebrated speech against the law of Leptĭnēs, and then made good his position on the rostrum. Two years afterwards he started on his political career. His object from the first was to restore the supremacy of Athens through her own resources, and to rally the Greek states round her against the common enemy, whom he had long recognized in Philip of Macedon. It was in 351 B.C. that he first raised his voice against the Macedonian king. Philip, invoked by the Thessalians to help them against the Phocians, had conquered the latter, and was threatening to occupy the pass of Thermŏpўlæ, the key of Greece Proper. In his first Philippic, Demosthenes opened the conflict between Greek freedom and the Macedonian military despotism. This contest he carried on with no other weapon than his eloquence; but with such power and persistence that Philip himself is reported to have said that it was Demosthenes and not the Athenians with whom he was fighting. On this occasion he succeeded in inspiring the Athenians to vigorous action. But his three Olynthiac orations failed to conquer the indolence and short-sightedness of his fellow-citizens, and their ally the city of Olynthus was taken by Philip in 348. In 346 he was one of the ambassadors sent to conclude a peace with Philip. His colleagues Philŏcrătēs and Æschĭnēs were bribed with Macedonian gold, and Demosthenes did not succeed in thwarting their intrigues, which made it possible for the king to occupy Thermopylæ, and secure therewith the approach to Greece. In his speech on the Peace he advises his countrymen to abide by the settlement. But the ceaseless aggression of the Macedonian soon provoked him again to action, and in the second and third Philippic (344 and 341) he put forth all the power of his eloquence. At the same time he left no stone unturned to strengthen the fighting power of Athens. His exertions were, on this occasion, successful: for in spite of the counter efforts of the Macedonian party, he managed to prevail on the Athenians to undertake a war against Philip, in the victorious course of which Pĕrinthus and Byzantium were saved from the Macedonian despotism (340). But it was not long before the intrigues of Æschines, who was in Philip's pay, brought about a

new interference on the king's part in the affairs of Greece. As a counter-move Demosthenes used his eloquence to persuade the Thebans to ally themselves with Athens: but all hope was shattered by the unhappy battle of Chærōnëa (B.C. 338), in which Demosthenes himself took part as a heavy-armed soldier. Greece was now completely

* DEMOSTHENES.
(Vatican Museum, Rome.)

in the hands of Philip. The Macedonian party tried to make Demosthenes responsible for the disaster; but the people acquitted him, and conferred upon him, as their most patriotic citizen, the honour of delivering the funeral oration over the dead. In 336, after Philip's death, Demosthenes summoned the Athenians to rise against the Macedonian dominion. But the destruction of Thebes by Alexander crippled every attempt at resistance. It was only through the venal intervention of Dēmādēs that Demosthenes, with his true-hearted allies and supporters Hypĕrīdēs and Lycurgus, escaped being given up to the enemy, as had been demanded. Demosthenes had been repeatedly crowned in public for his public services, and in 337 B.C. Ctēsĭphōn had proposed not only to give him a golden crown for his tried devotion to his country, but to proclaim the fact at the Dionysia by the mouth of the herald. Æschines had already appeared to prosecute Ctesiphon for bringing forward an illegal proposal. In 330 he brought up the charge again, meaning it no doubt as a blow against his bitterest enemy Demosthenes. Demosthenes replied in his famous speech upon the Crown, and won a brilliant victory over his adversary, who was thereupon obliged to go into exile at Rhodes. But in 324 his enemies, joined on this occasion by his old friend Hyperides, succeeded in humiliating him. Harpălus, the finance minister of Alexander, had fled to Athens with an immense treasure, and Demosthenes was accused of having taken bribes from him, condemned, and sentenced to pay a fine of 50 talents. Unable to pay this enormous sum, he was thrown into prison, whence he escaped to Ægīna, to be recalled and welcomed with trumpets in the following year after the death of Alexander. But the unfortunate issue of the Lamian war, which resulted in a Macedonian occupation of Athens and the dissolution of the democratic constitution, involved him in ruin. Condemned to death with his friends by the Macedonian party, he fled to the island of Calauria, near Trœzēn, and took sanctuary in the temple of Poseidon. Here, as Antĭpăter's officers were upon him, he took poison and died, Oct. 16, 322.

Sixty-five genuine speeches of Demosthenes were known in antiquity, and many others were falsely attributed to him. The collection which we possess contains sixty speeches, besides a letter of Philip to the Athenians, but some twenty-seven of these are suspected. The seventh, for instance, On the Island of Hălonnēsus, was written by a contemporary, Hēgēsippus. The genuineness of the six letters, and of fifty-six prŏœmĭa, or introductions to public speeches, which bear his name, is also doubtful. Among the genuine speeches the most

remarkable, both for the beauty of their form and the importance of their subjects, are the Olynthiacs, the Philippics, the orations on the Peace, on the Crown, on the Embassy (against Æschines), with those against the Law of Leptĭnēs, against Andrŏtĭōn, and against Meidĭās. The greatness of Demosthenes consists in his unique combination of honest intention with natural genius and thoroughly finished workmanship. He has all the qualities by which the other Greek orators are distinguished singly, and at the same time the power of applying them in the most effective way on each occasion as it arises. It is true that he had not the gift of free extempore speaking, or if he had, he did not cultivate it; he gave the most elaborate preparation to all his speeches, so that a witty contemporary said they smelt of the lamp. The consequence however is, that all he says shows the deepest thought and ripest consideration. There is the same finish everywhere, whether in the sobriety and acuteness of his argumentation, in the genial and attractive tone of his narrative, or in the mighty and irresistible stream of his eloquence, which no violence of passion ever renders turbid. With all his art, his language is always simple and natural, never far-fetched or artificial. The greatest of the Greek orators, Demosthenes was the centre of all rhetorical study among the Greeks and Romans, and was much commented upon by scholars and rhetoricians. Little, however, of these commentaries remains, except a collection of mediocre scholia, bearing the name of Ulpĭānus.

Dēmŏtæ. See DEMOS.

Dēnārĭus (Latin). A Roman silver coin so called because it originally contained 10 asses. In later times it = 16 asses = 4 sestertĭī = $\frac{1}{25}$ of an aurĕus. Its original weight was 4·55 gr. (= between 9d. and 10d.), from 207 B.C. to Nero, 3·90 (about 8½d.), after Nero's time 3·41 gr., the amount of pure silver being so reduced that it was worth only about 6d. Its value subsequently sank more and more, until at the beginning of the 3rd century A.D. it was worth only 3½d. When at the end of the 3rd century Diocletian introduced a new silver coin of full value according to the Neronian standard (the so-called argentĕus), the name denarius was transferred to a small copper coin (see COINAGE, ROMAN).

Dēō. See DEMETER.

Dēportātĭō. Banishment to a specified locality, generally an island. This form of exile was devised under the early Roman emperors. It involved loss of civil rights, and generally also of property.

Dĕsultōrēs. *See* CIRCUS.

Deucălĭōn. In Greek mythology, the son of Promētheus and Clўmĕnē, husband of Pyrrha, the daughter of Epimētheus, monarch of Phthia in Thessaly. Zeus having resolved to destroy the degenerate race of mankind by a great flood, Deucalion, by the advice of his father, built a wooden chest, in which he rescued only himself and his wife from the general destruction. After nine days he landed on Mount Parnassus and sacrificed to Zeus Phyxĭŏs (who sends help by flight). Inquiring of the oracle of Thĕmis at Delphi how the human race could be renewed, he received answer that Pyrrha and he should veil their heads, and throw behind them the bones of their mother. They understood the priestess to refer to stones, which they accordingly threw behind them; and the stones of Deucalion turned into men, those of Pyrrha into women. With this new race Deucalion founded a kingdom in Locris, where the grave of Pyrrha was shown. That of Deucalion was said to be visible at Athens in the ancient temple of the Olympian Zeus, which he was supposed to have built.

Dĕverra. One of the three goddesses worshipped among the Italian tribes. She was supposed to protect new-born children and their mothers against disturbance from the god Silvānus (*see* PICUMNUS).

Dĕversŏrĭum. *See* INNS.

Dĕvōtĭō (Latin). A religious ceremony, by virtue of which a general, whose army was in distress, offered up as an atonement to the gods below, and a means of averting their wrath, the army, city, and land of the enemy; or some soldier in the Roman army; or even himself, as was the case with the Dĕcĭĭ. The general, standing on a spear and with veiled head, repeated a solemn formula dictated to him by the Pontifex. If the city and land of the enemy were offered, the gods were solemnly invited to burn the land or city (*See* EVOCATIO). The fate of the devoted person was left in the hands of the gods. If he survived, an image at least seven feet high was buried in the ground and a bloody sacrifice offered over it; he was meanwhile held incapable in future of performing any other religious rite, either on his own behalf or on that of the state.

Dīa. *See* HEBE.

Diadem (*dĭădēmă*). The white fillet round the brow which was the emblem of sovereignty from the time of Alexander the Great. Cæsar refused it when offered him by Antōnĭus, and it was not, in consequence, worn by the Roman emperors, except in a few cases. But when the seat of government was removed to Byzantium, Constantine adopted the Greek emblem of royalty.

Diacrĭī. *See* SOLONIAN CONSTITUTION.

Dĭāna. An ancient Italian deity, whose name is the feminine counterpart of Iānus. She was the goddess of the moon, of the open air, and open country, with its mountains, forests, springs and brooks, of the chase, and of childbirth. In the latter capacity she, like Juno, bore the second title of Lūcīna. Thus her attributes were akin to those of the Greek Artĕmĭs, and in the course of time she was completely identified with her and with Hĕcătē, who resembled her. The most celebrated shrine of Diana was at Arĭcĭa in a grove (*nĕmus*), from which she was sometimes simply called Nĕmŏrensis. This was on the banks of the modern lake of Nemi, which was called the mirror of Diana. Here a male deity named Virbĭus was worshipped with her, a god of the forest and the chase. He was in later times identified with Hippŏlўtus, the risen favourite of Artemis, and the oldest priest of the sanctuary (*Rex Nemorensis*). He was said to have originated the custom of giving the priest's office to a runaway slave, who broke off a branch from a particular tree in the precincts, and slew his predecessor in office in single combat. In consequence of this murderous custom the Greeks compared Diana of Aricia with the Tauric Artemis, and a fable arose that Orestes had brought the image of that god into the grove. Diana was chiefly worshipped by women, who prayed to her for happiness in marriage or childbirth. The most considerable temple of Diana at Rome was in the Aventine, founded by Servius Tullius as the sanctuary of the Latin confederacy. On the day of its foundation (August 13) the slaves had a holiday. This Diana was completely identified with the sister of Apollo, and worshipped simply as Artemis at the Secular Games. A sign of the original difference however remained. Cows were offered to the Diana of the Aventine, and her temple adorned with cows, not with stags' horns, but it was the doe which was sacred to Artemis (*see* ARTEMIS).

Diæta. *See* HOUSE.

Diætētæ (Athenian). Public arbitrators, to whom the parties in a private suit might apply if they wished to avoid a trial before the Hēliastæ. For this object a considerable number of citizens 60 years of age were nominated. They received no salary, but a fee of a drachma (about 8d.) from each party, and as much from the complainant for every adjournment. In case of misconduct they could be called to account. The *Diætetæ* were assigned to the parties by lot by the magistrate who (according to the character of the case) would have presided in the court of the Heliæa. To this magistrate (in case the parties did not appeal to the Heliæa against it), the *Diætetēs* handed in the sentence he had delivered as the result of his investigation, to have it signed and published, and thus made legal. The name of *Diætetæ* was also given to private arbitrators named by agreement between the parties on the understanding that their decision was to be accepted without appeal.

Diāsia. A festival of atonement held by the whole population of Attica, on the 23rd of Anthestērīŏn (February to March), to Zeus Meilĭchĭŏs (the Zeus of propitiatory offerings). The offerings were bloodless, and consisted chiefly of cakes.

Diaulŏs. *See* GYMNASTICS.

Diazōmătă (Latin *præcinctĭōnēs*). The broad passages in the Greek theatre, which horizontally divided the successive row of seats into two or three flights (*see* THEATRE.)

Dicæarchus (*Dĭkaiarchŏs*). A Greek philosopher and author, a disciple of Aristotle. He was born at Messāna in Sicily, but lived mostly in Greece, and especially in the Peloponnese. He was the author of many works on geography, history, politics, and philosophy. One of his most important works was *The Life of Hellas*, in three books, which contained an account of the geography of Greece, its political development and the condition of its various states, its public and private life, its theatre, games, religions, etc. Only fragments of it remain. [The *De Re Publĭcā* of Cicero is supposed, with good reason, to be founded upon a work by Dicæarchus.] A badly written description of Greece, in 150 iambic *sēnārĭī*, bears the name of Dicæarchus, but (as the acrostic at the beginning shows) is really from the hand of a certain Dionysius, son of Callĭphōn. Three interesting and not unimportant fragments of a work on *The Cities of Greece* have also been wrongly attributed to him. Their real author appears to have been an unknown writer named Hērăclīdēs who flourished 280 B.C.

Dicastērĭŏn. *See* HELIÆA.

Dice (Games with). Games with dice were of high antiquity and very popular among the Greeks. They were usually played on a board with a vessel called a tower (*pyrgŏs, turrĭcŭla, frĭtillus,* etc.), narrower at the top than at the bottom, and fitted inside with gradually diminishing shelves. There were two kinds of games. In the first, three dice (*kўbŏs, tessĕra*), and in later times two were used. These were shaped like our dice and were marked on the opposite sides with the dots 1–6, 2–5, 3–4. The game was decided by the highest throw, and each throw had a special name. The best (3 or 4 × 6) was called *Aphrŏdītē* or *Vĕnus,* the worst (3 × 1) the dog (*kўŏn* or *cănis*). In the second, four dice (*astrăgălŏs* or *tălus*) were used, made of the bones of oxen, sheep or goats, or imitations of them in metal or ivory. They had four long sides, two of which, one concave and the other convex, were broad, and the other two narrow, one being more contracted than the other, and two pointed ends, on which they could not stand, and which therefore were not counted. The two broad sides were marked 3 and 4; of the narrow sides the contracted one was marked 6, and the wider one 1, so that 2 and 5 were wanting. As in the other game, so here, every possible throw had its name. The luckiest throw (*Venus*) was four different numbers, 1, 3, 4, 6; the unluckiest (*cănis*) four aces. Dicing as a game of hazard was early forbidden in Rome, and only allowed at the *Sāturnālĭa.* The penalty was a fine and *infămĭa.* The ædiles were responsible for preventing dicing in taverns. If a private individual allowed it in his house, he had no legal remedy for any irregularities that might occur. In spite of this, dicing was quite common at drinking bouts, especially under the empire. Indeed some emperors, *e.g.* Claudius, were passionate players. Others however did their best to check the evil. Justinian went so far as to allow a claim for the recovery of money lost at play.

Dictātor. The Latin term for a magistrate appointed for special emergencies, after auspices duly taken by the consuls on the commission of the senate. The dictator was never appointed for more than six months. The first instance of the appointment occurred in 501 B.C. The dictator was usually, though not always, chosen from the number of *consŭlārēs* or men who had held the office of consul. No plebeian was elected before 356 B.C. He was always nominated for a particular or specified purpose, on the fulfilment of which he laid down his office. He combined the supreme judicial with the supreme military power, and there was, originally, no appeal against his proceedings, even the *veto* of the tribunes being powerless against him. He was entirely irresponsible for his acts, and could therefore not be called to account on the expiration of his term of office. His *insignia* were the *sella cŭrūlis*, *tŏga prœtexta*, and 24 lictors, who represented the lictors of two consuls, and who even in the city bore axes in their bundle of rods, as a sign of the unlimited power of life and death. His assistant was the *măgister ĕquĭtum* (master of the horse), who was bound absolutely to obey his commands, and whom he had to nominate immediately after his own election. The original function of the dictator was military; but after 363 B.C. a dictator was occasionally chosen, in the absence of the consuls, for other purposes than dealing with external danger or internal troubles; especially to hold the games or religious festivities. The office gradually passed out of use, though not legally abolished. The last military dictator was appointed in 206 B.C., the last absolutely in 202 B.C. The dictatorships of Sulla and Cæsar, who was named perpetual dictator not long before his death, were anti-republican and unconstitutional. After Cæsar was murdered in 44 B.C., the office was abolished for ever by a law of Marcus Antōnius.

Dictymna. A goddess of the sea, worshipped in Crete. (*See* BRITOMARTIS.)

Dictȳs. (1) A poor fisherman on the island of Serīphus, who gave welcome to Dănăē and her son Perseus.

(2) *Dictys of Gnossŏs in Crete.* Alleged to have been the companion of Idŏmĕneus in the Trojan war, and author of a diary recording his experiences therein. The diary, written in Phœnician on palm leaves, was said to have been found in a leaden box in his grave in the time of Nero, and to have been translated into Greek at that emperor's command. The existence of this Greek version was doubted, but a certain Lucius Septīmĭus, of the 4th century A.D., gave out his *Dictys Crētensis Ephēmĕrĭs De Bello Troiāno* as a translation of it. This book, and the equally absurd one of Dărēs (*see* DARES), were the chief authorities followed by the mediæval poets who handled the story of Troy.

Dĭdascălĭa (*Dĭdaskălĭa*). A Greek word meaning (1) The performance of a drama. (2) The pieces brought forward for performance at a dramatic entertainment. (3) A board hung up in the theatre, with short notices as to the time and place of the contest, the competing poets, their plays and other successes, perhaps also the *Chŏrēgĭ*, and the most celebrated actors. These documents, so important for the history of the drama, were first collected and arranged by Aristotle, whose example was followed by the Alexandrian scholars Callīmăchus, Aristŏphănēs of Byzantium, and others. From these writings, also called *didascaliæ*, but now unfortunately lost, come the scanty notices preserved by grammarians and scholiasts upon the particular tragedies and comedies. Following the example of the Greeks the Romans provided the dramas of their own poets with *didascaliæ*, as for instance those attached to the comedies of Terence and the *Stichus* of Plautus.

Dīdō. Properly a surname of the Phœnician goddess of the moon, the wandering Astartē, who was also the goddess of the citadel of Carthage. The name of this goddess and some traits of her story were transferred to Elissa, daughter of the Tyrian king Muttōn (the Bēlus or Agēnōr of the Greeks). Elissa came from Tyre to Africa, where she founded Carthage. She was flying from her brother Pygmălĭŏn, the murderer of her husband and paternal uncle Sicharbaal or Sicharbas (called in Greek Acerbās and in Latin Sychæus). To escape wedding the barbarian king Iarbas she erected a funeral pyre and stabbed herself upon it. According to the later story, followed or invented by Vergil, the tragedy was due to her despair at her desertion by Æneās.

Didrachma. *See* COINAGE.

Dĭdȳmus. One of the most celebrated Greek scholars of antiquity. He was born at Alexandria in 63 B.C., but lived and taught in Rome. He was one of the chief representatives of the school of Aristarchus. He is said to have been the author of more than 3,500 works, and from his own industry and gigantic power of work was called *Chalkentĕrŏs* (the man with bowels of brass). Homer was the chief subject of his researches. His greatest work was a treatise of extraordinary care upon Aristarchus' edition of Homer, extracts from which are preserved in the Venetian *Scholia* to Homer. He wrote commentaries, not only on Homer, but on Hesiod, the lyric and dramatic poets, and the Attic orators, besides monographs and works of reference on literary history. The most valuable part of the information handed down in the grammatical lexicons and commentaries of the Byzantines is to be referred to him.

Diipŏlĭa. A festival celebrated in Athens on the 14th Scīrŏphŏrīŏn (June to July), to Zeus as the protector of the city. It was also called *Būphŏnĭa*, from the sacrifice of an ox connected with it. A labouring ox was led to the altar of Zeus in the Acropolis, which was strewn with wheat and barley. As soon as the ox touched the consecrated grain, he was punished by a blow on the neck from an axe, delivered by a priest of a particular family, who instantly threw away the axe and took to flight. In his absence the axe was brought to judgment in the Prytăneum, and condemned, as a thing polluted by murder, to be thrown into the sea. To kill a labouring ox, the trusty helper of man, was rigidly forbidden by custom. In the exceptional sacrifice of one at this festival, the ancient custom may be regarded as on the one hand excusing the slaughter, and on the other insisting that it was, nevertheless, equivalent to a murder.

Dīlectŭs. The levying of soldiers for military service among the Romans. In the republican age all the citizens who were liable to service assembled in the Capitol on the day previously notified by the Consuls in their *ēdictum*, or proclamation. The twenty-four *tribūni mīlĭtum* were first divided among the four legions to be levied. Then one of the tribes was chosen by lot, and the presence of the citizens ascertained by calling the names according to the lists of the several tribes. The calling was always opened with names of good omen (*see* OMEN). If a man did not appear, he would be punished according to circumstances, by a fine, confiscation of property, corporal punishment, even by being sold into slavery. Four men of equal age and bodily capacity were ordered to come forward, and distributed among the four legions, then another four, and so on, so that each legion got men of equal quality. As the proceeding was the same with the other tribes, each legion had a quarter of the levy for each tribe. No one man was excused (*văcātĭŏ*) from service unless he was over 46 years of age, or had served the number of campaigns prescribed by law, twenty in the infantry, ten in the cavalry, or held a city

office or priesthood, or had a temporary or perpetual dispensation granted on account of special business of state. In ancient times the levy of the cavalry followed that of the infantry, in later times it preceded it. On the oath taken after the levy *see* SACRAMENTUM.

About the year 100 B.C. Marius procured the admission of the *căpĭtĕ censĭ*, or classes without property, to military service (*see* PROLETARII). After this the legions were chiefly made up out of this class by enlistment; and though the liability to common military service still existed for all citizens, the wealthy citizens strove to relieve themselves of it, the more so, as after Marius the time of service was extended from twenty campaigns to twenty years. In 89 B.C. the Roman citizenship was extended to all the inhabitants of Italy, and all, therefore, became liable to service. The levies were in consequence not held exclusively in Rome, but in all Italy, by *conquīsītōres*. These functionaries, though they continued to use the official lists of qualified persons, assumed more and more the character of recruiting officers. They were ready to grant the *vacatio*, or exemption, for money or favour, and anxious to get hold of volunteers by holding out promises. The legal liability to military service continued to exist in imperial times, but after the time of Augustus it was only enforced in regard to the garrison at Rome, and on occasions of special necessity. The army had become a standing one, and even outside of Italy, except when a special levy of new legions was made, the vacancies caused by the departure of the soldiers who had served their time were filled up by volunteers. The levy was carried out by imperial commissioners (*dilectātōres*), whose business it was to test the qualifications of the recruits. These were, Roman citizenship—for only citizens were allowed to serve, whether in the legions, or in the guard and other garrison cohorts of Rome (*Cohortēs Urbānæ*)—physical capacity, and a certain height, the average of which was 5 feet 10 inches under the empire. For the republican age we have no information on this point.

Dīnarchus (*Deinarchŏs*). The last of the ten great Attic orators. He was born at Corinth about 361 B.C., and came early to Athens, where he became the pupil and friend of Theophrastus and Dēmētrius of Phălērum. After B.C. 336, and especially after the death of the great orators, he acquired wealth and reputation by writing speeches for others. He was involved in the ruin of his patron, Demetrius, and in 307 went into voluntary exile at Chalcis in Eubœa. It was fifteen years before he obtained permission to return, through the good offices of Theophrastus. Robbed of his property by the treachery of a friend, and nearly blind, he died at Athens, more than 70 years old. His speeches, which were very numerous (there were at least fifty-eight), are all lost, except three on the trial of Harpălus, one of which is directed against Demosthĕnēs. They do not give a favourable idea of his powers. In the opinion of the ancients his style had no individuality, but was an unsuccessful imitation, at one time of Lysias, at another of Hypĕrīdēs, at another of Demosthenes.

Dīnŏcrătēs (*Deinŏkrătēs*). A Greek architect, a native of Macedonia, who flourished in the second half of the 4th century B.C., and was thus a contemporary of Alexander the Great. On the commission of Alexander he superintended the foundation of Alexandria, and erected the funeral pyre of Hephæstīŏn, celebrated for its boldness and splendour. He is also said to have restored the temple of Artĕmīs at Ephesus, burnt down by Herostrătus. An idea of the boldness of his conceptions may be gathered from the fact that he proposed to represent Mount Athos in human form, with a city in one hand, and in the other a vessel from which the waters of the mountain flowed into the sea.

Dīnŏlŏchus (*Deinŏlŏchŏs*). See COMEDY.

Diocletian, Edict of. [An edict published by the Emperor Diocletian about 303 A.D., directing those engaged in the sale of provisions not to exceed certain fixed prices in times of scarcity. It is preserved in an inscription in Greek and Latin on the outer wall of the *cella* of a temple at Strătŏnīcēa (*Eski-hissar*) in Caria. It states the price of many varieties of provisions, and these inform us of their relative value at the time. The provisions specified include not only the ordinary food of the people, but also a number of articles of luxury. Thus mention is made of several kinds of honey. of hams, sausages, salt and fresh-water fish, asparagus and beans, and even *pernœ Menăpĭcœ* (Westphalian hams). At the time when the edict was published the *dĕnārĭus* was obviously much reduced in value, that coin appearing as the equivalent of a single oyster. The inscription was first copied by Sherard in 1709; it has been

elaborately edited by M. Waddington, with new fragments and a commentary, 1864; and by Mommsen in the third volume of the *Corpus Inscriptĭōnum Latīnārum.* Portions of the Greek copy and the Latin preamble were found at Platæa in 1888–9 during the explorations of the American School of Classical Archæology. In 1890, during the excavations of the British School of Archæology, several hundred lines of the Greek version of the decree were discovered at Mĕgălŏpŏlĭs, including a list of pigments with their prices. It has been edited anew by Mommsen and Blümner, 1893.— J. E. S.]

Dĭŏdōrus, surnamed *Sĭcŭlus*, or the Sicilian. A Greek historian, native of Agyrĭŏn, in Sicily, who lived in the times of Julius Cæsar and Augustus. After thirty years' preparation, based upon the results yielded by long travels in Asia and Europe, and the use of the plentiful materials supplied by residence in Rome, he wrote his *Biblĭŏthĕca*, an Universal History in 40 books, extending over a period of some 1,100 years, from the oldest time to 60 B.C. In the first six books he treated the primitive history and mythology of the Egyptians, the natives of Asia, and Africa, and the Hellenes. The next eleven embraced the period from the Trojan war to the death of Alexander the Great. The remaining 23 brought the history down to the beginning of Cæsar's struggle with Gaul. We still possess books 1–5 and 11–20 (from the Persian War under Xerxēs to 302 B.C.), besides fragments, partly considerable, of the other books. In the early books his treatment is ethnographical; but from the seventh book onwards, in the strictly historical part of his work, he writes like an annalist narrating all the events of one year at a time, with emphasis on the more important ones. It is obvious that this proceeding must rob the history of all its inner connection. He has other weaknesses. He is incapable of seizing the individual characteristics either of nations or of individuals, and contents himself with giving anecdotes and unconnected details. He follows his authorities blindly, without any attempt to criticize their statements. Then his work falls far short of the ideal which he himself sets up in his introduction. But it is none the less of great value as being one of the main authorities for many parts of ancient history, especially that affecting Sicily. In his style Diodorus aims at clearness and simplicity.

Dĭŏgĕnēs Laertius (*of Laertē in Cilicia*). A Greek author, who flourished about 150

A.D., the author of a work, in ten books, on the lives and doctrines of celebrated Greek philosophers. It is an uncritical compilation from books of earlier and later date, but the richness of the material gathered from lost writings gives it inestimable value for the history of philosophy. Books 1–7 embrace the Ionic philosophers from Thalēs onwards, Socrates, Plato, Aristotle and the Stoics down to Chrysippus. Books 8, 9 treat of the philosophers whom he includes under the name of Italian, Pȳthăgŏrās, Empĕdŏclēs, Hērăclītus, the Eleatics and Atomists, Prōtăgŏrās, Pyrrho and Epīcūrus, to the last of whom the whole tenth book is devoted.

Dĭŏgĕnĭānus. A Greek grammarian of Hēraclēa. In the middle of the 2nd century A.D. he made extracts in five books from the great collection of stories compiled about a century before by Pamphĭlus. These extracts form the foundation of the lexicon of Hēsȳchĭus. A collection of proverbs made by him is preserved in an abridged form.

Dĭŏmēdēs. (1) Son of Arēs and Cȳrēnē, king of the Bistŏnĕs. (*See* HERACLES.)

(2) Son of Tydeus and Dēïpȳlē, and one of the Epĭgŏni. After the death of his maternal grandfather Adrastus, king of Argos, he led 80 ships against Troy, accompanied by his trusty companions Sthĕnĕlus and Eurȳălus. He appears in Homer, like his father, as a bold, enterprising hero, and a favourite of Athēnē. In the battle which took place during the absence of Achilles she enables him not only to vanquish all mortals who came in his way, Ænēās among them, but to attack and wound Arēs and Aphrŏdītē. On his meeting with Glaucus in the thick of battle, *see* GLAUCUS 4. When the Achæans fly from the field, he throws himself boldly in the path of Hector, and is only checked by the lightning of Zeus, which falls in front of his chariot. In the night after the unsuccessful battle he goes out with Odysseus to explore, kills Dŏlōn, the Trojan spy, and murders the sleeping Rhēsus, king of Thrace, who had just come to Troy, with twelve of his warriors. In the post-Homeric story, he makes his way again, in company with Odysseus, by an underground passage into the acropolis of Troy, and thence steals the *Pallădĭum*. This, according to one version, he carried to Argos; according to another, it was stolen from him by the Athenian king, Dĕmŏphŏōn, on his landing in Attica. After the destruction of Troy, according to Homer,

he came safe home on the fourth day of his journey. His wife, Ægĭālē or Ægĭăleia (daughter or granddaughter of Adrastus), was, according to the later legend, tempted to unfaithfulness by Aphrodite in revenge for the wounds inflicted on her by Diomedes. To escape the fate of Agamemnon, Diomedes fled from Argos to Ætolia, his father's home, and there avenged his old grandfather Œneus on his oppressors. Hence he was driven by a storm to Italy, to king Daunus of Apulia, who helps him in war against the Messapians, marries his daughter Euippē, and extends his dominion over the plain of Apulia (called after him *Campĭ Dĭŏmēdēī*). According to one story, he died in Daunia, in another he returned to Argos, and died there; in a third, he disappeared in the islands in the Adriatic, named, after him, *Insŭlæ Dĭŏmēdēæ*, his companions being changed into the herons that live there, the birds of Diomedes. Diomedes was worshipped as a hero not only in Greece, but on the Italian coast of the Adriatic, where his name had in all probability become confused in worship with those of the native deities of horse-taming and navigation. The foundation of the Apulian city of Argȳrippa (later called Arpi) was specially attributed to him. In his native city, Argos, his shield was carried through the streets with the Palladium at the festival of Athene, and his statue washed in the river Inăchus.

(3) A Roman writer on grammar of the last part of the 4th century A.D. He was the author of an *Ars Grammătĭca*, in three books, founded on the same ancient authorities as the work of his contemporary Charisius, with whom he often agrees *verbatim*. His third book derives special value from the notices on literary history taken from Suetonius.

Dĭŏmeia. An Athenian festival in honour of Hērăclēs. (*See* HERACLES.)

Dĭōn (Lat. *Dĭŏ*). (1) *Dio Chrȳsostŏmus Cocceius.* A Greek rhetorician and philosopher, born of a respectable family at Prusa in Bithynia, about the middle of the 1st century A.D. He began his career by devoting himself to rhetoric. Driven from his native ocuntry by domestic intrigues, he lived for a long time in Egypt, where he obtained the favour of the future emperor Vespasian. Afterwards he lived in Rome under Domitian, until he was banished from Italy and Bithynia for his friendship with a person in high place who had incurred the suspicion of the emperor. The period of his banishment he spent, according to the command of the Delphic oracle, in distant travels through the northern regions of the Roman empire, as far as the Bŏrysthĕnēs, or Dnieper, and the Getæ. All this time he was studying philosophy, to which he had previously been averse, in spite of his friendship with Apollōnĭus of Tyăna. His leaning was in the direction of Stoicism. On the accession of his friend Cocceius Nerva (from whom he took the name *Cocceius*), he returned to Rome, where he spent the remainder of his days, with the exception of a short stay in Prusa. He was greatly honoured both by Nerva and his successor Trajan. His contemporaries called him *Chrysostomos* ("Golden mouth"), from his powers as a speaker, which he often displayed in public in Rome and elsewhere. Eighty of his speeches survive. They should rather be called essays on topics of philosophy, morals, and politics. He has talent, and refinement, and healthy moral tone. In his style he imitates the best models, especially Plato and Demosthenes, and his writings are on the whole, in spite of many defects, among the best literary productions of that age.

(2) *Dio Cassius* (or *Cassius Dio*) *Cocceiānus.* A Greek historian, grandson of Dio Chrysostomos, born at Nicæa, in Bithynia, 155 A.D. He came early to Rome with his father, Cassĭus Aprōnĭānus, a senator and high official. Here he received a careful education. In about 180 A.D. he became a member of the senate, and he was a long time in practice as an advocate. In 194 he was prætor, and afterwards consul. As proconsul he administered in succession the provinces of Africa, Dalmatia, and Pannonia. The strict order which he had maintained in Pannonia had drawn upon him the hatred of the undisciplined prætorians, who demanded his life. Alexander Sĕvērus, however, not only shielded him, but nominated him his colleague in the consulship of 229. At the same time he allowed him, for the sake of his own personal safety, to live outside Rome during his term of office. When this had expired the emperor, in consequence of his age and weak health, gave him leave to quit the public service and retire to his native city, where he ended his days. Here he completed his great work on Roman history, from the arrival of Æneās in Italy, to his own consulship in 229 A.D. This he had undertaken at the divine command, communicated to him in a dream. He spent twenty-two years upon it, ten on the preparation, and twelve on the execution. It contained 80

books, divided into decades. It gives only a sketch of the history down to Cæsar, but treats the empire in detail, special care being bestowed upon the events contemporary with the writer. Of the first thirty-five books we have only fragments; book 36 (the wars with the pirates and with Mithridates) is mutilated at the beginning; books 37-54 (down to the death of Agrippa) are tolerably complete; books 55-60, which come down to Claudius, are imperfect. The rest are preserved only in fragments, and in the extracts made by Iōannēs Xĭphĭlīnŏs, a Byzantine monk of the 12th century. These begin with book 35. The model taken by Dio for imitation was Polўbĭus, whom ·he only distantly resembles. He often repels the reader by his crawling flattery, his affected dislike of the republican champions, such as Cicero, Brutus, and Cassius, and his gross superstition. But his book is a work of enormous industry, and of great importance, especially for the hist⊃ry of his own time. His narrative is, generally speaking, clear and vivid, and his style is careful.

Dĭŏnē. In Greek mythology, the daughter of Ocĕănus and Tēthys, or, according to another account, of Urănus and Gaia. By Zeus she was mother of Aphrŏdītē, who was herself called Dione. At Dōdōna she was worshipped in Hēra's place as the wife of Zeus. Her name, indeed, expresses in a feminine form the attributes of Zeus, just as the Latin Juno does those of Jupiter. When the oracle of Dodona lost its former importance, Dione was eclipsed by Hera as the wife of Zeus, and came to be regarded as a nymph of Dodona.

Dĭŏnŷsĭa. A celebration in honour of Dĭonŷsus, which was held in Athens in a special series of festivals, namely:

(1) The *Oschŏphŏrĭa*, supposed to have been instituted by Thēseus on his return from Crete. This was celebrated in the month of Pyănepsĭōn (October to November), when the grapes were ripe. It was so called from the shoots of vine with grapes on them, which were borne in a race from the temple of Dionysus in Limnæ, a southern suburb of Athens, to the sanctuary of Athena Sciras, in the harbour town of Phalērum. The bearers and runners were twenty youths (*ĕphēbī*) of noble descent, whose parents were still living, two being chosen from each of the ten tribes. The victor received a goblet containing a drink made of wine, cheese, meal and honey, and an honorary place in the procession which followed the race. This procession, in

which a chorus of singers was preceded by two youths in women's clothing, marched from the temple of Athene to that of Dionysus. The festival was concluded by a sacrifice and a banquet.

(2) The *smaller*, or *rustic Dionysia*. This feast was held in the month Poseideon (December to January) at the first tasting of the new wine. It was celebrated, with much rude merriment, throughout the various country districts. The members of the different tribes first went in solemn processions to the altar of the god, on which a goat was offered in sacrifice. The sacrifice was followed by feasting and revelry, with abundance of jesting and mockery, and dramatic improvisations. Out of these were developed the elements of the regular drama. And in the more prosperous villages, pieces —in most cases the same as had been played at the urban Dionysia—were performed by itinerant troupes of actors. The festival lasted some days, one of its chief features being the *Askŏlia*, or bag-dance. The point of this was to dance on one leg, without falling, upon oiled bags of inflated leather. The *Hălŏa*, Harvest-home (or feast of threshing-floors) was celebrated at Athens and in the country in the same month to Dēmētĕr and Persĕphŏnē in common.

(3) The *Lēnœa*, or feast of vats. This was held at Athens in the month of Gamēlĭŏn (January to February), at the Lēnæŏn, the oldest and most venerable sanctuary of Dionysus in the city. After a great banquet, for which the meat was provided at the public expense, the citizens went in procession through the city, with the usual jesting and mockery, to attend the representation of the tragedies and comedies.

(4) The *Anthestērĭa*. Celebrated for three days in Anthestērĭŏn (February to March). On the first day (*Pĭthœgĭa*, or opening of casks) the casks were first opened, and masters and servants alike tasted the new wine. On the second, or *Feast of Beakers*, a public banquet was held, at which a beaker of new wine was set by each guest. This was drunk with enthusiasm, to the sound of trumpets. The most important ceremony, however, was the marriage of the *Băsĭlissa*, or wife of the *Archŏn Băsĭleus*, with Dionysus, the *Basilissa* being regarded as representing the country. The ceremony took place in the older of the two temples in the Lenæon, which was never opened except on this occasion. The last day was called *Chytroi*, or the

Feast of Pots, because on this day they made offerings of cooked pulse in pots to Hermes, as guide of the dead, and to the souls of the departed, especially those who had perished in the flood of Deucălĭŏn.

(5) *The great urban Dionysia*. This festival was held at Athens for six days in the month of Elăphēbŏlĭŏn (March to April) with great splendour, and attended by multitudes from the surrounding country and other parts of Greece. A solemn procession was formed, representing a train of Dionysiac revellers. Choruses of boys sang dithyrambs, and an old wooden statue of Dionysus, worshipped as the liberator of the land from the bondage of winter, was borne from the Lenæon to a small temple in the neighbourhood of the Acropolis and back again. The glory of this festival was the performance of the new tragedies, comedies, and satyric dramas, which took place, with lavish expenditure, on three consecutive days. In consequence of the immense number of citizens and strangers assembled, it was found convenient to take one of these six days for conferring public distinctions on meritorious persons, as in the case of the presentation of the golden crown to Demosthenes.

Dĭŏnȳsĭus. (1) A Greek *lŏgŏgrăphŏs*. (*See* LOGOGRAPHI.)

(2) *Dionysius Thrax*, or the Thracian. A Greek scholar, so called because his father was a Thracian. He lived at Alexandria, and was a disciple of Aristarchus. About 100 B.C. he wrote the first scientific Greek grammar in existence, on which a high value was set in antiquity. The work has come down to us, though not in its original form.

(3) *Dionysius of Hălĭcarnassus*. A Greek scholar and historian. He came to Rome about 30 B.C., and lived there for twenty-two years, probably as a professor of rhetoric, enjoying the society of many men of note. In these circumstances he devoted himself to studying the Roman language and literature, the historical literature in particular. The result of his studies was his *Roman Antiquities*, finished about 8 B.C., in all probability not long before his death. This was a history of Rome from the mythical age to the Punic Wars, with which the work of Pŏlȳbĭus begins. There were twenty books, of which we have 1–9 in a complete state, 10 and 11 in great part, but the rest only in fragments. The intention of its author was to give the Greeks a more correct and more favourable idea of the Roman

people, and the growth of its power, and thus to reconcile them to the Roman yoke. With this view he sets forth the wisdom and the good qualities of the founders of Rome. The book is founded on a thorough study of the authorities, and, in spite of its rhetorical tone and of many other defects, forms one of our chief sources of information upon ancient Roman history in its internal and external development. The other remaining works of Dionysius are partly on rhetoric, partly on literary criticism. The rhetorical works are: (a) *On the Arrangement of Words*, or on the different styles of Greek prose structure; (b) a treatise on rhetoric, which has certainly not come down to us in its original form. The critical writings are essays on the ancient Greek classics, particularly the orators, and among them Demosthenes; but also on Aristotle, Plato, and Thucӯdĭdēs. They are in part thrown into the form of letters to contemporary Romans of repute.

(4) *Dionysius of Alexandria*. A Greek poet of the 2nd century A.D. Two hymns of his have survived, one to the Muse Callĭŏpē, the other to Apollo. A special interest attaches to them from the fact that the principle of their composition has been preserved in ancient musical notation.

(5) *Dionysius Pĕrĭēgētēs*, or the describer of the earth. A Greek poet whose precise country and date have not been ascertained; it is certain only that he did not live earlier than the imperial age of Rome. His surviving work is a *Dēscriptĭō Orbis Terrārum*, or description of the earth, written in well-turned hexameters, and founded mainly on Erătosthĕnēs. This was much read, and translated into Latin by Avĭēnus and Priscian (see these names). To the later Greeks he was the geographer *par excellence*. The ancient *scholia* to his book, a paraphrase, and the commentary by Eustathius, testify to the interest which it excited. (On another author of a geographical poem of the same name, see DICӔARCHUS.)

Dĭŏnӯsus, sometimes **Dĭŏnӯsus** (*Greek*). The god of luxuriant fertility, especially as displayed by the vine; and therefore the god of wine. His native place, according to the usual tradition, was Thebes, where he was born to Zeus by Sĕmĕlē, the daughter of Cadmus. Semele was destroyed by the lightning of her lover, and the child was born after six months. Zeus accordingly sewed it up in his thigh till ripe for birth and then gave it over to Ino, the daughter of Semele. (*See* ATHAMAS.) After her death

Hermēs took the boy to the nymphs of Mount Nysa, or according to another version, to the *Hȳădĕs* of Dōdōna, who brought him up, and hid him in a cave away from the anger of Hēra. It cannot be ascertained where Mount Nysa was originally supposed to be. In later times the name was transferred to many places where the vine was cultivated, not only in Greece, but in Asia, India, and Africa. When grown up, Dionysus is represented as planting the vine, and wandering through the wide world to spread his worship among men, with his wine-flushed train (*thĭăsŏs*), his nurses and other nymphs, Satyrs, Sīlēnī, and similar woodland deities. Whoever welcomes him kindly, like Icărĭus in Attica, and Œneus in Ætolia, receives the gift of wine; but those who resist him are terribly punished. For with all his appearance of youth and softness, he is a mighty and irresistible god, strong to work wonders. A whole series of fables is apparently based upon the tradition that in many places, where a serious religious ritual existed, the dissolute worship of Dionysus met with a vigorous resistance. (*See* LYCURGUS, MINYADӔ, PENTHEUS, PRŒTUS.)

This worship soon passed from the continent of Greece to the wine-growing islands, and flourished pre-eminently at Naxos. Here it was, according to the story, that the god wedded Ariadnē. In the islands a fable was current that he fell in with some Tyrrhenian pirates who took him to their ship and put him in chains. But his fetters fell off, the sails and the mast were wreathed in vine and ivy, the god was changed into a lion, while the seamen throw themselves madly into the sea and were turned into dolphins. In forms akin to this the worship of Dionysus passed into Egypt and far into Asia. Hence arose a fable founded on the story of Alexander's campaigns, that the god passed victoriously through Egypt, Syria, and India as far as the Ganges, with his army of Silēni, Satyrs, and inspired women, the *Mœnădēs* or *Bacchantēs*, carrying their wands (*thyrsĭ*) crowned with vines and ivy. Having thus constrained all the world to the recognition of his deity, and having, with Hērăclēs, assisted the gods, in the form of a lion, to victory in their war with the Giants, he was taken to Olympus, where, in Homer, he does not appear. From Olympus he descends to the lower world, whence he brings his mother, who is worshipped with him under the name of Thȳōnē (the wild one), as Lētō was with Apollo and Artĕmis. From his mother he is called *Thyōneus*, a name which, with others of similar meaning, such as *Bacchŭs*, *Brŏmĭŏs*, *Euĭŏs*, and *Iacchŏs*, points to a worship founded upon a different conception of his nature.

In the myth with which we have been hitherto concerned, the god appears mainly in the character and surroundings of joy and triumph. But, as the god of the earth, Dionysus belongs, like Persĕphŏnē, to the world below as well as to the world above. The death of vegetation in winter was represented as the flight of the god into hiding from the sentence of his enemies, or even as his extinction, but he returned again from obscurity, or rose from the dead, to new life and activity. In this connexion he was called *Zagreus* ("Torn in pieces") and represented as a son of Zeus and his daughter Persephone, or sometimes of Zeus and Demeter. In his childhood he was torn to pieces by the Titans, at the command of the jealous Hēra. But every third year, after spending the interval in the lower world, he is born anew. According to the Orphic story, Athene brought her son's heart to Zeus, who gave it to Semele, or swallowed it himself, whereupon the Theban or younger Dionysus was born. The grave of Dionysus was shown at Delphi in the inmost shrine of the temple of Apollo. Secret offerings were brought thither, while the women who were celebrating the feast woke up *Licnītĕs ;* in other words, invoked the new-born god cradled in a winnowing fan, on the neighbouring mountain of Parnassus. Festivals of this kind, in celebration of the extinction and resurrection of the deity, were held by women and girls only, amid the mountains at night, every third year, about the time of the shortest day. The rites, intended to express the excess of grief and joy at the death and reappearance of the god, were wild even to savagery, and the women who performed them were hence known by the expressive names of Bacchæ, Mænads, and Thyiădĕs. They wandered through woods and mountains, their flying locks crowned with ivy or snakes, brandishing wands and torches, to the hollow sounds of the drum, and the shrill notes of the flute, with wild dances, and insane cries and jubilation. The victims of the sacrifice, oxen, goats, even fawns and roes from the forest, were killed, torn in pieces and eaten raw, in imitation of the treatment of Zagreus by the Titans. Thrace, and Macedonia,

and Asiatic Greece were the scene of the wildest orgies; indeed Thrace seems to be the country of their birth. In Asiatic Greece, it should be added, the worship of Dionysus-Zagreus came to be associated with the equally wild rites of Rhea (Cȳbĕlē), and Atys, and Sabus or Sabazius. (*See* SABAZIUS.) In Greece Proper the chief seats of these were Parnassus, with Delphi and its neighbourhood, Bœotia, Argos, and Lacŏnĭa, and in Bœotia and Laconia especially the mountains Cĭthærŏn and Tăȳgĕtus. They were also known in Naxos, Crete, and other islands. They seem to have been unknown in Attica, though Dionysus was

(1) BEARDED DIONYSUS AND SATYR.
(From the relief of the Reception of Dionysus by Icarius; Vatican, Louvre, and British Museum.)

worshipped at the Eleusinian mysteries with Persephone and Demeter, under the name of Iacchos, as brother or bridegroom of Persephone. But the Attic cycle of national festivals in honour of Dionysus represents the idea of the ancient and simple Hellenic worship, with its merry usages. Here Dionysus is the god who gives increase and luxuriance to vineyard and tree. For he is a kindly and gentle power, terrible only to his enemies, and born for joy and blessing to mankind. His gifts bring strength and healing to the body, gladness and forgetfulness of care to the mind, whence he was called *Lyæŏs*, the loosener of care. They are ennobling in their effects, for they require tending, and thus keep men employed in diligent labour; they bring them together in merry meetings, and inspire them to music and poetry. Thus it is to the worship of Dionysus that the dithyramb and the

(2) YOUTHFUL DIONYSUS AND SATYR.
(Rome, Vatican.)

drama owe their origin and development. In this way Dionysus is closely related, not only to Demeter, Aphrodite, Erōs, the Graces and the Muses, but to Apollo, because he inspires men to prophesy.

The most ancient representation of Dionysus consists of wooden images with the *phallus*, as the symbol of generative power. In works of art he is sometimes represented as the ancient Indian Dionysus, the conqueror of the East. In this character he appears, as in the Vatican statue called Sardănăpālus, of high stature, with a luxuriant wealth of hair on head and chin (*comp.* fig. 1). Sometimes again, as in numerous statues which have survived, he is a youth of soft and feminine shape, with a dreamy expression, his long, clustering hair confined by a fillet or crown of vine or ivy, generally naked, or with a fawn or panther skin thrown lightly over him. He is either reposing or leaning idly back with the Thyrsos, grapes, or a cup in his hand (fig. 2). Often, too, he is

surrounded by the fauns of his retinue, Mænads, Satyrs, Sileni, Centaurs, etc., or by Nymphs, Muses, Cupids, indeed in the greatest possible number and variety of situations. (*See* the engravings.) Besides the vine, ivy, and rose, the panther, lion, lynx, ox, goat, and dolphin were sacred to him. His usual sacrifices were the ox and the goat.

In Italy the indigenous god Līber, with a feminine Lībĕra at his side, corresponded to the Greek god of wine. Just as the Italian Cĕrēs was identified with Demeter, so these two deities were identified with Dionysus, or *Iakchŏs*, and Persephone, with whom they were worshipped under their native name, but with Greek rites, in a temple on the Aventine. (*See* CERES.) Liber or Bacchus, like Dionysus, had a country and an urban festival. The country festivities were held, with unrestrained merriment, at the time of grape-gathering and straining off the wine. The urban festival held in Rome on the 17th March, was called Lībĕrālĭa. Old women, crowned with ivy, sold cheap cakes (*lĭba*) of meal, honey, and oil, and burnt them on little pans

(3) * MÆNAD.
(Vase from Nocera, IV, No. 2419, Naples Museum.)

for the purchasers. The boys took their *tŏga vĭrīlis* or *toga libera* on this day, and offered sacrifice on the Capitol. Side by side with this public celebration, a secret worship, the *Bacchānālĭa*, found its way to Rome and into the whole of Italy. The

Bacchanalia were celebrated by men and women, in Italy outside the cities, in Rome in the sacred enclosure of Stĭmŭla or Semele. They were accompanied with such shameless excesses that in 186 B.C. they were put down, with unsparing severity, by a decree of the senate.

Dĭŏphantus. A Greek mathematician of Alexandria, who flourished probably about 360 B.C. He was the author of an *Arithmĕtĭca* in thirteen books, of which littlemore than the first six still remain. The book is the only Greek work upon algebra. Diophantus was the most considerable arithmetician in Greek antiquity.

Dĭoscŏrĭdēs (*Pedānĭŏs*). A Greek physician and man of science. He flourished about the middle of the 1st century A.D., and was the author of a work *De Mātĕrĭā Mĕdĭcā* in five books. For nearly 1700 years this book was the chief authority for students of botany and the science of healing. Two short essays on specifics against vegetable and animal poisons (*Alexĭpharmăca* and *Thērĭăca*) are appended to it as the sixth and seventh books : but these are probably from the hand of a later Dioscorides of Alexandria. A work on family medicine is also attributed to him, but is not genuine.

Dĭoscūrī, *i.e.* sons of Zeus, the horsetamer Castor, and Pŏlўdeucēs (Lat. *Pollux*) the master of the art of boxing. In Homer they are represented as the sons of Lēda and Tyndărĕōs, and called in consequence Tyndărĭdæ, as dying in the time between the rape of Helen and the Trojan War, and as buried in their father-city Lăcĕdæmōn. But even under the earth they were alive. Honoured of Zeus, they live and die on alternate days and enjoy the prerogatives of godhead. In the later story sometimes both, sometimes only Polydeuces is the descendant of Zeus. (*See* LEDA.) They undertake an expedition to Attica, where they set free their sister Hĕlĕna, whom Theseus has carried off. They take part in the expedition of the Argonauts. (*See* AMYCUS.) Castor, who had been born mortal, falls in a contest with Idas and Lynceus, the sons of their paternal uncle Aphăreus. The fight arose, according to one version, in a quarrel over some cattle which they had carried off ; according to another, it was about the rape of two daughters of another uncle Leucippus, Phœbē and Hilăīra, who were betrothed to the sons of Aphareus. On his brother's death Polydeuces, the immortal son of Zeus, prays his father to let him die too. Zeus permits

him to spend alternately one day among the gods his peers, the other in the lower world with his beloved brother. According to another story Zeus, in reward for their brotherly love, sets them in the sky as the constellation of the Twins, or the morning and evening star. They are the ideal types of bravery and dexterity in fight. Thus they are the tutelary gods of warlike youth, often sharing in their contests,and honoured as the inventors of military dances and melodies. The ancient symbol of the twin gods at Lacedæmon was two parallel beams, joined by cross-pieces, which the Spartans took with them into war. They were worshipped at Sparta and Olympia with Hĕrăclēs and other heroes. At Athens too they were honoured as gods under the name of Anăkĕs (Lords Protectors). At sea, as in war, they lend their aid to men. The storm-tossed mariner sees the sign of their beneficent presence in the flame at the mast-head. He prays, and vows to them the sacrifice of a white lamb, and the storm soon ceases. (*See* HELENA.) The rites of hospitality are also under their protection. They are generally represented with their horses Xanthus and Cyllărus, as in the celebrated colossal group of Monte Cavallo in Rome. Their characteristic emblem is an oval helmet crowned with a star.

The worship of Castor and Pollux was from early times current among the tribes of Italy. They enjoyed especial honours in Tuscŭlum and Rome. In the latter city a considerable temple was built to them near the Forum (414 B.C.) in gratitude for their appearance and assistance at the battle of the Lake Regillus twelve years before. In this building, generally called simply the temple of Castor, the senate often held its sittings. It was in their honour, too, that the solemn review of the Roman *ĕquĭtēs* was held on the 15th July. The names of Castor and Pollux, like that of Hercŭlēs, were often in use as familiar expletives, but the name of Castor was invoked by women only. They were worshipped as gods of the sea, particularly in Ostia, the harbour town of Rome. Their image is to be seen stamped on the reverse of the oldest Roman silver coins. (*See* COINAGE.)

Dīphĭlus. A poet of the new Attic comedy, a native of Sīnōpē, and contemporary of Menander. He is supposed to have written some 100 pieces, of which we have the titles and fragments of about 50.

The *Căsĭna* and *Rŭdens* of Plautus are modelled on two of Diphilus' plays; and Terence has adopted some scenes from one of them in his *Adelphi.* Diphilus took his subjects both from common life and from mythology. Both the judgments passed on him in antiquity, and his remaining fragments, justify us in recognising him as one of the most gifted poets of his age.

Diphrŏs. *See* CHAIRS.

Dipœnus. A Greek sculptor, born in Crete, who flourished in Argos and Sĭcўōn about 550 B.C. In conjunction with his countryman Scyllis he founded an influential school of sculpture in the Pělŏponnēsus. (*See* SCULPTURE.)

Diptĕrŏs. An architectural epithet descriptive of a temple surrounded by a double line of columns. (*See* TEMPLE.)

Diptўchŏn. This Greek word was applied in antiquity to a pair of writing tablets fastened together by rings, so that the inner sides, covered with wax, lay one upon the other. They were fastened sometimes by a strap, on the side opposite to the rings: sometimes by a string passed through two holes in the middle, and secured, if necessary, by seals at the back. (*See* the engravings under WRITING MATERIALS.) Two or more of the tablets (*Triptўcha, Polyptўcha*) were sometimes joined in the same way. They were used for notes, letters, and documents. Under the Empire much fancy and expense were lavished on them, the outer side being sometimes made of gold, silver, or magnificently carved ivory. This was especially the case after it became the fashion for consuls, and other high officials, to give presents of *diptycha* when entering upon office. For the diplomas made out on bronze *diptycha* for soldiers who had served their time, *see* MISSIO.

Diræ. *See* ERINYES.

Dirc3 (*Dirkē*). Wife of Lycus, who governed Thebes as guardian of Laïus. In revenge for her ill-treatment of their mother Antĭŏpē, the brothers Amphīŏn and Zēthus bound her to the horns of a bull and left her to be dragged to death (*see* cut). They threw her body into a spring near Thebes, which bore her name ever after.

Discus (Gr. *diskŏs*). (1) A flat piece of stone, or metal, shaped like a bean to fit the palm of the hand. As far back as the age of Homer it was a common thing for men to contend in throwing the discus, and the exercise was a favourite one in the *palæstræ* or *gymnăsĭa* of Greece in historical times. It was represented at the great festivals, but as part of the *pentathlŏn*, not as an independent exhibition (*see* GYMNASTICS). The thrower grasped the discus—the size and weight of which would vary according to circumstances—with the fingers of his right hand, with which he held the edge, letting the whole rest on the inner surface of the hand and lower arm. He then raised his arm backwards as far as the shoulder, and threw the disk forward in an arch. The longest throw won the prize. The exercise was taken up by the Romans under the Empire. It was a favourite subject with artists, the most celebrated statue of a *Discŏbŏlŏs* being that of Mўrōn (*see* cut,

ZETHUS.   DIRCE.   ANTIOPE.   AMPHION.   MOUNTAIN GOD.
Dionysiac snake and ivy.   Hound of Zethus and lyre of Amphion.

THE FARNESE BULL, BY APOLLONIUS AND TAURISCUS OF TRALLES.

(As restored by Guglielmo della Porta, Naples Museum.)

under Mўrōn). (2) The name was also applied to the oil-disk of a lamp. (*See* ILLUMINATION.)

Dis Păter (= *Dīvĕs Pater*, Father *Dives* or the rich). The ruler of the world below, worshipped by the Romans as the god who corresponded to the Greek Plūtŏ. His worship, like that of Prŏserpĭna, was first introduced in the early days of the Republic, at the command of the Sibylline books. Dis Pater had a chapel near the altar of

Sāturnus,and a subterranean altar on the Campus Martius in common with Prōserpīna. This was only opened when, as at the secular games, sacrifices were offered to both. The victims offered thus were black animals.

Dĭthÿrambŏs. A hymn sung at the festivals of Dĭonÿsus to the accompaniment of a flute and a dance round the altar. The hymn celebrated the sufferings and actions of the god in a style corresponding to the passionate character of his worship. In the course of time it developed into a special class of Greek lyric poetry. It was in Corinth that it first received anything like a definite artistic form, and this at the hands of Arīōn, who was therefore credited by the ancients with its actual invention. The truth probably is that he was the first who divided the festal song of the chorus into strŏphē and antistrŏphē, an arrangement from which tragedy took its rise. (*See* TRAGEDY.) Dithyrambs were sung at Athens twice in the year—at the great Dĭonÿsĭa in the spring, and at the Lēnæa in the beginning of winter. The chorus consisted of fifty persons, who stood in a circle round the altar. The dithyramb was further developed by Lāsŏs of Hermĭŏnē, the lyric poet and musician who lived about 507 B.C. at the court of the Pīsistrătĭdæ. By several innovations in music and rhythm, especially by a stronger and more complete instrumentation, this artist gave it greater variety and a more secular character. He also introduced the prize contests for the best dithyramb, and apparantly abolished the antistrophical division. Of the dithyrambs of his pupil Pindar fragments only have survived. With Lasos and Pindar, Simōnĭdēs and Bacchÿlĭdēs may be named as among the foremost dithyrambic poets of the time. At the dithyrambic contests the poets and the different tribes contended for the prize. Each had their chorus, brilliantly fitted out at great expense by the richer citizens. Besides the honour of the victory, the poet received a tripod; the chorus, and the people which he represented, an ox for the sacrificial feast. These performances were very popular for a long time; but as the new tendency developed itself, voices of authority made themselves heard, condemning them as involving a serious degeneracy in art. And there is no doubt that in the form which it assumed after the time of the Peloponnesian War, the dithyramb did violence to the older taste. More and more it lost the inner unity and beautiful proportion which that feeling required.

A continuous and rapid change of rhythm and mode was accompanied by an extraordinary boldness of diction, in keeping with the wild character of the composition. In the hands of inferior poets this often passed into turgidity and bombast, if not into mere nonsense. Solo pieces were inserted to relieve the choruses, the text was gradually subordinated to the music, and the dithyramb was thus gradually transformed into a kind of opera. Though the subjects of the poems had long ceased to be taken exclusively from the cycle of Dionysiac myths, they were never, of course, entirely out of harmony with the lyrical spirit of the dithyramb.

There was a very considerable number of dithyrambic poets. The best known are Mĕlănippĭdēs of Mĕlŏs (about 415 B.C.), who is generally held responsible for the degeneracy of the dithyramb, and the excess of instrumental music; his disciple Philoxĕnus of Cÿthēra, who died in 380; Tĭmŏthĕus of Mīlētus, who died in 357, and his contemporaries Pŏlyeidus ʼand Tĕlestēs. Of the whole literature we possess nothing but fragments.

Dĭus Fĭdĭus (Italian). The god of oaths and protector of the laws of hospitality and international dealing. (*See* SANCUS.)

Dīvīnātĭō (prevision of the future).

(1) In general the word is applied to all prophecy or foretelling in the simplest sense of the word. Among the Romans prophecy was based, not on inspiration, as with the Greeks, but on the observation of definite signs, such as the *ōmen* (or voice), the prodigies and the auspices taken note of by the augurs (*see* AUGURES). The science of the *hăruspĭcēs* (or the foretelling of events from the inspection of the carcases of sacrificial victims) was a later importation from Etruria. The ancient Romans were not familiar with the *divinatio* from *sortēs* or lots, which was common in many parts of Italy. The Sibylline books threw no light on future events. (*See* SIBYLS.) Towards the end of the republican period the sciences of the augurs and haruspices lost their significance, and the Greek oracles, in the various forms of their craft, with the Chaldæan astrology, came into vogue, and carried the fashion in the society of the Empire. (*Cp.* MANTIC ART.)

(2) In the language of Roman law, *divinatio* meant the legal inquiry for deciding who, among many advocates proposing themselves, was the fittest to undertake a prosecution, and the speeches by

which the various advocates tried to make good their competency for the task.

Dōdōna. In Epīrus. The ancient seat of the oracle of Zeus and Dīōnē, who was worshipped here as his wife instead of Hēra. The oldest sanctuary of the god was an oak tree, with a spring at its foot, sacred to Zeus, and probably mephitic. The will of Zeus was ascertained from the rustling of the oak leaves by the priests, whom Homer calls *Selloi*, and their grey-headed priestesses called *Pĕleiădĕs*. In later times oracles were taken at Dodona from lots, and from the ringing of an iron basin. In front of this basin there stood an iron statue of a boy, with a whip formed of three chains, from which hung some buttons which touched the basin. If the whip moved in the breeze, the buttons sounded against the basin. The oracle of Dodona had in early times the greatest name of all; but in later times, though it never lost its reputation, it was eclipsed by that of Delphi. It was still consulted, mainly indeed by the neighbouring populations, but sometimes also by the states of Athens and Sparta. It was in existence in the 2nd century A.D., and does not seem to have disappeared before the 4th.

Dŏkĭmăsĭa. The name used at Athens to denote the process of ascertaining the capacity of the citizens for the exercise of public rights and duties. If, for instance, a young citizen was to be admitted among the Ephēbī (*see* EPHEBI), he was examined in an assembly of his district, to find out whether he was descended on both sides from Athenian citizens, and whether he possessed the physical capacity for military service. All officials too, even the members of the senate, had to submit to an examination before entering upon their office. The purpose of this was to ascertain, not their actual capacity for the post, which was pre-supposed in all candidates, but their descent from Athenian citizens, their life and character, and (in the case of some offices which involved the administration of large sums) even the amount of their property. The examination was carried on in public by the archōns in the presence of the senate, and any one present had the right to raise objections. If such objections were held to be valid, the candidate was rejected; but he had the right of appeal to the decision of a court, which would take cognizance of the matter in judicial form. On the other hand, if he were accepted, any one who thought his claims insufficient had

the right of instituting judicial proceedings against him. If the decision was adverse, he would lose his office, and was further liable to punishment varying according to the offence charged against him, which might be, for instance, that of unlawfully assuming the rights of a citizen. A speaker in a public assembly might thus be brought before a court by any citizen, for no one not possessed of the full right of citizenship could legally address the people. The question might thus be raised whether the orator were not actually *ătĭmŏs*, or guilty of an offence which involved *ătĭmĭa*.

Dŏlĭchŏs. *See* GYMNASTICS.

Dŏlĭum. *See* VESSELS.

Dōnātīvum (Roman). A present of money made to the army. In the republican age donatives were distributed on the occasion of a triumph, the expense being defrayed out of the money raised by selling the spoil. Under the Empire it was usual for the emperor to grant a *donativum* on his accession. Tiberius on this occasion made a present of some £750,000 to the army; and the sum increased in later reigns. After the time of Claudius it became the fashion for the emperor to purchase the favour of the prætorians by a special largess.

Dōnātus (*Ǣlĭus*). A Roman scholar and rhetorician of about the middle of the 4th century A.D., and tutor of Jerome. He was the author of a Latin grammar (*Ars Grammătĭca*) in three books. This was much commented on by Servius, Pompeius, and others. His *Ars Mĭnor*, or short catechism on the eight parts of speech, survived long after the Middle Ages as the chief manual for elementary instruction. These works survive in their original form. He also wrote a valuable commentary on Terence, which we possess in an imperfect shape, the notes on the *Hĕautŏn Tĭmŏrū-mĕnŏs* being lost, and not in its original form. [He was also the author of a lost commentary on Vergil, which is often alluded to contemptuously by Servius.]

[**Dōnātus** (*Tĭbĕrĭus Claudĭus*). A commentator on the Æneid of Vergil, who probably lived in the 4th or early 5th century A.D. His work, which is mostly a prose paraphrase, survives in great part, but is of little value.—H. N.]

Dōrĭs. Daughter of Ōcĕănus, wife of the sea-god Nēreus, and mother of the Nērēĭdĕs. (*See* OCEANUS, NEREUS.)

Dosĭthĕus. A grammarian who flourished towards the end of the 4th century A.D. He wrote a Latin grammar for Greek boys, with a literal Greek translation, which was not fully completed. With this was bound up (whether by Dositheus himself is uncertain) a miscellany of very various contents by another author. This comprises (1) anecdotes of the Emperor Hadrian, (2) fables of Æsop, (3) an important chapter on jurisprudence, (4) mythological stories from Hўgīnus, (5) an abridgment of the Iliad, (6) an interesting collection of words and phrases from ordinary conversation.

Drachma (Greek). A weight and coin = 6 obols, $=\frac{1}{100}$ of a *mĭna* or $\frac{1}{6000}$ of a talent. Before the time of Solon it = 6·03 grs., or rather more than a shilling. After Solon it maintained the same value as a weight, but as a coin (the Attic dr.) it sank to 4·366 grs., about 8*d.* (*See* COINAGE.)

Drăcō. The standard of the Roman cohort. (*See* SIGNUM.)

Drăcontius (*Blossĭus Æmĭlĭus*). A Latin poet who lived and practised as an advocate at Carthage towards the end of the 5th century A.D. He was a man of real poetic gifts and considerable reading, but his style is spoiled by rhetorical exaggeration and false taste. His surviving works are : (1) a number of short epics upon subjects taken from the old mythology and school-room rhetoric. (2) An apólogetic poem (*Sătisfactĭŏ*) addressed in the form of an elegy to Guthamund, king of the Vandals, whose wrath he had excited by writing a panegyric on a foreign prince. (3) A Christian didactic poem in three books. This is a really poetical treatment of the story of the creation.

Drama. (1) *Greece.* In Athens the production of plays was a state affair, not a private undertaking. It formed a great part of the religious festival of the Dĭŏnŷsĭa, in which the drama took its rise (*see* DIONYSIA); and it was only at the greater Dionysia that pieces could be performed during the author's lifetime. The performances lasted three days, and took the form of musical contests, the competitors being three tragic poets with their tetralogies, and five comic poets with one piece each. The authority who superintended the whole was the archon, to whom the poets had to bring their plays for reading, and apply for a chorus. If the pieces were accepted and the chorus granted, the citizens who were liable for the *Chŏrēgĭa* undertook at their own cost to practise and furnish for them one chorus each. (*See* LEITOURGIA.) The poets

whose plays were accepted received ' an *honorarium* from the state. The state also supplied the regular number of actors, and made provision for the maintenance of order during the performances. At the end of the performance a certain number of persons (usually five), was chosen by lot from a committee nominated by the senate, to award the prizes (*Agōnŏthĕtœ*), and bound them by oath to give their judgment on the plays, the *chŏrēgĭ,* and the actors. The poet who won the first prize was presented with a crown in the presence of the assembled multitude—the highest distinction that used to be conferred on a dramatic author at Athens. The victorious *chŏrēgus* also received a crown, with the permission to

(1) *NIKE POURING A LIBATION BEFORE A CHORAGIC TRIPOD.

Inscribed Ἀκαμαντὶς ἐνίκα φυλή : Γλαύκων καλός.

(Panofka, *Musée Blacas*, pl. 1; now in British Museum.)

dedicate a votive offering to Dionysus. This was generally a tripod, which was set up either in the theatre, or in the temple of the deity, or in the "Street of Tripods," so named from this custom, an inscription being put on it recording the event (fig. 1). The actors in the successful play received prizes of money, besides the usual *honoraria.*

From the time of Sophocles the actors in a play were three in number. They had to represent all the parts, those of women included, which involved their changing their costume several times during the performance. The three actors were distinguished as *Prōtăgōnistēs, Deutĕrăgōnistēs,* and *Trĭtăgōnistēs,* according to the importance of their parts. If the piece required a fourth actor, which was seldom the case, the *choregus* had to provide one. The *choregus* had also to see to the position and equipment of the *persōnæ mūtæ*.

In earlier times it is possible that the persons engaged in the representation did not make a business of their art, but performed gratuitously, as the poets down to the time of Sophocles appeared on the stage. But the dramatic art gradually became a profession, requiring careful preparation, and winning general respect for its members as artists. The chief requirements for the profession were distinctness and correctness of pronunciation, especially in declamatory passages, and an unusual power of memory, as there was no prompter in a Greek theatre. An actor had also to be thoroughly trained in singing, melodramatic action, dancing, and play of gesture. The latter was especially necessary, as the use of masks precluded all play of feature. The actors were, according to strict rule, assigned to the poets by lot; yet a poet generally had his special *protagonistes*, on whose peculiar gifts he had his eye in writing the dramatic pieces.

The Athenian tragedies began to be known all over the Hellenic world as early as the time of Æschylus. The first city, outside of Attica, that had a theatre was Syracuse, where Æschylus brought out some of his own plays. Scenic contests soon began to form part of the religious festivals in various Greek cities, and were celebrated in honour of other deities besides Dionȳsus. It was a habit of Alexander the Great to celebrate almost every considerable event with dramatic exhibitions, and after him this became the regular custom. A considerable increase in the number of actors was one consequence of the new demand. The actors called themselves artists of Dionysus, and in the larger cities they formed permanent societies (*sy̆nŏdoi*) with special privileges, including exemption from military service, and security in person and property. These companies had a regular organization, presided over by a priest of their patron-god Dionysus, annually elected from among their members. A treasurer and officers completed the staff. At the time of the festivals the societies sent out their members in groups of three actors, with a manager, and a flute-player, to the different cities. This business was especially lively in Ionia and on the Euxine, the societies of Tĕōs being the most distinguished. The same arrangement was adopted in Italy, and continued to exist under the Roman Empire.

The universal employment of masks was a remarkable peculiarity of costume (*see* MASKS). It naturally excluded all play of feature, but the masks corresponded to the general types of character, as well as to the special types indicated by the requirements of the play. Certain conventionalities were observed in the colour of the hair. Goddesses and young persons had light hair, gods and persons of riper age, dark brown; aged persons, white; and the deities of the lower world, black. The height of the masks and top-knots varied with the age of the actors, and the parts they took. Their stature was considerably heightened in tragedies by the high boot (*see* COTHURNUS), and the defects in proportion corrected by padding, and the use of a kind of gloves. The conventionalities of costume, probably as fixed by Æschylus, maintained themselves as long as Greek tragedies were performed at all. Men and women of high rank wore on the stage a variegated or richly embroidered long-sleeved *chĭtŏn*, reaching to the feet, and fastened with a girdle as high as the breast. The upper garment, whether *hĭmătĭŏn* or *chlămy̆s*, was long and splendid, and often embroidered with gold. Kings and queens had a purple train, and a white *himation* with a purple border; soothsayers, a netted upper garment reaching to the feet. Persons in misfortune, especially fugitives, appeared in soiled garments of grey, green, or blue; black was the symbol of mourning, and so on.

In the Satyric Drama the costumes of the heroic characters resembled in all essentials what they wore in the tragedies, although, to suit the greater liveliness of the action, the *chiton* was shorter and the boot lower. In the Old Comedy the costumes were taken as nearly as possible from actual life, but in the Middle and New Comedy they were conventional. The men wore a white coat; youths, a purple one; slaves, a motley, with mantle to match; cooks, an unbleached double mantle; peasants, a fur or shaggy coat, with wallet and staff; panders, a coloured coat and motley over-garment. Old women appeared in sky-blue or dark yellow, priestesses and maidens in white; courtesans, in motley colours, and so on. The members of the chorus were masked and dressed in a costume corresponding to the part assigned them by the poet. (On their dress in the

Satyric Drama, *see* SATYRIC DRAMA.) The chorus of the comedy caricatured the ordinary dress of the tragic chorus. Sometimes they represented animals, as in the Frogs and Birds of Aristophanes. In the Frogs they wore tight dresses of frog-colour, and masks with a mouth wide open; in the Birds, large beaks, bunches of feathers, combs, and so on, to imitate particular birds. (*See* plate in *Journal of Hellenic Studies*, vol. ii, plate xiv B, copied in Haigh's *Attic Theatre*, p. 267.)

the manager received no compensation. But after performance the piece became his property, to be used at future representations for his own profit. In the time of Cicero, when it was fashionable to revive the works of older masters, the selection of suitable pieces was generally left to the director. The Romans did not, like the Greeks, limit the number of actors to three, but varied it according to the requirements of the play. Women's parts were originally played by men, as in Greece.

(2) * REHEARSAL OF A SATYRIC DRAMA.
(Mosaic from Pompeii, Naples Museum.)

(2) *Roman.* Dramatic performances in Rome, as in Greece, formed a part of the usual public festivals, whether exceptional or ordinary, and were set on foot by the ædiles and prætors. (*See* GAMES.) A private individual, however, if he were giving a festival or celebrating a funeral, would have theatrical representations on his own account. The giver of the festival hired a troupe of players (*grex*), the director of which, (*dŏmĭnus grĕgis*), bought a play from a poet at his own risk. If the piece was a failure,

Women appeared first in mimes, and not till very late times in comedies. The actors were usually freedmen or slaves, whom their masters sent to be educated, and then hired them out to the directors of the theatres. The profession was technically branded with *infămia*, nor was its legal position ever essentially altered. The social standing of actors was however improved, through the influence of Greek education; and gifted artists like the comedian Roscius, and Æsōpus the tra-

edian in Cicero's time, enjoyed the friend-
hip of the best men in Rome. The in-
tance of these two men may show what
rofits could be made by a good actor.
Roscius received, for every day that he
played, £35, and made an annual income of
ome £4,350. Æsopus, in spite of his great
xtravagance, left £175,400 at his death.
Besides the regular *honoraria*, actors, if
hought to deserve it, received other and
voluntary gifts from the giver of the per-
ormance. These often took the form of
inely wrought crowns of silver or gold
work. Masks were not worn until Roscius
made their use general. Before his time
actors had recourse to false hair of different
colours, and paint for the face. The cos-

Deceptive dreams issue from a gate of
ivory, true dreams through a gate of horn.
The gods above, especially Hermēs, have
authority over these dream-gods, and send
sometimes one, sometimes another, to mankind. On some occasions they create
dream-figures themselves, or appear in person under different shapes, in the chamber
of the sleeper. The spirits of the departed,
too, so long as they are not in the kingdom
of Hādēs, have the power of appearing to
the sleeper in dreams. These, the ideas
of the Homeric age, survived in the later
popular belief. Later poets call dreams the
sons of Sleep, and give them separate names.
Morpheus, for instance, only appears in
various human forms. Ikĕlŏs, called also

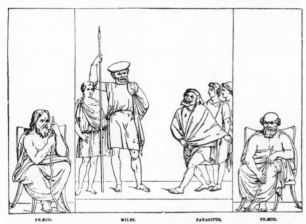

PRÆCO.   MILES.   PARASITUS.   PRÆCO.

(3) * SCENE FROM A ROMAN COMEDY (*Fabula Palliata*).
(Mural painting from Pompeii, Naples Museum.)

tume in general was modelled on that of
actual life, Greek or Roman. As early as
the later years of the Republic, a great
increase took place in the splendour of the
costumes and the general magnificence of
the performance. In tragedy, particularly,
a new effect was attained by massing the
actors in great numbers on the stage. (*See
further* THEATRE, TRAGEDY, COMEDY, and
SATYRIC DRAMA.)

Dreams (Greek *Oneiroi*). According to
Hesiod, Dreams are the children of Night,
and brothers and sisters of Death and
Sleep. Like these they are represented in
the Odyssey as dwelling in the far West,
near Ocĕănus, in the neighbourhood of the
sunset and the kingdom of the dead.

Phŏbētōr, or Terrifyer, assumes the shapes of
all kinds of animals as well as that of man :
Phantăsŏs only those of inanimate objects.
A god of dreams was subsequently wor-
shipped, and represented in works of art,
sometimes with Sleep, sometimes alone.
He was honoured especially at the seats
of dream-oracles and the health-resorts of
Asclēpĭus. (*See* ARTEMIDORUS, 2 ; INCU-
BATIO ; and MANTIC ART.)

Dress. *See* CLOTHING.

Drŏmŏs. *See* GYMNASTICS.

Dryădēs. *See* NYMPHS.

Duodĕcim Tăbŭlæ. *See* TWELVE TABLES.

Dŭŏvĭrī or **Dŭumvĭrī** (Italian). A board
or commission of 2 men, as *e.g.* the *duoviri
capĭtālēs perduellĭonis*, or *duoviri sac-*

rŏrum (see SIBYLS), duoviri viis purgandis (see VIGINTI SEX VIRI, 6). In colonies and mūnĭcĭpia, the title was borne by the two highest officials, who represented the the authority of the Roman consuls. (See MUNICIPIUM.)

Dŭpondĭus. See COINAGE.

Duris. (1) A Greek historian, a native of Samos, and a disciple of Theophrastus. For some time he was despot of Samos. In the first half of the 3rd century B.C. he wrote, besides other historical works, a comprehensive history, in twenty-three books, of Greece and Macedonia, from 370 to at least 281 B.C. He was also the author of Annals of Samos, in at least twelve books. Nothing but fragments of his writings remain, which show that they were no more than uncritical collections of material carelessly treated.

(2) A vase-painter; see VASES.

Duumviri. See DUOVIRI.

E

Eagle (ăquĭlă). The standard of a Roman legion, introduced by Marius: a silver (or, under the Empire, golden) eagle carried on a pole by the ăquĭlĭfĕr, or eagle-bearer, its wings spread out, and often a thunderbolt in its talons. Beneath it were frequently fixed in later times a flag (see VEXILLUM), and other ornaments, e.g. medallions with portraits of emperors and generals. Under the Republic, during peace, it was preserved in the ærārĭum; in camp it stood in a small chapel beside the prætōrĭum, was held in religious veneration by the soldiers, and regarded as affording sanctuary; in battle it was borne on the right wing of the legion, in the first century of the first cohort. From Augustus' time it bore the name and number of the legion (see the figs. under SIGNUM).

Ecclēsĭa (Greek). The assembly of the people, which in Greek cities had the power of final decision in public affairs.

(1) At Athens every citizen in possession of full civic rights was entitled to take part in it from his twentieth year upwards. In early times one ecclesia met regularly once a year in each of the ten prytanies of the senate (see BOULE), in later times four, making forty annually. Special assemblies might also be called on occasion. The place of meeting was in early times the market-place, in later times a special locality, called the Pnyx; but generally the theatre, after a permanent theatre had been erected. To summon the assembly was the duty of the Prỹtănēs, who did so by publishing the notice of proceedings. There was a special authority, a board of six Lĕxĭarchĭ (so called) with thirty assistants, whose business it was to keep unauthorized persons out of the assembly. The members on their appearance were each presented with a ticket, on exhibiting which, after the conclusion of the meeting, they received a payment of an

ŏbŏlus (about 1·3d.), in later times of three obols. After a solemn prayer and sacrifice, the president (Epĭstătēs) communicated to the meeting the subjects of discussion. If there were a previous resolution of the senate for discussion, he put the question whether the people would adopt it, or proceed to discuss it. In the debates every citizen had the right of addressing the meeting, but no one could speak more than once. Before doing so he put a crown of myrtle on his head. The president (but no one else) had the right of interrupting a speaker. If his behaviour were unseemly, the president could cut short his harangue, expel him from the rostrum and from the meeting, and inflict upon him a fine not exceeding 500 drachmæ (£16 13s. 4d.). Cases of graver misconduct had to be referred to the senate or assembly for punishment. Any citizen could move an amendment or counter-proposal, which he handed in in writing to the presiding Prytany. The president had to decide whether it should be put to the vote. This could be prevented, not only by the mere declaration of the president that it was illegal, but by any one present who bound himself on oath to prosecute the proposer for illegality. The speaker might also retract his proposal. The votes were taken by show of hands (cheirŏtŏnĭa). The voting was never secret, unless the question affected some one's personal interest, as in the case of ostracism. In such cases a majority of at least 6,000 votes was necessary. The resolution (psēphismă) was announced by the president, and a record of it taken, which was deposited in the archives, and often publicly exhibited on tables of stone or bronze. After the conclusion of business, the president, through his herald, dismissed the people. If no final result was arrived at, or if the business was interrupted by a sign from heaven, such as a storm or a hower of rain, the meeting was adjourned. Certain classes of business were assigned to the ordinary assemblies.

The functions of the *ecclesia* were :

(*a*) To take part in legislation. At the first regular assembly in the year the president asked the question whether the people thought any alteration necessary in the existing laws. If the answer were in the affirmative, the proposals for alteration were brought forward, and in the third regular assembly a legislative commission was appointed from among the members of the *Hēliœa* or jury for the current year (*see* HELIÆA). The members of this commission were called *Nŏmŏthĕtœ*. The question between the old laws and the new proposals was then decided by a quasi-judicial process under the presidency of the *Thesmŏthĕtœ*, the proposers of the new law appearing as prosecutors, and advocates, appointed by the people, coming forward to defend the old one. If the verdict were in favour of the new law, the latter had the same authority as a resolution of the *ecclesia*. The whole proceeding was called "Voting (*ĕpĭcheiro-tŏnĭa*) upon the Laws." In the decadence of the democracy the custom grew up of bringing legislative proposals before the people, and having them decided at any time that pleased the proposer.

(*b*) *Election of officials*. (*See* PROBOLE.) This only affected, of course, the officials who were elected by show of hands, as the *Strătēgi* and ministers of finance, not those chosen by lot. In the first *ecclesia* of every *prytănĭa* the archon asked the question whether the existing ministers were to be allowed to remain in office or not, and those who failed to commend themselves were deposed.

(*c*) The banishment of citizens by *ostracism*. (*See* OSTRACISM.)

(*d*) Judicial functions in certain exceptional cases only. (*See* EISANGELIA.) Sometimes, if offences came to its knowledge, the people would appoint a special commission of inquiry, or put the inquiry into the hands of the Areŏpăgus or the senate. Offences committed against officials, or against private individuals, were also at times brought before the assembly, to obtain from it a declaration that it did, or did not, think the case one which called for a judicial process. Such a declaration, though not binding on the judge, always carried with it a certain influence.

(*e*) In legal co-operation with the senate the *Ecclesia* had the final decision in all matters affecting the supreme interests of the state, as war, peace, alliances, treaties, the regulation of army and navy, finance, loans, tributes, duties, prohibition of exports or imports, the introduction of new religious rites and festivals, the awarding of honours and rewards, and the conferring of the citizenship [Aristotle, *Const. of Athens*, 43].

(2) At Sparta all the *Spartĭātœ*, or citizens in possession of full civic rights, were entitled to take part in the deliberations of the assembly from their thirtieth year onwards. The assembly was convoked once a month at the full moon by the kings, and later by the ephors as well. After 600 B.C. it met in a special building in the market-place at Sparta, the *Scias*, the members standing, not sitting, as in the Athenian *ecclesia*. Its business was to accept or reject proposals made by the *Gĕrūsĭa* or senate. (*See* GERUSIA.) It made its will known by acclamation, or, in doubtful cases, by separation of the parties into different places. The right of bringing forward proposals and speaking in the debates belonged only to the kings, the members of the *Gerusia*, and the ephors ; in all other cases special consent was required. The functions of the assembly were the election of the officials and senators to decide (in doubtful cases) on the regal succession, on war and peace, treaties, legislation, and other matters affecting the state.

Echidna. A monster and robber in Greek fable, half maiden, half snake, the daughter of Chrysaŏr and Callirrhŏē, or, according to another story, of Tartărus and Gææa. Her home was the country of the Arĭmi in Cilicia, where she brought forth to Typhœus a number of monsters, Cerbĕrus, Chĭmæra, Sphinx, Scylla, the serpent of Lerna, the Nemean lion, etc. (*See* TYPHŒUS.) She was surprised in her sleep and slain by Argos. (*See* ARGOS, 1.)

Echīon. One of the five Sparti who helped Cadmus to build Thebes ; husband of Agāvē, the daughter of Cadmus, and father of Pentheus. (*See* SPARTI.)

Echō. A Nymph, who by her chattering prevented Hēra from surprising her husband Zeus in the company of the Nymphs. Hera punished her by making it impossible for her either to speak first, or to be silent when any one else was speaking. She loved the beautiful Narcissus, but in vain, and pined away in grief till nothing remained of her but her voice.

Eclectics or "Selecters." The technical name in philosophy for philosophers who were attached to no particular school, but made a selection of favourite dogmas from the tenets of the different sects.

Eclogue (Gr. *Eclŏgē*). A selected piece of writing. Properly a poem taken out of a larger collection, ᴜnd so applied, under the Roman Empire, to a short poem, as an idyll or satire. The term was specially applied to the pastoral poems of Vergil and Calpurnǐus Sǐcŭlus.

Edictum. The Roman term for any written announcement made by a magistrate to the people. An *ēdictum* was sometimes temporary only, as, *e.g.*, the announcements of the public assemblies or games; sometimes it contained permanent enactments, as, for instance, the *edicta* of the censors against luxury. The name was especially applied to the proclamations issued by judical functionaries on assuming office, and stating the principles or rules which they intended to follow in the exercise of their authority. The *edicta* of the ædiles relative to the markets belong to this class. One kind of *edictum* was specially important in its bearing upon Roman law, the *edicium* of the prætor. In his *edictum* the prætor laid down the rules which he would observe in arranging the proceedings of the regular courts and of his voluntary jurisdiction, and in deciding cases which did not appear to be covered by the written enactments of the Twelve Tables, or later legislation. These *edicta*, written on wood, stone, or bronze, were in early times published only as occasion required, but in later times the prætors regularly promulgated them on entering upon their office. They prevented the fossilization of the law, and allowed the enactments of the Twelve Tables to adapt themselves in natural development to the changing circumstances of civic life and intercourse. It is true that the *edicta* had no force beyond the prætor's year of office, but, as every new prætor observed what was found in the *edicta* of his predecessors, a permanent nucleus of constantly repeated rules, called *edictum perpetuum* (or continuous edict), was formed in course of time. This became, for the later period, a recognised source of customary law, side by side with the *lĕgēs* proper. At length, under Hadrian, the mass of *edicta* was reduced to system by Salvǐus Jūlǐānus, and received the force of law at the imperial command. This body of law included the accepted *edicta* of the *prætor urbānus* and the other

prætors administering law in the provinces, of the proconsuls, proprætors, and ædiles. It was called *edictum perpĕtuum*, *iūs prætōrǐum*, or *ius hŏnōrārǐum*, the latter because its authors had held public offices (*hŏnōrēs*). On this collection the *Corpus Iūris* of Justinian is in great part founded. The emperor and imperial officials, as *præfectus urbǐ* and *præfectus prætōrǐō*, had also the right of issuing *edicta*.

Education. (1) *Greek*. The Dorians of Crete and Sparta followed a peculiar line in the matter of education. Throughout Greece generally the state left it to private effort; but in Sparta and Crete it came under the direct supervision of the community. At Sparta, as soon as a child was born, a commission of the elders of its tribe had to decide whether it should be reared or exposed. If it was weakly or deformed, it was exposed in a defile of Mount Tay̆gĕtus. Till his seventh year, a boy was left to the care of his parents. After this the *Paidŏnŏmŏs*, or officer presiding over the whole department of education, assigned him to a division of children of the same age called a *bua*. Several of such *buas* together formed a troop or *īla*. Each *bua* was superintended by a *Buāgŏrŏs*, each *īla* by an *Īlarchŏs*. Both these officers were elected from among the most promising of the grown up youths, and were bound to instruct the children in their exercises. The exercises were calculated to suit the various ages of the children, and consisted in running, leaping, wrestling, throwing the spear and discus, as well as in a number of dances, particularly the war dance or *Pyrrhǐchē* (*see* PYRRHIC DANCE). The dancing was under the constant superintendence of the *Paidonomos*, and five *Bidyæ* under him. The discipline was generally directed to strengthening or hardening the body. The boys went barefoot and bareheaded, with hair cut short, and in light clothing. From their twelfth year they wore nothing but an upper garment, which had to last the whole year. They slept in a common room without a roof, on a litter of hay or straw, and from their fifteenth year on rushes or reeds. Their food was extremely simple, and not sufficient to satisfy hunger. A boy who did not want to be hungry had to steal; if he did this cleverly, he was praised, and punished if detected. Every year the boys had to undergo a flogging at the altar of Artĕmǐs Orthǐa, as a test of their power to endure bodily pain. They were whipped all the blood flowed, and deemed it a disgrace to shew any sign of suffering. Reading and writing were left to private instructors; but music, and choral singing in particular, formed a part of the regular discipline. The understanding was assumed to be formed by daily life in public, and the conversation of the men, to which the boys were admitted. Every Spartan boy looked up to his seniors as his instructors and superiors; the consequence being that in Sparta the young behaved to their elders with more modesty and respect than in any other Greek city. Besides this, every man chose a boy or youth as his favourite. He was bound to set the boy an example of all manly excellence, and was regarded as responsible and punishable for his delinquencies. This public education and the performance of the regular exercises, under the superintendence of the *Bidyæ*, lasted till the thirtieth year. In the eighteenth year the boy passed into the class of youths. From the twentieth year, when military service proper began, to the thirtieth, the youth was called an *eirēn*. He was not regarded as a man, or allowed to attend the public assembly till his thirtieth year.

The girls had an education in music and gymnastic education similar to that of the boys, and at the public games and contests each sex was witness of the performances of the other. The girls' dress was extremely simple, consisting of a sleeveless tunic reaching not quite down to the knees, and open at the sides. In this, however, there was nothing which interfered with modesty and propriety of behaviour.

In Crete the system of education was generally similar to that of Sparta. But the public training did not begin till the seventeenth year, when the boys of the same age joined themselves freely into divisions called *ăgĕlai*, each led by some noble youth, whose father was called *ăgĕlătās*, and undertook the supervision of the games and exercises. It is probable that the young men remained in this organization till their twenty-seventh year, when the law compelled them to marry.

At Athens, as in Greece generally, the father decided whether the child should be reared or exposed. The latter alternative seems to have been not seldom adopted, especially when the child was a girl. If the education of a child was once fairly commenced, the parents had no power to put it out of the way. At the birth of a boy, the door of the house was adorned with

a branch of olive; at the birth of a girl, with wool. On the fifth or seventh day after birth the child underwent a religious dedication at the festival of the *Amphĭdrŏmĭa* ("running round"). It was touched with instruments of purification, and carried several times round the burning hearth. On the tenth day came the festival of naming the child, with sacrifice and entertainment, when the father acknowledged it as legitimate. To the end of the sixth year the boys and girls were brought up together under female supervision; but after this the sexes were educated apart. The girls' life was almost entirely confined to her home: she was brought up under the superintendence of women, and with hardly anything which can be called profitable instruction. The boy was handed over to a slave older than himself called *Pædăgōgŏs*. It was the slave's duty to watch the boy's outward behaviour, and to attend him, until his boyhood was over, whenever he went out, especially to the school and the gymnasium. The laws made some provision for the proper education of boys. They obliged every citizen to have his son instructed in music, gymnastics, and the elements of letters (*grammătă*), *i.e.* writing, reading, and arithmetic. They further obliged the parents to teach their boys some profitable trade, in case they were unable to leave them a property sufficient to maintain them independent. If they failed in this, they forfeited all claim to support from the children in old age. But with schools and their arrangements the state did not concern itself. The schools were entirely in private hands, though they were under the eye of the police. The elementary instruction was given by the *grammătistæ*, or teachers of letters, the teacher writing and the scholars copying. The text-books for reading were mostly poems, especially such as were calculated to have an influence on the formation of character. The Homeric poems were the favourite reading book, but Hesiod, Thĕognis, and others were also admitted. Collections of suitable passages from the poets were early made for the boys to copy, learn by heart, and repeat aloud. The higher instruction given by the *grammătĭkŏs* was also of this literary character.

Mathematics were introduced into the school curriculum as early as the 5th century, drawing not till the middle of the 4th century B.C. Instruction in music proper began about the thirteenth year.

The profound moral influence attributed to music in Greek antiquity made this art an essential part of education. It brought with it, naturally, an acquaintance with the masterpieces of Greek poetry. The instrument most practised was the lyre, from its suitableness as an accompaniment to song. The flute was held in less esteem.

The aim of education was supposed to be the harmonious development of mind and body alike. Instruction in gymnastics was consequently regarded as no less essential than in music, and began at about the same age. It was carried on in the *pălæstræ* (*see* PALÆSTRA) under the *paidŏtrĭbai*, who were, like the *grammătĭkoi*, private, not public instructors. The boys began their gymnastics in the *palæstra*, and completed them in the *gymnasia* under the superintendence of the *gymnastæ*. The *ĕphēbĭ*, in particular, or boys between sixteen and nineteen, practised their exercises in the *gymnasia*, till, in their twentieth year, they were considered capable of bearing arms, and employed on frontier service. At this point they became liable to enlistment for foreign service, and obtained the right of attending the meeting of the public assembly. Towards the end of the 5th century B.C. the class of *sophistæ*, or professors of practical education, arose. This gave the young men an opportunity of extending their education by attending lectures in rhetoric and philosophy; but the high fees charged by the *sophistæ* had the effect of restricting this instruction to the sons of the wealthy.

(2) *Roman.* Among the Romans the father was free, when the new-born child was laid before him, either to expose it, or to take it up, as a sign that he meant to rear it. He had also the right of selling his children, or putting them to death. It was not till the beginning of the 3rd century A.D. that the exposure of children was legally accounted as murder, nor did the evil practice cease even then. If the child was to be reared, it was named, if a boy on the ninth day after birth, if a girl, on the eighth. The day was called *dĭēs lustrĭcus*, or day of purification. A sacrifice in the house, accompanied with a feast, gave to the child's life a religious dedication. A box with an amulet was hung round the child's neck as a protection against magic (*see* BULLÆ). Official lists of births were not published until the 2nd century after Christ. In earlier times, in the case of boys, the name was not formally confirmed

until the assumption of the *tŏga vĭrĭlĭs* The child's physical and moral education was, in old times, regularly given at home under the superintendence of the parents, chiefly of the mother. The training was strict, and aimed at making the children strong and healthy, religious, obedient to the laws, temperate, modest in speech and actions, strictly submissive to their superiors, well behaved, virtuous, intelligent, and self-reliant. The girls were taught by their mothers to spin and weave, the boys were instructed by their fathers in ploughing, sowing, reaping, riding, swimming, boxing and fencing; in the knowledge necessary for household management; in reading, writing, and counting; and in the laws of their country. The Romans did not, like the Greeks, lay stress on gymnastics, but only carried physical exercises to the point necessary for military service. The contests and exercises took place in the *Campus Martĭus*, which, down to the time of the Empire, was the favourite arena of the youths. The state took as little care of mental as of physical education. If a man could not educate his children himself, he sent them to a master. From an early time there were elementary teachers (*littĕrātŏrēs*) at Rome, corresponding to the Greek *grammătistæ*. These were sometimes slaves, who taught in their masters' house for his benefit. Sometimes they were freedmen, who gave instruction either in families, or in schools, (*schŏlă* or *lūdus*) of their own. They received their salary monthly, but only for eight months in the year; no instruction being given between June and November. Boys and girls were taught together. The elementary instruction included reading, writing, and arithmetic; arithmetic being, as among the Greeks, practised by counting on the fingers. In later times grown up boys learned arithmetic with a special master (*calcŭlātŏr*), who was paid at a higher rate than the *litterator*. With the duodecimal system in use, arithmetic was regarded as very difficult. The reading lessons included learning the Twelve Tables by heart.

After the Second Punic War it became usual, at first in single families, and afterwards more and more generally, to employ a *litterator*, or *grammătĭcus*, to teach Greek The chief element in this instruction was the explanation of Greek poets, above all of Homer, whose writings became a school book among the Romans, as among the Greeks At the same time higher instruction was given in Latin as well, the text-book being the Latin Odyssey of Līvius Andrŏnīcus, ᵗerence, and in later times Vergil, Horace, and others. The exposition of these authors gave an opportunity of communicating a variety of information. Girls were educated on the same lines. The highest point in Roman education was attained by the schools of the rhetoricians, which came into existence before the end of the republican age. In these schools, as in those of the *grammătĭcī*, Greek was at first the only language taught. Since the time when Greek literature became the highest educational standard, boys, and sometimes girls, were taught Greek from their earliest years. They were put into the hands of a Greek *pædăgōgus*, or a Greek female slave, and learned the first rudiments from Greek schoolmasters. As the range of subjects widened, so as to include, among other things, music and geometry, more importance came to be attached to scholastic education. This tendency was strengthened by the increased demand for Greek culture which manifested itself under the Empire throughout the length and breadth of the Western provinces. Education was carried on on stricter lines as the old system of home training disappeared, mainly owing to the diffusion of an effeminate refinement, and the parents' habit of putting their children into the hands of Greek slaves.

After the time of Vespasian the higher public instruction began to be a matter of imperial concern. Vespasian paid away as much as £850 annually to the Latin and Greek rhetoricians in Rome. Hadrian founded the Äthēnæum, the first known public institution for the higher education, with salaried teachers (*see* ATHENÆUM). After his time philosophers, rhetoricians, and grammarians were publicly appointed to lecture in all the larger cities of the empire. They were maintained partly at the expense of the respective communities, partly by the emperors, and enjoyed in all cases certain immunities conferred by the State.

The ordinary educational course generally concluded with a boy's sixteenth or seventeenth year, though rhetorical instruction was sometimes continued far beyond this limit. And towards the end of the republican age, young men of intellectual ambition would often go to Greece to enlarge their sphere of culture.

On the 17th March, the festival of the *Lĭbĕrālia*, boys who had reached the age of puberty, or their fifteenth year, took off, in the presence of the Lares, their *bulla* and *toga prætexta*, or purple-edged toga, and put on the unadorned *toga virĭlis*. They were then, after a sacrifice at home, taken by their fathers or guardians, accompanied by friends and relations, to the forum, and enrolled in the lists of citizens. The boys were from this time, in the eyes of the law, capable of marriage, and bound to military service. They now entered upon their *tīrōcĭnĭum*, which was regarded as the last stage of education. (*See* TIROCINIUM.)

Egĕrĭa (Latin). A goddess of fountains, who was also a goddess of birth, and possessed the gift of prophecy. It was from her fountain in the sacred enclosure of the Cămēnæ, before the Porta Căpēna in Rome, that the Vestal Virgins brought the water necessary for the baths and purifications of their office. There was another fountain of Egeria in the precincts of Diāna at Arīcĭa. In Roman story Egeria was the consort and counsellor of king Numa, who used to meet her in a grotto in the precincts of the Camenæ. After the death of her beloved, she fled to the shrine of the Arician Diana, by whom, as her wailings disturbed the worship, she was changed into the fountain which bore her name. Married women worshipped her at Rome, as a goddess of childbirth.

Eidŏthĕa. A sea-goddess, daughter of Prōteus, the old man of the sea.

Eidyllĭŏn. *See* BUCOLIC POETRY.

Eilithȳĭa (Latin, *Ilīthȳĭa*). The Greek goddess of childbirth, daughter of Zeus and Hēra, according to whose will she makes childbirth easy or difficult. In Homer there is more than one goddess of the name. Just as Hera was herself often worshipped as a goddess of childbirth, so Artĕmis, goddess of the moon, was invoked under the title of Eilithyia; the moon, according to ancient belief, having had great influence upon the event. The oldest seat of the worship of Eilithyia was the island of Crete, where a grotto at Cnossus, consecrated to her, is mentioned in Homer. Next to this came the island of Dēlŏs, where she was also worshipped as a goddess of Destiny. She had sanctuaries and statues in many places, being represented as veiled from head to foot, stretching out one hand to help, and in the other holding a torch, as the symbol of birth into the light of the world.

Eirēnē (Latin, *Irēnē*). The Greek goddess of peace, one of the Hōræ. She was worshipped as goddess of wealth, and repre-

sented accordingly as a young woman with
Plūtus in her arms. (*See* PLUTUS.) Among
her other attri-
butes are the
cornucŏpĭa, the
olive branch,
Hermēs' staff,
and ears of corn
in her hand and
on her head.
The correspond-
ing deity among
the Romans was
Pax, to whom an
altar was set up
on July 4th, 13
B.C., on the re-
turn of Augustus
from Gaul.
Eirĕsĭōnē. *See*
PYANEPSIA.

Eisangĕlĭa
(Greek). Pro-
perly, an an-
nouncement made in presence of a legal
authority. In Attic jurisprudence *eisangelia* was a special form of public prosecution, instituted especially for offences
which appeared to inflict injury, directly
or indirectly, upon the state, but which it
was impracticable to prosecute under the
regular and customary procedure. The
accusation was put into writing and handed
in to the senate; if the senate received it,
the accused was arrested, or had to get
three persons to stand surety for him. But
if the charge were one of treason, or an
attack upon the constitution, this was not
allowed. If the voting on the guilt or
innocence of the accused were unfavourable,
the senate itself fixed the penalty, supposing it fell short of the amount which lay
within its competence (500 drachmæ or
£16 13s. 4d.). If not, the senate referred
the case at once to one of the courts of the
Hēlĭæa, or even to the *ecclēsĭa*, to which
the prosecutor might, indeed, have applied
from the first. If the *ecclesia* decided to
take up the case, the first thing it did was
to fix the penalty, in case there were no
legal provisions on this point. It then
either entered on the investigation and
decided the case, or handed it over to a
court of law. The name *eisangelia* was
also given to the prosecution of judges in
office for neglect of their duties; and to
certain charges lodged before the archons :
namely, charges against children for ill-
treatment of parents, against husbands for

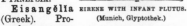

EIRENE WITH INFANT PLUTUS.
(Munich, Glyptothek.)

ill-treatment of heiresses, and against guar
dians for ill-treatment of their wards. (*See*
ARCHONS.)

Eisphŏrā (Athenian). An income-tax
levied only in extraordinary cases. It wa
based on the Solonian division of classe
into *Pentăcŏsĭŏmĕdimnī, Hippeis, Zeugĭtæ*
and *Thētĕs*, the last of whom were no
taxed at all. The taxable capital was esti
mated at twelve times a man's net incom
as estimated by himself. In the case of th
Pentacosiomedimni, with a minimum in
come of 500 drachmæ and minimum capita
of 6,000 drachmæ (=1 talent or £200
the whole property was treated as taxabl
capital (*tīmēmă*). In the case of th
Hippeis (300–3,600 drachmæ) five-sixths, i
that of the *Zeugĭtæ* (150–1,800 drachmæ
five-ninths or 1,000 drachmæ. The firs
instance of the levy of an *eisphora* oc
curred in 428 B.C. In 378 B.C. anothe
method of levying it was introduced unde
the archon Nausīnīcus. According to thi
the taxable capital of the highest clas
was fixed at one-fifth of the whole property
The resident aliens (*mĕtœcī*), as well as th
citizens, were liable to pay the *eisphora*
On the method of collecting it, *see* SYM
MORĬÆ.

Ekĕcheirĭa. The "truce of God" (lite
rally, "holding of hands"), observed i
Greece at the great festivals which wer
visited by strangers; *e.g.* the nationa
games, and the *Eleusīnĭa* in Attica. Thi
peace was proclaimed by heralds through
out Greece, to secure the visitors to th
games freedom in passing backwards and
forwards and security during the festival
In the case of the *Eleusinia* the truc
lasted 1½ months and ten days.

Elăphēbŏlĭa. A festival held at Athens
in the month Elăphēbŏlĭōn (March–April)
in honour of Artĕmis as goddess of the
chase and of game. (*See* ARTEMIS.)

Electra (Gr. *Elektra*). (1) Daughter o
Agămemnōn and Clytæmnēstra, sister o
Iphĭgĕnĭa and Orestēs. She saved Oreste
from the murderer of his father, and
assisted him afterwards in avenging hi
death. She married Pўlădēs, her brother'
friend, and became the mother of Mĕdōn
and Strŏphĭus.

(2) One of the Pleiădĕs, the mother (by
Zeus) of Dardănus, ancestor of the roya
house of Troy.

Electrum (Gr. *Elektrŏn*). This word ha
two meanings in antiquity. (1) A mixture
of gold and silver in the proportion of abou
4 : 1. (2) Amber, the use of which in orna-

nentation was known to the Greeks as arly as the Homeric age through their rade with Phœnicia. In later times, mainly hrough the overland trade, amber was »rought down from the Baltic to the nouths of the Po, and from thence farther outh. In the classical times it seems to save been only in exceptional cases that .mber was applied to the uses of art; and ss Greek influence increased, the taste for t disappeared in Italy. It was only to-vards the end of the republican age that t gradually came into favour again, and .hen as a material for ladies' ornaments, such as bracelets, pins and rings, and for .dorning bedsteads and similar furniture. Jnder the Empire it was more fashionable han it had ever been. The white, wax-oloured sort was accounted the worst, and vas only used for fumigation. The ruddy .mber, especially if transparent, found more avour; the bright yellow, of the colour of Falernian wine, was liked best of all. The satural colour was sometimes intensified or altered by artificial means.

Electryŏn (Gr. *Elektryŏn*). Son of Perseus and Andrŏmĕda, king of Mўcēnæ, father of Alcmēnē, the mother of Hērăclēs. (*See* AMPHITRYON.)

Elegy. The general term in Greek for any poem written in the elegiac metre, a combination of the dactylic hexameter and pentameter in a couplet. The word *ĕlĕgŏs* is probably not Greek, but borrowed from the Lydians, and means a plaintive melody accompanied by the flute. How it happened that the word was applied to elegiac poetry, the earliest representatives of which by no means confined it to mournful subjects, is doubtful. It may be that the term was only chosen in reference to the musical set-ting, the elegy having originally been ac-companied by the flute. Like the *ĕpŏs*, the elegy was a production of the Ionians of Asia Minor. Its dialect was the same as that of the *epos*, and its metre only a varia-tion of the epic metre, the pentămĕter being no more than an abbreviation of the hexămĕter. The elegy marks the first transition from the epic to lyric proper. The earliest representatives of the elegy, Callīnus of Ephĕsus (about 700 B.C.), and Tyrtæus of Aphidnæ in Attica (about 600), gave it a decidedly warlike and political direction, and so did Solon (640–559) in his earlier poems, though his later elegies have mostly a contemplative character. The elegies of Thĕognis of Mĕgără (about 540), though gnomic and erotic, are essentially

political. The first typical representative of the erotic elegy was Mimnermus of Cŏlŏphŏn, an elder contemporary of Solon. The elegy of mourning or sorrow was brought to perfection by Simōnĭdēs of Cĕŏs (died B.C. 469). After him the emotional element predominated. Antīmăchus of Cŏlŏphŏn (about 400) gave the elegy a learned tinge, and was thus the prototype of the elegiac poets of Alexandria, Phanŏclēs, Phīlētās of Cōs, Hermēsĭănax of Colophon, and Callīmăchus of Cўrēnē, the master of them all. The subject of the Alexandrian elegy is sometimes the passion of love, with its pains and pleasures, treated through the medium of images and similes taken from mythology, sometimes learned narrative of fable and history, from which personal emo-tion is absent.

This type of elegy, with its learned and obscure manner, was taken up and imitated at Rome towards the end of the Republic. The Romans soon easily surpassed their Greek masters both in warmth and sin-cerity of feeling and in finish of style. The elegies of Catullus are among their earliest attempts; but in the Augustan age, in the hands of Cornēlĭus Gallus, Prŏpertĭus, Tĭbullus, and Ovid, the elegiac style was entirely appropriated by Latin literature. Ovid in his *Fasti* showed how a learned subject could be treated in this metre. From his time onward the elegiac metre was constantly employed. In the later literature it was used, like the epic metre, for every possible subject, as, for instance, by Rutĭlĭŭs Namatĭānus in the description of his return from Rome to France (A.D. 416). In the 6th century A.D. the poet Maxĭmĭānus, born in Etruria at the beginning of the 6th century, is a late instance of a genuine elegiac poet.

Elephants. Indian elephants were first used in European warfare by the successors of Alexander for the purpose of breaking through the enemy's ranks. An elephant, if completely equipped, carried on its back, besides its driver, a tower or howdah, generally containing four archers. The Romans first learned their use in the war with Pyrrhus. In the Second Punic War they got possession of African elephants, the first which they turned to their own account, and used them against Philip of Macedon. But elephants never played so important a part in the Roman armies as they had in those of Alexander's successors. They were liable to panic if the enemy frightened them with firebrands or in any other way, and in this state became dangerous to friends as well as enemies. Combats of elephants, however, were always the central attraction in the fights of wild animals in the games of the circus, and, from the time of Augustus, the chariots which bore the images of the deified emperors were drawn by elephants in the solemn procession.

Eleusinia. The two mystic festivals of Dēmētēr and her daughter Persĕphŏnē (*Cŏrē*) celebrated in Attica. They took their name from the city of Eleusis, twelve miles distant from Athens. This was, from time immemorial, a seat of the worship of Demeter, instituted, it was said, by the goddess herself after the disappearance of her daughter. (*See* DEMETER.) The worship of Dionȳsus was early associated with that of the two goddesses of the earth, for Dionysus was himself a god of fertility, worshipped here under the name of Iakchŏs, as son of Zeus and Demeter or Persephone. The ritual of the Eleusinian service was supposed to have been ordained by Eumolpus (*see* EUMOLPUS). The conquest of Eleusis, which took place, according to the story, under king Erechtheus, gave Athens a right to take part in the solemnity, and the lesser of the two festivals was actually celebrated in Athens. Eleusis, however, continued to be the chief seat of the worship, and the highest priesthoods were hereditary in the Eleusinian families of the Eumolpĭdæ and Kērȳkĕs. The sanctity which shrouded the Eleusinian mysteries occasioned the foundation of *Eleusinia* on their model in other Greek cities. But the initiations at Eleusis were always accounted the most sacred and the most efficacious. The events celebrated in the mysteries were the descent of Persephone into the world below, and her return to light and to her mother. The former was celebrated at the greater Eleusinia between autumn and seed-time; the latter in spring at the lesser Eleusinia. The symbolical representation of both events had the same object. This was to excite and strengthen in the minds of the initiated, by means of the story of Persephone, the faith in the continuance of life, and a system of rewards and punishments after death. The right of initiation into the Eleusinian mysteries was in all probability restricted originally to inhabitants of Attica, but it was not long before it was extended to all Greeks. In later times, after their closer connexion with the Greeks, the Romans were also admitted. Barbarians were excluded, and so were all

who had been guilty of murder, or any other serious offence. The neophyte was proposed for initiation by an Athenian citizen who had himself been initiated. He was admitted first to the lesser mysteries at the lesser *Eleusinia*. At this stage the candidates were termed *Mystæ*, and were allowed to take a limited part in the greater *Eleusinia* the next autumn. They were not initiated, however, into the greater mysteries until the greater *Eleusinia* succeeding these; and after their initiation were called *ĕpoptæ*, or seers. The external arrangement of the festival was in the hands of the second archōn, or Archon Băsĭleus, who exercised a general superin tendence over the whole of the public wor ship. He was assisted by four overseers (*ĕpĭmĕlĕtæ*), two of whom were elected from the whole body of citizens, and two from the Eleusinian families of the Eumolpĭdæ and Kerykes.[1] The high-priestly officials, who carried out the liturgical functions at the celebration, were also chosen from these two families. The Hĭĕrŏphantēs, or chief priest, belonged to the house of Eumolpus. It was his duty to exhibit to the initiated the mysterious shrines, and probably to lead the performance of the hymns handed down from his ancestors. The Kēryx, or herald, was of the house of the Kērȳkĕs. He summoned the initiated, in the traditional form of words, to wor ship, pronouncing for them the form of prayer. The Dādūchŏs or torch-bearer, and the superinten dent of the sacri fice, were also im portant officials. The lesser Eleusinia were celebrated in the month Anthes tērĭōn, which

(1) *ELEUSINIAN PRIEST.
(Vase from Kertch; Gerhard,
Ges. Abh., taf. 77.)

corresponded roughly to February.

The service was performed at Agræ, a suburb of Athens on the Ilissus, in the temple of Demeter and Corē, and accom

---

[1] Keryx was, according to one account, repre sented as the son of Hĕrmēs and Aglaurŏs, daughter of Cecrops, according to another, one of the sons of Eumolpus.

anied by mystical rites, the nature of which is unknown. It was said to have been founded at the wish of Hĕrăclēs, who, being a stranger, was excluded by usage from the greater Eleusinia. The great Eleusinia were celebrated in the middle of Bŏĕdrŏmĭōn (roughly = September), for a space probably of nine days. The first days were devoted to the preparation for the main festival, bathing in the sea, sacrifices of purification, and the like. On the sixth day, the 20th Boedromion, the immense multitude of *mystœ*, in festal attire and crowned with myrtle, marched in procession along the sacred way to Eleusis, preceded by the image of Iakchos, who gave his name to the celebration. Much time

by the potion mixed of water, meal, and penny-royal, supposed to have been the first food tasted by Demeter after her reception in Eleusis. It was probably while these celebrations were going on that the *Epoptœ*, and the *Mystœ* who were called to their final initiation, took part in the mysteries proper. Mysterious rites were first, it would seem, performed in darkness, which threw the celebrants into a state of painful suspense and expectation. Then, in a dazzling light, and amid great splendour, the Hierophantes showed them certain shrines of the goddess and Iakchos, explaining their meaning; holy songs being meantime performed, partly by himself, partly by choirs with instrumental accom-

(2) * PLAN OF THE TEMPLE ENCLOSURE AT ELEUSIS.

A, outer *peribŏlŏs*; aa, inner *peribolos*; B, greater *propylœa*; C, lesser *propylœa*; D, Great Temple of the Mysteries, with portico of Philon (183 ft. × 37¼ ft.), and *Telesterion*, or interior of the temple (178 ft. × 170 ft.), with eight rows of seats, partly hewn out of the rock.—*Unedited Antiquities of Attica*, chap. i. 5.

was spent, partly in the performance of acts of devotion at the numerous holy places on the road, partly in merriment and banter; so that it was late in the evening before they arrived at the *Tĕlĕstĕrĭŏn*, or house of initiation, at Eleusis. This was a magnificent temple erected by Pĕrĭclēs in place of the ancient temple of Demeter, which had been burnt down in the Persian War. During the following nights various celebrations took place at those spots in Eleusis and its neighbourhood which were hallowed in the story of the goddess. In these were represented the sorrowful searching of the goddess for her lost daughter, and the mother's joy at finding her. The transition from sorrow and fasting to joy and festivity was symbolized

paniment. The climax of the whole was the sacred drama, a representation of the story of the three goddesses in the worlds above and below. The festival was brought to a close by a libation of water from two vessels in the shape of a top (*plēmŏchŏē*). The water was poured in the direction of east and west with mystical formulæ.

The ancients speak of the revelations made in the mysteries as having a beneficial influence on morality, pointing as they did to reward and punishment after death. They represent them further as giving comfort in the trials and sufferings of life, and as opening brighter hopes after death. It is certain that there were few citizens of Athens who were not initiated; many who neglected the rite early in life were initiated in old age. For in the popular belief the initiation conferred a claim to the joys promised in the mysteries to the good after death.

The Eleusinian mysteries maintained their position for a long time. Among the Romans, men of the highest rank, as, for instance, Hadrian and Marcus Aurelius, deigned to receive the initiation. When the Christian emperor Valentinian put an end to all religious celebrations by night, he excepted the *Eleusinia*, which continued in existence till they were abolished by Theodosius towards the end of the 4th century A.D.

Eleuthĕrĭa. A festival in honour of Erōs, celebrated at Samos. (*See* EROS.)

Eleven. *See* HENDEKA.

Elissa. *See* DIDO.

Elўsĭum. In Homer Elysium is a beautiful meadow at the western extremity of the earth, on the banks of the river Ocĕănus. Thither the favoured of Zeus, such as Rhădămanthys his son, and his son-in-law Mĕnĕlāus, are carried without having seen death. They live a life of perfect happiness, there is no snow, nor storm, nor rain, but the cool west wind breathes there for ever. Hesiod speaks of the islands of the blest by the Ocean, where some of the heroes of the fourth generation of men live a life without pain, and where the earth produces her fruits three times in the year. According to Pindar, all who have three times passed blamelessly through life live there in perfect bliss under the sway of Crŏnus and his assessor Rhadamanthys. Such are Cadmus and Pēleus, and Achilles through the intercession of his mother Thĕtis with Zeus. Like Cronus, the Titans, after their reconciliation with Zeus, dwell on these islands. In later times Elysium with its bliss was localized in the world below, and regarded as the abode of those whom the judges of the dead had pronounced worthy of it. (*Cp.* HADES, REALM OF.)

Emancĭpātĭō (Roman). The formal liberation of a son from the control (*mănus*) of his father. If the son were sold three times over, all the rights of his father came to an end. If then a father wished to make a son his own master (*sŭĭ ĭūris*), he made him over three times by *mancĭpātĭō* or a fictitious sale to a third person. The third person emancipated him the first and second time, so that he came again into the control of his father. After purchasing him a third time he either emancipated him him-

self, and thus became his *patrōnus*, or he sold him back to his father, to whom he now stood, not in the relation of a son, but *in mancĭpĭō*, so that the father could liberate him without more ado. In this case the father remained *patronus* of the son. The emancipated son did not, as in the case of adoption (*see* ADOPTION), pass into the *patria pŏtestās* of another, and therefore retained his father's family name. But he lost his right to inherit in default of a will.

Emăthĭōn. Son of Eōs and Tīthōnus, brother of Memnōn, from whom he seized the government of the Ethiopians. He was slain by Hērăclēs when travelling in search of the apples of the Hespĕrĭdĕs.

Emmĕleia. The serious and majestic dance of the chorus in the Greek Tragedy.

Empĕdŏclēs. A Greek philosopher and poet, born of a rich and noble family at Agrigentum in Sicily, about 490 B.C. Like his father, Mĕtōn, who had taken part in the expulsion of the tyrant Thrăsўdæus, he was an ardent supporter of the democracy. He lent his aid in destroying the aristocracy and setting up a democratic constitution, although his fellow-citizens offered him the kingly dignity. He was content with the powerful influence which he derived from his wealth, his eloquence, and extraordinary knowledge. His acquaintance with medicine and natural science was so great as to win him the reputation of a wonder-worker in his lifetime, and the position of a hero after his death. It was probably a political revolution which caused him, in advanced age, to leave his country and settle in the Peloponnese. He died about 430 B.C., away from Sicily. A later story represented him as having thrown himself into the crater of Ætna, that his sudden disappearance might make the people believe him a god. The truth, however, was said to have been revealed by the appearance of his shoes, thrown up by the volcano.

He was the author of propitiatory hymns, probably of a mystical and religious character; of a didactic poem on medicine; and of an epic poem in three books upon Nature. This last was his *chef d'œuvre*, and had a high reputation in antiquity, both for its contents, and for its form, in which the writer took Homer for his master. Considerable fragments of it remain, written in a sublime and pregnant style. His system is grounded upon the assumption of four unchangeable elements, fire (the noblest of all), air, earth, and water, and two opposing forces, Love which binds and attracts, and Hate which separates and repels. The formation of the world began when the elements, held together by Love, and separated by Hate, again tended to union under the influence of Love. The manifold minglings and separations of the elements originated in the different species, that of man included. Our perceptions arise from the particles which are thrown off by things, and stream in upon us through special pores or passages. As in our persons all the fundamental elements are united, we are enabled by their means to recognise what is homogeneous outside us. Our ideas are not pure, but compounded of the particles which pour in upon us and go out from us. The system of Empedocles often agreed with that of Pȳthăgŏrās. Both adopted the theory of transmigration, and the moral and ascetic doctrines connected with it. The propitiatory hymns above mentioned may well have been in harmony with these ideas.

Emptĭō. *See* BONORUM EMPTIO.

Encaustĭkē. The art of painting by burning in the colours. (*See* PAINTING.)

Encĕlădus. (*See* GIANTS.)

Encōmĭŏn (Greek). Originally the song sung by the chorus at the *kōmŏs* or festal procession held at the great national games in honour of the victor, either on the day of his victory, or on its anniversary. The word came afterwards to denote any song written in celebration of distinguished persons, and in later times any spoken or written panegyric whatever.

Endēïs. Daughter of Chīrōn and the Naiad Chărĭclō, wife of Æacus, mother of Pēleus and Tĕlămōn.

Endeixis. A term in Athenian jurisprudence, denoting a prosecution in notorious cases, as, for instance, against the Prȳtănēs, if they refused to put a question to the vote in the great assembly. It was especially employed against persons who, although lying under ătīmĭa, presumed to claim a share in civic rights, as (particularly) by instituting prosecutions, or appearing, speaking, and voting in the assembly [Aristotle, *Const. of Athens*, 29, 52, 63].

Endrŏmĭs (Greek). (1) A boot of leather or felt, rising as far as the calf or above it, and fitting close to the foot. In front it was open and fastened with straps. It was specially adapted for journeys or hunting, and consequently appears often in representations of Artĕmis and of the Ĕrīnȳĕs. Runners in races too, often wore it. (*See* ELEUSINIA, fig. 1, and ERINYS.) (2) A thick woollen rug (mentioned by Martial and Juvenal, iii 102).

Endȳmĭōn. In Greek mythology, the beautiful son of Aëthlĭŏs (or, according to another story, Zeus and Călȳcē), daughter of Æŏlus, king of Elis, father of Epēus, Ætōlus, and Pæōn, the first of whom won the government of the country by conquering in a race which his father had set on foot. He was loved by Sĕlēnē, the goddess of the moon, by whom he had fifty daughters. They were supposed to symbolize the fifty lunar months which intervened between the Olympic games. His grave was at Olympia. Another story made him a shepherd or hunter on Mount Latmŏs in Caria. Zeus bestowed on him eternal youth and eternal life in the form of unbroken slumber. Selene descended every night from heaven to visit and embrace the beautiful sleeper in his grotto.

Ennĭus (*Quintus*). The founder of the Hellenized type of Latin poetry. He was born 239 B.C. at Rŭdĭæ in Călăbrĭa, and was by descent a Græcised Messapian. He was probably educated at Tărentum, and served with the Romans in the Second Punic War in Sardinia, whence Cato took him to Rome in 204 B.C. His poetical talent here came to his aid, not in a pecuniary way (for he was in slender circumstances to the end of his life), but as an introduction to the favour of the great men. Among these must be mentioned the Scipios, and Fulvĭus Nŏbĭlĭor, who took him in his retinue to the Ætolian war in B.C. 189, and whose son procured him the citizenship five years later (184). A gouty affection did not prevent him from continuing his literary work to an advanced age. He was in his sixty-seventh year when he finished his *Annālēs*, and he put a tragedy on the stage shortly before his death. He died in 170 B.C., in his seventieth year. It was said that the Scipios placed his image in their family vault.

Ennius wrote poetry with success in a great number of styles. But in his own opinion, as well as in that of his fellow-citizens, his greatest work was his *Annales* in eighteen books. This was a chronological narrative of Roman history in verse. Like Nævius' *Bellum Pœnĭcum*, it began with the destruction of Troy, and came down to the poet's own times. In this poem Ennius created for the Romans their first national epic, the fame of which was only eclipsed by Vergil. But he did more. By the introduction of the Greek hexameter Ennius did much to further the future development of Latin poetry. His predecessor, Nævius, had continued to write in the native Saturnian metre, which was hardly capable of artistic development. But the practice of writing in the strict dactylic measure enabled the Latin poets to assimilate the other metrical forms presented by Greek literature.

Of the Annals we possess, relatively speaking, only a small number of fragments. Some of these can only be distinguished from prose by their metrical form; others are very fine, both in form and ideas. Ennius showed considerable capacity, too, as a writer of tragedies. His dramas, which were very numerous, were composed after Greek models, especially the tragedies of Euripides. More than twenty of these Euripidean plays are known to us by their titles and surviving fragments. He also wrote *prætextæ*, or tragedies on Roman subjects, as, for instance, the *Ambrācĭa*, representing the siege and conquest of this city by his patron Fulvius Nobilior. His comedies were neither so numerous nor so important as his tragedies. Besides these he wrote several books of *sătŭræ*, or collections of poems of various contents and in various metres. Several of his adaptations or translations of Greek originals were probably included in these : as, for instance, the *Hēdў-phăgētĭca*, a gastronomic work after Archestrătus of Gela ; *Epicharmus*, a didactic poem on the "Nature of Things"; *Euhē-mĕrus*, a rationalistic interpretation of the popular fables about the gods; *Præcepta* or *Protreptĭcŭs*, containing moral doctrines; and others of the same kind. There was a poem entitled *Scipio*, written in honour of the elder Afrĭcānus. Whether this was a *satura* or a drama is uncertain.

The memory of Ennius long survived the fall of the Republic. Even after literary taste had taken quite a different direction, he was revered as the father of Latin poetry, and especially as having done much to enrich the Latin language.

Ennŏdĭus (*Magnus Felix*). A Latin rhetorician and poet. He was born about 473 A.D. in the south of France, and died in 521 as bishop of Pavia. Among the other works, he wrote between 504 and 508 an extremely fulsome panegyric on Theodosius the Great, and a biography of Epiphanius, his predecessor in the see. Both these writings have a value for the historian. Besides these we have a collec-

tion of twenty-eight model speeches, some of which were really delivered : nine books of letters, and two of poems, sacred and secular. The first book of poems contains longer, the second shorter and occasional pieces. Both show a certain command of form.

Enŏmŏtĭa. A subordinate division of the *Lŏchŏs* in the Spartan army. (*See* Lochos and Mora.)

Enyălĭŏs. Epithet of Arēs. (*See* Ares.)

Enyō. (1) A Greek goddess of battle, companion of Arēs (*see* Ares), identified by the Romans with Bellōna. (*See* Ares, Bellona.) (2) One of the *Graiæ*. (*See* Graiæ.)

Eōs (Latin *Aurōra*). The Greek goddess of the dawn, daughter of the Titan Hypĕrīōn and Theia, sister of Hēlĭŏs and Sĕlēnē, by Astræus, mother of the winds, Argestēs, Zĕphўrŏs, Bŏrĕās and Nŏtŏs, the morning star *Hĕōsphŏrŏs*, and of the stars in general. Her hair is beautiful, her arms and fingers ruddy, her wings are white. She rises early from her couch on the Eastern Ocean, and in a saffron-coloured mantle, on a golden chariot drawn by white horses, she comes forth as her brother's herald to proclaim the rising of day to mortals and immortals. Loving all fresh and youthful beauty, she carries away Clītus, Cĕphălus, Orīōn and Tīthōnus, to whom she bears Memnōn and Emāthīōn. She is represented in works of art as hovering in the sky, or riding on her chariot, moving with a torch before Arēs, or sprinkling dew from a vase over the earth. *See* Memnon.

Epăphŏs. *See* Io and Belos.

Epēus (*Epeiŏs*). (*See* Trojan War.)

Ephēbī. The Athenian name for youths over the age of sixteen. The completion of a boy's sixteenth year was the occasion of a festival, at which the *ĕphēbus* made a drink offering to Hērăclēs, and entertained his friends with wine. His hair, hitherto worn long, was cut, and the locks dedicated to Apollo. For the two following years the *ephebi* were mainly employed in gymnastic exercises, and after that time the proper civic *ephebĭa* commenced. After an examination intended to test the genuineness of their civic descent and their physical capacity, the *ephebi* were entered on the list of their tribe, presented to the people assembled in the theatre, armed with spear and shield, and taken to the sanctuary of Agraulŏs at the foot of the citadel, where they bound themselves by a solemn oath to the service and defence of their country.

'or the two following years they served as
guards on the frontier. After the comple-
ion of their twentieth year they were admitted to the meetings of the assembly and
imployed in foreign service. Their dress
was the *chlămÿs* and the *pĕtăsus.*

Ephēgēsĭs. *See* APAGOGE.

Ephĕtæ. A judicial court of high antiquity at Athens, consisting of fifty-one
judges elected from the noblest Athenian
families. It gave decisions in cases of
murder at five different places, differing
according to the character of the case. If
the crime had a religious character, the
Archōn Băsĭleus presided. (*See* ARCHONS.)
Solon did not abolish this court, but handed
over to the newly organized Arēŏpăgus its
most important functions,—the power of
deciding cases of intentional murder, poisoning, malicious wounding, arson, and the like.
The nearest relations of the murdered person
were bound by religious sanction to avenge
his blood. At the funeral, and after that
in the market place, they uttered a solemn
denunciation, which bade the murderer keep
away from all public places, assemblies,
and sanctuaries, and to appear before the
court. The Archon Basileus, after the
charge had been announced and received,
repeated this denunciation. The preliminary
investigation, and determination of the place
where the court was to be held, followed
at three appointed times in three successive months. The case was not finally
dealt with till the fourth month. On the
first two days of the final trial the two
parties, after solemnly taking an oath, conducted their case in person. On the third
day judgment was given, in case the accused
had not gone into voluntary exile. If he
had, his property was confiscated, but he
was pursued no further. Intentional murder was punished with death, malicious
wounding with exile; the man's property
was confiscated in both cases. In the
court of Areopagus, if the votes of the
judges were equal, the accused was acquitted. If the homicide were legally allowed
(as, for instance, that of an adulterer)
or legally innocent (as in self-defence), the
case was investigated in the Delphĭnĭŏn, a
sanctuary of the Delphic Apollo; and only
a religious purification was exacted. Cases
of unintentional homicide, murder of an
alien, and instigation to murder, were taken
at the Pallădĭŏn, a sanctuary of Pallas.
Instigation to murder was punished with
banishment and confiscation of property,
the murder of an alien with banishment,

unintentional murder with banishment,
until the kinsmen of the murdered person
gave permission to the slayer to return. In
the time of Demosthenes it would seem
that the cases which used to be heard at
the Delphinion and Palladion were handed
over to the *Hēlĭastæ.* Thus the Ephetæ
had only two courts left them, that in
Phrĕatto, a place in the Piræus, near the
sea, and the Prytănĕum. The former had
only to judge in the rare event of a person
banished for unintentional homicide being
charged with intentional murder. As he
might not set foot on land, he was heard
standing in a ship, and if found guilty was
punished with banishment for life. At the
Prytaneum a regular court was held on inanimate objects and animals which had been the
cause of death to a human being. The president of the four old Ionic tribes removed the
object or the animal over the border. Again,
if a murder had been committed and the offender was undiscovered, this court had to
pronounce lawful sentence against him [Dem.
23 §§ 64–79; Aristotle, *Const. Athens*, 57].

Ephialtēs. *See* ALOADÆ.

Ephors (*Ephŏroi* = overseers.) A board
of five members at Sparta, elected annually
from all the citizens. It is said to have
been established by Lycurgus or king Theopompus (770 B.C.). The original intention
was that it should give decisions in private
matters, and represent the absent kings in
certain of their duties, especially the superintendence of the officials and of public
discipline. But their circle of authority
gradually widened, till it came to mean a
superintendence over the whole commonwealth, including the kings. The ephors
had the right of raising objections against
their actions, calling them, like other
officials, to account for their conduct, punishing them with fines and reprimands, and
even prosecuting them before the senate,
and threatening them with deposition and
death. They were the only citizens who
were not obliged to rise in the kings'
presence, a fact which gives a good idea of
the relative position of the two parties.
Besides the duty of opposing everything
which they thought adverse to the laws
and interests of Sparta, they had from early
times the right of summoning the deliberative and legislative assemblies, the *Gĕrūsĭa*
and *Ecclēsĭa,* to make proposals to them,
and take the lead in proceedings left to
their management. Two of them regularly
accompanied the kings on their campaigns.
It is probable also that they had the super-

intendence of the public treasure. In their capacity of protectors of the public discipline their authority extended itself to the minutest details of private life. In regard to the Helots and Pĕrīœcī it was still more absolute. Even on a *periœcus* they could pass sentence of death without trial. (*See* PERIŒCI.) On important occasions a majority of their votes was required. At the end of their annual office, on which they entered at the beginning of the Spartan year or at the time of the autumnal equinox, they were liable to be called to account by their successors. The year was dated by the name of the first Ephor on the board.

Ephŏrus. A Greek historian, born about 400 B.C. at Cȳmē, in Asia Minor. He lived to see the invasion of Asia by Alexander the Great in 334. Like Theopompus, he was a pupil of Isŏcrătēs, who, seeing that he was not likely to succeed as a public speaker, persuaded him to write history. He was the author of a Universal History, which omitted the mythical age, and began with the return of the Hērăclīdæ into the Peloponnese. It treated in thirty books the history of the Greek and barbarian world, during a space of 750 years, ending in 340 B.C. The last book is said to have been completed by his son Dēmŏph'ĭlus. The work was continued in the Alexandrian period by Diyllus of Athens, Psaŏn of Platæa, and Mĕnŏdŏtus of Perinthus. It was much read and used for the wealth and excellent arrangement of its material, which embraced geography, ethnography, mythology, and the history of civilization and literature. It met with much hostile criticism, but had its admirers, among whom was Polybius.

Epĭcastē. *See* JOCASTA.

Epĭcharmus. A Greek comedian, born in the island of Cŏs, about 540 B.C. When only a child of three months old he came with his father Hēlŏthălēs, a physician, to Megara in Sicily, where he died about 450 at the age of 90. Like his father, he is said to have been personally acquainted with Pȳthăgŏrās, and whether this is so or no, his philosophical attainments were not inconsiderable. It was Epicharmus who gave to the Doric comedy of Sicily its literary form. Thirty-five of his plays, written in the Doric dialect, are known to us by their titles, and a few meagre fragments have survived. They differed from the Attic comedy in having no chorus. Their subjects were taken partly from the stories of gods and heroes, which they burlesqued and caricatured, and partly from life. The plots seem to have been simple and the action rapid. The philosophical leanings of Epicharmus are shown in numerous sayings of deep practical wisdom. Plato said that Epicharmus was the prince of comedy, as Homer was of tragedy, a striking testimony to the perfection of his compositions in their own line. In his mythical comedy he was imitated by Dīnŏlŏchus of Syracuse,

Epĭcheirŏtŏnĭa. *See* ECCLESIA.

Epictētus (Gr. *Epiktētŏs*). A Greek philosopher, born at Hĭĕrăpŏlis in Phrygia. He lived a long time in Rome as a slave, in the house of Epaphrŏdītus, a favourite of Nero. Emancipated by his master, he became a professor of the Stoical system, which he had learned from the lectures of Mūsōnĭus Rūfus. When the philosophers were expelled from Rome by Domitian in 94 A.D., Epictetus went to Nīcŏpŏlis in Epīrus, where he lived as the master of a school until the reign of Hadrian (117 A.D.) He formed numerous disciples by free conversations after the manner of Socrates. Among these was Arrĭānus, to whom we owe an account of Epictetus' doctrine, for the master himself left nothing in writing. The main point on which he laid stress was the independence of the human mind of all external circumstances, such being not in our power. This freedom is to be attained by patience and renunciation. The duty of man is to find all his happiness within himself, and the power of which he should be most in awe is the deity in his own breast.

Epĭcūrus (Gr. *Epĭkourŏs*.) A Greek philosopher, founder of the Epicurean school, which was so named after him. He was born 342 B.C. in the Attic deme of Gargĕttus, and spent his early years in Samos, where his father had settled as a *clērūchus*. (*See* COLONIES, Greek.) While still young he returned to Athens, and there acquired by independent reading a comprehensive knowledge of previous philosophies. In 310 (*ætat.* 32) he began to teach philosophy, first in Mȳtĭlēnē, and afterwards in Lampsăcus. After 304 he carried on his profession at Athens. Here he bought a garden, in which he lived in retirement in a very modest and simple style, surrounded by his brother and his friends. He died (B.C. 268, *ætat.* 74) of calculus, after terrible sufferings. But to the last moment he never lost the tranquil serenity which had characterized his whole life. Such was his authority with his disciples that none of them ventured to make any innovation in his doctrines. His school continued to flourish in Athens, under fourteen masters, for 227 years; and much longer in other cities. His writings were remarkably numerous, and in parts very comprehensive. They were admired for their clearness, but their form was found fault with as too careless. Epicurus used to say himself that writing gave him no trouble. All that remains of them [exclusive of what may be gleaned from quotations in later writers], is: (1) a compendium of his doctrine in forty-four short propositions, written for his scholars to learn by heart. This we must, however, remember is not preserved in its original form. (2) Some fragments, not inconsiderable, but much mutilated and very incomplete, of his great work *On Nature*, in thirty books. These are preserved in the Herculanean *păpȳri*. (3) Three letters have survived from the body of his correspondence, besides his will. For his system, *see* PHILOSOPHY.

Epĭgămĭa (Greek). The right of contracting a valid marriage, with all its legal consequences. It was possessed only by citizens of the same state; aliens could only acquire it by special legal authorization, *i.e.*, a decree of the popular assembly. At Athens even the *Mĕtœci*, or resident aliens, were excluded from it. (*Comp.* CONUBIUM.)

Epĭgŏnī. The descendants of the seven princes who marched against Thebes: Ægĭăleus, son of Adrastus; Alcmæōn, son of Amphĭărāus; Dĭŏmēdēs, son of Tȳdeus; Prŏmăchus, son of Parthĕnŏpæus; Sthĕnĕlus, son of Căpăneus; Thersander, son of Pŏlȳnīcēs; Eurȳălus, son of Mĕcisteus. To avenge the slain, they marched against Thebes, under the leadership of Adrastus, ten years after the first Theban war (*see* ADRASTUS). Unlike their ancestors, they started with the happiest auspices. The oracle of Amphiaraus at Thebes promises them victory, and a happy return to all, that is, except Ægialeus the son of Adrastus, the only warrior who escaped in the previous war. In the decisive battle at Glisas, Ægialeus falls by the hand of Lăŏdămās, son of Etĕŏclēs, and leader of the Thebans. Laodamas is himself slain by Alcmæon. Part of the defeated Thebans, by the advice of Teirĕsĭās, fly before the city is taken, and settle in the territory of Hestĭæōtis in Thessaly, or among the Illyrian Enchĕli, where the government is in the hands of descendants of Cadmus (*see* CADMUS). The victors having conquered

and destroyed the city, send the best part of the booty, according to their vow, to the Delphic oracle. Thersander and his family are henceforth the rulers of Thebes.

Epigram. Properly = an inscription, such as was often written upon a tomb, a votive offering, a present, a work of art, and the like, to describe its character. Inscriptions of this sort were from early times put into metrical form, and the writer generally tried to put good sense and spirit into them. They were generally, though not always, written in the elegiac metre.

The greatest master of epigram was Sīmōnĭdēs of Cĕŏs, the author of almost all the sepulchral inscriptions on the warriors who fell in the Persian wars. His lines are remarkable for repose, clearness, and force, both of thought and expression. Fictitious inscriptions were often written, containing brief criticisms on celebrated men, as poets, philosophers, artists and their productions. The form of the epigram was also used to embody in concise and pointed language the clever ideas, or the passing moods of the writer, often with a tinge of wit or satire. The occasional epigram was a very favourite form of composition with the Alexandrian poets, and remained so down to the latest times. Some writers, indeed, devoted themselves entirely to it. Many of the choicest gems of Greek literature are to be found in the epigrams. The epigrammatists used other metres besides the elegiac, especially the iambic. In later times more complex and almost lyrical measures were employed. The Greek Anthology has preserved 4,500 epigrams, of the greatest variety in contents, and from the hand of more than 300 poets. (*See* ANTHOLOGY.) Among these are found some of the most celebrated names of ancient and of later times. A great number, too, are found in inscriptions.

Of all the Greek varieties of lyric poetry, the epigram was earliest welcomed at Rome. It lived on in an uninterrupted existence from Ennius till the latest times, being employed sometimes for inscriptions, sometimes for other and miscellaneous purposes. In the second half of the 1st century A.D. Martial handled it in various forms and with the power of a master. We also have a collection of epigrams by Luxŏrĭus (6th century A.D.). Many of such poems are preserved on inscriptions, besides a great quantity in manuscript, which in modern times have been collected into a Latin Anthology.

Epiklērŏs. *See* INHERITANCE (Athenian).

Epilēnĭŏs. *See* DANCING.

Epimělētæ (overseers.) The name given at Athens to commissioners nominated as occasion might require for the superintendence of departments. Some of these commissioners were regularly elected every year, as, *e.g.*, the ten *ĕpĭmĕlētœ* of the wharves, who were responsible for the care of the ships of war and equipments stored in the docks; and the ten commissioners of the *Empŏrĭŏn*, whose duty it was to enforce the laws relative to duties and commerce. For the commissioners of the revenue, *see* TAMIAS.

Epīmētheus. Brother of Prŏmētheus and husband of Pandōra. (*See* PROMETHEUS.)

Epīnīkĭŏn (Greek). A prize hymn sung by the chorus in honour of the victors at the great national games.

Epiŏnē. *See* ASCLEPIUS.

Episkȳrŏs. *See* BALL.

Epistātēs. *See* BOULE.

Epithălāmĭŏn (Greek). The wedding-hymn sung before the bridal chamber by a chorus of youths and maidens.

Epītīmia (Greek). The full possession of civic privileges, the opposite of *ătīmĭa*.

Epŏnȳmŏs (Greek). Properly the person after whom anything is named. This was in various Greek states the unofficial title of the magistrates after whom (in default of a generally received standard of chronology) the year was designated. In Athens this would be the first Archōn, in Sparta the first Ephor, in Argos the priestess of Hēra. When the *ĕphēbī*, at Athens, were enrolled in the list of the citizens who could be called out for military service, the name of the first archon of the year was attached. And when the citizens of various ages were summoned to military service, a reference was made to the archon *eponymos*, under whom they had been originally enrolled. The ancient heroes who gave their name to the ten tribes of Clīsthěnēs, and the heroes worshipped by the demes, were also called *eponymoi.* The statues of the former were in the market place, and it was near them that official notices were put up [Aristotle, *Const. of Athens*, 53].

Epōpeus. Son of Pŏseidōn and Cănăcē, the daughter of Æŏlus, brother of Alŏeus. He migrated from Thessaly to Sĭcȳōn, where he became king. He was killed by Lycus for the sake of Antĭŏpē, who, it was alleged, was mother of Zēthus by him.

Epoptæ. *See* ELEUSINIA.

Epŏs. (1) *Greek.* Many indications point to the fact that the oldest poetry of th Greeks was connected with the worship o the gods, and that religious poetry of mystical kind was composed by the priest of the Thracians, a musical and poetica people, and diffused in old times throug Northern Greece. The worship of th Muses was thus derived from the Thracians who in later times had disappeared from Greece Proper ; and accordingly the oldes bards whose names are known to th Greeks, — Orpheus, Mūsæus, Eumolpus Thămȳrĭs,—are supposed to have beer Thracians also. The current ideas on th nature and action of the gods tended mor and more to take the form of poetica myths respecting their birth, actions an sufferings. And thus those compositions of which an idea may be derived from some of the so-called Homeric hymns gradually assumed an epic character. I course of time the epic writers threw of their connexion with religion, and struck ou independent lines. Confining themselves n longer to the myths about the gods, the celebrated the heroic deeds both of mythica antiquity and of the immediate past. Thus in the Homeric description of the epic age while the bards Phēmĭus and Dēmŏdŏcu appear as favourites of the gods, to whon they are indebted for the gift of song, the are not attached to any particular worship The subjects of their song are not onl stories about the gods, such as the love of Arēs and Aphrŏdītē, but the events o recent times, the conquest of Troy by means of the wooden horse, and the tragica return of the Achæans from Troy. Singer like these, appearing at public festivals and at the tables of princes, to entertair the guests with their lays, must have existed early in Greece Proper. But i was the Ionian Greeks of Asia Minor wh first fully developed the capacities of epi poetry. By long practice, extending prob ably through centuries, a gradual progress was probably effected from short lays t long epic narratives ; and at the same time a tradition delivered from master to scholar handed on and perfected the outer form o style and metre. Thus, about 900 B.C epic poetry was brought to its highest perfection by the genius of Homer, the reputed author of the Iliad and Odyssey. After Homer it sank, never to rise again, from the height to which he had raised it.

It is true that in the following centuries a series of epics, more or less comprehensive, were composed by poets of the Ionic school n close imitation of the style and metre of Homer. But not one of them succeeded in coming even within measurable distance of their great master. The favourite topics of these writers were such fables as served either to introduce, or to extend and continue, the Iliad and Odyssey. They were called cyclic poets, because the most important of their works were afterwards put together with the Iliad and Odyssey in an epic cycle, or circle of lays.[1] The Cyprian poems (*Cypria*), of Stăsīnus, of Sălāmīs (Cyprus (776 B.C.), formed the introduction to the Iliad. These embraced the history of the period between the marriage of Pēleus and the opening of the Iliad. At about the same time Arctīnus of Milētus composed his *Æthĭŏpĭs* in five books. This poem started from the conclusion of the Iliad, and described the death of Achilles, and of the Ethiopian prince Memnōn, the contest for the arms of Achilles, and the suicide of Ajax. The *Destruction of Ilium*, by the same author, was in two books. By way of supplement to the Homeric Iliad, Leschēs of Mўtĭlēnē, either about 708 or 664 B.C., wrote a *Little Iliad*, in four books. This embraced the contest for the arms of Achilles, the appearance of Neoptŏlĕmus and Philoctētēs, and the capture of the city. The transition from the Iliad to the Odyssey was formed by the five books of *Nostoi* (*The Return of the Heroes*), written by Aglās of Trœzēn. The *Tĕlĕgŏnĭa*, by Eugammōn of Cŷrēnē (about 570), continued the Odyssey. This was in two books, embracing the history of Odysseus from the burial of the suitors until his death at the hands of his son Tĕlĕgŏnus. These poems and those of the other cyclics were, after Homer, the sources from which the later lyric and dramatic poets drew most of their information. But only fragments of them remain.

A new direction was given to epic poetry in Greece Proper by the didactic and genealogical epics of Hesiod of Ascra, about a hundred years after Homer. Hesiod was the founder of a school, the productions of which were often attributed to him as those of the Ionic school were to Homer. One of these disciples of Hesiod was Eumēlus of Corinth (about 750 B.C.), of the noble family of the Bacchĭādæ. But his poems, like those of the rest, are lost.

The most notable representatives of mythi-

cal epic poetry in the following centuries are Pisander of Cămīrus (about 640 B.C.), and Panyǎsis of Hălĭcarnassus (during the first half of the 5th century). In the second half of the 5th century Chœrĭlus of Samos wrote a *Persēĭs* on the Persian wars; the first attempt in Greece at a historical epic. His younger contemporary, Antĭmǎchus of Cŏlŏphōn, also struck out a new line in his learned *Thēbāĭs*, the precursor and model of the later epic of Alexandria. The Alexandrians laid great stress on learning and artistic execution in detail, but usually confined themselves to poems of less magnitude. The chief representatives of the Alexandrian school are Callĭmǎchus (about 250 B.C.), Rhiānus, Euphŏrĭōn, and Apollōnĭŭs of Rhodes. The latter made the futile attempt to return to the simplicity of Homer. His *Argōnautĭca* is, with the exception of the Homeric poems, the only Greek epic which has survived from the ante-Christian era. In the 200 years between the 4th and 6th centuries A.D., the mythical epic is represented by Quintus Smyrnæus, Nonnus, Collūthus, Tryphĭŏdōrus, Musæus, and the apocryphal Orpheus. Nonnus, Colluthus, and Tryphiodorus were Egyptians. Nonnus and Musæus, alone among these writers, have any claim to distinction. The talent of Nonnus is genuine, but undisciplined; Musæus knows how to throw charm into his treatment of a narrow subject. The whole series is closed by the *Ilĭăca* of Jōannēs Tzetzes, a learned but tasteless scholar of the 12th century A.D.

As Homer was the master of the mythical, so Hesiod was the master of the didactic epic. After him this department of poetry was best represented by Xĕnŏphǎnēs of Cŏlŏphōn, Parmĕnĭdēs of Elĕa, and Empĕdŏclēs of Agrigentum, in the 6th and 5th centuries B.C. In the Alexandrian period didactic poetry was much taken up, and employed upon the greatest possible variety of subjects. But none of its representatives succeeded in writing more than poetic prose, or in handling their intractable material with the mastery which Vergil shows in his Georgics. The period produced the astronomical epic of Arātŭs of Sīcўōn (about 275 B.C.), and two medical poems by Nīcander of Colophon (about 150). Under the Roman Empire more didactic poetry was produced by the Greek writers. Maxĭmus and the so-called Mănĕthō wrote on astrology. Dionysius Pĕrĭēgētēs on geography, Oppian on angling, and an imi-

---

[1] [Or perhaps because their style and treatment was conventional and without originality. Another meaning of the word *cyclicus*.]

tator of Oppian on hunting. The Alexandrian period also produced didactic poems in iambic *sēnărĭĭ*, as *e.g.* several on geography bearing the names of Dĭcæarchus and Scymnus, which still survive.

(2) *Roman.* The Romans probably had songs of an epic character from the earliest times; but these were soon forgotten. They had, however, a certain influence on the later and comparatively artificial literature, for both Līvĭus Andrŏnĭcus in his translation of the Odyssey, and Nævius in his Punic War, wrote in the traditional Italian metre, the *versus Sătŭrnĭus.* Nævius was, it is true, a national poet, and so was his successor Ennius, but the latter employed the Greek hexameter metre, instead of the rude Saturnian. To follow the example of Ennius, and celebrate the achievements of their countrymen in the form of the Greek epic, was the ambition of several poets before the fall of the Republic. A succession of poets, as Hostius, the tragedian Accius, and Furius were the authors of poetical annals. In this connexion we should also mention Cicero's epics on Marius and on his own consulship, besides the poem of Terentius Varro of Atax (*Ătăcīnus*) on Cæsar's war with the Sĕquăni (*Bellum Sĕquănĭcum*). Latin epics on Greek mythical subjects seem to have been rare in the republican age. At least we know of only a few translations, as that of the Iliad by Mattiŭs and Ninnius Crassus, and of the *Cyprĭa* by Lævīnus. Towards the end of the republican age it was a favourite form of literary activity to write in free imitation of the learned Alexandrians. Varro of Atax, for example, followed Apollonius of Rhodes in his *Argŏnautĭca*; others, like Helvius Cinna and the orator Licinius Calvus, preferred the shorter epics so much in favour with the Alexandrians. Only one example in this style is completely preserved, *The Marriage of Pēleus and Thĕtis,* by Catullus. This is the only example we possess of the narrative epic of the republic.

But in the Augustan age both kinds of epic, the mythic and the historical, are represented by a number of poets. Varius Rufus, Rabīrĭus, Cornēlĭus Sĕvērus, and Albĭnŏvānus Pĕdŏ, treated contemporary history in the epic style: Dŏmĭtius Marsus and Măcer turned their attention to the mythology. The Æneid of Vergil, the noblest monument of Roman epic poetry, combines both characters. Of all the epic productions of this age, the only ones which are

preserved intact are the Æneid, a panegyric on Messāla, which found its way into the poems of Tibullus, and perhaps two poems, the *Cŭlex* and *Cīris,* falsely attributed to Vergil.

In the 1st century A.D. we have several examples of the historical epic: the *Pharsālĭa* of Lucan, the *Pūnĭca* of Silius Ĭtălĭcus, a *Bellum Cīvīlĕ* in the satirical romance of Petrōnĭus, and an anonymous panegyric on Calpurnius Pīsō, who was executed for conspiracy under Nero, A.D. 65. The heroic style is represented by the *Argŏnautĭca* of Valerius Flaccus, and the *Thēbaid* and *Achillēid* of Statius, to which we may add the metrical epitome of the Iliad by the so-called Pindărus Thēbānus. The politico-historical poems of the succeeding centuries, by Publĭus Porfīrĭus Optātĭānus in the 4th century Claudian, Merobaudes, Sidonius Apollīnārĭs in the 5th, Priscian, Corippus, and Venantius Fortūnātus in the 6th, are entirely panegyric in character, and intended to do homage to the emperor or men of influence. Of all these poets, Claudian is the most considerable. He and Dracontius (towards the end of the 5th century) are among the last who take their subjects from mythology.

Didactic poetry, which suited the sober character of the Romans, was early represented at Rome. Here the Romans were in many ways superior to the Greeks. Appius Claudius Cæcus and the elder Cato were the authors of gnomic poetry. Ennius, the tragedian Accius, and several of his contemporaries, wrote didactic pieces, the satires of Lucilius and Varro were also in part didactic. It was however not till the end of the republican period that the influence of Greek literature gave predominance to the Greek epic form. It was then adopted by Varro of Atax, the orator Cicero, and above all by Lucretius, whose poem *De Rērum Nātūrā* is the only didactic poem of this period that has been preserved intact. In the Augustan age many writers were active in this field. Valgius Rūfus and Æmilius Macer followed closely in the steps of the Alexandrians. Grattius wrote a poem on hunting, a part of which still survives; Manilius an astronomical poem which survives entire. But the Georgics of Vergil throws all similar work, Greek or Latin, into the shade. Ovid employs the epic metre in his *Mĕtămŏphŏsēs* and *Hālĭeutĭca,* the elegiac in his *Fasti.*

In the 1st century A.D. Germānĭcus

translated Arātus. Columella wrote a poem on gardening; an unknown author (said to be Lucilius), the *Ætna*. The 3rd century produced the medical poem of Sammonĭcus Sĕrēnus, and that of Nĕmĕsiānus on hunting. In the 4th we have Ausŏnĭus, much of whose work is didactic; Pallādĭus on agriculture; an adaptation of Aratus and of Dĭonȳsius Perĭēgētēs by Avĭēnus, with a description of the sea-coasts of the known world in iambics; in the 5th, besides some of Claudian's pieces, a description by Rutilius Namatiānus in elegiacs of his return home. The book of Dionysius Periegetes was adapted by Priscian in the 6th century. A collection of proverbs, bearing the name of Cato, belongs to the 4th century. In most of these compositions the metrical form is a mere set off; and in the school verses of the grammarians, as in those by Tĕrentĭānus Maurus on metres, by an anonymous author on rhetorical figures, and on weights and measures, there is no pretence of poetry at all.

Epŭlōnēs (Masters of the Feast). The office of *epulo* was created 196 B.C. to relieve the Pontĭfĭcēs. It was, from the first, open to plebeians, and could be held with the great offices of state. The first duty of the *epulones* was to provide the banquets (*ĕpŭlum*) of the Capitoline deities (*see* LECTISTERNIUM). In later times they had also to provide for and superintend the public entertainments (*ĕpŭlæ*) of the people, when the senate dined on the Capitol. Such entertainments were always provided at the games given by private individuals, or by the state, on occasions of religious festivals, dedications of temples, assumptions of office, triumphs, funerals, birthdays in the imperial household, and the like. The *Collēgĭum epulonum* consisted originally of three members (*trēs vĭrī epulones*) and afterwards of seven (*septem viri epulones*), a name which it retained even after Cæsar had raised the number to ten. Its existence can be traced down to the end of the 4th century.

Equirrĭa. *See* MARS and SALĬI.

Equĭtēs (horsemen or knights). The *ĕquites* were originally a real division of the Roman army. At the beginning of the kingly period they were called *cĕlĕrēs*, and their number is said to have been 300, chosen in equal parts from the three tribes of the Ramnēs, Titiēs, and Lucĕrēs. A hundred formed a *centŭrĭa*, each *centuria* being named after the tribe from which it was taken. Thirty made a *turma*, and ten were under the command of a *dĕcŭrĭō*, while the whole corps was commanded by the *trĭbūnis cĕlĕrum*. During the course of the kingly period the body of *equites* was increased to six *centuriæ*, and the constitution of Servius Tullius finally raised it to eighteen. When the twelve new centuries were formed, consisting of the richest persons in the state, whose income exceeded that of the first class in the census, the corps of *equites* lost the exclusively patrician character which had hitherto distinguished it. At the same time its military importance was diminished, as it no longer formed the first rank, but took up a position on the wings of the *phalanx* (*see* LEGIO). The *equites*, however, retained both in the state and in the army their personal *prestige*. In the *cŏmĭtĭa* they voted first, and in *centuriæ* of their own. They were the most distinguished troops in the army. No other soldiers were in a position to keep two horses and a groom apiece, a costly luxury, although they received an allowance for the purchase and keep of their horse. After the introduction of the pay system they received three times as much as the ordinary troops; on occasion of a triumph three times the ordinary share of booty; and at the foundation of a colony a much larger allotment than the ordinary colonist. The 1,800 *equites ĕquō publĭcō*, or *equites* whose horse was purchased and kept by the state, were chosen every five years, at the census. The election was carried out in the republican period originally by the consuls, but in later times by the censors. After the general census was completed, the censors proceeded to review the *equites* (*rĕcŏgnĭtĭō*). They were arranged according to their tribes, and each of them, leading his horse by the hand, passed before the tribunal of the censors in the forum. All who had served their time, and who were physically incapacitated, received their discharge. If an *equĕs* were judged unworthy of his position, he was dismissed with the words: " Sell your horse " (*Vendĕ ĕquum*). If there were nothing against him, he was passed on with the words *Trādūc equum* (" lead your horse past "). The vacancies were then filled up with suitable candidates, and the new list (*album equitum*) read aloud. In later times, the *eques* whose name was first read out was called *princeps iŭventūtis* (*see* PRINCEPS).

During their time of service (ætat. 17–46) the *equites* were bound to serve in a number of campaigns not exceeding ten. Their service expired, they passed into the first censorial class. The senators alone among the *equites* were, in earlier times, allowed to keep their *equus publicus*, their name on the roll, and their rights as *equites* unimpaired. But of this privilege the senators were deprived in the time of the Gracchi. The number of the *equites equo publico* remained the same, as no addition was made to the sum expended by the state on the horses. Young men of property sometimes served on their own horses (*equo prīvāto*) without any share in the political privileges of the *equites*. After the Second Punic war the body of *equites* gradually lost its military position, and finally ceased to exist as a special troop. In the 1st century B.C. the members of the equestrian *centuriœ* only served in the *cŏhors prœtōrĭa* of the general, or in the capacity of military tribunes and *prœfecti* of cohorts.

The wealthy class, who were in possession of the large capital which enabled them to undertake the farming of the public revenues, and who consequently had the opportunity of enriching themselves still further, had long enjoyed a very influential position. In 123 B.C. the *lex iūdĭcĭārĭa* of Gaius Gracchus transferred to the possessors of the equestrian census (400,000 *sestertĭī*, or about £3,500) to right to sit on juries, which had previously belonged exclusively to members of the senate. Thus an *ordŏ ĕquester* or third order, standing between the senate and the people, was formed, which began to play an important part in politics. Its members were called *equites* even if they were not enrolled in the *centuriœ equitum*. The contests between the senate and the *equites* for the exclusive right to sit on the juries, continued with varying fortunes until the end of the Republic. Augustus allowed the *ordo equester* to continue in existence as a class in possession of a certain income; but the old fiscal and judicial system came to an end, and the *ordo* accordingly lost all its former importance. On the other hand, the *equites* proper rose into a position of great consideration. They were divided into six *turmœ*, headed by an imperial prince as *princeps iuventutis*. True, they had no further standing as a corporation: but the emperor employed them in a variety of confidential posts. The title *eques equo* [1] *publico* was necessary for the attainment of the office of military

tribune, and for a number of the most important military posts. The power of conferring or withdrawing the title came at length to rest with the emperor alone.

The review of the *equites*, which used to take place every five years, now became a mere ceremony, and was united by Augustus with the ancient annual parade (*transvectĭŏ*) of the 15th July. The *equites*, in full uniform, rode through the Forum to the Capitol, past the temple of Mars or *Hŏnŏs*. After the transference of the seat of government to Constantinople, the *turmœ equitum* sank into the position of a city corporation, standing between the senate and the guilds, and in possession of special privileges. The insignia of the *equites* were a gold ring and a narrow purple border on the tunic (*see* TUNICA). At the *transvectio* they wore the *trăbĕa*, a mantle adorned with purple stripes, and crowns of olive. From 67 B.C. the fourteen first rows were assigned to them *hŏnŏris causā*.

Erănŏs. The Greek term for an organized club or society, for the purposes of feasting and amusement, whose members were called *ĕrănistœ*. Sometimes it would be formed in connexion with the worship of particular deities. Sometimes, again, the object of an *eranos* would be mutual assistance by advances of money. The government encouraged these clubs, because their corporate character made it easier to settle with expedition any legal proceedings arising out of their affairs. Trials of this kind, for refusal to pay subscriptions, or to repay loans, had to be settled within a month.

Erătŏ. *See* MUSES.

Erătosthĕnēs. A Greek savant, born at Cȳrēnē in 275 B.C. He completed his philosophical education at Athens, where he made his first public appearance as a lecturer on philosophy. His learning won him such a reputation that Ptolemy III (Euergĕtēs) invited him in 247 B.C. to Alexandria, and made him librarian there in the place of Callĭmăchus. He is said to have died, after nearly losing his eye-sight, by voluntary starvation in 195 B.C. He was a master of science in all its branches—history, geography, geometry, astronomy, philosophy, grammar and poetry. As a writer he treated an astonishing variety of subjects, and won thereby the name of *Pentathlŏs* (or master in the five great exercises of the arena). It is said that he was the first person who assumed the name of *Philŏlŏgŏs*, or friend of science. His

---

[1] The state did not actually provide the horse.

greatest service consists in the fact that he was the founder of scientific geography. His greatest work was his *Gĕōgrăphĭca*, in three books. The first was upon physical geography, the second treated mathematical geography on the basis of the measurement of degrees, discovered by himself. The subject of the third was chorography, based upon a map of his own drawing. The work is unfortunately lost, and known only by what later writers, especially Străbo, have preserved. Historical investigation owes a great deal to the *Chrŏnŏgrăphĭa*, in which he undertook to found chronology on astronomy and mathematics. His comprehensive book on Ancient Comedy was a contribution to the history of literature. The *Cătălŏgoi* was a work on astronomy and mythology, in which were collected the fables of the ancient writers on the constellations, with an enumeration of the single stars in each group. A dry compendium, called the *Catastĕrismoi*, containing a mere enumeration of 44 constellations, with 475 stars, and the fables attached, is based on the great work of Eratosthenes. His poetical efforts were a short epic called *Hermēs*, and a celebrated elegy, the *Erĭgŏnē*. Besides the compendium above mentioned, and some fragments, we have a letter of Eratosthenes to Ptolemy Euergetes on the doubling of the cube, and an epigram on the same subject.

Erĕbŭs. In Greek mythology, the primeval darkness, springing, according to Hesiod, from Chaos, brother of Night, and father by her of Æthēr and Hēmĕra (day). The word is commonly used of the lower world, filled with impenetrable darkness.

Erechthēum (*Erechtheĭŏn*). The original sanctuary of the tutelary deities of Athens, Athēnē Pŏlĭas, (the goddess of the city), Pŏseidōn, and Erechtheus. It was situated on the Acrŏpŏlis. The old temple, said to have been built by Erechtheus, was burnt by the Persians in 480 B.C. The restoration was perhaps begun as far back as the time of Pĕrĭclēs, but, according to the testimony of an inscription in the British Museum (no. xxxv), was not quite finished in 409. The new temple was, even in antiquity, admired as one of the most beautiful and perfect works of the Attic-Ionic style. It was 65 feet long and nearly 36 broad; and was divided into two main parts. Entering through the eastern portico of six Ionic pillars, one came into the *cella* of Athene Polias, with an image of the goddess, and a lamp that was always kept burning. To the solid wall at the back was attached the Erechtheum proper. Here were three altars, one common to Poseidon and Erechtheus, the other to Hēphæstus and the hero Būtēs. Connected with this, by three doors, was a small front-chamber, with seven half columns adorning the western wall, and three windows between them. This chamber was approached through a hall attached to the north side of the temple, adorned with seven Ionic columns in front, and one on each side. Under this was a cleft in the rock, said to have been made by the stroke of Poseidon's trident during his contest with Athene for the possession of the Acropolis. Corresponding to this on the south side was a small hall, supported not by pillars, but by căryātĭdĕs. This was called the Hall of Cŏrē, and it probably contained the tomb of Cecrops. From it a step led down to a court, once walled round, in which were the Pandrŏsēum (*see* PANDRŎSŎS), the sacred olive tree of Athene, and the altar of Zeus Herkeĭŏs. On the east side, in front of the temple of Athene Polias, stood the altar on which the great hecatomb was offered at the Panathēnæa. (*See* plan of ACROPOLIS.)

Erechtheus. A mythical king of Athens. According to Homer he was the son of Earth by Hēphæstus, and brought up by Athēnē. Like that of Cecrops, half of his form was that of a snake—a sign that he was one of the aborigines. Athene put the child in a chest which she gave to the daughters of Cecrops, Agraulŏs, Hersē, and Pandrŏsŏs, to take care of; forbidding them at the same time to open it. The two eldest disobeyed, and in terror at the serpent-shaped child (or according to another version, the snake that surrounded the child), they went mad, and threw themselves from the rocks of the Acropolis. Another account made the serpent kill them. Erechtheus drove out Amphictyŏn, and got possession of the kingdom. He then established the worship of Athene, and built to her, as goddess of the city (*Pŏlĭas*), a temple, named after him the Erechtheum. Here he was afterwards worshipped himself with Athene and Poseidōn. He was also the founder of the Panathenaic festival. He was said to have invented the four-wheeled chariot, and to have been taken up to heaven for this by Zeus, and set in the sky as the constellation of the charioteer. His daughters were Orīthyia and Procris (*see* BOREAS and CEPHALUS). Originally identi-•fied with Erichthŏnĭus, he was in later times distinguished from him, and was regarded as his grandson, and as son of Pandīŏn and Zeuxĭppē. His twin brother was Būtēs, his sisters Procnē and Phĭlŏmēla. The priestly office fell to Butes, while Erechtheus assumed the functions of royalty. By Praxĭthĕa, the daughter of Cephissus, he was father of the second Cecrops (see PANDION, 2), of Mētīŏn (see DÆDALUS); of Crĕūsa (see ION), as well as of Prŏtŏgĕneia, Pandōra, and Chthŏnĭa. When Athens was pressed hard by the Eleusinians under Eumolpus, the oracle promised him the victory if he would sacrifice one of his daughters. He chose the youngest, Chthŏnĭa; but Protogeneia and Pandora, who had made a vow with their sister to die with her, voluntarily shared her fate. Erechtheus conquered his enemies and slew Eumolpus, but was afterwards destroyed by the trident of his enemy's father, Poseidon.

Ergănē. *See* ATHENE

Ergīnus. King of the Mĭnўæ of Orchŏmĕnus, son of Pŏseidōn (or Clŷmĕnus, according to another account), and one of the Argonauts. At the games of Poseidon at Onchēstŏs, Clymenus was killed by a stone thrown by a noble Theban. Erginus in consequence compelled the Thebans to pay him an annual tribute of 100 oxen for twenty years. Hērăclēs, on returning from his slaughter of the lions of Cĭthærōn, came upon the heralds who were collecting the tribute. He cut off their noses and ears, tied their hands round their necks, and told them that this was the tribute they might take back to their master. War broke out. Heracles armed the Thebans with the arms hanging in the temples, the Minyæ having carried off all the others ; slew Erginus, destroyed Orchomenus, and forced the Minyæ to pay double the tribute to Thebes. The sons of Erginus were the mythical architects Agămēdēs and Trŏphōnĭūs.

Erichthŏnĭus. (1) Son of Dardănus (see DARDANUS) and Bateia, father of Trōs. (2) *See* ERECHTHEUS.

Erĭgŏnē. Daughter of Icărĭŭs, who hanged herself for grief at the murder of her father, and was taken up to heaven as the constellation of the Virgin. (*See* ICARIUS.)

Erinna. A famous Greek poetess, a native of the island of Telos. She was a friend and contemporary of Sappho, with whom she lived in Mĭtўlēnē. She flourished about 600 B.C. and died at the age of nineteen. The poem by which she is best known is

the *Spindle* (*Elăkătē*) consisting of 300 hexameters. A few verses of this, and a few epigrams, are all of her writing which survives. A poem in five Sapphic strophes, addressed to Rome as the mistress of the world, is from the hand of a much later poetess, Melinnō, who probably lived in Lower Italy at the time of the war with Pyrrhus, or the First Punic War.

Erīnўĕs (Greek). The goddesses of vengeance. Homer speaks sometimes of one, sometimes of several, but without any definite statement about either number, name, or descent. Hesiod makes them the daughters of Gaia (Earth), sprung from the blood of the mutilated Urănus. According to others they were the daughters of Night

(*Nyx*) or of the Earth, and Darkness (*Skŏtŏs*). Euripides is the earliest writer who fixes their number at three, and considerably later we find them with the names Allēcto ("She who rests not"), Tīsĭphŏnē ("Avenger of murder"), and Mĕgæra ("The jealous one.") They are the avengers of every transgression of natural order, and especially of offences which touch the foundation of human society. They punish, without mercy, all violations of filial duty, or the claims of kinship, or the rites of hospitality ; murder, perjury, and like offences ; in Homer even beggars have their Erinys. The punishment begins on earth and is continued after death. Thus they pursue Orestēs and Alcmæōn, who slew their mothers, and Œdĭpūs for the murder of his father and marriage with his mother, without regard to the circumstances by which their offences were excused. Their principle is a simple one, "an eye for an eye, and a tooth for a tooth." In spite of their terrible attributes as goddesses of vengeance they were called *Semnai* (the honourable) and *Eumĕnĭdĕs* (the kindly). For the punishment of the evil secures the well-being of the good, and by pursuing and destroying transgressors the Erinyes prove themselves benevolent and beneficent. They were worshipped in Athens under the name of *Semnai*, and had a shrine on the Arĕŏpăgus, and the hill of Cŏlōnus. Fresh water and black sheep were offered to them in sacrifice. The terrible picture drawn of them by Æschylus in his *Eumenides*, as women like Gorgons, with snakes for hair, bloodshot eyes, grinding teeth, and long black robes with blood-red girdles, was softened down in later times. They appear as maidens of stern aspect, with snakes in their hair or round their girdles and arms, torches, scourges, or sickles in their hands, generally in the costume of huntresses, and sometimes with wings as a sign of the swiftness of their vengeance (*see* cut).

The Furies (*Fŭrĭœ* or *Dīrœ*) of the Roman poets are a mere adaptation of the Greek Erinyes. They are generally represented as torturing the guilty in the world below, but as sometimes appearing on earth, to excite to crime and throw men into madness.

Ĕrĭphȳlē. In Greek mythology, sister of Adrastus and wife of Amphĭărăŭs. (*See* ADRASTUS.) Bribed with a necklace by Pŏlȳnīcēs, she prevailed on her husband to take part in the war of the Seven Chiefs against Thebes, in which he met his death. (*See* AMPHIARAUS.) In revenge for this she was slain by her son Alcmæōn. (*See* ALCMÆON.)

Ĕrĭs. The goddess of discord, fighting, and quarrelling in the Greek mythology. In Homer she is sister and companion of Ares, and like him insatiate of blood ; in Hesiod she is daughter of Night, and mother of trouble, oblivion, hunger, pain, murder and carnage, brawls, deceit, and lawlessness. She was the only one among the gods who was not bidden to the marriage of Pēleus and Thĕtĭs. In revenge she threw a golden apple among the guests, and thus gave occasion for the Trojan War. (*See* TROJAN WAR.) Side by side with this destructive Eris was a beneficent Eris, the

sister, according to Hesiod, of the other. She was the personification of noble rivalry, and is represented as stimulating even dullards to exertion.

Ĕrōs. The god of love among the Greeks. His name does not occur in Homer ; but in Hesiod he is the fairest of the deities, who subdues the hearts of all gods and men. He is born from Chaos at the same time as the Earth and Tartărus, and is the comrade of Aphrŏdītē from the moment of her birth. Hesiod conceives Eros not merely as the god of sensual love, but as a power which forms the world by inner union of the separated elements ; an idea very prevalent in antiquity, especially among the philosophers. But according to the later and commoner notion, Eros was the youngest of the gods, generally the son of Aphrodite by Ares or Hermēs, always

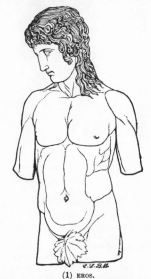

(1) EROS.

Probably as the *Genius of Death.* Ascribed to the time of Hadrian. Found at *Centocelle* (Rome, Vatican).

a child, thoughtless and capricious. He is as irresistible as fair, and has no pity even for his own mother. Zeus, the father of gods and men, arms him with golden wings, and with bow and unerring arrows, or burning torches. Antĕrōs, the god of mutual love, is his brother, and his companions are Pŏthŏs and Hĭmĕrŏs, the personifications of longing and desire, with

Peithō (Persuasion), the Muses, and the Graces. In later times he is surrounded by a crowd of similar beings, Erōtĕs or loves. (For the later legend of Eros and Psȳchē, *see* PSYCHE.)

One of the chief and oldest seats of his worship was Thespĭæ in Bœōtĭa. Here was his most ancient image, a rough, unhewn stone. His festival, the Erōtĭa or Erōtĭdĭa, continued till the time of the Roman Empire to be celebrated every fifth year with much ceremony, accompanied by gymnastic and musical contests. Besides this he was paid special honour and worship in the gymnasia, where his statue generally stood near those of Hermes and Hērăclēs. In the gymnasia Eros

(2) EROS.
(Rome, Capitoline Museum.)

was the personification of devoted friendship and love between youths and men ; the friendship which proved itself active and helpful in battle and bold adventure. This was the reason why the Spartans and Cretans sacrificed to Eros before a battle, and the sacred band of youths at Thebes was dedicated to him ; why a festival of freedom (*Eleuthĕrĭa*) was held at Samos in his honour, as the god who bound men and youths together in the struggle for honour and freedom ; and why at Athens he was worshipped as the liberator of the city, in memory of Harmōdĭus and Ăristŏgītōn.

In works of art Eros was usually represented as a beautiful boy, close upon the age of youth. In later times he also appears as a child with the attributes of a bow and

arrows, or burning torches, and in a great variety of situations. The most celebrated statues of this god were by Lȳsippus, Scŏpās, and Praxĭtĕlēs, whose Eros at Thespiæ was regarded as a master-piece, and unsurpassable. The famous torso in the Vatican, in which the god wears a dreamy, lovelorn air, is popularly, but probably erroneously, traced to an original by Praxĭtĕlēs (fig. 1). The Eros trying his bow, in the Capitoline Museum at Rome, is supposed to be the copy of a work by Lȳsippus (fig. 2).

The Roman god Āmor or Cŭpīdō was a mere adaptation of the Greek Eros, and was never held in great honour.

Ersē or Hersē. *See* CECROPS.

Erymanthian Boar. *See* HERACLES.

Erȳsichthōn. (1) Son of the Athenian Cĕcrops.

(2) Son of Trĭŏpās in Thessaly. For desecrating the sacred enclosure of Dēmētĕr, and felling an oak consecrated to the goddess, he was punished with insatiable hunger. Having consumed all that he had, he was supported by his daughter Mestra, to whom her lover Pŏseidōn had given the power of transferring herself into any shape that she liked. In various forms she continually got herself sold, and then returned to her father with the proceeds. At last Erysichthon was reduced to devouring his own limbs.

Erȳtheia. One of the Hespĕrĭdĕs.

Eryx. Son of Pŏseidōn (or, according to another account, of Būtēs) and Aphrŏdītē, who was worshipped on Eryx, a mountain in Sicily. He was king of the Ĕlȳmī in the neighbourhood of the mountain. Eryx was a powerful boxer, but was slain in a fight with Hērăclēs about a bull, which had run away from the latter, and which Eryx had appropriated.

Essēdărĭi. *See* GLADIATORES.

Essēdum. *See* CHARIOTS.

Etĕŏclēs. Son of Œdĭpūs king of Thebes and Iŏcastē, brother of Pŏlynīcēs and Antĭgŏnē. He broke the agreement he had made with his brother to give him the kingdom of Thebes for one year. Polynices accordingly organized the campaign of the Seven Chiefs against Thebes, and fell in single combat with Eteocles. (*See* ŒDIPUS *and* SEVEN AGAINST THEBES.)

Euadnē. Daughter of Iphĭs, wife of Căpăneus. Her husband fell before Thebes, and at his funeral she threw herself into the flames of the pyre and was consumed with the corpse.

Euandrŏs. *See* EVANDER.

Eubūlus. A Greek poet of the Middle Comedy, who flourished about 370 B.C. His plays were mainly on mythical subjects, and parodied the earlier tragedians, especially Euripides. One hundred and four pieces were attributed to him, of which only a few fragments have been preserved written in pure and well chosen language.

Euclīdēs (*Eukleidēs*). (1) A philosopher of Mĕgăra, a disciple of Socrates, and the founder of the Megarian school.

(2) A Greek mathematician who taught at Alexandria about 300 B.C. All that is known of his life is that he was held in much esteem, and won the high regard of king Ptolemy I. His labours in putting the discoveries of former mathematicians into order, completing them, and expounding them with matchless clearness and conciseness, won him the position of the founder of mathematical literature. We still possess his *Elements of Mathematics* (*Stoicheia*) which have been used until quite lately as the foundation of all geometrical text books. These are in 15 books; the 13th and 14th, however, are said to have been added by Hypsĭclēs of Alexandria about 160 B.C. Besides this, we have what are called his *Data*, or 95 geometrical propositions as an introduction to geometrical analysis, an astronomical work entitled *Phœnŏmĕna*, and a musical work on the division of the canon. Some other treatises, probably from the hands of other authors, have been attributed to Euclid. Such are the *Elements of Optics and Catoptrics*, and the *Introduction to Music*.

Eudēmus. A Greek philosopher, native of Rhodes. After Theophrastus he was the chief of Aristotle's disciples, and was the author of the seven books of *Eudemian Ethics*, which have come down to us among his writings.

Euhēmĕrus. A Greek writer, who flourished about 300 B.C. Under the title of *Hĭĕrā Anagrăphē*, or Sacred History, he wrote a work which purported to explain the whole mythology, on the theory of the apotheosis of men who by their bravery and cleverness had deserved well of mankind. Zeus, for instance, his kinsfolk and children, he represented as in reality an ancient family of Cretan kings. To prove his assertion he appealed to a representation of the whole primitive history of the world, from the time of Urănŭs onwards, given on a golden pillar in the temple of Zeus on the island of Panchæa. This, he said, he had discovered in the neighbourhood of India, when sailing round the coast of Arabia on the commission of king Cassander. The work of Euhemerus, of which only fragments now remain, was well known in Rome, where it was translated and adapted by Ennius. The method of rationalizing or analysing mythology into the history of human kings, heroes and adventurers, is called Euhemerism, after its founder.

Eulŏs. *See* DIONYSUS.

Eumæus. The faithful swineherd of Odysseus, who gave his master a friendly welcome on his return home in the guise of a beggar, and aided him in the slaughter of the suitors. (*See* ODYSSEUS.)

Eumēlus. *See* EPOS (1).

Euměnĭdēs. *See* ERINYES.

Euměnĭus. One of the Roman writers of panegyrics on the emperors. He was born about 250 A.D. at Augustŏdūnum (*Autun*) in Gaul; was tutor to Constantius Chlorus, and for a long time accompanied him on his campaigns. Later on, he settled in his native city, where he gave instruction in rhetoric. In 296 he delivered an oration on behalf of the restoration of schools (*Pro Restaurandīs Schŏlīs*). Besides this, three other speeches are attributed to him. These are panegyrics on Constantius Chlorus and Constantine, spoken at Trèves in 296, 310, and 311 A.D. His tact and cleverness distinguish him from the other panegyrical writers of that age.

Eumolpus. In Greek mythology, the son of Pŏseidōn and Chĭŏnĕ, the daughter of Bŏrĕās and Orīthўia. After his birth he was thrown by his mother into the sea, but his father rescued him and brought him to Æthiopia, to his daughter Benthĕsĭkўmē. When he was grown up, Endīus, the husband of Benthesikyme, gave him one of his daughters in marriage, but he desired the other as well, and was accordingly banished, and came with his son Ismărus or Immarādus to the Thracian king Tĕgyrĭus in Bœotia. As successor to this king he marched to the assistance of his friends the Eleusinians against the Athenian Erechtheus, but was slain with his son. (*See* ERECHTHEUS.) According to another story, Immaradus and Erechtheus both fell, and the contending parties agreed that the Eleusinians should submit to the Athènians, but should retain the exclusive superintendence of the mysteries of Eleusis, of which Eumolpus was accounted the founder. He was also spoken of as a writer of consecrational hymns, and as having discovered the art of cultivating the vines and trees in general. The Eumolpĭdæ, his descendants, were the hereditary priests of the Eleusinian ritual.

Eunăpĭus. A Greek rhetorician, born at Sardis in 347 A.D. In 405 he wrote biographies of twenty-three older and contemporary philosophers and sophists. In spite of its bad style and its superficiality, this book is our chief authority for the history of the Neo-Platonism of that age. We have also several fragments of his continuation of the chronicle of Herennĭus Dexippus. This continuation, in fourteen books, covered the period from 268 to 404 A.D., and was much used by Zosĭmus.

Eunēus. *See* JASON and HYPSIPYLE.

Eunŏmĭa. *See* HORÆ.

Eupătrĭdæ. The members of the ancient noble families of Attica. After the abolition of royal power they found themselves in exclusive possession of political rights, and distinguished from the *Gĕŏmŏrī* or agriculturists, and the *Dēmĭurgī* or mechanics. The constitution of Solon deprived them of this privilege. But their landed property, and the priestly dignities which they had possessed of old, assured them a certain influence for a considerable time.

Euphēmus. Son of Pŏseidōn and Eurōpa, daughter of Tītўus, husband of Lăŏnŏmē, the sister of Hēraclēs. His father conferred on him the gift of moving so swiftly over the sea that his feet remained dry. He was originally one of the Mīnўæ of Pănŏpeūs in Phōcis, but afterwards settled on the promontory of Tænărum in Lăcōnĭa, and took part in the Calydonian hunt and the expedition of the Argonauts. When the Argonauts came to the lake of Trītōn, Triton gave Eumolpus a clod of earth, and Mēdēa prophesied that if he threw this into the entrance of the lower world at Tænarum, his descendants of the tenth generation would be masters of Libya. The clod, however, was lost in the island of Thēra, and his descendants were compelled to hold possession of this island, from which at length, in the seventeenth generation, Battus came forth and founded Cўrēnē in Libya.

Euphŏrĭōn. (1) Son of Æschylus, the great tragedian. He flourished about 450 B.C., and after his father's death put on the stage four of his pieces, which had not yet been performed, and gained the prize. He also exhibited tragedies of his own, not without success.

(2) A Greek poet and writer of the Alexandrian age and in the Alexandrian style. He was born about 276 B.C., at

Chalcis in Eubœa, and died holding the post of librarian at the court of Antiochus the Great, king of Syria. Besides works [on mythology and history] in prose, he wrote epics, elegies, and epigrams in obscure and unfamiliar language. His poems were much valued by the Romans. Cornelius Gallus, in particular, thought very highly of them, and took him as his model in his own elegies.

Euphrānōr. A Greek artist, born at Corinth about 360 B.C. He was equally distinguished as a painter, and as a sculptor in bronze and marble. He also wrote a treatise on symmetry and form. Among his statues one of the most celebrated was the Păris, in which it was easy to recognise the threefold character : the judge of divine beauty, the lover of Helen, and the slayer of Achilles. In his paintings, if we may believe the ancients, he was the first who gave true expression to the grandeur and dignity of divine and hēroic form. [Pliny, *N. H.* xxxiv 27, xxxv 128.]

Euphrŏsўnē. (*See* CHARĬTES.)

Eupŏlis. Eupolis is coupled with Aristophanes as a chief representative of the Old Attic Comedy. He was born about 446 B.C., and died before the end of the Pelponnesian War. He made his first appearance as a dramatist in his seventeenth year, and carried off the prize seven times. According to a badly attested story, he was drowned in the sea by Alcĭbĭădēs in revenge for his treatment of him in one of his plays. We still have the titles, and some fragments, of fifteen of his pieces. He was at first on terms of intimate friendship with his contemporary Aristophanes, but an estrangement afterwards set in, and the two poets attacked each other with great bitterness. Eupolis is praised by the ancients for the splendour of his imagination, the coherence with which his plots are developed, the high quality of his patriotism, the grace and majesty of his language, and the telling character of his wit. The fragments that remain show great mastery of form. Like Aristophanes, he made an attempt to stem the current of moral degeneracy setting in at his time.

Eupompus. A Greek painter, native of Sĭcўŏn, who flourished about 400 B.C. He was the founder of the Sicyonian school of painting. which laid great emphasis on professional knowledge. [Pliny, *N. H.* xxxv 75.]

Eurĭpĭdēs. The third of the three great Attic tragedians. He was born in the island of Sălămīs. in 480 B.C., on the very day of the great battle. His father Mnēsarchus is said to have been a tradesman or tavern-keeper, his mother Clītō a seller of herbs. His parents, however, must have had some means, judging by the fact that they gave him a careful gymnastic education to fit him for the athletic contests. This was because they had misinterpreted an oracle given them before his birth which promised the child crowns of victory. Euripides is said in his boyhood really to have gained the prize in a public contest of this kind, but in fact he was destined to win victories in a very different arena. He associated much with the philosophers Anaxăgŏrās and Socrates, with the latter of

* BUST OF EURIPIDES.
(Naples Museum.)

whom he enjoyed an intimate friendship during the whole of his life. He also had instruction from the sophists Protăgŏrās and Prŏdĭcus. Thus he received the best of education in philosophy and rhetoric. It was in his twenty-fifth year (B.C. 455) that he first put a tetralogy on the stage. He did not win a prize till his forty-third year, and seems indeed to have been victorious only four times in all; but he was none the less indefatigable in writing tragedies. He took a lively interest in the important events and the public questions of the time; but personally he kept aloof from

public life, avoided society, and lived mostly in the enjoyment of an excellent library, amid his studies and poetical creations.

He was twice unfortunate in his marriage, a fact which may have encouraged him in his surly, unsociable ways. His first wife, Chœrĭlē, he had to divorce for infidelity. She bore him three daughters, the youngest of whom, who was named after her mother, put several of her father's tragedies on the stage after his death. His second wife, Mĕlĭtō, parted from him at her own desire. In 409, at the age of 71, he left Athens; it was said to get away from the ceaseless attacks of the comedians, and from his domestic troubles. He went to Magnēsĭa in Thessaly, where he was received as a guest of the city. Thence he went on to Pella to the court of Archĕlāus, king of Macedonia, who had gathered round him a number of poets and artists, and who treated him with great respect. Here he spent the last two years of his life and died B.C. 405. According to a story for which there is little authority, he was torn to pieces by a pack of hounds when returning from a nocturnal festivity.

The number of his tragedies is variously given as seventy-five, seventy-eight, and ninety-two. Eighteen have come down to us: the *Alcēstis*, *Andrŏmăchē*, *Bacchœ* (or the arrival of Dĭonȳsus at Thebes and the murder of Pentheus), *Hēcŭba*, *Hĕlĕna*, *Electra*, the *Hērăclīdœ* (or Dēmŏphŏŏn of Athens protecting the descendants of Hērăclēs against the persecution of Eurystheus); *Heracles in Madness*, the *Suppliants* (or the mothers of the Seven Chiefs who had fallen before Thebes, at whose prayers Theseus compelled the Thebans to bury the dead heroes); *Hippŏlȳtus*, *Iphĭgĕnĭa at Aulis*, *Iphĭgĕnĭa among the Tauri*, *Iŏn*, *Mēdĕa*, *Orestēs*, *Rhēsus*, the *Trŏădĕs* (or the royal house of Troy after the conquest of the city); the *Phœnissœ* (so called after the chorus of Phœnician maidens, an incident in the story of Etĕŏclēs and Pŏlȳnīcēs); and a satyric drama, the *Cyclops*, the only example of this style of composition which has survived. The earliest of these pieces in point of time is the *Alcestis*, performed in B.C. 438. It is also noticeable because, although not a satyric drama in the proper sense, it has comic features towards the end, and was actually performed at the end of a tetralogy in place of a satyric drama. The *Bacchœ*, on the other hand, was written in Macedonia in the poet's last years, and performed after his death at the same time as the *Iphigenia at Aulis*. The genuineness of the *Rhesus* was doubted even in antiquity. A great number of fragments have survived from about sixty pieces, and in particular from the *Phäethōn*.

The tragedies of Euripides are of very unequal merit. Some of them, for instance the *Hippolytus* and the *Bacchæ*, attain the lofty style of Sophocles, others approach it, as the *Medea* and *Iphigenia in Tauris*. But others, as for instance the *Andromache* and *Electra*, are very carelessly put together. His strong point is not artistic composition, well contrived disposition, or the coherent design which gives the inner motive of the action. It is sufficient, in support of this statement, to call attention to his habit of prefixing to every piece a prologue, explaining the story to the spectators, and connected loosely (if at all) with the play; to the very slight connexion between the chorus and the action, and to his liking for bringing in a *deŭs ex māchĭnā* to cut a difficult knot. On the other hand, it must be allowed that Euripides is a master in the art of devising pathetic situations, and shows extraordinary power in representing human passion, especially the resistless might of love in the case of women.

In his religious views he differs essentially from Æschylus and Sophocles. With Euripides the gods are not moral powers, and fate is not so much the result of a higher dispensation as a perverseness of accident. The lack of grandeur is also a point which distinguishes him from his great predecessors. Instead of their sublime ideas he gives us maxims of worldly wisdom, often to all appearance dragged in without occasion. The motives of action are not so pure as in Æschylus and Sophocles, and the characters of the heroes are not raised above the level of ordinary life, but brought down to it. So fond is he of giving prominence to the faults of women, that he has been called a woman-hater. He pays more attention to the course of politics than his predecessors, and is indeed influenced by political considerations in his sketches of character. In deference to the democratic leanings of his public, he makes his kings cruel tyrants, without dignity or majesty, and the heroes of the Peloponnese, in particular, he treats with unconcealed dislike. His dialogues are often overloaded with rhetoric and sophistical dialectic. But, in spite of all these faults, for which the spirit of the age is mainly responsible, he is a great poetical

genius. He was very popular with his contemporaries, and has been still more so with succeeding generations. The tragedians of the next age made him their model and pattern without qualification, and the Roman poets preferred paraphrasing his dramas to those of the other tragedians.

Eurōpē (Lat. *Eurōpa*). A figure in Greek mythology. In Homer she is the daughter of Phœnix, in the later story of the Phœnician Agēnōr, and sister of Cadmus. Zeus, in the shape of a bull, carried her over the sea to Crete, where she bore him Mīnōs, Rhădămanthȳs, and according to the later legend, Sarpēdōn also. Zeus left her with Astĕrĭōn, king of Crete, who brought up her sons and left them his kingdom. She was worshipped in Crete under the name of Hellōtis, especially at Gortyn, where she was supposed to have been wedded with Zeus, and to have borne him her sons. A festival called Hellōtia was held in her honour, at which her bones were carried in a wreath of myrtle.

Eurўălē. *See* GORGON.

Eurўălus. Son of Mēcisteus, one of the Epĭgŏnī, and with Sthĕnĕlus, the companion of Dĭŏmēdēs before Troy.

Euryclēa (*Eurykleia*). The nurse of Odysseus, who brought up his son Tēlĕmăchus. When her master had returned home in the disguise of a beggar, she recognised him by a scar while bathing his feet. On a hint from him she kept silence, and afterwards was the first who brought to Pēnĕlŏpē the news of her husband's return and of the slaughter of the suitors.

Eurўdĭcē. *See* ORPHEUS.

Eurўnŏmē. *See* CHARITES.

Eurўpўlus. (1) Son of Pŏseidōn and Astȳpălæa, king of the Mĕrŏpĕs of Cōs. He was slain by Hērăclēs, who had been driven on to the coast on his return from Troy. The struggle was a hard one, but Heracles was assisted by Zeus. The daughter of Eurypylus, Chalcĭŏpē, became mother of Thessălus by Heracles.

(2) Son of Tēlĕphus and Astȳŏchē. Astyoche, bribed by her brother Priam with the present of a golden vine, persuaded Eurypylus to bring the last succour to the Trojans shortly before the fall of the city. After performing deeds of bravery, he fell at the hand of Neoptŏlĕmus.

(3) Son of Euæmōn, king of Ormĕnĭŏn in Thessaly, one of the suitors of Helen. He was among the bravest of the Greek heroes who fought before Troy, and of his own accord offered to engage Hector in single

combat. In the later story he appears in connexion with the worship of Dĭonȳsus. At the division of the Trojan spoil he received an image of Dionysus, made by Hēphæstus, and presented to Dardănus. This had been kept in a chest as a Pallădĭum. When Eurypylus opened the chest and beheld the image he fell into a madness. The Delphic oracle promised that he should be healed if he dedicated the image in a spot where men offered barbaric sacrifices. Accordingly he dedicated it at Arŏë in Achaia, where an offering of the fairest youth and fairest virgin was made annually to Artĕmĭs. The bloody act was abolished, and the gentle service of Dionysus introduced in its place.

Eurÿsăcēs (*Eurÿsăkēs*). Son of Ajax and Tecmēssa. *See* AJAX (2).

Eurystheus. Son of Sthĕnĕlus and Nĭcippē. (*See* PERSEUS.) He was king of Mўcēnæ, and through the cunning of Hēra got power over Hērăclēs, and imposed upon him the celebrated twelve labours. In pursuing the children of Heracles, and attempting to bring about by force their expulsion from Attica, he was defeated and slain in his flight by Hyllus. (*See* HYLLUS.)

Eurȳtus. (1) Son of Mĕlăneus, father of Iphĭtus and of Iŏlē, king of Œchălĭa in Thessaly or Messenia. According to a later story he dwelt in Eubœa. He was one of the most famous archers in antiquity. According to Homer he ventured to challenge Apollo to a contest of skill, and was slain in his youth for his presumption. In the later story he and his son Iphitus are slain by Hērăclēs, his former disciple in archery, for having insolently refused him his daughter Iole in marriage. (*See* HERACLES.) Iphitus gave his bow to Odysseus, who slew the suitors with it.

(2) One of the *Mŏlĭŏnĭdæ* (*see* MOLIONIDÆ).

Eusĕbĭus. The father of ecclesiastical history. He was born at Cæsărēa in Phœnicia in 264 A.D. In 315 he became bishop of that city, and died in 340. He was one of the most learned men of his time, and holds a high position both among the historians and the apologists of Christianity. His greatest work is his Church History. This work is in ten books, beginning with the rise of Christianity, and coming down to 314 A.D. It was much used by later writers, and was, about 403 A.D., translated into Latin by Tyrannius Rufīnus of Aquīlēĭa, who continued it down to the death of Theodosius (A.D. 395). The apologetic writings of

Eusebius are the *Præpărătĭō Evangĕlĭca* in fifteen books, and the *Dēmonstrătĭō Evangĕlĭca* in twenty. They are both, but especially the former, a rich storehouse of information on antiquity, particularly on the philosophy and religion of the Greeks. Of still greater importance is his Chronicle (*Chrŏnĭcŏn*), a work founded upon extracts from the now lost writings of previous historians. Its first book, the *Chrŏnŏgrăphĭa*, contains a general ethnographical history of the world, arranged from the creation to 325 A.D. The second, called the *Chronological Canon*, consisted of parallel chronological tables of the names of rulers and the most important events since 2017 B.C. Only fragments of the original work remain ; but we have both books in an Armenian translation, and the second in the Latin version of Hĭĕrŏnȳmus. Among the other works of Eusebius we may mention : (1) A sketch of the topography of Palestine, in two books. The second alone survives, both in the original and in the translation of Hieronymus. (2) A biography, in four books, of the emperor Constantine, who had shown favour to Eusebius and had been baptized by him. This work is strongly coloured by personal feeling. (3) A panegyric on Constantine.

Eustăthĭus. (1) *Eustathius Măcrembŏlīta*, a Greek writer of romance. He was a native of Constantinople, and belonged to the upper class. His *floruit* is perhaps to be assigned to the 9th century A.D. He was the author of a rather tasteless love story, in eleven books, about Hysmīnĭăs and Hysmīnē.

(2) *Eustathius of Constantinople*, appointed archbishop of Thessălŏnĭca in 1160 A.D. Previously to this he had been a deacon, and professor of rhetoric in his native city, and had written a comprehensive commentary on the Homeric poems. The commentary, which is characterized by learning remarkable for that age, is made up of extracts from older writers, and is therefore of great value. A commentary by the same author on Dĭonȳsĭus Pĕrĭēgētēs, and a preface to a commentary on Pindar, have also survived.

Euterpē. *See* MUSES.

Euthȳna (a giving of account). All officials at Athens without exception were bound, at the expiration of their term of office, to give an account of their administration. The authorities to whom it was given were the *Lŏgistæ*, supported by ten *Euthȳnī*. (*See* LOGISTÆ.) Within thirty days after the term of office had come to an end, these functionaries issued, to all whom it might concern, a public notice to lay before them any complaints they might have to make against the retiring officials. In case such complaints were made, the matter was brought to an issue by legal procedure. No official was allowed to leave the country, or take any measure affecting his property, or take another office, before his account was given [Aristotle, *Const. of Athens*, 48].

Eutrŏpius. A Roman historian who took part in the expedition of Julian against the Parthians in 363 A.D. In 378, under Valentinian, he wrote and dedicated to this emperor a sketch of Roman history (*Brĕvĭărĭum ab Urbe Condĭtā*) in ten books, from the earliest times to the death of Jovian in 364. The language is simple, and the narrative intelligent and impartial. The work was useful and concise, and became very popular. Succeeding writers down to the Middle Ages, and especially Hĭĕrŏnȳmus and Orosĭus, used it a great deal. It was several times turned into Greek, indeed as early as 380 by Pæänĭŏs, whose translation has been preserved almost entire. The work of Eutropius was enlarged and continued by Paulus Dĭăcŏnus, who, in the last part of the 8th century A.D., added six books to it. It was also used in the *Histŏrĭa Miscella*, or Collective History, and has continued to be a favourite school book down to our own day.

Evander (Gr. *Euandrŏs*, the good man), a figure in Latin mythology. He was said to be the son of Hermēs and an Arcadian nymph. Sixty years before the Trojan War he led a Pelasgian colony to Lătium from Pallantĭŏn in Arcadia, and founded a city Pallantēum near the Tiber, on the hill which was afterwards named after it the Palatine. Further it was said that he taught the rude inhabitants of the country writing, music, and other arts; and introduced from Arcadia the worship of certain gods, in particular of Pan, whom the Italians called Faunus, with the festival of the Lupercālĭa which was held in his honour. Evander was worshipped at Rome among the heroes of the country (*see* INDIGITES), and had an altar on the Aventine hill. But the whole story is evidently an invention of Greek scholars, who derived the *Lupercalia* from the Arcadian *Lȳcœa*. The name *Euandros* is a mere translation of the Italian *Faunus*, while Carmenta is an ancient Italian goddess.

Pallas, the son of Evander, is in like manner a creation of the poets. In Vergil he marches, at the command of his father, to assist Ænēās, and falls in single combat with Turnus.

Eventus, or properly *Bŏnus Eventus* (lucky or happy event). In Roman religion, a god of rural prosperity, like the Greek *Agăthŏdæmōn*, whose image was in later times transferred to the Italian deity. In the course of time *Bonus Eventus* gained the more general meaning of the friendly fortune which secures a lucky issue to undertakings. The god had a temple of his own on the *Campus Martius*, in the neighbourhood of the Pantheon.

Evŏcātī (those who are summoned or called out). The term applied in the Roman army to soldiers who had served their time and obtained their dismissal, but who, on the general summoning them by name, returned to the service on condition of receiving certain privileges. These were, exemption from all service except in battle, a rank and pay equal to those of the centurions, and prospect of advancement. The enlistment of *evocati* was especially common in the civil wars. Sometimes they were distributed in the legion, sometimes they formed a special and select troop, divided into *centŭrĭæ*. We sometimes find them, in isolated instances, under the early Empire. On the difference between them and the *vĕtĕrānī*, *see* VETERANI.

Evŏcātĭō (calling out). The term for the solemn summons given to the tutelary gods of a besieged city to leave it, and to migrate to Rome. The Romans always vowed, at the same time, to build them a temple at Rome. An example of a deity " evoked " in this way was Jūnō Rēgīna, who was originally worshipped at Veii, but afterwards had a temple in Rome on the Aventine.

Exĕcūtĭō. *See* BONORUM EMPTIO.

Exĕdra. An alcove, or semi-circular extension of the colonnade in a Greek *gymnăsĭum*. It was furnished with seats on which the philosophers usually sat to talk with their disciples. In private houses the *exedra* was a room intended for conversation, fitted with a bench running round the wall.

Exercĭtus. *See* STIPENDIUM, CASTRA, LEGION, DILECTUS, SACRAMENTUM.

Exĭlium (= banishment). (1) *Greek.* Among the Greeks exile was the legal punishment for homicide (*see* EPHETÆ). It was also, at times, a political measure, adopted especially in times of civil disturbance, and might carry with it *ātīmīa* and loss of property, except in the case of ostracism (*see* OSTRACISM).

(2) *Roman.* Among the Romans there was, originally, no such thing as a direct expulsion from the city. But a man might be cut off from fire and water, the symbol of civic communion, which of course practically forced him to leave the country. This *interdictīŏ āquœ et ignis* was originally inflicted by the *comītīa centŭrīāta*, and later by the permanent judicial commissions appointed to try certain serious offences, as, for instance, treason, arson, and poisoning. In case of the capital charge the accused was always free to anticipate an unfavourable verdict, or the *interdictio aquœ et ignis*, by withdrawing

into voluntary exile. The *exilium* involved the lesser *dēmĭnūtĭŏ cāpĭtĭs*, or loss of citizenship, if the banished person became citizen of another state; or if the people declared the banishment to be deserved; or if the *interdictio aquœ et ignis* was pronounced after he had gone into exile. It was only in very serious cases that a man's property was also confiscated. Real banishment was first inflicted under the Empire. (*See* DEPORTATIO and RELEGATIO.)

Exŏdĭum. A play of a lively character acted on the Roman stage at the end of a serious piece. It corresponded in character to the satyric drama of the Greeks. The place of the *exodium* was originally taken by the dramatic *sătŭra*, and later by the *Atellāna* and *Mīmus*.

Exōmĭs. *See* CHITON.

F

Făbĭus Pictŏr. *See* ANNALISTS.

Fabrī. The mechanics, carpenters, smiths, etc., in the Roman army. After the end of the republican age they formed an independent corps in every army, and were employed especially in the restoration of bridges, siege and defence works, artillery, etc. They were under the command of the *prœfectus fabrum*, or chief engineer, who was chosen by the general in chief, and was immediately responsible to him.

Făbŭla Pallĭāta and Tŏgāta. *See* COMEDY.

Fămĭlĭa. The Latin name for a household community, consisting of the master of the house (*păter fămĭlĭās*), his wife (*māter familiās*), his sons and unmarried daughters (*fĭlĭī* and *fīlĭœ familiās*), the wives, sons, and unmarried daughters of the sons, and the slaves. All the other members of the family were subject to the authority of the *pater familias*. (For the power of the husband over his wife, *see* MANUS.) In virtue of his paternal authority (*patrĭa pŏtestās*), the *păter familias* had absolute authority over his children. He might, if he liked, expose them, sell them, or kill them. These rights, as manners were gradually softened, were more and more rarely enforced; but they legally came to an end only when the father died, lost his citizenship, or of his own will freed his son from his authority. (*See* EMANCIPATIO.) They could, however, be transferred to another person if the son were adopted, or the daughter married. A son, if of full age, was not in any way interfered with by the *patria potestas* in the exercise

of his civil rights. But in the exercise of his legal rights as an individual, he was dependent always on his father. He could, for instance, own no property, but all that he acquired was, in the eye of the law, at the exclusive disposal of his father. The *pater familias* alone had the right of making dispositions of the family property by mortgage, sale, or testament.

Family Names. *See* NAMES.

Fannĭus. *See* ANNALISTS.

Farmers of Public Taxes. *See* PUBLICANI and TELONÆ.

Farnese Bull. *See* DIRCE.

Fascēs. The Latin name for a bundle of rods of elm or birch, tied together by a red strap, and enclosing an axe, with its head outside. The *fasces* were originally the emblem of the king's absolute authority over life and limb, and as such passed over to the high magistrates of the Republic. In the city, however, the latter had to remove the axe and to lower the rods in the presence of the popular assembly as the sovereign power. The lowering of the *fasces* was also the form in which the lower officials saluted the higher. The king was preceded by lictors bearing twelve *fasces*, and so were the consuls and proconsuls. The proconsuls, however, were, since the time of Augustus, only allowed this number if they had actually been consuls previously. The dictator had twenty-four *fasces*, as representing the two consuls, and his *măgistĕr ĕquĭtum* had six. Six was also the number allotted to the proconsuls and proprætors outside the city, and in the imperial age to those proconsuls who had provinces in virtue of their having held the prætorship. The prætors of the city had two, the imperial legates administering particular provinces had five *fasces*. One was allotted to the *flāmĕn Dĭālis*, and (from or after B.C. 42) to the Vestal Virgins. *Fasces* crowned with bay were, in the republican age, the *insignia* of an officer who was saluted as *Impĕrātor*. During the imperial age, this title was conferred on the emperor at his accession, and soon confined exclusively to him. The emperor was accordingly preceded by twelve *fasces laurĕātī*. The lictors held their *fasces* over the left shoulder. But at funerals, the *fasces* of a deceased magistrate, and his arms, were carried reversed behind the bier.

Fascĭnum (Latin). Enchantment by the evil eye, words, or cries, exercised on persons (especially children), animals, and things, as, for instance, on a piece of ground. The word was also applied to the counter-charm, by which it was supposed that the enchantment could be averted, or even turned against the enchanter. Amulets of various kinds were employed as counter-charms. They were supposed either to procure the protection of a particular deity, or to send the enchanter mad by means of terrible, ridiculous, or obscene objects. The name *fascinum* was thus specially applied to the *phallus*, which was the favourite counter-charm of the Romans. An image of this *fascinum* was contained in the *bulla* worn as an amulet by children, and was also put under the chariot of a general at his triumph, as a protection against envy.

Fastī (*dĭēs*). (Roman.) Properly speaking, the court-days, on which the prætor was allowed to give his judgments in the solemn formula *Do Dīco Addīco*, and generally to act in his judicial capacity. The name was further applied to the days on which it was lawful to summon the assembly and the senate (*dĭēs cŏmĭtĭālēs*). For these days might be used as court days in case the assembly did not meet: while on *dies fasti* proper no meeting of the *comitia* could take place. The opposite of *dies fasti* were the *dies nĕfasti*, or days on which on account of purifications, holidays, *fĕrĭœ*, and on other religious grounds, the courts could not sit, nor the *comitia* assemble. (*See* FERIÆ.) The *dies rĕlĭgĭōsī* were also counted as *nefasti*. (*See* RELIGIOSI DIES.) Besides the 38–45 *dies fasti* proper, the 188–194 *dies comitiales*, the 48–50 *dies*

nefasti, and 53–59 *dies religiosi*, there were 8 *dies intercīsī*, which were *nefasti* in the morning and evening because of certain sacrifices which took place then, but *fastī* for the remaining hours. There were also 3 *dies fissi* (split days), which were *nefasti* until the conclusion of a particular proceeding; *e.g.* the removal of the sweepings from the temple of Vesta on June 15th, but *fasti* afterwards.

The division of days into *fasti* and *prŏfesti*, or holidays and workdays, only affected private life, though many *dies nefasti*, as *feriœ*, would be identical with *dies fasti*.

The list of the *dies fasti* was of immense importance as affecting legal proceedings, and indeed all public life. For a long time it was in the hands of the *pontĭfĭcēs*, and was thus only accessible to the patricians; but at last, 304 B.C., Gnæus Flāvĭus published it and made it generally accessible. This list, called simply *Fasti*, was the origin of the Roman calendar, which bore the same name. In this calendar the days of the year are divided into weeks of eight days each, indicated by the letters A—H. Each day has marks indicating its number in the month, its legal significance (F = *fastus*, N = *nefastus*, C = *comitiālis*, EN = *intercisus*). The festivals, sacrifices, and games occurring on it are also added, as well as notices of historical occurrences, the rising and setting of the stars, and other matters. No trace remains of any calendar previous to Cæsar; but several calendars composed after Cæsar's reform have been preserved. Ovid's *Fasti* is a poetical explanation of the Roman festivals of the first six months. We have also many fragments of calendars, painted or engraved on stone, belonging to Rome and other Italian cities; for it was common to put up calendars of this kind in public places, temples, and private houses. There are two complete calendars in existence, one an official list written by Fūrĭus Dĭŏnȳsĭus Phĭlŏcălus in 354 A.D., the other a Christian version of the official calendar, made by Pŏlĕmĭus Silvĭus in 448 A.D.

The word *Fasti* was further applied to the annual lists of the triumphs, high officials, consuls, dictators, censors, and priests. These lists were originally, like the other *fasti*, made out by the *pontifices*. Some fragments of them have survived, among which may be mentioned the *Fasti Căpĭtŏlīnī*, so called from the Roman Capitol, where they are now preserved.

They were originally, in 36–30 B.C., engraved on the marble wall of the *Rēgĭa*, or official residence of the *Pontĭfex Maxĭmus*, and afterwards continued first to 12 B.C., and afterwards to 13 A.D.

Fātă. *See* MŒRÆ (PARCÆ), NEMESIS, TYCHE, FORTUNA.

Fātŭus. *See* FAUNUS.

Faucēs. *See* HOUSE.

Faunālĭă. *See* FAUNUS.

Faunus. "The well-wisher" (from *făvēre*) [or perhaps "the speaker" (from *fārī*)]. One of the oldest and most popular deities, who was identified with the Greek Pan on account of the similarity of their attributes. (*See* PAN.) As a good spirit of the forest, plains, and fields, he gave fruitfulness to the cattle, and was hence called *Inŭŭs*. With all this he was also a god of prophecy, called by the name of *Fātŭus*. He revealed the future in dreams and strange voices, communicated to his votaries while sleeping in his precincts upon the fleeces of sacrificed lambs. A goddess of like attributes, called *Fauna* and *Fatua*, was associated in his worship. She was regarded sometimes as his wife, sometimes as his daughter (*see* BONA DEA). Just as Pan was accompanied by the *Pănĭskoi*, or little Pans, so the existence of many *Fauni* was assumed besides the chief *Faunus*. They were imagined as merry, capricious beings, and in particular as mischievous goblins who caused night-mares. In fable Faunus appears as an old king of Latium, son of Pĭcus, and grandson of Sāturnus, father of Lătīnus by the nymph Mărīca. After his death he is raised to the position of a tutelary deity of the land, for his many services to agriculture and cattle-breeding. Two festivals, called *Faunālĭa*, were celebrated in his honour, one on the 13th of February, in the temple on the island in the Tiber, the other on the 5th of December. The peasants brought him rustic offerings and amused themselves with dancing.

Făvōnĭus. *See* ZEPHYRUS.

Fēlĭcĭtās. The personification of good fortune among the Romans. She was worshipped in various sanctuaries in Rome, her attributes being the cornucopia and the herald's staff.

Fērālĭa. The last day of the Roman festival called the Părentālĭa. (*See* MANES.)

Fērĭæ (Latin). Holidays, dedicated to the worship of some deity. A distinction was drawn between *feriæ prīvātæ*, or holidays observed by *gentēs*, families, and individuals, and *feriæ publĭcæ*, or public holidays. Public holidays were either fixed or movable, or occasional. The fixed holidays (*feriæ stătīvæ*), were forty-five in number, and were celebrated every year on a definite day and registered accordingly in the calendar. The movable holidays (*feriæ conceptīvæ*) were also annual, but were held on changing days, and had therefore to be announced beforehand by the consuls, or in their absence by the prætor. The occasional holidays (*impĕrātīvæ*) were commanded on special occasions by the authorities with the consent of the *pontĭfĭcēs*. Such were, for instance, the *supplĭcātĭōnēs*, a solemn service to the gods to celebrate a victory or the like. One of the principal movable festivals was the *Fērĭæ Lătīnæ*. This was originally a celebration by the Latin race held on the Alban mountain in honour of Jupiter Lătĭāris. It was subsequently transformed by Tarquinius Superbus into a festival of the Latin League. Its most notable ceremony consisted in the sacrifice of white bulls, a portion of whose flesh was distributed to each of the cities of the league represented at the sacrifice. If any city did not receive its portion, or if any other point in the ceremonial was omitted, the whole sacrifice had to be repeated. Originally it lasted one day, but afterwards was extended to four. It was then celebrated in part on the Alban hill by the Roman consuls, in presence of all the magistrates: in part on the Roman Capitol, a race being included in the performance. It was announced by the consuls immediately after their assumption of office, nor did they leave Rome for their provinces until they had celebrated it. The date therefore depended on that of the assumption of office by the higher magistrates.

Fērōnĭa. An old Italian goddess, of Sabine origin, but also much worshipped in Etrūrĭa. She seems originally to have been regarded in the same light as Flōra, Lībĕra, and Vĕnus. The Greeks called her a goddess of flowers ; on coins she is represented as a girl in the bloom of youth, with flowers in her hair. She was also worshipped as the goddess of emancipation from slavery. She had a very celebrated shrine at the foot of Mount Sōractĕ in Etruria, where the whole neighbourhood used to bring her rich votive offerings and the firstfruits of the field. The annual festivals served as fairs, such was the crowd of people who flocked to them. The mythical king Erūlus of Præneste was regarded as her son. He had three lives, and had to be slain three times by Evander in consequence.

Fescennīnī (*lūdī*). Rural festivals, of great antiquity, held by the population of Etruria and Latium, and named, from some cause which cannot now be ascertained, from Fescennīum in South Etruria. At harvest festivals, at the feast of Silvānus, and others of the kind, and at weddings, the young men would appear in rough masks or with faces painted with vermilion, bantering each other for the amusement of the spectators in rude and indecent jests. These were thrown into a rough kind of metre, originally no doubt the Saturnian. The Italians had at all times a keen sense of the ridiculous, and a love for personal attack; tendencies which were much encouraged by their gift for improvization, and pointed repartee. In Rome these games were taken up by the young men at public festivals, and combined with a comic imitation of the religious dances introduced from Etruria in 390 B.C. to avert a pestilence. In this form they are supposed to have given birth to the dramatic *sătŭra*. (*See* SATURA.) The license of personal abuse ended by going so far that it had to be restrained by a law of the Twelve Tables. The *Fescennīnī versūs* were gradually restricted to weddings, and the word came to mean the merry songs sung when the bride was brought home.

Festus. (1) Sextus Pompeius Festus; a Roman scholar, who probably flourished in the 2nd century A.D. He made an abridgment of the great lexical work of Verrius Flaccus, *De Verbōrum Signĭfĭcātū*, using at the same time other works of the same author. The abridgment, arranged in alphabetical order, and containing twenty books, superseded its original. Of Festus' own work we have only the second half (the letters M–V) in a very imperfect state. The rest is preserved in a meagre epitome made by the priest Paulus, in the age of Charles the Great. Slight as are these remains of the original work of Verrius, they are very valuable for the fulness of select grammatical and antiquarian notices which they contain.

(2) A Roman historian, who about 369 A.D. wrote an abridgment of Roman history (*Brĕvĭārium Rērum Gestārum Pŏpŭlī Rōmānī*) founded partly on *Eutrŏpĭus*, partly on *Flōrus*, and dedicated to the emperor Valens.

Fētĭālēs (Latin). A body of men whose business it was to maintain the forms of international relationship. The institution was universal in Italy. In Rome its introduction was ascribed to Numa or Ancu Martīus. Here the *fetiales* formed a *collēgĭum* of twenty' members elected for life, and filled up vacancies in their body by co-optation. They were in early time exclusively patricians, but at all times i was necessary that they should belong te the highest classes. Their duties were, in case of conflicts arising with other nation to give an opinion, based on the merits o the case, upon the question of war o peace; to give, or to demand in person satisfaction by delivering up the guilty individual, to declare war or conclud peace, and to give the sanction of religion to both acts. On all these occasions they went out wearing their sacerdotal dress and the *insignia* of their office. Before them one of the members of the *collēgĭum* carried the sacred plants which they had gathered on the Capitol after asking permission of the magistrate on whose commission they were acting, king, consul, o prætor. If satisfaction was to be demanded from another nation, a number of *fetiales* was sent under the leadership of a speaker the *păter patrātus*, with the forms of a special ceremonial. Supposing satisfaction given, they took the offender with them, and parted in peace; if the other party asked for time to consider the matter, this was granted to ten days and extended to thirty If, after this, satisfaction were not given, the speaker made a solemn protest, adding that the Roman people would now take the matter into its own hands. Supposing now that war were decided on, the speaker in presence of at least three witnesses uttered the solemn declaration, and threw a bloody lance into the enemy's territory After the war with Pyrrhus this ceremony was performed at the Column of War near the temple of Bellōna, and the declaration of war was carried to the general in command according to the form prescribed by the law of the *fetiales*. If it was in contemplation to bring the war to a close, and the enemy had not made an unconditional surrender, the *fetiales*, with the authority of a *sĕnātūs consultum*, and in the name of the State, either concluded a truce for a definite number of years, or a formal alliance. The general, if he made peace without the consent of the Roman people did so on his own responsibility and with out binding the State. If the people were dissatisfied with the terms, the *fetiales*

elivered the general up, naked and hand-
ound, to the enemy. In case of the
liance being concluded, the *pater patratus*
ook a flint stone, which was preserved in
the temple of Jūpĭter Fĕretrĭus, and slew a
wine therewith, first reading out the terms
of the alliance, and then appealing to Jupiter,
a case the Roman people maliciously broke
the treaty, to smite them as he would
nite the animal. He then signed the
ocument, which bound the *collegium* of
etiales to see that the treaty was observed.
t was also usual for the civil magistrate
a make oath by Jupiter, Mars, and
uĭrīnus, on a sceptre which was likewise
aken from the temple of Jupiter Feretrius.
ince the Second Punic War there is but
ttle mention of the action of the *fetiales*,
ut its existence can be traced as late as the
iddle of the 4th century A.D.

Fibŭla (Greek *pĕrŏnē*). A clasp for
astening garments, resembling our brooches

FIBULÆ.
(Grivaud de la Vincelle, *Arts et Métiers*, pl. xli, xliii.)

r safety-pins. It consisted of a hoop and
needle, sometimes elastic, sometimes fixed
y a joint. Some *fibulæ* were in the shape
f buckles. (*See* illustrations.)

Fĭdēs. The Roman personification of
onour in keeping word or oath. As *Fides
ublĭca*, or Honour of the People, this
oddess had a temple on the Capitol,
ounded by king Numa, to which the
amĭnēs of Jūpĭter, Mars, and Quĭrīnus rode
a a covered chariot on the 1st of October.
t the sacrifice they had their right hands
rapped up to the fingers with white
ands. The meaning of the covered chariot
as that honour could not be too carefully
rotected : of the covered right hand, that
ae right hand, the seat of honour, should
e kept pure and holy. The goddess was
apresented with outstretched right hand
nd a white veil. Her attributes were ears
f corn and fruits, joined hands, and a
irtle-dove.

Fire, God of. *See* HEPHÆSTUS **and**
ULCANUS.

Firmĭcus Māternus (*Iūlĭus*). (1) A
heathen writer, a native of Sicily. About
354 A.D. he published, in eight books, a
work on astrology (*Mäthĕsĕŏs Librī VIII*)
which he had begun under Constantine.
It gives a vivid picture of the gross superstition of that age with regard to the supposed influence of the stars in human
fortunes.

(2) Another writer of the same time, and
of the same age, was a convert to Christianity, who, about 347 A.D., published a work
on the error of the heathen religions (*De
Errōrĕ Prŏfānārum Rĕlĭgĭŏnum*) in which
he called on the emperors Constantĭus and
Constans to extirpate the last remains of
heathenism.

Fiscus. The emperor's private purse, as
distinguished from the public treasury
(*ærārĭum*). It was instituted by Augustus,
and was under the exclusive control of the
emperor. The chief sources from which it
was replenished were the entire revenues
of the imperial provinces, the produce of
unclaimed estates, and of confiscations.
The main items of fiscal expenditure were
the army, the fleet, and war material, the
salaries of officials, the provision of corn
for Rome, postal communication, and the
public buildings. For the officials who
administered the *fiscus*, *see* PROCURATOR.

Flābellum. A fan. *See* CLOTHING.

Flāmĕn (from *flāre ;* one who blows or
kindles the sacrificial fire). The special
priest of a special deity among the Romans.
There were 15 *Flāmĭnēs ;* three higher
ones (*Flamines māiōrēs*) of patrician rank :
these were the *flamen Dĭālĭs* (of Jupiter),
Martĭālĭs (of Mars), and *Quĭrīnālĭs* (of
Quĭrīnus). The remaining 12 were *flamines
mĭnōrēs*, plebeians, and attached to less
important deities, as Vulcānus, Flōra,
Pōmōna, and Carmenta. Their office was
for life, and they could only be deprived of
it in certain events. The emblem of their
dignity was a white conical hat (*ăpex*),
made out of the hide of a sacrificed animal,
and having an olive branch and woollen
thread at the top. This the *flamines* were
obliged to wear always out of doors, indeed
the *Flamen Dialis* had originally to wear
it indoors as well. They were exempted
from all the duties of civic life, and excluded at the same time from all participation in politics. In course of time, it is
true, they were allowed to hold urban
offices, but even then they were forbidden
to go out of Italy.

The *Flamen Dialis* was originally not

allowed to spend a night away from home: in later times, under the Empire, the Pontífex could allow him to sleep out for two nights in the year. Indeed, the *Flamen Dialis*, whose superior position among the flamens conferred upon him certain privileges, as the *tŏga prœtexta*, the *sella cŭrūlĭs*, a seat in the senate, and the services of a lictor, was in proportion obliged to submit to more restrictions than the rest. He, his wife, their children, and his house on the Palatine were dedicated to this god. He must be born of a marriage celebrated by *confarrĕātĭŏ*, and live himself in indissoluble marriage. (*See* MARRIAGE.) If his wife died, he resigned his office. In the performance of his sacred functions he was assisted by his children as *cămillĭ*. (*See* CAMILLUS.) Every day was for him a holy day, so that he never appeared without the *insignia* of his office, the conical hat, the thick woollen *toga prœtexta* woven by his wife, the sacrificial knife, and a rod to keep the people away from him. He was preceded by his lictor, and by heralds, who called on the people to stop their work, as the flamen was not permitted to look upon any labour. He was not allowed to cast eyes on an armed host, to mount, or even to touch, a horse, to touch a corpse, or grave, or a goat, or a dog, or raw meat, or anything unclean. He must not have near him, or behold, anything in the shape of a chain. Consequently there must be no knots, but only clasps, on his raiment; the ring on his finger was broken, and any one who came into his house with chains must instantly be loosened. If he were guilty of any carelessness in the sacrifices, or if his hat fell off his head, he had to resign. His wife, the *flămĭnĭca*, was priestess of Jūno. She had, in like manner, to appear always in her *insignia* of office, a long woollen robe, with her hair woven with a purple fillet, and arranged in pyramidal form, her head covered with a veil and a kerchief, and carrying a sacrificial knife. On certain days she was forbidden to comb her hair. The chief business of the flamens consisted in daily sacrifices: on certain special occasions they acted with the Pontĭfĭcēs and the Vestal Virgins. The three superior flamens offered a sacrifice to *Fĭdēs Publĭca* on the Capitol on the 1st October, driving there in a two-horse chariot. During the imperial period *flamines* of the deified emperors were added to the others.

Flămĭnĭca. *See* FLAMEN.

Flāvĭānum Iūs. *See* JURISPRUDENCE.

Fleet. *See* SHIPS, WARFARE, and CLASSIARII.

Flōra. A goddess, originally Sabine, of the spring and of flowers and blossoms in general, to whom prayers were offered for the prospering of the ripe fruits of field and tree. She was also regarded as a goddess of the flower of youth and its pleasures. Her worship was said to have been introduced into Rome by the Sabine king Tĭtus Tātĭus, and her special priest, the *Flămĕn Flōrālĭs*, to have been appointed by Numa. A temple was erected to her in the *Circus Maxĭmus* in 238 B.C. At the same time theatrical festival, the *Flōrālĭa*, was instituted at the behest of the Sibylline books. At this feast the men decked themselves and their animals with flowers, especially roses; the women put aside their usual costume, and wore the gay dresses usually forbidden. The scene was one of unrestrained merriment. From 173 B.C. the festival was a standing one, and lasted six days, from April 28, the anniversary of the foundation of the temple, to May 3. For the first five days of the games, for the superintendence of which the curule ædiles were responsible, there were theatrical performances, largely consisting of the very indecent farces called mimes. On the last day goats, hares, and other animals were hunted in the circus. The people were regaled during the games with porridge, peas, and lentils.

Flora was in later times identified with the Greek Chlōrĭs (*see* HORÆ). In works of art she was represented as a blooming maiden, decked with flowers.

Flōrus (*Iūlĭus*). (1) A Roman historian of the time of Hadrian, 117–138 A.D. He wrote, in two books, a history of the wars of Rome, from the time of the kings to the closing of the temple of Janus under Augustus (25 B.C.). In the title, as we have it, the book is called an excerpt from Livy (*Epĭtŏmē de Tĭtĭ Lĭvĭĭ bellōrum omnĭum annōrum DCC*). But this is not an adequate description of it. Florus, it is true, has used Livy a great deal, though not exclusively, and the work is really a panegyric on the greatness of Rome. It is the production of rhetoricians, as is shown by the tasteless and inflated language, with its poetical echoes of Vergil and Horace, and its tendency to exaggeration. Numerous gross errors testify to the insufficiency of the writer's knowledge. Worthless as it is, the book was much read and quoted in the Middle Ages.

(2) A Roman poet, who was on familiar terms with Hadrian, and who has left a few pieces. He is probably to be identified with the African rhetorician and poet Publius Annius Florus, the author of a dialogue, which still survives, on the question whether Vergil is an orator or a poet.

Flute (Gk. *aulŏs* = pipe, Lat. *tībĭa* = shin-bone). This was, in antiquity, an in-

(1) PHRYGIAN DOUBLE FLUTE.
(*Museo Pio Clement.*, *V*, tailpiece.)

trument resembling the modern clarionet, made of reed, box, bay, ivory, or bone. Its invention was ascribed to Athēnē (*see* MARSYAS). The wind was introduced by a mouthpiece, with one or two tongues, put on at every performance. In addition to the holes at the mouth it often had holes at the sides provided with stops. Besides the single flute, the double flute was sometimes used, especially at theatrical performances, funerals, sacrifices, and festal processions. This consisted of two flutes played at the same time by means of either one or of two separate mouthpieces. The two flutes together had as many notes as the *Sÿrinx* (*see* SYRINX). The right hand played the bass flute (*tĭbĭa dextra*), the left hand the treble (*tĭbĭa sĭnistra*). The two flutes were either of equal length and similar form, or unequal length and similar form, or unequal length and dissimilar form. In the Phrygian double flute, one pipe was straight, the other larger and bent at the end like a horn (see fig. 1). It is a peculiarity of Greek and Roman flutes that they were sometimes provided with a check-band covering the mouth, its opening fitted with metal. Through this opening were fixed the mouthpieces of the double flute (fig. 2). The long pipe is also an invention of the ancients.

Fons or **Fontus**. The Roman god of springs, son of Jānus and Jūturna, who had an altar in Rome on the Jānĭcŭlum. A special festival, the *Fontĭnālĭa*, was held

in his honour on the 13th October, at which garlands were thrown into the springs, and laid round the wells.

Fools, Feast of. *See* FORNACALIA.

Fordĭcīdĭa or **Hordĭcīdĭa.** A festival celebrated in Rome in honour of Tellūs, goddess of the earth, on 15th April. (*See* TELLUS.)

Fornācālĭa. A Roman festival held in February in honour of Fornax, the goddess of ovens. It was said to have been founded by Numa, and may be described as a thanksgiving for the earliest enjoyment of the newly gathered corn. It was held in the Forum by the Cūrĭæ, or ancient unions of kinsmen, under the superintendence of the *Cūrĭŏ Maxĭmus*, or president of the masters of the *curiæ*. Corn was baked in ovens in the ancient fashion. All who missed the festival were called fools (*stulti*), as being supposed not to know which was their *curia*, and had to make an offering at the so-called Feast of Fools (*stultōrum fērĭæ*) on the 17th February, the day of the *Quĭrĭnālĭa*.

Fortūna. The goddess of good luck, wor-

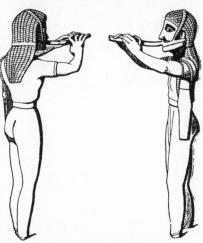

(2) *FLUTE-PLAYER WITH MOUTHPIECE.
Bronze, from Dodona (Carapanos, pl. 10.)

shipped from remote antiquity in Italy. Her worship was supposed to have been introduced into Rome by king Servius Tullius, popularly believed to be her favourite and confidant. He was said to have founded her oldest sanctuaries, as, for instance, that of *Fors Fortuna*, or lucky chance, on the right bank of the Tiber below Rome. To this a pilgrimage was made down the stream by land and water on the anniversary of its foundation (June 26). As time went on, the worship of Fortuna became one of the most popular in Italy. She was worshipped at a great number of shrines under various titles, given according to various circumstances of life in which her influence was supposed to have effect. These titles were *Fortuna Prīmĭgĕnĭa*, who determines the destiny of the child at its birth; *Fortūna Publĭca* or *Pŏpŭlī Rōmānī*, the tutelary goddess of the state; *Fortuna Cæsărĭs* or *Augusta*, the protectress of the emperor; *Fortuna prīvāta*, or of family life; *Fortuna patrĭcĭa, plēbeia, ĕquestrĭs*, of the different orders, classes, and families of the population; *Fortuna lībĕrum*, of children; *vir-gĭnālĭs*, of maidens, *mŭlĭĕbrĭs*, of women; *Fortuna vīrīlĭs* was the goddess of woman's happiness in married life, of boys and of youths, who dedicated to her the first cuttings of their beards, calling her from this *Fortuna barbāta*. Other epithets of *Fortuna* were *victrix*, or giver of victory; *dux* or *cŏmĕs*, the leader or attendant; *rĕdux*, who brings safe home; *tranquilla*, the giver of prosperous voyages. This *Fortuna* was worshipped with *Portūnus* in the harbour of Rome. There were also *Fortuna bŏna* and *māla*, good and evil Fortune; *blanda* or flattering, *obsĕquens* or yielding, *dūbĭa* or doubtful, *viscāta* or enticing, *brĕvĭs* or fickle, and *mănens* or constant. Trajan at last founded a special temple in her honour as the all-pervading power of the world. Here an annual sacrifice was offered to her on New Year's Day. In works of art she was represented with the same attributes as the Greek *Tўchē (see* TYCHE). *For-tuna*, in her general character as a goddess of Nature and Fate, had an ancient and celebrated temple, in which oracles were delivered, at Prænestĕ and Antĭum (*see* cut).

*GODDESSES OF FORTUNE.
(Fortunæ Antiates, coin of gens Rustia, from Gerhard, Ant. Bildw. taf. iv, 3, 4.)*

Fŏrum (Latin). An open space used for political meetings, judicial proceedings, and traffic. In Rome the oldest forum was the *Forum Rōmānum*, afterwards the Campo

Vaccino, a long and irregular four-side space, lying between the Capitol and tl Palatine, in the direction of WNW. an ESE (*see* plan, p. 241). In the course of tin it was surrounded with temples, publ buildings, and basilicas. It was originall used as a market place, but was earl monopolised for public purposes. Ther were, however, shops and stalls along tl northern and southern sides, where a active trade was carried on. Here, i particular, the money-changers carried o their business. The *Forum* was divide into the *Cŏmĭtĭum* with the *Rostra* speaking platform, and the *Forum* prope where the Romans habitually spent muc of their morning transacting private public business. (*See* COMITIUM and Ro TRUM.) Under the Empire a number other *fora* sprang up in its neighbourhoo which were used for legal and other bus ness. They were adorned with great magn ficence, having a temple in their midst, an colonnades round them, which were ope for ordinary traffic. There were thus *For* of Cæsar, Augustus, Vespasian, Nerva, an Trajan, the last the largest and most sple did of all (*see* plan, p. 241). There wer besides, several fora for market busines as the Forum *bŏărĭum* or cattle-market, *p cārĭum* or fish-market, *hŏlĭtōrĭum*, or veg table-market, and so on. The word *foru* was also applied to any place which forme the local centre of commerce and jurisdi tion: so that such local names as *Foru Iūlĭī* (now Frejus) were very common.

Freedmen. The emancipation of slav was tolerably common, both among Greel and Romans. The Greeks had no speci legal form for the process, and consequent no legal differences in the *status* of free men. At Athens they took the positic of resident aliens, and lay under certai obligations to their liberators as patron They could be called to legal account f any injury done to their patrons, and condemned could be given back to them slaves, or sold by the state. In the latte case the price was paid to their liberators.

Among the Romans emancipation (*mănn missĭō*) was a lucrative proceeding for tl State, as a tax of 5 per cent. on the valu of the slave was paid on his being set fre Emancipation was either formal or info mal. (1) Of formal emancipation ther were three kinds: (*a*) the *manumissio vi dictā*, in which the owner appeared wit the slave before an official with judicia authority, who in later times would gene ally be the prætor or governor of the province. A Roman citizen, usually one of the magistrates' lictors, laid a staff (*vindicta*) on the slave's head and declared him free. The master, who was holding the slave with his hand, thereupon signified his consent, and let him go, as a symbol of will. Here the master declared his slave free in his will, or bound his heir to emancipate him. The heir might adopt the formal or informal process. Constantine added a new form, the *manumissio in ecclēsĭā*, or emancipation in the church in presence of the congregation. (2) Informal

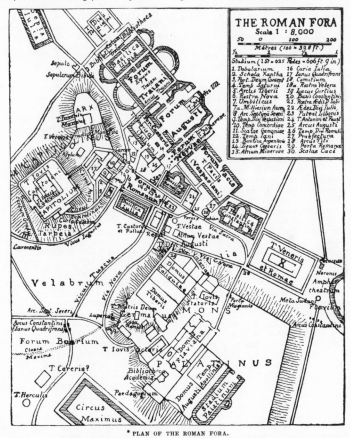

* PLAN OF THE ROMAN FORA.

(From Droysen's *Historischer Handatlas*, 1886, p. 11, with slight alterations.)

liberation (*mănŭ mīsĭt*). This formality was in later times restricted to the simple declaration of the master in the presence of the magistrate. (*b*) The *manumissio censu*, in which the master enrolled the slave's name in the list of citizens. (*c*) The *manumissio testāmentō*, or manumission by emancipation took place in virtue of an oral declaration on the part of the master, in presence of friends (*inter ămĭcŏs*), or by letter (*pĕr epistŭlam*), or by inviting the slaves to the master's table.

The freedmen were called *lībertī* in relation to the liberator (e.g. *libertus Cæsăris*)

and *lībertīnī* in their legal relation to the
State. After formal emancipation they at
once became Roman citizens, and members
of the urban tribes and of the lowest classes
in the *centŭrĭœ*, with full right of voting.
But, not being free born, they were not
eligible to office, and were excluded from
military service. The latter was, however,
the case only till the 1st century B.C. They
obtained the right to be enrolled in the
country tribes several times in the republican period, but not permanently till the
imperial age. Their descendants, however,
were, as being free-born (*ingĕnŭī*), admitted into all the tribes, and in the second,
or at least in the third generation, eligible
to office. Informal emancipation conferred
only practical freedom without civic rights.
It was not until 17 A.D., under Tiberius,
that freedmen of this kind won the *com-
mercĭum*, or the right of acquiring and
transferring property. Even then they had
no power of testamentary bequest, and their
property, at their death, went to their
liberators. It was permissible, however,
to pronounce a formal emancipation after
their death.

To obviate abuses, and to check the
excessive increase in the number of freedmen, the right of manumission was limited
in several directions under Augustus.
Among other things, if a slave under thirty
years of age was to be manumitted *vindicta*, a proof of sufficient reason was
required; and, in case of testamentary
manumission, the number was limited to a
certain proportion of the whole number of
slaves, and never allowed to exceed 100.

A mutual obligation continued to exist
between the freedman and his liberator,
based on the fact that the freedman belonged to the family of his patron. This
is seen in the circumstance that the freedman assumed the *nōmĕn* and the *prœnōmĕn*
of his patron. In and after the 1st century
B.C. we generally find a Greek *cŏgnōmĕn*
added. A well-known freedman of Lŭcĭus
Cornēlĭus Sulla, for instance, was called
Lucius Cornelius Epĭcădus. The *pătrōnus*
was bound on his side to care for his *libertus*, and in consequence either retained him
altogether in his home and service, or supplied him with a farm and capital to start
it; buried him in the family tomb after his
death, and took charge of his children if
not grown up. On the other side the freedman was bound to support his *patronus*,
in case of need, out of his own resources,
and if he was reduced to poverty, to main-

tain him. If he died childless, his patron
inherited his property. But the rights o.
the patron in respect of his freedman did
not pass to the patron's heirs. If the freedman neglected his duties, he was liable to
severe punishment. In special cases, at least
under the Empire, he might be sold for his
patron's profit, or given back to him as a slave.

Frīgĭdārĭum. *See* BATHS.

Frontīnus (*Sextus Iūlĭus*). A Roman
writer, born about 40 A.D. He was one
of the urban prætors under Vespasian, and
consul for the first time in 74. After this
he fought with distinction in Britain until
78, first under Pĕtīlĭus Cĕrĕālis, and then
as his successor. Under Domitian he kept
aloof from public life. He was recalled by
Nerva, who in 97 appointed him to the
important office of superintendent of the
aqueducts (*cūrātor ăquārum*). He was
also made a second time consul, and a third
time under Trajan, two years later (100).
Under Trajan he was also made augur, and
was succeeded in the office by the younger
Pliny. He died in 103 or 104, much esteemed by his contemporaries. His surviving works are (1) a collection, in three
books, of typical instances of military stratagems taken from Greek and Roman history.
This was intended as an additional chapter
to a lost work on military science, which
he had written under Domitian. A fourth
book has been rightly judged spurious, and
the work of a later age. (2) Selections
from a treatise on land-surveying in two
books (*De ăgrōrum qŭālĭtāte* and *De con-
trōversĭīs agrorum*), likewise written under
Domitian. (3) The interesting treatise on
the aqueducts of Rome (*De aquīs urbis
Rōmœ*), in two books. The occasion of his
writing this work was his tenure of the office
of *curator aquarum ;* but it was not published till the time of Trajan. It is a history and description of the water supply
of Rome, containing also the laws affecting
its use and maintenance.

Frontō (*Marcus Cornēlĭus*). The most
celebrated orator in the age of the Antonines, born at Cirta in Numidia, about
100 A.D. As an advocate and speaker at
Rome, he earned not only considerable
wealth and reputation, but the favour of
Hadrian and Antōnīnus Pĭus, who entrusted
him with the education of the imperial
princes Marcus Aurēlius and Lucius Vērus.

In 143 he was consul for two months,
but his health was too weak to allow of
his administering a province as proconsul.
This ill-health, and many family misfor-

nes, embittered the last years of his life. e died about 170. He was much admired y his contemporaries, some of whom formed school of their own bearing the name of 'rontōnĭānĭ, and this reputation survived fter his death. Accordingly he used to be egarded as one of the chief representatives f Roman eloquence. But the discovery of art of his writings in 1815 dispelled the lusion. The recovered writings consist ainly of the correspondence, the greater art of which they preserve, between Fronto nd the members of the imperial family, specially with Marcus Aurelius as prince nd emperor. A number of the letters are vritten in Greek. Besides these we have a ew fragments of historical works, and some hetorical declamations. Of the speeches nly a few meagre fragments remain. The haracter of Fronto, as revealed in these vritings, is that of a man of some knowledge, onourable and independent, but vain and orné. His main ambition is to pave the vay for the regeneration of the Latin anguage; and this, not by a study of the lassical models, but by quarrying in the vorks of the ante-classical writers. Their ntiquated expressions he revives, and uses n the most tasteless manner to clothe he poverty of his own thoughts. But is letters are of some value as con-ributing to our knowledge of the ge and the persons then living.

Fruit, Gods of. *See* VERTUMNUS, HORÆ, and POMONA.

Fulcra. [The ends of the frame-work on which the pillows of a couch r the cushions of a chair were placed, esembling the head of a modern sofa. They are invariably ornamented with nlaid bronze, sometimes of the rich-st kind, and are always surmounted by bronze ornaments representing the head and shoulders of a mule or ass, curning sideways and backwards, with ears put down and a vicious expression. The head is in almost every case decorated with a garland of vine-leaves entwined with tendrils and bunches of grapes, while the shoulders are covered with a curious leather collar, the top of which is turned down just where it joins the shaggy skin of some wild animal which is thrown over it. For the head of the ass is sometimes substituted that of a boy, or the head and neck of a goose. The lower part is decorated with a round boss from which springs a bust of a *genius* in full relief, or of some

youthful divinity, such as Bacchus or Hercules. The framework to which these ornaments are attached is described in Juvenal xi 93–98. The *genius fulcri* is mentioned *ib.* vi 22. Cp. Vergil, *Æn.* vi 604; Ovid, *Ep. Pont.* iii **3**, 14; Propert. iv 7, 3: 8, 68; Suetonius, *Claud.* 32; Pliny, *N. H.*, xxxiv 9; Ammianus xxviii 1, 47, *plūmĕum fulcrum*; Hyginus, *fab.* 274, "*Antiqui autem in lectis tricliniaribus in fulcris capita asellorum vite alligata habuerunt*"]. W. C. F. Anderson in *Classical Review*, 1889, 322.

Fulgentĭus (*Fābĭus Plancĭădēs*). A Latin grammarian, a native of Carthage, who wrote towards the end of the 5th century A.D. His works include, among other things, an allegorical interpretation of the ancient mythology in three books (*Mȳthŏlŏgĭæ*), the form of which reminds us of Martĭānus Căpella (*see* MARTIANUS CAPELLA), an exposition of the Æneid (*Vergĭlĭāna Con-tĭnentĭa*), and an explanation of strange and antiquated words illustrated by forged citations (*Expŏsĭtĭō Sermōnĭs Antīquī*).

Fullers (Gk. *gnăpheus*, Lat. *fullō*). The fuller's trade was one of the most import-ant and most widely extended in Greek and

* MURAL PAINTING FROM THE FULLER'S SHOP, POMPEII.
(Overbeck, fig. 193.)

Roman antiquity. It embraced all the processes, now distributed among different trades, necessary for converting the web into cloth, the chief material used by the ancients for clothing. Again, it was usual to send clothes to the fuller for cleaning and working up. Clothes when sent to be cleaned were stamped with the feet in pits or troughs filled with warm water and substances which separated the fat from them, as urine, nitre, and fuller's earth. If the object was to felt the web, and make it thicker and stronger, the same process was gone through, and the cloth was then beaten with rods, washed out in clean water, dried, carded with a kind of thistle or with the skin of a hedgehog, fumigated with sulphur, rubbed in with fuller's earth to make it whiter and stronger, and finally dressed by brushing, shearing, and pressing. The fuller's earth, when well rubbed in, prevented the clothes from getting dirty too soon, and freshened up the colours which

the sulphur had destroyed. Some frescoe preserved on the walls of an ancient fuller shop at Pompeii give a clear notion of th different processes. The *fullōnēs* at Rom formed one of the oldest guilds. Like a mechanics, they worshipped Mĭnerva t their tutelary goddess, and took a prominee part in her chief festival, the *Quinquātri*

Fundĭtōrēs (*funda*, a sling). The ligh armed slingers in the Roman army. The were usually raised by recruiting, or co tributed by the allies.

Fūrĭæ. *See* ERINYES.

Fustĭbălus. *See* SLINGS.

G

Gæa (Gr. *Gaia* or *Gē*). The Greek goddess of the Earth. According to Hesiod she came into being after Chaos, and brought forth of herself the sky (*Ourănŏs*), the mountains, and the sea (*Pontŏs*). By Urănus she was mother of the Titans, *Cyclōpĕs* and *Hĕcătoncheirĕs*. From the blood of her mutilated husband sprang the Erīnyĕs, Giants and Melian nymphs: to Pontus she bore Nereus, Thaumās, Phorcўs, Cētō and Eurўbĭa. Other terrible beings, such as the giants Tўphōn, Antæus and Tĭtўus, were her offspring, as also the *autŏchthŏnĕs* (aborigines) such as Erechtheus and Cĕcrops. In Homer she is invoked with Zeus, the Sun, Heaven and Hell as a witness to oaths, and worshipped with the sacrifice of a black lamb. But she was especially honoured as the mother of all, who nourishes her creatures and pours rich blessings upon them. In Athens, in particular, she was worshipped as *Kourŏtrŏphŏs*, or the nourisher of children, and at the same time as the goddess of death, who summons all her creatures back to her and hides them in her bosom. She was honoured also as the primeval prophetess, especially in Delphi, the oracle of which was at first in her possession as the power who sent forth the vapours which inspired the seer. The corresponding Roman goddess was *Tellūs*. (*See* TELLUS.)

Gaius. One of the most accomplished professors of Roman law and writers on the subject. He was a native of the Asiatic provinces, and spent his days in Rome under Hadrian, Antōnīnus Pĭus, and Marcus Aurēlĭus (about 110–180 A.D.). His writings were numerous : but we possess in a tolerably complete form nothing but his *Instĭtūtĭōnēs*, or introduction to the private law of the Romans. This was discovered in 1816, having before been known in quota-

tions only. The work is in four books, th first of which treats of the family, the s cond and third of property, and the fourt of legal procedure. Popular and intelligibl without being superficial, it was a favouri handbook of law, and served as a foundatio for the *Instĭtūtĭōnēs* of Justinian.

Gălătēa (the milk-white). A sea-nymp daughter of Nēreus and Dōris. According t a Sicilian story, which the poets Philoxēnu and Theocrĭtus have made famous, she wa pursued by the uncouth monster Pŏlўphe mus, being herself in love with the beauti ful Acĭs. The jealous giant crushes Acis wit a rock, and the nymph changes her belove into the Sicilian river which bears his name

Gălēnus (Gr. *Galēnŏs ; Claudius*) was th most celebrated physician in antiquit after Hippŏcrătēs, and at the same tim one of the most prolific among ancien writers. He was born at Pergămŏn i 131 A.D., received a careful education i philosophy, and afterwards devoted him self to medical studies in his native cit at Smyrna, Corinth, and Alexandria. H returned to Pergamon in 158, and under took the medical treatment of gladiators as giving him the best opportunity fo increasing his stock of surgical know ledge. In 164 he moved to Rome, and her won a considerable reputation by his suc cess in practice and his public lectures o anatomy. After three years he was drive by the attacks of jealous rivals to leav Rome. He undertook scientific journey through Greece and Asia, and then settle again in his native city. But he was soo recalled by the emperors Marcus Aurēlĭu and Lūcĭus Vērus, and in 170 appointed private physician to the young Commŏdus He died in his seventieth year, after winning the high esteem of his contemporaries.

Part of his writings were destroyed in a fire; in all 125 of his books are lost. About 100 of his genuine treatises have been preserved: of 19 we have fragments, more or less considerable; the genuineness of 18 is doubted, 24 are spurious. Many have not yet been printed, while others exist only in Latin, Syriac, Hebrew and Arabic translations. For during the Middle Ages, down to the 16th century, the authority of Galen was, throughout the East and West, held, especially by the Arabians, to be unassailable. A prolific writer like Galen was naturally careless of his style.

His writings leave no branch of medicine untouched. They comprise anatomy, physiology, pathology, pharmacology, and treatment. Among them should be mentioned the following: *On Anatomical Procedure*, in 9 books; *On the Use of Parts of the Human Body* (17 books); *On the Parts Affected* (6 books); *On the Composition of Medicines* (three works, including 26 books); *On Method in Therapeutics* (14 books). His book on medicine, a complete sketch of therapeutics, was immensely popular. He was also the author of 18 books of commentaries on Hippocrates, whom he claimed as his master. These still survive. His books contain important notices on the history of philosophy, of which he professes his knowledge and enthusiastic admiration. Some of his writings deal specially with this subject.

Galli. *See* RHEA.

Gallus. *See* CORNELIUS, 2.

Games. (1) *Public.* Among the Romans public games were intimately connected with religious worship. (For the public games of the Greeks, *see* ISTHMIAN, NEMEAN, OLYMPIAN, PYTHIAN GAMES.) The Roman *lūdī*, originally races, appear first in the worship of Mars and Consus, the tutelary deities of horses and mules. But it was also a very ancient custom to celebrate *ludi vōtīvī*, or games vowed on special occasions, particularly in time of war. Such games were usually vowed to Jupiter, the greatest deity of the Romans. These exceptional celebrations were so often repeated that they at length passed into regular annual festivals (*ludi stătī*). The number of these games gradually increased, and so did their duration. At the end of the republican period there were seven sets of games, which occupied 65 days; in the middle of the 2nd century A.D. 135 days were given up to them, and in 354 A.D. as many as 175. In old times the games only lasted part of the day; but they gradually began to take up the whole

day from early morning onwards. At a later period they went on in many cases into the night, requiring artificial illumination. The Roman ritual was very strict, and it happened pretty often that in consequence of some accidental interruption or trivial oversight, an *instaurātĭō* or repetition of the spoiled day, if not of the whole festival, would be ordered, lest the gods should have any cause for anger.

The different *collēgĭa* of the priests were responsible for superintending the games, prescribed in honour of their respective divinities. But in the case of festivities vowed by the State, this duty fell to the high magistrates; at first to the consuls, afterwards (and almost exclusively) to the ædiles, and after Augustus to the prætors. The expenses were provided for by a certain sum of money paid over from the public treasury to the giver of the games. For the *Ludi Rōmānī*, the greatest of all the festivals, this sum amounted, during the period preceding the Punic wars, to about £1,800. After this period it reached some £3,000, and by 51 A.D. had risen to £8,750. At the same time the givers of the games had to make larger supplementary contributions. The demands of the public were so extravagant that in course of time the amount of this private expenditure increased enormously, especially in the last century B.C. Augustus, indeed, tried to check it; but he was obliged to allow his prætors to spend three times as much on the games as was paid for the public treasury. Under the Empire many enactments were issued to restrict the expenditure on the games by law, but no permanent effect was produced. Even after the 4th century A.D. the expense rose to as large a sum as from £50,000 to £150,000. The oldest games were those of the circus, consisting mainly of horse-races and chariot-races, with gymnastic contests, to which others were added in course of time. (*See* CIRCUS.) After 364 B.C. dramatic representations were introduced from Etruria. These were in 240 B.C., and onwards, exchanged for regular theatrical performances (*see* LIVIUS ANDRONICUS). Contests of gladiators, also from Etruria, were fashionable after 264 B.C. But these were only exhibited, during the republican period, at funeral games, private and other entertainments (*see* GLADIATORES).

The following regular festivities were introduced in the republican period, and continued in existence until the latest times: (1) The *Ludi Romani*. These were the oldest games of all, and were, in strictness, celebrated in honour of Jupiter by victorious generals at their triumphs; hence it was that they included, as a special feature, a procession (*pompa*) from the Capitol to the Circus; a part of the performance which seems afterwards to have been embodied in the other games of the circus. Originally they lasted only one day; but in course of time they absorbed more and more time, till in the Ciceronian age they went on for fifteen (September 4–19). After the death of Cæsar another day was added in his honour. After the introduction of theatrical performances, several days were taken up with them. The curule ædiles were, in the republican period, responsible for the management. (2) *Ludi plēbēī.* These originally lasted one day, but afterwards fourteen, November 4–17. They were given in the *Circus Flāmĭnĭus* under the direction of the plebeian ædiles, and early included dramatic entertainments. (3) *Ludi Cĕrĕālēs*, given under the direction of the plebeian ædiles in honour of Ceres, the tutelary goddess of the *plebs.* The date was originally April 19, afterwards April 12–19. (4) *Ludi Apollĭnārēs*, or in honour of Apollo. These were introduced during the Second Punic War, and celebrated ♦riginally on July 13, continuing afterwards from July 6–13. On the last day only were there any performances in the circus; the rest of the festival was given up to the drama. These were the only games for which, in the republican period, the prætor was responsible. (5) *Ludi Mĕgălensēs*, in honour of the Magna Māter, introduced 204 B.C. and held at first on April 4, afterwards from April 4–10. (*See* RHEA.) They included performances both in the theatre and in the circus. They were under the management of the curule ædiles, and the same remark applies to (6) the *Ludi Flōrālēs*, from April 28 to May 3. (*See* FLORA.) During the imperial period the number of permanent festivals was largely increased. The birthday of Augustus, for instance (September 23), was regularly celebrated with *ludi circenses*, and the *ludi Augustālēs* (October 3–12) were instituted in honour of his memory.

Side by side with the public games, private performances were often given by societies, families, and individuals on special occasions, such as those of births, marriages, or funerals. Sometimes the object would be merely to please the public: sometimes to raise money. The giver of the entertainment had, like the superintendent of the public games, the privilege of lictors and the *tŏgă prætexta.* Charges for admission were made or not according to the occasion. But the admission to the public games was free, it being always understood that special seats were reserved for the magistrates, priests, senators, *ĕquĭtēs*, and particular families and individuals. (*See* AMPHITHEATRE, CIRCUS, GLADIATORES, SEA-FIGHTS, THEATRE, WILD BEASTS.)

Of social games the ancients, and especially the Greeks, had plenty. The *cottăbus*, so popular at Greek banquets, the games of ball, of which both Greeks and Romans were fond, and the games with dice, are described in separate articles. A game of draughts (*petteia*) appears as early as Homer, and was said to have been the invention of Pălămēdēs. But we have no knowledge of its nature and rules, and have

"GAME OF "ODD AND EVEN."
(Vase painting, Paris; *Arch. Zeit.* 1871, taf. 56, 3).

very scanty information about the similar games played in later times. The "game of cities" seems to have resembled our chess or draughts. The board was divided into spaces, and movements made upon it with stones; the object being to get your opponent into check. The Romans had several games of the sort, among which the *ludus lātruncŭlōrum*, or game at soldiers, is to a certain extent known. This was a game of siege. The men (*calcŭli*) were divided into privates (*mandræ*) and officers (*latrōnēs*), and the object was to take or to get your adversary's stones in check. In the *ludus dŭŏdĕcim scriptōrum*, or game of 12 lines, dice were used. The dice-board was divided into 24 spaces by 12 parallel lines intersected by a line at right angles. Each side had 15 men, one set being black and the other white. Before each move the dice were thrown, and the move determined by the number which turned up. A very favourite game was Odd and Even (Gk. *artĭasmŏs*, Lat. *lūdĕrĕ păr impăr*). You held out so many fingers, and put so many coins, pebbles, or nuts in your hand, and made your adversary guess whether the number was odd or even. The Roman children, and indeed their elders, were very fond of various games with nuts.

Gănўmēda. *See* HEBE.

Gănўmēdēs. The son of Tros, king of Dardănĭa, brother of Ilus and Assărăcus. According to Homer he was carried away by the gods for his beauty, to be the cup-bearer of Zeus, and one of the immortals. In the later legend he is carried away by Zeus himself in the shape of an eagle, or by the eagle of Zeus. To make amends to his father, Zeus presented him with four immortal horses for his chariot. Ganymedes was afterwards regarded as the genius of the sources of the Nile, and the astronomers made him into the constellation *Aquărĭus.* The rape of Ganymede was represented in a group by the sculptor Lĕŏchărēs (*see* LEOCHARES).

Gargĭlĭus Martĭālĭs flourished in the 3rd century A.D. and was the author of a great work, based upon Greek and Latin sources, on agriculture and veterinary science. Considerable fragments remain, dealing with the treatment of cattle (*De Cūrā Bŏum*) and the medical uses of herbs and fruit (*Mĕdĭcīna ex Hŏlĕrĭbŭs et Pōmīs*).

Gĕlānōr. A descendant of Inăchus king of Argos. When Dănăus, likewise a descendant of Inachus, came to Argos, and laid claim to the sovereign power, the citizens were doubtful in whose favour they should decide. While they were hesitating, a wolf fell upon the cattle which were feeding before the city, and killed the bull who was defending them. The citizens regarded this as a sign from heaven,

and, interpreting the wolf as meaning Danaus, they compelled Gelanor to retire in his favour. (*See* DANAUS.) In the *Supplĭcēs* of Æschylus, Pĕlăsgus is king of Argos. He gives Danaus a friendly welcome, and defends him against the sons of Ægyptus. But he is vanquished by them, retires from the sovereignty spontaneously in favour of the stranger, and leaves the country.

Gellĭus. (1) *Gnæus. See* ANNALISTS.

(2) *Aulus.* A Roman writer of the age of the Antonines, about 130–170 A.D. After receiving his education in rhetoric at Rome, he went to Athens, in his thirtieth year or thereabouts, to study philosophy. Here he saw much of Hērōdēs Attĭcus. Besides studying philosophy, he spent the long winter nights in wide and various reading, which he took up again with ardour after his return to Italy. From the material thus collected he composed the twenty books of his *Noctēs Attĭcæ*, written in remembrance of his days at Athens. One book, the eighth, is lost, and only the headings of the chapters remain. The remaining nineteen are a series of excerpts, loosely strung together, from all kinds of Greek and Latin authors, especially the ante-classical writers. They also contain a mass of information, and a number of opinions orally delivered by contemporary scholars. The whole forms a valuable storehouse of notes on questions of historical, antiquarian, and literary interest. Gellius' style is sober, and, like that of an admirer of Frontō (*see* FRONTO), full of archaic expressions.

Gems (*Gemmæ*). The art of cutting precious stones was early learned by the

(1)	(2)
* ATHENE, BY ASPASIOS.	* THE "STROZZI" MEDUSA, BY SOLON.
(Red jasper, in Vienna Cabinet.)	(Chalcedony, in British Museum Cabinet, no. 1256.)

Greeks from the Egyptians and Orientals, who had practised it from remote antiquity. The cuttings were originally only concave, and the gems set in rings and used as seals. Cameos, or stones carved in relief, first came

into use, it would seem, in the time of
Alexander the Great, and were used for ornament. For cameos precious stones of
various colours were used, especially the
onyx. The layers of the stone were so

(3) ARTEMIS. (4) PERSEUS.

GEMS FROM POMPEII.
(Naples Museum.)

treated, that the figures stood out bright on
a dark ground. Mnēsarchus of Sămos, the
father of the philosopher Pȳthăgŏrăs (about
600 B.C.) is the oldest Greek jeweller whose
name has come down to us. In the 4th
century B.C. the most celebrated master was
Pyrgŏtĕlēs, the only artist whom Alexander
the Great would allow to cut his likeness.
In the age of Augustus we hear of Dĭoscŏrĭdēs, who cut the emperor's likeness on
a stone which was used as a seal by the succeeding Cæsars. The Etruscans and Romans
took up the art very early, but never attained
the same perfection as the Greeks.

(5) DANCING SATYR. (6) SATYR WITH INFANT DIONYSUS.

CAMEOS.
(Naples Museum.)

The fancy for making collections of beautiful gems arose as early as the 1st century
B.C. The intaglios, or cut stones, have come
down to us in greater numbers than any of
the monuments of ancient art. Those which
belonged to the advanced periods of style
present examples of the most beautiful
workmanship, the most original composition,
and the most interesting subjects, the lat-

ter being mainly taken from mythology.
Among the remaining Greek cameos an
important place, both for size and beauty,
must be given to the Gonzaga Cameo in St
Petersburg. This, it has been conjectured,
represents the bust of Ptolemy Phĭlădelphus
and Arsĭnŏē, his sister and wife; [but it
more probably commemorates Nero and
Agrippina, fig. 7.] The largest and most

(7) * THE " GONZAGA " CAMEO, NERO AND AGRIPPINA.
(Sardonyx of 3 strata, 6×5 inches, Russian Imperial
Cabinet.)

splendid of the cameos which have come
down to us from the Roman period are those at
Vienna (fig. 8) and Paris, representing, in
groups and figures, the family of Augustus.

(8) * THE GEMMA AUGUSTEA, AT VIENNA.

Augustus and Livia receiving Drusus and Tiberius on
their return from their Vindelic and Rhætian campaigns.
(Sardonyx of 2 strata, 9×8 inches, Vienna cabinet.)

Whole vessels were sometimes made of
single stones, and adorned with reliefs.
An instance is the Mantuan vase now at

Brunswick, 6⅝ inches high, 2⅓ inches thick, consisting of a single onyx. The lid, handle and base are of gold. Two parallel lines of gold divide the surface into three parts, the midmost of which has twelve figures, representing the festival of the Thesmŏphŏrĭa, in three groups; while the highest and lowest are adorned with leaves, flowers, ears of corn, fruits, bulls' heads, and other objects connected with the worship of Dēmētĕr. Works of this kind are sometimes made of coloured glasses. The most celebrated instance of this sort is the Portland Vase now in the British Museum. Its height is about 10 inches. The material is a dark blue transparent glass, with beautiful reliefs in white opaque enamel (fig. 9). [See

PELEUS. THETIS. POSEIDON.
EROS.
(9) * THE PORTLAND VASE.
(British Museum.)

Catalogue of Engraved Gems in the British Museum, 1888, pp. 225–8; and (on the subject in general) *Introduction*, pp. 1–38.]

Gĕnĭus (= creator, begetter). The Italian peoples regarded the Genius as a higher power which creates and maintains life, assists at the begetting and birth of every individual man, determines his character, tries to influence his destiny for good, accompanies him through life as his tutelary spirit, and lives on in the *Lărēs* after his death. (*See* LARES.) As a creative principle, the Genius is attached strictly speaking, to the male sex only. In the case of women his place is taken by Juno, the personification of woman's life. Thus, in a house inhabited by a man and his wife, a Genius and a Juno are worshipped together. But in common parlance it was usual to speak of the Genius of a house,

and to this Genius the marriage bed was sacred. A man's birthday was naturally the holiday of his attendant Genius, to whom he offered incense, wine, garlands, cakes, everything in short but bloody sacrifices, and in whose honour he gave himself up to pleasure and enjoyment. For the Genius wishes a man to have pleasure in the life he has given him. And so the Romans spoke of enjoying oneself as indulging one's Genius, and of renunciation as spiting him. Men swore by their Genius as by their higher self, and by the Genius of persons whom they loved and honoured. The philosophers originated the idea of a man having two Genii, a good and a bad one; but in the popular belief the notion of the Genius was that of a good and beneficent being. Families, societies, cities and peoples had their Genius as well as individuals. The Genius of the Roman people (*Genius Publĭcus*, or *Pŏpŭli Rōmāni*) stood in the forum, represented in the form of a bearded man crowned with a diadem, a cornucopia in his right hand, and a sceptre in his left. An annual sacrifice was offered to him on the 9th October. Under the Empire the Genius of Augustus, the founder of the Empire, and of the reigning emperor, were publicly worshipped at the same time. Localities also, such as open spaces, streets, baths, and theatres, had their own Genii.

* HARPOCRATES, AND SNAKE AS GENIUS LOCI.
(*Pitture d'Ercolano*, i 207.)

These were usually represented under the form of snakes (*see* cut); and hence the common habit of keeping tame snakes.

Gennētæ. This was the Athenian term for the members of the 360 ancient families (*gennæ*), thirty of which made up one of the twelve *phrātrĭæ* of the four old Ionic tribes. These families consisted of some thirty houses, who referred their origin and name to a common ancestor, and observed a common worship, with special priests to superintend it. The objects of this worship were Zeus Herkeiŏs (the god of house and home), Apollo Pătrŏŏs (the god of the family), the hḗrŏs of the family, and other tutelary deities. Supposing that a family worship rose to the dignity of a state ceremony, the priestly office remained hereditary in the family (genna). If there were no nearer relations, the members of the genna had a law of inheritance which they observed among themselves. Maintained by these religious and legal ties, the gennœ and the phratriœ survived the old Ionic tribes, after the abolition of the latter by Cleis-thĕnēs. The president of the genna super-intended the enrolment of new members into it at the feast of the Apătūrĭă, the occasion on which the new members of the phratriœ were also enrolled. (See APA-TURIA.) A citizen who did not belong to a genna could only become member of one by adoption, and under certain conditions.

Gens (Latin). A family (in the widest sense of the word) descended on the male line from a common ancestor, and therefore bearing a commcn name. So long as the patricians were the only citizens with full rights, there could of course be no gentēs not patrician. The oldest gentes belonged to the tribes of the Latin Ramnēs and the Sabine Tĭtĭēs. Besides these there were the gentes belonging to the Alban families, brought to Rome by King Tullus Hostĭlĭus; and embodied by the other gentes in the community as a third tribe, the Lŭcĕrēs. These, the most ancient, were called gentes māiŏrēs as distinguished from the gentes mĭnŏrēs, which included the plebeians whom Tarquĭnĭus Priscus raised to the rank of patricians. There were in later times in-stances of plebeian gentes being raised to patrician rank: but these became rarer and rarer, so that the number of patrician gentes was very much reduced. During the last years of the Republic we hear of only fourteen still in existence, including thirty fămĭlĭœ (or families in the narrower sense). Many large gentes were divided into houses (stirpēs) who had a common cŏgnŏmen in addition to the name of their gens; thus the gens Cornēlĭă included the Cornelii Malŭgĭnensēs, Cornelii Cossi, Cornelii Scīpĭŏnēs, Cornelii Rūfīnī, Cornelii Len-tŭli, Cornelii Dŏlăbellœ, Cornelii Cethēgi, Cornelii Cinnœ, Cornelii Sullœ. Among

the plebeians, as among the patricians, the fămĭlĭa naturally developed into a larger circle of relationship; but gentes in the old sense were not formed by the process. Though the plebeian had his gentile name, and afterwards his cognomen, he had not the real ius gentĭlĭcĭum.

All gentĭlēs or members of a gens had a right to its common property, which in-cluded a common burial-place. They also had a testamentary law of their own which lasted on into the imperial period. When the member of a gens died without heirs of his body, the next to inherit (as in the case of the plebeians) were the ăgnătī, or gentiles on the male side, who could prove their relationship: failing these, the gentiles divided the inheritance. The existence of this law rendered it, in old times, necessary to obtain the consensus of the whole gens in cases of adoption and testamentary be-quest. Another consequence of it was, that it was the duty of the gentiles to provide a cūrătŏr for insane persons and spendthrifts, and a guardian for minors.

Every gens had its meetings, at which resolutions were passed binding its indi-vidual members in matters affecting the gens. It was a decree of the gens Manlĭa, for instance, which forbade any one of its members to bear the prœnŏmĕn Marcus. As every fămĭlĭa, whether patrician or plebeian, had certain sacrifices which it was bound to perform, so had every gens, as a larger or extended fămĭlĭa. All members of the gens were entitled, and indeed bound, to take part in the sacra gentilicia, or com-mon worship of the gens. These sacra ceased to exist with the extinction of a gens: and if a member of a gens left it, this right and duty also came to an end. It should be added that certain public religious services were assigned to particular gentes, that of Hercŭlēs, for instance, to the gens Pīnărĭa.

Geography. Geographical research and literature took their rise, like historical literature, among the Ionians of Asia Minor. Their extended commerce and their activity in founding colonies enlarged their geo-graphical horizon. The necessity was thus felt of utilizing and registering the know-ledge already acquired for the purpose of discovering the form and constitution of the earth. The first attempt at sketching a map of the world was made by Aristăgŏrās of Mīlĕtus about 550 B.C. His kinsman Hĕcătæus, one of the writers called Logŏgrăphī, who flourished about fifty years later, corrected and enlarged this map, and added a commentary. (*See* LOGOGRAPHI.) This commentary, of which only fragments are preserved in quotations, is the oldest piece of purely geographical writing in Greek. The geographical chapters in the history of Hērŏdŏtus (about 450 B.C.) compensate us to a certain extent for the loss of this work, and of the other works of the *Logographi* on history and geography. But they only treat the eastern half of the known world. It became indeed, in the absence of a regular tradition of geographical science, a usual thing for historians to insert geographical disquisitions into their works. The writings of Thūcȳdĭdēs, Xĕnŏphōn, Ctēsĭās, Ephŏrus, Thĕŏpompus, Tīmæus, and others down to Polybius, afford examples of this.

The first purely geographical work which has come down to us in a complete state is the *Pĕrĭplūs* bearing the name of Scylax, written in the first part of the 4th century B.C. This is a description of the coast of the Mediterranean. About the same time the astronomer Eudoxus of Cnĭdus made a great advance in the theory of physical geography. He was the first who adduced mathematical proof of the spherical shape of the earth, which had been asserted before his time by Pȳthăgŏrās. The division of the globe into five zones (two frigid, two temperate, and one torrid) is also due to him. About 330 B.C. Pȳthĕăs of Massĭlĭa explored towards the N.W. as far as the northern end of the British Islands and the coasts of the German Ocean. About the same time the campaigns of Alexander the Great opened up Asia as far as India to Greek research. Nĕarchus made a report of exceptional value on his coast voyage from the Indus to the Euphrates. All these discoveries were embodied, about 320 B.C. in a new map by Dĭcæarchus of Messāna, a disciple of Aristotle. He was the first savant who treated physical geography in a scientific manner. He assumed the existence of a southern hemisphere, and made an estimate of the earth's circumference, to which he gave the exaggerated measurement of 40,000 miles. His map remained for a long time the standard work of the kind. The southern and eastern parts of India were still further opened out under Alexander's successors, in consequence of the campaigns of the Sĕleucĭdæ, and several journeys undertaken by ambassadors, among which that of Mĕgasthĕnēs should be mentioned. The commercial expeditions of the Ptolemies

brought in fresh knowledge of the coasts of Arabia and E. Africa.

The first man who arranged the mass of geographical materials hitherto collected, into a really scientific system, was Erătosthĕnēs of Cȳrēnē (about 276–175 B.C.). His materials he found in the rich collections of the Alexandrian library, Alexandria being then the central point of the commerce of the world. He was fully equipped for his task by his acquirements both in physical science and mathematics, and in history and philology. He endeavoured for the first time to estimate the earth's circumference by a measurement of degrees carried out over a space of 15 degrees of latitude. The imperfection of his method brought out too large a quantity, 25,000 geographical miles. The name of Hipparchus of Nīcæa (about 140 B.C.) marks a considerable advance. He may be called the founder of mathematical geography, as he applied geographical length and breadth to determine the position of places on the earth's surface. He also superseded the rectangular and equidistant projection of parallels and meridians, hitherto used in maps, by a projection which, with few modifications, is identical with the one now in use. The parallels were represented by segments of a circle, the meridians by straight lines or curves, corresponding with the portion of surface to be represented, drawn at distances corresponding to the actual distances on the surface of the globe. The estimate of the earth's circumference which was accepted as correct down to the 10th century A.D., was that of Pŏsīdōnĭŭs of Apămĕa (about 90 B.C.). Taking as his basis the measurement of the shortest distance from Alexandria to Rhodes, he brought out the result as 18,000 geographical miles, instead of 21,600 (or about 25,000 English miles.)

Only fragments remain of the writings of these geographers, and others contemporary with them. But we possess the great work of Străbō of Amaseia, finished about 20 A.D., the most important monument of descriptive geography and ethnology which has come down from Greek antiquity. Thanks to the Roman conquest, he was in a position to give a more accurate description of the West than his predecessors. Up to this time all that the Romans had done for geographical research was to open up Western Europe and Northern Africa to the Greek savants. An immense service was rendered to science by Agrippa, under the direction of Augustus.

He measured and indicated on a map the distance between the stations on the great military roads and along the coasts of the Roman empire, thus contributing enormously to our knowledge of ancient topography, and laying a foundation for our maps. These *data* formed the basis of a new map of the world, which was first set up in Rome. Numerous copies were probably taken for the larger cities of the empire, and smaller portable ones distributed among the military and the administrating officials. It is probably upon copies of this kind that the *Tăbŭla Peutingĕrĭăna* and the *Itĭnĕrārĭa* are based. (*See* PEUTINGER ; ITINERARIA.)

In the 1st century A.D. much was added to geographical knowledge by the expeditions of the Romans into the interior of North Africa and the North of Europe. The most important literary works of the Romans on geography belong to this period. These are (1) the compendium of Pompōnĭus Mēla ; (2) the geographical books of Pliny the Elder's great encyclopædia, a dreary uncritical compilation, but the only representative we have of a number of lost works; (3) the *Germānĭa* of Tacitus, an essay mainly of an ethnographical character. The last great contribution made to geographical science in antiquity is the work of the Alexandrian astronomer Ptolemy (about 140 A.D.). This consists mainly of lists of the places marked in the current maps which he makes his authorities, with their latitude and longitude. After Ptolemy, the geographical literature of the Greeks and Romans alike has nothing to show but compilations and extracts. Towards the end of the 6th century, Stĕphănus of Byzantium compiled a dictionary of geography, which is valuable for the quantity of information taken from the older and lost writings which it embodies. The book of Pausănĭas (about 175 A.D.) is valuable as bearing on the special topography of Greece.

Gĕōmŏrī. In many Doric states, particularly in Syracuse, this term denoted the territorial aristocracy. But in Athens it was applied to the landed commonalty, distinguished from the *Eupătrĭdæ*, or nobles, on the one side, and the *Dēmĭūrgĭ*, or mechanics, on the other.

Gĕōpŏnĭcī. The ancient writers on agriculture : for instance (among the Greeks), the philosopher Dēmŏcrĭtūs, and in later times, Xĕnŏphōn, in his *Œcŏnŏmĭcus*. No other Greek works of the kind have come

down to us, except the collection called *Geoponica.* This consists of twenty books, and contains extracts from writers of the most widely distant periods. The compiler was a Bithynian, Cassĭānus Bassus, who lived about the middle of the 10th century A.D., and undertook the work at the suggestion of the Emperor Constantine VII. He based it upon a collection of extracts made by a certain Vindānĭŏs Anătŏlĭŏs. Agriculture was held in high esteem by the Romans, and the subject was in consequence a favourite one with their men of letters. A number of their works on it have come down to us : the *Res Rustĭca* of the elder Cato, a similar work by the encyclopædic scholar, Marcus Tĕrentĭus Varrō, the *Georgics* of Vergil, and after Christ the writings of Columella, Gargilĭus Martĭālĭs, and Pallădĭus. The *Georgics* of Vergil are a poem : and one book of Columella is in verse.

Germānĭcus Cæsăr. The son of Nero Claudius Drusus, adopted son of his uncle Tiberius, and grandson of Livia, the wife of Augustus. He was celebrated for his campaigns against the Germańs. He was born 15 B.C., and died 19 A.D. Distinguished as much for culture as for military accomplishments, he was an orator and author as well as a general. Ovid, who dedicated to him the 2nd edition of his *Fasti*, praises his poetry. His paraphrase of the *Phænŏmĕna* of Arātus in 725 lines, and three fragments (246 lines) of a paraphrase of the same writer's *Prŏgnŏstĭca*, still survive. They are remarkable for knowledge, command of metre, and a pleasant style. The *Phæno- mena* are dedicated to Tiberius, and described by the author himself as the work of a beginner. These poems used erroneously to be attributed to Domitian, who did not take the title of Germanicus until he was emperor. Three collections of *scholia* upon them, by no means without value, have also survived.

Gĕrūsĭa (council of old men, *Gĕrontĕs*). The supreme deliberative authority among the Spartans, according to the constitution of Lycurgus. It consisted of twenty-eight men of at least sixty years of age, called *Gerontes*, elected by the public assembly for life. The meetings of the *Gerusia* were presided over by the two kings, who had the right of voting. The number of the council thereforeamounted to thirty. It was their duty to deliberate beforehand on all important affairs of state, and prepare preliminary resolutions upon them, to be voted upon by the public assembly. They had also jurisdiction in the case of all offences which were punishable by death or loss of civil rights. They sat in judgment, if necessary, even on the kings, in later times associating the ephors with them in this function. Their authority, like that of the kings, suffered considerable restriction at the hands of the ephors. They had a similar position in the Cretan constitution, according to which only the members of the highest magistracy, called the *Cosmoi*, or regulators, could enter the council, and that after a blameless term of administration.

Gĕrўŏn, or **Gĕrўŏnēs.** A giant with three bodies and powerful wings, the son of Chrȳsāōr and Callirrhŏē. He dwelt in the island of Erytheia, lying in the ocean, in the extreme west; and was the possessor of a herd of red cattle, watched by the shepherd Eurytĭōn, and a two-headed dog called Orthrŏs. It was one of the twelve labours of Hērăclēs to carry off these cattle, and after a violent contest to slay the pursuing Geryon with his arrows.

Gĭgantĕs (Giants). In Homer the *Gigantes* are a wild and gigantic race of aborigines, kinsmen of the gods, as are the Cўclōpĕs and Phæacians. With their king Eurўmĕdōn, they are destroyed for their wickedness. Hesiod makes them the sons of Gæa, sprung from the blood of the mutilated Urănus. Neither Hesiod nor Homer know anything of their struggle with the gods (*Gĭgantŏmăchĭa*), the story of which seems to be a reflexion of the myth of the Titans, and their contest with the gods, and to be associated with local legends. The two are often confused by later poets. The place of the contest was Phlegra, or the place of burning. Phlegra was always localized in volcanic regions. In the earlier stories it is on the Macedonian peninsula of Pallēnē; and in later times on the Phlegræan plains in Campania between Cūmæ and Căpŭa, or again at Tartēssus in Spain. Led on by Alcўŏneus and Porphўrĭōn, they hurled rocks and burning trunks of trees against heaven. But the gods called Hērăclēs to their assistance; a prophecy having warned them that they would be unable to destroy the giants without the aid of a mortal. Heracles slew not only Alcyoneus, but gave the others, whom the gods had struck down, their *quietus* with his arrows. As Encĕlădus was flying, Athēnē threw the island of Sicily upon him. Pŏlўbōtes was buried by Pŏseidōn under the island of Nĭsȳrŏs, a piece of the island of Cōs, which Poseidon had broken off with his trident, with all

the giants who had fled there. Besides these, the following names are given among others : Agrĭŏs, Ephĭaltēs, Pallas, Clўtĭŏs, Eurўtŏs, Hippŏlўtŏs, Thŏōn.

In the oldest works of art the Giants are represented in human form and armed with harness and spears. But in course of time their attributes became terrific, awful faces, long hanging hair and beard, the skins of wild animals for garments, trunks of trees and clubs for weapons. In the latest representations, but not before, their bodies end in two scaly snakes instead of feet (*see* cut). In the *Gĭgantŏmăchĭa* of

GIANT IN CONFLICT WITH ARTEMIS.

Cp. Giant to right of Pergamene Sculptures, fig. 1.

(Roman relief in Vatican Museum.)

Pergămŏs, the grandest representation of the subject in antiquity, we find a great variety of forms; some quite human, others with snakes' feet and powerful wings, others with still bolder combinations of shape; some are naked, some clothed with skins, some fully armed, and others slinging stones. (*See* PERGAMENE SCULPTURES.)

Glădĭātŏrēs. The Latin name for the combatants who fought each other for life or death at the public shows. They first appear in Rome in 264 B.C., and only at the celebrations of private funerals, or in games given in memory of a private individual. Entertainments of this kind were often provided for in wills. The custom, like others of the same kind, seems to have come from Etruria, where it was a survival of the human sacrifices formerly usual at funerals. These gladiatorial contests soon became a very favourite form of popular entertainment, and in the last century of the republic were held to be an excellent means of winning the favour of the populace at elections. Indeed, custom at length imposed an obligation on some magistrates, for instance on the ædiles, to give gladiatorial games on their assumption of office; and they would try to outbid each other in the number of contending couples and in general expenditure. From Rome the fashion soon spread into the provinces. Campania was the part of Italy where it most prevailed. It was not, however, till the time of Domitian that quæstors designate were regularly compelled to give the great gladiatorial exhibitions, which occupied ten days in the month of December. In the Western Empire they survived at least down to the beginning of the 5th century A.D.

They were at first given in the forum, but afterwards generally in the amphitheatres (see AMPHITHEATRE), and in the circus, if the exhibition was to be on a very large scale. The gladiators were sometimes condemned criminals; but it must be remembered that originally Roman citizens could not be sentenced to the arena, and it was not till later times that this punishment was extended to criminals of low condition. Sometimes they were prisoners of war, slaves, or volunteers. Under the Empire it was not so uncommon, even in the upper classes, to volunteer as a gladiator. Sometimes the step was the last refuge of a ruined man ; sometimes the emperor would force a man to it. These volunteers were called *auctōrātī* (= bound over), to distinguish them from the rest; their pay was termed *auctōrāmentum*. Troops of gladiators were sometimes owned by Romans in good society, who often, towards the end of the republican age, employed them in streetfights against their political opponents. Sometimes they were the property of speculators, who often carried on at the same time the disreputable trade of a fencing master (*lănista*). These men would hire out or sell their gladiators to persons who were giving their shows, or would exhibit them for money to the public on their own account.

The gladiators were trained in special schools (*lŭdī*). Under the Empire things went so far that the emperors kept schools of their own under the supervision of *prŏcūrātōrēs* of equestrian rank. After Domitian's time there were four of these in Rome. A building for this purpose, large enough for a hundred gladiators, is preserved in Pompeii. To strengthen their muscles they were put on a very nourishing diet.

Every style of fighting had its special professor (*doctor* or *măgister*), and the gladiator was usually instructed only in one style. The novice (*tīrō*) began with fence-practice against a wooden stake, at first with light wooden arms, but afterwards with weapons of full weight.

If a man were intending to give a show of gladiators (*mūnus glădiătōrĭum*) he advertised it by notices (*prŏgrammăta*) put up on the walls of houses, numerous copies of these being at the same time widely distributed. These notices stated the date and occasion of the show, the name of the giver (*ēdĭtor*), the number of pairs of gladiators, and the different kinds of combats. The performance began with a gala procession (*pompa*) of the gladiators to the arena and through it. Then came the testing of the weapons by the *editor*, who, though he might be a private individual, had the right of wearing the *insignia* of a magistrate during the show. A preliminary skirmish or *prŏlūsĭō*, with wooden swords and darts, next took place, till the trumpets sounded, and the serious fighting began. This took place to the accompaniment of music in a space measured out by the fencing master. The gladiators sometimes fought, not in pairs, but in troops. The timid were driven on with whips and red-hot irons. If a gladiator was wounded in single combat, he raised his fore-finger to implore the mercy of the people, with whom, after the last years of the republic, the giver of the games usually left the decision. The sign of mercy (*missĭō*) was the waving of handkerchiefs : the clenched fist and downward thumb indicated that the combat was to be fought out till death. Condemned criminals had no chance of mercy. The slain, or nearly slain, were carried on the biers which stood ready for them, to a particular door (*porta Lĭbĭtĭnensĭs*), into a place where they were stripped (*spŏlĭārĭum*). There, if they had not actually expired, they were put to death. The victors received palms, with branches adorned with fillets. Under the Empire they sometimes got presents of money as well. If a gladiator, by repeated proofs of cleverness and bravery, succeeded in gaining the favour of the people, he was, at the public request, presented with a kind of wooden rapier (*rŭdĭs*),[1] as a token that he was now free from all further service. In this case he was called *rŭdĭārĭus*. This

---

[1] The swords used by gladiators often resembled rapiers : *see* fig. 1.

did not make him an absolutely free man; but if he chose to fight again, he did so as a free man, and could accordingly claim a high remuneration.

Gladiators were armed in various styles, as the pairs of combatants were usually armed, not with the same, but with different against the *retiarius*, was armed in Gallic fashion with helmet, sword and shield, and named after the figure of a fish (*mormўlŏs*), which adorned his helmet. The *Samnīs*, or Samnite, was so called after his Samnite equipment. This consisted of a large shield (*scūtum*), a sleeve of leather or metal on

(1) GLADIATORIAL HELMETS AND SWORDS.
(From Pompeii.)

weapons. The weapons of gladiators, and notably their helmets, were quite different in form from the arms of soldiers (*see* fig. 1). Gladiators were classed according to their equipment. Thus the *rētĭārĭus*

(2) SECUTOR, RETIARIUS, AND LANISTA.
(Mosaic in Madrid Library.)

was armed with a net, was bareheaded, and had nothing on but a short tunic and a girdle; his left arm was in a sleeve; his arms were a net (*iăcŭlum*), a trident (*fuscĭna*), and a dagger. The net he tried to throw over his pursuing adversary, and to despatch him with dagger or trident, if successful. The *sĕcūtor*, or pursuer, was so called, because he was generally set to fight with the *retiarius*, who retired before him (fig. 2). He was as lightly equipped as his adversary, but armed with helmet, sword, and shield. The *myrmillō* (fig. 3), who was also often matched

the right arm, with a shoulder piece (*gălērus*) rising above the shoulder, a girdle, a greave on the left foot, a visored helmet with crest and plume, and a short sword. The *Thrax*, or Thracian, wore, like his countrymen, a small round shield (*parma*) and a dagger (*sĭca*) curved in the form of a sickle, or bent at right angles. In other respects his equipment was more complete than the Samnite's, for he had greaves on both legs. The *hoplŏmăchus*, or heavily armed gladiator, wore a breastplate, as well as visored helmet and greaves. In later times the place of the *retiarius* was sometimes taken by the *lăquĕărĭus*, who wore the same light armour, but carried a short sword and a noose

(3) MYRMILLO.
(Rome, Palazzo Doria.)

(*lăquĕus*), which he threw over his adversary and pulled him to the ground. The *dĭmăchœri*, or men who fought with two swords, are also apparently the production of a later time. The *essĕdārĭi* (from *essĕdum*, a British war-car with two horses) fought in chariots. The *andăbătœ* (fig. 4) fought on horseback, armed with small round shield and spear (*spĭcŭlum*), and a visored helmet without eyeholes, and charged each other in the dark.

(4) ANDABATÆ.
(From the Amphitheatre, Pompeii.)

There are many representations of gladiatorial combats in works of art, the most comprehensive of which is a large bas-relief in Pompeii. [Overbeck's *Pompeii*, figs. 106–112; or Schreiber's *Bilderatlas*, I xxx figs. 2–8.]

Glădĭus. The Roman military sword, which was attached to a shoulder-strap round the neck, or to the girdle round the waist. The common soldiers wore it on the right side; the officers, having no shield like the common soldiers, on the left. It was a short, sharp, two-edged weapon, used more for thrusting than cutting. In the republican period it was only worn by magistrates when acting as military officers; but under the Empire it was the emblem of imperial power, and in consequence one of the *insignia* of the emperor and the commanders nominated by him. After the introduction of the sword instead of the axe in executions, the *iŭs gladiī* was the term expressing the full criminal jurisdiction conferred by the emperor on the provincial governors.

Glass (Gr. *hўălŏs*, Lat. *vĭtrum*). Glass was for a long time procured by the Greeks and Romans from Phœnicia and Egypt, where its manufacture had been carried on since very ancient times, and the art had reached an uncommon degree of perfection. The ancients produced glasswork of great beauty, both in form and colours. In later times it was the manufacturers of Alexandria whose reputation stood the highest. The manufacturers carried on, down to the times of the later Empire, a considerable export trade in coloured blown-glass and mosaics. It is uncertain whether the Greeks manufactured their own glass in more ancient times. It was certainly a very costly article down to the time of the Peloponnesian War, and only came into general use at a late period.

In Italy the manufacture of glass began at the commencement of the imperial period, first in Campania and afterwards in Rome, where they were ambitious of surpassing the art of Alexandria. From Italy it spread to Gaul and Spain and the more distant provinces, and before long, glass cups, saucers, and bottles became an ordinary part of household furniture. The remains discovered at Hercŭlānĕum and Pompeii show that glass windows were not unknown in the imperial age. The ancients were familiar with the manufacture of pure, white, transparent, crystal glass, which was much in request, as well as with the art of colouring glass in every tint. They could imitate every kind of stone, produce varying prismatic tints, and spread layers of different colours upon each other. The art of cutting and polishing glass was very advanced. From bits of glass, cut and polished, were made great numbers of mock pearls, or mock precious stones, and pastes, which were worn, instead of real stones, in rings, cut in intaglio or relief. The most important productions of art were: (1) the *vāsa dĭătrēta*. In these cups the outer side was made of filigree work, cut out of the hard mass. The outer network was of a different colour from the ground, with which it was connected by nothing but slender glass stalks. (2) The vessels which exhibit reliefs of white opaque glass on a dark and transparent ground, like the celebrated Portland Vase (*see* GEMS). Glass tablets, intended for mural decoration, were sometimes ornamented with reliefs of this kind.

Glaucē (*Glaukē*), also called Crĕūsa. The daughter of Crĕŏn king of Corinth, who was betrothed to Jāsōn, and slain out of jealousy by Mēdēa by means of a poisoned robe. (*See* ARGONAUTS, conclusion.)

Glaucus (*Glaukŏs*). (1) A god of the sea, therefore commonly called *Pontĭŏs*, who possessed the gift of prophecy. Originally a fisherman and diver of Anthēdōn in Bœōtĭa, he once chanced to eat of a herb which he had seen fish feed on to refresh themselves when tired. It drove him mad, and he threw himself into the sea, on which he was changed into a sea-god by Ocĕănus and Tēthys. According to another story he threw himself into the sea for love of the young sea-god Mĕlĭcertēs, with whom he was sometimes identified. He was also said to have been the builder and the pilot of the *Argō*, and to have been changed into a god in a wonderful way after the battle of the Argonauts with the Tyrrhenians.

According to common belief he visited all the coasts and islands of the Mediterranean every year, prophesying, and lamenting that he could not die. He, and the Nērēïdĕs with him, were said to have uttered oracles in Dēlŏs. The stories had much to tell of his loves, notably of those of Scylla and Circē. He was represented in works of art as an old man with a fish's tail, with sea-blue scales, long hair and beard, and breast covered with sea-weed and shells.

(2) Son of the Cretan Mīnōs and Pāsĭphăē. When playing in his infancy he fell into a jar of honey, and was stifled. His father, after a vain search for him, was told by the Cūrētĕs that only one person could find the child and bring him to life again. That was the man who should devise a suitable comparison for a cow in his herd, which became white, red, and black, alternately at intervals of four hours. The seers of the country being unable to solve the difficulty, Minos called in the seer Pŏlўīdus of Argos, the great-grandson of Mĕlampūs. He read the riddle by comparing the cow to a blackberry or mulberry, which is white, red, and black at various stages of its growth. The corpse of the child he found by aid of the flight of a bird. Professing himself unable to revive the corpse, Minos, in anger, ordered him to be shut up with it in a vault. A snake crept up to the corpse, and Polyidus killed it: he then saw another snake revive its dead fellow by laying a herb upon it. With this herb he brought the dead child to life again. Finally Minos compelled him to teach the boy the art of prophecy. But on his return to Argos, Polyidus made the child spit into his mouth, which caused him to forget all that he had learned.

(3) King of Corinth, son of Sīsўphus and father of Bellĕrŏphontēs. At the funeral games of Pĕlĭās in Iolcus, he was thrown and torn to pieces by his own horses, which Aphrŏdītē in her wrath had driven mad. His ghost was said to appear to the horses racing at the Isthmian games and terrify them. He was accordingly worshipped on the Isthmus, under the name of Tăraxippŏs, or Terrifier of Horses.

(4) Great-grandson of (3): grandson of Bellerophontes, and son of Hippŏlŏchus, prince of the Lycians. With his kinsman Sarpēdōn, he was leader of the Lycian auxiliaries of Priam, and met Dĭŏmēdēs in the mêlée. The two chieftains recognised each other as friends and guests of their grandfather Bellerophontes, and Œneus,

and exchanged armour, Glaucus parting with his golden suit for the brazen arms of Diomedes. When the Greek entrenchments were stormed, Glaucus had reached the top of the wall when he was put to flight by an arrow shot by Teucer. He protected Hector when wounded by Achilles; with Apollo's aid he avenged Sarpedon, and took a prominent part in the struggle for the body of Patroclus. He finally met his death at the hand of Ajax.

Glўcōn. An Athenian artist, who probably flourished in the 1st century B.C. He executed the famous colossal statue of the *Farnese Hercules*, now at Naples (*see* HERACLES).

Gnōmōn. The Greek term for the sundial, the use of which in Greece is said to date from Anaxĭmĕnēs or Anaxīmander (500 B.C.) The first sundial used in Rome (*sōlārĭum*) was brought there in 263 B.C. from Cătăna in Sicily, and set up in public. It was not, however, till 164 B.C. that one adapted to the latitude of Rome was constructed. From that time the use of sundials became so common throughout the empire, that it was assumed in legislation during the imperial period, and all private business was regulated by the hours marked on the dial.

Gold and Ivory, Art of Working in. The Greeks had a peculiar process of making statues of their gods, in which the unclothed parts were of ivory, the hair and raiment of gold. It was applied exclusively to colossal statues, and was in special vogue in the 5th century B.C., when Phĭdĭās showed himself an unrivalled master in the art. A clay model was sawn into pieces, in correspondence with which the parts of the statue were composed of ivory plates, made by a process (now lost) of softening and extending the material. This was done by sawing, scraping, and filing. The separate pieces were then fastened with isinglass on a solid nucleus of clay, gypsum, or dried up wood. The next step was to work over the surface of the ivory plates, to smooth over inequalities, and so on. Finally the gold portions, which had been finished separately, were laid on. Special care was required to keep the pieces of ivory together. Oil was much used to keep them in a state of preservation. The statue of Zeus by Phidias at Olympĭa was found, fifty or sixty years after it was finished, to be in so dislocated a state that a complete restoration was necessary [Pausanias v 11 § 10; iv 31 § 6].

Gorgĭăs. (1) A Greek sophist and rhetorician, a native of Lĕontīnī in Sicily. In 427 B.C., when already advanced in years, he came to Athens on an embassy from his native city, to implore aid against the Syracusans. The finished style of his speaking excited general admiration. He was successful in the object of his mission, and immediately returned home. But he soon came back to Athens, which he made his headquarters, travelling through Greece, like the other Sophists, and winning much popularity and emolument from a large number of disciples. He survived Socrates, who died in 399, and ended his days at Làrissa in Thessaly in his hundredth year.

His philosophy was a nihilistic system, which he summed up in three propositions: (*a*) nothing exists; (*b*) if anything existed, it could not be known; (*c*) did anything exist, and could it be known, it could not be communicated. He declined to assume the name of Sophist, preferring that of rhetorician. He professed to teach not virtue, but the art of persuasion; in other words, to give his disciples such absolute readiness in speaking, that they should be able to convince their hearers independently of any knowledge of the subject. He did not found his instruction on any definite rhetorical system, but gave his pupils standard passages of literature to learn by art and imitate, practising them in the application of rhetorical figures. He appeared in person, on various occasions, at Delphi, Olympia, and Athens, with model speeches which he afterwards published. It must not be forgotten that it was Gorgias who transplanted rhetoric to Greece, its proper soil, and who helped to diffuse the Attic dialect as the literary language of prose. Two highly rhetorical exercises, the genuineness of which is doubtful, have come down to us under his name,—the *Encōmĭum of Helen*, and the *Defence of Pălămēdēs* against the charge of high treason brought against him by Odysseus.

(2) A Greek rhetorician of the second half of the 1st century B.C. He was tutor to the younger Cicero, and was the author of a treatise on the figures of speech, which is in part preserved in a Latin paraphrase by Rutīlĭus Lŭpus. (*See* RUTILIUS LUPUS.)

Gorgō (Gorgons). Homer makes mention of the terrible head of the Gorgon, a formidable monster. This head is a terror in Hādēs, and in the ægis or breastplate of Zeus. Hesiod speaks of three Gorgons; Sthĕnō (the mighty), Euryălē (the wide-

wandering), and Mĕdūsa (the queen). They are the daughters of the aged sea-god Phorcys and Kētō, and sisters of the Graiæ (*see* GRAIÆ). They dwell on the farthest shore of Ocean, in the neighbourhood of Night and of the Hespĕrĭdĕs. They are awful beings, with hair and girdles of snakes, whose look turns the beholder to stone. They are also often represented with golden wings, brazen claws, and enormous teeth. Medusa is mortal, but the other two immortal. When Perseus cuts off Medusa's head, Chrȳsāōr and the winged horse Pēgăsus, with whom she was with child by Poseidōn, spring forth from the streaming blood. The head was given by Perseus to Athēnē, who set it in her shield. Hērăclēs received a lock of the hair from Athene as a present. When endeavouring to persuade Cĕphălus of Tĕgĕa to take part in his expedition against Hippŏcŏōn of Sparta, the king requested that he feared an attack from his enemies the Argives in Heracles' absence. Heracles accordingly gave to Stĕrŏpē, the daughter of Cephalus, the lock of Medusa's hair in a brazen urn, bidding her, in case the enemy approached, to avert her head and hold it three times over the walls, for the mere aspect of it would turn the enemy to flight. In consequence of the belief in this power of the Gorgon's head, or *Gorgŏneiŏn*, to paralyse and terrify an enemy, the Greeks carved images of it in its most terrifying forms, not only on armour of all sorts,

(1) ARCHAIC HEAD OF MEDUSA. (*Cp.* SCULPTURE, fig. 1).
(*Antefixum of terra-cotta*, found S.E. of Parthenon, 1836, published in colours by Ross, *Arch. Aufs.* I vii.)

especially shields and breastplates, but also on walls and gates (*see* fig. 1). Thus, on the south wall of the Athenian Acropolis, a large gilded *Gorgoneion* was set on an ægis [Pausanias, i 21 § 4]. In the popular belief the Gorgon's head was also a means of protection against all enchantment, whether of word or act, and we thus find it throughout Greek history employed as a powerful amulet, and often carved with graceful settings on decorative furniture and costly ornaments. But the Greek artists, with their native sense of beauty, knew, even in the case of the Gorgon, how to give adequate expression to the idea which lay at the root of the story. The story said that Medusa had been a fair maiden, whose luxuriant hair had been turned by Athene into snakes in revenge for the desecration of her sanctuary. Accordingly the head of Medusa is represented in works of art with a countenance of touching beauty, and a wealth of hair wreathed with snakes. The face was imagined as itself in the stillness of death, and thus bearing the power to turn the

(2) RONDANINI MEDUSA.
(Munich, Glyptothek.)

living to stone. The most beautiful surviving instance of this conception is the Rondanini Medusa now at Munich (fig. 2).

Gortȳn, Law of. [An archaic Greek inscription discovered in 1884 by Halbherr, in the bed of a mill-stream at Hagios Deka in Crete, the site of the Greek city of Gortyn. After many difficulties, the whole of it was copied and published at the end of the year. It was found to be inscribed in 12 columns on the inside wall of a circular building about 100 feet in diameter, which was probably a theatre, and covers a space of about 30 feet in length, to a height of between 5 and 6 feet from the ground. The lines are written alternately from left to right and from right to left. Two fragments of it had been discovered before, one of them being in the Louvre at Paris, and with the addition of these fragments the inscription was found to be practically complete. It contains a collection of laws regulating the private relations of the inhabitants of Gortyn. These laws deal chiefly with such subjects as Inheritance, Adoption, Heiresses, Marriage and Divorce, and incidentally afford much information on the slave system, the tenure of land and property, the organization of the courts, and other matters of interest. Its chief value is perhaps· as throwing light upon the laws of the earlier Athenian legislators. The inscription is probably to be dated a few years before 400 B.C.]—C. A. M. Pond.

Graiæ, *i.e.* the gray-haired women, were in Greek mythology, the protectresses of the Gorgons, and, like them, the daughters of Kētō and Phorcȳs, the aged god of the seas. Hesiod knows of only two, Pephrēdō and Enȳō; the later story adds a third, Deinō. Their very names suggest panic and terror. Born with gray hair, and having only one eye and tooth between them, which they pass from one to the other, they are the very personifications of old age. Perseus found it easy to rob them of their tooth. Their dwelling-place was in the boundary of the Gorgonian plain at the farthest end of Libya, where no sun or moon ever shone.

Grammăteus. The Greek word for a writer, secretary, or clerk. At Athens the officials had numerous clerks attached to them, who were paid by the state and belonged to the poorer class of citizens. But there were several higher officials who bore the title of *Grammateus.* The Boulē or senate, for instance, chose one of its members by show of hands to be its clerk or secretary for one year. His duty was to keep the archives of the senate. So, too, a secretary was chosen by lot from the whole number of senators for each prȳtăny, to draft all resolutions of the senate. (*See* PRYTANY.) His name is therefore generally given in the decrees next to that of the president and the proposer of the decree. The name of the *grammateus* of the first prytany was also given with that of the *archŏn,* as a means of marking the year with more accuracy. At the meetings of the Ecclesia a clerk, elected by the people, had to read out the necessary documents. The office of the *antĭgrăpheis,* or checking clerks, was of still greater importance. The *antigrapheus* of the senate, elected at first by show of hands, but afterwards by lot, had to take account of all business affecting the financial administration. The *antigrapheus* of the administration had to make out, and lay before the public, a general statement of income and expenditure, and exercised a certain amount of control over all financial officials. In the Ætolian and Achæan federations the *grammateus* was the highest officer of the League after the *strătēgī* and *hipparchī*.

Grammătĭca [sometimes rendered in Latin by *littĕrātūra*].

1. *Greece.* The term *grammatica*, in the scientific sense, included, in antiquity, all the philological disciplines, grammar proper, lexicography, prosody, the lower and higher criticism, antiquities, everything, in short, necessary to the understanding and explanation of *grammăta*, or the treasures of literature, whether their form or their matter be in question. It was first developed into a special science during the Alexandrian age, in Alexandria and Pergămŏn, where the great libraries gave ample opportunity for philological studies on the scale above indicated. It was the restoration of the text of the Homeric poems, and the explanation of their words and contents, that primarily exercised the wits of the scholars. Hesiod, the lyric poets, the dramatists, and certain prose writers next engaged their attention. The progress and development of philology is marked by the names of Zēnŏdŏtus (about 280 B.C.), Aristŏphănēs of Byzantium (260–183), and Aristarchus (about 170), the three chief representatives of the Alexandrian school. To these must be added Crătēs (about 160), the head of the school of Pergamon, and the opponent of the Alexandrians. The name of Aristarchus represents the highest point of philological learning and criticism in antiquity. He was the founder of the celebrated school of the Aristarcheans, which continued to exist and to maintain an uninterrupted tradition, down to the first century of the imperial age. His disciple Dĭonȳsĭus Thrax wrote the oldest manual of grammar that we possess. By far the most celebrated of the later Aristarcheans was Dĭdȳmus, born about 63 B.C. His writings are the chief foundation of the Byzantine collections of *schŏlĭa*.

The science of *grammatica* gradually narrowed its scope till it confined itself to grammar in the restricted sense of the word, namely, accidence and syntax, combined with lexical researches into the dialects, and into the usages of special periods of literature, and special groups of authors. The most eminent scholars of the Empire are Apollōnĭus Dyscŏlus (about 150 A.D.), who endeavoured to reduce the whole of empirical grammar to a system, and his son, Ælĭus Hērōdĭānus, a still more important personage. The writings of the latter form one of the chief authorities of the later grammarians, such as Arcădĭus. The lexical writings of the earlier scholars were often very comprehensive, and have only survived in fragments, or in later extracts, such as that of Hēsȳchĭus. They had consisted mainly in collections of glosses, or strange and antiquated expressions. But in the 2nd century A.D. the influence of the reviving sophistic literature and education turned the attention of lexicographers to the usage of the Attic writers. This tendency is represented in the surviving works of Pollux, Harpŏcrătĭōn, and others. To the same period belongs Hephæstĭōn's manual of prosody, which is the only complete treatise on this subject. Athenæus, at the beginning of the 3rd century, wrote a work (the *Deipnŏsŏphistœ*) of inestimable value to the student of antiquities. Longīnus, who died 273 A.D., may be regarded as the last considerable scholar of the ancient world. The later grammarians restricted themselves to compiling extracts from the works of earlier ages.

(2) *Rome.* After the middle of the 2nd century B.C., a lively interest in the history of literature and the study of language arose in Rome. It had been excited by the lectures on Greek authors given by Crates during his sojourn in Rome as ambassador (B.C. 159). Not only writers of repute, such as Accius and Lucilius, but men like Ælĭus Stĭlō, a member of the equestrian order, who was actively engaged in public life, took up these studies with eagerness. What was afterwards known of the primitive Latin language we owe mainly to Ælius Stilo. He was the master of the great encyclopædist Marcus Terentĭus Varrō, Cicero's contemporary. This great scholar left his mark on every department of philological research, and his writings were the storehouse from which the following generations mainly drew their information. Besides Varro, other men of mark occupied themselves with grammatical study in the Ciceronian age, notably Nigĭdĭus Fĭgŭlus. Julius Cæsar was the author of a treatise on accidence. There were numerous scholars in the Augustan age, among whom Verrĭus Flaccus and Hȳgīnus deserve especial notice. In the 1st century A.D. we have Remmĭus Pălæmŏn, Asconĭus Pĕdĭānus, Vălĕrĭus Prŏbus, and the elder Pliny. It was Remmius Palæmon who is mainly responsible for having made Vergil the centre of scholastic instruction for the Latin world, as Homer was for the Greek. During the 2nd century, under Hadrian and the Antonines, we notice a

revived interest in the older literature. This period is distinguished by the names of Suētōnïus, Terentïus Scaurus, and Aulus Gellïus. Suetonius aspired to the many-sided learning of Varro, and, like Varro, was much quoted by later writers.

After this time the grammarians tend more and more to confine their studies to points of language, to abandon independent research, and to depend on the labours of their predecessors. The chief value of their writings consists in the fact that they have preserved some fragments of ancient learning. Their extracts are usually made for school purposes, and put together in *artēs*, or manuals of accidence, orthography, prosody, and metre. Such are the books of Mārïus Victōrīnus, Dōnātus, Servïus, Charī-sïus, Diomēdēs, who are all assigned to the 4th century A.D. Nōnïus Marcellus belongs to the same period. He is the author of a work (*De Compendïōsā Doctrīnā*) which, though dreary and uncritical, is invaluable for the stores of old Latin which it has preserved. The 6th century is marked by the name of Priscian. We may further notice Tĕrentïānus Maurus, the author of a versified treatise on metre in the 3rd century; Macrŏbïus, who in the 5th century composed a miscellany of antiquities called *Sāturnālïa;* and Isidore, Bishop of Seville, in the 7th century, whose *Orīgïnēs* is the last work founded on a real study of ancient authorities.

Grammăticus (Gr. *Grammătï-kŏs*). *See* EDUCATION.

Grammătistēs. *See* EDUCATION.

Grānïus Lïcïnïānus. A Roman historian, who probably flourished in the 2nd century A.D. He was the author of a work compiled in the style of *annālēs*, ending with the death of Cæsar. Some considerable fragments have been found in modern times of books 28–36, covering the history of the years 163–78 B.C.

Grăphē. *See* JUDICIAL PROCE-DURE.

Grātïæ, or *Graces. See* CHARITES.

Grātïus [better *Grattïus*] **Fălis-cus.** A Roman poet, contemporary with Ovid. He was the author of a poem on the chase (*Cÿnĕgĕtïcōn*), of which only the first book has been preserved, and that mutilated towards the close. The fragment consists of some 535 hexameters, in which the subject is treated

with much talent in an even and classical style, but with considerable dryness in many parts. Grattius has been styled *Faliscus* because, in one passage, he apparently indicates that the Falisci were his countrymen.

Grōma. The measuring instrument used by land surveyors, who were called *Grōmā-tïcī* from it. *See* AGRIMENSORES.

Gustātïō. *See* MEALS.

Gÿnaikōnītïs. *See* HOUSE.

Gymnăsïarchïa. *See* LEITOURGIA (2).

Gymnăsïum (Gr. *Gymnăsïŏn*). The Greek name for the place where the youths who had already passed through the *pălæstra* performed their gymnastic exercises. (*See* PALÆSTRA.) Such was the importance which the Greeks attached to physical training, that no city in Greece proper, and no Greek colony, was without its *gymnasium*. There were several in the larger cities. Athens, for instance, in the time of its greatness, possessed three, all situated outside the city, the *Acădēmïa*, the *Lÿcæum*, and the *Cÿnŏsargēs*. In later times there were even more. It was in the *gymnasia* that the *ĕphēbī* went through the two years' course of exercises which were to fit them for military service.

The simplest form of a *gymnasium* was that of a court surrounded by columns

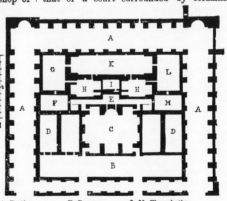

A. Portico.
B. Palæstra.
C. Ephebeion.
D. Dressing-rooms.
E. Passage.
F, G. Cold baths.
H, H. Hot baths.
L, M. Warm baths.
Near I. Staircase to *laconicum*.
K. Ball-alley.

* GYMNASIUM AT EPHESUS.
(*Ionian Antiquities*, ii, pl. 40.)

(*pĕristÿlïŏn*). This served for the exercises in leaping and running. Covered spaces were attached for wrestling. Owing to the great variety of gymnastic exercises, and the increasing inclination of grown men to look on at them and take part in them, the *gymnasia*, often adorned with beautiful sculptures, grew in extent and splendour of equipment. (*See* cut.)

The great court comprised a number of spaces serving a variety of purposes: for instance, the *ĕphēbeiŏn*, or hall where the *ephebi* practised, rooms for dressing and anointing, sanding or dusting the body, cold-water baths and dry *sūdātōrĭa*, spaces for playing at ball, open and covered passages for running, wrestling, or walking. Attached to the colonnades on the outside were semicircular niches, furnished with stone seats, called *exedræ*. In these philosophers and rhetoricians would sit and talk with their disciples. A *stădĭŏn*, with a space for spectators to look on, and walks planted with trees, were often attached to the *gymnasium*. The whole was under the superintendence of a *gymnasiarchŏs*. The conduct of the youths was under the supervision of *sŏphrŏnistœ*. At Athens these officers were ten in number, and elected annually. The exercises were directed by the *gymnastœ*. For similar arrangements under the Roman empire *see* THERMÆ.

Gymnastics. I *Grecian.* The art of physical exercises, so called because the Greeks practised them unclothed (*gymnŏs*). Various exercises of the kind, carried on in view of contests on festive occasions, are mentioned as early as Homer. After the Homeric time they were, at all periods, widely practised among the Greeks, and more so after they were legally prescribed as part of the regular educational course, especially at Athens and Sparta. They were, moreover, actively encouraged by the great national games, particularly the Olympian games, of which they formed the chief part. Hērăclēs and Hermēs were the tutelary gods of gymnastics, which attained in Athens their highest and most varied development. The object of the art was to develop the body harmoniously in health, activity, and beauty. Boys went through certain preliminary stages of gymnastics in the *palœstrœ*, and carried on their further training to perfection in the *gymnăsĭa*. (*See* GYMNASIUM.)

The different kinds of exercises were as follows: (1) Running (*drŏmŏs* or *stădĭŏn*). This was the oldest of all, and for a long time the only one practised in the public games. In later times, indeed, it stood at the head of the list. The course was either single (*stadion*, nearly the eighth of a mile), or double (*dĭaulŏs*). The runner was some-

times equipped with helmet and greaves, but in later times only with the latter. The hardest of all was the long course or *dŏlĭchŏs*. This was a distance of 24 *stadia*, between two and three English miles, which had to be run without stopping.

(2) Leaping (*halmă*). This included the high and wide jump, and jumping downwards. To strengthen the power of spring and secure the equilibrium of the body, especially in leaping downwards, it was common to use pieces of iron called *haltērĕs*, not unlike our dumb-bells.

(3) Wrestling (*pălē*). This was the *pièce de résistance* of the Greek gymnastic. The combatants were allowed certain tricks which are now forbidden, as throttling, pushing, and twisting the fingers. Standing upright, each wrestler tried to throw the other down, and if one of them was thrown thrice, he was regarded as beaten, unless the contest was continued on the ground. In this case the one who was thrown tried to get up, while the other tried to hinder him, until he owned himself vanquished.

Before all gymnastic exercises the body was well rubbed with oil to make the limbs supple. But before wrestling it was also sprinkled with dust, partly to afford a firm hold, partly to prevent excessive perspiration.

(4) *Discŏbŏlĭa*, or throwing the *discus*. (*See* DISCUS.)

(5) Throwing the javelin (*ăkontismŏs*).

(1) * METHOD OF DISCHARGING THE JAVELIN WITH
THE AID OF AN *ammentum*, OR THONG.
(Vase in British Museum : *Rev. Arch.*, 1860, ii 211.)

These five exercises together formed the *pentathlŏn*, or set of five, in which no one was accounted victorious who had not conquered in all. Besides these there was

(6) The dangerous game of boxing (*pyx, pygmē*). In this the combatants struck out with each hand alternately, their hands being bound round with thongs so as to leave fingers and thumb free to form a clenched fist (*see* engraving). Athletes often fitted the thongs with strips of sharp and hardened

leather, or with nails and leaden knobs. The blow was directed against the upper part of the body, head, and face.

(2) BOXER.
(Dresden.)

(7) The *Pancrătĭŏn* was a combination of boxing and wrestling, but nothing was worn on the hands, and the blow was delivered, not with the clenched fist, but with the fingers bent. This exercise was not introduced into the public games until 650 B.C. Indeed, the two latter exercises were generally confined to the professional athletes. (*See* ATHLETES.) In Sparta they were not practised at all.

II *Roman.* Among the Romans from the oldest times until the imperial period, the youths used to assemble for exercises in the Campus Martius, the object of the exercises being exclusively to prepare them for military service. (*See* EDUCATION.) The Greek gymnastic was not introduced at Rome until the decline of Roman tradition had set in, and professional athleticism had

become fashionable. The Roman sense of propriety was offended by the Greek practice of exercising unclothed, and the only game which they really adopted was that of throwing the *discus*.

Gymnētæ (troops without defensive armour). A name for the different sorts of sharpshooters employed in the Greek armies after the Persian Wars, in place of the light-armed slaves. It was only after the expedition of the Ten Thousand that they came to form an essential part of a Greek army. They were generally recruited from the barbarous nations who were specially distinguished in the use of particular missiles. The archers (*toxŏtæ*), for instance, were generally Cretans, the slingers (*sphendŏnētæ*) Rhodians and Thessalians, while the javelin men (*ăkontistæ*) were taken from the semi-Hellenic populations in the west of Greece, notably the Ætolians and Acarnanians. The common characteristic of all these troops was the absence of all defensive weapons. It was among the Lacedemonians that they were introduced latest. Alexander the Great had a corps of 2,000 of them, with which he opened his campaign against the Persians. Half of these were spearmen, taken from the Agrĭānī, in the mountains of northern Macedonia; the other half archers, from the lowest class of the Macedonian population.

Gymnŏpaidĭa. A great festival held at Sparta from the 6th to the 10th of July. It was an exhibition of all kinds of accomplishments in gymnastics, music, and dancing, given by boys, youths, and men for the benefit of the citizens and of the numerous strangers who flocked to Sparta for the occasion, and were hospitably entertained there. Festal hymns were written for the occasion, in honour not only of the gods but of brave citizens, notably those who had fallen at Thy̆rĕa, and later at Thermŏpy̆læ.

H

Hādēs (originally *Ăĭdēs* or *Ăĭdōneus*, i.e. "the Invisible"). In Greek mythology, the son of Crŏnus and Rhea, who received the dominion of the lower world at the division of the universe after the fall of Cronus, his brothers, Zeus and Pŏseidōn, being made lords respectively of the sky and sea. With his queen Persĕphŏnē he held sway over the other powers of the infernal regions, and over the ghosts of the dead.

The symbol of his invisible empire was the helmet that made men invisible. This was given to him by the Cyclōpĕs to aid him in the battle of the gods with the Giants. Originally he was, to all appearance, conceived as bringing down the dead himself to the lower world in his chariot, or as driving them down with his staff; but in the later belief, the office of conductor of souls belonged to Hermēs. Hades is the enemy of all life, heartless and inexorable, and hated, accordingly, by gods and men. Sacrifice and prayer are of no avail with him, and he is therefore only worshipped on exceptional occasions. But, like Persephone, he was sometimes represented in a milder light, being called Plūtō, or the giver of wealth. This because it is from the depths of the earth that corn and its attendant blessings are produced. As old as Hesiod is the advice to the plougher to call upon the Zeus of the lower world, as well as upon Dēmētēr.

HADES ENTHRONED, WITH CERBERUS.
(Rome, Villa Borghese.)

The most celebrated of the myths referring to Hades is that of the rape of Persephone. In works of art he is represented as resembling his brothers Zeus and Poseidon, but with gloomy features and hair falling over his brow, the key of the infernal world in his hand, and the dog Cerbĕrus at his side. Sometimes he appears as a god of agriculture, with a cornucopia, or a two-pronged pickaxe. The plants sacred to him were the cypress and the narcissus; black sheep were offered to him in sacrifice.

The word *Hades* is also a general term for the lower regions. By the Romans Hades was identified partly with *Orcus*, partly with *Dīs păter*.

Hades, Realm of. According to the belief current among the Greeks, the world of the dead, or the spacious abode of Hādēs, with its wide doors, was in the dark depths of the earth. In the Odyssey, its entrance and outer court are on the western side of the river Ocĕănus, in the ground sacred to Persĕphŏnē, with its grove of barren willows and poplars. Here is the abode of the Cimmerians, veiled in darkness and cloud, where the sun never shines. The soil of this court, and indeed of the lower world in general, is a meadow of asphodel, an unattractive weed of dreary aspect usually planted on graves. The actual abode of the subterranean powers is Erĕbŏs, or the impenetrable darkness. In later times entrances to the lower world were imagined in other places where there were cavernous hollows which looked as if they led into the bowels of the earth. Such places were Hermĭŏnē and the promontory of Tænărum in the Peloponnese, Hērăclĕa on the Euxine, and Cūmæ in Italy, where the mythical Cimmĕrĭī were also localized. The lower world of Homer is intersected by great rivers, the Styx, the Achĕrōn (river of woe), Cōcȳtus (river of cries), a branch of the Styx, Phlĕgĕthōn and Pȳrĭphlĕgĕthōn (rivers of fire). The last two unite and join the waters of the Acheron. In the post-Homeric legend, these rivers are represented as surrounding the infernal regions, and another river appears with them, that of Lēthē, or oblivion. In the waters of Lethe the souls of the dead drink forgetfulness of their earthly existence. The lower world once conceived as separated from the upper by these rivers, the idea of a ferryman arose. This was Chărōn, the son of Erebos and of Nyx, a gloomy, sullen old man, who takes the souls in his boat across Acheron into the realm of shadows. The souls are brought down from the upper world by Hermēs, and pay the ferryman an *ŏbŏlŏs*, which was put for this purpose into the mouths of the dead. Charon has the right to refuse a passage to souls whose bodies have not been duly buried. In Homer it is the spirits themselves who refuse to receive any one to whom funeral honours have not been paid. At the gate lies the dog Cerbĕrus, son of Tȳphāōn and Echidna. He is a terrible monster with three heads, and mane and tail of snakes. He is friendly to the spirits who enter, but if any one tries to get out he seizes him and holds him fast.

The ghosts of the dead were in ancient times conceived as incorporeal images of their former selves, without mind or consciousness. In the Odyssey the seer Tīrĕsĭās is the only one who has retained his consciousness and judgment, and this as an exceptional gift of Persephone. But they have the power of drinking the blood of animals, and having done so they recover their consciousness and power of speech. The soul therefore is not conceived as entirely annihilated. The ghosts retain the outer form of their body, and follow, but instinctively only, what was their favourite pursuit in life. Orīon in Homer is still a hunter, Mīnōs sits in judgment, as when

that Homer several times mentions that the Erīnyĕs punish perjurers after death. We are forced then to conclude that the ancient belief is, in this instance, found side by side with the later and generally received idea, that the dead, even without drinking blood, preserved their consciousness and power of speech. Connected with it is the notion that they have the power of influencing men's life on earth in various ways. The most ancient belief knows nothing of future

MEGARA AND HER SONS.
HUSBAND, WIFE, AND CHILD.   ORPHEUS.   PERSEPHONE AND HADES.   MEDEA (OR DIKE), PEIRITHOUS, AND THESEUS.
SISYPHUS.   ERINYS.   HERMES.   HERACLES.   CERBERUS.   TRIPTOLEMUS, ÆACUS, AND RHADAMANTHYS.
                                                                              ERINYS.   TANTALUS.

* THE REALM OF HADES.
(Vase from Canosa: Munich, Pinakothek, No. 849.)

alive. Perhaps the punishments inflicted in Homer on Tĭtўus, Tantălus, and Sīsўphus (for Ixīon, the Dănăĭdĕs, Peirĭthŏüs, and others belong to a later story) should be regarded in this light. The penalties inflicted on them in the upper world may be merely transferred by Homer to their ghostly existence. For the idea of a sensible punishment is not consistent with that of an unconscious continuance in being. It must be remembered, at the same time,

rewards of the righteous, or indeed of any complete separation between the just and the unjust, or of a judgment to make the necessary awards. The judges of the dead are in the later legend Minos, Rhădămanthўs, Æăcus, and Triptŏlĕmus. It was a later age, too, which transferred Elўsĭum and Tartărus to the lower world, Elysium as the abode of the blessed, and Tartarus as that of the damned. In the earlier belief these regions had nothing to do with the realm of Hādēs (*see* HADES). The name *Tartărus* was in later times often applied to the whole of the lower world. The ghosts of those who had lived a life of average merit were imagined as wandering on the asphodel meadow.

In general it must be said that the ancient ideas of a future life were always subject to considerable changes, owing to the influence of the doctrines taught in the mysteries, and the representations of poets, philosophers, sculptors, and painters (*see* POLYGNOTUS). The general tendency was to multiply the terrors of Hades, especially at the gates, and in Tartarus. (For the deities of the lower world *see* HADES, PERSEPHONE, and ERINYES.) The Greek beliefs on the subject found their way to Rome through the instrumentality of the poets, especially Vergil. But they did not entirely supplant the national traditions. (*See* ORCUS, MANIA, MANES, LARES, *and* LARVÆ.)

and dedicated it to some deity, generally to Apollo, or the gods of their rivers, or the Nymphs, who were regarded as the protectresses of youth. But a free Athenian citizen did not wear his hair very short, or he would have been mistaken for a slave, who would be obliged to do so. Down to the time of Alexander the Great, a full beard was regarded as a mark of manly dignity. After this it became fashionable to shave the face quite smooth, and only philosophers wore beards, to mark their antagonism to the general custom. The Romans too, in ancient times, wore long hair and beards. It was not till 300 B.C., when the first hair-cutter (*tonsor*) came to Rome from Sicily, that they began to cut both. The younger Scipio is said to have been the first Roman who shaved every day. In course of time it became the fashion to make a festival of the day when the beard was first shaved. Young men, however,

(1) COIFFURES OF GREEK LADIES.
(From terracottas, Stackelberg's *Gräber der Hellenen*, taf. lxxv, etc.)

Hæmŏn. *See* ANTIGONE.

Hair, mode of wearing. The Greeks of the oldest times regarded long hair in a man as an ornament, and only cut it as a sign of mourning. Among the Spartans it was usual for boys to wear their hair short, and to let it grow when they attained the age of *ĕphēbī*. At Athens, down to the Persian Wars, the hair was worn long, and fastened up into a knot (*krōbўlŏs*) by a needle in the form of a grasshopper. In later times, however, the Athenian boys had their hair cut when they became *ephebi*,

would sometimes wear a neatly cut beard, and only men over forty would shave. To let the beard grow was a sign of mourning. In the first half of the 2nd century A.D. the emperor Hadrian brought full beards into fashion again; and if we may trust the coins, it continued among his successors, with few exceptions, until Constantine. From his time, however, the emperors appear almost without exception without a beard.

The beard was removed not only with razors and scissors, but with tweezers and hair-destroying compositions. The hair of the head was artificially treated with oils and hot irons. From the middle of the 2nd century A.D. to the time of Constantine it was the established custom to cut the hair quite short, after the fashion of athletes and Stoic philosophers. As Greeks and Romans usually went bareheaded, good manners required particular attention to be paid to the hair and beard. Hence a great demand arose for barbers, part of whose business it was to trim the nails, remove warts, and so on. The barbers' shops were much frequented, and became the favourite resort for people in quest of news and gossip.

The Greek women, to judge by existing monuments, followed an extraordinary variety of fashions (fig. 1, *a–h*). The point seems generally to have been to cover the forehead as much as possible. One of the commonest modes of wearing the hair was to draw it back over the head and ears, and let it simply hang down, or fasten it in a knot with a band and a needle. The bands of cloth or leather, wound round the front of the head to fasten the front and back hair, were often made to support a pointed metal plate called *stĕphănē*. This was a broad strip of metal resembling a diadem, and richly ornamented. It sometimes appears as an independent ornament, especially on the images of goddesses (fig. 1, *c, d, f, g*). There were several kinds of fastenings, by which the hair was artistically arranged; for instance, the *sphendŏnē*, so called from its likeness to a sling, being broad in the middle and narrow at the end. The hair was often worn in nets (*kekrў-phălŏs*), bags (*sakkŏs*), and handkerchiefs wrapped round it in the shape of a cap. Greek ladies were early acquainted with the use of artificial appliances, such as fragrant oils, curling irons, and the like.

(2) COIFFURES OF IMPERIAL ROMAN LADIES.

The Roman matrons, in ancient times, tied up their hair with a fillet (*vitta*) in a tower-shaped top-knot (*tŭtŭlus*); but un-married women wore their hair in as simple a style as possible. It was, in general, merely parted, or fastened up in a knot on the neck, or woven in tresses arranged round the front of the head. Brides wore their hair in a peculiar fashion, arranged in six braids, and wrapped in a red handkerchief. To attract attention by an unusual *coiffure* was thought to be in bad taste. But, towards the end of the republican age, the old-fashioned simplicity in dressing the hair disappeared, as it did in other

SABINA.   FAUSTINA, FROM POMPEII.   IULIA DOMNA.

(3) *COIFFURES OF IMPERIAL ROMAN LADIES
(FROM COINS).

matters of dress. Foreign arts, especially those of Greece and Asia, found more and more acceptance. During the imperial period, when the arrangement of the hair

a, b, c, h, i, k. Ivory hair-pins.   *f.* Bronze comb.
e. Pomatum-box, with resting Cupid.   *d, g.* Hand mirrors.

(4) HAIR-PINS, ETC.
(From Pompeii.)

formed a most important part of a lady's toilet, no rule was observed but what individual caprice and varying fashion dictated, and the wildest and most tasteless fashions were introduced. False hair came into use, as well as ointment and curling irons. False hair was used sometimes in making up the high *coiffures* at one time in fashion, and sometimes for *perruques*. Light colours were the favourite ones for *perruques*, and hence a regular trade was set up in the hair of German women. Sometimes, following a Greek fashion, Roman ladies tried, by artificial means, to give their own dark hair a fair or a ruddy complexion. A corrosive soap, imported from Gaul, was specially used for this purpose. Besides ribbons and fillets, needles, often richly ornamented, of ivory, bone, bronze, silver, and gold, were used to fasten the hair. To protect the hair, Roman ladies wore nets (*rētǐcŭlum*), often of gold thread, kerchiefs (*mitra*), and caps (*cǎlantǐca*), made of various materials, sometimes of bladders. In wealthy houses male and female slaves, trained by special masters, were kept for dressing the hair. (*See* the engravings.)

Halcȳŏnē. *See* ALCYONE.

Halia. *See* HELIOS.

Handicraft. Examples of handicraft applied to the ordinary needs of life occur in the mythical ages of Greece. Among the gods of Olympus, Hēphæstus represents this kind of industry, and the oldest craftsmen are represented as divine beings appearing on earth, as in the instance of the Idæan Dactȳlī and the Telchīnēs in Crete. In the Homeric poems, which are the production of an age fairly advanced in culture, the number of craftsmen properly so called is very small. (*See* DEMIURGI.) The only ones mentioned are builders, carpenters, potters, and workers in leather and metal. The development of the mechanical arts in Greece was immensely indebted, in ancient times, to foreign influence, especially that of the East; for Eastern civilization was far older than Hellenic. The greater part of the trade carried on in Greek waters was in the hands of the Phœnicians, and it was, consequently, Phœnician manufacture which the Hellenes took as a model for imitation, so soon as they thought of widening the sphere of their own industries, and bringing them to perfection. Since the 6th century B.C., or thereabouts, the definite impress of Asiatic manufacture disappears, and Greek trade, supported by a rapidly developing art, takes its own time. Not that it lost all contact with foreign work, for not only did the colonies keep up an active communication with the non-Hellenic world, but foreign craftsmen took up their permanent residence in Greek towns, such as Athens and Corinth.

Manual labour, like every lucrative occupation, was generally held in low esteem among the Greeks, and especially among the Dorian tribes. But this state of opinion must have grown up comparatively late, as there is no trace of it in Homer or Hesiod. On the contrary, the Homeric princes do not think it beneath them to undertake the work of craftsmen. In later times we find the free citizens of many states entirely declining all manual labour. In Sparta, for instance, the handicrafts were only practised by the *pĕrǐœcī* and helots, and mechanics were excluded from civic rights. At Athens all citizens were equal in the eyes of the law, and it was expressly forbidden to reproach a man for the character of his vocation, whatever it might be. The poorer citizens were compelled by law to practise some trade or other, and it was quite usual to engage in commerce. But still, in the opinion even of the wisest statesmen, mechanical labour was physically, intellectually, and morally prejudicial. The petty anxieties which it involved were held to be incompatible with the tone and culture demanded by the active life of the citizen, with the qualities which would enable him to join in deliberation on great affairs of state, and conduct public business with honesty and intelligence. It was thought, in fact, that all manual labour should be left to slaves and freedmen. Much of the mechanical industry of Athens was, accordingly, in the hands of slaves, freedmen, and resident aliens.

The slaves worked sometimes on their own account, paying a certain amount of their earnings to their master; sometimes entirely for the profit of their masters, the latter taking no active part in the business; sometimes they acted as assistants to the citizens and resident aliens who carried on a business of their own. But in industrial cities the great mass of slaves was employed in factories, the owners of which left the superintendence of the work to a head man, usually himself a slave or freedman, reserving for themselves only the general management and the financial control of the business. The immense masses of slaves kept at Athens and Corinth, and in Ægīna and Chīos, show how numerous the factories were in industrial cities. The manufacture of metal wares, pottery, and other objects which could not be made at home, was the most extended of all. The division of labour kept pace with the development of trade and manufacture. This fact may partly explain how it is that, in spite of the comparative simplicity of their tools, the Greek craftsmen attained, especially in works of art, such admirable perfection of technical detail.

In ancient Greece it would appear that there were no trade-guilds and corporations in the proper sense. But among the Romans these societies were an institution of old standing, the foundation of which was attributed to king Numa, like that of many others which had existed from time immemorial. The guilds of craftsmen (*collēgia ŏpĭfĭcum*), included flute-players, goldsmiths, coppersmiths, carpenters, fullers, dyers, potters, and shoemakers. There was originally a ninth *collegium*, which embraced all not included in the other eight; but in later times these, with the new industries that gradually arose, combined into special guilds. The object of the guilds undoubtedly was to maintain an unbroken tradition, and to watch over the common interest. But there seems to have been no compulsion exercised to make men join a guild.

The Romans, like the Greeks, seem to have thought that there was something objectionable in mechanical labour; but it is uncertain whether the prejudice was of really old standing. It must be remembered that the Servian constitution threw the burden of military service entirely upon the landowners. Thus the craftsmen, who as a rule had no landed property, were practically, though not legally, excluded from the army. From this circumstance may have arisen the low estimation in which manual industry was consequently held. It was partly owing to this state of opinion that peasants, when they lost their land, were unwilling to win their bread as mechanics, and preferred to adopt the dependent position of clients, living on public alms and the bribes of candidates at elections. In Rome, as in Greece, the handicrafts tended more and more to pass into the hands of strangers, freedmen, and slaves. In wealthy houses most of the necessary manual work was done by slaves, whose talents were often, as in Greece, turned to account by their masters. They were often employed in manufactures, and especially in such branches of industry as could be combined with agriculture, tile-making for instance, pottery, dying, tanning, felt-making, etc. No social stigma attached to manufacture in Rome any more than in Greece; indeed in the imperial age even the emperors and the members of the imperial household would, without scruple, invest their private capital in industrial undertakings of this sort. After the fall of the republic, and throughout the imperial age, Rome was the centre of the whole commercial activity of the ancient world, though the Romans made no special contribution to industrial progress. Having in former ages been dominated by Etruscan

influence, Roman industry was in later times dependent on the art of the Eastern world, and especially of Greece.

Hannō. A Carthaginian, who, about 500 B.C., undertook a voyage of discovery along the west coast of Africa, and penetrated beyond the Senegal. He put up a tablet in the temple of Bel at Carthage, describing his journey in the Phœnician language. A Greek translation of this document (*Hannōnis Pĕrĭplūs*), of uncertain date, still survives, and is one of the oldest memorials of ancient geographical science.

Har. *See* HOROS.

Harmŏnĭa. The daughter of Arēs and Aphrŏdītē, and wife of Cadmus. (*See* CADMUS.) At her marriage all the gods were present on the Acropolis of Thebes, and offered her their wedding gifts. Cadmus gave her a costly garment and a necklace, the workmanship of Hēphæstus, which he had received from Aphrodite, or (according to another account), from Eurōpa. These gifts, so the story runs, had everywhere the fatal property of stirring up strife and bloodshed. It was with them that Polyneicēs corrupted Eriphȳlē, who drove her husband to his destruction in the Theban War, and was murdered in revenge by her son Alcmæōn. It was for their sake that Alcmæon and Phēgeus and his sons were slain. (*See* ALCMÆON and PHEGEUS.) The jewels were at length deposited by the sons of Alcmæon in the sanctuary of Delphi. According to a later story Phaÿllus, a leader of the Phocians in the war against Philip of Macedon, carried off, among other treasures, the necklace of Harmonia, and gave it to his mistress, the wife of Aristōn of Œta. But her youngest son set fire to the house in a fit of madness, and the mother, with the necklace, was consumed.

Harmostæ ("regulators"). A board consisting of twenty members, at Sparta; probably a kind of higher police, whose duty it was to maintain a supervision over the districts inhabited by the *pĕrĭœcĭ*. After the Peloponnesian War the name was given to the officials who were sent into the conquered cities to command the garrisons, and to see that the oligarchical constitution was maintained.

Harpastum. *See* BALL, games with.

Harpŏcrātēs. *See* HOROS.

Harpŏcrătĭōn (*Valerius*). A Greek scholar of Alexandria, who lived probably in the 2nd century A.D. He was the author of a lexicon to the ten great Attic orators, which has survived, though in a very fragmentary form. It contains, in alphabetical order, notes on the matters and persons mentioned by the orators, with explanations of the technical expressions; thus forming a rich store of valuable information on matters of history, literature, and the constitution and judicial system of Athens.

Harpyïæ. The Harpies were originally the goddesses of the sweeping storm, symbolic of the sudden and total disappearance of men. Homer only names one of them, Pŏdargē, or the swift-footed, who, in the shape of a mare, bore to Zĕphȳrus the horses of Achilles. In Hesiod the Harpies appear as winged goddesses with beautiful hair, daughters of Thaumās and Electra, sisters of Iris, with the names of Aëllō and Okȳpĕtē. In the later story their number increased, their names being Aëllŏpūs, Okȳthŏē, Nikŏthŏē, and Cĕlæno. They are now represented as half-birds, half-maidens, and as spirits of mischief. In the story of the Argonauts, for instance, they torment Phineus by carrying off and polluting his food till they are driven off by Cālāïs and Zētēs, and either killed or banished to the island of the Strŏphădĕs, where they are bound on oath to remain. (*Cp.* SCULPTURE, fig. 4.)

Hăruspex. An Etruscan soothsayer, whose function it was to interpret the divine will from the entrails of sacrificial victims, to propitiate the anger of the gods as indicated by lightning or other marvels, and to interpret their significance according to Etruscan formulæ. This art had long been practised in Etruria, and was referred to a divine origin. In the course of the republican era it found a home in the private and public life of the Romans, winning its way as the native priesthoods, entrusted with similar functions, lost in repute. From the time of the kings to the end of the republic, *haruspĭcēs* were expressly summoned from Etruria by decrees of the senate on the occurrence of prodigies which were not provided for in the Pontifical and Sibylline books. Their business was to interpret the signs, to ascertain what deity demanded an expiation, and to indicate the nature of the necessary offering. It then lay with the priests of the Roman people to carry out their instructions. Their knowledge of the signs given by lightning was only applied in republican Rome for the purpose of averting the omen portended by the flash. (*See* PUTEAL.) But under the Empire it was also used for consulting the

lightning, either keeping it off, or drawing it down. From about the time of the Punic Wars, *haruspices* began to settle in Rome, and were employed both by private individuals and state officials to ascertain the divine will by examination of the liver, gall, heart, lungs, and caul of sacrificial victims. They were especially consulted by generals when going to war. Their science was generally held in high esteem, but the class of *haruspices* who took pay for their services did not enjoy so good a reputation. Claudius seems to have been the first emperor who instituted a regular *collēgĭum* of Roman *haruspices*, consisting of sixty members of equestrian rank, and presided over by a *haruspex maxĭmus*, for the regular service of the State. This *collegium* continued to exist till the beginning of the 5th century A.D.

Hasta. The Roman lance. In the earlier times of the army the four first classes in the Servian constitution, and in later times, the *trĭārĭī*, or hindmost rank, were armed with this weapon. (*See* LEGION.) At length, however, the *pĭlum* was introduced for the whole infantry of the legion. (*See* PILUM.) To deprive a soldier of his *hasta* was equivalent to degrading him to the rank of the *vēlĭtēs*, who were armed with javelins. A blunt *hasta* with a button at the end (*hasta pūra*) continued to be used in later times as a military decoration. The *hasta* indeed was employed in many symbolical connexions. The *fētĭālĭs*, for instance, hurled a blood-stained *hasta* into the enemy's territory as a token of declaration of war, and if a general devoted his life for his army he stood on a *hasta* while repeating the necessary formula. The *hasta* was also set up as a symbol of legal ownership when the censor farmed out the taxes, when state property, booty for instance, was sold; at private auctions (hence called *sŭbhastātĭonēs*), and at the sittings of the court of the *centumvĭri*, which had to decide on questions of property.

Hēbē. Daughter of Zeus and Hēra, goddess of eternal youth. She was represented as the handmaiden of the gods, for whom she pours out their nectar, and the consort of Hēraclēs after his apotheosis. She was worshipped with Heracles in Sĭcȳōn and Phlīūs, especially under the name Gănȳmēdē or Dia. She was represented as freeing men from chains and bonds, and her rites were celebrated with unrestrained merriment. The Romans identified Hēbē with *Iŭventās*, the personication of youthful manhood. As representing the eternal youth of the Roman state, *Iuventas* had a chapel on the Capitol in the front court of the temple of Minerva, and in later times a temple of her own in the city. It was to Jupiter and Juventas that boys offered prayer on the Capitol when they put on the *tŏga vĭrīlis*, putting a piece of money into their treasury.

Hĕcătæus. A Greek *lŏgŏgrăphŏs* or chronicler, born of a noble family at Mīlētus, about 550 B.C. In his youth he travelled widely in Europe and Asia, as well as in Egypt. At the time of the Ionian revolt he was in his native city, and gave his countrymen the wisest counsels, but in vain. After the suppression of the rising, he succeeded by his tact and management in obtaining some alleviation of the hard measures adopted by the Persians. He died about 476. The ancient critics assigned him a high place among the Greek historians who preceded Herodotus, though pronouncing him inferior to the latter. His two works, of which only fragments remain, were : (1) A description of the earth, which was much consulted by Herodotus, and was apparently used to correct the chart of Anaximander; and (2) a treatise on Greek fables, entitled *Genealogies*.

Hĕcătē. A Greek goddess, perhaps of non-Hellenic origin. She is unknown to Homer, but in Hesiod she is the only daughter of the Titan Persēs and of Astĕrĭa, the sister of Lētō. She stands high in the regard of Zeus, from whom she has received a share in the heaven, earth, and ocean. She is invoked at all sacrifices, for she can give or withhold her blessing in daily life, in war, in contests on the sea, in the hunting field, in the education of children, and in the tending of cattle. Thus she appears as a personification of the divine power, and is the instrument through which the gods effect their will, though themselves far away. In later times she was confused with Persĕphŏnē, the queen of the lower world, or associated with her. Sometimes she was regarded as the goddess of the moon or as Artĕmis, sometimes she was identified with foreign deities of the same kind. Being conceived as a goddess of night and of the lower world, she was, as time went on, transformed into a deity of ghosts and magic. She was represented as haunting crossways and graves, accompanied by the dogs of the Styx, with the spirits of the dead and troops of spectral forms in her train. She lends powerful aid to all magical incantations and witches' work. All enchanters and enchantresses are her disciples and *protégés;* Mēdēa in particular is regarded as her servant. She was worshipped in private and in public in many places, for instance Samothrace, Thessaly, Lēmnŏs, Athens, and Ægīna. Her

HECATE.
(Rome, Capitoline Museum.)

images were set up in the front of houses and by the road-side, with altars in front of them, and a roof above them. On the last day of the month, which was sacred to her, offerings were made to her in the crossways of eggs, fish, and onions. The victims sacrificed to her were young dogs and black she-lambs and honey.

In works of art she is usually portrayed in three forms, represented by three statues standing back to back. Each form has its special attributes, torches, keys, daggers, snakes, and dogs. In the *Gĭgantŏmăchia* of Pergămŏn she appears with a different weapon in her three right hands, a torch, a sword, and a lance. (*See* PERGAMENE SCULPTURES.)

Hĕcătombē (Greek). The original meaning of the word was a sacrifice of a hundred oxen; but in early times it was applied generally to any great sacrifice, without any idea either of oxen or a definite number. Such great sacrifices were especially common in the worship of Zeus and Hēra.

Hĕcătŏncheirēs (" the hundred-handed ones "). In Hesiod they are three giants, each with a hundred arms and fifty hands, sons of Urănus and Gæa. Their names are Briărĕŭs, Cottus, and Gȳēs. Owing to their hostile attitude to him, their father kept them imprisoned in the bowels of the earth. But on the advice of Gæa, the gods of Olympus summoned them from their prison to lend assistance against the Titans, and, after their victory, set them to watch the Titans, who had been thrown into Tartărus. Homer mentions Briareus, called by men Ægæōn, as the son of Pŏseidōn, and mightier than his father. Briareus was summoned to the aid of Zeus by Thĕtis, when Hēra, Poseidon, and Athēnē were wishing to bind him.

Hectŏr. The eldest son of Prĭămŭs and Hĕcăbē, husband of Andrŏmăchē and father of Astȳănax. In Homer he is the most prominent figure among the Trojans, as Achilles is among the Greeks, and is evidently a favourite character with the poet. He has all the highest qualities of a hero, unshaken spirit, personal courage, and wise judgment; but he is also a most affectionate son, and the tenderest of fathers and husbands. This trait is most touchingly exhibited in the celebrated scene in the sixth Iliad, where he takes leave of Andromache. Moreover, he is a favourite of the gods, especially of Apollo. He clearly foresees his own death, and the destruction of his native city; but he does not allow the thought to unnerve his courage and force for a moment. The Trojans love and revere him as the shepherd of his people; his enemies fear and respect him, and even Achilles cannot meet him without some apprehension. He is always to be found where the battle rages most furiously, and he does not hesitate to meet the chiefest heroes of the Greeks in single combat. Ajax the son of Tĕlămōn is his especial foe. In the absence of Achilles he reduces the Greeks to the direst straits, storms their defences, and sets their ships on fire. Pătroclus, who opposes him, he slays with the aid of Apollo. But his destiny at length overtakes him. In spite of the entreaties of his parents and his wife, he goes out to meet Achilles in his wrath. He is suddenly seized with the agony of terror; his terrible foe chases him three times round the walls of the city; Zeus mourns for him; but when his life and that of his enemy are weighed in the balance, Hector's scale sinks, Apollo leaves him, and he falls by the spear of Achilles before the eyes of his people. Achilles flings his corpse into the dust in front of Patroclus' bier, to be devoured by dogs and birds. But Aphrŏdītē anoints the body with ambrosia, and thus saves it from corruption. Achilles drags it three times behind his chariot round the grave of Patroclus, but Apollo preserves it from mutilation. At length, at the command of Zeus, Achilles delivers up the body to Hector's aged father, to be laid out in the court of the palace, and afterwards burnt on a funeral pyre. In later times Hector was worshipped as a hero by the inhabitants of Ilium, who offered sacrifices at his grave.

Hĕcŭba (Gr. *Hĕkăbē*). The daughter of the Phrygian Dȳmăs, or, according to another story, of Cisseus, and wife of Priam. (*See* Priamus.) After the fall of Troy she was made a slave, and fell to the lot of Odysseus. Her son Pŏlȳdōrus had been slain by Pŏlȳmēstōr, king of Thrace, on whom she took vengeance by putting out his eyes on the Thracian coast. On this she was changed into a dog, and threw herself into the sea. Her tomb served as a landmark for sailors.

Hĕgĕmŏnē. *See* Charites.

Hegemony (Gr. *hĕgĕmŏnĭa*, or "leadership"). This was the Greek name for the supremacy assumed by a single state in a confederacy of states, and with it the direction, more or less absolute, of the business of the confederacy. In the language of Athenian law *hegemonia* meant the presidency in the courts, which belonged in different cases to different officials. Their business was to receive the charge, make the arrangements for the trial, and preside while it was going on.

Hēgēsĭăs. A Greek orator, born in Magnesia on Mount Sĭpȳlus in the first half of the 3rd century B.C. He was the founder of what was termed the Asiatic style of oratory. (*See* Rhetoric.)

Hēgēsippus. (1) An Athenian statesman and orator, a contemporary of Demosthenes, whose political opinions he shared. He is the author of the speech *On the Island of Halonnēsŏs*, which was falsely attributed to Demosthenes.

(2) *See* Josephus.

Hĕlĕna. The divinely beautiful daughter of Zeus and Lēda, the wife of Tyndărĕŏs of Sparta; sister of the Dĭoscūrī and of Clȳtæmnēstra. The post-Homeric story represented her as carried off, while still a maiden, by Thēseus, to the Attic fortress of Aphidnæ, where she bore him a daughter Iphĭgĕneia. She was afterwards set free y her brothers, who took her back to Sparta. She was wooed by numbers of suitors, and at length gave her hand to Měnělăŭs, by whom she became the mother of one child, Hermīŏnē. In the absence of her husband she was carried away to Troy by Paris the son of Prĭămus, taking with her much treasure. This was the origin of the Trojan War. The Trojans, in spite of the calamity she had brought upon them, loved her for her beauty, and refused to restore her to her husband. She, however, lamented the fickleness of her youth, and yearned for her home, her husband, and her daughter. After the death of Paris she was wedded to Dēïphŏbus, assisted the Greeks at the taking of Troy, and betrayed Dēïphobus into Menelaus' hands. With Menelaus finally she returned to Sparta after eight years' wandering, and lived thenceforth with him in happiness and concord.

According to another story, mainly current after the time of Stēsĭchŏrus, Paris carried off to Troy not the real Helena, but a phantom of her created by Hēra. The real Helena was wafted through the air by Hermēs, and brought to Prōteus in Egypt, whence, after the destruction of Troy, she was taken home by Menelaus. (See PROTEUS.) After the death of Menelaus he was, according to one story, driven from Sparta by her stepsons, and fled thereupon to Rhodes to her friend Polyxō, who hanged her on a tree. Another tradition represented her as living after death in wedlock with Achilles on the island of Leucē. She was worshipped as the goddess of beauty in a special sanctuary at Therapnē in Laconia, where a festival was held in her honour. She was also invoked like her brothers the Dioscuri, as a tutelary deity of mariners. (See DIOSCURI.)

Hělěnus (*Hělěnŏs*). The son of Priam and Hěcŭba, who, like his sister Cassandra, was endowed with the gift of prophecy. When Dēïphŏbus, after the death of Paris, took Hělěna to wife, Helenus went over to the Greeks; or (as another story has it) was caught by Odysseus in an ambush. He revealed to the enemy the fact that Troy could not be taken without the aid of Něoptŏlěmus and Phǐlŏctētēs; and he is also said to have suggested the plan of outwitting the Trojans by means of the wooden horse. After the fall of Troy he was carried away by Neoptolemus, and advised him to settle in Epīrus. After his death Helenus took Andrŏmăchē to wife, and became king of the Chaonians.

Hělĭæa. The name of the great popular Athenian law-court, instituted by Solon. The word was also applied to the locality in which the greatest number of its members, and sometimes all of them, assembled. The number of the *Hělĭastæ*, or members of the court, or jurors, was, in the flourishing period of the democracy, 6,000, 600 being taken from each tribe (*phȳlē*). The choice of the *Hělĭastæ* was determined by lot, under the presidency of the archons. No one was eligible who was not a fully qualified citizen, and over thirty years of age. On their election, the Heliasts took the oath of office, and were distributed into ten divisions of 500 each, corresponding respectively to the ten tribes. The remaining 1,000 served to fill up vacancies as they occurred.

Every Heliast received, as the emblem of his office, a bronze tablet, stamped with the Gorgon's head [or with an owl surrounded by an olive-wreath: Hicks, *Hist. Inscr.* No. 119], his name, and the number of his division. The different courts were mostly situated near the *ăgŏra*, and distinguished by their colour and their number. On court-days the *Thesmŏthětæ* assigned them by lot to the different divisions of the Heliasts. Every Heliast was then presented with a staff bearing the number of his court, and painted with its colour. On entering the room he received a ticket, which he exhibited after the sitting and thereupon received his fee. This system of paying the jurors was introduced by Pěrĭclēs, and the fee, originally an *ŏbŏlŏs* (about 1½*d.*), was afterwards increased to three obols.

In some instances only a part of one division of the jurors would sit to try a case; but in important cases several divisions would sit together. Care was always taken that the number should be uneven. The jurisdiction of the *Helĭæa* extended to all kinds of suits. In public causes it acted as a court both of first instance and of final appeal. For private causes it was originally only a court of appeal; but in later times these suits also came to be brought before it in the first instance.

Hělĭastæ. *See* HELIÆA.

Hělĭŏdōrus (*Hělĭŏdōrŏs*). A Greek writer of romance, born at Emēsa in Phœnicia. He was a pagan Sophist, who probably flourished in the second half of the 3rd century A.D. At one time he was erroneously identified with another Heliodorus, bishop of Tricca in Thessaly, who flourished about 390 A.D. A romance of his called *Æthĭŏpĭca,* in ten books, has come down to us. Its subject is the strange story of Thēägĕnēs the Thessalian and Chărĭclĕa, the daughter of the king of Æthiopia. This book served as a model for most of the later Greek writers of romance, and may be classed with the novel of Longus as one of the best specimens of this kind of literature which Greek antiquity has to show. It is remarkable for original power, clear sketches of character, beauty of drawing, and moral intention; the style is pure, simple, and elegant.

Hēlĭŏs. In Greek mythology, the Sungod, son of the Titan Hўpĕrīŏn (whose name he bears himself in Homer) and the Titaness Theia; brother of Sĕlēnē (the Moon) and Eōs (Dawn). The poets apply the name Tītăn to him in particular, as the offspring of Titans. He is represented as a strong and beautiful god, in the bloom of youth, with gleaming eyes and waving locks, a crown of rays upon his head. In the morning he rises from a lovely bay of the Ocean in the farthest East, where the Ethiopians dwell. To give light to gods and men he climbs the vault of heaven in a chariot drawn by four snow-white horses, breathing light and fire; their names are Eōŏs, Æthĭops, Brontē, and Stĕrŏpē. In the evening he sinks with his chariot into the Ocean, and while he sleeps is carried round along the northern border of the earth to the East again in a golden boat, shaped like a bowl, the work of Hēphæstus. He is called Phăĕthōn, from the brilliant light that he diffuses; he is the All-seer (Pănoptēs) because his rays penetrate everywhere. He is revealer of all that is done on earth; it is he who tells Hephæstus of the love of Arēs and Aphrŏdĭtē, and shows Dēmētĕr who has carried off her daughter. He is accordingly invoked as a witness to oaths and solemn protestations.

On the island of Trĭnăcrĭa (Sicily) he has seven flocks of sheep and seven herds of cattle, fifty in each. It is his pleasure, on his daily journey, to look down upon them. Their numbers must not be increased or diminished; if this is done, his wrath is terrible. (See ODYSSEUS.) In the 700 sheep and oxen the ancients recognised the 700 days and nights of the lunar year. The flocks are tended by Phăĕthūsa (the goddess of light) and Lampĕtĭē (the goddess of shining), his daughter by Nĕæra.

By the ocean Nymph Persē or Persēïs he is father of Æētēs, Circē, and Pāsĭphăē, by Clўmĕnē the father of Phăĕthōn, and Augĕās was also accounted his son. His children have the gleaming eyes of their father.

After the time of Euripides, or thereabouts, the all-seeing Sun-god was identified with Apollo, the god of prophecy. Helios was worshipped in many places, among which may be mentioned Corinth and Elis. The island of Rhodes was entirely consecrated to him. Here an annual festival (Halia) was held during the summer in his honour, with chariot-racing and contests of music and gymnastics; and four consecrated horses were thrown into the sea as a sacri-

HELIOS.
(Metope from temple of Athena, probably of 2nd century B.C., at the Greek city of Ilium, *Hissarlik*.)

fice to him. In 278 B.C. a colossal bronze statue, by Chărēs of Lindus, was erected to him at the entrance of the harbour of Rhodes. Herds of red and white cattle were, in many places, kept in his honour. White animals, and especially white horses were sacred to him; among birds the cock, and among trees the white poplar.

The Latin poets identified Helios with the Sabine deity Sōl, who had an ancient place of worship on the Quirinal at Rome and a public sacrifice on the 8th of August But it was the introduction of the ritual of Mithrās which first brought the worship of the sun into prominence in Rome. (See MITHRAS.)

Hellănīcus (*Hellănĭkŏs*). One of the Greek *lŏgŏgrăphī* or chroniclers, born at Mўtĭlēnē in Lesbos about 480 B.C. He is said to have lived till the age of 85, and to have gone on writing until after B.C. 406. In the course of his long life he composed a series of works on genealogy, chorography, and chronology. He was the first writer who attempted to introduce a systematic chronological arrangement into the traditional periods of Greek, and especially Athenian, history and mythology. His theories of the ancient Attic chronology were accepted down to the time of Erătosthĕnēs.

Hellănŏdīcæ (*Hellănŏdĭkai*). *See* OLYMPIC GAMES.

Hellē. In Greek mythology, daughter of Athămās and Nĕphĕlē. (*See* ATHAMAS.)

Hellēnŏtămĭæ. The name of a board of ten members, elected annually by lot as controllers of the fund contributed by the members of the Athenian confederacy. The treasure was originally deposited at Dĕlŏs, but after B.C. 461 was transferred to Athens. The yearly contributions of the cities owning the Athenian supremacy amounted at first to 460 talents (some £92,000); during the Peloponnesian War they increased to nearly 1,300 talents (£260 000).

Hellŏtĭs. *See* EUROPE.

Helmets. Helmets were, in antiquity, made sometimes of metal, sometimes of leather. A metal helmet was in Greek called *krănŏs*, in Latin *cassĭs ;* a leather one in Greek *kўnē*, in Latin *gălĕa*. Leather helmets were sometimes finished with metal work.

(1) Three forms of the Greek helmet may be distinguished. (*a*) The Corinthian visored helmet, which Athēnē is represented as wearing on the coins of Corinth. This had a projecting nose-guard, a long or short neck-piece, and two side-pieces to protect the cheeks. An opening, connecting with the two eye-holes, was left for the nose and mouth. The helmet was, except in battle, thrown backwards over the head. (*b*) the Attic helmet, represented on Attic coins as the only one worn by Athene. The neck-piece fits close to the head ; the cheek-pieces are either fixed immovably to the head-piece, or can be moved up and down by means of joints ; in front of the head-piece, extending from ear to ear, was a guard, sometimes arranged for putting up or down, and thus acting as a screen for the face. (*c*) The simple cap, worn chiefly by

the Arcadians and Lacedæmonians. This sometimes had a projecting brim, sometimes not. The skull was protected either by a cone of varying form, or by a guard running

GREEK HELMETS.

over the top of the helmet. This was often adorned with a plume of horsehair or feathers.

(2) *Roman.* The engravings will give a sufficient idea of the different varieties of Roman helmets. For the visored helmets of the gladiators *see* GLADIATORES. The stan-

dard-bearers, during the imperial period, wore, not a helmet, but a leather cap.

ROMAN HELMETS.

Helots (Gr. *Heilōtai* or *Hĕlōtai*). This name was given at Sparta to those among the original inhabitants of Lacōnia who lost their land and freedom at the Dorian conquest. (For the others, *see* PERIŒCI.) It is not certain what the word originally meant. Some scholars have explained it as " prisoners of war " ; others have derived it from *Hĕlŏs*, the name of a city supposed to have been conquered in consequence of an insurrection. This view was held in antiquity. The Helots were slaves of the state, which assigned them to individual citizens to cultivate their lands. Their employers had no power to kill them, to sell them, or to set them free. The law fixed a certain proportion of the produce in barley, oil, and wine, which the Helots were bound to pay over to the landowner. The rest was their own property, and a certain degree of prosperity was therefore within their reach. A Helot was liable to be called upon for personal service by any Spartan, even if not attached to his estate ; but no authority save that of the state could either set him free or remove him from the soil to which he was bound.

In war, the Helots were employed sometimes as shield-bearers to the heavy-armed troops, sometimes as archers and slingers, sometimes in other subordinate capacities. After Sparta had become a naval power, they were used as pilots and marines ; but they were seldom admitted to the ranks of the heavy-armed infantry. For distinguished merit in the field they might be set free, and a special class called *Nĕŏdā-mōdēis* was formed of these liberated Helots.

The *Neodamodeis*, however, had no civil rights ; and indeed it was but seldom that a Helot ever became a Spartan citizen. The children of Spartan fathers and Helot mothers, called *Mŏthăkĕs*, were free, and brought up with the young free Spartans. In many cases, through a species of adoption on the father's part, they obtained the citizenship.

The Helots formed a very numerous body, amounting to more than half of the whole Lacedæmonian population (400,000). As they were in a state of chronic discontent, they were, in times of danger, a source of anxiety to the Spartans, and the object of constant vigilance. Hence the institution of the *Crypteia*, which used to be erroneously represented as a chase of the Helots. The fact is that, before being admitted to military service proper, the young Spartans were annually commanded by the ephors to scour the country, seize on any objects of suspicion, and, in particular, to keep an eye on the Helots, and put any Helot, whom they had reason to distrust, out of the way without more ado.

Hendĕkă ("The Eleven "). The term applied at Athens to a band consisting of ten members, chosen by lot, and their secretary. Their duty was to superintend the prisons, receive arrested prisoners, and carry out the sentences of the law. The capital sentence was executed by their subordinates. They also had penal jurisdiction in the case of delinquents discovered in the act of committing offences punishable with death or imprisonment. If they pleaded guilty, the Eleven inflicted the punishment at once ; if not, they instituted a judicial inquiry and presided at the decision of the case. They had the same power in the cases of embezzlement of confiscated property, of which they had lists in their possession.

Hĕphæstĭŏn. A Greek soldier, a native of Alexandria, who flourished about the middle of the 2nd century A.D., and was tutor to the emperor Vērus before his accession. He wrote a work on prosody, in forty eight books, which he first abridged into eleven books, then into three, and finally into one. The final abridgment, called a manual (*Encheirĭdĭŏn*) has come down to us It gives no more than a bare sketch of prosody, without any attempt at theoretical explanation of the facts ; but it is, nevertheless, of immense value. It is the only complete treatise on Greek prosody which has survived from antiquity, and it quotes verses from the lost poets. Attached to i is a treatise on the different forms of poetry and composition, in two incomplete versions. The manual has a preface (*Prŏlĕgŏmĕna*) by Longīnus, and two collections of *schŏlia*.

Hēphæstus (*Hēphaistŏs*). In Greek mythology, the god of fire, and of the arts which need fire in the execution. He was said to be the son of Zeus and Hēra, or (according to Hesiod) of the latter only. The boy was ugly, and lame in both feet, and his mother was ashamed of him. She threw him from Olympus into the ocean,

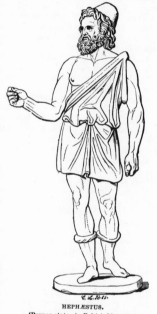

HEPHÆSTUS.
(Bronze statue in British Museum.)

where he was taken up by Eurȳnŏmē and Thĕtĭs, and concealed in a subterranean cavern. Here he remained for nine years, and fashioned a number of exquisite works of art, among them a golden throne with invisible chains, which he sent to his mother by way of revenge. She sat down in it, and was chained to the seat, so fast that no one could release her. On this it was resolved to call Hephæstus back to Olympus. Arēs wished to force him back, but was scared off by his brother with fire-brands. Dīonȳsus at length succeeded in making

him drunk, and bringing him back, in this condition, to Olympus. But he was destined to meet with his old mishap a second time. There was a quarrel between Zeus and Hera, and Hephæstus took his mother's part; whereupon Zeus seized him by the leg and hurled him down from Olympus. He fell upon the island of Lēmnŏs, where the Sintians, who then inhabited the island, took care of him and brought him to himself. From this time Lemnos was his favourite abode. His lameness was, in the later story, attributed to this fall.

The whole story, the sojourn of Hephæstus in the cavern under the sea, and his fondness for Lemnos, is, in all probability, based upon volcanic phenomena; the submarine activity of volcanic fires, and the natural features of the island of Lemnos. Here there was a volcano called Mŏsychlŏs, which was in activity down to the time of Alexander the Great. The friendship existing between Dionysus and Hephæstus may be explained by the fact that the best and finest wines are grown in the volcanic regions of the South.

As a master in the production of beautiful and fascinating works of art, Hephæstus is in Homer the husband of Chărĭs, and in Hesiod of Aglāïa, the youngest of the Graces. (*See* CHARITES.) The story of his marriage with Aphrŏdītē was not, apparently, widely known in early antiquity. Through his artistic genius he appears, and most especially in the Athenian story, as the intimate friend of Athēnē. In Homer he lives and works on Olympus, where he makes palaces of brass for himself and the other deities. But he has a forge also on Mount Mosychlos in Lemnos; the later story gives him one under Ætna in Sicily, and on the sacred island, or island of Hephæstus, in the Lipari Islands, where he is heard at work with his companions the Cyclōpēs. All the masterpieces of metal which appear in the stories of gods and heroes, the ægis of Zeus, the arms of Achilles, the sceptre of Agămemnŏn, the necklace of Harmŏnĭa, and others, were attributed to the art of Hephæstus. To help his lameness he made, according to Homer, two golden maidens, with the power of motion, to lean upon when he walked.

He was much worshipped in Lemnos, where there was an annual festival in his honour. All fires were put out for nine days, during which rites of atonement and purification were performed. Then fresh fire was brought on a sacred ship from

Dēlŏs, the fires were kindled again, and a new life, as the saying went, began. At Athens he was worshipped in the Academy, in connexion with Athēnē and Prŏmētheus (*see* PROMETHEUS). In October the smiths and smelters celebrated the *Chalkeia*, a feast of metal-workers, in his honour and that of Athene; at the *Apătūrĭa* sacrifices were offered to him, among other gods, as the giver of fire, and torches were kindled, and hymns were sung; at the *Hephœstĭa*, finally, there was a torch-race in his honour. In works of art he is represented as a vigorous man with a beard, equipped, like a smith, with hammer and tongs; his left leg is shortened, to show his lameness (*see* engraving). The Romans identified him with their Vulcānus (*see* VULCANUS).

Hēra. In Greek mythology, the queen of heaven, eldest daughter of Crŏnŭs and Rhea, sister and lawful consort of Zeus. According to Homer, she was brought up in her youth by Ocĕănŭs and Tēthўs. But every place in which her worship was localized asserted that she was born there, and brought up by the Nymphs of the district. She is said to have long lived in secret intimacy with Zeus, before he publicly acknowledged her as his lawful consort. Her worshippers celebrated her marriage in the spring time. In the oldest version of the story it took place in the Islands of the Blessed, on the shore of the Ocean stream, where the golden apple tree of the Hespĕrĭdĕs sprang up to celebrate it. But this honour, too, was claimed by every place where Hera was worshipped. According to one local story, Zeus obtained the love of Hera by stealth, in the form of a cuckoo.

Hera seems originally to have symbolised the feminine aspects of the natural forces of which Zeus is the masculine representative. Hence she is at once his wife and his sister, shares his power and his honours, and, like him, has authority over the phenomena of the atmosphere. It is she who sends clouds and storms, and is mistress of the thunder and the lightning. Her handmaids are the Hōræ or goddesses of the season, and Iris, the goddess of the rainbow. Like Zeus, men worship her on mountains, and pray to her for rain. The union of sun and rain, which wakes the earth to renewed fertility, is symbolised as the loving union of Zeus and Hera. In the same way a conflict of the winds is represented as the consequence of a matrimonial quarrel, usually attributed to the jealousy of Hera, who was regarded as the stern protectress of honourable marriage. Hence arose stories of Zeus ill-treating his wife. It was said that he scourged her, and hurled Hēphæstus from heaven to earth when hurrying to his mother's assistance; that in anger for her persecution of his son Hērăclēs, he hung her out in the air with golden chains to her arms and an anvil on each foot. There were also old stories which spoke of Hera allying herself with Athēnē and Pŏseidōn to bind Zeus in chains. Zeus was only rescued by the Giant Ægæōn, whom Thĕtĭs called to his assistance. The birth of Athene was said to have enraged Hera to such a pitch that she became the mother of Typhōn by the dark powers of the infernal regions. In fact, this constant resistance to the will of Zeus, and her jealousy and hatred of her consort's paramours and their children, especially Heracles, becomes in the poets a standing trait in her character.

In spite of all this, Homer represents her as the most majestic of all the goddesses. The other Olympians pay her royal honours, and Zeus treats her with all respect and confides all his designs to her, though not always yielding to her demands. She is the spotless and uncorruptible wife of the King of Heaven; the mother of Hephæstus, Arēs, Hēbē, and Ilĭthŷīa, and indeed may be called the only lawful wife in the Olympian court. She is, accordingly, before all other deities the goddess of marriage and the protectress of purity in married life. She is represented as of exalted but severe beauty, and appears before Paris as competing with Aphrodite and Athene for the prize of loveliness. In Homer she is described as of lofty stature, large eyes, white arms, and beautiful hair. On women she confers bloom and strength; she helps them, too, in the dangerous hour of childbirth. Her daughters Hēbē and Ilithyia personify both these attributes.

In earlier times Hera was not everywhere recognised as the consort of Zeus; at the primitive oracle of Dōdōna, for instance, Diōnē occupies this position. The Pĕlŏponnēsus may be regarded as the earliest seat of her worship, and in the Homeric period, Argos, Mўcēnæ, and Sparta are her favourite seats. Of these, according to the poet, she is the passionate champion in the Trojan War. In later times the worship of Hera was strongly localized in Argos and Mycenæ. At Argos she took the same commanding osition as Athene at Athens, and the year vas dated by the names of her priestesses. ‹etween these cities was situated the

(1) FARNESE HERA.
(Naples Museum.)

(2) LUDOVISI HERA.
(Rome, Villa Ludovisi.)

‹ēræum (*Hēraiŏn*), a temple held in great ›nour (*see* HERÆA). At Corinth she was ›e goddess of the stronghold. At Elĭs a

garment was offered her every five years by sixteen ladies chosen for the purpose, and the maidens held a race in her honour on the race-course at Olympia. Bœotia had its feast of the *Dædăla* (see DÆDALA); Samŏs its large and splendid temple, built by the famous Pŏlÿcrătēs. The cuckoo was sacred to her as the messenger of spring, the season in which she was wedded to Zeus; so were the peacock and the crow, and among fruits the pomegranate, the symbol of wedded love and fruitfulness. Hecatombs were offered to her in sacrifice, as to Zeus.

(3) * BARBERINI HERA.
(Rome, Vatican.)

In works of art she is represented as seated on a throne in a full robe, covering the whole figure. On her head is a sort of diadem, often with a veil; the expression of the face is severe and majestic, the eyes large and wide open, as in the Homeric description. The ideal type of Hera was found in the statue by Pŏlÿclītus in the temple at Argos. This was a colossal image, in gold and ivory, representing the goddess on her throne, her crown adorned with figures of the Graces and the Seasons, a pomegranate in one hand, and in the other a sceptre with the cuckoo on the top. The

Farnese Juno at Naples, and the *Ludovisi Juno* in Rome, are copies of this work (*see* figs. 1 and 2). The Romans identified Hera with their own Jūnō. (*See* JUNO.)

Hērăclēs (*Hērăklēs*) = renowned through Hēra; Latin *Hercŭlēs*. Heracles is not only one of the oldest heroes in the Greek mythology, but the most illustrious of all. Indeed, the traditions of similar heroes in other Greek tribes, and in other nations, especially in the East, were transferred to Heracles; so that the scene of his achievements, which is, in the Homeric poems, confined on the whole to Greece, became almost extensive with the known world; and the story of Heracles was the richest and most comprehensive of all the heroic fables.

Heracles was born in Thebes, and was the son of Zeus by Alcmēnē, the wife of Amphĭtrўōn, whose form the god assumed while he was absent in the war against the Tēlĕbŏī. On the day which he should have been born, Zeus announced to the gods that a descendant of Perseus was about to see the light, who would hold sway over all the Perseidæ. Hera cunningly induced her consort to confirm his words with an oath. She hated the unborn son as the son of her rival, and (in her capacity as the goddess of childbirth) caused the queen of Sthĕnĕlus of Mўcēnæ, a descendant of Perseus, to give birth prematurely to Eurystheus, while she postponed the birth of Heracles for seven days. Hence it was that Heracles, with his gigantic strength, came into the service of the weaker Eurystheus. Hera pursued him with her hatred during the whole of his natural life. Heracles and his twin brother Iphĭclēs, the son of Amphitryon, were hardly born, when the goddess sent two serpents to their cradle to destroy them. Heracles seized them and strangled them. The child grew up to be a strong youth, and was taught by Amphitryon to drive a chariot, by Autŏlўcus to wrestle, by Eurўtus to shoot with the bow, and by Castōr to use the weapons of war. Chīrōn instructed him in the sciences, Rhădămanthўs in virtue and wisdom, Eumolpus (or according to another account Līnus) in music. When Linus attempted to chastise him, Heracles struck him dead with his lute. Amphitryon accordingly, alarmed at his untamable temper, sent him to tend his flocks on Mount Cĭthærōn.

It was at this time, according to the Sophist Prŏdĭcus, that the event occurred which occasioned the fable of the "Choice of Heracles." Heracles was meditating in solitude as to the path of life which he should choose, when two tall women appeared before him, the one called Pleasure, the other called Virtue. Pleasure promised him a life of enjoyment, Virtue a life of toil crowned by glory. He decided for Virtue. After destroying the mighty lion of Cithæron, he returned, in his eighteenth year, to Thebes, and freed the city from the tribute which it had been forced to pay to Ergīnus of Orchŏmĕnus. Crĕōn, king of Thebes, gave him, in gratitude, his daughter Mĕgăra to wife. But it was not long before the Delphic oracle commanded him to enter the service of Eurystheus king of Mўcēnæ and Tĭryns, and perform twelve tasks which he should impose upon him. This was the humiliation which Hera had in store for him. The oracle promised him, at the same time, that he should win eternal glory, and indeed immortality, and change his present name Alcæus or Alcides[1] for Heracles (renowned through Hera). Nevertheless, he fell into a fit of madness, in which he shot down the three children whom Megara had born him. When healed of his madness, he entered into the service of Eurystheus.

The older story says nothing of the exact number (twelve) of the labours of Heracles. The number was apparently invented by the poet Pīsander of Rhodes, who may have had in his eye the contests of the Phœnician god Melkart with the twelve hostile beasts of the Zodiac. It was also Pisander who first armed the hero with the club, and the skin taken from the lion of Cithæron or Nĕmĕa. Heracles was previously represented as carrying bow and arrows, and the weapons of a Homeric hero.

The twelve labours of Heracles are as follows: (1) The contest with the invulnerable lion of Nemea, the offspring of Typhōn and Echidna. Heracles drove it into its cavern and strangled it in his arms. With the impenetrable hide, on which nothing can make any impression but the beast's own claws, he clothes himself, the jaw covering his head. (2) The hydra or water snake of Lerna, also a child of Typho and Echidna. This monster lived in the marsh of Lerna, near Argos, and was so poisonous that its very breath was fatal. It had nine heads, one of which was immortal. Heracles scares it out of its lair with

[1] He was called *Alcæus* (*Alkaiŏs*) from his paternal grandfather; *Alcĭdēs* (*Alkĭdēs*) from *alkē*, strength.

burning arrows, and cuts off its heads; but for every head cut off two new ones arise. At length Iŏlăŭs, the charioteer of Heracles and son of his brother Iphicles, sears the wounds with burning brands. Upon the immortal head he lays a heavy mass of rock. He anoints his arrows with the monster's gall, so that henceforth the wounds they inflict are incurable. Eurystheus refuses to accept this as a genuine victory, alleging the assistance offered by Iolaus. (3) The boar of Erўmanthus, which infested Arcadia. Heracles had been commanded to bring it alive to Mycenæ, so he chased it into an expanse of snow, tired it out, and caught it in a noose. The mere sight of the beast threw Eurystheus into such a panic, that he slunk away into a tub underground, and bid the hero, in future, to show the proof of his achievements outside the city gates. (On the contest with the Centaurs which Heracles had to undergo on his way to the chase, see PHOLUS and CHIRON.) (4) The hind of Mount Cĕrўneia, between Arcadia and Achaia. Another account localizes the event on Mount Mænălus, and speaks of the Mænalian hind. Its horns were of gold and its hoofs of brass, and it had been dedicated to Artĕmis by the Pleiad Taўgĕtē. Heracles was to take the hind alive. He followed her for a whole year up to the source of the Ister in the country of the Hyperboreans. At length she returned to Arcadia, where he wounded her with an arrow on the banks of the Lādōn, and so caught her. (5) The birds that infested the lake of Stymphǎlus, in Arcadia. These were man-eating monsters, with claws, wings, and beaks of brass, and feathers that they shot out like arrows. Heracles scared them with a brazen rattle, and succeeded in killing part, and driving away the rest, which settled on the island of Arētĭăs in the Black Sea, to be frightened away, after a hard fight, by the Argonauts. (6) Heracles was commanded to bring home for Admētē, the daughter of Eurystheus, the girdle of Hippŏlўtē, queen of the Amazons. After many adventures he landed at Thĕmiscўra, and found the queen ready to give up the girdle of her own accord. But Hera spread a rumour among the Amazons that their queen was in danger, and a fierce battle took place, in which Heracles slew Hippolyte and many of her followers. On his return he slew, in the neighourhood of Troy, a sea-monster, to whose fury king Lăŏmĕdōn had offered up his daughter

Hēsĭŏnē. Laomedon refused to give Heracles the reward he had promised, whereupon the latter, who was hastening to return to Mycenæ, threatened him with future vengeance (see LAOMEDON). (7) The farm-yard of Augeās, king of Elis, in which lay the dung of 3,000 cattle, was to be cleared in a day. Heracles completed the task by turning the river Alphēus into the yard. Augeas now contended that Heracles was only acting on the commission of Eurystheus, and on this pretext refused him his promised reward. Heracles slew him afterwards with all his sons, and thereupon founded the Olympian games (see AUGEAS). (8) A mad bull had been sent up from the sea by Pŏseidōn to ravage the island of Crete, in revenge for the disobedience of Mīnŏs (see MINOS). Heracles was to bring him to Mycenæ alive. He caught the bull, crossed the sea on his back, threw him over his neck and carried him to Mycenæ, where he let him go. The animal wandered all through the Peloponnese, and ended by infesting the neighbourhood of Mărăthōn, where he was at length slain by Thēseus. (9) Dĭŏmēdēs, a son of Arēs, and king of the Bistŏnĕs in Thrace, had some mares which he used to feed on the flesh of the strangers landing in the country. After a severe struggle, Heracles overcame the king, threw his body to the mares, and took them off to Mycenæ, where Eurystheus let them go. (10) The oxen of Gērўŏnēs, the son of Chrysāŏr and the ocean Nymph Callirrhŏē, was a Giant with three bodies and mighty wings, who dwelt on the island of Erўthēa, in the farthest West, on the borders of the Ocean stream. He had a herd of red cattle, which were watched by the shepherd Eurўtĭŏn and his two-headed dog Orthrŏs, a son of Typhon and Echidna. In quest of these cattle, Heracles, with many adventures, passes through Europe and Libya. On the boundary of both continents he sets up, in memory of his arrival, the two pillars which bear his name, and at length reaches the Ocean stream. Oppressed by the rays of the neighbouring sun, he aims his bow at the Sun-god, who marvels at his courage, and gives him his golden bowl to cross the Ocean in. Arrived at Erythea, Heracles slays the shepherd and his dog, and drives off the cattle. Mĕnœtĭus, who tends the herds of Hādēs in the neighbourhood, brings news to Geryones of what has happened. Geryones hurries in pursuit, but after a fierce contest falls before the arrows of

Heracles. The hero returns with the cattle through Iberia, Gaul, Liguria, Italy, and Sicily, meeting everywhere with new adventures, and leaving behind him tokens of his presence. At the mouth of the Rhone he had a dreadful struggle with the Lĭgўĕs; his arrows were exhausted, and he had sunk in weariness upon his knee, when Zeus rained a shower of innumerable stones from heaven, with which he prevailed over his enemies. The place was ever after a stony desert plain (*see further* CACUS and ERYX). Heracles had made the circuit of the Adriatic and was just nearing Greece, when Hera sent a gadfly and scattered the herd. With much toil he wandered through the mountains of Thrace as far as the Hellespont, but then only succeeded in getting together a part of the cattle. After a dangerous adventure with the Giant Alcўŏneus, he succeeded at length in returning to Mycenæ, where Eurystheus offered up the cattle to Hera (*see* ALCYONEUS). (11) The golden apples of the Hespĕrĭdĕs (*see* HESPERIDES). Heracles is ignorant where the gardens of the Hesperides are to be found in which the apples grow. He accordingly repairs to the Nymphs who dwell by the Erĭdănus, on whose counsel he surprises Nēreus, the omniscient god of the sea, and compels him to give an answer. On this he journeys through Libya, Egypt, and Ethiopia, where he slays Antæus, Būsīrĭs, and Emăthĭŏn (*see* under these names). He then crosses to Asia, passes through the Caucasus, where he sets Prŏmētheus free, and on through the land of the Hўperbŏrĕans till he finds Atlas. Following the counsel of Prometheus, he sends Atlas to bring the apples, and in his absence bears the heavens for him on his shoulders. Atlas returns with them, but declines to take his burden upon his shoulders again, promising to carry the apples to Eurystheus himself. Heracles consents, and asks Atlas to take the burden only a moment, while he adjusts a cushion for his head; he then hurries off with his prize. Another account represents Heracles as slaying the serpent Lădōn, who guards the tree, and plucking the apples himself. Eurystheus presents him with the apples; he dedicates them to Athene, who restores them to their place. (12) He brings the dog Cerbĕrus up from the lower world. This is the heaviest task of all. Conducted by Hermēs and Athene, he descends into Hades at the promontory of Tænărum. In Hades he sets Theseus free,

and induces the prince of the infernal regions to let him take the dog to the realms of day, if only he can do so without using his weapons. Heracles binds the beast by the mere strength of arm, and carries him to Eurystheus, and takes him back again into Hades.

His task is now ended, and he returns to Thebes. His first wife, Mĕgăra, he weds to his faithful friend Iolaus, and then journeys into Œchălĭă[1] to king Eurўtus, whose daughter Iŏlē he means to woo. The king's son Iphĭtus favours his suit, but Eurytus rejects it with contempt. Soon after this Autŏlўcus steals some of Eurytus' cattle, and he accuses Heracles of the robbery. Meanwhile, Heracles has rescued Alcēstis, the wife of Admētus, from death. Iphitus meets Heracles, begs him to help him in looking for the stolen cattle, and accompanies him to Tiryns. Here, after hospitably entertaining him, Heracles throws him, in a fit of madness, from the battlements of his stronghold. A heavy sickness is sent on him for this murder, and Heracles prays to the god of Delphi to heal him. Apollo rejects him, whereupon Heracles attempts to carry away the tripod. A conflict ensues, when Zeus parts the combatants with his lightning. The oracle bids Heracles to hire himself out for three years for three talents, and pay the money to Eurytus. Hermes puts him into the service of Omphălē, queen of Lydia, daughter of Iardănus, and widow of Tmōlus. Heracles is degraded to female drudgery, is clothed in soft raiment and set to spin wool, while the queen assumes the lion skin and the club. The time of service over, he undertakes an expedition of vengeance against Laomedon of Troy. He lands on the coast of the Troad with eighteen ships, manned by the boldest of heroes, such as Tĕlămōn, Pēleus, and Oïclēs. Laomedon succeeds in surprising the guard by the ships, and in slaying Oïcles. But the city is stormed, Telamon being the first to climb the wall, and Laomedon, with all his sons except Pŏdarcēs, is slain by the arrows of Heracles. (*See* PRIAMUS.) On his return Hera sends a tempest upon him. On the island of Cōs he has a hard conflict to undergo with Eurўtĭŏn, the son of Pŏseidōn, and his sons. Heracles is at first wounded and forced to fly, but prevails at length with the help of Zeus.

After this Athene summons the hero to

---

[1] In Thessaly or Messēnĭa; according to a later story, in Eubœa.

the battle of the gods with the Giants, who are not to be vanquished without his aid. (*See* GIGANTES.) Then Heracles returns to the Peloponnese, and takes vengeance on Augeas and on Nēleus of Pylos, who had refused to purify him for the murder of Iphitus. (*See* AUGEAS, MOLIONIDÆ, NELEUS, and PERIDYMENUS.) In the battle with the Pylians he goes so far as to wound Hades, who had come up to their assistance. Hippŏcŏōn of Sparta and his numerous sons he slays in revenge for their murder of Œŏnus, a son of his maternal uncle Lĭcymnĭus. In this contest his ally is king Cēpheus of Tĕgĕa, by whose sister Augē he is father of Tēlĕphus. Cepheus with his twenty sons are left dead on the field.

Heracles now wins to wife Dēĭănĭra, the daughter of Œneus of Călȳdōn. (*See* ACHĒLŌUS.) He remains a long time with his father-in-law, and at length, with his wife and his son Hyllus, he passes on into Trāchīs, to the hospitality of his friend Ceyx. At the ford of the river Evēnus he encounters the Centaur Nessus, who has the right of carrying travellers across. Nessus remains behind and attempts to do violence to Deianira, and Heracles shoots him through with his poisoned arrows. The dying Centaur gives some of his infected blood to Deianira, telling her that, should her husband be unfaithful, it will be a means of restoring him. Heracles has a stubborn contest with Theiŏdămās, the king of the Drȳŏpĕs, kills him, and takes his son Hȳlās away. (*See* HYLAS). He then reaches Trachis, and is received with the friendliest welcome by king Ceyx. From hence he starts to fight with Cycnus (*see* CYCNUS); and afterwards, at the request of Ægĭmĭus, prince of the Dorians, undertakes a war against the Lapithæ, and an expedition of revenge against Eurytus of Œchalia. (*See* above.) He storms the fortress, slays Eurytus with his sons, and carries off Iole, who had formerly been denied him, as his prisoner. He is about to offer a sacrifice to his father Zeus on Mount Cēnæum, when Deianira, jealous of Iole, sends him a robe stained with the blood of Nessus. It has hardly grown warm upon his body, when the dreadful poison begins to devour his flesh. Wild with anguish, he hurls Lĭchās, who brought him the robe, into the sea, where he is changed into a tall cliff. In the attempt to tear off the robe, he only tears off pieces of his flesh. Apollo bids them take him to the top of Œta, where he has a great funeral pyre built up for him. This he ascends; then he gives Iole to his son Hyllus to be his wife, and bids Pœäs, the father of Phĭloctētēs, to kindle the pyre. According to another story, it is Philoctetes himself, whom Heracles presents with his bow and poisoned arrows, who performs this office. The flames have hardly started up, when a cloud descends from the sky with thunder and lightning, and carries the son of Zeus up to heaven. Here he is welcomed as one of the immortals. Hera is reconciled to him, and he is wedded to her daughter Hēbē, the goddess of eternal youth. Their children are Alexĭărēs (Averter of the Curse) and Anĭkētŏs (the Invincible). The names merely personify two of the main qualities for which the hero was worshipped.

About the end of Heracles nothing is said in the Iliad but that he, the best-loved of Zeus' sons, did not escape death, but was overcome by fate, and by the heavy wrath of Hera. In the Odyssey his ghost, in form like black night, walks in the lower world with his bow bent and his arrows ready, while the hero himself dwells among the immortals, the husband of Hebe. For the lives of his children, and the end of Eurystheus, *see* HYLLUS.

Heracles was worshipped partly as a hero, to whom men brought the ordinary libations and offerings, and partly as an Olympian deity, an immortal among the immortals. Immediately after his apotheosis his friends offered sacrifice to him at the place of burning, and his worship spread from thence through all the tribes of Hellas. Dĭŏmus the son of Colyttus, an Athenian, is said to have been the first who paid him the honours of an immortal. It was he who founded the gymnasium called *Cȳnŏsargĕs*, near the city. This gymnasium, the sanctuary at Marathon, and the temple at Athens, were the three most venerable shrines of Heracles in Attica. Diomus gave his name to the Diomeia, a merry festival held in Athens in honour of Heracles. Feasts to Heracles (*Heracleia*), with athletic contests, were celebrated in many places. He was the hero of labour and struggle, and the patron deity of the *gymnasium* and the *palœstra*. From early times he was regarded as having instituted the Olympic games; as the founder of the Olympic sanctuaries and the Olympic truce, the planter of the shady groves, and the first competitor and victor in the contests. During his earthly life he had been a helper of gods and men, and had set the earth free from monsters and rascals. Accordingly he was invoked in all the perils of life as the saviour (*Sōtēr*) and the averter of evil (*Alexĭkăkŏs*). Men prayed for his protection against locusts, flies, and noxious serpents. He was a wanderer, and had travelled over the whole world; therefore he was called on as the guide on marches and journeys (*Hēgĕmŏnĭŏs*). In another character he was the glorious conqueror (*Kallĭnĭkŏs*) who, after his toils are over, enjoys his rest with wine, feasting, and music. Indeed, the fable represents him as having, in his hours of repose, given as striking proofs of inexhaustible bodily power as in his struggles and contests. Men liked to think of him as an enormous eater, capable of devouring a whole ox; as a lusty boon companion, fond of delighting himself and others by playing the lyre. In Rome he was coupled with the Muses, and, like Apollo elsewhere, was worshipped as *Mūsāgĕtēs*, or master of the Muses. After his labours he was supposed to have been fond of hot baths, which were accordingly deemed sacred to him. Among trees, the wild olive and white poplar were consecrated to him ; the poplar he was believed to have brought from far countries to Olympia.

Owing to the influence of the Greek colonies in Italy, the worship of Hercules was widely diffused among the Italian tribes. It attached itself to local legends and religion; the conqueror of Căcus, for instance, was originally not Hercules, but a powerful shepherd called Garănŏs. Again, Hercules came to be identified with the ancient Italian deity Sancus or Dīus Fĭdĭus, and was regarded as the god of happiness in home and field, industry and war, as well as of truth and honour. His altar was the *Ara Maxĭma* in the cattle-market (*fŏrum bŏārĭum*), which he was believed to have erected himself. (*See* CACUS.) Here they dedicated to him a tithe of their gains in war and peace, ratified solemn treaties, and invoked his name to witness their oaths. He had many shrines and sacrifices in Rome, corresponding to his various titles *Victŏr* (Conqueror), *Invictus* (Unconquered), *Custōs* (Guardian), *Dēfensŏr* (Defender), and others. His rites were always performed in Greek fashion, with the head covered. It was in his temple that soldiers and gladiators were accustomed to hang up their arms when their service was over. In the stone-quarries the labourers had their *Hercules Saxārĭus* (or Hercules of the

stone). He was called the father of Lătīnus, the ancestor of the Latines, and to him the Roman *gens* of the Făbĭī traced their origin. The ancient *gens* of the *Pŏtĭtĭī* were said to have been commissioned by the god in person to provide, with the assistance of the *Pĭnārĭī*, for his sacrifices at the *Ara Maxĭma*. In 310 B.C. the Potitii gave the service into the hands of state slaves. Before a year had passed the flourishing family had become completely extinct.

In works of art Heracles is represented as the ideal of manly strength, with full,

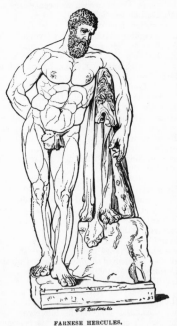

FARNESE HERCULES.
(Naples Museum.)

well knit, and muscular limbs, serious expression, a curling beard, short neck, and a head small in proportion to the limbs. His equipment is generally the club and the lion's skin. The type appears to have been mainly fixed by Lўsippus. The *Farnese Hercules*, by the Athenian Glўcōn, is probably a copy of one by Lysippus. Hercules is portrayed in repose, leaning on his club, which is covered with the lion's skin (see engraving, and article GLYCON). The Hercules of the Athenian Apollōnĭus, now only a torso, is equally celebrated. (See APOLLONIUS.) Compare also the copy of a head of Heracles on a *tĕtrădrachmŏn*, of which there is an engraving under the article COINAGE.

Hērăclīdēs (*Hērăkleidēs*). Surnamed *Pontĭcus*. A Greek philosopher, born at Hērăclēa in Pontus about 380 B.C. He came early to Athens, where he became a disciple of Plato and Aristotle, and had made a reputation by about 340 B.C. He was the author of some sixty works in a great variety of subjects: philosophy, mathematics, music, grammar, poetry, political and literary history, and geography. He was a learned and interesting writer, but somewhat deficient in critical power. We have a few fragments of his works remaining, besides an extract from a book on Constitutions which bears his name. But as no such treatise is elsewhere attributed to him, this must probably be regarded as a selection from some of his other writings.

Hērăclītus (*Hērăkleitŏs*) of Ephesus. A Greek philosopher, who lived from about 535-475 B.C., during the time of the first Persian domination over his native city. As one of the last of the family of Androclus the descendant of Codrus, who had founded the colony of Ephesus, Heraclitus had certain honorary regal privileges, which he renounced in favour of his brother. He likewise declined an invitation of king Darius to visit his court. He was an adherent of the aristocracy, and when, after the defeat of the Persians, the democratic party came into power, he withdrew in ill-humour to a secluded estate in the country, and gave himself up entirely to his studies. In his later years he wrote a philosophical treatise, which he deposited in the temple of Artĕmis, making it a condition that it should not be published till after his death. He was buried in the market-place of Ephesus, and for several centuries later the Ephesians continued to engrave his image on their coins.

His great work *On Nature*, in three books, was written in the Ionian dialect, and is the oldest monument of Greek prose. Considerable fragments of it have come down to us. The language is bold, harsh, and figurative; the style is so careless that the syntactical relations of the words are often hard to perceive; and the thoughts are profound. All this made Heraclitus so difficult a writer, that he went in antiquity by the name "the obscure."

Knowledge, according to Heraclitus, is based upon perception by the senses. Perfect knowledge is only given to the gods, but a progress in knowledge is possible to men. Wisdom consists in the recognition of the intelligence which, by means of the universe, guides the universe. Everything is in an eternal flux; nothing, therefore, not even the world in its momentary form, nor the gods themselves, can escape final destruction. The ultimate principle into which all existence is resolvable is fire. As fire changes continually into water and then into earth, so earth changes back to water and water again to fire. The world, therefore, arose from fire, and in alternating periods is resolved again into fire, to form itself anew out of this element. The division of unity, or of the divine original fire, into the multiplicity of opposing phenomena, is "the way downwards," and the consequence of a war and a strife. Harmony and peace lead back to unity by "the way upwards." Nature is constantly dividing and uniting herself, so that the multiplicity of opposites does not destroy the unity of the whole. The existence of these opposites depends only on the difference of the motion on "the way upwards" from that on "the way downwards"; all things, therefore, are at once identical and not identical.

Hēræa. A festival held at Argos every five years in honour of Hēra, the goddess of the country. The priestess of Hera drove, in a car drawn by white oxen, to the Hēræum, or temple of the goddess, situated between Argos and Mўcēnæ. Meantime the people marched out in procession, the fighting men in their arms. There was a great sacrifice of oxen (*hĕkă-tombē*), followed by a general sacrificial banquet and games of all sorts. A special feature of these was a contest in throwing the javelin, while running at full speed, at a shield set up at the end of the course. The victor received a crown and a shield, which he carried in the final procession

Herald. *See* CERYX and PRÆCO.

Herald's Staff (Gr. *kērўkeiŏn;* Lat. *cădū-cĕŭs*). An attribute of Hermēs (*q.v.*).

Hermæ. Pillars, smaller at the base than at the summit, which terminated generally with a head of Hermēs. In the earliest times, Hermes (in whose worship the number 4 played a great part) was worshipped [especially in Arcadia, *see* Pausanias, viii 4 § 4; *cp.* iv 33 § 4] under the form of a simple quadrangular pillar of marble or wood, with the significant mark of the male sex. As art advanced, the pillar was surmounted, first with a bearded head, and afterwards with a youthful head of the god. *Hermes* being the god of traffic, such pillars were erected to him in the streets and squares of towns; in Attica, after the time of Hipparchus, the son of Pisistrătus, they were also erected along the country roads as mile-stones. Sometimes they were inscribed with apophthegms and riddles, in addition to directions as to the way; [sometimes also with inscriptions in honour of those who had fought bravely for their country, Dem., *Lept.*, 112; Æschines, *Or.* 3 § 183.] In Athens there was an especially large number of them; in the market-place to the N.W. of the Acropolis, the *Hermœ,* erected partly by private individuals and partly by corporations, formed a long colonnade extending between the Hall of Paintings (*stŏā poikĭlē*) and the King's Hall (*stoa băsĭleiŏs*). Accordingly, the latter was sometimes called the Hall of *Hermœ.* When the heads of other divinities (such as Athēnē, Hērăclēs, Erōs) were placed on such pillars, these were then called *Hermathēnē, Hermērăclēs, Hermĕrōs.*

Hermăgŏrās. *See* RHETORIC, *Greek,* near end.

Hermăphrŏdītŭs. In Greek mythology, the son of Hermēs and Aphrŏdītē, born on Mount Ida, and endowed with the beauty of both deities. When a grown youth, he was bathing in the Carian fountain of Salmăcis; and the Nymph of the fountain, whose love he rejected, prayed the gods that she might be indissolubly united with him. The prayer was answered, and a being sprang into existence which united the qualities of male and female. The fable probably arose from the inclination, prevalent in the Eastern religions, towards confusing the attributes of both sexes. In Cyprus, for instance, a masculine Aphrŏdītŏs, clad in female attire, was worshipped by the side of the goddess Aphrodite. Figures of hermaphrodites are common in art.

Hermēs. Son of Zeus and of the Naiad Maia, daughter of Atlas. Immediately after his birth upon the Arcadian mountain of Cyllēnē, he gave proof of his chief characteristics, inventiveness and versatility, united with fascination, trickery, and cunning. Born in the morning, by mid-day he had invented the lyre; in the evening he stole fifty head of cattle from his brother Apollo, which he hid so skilfully in a cave that they could not be found; after these exploits he lay down quietly in his cradle. Apollo, by

means of his prophetic power, discovered the thief and took the miscreant to Zeus, who ordered the cattle to be given up. However, Hermes so delighted his brother by his playing on the lyre that, in exchange for it, he allowed him to keep the cattle, resigned to him the golden staff of fortune and of riches, with the gift of prophecy in its humbler forms, and from that time forth became his best friend. Zeus made his son herald to the gods and the guide of the dead in Hādēs. In this myth we have allusions to several attributes of the god.

In many districts of Greece, and especially in Arcadia, the old seat of his worship, Hermes was regarded as a god who bestowed the blessing of fertility on the pastures and herds, and who was happiest spending his time among shepherds and dallying with Nymphs, by whom he had numberless children, including Pan and Daphnis. In many places he was considered the god of crops; and also as the god of mining and of digging for buried treasure. His kindliness to man is also shown in his being the god of roads. At cross-roads in particular, there were raised in his honour, and called by his name, not only heaps of stones, to which every passer by added a stone, but also the quadrangular pillars known as *Hermæ (q.v.)* At Athens these last were set up in the streets and open spaces, and also before the doors. Every unexpected find on the road was called a gift of Hermes (*hermaiŏn*). Together with Athēnē, he escorts and protects heroes in perilous enterprises, and gives them prudent counsels. He takes special delight in men's dealings with one another, in exchange and barter, in buying and selling; also in all that is won by craft or by theft. Thus he is the patron of tradespeople and thieves, and is himself the father of Autŏlўcus (*q.v.*), the greatest of all thieves. He too it is who endowed Pandōra, the first woman, with the faculty of lying, and with flattering discourse and a crafty spirit. On account of his nimbleness and activity he is the messenger of Zeus, and knows how to carry out his father's commands with adroitness and cunning, as in the slaying of Argos (the guard of Io), from which he derives his epithet of Argos-Slayer, or *Argeiphontēs.* Again, as Hermes was the sacrificial herald of the gods, it was an important part of the duty of heralds to assist at sacrifices. It was on this account that the priestly race of the *Kērỹkēs* claimed him as the head of their family (*see* ELEUSINIA). Strength of voice and excellence of memory were supposed to be derived from him in his capacity of herald. Owing to his vigour, dexterity, and personal charm, he was deemed the god of gymnastic skill, which makes men strong and handsome, and the especial patron of boxing, running, and throwing the *discus;* in this capacity the *pălœstrœ* and *gymnăsĭa* were sacred to him, and particular feasts called *Hermaia* were dedicated to him. He was the discoverer of music (for besides the lyre he invented the shepherd's pipe), and he was also the god of wise and clever discourse. A later age made him even the inventor of letters, figures, mathematics, and astronomy. He is, besides, the god of sleep and of dreams; with one touch of his staff he can close or open the eyes of mortals; hence the custom, before going to sleep, of offering him the last libation. As he is the guide of the living on their way, so is he also the conductor of the souls of the dead in the nether-world (*Psўchŏpompŏs*), and he is as much loved by the gods of those regions as he is by those above. For this reason

sacrifices were offered to him in the event of deaths, *Hermœ* were placed on the graves, and, at oracles and incantations of the dead, he was honoured as belonging to the lower world; in general, he was accounted the intermediary between the upper and lower worlds. His worship early spread throughout the whole of Greece. As he was born in the fourth month, the number four was sacred to him. In Argos the fourth month was named after him, and in Athens he was honoured with sacrifices on the fourth of every month. His altars and images (mostly simple *Hermœ*) were in all the streets, thoroughfares, and open spaces, and also at the entrance of the *palœstra.*

In art he is represented in the widely varying characters which he assumed, as a shepherd with a single animal from his

(1) HERMES LOGIOS.
Hermes as patron of the Art of Rhetoric.
(Rome, Villa Ludovisi.)

flock, as a mischievous little thief, as the god of gain with a purse in his hand (*cp.* fig. 1), with a strigil as patron of the *gymnasia*, at other times with a lyre, but oftenest of all as the messenger of the gods.

He was portrayed by the greatest sculptors, such as Phīdĭăs, Pŏlўclītus, Scŏpas, and Praxĭtĕlēs, whose Hermes with the infant Dĭonўsus was discovered in 1877, in the temple of Hera, at Olympia. (*See* PRAXI-TELES, and SCULPTURE, fig. 10.) In the older works of art he appears as a bearded and strong man ; in the later ones he is to be seen in a graceful and charming attitude, as a slim youth with tranquil features, indicative of intellect and good will. His usual attri-butes are wings on his feet, a flat, broad-brimmed hat (*see* PETASUS), which in later times was ornamented with wings, as was also his staff. This last (Gr. *kērўkeĭŏn ;* Lat. *cādūcĕus*, fig. 2) was ori-ginally an enchanter's wand, a symbol of the power that pro-duces wealth and prosperity, and also an emblem of influence over the living and the dead. But even in early times it was regarded as a herald's staff and an emblem of peaceful inter-course ; it consisted of three shoots, one of which formed the handle, the other two being (2) CADUCEUS. intertwined at the top in a knot. The place of the latter was afterwards taken by ser-pents ; and thus arose our ordinary type of herald's staff. By the Romans Hermes was identified with MERCURIUS (*q.v.*).

Hermēsĭānax, of Cŏlŏphōn in Ionia ; a Greek elegiac poet, who lived in the time of Alexander the Great, about 330 B.C., and was a scholar and friend of Phīlētās. He composed erotic elegies in the style of those by his compatriot Antīmăchus. The three books containing his compositions he en-titled *Lĕontĭŏn*, after his mistress. A frag-ment of ninety-eight lines of the third book has been preserved, in which love-stories of poets and wise men from Orpheus down to Philetas are treated in a rather unconnected manner, but not without spirit.

Hermĭŏnē. The only child of Menelāus and Helen. She was married to Neoptŏlĕ-mus the son of Achilles, immediately on her father's return from Troy, in fulfilment of a promise he had made there. According to a post-Homeric tradition, she had been previously promised to Orestes ; he claimed her on the ground of his prior right, and on his claim being refused by Neoptolemus, killed his rival with his own hands, or at any rate compassed his death, at Delphi. Orestes took Hermione to his home, and had by her a son, Tisămĕnus.

Hermippus. A Greek poet of the Old

Comedy, an elder contemporary of Aristo-phanes and a bitter opponent of Pericles, whose mistress, Aspasia, he prosecuted on a charge of atheism. Only a few fragments of his dramas, as also of his libellous iambic poems, after Archilochus' manner, have been preserved ; they are remarkable for the cleverness of their style.

Hermŏgĕnēs. A Greek rhetorician of Tarsus in Cilicia, who flourished in the middle of the 2nd century A.D. He came to Rome as a rhetorician as early as his fifteenth year, and excited universal admi-ration, especially on the part of the emperor Marcus Aurelius. In his twenty-fourth year he lost his memory, and never recovered it, though he lived to a great age. His work on Rhetoric, which still exists, enjoyed a remarkable popularity, and was for a long time the principal text-book of rhetoric ; it was also epitomised, and was the subject of numerous commentaries. The work itself consists of five sections : (1) On points at issue in legal causes ; (2) On the art of dis-covering arguments; (3) On the various forms of oratorical style; (4) On political orations in particular, and on the art of eloquent and effective speaking ; (5) the last section consists of rhetorical exercises (*Prŏgymnasmătă*), which were cast into a fresh form by Aphthŏnĭus (*q.v.*), and trans-lated into Latin by Priscian.

Hērō. *See* LEANDER.

Hērōdēs Attĭcus (the name in full is *Tiberius Claudius Attĭcus Herodes*). A celebrated Greek rhetorician, born about A.D. 101, at Marathon. He belonged to a very ancient family, and received a careful edu-cation in rhetoric and philosophy from the leading teachers of his day. His talents and his eloquence won him the favour of the emperor Hadrian, who, in A.D. 125, ap-pointed him prefect over the free towns of the Province of Asia. On his return to Athens, about 129, he attained a most exalted position, not only as a teacher of oratory, but also as the owner of immense wealth, which he had inherited from his father. This he most liberally devoted to the sup-port of his fellow citizens, and to the erec-tion of splendid public buildings in various parts of Greece. He had just been *archōn*, when in 140 he was summoned to Rome by Antoninus Pius, to instruct the imperial princes, Marcus Aurēlĭus and Lūcĭus Vērus, in Greek oratory. Amongst other marks of distinction given him for this was the consulship in 143. His old age was sad-dened by misunderstandings with his fellow citizens and heavy family calamities. He died at Marathon in 177. His pre-eminence as an orator was universally acknowledged by his contemporaries; he was called the king of orators, and was placed on a level with the great masters of antiquity. His reputation is hardly borne out by an unimportant rhetorical exercise (*On the Constitution*) calling on the Thebans to join the Peloponnesians against Archelaus, king of Macedonia. This has come down to us under his name, but its genuineness is not free from doubt. Numerous inscriptions still remain to attest his ancient renown; and out of the number of his public buildings, there is still standing at Athens the *Odeum*, a theatre erected in memory of his wife Regilla.

Hērōdiānus. (1) A Greek historian, about 170–240 A.D., who lived (for a time at any rate) in Rome, and filled offices both at court and in the state. We still possess his history of the Roman emperors, from the death of Marcus Aurelius to the accession of Gordianus III (180–238); it is distinguished by its impartiality, and its clear and pleasing style.

(2) *Ælius Hērōdiānus.* A Greek scholar, son of Apollōnius Dyscŏlus (*q.v.*), born at Alexandria; he flourished in the second half of the 2nd century A.D., and after the completion of his education, went to Rome, where he long lived in confidential intercourse with Marcus Aurēlius, and received the Roman citizenship. He died in his native town. In a large number of treatises he extended in every direction the work begun by his father in the investigation of grammar, and in reducing it to a systematic form. Of his activity as an author numerous evidences have come down to us in the shape of extensive fragments of his works.

Hērŏdŏtus. The famous Greek historian, called the Father of History, born about 490–480 B.C., at Halicarnassus in Asia Minor. He was of noble family, being the son of Lyxēs and Dryō (or Rhoiō). Like his uncle, the poet Panyasis (*q.v.*), he fled in 460 to the island of Samos, having been expelled from his native town by the tyrant Lygdămis. From this spot he seems to have completed his great travels, which he had already begun when at Halicarnassus. These travels were most extensive: he traversed Asia Minor, the interior of Asia nearly as far as Susa, the Græco-Asiatic islands, Egypt as far as Elephantīnē, Cȳrēnē, the shores of the Euxine as far as

the Caucasus and the mouth of the Danube, as well as Greece and the neighbouring countries. Having returned with his uncle to Halicarnassus, he took part in the expulsion of Lygdamis (about 450), but, probably in consequence of political intrigues, he fell into disgrace with his fellow townsmen, and was again compelled to quit his native country.

In 445 he betook himself to Athens in order to take part in the projected colonization of Thurii in Southern Italy. Here he gave public readings from the works which he had begun to compose in Samos (probably the portions relating to the Persian War). They met with such applause that he was rewarded with a present of ten talents (£2,000) from the public treasury. He is also said to have given similar recitations elsewhere—at the festal assembly of the Greeks at Olympia, and also at Corinth and Thebes. We are told that at one of these recitals Thucydides was present as a boy, and was so affected that he shed tears and resolved to devote himself to the writing of history. [See, however, Dahlmann's *Life of Herodotus*, chap. ii, sect. ii.] Herodotus was in close intercourse with the leading men of the day. In Athens, which he seems to have often visited, after having settled at Thurii (443), he knew Pericles and the poet Sophocles, who composed a special poem in his honour in 442. It was doubtless there that he was prompted to mould the materials of his history into a complete and artistic whole. He carried forward this plan at Thurii; but it is probable that his death, which occurred about 424, prevented his finishing his grand design.

This work (which the Alexandrine critics divided into nine books, named after the nine Muses), marks the beginning of real historical writing among the Greeks. The industry of the earlier historical writers (known as *Lŏgŏgrăphi, q.v.*) had contented itself with collecting material for a limited purpose, such as histories of towns and families, arranged in an uncritical and inartistic manner. It is the merit of Herodotus, that, by his study of the existing literature and by his travels, he collected historical, geographical, and ethnographical materials relating to the greater part of the then known world, that he sifted them with some critical discernment, that he arranged them under leading topics, and set them forth in an original and attractive form. The true scope of the work, which embraces a period of 320 years down to the battle of Mўcălē (479), is the struggle between the Greeks and the barbarians; with this leading thread of his narrative are inwoven, in a countless number of episodes, descriptions of the countries and races, more or less closely connected with the principal events of the story, so that the result is a complete picture of the known world as it then existed. In subordination to this general object, the whole narrative is inspired with the one guiding thought, that all history is determined by a moral government of the world, ordained by a Providence which rules the destinies of man ; and that every exaltation of man above the limits fixed by the eternal law of heaven excites the jealousy of the gods, and draws down an avenging Nemesis on the head of the guilty one himself, or his descendants.

His veracity shows itself in the sharp distinction he draws between personal observation, oral information, and mere conjecture; his impartiality, his just recognition of praiseworthy qualities (even on the side of the enemy), is displayed in his frank censure of political or moral failings which he thinks he perceives in his friends ; while his nobility of character is evinced by his hearty delight in all that is good and beautiful.

Although by race Herodotus belonged to the Dorians, he nevertheless made use of the Ionic dialect which had been employed by his predecessors, the *lŏgŏgrăphĭ*, though at times he mingles it with Epic, Doric, and Attic forms. His simplicity of style recalls that of the *logographi*, but he far excels them in clearness and general intelligibility of composition, in a pleasing flow of language, in an epic, and often even redundant, fulness of expression, and above all in a genius for narrative, which he shows in the vivid description of the most diverse events.—A biography of Homer, written in the Ionic dialect, bears the name of Herodotus; it is really the work of a rhetorician at the beginning of the 1st century of our era.

Hērŏn. A Greek mathematician of Alexandria, about the middle of the 3rd century B.C., the well-known inventor of *Heron's ball* and *Heron's fountain*. Of his *Introduction to Mechanics*, the most comprehensive work of antiquity on the theory of that science, only extracts are preserved in Pappus. We also possess his disquisitions on presses, on the contrivance of automa-

tons, and on the construction of catapults and other engines for projectiles.

Hērŏŏn. The shrine of a hero. (*See* HEROS.)

Hērŏphĭlē. The Erythræan Sibyl. (*See* SIBYLLÆ.)

Hērŏs (*Gr.*). A hero. This is in Homer a descriptive title given specially to princes and nobles, but also applied to men of mark sprung from the people. Hesiod reserves the name for mortals of divine origin, who are therefore also known as demigods. Many of these he places on the Islands of the Blessed, where under the sovereignty of Crŏnus (Krŏnŏs), they lead a life of happiness. Hesiod makes no allusion to the influence of heroes upon the life of man, or to the worship due to them in consequence. But in later times this belief spread throughout the whole of Greece. The heroes are in most respects like men and suffer death ; but death puts them in a more exalted rank, and they then have power to do men good as well as harm. The most distinguished warriors of prehistoric times were accounted heroes, being generally regarded as the offspring of gods by mortal women ; to their souls another destiny was accordingly assigned than that allotted to the souls of mortals. But even amongst the heroes of old time there were some who, without being children of the gods, nevertheless so distinguished themselves by their virtue, that they appeared to participate in the divine nature, and therefore to deserve a higher distinction after death. Even in later times such men were not unknown, when personages recently deceased were actually exalted to the ranks of heroes, as in the case of Lĕŏnĭdās at Sparta, and Harmŏdĭus and Aristŏgeitōn at Athens. The founders of colonies were especially considered worthy of worship as heroes; when the true founder was unknown, then some appropriate hero was selected instead. Formerly there were many such fictitious heroes; to this class properly belong all the titular ancestors of the noble and priestly families of Attica, and the founders of particular arts and trades, as Dædălus. Many heroes of historical times were originally gods, who, in course of time, were divested of their primitive dignity. There was no town or district of Greece in which a host of heroes was not worshipped by the side of the higher divinities; many as special tutelary spirits of the country, others as the heroes of the country, as the Dioscŭri at Sparta, the Æacĭdæ at Ægīna, and

Theseus in Attica. There were festivals in their honour everywhere, many of them small and unimportant, and only celebrated in a restricted circle, others observed by the state as festivals of the people in general, and not a whit inferior, in wealth of equipment, to the most important festivals in honour of the gods. This was especially the case with the heroes of the country. Many heroes had shrines, known as *Hērōa*, which were generally erected over their graves. The altars of heroes were lower than those of gods, and were commonly designated sacrificial hearths; they were generally on a level with the ground, and on the west side, the region of the nether world, were provided with a hollow into which the libations were poured. Like offerings to the dead, these consisted of honey, wine, water, milk, oil, and blood which had been shed by sacrificial victims; the flesh of the animals sacrificed was burnt. In the period of decadence it became customary to treat the living with heroic honours. Such honours were paid to the Spartan Lȳsander by the towns in Asia Minor, and were afterwards accorded to kings, *e.g.* to Antȳgŏnus and his son Dēmētrius at Athens.

Hērsē. *See* ERSE.

Hesiod (*Hēsĭŏdŏs*). The earliest epic poet of Greece (next to Homer), whose writings have actually come down to us. Even the ancients themselves had no clear views of his date, some making him the contemporary of Homer and others even still older. He certainly lived after Homer, probably about the beginning of the Olympiads in 776 B.C. His poems contain incidentally a few allusions to the circumstances of his life. According to them he was born at Ascra in Bœotia, near Hĕlĭcōn, where his father Dius had settled as an emigrant from the Æolic Cyme (*Kūmē*) in Asia. At his father's death he was involved in a dispute with his younger brother Perses about his patrimony. This was decided against him by the verdict of the judges, who had been bribed by the younger brother. Disgust at the injustice he had suffered, and a renewal of the dispute with his brother, appear to have determined him to forsake his native land and to settle at Naupactus. According to a tradition he was murdered at the Locrian town of Œnĕŏn by the sons of his host, on a false suspicion; but, by command of the Delphic oracle, his bones were brought to Orchŏmĕnus, where a monument, with an inscription, was erected

to him in the market-place. In ancient times a series of epic poems bore his name, and were attributed to him as the representative of the Bœotian and Locrian school of poetry, in contrast to the Ionian and Homeric school. Three poems of his have been preserved : (1) The *Works and Days*, which consists of myths, fables, and proverbs, interwoven with exhortations to his brother, who, having lost by extravagance his share of the· patrimony, was now threatening him with a new law-suit. The poet here recommends him to abstain from his unrighteous proceedings, and by honourable toil to gain fresh wealth for himself. He therefore lays down for his guidance all manner of precepts, on agriculture, domestic economy, navigation, etc., and specifies the days appropriate for every undertaking. Although this poem is deficient in true artistic finish, it was highly valued by the ancients on account of its moral teaching. (2) The *Theogony*. An account of the origin of the world and of the birth of the gods, which, in its present shape, is composed of different recensions, together with many later additions. Next to the Homeric poems, it is the most important source of our knowledge of the views of the Greeks of the earliest times as to the world and the gods. (3) The *Shield of Hērăclēs*. A description of the shield of Heracles, wrought by Hēphæstus, to arm the hero in his conflict with Cycnus (*q.v.*), son of Ares. It is a weak imitation of the Homeric account of the shield of Achilles, and is certainly not the work of Hesiod. As an introduction, a number of verses are borrowed from a lost poem by Hesiod, of genealogical import,—a list of the women whom the gods had made the mothers of the heroic families of Greece.

The poetry of Hesiod, although composed in the same form as that of Homer, never approaches it in grace and beauty. On the contrary, it is wanting in artistic form and finish, and rarely affords any real enjoyment. Nevertheless it betokens an important advance in the development of the Greek intellect, from the naïve simplicity of its attitude in Homeric times, to the speculative observation of the world and of human life. It contains the germs of lyric, as also of elegiac, iambic, and aphoristic poetry.

Hēsĭŏnē. Daughter of Lāŏmĕdōn, king of Troy, and of Leucippē. By her death she was to appease the wrath of Pŏseidōn, who, on account of her father's breaking his word, was devastating the land with a marine monster. Heracles destroyed the monster and set the maiden free; but Laomedon wanted to break his promise to the hero, and to deprive him of his stipulated payment. So Heracles took Troy, slew Laomedon and his sons, and gave Hesione to his companion Tĕlămōn, to whom she bore a son, Teucer.

Hespĕrĭdĕs. According to Hesiod, the daughters of Night; according to later accounts, daughters of Atlas and of Hespĕrĭs. Their names were *Æglē*, *Arĕthūsa*, *Erȳtheia*, *Hespĕrĭa*. They dwell on the river Ocĕănus, near Atlas, close to the Gorgons, on the borders of eternal darkness, in the garden of the gods, where Zeus espoused Hera. Together with the hundred-headed dragon Lādōn, the son of Phorcys or Typhon, they guard the golden apples which *Gœa* (or Earth) caused to grow as a marriage gift for Hera. (*See* HERACLES.)

Hestia. The goddess of the hearth, which is the emblem of the settled home. She is deemed the founder and maintainer of the family and the state, of civic concord and of public reverence for the gods. She is the daughter of Cronus (Krŏnŏs) and of Rhea; sister of Zeus, Pŏseidōn, Hādes, Hēra, and Dēmētēr; one of the twelve Olympian deities, from whom she is distinguished by the fact that, as the abiding goddess of the household, she never leaves Olympus. In Homer the sanctity of the hearth is indeed recognised, but as yet we find no mention of the goddess. It is a matter of discussion whether this was by accident, or because in that period the personification of the worship of the hearth had not attained its full perfection. Having been wooed by Apollo and Poseidon, she took an oath of perpetual virginity; so Zeus granted her the honour of being worshipped, as a tutelary goddess, at every hearth, in human habitations as well as in the temples of the gods, and of being called to mind amid libations at the beginning and end of every sacrifice and every festal entertainment. Hence it was that every sacrifice began and ended with a libation to Hestia, so that she had a share in all festivities; and in every prayer, as well as in all the public forms of solemn oaths, her name was recited before the name of any other god. Just as in the home her consecrated hearth formed the central point of family life, at which family festivals were celebrated and where both strangers and fugitives found a hospitable asylum, so also in the *Prytaneiŏn*, or townhall, where the sacred fire was ever

burning, her hearth was the centre of the life of the city, indeed of the whole state, and of the colonies which had gone forth from it. Here, as representative of the state, the highest officials sacrificed to her, just as in every private house the father or mother of the family provided for her worship. Here also were held the public deliberations, and the public banquet given to deserving citizens and to foreign ambassadors. Hither repaired all who besought the protection of the state. Hence also did the colonists, bound for distant shores, take the fire for the public hearth of their new community. In some respects,

THE GIUSTINIANI HESTIA.
(Rome, now in the *Torlonia Museum*.)
[In the original the left hand is nearer the shoulder; the forefinger modern.]

the centre of the religious life of Greece was the fire on the hearth of Hestia in the Delphic temple, where was the sacred *omphălŏs* (or navel), which the Greeks considered to be the central point of the inhabited earth. Hestia stands in close connexion with Zeus as the guardian of the law of hospitality and of the oath. She was also much associated with Hermēs and often invoked in conjunction with him; Hestia, as the goddess of gentle domesticity, and Hermes, as the restless god of trade on the public streets and roads, representing between them the two principal varieties of human life. According to a view that afterwards became current, under the influence of philosophers and mystics, she was regarded as personifying the earth, as the fixed centre of the world, and was identified with Dēmētēr and Cÿbĕlē. The corresponding deity among the Romans was Vesta (*q.v.*). The statues placed in the *Prÿtănĕia* represented her, in accordance with her nature, as a being with grave and yet gentle expression, sitting or standing in an attitude of rest, with a sceptre as her attribute. The most celebrated of her existing statues is known as the *Giustiniani Vesta* (*see* cut); a form robed in simple drapery, with hair unadorned and wearing a veil; her right hand rests on her hip, and her left hand, which is pointing upwards, once held a long staff as her sceptre.

Hēsÿchĭŭs. A Greek grammarian of Alexandria, who lived probably towards the end of the 4th century A.D. He composed, with the assistance of the works of earlier lexicographers (especially that of Diogĕnĭānus), a lexicon, which has come down to us in a very confused form, but is nevertheless among the most important sources of our knowledge of the Greek language, and throws much light on the interpretation and criticism of Greek poets, orators, historians, and physicians.

Hetæræ (Gr. *hĕtairai*). A euphemism for courtesans carrying on their profession chiefly at Corinth and Athens. In the former place they were connected with the worship of Aphrŏdītē; in the latter they were introduced by an ordinance of Solon, who intended thereby to obviate worse evils that imperilled the sanctity of the marriage-bond and the chastity of domestic life. The intercourse of unmarried men with *hetæræ* was by no means considered immoral; in the case of married men it was disapproved by custom, which, after the Peloponesian War, became more and more lax in this as in other respects. The *hetæræ* who were kept in special establishments and on whom the state levied a tax, were all female slaves; on the other hand, the women called *hetæræ* in a narrower sense, who carried on their trade independently, were drawn chiefly from the ranks of foreigners and freedwomen. It was quite unexampled for any Athenian citizen's daughter to become a *hetæra*. The important position they assumed in the social life of Athens after the Peloponnesian War is easily gathered from the later Attic Comedy, as the plot of the pieces generally turns upon the adventures of a *hetæra*. As custom debarred all respectable women and girls from the society of men, the female element in the latter was represented exclusively by *hetæræ*, many of whom became famous by possessing the mental culture from which the female citizens were debarred by their education and by their secluded life. Thus they were able to attract even men of eminence. *Aspăsĭa* of Mīlētus was able to make her house at Athens the meeting-point of the most remarkable men of her day; among them even a Socrates and a Pericles, and the latter deserted his wife to marry her.

Courtesans (called in Latin *mĕrĕtrīcēs*) were tolerated in Rome as in Greece; and no objection was raised to the intercourse of unmarried men with these persons. They were under the charge of the ædiles, and from the time of Caligula they had to pay a tax to the imperial exchequer. Steeped as they were in infamy, the law even refused to accept their testimony as valid. They were distinguishable from respectable women by their costume; they wore neither *stŏla* nor *palla*, but a shorter tunic without fringe, over which was a toga of darker colour; they were not permitted to adopt the characteristic head-gear of matrons. In the best times the trade was only carried on by slaves and freedwomen, but afterwards by free-born women also.

Hetæri (Gr. *hĕtairoi*) ("companions"). The designation of all free Macedonians who were ready to join in the defence of their country; especially the noblemen who composed the heavy cavalry, as contrasted with the infantry (Gr. *pĕzĕtairoi*) of the royal guard [*see* Thirlwall, *H. G.*, v, p. 179].

Hetæriæ (Gr. *hĕtairĭai*). The common name in Greece for all associations having any particular object, but chiefly for political clubs, often of a secret character, for the advancement of certain interests in the state. In many cases their members only aimed at assisting one another as candidates for public office or in lawsuits; but occasionally they also worked for the victory of their party and for a change in the constitution.

Hĭĕrŏdūlī (Gr. *-oi*), (temple servants). The name for all who were closely connected with the service of a sanctuary, and especially such as were bound to perform certain services, obligations, and duties to the same, and in part lived as a kind of bondmen upon its land. We find them forming a considerable population in Asia; *e.g.* at Cōmāna in Cappadocia, there were more than 6,000 of them, who with their descendants belonged as slaves to the goddess called Enyō by the Greeks. They served as labourers on the estates of the temple, and performed the humblest offices as hewers of wood and drawers of water. The Delphic sanctuary of Apollo had similar ministrants from a very early date, as had also the temple of Aphrodite on Mount Eryx in Sicily. In the same manner Aphrodite of Corinth, in the flourishing times of that that city, had over 1,000 girls dedicated to her service; they added brilliancy and lustre to her worship, and living as *hetairai* they paid a portion of their earnings to the goddess as tribute.

Hĭĕrŏmēnĭă. The Greek term for the holy time of the month, *i.e.* that portion of each month which was kept as a festival. It differed in the several months according to the number and duration of the festivals. During this time there was a suspension of all business and even of lawsuits, and executions and warrants were in abeyance; in short, everything that was likely to interrupt the universal peace and the celebration of the festival was set on one side. For the greater feasts a "truce of God" was proclaimed. (*See* EKECHEIRIA.)

Hĭĕrŏmnēmōn. The recorder or officer in charge of sacred business at the meetings of the Amphictyonic Council. (*See* AMPHICTYONS.)

Hĭĕrŏnўmŭs. (1) A Greek historian born at Cardia in Thrace; he fought under Alexander the Great, and after his death attached himself to his compatriot Eumĕnēs. They were both captured in B.C. 316, but Hieronymus found favour with Antĭgŏnus and was appointed governor of Syria. Dēmētrius, the son of Antigonus, entrusted him with the governorship of Bœotia. He survived Pyrrhus (*ob.* 272), and died, at the age of 104, at the court of Antigonus Gŏnātās. At an advanced age he composed a history of the Dĭădŏchi and their successors down to and beyond the death of Pyrrhus; which, although of small value in point of style, was an original work of great value, and the foundation of all the accounts of the successors of Alexander that have come down to us. The work exists in fragments only.

(2) Best known as *Saint Jerome.* One of the most famous of the Latin Fathers

of the Church. He was born at Stridōn on the borders of Dalmatia and Pannonia, about A.D. 340. He was the son of respectable and wealthy Christian parents, and received in Rome and Trèves a secular education in rhetoric and philosophy. In 374, during a journey in the East, he was alarmed by a dream, which led to his withdrawing from the world and living as a hermit in the Syrian desert. After five years he left his retirement and lived in Antioch, Constantinople, and Rome, till he settled at Bethlehem in 386. He there founded a monastery and a school of learning, and he ended an active life in 420. Among his numerous works mention must be made of his translation and continuation (in 380 B.C.) of the Greek Chronological Tables of Eusebius (*q.v.*); this is of great value for the history of Roman literature, owing to its quotations from the work of Suetonius *De Vĭrīs Illustrĭbus*, which was then extant in its complete form. In imitation of the latter and under a similar title he wrote a work on Christian Literature. He also wrote the well-known Latin version of the Bible known as the Vulgate, which is, strictly speaking, a revision, and in part a new version, of an older translation.

Hierophant (Gr. *hĭĕrŏphantēs*, "discloser of sacred things"). The chief priest in the Eleusinian mysteries (*see* ELEUSINIA.) He was always a member of the family of the Eumolpĭdæ. It was his duty to exhibit to the initiated the sacred symbols of the mysteries, and at the same time probably to chant the liturgic hymns originally derived from his ancestor, the Thracian bard Eumolpus.

Hieropœi (Gr. *hĭĕrŏpoioi*, "managers of the sacrifices"). The Greek term for certain officials, who, besides having the care of the sacrifices, had also the superintendence of the economic details of the sanctuary, and the charge of the money and treasures of the temple. In Athens, besides such officials attached to the several temples, there was a board of ten men, yearly appointed by lot, who had to attend to the celebration of the extraordinary and quinquennial sacrifices, the cost of which was defrayed by the public treasury. Another college of three or ten *hieropœi*, appointed by the Areopagus, superintended the sacrifices offered to the Eumĕnĭdĕs by the state.

Hieroscopy (Gr. *hĭĕrŏskŏpĭa*, "viewing the sacrifice"). A form of divination by means of the entrails of sacrificed beasts. (*See* MANTIKE.)

Hĭlărŏträgœdia (lit. " gay and lively tragedy "). A species of comedy invented by Rhinthon of Tarentum, and consisting of a travesty of tragic themes. (*See* RHINTHON.)

Hildesheim, the Treasure of. A number of drinking vessels, plates, and cooking utensils of silver, most of them embossed in high relief, found at Hildesheim in 1868. These important products of Roman art, of the time of Augustus, are now among the chief attractions of the Berlin Museum. They probably belonged to the table service of some wealthy Roman, and had been hidden in the ground by Germans who had taken them as the spoils of victory. Artistically the most important pieces are a bowl shaped like a bell, and gracefully decorated externally with arabesques and figures of children (*see* cut), and four magnificent saucers decorated with a gilt Minerva seated on a rock, and half-length figures of the young Hercules slaying the serpents, and of Cўbĕlē and of Attis; also two cups

ROMAN MIXING-BOWL.
(Found at Hildesheim, now in Berlin Museum.)

adorned with masks and all kinds of emblems of the worship of Bacchus.

Hĭmätĭŏn. Part of the outdoor dress of Greeks of free birth, worn over the *chĭtōn*, and reaching at least as far as the knees. It was an oblong piece of drapery, one end of which was first thrown over the left shoulder, then brought forward and held fast by the left arm; the garment was then drawn over the shoulder to the right side in such a manner that the right side was completely covered up to the shoulder, according to the more elegant fashion (fig. 1). Otherwise it went on under the

right arm, and left the right shoulder exposed. Women wore the *himation* in the same manner, but some drew it over their

(1) From a vase-painting (Gerhard, *Arch. Zeitung*, 1848, taf. xiii.)

(2) Terra-cotta in Stackelberg's *Gräber d. Hellenen*, taf. lxvii.

HIMATION.

head, so as to leave only the face visible (fig. 2). *See* CHLAMYS and TRIBON.

Hĭmĕrĭŭs. A Greek Sophist, born at Prusa in Bithynia, about 315 A.D., and educated at Athens, where, after extending his knowledge by travelling, he became a teacher of rhetoric. As such, he was so successful that he received the rights of citizenship, and became a member of the Areopagus. Among his pupils were Basil the Great and Gregory of Nazianzus; for, although himself a pagan, nevertheless, like Libanius, he exhibited no animosity against Christians. He was summoned to Antioch by Julian, and appointed his private secretary. On the emperor's death (363), he returned to his earlier occupation at Athens, and there died, after becoming blind in his old age, about 386. Of his speeches and declamations twenty-four exist in a complete form, ten in fragments, and thirty-six in the summaries and excerpts preserved by Photius. His style is ornate, turgid, and overladen with erudition. He owes his special importance solely to the fact that his speeches contain materials for the history of the events and of the manners of his time.

Himĕrŏs. The personification of longing and desire, and companion of Erōs (*q.v.*).

Hippāgrĕtæ. The three officers chosen at Lacedæmon by the ephors to command the horsemen who formed the bodyguard of the kings.

Hipparch (Gr. *hipparchŏs*). The Greek name for a commander of cavalry (*see* HIPPEIS). In the Ætolian and Achæan leagues, this name was borne by an officer charged with other functions besides, who was in rank second only to the *strătēgŏs*.

Hipparchus. A Greek mathematician, the founder of scientific astronomy, born at Nicæa in Bithynia, lived chiefly at Rhodes and Alexandria, and died about B.C. 125. He discovered the precession of the equinoxes, settled more accurately the length of the solar year, as also of the revolution of the moon, and the magnitude and distances of the heavenly bodies. He placed mathematical geography on a firmer basis, by teaching the application of the latitude and longitude of the stars to marking the position of places on the surface of the earth. Of his numerous writings we only possess his commentary on the *Phœnŏmĕna* of Eudoxus and Arātus, and a catalogue of 1,026 fixed stars.

Hipparmostēs. A leader of the Spartan cavalry. (*See* HIPPEIS.)

Hippeis. The Greek term for riders and knights. (1) Among the Athenians, the citizens whose property qualified them for the second class. (*See* SOLONIAN CONSTITUTION.) (2) Among the Spartans, the royal guard of honour, consisting of 300 chosen Spartan youths under the age of thirty, who, although originally mounted, afterwards served as heavy-armed foot-soldiers.

The cavalry of *Athens*, which was first formed after the Persian War, and then consisted of 300 men, from the Periclean period onwards consisted of 1,200 men, *viz.* 200 mounted bowmen (*hippotoxŏtæ*), who were slaves belonging to the state, and the 1,000 citizens of the two highest classes. They were kept together in time of peace, and carefully drilled; at the great public festivals they took part in the processions. They were commanded by two *hipparchi*, each of whom had five *phŷlai* under him and superintended the levy. Subordinate to these were the ten *phylarchi* in command of the ten *phylai*. Both sets of officers were drawn from the two highest

classes. It was the duty of the council to see that the cavalry was in good condition, and also to examine new members in respect of their equipment and their eligibility. (*See* BOULE.)

The number of horsemen to be despatched to the field was determined by the decree of the popular assembly. Every citizen-soldier received equipment-money on joining, and during his time of service a subsidy towards keeping a groom and two horses; this grew to be an annual grant from the state, amounting to forty talents (= £8,000 in intrinsic value), but regular pay was only given in the field.

At Sparta it was not until B.C. 404 that a *regular* body of horse was formed, the cavalry being much neglected as compared with the infantry. The rich had only to provide horses, equipment, and armour; for the actual cavalry service in time of war, only those unfitted for the heavy-armed infantry were drafted off and sent to the field without any preliminary drill. In later times every *mŏra* of heavy-armed infantry seems to have had allotted to it a *mora* of cavalry, of uncertain number. By enlisting mercenaries, and introducing allies into their forces, the Spartans at length obtained better cavalry.

The utility of the Greek citizen-cavalry was small on account of their heavy armour, their metal helmet, and their coat of mail, their kilt fringed with metal flaps, their cuisses reaching to the knee, and their leather leggings. They did not take shields into action. As weapons of offence they had the straight two-edged sword and a spear, used either as a lance or a javelin. Shoeing of horses was unknown to the Greeks, as was also the use of stirrups. If anything at all was used as a saddle, it was either a saddle-cloth or a piece of felt, which was firmly fastened with girths under the horse's belly. The Thessalians were considered the best riders. Cavalry became really important for the first time in the Macedonian army under Philip and his son Alexander the Great. Although in earlier times the number of horsemen in the Greek forces was only very small, in the army which Alexander marched into Asia they formed nearly a sixth part of the infantry. The Macedonian cavalry was divided into heavy and light, both consisting of squadrons (*ilai*) of an average strength of 200 men. Of the heavy cavalry the choicest troops were the Macedonian and Thessalian horsemen, armed in the

Greek fashion, who were as formidable in onslaught as in single combat; in order and discipline they far surpassed the dense squadrons of the Asiatic cavalry, and even in attacking the infantry of the enemy they had generally a decisive effect. The light cavalry, which was constituted under the name of *prŏdrŏmoi* (skirmishers), consisted of Macedonian *sarissŏphŏroi*, so called from the *sarissa*, a lance from 14 to 16 feet long [Polybius, xviii 12], and of Thracian horsemen. The heavy-cavalry men had each a mounted servant and probably a led horse for the transport of baggage and forage. In the time after Alexander there came into existence what were called the *Tarentīnī ĕquĭtēs*, or light-armed spearmen, with two horses each [B.C. 192, Livy, xxxv 28, 29].

Hippĭăs. A Greek Sophist of Elis and a contemporary of Socrates. He taught in the towns of Greece, especially at Athens. He had the advantage of a prodigious memory, and was deeply versed in all the learning of his day. He attempted literature in every form which was then extant. He also made the first attempt in the composition of dialogues. In the two Platonic dialogues named after him, he is represented as excessively vain and arrogant.

Hippŏcampus. A fabulous marine animal, shaped like a horse, but having a curved and fish-like tail. The gods of the sea are often represented as riding or sitting on such animals.

Hippŏcŏŏn. Son of Œbălus of Sparta and of the Nymph Băteia, drove his brothers Tyndărĕŏs and Icărĭus from home. Afterwards, in consequence of his slaying the young Œōnus, a kinsman of Hērăclēs, he himself, with his twenty sons, was slain by Heracles in alliance with king Cēpheus of Tĕgĕa. Tyndareos was thereby restored to the inheritance of his father's kingdom.

Hippŏcrătēs, the famous Greek physician, was born in the island of Cōs (an ancient seat of the worship of Asclēpius), about 460 B.C. He was the son of Heracleidēs and of Phænărĕtē, and sprang from the race of the Asclēpĭădæ, a priestly family, who in the course of time had gathered and preserved medical traditions, which were secretly handed down from father to son. Like many of the Asclepiadæ, he exercised his art whilst travelling in different parts of Greece. He is said to have been at Athens at the time of the Peloponnesian War, and to have taken advantage of the instructions of the Sophists Gorgias and Prodĭcus;

Democrĭtus of Abdēra is also named as one of his teachers. The value he himself set upon philosophic education is proved by his remark that "a philosophic physician resembles a god." Towards the end of his life he lived chiefly in Thessaly and on the island of Thasos. He died about 377 B.C. (or later) in the Thessalian Larissa, where his tomb was to be seen as late as the 2nd century A.D. All through his long life his activity was unceasing in its efforts to increase the amount of his knowledge on all subjects, by both practical and theoretical investigations. He was the founder of the school of a scientific art of healing, and, as in the case of Homer, numerous writings of unknown authorship, proceeding from the school which followed his system, were attributed to him. Seventy-two works, great and small, in the Ionic and old Attic dialects, bear his name, and, apparently, formed a single collection, even before they came under the consideration of the critics of Alexandria. But it is clear that, as the ancients themselves were aware, only a small portion, which can no longer be precisely defined, really belongs to him. It is highly probable that his nearest relations, who were also distinguished physicians, contributed their share to the collection, and that it contains works by his sons Thessălus and Drăcōn, his son-in-law Pŏlўbus, and his two grandsons, the sons of Thessalus and Dracon, who bore his own name. The best known of these works are the *Aphorisms*, which, in antiquity and in mediæval times, were held in high esteem, and have been freely commented on by Greeks, Romans, and Arabians; they consist of short sentences upon the nature of illnesses, their symptoms and crises, and their final issue. One of his writings which is of general interest, and is in all respects among the best, is that on the influence of the climate, the water, and the configuration of a country upon the physical and intellectual life of its inhabitants. In the second portion of this work we find the first beginnings of a comparative ethnography, which at once surprises us by the acuteness and intelligence of its observation, and attracts us by the simplicity and clearness of its style.

Hippŏcrēnē (= "the fountain of the steed "). The fount of the Muses, which was struck out of Mount Hĕlĭcōn, in Bœotia, by the hoof of the winged steed Pēgăsus. (*See* MUSES and PEGASUS.)

Hippodameia (Lat. *Hippŏdămīa*). (1)

The daughter of Œnomäus and the wife of Pělops (*q.v.*).

(2) A daughter of Atrax, one of the Lăpīthæ. It was at her marriage with Pīrīthŏus (*q.v.*), that the combat between the Centaurs and Lapithæ took place.

Hippodămus. A Greek Sophist, born at Milētus in the second half of the 5th century B.C. He was the first inventor of a system of laying out towns on geometrical principles. This was carried out, under his direction, in the laying out of the Piræus, the harbour-town of Athens, and also at the building of Thurii (B.C. 444) and of Rhodes (408); it was also used in subsequent times in the foundation of new towns.

Hippodrome (*Hippŏdrŏmŏs*). The Greek name for the racecourse for horses and chariots. It was about 400 yards long and 125 broad. The two long sides were meant for spectators. At one of the narrow ends was the starting-point; the other end was of semi-circular form. In front of the middle of the latter was the goal; at Olympia a round altar of *Taraxippŏs* (possibly a demon who terrified horses). The drivers had to pass round this after they had driven down one of the long sides; then they turned back and went up the other long side to a second goal, situated near the starting-point. At Olympia this goal bore a statue of Hippodameia. Here they turned round and drove back again. Racing chariots with full-grown horses had to cover this circuit twelve times; and with young horses (according to a later custom) eight times. The name of *Hippodrome* was also given to the race-courses laid out in Grecian countries in the time of the Romans, after the pattern of the Roman circus (*q.v.*). The most famous of these was that at Byzantium, which was begun by Septimius Sevērus, and finished by Constantine.

Hippŏlўtē. Queen of the Amazons, daughter of Ares and of Otrēra; slain in battle by Hēráclēs, when he went at the bidding of Eurystheus to fetch the girdle given her by Ares. (*See* HERACLES.)

Hippŏlўtus. Son of Theseus and of the Amazon Antĭŏpē. When he spurned the love of his step-mother Phædra, she slandered him to her husband Theseus, who begged his father Pŏseidōn to avenge him. While Hippolytus was driving along the seashore, his horses were frightened by a bull sent forth from the water by Poseidon, and he was thrown from his chariot and killed. Phædra, conscious of the wrong that she had done, killed herself. A later

legend describes Hippolytus as a chaste huntsman and a favourite of Artĕmis, who was raised from the dead by Æsculapius and taken by the goddess to the sacred grove of Diana at Arīcia in Latium, where he was worshipped with the goddess under the name of Virbius. (*See* DIANA.)

Hippomĕnēs. The lover of the Bœotian Atalante (*q.v.*).

Hippōnax. A Greek iambic poet of Ephesus, who about 540 B.C. was banished to Clazŏmĕnæ by Athēnăgŏras and Cōmās tyrants of his native city. At Clazomenæ two sculptors, Būpălus and Athēnĭs, made the little, thin, ugly poet ridiculous in caricature, who avenged himself in such bitter iambic verses that, like Lycambēs and his daughter, who were persecuted by Archĭlŏchus, they hanged themselves.

The burlesque character of the poems which he composed in the Ionic dialect found an appropriate form in his favourite metre, which was probably invented by himself. This metre is known as the *Chŏlĭambus* ("the halting iambus"), or the *Scāzōn* (lit. "limping"), from its having a spondee or trochee in the last place, instead of the usual iambic foot. He is also supposed to have been the first to produce parodies of epic poetry. Of his poems we have only a few fragments.

Hippŏthŏōn. Son of Pŏseidōn and Alŏpē, the daughter of Cercўōn of Eleusis. After his birth he was exposed by his mother and suckled by a mare, until some shepherds found him and reared him. Alŏpē (who had been imprisoned for life by her father) was transformed into a spring bearing her own name at Eleusis. When Theseus (*q.v.*) overcame Cercyon in wrestling, and killed him, he restored to Hippothoon the inheritance of his grandfather. He was afterwards honoured as the hero of the Attic tribe that bore his name.

Hippŏtoxŏtæ. A name given at Athens to à corps of mounted archers, composed of slaves belonging to the state. (*See* HIPPEIS.)

Hippўs (of Rhēgium). One of the Greek *Logographi* (*q.v.*).

Hirtius (*Aulus*). A friend of Cæsar, and one of his companions in arms. He completed Cæsar's *Commentārĭĭ* on the Gallic War by adding an eighth book. According to the dedication to Cornēlius Balbus prefixed to that book, he contemplated the continuation of Cæsar's account of the Civil War to Cæsar's death. This intention he never carried out, as he fell in battle at

Mŭtĭna, 14th April, 43 B.C., when he was consul. Of the three works, the *Bellum Alexandrīnum, Bellum Afrĭcum,* and *Bellum Hispānĭense,* which have come down to us with Cæsar's Commentaries, the first may have been written by him. Of the other two, it has been conjectured that they were composed at his request, in preparation for his intended work on military commanders, and that having been found at his death among his papers, they were added, with his own writings, to the works of Cæsar himself. (*See* CÆSAR.)

History. (I) The composition of history, and indeed of all prose among the Greeks, originated with the Ionians of Asia Minor, who also created the *ĕpŏs,* the elegy, and iambic poetry. It was among them that, in the 6th century B.C., the *Logogrăphī* (*q.v.*), made their appearance. These writers treated the materials supplied by family and local stories in a style which gradually approached more and more to prose, but without any attempt at critical investigation or scientific arrangement. The most considerable writers in this style are also its latest representatives, HĔCĂTÆUS of Miletus, HELLĀNĪCUS of Lesbos. The latter was a contemporary of HĒRŎDŎTUS of Halicarnassus (about 485–424 B.C.), the Father of History. His work, written like the others in the Ionic dialect, was founded upon a vast collection of historical and geographical material gathered in distant travels, and through the researches of many years. This mass of information he has, with great art, moulded into a homogeneous work, the main theme of which is the struggle of the Greeks against the barbarians. The narrative is simple, but always attractive. The line of historians who wrote in the Attic dialect is headed by the Athenian THŪCȲDĬDĒS, whose history of the Peloponnesian War is a masterpiece of the first order, grand alike in style and in matter. A continuation of Thucydides was written by his countryman XĔNŎPHŌN (about 431–355 B.C.) in his *Hellēnĭca;* in his *Anăbăsĭs,* Xenophon described the famous retreat of the Ten Thousand in a style as masterly as his generalship. In the *Cȳropœdĭa* he gives a picture, idealized indeed, but not without foundation in fact, of the history of Cyrus. His contemporary CTĒSIAS of Cnĭdus, writing in Ionic Greek, introduced his countrymen to the history of the Persian empire. At the same time PHILISTUS of Syracuse, an imitator of Thucydides, compiled the history of Sicily from the earliest times down to his own. In the second half of the 4th century B.C. appeared two celebrated historians, THEOPOMPUS of Chioś and EPHŎRUS of Cyme, both disciples of the rhetorician Isocrates. The chief work of Theopompus was a history of Philip of Macedon, from his accession to his death. Ephorus, in a great work embracing the whole course of events from the invasion of the Peloponnesus by the Heraclidæ, to 345 B.C., was the first writer who attempted a universal history. To this period belong the numerous chronicles of Attic history, called *Atthĭdĕs* (*see* ATTHIS). In these comparatively little regard is paid to style, less certainly than is paid by the historians just mentioned as succeeding Xenophon. The period of Alexander the Great and his successors was very fertile in historical writing. We may mention CALLISTHĔNĒS, ARISTŎBŪLUS, CHĂRĒS, ONĒSICRĬTUS, CLITARCHUS, and HĬĔRŎNȲMUS (*q.v.*), who narrated contemporary events in a style sometimes plain and simple, sometimes exaggerated. This was the age of the Sicilian TĪMÆUS, whose great work on the history of his native island won him little recognition, but who simplified chronology by introducing the method of reckoning by Olympiads, and thus established a lasting claim on the gratitude of historians. Among the better histories should be named the great work of PHȲLARCHUS (about 210 B.C.), which began at the invasion of the Peloponnesus by Pyrrhus, and ended at the death of Clĕŏmĕnēs.

The Alexandrian scholar ERĂTOSTHĔNĒS conferred an immense boon on historical investigation by his attempt to place chronology on the firm scientific foundation of mathematics and astronomy. His labours were continued by APOLLŎDŌRUS, whose *Chrŏnĭca* was the most important work on chronology produced in antiquity. This was a brief enumeration of the most important events, from the taking of Troy, which he dated B.C. 1183, till his own time (B.C. 144). Only isolated fragments of the histories written after Xenophon have, in the great number of instances, come down to us. But we have a considerable part of the work of POLYBIUS of Mĕgălŏpŏlis (died about 122). This was a general history of the known world from the beginning of the second Punic War to the destruction of Carthage. Its style has no just claim to artistic merit, but its contents make it one of the most remarkable of ancient Greek histories. In about 40 B.C. the Sicilian writer DIODŌRUS compiled a valuable general history from the works of Greek and Roman writers now lost. A considerable part of this still remains. NĬCŎLÀUS of Damascus, who lived a little later, was the author of a great general history, of which we have considerable fragments. DĬŎNȲSĬUS of Hălĭcarnassus composed, a few years before Christ, his *Roman Archæology*, about half of which has survived. This was the ancient history of Rome down to the first Punic War, written with taste and care. In the second half of the 1st century A.D. the Hebrew JOSÉPHUS wrote his *Jewish Archæology* and his *History of the Jewish War*. At the beginning of the 2nd century PLUTARCH of Chærŏnĕa produced his excellent biographies of famous Greeks and Romans. In the course of the same century appeared the *Anăbăsis* of Alexander the Great, written after the best authorities by ARRIAN of Nicomedīa, the *Strătĕgĕmătă* of the Macedonian POLYÆNUS, a number of examples of military stratagems collected from older writers; and a part of the *Roman History* of the Alexandrian APPIAN, ethnographically arranged. At the beginning of the 3rd century DĬO CASSIUS of Nicæa conceived and executed his great work on Roman history, which has unfortunately come down to us in a very mutilated form. His younger contemporary, HÉRŎDĬÀNUS, wrote an interesting *History of the Cæsars*, which still survives, from the death of Marcus Aurelius to Gordian. Ancient chronology is much indebted to the *Chronicle* of EUSÉBIUS, bishop of Cæsarea. This was written in the 4th century A.D., and only survives in translations. Among later writers we may mention ZŌSĬMUS (in the second half of the 6th century), the author of a history of the emperors, from Augustus to 410 A.D.

(II) *Ancient Roman History.* The beginnings of Roman history go back to about 200 B.C. The form of composition was, until the first half of the 1st century B.C., almost exclusively that of annals, and the historians previous to that date are, in consequence, usually comprised under the term annalists. (For the special representatives of this style, *see* ANNALISTS.) They confined themselves exclusively to the history of their country in its widest extent, from the earliest times to their own. In later times, but not till then, Roman historians undertook to write on the events of special periods, generally on those of their own time. The early annalistic writers had no style. It is not until the knowledge of Greek literature and the development of rhetorical style has reached a higher stage, in the second half of the 2nd century B.C., that any attempt at good writing is discernible. The first indication of such an attempt is the tendency to rhetorical ornamentation. In the Ciceronian age, the art of prose writing had greatly advanced, and many men of mark devoted themselves to history. Some endeavoured to include foreign history within the lines of their narrative. This was the case, for instance, with CORNÉLIUS NĔPOS, in his great biographical work, *De Vĭrīs Illustrĭbus*. The biographies which remain are mostly those of non-Roman generals. CÆSAR and SALLUST surpass all the other historical writers of this period both in form and matter. Sallust is an imitator of Thucydides, and the first Roman historian who can lay any claim to finished execution. The other historians of this period whose works have come down to us are HIRTĬUS, who continued Cæsar's *Commentărĭī*, and the authors of the Alexandrian, African, and Spanish Wars.

The Augustan age produced the Roman history of LIVY, a work as remarkable for its comprehensiveness as for its literary finish. The greater part of it is unhappily lost. The first general history written in Latin, by TROGUS POMPEIUS, belongs to the same period. This is only preserved in an epitome by JUSTÍNUS. The 1st century A.D. was fruitful of historical literature, but only a certain number of writings have survived: a short sketch of Roman history by VELLEIUS PATERCŬLUS, which is unduly influenced by the spirit of court adulation; a collection of historical anecdotes by VALERIUS MAXIMUS; a very rhetorical history of Alexander the Great, by CURTIUS RUFUS; and a number of instances of military stratagems by JULIUS FRONTÍNUS. The great history of the empire comprised in the *Annălĕs* and *Histŏrĭœ* of TĂCĬTUS, one of the most important monuments of Roman literature, was written partly in the 1st and partly in the 2nd century A.D. In the beginning of the 2nd century A.D. we have SUETONIUS' *Lives of the Cæsars*, and the panegyrical account of Roman history by FLORUS.

After this period, Suetonius becomes the model of historians, and their favourite subject the doings of the emperors and the imperial court. These lost writings were the main sources of the *Historia Augusta*, a collection of biographies of the emperors from Hadrian to Numerian (117-284 A.D.).

'he compilation is rude and uncritical, but
istorically important. It is the work of six
ifferent authors belonging to the end of the
rd and the beginning of the 4th centuries
.D. Soon after the middle of this century,
AURĒLIUS VICTOR wrote a short history of
he Cæsars, and EUTRŎPIUS and FESTUS
pitomes (*brĕvĭārĭa*) of all Roman history.
'he clearness and simplicity of Eutropius'
ook has maintained its popularity down to
nodern times. AMMĬĀNUS MARCELLĪNUS
ises far above the heads of his contem-
oraries. He was a Greek by birth, and
wrote a continuation of Tacitus from 96–378
..D., only the second half of which has
ome down to us. After him begins the
poch of Christian historians, *e.g.* SULPĬCIUS
ĒVĒRUS and OROSIUS. Special mention
hould be made of HIERŎNŸMUS, who trans-
ated and made additions to the *Chronicon*
f Eusebius.

Homer (Gr. *Hŏmērŏs*). (1) The poet,
whose name is borne by the two oldest and

(1) * BUST OF HOMER.
(Sanssouci Palace, Potsdam.)

t the same time grandest monuments of
he Greek genius, the epic poems called
he Iliad and the Odyssey. Concerning the
ersonality of the poet, his country, and
is time, we have no trustworthy infor-
nation. Even the personal existence of
ne poet has been disputed, and it has
ften been attempted to prove, from the
neaning of the name, that he was not an
ndividual, but an ideal type. It has been
held that Homer means either *orderer* or
comrade, and it has been supposed that
in the former case the name indicates the
ideal representative of the epic poem in its
unified and artistically completed form,
whilst the other explanation is suggestive
of an ideal ancestor and patron of an exclusive order of minstrels. But as Homer
is a proper name, simply meaning *hostage*,
without any connexion with poetry, there
is nothing in the name itself to give
occasion to any doubt as to the existence
of Homer as an historical personage. In
antiquity seven places contended for the
honour of being his birthplace : Smyrna,
Rhodes, Cŏlŏphōn, Sălămīs (in Cyprus),
Chios, Argos, and Athens ; yet there is no
doubt that the Homeric poems originated
on the west coast of Asia Minor, and the
older tradition is fairly correct in fixing on
the Æolian Smyrna as his home, and on
the Ionian island of Chios as the place where
his poetry was composed. The Æolic colouring of the Ionic dialect, which forms the
foundation of Homeric diction, agrees with
this ; as also the fact that at Chios for centuries afterwards there was a family called
the *Hŏmērĭdæ*, who, called after his name,
claimed descent from him and occupied
themselves with the recitation of his poetry.

As to the time when the poet lived, all
the views of early investigators, founded on
chronological considerations, differ widely
from one another. However, this much
seems certain, that the period in which
epic poetry attained the degree of perfection to which Homer brought it does not
fall either before B.C. 950 or after 900. Of
the various traditions respecting Homer, we
need only state that his father's name was
Mĕlēs, that in his old age he was blind,
and that he died on the small island of Ios,
where his grave was shown, and on it yearly,
in the month called after him Hŏmērĕōn, a
goat was sacrificed to the poet, who was
worshipped as a hero. Perhaps the story
of his blindness arose from fancying that
Dēmŏdŏcŭs, the blind singer in the Odyssey,
was a prototype of Homer. A trustworthy
corroboration of this was supposed to be
found in the fact that the author of the
hymn to the Delian Apollo, which the voice
of antiquity unhesitatingly described to
Homer, represented him as blind and living
on the island of Chios. The importance of
Homer rests in the fact that, while using
the fixed forms of poetic diction and metre
which had been fashioned by his predecessors, he was able to raise epic song to

the definite level of epic poetry with its systematic arrangement and its artistic elaboration.

The two epics which bear his name, the *Iliad* and the *Odyssey*, both of which at a late period were divided into twenty-four books, deal with the legends of Troy. The *Iliad* traverses an interval of fifty-one days out of the tenth year of the Trojan War, according to a simple plan with a consecutive account of the events of the time. Beginning with the wrath of Achilles at being deprived of his captive, the maiden Brīsēïs, at the command of Agamemnon, it narrates the ever-increasing distress which the indignant hero's withdrawal from the battle brings upon the Greeks in their fights on the Trojan plain, around the walls, and near the naval camp. This gives a suitable opportunity for describing the other heroes down to the fall of Patroclus, which is the turning-point of the poem. Then follows the reconciliation of Achilles, his avenging his slain friend by killing Hector, and the funeral games in honour of Patroclus. The poem comes to a tragical conclusion with the surrender and burial of the body of Hector. The *Odyssey* similarly deals with a multitude of incidents connected with the return of Odysseus to his home, all of which take place in the narrow interval of forty days, but according to a highly artistic and complex plan. In contrast to the two main portions of the Iliad, the Odyssey consists of four parts. The first describes the adventures of Tēlĕmăchus, who is oppressed by the suitors of his mother Pēnĕlŏpē, and sets off on a journey to Nestor at Pylos and Menelāus at Sparta, in quest of his father. Thus the poet finds occasion to give an account of the different fates of the Greek heroes on their return home. The second part describes the adventures of Odysseus in his voyage from Ogȳgĭa, the island of Calypso, his stay among the Phæacians (connected with which is the hero's own account of his wanderings on his voyage from Troy down to his landing at Ogygia), and, lastly, his arrival at Ithaca. The third part contains his visit to the hut of the swineherd Eumæus, his recognition by Telemachus (who has returned home) and by his faithful servant, and the planning of vengeance on the suitors. The fourth part contains the carrying out of the ve igeance, and the whole is brought to a peaceiul conclusion by the re-union of the hero with his wife Penelope and his aged father Laërtēs.

By means of professional reciters, who went from city to city and were called *rhapsōdoi* (*q.v.*), the Homeric poems found a rapid circulation, not only in their Asiatic home, but also in Greece and its western colonies. They were introduced into Sparta by Lycurgus [Plut., *Lyc.* 4], who learned their existence in his travels, at Samos from the descendants of Crĕŏphȳlus, a poet reputed to have been a friend and relation of Homer. In 753 B.C., twenty-three years after the commencement of the Olympiads they were, in fact, the common property of all Greeks.

At the recitations given by the *rhapsodo* at many places during festivals, the great bulk of the poems from the very first necessitated a regular division of the subject into suitable portions, in order to give intervals of rest not only to the reciters but also to the audience. Hence arose the division into separate lays called *rhapsodies* with distinctive titles, which were still in use at a later date, when both poems were divided into twenty-four books. It soon became customary to recite single rhapsodies, some being especial favourites and considered more suitable than others for showing the special talents of individual rhapsodists to advantage. Thus it happened that some portions easily fell into oblivion and gaps arose in the oral tradition of the poems. On the other hand, the rhapsodists could not avoid giving a certain finish and completeness to their favourite pieces, and even permitted themselves to make alterations and additions where they saw fit. To Athens belongs the honour of having arrested the ever increasing confusion caused by these practices. Solon was the first to order that the rhapsodists at their public recitals should keep closely to the traditional text of the poems. Pīsistrătus (about B.C. 535 made, by means of a committee of several poets, headed by Onomacrītus (*q.v.*), a collection of the scattered lays and a revision of the text, founded on extant copies and on the oral traditions of the rhapsodists [Cic., *De Orat.* iii 137 and Pausanias, vii 26 are the earliest authorities for this vague and doubtful story.]

Either Pisistratus or his son Hipparchus made the regulation that the rhapsodists in their competitions at the Panathenaic festival, should recite in consecutive order and completeness the Homeric poems which had been thus restored to their proper form. To this revision, which could

nly partially counteract the gradually
ncreasing corruption of the text, we may
probably trace the copies of the Homeric
poems which were afterwards in existence
in various parts of Greece. In course of
time these also in their turn underwent
many arbitrary alterations, chiefly at the

joyed both the means and the opportunity
in the collection of ancient manuscripts of
the poet in the Library of Alexandria.
The beginning was made by ZĒNŎDŎTUS of
Ephesus, who was succeeded by ARISTO-
PHĀNES of Byzantium, whose pupil ARIS-
TARCHUS (q.v.), by his dition of Homer,

(2) * APOTHEOSIS OF HOMER.

(Relief found at Bovillæ. Now in British Museum.)

ands of the learned who sought to im-
rove the text. The first to do this were
he Alexandrine scholars, who found in
Homer a central point for their philo-
ogical studies, and practised a methodical
riticism of the text, for which they en-

reached the highest point that the ancients
ever attained in philological criticism. The
editions of these Alexandrine critics were
founded on the redaction by Pisistratus,
and are themselves the origin of our present text of the Homeric poems.

From that time forward down to the latest times of Greek antiquity, Homer never ceased to be a theme for learned disquisition, which is attested for us by numerous remains still in existence. Even in ancient times scholars occupied themselves with the question whether the Iliad and the Odyssey were composed by the same poet. This question was fully justified by the fact that the name of Homer had long been recognised as a collective term, and had included a long series of epics formed on his model, the true authorship of which was only gradually discovered; and it did not escape observation that the Odyssey, in its more artistic design, as well as in relation to social, moral, and religious life, belonged to a more advanced stage of development than the Iliad. Thus, in ancient times, those who are known as *Chōrīzontĕs* (or " Separaters "), headed by the grammarians Xĕnōn and Hellānīcus, probably belonging to the beginning of the Alexandrine period, held that the Odyssey was composed by a later poet. Even modern scholars have shared this view, while others, relying on the essential correspondence of tone, language, and metre, attribute less importance to the points of divergence, and explain them as due to the difference in the aim of the two poems as well as in the poet's time of life. With all our admiration of the art and beauty of the Homeric poems, it is not to be denied that they do not stand throughout on the same level of perfection, but that, by the side of the most magnificent passages, there are others which are dull and less attractive, and interruptions of the narrative and even contradictions are not wanting. Such blemishes did not escape the observation of the Alexandrine scholars, who met objections of this kind by assuming frequent interpolations, not only of single lines, but of whole passages ; *e.g.* they held that the second half of the last book but one, and the whole of the last book of the Odyssey, were spurious.

In modern times many explanations of these defects have been put forward. In the first place F. A. Wolf [1795] observed that in the time of Homer the art of writing was not yet practised to such an extent as to be employed for literary purposes ; and held that it was impossible even for the highest genius, with the aid of memory alone, either to produce such comprehensive works, and to transmit them to others. On these grounds he held that the Iliad and Odyssey received their existing form for the first time, in the time of Pisistratus when the old lays on the Trojan War, whic had hitherto been preserved by oral tradi tion alone, were fixed by means of writing and collected and united into two grea wholes. He has been followed by others wh have endeavoured to dissect the Iliad i particular into its separate and originall independent lays. Others hold that Homer' two poems consisted of compositions c moderate length ; the *Wrath of Achille* and the *Return of Odysseus*, which, b amplifications, improvements, and altera tions, have resulted in the existing Odysse and Iliad. Others again, instead of assum ing a larger number of single lays, assum a combination of small epic poems, a *Achillēis* and an *Iliad*, thus resulting in th present *Iliad*, and a *Tĕlĕmăchĭa* and *Return of Odysseus* in the present *Odysse* On the other hand, many important authori ties maintain that, granting the possibilit of a utilization of previously existing lay the Odyssey and Iliad, from the ver beginning, respectively constituted a unite whole ; but that, soon after their first com position, they underwent manifold revisio and amplification, until they received, befor the beginning of the Olympiads, the essen tial form which they still retain. Certai it is that, after the first Olympiad, longe epic poems were composed on the mode of the Iliad and Odyssey, and in continua tion of them ; and it cannot be denied that long before this period, the art of writin had been extensively employed in Greece It is also beyond contradiction that, apar from corruptions which arose from late alterations, dissimilarities in the treatmen of the several parts, as well as many in consistencies, may have existed in the poem even in their primitive form. In spit of such blemishes of detail, the Homeri poems remain unsurpassed as works of art which have had an incalculable influenc not only upon the development of literatur and art, but also upon the whole life o the Greeks, who from the earliest time regarded them as the common property o the nation, and employed them as the foun dation of all teaching and culture. Eve now, after nearly 3,000 years, their in fluence remains unimpaired.

Besides the *Iliad* and *Odyssey*, we sti possess under the name of Homer : (*a*) *F* collection of *Hymns:* five of greater lengt on the Pythian and Delian Apollo, Hermēs Aphrŏdītē, and Dēmētēr.; and twenty-nin shorter poems on various gods. These are really *prŏœmia*, or introductions, with which the rhapsodists prefaced their recitations. Their object is to praise the god at whose festival the recitation took place, or who was specially honoured in the town where the rhapsodist presented himself. Perhaps even the choice of the introduction may have been influenced by the contents of the subsequent poem. If these poems did not originate with Homer, at any rate they are the compositions of rhapsodists of the Homeric school, called *Hŏmē-rĭdæ*. Thus the rhapsodist Cȳnæthus of Chios (about B.C. 504) is named as the author of the hymn to the Delian Apollo. The collection appears to have been prepared for the use of the rhapsodists in Attica, with a view to selections being made from it at pleasure. (*b*) Sixteen small poems called *Epĭgrammăta*, remains of an older poetry, two of which are lays in a popular style: the *Kămīnŏs*, or "potter's oven " (in which the blessing of Athēnē is invoked on a batch of earthenware, when placed in the furnace), and a kind of begging song, called the *Eĭrĕsĭōnē* (lit. a harvest-wreath wound round with wool). (*c*) The *Bătrăchŏmўŏmăchĭa*, the Battle of the Frogs and Mice, a parody of the Iliad, is generally attributed to Pigrēs, the brother of the Carian queen Artĕmīsĭa, so well known in connexion with the Persian Wars. The ancient satirical epic poem called the *Margītēs* (" the dolt ") has been lost. Its great antiquity may be inferred from its having been assigned to Homer as early as the time of Archĭlŏchus *ob.* 676 B.C.) [On Homer, *see* Prof. Jebb's *Introduction*.]

(2) A poet of Hĭĕrăpŏlis in Caria, son of the poetess Mœro, born in the first half of the 3rd century B.C. He was one of the seven tragic poets of the Alexandrine *Pleiad* (*q.v.*).

Hŏmoioi (=" Peers "). A name given to the Spartĭatæ (*q.v.*) in allusion to their having equal political rights with one another.

Hŏnōs and Virtūs. The Latin personifications of honour and warlike courage. [Cic., *Verr.* ii 4, 121.] Marcus Marcellus, the famous conqueror of Syracuse (B.C. 212), added to an already existing shrine dedicated to *Honos* another to *Virtus*, and united them both in one building, which he adorned with the masterpieces of Greek art which he had carried off from Syracuse. Marius built a second temple from the booty gained in the Cimbrian War (B.C.

101). Upon coins they are both represented as youthful figures, with tresses; *Honos* with a chaplet of bay-leaves and cornucopia, and *Virtus* with a richly ornamented helmet.

Hoplites. The heavily armed foot-soldiers of the Greeks, who fought in serried masses (*see* PHALANX). Their weapons

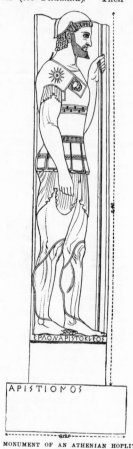

* MONUMENT OF AN ATHENIAN HOPLITE.
(Athens.)

consisted of an oval shield suspended from the shoulder-belt, and wielded by means of a handle, a coat of mail (*see* THORAX), a helmet and greaves of bronze, and sometimes a lance about six feet long, and a short sword. The Spartans, who fought with

shields large enough to cover the whole
man, appear to have worn neither cuirass
nor greaves. The whole equipment, weighing close on 77 lbs., was worn only in battle;
on the march the greater part of it was
carried by a slave. An idea of the equipment of an Athenian hoplite [about 500
B.C.] may be derived from the accompanying
illustration of the monument to the Athenian Aristīōn [found near Mărăthōn, but
probably of earlier date than 490]. The
weapons of the Macedonian hoplites, or
phălangītæ, were a circular shield with a
bronze plate, about two feet in diameter,
and about twelve pounds in weight, a
leather jerkin with brass mountings and
ornaments, light greaves, a round felt hat
(*see* CAUSIA), a short sword, and the Macedonian sarissa (*q.v.*).

Hoplŏmǎchī. *See* GLADIATORES.

Horace (*Quintus Hŏrātius Flaccus*).
The well-known Roman poet, born 8th Dec.,
B.C. 65, at Vĕnŭsia, on the borders of Apulia
and Lucania, where his father, who was a
freedman, possessed a small property, and
filled the office of a collector (*coactor*). To
give his son a better education, he betook
himself to Rome, and
here Horace received a
training similar to that
of the sons of wealthy
knights and senators,
under his father's eye,
who watched over him
with a touching solici-
tude. At first he studied
under the grammarian
Orbĭlĭus Pŭpillus of
Bĕnĕventum, whose
flogging propensities
Horace rendered proverbial. To complete
his education, and especially to study
philosophy, Horace resorted to Athens in
B.C. 45; but towards the end of the summer
of B.C. 44, when Brutus, after the murder
of Cæsar, appeared at Athens, Horace, like
most of the young Romans studying there,
joined him in his enthusiasm for the cause
of liberty. At the defeat at Philippi in
42, where he fought as a military tribune,
he saved himself by flight, and fortunately
reached Italy in safety. It is true that
he met with favour, but he found himself
absolutely without means, as the property
of his father, who had probably died in
the interval, had been confiscated. To gain
a livelihood, he managed to get a clerkship in the quæstor's office (*see* SCRIBÆ).
It was at this period that, emboldened (as

* HORACE.
(From a gem in the
British Museum.)

he himself says) by his poverty, he first
appeared as a poet. His own bent and pre-
disposition led him at that time to satire, in
which he took Lūcīlius for his model, and
to iambic poetry after the manner of Archī-
lŏchus. His first attempts gained him the
acquaintance of Vergil and Vărius, who
commended him to their influential patron
Mæcēnas. The latter allowed the poet to
be introduced to him (about 38 B.C.), but
for fully nine months paid no attention to
him, until he once more invited him to his
house, and admitted him to the circle of
his friends. In course of time there grew
up a very intimate friendship between
Mæcenas and Horace. About 35 B.C. the
poet dedicated to him, under the title of
Sermōnēs, the first collection of his *Satires*,
which up to then had been published
separately; and about 33 he received from
Mæcenas the gift of a small estate in the
Sabine district, which from that time
forward was his favourite abode. In the
year B.C. 30, or perhaps in the beginning of
B.C. 29, Horace published his second book
of *Satires;* and (nearly simultaneously) his
collection of iambic verses, or *Epodes*, appeared. In the following years he specially
devoted himself to lyric poetry, taking the
Æolic poets for his model, and having the
merit of being the first who found for their
forms of verse a home on Roman ground.
About 23, he published his first collection of
Odes (*Carmĭna*) in three books, which were
all dedicated to Mæcenas. [But some of
the Odes were written before B.C. 29, so that
in respect to the date of composition, as
distinguished from that of publication, the
collections of Odes and Epodes overlap.
See Prof. Nettleship's *Lectures and Essays*,
pp. 156–163.] The Odes were followed by
a continuation of the conversational *Satires*
or *Sermones* in a new form, that of letters,
each addressed to one person, and called
the *Epistŭlæ*.

Through Mæcenas Horace made the acquaintance of Augustus. The ex-republican
and soldier of freedom had shown at first
but little sympathy for him; but afterwards, having learned to recognise that
the only chance of the salvation of the
state lay in the rule of a monarch, and having seen Augustus successfully engaged in
restoring the country to tranquillity and
prosperity at home, and to its ancient prestige abroad, he was completely reconciled
to the emperor, and in several of his Odes
paid a high tribute to his merits. Nevertheless, he was always anxious to maintain

an attitude of independence towards the emperor, and excused himself from accepting the tempting offer of Augustus to enter his service as private secretary and to form one of his suite. But he did not entirely decline to carry out his wishes. It was by his desire that (about B.C. 17) he composed, for the festival of the Secular Games, the hymn to Apollo and Diana, known as the *Carmĕn Sœcŭlārĕ*. He also celebrated the victories of the emperor's step-sons, Tiberius and Drusus, in several Odes (B.C. 15), which he published with some others as a *fourth book of Odes* (about 13 B.C.) As Augustus had complained that Horace had made no mention of him in his earlier Epistles, the poet addressed to him a composition which stands first in the *second book of Epistles*, probably published shortly before his death. The famous *Epistŭla ad Pisōnes*, commonly called the *Ars Poetica*, is often reckoned as the third epistle of the second book [but probably belongs to an earlier date]. The poet died 27th November, B.C. 8, and was buried on the Esquiline, near to his recently deceased friend, Mæcenas.

Horace, as he was himself aware, is not a poet whò soars to lofty heights; on the contrary his nature is essentially reflective, and with him taste and fancy are always under the control of reason. In his lyrical poems he began with more or less free imitations of Greek models, and gradually advanced to independent compositions in the Greek form. Their merits do not

art with which both diction and metre are handled. In the poems of a higher style which he composed by desire of Augustus, or under the influence of the times in which he lived, the expression rises to actual loftiness, but the spirit of deliberate purpose is generally prominent. He succeeds best in those of his Odes in which, following his own bent, without any external prompting, he treats of some bright and simple theme, such as love or friendship. His personality reflects itself most vividly in his Satires and in his Epistles, which often have a similar aim. Following the method of Lucilius, he here gives his personal impressions of social and literary matters in a form that is more natural, and at the same time more artistic, than his predecessor's, and in a style that approaches the language of everyday life. At first his Satires, like his Epodes, were not without a pungency corresponding to a bitterness of feeling due to the circumstances of his life; but as his temper became calmer, they assume a more genial and less personal complexion. In the Epistles, the poet shows himself the exponent of a mild, if not very deep, philosophy of life. From an early date Horace's poems were used in Roman schools as a text-book, and were expounded by Roman scholars, especially by Acron and Porphÿrĭŏ (*q.v.*, 6).

Hōræ. The goddesses of order in nature, who cause the seasons to change in their regular course, and all things to come into

* THE HORÆ BRINGING WEDDING GIFTS TO PELEUS.
(Paris, Louvre.)

consist in warmth of feeling or depth of thought, but in the perspicuity of their plan, the evenness of their execution, and the

being, blossom and ripen at the appointed time. In Homer, who gives them neither genealogy nor names, they are mentioned as handmaidens of Zeus, entrusted with the guarding of the gates of heaven and Olympus; in other words, with watching the clouds. Hesiod calls them the daughters of Zeus and Thĕmĭs, who watch over the field operations of mankind; their names are *Eunŏmĭa* (Good Order), *Dĭkē* (Justice), and *Eirēnē* (Peace), names which show that the divinities of the three ordinary seasons of the world of nature, Spring, Summer, and Winter, are also, as daughters of Themis, appointed to superintend the moral world of human life. This is especially the case with *Dike*, who is the goddess who presides over legal order, and, like Themis, is enthroned by the side of Zeus. According to Hesiod, she immediately acquaints him with all unjust judicial decisions, so that he may punish them. In the tragic poets she is mentioned with the Erīnȳĕs, and as a divinity who is relentless and stern in exacting punishment. (*See* ASTRÆA.) At Athens, two *Horæ* were honoured: *Thallō*, the goddess of the flowers of spring; and *Carpō*, the goddess of the fruits of summer. Nevertheless the Horæ were also recognised as *four* in number, distinguished by the attributes of the seasons. They were represented as delicate, joyous, lightly moving creatures, adorned with flowers and fruits, and, like the Graces, often associated with other divinities, such as Aphrŏdītē, Apollo, and Hēliŏs. As the Hora specially representing spring, we have *Chlōris*, the wife of Zĕphȳrus, and goddess of flowers, identified by the Romans with *Flora* (*q.v.*).

Hordĭcīdia. *See* FORDICIDIA and TELLUS.

Hormŏs. A chain-dance (*see* DANCE).

Hortensius (*Quintus;* surnamed *Hortălus*). A distinguished Roman orator, B.C. 114–50. For a considerable time he had no rival in the Forum, owing to his brilliant genius and his remarkably retentive memory. Possessing vast means, he gave himself up to the enjoyments of life, and allowed his somewhat younger contemporary, Cicero, completely to outstrip him. [Down to about 63 B.C. Hortensius represented the *nōbĭlēs,* as against Cicero; but afterwards the two orators were generally on the same side.] He also tried his hand as a writer of history and as a poet. Of his writings we have only meagre notices. [Cic., *Brutus,* §§ 301–303.]

Hŏrus (Egyptian *Har*). An Egyptian god, the son of Osīris and Isis. At the death of his father he was still a child but when he had grown to be a stalwart youth (*Harver,* i.e. a "stronger Horus") he overcame and captured Typhōn, the murderer of his father, after a combat lasting over many days, and handed him over to Isis, who, however, let him go free. By the Egyptians he was deemed the victorious god of light (who overcame darkness, winter, and drought), and was identified with Apollo by the Greeks. He is often represented with the head of a hawk, which was sacred to him. He must be distinguished from a younger *Horus* the *Harpŏcrătēs* of the Greeks (in Egyptian *Harpechruti,* i.e. "Har the child"), who was received by Isis from Osiris in the under-world, and is the representative of the winter-sun, and also the image of early

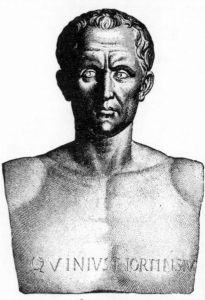

* HORTENSIUS.
(Rome, Villa Albani.)

vegetation, and therefore identified with Priăpus. Statues represent him as a naked boy with his finger on his mouth (*see* fig. 2 under ISIS). Misunderstanding this symbol of childhood, the Greeks made him the god of Silence and Secrecy. Afterwards, in the time when mysteries were in vogue, his worship was widely extended among the Greeks, and also among the Romans.

House. The *Greek* house (*see* plan, fig. 1) was divided into two chief parts, one of which was assigned to the men (*andrŏnītĭs*) and the other to the women (*gўnaikōnītĭs* or *gўnaikeiŏn*). The women's division was situated at the back of the house, and sometimes in the upper story if there was one.

(1) PLAN OF OLDEST TYPE OF GREEK HOUSE WITH ONE COURT.

(Designed by Guhl.)

a, a, a. Workrooms for the maid-servants.
b, Bedroom of the master of the house.
c, Hall.
d, d, d, d, d, d, d, d, Store-rooms, bedrooms, etc.
e, Courtyard.
f, Passage.
g, g, g, g, Shops.

The door of the house opened inwards. It was placed sometimes in a line with the *façade,* sometimes in a small recess called the *prŏthўrŏn* or *prŏpўlaiŏn.* In front of this there often stood an altar belonging to the house and consecrated to Apollo Agyieus, or the god of streets. In the interior, on both sides of the vestibule, were the doorkeeper's room and other chambers for work and business. The vestibule led into an open court (*aulē*) surrounded on three sides with columns. In the middle of this was the altar of Zeus *Herkeiŏs,* the

patron deity of domestic life. At the sides were chambers for eating and sleeping, storerooms, and cells for slaves, which, like the front rooms, opened into the court. But the slaves sometimes lived in an upper story, co-extensive with the whole house. On the side of the court opposite the vestibule there were no columns, but two pilasters at some distance from each other marked the entrance of a hall called *prostăs* or *parastăs,* which measured in breadth two-thirds of the distance between the pilasters. Here the family met at their common meals and common sacrifices; here, too, in all probability stood the hearth or sanctuary of Hestia. On one side of the *parastas* was the *thălămŏs* or sleeping room for the master and mistress of the house. On the other side was the *amphĭthălămŏs,* where the daughters probably slept. In the under wall of the *parastas* was a door called *mĕtaulŏs* or *mĕsaulŏs,* which led into the workroom of the female servants. Large houses had a second court, *pĕristўlŏn,* entirely surrounded by columns. The roof of the Greek house was generally, though not always, flat; the rooms were mostly lighted through the doors which opened into the court.

The ancient *Roman* dwelling house (fig. 2) consisted of a quadrangular court called *ātrĭum* (from *āter,* black), because the walls were blackened by the smoke from the hearth. The *atrium* was entered by the door of the house, and was the common meeting place for the whole family. It was lighted by an opening in the tiled roof, which was four-sided and sloped inwards. This opening was called the *complŭvĭum,* and served both as a chimney for the hearth and as an inlet for the rain, which fell down into the *implŭvĭum,* a tank sunk in the floor beneath. There was also, in more ancient times, a subterranean cistern (*pŭtĕus*) into which the rain out of the *impluvium* was collected. But in later times the water was carried off by pipes underground. At the back of the *impluvium* was the hearth with the *Pĕnātēs.* At the side of the *atrium* was the room used for cooking, for meals, and for sacrifices. In the wall fronting the entrance was the marriage-bed and the master's money-chest. The mistress of the house sat in the *atrium* with her maids, spinning, weaving, and generally superintending the household. It was in the *atrium* that the family received their clients and friends, that the dead were laid out in state, and memorials of the departed were hung on the wall. Gradually it became the fashion to attach small rooms

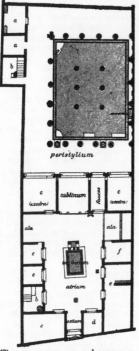

(2) PLAN OF THE CASA DE' CAPITELLI FIGURATI, POMPEII.

a, a, Store-room and servants' room.
b, b, Flight of steps.
c, c, Reception rooms.
d, Porter's lodge.
e, e, e, e, Day rooms.

to the two sides as far as the hearth. These rooms had no light except that obtained from the *atrium*. But the space at the back was left quite free, and extended in its full width in two wings (*ālæ*) behind these side chambers on right and left. In aristocratic houses the busts of the ancestors were set up in these wings. The marriage-bed was also removed from the wall against which it stood; the wall was broken through, and the *tablīnum* erected against it originally a wooden shed, which

at the back in summer, but closed in winter by a partition. The *tablīnum* was used as the master's office. In later times a garden surrounded by side buildings and covered colonnades, was added at the back of the house. This was called *pěristȳlium*, and was, as the name and the whole plan of it shows, an imitation of the Greek arrangement. The dining rooms, sleeping apartments, and living rooms (*trǐclīnium, cǔbǐcǔlum, diæta*) were transferred into the side buildings, as were also the entertaining room (*exědra*) and the hall (*œcus*), and above all the storerooms, hearth, and kitchen. The private chapel (*sacrārǐum* or *lǎrārǐum see* LARES) was also generally situated in the *peristylium.* The entrance into this from the atrium was through corridors (*faucēs*) situated near the *tablīnum.* The *atrium* now served merely as a state reception room. It was splendidly decorated with pillars and other ornaments, and had a table (*curtǐbǔlum*) in the middle to represent the hearth. If the roof was simply supported on beams, the *atrium* was called *tuscānǐcum* (fig. 3); if the *compluvium* was supported on four columns, *tetrastȳlum*; if the roof-beams were let into the wall on one side, and supported on a column apiece on the other, it was styled *cŏrinthǐum.*

Great houses, like temples and large tombs, generally had a kind of entrance hall or *vestǐbǔlum* [*ve, stǎbǔlum,* or an outside standing-place], raised above the street and approached by steps. This space was often adorned with arms taken in war, statues, colonnades, and flower-beds. It was here that visitors assembled for morning calls. In ordinary houses there was either no *vestibulum* or only an indication of one, effected by throwing the door a few steps back into the house. The door opened outwards, and generally consisted

(3) *ATRIUM* IN THE HOUSE OF PANSA, POMPEII (LOOKING THROUGH INTO THE *TABLINUM* AND *PERISTYLIUM*); RESTORED.

This was | of two wings; but sometimes, if the entrance was a wide one, of several folds

It did not move on hinges, but on pegs let into the threshold above and below. The door led immediately into the *ostĭum*, a space opening directly into the *atrium*. At the side of the *ostium* was the room of the doorkeeper (*iānĭtor*), with other rooms, which were sometimes let out as shops.

The Roman house was originally calculated only for one story, but in course of time a second story became usual. As the dining-room was generally in this part of the house, all the rooms in the upper story were called *cēnācŭla*. The upper story was approached by steps in the form of a ladder, and was lighted by openings which could be closed by shutters. Some of these windows were pierced in the outer wall, and some in the inner wall, carried round the roofs of the *atrium* and *peristylium*. There were three-storied houses in Rome as early as the end of the Republic. The upper stories were let to tenants, and as early as the time of Augustus it was found necessary to limit the height of the street frontage to 70 Roman feet, a maximum which was afterwards lowered to 60 feet. The roof was of tiles, and sometimes pointed and sloping on the four sides, sometimes flat, in which case it was often ornamented with flowering plants and shrubs. A flat roof of this sort was called *sōlārĭum*. The ancients heated their houses by means of portable fireplaces, braziers, and sometimes stoves. The Romans in the north of Italy, Gaul, and Germany used hot air for the purpose. (*See* BATHS.) Large lodging-houses were found both in Greek and Roman cities, the Greek name for such a house being *sўnoikĭa* and the Latin name *insŭla*.

Household Gods. *See* LARES and PE-NATES.

Hyăcinthus. Son of king Amyclās, of Amyclæ in Laconia, and of Dĭŏmēdē. He was beloved for his beauty by Apollo and Zĕphўrus. As Apollo was one day teaching the boy how to play at quoits, on the banks of the river Eurōtas, the wind-god in his jealousy drove the quoit with such violence against the head of Hyacinthus, that the blow killed him. From his blood Apollo caused a flower of the same name to spring up, with the exclamation of woe, AI, AI, marked upon its petals. Hyacinthus, like Adōnis, is a personification of vegetation, which flourishes in the spring-time, but is scorched and killed by the glowing heat of the summer sun, which is symbolized by the quoit or *discus*. Like other festivals in honour of nature, the festival of the Hyacinthia, celebrated by the Spartans at Amyclæ for three days in July, down to the time of the Roman emperors, was connected with the expression of grief at the death of vegetation, of joy over the harvest, and of cheerful trust in the re-awakening of nature. On the first day, which was dedicated to silent mourning, sacrifice to the dead was offered at the grave of Hyacinthus, which was under the statue of Apollo in the temple at Amyclæ. The following day was spent in public rejoicing in honour of Apollo, in which all the populace, including the slaves, took part. They went in festal procession with choruses of singing boys and girls, accompanied by harps and flutes, to the temple of Apollo, where games and competitions, sacrifices and entertainments to one

(4) LONGITUDINAL SECTION OF THE HOUSE OF PANSA, POMPEII.

another took place, and a robe, woven by the Spartan women, was offered to the god.

Hўădĕs ("the raining ones"). Daughters of Atlās and of Æthra, and sisters of the Pleiădĕs : their number varies between two and seven. Being Nymphs who supplied nourishment by means of moisture, they were worshipped at Dōdōna as nurses of Zeus or of the infant Dionўsus. As a reward for this they were placed in the sky as stars. At their rising about the same time as the sun, between May 7 and 21, rainy weather usually began. *Hyades* is naturally derived from the verb " to rain "; but the Romans, wrongly supposing it came from the Greek for " a pig," called the constellation " the little pigs " (*sŭcŭlæ*).

Hydria (*Greek*). A kind of vessel for holding water. (*See* VESSELS.)

[**Hydrĭăphŏrĭa** (*Greek*). " The carrying of a waterpot," a service performed by the wives of resident aliens at the *Panăthēnæa*.]

Hўgĭeiă. In Greek mythology, the goddess of Health, daughter of Æsculapius (Gr. *Asklēpĭŏs*), with whom she is often worshipped. In works of art she is represented by his side, as a maiden of kindly aspect, with a serpent, to whom she is giving drink from a saucer (*see* cut). By the Romans she was identified with *Sălūs.*

HYGIEIA.
(Found at Ostia, 1797; in the Hope Collection, Deepdene, Surrey.)

Hygīnus. (1) *Gaius Iūlius.* A Roman scholar, a native of Spain, and a freedman of Augustus, who appointed him librarian of the Palatine Library. His versatility as an author reminds us of Varro, for works of his are mentioned bearing on historical, antiquarian, geographical, theological, and agricultural subjects. Under the name of Hyginus we possess two schoolbooks of mythology; both are the production of the same author, but it is somewhat doubtful whether they are really written by the Roman scholar, or are only extracts from the genuine works or fresh versions of them. They are; (*a*) the *Făbŭlārum Lĭber,* a collection of 277 legends, which are not without value for the mythology and history of the Greek drama, as the author has made use of the tragedians in his compilation; (*b*) an incomplete work, *De Astrŏnŏmĭā,* in four books, commonly called *Pŏētĭca Astrŏnŏmĭca,* consisting of the elements of astronomy with an account of the constellations and the myths relating to them, mainly after Eratosthĕnēs.

(2) *H. Grōmătĭcus* (the land-surveyor,

from *grūma,* a surveyor's measuring rod). He composed under Trajan, about A.D. 10[?] several books on the surveying of land. I[t] is doubtful whether the work on Roma[n] castrametation, entitled *De Mūnītĭōnĭbu[s] Castrōrum,* should be really attributed t[o] him. The beginning and the end are alik[e] lost. It is the chief source of our knowledge of the subject. It was probably composed early in the 3rd century A.D.

Hўlās. Son of Theiŏdămās, king of the Drўŏpĕs, and of the Nymph Mĕnŏdĭcē. He was a favourite of Hērăclēs, whom he accompanied on the Argonautic expedition. When Heracles disembarked upon the coast of Mysia to cut himself a fresh oar, Hyla[s] followed him to draw water from a fountain, the Nymphs of which drew the beautifu[l] youth down into the water. The Argonaut[s] having gone on their way, Heracles, wit[h] his sister's son Pŏlўphēmus, remaine[d] behind to search for him. On failing t[o] find him, he did not leave until he had take[n] hostages from the Mysians, and made the[m] promise that they would produce the bo[y] either dead or alive. After that the inhabitants of Cĭŏs (founded by Polyphemus an[d] afterwards called Prusias) continuall[y] sought for Hylas, and sacrificed to hi[m] every year at the fountain, and thrice calle[d] him by name.

Hyllus. The son of Hērăclēs and Dēĭănīra, husband of Iŏlē. When he, and th[e] rest of the children of Heracles, at thei[r] father's death, were pursued everywhere b[y] the enmity of Eurystheus, they at last fou[nd] succour from Theseus, or his son Dēmŏphŏ[n]. When Eurystheus drew near with hi[s] army to compel the Athenians to give the[m] up, Măcărĭa, daughter of Heracles, freel[y] offered herself up as a sacrifice for he[r] brethren, who, aided by the Athenians, defeated the enemy, Eurystheus bein[g] slain as a fugitive by Hyllus himsel[f]. Having withdrawn from Attica to Thessaly, Hyllus was adopted by the Dorian princ[e] Ægĭmĭus, whom Heracles had once assiste[d] in the war between the Lăpĭthæ and th[e] Drўŏpĕs, under promise of his abdicatio[n] of the royal power, together with a thir[d] part of the kingdom. Thus the rule ove[r] the Dorians passed to him and his descendants. When commanded by the Delphi[c] oracle to attempt to conquer the king[-] dom of Eurystheus immediately after "th[e] third fruit," he endeavoured after the laps[e] of three years to invade the Peloponnesus by way of the Isthmus. He was, however, repulsed by Atreus, the successor of Eurys[-] theus, and fell in single combat with Echĕmŭs, king of Tĕgĕa. It was in the "third generation" after him that the sons of his grandson Aristomăchus, *viz.* Tĕmĕnus, Cresphontēs, and Aristodēmus, at last conquered the Peloponnesus, which was then under the rule of Tīsămĕnus, son of Orestēs.

Hўmēn (Gr. *Hўmĕnaiŏs;* Lat. *Hўmĕnœus*). The Greek god of marriage and of the marriage-song (named after him). He is sometimes described as the son of Apollo and a Muse (either Terpsĭchŏrē, Urănĭa, or Callĭŏpē), who had vanished on his own weddingday, and was consequently always sought for at every wedding. He is also described as a son of the Thessalian Magnēs and of the Muse Clio, and as beloved by Apollo and Thămўris; or as the son of Dionўsus and Aphrŏdītē, who lost his voice and life while singing the nuptial song at the marriage of Dionysus and Ariadnē. According to Attic tradition, he was an Argive youth who, in the disguise of a girl, followed to the feast of Dēmētēr at Eleusis a young Athenian maiden whom he loved without winning the consent of her parents. Hymenæus and some of the maidens who were celebrating the festival, were carried off by pirates, whom he afterwards killed in their sleep, and henceforth became the champion of all women and damsels. In art he is represented like Erōs, as a beautiful, winged youth, only with a more serious expression, and carrying in his hand the marriage torch and nuptial veil. The marriage-song called *Hymenæus,* which is mentioned as early as Homer, was sung by young men and maidens, to the sound of flutes, during the festal procession of the bride from the house of her parents to that of the bridegroom. In character it was partly serious and partly humorous. The several parts always ended with an invocation of Hymenæus. (*See* EPITHALAMIUM.) On the Roman god of weddings, *see* TALASSIO.

Hymnus generally meant among the Greeks an invocation of the gods, especially in the form of an ode sung by a choir, to the accompaniment of the *cĭthăra,* while they stood round the altar.

Hypæthral Temple A temple not covered by a roof. (*See further under* TEMPLE.)

Hўpaspistæ. The shield-bearers in the Greek army, who followed the heavyarmed warriors and carried a portion of their burdensome equipment, principally the shield, the necessary baggage, and the usual provision for three days. Among the Macedonians the light infantry were so called to distinguish them from the heavy *Phalangĭtæ* (*see* HOPLITES), and the archers. They wore a round felt hat (*see* CAUSIA), a linen jerkin, and had a long dagger and a short hand-pike. They were a standing body of 6,000 men, and in war formed the king's bodyguard. (*See* AGEMA.)

Hўperbŏrĕī, lit. "dwellers beyond the north wind" (*Bŏrĕas*). A people of Greek legend, whose existence was denied by some of the ancients, while others endeavoured to define their position more precisely. They were said to dwell far away in the north, where the sun only rose and set once a year, a fancy due, perhaps, to some dim report of the long arctic summer day. The fruits of the earth ripened quickly with them; they lived in unbroken happiness, knowing no violence or strife, and reached the age of 1,000 years; any who were weary of life casting themselves from a sacred rock into the sea. The myth is connected with the worship of the god of light, Apollo, who during the dark winter was supposed to visit them, as his priestly people, in a chariot drawn by swans; returning to Delphi for the summer. There was a tradition in Dĕlŏs, that in earlier times they used to send to that island the firstfruits of their harvests by way of Dōdōna, Thessaly, and Eubœa.

Hўpĕrīdēs (Gr. *Hўpĕreidēs*). One of the Ten Attic Orators, born about B.C. 390, son of the Athenian Glaucippus. He was a pupil of Plato and Isŏcrătēs, and won for himself an important position as a forensic and political orator, although his private life was not unblemished. As a statesman, he decidedly shared the views of Demosthenes, and was his steadfast ally in the struggle against the Macedonian party. It is true that he afterwards [B.C. 324] took part in the prosecution of Demosthenes, when accused of having taken bribes from Alexander's treasurer, Harpălus, and that he contributed to his condemnation on that charge. After the destruction of Thebes by Alexander [335] it was only with difficulty that he and Demosthenes escaped being given up to the Macedonians. After the death of Alexander [323] he was the chief instigator of the Lamian War, at the unfortunate conclusion of which he and Demosthenes (who had been reconciled to one another in the meantime) and other patriots were condemned to death by the Macedonian party. He fled for sanctuary to a temple in Ægīna, but was dragged away from it by force, and by order of Antipater put to death at Corinth in 322. Of the seventy-seven speeches which were known to antiquity as the work of Hyperides, only a few fragments were known until recent times; but in 1847, in a tomb at Thebes, in Egypt, extensive fragments were found of his speech *Against Demosthenes*, together with a speech *For Lўcŏphrōn* and the whole of his speech *Against Euxĕnippus*. In 1856 there was a further discovery in Egypt of an important part of the *Funeral Oration* delivered in 322 over those who had fallen in the siege of Lămĭa. [The conclusion of the speech *Against Phĭlippĭdēs* and the whole of that *Against Athēnŏgĕnēs* were first published in 1891].

Though the speeches of Hyperides never attain to the force and depth of those of Demosthenes, nevertheless they were valued highly on account of the skill of their construction and the grace and charm of their expression.

Hўpĕrīōn. One of the Titans (*q.v.*), father of the Sun-god Helios, who himself is also called Hyperion in Homer.

Hўpermnēstra. The only one of the daughters of Danaus who spared her husband, Lynceus. (*See* DANAUS.)

Hўpĕrŏŏn. The upper story of a Greek house. (*See* HOUSE.)

Hypnŏs. The god of sleep. (*See* SLEEP.)

Hўporchēma. A species of lyric, choral song in lively rhythms; its subject was generally gay, and contained imitative dance movements. Like the pæans, these choral odes were mostly sung in honour of Apollo.

Hўpŏscēnium. *See* THEATRE.

Hypsĭpўlē. Daughter of Thŏās of Lēmnŏs. The Lemnian women had, from jealousy, killed all the men of the island; Hypsipyle alone spared her father Thŏās, having been the means of aiding his flight. When the Argonauts landed at Lemnos and married the women, Hypsipyle bore twin sons to Jason: *Eunēus*, who in Homer figures as king of Lemnos and carries on trade with the Greeks before Troy; and *Thoas*, who is sometimes described as a son of Dionўsus. When the news of her father's escape was rumoured among the Lemnian women, Hypsipyle was forced to flee for her life, and was captured by pirates, who sold her to Lycurgus of Nĕmĕa. There, as the nurse of Opheltes, the infant son of the king, she accidentally caused his death (*see* SEVEN AGAINST THEBES), and was exposed to the greatest danger, from which she was only rescued by the intervention of her sons who were sent to her aid by Dionysus.

I

Ĭacchus. A name under which Dionysus was honoured, together with Dēmētēr and Persĕphŏnē, at the Eleusinian Mysteries. (*See* DIONYSUS, PERSEPHONE, and ELEUSINIA.)

Iambic Poetry. Iambic poetry, like the elegiac poetry which was also nearly contemporaneous with it and was similarly cultivated by the Ionians of Asia Minor, forms a connecting link between epic and lyric poetry. While elegy however is directly connected, both in metrical form and expression, with epic poetry, iambic poetry is in direct contrast to it, both as regards subject-matter, diction and metre. The difference between the subject-matter of the two is as marked as the distinction was between tragedy and comedy in later times. While the aim of epic poetry is to awake admiration for its heroes, iambic poetry strains all the resources of art and irony, sarcasm and satire, to hold up the faults and weaknesses of human nature to mockery and contempt. This form of

poetry, in keeping with its subject, confined itself to the simple, unadorned language of everyday life, and made use of the pliant iambic metre, which lent itself readily to such language, and had long been popularly employed to clothe in a poetic garb the raillery which formed part of the rustic feasts of Demeter. This custom, as well as the application of the word *iambus* to verses of this kind, was traced to the Thracian maiden *Iambē* (also called the daughter of Pan and Echo). When the goddess Dēmētēr was plunged in grief for the loss of her daughter Persĕphŏnē, on entering the house of Cĕlĕŭs at Eleusis, it was the jests of Iambe that forced her to smile and restored her appetite.

Iambic poetry was brought to artistic perfection by *Archĭlŏchus* of Părŏs (about 700 B.C.). He did not remain satisfied with the simple repetition of the same iambic verse, but invented the most varied forms, linking the longer iambic measures with the shorter, as well as with dactylic metres, and thus forming epodes. Instead of the iambus ($\smile$ -), he also made use of its inverted form, the trochee (- $\smile$). Further representatives of this class were his younger contemporary *Sĭmōnĭdēs of Amorgus*, and *Hippōnax* of Ephesus (about 540 B.C.), the inventor of the metre called the *chōliambus* or *scāzōn iambus*, the "lame" or "limping iambus," in which the last iambic foot is replaced by a trochee, which as it were limps at the end of the verse and gives it a comic effect. *Solon* employed the iambic form in justifying his political aims in the face of his opponents. Of the later iambic writers may be mentioned *Hērōdēs* or *Hērondās*, whose extant poems (*editio princeps*, 1891), may be assigned to the 3rd century B.C. He was the composer of mimes in iambic metre, a kind of imitative pourtrayal of manners in choliambic verses, similar to those of the Roman *Gnæus Mătĭus* in the 1st century B.C. From the middle of this century onwards lampoons in iambic verse became common among the Romans. Its earliest representatives included *Fŭrĭus Bĭbăcŭlus*, *Catullus*, and also *Horace*, who in his epodes imitated the metres of Archilochus. Under the Empire, a few poems by *Martial* and *Ausōnius* belong to this class.

Iamblĭchus. (1) A Greek writer of romances, born in Syria, who composed in the second half of the 2nd century A.D. a romance in sixteen books, called, from the scene of the greater part of the story, *Băbўlōnĭca*. It relates the love-adventures of Rhŏdănēs and Sinōnis. We only possess an epitome of it by Phōtius.

(2) A Greek philosopher from Chalcis in Syria, a pupil of Porphўrius, and the founder of the Syrian school of Neo-Platonic philosophy. He died about 330 A.D. He employed the Neo-Platonic philosophy entirely in the service of polytheistic religion, and mingled it with Oriental superstition, which he endeavoured to justify on speculative grounds. He even taught that divination and magic were necessary to bring about a re-absorption into the Deity. He himself had the reputation of working miracles, and was highly venerated by his disciples. Of his work in ten books on the Pythagorean philosophy, we still possess four parts, including a life of Pythagoras, an uncritical and careless compilation from the works of earlier writers. A work, formerly attributed to him, on the theology of arithmetic, setting forth the mystic lore of numbers according to the later Pythagoreans and Platonists, is not written by him, any more than the work on the Mysteries of Egypt. Both however belong to his school.

Iăpĕtŭs. Son of Urănus and Gæa, a Titan, who, either by Clўmĕnē or Asia, the daughter of Ocĕănus, became the father of Atlas, Mĕnœtius, Prŏmētheus, and Epĭmētheus. He was thrown into Tartărus, with his son Menœtius, on account of his rebellion against Zeus.

Iăsĭōn (or *Iăsĭus*). A favourite of Dēmētēr, who in Crete became by him the mother of Plutus. Zeus accordingly killed Iasion with a flash of lightning.

Ibўcus. A Greek lyric poet of Rhēgium in Lower Italy, about 530 B.C. Like Anacreon, he led a wandering life, and spent much of his time at the court of Pŏlўcrătēs of Samos. According to his epitaph, he died in his native town; according to the legend made familiar by Schiller's poem, he was slain on a journey to Corinth, and his murderers were discovered by a flock of cranes. His poems, which were collected into seven books, survive in scanty fragments only. They dealt partly with mythological themes in the metres of Stēsĭchŏrus and partly with love-songs in the spirit of Æolic lyric poetry, full of glowing passion and sensibility. It was mainly to the latter that he owed his fame.

Icărĭus. (1) The hero of the Attic deme of Icaria. Under the reign of Pandīōn he received the vine from Dionўsus in return for his hospitable reception of the god. As he went about the land with skins full of wine, in order to spread the cultivation of the vine, and some shepherds became intoxicated on the new drink, their companions, thinking they had been poisoned, slew him and either cast his body into a dry brook or buried him under a tree on Mount Hymettus. His daughter *Erĭgŏnē* found it after a long search, being led to the spot by her faithful dog *Mæra ;* and hung herself on the tree. Dionysus punished the land with a plague, and the maidens with madness, so that they hanged themselves after the manner of Erigone. To expiate the guilt of slaying Icarius and to avert the curse, the festival of the *Aiōra* (the "swing") was founded in her honour. During this all sorts of small images were hung on the trees and swung, and fruits were brought as an offering to the father as well as to the daughter. Icarius was placed among the constellations as *Bŏōtēs* or *Arctūrus*, Erigone as *Virgo*, and Mæra as *Prŏcўōn*.

(2) Son of Œbălus of Sparta. By the

Nymph Pĕrĭbœa he was the father of Pēnĕlŏpē, wife of Odysseus.

Īcărus. Son of Dædălus. While he and his father were flying away from Crete by means of waxen wings, in spite of his father's warnings, he flew too near the sun, so that the wax melted and he sank into the sea and was drowned. After him the island where his body was washed ashore and buried by Hēráclēs was called *Icaria*, and the surrounding sea, the "Icarian Sea."

Īcĕlus. A dream-god. (*See* DREAMS.)

Ichthyocentaurs. *See* TRITON.

Ictīnus. One of the most famous architects of Greece; he flourished in the second half of the 5th century B.C. and was a contemporary of Pericles and Phīdīās. His most famous works were the Parthĕnōn on the Acropolis at Athens, and the temple of Apollo at Bassæ, near Phīgălīa in Arcadia. Of both these edifices important remains are in existence. Most of the columns of the temple at Bassæ are still standing. In the judgment of the ancients, it was the most beautiful temple in the Peloponnesus, after the temple of Athēnē at Tĕgĕa, which was the work of Scŏpās. [Pausanias, viii 41 § 8.]

Idæan Dactylī (Gr. *Daktŭloi*). Fabulous beings in Greek mythology who had their original home in Phrygian Ida, but were afterwards transferred by legend to the mountain of the same name in Crete, and were confounded with similar beings called the *Telchīnĕs, Cŭrētĕs, Căbīri,* and *Cŏrybantĕs,* who were all fabulous beings in the service of Rhea Cybĕlē (the "Idæan Mother"). They were accredited with having discovered, and having been the first to work, iron and copper; with having introduced music and rhythm into Greece; and with being possessed of magic power. Three of the Phrygian Dactyli had names: *Celmis* (the smelter), *Damnămĕneus* (the hammer), and *Acmōn* (the anvil). Among the Cretan Dactyli, who were five, ten, and even more in number, was the "Idæan Hēráclēs," a personification of the procreative powers of nature, who also afforded magical protection against perils.

Īdās and Lynceus. Sons of Aphăreus of Messēnia and of Arēnē; a pair of brothers as heroic and as inseparable as their cousins Castor and Pollux (Pŏlydeucēs). The Nymph Marpĕssa, daughter of the Acarnanian river-god Euēnus, was wooed by Apollo, when Idas carried her off in a winged chariot given him by Pŏseidōn.

When Apollo overtook the fugitives in Messenia, Idas, who was then "the strongest of living men" [Homer, *Il.* ix 556], stretched his bow against Apollo. Zeus interposed and gave the damsel her choice of suitors; she decided in favour of the mortal, as she feared Apollo would desert her. After that the god hated her; she herself and her beautiful daughter Cleopatra or Alcyŏnē, wife of Mĕlĕager, and their daughter, all died young, and brought misfortune on those that loved them. Idas and the keen-sighted Lynceus, who could even see into the heart of the earth, joined in the Calydonian Hunt and the Argonautic expedition. They met their end fighting Castor and Pollux, with whom they had been brought up. As they were all returning from a raid into Arcadia, Idas was appointed to divide the cattle they had captured; he divided an ox into four portions and decided that whosoever devoured his portion first was to have the first half of the spoil, and he who finished his next, the second half. He finished his own and his brother's share first, and drove the cattle away. The Dīoscūrī were enraged and hid themselves from the brothers in a hollow oak-tree; but the keen sight of Lynceus detected their lurking-place and Idas stabbed Castor in the tree. Thereupon Pollux pierced Lynceus through, while Idas was slain by the lightning of Zeus. For another account of the origin of the quarrel, *see* DIOSCURI.

Idmōn. Son of Apollo and of Astĕrīē, daughter of Cŏrōnus; a seer who took part in the Argonautic expedition, although he foresaw that it would lead to his own death. He was killed by a wild boar in the land of the Mărĭandynī, in Bithynia. He was worshipped as a hero by the inhabitants of the town of Hērácleia in Pontus, which was built around his grave by command of Apollo.

Īdŏmĕnĕūs. The son of Deucălīon of Crete, and grandson of Mīnōs. Being one of Helen's suitors, he and Mērĭŏnēs, the son of his half brother, went with eighty ships to Troy, where he appears in Homer as among the bravest of heroes. He is described [in *Od.* iii 191] as one of those who safely returned to his native land. According to a later story, he was caught in a storm on his way home, and vowed to Pŏseidōn that, if he returned in safety, he would sacrifice to the god whatever he should first meet on his landing. His son came out to meet him, and was accordingly sacrificed ; a plague thereupon broke out, he was banished by the Cretans, and betook himself to Calabria. He afterwards withdrew to Cŏlŏphōn in Asia, where he is said to have been buried. His tomb, however, was shown by the Cretans at Cnōsus, where he was worshipped as a hero.

Īdūs. The thirteenth or fifteenth day of the Roman month (*see* CALENDAR). It was sacred to Jupiter.

Idyll (in Greek *eidylliŏn*, diminutive of *eidōs*, "form," "a small picture"). A poetic sketch of character, specially in connexion with pastoral life. (*See further under* BUCOLIC POETRY.)

Īlē ("a troop"). (1) The Spartan term for a company of boys of the same age, who were brought up together. (*See* EDUCATION.) (2) In the organization of the Macedonian army, a squadron of cavalry, generally 200 strong, under the command of an *ilarchus*. (*See* HIPPEIS.)

Īlĭa. Daughter of Æneas and Lavīnīa. According to the legend, Romulus and Remus were her sons by Mars. (*See* ÆNEAS and RHEA SILVIA.)

Iliad. *See* HOMER and TROJAN WAR.

Īlĭŏnē. Daughter of Priam and Hĕcŭbă, and wife of the Thracian prince Pŏlў-mēstŏr. Her youngest brother Pŏlўdōrus was entrusted to her care by her parents, and she brought him up as her own son, while she gave out that her own son Deï-phīlus or Deïpўlus was Polydorus. When Polymestor (who was bribed by the Greeks) murdered the supposed Polydorus, Ilione blinded and killed him.

Īlīthyia. *See* EILEITHYIA.

Īlus. The son of Trōs, and great-grandson of Dardănus, brother of Assărăcus and Ganymede, and father of Lăŏmĕdŏn. He once went from his native town of Dardania upon Mount Ida to Phrygia, where he was victorious in an athletic contest held by the king of the country. Beside fifty youths and fifty maidens, the prize of the contest, the king gave him, at the command of an oracle, a spotted cow, and told him there to found a city on the spot where she lay. He accordingly founded on the hill of the Phrygian Atē, the town which after him was called *Ilĭŏn*, and also *Troy* (Gr. *Troïa*) after his father. When he demanded a sign of Zeus, on the following morning he found the *Pallădĭum* before his tent.

Īmāgĭnēs. The Roman portrait masks of deceased members of a family; they were made of wax and painted, and pro-

bably fastened on to busts. They were kept in small wooden shrines let into the inner walls of the *ātrĭum*. [The design of the funeral monument represented in the accompanying cut has been obviously suggested by this method of enshrining the bust.] Inscriptions under the shrines recorded the names, merits, and exploits of the persons they referred to. The images were arranged and connected with one another by means of coloured lines, in such a way as to exhibit the pedigree (*stemma*) of the family. On festal days the shrines were opened, and the busts crowned with bay-leaves. At family funerals, there were

* MEMORIAL BUST OF A ROMAN LADY.
(Rome, Lateran Museum.)

people specially appointed to walk in procession before the body, wearing the masks of the deceased members of the family, and clothed in the *insignia* of the rank which they had held when alive. The right of having these ancestral images carried in procession was one of the privileges of the nobility. [Polybius, vi 53; Pliny, *N. H.*, xxxv 2 §§ 6, 7; Mommsen, *Rom. Hist.*, book iii, chap. xiii.]

Impĕrātor (commander-in-chief). A Roman title, originally the designation of each separate possessor of an independent command (*imperium*). In the course of time it became customary to assume the title after a man had gained his first great victory, usually after having been greeted as imperator either by the soldiers on the battlefield, or by the decree of the senate. Under the Empire the title, which was seldom conferred by Augustus, was granted for the last time by Tiberius 22 A.D. It was usually followed by a triumph, and ceased when the triumph was over. As a permanent title, it was first assumed by Cæsar, whose adopted son and heir Octavian bore it as an inherited *cognōmen*, and from the year B.C. 40 onwards, according to a custom that arose at that time, substituted it for his previous *prænomen* Gaius, thus becoming *Imperator Cæsar*, instead of *Cæsar Imperator*. His immediate successors, Tiberius, Călĭgŭla, and Claudius abstained from using this *prænomen ;* Nero used it frequently, but it first became permanent with Vespasian. The emperors also took the title *Imperator*, in its earlier signification, after a victory won by themselves or on their behalf.

Impĕrĭum. The full kingly power among the Romans, the royal authority over all members of the state. It was conferred on the newly elected king by the *cŏmĭtĭa cūrĭāta*, a formal assembly of the patricians comprising the *cūrĭœ*, and it consisted of the rights of levying the citizens for military service, of leading the army, of celebrating a triumph, of exercising civil and criminal jurisdiction, and of inflicting punishment on the citizens, whether corporal or capital, or such as affected either their property or their liberty. A symbol of this authority was the axe and the bundle of rods borne by the lictors. (*See* FASCES.)

At the establishment of the Republic the *imperium* was transferred to the two consuls, as the successors of the kings; but the full power of the *imperium* was then limited by the fact that both possessed the same power, and that, in the penalties they inflicted in times of peace, they were subject to the right of appeal (*see* PROVOCATIO), and to the intervention of the tribunes of the people, after the institution of that office. When the consulship was deprived of its civil jurisdiction and the prætorship instituted for this purpose, the prætors also received the *imperium ;* nevertheless it was more limited (*mĭnŭs*) than that of the consuls, who, in contrast with the prætors and all other magistrates except the tribunes, had the right of ordering and forbidding. The *imperium* in its undivided and unlimited form was conferred on those who in exceptional cases

were appointed dictators. It was also possessed by the *interrex*, but for five days only. For consuls and prætors the *imperium* could be "prorogued," *i.e.* prolonged beyond their time of office; but the *imperium* thus prolonged was *fīnĭtum*, i.e. bounded within the limits of their province. In the Republic it could also be conferred by means of the *comitia curiata*, but this act fell into a mere formality. Under the Empire the term *imperium* included the highest military authority, which resided in the emperor and was the foundation of all his power. It was taken up either at the instance of the senate or the troops. Its full validity depended on its recognition by both.

Implŭvĭum. A depression in the floor of the Roman *atrium* made for the purpose of receiving the rain which came in through the open roof. (*See* HOUSE.)

Īnăchus. The most ancient king of Argos, properly the god of the river of the same name, son of Ocĕănus and Tēthys, and father of Phŏrōneus and Io. After the flood of Deucălīon, he is said to have led the inhabitants down from the mountains to the plains, and when Pŏseidōn and Hēra contended for the possession of the land, he decided in favour of the latter. In punishment for this Poseidon made the rivers of Argos suffer from a scarcity of water.

Incŭbărĕ (Gr. *enkoimāsthai*). Specially used of sleeping in a sanctuary where oracular responses were sought through dreams or necromancy. (*See* ORACLES.) It was with a view to obtaining in a dream a revelation either from the god of the sanctuary, or by conjuring up the spirit of some dead person. Certain preliminaries had generally to be performed, in particular the sacrifice of some animal, on whose skin it was often customary to sleep. These incubations, which were in vogue among the Greeks from the earliest times, but were not extensively practised among the Romans until under the Empire, generally took place in the temple of Æsculapius, the god of healing.

Indĭgĕtēs. Roman deities of uncertain import. They appear to have been local heroes, who ranked beneath the gods, such as Evander, Æneas, and Romulus.

Indĭgĭtāmenta. The Latin term for an official collection of forms of prayer belonging to the *libri pontĭfĭcĭi* (*see* PONTIFEX). In them were set forth the various powers of each god who was to be summoned to aid in particular cases; and none of these divinities could be passed over, if the prayer was to receive a favourable answer. Only those portions of the collection were made public which bore direct reference to private life; prayers at marriages, at births, for a blessing on the children at different times of life, and for the beginning of all kinds of work, especially agriculture. (The names of the gods of earliest childhood were as follows: *Pŏtīna* and *Edūca*, who taught the child when weaned to eat and drink; *Cŭba*, who protected the child when taken out of the cradle and put to bed; *Ossipāga*, who strengthened the bones; *Carna*, who strengthened the flesh; *Levāna*, who helped it to rise from the ground; *Stătānus*, *Stătĭlīnus*, or *dea Stătīna*, who taught it to stand; *Abeōna* and *Adeōna*, who supported its first walking; *Făbŭlīnus*, *Farīnus*, who assisted it to talk.) All collective occupations, all parts of the house, all different spots had their particular gods, who were invoked in these forms of prayer. Often the various names only indicate the different characteristics of a single divinity; e.g. *Maia* was invoked under the names of *Bona*, *Fauna*, *Ops*, and *Fătŭa*. In course of time the different attributes came to be regarded as separate divinities. [The names of the above divinities are quoted from Varro, *Antiquitates Rerum Divinarum*, by Tertullian, *Ad Nat.* ii 11, 15 (and *De Anima* 37, 39); and by Augustine, *De Civitate Dei*, iv 11, 21 (and iv 8, 10; vi 9, vii 23).]

Infămĭa. The Latin term for the loss of certain political rights; resembling, but not identical with, *dēmĭnūtio căpĭtĭs* (*q.v.*). It was the direct consequence of dishonourable conduct, or of some shameless act (such as a widow not observing the usual year of mourning, bigamy, bankruptcy, going on the stage, or becoming a gladiator, pandering, or becoming a prostitute, etc.). It also resulted from a condemnation for felony, robbery, fraud, embezzlement of a deposit, whether belonging to a society or a ward, or in fact for any criminal offence. The *infamis* was expelled from his tribe, lost his vote and his capacity for filling public offices (*iūs suffrāgĭī* and *ius hŏnōrum*), and could not appear in a court of law either on his own account or on behalf of another. (*Cp.* ATIMIA.)

Inheritance. (1) *Greek* (Athens). If a person died intestate, leaving sons, all of equal birthright, and none of them disinherited, the sons inherited the property

in equal parts, the eldest probably receiving the same share as the rest. If there were daughters, they were provided for by dowries, which, in case they were divorced or childless after marriage, went back to the remaining heirs. If a man had no sons of his own, he usually adopted a son to continue the family and the religious worship connected with it. If he had daughters he would marry one of them to the adopted son; in this case the chief share of the inheritance would fall to this married daughter and her husband, the rest receiving dowries. If there were only daughters surviving, the succession passed to them. In such a case the next of kin had a legal right to one of the heiresses, (*ĕpĭclērŏs*) and could claim to marry her, even if she had married some one else before receiving the inheritance. And poor heiresses, on the other hand, had a legal claim on their nearest of kin either for marriage, or for a provision suitable to their circumstances. If a man had married an heiress, he was bound by custom and tradition, if he had sons, to name one as heir to the property which had come with his wife, and thus to restore the house of the maternal grandfather. Children born out of wedlock were illegitimate, and had no claim on the father's estate. If a man died intestate, leaving no heirs either of his body or adopted, his nearest relations in the male line inherited, and in default of these, those in the female line as far as the children of first cousins. Any one thinking he had a legal claim to the inheritance made an application to the *archŏn* to hand it over to him. The application was posted up in public, and read out in the following *ecclēsia*. The question was then asked whether any one disputed the claim, or raised a counter-claim. If not, the archon assigned the inheritance to the claimant; otherwise the matter was decided by a lawsuit. Even after the assignment of an inheritance, it might be disputed in the lifetime of the holder, and for five years after his death. The claim of the nearest relation to an heiress was in the same way lodged with the archon and ratified before the assembly.

(2) *Roman*. If a man died intestate leaving a wife and children of his body or adopted, they were his heirs (*sŭī hērēdēs*). But this did not apply to married daughters who had passed into the *mănus* of their husbands, or the children who had been freed by emancipation from the *pŏtestās* of their

father. If the man left no wife or children, the *agnāti*, or relations in the male line, inherited, according to the degree of their kinship. If there were no *agnati*, and the man was a patrician, the property went to his *gens*. The *cōgnātī*, or relations in the female line, were originally not entitled to inherit by the civil law. But, as time went on, their claim was gradually recognised more and more to the exclusion of the *agnati*, until at last Justinian entirely abolished the privilege of the latter, and substituted the principle of blood-relationships for that of the civil law. Vestal Virgins were regarded as entirely cut off from the family union, and therefore could not inherit from an intestate, nor, in case of their dying intestate, did the property go to their family, but to the state. But, unlike other women, they had unlimited right of testamentary disposition. If a freedman died intestate and childless, the *patrōnus* and his wife had the first claim to inherit, then their children, then their *agnati*, and (if the *patronus* was a patrician) then his *gens*. In later times, even if a freedman, dying childless, left a will, the *patronus* and his sons had claim to half the property. Augustus made a number of provisions in the matter of freedmen's inheritance. The civil law made it compulsory on a man's *sui heredes* to accept an inheritance whether left by will or not. But as the debts were taken over with the property, the *edictum* of the prætor allowed the heirs to decline it. *A fortiori*, no other persons named in the will could be compelled to accept the legacy. (*See* WILL.)

Inns did not come into existence in Greece until the times when, in consequence of the increase of traffic, the custom of hospitality, which was formerly practised on an extensive scale, became more and more confined to cases where it was either inherited or was the subject of special agreement on both sides. Besides private inns (*pandōkeia*), which offered food as well as shelter to strangers, public inns, which at least gave shelter and night-quarters, were to be found in some places, especially where great crowds of men were accustomed to assemble for the celebration of festivals, and also near temples which were much visited. The profession of an inn-keeper was little esteemed, still less that of a tavern-keeper, whose bar (*kăpē-leiŏn*) it was not considered proper for respectable people to frequent [Isocr., *Areop.* 49]; in Athens a visit to a tavern was even

sufficient to lead to expulsion from the Areopagus.

In Rome, as in most parts of Italy, there were inns for travellers (*dēversōrĭa*) at least as early as the 2nd century B.C. On the great high-roads taverns were built on speculation by landowners resident in the neighbourhood, and were either let out, or kept for them by slaves. With the increase of traffic, stations for changing horses (*mūtātĭō*) and for night-quarters (*mansio*) began to be placed on the high-roads of all the provinces. Cook-shops (*pŏpīnæ*) and taverns (*caupōnæ*) were seldom frequented by any but the commonest people. Those who kept them were just as much despised as in Greece, and were actually considered by the law as under a ban. Even in antiquity it was the custom to make inns known by a sign-board (*insigne*). Thus in Pompeii an inn has been discovered with the sign of an elephant.

Inō. Daughter of Cadmus, and wife of Athămās (*q.v.*). Being followed by the latter when he had been seized with madness, she fled to the cliff Mŏlūrĭs, between Mĕgărā and Corinth, and there threw herself into the sea with her infant son Mĕlĭ-certēs. At the isthmus, however, mother and child were carried ashore by a dolphin, and, from that time forward, honoured as marine divinities along the shores of the Mediterranean, especially on the coast of Megara and at the Isthmus of Corinth. Ino was worshipped as *Leucŏthĕa*, and Melicertes as *Pălæmōn*. They were regarded as divinities who aided men in peril on the sea. As early as Homer, we have Ino mentioned as rescuing Odysseus from danger by throwing him her veil [*Od.* v 333–353]. Among the Romans Ino was identified with *Mătūta* (*q.v.*).

Insŭla. *See* HOUSE, near the end.

Intercessĭō. (1) The Latin term for the interference of a higher officer with some public act on the part of one lower in rank, *e.g.* calling a meeting of the commons. The tribune of the people could thus interfere with the prætor, quæstor, and ædile. Thus it was even open to the tribunes of the people to refuse a triumph to a consul or a prætor. (2) The quashing of an official act. As in (1), this might be issued by a higher official against a lower one ; and also by one colleague against another, *e.g.* by tribune against tribune. It was necessary that the *intercessio* should be made in person, and in general immediately after the act in question. It was employed against judicial decisions, administrative ordinances (solely on the appeal of the person concerned); also against decrees of the senate and motions in the popular assembly. The later species of *intercessio* early became a special right of the tribunes (*q.v.*).

Intercidōna. The name given by the Italian tribes to one of the three divinities who, during child-bed, protected mother and child from being tormented by the wood-god Silvānus. (*See* PICUMNUS.)

Interdictĭō Aquæ et Ignis. The Roman term for exclusion from the common use of fire and water, which were the symbols of the community. (*See* EXILIUM.)

Interest (Gr. *tŏkoi ;* Lat. *fēnus* or *ūsūra*). In Greece the rate of interest on invested capital was not restricted by law, but was left entirely to arrangement between the parties concerned. The average rate, compared with that usually given at the present day, was very high, far higher than the rent either of houses or land. This is partly explained by the proportionately greater scarcity of ready money, and by the fact that it was difficult to accumulate a large amount of capital.

In the time of Demosthenes 12 per cent. was regarded as a rather low rate of interest, and higher rates, up to 18 per cent., were quite common. In bottomry the ordinary rate of interest at Athens was 20 per cent. In the event of failure in the payment of interest due, compound interest was charged. In the computation of interest two different methods were employed. It was usual to specify either the sum to be paid by the month on every mina (equal in intrinsic value of silver to £3 6s. 8d.), or the fraction of the principal which was annually paid as interest. Capital therefore was said to be invested at a *drachma*, if for every *mina* (100 *drachmœ*) there was paid interest at the rate of one *drachma*, i.e. one per cent. monthly, and consequently 12 per cent. per annum. Or again, if 12½ per cent. yearly interest was to be paid, the capital was said to be invested at "one-eighth." In most cases the interest appears to have been paid monthly, and on the last day of the month; but payment by the year was not unknown. In bottomry the interest was according to the terms of the contract.

In *Rome*, as at Athens, the rate of interest was originally unrestricted, and it was not until after hard struggles that, by the laws of the Twelve Tables, a regular yearly rate of interest at one-twelfth of the capital, or

8⅓ per cent., was established. But this and subsequent legal limitations were all the less effectual for putting down usury, because they were valid in the case of Roman citizens only, and not in that of foreigners. Usury was accordingly practised under the name of foreigners up to the end of the 2nd century B.C., when the laws against it were extended so as to include aliens. Through intercourse with Asia and Greece, a change in the payment of interest was gradually introduced, which in the first half of the 1st century B.C. was generally adopted. Capital was no longer lent by the year, but by the month, and monthly interest was paid, on the first day of each month; notice of intention to call in the loan was given on the Ides (the 13th or 15th day of the month), and reimbursement took place on the first day of the following month. The regular rate of interest with this reckoning was 1 per cent. monthly, or 12 per cent. per annum. The accumulation of large fortunes in Rome at the end of the Republic considerably lessened the rate of interest on safe investments. The chief field for usury was then the provinces, whose inhabitants were compelled by the exorbitant imposts to be continually raising loans at any price. The custom, long permitted, of adding the year's unpaid interest to the principal, was first forbidden by the later Roman law. Justinian permanently fixed the rate of interest in ordinary investments at 6 per cent., in commercial enterprises at 8 per cent., and in bottomry, in which it had previously been unlimited on account of the risk incurred by the stock on long voyages, at 12 per cent.

Internundĭnum. The Roman week. (*See* NUNDINÆ and CALENDAR.)

Interrēgēs. The name given by the Romans to the senators who, between the death of one king and the election of another, held regal authority, during the *interregnum*, for successive periods of five days each. One of these *interrēgēs* had to conduct the election itself. Even under the Republic an *interrex* was nominated by the senate to hold the *cŏmĭtĭa* for the election of consuls, whenever the consuls had died, or resigned, or if the election had not been completed by the end of the year. If five days did not suffice, the retiring *interrex* named another to succeed him.

Ĭnŭŭs. *See* FAUNUS.

Ĭō. The beautiful daughter of Ināchus, and the first priestess of Hēra at Argos. As Zeus loved her, she was changed by the jealousy of Hera into a white heifer, and Argus of the hundred eyes was appointed to watch her. When Hermēs, at the command of Zeus, had killed Argus, Hera maddened the heifer by sending a gad-fly which perpetually pursued her. Io thus wandered through the continents of Europe and Asia, by land and by sea. Each of the different straits she swam across was named after her *Bospŏrus*, or Ox-ford. At last in Egypt she recovered her original shape, and bore Ĕpăphus to Zeus. Libya, the daughter of Epaphus, became by Pŏseidōn the mother of Bēlus, who in turn was father of Ægyptus, Dănăus, Cēpheus, and Phīneus. The Greek legend of Io's going to Egypt is probably to be explained by her having been identified with the Egyptian goddess Isis, who is always represented with cow's horns. Io (" the wanderer ") is generally explained as a moon-goddess wandering in the starry heavens, symbolized by Argus of the hundred eyes; her transformation into a horned heifer represents the crescent moon.

Ĭŏbătēs. A king of Lycia, father of Anteia, and son-in-law of Prœtus, king of Tīryns, by whom he was commissioned to kill Bellĕrŏphōn (*q.v.*).

Ĭŏcastē. The mother and also the wife of Œdĭpūs (*q.v.*).

Ĭŏlāus. Son of Iphĭclēs, the half-brother of Hērăclēs, and the faithful companion and charioteer of that hero. For his help in destroying the Lernæan hydra and in the fight with Cycnus, Heracles transferred to him his first wife Mĕgăra. The friendship he had devoted to the father he continued to the children of Heracles in defending them against Eurystheus. As the comrade of Heracles he was worshipped beside him in Thebes, where the gymnasium was named after him, and where the inhabitants used to swear by his name.

Ĭŏlē. Daughter of Eurytus of Œchălĭa. She came into the power of Hērăclēs as a captive of war, and was on his death (of which she was the innocent cause) married to his son Hyllus. (*See* HERACLES.)

Ĭŏn. (1) According to the Attic story, the son of Apollo and Crĕūsa, daughter of the Athenian king Erechtheus. He was exposed at his birth by his mother in a grotto on the cliff of the Acrŏpŏlĭs, whence he was taken by Hermēs to Delphi and brought up by the Pythian priestess to be an attendant in his father's temple. Creusa afterwards married Xūthus, who had migrated from Thessaly, and was son of Hellēn and brother of Æŏlus and Dōrus.

As this marriage was childless, the pair went to Delphi to consult the god as to the cause. Xuthus received the command to consider as his son the first person he should meet in front of the temple. This happened to be Ion, who had meanwhile grown up, and was at once accepted by Xuthus as his son. But Creusa, fancying he was her husband's son by a former union, resolved to poison him. Ion detects her design in time and would have killed Creusa, who however takes refuge at the altar of the god. Then the Pythian priestess produces the cradle in which he had been exposed as an infant, and thus brings about recognition and reconciliation between mother and son. Ion married Hĕlĭcē, the daughter of Sĕlīnus, king of the Ægialeans on the north coast of the Peloponnesus. At the death of this king he became monarch of the land, and the inhabitants assumed the name of Ionians after him. Afterwards being called upon by the Athenians to help them against Eumolpus and the Eleusinians, he conquered the enemy and was made king of Athens. From the four sons who are attributed to him, Hŏplēs, Gĕlĕōn, Ægĭcŏrēs, and Argădēs were descended the four Ionic tribes.

(2) *Of Chios.* A Greek author of rare versatility for his time. He composed historical writings, among them a kind of memoirs of men of mark he had met, such as Sophocles; also lyric poems of the most varied types, and thirty or forty tragedies which were more remarkable for elegance and erudition than for elevation of style. When in B.C. 452 he won a dramatic victory at Athens, he is said to have presented every Athenian with a flask of Chian wine. He died at Athens in 422 B.C. We only possess scanty fragments of his works.

Ĭŏphōn. The son of Sophocles, and, like his father, a tragic poet. (*See* SOPHOCLES.)

Iphĭănassa. *See* IPHIGENIA.

Iphĭclēs. Son of Amphĭtryon and Alcmēnē, half-brother of Hērăclēs and father of Iŏlāus. He took part in the Calydonian Hunt and also in many of his brother's expeditions, especially against Ergīnus, Augeas, Lāŏmĕdōn, and Hippŏcŏōn. He either fell in the fight against the sons of Hippocoon or was wounded in battle against the Mŏlĭŏnĭdæ at Phĕnĕŭs in Arcadia, where he was afterwards worshipped as a hero.

Iphĭclus. Son of Phylăcus of Phylăcē in Thessaly, father of Pŏdarcēs and Prōtĕsĭlāus. He took part in the Argonautic expedition and in the funeral games in honour of Pĕlĭas. Here he outstripped all his competitors, being so swift of foot that he could pass over a cornfield without bending the ears, and could run over the sea without wetting his feet. On his herds of cattle and his powers of healing, *see* MELAMPUS.

Ĭphĭgĕnĭă (Gr. *Iphĭgĕneia*, in Homer *Iphĭănassa*). Daughter of Agămemnon and of Clўtæmnēstra, or (according to another account) of Thēseus and Helen (*q.v.*), and brought up Clytæmnestra as her child. When the Greek ships were detained at Aulis by the calm caused by the wrath of Artĕmis against Agamemnon for killing a hind sacred to that goddess, and boasting that he was superior to her in the chase, the seer Calchās announced that the goddess could only be appeased by the sacrifice of Iphigenia. According to another story, Agamemnon had vowed, before the birth of Iphigenia, that he would sacrifice to the goddess whatever the year brought forth that was loveliest, but had neglected to keep his vow. After a long struggle Agamemnon finally gave way to the pressure put upon him by Mĕnĕlāus, and sent for his daughter to come to Aulis under the pretext of betrothing her to Achilles. During the sacrifice Artemis substituted a hind for her, and carried her off in a cloud to the land of the Tauri [the modern *Crimea*], where, as priestess of the goddess, it fell to her lot to offer up as victims all strangers who were shipwrecked on the

* SACRIFICE OF IPHIGENIA.
(Mural painting from Pompeii. Naples Museum.)

coast. Orestēs, who, commanded by the oracle, had gone there to bring to Attica the image of the goddess, was on the point of being sacrificed by her, when she recognised him as her brother and allowed herself to be carried off by him together with the image. At Delphi her sister Electra wanted to put her eyes out, on hearing that the Tauric priestess had slain Orestes; but was prevented from doing so by her brother's arrival. She is said

to have brought the image of the Tauric
Artemis to the Attic deme of Braurōn, and
to have died and been buried there as its
priestess. She was even introduced into
Attic legend as daughter of Theseus and
Helen. In other places also, such as
Sparta, the image was shown, and she was
regarded as a priestess who had brought it
to Greece from among the Scythians. In
all probability Iphigenia was originally a
designation of Artemis herself, and out of
this epithet of the goddess the personality
of the priestess was in time evolved. Her
grave was also shown at Mĕgăra. According
to another legend, she is said to have been
made immortal by Artemis, and to have
lived on in the island of Leucē as the wife
of Achilles under the name of *Orsĭlŏchĭa.*

Iphĭtus. Son of Eurȳtus of Œchălĭa,
and a friend of Hērăclēs, who, in a fit of
madness, hurled him down headlong from
the battlement of his castle at Tiryns.
(*See* HERACLES.)

Irēnē. *See* EIRENE.

Iris. The daughter of Thaumās and of
Electra, and a sister of the Harpies. She
is the personification of the rainbow which
unites heaven and earth. As a virgin goddess, swift as the breeze and with wings
of gold, she is the messenger of the gods,
especially of Zeus and Hēra, and, according
to later writers, exclusively of the latter.
She bears their behests from the ends of
the earth even to the river Styx, and into
the depths of the sea. As a messenger
of the gods she resembles Hermēs, and
therefore carries the herald's staff of that
divinity.

Isæus. The fifth of the Ten Attic Orators,
a pupil of Isocrătēs ; born before B.C. 400
at Chalcis in Eubœa. He lived to the
middle of the 4th century at Athens, probably as a resident alien (*mĕtoikŏs*), writing
forensic speeches for other people and giving
instruction in rhetoric. Demosthenes was
for several years his pupil. Of the sixty-
four speeches attributed to him by antiquity, we have (besides some not unimportant fragments) eleven speeches dealing
with matters relating to inheritance, and
therefore of great importance as throwing
light upon Attic private law. In his style
he most closely resembles Lysias, to whom
he is inferior in natural elegance, while he
surpasses him in oratorical skill.

Isĭdōrus. A Spaniard who, from the
beginning of the 7th century, was bishop
of Seville (in Latin *Hispălis*, whence he is
called *Hispalensis*). He died about 636

A.D. He possessed a width of reading
which was remarkable for his time, and an
extraordinary faculty for collecting information. Next to Bŏēthius and Cassiodōrus,
he exercised the most important influence
upon the general culture and literature of
the Middle Ages. Besides works on
grammar, theology, and history (including
a Chronicle of the World to his own day,
and histories of the Goths, Vandals, and
Suevi), he composed in the last years of
his life his greatest and most important
work, an immense but imperfect encyclopædic survey of all knowledge, in twenty
volumes, entitled the *Etȳmŏlŏgĭœ* or
Ŏrīgĭnēs, from its often very capricious
and marvellous explanations of the various
subjects of which it treats. Though it is
only a vast congeries of collected excerpts,
devoid of a single original idea, it is nevertheless important owing to the variety of its
contents and its citations from writings now
lost, such as those of Suetonius. Another
work, which is similarly a compilation, but
was greatly used in the Middle Ages, is his
De Nātūrā Rērum, a handbook of natural
history.

Isĭs. The divinity most extensively
worshipped, with her brother and husband
Osīris, by the Egyptians, among whom she
represented the feminine, receptive, and
producing principle in nature. As the
goddess of procreation and birth her symbol
was the cow. On monuments she is mostly
represented as of youthful appearance with
a cow's horns on her head, between the
horns the orb of the moon, and with a
sceptre of flowers and the emblem of life
in her hands (fig. 1). Her greatest temple
stood at Būsīris (i.e. *Pe-Osiri,* or Abode of
Osiris) in the midst of the Delta of the
Nile, where, amidst the fruitful fields, the
inhabitants worshipped the mightiest god
and goddess with ceremonies which typified
the search and discovery of Osiris by his
mourning wife after his murder by Typhōn.
Like Osiris she was a divinity who ruled
over the world below. In the course of the
fusion of religions which took place under
the Ptolemies, Isis and Osiris were confounded with all manner of Asiatic and
Greek gods. In process of time she became
in her power the most universal of all
goddesses, ruling in heaven, on earth,
and on the sea, and in the world below,
decreeing life and death, deciding the
fate of men, and dispensing rewards and
punishments. Her worship spread over
Greece, and after the second Punic War

obtained a firm footing in Rome in spite of repeated interference by the State. In

(1) EGYPTIAN ISIS AND HORUS (HARPOCRATES).
(Berlin Museum.)

the days of the Empire it obtained recognition by the State and established itself in all parts of the Roman dominions. The attractiveness of the service of Isis lay in the religious satisfaction which it was calculated to insure. Through abstinence from food and from sensual pleasures, and through expiations and purifications, it promised to lead its votaries to sanctification of life and to a true perception of the life divine. The ritual consisted in part of a morning and evening service to the god, partly in annual festivals celebrated in spring at the return of the season for navigation, and also in the late autumn before the advent of winter. At the former festival, held on the 5th of March, and called the ship of Isis (*Isĭdĭs nāvĭgĭum*), in recognition of her being the patroness of navigation, and inventress of the sail, the people in general, with the devotees and priests of Isis, went in solemn procession down to the seashore, where a sailing vessel painted in the Egyptian manner and laden with spices, was committed to the sea. [Apuleius, *Met.* xi 8–17, esp. 11; Firmicus Maternus, *De Err. Prof. Relig.* 2.] The other feast was emblematic of the grief of Isis at her loss and her joy at finding again her husband Osiris and her son Hōrus. Besides these popular feasts there were also certain special *mysteries* of Isis, which in all their essentials were borrowed from the Eleusinian mysteries of Dĕmētēr. In these, all who were called thereto by the goddess in a dream were admitted to the select circle of the worshippers of Isis. These devotees, like the priests, were recognised by their linen robes and their shaven heads, and had to devote themselves to an ascetic life. Oracular responses received in dreams were as much associated with the temples of Isis as with those of Sĕrāpis (*q.v.*). In Greek art the goddess is represented as similar to Hēra. Her attributes are a serpent, a cornucopia, ears of corn, lotus, moon and horns, as well as the *sīstrum*, a metal rattle, specially employed in her service (fig. 2).

(2) ROMAN ISIS AND HORUS (HARPOCRATES).
(Munich, Glyptothek.)

Ismēnē. A daughter of Œdĭpūs (*q.v.*).

Īsŏcrătēs. The fourth among the Ten Attic Orators, was born at Athens B.C. 436. He was the son of Thĕŏdōrus, the wealthy proprietor of a flute manufactory, who provided for his son's receiving a careful education. Accordingly he had the advantage of being instructed by Prŏdĭcus, Prŏtăgŏras, Thērămĕnēs, and (above all) Gorgĭas; his character was also moulded by the influence of Sōcrătēs, although he never belonged to the more restricted circle of his pupils. Bashfulness and a weak voice prevented him from taking part in public life. After the fall of the Thirty, as his father had lost his means in the calamitous years that closed the Peloponnesian War, he turned his attention to composing forensic speeches for others. After having taught rhetoric at Chios [possibly about 404 B.C.], he returned to Athens in 403, and there opened a regular school of rhetoric about 392. It was largely attended by both Athenians and non-Athenians, and brought him in considerable wealth. The total number of his pupils has been given at one hundred, including Tīmŏthĕus, the son of Cŏnōn, the orators Isæus, Hўpĕrīdēs, and Lycurgus, and the historians Ephŏrus and Theopompus. Isocrates also had friendly relations with foreign princes, especially with Evăgŏrās of Cyprus and his son Nīcŏclēs, who loaded him with favours. He kept himself completely aloof from any personal share in the public life of his day ; yet he attempted to influence the political world, not only within the narrow bounds of his native land, but also throughout the whole of Greece, by a series of rhetorical declamations, not intended to be delivered, but only to be read. This he did in the first place in his *Pănēgўrĭcus*, which he published in 380 B.C., after spending ten or (according to another account) as many as fifteen years over its preparation. This is a kind of festal oration eulogising the services of Athens to Greece, exhorting the Spartans peacefully to share the supremacy with Athens, and calling on the Greeks to lay aside all internal dissensions and attack the barbarians with their united strength. In the ninetieth year of his age, in a discourse addressed to Philip, in 346 B.C., he endeavours to induce that monarch to carry out his policy by reconciling all the Greeks to one another, and leading their united forces against the Persians. Other discourses relate to the internal politics of Athens. Thus, in the *Arĕŏpăgĭtĭcus*, he recommends his fellow citizens to get rid of the existing weaknesses in their political constitution by returning to the democracy as founded by Solon and reconstituted by Clīsthĕnēs, and by reinstating the Areopagus as the supreme tribunal of censorship over public decorum and morality. He retained his mental and bodily powers un-

impaired to an advanced age, and in his ninety-eighth year completed the *Pănăthĕnăĭcus*, a discourse in praise of Athens. He lived to see the total wreck of all his hope for a regeneration of Greece, and died B.C. 338, a few days after the battle of Chærŏnēa He is said to have died of voluntary starvation, owing to his despair at the downfall of Greek liberty; [but this account of his death, familiarised by Milton in his fifth English sonnet, must be considered as doubtful.]

There were sixty compositions bearing his name known to antiquity, but less than half that number were considered genuine Of the twenty-one which have come down to us, the first, the *Letter to Dēmŏnĭcus*, is often regarded as spurious, [but there is no reason to doubt the genuineness of nine of the ten other *Letters*. It is only the letter prefixed to the nine in the older edition that is not genuine, having been really written by Theophylact Simocatta early in the 7th century A.D.] Of the speeches, six are forensic orations, written to be delivered by others; the rest are declamations, chiefly on political subjects. By his mastery of style, Isocrates had a far-reaching influence on all subsequent Greek prose, which is not confined to oratorical composition alone His chief strength lies in a careful choice of expression, not only in his vocabulary but also in the rhythmical formation of his flowing periods, in a skilful use of the figures of speech, and in all that lends euphony to language. [Even in Latin, the oratorical prose of Cicero is, on its formal side, founded chiefly on that of Isocrates Modern literary prose has, in its turn, been mainly modelled on that of Cicero, and thus the influence of Isocrates has endured to the present day.]

Isŏtĕlĭa (" equality in tax and tribute "). At Athens, the position of partial equality with the citizens which was granted to the more deserving of the *mĕtœci* (*q.v.*).

Isthmian Games. One of the four great national festivals of the Greeks, held on the Isthmus of Corinth, in a grove of pine trees sacred to Pŏseidōn, near the shrines of the Isthmian Poseidon and of Mĕlĭcertēs. From B.C. 589, they were held in the first month of spring, in the second and fourth years of each Olympiad. According to legend, the Isthmian Games were originally funeral games in memory of Melicertes (*q.v.*) ; another tradition relates that they were established by Thēseus either in honour of Poseidon, or in commemoration of his victory over Scīrōn and Sĭnĭs. In any case, the Athenians were specially interested in the festival from the earliest times. It was alleged that, from the days of Theseus downwards, they had what was called the *prŏĕdrĭa*, the right of occupying the most prominent seats at the games, and, in accordance with a law attributed to Solon, they presented to those of their citizens who were victors in the contests a reward

Corinth (B.C. 46) it was restored to that city. The contests included gymnastic exercises, horse-races, and competitions in music. The two former differed in no essential way from the Olympian Games (*q.v.*); in the third, besides musicians, poets of either sex contended for the prize. Besides the customary palm, the prize in Pindar's time consisted of a wreath of dry *sĕlĭnŏn* [often translated " parsley," but

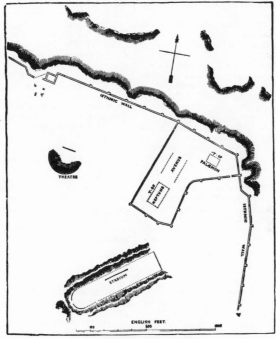

* SITE OF THE ISTHMIAN GAMES.

The Isthmian stadium, and sacred inclosure containing the temples of Poseidon (Neptune) and Melicertes (Palæmon).
After Leake's *Travels in the Morea*, vol. iii, pl. 3.

amounting to 100 *drachmæ*. [The only occasion when Socrates was absent from Athens, except with the army, was to attend this festival.] The inhabitants of Elis were completely excluded from the games, being debarred from either sending competitors or festal envoys. The Corinthians had the presidency, which was transferred to the Sicyonians after the destruction of Corinth (B.C. 146), but at the rebuilding of

more probably identical with the " wild celery," *ăpĭum grăvĕŏlens*. The *selinon* was a symbol of funeral games]. After the destruction of Corinth, a crown of pine leaves was substituted for it. The games long continued to be held, even under the Roman Empire. [*Cp.* Plutarch, *Timoleon*, 26, and *Sympos.* v 3, 1–3.]

Ĭtĭnĕrārĭa. The Roman term for (1) compendious lists of the names and distances of the different stations on the public roads, after the manner of our road-books (*itineraria adnŏtāta* or *scripta*); or (2) chartographic representations similar to our travelling maps (*itineraria picta*). Of the former kind we have

(1) the two *Antonine Itineraries*, the basis of which belongs to the time of the emperor Antŏnīnus Caracalla; but the edition which has come down to us dates from the beginning of the 4th century. They contain lists of routes by land and sea in the Roman empire.

(2) The *Itinerarium Burdĭgālense* or *Hĭĕrŏsŏlўmĭtānum*, 333 A.D., the route of a pilgrimage from Burdĭgăla (Bordeaux) to Jerusalem.

(3) The *Itinerarium Alexandri*, an abstract of the Persian expedition of Alexander the Great, drawn up mainly from Arrian for the expedition of the emperor Constantius against the Persians (A.D. 340–345).

Of the other kind of itineraries, in the form of maps, we have a specimen in the Peutinger Map, *tăbŭla Peutingeriana*, now in Vienna. It received its name from its former possessor, Konrad Peutinger, a councillor of Augsburg. It was painted at Kolmar in 1265 on the model of an original map which dates back to the middle of the 3rd century A.D. It consists of twelve broad strips of parchment, on which are delineated all those parts of the world which were known to the Romans: only the pieces which should contain Spain and Britain are lost [with the exception of part of Kent.] It is disproportionately elongated in the direction of east to west, the ratio of its height to its breadth being 1 : 21. The distances from town to town are marked on lines running from east to west, and the relative sizes of the towns indicated by distinctive marks. [A cheap and excellent *facsimile* was published by O. Maier of Ravensburg in 1888.]

Ītўlus (*Ĭtys*). See AËDON, PROCNE.

Īŭlus. See ASCANIUS.

Ixīōn. Son of Phlĕgўās (or of Arēs), and king of the Lăpĭthæ. By Dia he was the father of Pīrĭthŏüs (who, according to Homer, however, was a son of Zeus). He attempted to withhold from his father-in-law, Dēïŏneus, the bridal gifts he had promised. Deïoneus accordingly detained the horses of Ixion. The latter invited him to his house and threw him into a pit filled with fire. When Zeus not only purified him from this murder, but even invited him to the table of the gods, he became arrogant and insolent, and even sought to win the love of Hēra. Zeus thereupon formed of the clouds a phantom resembling Hera, and by it Ixion became the father of the Centaurs. On his boasting of the favours he imagined the goddess to have granted him, Zeus caused him to be punished for this crime by being fastened to a wheel, on which he was to turn in terror for evermore in the world below.

J

Jānus. A god peculiar to the Italians, with no corresponding divinity among the Greeks. Even the ancients were by no means clear as to his special significance; he was, however, regarded as one of the oldest, holiest, and most exalted of gods. In Rome the king, and in later times the *rex sacrōrum* (*q.v.*), sacrificed to him. At every sacrifice, he was remembered first; in every prayer he was the first invoked, being mentioned even before Jupiter. In the songs of the Sălĭī he was called the good creator, and the god of gods; he is elsewhere named the oldest of the gods and the beginning of all things. It would appear that originally he was a god of the light and of the sun, who opened the gates of heaven on going forth in the morning and closed them on returning at evening. In course of time he became the god of all going out and coming in, to whom all places of entrance and passage, all doors and gates, were holy. In Rome all doors and covered passages were suggestive of his name. The former were called *iānŭæ;* over the latter, the arches which spanned the streets were called *iāni*, a term perhaps symbolical of the vault of heaven. Many of these were expressly dedicated to him, especially those which were situated in markets and frequented streets, or at crossroads. In this case they were adorned with his image, and the double arch became a temple with two doors, or the two double arches a temple with four. He was generally represented as a porter with a staff and a key in his hands, and with two bearded faces placed back to back and looking in opposite directions (*see* cut). He is also the god of entrance into a new division of time, and was therefore saluted every morning as the god of the breaking day (*pătĕr mātūtīnus*); the beginnings of all the months (the calends) were sacred to him, as well as to Juno; and, among the months, the first of the natural year, which derived from him its name *Iānŭārius*. For sacrifices on the calends twelve altars were dedicated to him; his chief festival, however, was the 1st of January, especially as in B.C. 153 this was made the official beginning of the new year. On this day he was invoked as the god of good beginnings, and was honoured with cakes of meal called *ianuæ;* every disturbance, every quarrel, was carefully avoided, and no more work was done than was necessary to make a lucky beginning of the daily business of the year; mutual good wishes were exchanged, and people made presents of sweets to one another as a

HEAD OF JANUS.
(On a Roman as.)

good omen that the new year might bring nothing but that which was sweet and pleasant in its train (*see* STRENÆ). The newly chosen consuls and the other officials together with the senate and the knights went up to the Capitol to offer to Jupiter a festal sacrifice of white cattle and to pray for the safety of the State. Under the Empire the 3rd of January was substituted as the day for offering vows for the prosperity of the imperial house. The origin of all organic life, and especially all human life, was referred to him; he was therefore called *consivius* (sower). From him sprang all wells, rivers, and streams; in this relation he was called the spouse of Jūturna, the goddess of springs, and father of Fontus, the god of fountains. As the god of coming and going and of traffic, he had power not only on land, but also on sea; he was therefore

described as the husband of the sea-goddess Vĕnīlia and as the discoverer of the art of shipbuilding. For this reason the Roman *as* bore the impression of a ship on the obverse of the head of Janus (*see* COINAGE, fig. 7). His authority extended as much over war as over peace. In connexion with war he was known in the fane founded by Numa near the ancient Forum, as *Ianus Quĭrīnus.* When war was declared, the consul opened the double doors of this sanctuary and summoned the Roman youths capable of bearing arms to march through it with him. As long as war continued, the doors stood open, but on the declaration of peace they were closed. From the time of Numa to the year of the birth of Christ, this happened on four occasions only, and twice in the reign of Augustus. While Janus appears as the most ancient of the Roman gods, he is at the same time named as the most ancient king of the land, who dwelt upon the Jānĭcŭlum on the right bank of the Tiber, and erected a temple to the gods and gave a friendly reception to Saturn. In very late times, he is represented with a bearded and an unbearded face; and, instead of his having the usual attributes of the key and staff, the fingers of his right hand exhibit the number 300 (CCC), and those of his left hand the number of the remaining days of the year (LXV).

Jāsōn. The son of Æsōn, and leader of the Argonauts (*q.v.*), husband of Mēdēa.

Jĕiūnĭum. The first breakfast among the Romans (*see* MEALS). On *Ieiunium Cĕrĕris,* the fast of Ceres, *see* CERES.

Jewellery. *See* TOREUTIC ART.

Jocasta. *See* IOCASTE.

Jordānĕs. An Alanian by birth, and probably bishop of Crŏtōna. He wrote two historical works: (1) a compendium of Universal History down to 552 A.D.; (2) an abstract of Cassiodōrus' History of the Goths (*De Rēbus Gĕtĭcīs*), which, though done in a cursory and unskilful manner, is nevertheless of great value, owing to the loss of the original work.

Jōsĕphus (*Flāvius*). Born at Jerusalem, A.D. 37, of a respectable priestly family. He received a scholarly education, and in 63 went to Rome, where he gained the favour of Poppæa, the wife of Nero. After having returned to his native land, he endeavoured in vain to check the revolt of his own people against the Romans; thereupon he himself joined the rebellion, but, while in command of Galilee, was taken prisoner by the Romans. He was freed from this after two years' captivity, owing to his having prophesied the coming reign of Vespasian, from whom he took the family name of Flavius. After having been present at the siege of Jerusalem, in the suite of Titus, he lived in Rome until his death about 93, devoting himself to learned studies and literary activity. His works, which are written in Greek, are: (1) *The History of the Jewish War*, in seven books, originally composed in Syro-Chaldee, but translated into Greek at the request of Titus. It is remarkable for its masterly delineation of events in which he himself took part or of which he was an eye-witness. (2) *The Jewish Antiquities*, in twenty books; a history of the Jews from the creation down to the twelfth year of Nero (A.D. 66), written with the object of making a favourable impression on the Greeks and Romans. (3) An *Autobiography*, to complete the Jewish History. (4) A treatise in defence of his *Jewish Antiquities* against the attacks of a scholar named *Apīon*. The *Eulogy of the Maccabees* is probably spurious. There is a Latin version of the *History of the Jews*, dating from the end of the 4th century A.D., under the name of *Hēgēsippus*, a corruption of *Josephus*.

Jūdex. In the Roman constitution a general designation of all judges, whether officials exercising judicial functions or individuals in a private position, entrusted on oath with the duty of deciding in either civil or criminal trials. For standing and for extraordinary *criminal courts* (*see* QUÆSTIO) the *iūdĭcēs* were at first chosen from the number of the senators by agreement of the parties concerned. Gaius Gracchus first introduced a list of *iudices* (*album*) for the permanent tribunals (*quæstĭōnes perpĕtŭæ*). At first this list was permanent, but afterwards it was published annually by the *prætor urbānus*, who had to swear that he would be impartial in his selection of names. Under the Empire, as long as the *quæstiones perpetuæ* existed, it was published by the emperor, who nominated the *iudices* to hold office for life, and from time to time revised and completed the list. By the *lex Sempronia* of Gaius Gracchus, B.C. 123, the office of judge was taken away from the senators, who had held it previously, and transferred to the possessors of the knight's census (the *ēquĭtēs*). In B.C. 80 a *lex Cornēlia* of L. Cornelius Sulla restored it to the Senate. In B.C. 70 the office was equally divided between the senators, the knights, and the *tribūni ærārii*. These last were once more excluded by Cæsar. Augustus formed four *dĕcŭrĭæ*, or divisions, of *iudices*. Of these the first three were obliged to possess the knight's census, and the last the half of it. Caligula added a fifth *decuria*.

Under the Empire the judicial functions, hitherto confined to certain definite classes, 'had become so general in their obligations, that it was considered a privilege to be freed from them. This exemption was granted to a man with many children, and, afterwards, to those following the professions of grammarians and teachers. The requisite qualifications, apart from that of property, were that a person should be by birth a citizen, and not less than thirty years of age (after Augustus, not less than twenty-five). The other requirements were bodily and mental capacity, an unblemished reputation, and a long residence in Italy. Under the Republic, the number of those who were sworn in varied at different times; under the Empire it was fixed at 4,000, and later at 5,000. For every court of justice the judges were taken from the general list by lot, and out of this special list the presiding magistrate appointed a definite number for each trial. Out of these a certain number might be challenged and rejected by either side; perhaps the president filled up the vacancies by again drawing lots. The swearing in took place before the trial. When the number of the prætors appointed for the *quæstiones* was not sufficiently large, a *iudex quæstionis* was appointed, generally one who had served as ædile.

In civil cases it was customary from early times for the judicial magistrates, *i.e.* the prætors, to depute the investigation and decision to a person instructed by them and appointed by consent of both sides. From the time of Augustus a single judge (*iudex unus*) was appointed in each case from the general *album* of sworn *iudices*, but for certain cases several judges were introduced. (*See* RECUPERATORES, and JUDICIAL PROCEDURE, II, below.) The *iudices centumvĭri* formed the single great judicial body for trying civil cases. (*See* CENTUMVIRI.) Concerning the *iudices lītĭbus iudicandīs*, who were also appointed in civil cases, *see* VIGINTI-SEX VIRI.

Judicial Procedure. (I) *Athenian.* A clear distinction was drawn at Athens between public and private actions. But it must be remarked that the public actions ncluded more offences than those which directly affected the State. Injuries to individuals might form matter for a public prosecution, if (as, e.g., in a case of theft or damage to property) the wrong to a citizen in his honour or property admitted of being viewed as an attack upon the honour of the citizens or the security of property in general. The difference, both in public and private actions, was essential, whether we consider (a) the right of prosecution, or (b) the consequences of condemnation.

(a) Any one might institute a public prosecution, even if he had himself suffered no wrong. The only condition was that he must be of full age and in possession of all civic rights. It was only in cases of murder that the right of prosecution was limited to the relations of the murdered person. Private prosecutions, on the other hand, could only be undertaken by the injured person or his legal representative, in the case of a ward by his guardian, in that of a married woman by her husband, in that of strangers by their prŏxĕnŏs, in that of resident aliens by their patrons.

(b) In the case of public prosecutions, if a fine was inflicted the amount went into the public treasury; in the case of a private prosecution, to the prosecutor. At public trials other penalties than fines could be inflicted: death, imprisonment, deprivation of civic rights, banishment with confiscation of property. This was not the case in private causes, though in them the State had the right of increasing the penalty. For instance, a prosecution for false witness was not public, but private; yet if a person was convicted three times, the State could inflict deprivation of civil rights. In public causes the prosecutor ran the risk of being himself fined 1,000 drachmæ (£33 6s. 8d.) if he failed to carry at least one-third of the votes of the jurymen: besides which he lost his right of instituting a similar action again. In private causes the prosecutor, if he failed to establish his case, was fined in an amount generally equal to one-sixth of the sum in dispute. A distinction was drawn between assessed and non-assessed causes. The non-assessed were those in which the amount of the fine was already fixed by law, and any further estimate was therefore unnecessary: the assessed causes were all those in which the amount of fine had to be settled according to the character of the offence, or the magnitude of the damage: in other words, those which required that the punishment should be fixed

for the occasion. Besides those prosecutions, the object of which was to get a person punished for an actual breach of law, there were others which merely aimed at settling a disputed right. These were naturally, for the most part, private causes: but there were public prosecutions of this kind as well. For instance, any one who proposed and carried a new law was liable for a whole year after it had passed to prosecution and punishment for making an illegal proposal. But after the year had elapsed his personal responsibility came to an end, and only the new law could be attacked. Private causes could be settled by arrangement, but the law forbade the accuser in a public cause to drop the case. If he did, he was liable to the same punishment as if he had failed to carry one-third of the votes. This was the principle, but it was not always carried out in practice. In certain public causes in which a reward was offered by the State, the prosecutor, if successful, received a share of the fine. The costs of private causes (prўtăncia) were paid by both parties in advance, and returned to the successful suitor by his adversary. These fees amounted, if the sum in dispute were less than 1,000 drachmæ (£33 6s. 8d.), to three drachmæ (about 2s.); if greater, to thirty drachmæ, or about £1. The costs of public prosecutions were not paid by the accused. They were paid by the accuser in one case only; namely, if, in the event of the accused being condemned, the accuser received part of the fine imposed. In testamentary suits, supposing a person to claim an inheritance already assigned to another, or to lay exclusive claim to one which was claimed by several others, the tenth part of the amount was deposited before the trial. If the suit was instituted against the State, supposing the question affected confiscated property, a fifth part of the amount was deposited. The successful litigant in either case received the amount deposited.

As above mentioned, the Athenian law allowed the prosecutor, in many cases, to institute the same suit in various forms. A case of personal injury might be treated either as a private action for assault or as a public action for outrage. In the latter case the prosecutor could make no claim for personal compensation. If the injury was accompanied by aggravating circumstances, supposing, for instance, that the person injured were performing a public function, either form of action was open.

Private actions were often decided by *Diaitĕtai*, or arbitrators (*see* DIÆTETÆ); an important body. For the convenience of persons living outside Athens, thirty (in later times 'forty) local magistrates were appointed by lot, whose business it was to go from place to place and decide petty cases of debt or damage or assault. In cases of murder the jurisdiction belonged to the *Ĕphĕtæ*, in certain other cases to the Senate, the *Ecclēsīa*, the *Strătēgī*, the *Archons*, and the *Eleven* (*see* HENDEKA). The greater number of cases came before the court of the *Hēlīæa* (*see* HELIÆA).

The most general name for a public charge was *grăphē*, or a statement in writing. The *graphe* was only resorted to in cases of offences already recognised by law, and was always brought before a court of law, never before a political body such as the senate or public assembly. On the special forms of public prosecution, *see* APAGOGE, EISANGELIA, ENDEIXIS, PHASIS, PROBOLE. *Dīkē* (suit) was the term for a civil process. Under both forms of action the proceedings were very much the same. Except in certain cases affecting the religious mysteries, they were public, and involved a great many formalities. By way of introducing his case the prosecutor applied to the president of the court, who fixed the date for the preliminary investigation. The summons was made by the prosecutor in a public place and in the presence of witnesses. Aliens were obliged to give security for their appearance; citizens were not, except in case of *ăpăgōgē*, *endeixis*, or *eisangĕlīa*. And in these cases a special summons was sometimes dispensed with, and the accused might be immediately arrested. The charge having been handed in, the presiding judge decided, when the day mentioned in the summons came round, whether he should admit it or not. Various reasons might lead him to dismiss it: the non-appearance of the accused, there being no sufficient evidence to show that he had been summoned; or if the accuser appeared on the whole not justified in bringing the charge; or if the forms were not duly observed. If the charge were admitted, it was publicly posted up on a tablet in the neighbourhood of the court, with a notification of the day when the trial would come on. If the accuser failed to appear on the appointed day, the charge fell through *ipso facto;* if the accused failed without putting in a valid plea for postponement, he was pro-

ceeded against *in contŭmāciam*. If the parties came into court, they were both put on their oath, the accuser with respect to his charge, the accused with regard to his answer. They then paid the court fees.

The accused generally tried, if possible, to prevent the trial coming on. There were many ways of doing this. He might, or another might for him, dispute the admissibility of the charge on various grounds; *e.g.* the legal inability of the prosecutor to prosecute, limitation, want of jurisdiction on the part of the authorities, absence of any law to serve as a basis for the charge, and so on. A witness was usually put forward in cases of disputed inheritance, to prove that the prosecutor had no claim. In either case the trial was postponed until a decision had been come to upon the objection raised by the accused or upon the charge of false testimony brought by him against the witness. If the decision went against the accuser he was obliged to retire from the case. After a decision was given on the objection raised by the accused, the party to whom it was unfavourable had to pay his adversary a fine amounting to a sixth part of the value of the object in dispute.

All the material necessary for the trial, the passages to be quoted from laws, documents, and testimony, had to be prepared by the parties. The evidence consisted of written statements which were given in among the records. The witnesses who were responsible for these might either have made them in person before the magistrates, or in their absence before other witnesses. The witnesses were either willing or unwilling. If a person had at first offered to give evidence and afterwards refused to do so, he might be prosecuted by the person affected by his conduct. If any person, even without having bound himself to appear, refused to give evidence after being formally summoned by the herald, he had to pay into the public treasury a fine of 1,000 *drachmæ*.

The statements of slaves were only accepted as evidence when given under torture in the presence of witnesses, who had to take them down. The owners of slaves offered to submit them to the torture, either on their own will or on the demand of the opposite party, with which, however, they were not bound to comply. The oath was regarded as the ultimate test of truth. It might either be taken by both parties on their own proposal, or be exacted by one party from the other. The taking of the oath or the refusal to take it was put into writing as evidence and enrolled among the archives. These documents were kept by the magistrate in a sealed box, and brought by him into court on the day of trial. In certain cases, such as those relating to commerce, mining, and dowries, the duration of the proceedings was legally limited to thirty days; but in other causes trials would sometimes drag themselves out through a whole year. If one of the parties failed to appear in court on the day appointed, his reason had to be stated on oath by a representative. The other party was free to declare on oath that the reasons alleged were insufficient: if the judge took this view, the proceedings went on *in contumaciam,* and the absent party lost in the suit. In the opposite case the accuser had to propose another date for the trial. In private cases an arrangement might be come to, even in court. The charge and the answer having been read by the clerk, both parties delivered their speeches. These had often been composed for them, for according to strict law the parties could not be represented by advocates. In practice, however, they often contented themselves with a short introductory address of their own, and then asked for permission to employ an advocate.

The first speech and reply were often followed by a second, but the whole number of speeches on each side was not allowed to exceed a certain time measured by the water-clock. The pieces of written evidence were read out by the clerk, during the speaking, in their proper places, but the time which they took was not counted against the speaker. The judge alone had the right of interrupting the speaker. It was usual to introduce the witnesses of parents, wives, children, and influential persons. The voting was secret. Every judge received a black and white pebble (the black for condemnation and the white for acquittal), and put the pebble which indicated his vote into a metal urn, and the other into a wooden one. Stones bored through or left entire, mussel shells, beans, or metal balls were also used for voting.

The verdict was decided by the majority of votes: if they were equal, the accused was acquitted. If the cause was assessed (*ăgōn tĭmētŏs*), a second voting followed, to decide between the punishment proposed by the accuser and the counter-proposal of the accused. There was no appeal, at least against the decision of the public court

of the *Hēlĭastœ.* The utmost that was possible was to get the verdict set aside by proving that the proceedings *in contumaciam* had been illegal, or that the winner had gained the case by suborning false witnesses. The magistrates were, in the case of public actions, responsible for carrying out the punishment. Capital sentences were usually carried out (by poison or strangulation) in prison by the executioner commissioned by the Eleven. (*See* HENDEKA.) The corpses of great criminals were thrown down a precipice or removed over the border. If the sentence were banishment, the condemned person had to leave the country within a certain time at the peril of his life; his property was confiscated. If *ătĭmĭa* were inflicted, and the condemned person attempted to usurp the rights of which he had been deprived, he was liable to severe, even to capital punishment. In case of a fine being inflicted, a man was *ătĭmŏs* till it was paid: if he failed to pay by the time appointed, he was liable to a double punishment, and ultimately to the confiscation of his property. If the amount of his property exceeded the fine, the surplus was returned to him; if it fell short of it, he and his descendants were debtors to the State and *atimoi.* Imprisonment seems to have served only as an increase of sentence or as a means of enforcing sentence. Loss of freedom and sale were only inflicted on non-citizens for usurping civic rights. In private actions the ultimate means of compelling the condemned person to the fulfilment of his obligation was an executory mandate, by which he was declared a debtor to the State in the same sum that he owed the prosecutor, and made *atimos* till it was paid.

(II) *Roman.* Criminal jurisdiction, until the establishment of the Republic, belonged to the kings, and on their commission to the *quœstōrēs parrĭcīdĭī* and the *duo vĭrī perduellĭōnĭs.* (*See* PARRICIDIUM; PERDUELLIO.) After the expulsion of the kings it passed over immediately to the consuls, until the public courts (*iūdĭcĭa pŏpŭlī*) were gradually developed. In capital cases, even in the time of the kings, an appeal was allowed, as an act of grace, from their verdict to the representative assembly, at first to the *cŏmĭtĭa cūrĭāta,* and after Servius Tullius to the *comitia centŭrĭāta.* (*See* PROVOCATIO.) After the establishment of the Republic, it was, in 509 B.C., legally provided that an appeal might be made, in capital cases, from the sentence of the magistrate to the decision of the *comitia centuriata* as a court of appeal. Condemned persons, as a rule, naturally made use of this right, and the magistrates consequently brought their verdict before the *comitia centuriata*, in the form of a charge with reasons to support it. Thus these *comitia* acquired a jurisdiction, dependent, it is true, on a previous judgment of the magistrates, and limited to capital cases which admitted of appeal. The jurisdiction of the *comitia trĭbūta* was developed in the same way. At first these *comitia* had merely served as a court of appeal against the fines imposed by the tribunes for violation of their authority. (*See* MULTA.) But they soon acquired jurisdiction in all cases involving fines, and quite overshadowed the *comitia centuriata* in importance. The judicial power of the latter was gradually more and more restricted by the increasing habit of referring cases of common offences to exceptional commissions (*quæstiones extraordĭnārĭæ*. At last trials for *perduellio* were the only ones in which they retained their judicial competence. But the greatest possible number of cases were brought before the *comitia tributa*, notably those of a political character in which illegal or mischievous administration was in question. Only the name of *perduellio* was avoided. The distinction between the judicial competence of the two assemblies was founded, not so much on differences in the offences, as in those of the penalties. Whether the *comitia centuriata* or *comitia tributa* were to take cognisance of an offence depended on the light in which the magistrates regarded it. If they thought less seriously of it, it would go before the *comitia tributa*, which had only the power of inflicting fines to the amount of half the property: if more seriously, before the *comitia centuriata*, which could only pass capital sentences : in early times death, in later times the *interdictĭo ăquæ et ignis*, and the confiscation of property which accompanied them. (*See* EXILIUM.)

The proceedings in the assembly were opened by the accusing magistrate. In the *comitia centuriata* this would be a consul or prætor, in the *comitia tributa* a tribune, ædile, or quæstor. The trial began with the *dĭĕī dictĭō*, or fixing of a day for the proceedings. The accused was then either put into prison, or left free on giving bail for his appearance. To give the people some means of arriving at a conclusion on the guilt or innocence of the accused, a preliminary investigation was held in three *contĭōnēs* at intervals of some days. Before these the accused was allowed to defend himself against the charge of the magistrate. At the last *contio* the magistrate pronounced a provisional verdict, which (if adverse) was taken as a definite charge. At the same time he fixed the day for the meeting of the *comitia*, always allowing an interval of thirty days. At the meeting of the *comitia*, supposing nothing had occurred to stop the proceedings—*i.e.* supposing the accused had gone into voluntary exile, or a tribune had interposed his *veto*, or the accuser had withdrawn the charge—the accuser made his proposal (*rŏgātio*) to punish the accused. Thereupon the accused (or his advocate) spoke in his defence, the evidence of the witnesses who had been previously called was shortly gone through, and the proofs laid before the assembly. Finally the votes were taken in the usual manner, and the result at once made known. A prosecution which remained unfinished at the expiration of the appointed time was not continued, but the accusêd was regarded as acquitted. The condemnation of the accused was followed by the immediate infliction of the penalty. The sentence could only be reversed by a subsequent resolution of the people. (*See* RESTITUTIO.) The popular tribunals fell gradually into disuse : the standing judicial courts or *quæstiones* arose, the first of which was instituted in B.C. 149. In Cicero's time there were eight of these commissions, each presided over by a prætor or his representative. These courts were respectively appointed to try the following offences : (1) *Rĕpĕtundæ*, or official extortion ; (2) *Māiestās*, or treason against the majesty of the State ; (3) *Pĕcŭlātus*, or embezzlement ; (4) *Ambĭtus*, or attempt to gain office by unlawful means ; (5) *Vīs*, or violence ; (6) *De Sĭcārĭīs*, or murder ; (7) *Adultĕrium*, or adultery ; (8) *Falsum*, or forgery. (*See* AMBITUS, MAIESTAS, PECULATUS, REPETUNDÆ, VIS.) Any citizen, not an official, might bring the charge. On the proceedings, *see* QUÆSTIO.

The *comitia tributa* were, after this, only set in motion in cases for which there was no *quæstio perpetua*, or for which it was thought improper to institute a *quæstio extraordĭnārĭa*. The popular tribunals of the *comitia* came to an end with the Republic, but the *quæstiones* continued until the 2nd century A.D. to act as the regular criminal courts. Under the Empire the

enate and the emperor had an extra-
rdinary jurisdiction in criminal cases.
The senatorial court, which met under the
residency of the consuls, followed the pro-
edure of the *quæstiones*, but its proceed-
ngs were not public. The cases which
t tried were usually those which affected
ersons of high standing charged with
olitical or official offences. The decision
f the court took the form of a *sĕnātūs
onsultum*, but had all the force of a legal
entence. The emperor, in virtue of his
ribunician authority, had the power of
eutralizing it by his veto. An interval
f ten days occurred between sentence and
xecution, in pursuance of an order of
Tiberius made in 22 A.D. But up to that
ime the sentence was carried out immediately after being passed, even in capital
ases. Capital punishment had in the re-
ublican times been practically abolished,
ut was at once reinstated under the
mperial *régime*. The emperor himself
isually exercised his jurisdiction only over
is own procurators and the higher officers
f the army, notably in the case of strictly
iilitary offences. He acted as sole judge
ven when he invited the assistance of a
ury (*consĭlĭum*). No formal act of accusa-
ion was required. Cases which he was
unwilling to settle himself he would gene-
ally hand over to the *quæstiones* or the
enatorial tribunals. The power of inflict-
ng sentence of death on Roman citizens
vas confined originally to the emperor and
enate; but in later times the emperor, by
a special mandate, transferred it for purposes of provincial administration, to the
governors of the provinces, whose jurisdiction extended to all citizens, with the
xception of the high military officers,
enators, and the *dĕcŭrĭōnēs* of a *mŭnĭ-
ĭpĭum*. (*See* DECURIO, 2.) The criminal
jurisdiction in Rome and its neighbourhood
for a radius of 100 miles was given to the
præfectus urbi, whose court ended by
becoming the chief criminal court in the
capital. The rest of Italy was placed under
the jurisdiction of the præfect of the Prætorian Guard. From the decision of these
representatives of the imperial authority an
appeal was allowed to the emperor. But,
after the 3rd century A.D., the appeal
mostly came before the præfect of the body-
guard, whose judgment was generally final.
The senatorial court came finally to acting
only on the motion of the emperor.

The Roman civil jurisdiction, like the
criminal, belonged originally to the king,
from whom it passed to the consuls. With
them it remained until a special magistracy, the prætorship, was instituted for it.
(*See* PRÆTOR.) According to ancient usage,
the highest judicial authorities did not
superintend the case from beginning to end.
Their action was usually confined to the
preparation of the case and such measures
as its course made absolutely necessary, as
(supposing their interference was required)
in ordering execution of sentence. The
investigation proper, and the passing of
judgment, they as a rule handed over
(with the consent of the parties) either to
a single judge (*see* JUDEX) or *rĕcŭpĕrātōrēs*
(*see* RECUPERATORES) appointed for the
occasion, or to the judicial *collegia* of the
iudices decemviri and *centumviri*, appointed, independently of special cases, for
the whole year. As an introduction of the
case, the plaintiff (*pĕtĭtor*) was required to
bring the defendant (*rĕus*) before the tribunal of the magistrate (*in iūs*). In the case
of the prætor, this would be his tribunal
in the Forum. If the accused failed either
to obey the personal summons of the plaintiff (*in ius vŏcātĭō*) or to appear by his
representative (*vindex*), the plaintiff could,
after calling a witness to attest that his
summons was in order, take him before
the prætor by force. In later time, to meet
the cases in which the accused was unable
to answer the summons immediately, the
vadimonium was introduced. This was
a promise, given by the accused on the
security of sureties, that he would appear
in court on a certain day, or if he failed
would pay a sum of money, the amount
of which depended on the nature of the
question in dispute. The proceedings *in
iure*, or before the magistrate, took place
according to certain definite formal rules,
the so-called *lĕgĭs actĭōnēs*, the commonest
of which was the *actio sacrāmentĭ*. This
was accompanied by the utterance of a
solemn formula partly by the magistrate,
partly by the parties, and by certain symbolical acts. The smallest departure from
the traditional formula involved the loss of
the suit. The trial thus commenced, the
next step was the *iudicis dātĭō*, or appointment of a judge to try it. The case came
on before the appointed *iudex* (*in iudicio*)
on a day appointed. It was first shortly
stated; the parties or their advocates made
their speeches, the evidence was tested and
judgment pronounced.

The cumbrous machinery of the *lĕgĭs
actiones* gave way afterwards, in all cases

but a few, to the procedure by *formŭla*. The *formula* was a document written out by the prætor, in which he, after hearing the parties, summed up the points of the accusation and the replies of the accused, appointed the judge, and gave him the materials for investigation and judgment. The proceedings *in iu̇dicio* were then opened with the production of the *formula*. The question of the debt being settled, the judge proceeded to make a valuation of the object in dispute, in case a definite amount had not been mentioned in the formula. On the procedure in case of default, *see* CONTUMACIA. The judgment was irreversible. It was only in certain exceptional cases, notably if it appeared that any deception or force had been employed, that the magistrate who had appointed the judge, or his successor in office, could set it aside by *restĭtūtĭō in intĕgrum*. If the condemned party refused to make the payment, the magistrate who had prepared the ˙case could order personal arrest or seizure of goods. (*See* MANUS INIECTIO and BONORUM EMPTIO.)

The only weapon against abuse of judicial authority in the republican age was the right of appeal to a magistrate with the power of *veto*. (*See* APPELLATIO.)

The system of civil jurisdiction continued to exist in the imperial period, though with many modifications in detail, until the 3rd century A.D. After that, the exceptional procedure (*extrā ordĭnem*) in which the magistrate superintended the case till its conclusion and pronounced judgment at the end of it, became the usual one. The emperor, as supreme judge, had the power of deciding every case, criminal or otherwise, if his decision was appealed to. Further, he could interfere by his decree during the course of the trial, and either quash the verdict himself, or lay the appeal for decision before an authority constituted by himself for the purpose. In later times this authority was the *præfectus urbi*. A further appeal from this authority back to the emperor was allowed.

Jūdĭcium. The Latin name for a court : *iudicium pŏpŭli*, a court in which the *populus* acted as *iūdĭcēs*. *Iudicium prīvātum*, a civil, *iudicium publĭcum*, a criminal court; *iudicium dŏmestĭcum*, a family court. (*See* JUDICIAL PROCEDURE.)

Jūgĕrum. The unit of superficial measure among the Romans. A rectangle 240 Roman feet in length and 120 feet broad = 28,800 Roman square feet = rather more

than half an English acre of 43,560 square feet. Two hundred *iŭgĕră* form one *cen-tŭrĭa* [about 132 acres].

Julian Calendar. *See* CALENDAR.

Jūlĭānus. (1) *Salvius.* An eminent Roman jurist, born in Africa, who lived in the days of Hadrian. Besides many original works which were long held in high esteem he compiled at the command of the emperor in 131 A.D., a systematic collection of Edicts of the Prætors, beginning with the republican time (*edictum perpĕtŭum*). This was the first scientific collection of Roman legal documents. Numerous fragments of his works are quoted in the Digest. *Cf.* CORPUS JURIS CIVILIS (2).

(2) *Flavius Claudius*, "the Apostate. Born at Constantinople A.D. 331 ; he was the son of Julius Constantius, a brother of Constantine the Great. In spite of his early monastic education, he was so strongly prepossessed against the Christian religion owing to the murderous deeds of his own family, the persecutions he suffered at the hands of his cousin Constantius, and his own intercourse with the most renowned Sophists both in Nĭcŏmēdīa and at Athens, that, on his elevation to the imperial throne in 361, he attempted to drive out Christianity, and to restore Paganism on the foundation of Neo-Platonic philo-sophy. His attempts were however cut short by his death in the war against the Persians. We still possess eight essays written by him in Greek, in the form of speeches; seventy-eight letters of the most varied contents, valuable as throwing light on his character and his aims ; and two satirical writings : (i) *The Cæsars, or the Banquet*, a brilliant criticism on the Roman emperors, from Cæsar downwards, in the form of Varro's Menippean satires ; (ii) the *Mĭsŏpōgōn* (Beard-Hater), a satire directed against the inhabitants of Antioch, who had cast ridicule on his beard and his philosophic garb. Of his work directed against the Christians and their religion, which he composed in Antioch before the expedition against the Persians, only extracts and fragments survive. Julian is one of the cleverest, most cultivated and elegant writers of the period after the birth of Christ.

Jūlĭus Căpĭtōlīnus. A Roman historian (*See* SCRIPTORES HISTORIÆ AUGUSTÆ.)

Jūlĭus Vălĕrius. The Latin translator of the romance of pseudo-Callisthĕnēs on Alexander the Great. (*See* CALLISTHENES.)

Jūnĭus Cordus. A Roman historian. (*See* SCRIPTORES HISTORIÆ AUGUSTÆ.)

Jūnō (i.e. *Iovino*, a feminine form corresponding to *Iŏvis* contained in *Iūpĭter*). In the Italian mythology, the queen of heaven and of heavenly light, especially that of the new moon; the wife of Jupiter. After she had been identified with the Greek Hēra (*q.v.*), she was regarded as the daughter of Sāturnus (who was identified with Crŏnus), and as sister of her husband. In Italy, as the queen of womankind, she was the representative of woman in general, to such a degree that, as every man had his *Gĕnĭus*, so every woman had her *Iuno*, to whom she offered sacrifice and by whom she swore. It was as *Iuno Lūcīna* (the bringer of light) that she was worshipped from the most ancient times and in many parts of Italy. As such, she was the goddess of the beginnings of all the months, and on the calends, at Rome, the *rex sacrorum* and his wife made regular sacrifices to her. As all goddesses of light are also goddesses of birth (the appearance of the light from out of the darkness being looked on as a birth), under the same name of *Lucina* she was honoured as the mightiest of the goddesses of birth. Her temple at Rome, in a sacred grove, was one of the most ancient and venerated. By a custom dating back to Numa, a piece of gold was placed in her treasury there at the birth of every male child. The *Mātrōnālia* (*q.v.*) was the most famous feast of the goddess. It was celebrated by the Roman matrons and virgins on the 1st March. At this festival the goddess was represented veiled, with a flower in her right hand, and an infant in swaddling clothes in her left. Another ancient worship highly honoured throughout Italy was that of *Iuno Sōspĭta* (the Saviour), whose ancient grove and temple at Lānŭvĭum was deemed sacred at Rome, which itself had two temples to this divinity. At an appointed time in every year the Roman consuls offered a sacrifice to the Juno at Lanuvium. The image of the goddess at that place wore, over the robes of a matron, a goatskin which served as helmet and cuirass, with a shield held in one hand and a spear brandished in the other. This worship assigned to the goddess who presided over the life of woman the character of a divinity of protecting power.

Iuno Cŭrītis, or *Quĭrītis* (*i.e.* armed with a spear), who was specially worshipped by the Sabines, was also a warlike goddess. As goddess of marriage Juno was invoked at weddings under many names. As *Dŏmĭdūca* she conducts the bride into the bridegroom's house; as *Unxĭa* she anoints the doorposts as a sign of good omen at her reception; as *Cinxĭa* she ties and unlooses the marriage girdle; and as *Pronūba* and *Iŭga* she is the foundress of marriage. On the citadels of towns, which were deemed to be under her particular protection, she was specially worshipped by matrons, either with Jupiter, or alone, as *Iuno Rēgĭna*, being the wife of *Iūpĭter Rex* and the highest celestial goddess. In this capacity she had her chief temple at Rome, on the Capitol, close to Jupiter. It was there that the well-known geese were kept, which were sacred to her as being prolific and domesticated creatures. Another highly honoured fane of *Iuno Regina* was on the Aventine, to which her worship had been transplanted from Veii after the destruction of that city. There was also a temple on the Capitol dedicated to *Iuno Mŏnēta* ("the admonisher"), in gratitude (it was said) for her salutary admonitions [Cic., *De Divinatione*, i 45 § 101]. Money derived from the goddess its designation *Moneta*, as it was coined in the temple of *Iuno Moneta*. Another most ancient Roman worship was that of *Iuno Caprŏtīna* (Juno of the goat). This was celebrated by the festival held by female slaves on the 7th July, called *Nōnæ Caprotinæ*. (*See* CAPROTINA.) In the third Punic War the worship of *Iuno Cœlestis* was brought into Rome from Carthage. This was the ancient tutelary goddess of Carthage, strictly speaking the Astarte of the Phœnicians. When Carthage was restored under the Empire, her worship flourished anew. Not only the goose, but also the raven that loves the heights, was sacred to her as the protectress of citadels.

Jūpĭtĕr (*Iuppĭtĕr*). In the Italian mythology, the highest god in heaven, corresponding to the Greek Zeus (*q.v.*), with whom he was identical, not only in his nature, but also in his name. For Jupiter is compounded of *Iŏvĭs* (an older form is *Diovis*) and *păter*; Zeus stands for *Dieus* (Indian *Diaus* = " the bright heaven "). As in course of time the Italian god became identified with the Greek, he was regarded as a son of Saturn and of Ops, the deities deemed to correspond to the Greek Urănus and Rhea respectively. From Jupiter comes all that appears in the heavens. As *Lūcĕtius* (from *lux*, "light ") he is the bringer of light, the cause of the dawn of day, as well as of the full moon at night. Just as the calends (1st) of each month are sacred to Juno, so the ides (13th or 15th), which are full-moon days, are sacred to Jupiter. On these his special priest, the *flāmĕn dĭālis*, offers him the *Idūlia*, a sacrifice of a white lamb. While he watches over fair weather, he also controls all other weather; as *Fulgŭrātor* and *Fulmĭnātor* ("flasher of lightning ") and as *Tŏnans* or *Tŏnitrŭālis* ("thunderer ") he brings down those fearful storms which were familiar to Rome; as *Plŭvius* he sends a fertilizing rain. Any place, or thing, struck by lightning was supposed to be sacred to Jupiter as having been taken possession of by him, and thus it needed a particular dedication. (*See* PUTEAL.) As the god of rain, there was instituted in his honour at Rome a festival of supplication, called *ăquælĭcĭum*. In this the *pontĭfĭcēs* brought into Rome from the temple of Mars outside the *Porta Căpēna* a cylindrical stone called the *lăpĭs mānālĭs* (rain-stone), while the matrons followed the procession with bare feet, as did also the magistrates, unaccompanied by their *insignia*. In the same character he was appealed to by the country-folk, before sowing time and in the spring and autumn, when a sacrificial feast was offered to him. He and Juno were worshipped before the commencement of the harvest, even before any sacrifice to Ceres. Throughout all Latium, the feast of the *Vīnālĭa* (*q.v.*) was celebrated in his honour as the giver of wine; and at the commencement of the vintage season he was offered a lamb by the *flamen Dialis*. He was honoured in all Italy, after Mars, as the decider of battles and giver of victory; this was specially the case at Rome, where, as early as the days of Rŏmŭlus, shrines were founded to him as *Stător* ("he who stays flight ") and *Fĕretrius* (to whom the spoils taken by a Roman general in the field from a hostile general were offered. *See* SPOLIA). He watches over justice and truth, and is therefore the most ancient and most important god of oaths; he was specially called on by the *fĕtĭālēs* (*q.v.*) as a witness at the ceremonies connected with treaties of peace. Not only the law of nations, but also the law of hospitality, is under his special protection, and while he causes his blessing to fall on the whole country, he is also the god of good fortune and blessing to the family. His gracious power does not confine itself to the present alone; by means of signs comprehensible to experts, he reveals the future (*see* AUSPICIA) and shows his approval or disapproval of a contemplated undertaking.

He was worshipped of old on the Alban Hill, by the Latin people, as their ancestral god, under the name of *Iuppiter Lătiāris* (or *Lătiālis*); at the formation of the Latin league he was honoured as the god of the league by a sacrificial feast, which they all held in common; even after its dissolution the sacrifice was continued under the superintendence of the consuls. (*See* FERIÆ.) The chief seat of his worship in Rome was the Capitol, where he was honoured as the ideal head of the State, as the Increaser and Preserver of Roman might and power, under the name of *Iuppĭter Optĭmus Maxĭmus* ("Best and Greatest "). It was there that his earthenware image was enthroned, with the thunderbolt in its right hand. It stood in the centre of the temple begun by Tarquĭnius Sŭperbus, the last of the kings, and finished and dedicated in the first year of the Republic. In the pediment of the temple was the *quadrīga*, the attribute of the god of thunder, while the chambers to the left and right were dedicated to Juno and to Minerva respectively. Here the consuls, at their entry into office and their departure to war, made their solemn vows; hither came the triumphal procession of the victor, who was clad in the festal garb of the god, and who, before offering to Jupiter the customary thank-offering of white oxen, prayed to his image and placed in his lap the laurel-wreath of victory bound about the *fascēs*. Hither poured in, to adorn the temple and to fill its treasures, countless multitudes of costly votive offerings from the State, from generals and private citizens, and from foreign kings and nations. When, after its existence for 400 years, the ancient temple was destroyed by fire in B.C. 83, it was rebuilt on its original plan but with increased magnificence (B.C. 78). The image of the god was a copy in gold and ivory of the Olympian Zeus (*q.v.*). The temple was burnt down again A.D. 70, and Vespasian had scarcely restored it when a fresh fire burnt it down A.D. 80, whereupon Domitian in A.D. 82 erected the temple which continued to stand as late as the 9th century.

As was natural for the most exalted god of the Roman State, he had the most splendid festivals in his honour. Amongst the greatest of these were the *lūdī Rōmānī*, the *ludi magni*, and the *ludi plĕbeii*. (*See* GAMES.) Under the Empire the Capitoline Jupiter was recognised as the loftiest representative of the Roman name and State, whose vicegerent on earth was the emperor. As his worship gradually spread over the whole empire, he finally became the representative of the pagan world in general. He was often identified with the native gods of the provinces, including the sun-god of Hēliŏpŏlĭs and Dŏlĭchē in Syria, who, from the 2nd and 3rd centuries A.D., was worshipped far and wide under the name of *Iuppiter Heliopolītānus* and *Dolichēnus*. Antonīnus built for the former the magnificent temple of Heliopolis, or Baalbec. He was similarly identified with various Celtic and German gods, especially those who were worshipped on Alpine mountain-tops as protectors of travellers. As an example of the latter we have *Iuppiter Optimus Maximus Pœnīnus*, whose seat was on the Great St. Bernard.

Jurisprudence. The science of law is the one branch of Roman literature which had a purely national development. From an early date there were definite legal ordinances in Rome, and shortly after the expulsion of the kings a collection of *lēgēs rēgiœ* was made by a certain Gaius Pāpīrius. These consisted of archaic customary laws of a strongly sacerdotal character, and arbitrarily attributed to individual kings (known as the *Iūs Pāpīriānum*). However, the foundation of the collective legal life of the Romans was primarily the well known law of the Twelve Tables, B.C. 451-450. (*See* TWELVE TABLES.) This put an end to the want of a generally known law; for the knowledge of previous legal decisions, like the whole of the judicial procedure, had been hitherto kept in the exclusive possession of the patricians. The administration of the law remained as formerly in the hands of the patricians alone, for they kept from the plebeians all knowledge of the *dĭēs fastī* and *nĕfasti*, i.e. the days on which legal proceedings might or might not be taken, as also the forms of pleading which were regularly employed (*lēgĭs actĭōnēs*). The latter were so highly important that the least infraction of them would involve the loss of the cause. This condition of things existed for a long time, until *Appius Claudius Cœcus* drew up a calendar of the days on which causes could be pleaded, and a list of the forms of pleading. These were made public about 304 B.C. by his secretary, Gnæus Flāvius, after whom they were then called *Ius Flaviānum*. By these means a knowledge of the law became generally attainable. It soon had eminent representatives among the plebeians in the

persons of *Publius Semprōnius Sŏphus* and *Tĭbĕrius Coruncānĭus*. In ancient days, however, the work of the jurists was purely practical. It was considered an honourable thing for men learned in the law to allow people to consult them (*consŭlĕre*, hence *iuris*, or *iure consulti*) either in the Forum or at appointed hours in their own houses, and to give them legal advice (*responsa*). It was mainly by a kind of oral tradition that the knowledge of law was handed down, as the most eminent jurists allowed younger men to be present at these consultations as listeners (*audītōrēs* or *discĭpŭlī*). The beginning of literary activity in this department, as in others, dates from the second Punic War. It begins with the earliest exposition of existing law. *Sextus Ælius Cātus* published in 204 B.C. a work named *Tripertīta* (from its being divided into three parts) or *Ius Æliānum*, which consisted of the text of the laws of the Twelve Tables together with interpretations, and the legal *formŭlœ* for carrying on suits. From the middle of the 2nd century it became common to make collections of the *responsa* of eminent jurists, and to use them as a source of legal information. Among others, *Marcus Porcius Cāto*, the son of Cato the Elder, made a collection of this kind. In some families knowledge of the law was in a measure hereditary, as in those of the Ælii, Porcii, Sulpĭcii, and Mūcii. A member of the last family, the pontifex *Quintus Mūcius Scœvŏla* (died B.C. 82), was the first who, with the aid of the formal precision of the Stoic philosophy, gave a scientific and systematic account of all existing law, in his work, *De Iure Cīvīli*. *Servius Sulpĭcius Rufus*, the contemporary and friend of Cicero, further advanced this new and more methodical treatment of law by his numerous writings and by training up pupils, such as *Aulus Ofilius* and *Publius Alfēnus Vārus*. The former rendered great assistance to Cæsar in his scheme for forming the whole of the *Ius Civile* into a single code. Besides these there were several eminent jurists at the close of the Republic: Gaius Trēbātius Testa, Quintus Ælius Tŭbĕro, Gaius Ælius Gallus, and Aulus Cascellius.

While under the Republic the learned jurist had held an inferior position to the orator in influence and importance, there is no doubt that under the Empire public eloquence became subordinate, and the position of the jurists was the most coveted and influential in the State, especially when

Augustus decreed that the opinions of jurists authorized by the head of the State were to have the validity of law. It was from the jurists as advisers of the emperor that all legislation now proceeded. They had access to all the highest offices of the court and of the State. Accordingly the men of the highest gifts and character betook themselves naturally to this profession, and even introduced into the laws an increased unity, consistency, and systematic order. Under Augustus two jurists were pre-eminent, *Quintus Antistius Lăbĕŏ* and *Gaius Atēius Căpĭtŏ*, the founders of the two later schools, named, after their pupils Sempronius Prŏcŭlus and Masurius Sabīnus, the *Proculiăni* and *Sabīni* respectively. Labeo sought to extend his professional knowledge, whilst Capito held fast to the traditions of former jurists.

The first scientific collection of laws was made under Hadrian by the Sabinian lawyer *Salvius Iuliánus*, with his *Edictum Perpetuum*, a classified collection of the prætorian edicts from the times of the Republic. (*See* EDICTUM.) *Sextus Pompōnius*, his somewhat younger contemporary, composed amongst other things a history of the law till the time of Hadrian.

Under the Antonines jurisprudence was able to claim a remarkable representative in the Asiatic *Gaius*, but it received its completion and conclusion in the first half of the 3rd century A.D., through *Æmilius Păpīniănus, Domitius Ulpiănus,* and *Iulius Paulus.* After their time there were no jurists of great and original capacity. In the 4th century literary activity revived again, but confined itself to the collection of legal authorities, especially that of imperial ordinances. Thus the *Cŏdex Theodōsiănus,* finished in A.D. 438, contains an official record of all the enactments decreed by the emperors from the time of Constantine. Under *Justinian I* (527-565 A.D.) the last and most complete Roman collection of laws was made, under the name of the *Corpus Iuris Civilis* (*q.v.*).

Justĭniănus. *See* CORPUS JURIS CIVILIS.

Justīnus. A Latin author, who composed, probably in the 2nd century A.D., an abstract, still extant, of the Universal History of Pompeius Trogus (*Trogi Pompēi Histŏrĭārum Philippicārum Epitŏma*). It enjoyed a great reputation in the Middle Ages. Of the circumstances of his life nothing is known.

Jūstĭtĭum. The term by which the Romans designated a legal vacation, or cessation from business in the courts of justice, in the sittings of the senate, and even in private life, when all the shops were closed. This took place on extraordinary occasions, such as famine, or during the perils of war, and, under the Empire on the death of a member of the imperial family. It was decreed by the highest magistrate present in Rome, subject to the approval of the senate. When the occasion had passed by, it was removed by a special edict on the part of the magistrate.

Jūturna. An old Latin goddess of fountains, sometimes said to have been beloved by Jupiter, from whom she received the dominion over all the rivers and waters of Latium. She is also called the wife of Janus, and by him the mother of Fontus the god of springs. Vergil makes her the sister of Turnus of Ardĕa, king of the Rŭtŭli, probably in allusion to a spring named after her in the country between Ardea and Lavīnium. Besides the pond of Juturna in the Forum at Rome, there was also a spring bearing her name in the Campus Martius, the water of which was considered sacred and salutary, and was therefore employed in all sacrificial rites and services, and also used by sick people. On January 11th, the anniversary of the day on which her temple was erected in the Campus Martius by Lutatius Catulus, all workmen engaged on aqueducts and the like celebrated the *Juturnalia.* As a goddess who dispenses water, she was, together with Vulcan, specially invoked at the breaking out of fires. [*Iuturna* = *Dĭūturna*.]

Jŭvĕnālis (*Dĕcĭmus Iūnius*). The great Roman satirist, born at Aquīnum, a town of the Volscians, about 47 A.D. According to the accounts of his life which have come down to us, he was the son, either real or adopted, of a wealthy freedman, and spent the first half of his life in Rome engaged in declamatory exercises more for pleasure than as a preparation for the Forum or the schools. He continued there until he became a knight. In an inscription of the time of Domitian he is named as *duumvir* and as a *flamen* of Vespasian in his native town, and also as tribune of the first Dalmatian cohort. The command of a cohort is also specified in the accounts already mentioned. According to these he was sent into banishment under the pretence of military distinction, because in a satirical composition he had taken the liberty of denouncing the political influence of a favourite comedian of the emperor

s to the place and date of his banishment,
ne accounts vary between Britain and
gypt, and also between the last years of
Domitian (against which theory there are
weighty objections) and the reigns of either
rajan or Hadrian. In any case he died
fter 127 A.D., according to one account, in
ne eighty-second year of his life, or about
30, the cause being grief at his exile. By
thers he is made to return to Rome before
is death. We possess sixteen satires by
im, which the grammarians have divided
nto five books. In these he delineates with
noral indignation and with pitiless scorn the
niversal corruption of society, particularly
n the times of Domitian, painting its vices
n all their nakedness and ugliness with
he most glaring colours. His composition
s often concise to the verge of obscurity,
nd by its strong rhetorical colouring be-
rays his earlier studies. In his own day,
nd afterwards, his satires enjoyed great
popularity, and were held in high repute
ven in the Middle Ages. Owing to his
bscurity he early attracted the attention
f learned men of old, and we still possess
he remains of their industry in a collection
f Scholia. [About the life of the poet

nothing certain can be really ascertained
except from the hints given in his own
writings. The biographies which have
come down to us must be used with extreme caution: and it is not at all certain
that the inscription mentioned above refers
to him at all.]

Jŭvencus (Gaius Vettius Aquĭlius). A
Christian Latin poet and a presbyter in
Spain. About 330 he composed a poetic
version of the gospel narrative (Histŏria
Evangĕlĭca) in four books; he also cast the
books of Moses and Joshua [and Judges] into
the form and phraseology of the Roman epic
poets. This seems to have been the earliest
attempt to make the Christian literature
rival the pagan in beauty of form, and to
supplant and supersede heathen poetry as
a means of education. [The epic paraphrase
of the Heptateuch is now no longer ascribed
to Juvencus, but to Cyprian, not the bishop
of Carthage, but a Gaul of the 6th century,
in all probability the third bishop of Toulon.
(The Latin Heptateuch, critically reviewed
by Prof. Mayor, pp. xxxiv-xlii). See
CYPRIAN, 2.]

Jŭventas. The Roman goddess of youth.
(See HEBE.)

K see C

Knights. See EQUITES and HIPPEIS.

L

Labdăcus. Son of Pŏlўdōrus, grandson of
Cadmus, and father of Lāïus (q.v.).

Lăbĕrĭus (Dĕcĭmus). The originator and
leading representative of the mime (q.v.) as
a form of literature; born about 105 B.C.
Being a Roman knight with a strong love
of freedom, he roused the wrath of the
dictator Cæsar; accordingly in B.C. 45
he latter compelled him to appear on the
stage at the age of sixty, and to compete
with his rival Publilius Syrus. In the pro-
ogue to the piece, one of the most beautiful
monuments of Roman literature which have
come down to us, Laberius complains bit-
erly of the indignity put upon him. His
appearing as an actor involved the loss of
knightly rank, which in this case, however,
was restored to him by Cæsar. He died
t Pŭtĕŏli in 43. Apart from the prologue
already mentioned, we have only unimpor-
ant fragments of more than forty of his
mimes These bear witness to the origina-
ity of his wit and the vigour of his style.

Lăcerna. The Latin term for a coarse,
dark-coloured cloak, fastened on the shoulder
by a brooch, which was in use as a protection against rain. It was provided with a
hood. In later times the name was given
to a light and elegant mantle, either white or
dyed in Tyrian purple, which was worn over
the toga to complete the costume at games
or other outdoor occasions. In the time of
Augustus, who forbade its use in the Forum
or Circus, it formed part of the military
uniform. It was afterwards commonly
worn even in Rome itself.

Lăchĕsis (Greek). One of the three
goddesses of fate. (See MŒRÆ.)

Lăcŏnĭcum. A species of dry sweating-
bath, introduced from Greece by the Romans
towards the end of the Republic. It was
specially used to correct the effects of
excessive indulgence at the table, by inducing severe perspiration; at the conclusion
of the process it was usual to take either a
cold plunge or a shower-bath. The dry

sweating-bath was taken in a small, circular room, covered with a cupola, and capable of being raised to a high degree of temperature. Its sole light was admitted through a hole in its vaulted roof. Under this opening there hung on chains a bronze shield (*clĭpeus*), by elevating and depressing which it was possible to regulate the temperature.

Lactantĭus (*Firmĭānus*). A pupil of Arnŏbius, summoned by Diocletian to teach rhetoric in the school of Nīcŏmēdīa in Bithynia. Here he embraced Christianity (before A.D. 303), and in his old age (about 317) he became the teacher, in Gaul, of Crispus, the son of Constantine the Great. He is remarkable above all Christian authors for the purity and smoothness of his style, for which he was indebted to the careful study of Cicero, so much so indeed, as to have earned the title of the Christian Cicero. His great work is the "Introduction to Divine Knowledge" (*Divinæ Institūtiōnes*), in seven books. A poem on the phœnix, in eighty-five couplets, is also ascribed to him; but this ascription is doubtful.

Lăcūnārĭa (*Lăcŭārĭa, Lăquĕārĭa*). The Latin name for the panelled ceilings of rooms which were formed by placing planks across the beams of the roof, whereby hollow spaces were produced. These spaces were covered with wood or ivory, or ornamented with sculptured reliefs or pictures; occasionally they were even gilded or inlaid with plates of gold. [Horace, *Odes*, ii 18, 1.] In banqueting-rooms they were sometimes so formed that the panels could be slipped aside to let flowers, wreaths, and other complimentary presents fall in showers on the guests below. [Suetonius, *Nero*, 31.]

Lādōn. The hundred-headed dragon, who watched over the garden of the Hespĕrĭdĕs (*q.v.*); the son of Phorcys (or of Typhōn) and of Cētō. He was slain by Hērăclēs when he went to fetch the golden apples.

Læna. An ancient Roman garment. It was a woollen mantle, fastened by a brooch, of a coarse, shaggy material, twice as thick as an ordinary *tŏga*. Under the Empire it was very generally worn as an outer cloak by all classes of society, especially on going out to supper.

Lăërtēs. King of Ithăca, and son of Arcĭsius, a son of Zeus. He was the husband of Anticleia and father of Odysseus (*q.v.*).

Læstrȳgŏnĕs. In Homer, a race of giants and cannibals dwelling in the distant north, where the nights are so short that the shepherd driving his flock out meets the

shepherd who is driving his flock in. The city was Tēlĕpȳlus, founded by Lămus. When Odysseus (*q.v.*) came there on his wanderings, their king was Antĭphātēs. The later Greeks placed the home of the Læstrygonians in Sicily, to the south of Etna, near the town of Leontīni; the Romans, on the southern coast of Latium near Formiæ. [Homer, *Od.* x 82, 106; Thuc., vi 2; Cic., *Ad Atticum* ii 13; Horace, *Odes* iii 16, 34.] (*See* PAINTING, fig. 5.)

Lævĭus. A Roman epic and lyric poet (*See* EPOS and LYRIC POETRY.)

Lăgœna, Lăgŏna; Lăgȳnŏs. *See* VESSELS

Lāĭus. The son of Labdăcus, grandson of Pŏlȳdōrus, and great-grandson of Cadmus. When his guardian Lycus was banished or slain by Amphīon (*q.v.*) and Zēthus, he fled to Pĕlops. At the death of the usurpers he ascended the throne of his fathers and married Jŏcasta. (*See* ŒDIPUS.)

Lampădēdrŏmĭa. *See* TORCH-RACE.

Lamprĭdius. One of the *Scriptores Historiæ Augustæ* (*q.v.*).

Lamps. *See* LIGHTING.

Lancea. *See* LEGION, *near end.*

Lănista. The Roman name for a fencing-master or trainer of gladiators. (*See* GLADIATORES.)

Lantern of Demosthenes. A mediæval name for the monument of Lysicrates (*q.v.*)

Lanterns. *See* LIGHTING.

LAOCOON AND HIS SONS.
(Rome, Vatican.)

Lāŏcŏŏn. According to the post-Homeric story, a priest of Apollo. He had displeased that god by marrying against his wishes and, when the Greeks had departed for a time from Troy, leaving the wooden horse behind them, he again offended, by serving as a priest on the occasion of the sacrifice offered to Pŏseidōn. Accordingly, in the midst of the sacrificial feast, the god sent two serpents who strangled Laocoon and one of his sons. In Vergil's account [*Æn.* ii 230] Laocoon draws down upon himself the wrath of Athena, not only for warning the Trojans against the guile of the Greeks, but for piercing with a spear the flank of the horse dedicated to the goddess. Whilst he was sacrificing to Poseidon on the beach, Athena caused two snakes to emerge from the sea and strangle the father and both of his sons. This incident has been represented in the famous group of sculpture (*see* cut), the work of the Rhodian artists Agēsander, Pŏlȳdōrus, and Athēnŏdōrus, which was found in 1506 amid the ruins of the house of the emperor Titus at Rome. It is now in the Belvedere court of the Vatican Museum. (*Comp.* SCULPTURE.)

Lāŏdămeia. (Lat. -*ĭa*). The daughter of Acastus, and wife of Prŏtĕsĭlāus (*q.v.*). She was celebrated for her attachment to her husband, whom she followed to death of her own free will.

Lāŏmĕdōn. Son of Ilus and Eurȳdĭcē, father of Priam, Tithōnus, and Hēsĭŏnē, and king of Ilium. Apollo and Pŏseidōn served him for wages, the former pasturing his flock on Mount Ida, while the latter, either alone or with the help of Apollo and Æăcus (*q.v.*), built the walls of the town. But Laomedon defrauded the gods of the payment that had been agreed upon. Apollo therefore visited the land with a plague, and Poseidon sent a sea-monster, to whom the king was forced to offer his daughter Hesione. Hērăclēs, on his way back from the Amazons, found the maiden chained to a rock in the sea, and he offered to kill the monster if he were given the magic horses which Zeus had bestowed on Trōs in exchange for Ganymede, whom he had carried off. Laomedon agreed to this, but again broke his promise. Accordingly Hērăclēs (*q.v.*) subsequently waged

war against him, and after capturing the city, slew him and all his sons, except Priam.

Laquearia. *See* LACUNARIA.

Laquearius. *See* GLADIATORES.

Lara. *See* MANIA.

Lărārium. The shrine of the *Lărēs.* (*See* LARES.)

Lărēs (*i.e.* lords). The Latin name for the good spirits of the departed, who even after death continue to be active in bringing blessing on their posterity. The origin of the worship of the *Lares* is traced to the fact that the Romans buried their dead in their own houses, until it was forbidden by the laws of the Twelve Tables. Every house had individually a *lar fămĭlĭāris*, who was the "lord" or tutelary spirit of the family; his chief care was to prevent its dying out. His image, habited in a *tŏga*,

* ALTAR OF LARES COMPITALES.
(Pompeii.)

stood between the two *Pĕnātes*, in the *lărārium* or shrine of the *Lares*, beside the household hearth, which in early days was in the *atrium ;* the group as a whole was also commonly called either the *Lares* or the *Pĕnātēs.* The ancient Roman and his children saluted it daily with a morning prayer and an offering from the table; for, after the chief meal was over, a portion of it was laid on the fire on the hearth. When the hearth and the *Lares* were not in the eating-room, the offering was placed on a special table before the shrine. Regular sacrifices were offered on the calends, nones, and ides of every month and at all important family festivities, such as the birthday of the father of the family, the assumption by a son of the *tŏga vĭrīlis,* the marriage of a child, or at the reception of a bride, or the return of any member of the family after a long absence. On such occasions the *Lares* were covered with garlands and cakes and honey; wine and incense, and animals, especially swine, were offered up. Out of doors the *Lares* were also honoured as tutelary divinities, and in the chapels at the cross-ways (*compĭta*) there were always two *lares compĭtālēs* or *vicōrum* (one for each of the intersecting roads) which were honoured by a popular festival (*Compĭtālia*) held four times a year (*cp.* cut). Augustus added to the *Lares* the *Gĕnĭus Augusti,* and commanded two regular feasts to be held in honour of these divinities, in the months of May and August. Further, there were *Lares* belonging to the whole city (*lares prœstĭtēs*). They were invoked with the mother of the *Lares,* also called Lara, Larunda, or Mania (*q.v.*), and had an ancient altar and temple to themselves in Rome. The *Lares* were invoked as protectors on a journey, in the country, in war, and, on the sea. In contrast to these good spirits we have the *Larvæ* (*q.v.*).

Larunda. *See* MANIA.

Larvæ. In Roman belief the *Larvæ,* in contrast to the *Lares* (the good spirits of the departed), were the souls of dead people who could find no rest, either owing to their own guilt, or from having met with some indignity, such as a violent death. They were supposed to wander abroad in the form of dreadful spectres, skeletons, etc., and especially to strike the living with madness. Similar spectres of the night are the *Lĕmŭrēs.* To expel them from the house, peculiar expiatory rites were held on three days of the year, the 9th, 11th, and 13th of May, the *Lĕmŭrĭa,* when all the temples were closed, and marriages avoided.

Lasus (Gr. *Lasos*). A Greek dithyrambic poet. (*See* DITHYRAMBOS.)

Lātĭfundium. The Latin term for an extensive landed estate which was worked by means of slaves. Lands of the State (*see* AGER PUBLICUS) taken into permanent use by *occŭpātĭō* formed the foundation of these properties, and their possessors enlarged them by obtaining contiguous property either by purchase or by forcible appropriation. This system of *latifundia* gradually caused the utter ruin of the Italian peasantry, and involved in it the general destruction of the community [*Lati fundia perdĭdērĕ Itălĭam,* Pliny, *N. H.* xviii 35].

Lătīnī. The name originally given by the Romans, in the language of constitutional law, to those who belonged to the Latin league. At its dissolution, in B.C 338, they did not receive the right of Roman citizenship, but entered into the condition of dependent *sŏcii* (*q.v.*); they had a definite precedence over the other *socii,* possessed the *commercium* (*q.v.*), and the right of settlement in Rome, and their attainment of the right of citizenship was materially facilitated. They received this when they had once filled any annual public office in their community, or when, on settling in Rome, they left a son behind them in the colony to which they belonged. After the right of citizenship had been given to all the inhabitants of Italy (B.C 89), this *iūs Latii,* or Latin Right, became useless for Italy; it was even given by many of the emperors to communities in the provinces, and A.D. 212 all free inhabitants of the empire received the right of citizenship. After this time the only *Latini* remaining were those called the *Latini Iūniāni,* slaves who had been informally set at liberty, and who were allowed this privilege from the time of Tiberius.

Lătīnus. Son of Faunus and of the Nymph Mărīca (according to another story, of Hercules and Fauna, or of Odysseus and Circē) He was king of Latium, and father of Lavīnia, the wife of Æneas (*q.v.*).

Lătōna. *See* LETO.

Lăvātrīna. *See* BATHS.

Lăverna. The Roman patroness of thieves There was an altar dedicated to her at the gate named after her the *Porta Lavernālis*

Lavīnĭa. Daughter of Lătīnus, and wife of Æneas (*q.v.*).

Lĕander (Gr. *Lĕandrŏs*). A youth of Abȳdŏs, on the Hellespont, whose story was very celebrated in ancient times, and was the theme of a minor epic poem by Musæus (*q.v.*). He was in love with Hērō (*q.v.*), and every night swam across the Hellespont to visit her in her solitary tower at Lesbos. He was guided by a light in the tower, and on its being extinguished in a night of tempest, he lost his life in the waves. When Hero saw his corpse washed up the next morning on the shore, she threw herself down from the tower, and was thus killed.

Lĕarchus. The son of Athămās (*q.v.*) and Inō. He was killed by his father in a fit of madness.

Lectica. *See* LITTERS.

Lectisternium. A festival of Greek origin, first ordered by the Sibylline books in 399 B.C. It was held on exceptional occasions, particularly in times of great distress. Images of the gods (probably portable figures of wood draped with robes, and with their heads made of marble, clay, or wax) were laid on a couch (called the *lectus* or *pulvīnar*). A table was placed before them, on which was laid out a meal, always a free-will offering. At the first *Lectisternia*, there were three *lectī* arranged for three pairs of non-Roman divinities ; Apollo and Lātōna, Hērăclēs and Artĕmis (Diana), Hermēs (Mercurius) and Pŏseidōn (Neptune). Afterwards, this sacrifice was offered to the six pairs of Roman gods, who corresponded to the twelve great gods of the Greeks : Jupĭter, Juno, Neptune, Minerva, Mars, Venus, Apollo, Diana, Vulcan, Vesta, Mercury, and Ceres. These banquets to the gods generally took place at festivals of prayer and thanksgiving, which were called *Supplĭcătĭōnēs* (*q.v.*), and were performed in the market-places or at appointed temples, in which the arrangements for the purpose were on a permanent footing. It was customary to have connected with this a domestic feast, to which both strangers and friends were invited, and in which even those imprisoned for debt were allowed to participate. From the commencement of the 3rd century B.C. a banquet was regularly given to the three Capitoline divinities, Jupiter, Juno, and Minerva, on every 13th of November, in conjunction with the plebeian games. Under the Empire the celebration was on the 13th of September, and was associated with the Roman games. From B.C. 196 it was provided by the College of *Epŭlōnēs* (*q.v.*). The images of the three gods were decked with curls, anointed, and tricked out with

colours. Jupiter was placed reclining on a cushion, with a goddess on each side of him seated on a chair ; and the divinities were invited to a banquet, in which the whole senate participated.

Lēcȳthus (Gr. *lēkŭthŏs*). An oil-flask. (*See* VASES *and* VESSELS.)

Lēdă. Daughter of Thestius, and sister of Althæa, and wife of Tyndărĕōs. According to Homer it was by Tyndareos that she became the mother of Castor and Pollux (Polydeuces), and also of Clȳtæmnēstra, while Helen was her daughter by Zeus. Generally, however, Helen and Pollux are described as children of Zeus, Clytæmnestra and Castor as those of Tyndareos. According to the later story, Zeus approached Leda in the shape of a swan, and she brought forth two eggs, out of one of which sprang Helen, and out of the other Castor and Pollux.

Lēgātī. The Roman term for (1) ambassadors who, under the Republic, were chosen by the senate from among the most distinguished senators and provided with instructions and proper remuneration. On their return they had to hand in a report to the senate.

(2) Persons appointed, as above, by the senate, to accompany the generals and the governors of provinces. Three or more could be appointed, according to the necessity of the case. They were of senatorial rank, and were bound to carry out the commands of their superior officer, who was responsible for them. In his absence they took his place as *legati pro prætōre*. Under the Empire this title was also given to those who assisted in the duties of jurisdiction and government in the senatorial provinces. On the other hand, the *legati Augusti pro prætore* were nominated by the emperor himself, without any specified limit of time, to act as governors over imperial provinces in which there was an army. They were divided into *consular* and *prætorian legati*, according as the authority delegated to them extended over several legions or only one. Besides these there were *legati lĕgĭōnum*, appointed according to the number of the legions. They were men of senatorial rank, and had the command of the several legions, and of the auxiliary troops belonging to them.

Legion (*Lĕgĭo*). In the time of Rŏmŭlus the united armed forces of Rome went by this name. The legion consisted of 300 knights (*cĕlĕres*) under the command of a *tribūnus celerum*, appointed by the king, and 3,000 foot soldiers, under the command of three *tribuni militum*. Each of the three ancient tribes provided a third of this force and one tribune. With the increase of the military forces of Rome the name of *legio* was given to each of the sub-divisions equivalent in numbers to the original army.

The military system of king Servius Tullius made the infantry the most important part of the military forces, instead of the cavalry as heretofore. The five classes included in the *census* (*q.v.*) were obliged to serve in the army at their own expense; those who were not comprised in these classes, *viz.* the *proletarii*, were freed from service, and, when they were enlisted, received their equipment from the State. The *iuniores*, those who were from 17 to 46 years old, were appointed for field service, and the *seniores*, those from 47 to 60, for the defence of the city.

The first and second lines of the legion, drawn up in unbroken order like the Greek phalanx, consisted of citizens of the first class, equipped with helmet, cuirass, round shield (*clipeus*), and greaves, all of bronze. The third and fourth lines were from the second class, and had no cuirass, but had the helmet and greaves and large oblong shields (*scutum*). The fifth and sixth were armed similarly, but without greaves, and were drawn from the third class. The fourth class was armed with the *scutum* as its only weapon of defence, but, like the others, provided with spear (*hasta*) and sword. It either filled the seventh and eighth lines, or, with the fifth class, formed the *rorarii*, who opened the battle with slings and other light missiles.

An important alteration, ascribed to Camillus (about B.C. 390), was the abolition of the phalanx and introduction of the *manipular* formation, which prevailed till the time of Marius (end of the 2nd century B.C.). In the flourishing days of the Republic, the normal strength of a legion, which could be increased in time of need, consisted of 300 knights (*equites*), and 4,200 foot soldiers (*pedites*). In respect to the weapons used, the latter were divided into four kinds, according to their length of service and familiarity with warfare. (1) 1,200 *hastati*, all in early manhood; (2) 1,200 *principes*, in the full vigour of life; (3) 600 *triarii*, who were proved veterans; and (4) 1,200 *velites*, who were lightly armed, and were drawn from the lowest classes of the census. The three first classes had a bronze helmet (*cassis*) with a

lofty plume of feathers, a *scutum*, a leathern cuirass (*lorica*, *q.v.*), greaves and a sword (*gladius*), which, after the second Punic War was of the Spanish kind, being short, strong, and two-edged, fitted for thrusting rather than cutting, and worn on the right side. There was also a spear, which in the two first divisions was a *pilum* (*q.v.*), and among the *triarii* a lance [Polyb. vi 23]. The *velites* were armed with a leather helmet (*galea*), a light shield (*parma*), and a sword and several light javelins. The 3,000 heavily armed men were divided into 30 *manipuli*, numbering 120 men each among the *hastati* and *principes*, and 60 each among the *triarii*, and were again subdivided into two bodies called *centuriae*, and led by centurions (*q.v.*). Of the 1,200 *velites*, 20 were allotted to each century, and they formed the final complement of each maniple. On the field of battle the maniples were drawn up in open order, separated laterally from one another by intervals corresponding to the breadth of each maniple in front. The arrangement of the maniples would thus resemble that of the black squares on a chessboard. They fell into three divisions; the *hastati* in the front rank, with the *principes* behind them, and the *triarii* in the rear. If the first division, the *hastati*, were compelled to give way, then the second division, the *principes*, advanced through the intervals left by the maniples of the first division; if the *principes* in their turn had to retreat, then the third division, the *triarii*, who had been previously kneeling, protected by their shields, allowed the *hastati* and *principes* to fall back into the intervals separating the maniples of the *triarii*, and themselves closing their ranks pressed forward to meet the enemy. The 300 knights of the legion were divided into 10 *turmæ* of 30 men each, and were equipped with a bronze cuirass, leathern greaves, helmet, shield, a long sword for attacking, and a long lance provided at both ends with an iron point. Each *turma* was under three decurions and three under officers (*optiones*). The legion as a whole was under the command of six *tribuni militum* (*q.v.*)

The consular army consisted of two legions. Four legions were regularly levied in each year; in other words, 16,800 foot soldiers and 1,200 cavalry. This levy of citizens was further swelled by the allies (*socii*), a body of 20,000 foot soldiers and 3,600 cavalry, thus adding to each of the two consular armies 10,000 foot soldiers and 1,800 cavalry. The former were in twenty cohorts (*see* COHORS), each consisting of 420 men. Ten of these cohorts fought on the right wing, and ten on the left wing of the legions. Besides these, four cohorts of 400 men each were formed into a picked body. The cavalry were in six squadrons (*see* ALA, 1) of 300 men each. Four of these belonged to the main army, and two to the picked body. In wars beyond the limits of Italy there were also auxiliary forces (*auxīlia*), consisting either of soldiers raised in the country where the war was being carried on, or of light-armed troops furnished by allied kings and nations. Besides the ordinary component parts of the legion there was also the bodyguard of the commander-in-chief, the *cŏhors prætōria*. (*See* COHORS.)

In the course of the 1st century B.C. the organization of the legion was essentially altered. In the first place, in the time of Mārius, the census ceased to be the basis of the levy, and all the citizens collectively were placed on the same footing in respect to their military service and the uniform which they wore. All the soldiers of the legion alike received the heavy equipment and the *pilum*, while the light-armed *velites* were done away with. After the right of citizenship had been conferred on the Italian allies, these no longer formed a separate part of the legions, but were incorporated with them. Thus the Roman army now consisted only of heavy-armed legions and of light-armed auxiliary troops. The latter were partly raised in the provinces and divided into cohorts, and partly enlisted as slingers and archers. The cavalry of the legions ceased to exist. Like the light-armed soldiers, the whole of the cavalry consisted of auxiliary troops, who were partly enlisted and partly levied from the provinces, while some were supplied according to agreement by allied nations and princes. A further important novelty introduced by Marius was the use of the cohort-formation, instead of the maniple-formation, which broke up the front too much. The legion was now divided into ten cohorts, in each of which there were three maniples of *hastati, principes*, and *triarii*, designations which now only concern the relative rank of the six centurions of the cohort. The customary battle array was in three divisions, the first being formed of four cohorts, and the second and third of three each. Again, while in earlier times the obligation of service extended at the

most in the infantry to twenty campaigns and in the cavalry to ten, from the days of Marius the soldier remained uninterruptedly for twenty years with the army; an earlier dismissal being only exceptional. For this reason the well-to-do classes sought to withdraw themselves from the general military service, and it thus came to pass that the legions were for the greater part manned by means of conscriptions from the lowest strata of the burgher population of Italy, in which the service was regarded simply as a means of livelihood. Thus from the original army of citizens there was gradually developed a standing army of mercenaries. Under the Empire we find what is really a standing army, bound to the emperor by oath (*see* SACRAMENTUM); apart from the legions this army consisted of the *auxilia* (*q.v.*), the guards stationed in Rome and the neighbourhood (*see* PRÆ-TORIANI), and the city-cohorts (*see* COHORS), the artillery and the corps of workmen (*see* FABRI), the marines (*see* CLASSIARII), and the municipal and provincial militia. The legions are now once more provided with a corps of cavalry 120 strong, and are designated not only by numbers, but also by distinctive names. Together with the auxiliary troops they form the garrison of the imperatorial provinces under the command of the imperatorial *lēgāti lĕgĭōnum* (*see* LEGATI), whose place was taken in the middle of the 3rd century by the *præfecti legionum* (*see* PRÆFECTI). The strength of the legion now amounted to 5–6,000 men, raised partly by a regular levy, partly by drawing recruits from the Roman citizens of all the provinces beyond the bounds of Italy. As under the Republic, it was divided into 10 cohorts of 6 centuries each; the first cohort was, however, twice the strength of the remainder. It was not until the second half of the 3rd century A.D. that a new division of the 10 cohorts into 55 centuries came into use, with 10 centuries in the first cohort, and 5 in each of the rest. At the death of Augustus, the number of the legions was 25; it was then increased to 30, and this number was maintained until the end of the 2nd century, when three new legions were added by Septimius Sevērus. From the beginning of the 4th century it gradually rose to about 175, each of them, however, mustering a considerably smaller contingent. In course of time, and especially after the 2nd century, owing to the conflicts with the barbarians, the legion was drawn up more and more after the manner of the Greek phalanx, without intervals in its line and with a division of troops in its rear. In its equipment there was an important alteration beginning with the second half of the 3rd century, when all the soldiers of the legion carried long swords (*spāthœ*), and the first five cohorts two *pīla*, one larger and another smaller, while the last five had *lancĕœ*, or javelins serving as missiles, and fitted with a leather loop to help in hurling them with precision.

The military music of the Romans was provided by *tŭbĭcĭnēs* (*see* TUBA), *cornĭcĭnes* (*see* CORNICEN), *bŭcĭnātōres* (*see* BUCINA), and *lĭtĭcĭnes* (*see* LITUUS, 2). On standards or ensigns, *see* SIGNUM and VEXILLUM. On levy, oath of allegiance, pay, and discharge from service, *see* DILECTUS, SACRAMENTUM, STIPENDIUM, and MISSIO. The accompanying cut (from the Column of Trajan) represents the soldiers of a legion on the march,

ROMAN LEGIONARIES ON THE MARCH.
(Relief from the Column of Trajan, Rome.)

carrying their helmets close to the right shoulder, and their kit at the top of a pole resting on the left.

Leitourgīa (*i.e.* "service performed for the public"). A term applied at Athens to either an ordinary or extraordinary service, which the State imposed on its wealthier citizens in accordance with a regular rotation. The *ordinary* services, which citizens whose property amounted to more than three talents [£600] were required to perform, are: (1) the *Chŏrēgĭa*, the most ex-

pensive service of this kind, involving the equipment of a chorus (*q.v.*) for its musical competitions at public festivals, which were accompanied by theatrical and musical performances. (2) The *Gymnăsĭarchĭa*, which imposed the obligation of training in the Gymnasia the competitors for the gymnastic contests, supplying them with proper diet while they were in training, and providing at the games themselves for the requisite arrangement and decoration of the scene of the contest. The most expensive type of this form of service was the *lampădarchĭa*, the equipment of the torch race (*q.v.*), which in one instance [recorded in Lysias Or. 21 § 3] cost twelve *mĭnœ* [£40]. (3) The *Archĭthĕōrĭa*, or superintendence of the sacred embassies (*thĕōrĭœ*) sent to the four great national festivals, or to Delos and other holy places. In this case the State contributed part of the expense. There were other *leitourgiai* confined to the separate tribes and demes, such as the entertainment of members of the clan on festal occasions.

The most expensive óf all was the *extraordinary leitourgia* called the *trĭērarchĭa*, which was necessary only [or rather mainly] in times of war. This involved the equipment of a ship of war, and was required of the wealthiest citizens only. Before the Persian Wars the equipment of the forty-eight to fifty ships of the Athenian navy of that time devolved on the *naucrārĭo* (*q.v.*). When the number of the fleet was increased, the necessary number of trierarchs was nominated in each year by the *strătēgī.* The State provided the vessel, *i.e.* the hull and mast; and every trierarch had to fit out this vessel with the necessary equipment, to keep it in readiness for the year, and to man it with a complete crew of oarsmen and others. The State supplied pay and provision for the crew, though th[e] sum paid did not always suffice for th[e] purpose; it afterwards supplied the furni ture of the vessel also. To lighten th[e] expense, which amounted to between fort[y] *mĭnœ* and a talent (£133–£200), it becam[e] allowable, about 411 B.C., for two person[s] to share it. Afterwards, in 358, twent[y] *symmŏrĭœ* (*q.v.*) were instituted, *i.e.* com panies consisting of sixty citizens each with a committee of the 300 wealthies[t] citizens at their head; the 300 distribute[d] the expense over the individual *symmŏrĭ*[a] in such sort that the cost of a single trirem[e] was shared by a greater or less number [of] citizens. Lastly, about B.C. 340, the inc[ome] dence of the burden was regulated by a law introduced by Demosthenes, whereby all citizens, with the exception of the poorer classes, bore the expense in proportion to their property. Thus property [or rather, taxable capital] amounting to ten talents imposed the obligation of equipping one vessel, twenty talents two vessels, and so on. Those who had less than ten talents were to club together and to make up that amount among them.

The time of service lasted, as has been already stated, for one year. On its expiration, the trierarch, who had looked after the vessel, was responsible to the *Lŏgistæ* (*q.v.*) for the condition of the vessel, and had to hand in his account of the expenditure of the sums paid by the State.

*GANYMEDE AND THE EAGLE.
(Rome, Vatican Museum.)

Another board, the *ĕpĭmĕlētai* of the *nĕōrĭă* (the inspectors of the dockyards), superintended the regular fulfilment of the duties of the trierarchs, and were armed for this purpose with compulsory powers.

No one was compelled to undertake more than one *leitourgia* at the same time, or two in two immediately successive years. The only persons exempt from the trierarchy were the archons, unmarried "heiresses," and orphans up to the end of the first year after they had come of age. The obligation to see that the *leitourgia* was discharged in each particular case fell on the tribe concerned. If any one considered that he had been unfairly chosen for this duty, and a wealthier person passed over, he could resort to the form of challenge to exchange properties known as the *antidŏsis* (*q.v.*). [*Cp.* Introduction to Demosthenes, *Adv. Leptinem*, ed. Sandys, pp. ii–xviii.]

Lĕmŭrēs. Ghosts. (*See* LARVÆ.)

Lēnæa. A festival in honour of Dĭonȳsus. (*See* DIONYSIA, 3).

Lĕŏchărēs. A Greek sculptor, of Athens, who (about 350 B.C.) was engaged with Scŏpās in the adornment of the Mausōlēum (*q.v.*) of Halicarnassus. One of his most famous works was the bronze group of *Ganymede and the Eagle*, a work remarkable for its ingenious composition, which boldly ventures to the verge of what is allowed by the laws of sculpture, and also for its charming treatment of the youthful form as it soars into the air. It is apparently imitated in the well-known marble group in the Vatican (*see* cut).

Lernæan Hydra. *See* HERACLES.

Lesbōnax. A Greek rhetorician who lived early in the 1st century of our era. He composed political declamations on imaginary topics. Two of these have come down to us, exhorting the Athenians in the Peloponnesian War to be bold in battle against the Thebans and the Spartans.

Lēthē ("the river of oblivion"). A river of Hades (*q.v.*), out of which the souls of the departed drink oblivion of all their early existence.

Lētō (Lat. *Lātōna*). Daughter of the Titan Cœus and Phœbe. According to Hesiod [*Theog.* 406], she was the "dark-robed and ever mild and gentle" wife of Zeus, before he was wedded to Hēra, and the mother of Apollo and Artĕmis. According to a later legend she is only the mistress of Zeus after he is wedded to Hera; when about to give birth to her children, she is pursued from land to land till at last she finds rest on the desolate island of Ortȳgĭa (Dĕlŏs), which, up to that time, had floated on the sea, but was thereafter fixed firmly on four pillars of adamant. As mother of Apollo and Artemis, she dwells in Olympus. Her devoted children exact vengeance for her on Nĭŏbē (*q.v.*). The giant Tĭtȳus, for attempting to offer violence to her, is punished for evermore in the world below. She is for the most part worshipped in conjunction with Apollo and Artemis.

Letters. Letters were written on tablets (*see* DIPTYCHON) or small rolls of papyrus, the address being put on the outside. They were tied up with a thread, and the knot was sealed with wax. In wealthy Roman families special slaves or freedmen (*ab epistŭlīs*) were kept for writing the correspondence, and carrying the letters : the latter were called *tăbellārĭī*.

Leucŏthĕa. The name of the deified Ino.

Lĕxiarchs (Gr. *lĕxiarchoi*). At Athens, a board of six members, who, with thirty assistants, saw that only properly qualified persons attended meetings of the *ecclēsia.* They also entered young citizens on the list of their deme when they came of age.

Lĭbănĭus. A Greek rhetorician of Antioch in Syria, born 314 A.D. His education was begun in his native city and completed at Athens, where he became a public teacher at the early age of 25. Called from Athens to Constantinople in 340, he met with extraordinary success; at the same time he excited the envy of his rivals, whose slanders led to his expulsion in 342. After being actively engaged for five years as a public teacher in Nĭcŏmēdĭa in Bīthȳnĭa, he was recalled to Constantinople, where he was again remarkably popular, but found himself compelled by the continued persecutions of his detractors to leave the capital once more in 353. He withdrew to his native city of Antioch, where he was for many years actively employed in the exercise of his profession and in promoting the interests of his fellow citizens; but even here he was much persecuted by his opponents. Apart from bodily sufferings caused by his being struck by a flash of lightning, his old age was saddened by the decline of learning and the fall of paganism, which he had foreseen would follow the lamented death of his admirer and patron, Julian. He died about 393, honoured and admired by his pupils, among whom were included Christians such as Basil the Great and John Chrysostom; for, although he was enthusiastically devoted to the old religion, he was so tolerant in his relations to the adherents of Christianity, that he imparted his instructions to Christians and pagans alike. He himself gives us information about his life and work in a series of letters and in a speech " on his own fortune," written in his sixtieth year, but completed at a later date. He was conspicuous among his contemporaries, not only for his comprehensive culture and intellectual ability, but also for his productivity. We still possess sixty-seven of his speeches, the majority of which refer to the events of his time, and materially add to our knowledge of them ; also fifty declamations ; a considerable series of rhetorical exercises of various kinds, among them narratives, sketches of character and descriptions of works of art (some of them important in connexion with the history of ancient art), and also arguments to the speeches of Demosthenes. We have further about 2,000 letters addressed to friends, pupils, rhetoricians, scholars, statesmen, etc., which give us a vivid picture of his times. A fourth part of them, however, only exist in a Latin translation, and some of them are of doubtful genuineness. Indeed many of the writings that bear his name do not really belong to him. His style, which is formed on the best Attic models, is pure and has a certain elegance, although it is not always free from the affected and unnatural mannerism of his age.

Lĭbĕr. The Italian god of wine, identified with the Greek *Dĭonȳsus* (*q.v.*).

Lĭbĕra. The wife of the Italian wine-god Liber; identified with the Greek *Persĕphŏnē.* (*See* DIONYSUS, last par.)

Lĭbĕrālĭa. The Roman festival of the wine-god Liber. (*See* DIONYSUS.)

Lĭbertās. Among the Romans, the personification of Liberty ; she had a temple on the Aventine. Her name was also given to the *Atrĭum Lĭbertātis*, a place of public business which served, amongst other purposes, as an office of the censors. After it had been burnt down under Augustus, it was rebuilt by Asinius Pollio, and the first public library in Rome was established within its walls. On coins Libertas is represented as a beautiful and richly adorned matron. At the end of the Republic, after the assassination of Cæsar, she appears with a dagger and a cap of Liberty (*see* PILLEUS and coin *under* BRUTUS).

Lĭbertī, Lĭbertīnī. *See* FREEDMEN.

Lĭbĭtīna. An ancient Italian goddess of voluptuous delight and of gardens, vineyards, and vintages, originally connected with Venus, and therefore often called *Venus Libitina.* She was also regarded as the goddess of death and of the departed, and was therefore afterwards identified with Prŏserpĭna. By an ancient ordinance, ascribed originally to Servius Tullus, for every person who died in Rome a piece of money was deposited in her temple. Everything requisite for burials was kept there, and had to be bought or borrowed from it.

Libraries. In the earlier times libraries among the Greeks, were only possessed by private individuals, such as Euripides Aristotle, and Theophrastus. Tradition attributed the establishment of a public library at Athens to Pīsistrătus in the 6th century B.C. This was said to have been carried off by Xerxes, and afterwards restored by the Syrian Seleucus Nicănor. The greatest library known in antiquity was that founded by the first Ptolemy at Alexandria, which is said to have contained 400,000 volumes. Next to this, the most important was that of the kings of Per-gămŏn, said to have contained 200,000 volumes. This library was presented by Marcus Antŏnius to Clĕŏpătra, when the best part of the library at the Museum of Alexandria was burnt down at the taking of the town by Cæsar. There was a second library at Alexandria in the Sĕrăpĕum.

The first libraries which were formed at Rome were Greek, as, for instance, those of Æmilius Paullus, Sulla, and Lūcullus, who had brought them to Rome as booty after their wars in Macedonia, Athens, and Asia Minor. From the middle of the last century of the Republic it became the fashion in wealthy families to form libraries; in country houses, especially, they were regarded as indispensable.

Cæsar had formed the plan of founding a public library in Rome, and of setting Varro to make a collection of Greek and Latin books. The first public library of Greek and Latin books was actually set up in the time of Augustus by Asĭnius Pollio in the ātrĭum of Lībertās. Augustus him-self founded two more, the Octavian library in the portico of Octavia, and the Palatine in the temple of the Palatine Apollo. The most celebrated of those founded by the later emperors was the byblĭŏthēca Ulpia of Trajan. In the later imperial period there were twenty-eight public libraries in Rome. There were some very considerable private collections, for instance, that of Serēnus Sammŏnicus, the tutor of Gordian, which consisted of 62,000 volumes. 1,700 rolls have been found in a library discovered during the excavations at Herculaneum.

Librārĭus. The Latin name for a book-seller. (*See* BOOKS AND BOOK-TRADE.)

Liburna. A kind of light war-vessel, with two banks of oars and of little draught. Its shape was long and narrow, pointed at both ends. The pattern was taken by the Romans from the Liburnians, a piratical tribe on the Dalmatic coast. (*See* SHIPS.)

Lĭchās. The attendant of Hĕrăclēs (*q.v.*), who brought him from Dēĭănīra the poisoned garment, and was hurled by him into the sea, where his body became a rock.

Lĭcĭnĭus Măcer. *See* ANNALISTS.

Lictors (*Lictōrēs*). Attendants who bore the *fascēs* (*q.v.*) before Roman magistrates who had a right to these *insignia*. They were generally freedmen, and formed in Rome a corps consisting of three dĕcŭrĭœ under ten presidents. From these decurĭœ, the first of which was exclusively reserved for the consuls, the magistrates in office drew their lictors, while the provincial office-bearers nominated their own for their term of power. There was besides another decuria of thirty lictores cūrĭātĭ to attend on the public sacrifices, to summon the cŏmĭtĭa cūrĭāta, and, when these meetings became little more than formal, to repre-sent in them the thirty curĭœ ; from this decuria probably were also chosen the lictors of the flāmen diālis and of the Vestals. It was the duty of the lictors to accompany the magistrate continually, whenever he appeared in public. On these occasions they marched before him in single file, last in order and immediately preceding him being the lictor proxĭmus, who was superior in rank. All passers by, with the exception of matrons and Vestals, were warned by the lictors to stand aside and make due obeisance. The space required for official purposes was kept clear by them. Sentences of punishment were also executed by them. Their dress corresponded to that of the magistrate; inside the city the tŏga, outside, and in a triumph, the red military cloak.

Lighthouse. *See* PHAROS.

Lighting. In the earliest times the rooms of the Greeks were lighted by means of pans filled with dried chips of logs, and strips of resinous wood, or long deal staves tied together with bands of bast, and the like. In later times torches were made of metal or clay cases filled with resinous sub-stances. Or again, wooden staves dipped in pitch, resin, or wax were tied close together and inclosed in a metal casing, inserted in a saucer to catch the ashes and drops of resin. These torches were either carried by a handle under the saucer, or had a long shaft and a stand to set them up on. Resinous torches were in use among the Romans also, in early and later times. They used besides a dry wick of linen or oakum dipped in wax or tallow. Oil lamps, however, were no sooner invented than they became the most general medium of illumination among both Greeks and Romans. The lamp consisted of two parts : (1) A saucer for the oil, sometimes round, sometimes oval, sometimes angular, with a hole in the top for pouring in the oil, often shut with a lid. (2) The wick-holder, a projecting socket (Gr. *myxa;* Lat. *rostrum*).

(1 and 2) GREEK TERRACOTTA LAMPS.
(Stackelberg's *Gräber der Hellenen*, taf. lii.)

Sometimes there was a second hole on the surface of the oil-vessel, through which the wick could be pushed up by means of a needle. If the lamp was to be carried, it

images of gods, stories from mythology, scenes of warlike and domestic life, of the circus and the amphitheatre, animals, arabesques, etc. (fig. 3). Some lamps are themselves formed in the shape of gods, men, or objects of different kinds (*e.g.* fig. 3, *b, i*). The bronze lamps are specially distinguished by elegance and variety. The opening through which the oil was poured in being small, they had vials specially made for the purpose, with thin necks and a narrow mouth. Special instruments were made for trimming and pulling up the wick · little tongs, or hooked pins, which were sometimes fastened by a chain to the handle. No method of preventing the smoking of the lamps was known to the ancients. Lanterns were made of trans-

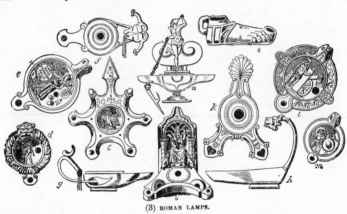

(3) ROMAN LAMPS.

Guhl and Koner, fig. 460.
a Museo Borbonico, IV lviii; *f, g, h, i,* ib VI xlvii, xxx; *b, c, d, e, l, m,* Passerius, *Lucernæ fictiles,* I 30, 27, II 6, I 6, II 29, 96; *k,* Bellori, *Antiche Lucerne.*

had a handle; if to be hung up, it was furnished with one or more ears, to which chains were attached. There were lamps with two, three, four, and sometimes as many as twenty wicks; these were hung up on the roof or set up on a high stand. The material of ancient lamps was clay, mostly of the red sort, and the manufacture of clay lamps formed a principal branch of Italian pottery. (Greek lamps of this material are represented in figs. 1, 2.) The next in frequency is bronze; it is not so common to find lamps of other metals, alabaster or glass. The numerous Roman lamps still preserved generally exhibit ornaments in relief of the most various kinds on the surface and on the handle:

parent materials, such as horn, oiled linen, and bladders: the use of glass came in later. (*See also* CANDELABRUM.)

Linus (Gr. *Līnŏs*). A hero representing probably a god of the old Greek nature-worship; his death, symbolic of the flagging vegetation during the heat of the dog-days, was hymned in widely known laments. The lament for Linus is mentioned as early as Homer [*Il.* xviii 570]. In Argos an ancient festival of Linus was long continued. Here he was said to be the son of Apollo and the princess Psămăthē. Born in secret and exposed by his mother the child grew up at a shepherd's among the lambs, until torn in pieces by dogs. Psamathe, however, on the news of what had happened, was put to death by her father. Apollo in wrath sent against the land a monster in female form, named Poinē. By this monster mothers were robbed of their children, nor were the Argives freed from the curse until, by the bidding of the oracle, they appeased Apollo by building a temple, and establishing an expiatory festival in honour of the boy and his mother. This was celebrated in the dog-days, in what was hence called the "Month of Lambs," as the "Feast of Lambs" (*Arnēis*) or the "Slaying of Dogs" (*Cÿnŏphŏntĭs*), whereat lambs were sacrificed, and the dogs which ran about free were slain, while women and children lamented Linus and Psamathe in mournful songs. In other places, *e.g.* in Thebes, on Hělĭcōn, and on Olympus, Linus, as son of Amphĭmărus and the Muse Urania, was known as a minstrel, the inventor of the Linus-song, who met with an early death, and whose grave was pointed out in different places. He was said to have challenged Apollo to a contest, and for that reason to have been slain by the god. On Hělĭcōn, the mountain of the Muses, his statue was placed in a grotto, where year by year, before the sacrifice to the Muses, a sacrifice for the dead was offered up to him. In later times he was described as the teacher of Heracles, who, when reprimanded, slew him with the lyre.

Lions, Gate of,·at Mÿcēnæ. *See* ARCHITECTURE, fig. 2.

Lītai. *See* ATE.

Literature (general view).

GREEK LITERATURE.

Period I. From Homer to the time of the Persian Wars.

(900–500 B.C.)

The first efforts of Greek *poetry,* which were made in the mother-country in Europe, and of which we have only legendary tradition, received their earliest artistic form in the Ionian colonies in Asia Minor. Here was developed first of all the *Heroic Ĕpŏs.* In the great poems which bear the name of HOMER, and are the oldest monuments of Greek literature (about 900 B.C.), we find epic poetry already in a stage of perfection never subsequently attained. As an Ionic school of poets (the Cyclic poets) attached itself to Homer, so in Greece itself, the Bœotian HESIOD (about 800 B.C.), with his didactic and genealogical epics, became the founder of the Bœotian School. The last epic writer of note in this period is PĪSANDER of Cămīrus (about 640 B.C.). Elegiac and

iambic poetry, like epic, owe their origin to the Ionians, the former represented by CALLĪNUS (about 700 B.C.), TYRTÆUS (about 680), MIMNERMUS (about 600), SŎLŌN (died 559), THĔOGNIS (died about 500), and SĬMŎNĬDĒS OF CĔŌS (died 468); the latter by ARCHĬLŎCHUS (about 700), SIMONIDES OF AMORGUS (about 650), and HIPPŌNAX (about 540 B.C.). The true lyric or melic poetry was developed after the Æolian TERPANDER (about 675 B.C.) had originated in the classical Greek music. Among the Æolians in Lesbos it assumed the form of a strophic poem, and among the Peloponnesian Dorians of a choric song, composed of *strŏphē, antistrŏphē,* and *ĕpōdŏs.* The great masters of the Æolian school of lyric poetry are the Lesbians ALCÆUS and SAPPHO (about 600 B.C.), and the Ionian ANĂCRĔŌN (about 530 B.C.); an echo of the Æolian lyric poetry remained, when it was already silent in its native home, in what were called *Scŏlĭă.* The development of the choral form of lyric poetry, which soon spread over the whole of Greece, is marked by ALCMĀN (about 660), STĒSĬCHŌRUS (about 600), and IBŸCUS (about 540). Its perfection was reached in the time of the Persian War by Simonides of Ceos, mentioned above, and PINDAR (died 442). From the dithyramb (a perversion of the choral lyric, which was given artistic form by ARĪŌN, about 600 B.C.) was developed in Attica, from the second half of the 6th century onwards, the drama with its three divisions, tragedy, comedy, and satyric play.

As poetry developed itself first among the Ionians, so also did *prose,* which had its beginning about the middle of the 6th century, in the era of the Seven Sages. At this time ÆSOP created in prose the fables about animals known by his name, and PHĔRĔCŸDES OF SYROS composed the earliest prose work. The subject of this was philosophical. Philosophy was actually founded, on the one hand, by THĂLĒS of Milētus (died about 550), ANAXĬMANDER (died 547), and ANAXĬMĔNĒS (died 502), the founders of the Ionic school; on the other hand, by PŸTHĂGŎRĂS of Sămos (died 504 B.C.), who established his philosophy in Magna Græcia. At the same time the first attempts at historical composition were made in Ionia by writers whom we know as the *Lŏgŏgrăphĭ.*

Period II. The Attic Era.

(500–300 B.C.)

The wonderful impulse which the whole life of the Greek nation received from the Persian Wars showed itself in no place with greater force than at Athens, which, under the guidance of Pericles in particular, became the centre of all intellectual effort. In *poetic literature* the first place was now taken by the Attic drama, which reached its highest level and maintained it until the close of the 5th century. Tragedy was represented by ÆSCHYLUS (died 456), SŎPHŎCLĒS (died 405), and EURĪPĪDĒS (died 405); what is known as old or political comedy by CRĀTĪNUS, EUPŎLIS, and ARIS-TŎPHĂNĒS (died about 388 B.C.). While in the 4th century tragedy followed practically the traditional path, the poets of the Middle Comedy, at the head of which stand ANTĬPHĂNĒS and ALEXIS, found themselves compelled to turn their attention more and more away from public life, which had formed the subject of the older comic writers. Finally the New Comedy (probably from 330 on) under DĪPHĬLUS, PHĬLĒMŌN, and MĔNANDER (died 290) took completely the form of a comedy of manners. The other branches of poetry were almost entirely thrown into the shade.

Didactic poetry received important contributions about the beginning of this period from the Eleatic philosophers XĔNŎPHĂNĒS (died about 470) and PARMĔNĬDĒS (died about 450); also from EMPĔDŎCLĒS (died about 430 B.C.). The attempts of PANYASIS (died about 450) and of ANTĬMĂCHUS (about 400) to revive the heroic Epos, and that of CHŒRĬLUS to found the historic, were fruitless. The elegy attained still less of independent importance than epic poetry.

Lyric poetry had, besides Simonides and Pindar, whose career extends into this period, an eminent exponent in BACCHȲLĬDĒS (about 450 B.C.); in later times, the only class of melic composition which showed any vitality was the dithyramb, under the new form of melodrama, in which PHĬLŎXĔNUS (died 380) and TĪMŎTHĔUS (died 357 B.C.) especially distinguished themselves.

In the domain of *prose* the Ionic dialect held undisputed mastery at the beginning of this period: in it were composed the works of the philosophers HĒRACLĪTUS (died about 475), ĂNAXĂGŎRĂS (died about 428), and DĒMŎCRĬTUS (died about 370), besides those of HĒRŎDŎTUS (died about 424) the "Father of History," the first to give an artistic form to prose-narrative, and HIPPŎCRĂTĒS (died about 377 B.C.) the founder of medical science. In Attic, the dialect of Athens, which was to become the general language of prose, the greatest influence on the artistic development of prose style was

exerted by the Sophists, especially PRO-TĂGŎRĂS and GORGĬĂS. The stimulus which they gave was turned to the account of practical oratory first by ANTĬPHŌN (died 411), the pioneer of the "Ten Attic Orators." He was followed by ANDŎCĬDĒS (died 344); LȲSĬĂS (died 360), the first really classical orator; ISŎCRĂTĒS (died 338), the father of rhetoric as an art; ISÆUS (died 350); DĒMOSTHĒNĒS (died 332 B.C.), who represents the most perfect form of Attic oratory, with ÆSCHĬNĒS, HȲPĔRĬDĒS, LȲCURGUS, and DINARCHUS, his contemporaries. While, on the one hand, it was only in the time of the decline of Greek freedom that Attic oratory reached its highest point (from which, after Demosthenes, it soon declined), in Attic historical composition, on the contrary, there stands at the very beginning an achievement never paralleled by Greek literature in this line—the History of THŪCȲDĬDĒS (died not later than 396). After him the most noteworthy representatives of this department are, for this period, his fellow countryman XĔNŎPHŌN (died about 350), and his younger contemporaries THĔŎPOMPUS and ĔPHŎRUS, neither of whom was of Attic origin, though both of them were pupils of Isocrates.

In philosophy Athens won a leading position through SŎCRĂTĒS (died 399). Of his numerous pupils (Euclīdēs, Aristippus, Antisthĕnēs, Xenophon), PLATO (died 348 B.C.) was the founder of the Academic school, and both as philosopher and as prose-writer did ever-memorable service. The same is true of Plato's pupil ARISTOTLE (died 322), the founder of the Peripatetic school, whose literary activity extended over the most widely different branches of knowledge. Outside the domain of philosophy he made a marked advance in his contributions to the natural sciences. He was followed by a succession of pupils, who made further progress in the separate departments of science. THĔŎPHRASTUS (died 287), for example, did much for the natural sciences, especially botany, ARISTŎXĔNUS (about 330) for music, DICÆARCHUS (about 320 B.C.) for geography. To the close of this period belong the philosophers PYRRHO (died about 275), ZĒNŌ (about 300), and ĔPĪCŪRUS (died 268 B.C.), the founders of the Sceptic, Stoic, and Epicurean schools respectively.

Period III. The Alexandrian Era.
(300–30 B.C.)

After the downfall of Greek liberty, Athens remained the city of philosophers, but Alexandria became the true intellectual capital of the Hellenic world and the head-quarters of its erudition. This it owed to its position as metropolis of the Ptolemaic dynasty in Egypt, and to the encourage-ment given by the Ptolemies to scientific studies, especially by the establishment of the great Library and of the Museum. The great achievements of the earlier periods were the genuine outcome of the national spirit; but, when the nation no longer existed, literature became more and more the business of the learned, so that even poetry assumed a pedantic dress. As re-gards *poetry*, at the beginning of this period the New Comedy still existed and endured for a time, but then expired. Tragedy also enjoyed a brief after-glow, in the poets of what is known as the Alexandrine Pleiad. Scarcely anything is known of lyric poets from this period, whereas epic poetry was again taken up and both its branches found numerous followers. The first, or narrative, branch took the form of short epic tales by CALLĪMĂCHUS (died about 240), ĂPOLLŌNĬUS RHŌDIUS (died about 190), RHĪĀNUS (about 230 B.C.). The poets of the other, or didactic, branch, ĂRĀTUS (about 270), NĬCANDER (about 150 B.C.), and others, eagerly devoted themselves to popularising less known branches of knowledge (astronomy, medi-cine, etc.).

A new field for epic poetry was even dis-covered during this period, in the bucolic or pastoral poems, which were native to Sicily, and were given artistic form by THĔOCRĬTUS (about 270 B.C.). In elegiac poetry good service was done, especially by Callimachus, mentioned above, the true founder of the erotic elegy. The same may be said of Epigrams.

In the department of *prose* the Alexan-drine epoch evinced astounding fertility, but form was for the most part neglected. Of the numerous historians of this time, the earlier of whom mostly described the deeds of Alexander the Great, *e.g.* CLITARCHUS (about 300), the most noteworthy are TĬMÆUS (died 256) and PŎLȲBĬUS (died 122). Besides history itself, its various subsidiary sciences were eagerly cultivated ; for example, geography and chronology, which received from ĔRĂTŎSTHĔNĔS (died about 195) their scientific form, and the latter of which especially was further de-veloped by ĂPOLLŌDŌRUS (about 140 B.C.). Literary criticism grew into an independent science and flourished under the scholars of Alexandria and Pergămus, as ZĔNŎDŎTUS

(about 275), ARISTŎPHĂNĔS of Byzantium (died about 185), CRĂTĔS (about 170), but above all ARISTARCHUS (died about 153 B.C.). Considerable progress was also made in the exact sciences, in mathematics by EUCLĪDĔS (Euclid, about 300) and ARCHĪ-MĒDĔS (died 212), in astronomy by Eratos-thenes, just mentioned, and especially by HIPPARCHUS (died about 125 B.C.) who established astronomy as a science. Simi-larly the science of medicine attained great perfection in Alexandria, in particular under HĔRŎPHĬLUS and ĔRĂSISTRĂTUS. In philosophy also great literary activity was shown by the various schools, without, how-ever, much speculative progress. Practical oratory existed only in certain free com-munities of Asia and in Rhodes, nor had it any literary importance. On the other hand the science of rhetoric received a great impetus about the end of the 2nd century, chiefly by the services of HER-MĂGŎRĂS (about 120 B.C.).

Period IV. The Roman Era.
(30 B.C. to 529 A.D.)

(30 B.C.) All the Greek provinces of Europe, Asia, and Africa became incorporated in the Roman Empire. Thus to the centres of learn-ing which had hitherto existed in Athens and Alexandria, was added a new centre in Rome, the capital of the world. Greek scholars of every kind flocked from every quarter to Rome. Nor did they only stimulate the rising intellect of Rome, but themselves received much intellectual ad-vantage. Whereas Roman literature after the end of the 1st century A.D. was sinking rapidly and inevitably to its decline, Greek literature received a fresh start from the favour shown to it by the emperors of the 2nd century. It received a further impetus by the contest—the unavailing contest—against Christianity, the victory of which confined Hellenism within ever narrower limits, until its destruction was sealed by the emperor Justinian, when, in 529, he closed the pagan schools in Athens, their last refuge. *Poetry* takes a subordinate position in this epoch. The Epigram alone remained in constant use, and during this period much good work was done in this line.

Didactic poetry is represented chiefly by OPPIAN (2nd century), and the fabulist BABRIUS (beginning of 3rd century ?) nar-rative epic by QUINTUS SMYRNÆUS (4th century ?), and the Egyptian NONNUS (5th century) the founder of a school of his own, to which, besides TRȲPHĬŎDŌRUS and COLLȲTHUS, belongs the charming MŪSÆUS. In *prose*, history had numerous representatives; *e.g.* DĬŎDŌRUS and DĬŎNȲSĬUS of Hălĭcarnassus, who both belong to the beginning of this period, PLUTARCH, ARRIAN, and APPIAN in the 2nd century, DIO CASSIUS and HĔRŎDIAN in the 3rd, ZŌSĬMUS in the 5th, and others. In geography important work was done by STRĂBO (about 20 A.D.) and PTŎLĔMY (about 150 A.D.). The latter's contemporary, PAUSĂNĬĀS, did meritorious work in a narrower sphere. Ptolemy's services to geography were equalled by his services to astronomy, of which, as of the other exact sciences, Alexandria was the headquarters. Among mathematical writers, THĔŌN, NĬCŎMĂCHUS, DĬŎPHANTUS, and PAPPUS must be mentioned; of physicians DĬOSCŎRĬDĒS, SŌRĀNUS, and above all GALEN (second half of 2nd century). In "grammar," which was now more and more confining itself to the subject of language, the Alexandrines APOLLONIUS DYSCŎLUS and his son HĔRŌDIAN (2nd century) are conspicuous. Among the numerous authors of compilations, ATHĒNÆUS (about 200), and STŎBÆUS (about 500) are the most meritorious. To rhetoric valuable service was rendered in this period. The revival of rhetoric after the standard of the Attic orators was the aim of Dionysius of Halicarnassus (already mentioned). The most important work in this department was done by HERMŎGĔNĒS (2nd century). Grammatical and rhetorical studies were favoured by the direction taken from the beginning of the 2nd century by the later sophistical school. This school aimed at attaining the masterly command of prose expression as shown in its fairest form by the Attic orators, and that in very different spheres, but mainly in oratory. The chief representatives of this tendency in its period of greatest vigour, the 2nd century, are DIO CHRYSOSTOM, ÆLIUS ARISTĬDĒS, LUCIAN, and ÆLIAN; in the 3rd, PHĬLOSTRĂTUS; in the 4th, HĬMĔRIUS, LĬBĀNIUS, the emperor JULIAN, THĔMISTIUS, SȲNĔSIUS. Among the peculiar products of this time may be mentioned the fictitious letters, written especially by ALCĬPHRŌN (2nd century) ánd ARISTÆNĒTUS (5th century), and the love romances of XĔNŎPHŌN OF EPHESUS, HĒLĬŎDŌRUS, LONGUS, ACHILLĒS TATIUS, and CHĂRĬTŌN. Philosophy in the first two centuries of the imperial times moves on the whole in its old channels and has a generally popular character; as in the writings of PLUTARCH,

ARRIAN, and GALEN, who have already been mentioned under other branches, of SEXTUS EMPĪRĬCUS, the emperor MARCUS AURĒLIUS, and others. A new and final departure was taken by philosophy from the 3rd century onwards in Neo-platonism, founded by PLŌTĬNUS, and carried on chiefly bv PORPHȲRĬUS, IAMBLĬCHUS, and PRŎCLUS.

ROMAN LITERATURE.

Period I. Archaic Literature.

From Livius Andronicus to Cicero.

(240–80 B.C.)

Poetry. Although many beginnings had been made by the Romans from which a national poetry might have been developed, for instance, ritual hymns, songs in praise of ancestors, dramatic dialogues of rude fun and rough wit (*see* FESCENNINI), yet the national mind had shown little aptitude for intellectual interests, and so was unable to complete this development and create an independent poetic literature. Instead of this, Roman poetry formed itself entirely upon Greek poetry, which had already been perfected in all its main branches. And although the first kind of literature to be introduced into Rome was the drama—precisely that kind which marked the culminating point of poetical composition—this was not due to any intellectual cravings on the part of the Romans, but to the fact that in this particular branch there existed a point of contact. For a considerable time past the diversions offered to the populace at the public games had included a dramatic representation, in place of which dramas modelled after Greek types were successfully substituted. This attempt was first made by LĪVIUS ANDRŎNĬCUS, a Greek from Southern Italy, who, from 240 B.C. onwards, brought on the stage tragedies and comedies formed on Greek originals. He also kindled an interest in epic poetry by translating the Odyssey of Homer into the national metre, the Saturnian verse. Livius was soon succeeded, both in dramatic and epic poetry by others, who carried on what he had begun. It shows, however, how little root poetry really had in the life of the people, that for a long time the poets, like Livius himself, were foreigners and received little consideration for their performances. In tragedy the poets who succeeded him confined themselves to the adaptation of Greek dramas; in the *prætexta*, which treated Roman materials in the Greek dramatic form, only solitary attempts were made by the chief Roman tragedians of the Republic, ENNIUS (died 170), PĀCŬVIUS (died 130), ACCIUS (died about 100). They had been introduced by NÆVIUS, who was a prolific writer of tragedies, and still more of comedies, from 235 B.C. onwards. The reproduction of Greek originals in the form of comedies, which were known as palliātœ, is best represented by PLAUTUS (died 184), CÆCĬLIUS (died 166), and TERENCE (died 158 B.C.). This also soon passed over into the representation of Roman life under Greek forms, cōmœdiœ tŏgātœ; and, after palliātœ had ceased to be written, these attained greater perfection under AFRĀNIUS (second half of 2nd century B.C.). Towards the end of this period a popular farce, the Atellāna, received artistic form from POMPŌNIUS and NŎVIUS. It was followed, probably about 50 B.C., by the mīmus, also originating in popular buffoonery, as treated by LĂBĒRIUS and PUBLILIUS SȲRUS.

NÆVIUS endeavoured to give a national direction to epic as well as to tragic poetry, by his poem on the first Punic War, written in Saturnian verse. This attempt was crowned with success; for, with unimportant exceptions, the epic poems of the whole period were directed to the celebration of the achievements of Rome. His immediate successor ENNIUS took Homer as his model; he introduced the Greek hexameter, and became in consequence the founder of the classic Roman epic. In this period also the only peculiar creation of Roman poetry, the satire, was initiated by Ennius; but its form and spirit were materially changed by LŪCILĬUS (died about 108 B.C.). The only complete monuments of the archaic poetry of Rome that are still extant are the comedies of Plautus and Terence.

While the literary poetry of Rome was thus founded and developed by writers of foreign extraction, prose owes its literary origin to a native Roman; although considerably influenced by Greek models, it was mainly developed by the Romans themselves. The most important monument of prose composition which the Romans inherited from ancient times was the Laws of the Twelve Tables (451 B.C.), the foundation of the Roman legal system. When the Romans, about 200 B.C., first attempted to write history, their own tongue appeared to them so ill-adapted for the purpose that they used Greek.[1] The creator of literary

[1] Dionysius, Ant. Rom. i 6, mentions Fabius as one of the historians who had written in Greek

prose-Latin was the well-known CĂTO (died 149). He employed his mother-tongue for the most diverse varieties of prose writing, —history, speeches, and learned treatises of every kind. From his time onwards there was much activity in the provinces both of history and oratory. The most numerous class of historical writers, called, from their mode of treating the subject, the Annalists, did not succeed, however, in making any substantial progress in the art of history. Oratory, on the other hand, thanks to the constant practice provided by public life, and the influence of Greek rhetoric, which was becoming daily of greater importance, made important progress, especially as represented by GAIUS GRACCHUS (died 121), CRASSUS (died 91), and ANTŌNIUS (died 81 B.C.) Jurisprudence was the only science which was independently developed by the Romans; but literary criticism, as well as rhetoric, both introduced by Greeks about the latter half of the 2nd century B.C., were cultivated,—the former even by men of note, as for example ÆLIUS STĬLO. Cato's book on husbandry, and (at the end of this period) the treatise on rhetoric often ascribed to Cornificius, are the only monuments of the prose literature of this time which have come down to us entire.

Period II.   Classical Literature.
From Cicero to the death of Augustus.
(80 B.C. to 14 A.D.)

This is known as the golden age of Roman literature. The first place in the earlier half of the period, i.e. down to the fall of the Republic, is taken by oratory. This attained its highest perfection in the hands of CICERO and his rival orators, HORTENSIUS, CÆSAR, and others. Cicero is the creator of classical prose: his supremacy was not confined to oratorical compositions, but was maintained in his dissertations on rhetoric and philosophy. By the latter he laid the foundations of Roman philosophical literature, which however remained entirely dependent on Greek models. History was conspicuously represented by CÆSAR (died 44) and SALLUST (died 36 B.C.), the first great Roman historians, beside whom CORNĒLIUS NĒPŌS only deserves mention for his

on the early legends of Rome; but Cicero always speaks of him with Cato as exemplifying the baldness of early Latin prose. In the De Divinatione i 43, he refers to the Grœci Annales of Fabius Pictor, which does not necessarily or naturally mean " annals written in Greek."—Prof. Nettleship's Essays, p. 340.

attempt to bring foreign history also into the field. VARRO (died 27 B.C.), the most productive of Roman authors, laboured in the most diverse paths: his writings on grammar, on literary subjects, and on antiquities were admired for centuries.

Poetry was entirely thrown in the shade by prose. Dramatic poetry is only represented by the *mīmus*, which imitated the license of the capital and was now, as has been stated, elaborated into literature. The *Sătūræ Mĕnippēæ* of the above-mentioned Varro and the didactic philosophical poem of LUCRĒTIUS (died 55) are of conspicuous merit. The latter still maintained the style modelled on Homer by Ennius; but, beside this, a new departure in epic poetry now appeared. The learned and polished Alexandrine Greek poets were the models for this, of which a solitary specimen is extant in an *ĕpyllĭum* of CĂTULLUS (died about 54 B.C.), the *ĕpĭthălămĭum* of Pēleus and Thĕtis. He is perhaps the most richly endowed of Roman poets, and is the first conspicuous writer of Latin lyrics. Lyric poetry was the most alien to the Roman character, and was only beginning to make its way about this time in the forms of iambic poetry, epigrams, and elegiacs. For these too the Alexandrine poets are the type. After the downfall of the Republic, in proportion as public life sank into the background, the interest of the educated classes was increasingly absorbed in literary efforts which were favoured in every way by the emperor Augustus himself, and by men of eminence like Mæcēnas, Messalla, and Asīnius Pollio. (*See* RECITATIONS.)

As political events caused oratory and history to recede into the background, the first place in literature was again taken by poetry, which in the time of Augustus attained its highest point in the emulous attempts of the poets to reach Greek perfection in form. The most prominent poetic writers of this age are: VERGIL (died 19 B.C.), who, beginning with imitations of the bucolic poetry of Theocritus, surpassed the Greeks in didactic poetry, and in his *Æneid* fashioned for the Romans a national epic; HORACE (died 8 B.C.), who gave new life to the satiric poetry of Lucilius, and naturalized in Rome the metrical forms of the Æolic odes; and the elegiac writers, TĬBULLUS (died 19 B.C.), PRŌPERTIUS (died 15 B.C.), and OVID (died 17 A.D.). The last-named also applied his perfection of form to didactic poetry with brilliant results. Dramatic poetry alone failed to prosper, as the popular interest

was entirely absorbed by the *Pantŏmīmus*, which, with its gorgeous displays, was just coming into being.

Meanwhile, in the realm of *prose* composition, the most brilliant contribution of this time is the work of LIVY (died 17 A.D.) which comprised the complete history of Rome. Beside him may be mentioned POMPEIUS TROGUS, the compiler of the first Latin universal history. Under the Empire, oratory lost day by day its political importance, and in practice was confined to the senatorial debates, which were entirely under imperial guidance, and to civil lawsuits. Its natural field now became the schools of the rhetoricians, in which it sank to mere flowery declamation. A living picture of the proceedings in them at this time is given by the descriptions of the ELDER SENĔCA, which were not reduced to writing till the following period (he died about 37 A.D.). After poetry most interest was taken in criticism, in which VERRIUS FLACCUS and HYGĬNUS achieved the most important results. Of the practical sciences, geography was advanced by the mensuration of the Roman empire accomplished by Agrippa, and the edifices erected by Augustus gave rise to the instructive work of VITRUVIUS on architecture (about 15 B.C.).

Period III. The Silver Age.
From Tiberius to the death of Trajan.
(14–117 A.D.)

Under the influence of the schools of rhetoric (which had become one of the most important means of education), both the poetic and the prose literature of this epoch show a tendency to the rhetorical and declamatory style. Both alike endeavour to produce effect by what is interesting and novel, rather than to give pleasure by elegance and taste. Poetry became rhetorical and prose poetic. A goodly array of poetic works has come down to us from this period. Epic is represented in its didactic branch by GERMĀNĬCUS (died 19 A.D.) and the poets whom we know as MĂNĪLĬUS and LŪCĬLĬUS (*Scriptor Ætnæ* about 75 A.D.); in its historic, by LUCAN (died 65) and SĬLĬUS ĬTĂLĬCUS (died 101); in its heroic, by VĂLĔRĬUS FLACCUS (died about 90) and STĀTĬUS (died 96 A.D.), who is also the most eminent lyric writer. Bucolic poetry is represented by CALPURNĬUS SĬCŬLUS (about 55 A.D.). The satiric poetry of Horace was continued by PERSĬUS (died 62) and JUVENAL (died about 130).

A new kind of literature, in the form of poetic fables, was introduced into literature by PHÆDRUS (died about 40), and MARTIAL (died 102 A.D.) elaborated the epigram as an independent branch of poetry. The tragedies of SĔNĔCA (died 65 A.D.) are not intended for the stage, on which mimes and pantomimes alone bore sway, but are simply declamatory exercises. The most important prose writers of the time are the same Seneca, who composed numerous philosophical treatises; PĔTRŎNĬUS (died 67) with his satirical novel; the ELDER PLINY (died 79) with his gigantic Natural History; QUINTILIAN (died about 118), who, in his *Instĭtūtĭŏ Ŏrātŏrĭa*, sought to cause a reaction to the old models in oratory; the great historian TĂCĬTUS (died about 120); and the YOUNGER PLINY (died about 114 A.D.) with his Letters and the Panegyric on Trajan, the pattern of the later Panegyrics. Beside these must be mentioned the writers of research, VELLEIUS PĂTERCŬLUS and VĂLĔRIUS MAXĬMUS (both about 30), CURTIUS RŪFUS (about 40), FRONTĬNUS (died about 104), who was also an active contributor to technical literature, the geographer POMPŌNIUS MELA (about 40), the physicians CELSUS (about 30) and SCRIBŌNIUS LARGUS (about 45), the writer on husbandry CŎLŬMELLA (about 65), the grammarian REMMIUS PĂLÆMŌN (about 50), the textual critic PRŎBUS (about 65), and the commentator ASCŌNIUS PĔDĬĀNUS (died 88 A.D.).

*Period IV. The Literature in its Decline. From Hadrian (117 **A.D.**) to the 6th century.*

Of the numerous poets of this period only a few, and those belonging to the later time, are of special interest; *e.g.* AUSŎNIUS (4th century), CLAUDIAN, NAMĀTIĀNUS, DRĂCONTĬUS (5th century). In *prose* literature, from the time of Hadrian, jurisprudence takes a prominent position. It was mainly represented by GAIUS, PAPINIAN, ULPIAN, and PAULUS (2nd to 3rd century), and a magnificent completion was given to their labours by the *Corpus Iūris Cīvīlis* compiled under Justinian I (6th century). Among the historians the most noteworthy are SUETŌNĬUS (2nd century), who was also the compiler of numerous writings on archæology, literary criticism, and grammar, which were no less eagerly read by subsequent generations than Varro's; and AMMĬĀNUS MARCELLĪNUS (4th century). The rest, such as FLŌRUS (2nd century), the

Scriptōres Histŏrĭæ Augustæ (3rd and 4th centuries). JUSTIN, AURĒLIUS VICTOR, EUTRŎPIUS, etc., are only epitomizers. From the 4th century onwards the influence of Christianity made itself felt in this subject, as with SULPĬCIUS and OROSIUS. In the 2nd century FRONTO gave a new direction to oratory by reverting to the writers of the archaic era. In this he was followed by the rhetorician APŬLEĬUS, the writer of a humorous and fanciful novel of character, one of the most interesting products of the period. Gaul was from the end of the 3rd century the headquarters of oratory, in which the panegyric style predominates, as in the collection called the *Panegyricī Lătīnī*, and in SYMMĂCHUS (end of 4th century), who, as well as SĬDŎNĬUS APOLLĬNĀRIS (5th century), is also known by his letters. Besides Suetonius already named, grammar found numerous votaries, who were, however, more remarkable as zealous compilers than as original investigators. GELLIUS (2nd century), NŌNIUS (3rd century), DŌNĀTUS, CHĂRĬSIUS, DĬŎMĒDES, SERVIUS (4th century), MACRŎBIUS (5th century), and PRISCIAN (about 500 A.D.) may be cited. Works on the educational curriculum were written by MARTIĀNUS CĂPELLA (5th century) and CASSĬŎDŌRUS (6th century). The above-mentioned Apuleius and also BŎĒTHĬUS (6th century) are worthy of mention as philosophic writers. As representatives of other subjects may be adduced CENSŌRĪNUS (3rd century) and FIRMĬCUS MĀTERNUS (4th century) for astrology; VĒGĔTĬUS RĔNĀTUS (4th century) for tactics; PALLĂDIUS (4th century) for husbandry; CÆLIUS AURĒLIĀNUS and MARCELLUS EMPĬRĬCUS (5th century), for medicine.

Littĕrātor. The Roman designation of an elementary instructor (*see* EDUCATION, 2).

Littĕrātus. The Roman term for the teacher who imparted the higher branches of knowledge (Suetonius, *De Grammaticis*, §§ 4, 12).

Litters, in ancient Greece, were for the most part used only for the conveyance of sick people and women; in other cases their use was regarded as a luxury. Among the Romans they appear to have first come into vogue along with the other luxuries of Asia after the victory over the Syrian king, Antĭŏchus the Great (B.C. 190). They were used principally in the country and upon journeys. As in Greece, so in Rome, where driving was only exceptionally allowed (*see* CHARIOTS, 2), their use was at first confined to invalids and women; but when men also began to use them in the town, they formed in the first instance a privilege of certain classes, until in the course of the imperial time they came into general use. Two kinds were distinguished: (1) the *lectīca*, resembling a *palanquin*, adapted for lying down: this was a framework spanned by girths and with a bolster and pillow; and (2) the *sella*, a sedan chair, for one or two persons, which was used particularly by the emperors and *consŭlārēs*. Both kinds were provided with an arched covering, which could be closed up, even at the sides, by means of curtains or windows made of thin plates of talc [*lăpĭs spĕcŭlāris*, Juv. iv 21, iii 242]. The litter was carried upon poles, which were either low and therefore hung in straps, or else rested upon the shoulders of the bearers, who were two, four, six, and even eight, according to its size. In distinguished houses special slaves (*lectĭcārĭi*) of particularly powerful bodily frame, in later times especially Cappadocians, were kept for this purpose; these used to wear a red livery. For those who could not afford the expense of a private litter, there were also hack-litters. In the later imperial time a litter called a *basterna* came into fashion, which was carried by two mules in shafts before and behind.

Liturgia. *See* LEITOURGIA.

Litŭus. (1) The Roman term for the augur's wand. It was a staff hooked at the upper end; with it the augur marked out the sacred region (*templum*) for the observation of birds (*see* cut and *cp.* AUGURES). (2) The signal-trumpet of the cavalry, bent at the lower end; it was blown by the *lĭtĭcen*, and emitted a clear, shrill note (*cp.* TUBA).

AN AUGUR'S WAND.

Lĭvĭus. (1) *Lĭvĭus Andronīcus*, the founder of Roman epic and dramatic poetry. He was by birth a Greek of Southern Italy, and was brought as a slave to Rome, after the conquest of Tarentum in 272 B.C., while still of tender age. His master, a Livius, whose name he bears, gave him his liberty, and he imparted instruction in the Greek and Latin languages. This employment probably gave occasion for his translation of the Homeric Odyssey into Saturnian metre; in spite of its imperfections, this remained a school-book in Rome for centuries. In 240 B.C. he brought on the Roman stage the first drama composed after a Greek model, and with such success that thenceforward dramatic poetry was

well established in Rome. According to ancient custom he appeared as an actor in his own pieces. His dramatic compositions, tragedies, and comedies were faithful but undoubtedly imperfect translations of Greek originals. He attempted lyric poetry also, for he was commissioned by the State to write a march in honour of *Iūnō Rēgīna* Scanty remains of his works are all that have come down to us.

(2) *Tĭtus Lĭvĭus*, the celebrated Roman historian, was born at Pătăvĭum (59 B.C.), apparently of good family. He was carefully educated, and betook himself early (certainly before 31 B.C.) to Rome, where he soon became acquainted with the most distinguished men of the time. Even Augustus entertained friendly relations towards him in spite of his openly expressed republican convictions, for which he called him a partisan of Pompey. He does not seem to have taken public office, but to have lived exclusively for literature. Esteemed by his contemporaries, he died in his native town in 17 A.D. He must have begun his great historical work between 27 and 25 B.C.; it can only have been completed shortly before his death, as he did not publish the first twenty-one books until after the death of Augustus (14 A.D.). He recounts the history of Rome in 142 books, extending from the foundation of the city (whence the title *Ab Urbe Condĭtā librī*) to the death of Drūsus (9 A.D.). His own death must have prevented its continuation to the death of Augustus, as he doubtless proposed. He published his work from time to time, in separate parts. He arranged his material—at least for the first ninety books—as far as possible in decads (portions consisting of ten books), and half-decads; the division into decads was however first carried through in the 5th century, probably for convenience of handling so vast a series of books. There still remain only the first decad (to 293 B.C.), the third, fourth, and half of the fifth decad (218–167); of the remainder, with the exception of a fairly large portion of book 91, only inconsiderable fragments. We also possess from an unknown pen, summaries (*pĕrĭŏchæ*) of all the books except 136 and 137, and a scanty extract from the account of the portents (*prōdĭgĭa*), which appeared in 249 B.C. and following year; this is by a certain Iūlĭus Obsĕquens, and perhaps dates from the 4th century.

Livy's importance rests more on the magnitude of his patriotic undertaking and the style of his narrative than upon his thoroughness as a historic inquirer. His preliminary studies were inadequate, and his knowledge of Roman law, and still more of the military system of Rome, was insufficient. He was content to select what seemed to him the most probable and reasonable statement from the authorities which happened to be familiar and accessible to him, without regard to completeness, and without severely scrutinising their value,—a method which necessarily led to numerous inaccuracies and serious errors. Primarily, his great aim was not critical research into the history of his country. He desired rather by a lively and brilliant narrative, which should satisfy the more exacting taste of the time, to rekindle the flagging patriotism of his countrymen, and to raise his politically and socially degraded contemporaries to the level of their ancestors' exploits. And his narrative in fact deserves the fullest admiration, especially for its descriptions of events and the actors in them, and for the speeches which are inserted in the work. The latter show his rhetorical training in all its brilliance. His language is choice and tasteful, although in details it marks a decline from the strictly classical standard. Asinius Pollio, in allusion to the author's birthplace, charged it with a certain *pătăvī-nĭtas*. This can only mean a provincial departure from the peculiar language of the metropolis, which is to us no longer perceptible. Livy's work enjoyed the greatest renown down to the latest days of Roman literature, and has been the great mine of information for knowledge of the past to all succeeding generations.

Lŏchăgŏs (*Greek*). The commander of a *lŏchŏs* (*q.v.*).

Lŏchŏs. The Greek designation of a body of foot soldiers. Among the Spartans, it denoted in early times the largest divisions into which the whole population capable of bearing arms was grouped. Each of these [according to Thucydides v 68, *cp.* 66] comprised four *pentēcostўĕs* of four *ĕnŏmŏtĭœ* each [an *ĕnŏmŏtĭă* containing on an average thirty-two men]. The name also denoted the individuals comprised therein; later, [Xenophon, *Rep. Lac.* ii 4], it was the name of the four sub-divisions of a *mŏra* (*q.v.*). In Greek mercenary troops, a *lochos* was a company of 100 men under a separate commander. Several of these companies were united under the superior command of a *strătēgŏs* (*q.v.*).

Lŏgeiŏn ("speaking-place"), *see* THEATRE.

Lŏgistæ ("auditors of accounts"). The name given at Athens to a board consisting originally of thirty, subsequently of ten members, who, in conjunction with another board, the ten *euthўnĭ*, and their twenty assessors, received from magistrates, at the expiry of their term of office, the accounts of their administration. (*See* EUTHYNA.) This was especially important with those magistrates through whose hands public money passed. Both boards were originally chosen by show of hands; later by lot. One member was elected from each *phўlē*, the assessors of the *euthyni* were appointed by free choice. The *logistœ* were the supreme authority to whom outgoing magistrates submitted their accounts. The *euthyni* examined the several details, notified, when necessary, those who were liable, and returned the accounts to the *logistœ* with a report on their merits. Magistrates who had nothing to do with public money only gave an assurance to the *logistœ* that they had received and paid nothing. If the accounts were approved, and no charge was brought after the public proclamation by the *logistœ*, they gave the magistrate his discharge. In the other alternative they referred the case to a court of justice in which they were themselves presidents. The prosecution was entrusted to ten *sўnēgŏri* or counsel for the State, who were chosen by lot and sat with the *logistœ*. The final decision rested with the Heliastic court. (*See* HELIÆA.)

Lŏgŏgrăphī (Gr. *lŏgŏgrăphoi*, i.e. writers in prose). The name given to the oldest Greek historians, who by their first attempts at disquisitions in prose marked the transition from narrative poetry to prose history. As in the case of epic poetry, so these earliest historical writings emanated from Ionia, where the first attempts at an exposition of philosophic reflexions in prose were made at about the same time by Phĕrĕcўdēs, Anaxĭmander, and Anaxĭmĕnēs; and, in both cases alike, it was the Ionic dialect that was used. This class of writing long preserved in its language the poetic character which it inherited from its origin in the epic narrative. It was only by degrees that it approached the tone of true prose. It confined itself absolutely to the simple telling of its story, which was largely made up of family and local traditions. It never classified its materials from a more elevated point of view, or scrutinised them with critical acumen The logographers flourished from about 550 B.C. down to the Persian Wars. Their latest representatives extend, however, down to the time of the Peloponnesian War. When true history arose with Hērŏdŏtus, they soon lapsed into oblivion, whence they were rescued in Alexandrian days. Many of the works ascribed to them were however believed to be spurious, or at least interpolated. We possess fragments only of a few. The larger number of the historic writers who are described as logographers were Asiatic Greeks, *e.g.* CADMUS of Milētus, author of a history of the founding of Mīlētus and the colonization of Ionia (he lived about 540 B.C., and was considered the first writer of historic prose); further, DĬŎNȲSĬUS of Miletus, a writer of Persian history, HĔCĀTÆUS (*q.v.*) of Miletus (550–476), XANTHUS of Sardis (about 496), a writer of Lydian history, HELLĀNĬCUS (*q.v.*) of Lesbos (about 480–400), CHĂRON of Lampsăcus (about 456), a compiler of Persian history and annals of his native town, PHĔRĔCȲDĔS of the Carian island Lĕrŏs (died about 400 B.C.), who lived at Athens, and in his great collection of myths in ten books treated chiefly of the early days of Attica. Some belonged to the colonies in the West, *e.g.* HIPPȲS of Rhēgium, at the time of the Persian War the oldest writer on Sicily and Italy. The only representative from Greece itself is ACŪSĬLĀUS of Argos in Bœotia, the author of a genealogical work.

Longīnus (*Cassius*). A Greek rhetorician, born at Athens about 213 A.D., who studied Neoplatonism at Alexandria, and practised as teacher of philosophy, grammar [*i.e.* literary criticism], and rhetoric, in his native city, from about 260, until the accomplished queen Zĕnŏbĭa of Palmȳra summoned him as minister to her court. As he persuaded her to resist the Roman yoke, the emperor Aurelian caused him to be executed after Zenobia's overthrow in 273. He possessed such an extent of learning, that Eunāpius called him a living library and a walking museum. His versatility is proved by compositions on philosophy, grammar, rhetoric, chronology, and literature. Of these, only fragments are extant, for example, the introduction to a commentary on Hēphæstīon's handbook of metres, and a short Rhetoric incomplete at the beginning. A brief treatise *On the Sublime*, commonly ascribed to him, is more probably to be assigned to an unknown writer about the Christian era. It treats and illustrates by classic examples the characteristics of the lofty style from a philosophical and æsthetic point of view. It is written in a vigorous manner.

Longus, who probably lived in the 3rd century A.D., was the author of a Greek pastoral romance, *Daphnis and Chlŏĕ*, in four books. It is considered the best of all ancient romances which have come down to us, on account of its deep and natural feeling, its grace of narrative, and the comparative purity and ease of the language. It has often been imitated by Italian, French, German, and English writers. [The rare translation by John Day of the French version of Amyot was reprinted in 1890.]

Lōrīca. (1) The leathern corselet of the Roman legionary. It consisted of thongs (*lŏra*) of shoe-leather faced with metal. These were fastened one upon another in such a way that they formed a covering for the body with two shoulder-pieces. Below the latter a plate of iron $9\frac{1}{2}$ inches square, was placed over the region of the heart

ROMAN LEGIONARY WEARING THE LORICA.
(Arch of Severus.)

(*see* cut). Of the early citizen-soldiers, the more wealthy wore also coats of chain-armour (*lorica hāmāta*), and corselets of mail (*lorica squāmāta*), in which the joints were further covered with metal plates; the latter were also worn by the prætorians in imperial times.

(2) The breastworks on walls and on redoubts.

Lot, Election by. *See* OFFICIALS.

Lōtŏphăgī (*i.e.* Lotus-eaters). A people on the north coast of Africa, mentioned as early as Homer [*Od.* ix 84]. They lived on the fruit of the lotus. (*Cp.* ODYSSEUS.)

Love, God of, *see* EROS; Goddess of, *see* APHRODITE and VENUS.

Lucan (*Marcus Annæus Lūcānus*). A
Roman poet, born 39 A.D. at Cordova in
Spain. He was grandson of Sĕnĕcă the rhetorician, and nephew of Seneca the philosopher. He was brought up in Rome from
the first year of his age, and excited attention at an early date by his rhetorical and
poetic powers. On the recommendation of
his uncle, Nero conferred on him the quæstorship while yet under the legal age, and
admitted him to favour. The applause
however which his poems received soon
aroused the jealousy of the emperor, who
was particularly conceited about his own
poetic abilities. Accordingly he was forbidden for the future to recite his poems
in public, or to appear on the platform.
This inspired the poet with such animosity
that he took part in Piso's conspiracy.
When it was detected, he sought at first
to save himself by the most abject entreaties, by denouncing his fellow conspirators, and even by falsely accusing his
mother Acilia. Being nevertheless condemned to die, he himself caused his veins
to be opened, and thus perished (65 A.D.).
Of his numerous compositions, the *Phar-
sālia*, an unfinished epic in ten books, is
extant. It is an account of the civil war
between Cæsar and Pompey, extending
beyond the battle of Pharsālus and down
to the capture of Alexandria. It maintains such strict chronological order and
exactitude of detail, that it was a question after his death whether he deserved
to be reckoned a poet at all. [Petronius
118 and, at a later date, Servius, *Ad Æn.*
i 382. *Cp.* Dryden's preface to *Annus
Mirabilis*, quoted in Heitland's *Introd.* to
Lucan, ed. Haskins, p. xix.]

Lucan represents himself in his poem as
an enthusiastic lover of the lost days of
liberty, and in that capacity extols Pompey,
to the unjust disparagement of Cæsar. His
narrative displays some talent, but also an
inability to give his materials a more than
merely outward poetical form. It is moreover turgid, rhetorical to a degree, and its
pathos smacks of declamation. Remains of
the literary activity which made him its
object in olden times are extant in two collections of *scholia*.

Lŭcĕrēs. One of the three old patrician
tribes in Rome. (*See* PATRICIANS.)

Lŭcerna (a lamp). *See* LIGHTING.

Lucian (Gr. *Loukĭānŏs*). One of the most
interesting of Greek writers, born about
120 A.D. at Sămŏsătă, on the Euphrates in
Syria. Owing to the poverty of his parents,

he was apprenticed to a stonemason; but,
thanks to his irresistible eagerness for
higher culture, contrived to devote himself
to the art of rhetoric. After practising
for some time as an advocate, he traversed
Greece, Italy, and Southern Gaul in the
guise of a sophist, and gained wealth and
renown by his public declamations. In
his fortieth year he removed to Athens,
to devote himself to the study of philosophy, and attached himself closely to the
Stoic Dēmōnax. In his old age the state
of his finances compelled him once more to
travel as a professional orator. At last,
when far advanced in years, he was given
an important and influential post in the
administration of justice in Egypt, this he
seems to have retained till death.

Under his name we still possess more
than eighty works (including three collections of seventy-one shorter dialogues).
Twenty of these are, however, either certainly spurious or of doubtful authenticity.
They date from every period of his life,
the best and cleverest from the time of his
sojourn in Athens. They fall into two
classes, rhetorical and satirical. Of the
latter the majority are in dramatic form,
recalling in dialogue and outward dress
the Old Comedy, of which Lucian had a
thorough knowledge, and to which his
genius was closely akin. These writings
present an admirable picture of the tendencies and the absurdities of the time.
In the field of religion, he directed his
mockery (especially in the *Dialogues of
the Gods*) against the tenets of the popular religion, the artificial revival of which
was attempted in the time of Hadrian and
the Antonines. He further attacked the
popular conceptions of life after death in
the *Dialogues of the Dead.* He assails
with special bitterness the superstitions
which had penetrated from the East,
among which he reckons, it is true, Christianity, but without any real knowledge
of its nature. In *Pĕrĕgrīnus Prōteus*, he
attacks mystical enthusiasm; in *Alexander,
or the Prophet of Lies*, the impostors and
oracle-mongers who preyed upon the superstition of the time, which he portrays in
a masterly style in his *Lover of Lies* and
his *True Stories* (*Vēræ Histŏrĭæ*). Another
object of his satiric lance was the current
philosophy, in which he had sought relief
when sated with rhetoric. He had only
found in it, however, a petrified dogmatism,
a passion for strife and disputation, with
the most absolute contradiction between

theoretical teaching and the practice of life. This was true even of the Stoics, and still more of the Cynics, whose meanness and love of pleasure, which they concealed under a pretended absence of personal wants, he is never weary of deriding.

Especially instructive for his attitude towards philosophy and his general view of life are the *Auction of Philosophers*, the *Fisherman* (with his defence of the latter), and *Chărōn, or the Spectator of the World.* All these are works of marked ability. The last named is a brilliant exposition, from his negative point of view, of the vanity of all human existence. He even exposes his own class, the Sophists, for attempting to conceal their miserable poverty of intellect by their bold readiness of tongue, and by their patchwork of fragmentary quotations borrowed from the writers of antiquity. In fact, there is scarcely a side of the literary and social life of the time that he does not attack in its weak points, confining himself, however, for the most part to demonstrating what ought not to be, without showing how the existing evils were to be cured. To sit in judgment on the false culture and want of taste in his contemporaries, he was certainly fitted above all others; for, apart from a wide range of knowledge, he possessed keen observation, and an unusual measure of wit and humour. He had moreover an extraordinary gift of invention, remarkable aptitude for vivid delineation of character, and a singular grace and elegance. In spite of his Syrian origin, his zealous study of the best models gave him a purity of language which for his time is remarkable.

Lŭcīlius. (1) *Gaius Lucilius*, founder of Roman satire, was probably born 180 B.C. at Suessa Aurunca in Campania, of a distinguished and wealthy Latin equestrian family. He afterwards settled in Rome, where his Latin origin excluded him from a political career. Owing partly however to his excellent education, partly to his family connexions (being Pompey's grand-uncle on the mother's side), he was on friendly terms with the most distinguished men. In particular, he lived with the younger Scipio and his friend Lælius in the closest intimacy. He accompanied the former during the Numantine War, and died in Naples, 103 B.C.—His satires, in thirty books, were much esteemed in the time of the Republic and later. We possess numerous but inconsiderable fragments, from which, however, can be gathered their original

position in the general scheme of his work. Each book certainly contained a number of separate poems which, at least in books xxvi–xxx (the first written and published), were composed, like the satires of Ennius, in various metres. In most of the books, however, only a single metre was used, by far the most common being the dactylic hexameter (bks. i–xx and xxx), which from Horace's time became the ordinary metre for satire. The contents of the satires were exceedingly varied : all occurrences of political, social, and learned life were brought by him within the range of his discussion. He even touched upon his own experiences and his studies on literary, antiquarian, grammatical, and orthographical questions. His severest censure and most pitiless mockery were directed, not only against the vices and absurdities of the time in general, but also against particular individuals without any respect of persons On the other hand, true merit received his warmest praise. His satires must have given, on the whole, a true and lively picture of the time. On metrical form and on style he does not seem to have set much store ; it is apparently only in its metrical setting that his language differs from the daily tone of educated circles. To the latter we may also probably ascribe the incorporation of so many fragments of Greek. His writings early became an object of study to the learned of Rome, and they also remained models to subsequent satirists, especially Horace.

(2) *Lucilius Iunior*, friend of the philosopher Seneca, is supposed by a common but not improbable assumption to be the author of *Ætna*, a didactic poem in 645 hexameters. Suetonius, in his life of Vergil, says of that poet, *Scripsit etiam de qua ambīgǐtur Ætnam.* It treats of Etna and its wonders, and was composed before the eruption of Vesuvius in 79 A.D.

Lŭcīna. The Roman title of Juno (*q.v.*) as the goddess of light and of child-birth ; later also of Diana in similar acceptation.

Lŭcrētius Cărus (*Titus*). A Roman poet, born at Rome about 98 B.C. and died by his own hand, in 55. He composed for his friend Memmius, the orator and poet, a didactic poem in hexameter verse concerning the nature of things (*De Rērum Nātūrā*) in six books. The teaching of Epǐcūrus forms the main subject, the example of Empědŏclēs prescribed the poetic form, and the mode of treatment was modelled on Ennius. The ostensible object of the work is to prove by a profound investigation of the world of nature that all comes to be, exists, and perishes by eternal law, without any interference of supernatural powers, and hence to set men free from their fearful torture, terror, and superstition. The first elements of all existence are the imperishable atoms which move in infinite space (book i). By union of these come into existence not only the material world (ii), but also soul and spirit, which consequently perish as soon as a dissolution of the atoms takes place (iii); perception, sensation, and thought are mental processes, occasioned by images which are ceaselessly being emitted by the surfaces of things (iv). Book v treats of the formation of the world, vi of single natural phenomena. This work is the only considerable composition in epic verse which has come down to us from the time of the Republic. It is also the first attempt at a systematic treatment of Greek philosophy in the Latin tongue. The greatest admiration is due to the art with which Lucretius gives poetic form to his unpoetical subject, and adapts to his purpose a language which had hitherto been little exercised on such topics. The matter causes the exposition to be often dry, but frequently it rises to a magnificent beauty, as in the famous description of the Athenian plague at the end of the poem. The scientific zeal with which the whole is imbued, and which stands aloof from all frivolity, must inspire respect. He expresses himself with simplicity and power, and his language has an antique colouring. He was prevented by death from putting the finishing touches to his work [or even from completing it. Thus there is nothing on the subject of ethics, which could not properly be omitted in an exposition of the teaching of Epicurus]. It is true that Cicero revised it before publication, yet the condition in which we have it is in great measure defective.

*LUCRETIUS.
(From a black agate, formerly in Dr. Nott's collection.)

Lūdi. *See* GAMES.

Lūna. The Italian goddess of the moon. She had in Rome an ancient sanctuary on the Aventine, in which as goddess of the month she received worship on the last day of March, which was the first month of the old Roman year. As *noctilūca*, "lamp of the night," she had a temple on the Palatine, which was illuminated at night.

Lŭpercālia. A festival held in Rome from time immemorial on February 15. It was in honour of Faunus, who was worshipped under the name *Lŭpercus* in the *Lŭpercal*, a grotto in the Palatine Mount. The object of the festival was, by expiation and purification, to give new life and fruitfulness to fields, flocks, and people. The cult was originally administered by two confraternities, which were chosen from the members of the Fabian and Quintilian families, and were named in consequence *Luperci Făbĭāni* and *Luperci Quintĭlĭānĭ*. To these was added in 44 B.C. that of the *Luperci Iūlii* in honour of Cæsar. In consequence of the civil wars the cult fell into desuetude, but was renewed by Augustus. In imperial times the members of these *collēgia* were commonly of equestrian standing, and retained the name of *Luperci* even after leaving the body. The festival was observed until 494 A.D., in which year Bishop Gelasius I changed it into the Feast of the Purification. The procedure at the *Lupercalia* was as follows. After the *flāmen Dĭālis* had sacrificed some he-goats and a dog, two youths were touched on the forehead with a knife, smeared with the blood of the goats. It was then immediately wiped off with wool dipped in milk, whereupon they were bound to laugh. After the sacrificial feast the *Luperci*, crowned and anointed, and naked, except for an apron of goatskin, ran round the ancient city on the Palatine with thongs cut from the skin of the sacrificed goats in their hands. On their course women used to place themselves in their way to receive blows from the thongs, which was believed to be a charm against barrenness. The thongs were called *fĕbrŭa*, from the old word *fĕbrŭārĕ*, "to purify"; the day, *dies fĕbrŭātus*, "the day of purification"; and the whole month, *fĕbrŭārĭus*, "the month of purification."

Lŭstrum, among the Romans, was the purification, or absolution from sin, of the entire people. It took place at the close of each *census* (*q.v.*), commonly in May of the year following the censors' accession to office. The host of the people, horse and foot, in their newly constituted classes, was drawn up in full armour on the Campus Martius under the leadership of the censor to whom this duty fell by lot. The *Suove-*

taurīlĭa, a pig, ram, and bull, was carried three times round the whole army, and thereupon sacrificed to Mars, accompanied by a prayer of the censor in which he besought that the power of the Roman people might be increased and magnified, or as it ran later, might be maintained entirely undiminished. The censor then led the army under his banner to the city gate, where he dismissed them, while he himself, as a token of the completed *lustrum*, drove a nail into the wall of a temple and deposited the new roll of citizens in the *Ærārĭum* (or Treasury) of the people.

Luxŏrius. A Roman epigrammatic poet, who lived in Africa about the beginning of the 6th century A.D., during the Vandal domination. He sought to imitate Martial. We still possess eighty-eight of his epigrams, which are often coarse and always dull.

Lȳæus ("Care-dispeller"). A name of Dionysus.

Lȳcæa (Gr. *Lŭkaia*). A festival celebrated in honour of Zeus on the Lycæan Mount (Gr. *Lŭkaiŏn*) in Arcadia. In the sacred inclosure on its highest peak, where, according to popular belief, no object cast a shadow, there was an altar of heaped up earth, and before it two columns with gilt eagles on top of them, looking to the east. At the festivals, probably celebrated every ninth year, the priests, who alone were allowed to enter the precincts, offered mysterious sacrifices to the god, including a human sacrifice. These were said to have been instituted by Lȳcāōn (*q.v.*), and were kept up till the 2nd century A.D. The man who had been chosen by lot to perform the sacrifice was afterwards compelled to flee, and wandered about for nine years; like Lycaon, in the shape of a wolf, so the people believed. In the tenth he was allowed to return and regained his human form, *i.e.* the taint was removed. Besides the festival there were also athletic contests.

Lȳcāōn. Mythical king of Arcadia, son of Pĕlasgus and Mĕlĭbœa (daughter of Ocĕănus) or Cyllēnē, and father of Callisto. He is said to have founded on Mount Lycæum the town Lȳcŏsūra, the oldest that Hĕlĭŏs looked upon, and to have sacrificed a child to Zeus on the altar he had raised on the highest peak of the mountain, on account of which he was changed into a wolf (*see* LYCÆA). Another legend relates that he had fifty impious sons. When Zeus came to them in the guise of a beggar

in order to put their contempt of the gods to the test, they followed the advice of Mænălus, the eldest, and set before him the entrails of a boy which had been mixed with the sacrifice. The god however threw the table over and killed Lycaon and his sons with lightning, with the exception of Nyctĭmus, the youngest, whom Gæa saved by firmly holding the right hand of Zeus. During the reign of Nyctimus the deluge connected with the name of Deucălĭōn covered the land as a punishment for the impiety of Lycaon and his sons.

Lȳcĭus. Epithet of Apollo (*q.v.*).

Lȳcŏmēdēs. King of Scȳros, the murderer of Thēseus (*q.v.*). Achillēs grew up among his daughters; the son of Achilles and of one of these, Dēĭdămeia, was Nĕŏptŏlĕmus.

Lȳcŏphrōn. A Greek grammarian and poet, a native of Chalcis in Eubœa, who lived in the first half of the 3rd century B.C. at Alexandria, where Ptolemy Phĭlădelphus entrusted him with arranging for the library the works of the Greek comic poets. As a result of this occupation, he produced a voluminous and learned work on Greek Comedy. He himself wrote tragedies, and was counted one of the Pleiad, the seven Alexandrine tragedians. Of his works there remains a poem in 1,474 iambic verses, entitled *Alexandra* or *Cassandra*, which is rendered almost unreadable by the obscurity of its language and by its pedantic display of learning. It consists of a long monologue, in which Cassandra prophesies the fall of Troy and the fates of the heroes of the Trojan War, with allusions to the universal empire of Alexander the Great.

Lȳcurgus. (1) Son of Drȳās, king of the Thracian Edōni, threatened Dĭonȳsus with a scourge when he was wandering about on the Mount Nȳsa with his nurses, which made them let the holy implements fall to the ground, while the god sought shelter with Thĕtis in the sea. The gods punished him with blindness and an early death [*Il.* vi 130–140]. According to another legend, he was made mad by Dionysus and cut off his son's limbs, imagining that he was pruning the shoots of a vine. In accordance with the god's prophecy that his death alone could deliver the land from its temporary barrenness, he was led by the Edoni to Mount Pangæus, where Dionysus caused him to be torn to pieces by horses.

(2) One of the Ten Attic Orators, born about B.C. 390 at Athens, of a noble family, pupil of Plato and Sōcrătēs. With Dēmos-

hēnēs and Hȳpĕrīdēs he was a principal representative of the patriotic party, and directed his exertions especially to the improvement of the internal affairs of Athens. During his administration of the finances, a period of twelve years (338–326), he won great credit by increasing the revenues of the state and the military strength of Athens, by beautifying the city with magnificent buildings, such as the completion of the theatre of Dīŏnȳsus, and the building of the Panathenaic Stădĭum, and by causing copies of the plays of Æschylus, Sŏphŏclēs, and Eurīpĭdēs to be preserved in the public archives. He died in 329, and was interred at the public expense. The Athenians did honour to his memory by raising a statue of bronze in his honour on the market-place and by a decree which is still extant [Hicks, *Greek Historical Inscriptions*, No. 145]. His speeches, of which the ancients possessed fifteen, laborated with the greatest care, were remarkable for their serious moral tone and noble manner, though they were wanting in grace of form, and apt to become tedious owing to frequent digressions. These merits and defects are exemplified in the only speech of his now extant, that *against Lĕŏcrătēs.*

Lȳcus. (1) Son of Pŏseidōn and the Pleiad Cĕlænō, married to Dircē. He took over the government of Thebes after his brother Nycteus, for Labdăcus, who was a minor; and, after the death of Labdacus, or his son Lāĭus. He was either killed by Amphīōn (*q.v.*) and Zēthus, or (according to another account) handed the government of Thebes over to them at the behest of Hermēs.

(2) Son of Pŏseidōn, tyrant of Thebes, killed by Hēräclēs for murdering his father-in-law Crĕŏn during his absence, and for plotting against his wife Mĕgărä and his children.

Lȳdus (*Ioannes Laurentius*). A Greek writer, born at Phĭlădelphĭa in Lydia 490 A.D. At the age of twenty-one he went to Constantinople in order to study philosophy, entered the service of the State, and rose to high office. About 552 he was dismissed by Justinian and took a post as teacher in the imperial school. Here he devoted himself to literature, and died at a great age in 565. We still possess some of his writings, which are derived from ancient sources lost to us: (1) on the State offices of Rome *De Măgistrătĭbus*); (2) on portents in the sky, etc., and the doctrine of auguries (*De*

Ostentīs); (3) extracts from a work on the Roman months and the festivals held in them (*De Mensĭbus*).

Lygdămus. A Roman poet. *See* TIBULLUS.

Lynceus. (1) Son of Ægyptus, husband of Hȳpermnēstra, the daughter of Dănăus(*q.v.*).

(2) Brother of Idas. (*See* IDAS AND LYNCEUS.)

Lȳrä. A stringed musical instrument, said to have been invented by Hermēs, who stretched four strings across the shell of a tortoise. In historical times a whole tortoise-shell was used for the sounding-bottom, the curved horns of a goat or pieces of wood of a similar shape were inserted in the openings for the front legs, and joined near the upper ends by a transverse piece of wood called the yoke. On the breast-plate of the shell was a low bridge, across which

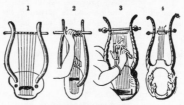

FORMS OF THE LYRE.

1. Tischbein, *Peintures des Vases antiques.*
2. De Laborde, *Collect. d. Vases gr.*, I, pl. 11.
3. *Museo Borbonico*, X, tav. liv.
4. *Ibid.* XI, tav. xxxi.

the strings (usually seven) ran all at the same height to the yoke, and were either simply wound round it or fastened to pegs , at the other end they were tied in knots and fastened to the sounding board. It was ordinarily played with the left hand, while to produce louder and longer notes the strings were struck by the right hand with the plectrum, the point of which was usually like the leaf of a tree, and sometimes in the shape of a heart or like a little hammer (*see* fig. 3 of the cuts, which represent various forms of the lyre). *Cp.* CITHARA and SAMBUCA.

Lyric Poetry. While among the *Greeks* elegiac and iambic poetry (*q.v.*), which forms the transition from epic to lyric composition, was practised by the Ionians, lyric poetry proper, or, as it was more commonly called, melic poetry (*mĕlŏs*, a song), *viz.* the song accompanied by music, was cultivated by the Æolians and Dorians. This is due to the talent for music peculiar to these races. That playing on stringed instruments and singing were cultivated even in mythical times in Æolia, in the island of Lesbos, is shown by the legend that the head and lyre of Orpheus, who had been torn to pieces by Thracian women, were washed ashore on that island, and that the head was buried in the Lesbian town of Antissa. Antissa was the native place of TERPANDER, who gave artistic form to the *nŏmŏs* (*q.v.*), or hymn to Apollo, by elaborating the laws of its composition. Settling at Sparta in B.C. 676, he laid down the foundation of Dorian music. While he had closely followed Homeric poetry in the texts which he wrote for his musical compositions, there afterwards arose a greater variety in the kinds of songs, corresponding to the greater variety of musical forms, springing from the foundation laid by him. In the *Æolian* lyric the pathetic prevails, as might be expected from the passionate nature of the people; the feelings of love and hatred, joy and sorrow are their principal themes. As to the metrical form we find short lines with a soft, melodious rhythm, which make up a small number of short strophes. They are written in the Æolic dialect; we may suppose that they were solos sung to the accompaniment of stringed instruments. In Lesbos the Æolian lyric was brought to its highest perfection by ALCÆUS of Mȳtĭlēnē (about 600), and by his contemporary SAPPHO, also a Lesbian, and teacher of the poetess ERINNA. The joyous poems of ANĂCRĔON of Tĕŏs (born about 550), whose subjects are love and wine, were also in the Æolian style, but in the Ionic dialect. An echo of the Æolian lyric are the *scŏlia* (*q.v.*).

It was among the *Dorians*, however, that the lyric poetry of the Greeks reached the highest degree of its development. It is also called choral lyric, because the Dorian songs were intended to be sung at the public festivals, especially those of the gods, by a dancing choir to the accompaniment of stringed instruments and flutes. Intended therefore to be public, it naturally had on the whole an earnest, objective character, and is thus distinguished from the Æolian lyrics that expressed the personal feelings of the poet. Their form shows further points of difference. Instead of the diminutive Æolian strophes of short lines, unsuitable for dancing, the Dorian lyrics have ampler strophes, usually with longer lines, and the combination of strophes is again subdivided into strophe, antistrophe, and epode, of which the first two are exactly

parallel, while the last differs from both in its structure. While the number of the Æolian metres is fixed, every Dorian song has its own metre, the rhythm of which depends on the tune suitable to the subject. As to the kinds of songs we also find great variety in the Dorian lyric: there are *pœans*, *hȳporchēmata*, *hymns*, *prŏsŏdĭa*, *parthĕnĭa*, *dithyrambs*, *encōmĭa*, *ĕpĭnīcĭa*, *hȳmĕnæa*, *ĕpĭthălămĭa*, *thrēnoi* (*q.v.*); drinking songs and love songs are also not wanting. They are written in the old epic dialect, influenced by Doric.

With regard to their historical development: ALCMĀN (about 660), a Lydian who had become a citizen of Sparta, was the first to compose longer and more varied poems on the lines laid down by Terpander and his school. The Dorian lyric received its later artistic form from the Sicilian STĒSĬCHŎRUS of Hĭmĕrā (about 600), whose contemporary ARĪON first gave a place in literature to the dithyramb. (*See* DITHYRAMBOS.) In the 6th century choral poetry became the common property of all Greeks, and so flourished more and more. Of its older representatives we have still to mention IBȲCUS of Rhēgium (about 540), in whose choral songs the erotic element prevails. This class of poetry was brought to its greatest perfection at the time of the Persian Wars by SĬMŌNĬDĔS of Cĕŏs, by his nephew, BACCHȲLĬDĔS, and above all by PINDAR of Thebes. Besides these TĬMŎCREŌN of Iālȳsus, and the poetesses MYRTIS, CŎRINNA, PRAXILLA, and TĒLĒSILLA deserve mention. Of the productions of Æolian and Dorian lyric poetry only fragments have been preserved, except the epinician odes of Pindar.

With the *Romans*, the first attempts to imitate the forms of the Greek "melic" date from the last years of the Republic. LÆVIUS wrote mythological poems in a great variety of metres, the *Erŏtŏpœgnĭa* ("Diversions of Love"), which however seem to have attracted little attention. CĂTULLUS also wrote some poems in "melic" measures. This kind of poetry was perfected in the age of Augustus by HORACE, who introduced the forms of Æolian lyric. None of the succeeding poets were of even secondary importance, in spite of the great skill with which they handled the various melic metres; one of them, the Christian poet PRŪDENTIUS, wrote as late as the 4th century. The Dorian lyric never obtained a footing among the Romans.

Lȳsĭăs, in point of time the third of the Ten Attic Orators, was born at Athens about

B.C. 445. He was a son of the rich Syracusan Cĕphălus, who had been invited by Pericles to settle at Athens. At the age of fifteen he went with his two brothers to Thŭrii, in South Italy, and there studied under the Syracusan rhetorician Tīsĭäs. He returned to Athens in 412, and lived in the Piræus in comfortable circumstances, being joint possessor, with his eldest brother Pŏlĕmarchus, of several houses and a manufactory of shields, where 120 slaves were employed. Under the rule of the Thirty Tyrants, however, the brothers were accused in 404 of being enemies to the existing government; their property was confiscated and Polemarchus executed, while Lysias with the greatest difficulty managed to escape to Mĕgără. After the fall of the Thirty, in which he had eagerly co-operated, he returned to Athens, and gave his time to the lucrative occupation of writing legal speeches for others, after obtaining high repute as an orator, in 403, by his accusation of Erătosthĕnĕs, the murderer of his brother. He died in his eighty-third year, esteemed by all.

Of the 425 speeches to which the ancients assigned his name, but of which the greater number (233) were regarded as not genuine, there remain—besides numerous and sometimes considerable fragments—thirty-one, though they are not all quite complete; and of these five must be looked upon as certainly not genuine, and four others are open to grave suspicion. Only one of these speeches, that against Eratosthenes, mentioned above, was delivered by Lysias in person. He is the first really classical orator of the Greeks, and a model of the *plain style*, which avoids grandiloquence and seeks to obtain its effect by a sober and clear representation of the case. The ancient critics justly praised the purity and simplicity of his language, the skill shown in always adapting style to subject, the combination of terseness with graphic lucidity of description, particularly noticeable in narrative, and, lastly, his power of painting character.

Lȳsĭcrătĕs, Monument of, at Athens. One of the most graceful relics of Greek antiquity, raised in memory of a victory in the dramatic contests won by Lysicrates when he was *chŏrēgus* (*see* CHORUS) in B.C. 334. From a slender square basement, [12 feet high by 9 feet wide] rises a small but elegant round temple; six engaged Corinthian columns surround its circular wall and support the entablature, on the frieze of which there is a delicate and life-like representation of a scene in the legend of Dĭonȳsus (the changing of the Tyrrhenian pirates into dolphins, for having by mistake laid hands on the god). Over the entablature is a flat dome made of a single block of marble, and from the centre of the roof rises a finial of acanthus leaves, formerly crowned by the tripod which was the prize of victory. The monument is thirty-five feet high, and the diameter of the inside is about six feet. The reliefs of the frieze are of great value, as they belong to the new Attic school of Scŏpäs and Praxĭtĕlĕs. According to a tradition (which is without foundation) that Demos-

THE CHORAGIC MONUMENT OF LYSICRATES, ATHENS.

thenes used to study here, the monument used to be called the Lantern of Demosthenes. [This name was familiar to Michael Akominatos, in the second half of the 12th century; Gregorovius, *Mirabilien der Stadt Athen*, p. 357. The true name was first restored by Transfeldt about 1674, id. *Athen im Mittelalter*, ii 357.]

Lȳsippus, of Sĭcȳŏn. One of the most famous Greek artists, a contemporary of Alexander the Great; was originally a worker in metal, and taught himself the art of the sculptor by studying nature and the *canon* of Pŏlȳclītus (*q.v.*). His works, which were said to amount to 1,500, were all statues in bronze, and were remarkable for their lifelike characterization and their careful and accurate execution, shown particularly in the treatment of the hair. He aimed at representing the beauty and harmony more especially of the male human body; and substituted for the proportions of Polyclitus a new ideal, which kept in view the effect produced, by giving the body a more slender and elegant shape, and by making the head smaller in comparison with the trunk, than is the case with the actual average man. The most famous among his statues of gods were the colossal forms of Zeus and Hēraclēs, at Tarentum (of which the former was second in size only to that at Rhodes, while the latter was afterwards brought to the Capitol at Rome, and then to the Hippodrome at Constantinople, where it was melted down in A.D. 1022), and, lastly, the sungod on the four-horse chariot at Rhodes [Pliny, *N. H.*, xxxiv §§ 40, 63].

The first example of pure allegory in Greek art was his *Cairŏs*, the Favourable Moment; a delicate youth with modest look standing on a ball, with his feet winged, and holding shears and a balance in his hands. The hair hung down in front, while it was so short behind that it could not be grasped [*Anthol. Gr.* ii 49, 13; Callistratus, *Statuæ*, 6].

By far the greater number of his statues were portraits; of these the various representations of Alexander the Great from boyhood onwards were of marked excellence [Pliny, *l.c.* 64]. Indeed, the king would have no sculptor but Lysippus to represent him, even as he would have no other painter than Apelles [Pliny, *N. H.*, vii 125; Horace, *Epist.* ii 1, 240; Cicero, *Ad Fam.* v 12, 13].

Among his large groups were Crātērus saving the life of Alexander chasing the lion [Pliny, xxxiv 64], and the portraits of twenty-five horsemen and nine foot soldiers who fell at the first assault in the battle

of the Granīcus [Arrian, *Anab.* i 16 § 7; Plutarch, *Alex.* 16]. The excellent copy in marble, at the Vatican, of the *Apoxyŏmĕnŏs*,

* MARBLE COPY OF THE APOXYOMENOS OF LYSIPPUS.
(Rome, Vatican Museum.)

a youth removing the dust of the palæstra with a strigil, affords an idea of his skill in representing beautiful and perfectly developed bodies of delicate elasticity and graceful suppleness [Pliny, xxxiv 62].

M

Māchaira. A one-edged sword, slightly curved, in use among the Greeks. For further information, *see* SWORD.

Māchāōn and Pŏdălīrius. The sons of Asclēpius and Ēpĭōnē, skilled in the art of healing, took part in the expedition to Troy with thirty Thessalian ships, and were there the physicians of the Greeks, besides fighting valiantly. According to post-Homeric legends Machaon was slain by Eurўpўlus, the son of Tēlĕphus, and his corpse was brought by Nestor to Messenia, where, at Gĕrēnia, he had a sepulchre and a temple in which cures were effected. Podalirius, who recognised the madness of Ajax by his burning eyes, stayed with Calchās from the fall of Troy to his death, and then settled at Syrnŏs in Caria; he had a *hērŏōn* in Apulia, close to that of Calchas.

Macrŏbius (*Ambrŏsius Theodŏsius*). A man of high rank, and, according to his own account, not a born Roman, and probably a

pagan, who wrote, in the beginning of the 5th century after Christ, two extant works: (1) a commentary on Cicero's Dream of Scipio (*Somnium Scīpĭōnis*, from the sixth book of the *De Republĭcā*); and (2) an antiquarian compilation in seven books, treating of a number of historical, mythological, grammatical, and antiquarian subjects, in the form of table talk, at a celebration of the *Sāturnālĭa;* hence the title, *Convīvia Saturnalia.* Macrobius has gathered his information from various authors, especially Gellius, whom, however, he does not mention any more than his other authorities.

Mænads (Gr. *mainādĕs*) "the frenzied ones." Women in Bacchic ecstasy, who formed part of the train of Dionysus (*q.v.* fig. 3; *cp.* VASES, fig. 13).

Magister Equĭtum. The assistant of the dictator, nominated by him immediately after his own appointment, and bound to obey him unconditionally, representing him in his absence, or when otherwise prevented. He owed his name ("Master of the Horse") to the fact that it was part of his office to command the cavalry in battle, while the dictator was at the head of the infantry. As the *insignia* of his magistracy he had the *sella cŭrūlis*, the *prœtexta*, and six lictors.

Măgistrātŭs. A term used by the Romans both to designate the magistracy and the person who held it. The magistrates of the Republic were partly ordinary, chosen at regular intervals: *consŭlēs, censōres, prœtōres, œdīles cŭrūles, quœstōres, trĭbunī plēbĭs*, and *œdīles plēbĭs;* partly extraordinary, chosen only under special circumstances, the principal being *dictātor, măgister ĕquĭtum*, and *interrex*. Among these the consuls, prætors, and dictator are distinguished from the others by the possession of the *impĕrium* (*q.v.*) derived from the regal power (the *interrex* had it for five days only); they and the censors, who, without possessing the *impeňium*, derived their duties from the regal power, constitute the higher magistrates, *magistratus māiōres*, while the rest are the lower, *mĭnōres*, with the exception of the tribunes, who have a position of their own. For those offices, which could originally be held by patricians alone, the term *patrician* was preserved, even after they had become accessible to the plebeians. The *plebeian* offices also, the tribunate and plebeian ædileship, do not designate any political contrast after plebeians and patricians had been made legally equal, although only plebeians could hold them. Another distinction is that into *magistratus curules* and *non curules*, which refers to the right of having a *sella curulis* (*q.v.*). This and the *tŏga prœtexta*, a white *toga* edged with purple, were accorded to the higher magistrates, the *œdiles curules* and the *magister equitum*. Only the *magistratus cum imperio* and the *magister equitum* were permitted to have lictors with the *fasces* (*q.v.*). All the magistrates were elected, except the *dictator* and the *magister equitum;* the *magistratus maiores* at the *cŏmĭtĭa centŭrĭāta*, the rest at the *comitia trĭbūta*. Every magistrate had the right to call the people to a *contĭo* (*q.v.*), to issue edicts, which had the force of laws as long as his authority (*pŏtestās*) lasted, to take auspices which were binding for the district within his jurisdiction, and to exercise a limited right of punishment; the higher magistrates and the tribunes had the power, generally

speaking, of convoking the comitia and the senate (*cp.* IMPERIUM). The power of the magistrates was limited by the senate, the intercession of the tribunes and of magistrates of equal or higher rank, the right of appeal of the citizens, and the liability to give account after retirement from office; for no charge could be brought, at any rate against the higher magistrates, as long as they held it.

The following were the conditions for obtaining an office: (1) Personal application before the election, the right of rejection being in the hands of the magistrate who directed them (a consul in the case of the higher magistrates, a tribune for the plebeian, a consul—afterwards also the prætor of the city—for the rest). (2) Eligibility, dependent on membership of a citizen family, full possession of personal liberty and honorary rights (*see* INFAMIA), and the absence of bodily blemish (note also that patricians could not hold plebeian offices). (3) A minimum age for each office, at first according to a certain tradition, then regulated by law, so that in Cicero's time a candidate for the quæstorship had to be in his 30th year at least; in his 37th for the curule ædileship; in his 40th for the prætorship; and in his 43rd for the consulship. (4) At this time also the traditional order of the above-mentioned offices was considered law, and a man was compelled to hold the lower office before he could proceed to the higher, except that the ædileship could be neglected. (5) An interval of two years had to elapse between the ædileship, prætorship, and consulate, and of one year between the tribunate and any other office. (6) Ten years had to elapse before the same office could be held again; in this, and with regard to age, order of offices, and intervals between them, exceptions were permitted under special circumstances.

The date of the elections was fixed by the senate; in Cicero's time they usually took place in July [*Ad Att.* i 16; *Ad Fam.* viii 4]. From B.C. 153 the magistrates, whose names were solemnly announced (*rĕnuntĭātĭo*) at the end of the elections, mostly entered upon their office on January 1st. (*See articles on the individual magistrates.*) Just as on this occasion they swore to keep the laws, so at the end of their term of office, which was a year, except in the case of the censors, the dictator, and the *magister equitum* (*q.v.*), they affirmed on oath before a *contio*, that they had done nothing contrary to the laws. The officials elected to an office vacated before the end of the year (*suffecti*) simply held it for the remainder of that year. The only thing that could legally compel a magistrate to resign before the end of his time was a formal error in the taking of the auspices at the elections.

The magistrates received no salaries whatsoever, but they were indemnified for official expenses within the town (*e.g.* for the games) or without it; those officials more especially who were going to the provinces as procurators received a sufficient sum from the treasury for their equipment and the support of themselves and their suite. Under the Empire the old magistracies continued to exist, though their authority was considerably limited; *cp.* the several articles, and for their election, *see* COMITIA (*end*). Besides these, numerous new offices came into existence, especially the various *præfecti* (*q.v.*), some of whom received an actual salary.

The magistracies were completely remodelled by Diocletian and Constantine, especially with regard to their pay; all imperial officials received salaries, while the municipal did not. *Cp.* the several articles mentioned in the beginning.

Magna Mater. A Roman name of the goddess Rhea (*q.v.*).

Magnes. One of the first founders of Attic Comedy. (*See* COMEDY.)

Maia. Daughter of Atlas and Pleïŏnē, one of the Pleiads (*q.v.*), mother of Hermēs by Zeus. The Romans identified her with an old Italian goddess of spring, *Maia Mâiestâs* (also called *Fauna, Bŏna Dea, Ops*), who was held to be the wife of Vulcan, and to whom the flamen of that god sacrificed a pregnant sow on the 1st of May.

Mâiestâs. Denoted among the Romans the sovereign power of the people and the State, or that of the emperor. To detract from this sovereign power was a crime (*crimen mĭnûtæ mâiestâtis*). Originally the term *perdŭellio* (*q.v.*) included all offences of this kind; distinctions were first made in B.C. 100 by the *Lex Apŭlēïa*, which declared some offences to be treason that had previously been regarded as *perduellio*, such as hindering the tribunes and exciting to sedition. The idea of treason was considerably extended by the *Lex Cornēlïa* of the dictator Sulla in B.C. 80, which made it include inciting to sedition, hindering a magistrate in the exercise of his functions, and acting in a manner prejudicial to the

Roman prestige or beyond the limits of one's authority. It also instituted a permanent lawcourt (*see* QUÆSTIO PERPETUA) to take cognisance of such cases; and made exile (*interdictio aquæ et ignis*) the penalty. (*See* EXILIUM.) Cæsar's *Lex Iulia*, B.C. 46, made *perduellio* pass over into *crimen maiestatis*, which was held to cover all actions prejudicial to the State and the existing constitution (such as treason, plots, conspiracies, sedition, illegal assumption of authority). The Julian Law also formed the basis for punishing offences of this kind under the Empire; to these were now added all those against the person and the authority of the emperor. The term was very elastic, and received whatever interpretation the emperor preferred, so that when a charge, *e.g.* that of embezzlement (*see* REPETUNDARUM CRIMEN), was brought against a man, he could often be also charged with the *crimen maiestatis*, especially as the accusers were rewarded if the offence was proved. After the closing of the *quæstiones* these cases were decided by the senate; later still, the emperor was judge, or entrusted them to the *præfectus urbi*. The regular penalty was confiscation, and sometimes banishment or death. Charges of treason could be brought or the trial could be continued, even after the death of the accused; and in the most serious cases the penalty had to be borne by the children, in accordance with a decree of the emperor, and even with the law at a later period.

Mamers. *See* MARS.

Mamertinus (*Claudius*). A Latin panegyrist, the author of a speech addressed to the emperor Julian on January 1st, A.D. 362, at Constantinople, thanking him for conferring the consulate on him. It gives a pretty accurate picture of the personality of the emperor and of his administration. An older Mamertinus is assumed to be the author of two panegyrics in praise of Maximinianus, co-regent with Diocletian, which were delivered in 289 and 291 at Trèves.

Mâmûrius. The mythical maker of the *ancilia*. (*See* ANCILE.)

Mâna Gĕnïta. *See* MANIA.

Mancĭpâtĭo (*lit.* a taking with the hand). A formal mode of purchase among the Romans, which seems to go back to a time when the price of purchase was weighed out in bars of copper. In the presence of six Roman citizens of the age of puberty, one of whom, called the *librïpens* (weigher), held a copper balance, the pur chaser took hold of the thing and uttered certain prescribed words. He then struck the balance (*libra*) with a small piece of copper (*œs* or *rauduscŭlum*), which he gave to the seller as symbol of the price. This mode of purchase *per œs et libram* was employed in the case of *res mancĭpi*, i.e. estates in Italy or provinces with Italian iaw, in the country or in towns, slaves, and domestic animals and beasts of burden needed for agricultural purposes; also in a certain kind of testaments, in the form of marriage called *coëmptio*, and in transferring one's power over a person (*manus*) to another. (*See* ADOPTION, EMANCIPATIO, and MANCIPIUM.)

Mancĭpĭum. The right of possession obtained through *mancipatio* (*q.v.*), and the possession itself, which none but the head of the family has a right to dispose of. *Hŏmĭnes lībĕri in mancipio* are free men, whom their father has given into the power of another man by *mancipatio*, e.g. in compensation for some damage they have done to the latter. Their position differed from that of slaves in this, that they retained the right of personality, could complain if their masters treated them badly, and regained all the rights of a freeborn man on leaving their position of dependence. This was effected in the same way as the liberation of slaves *vindictā, censu,* and *testamento*. (*See* FREEDMEN.) After the repeal of the severe laws making imprisonment the penalty of convicted debtors, the same relation as that mentioned above existed between debtor and creditor, until the money was paid.

Mānēs (*i.e.* the good). A name given by the Romans to the spirits of the dead, which were held to be immortal like the gods, and hence designated as such (*dii manes*). They dwell below the earth, and only come forth at certain seasons of the year. On the *Mons Pălātīnus* at Rome, there was, as in other Italian towns, a deep pit with the shape of an inverted sky, known as *mundus*, the lowest part of which was consecrated to the infernal gods and also to the Manes, and was closed with a stone, *lăpĭs mānālis*, thought to be the gate of the nether world. This stone was lifted up three times a year (August 24th, October 5th, November 8th), and the Manes were then believed to rise to the upper world: on this account those days were *rēlĭgĭōsi*, i.e. no serious matter might be undertaken on them. Sacrifices were offered to them as to the dead; water, wine, warm milk, honey, oil, and the blood

of black sheep, pigs, and oxen, were poured on the grave; ointments and incense were offered; and the grave was decked with flowers, roses and violets by preference. Oblations, which chiefly consisted of beans, eggs, lentils, bread and wine, were placed on the grave, and the mourners partook of a meal in its neighbourhood. Besides the private celebrations there was also a public and universal festival, the *Părentālia*, which lasted from the 13th to the 21st of February, the last month of the older Roman year; the last day had the special name *Fĕrālia*. During these days all the temples were closed, marriages were prohibited, and the magistrates had to appear in public without the tokens of their office. The festival of the dead was followed by that of the relations on February 22nd, called *Caristia*. This was celebrated throughout the town by each individual family, the members of which exchanged presents and met at festal banquets.

Mănĕthōn (or *Manĕthōs*). An Egyptian of Sĕbennytus, who lived in the second half of the 3rd century B.C. He was high priest at Hēlĭŏpŏlis in Egypt, and wrote in Greek a history of his native country from the oldest times to its conquest by Alexander the Great, founded on the sacred records of the Egyptians. Recent hieroglyphic discoveries have confirmed the authority of this work against the doubts and suspicions previously entertained, and show it to have been compiled from good sources: only a third of the kings' names and some fragments have been preserved by later writers. He has been wrongly considered the author of a Greek poem in six books, treating of the influence of the constellations on the fates of men, entitled *Apŏtĕlesmătĭca ;* various parts of it seem to have been written by different authors between the 3rd and 5th century after Christ.

Mānĭa. An old Italian goddess of the Manes, *i.e.* the dead, also called *Lara, Larunda, Muta* (the dumb), *Māna Gĕnĭta,* who was held by some to be the mother or grandmother of the good *Lărēs,* by others of the evil *Larvœ.* Originally daughter of the river-god Almo, and called Lara, she was deprived of her tongue by Jupiter, because she had betrayed his love for the Nymph Juturna, and was condemned to be the Nymph of the marshy waters in the realm of the speechless. On the way to the nether world Mercury fell in love with her, and the Lares were her offspring   In early times boys are said to have been sacrificed to her, to insure the prosperity of a family. At a later period heads of poppies and garlic were offered to her, and woollen dolls, *maniæ*, called after her, were suspended on the doors as a protection. As *Mana Genita* she received the sacrifice of a dog and was implored not to let any of the family become a " good one," *i.e.* die. In the course of time Mania became a bogy with which children were threatened.

Mānīlius. The reputed author of a Latin didactic poem about astronomy and astrology (*Astrŏnŏmĭca*), in five books, the first of which was written under Augustus, after the battle in the *Saltus Teutoburgiensis*, 9 A.D., and the fifth under Tiberius. The first two books treat of astronomy as the foundation of astrology; the rest, of the influence of constellations on human destiny. The author certainly intended to write a sixth book, but it has either been lost or was never written. The poet, who shows extensive knowledge, frequently boasts of having been the first among Roman poets to treat the subject, and handles his difficult theme with a dexterity and a moral earnestness that recall Lucretius, whose language he has frequently imitated. In metrical skill he is on a par with the best poets of the Augustan age.

Mānĭpŭlus. A subdivision of the Roman legion (*q.v.*), which had thirty of them (three in each of the ten cohorts). The *manipulus* consisted of two centuries.

Mantīkē (sc. *technē*) is the name given by the Greeks to the gift or *art of divination.* The belief of the ancients, that it was possible to find out what was hidden or what was going to happen, sprang from the idea that the gods, when implored by prayer, or even when unimplored, graciously communicated revelations to men, by means of direct inspiration or through signs requiring interpretation. Hence the ancients distinguished between *natural* and *artificial divination.*

Divination is *natural*, when a man receives the inspiration of the divinity in a dream or in an ecstatic state. The belief in divine inspiration in dreams is of the greatest antiquity (*see* DREAMS), and continued to be held when the natural causes of dreams had been ascertained. The meaning of prophetic dreams cannot, however, always be immediately comprehended ; they are mostly symbolical and therefore require an interpretation. As a guide to this, there arose in the course of time certain rules resulting from experience, which

produced a special art, that of interpreting dreams, of which some idea is given by the *Oneirŏcrĭtĭca*, on the interpretation of dreams, by Artĕmĭdōrus (*q.v.*). Similarly, the dreams obtained by sleeping at holy places (*incŭbātĭo*, *see* INCUBARE), which were always considered prophetic, usually needed a priest to interpret them.

The power of more or less clearly seeing in waking hours things concealed from ordinary vision was believed by the Greeks to be a special gift of Apollo. It is from him that Homer makes Calchās receive his revelations, although no mention is made of his being in the ecstatic state usually connected with this kind of soothsaying. At the oracles this state was usually produced by external influences (*see* ORACLES) ; women were held to be particularly susceptible to them. Besides oracles and persons reputed to be inspired, use was made of various collections of older oracular sayings and pretended predictions of prophets and prophetesses of former times. Such collections were not only in the possession of states and priesthoods, but also in that of private individuals, called *chrēsmŏlŏgī*, who drew on their store when paid to do so by those who believed in them, and often also explained the dark sayings. Like the prophets by immediate inspiration, those also were called seers who interpreted according to certain rules the divine signs, which formed the subject of the *artificial* variety of the art of divination.

From the very oldest times special importance was attached to omens of birds (whether in answer to prayer or not), which were discriminated from one another by various rules, with regard partly to the kind of birds, partly to the manner of their appearing ; *e.g.* direction (favourable from the right, unfavourable from the left), flight, alighting, singing, and anything else they did. The principal birds consulted were the birds of prey that fly highest and alone, the eagle (the messenger of Zeus), the heron, the hawk, the falcon, and the vulture ; in the case of ravens and crows the cawing was an omen.

Second in importance were the various phenomena of the sky considered as divine signs. Whether thunder and lightning were favourable or not was also decided by the direction, right or left, from which they came. At Sparta shooting stars were thought to show that the gods were displeased with the kings. Eclipses of the sun and moon, comets, and meteors were signs that inspired terror. Prophesying from the stars however did not become known in Greece till the time of Alexander the Great.

In important enterprises, especially in war, recourse was had to an examination of the condition of sacrificed animals or *hĭĕro-scŏpĭa;* oxen, sheep, and also pigs being most frequently the victims. The points observed were: normal or abnormal nature of the entrails, especially the liver, with the gall-bladder, and also the heart, spleen, and lungs. The various kinds of entrails and their abnormal conditions were made the subject of a highly elaborate system, so that no Greek army could dispense with a skilled interpreter of signs. When the omens were unfavourable, the sacrifice was repeated till they were favourable, or the enterprise was postponed. The manner too in which animals went to be sacrificed, whether willingly or with reluctance, etc., was looked upon as an omen, as also the way in which the sacrifice burnt on the altar, the burning of the flame itself, the rising or sinking of the smoke, etc. These signs drawn from fire were the subject of *pyrŏmantcia.*

There was indeed a general inclination to regard all striking and unusual events as hints from the gods, and to interpret them oneself, or to have them interpreted by skilled seers. From ancient times the chance utterances of others were thought to be prophetic in so far as they applied to the circumstances of the moment. For such omens also the gods were asked. Besides these, lots and dice were used for predictions. There were many other artificial varieties of the art of divination, some of them very strange, which were in special favour in the lower classes of the people and in later times; as, for instance, soothsaying with a sieve suspended by threads, for the purpose of finding out thieves or remedies for illness, etc., that name being thought the one required at mention of which the sieve ceased to turn round. As early as Aristotle allusion is made to *chiromancy,* or palmistry. For the Roman methods of prophecy, *see* DIVINATIO.

Manto. Daughter of the seer Tīrĕsĭas, was herself a prophetess, at first of the Ismenian Apollo at Thebes. After the capture of the town by the Epĭgŏni she was presented to the oracle at Delphi as part of the booty, and sent by the god to Asia, in order to found the oracle of the

Clarian Apollo in the neighbourhood of what was afterwards Cŏlŏphōn. Here she bore Mopsus (*q.v.*, 2) to the Cretan seer Rhăcius.

Mantuan Vase. *See* GEMS.

Mănŭmissĭō. Freeing of slaves. *See* FREEDMEN.

Mănŭs, in its wider sense, is the name given by the Romans to the power of the chief of a family over the whole of that family, especially the power of the husband over his wife, whose person and property were so completely his own, that he was legally responsible for her actions, but at the same time had the right to kill, punish, or sell her. As in this respect, so also with respect to the right of inheritance, the wife was placed on a level with the children, as she obtained the same share as they. For marriages without *manus, see* MARRIAGE.

Mănŭs Iniectĭō (laying the hand on). In the oldest Roman legal procedure a kind of execution levied on the person of one who had been condemned to pay a certain sum. If this was not done within thirty days of the condemnation, the plaintiff could seize the debtor and bring him before the prætor, who handed him over to the creditor with the word *addĭcō* (I hand over), unless he paid there and then, or a *vindex* came forward to pay for him or to show there was no ground for complaint. The creditor kept the debtor in chains at his house for sixty days; if his claims had not been satisfied during this period, he might kill him or sell him as a slave in foreign parts. From the 4th century onwards a less severe arrangement was usual; the relation of the *addictus* to his creditor was that of a *hŏmo lĭber in mancĭpĭo.* (*See* MANCIPIUM.)

Marcellus Empĭrĭcus (so called from his empirical work on medical remedies), of Burdĭgălă (*Bordeaux*). Marshal of the household (*magister offĭcĭōrum*) to Thĕŏdosius I, compiled about A.D. 410 a dispensatory for the poor, which was chiefly founded on Scribonius Largus (*q.v.*), with many superstitious additions.

Marciānus. A Greek geographer, who lived at Hērăclēa in Bithȳnia. With the aid of the best sources of information from Hanno and Scȳlax down to Ptŏlĕmæus, he compiled, about 400 A.D., a description of the Western and Eastern ocean in two books, not completely preserved. It is of particular importance for ancient geography, as the distances in stadia are given.

Marcus Aurelius. *See* ANTONINUS (1).

Marius Maxĭmus. Latin historian. (*See*

SCRIPTORES HISTORIÆ AUGUSTÆ and SUETONIUS).

Market. *See* AGORA and FORUM.

Market, Clerks of the (*see* AGORANOMUS).

Marpēssa. Daughter of the river god Euēnus, and wife of Idas. (*See* IDAS AND LYNCEUS.)

Marriage. (I) *Greek.* The principle of monogamy was predominant as early as the Homeric age. The Homeric poems represent the son as leaving the choice of a wife to his father, and the father as disposing at will of his daughter's hand. The suitor usually offered to pay the girl's father a certain number of oxen or other objects of value. The daughter on her side received a suitable provision from her father. This property had to be restored to the wife on the death of her husband, unless his heirs wished otherwise. Marriages were valid between persons of different station as well as between persons of the same station. The marriage festivities included a banquet given by the father of the bride. The bride was conducted in festal procession with torches to the house of her husband, a bridal song, the *Hymĕnæus*, being meanwhile sung with dances by the youths who accompanied her. The mistress of the house held a position equal to that of the man with whom she was associated for life, and was treated with the same consideration in her sphere as her husband in his. The husband was allowed by custom to have concubines, whose children were brought up in the house of their father with those of the lawful wife. But they received only a small share of the property, which the legitimate children divided among themselves by lot after their father's death. Illegitimate children incurred no disgrace, and the sons borne by a slave to a free man were accounted free.

Later times. Athens. In Athens a girl's life was so completely confined to her home that love was very seldom the prelude to marriage. The parents made the choice for their children, equality of birth and property being the chief considerations. No marriage was valid unless both parties were children of Athenian citizens, and no children were legitimate unless born of such a marriage. If either wife or husband were of non-Athenian extraction, the marriage was accounted as no better than concubinage, and the children were illegitimate. Every legal marriage was preceded by a formal betrothal, at which the agreements were settled and the amount of the dowry determined. If an heiress were left fatherless, the man next in order of inheritance was entitled to claim her in marriage; if she were poor, and so unable to obtain a husband, he was bound to make her a provision within an amount fixed by law. Weddings were held by preference in the seventh month of the Athenian year, which was thence called Gămēlĭŏn (Jănuary–February). A wedding was preceded by certain preliminary rites called *prŏtĕleia*, consisting of prayers and sacrifices offered to the deities of marriage, especially to Hēra. The bride was conducted to the Acrŏpŏlĭs by her parents into the temple of Athēnē, goddess of the city, whose blessing they prayed for with offering of sacrifice. On the wedding-day the bride and bridegroom bathed in water brought at Athens from the spring Callirrhŏē, and in all other cities from some special river or spring. The water was fetched by a male or female relation of youthful age. The bride's father provided a wedding banquet, to which the women, usually excluded from the gatherings of men, were invited. The men and women sat at separate tables, the bride being veiled. In the evening the bride was formally conducted to her new home on a carriage drawn by mules or oxen. She took her place, surrounded by various kinds of household furniture, between the bridegroom and the conductor of the bride, a confidential friend of the bridegroom. If the bridegroom had been previously married, he did not bring his bride home himself, but was represented by his friends. The carriage was followed by the friends and relatives, singing the marriage hymn to the accompaniment of flutes. Among them was the bride's mother, bearing the wedding torch, kindled at her own hearth; other torches preceded and followed. At the door of the bridegroom's house, which was adorned with green branches, the bridegroom's mother met the pair with torches in her hand. The bride and bridegroom now entered the house amid the cheers of its inmates, who, by way of a lucky omen, rained upon them a shower of all kinds of fruits and sweetmeats. The bride ate a quince, the symbol of fertility. At this point there was often a supper. The bride was then conducted by an elderly female relation, called the Nympheutrĭa, to the bridal chamber, which the latter had adorned, and here given to the bridegroom. Songs, called *ĕpĭthălămĭa*, were sung by the guests before the doors of the chamber. The next two days were taken up with the sending of wedding presents, and it was only after these days had passed that the young bride appeared unveiled. It was now the duty of the husband to enroll his wife in his *phrātria*, and have his marriage registered: a sacrifice and a banquet forming part of the ceremonies. If these formalities were neglected, doubts might be subsequently raised as to the validity of the marriage. A representation of the ceremonies preliminary to a Greek marriage may be seen in the painting called the *Aldobrandini Wedding*. (*See* cut under PAINTING, fig. 4.) The usages were similar in the other Greek cities. The Spartans had some peculiarities, one of which was that the bridegroom had to get possession of his bride by an act of violence, carrying her off from among her companions, who had to offer a more or less serious resistance. He then brought her to the house of a female relation, who took her to the bridal chamber, cut off her hair and clothed her in male attire, and then introduced the bridegroom. Greek custom allowed of marriage between half brothers and half sisters, when not descended from the same mother. Girls generally married early, sometimes when not older than fourteen.

The women lived in a separate part of the house, situated in the upper story or at the back. To this the unmarried daughters were confined, and no men, except the nearest relatives, were allowed to enter it. The life of a Greek woman was entirely taken up with household management, for which she was responsible to the fullest extent. Her appearance in public was regulated by certain limitations of general custom and of law, which in many places were strictly enforced by a special authority. It was only at family festivals and the great religious celebrations that they mixed freely in men's society; at the ordinary meals of the men they were never allowed to be present. Their position was in most states a subordinate one. The general opinion was that women were, not only physically, but intellectually and morally, inferior to men, that they required guidance and superintendence, and were only to a slight extent in sympathy with higher interests. They were all their life precluded from the legal acquisition of property. Sparta was an exception. Here the training of the women was assimilated to that of the men. The Spartan woman

was accustomed from her youth up to account herself a citizen, to take a lively interest in all public affairs, and even in matters which elsewhere were deemed to be quite outside the sphere of women's judgment. Thus women in Sparta acquired a considerable influence, and much importance was attached to their approval or disapproval. But even in Sparta the life of married women was mostly confined to their own houses, nor were they so free as the unmarried girls to mingle in men's society. The married women, unlike the unmarried girls, could not appear in public unveiled. — In Sparta dowries were forbidden by law, but in Athens they were an important element in society. The husband had only the usufruct of the dowry, it did not become his property. Everything else that the wife brought into the house was regarded as her personal property, though she had by no means the free disposal of it. If the husband died first, the wife, if she had no children, would return with her dowry to her relations on the father's side: if there were children, she was free to remain with them in her husband's house. The property of father and mother came to the sons as soon as they were of age, up to which time it was administered for them by guardians. Divorce might take place at the mere pleasure of the husband, but he had to repay the dowry, unless the wife had given any legal ground for his action, as, *e.g.*, by the commission of adultery. The wife could not separate from her husband against his wish without a judicial decision. To obtain this she had to hand in to the archon a written statement of the grounds on which she sought a divorce. If the wife was guilty of adultery, the husband was bound to divorce her; if he failed, his reputation suffered as much as that of the adulteress herself. The injured husband was legally allowed to kill the adulteress on the spot. Not to marry was in Sparta accounted a violation of civil duty, and punished by a sort of *ătīmīa*. An old bachelor was not admitted to the public festivals, such as the *Gymnŏpœdīa*. He had, at the command of the ephors, to walk round the market in a single shirt, singing against himself the while a mocking ditty in which he owned the justice of his punishment for disobedience to the laws. Nor had he any claim to being greeted with the marks of deference with which the old were generally received by the young.

(II) *Roman.* Among the Romans a lawful marriage could only be contracted by persons who were politically entitled to do so. The right of contracting a lawful marriage was at first confined to the patricians, until in 445 B.C. the law of the tribune Canuleius opened it to all Roman citizens. The Latins received it on being admitted to the Roman citizenship; in later times it was extended in like manner to all the Italians, and finally Caracalla conferred it on all the inhabitants of the Roman empire. If only one party to the marriage were a Roman citizen, the marriage was invalid: the children took the position of the mother, unless she were a citizen. Marriages within the sixth degree of relationship were originally forbidden. In later times they were allowed as far as the fourth degree, and after 49 A.D. within certain limitations as far as the third. It was originally the parent's business to arrange the marriage of the children, but the consent both of son and daughter was absolutely necessary. There were two methods of concluding a marriage. The woman might come into the power (*mănus*) of her husband: in this case she passed into his family, the property she brought with her became his, and she acquired the right of inheritance in his family. Or she might remain in the *manus* of her own father and in possession of her own rights of property. A marriage of the first kind might be contracted in three ways:

(1) By *confarrĕātĭō.* This ceremony was so called from the offering of a cake of spelt, made to Jupiter in the presence of the *pontĭfex* and *flāmen Diālis,* with ten witnesses. This was the ancient patrician form of marriage. Towards the end of the republican age it became obsolete except in case of the most sacred priesthoods of the State. (2) By *ūsus.* If the woman lived for a year in her husband's house without absenting herself from him for three nights. (3) By *coĕmptĭŏ,* or a symbolic sale. (*See* COEMPTIO.) In this case the father delivered his daughter to her husband as a piece of property, she at the same time declaring her consent. The conclusion of the marriage was preceded by the betrothal. In this ceremony the bridegroom gave the bride earnest-money, as in other cases of contract, or a ring in its stead.

The wedding-day was always carefully chosen, certain seasons of the year being deemed inappropriate on religious grounds.

These unlucky periods were the whole of May, the first half of March and of June, all the *dĭēs rĕlĭgĭōsi* and the calends, nones, and ides. The bridal garment consisted in a white *tŭnĭca,* a robe woven in ancient fashion from top to bottom, and fastened by a woollen girdle with a peculiar knot. The bride's hair was arranged in six locks (*crīnĕs*), and in it she wore a garland of flowers of her own gathering: her head was covered with a red veil. A victim was sacrificed, the auspices taken, and the marriage contract completed. A married lady then led the bride and bridegroom together: they took each other's hands, a prayer was addressed to the gods of marriage, and a sacrifice offered by the newly married pair, generally on one of the public altars. A feast was held in the bride's house, and at nightfall the bride was carried off with a show of violence from the arms of her mother and conducted to her new house in festal procession, preceded by a flute-player and torch-bearer, to the singing of Fescennine verses and the wedding cry *talasse.* (*See* FESCENNINI, and *cp.* TALASSIO.) Two boys, whose fathers and mothers were still living, walked at her side; a third lighted her way with a torch of white-thorn, which was accounted a charm against magic; a spindle and thread were carried after her. The bridegroom threw walnuts to the boys in the street as a token that he was bidding adieu to the amusements of childhood. Arrived at the house, the bride anointed the doorposts with oil and fat, and decked them with woollen fillets. She was then lifted over the threshold into the *ātrium,* her future abode, where stood the marriage bed. Here her husband welcomed her into the partnership of fire and water, that is to say, of domestic life and worship. Here also she offered a prayer to the gods for a happy marriage. A feast was given on the next day by her husband, called *rĕpŏtĭa.* At this, in her new position as a married lady she welcomed her relations, who brought her their presents, and offered her first sacrifice to the *Pĕnātēs.*

The position of a married woman among the Romans was much better than it usually was among the Greeks. She was indeed subordinate to her husband, but shared the management of the house with him. She was free in her house, not confined to a special part of it. She had no menial offices to perform, not even cooking, and her time was devoted to the management of the house, to weaving and spinning with her maid-servants in the *atrium*, and to the training of her children. She was addressed as *dŏmĭnă* (mistress) by all the members of her household, even her husband, and their conduct towards her was regulated by certain rules of etiquette. On the 1st of March, the *mātrōnālĭa*, she received congratulations and presents from the whole household. Her birthday, too, was observed with due festivities. She took a personal interest in her husband's pursuits, and was consulted by him on all occasions that concerned the family. In public she was treated with great respect, place was made for her, and no hand might be laid upon her, not even by the officers of the law. She might appear at religious services, at meals (where she remained sitting and took no wine), in the theatre, and even in the courts, whether to give evidence, or to offer intercession for a relative charged with an offence. After her death she was honoured by a public panegyric. The strictness of the social code which regulated the behaviour of women at home and abroad, and the respect in which they were held, maintained the sanctity of marriage for a long time inviolate.

The second Punic War was followed by a state of social corruption, which extended to the female sex, the degradation of which was completed by the dissolution of moral ties brought about by the civil wars. One symptom of the loosening of family life was the increasing number of marriages which did not bring the wives into the power of their husbands, and left them the control of their property. Under the Empire no other kind of marriage survived. Another symptom which appeared, even in the later days of the Republic, was the increasing number of divorces, and the growing unwillingness to marry. In the first five centuries of the city divorces must have been rare. Marriages contracted by *confarreatio* seem originally to have been dissoluble only in case of certain definite offences on the part of the wife. Such were adultery, child-murder, making of false keys, and drinking of wine. In these cases the family council pronounced sentence of death, the execution of which was preceded by a solemn act of *diffarreatio*. The marriages of priests, contracted by *confarreatio*, remained always indissoluble. In early times the dissolution of a marriage for a trivial reason drew down upon it the reproof of the censor. But as time went on divorces became not only more frequent, but more capricious, until at length the mere expression of a desire for separation on the part of husband or wife was sufficient. If the fault was on the husband's side, the wife's dowry was returned to her: if not, certain deductions were made. In case of adultery on the wife's part, the husband had, in ancient times, the right of keeping back the whole dowry, but this law was afterwards relaxed. The censors had, originally, the power of punishing with a pecuniary fine a citizen who refused to marry, but the disinclination to marry grew to such a pitch that neither punishment of the offence, nor rewards offered to the parents of numerous families, could check it. As far back as 131 B.C. the censor Metellus had spoken of marriage as a necessary burden to be borne for patriotic motives. Augustus endeavoured to check the course of opinion by legislation affecting property: unmarried persons were not permitted to inherit at all, and childless couples were allowed to receive only half of their legacies, while parents, especially parents of three or more children, were favoured by various privileges and advantages. Divorces were not to take place, unless accompanied with certain forms and prescriptions. But these laws produced only a superficial effect. The moral standard was not raised, but society sank, under the Empire, to the lowest depth of corruption.

Mars (also *Māvors*, *Māmers*). With Jupiter the principal deity of the inhabitants of Italy, and therefore honoured with particular reverence by the Latins and Romans from the very earliest times, especially as the latter regarded him as the father of Romulus, the founder of Rome. He was held to be the son of Juno, who bore him in consequence of touching a wonderful spring-flower, and the husband of Nĕrĭŏ or Nĕrĭēnē, a goddess of strength. Through the emphasising of one of his attributes he gradually came to be considered as, above all, the god of war; for originally he is at the same time one of the mightiest gods of nature, who accords fertility and protection to fields and herds.

The first month of the old Roman year was dedicated to him as the fertilizing god of spring; in the very ancient chant of the Arval brothers (*q.v.*), at the May-day festival of the Dĕa Dĭa, the help and protection of Mars were demanded. In earlier times he was also invoked at the hallowing of the fields (*see* AMBARVALIA), that he might bless the family, the field and the cattle, and keep off sickness, bad weather, and all else that did harm. (*Cp.* ROBIGUS.) In later times the names of Cērēs and Bacchus were substituted for his on this particular occasion. At the festival on 15th October (*see below*) a horse was sacrificed to him to insure the fair growth of the seed that had been sown. As god of war he had the special name *Gradīvus*, the strider, from the rapid march in battle [1] (*cp.* QUIRINUS), and his symbols were the ravenous wolf, the prophetic and warlike woodpecker, and the lance. When war broke out, the general solemnly invoked his aid, by smiting his holy lance and the holy shields (*ancīlīa* —*see* ANCILE) with the cry, Mars, awake! (*Mars vīgĭlā!*) Many sacrifices were also offered to him during the campaign and before battle; and in his name military honours were conferred. The Field of Mars (*Campus Martius*) was dedicated to him as the patron god of warlike exercises; contests with battle-steeds, called *Equirria*, were there held in his honour on the 27th February, 14th March, and 15th October. On the last-mentioned day the horse on the right of the victorious team was sacrificed on his altar in the Field of Mars; it was known as the horse of October (*October ĕquus*), and its blood was collected and preserved in the temple of Vesta, and used at the Pălīlia for purposes of purification. The cult of Mars was entrusted to a special priest, the *flamen Martialis* (*see* FLAMEN), and the college of the *Sălii* (*q.v.*), which worshipped him more particularly as god of war. His principal festival was in March, the month sacred to him. As early as the time of king Tullus Hostilius, *Păvor* and *Pallor*, Fear and Pallor, are said to have been worshipped as his companions in the fight, in sanctuaries of their own. Augustus caused him to be honoured in a new form, as *Mars Ultor* (avenger of Cæsar), in the magnificent temple in the *Forum Augusti*, consecrated B.C. 2, where statues of him and of Venus, as the two divine ancestors of the Julian family, were set up. In later times he was identified completely with the Greek *Arēs* (*q.v.*).

Mars, Field of. *See* CAMPUS MARTIUS.

Mars' Hill. *See* AREOPAGUS.

---

[1] It has recently been proposed to connect it with *grand-is, grand-ire,* and to explain it as an epithet of growth (Mr. Minton Warren, in *American Journal of Philology,* iv 71).

Marsȳās. A Sīlēnus of Phrygian legend (really god of the river of the same name near the old Phrygian town Cĕlænæ), son of Hyagnis. He was the typical player on the flute. Among the Phrygians the flute entered into the worship of Cȳbĕlē and Dīonȳsus, and Marsyas is said to have instructed Olympus in playing upon that instrument. According to a Greek legend, Athēnē had invented the flute, and then cast it aside because it distorted the features of the player. Marsyas took it up, and became so skilful as to challenge Apollo, the patron god of the lyre. The Muses having declared him vanquished, the god flayed him; his skin was hung up in the cave from which the river Marsyas issued, and was said to move about joyfully when a flute was played. King Mĭdās, who had decided in his favour, received as punishment from Apollo a pair of donkey's ears. The contest was a favourite subject in art.

Martiālis (*Marcus Vălĕrius*). The Roman epigrammatist, born at Bilbĭlis in Spain between A.D. 40 and 43. He was originally intended for the law, and was sent to Rome in Nero's reign to complete his studies, but devoted himself to poetry, which obtained for him the favour of Titus, Domitian, and the great men of Rome, and thus insured him a livelihood. On returning in 98 under Trajan to Bilbilis, after a stay of thirty-four years in the capital, he was so poor that the younger Pliny [Ep. iii 21] had to give him pecuniary assistance for the journey. Though his skill as a poet won him patrons in his native country, and even an estate from the wealthy Marcella, yet he yearned for the bustle of the capital. He died about 102.—Martial is the creator of the modern epigram, and the first ancient poet who exclusively cultivated the epigram as a separate branch of literature. Besides a small collection of epigrams about public shows under Titus and his successor (*Lĭber Spectācŭlōrum*), we possess a much larger collection in fourteen books, of which only two (xi and xii) were not published under Domitian. He depicts, usually in elegiac or iambic verse, the corrupt morals of his degenerate times with brilliant and biting wit and with the metrical skill of Ovid, but without any moral seriousness, and with evident pleasure in what is coarse. A particularly distasteful effect is produced by his fulsome flattery of patrons in high positions, especially Domitian, in whom he manages to discover and to admire every virtue that a man and a prince could possibly possess. His epigrams were much read by the ancients. They have many points of excellence, and they throw a vivid light on the manners and customs of the Silver Age of Latin literature.

Martĭānus Căpella, of Madaura in Africa, apparently a pagan; a lawyer at Carthage. He compiled before 439 A.D. (when Genseric took Carthage) an encyclopædia of the liberal arts, entitled, "The Marriage of Philology and Mercury" (*Nuptiæ Phĭlŏlŏgĭæ et Mercŭrii*), in nine books, a medley of prose and verse on the pattern of the Menippean Satires of Varro, to whom he is also otherwise indebted. The first two books contain the allegory: Mercury marries the maiden Philologia, and among the presents he gives her are seven maidens, the liberal arts: Grammar, Dialectic, Rhetoric, Geometry, Arithmetic, Astronomy, and Harmony (Music); each of these delivers her teaching in the following books. The style is partly dry and partly bombastic. In the earlier Middle Ages the book was for a long time the principal basis of school education in general, and exerted great influence on

the pupil of the actor concealed under the mask; similarly, in the masks of tragedy (figs. 1–4), the hole for the mouth was only a little larger than sufficed to let the sound pass through; while the masks of comedy (figs. 6–10) had lips that were distorted far apart, and in the form of a round hole, so as to make the voice louder. By moulding and painting them in different ways, and variously arranging the hair of the head and the beard, the masks were made to represent many different types of character, men and women of various ages, slaves, etc; the expression also was made to agree with the dominant nature of the parts [Pollux, iv 133–154].

Among the Romans, masks were at first only used at the *Atellānæ* (q.v.), popular farces acted by amateurs; they were not introduced on the stage till the 2nd century B.C., and were not generally employed before the time of the celebrated actor Roscius, an older contemporary of Cicero. After that time, the mimes seem to have been the only actors without masks.

Mātrōna. A name applied by the

MASKS.
1–4 Masks used in Tragedy. 5 Mask used in Satyric Dramas.
6–10 Masks used in Comedy.
(Wieseler, *Theater-gebäude*, etc., taf. v.)

Masks (Gr. *prŏsōpă*, Lat. *persōnæ*). An indispensable part of the equipment of a Greek actor. Their use, like the drama itself, goes back to the mummery at the festivals of Dionўsus, in which the face was painted with lees of wine or with vermilion, or covered with masks made of leaves or the bark of trees. The development of the drama led to the invention of artistic masks of painted linen which concealed not only the face, but the whole head, a device ascribed to Æschўlus. The opening for the eyes was not larger than

Romans to every honourable married woman. She enjoyed the highest esteem; the way was cleared for her in the street, in which she might not appear unaccompanied, and she was not allowed to be touched even when cited before a law court. She was distinguished by the long white *stŏla*, the cloak called *palla*, and her hair divided into six plain plaits, with woollen ribbons (*vittæ*) wound round it.

Mātrōnālĭa. A festival celebrated by Roman matrons on the 1st of March, the anniversary of the foundation of the temple of Juno Lūcīna on the Esquiline. In the houses sacrifices and prayers were offered for a prosperous wedlock, the women received presents from the men and waited on the slaves, just as the men did at the *Saturnalia*. In the temple of the goddess, women and girls prayed to her and to her son Mars, and brought pious offerings.

Mātūta (usually *Māter Mātūta*). An old Italian goddess of dawn and of birth, also goddess of harbours and of the sea, and hence identified with the Greek Leucŏthĕa. In her temple at Rome in the *Forum Boārium*, on the 11th of June, the *Mātrālia*, or festival of mothers, was cele-

honour of king Mausōlus of Caria (died B.C. 352) by his wife Artĕmīsia, and counted by the ancients one of the seven wonders of the world. [According to Pliny, *N. H.* xxxvi §§ 30, 31], it consisted of an oblong substructure surrounded by thirty-six columns, with a circuit of 440 feet, crowned by a pyramid diminishing by twenty-four steps to its summit, on which stood a marble *quadrīga*, the work of Pythis [or Pȳthius, Brunn, *Gr. Künstler,* ii 377, ed. 1]. The height of the whole building, gorgeous with the most varied colours, was 140 feet. Sătȳrus

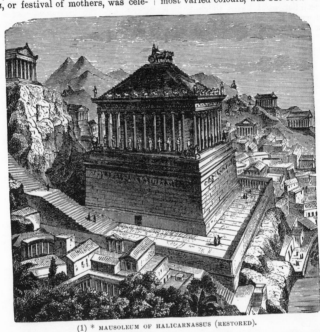

(1) * MAUSOLEUM OF HALICARNASSUS (RESTORED).

brated in her honour by the women of Rome; no slaves were admitted to it, and only a matron who had not been married before was allowed to place a wreath on the statue of the goddess. The women first prayed for the well-being of their nephews and nieces, and then for that of their own children. This custom was referred to the myth of Ino-Leucothea, who tended Dīonȳsus, the son of her sister Sĕmĕlē.

Mausŏlēum (Gr. *Mausōlcĭŏn*). A splendid sepulchre at Halicarnassus, built in

and Pythius were the architects, and the sculptures on the four sides were executed by Scŏpās, Bryaxis, Tīmŏthĕus, and Lĕŏchărēs. In the 12th century after Christ the work was still in a good state of preservation; in succeeding centuries it fell to pieces more and more, until the Knights of St. John used it as a quarry [from the time when they built their castle on the site of the old Greek acropolis in 1402, down to the repair of their fortifications in 1521, when they made lime of its marble sculptures. In 1845, a number of reliefs were extracted from the walls of the castle and placed in the British Museum.] In 1857 the site was discovered by Newton, acting under a commission from the English

at Halicarnassus, etc., 1862; *Travels and Discoveries*, ii 84-137].

The Romans gave the name of *Mausoleum* to all sepulchres which approached

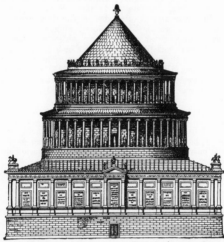

(2) MAUSOLEUM OF HADRIAN AT ROME (RESTORED).

government, and the sculptures thus unearthed [including the statue of Mausolus

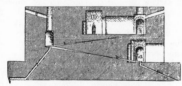

(3) SECTION OF HADRIAN'S MAUSOLEUM.
a. Entrance, with Statue of Hadrian.
b. Ventilating Passage.   d. Ventilating Channel.
c. Central Tomb-chamber.   f. Drainage Outlet.

(4) GROUND-PLAN OF
HADRIAN'S MAUSOLEUM.

and important fragments of the marble *quadriga*] were removed to the British Museum [Newton's *History of Discoveries*

that of Mausolus in size and grandeur of execution, as, for instance, (1) that erected by Augustus for himself and his family, the magnificence of which is attested by the still extant walls inclosing it; and (2) the sepulchre of Hadrian, which is in part preserved in the castle of *S. Angelo*, a circular building of 220 feet in diameter and 72 feet high, resting on a square base, the sides of which are almost 100 yards long. It was originally covered with Parian marble, and profusely ornamented with colonnades and statues; and probably had a pyramid on the top (*cp.* figs. 2-4).

Mavors. *See* MARS.

Maximiānus of Etruria, a Latin poet in the beginning of the 6th century after Christ. He is the author of six amatory elegies, modelled on classical poets, from whom he borrowed largely.

Maximus. (1) of Tyre. A Greek rhetorician and adherent of the Platonic philosophy, in the second half of the 2nd century after Christ. Forty-one rhetorical lectures of his on philosophical subjects of general interest are extant; the style is neat and scholarly.

(2) The author, otherwise unknown, of an astrological poem about the positions of the

stars which are favourable for various undertakings; only fragments of this are preserved. It is probable that he lived under
the early Empire.

Meals. The GREEKS had three during
the day; (1) the first breakfast, *acrātisma*,
consisting of bread which was dipped into
unmixed wine; (2) the second breakfast, or
luncheon, *ārĭstŏn*, eaten about noon and
consisting of warm dishes; and (3) the
principal meal, *deipnŏn*, which took place
before sunset. In the Homeric times, men
sat down when eating, a custom preserved
by the Cretans. In later times men reclined
at the table, usually only two together on
a couch (Gr. *klīnĕ*), in such a way that the
left arm was supported on a cushion while
the right arm remained free. The women
and children, who were, however, excluded
from real banquets, sat on stools; the former
might also sit on the couch at their husbands' feet. Before the meal, slaves took
off the sandals of the guests and washed
their feet; water and a towel was then
handed to them for washing their hands,
and this was repeated after the meal, as no
knives and forks were used; there were
only spoons, usually of metal. While eating
they cleaned their hands with the crumb of
bread or with a kind of dough. The common
food of the lower classes was the *māza*, a
paste of barleymeal dried in a dish, and
moistened before it was eaten; properly
baked bread of wheatmeal was considered
a comparative delicacy. As relish (*ŏpsŏn*)
they had salad, leeks, onions, beans, lentils,
and meat variously prepared; and especially fish, mostly from the sea, which in
later times formed the chief object of the
gourmand's attention. After the meals
the tables were cleared away (every pair
of guests usually having a table to itself),
the remnants that had fallen to the ground
were swept up, and the hands were washed
with scented soap; then a libation of un-
mixed wine was drunk in honour of the
good genius (*see* AGATHODÆMON)—none was
served during the meal—and the hymn of
praise (*see* PÆAN) was sung. After the
tables had been changed and the dessert,
consisting of fruit, cheese, cakes sprinkled
with salt, etc., had been served, the *sympŏsĭum*, or the drinking-bout, began.

The wine was diluted with warm or cold
water; in the latter case snow was frequently
used to cool it. It was deemed barbarous
to drink unmixed wine, and a mixture of
equal parts of wine and water even was
uncommon, the usual proportion of water to

wine was 3 : 1. They were mixed in a large
bowl (*krātēr*), from which it was poured
into the goblets by means of a ladle. First
three mixing-bowls were filled, and from
each of them a libation was offered, the first
to the gods of Olympus, the second to the
heroes, the third to Zeus the Saviour. How
the drinking was to be carried on (*e.g.* how
many goblets each guest should have) was
settled by a president, who was chosen by
the others or by casting the dice, and called
the king (*băsĭleus*) or master of the feast
(*sympŏsĭarchus*); he also enforced penalties,
such as emptying a goblet at a single
draught. The guests amused themselves
with merry talk and riddles, impromptu
songs (*see* SCŎLIA), games, more especially
the *cottăbus* (*q.v.*), mimetic dances, the
playing of women on flutes and lyres, etc.
The bout was terminated by a libation to
Hermēs. For the meals of the Spartans,
cp. SYSSITIA.

The ROMANS also had three meals during
the day. Breakfast, *iēiūnĭum* or *iantācŭ-
lum*, at about 9; followed in early times by
the principal meal (*cēna*) at 12, and by the
vesperna in the evening; but afterwards
the multiplied occupations of city life, that
extended over the early hours of the afternoon, necessitated a different arrangement;
lunch, *prandium*, was accordingly taken at
noon, and the *cena* after bathing, at about
3. The *ieiunium* consisted of bread
dipped in wine or eaten with honey, salt, or
olives, the *prandium* of a plentiful supply
of warm and cold viands, with wine. At
the *cena* originally nothing was eaten but
the peculiarly Roman *puls*, a kind of porridge, and other simple food, especially
common vegetables; meat was not usually
eaten, and prolonged dinners were only
permissible on grand occasions. From the
2nd century B.C. onwards the importation
of dainties from every country to Rome
made extravagance in eating so universal
that it was vainly attempted to check it by
law, and at the same time the *cena* was
prolonged over the whole of the latter end
of the day; it was looked upon as a remarkable instance of economising time,
when it was told of a man like the older
Pliny that he only spent three hours reclining at table [*Letters* of the Younger
Pliny, iii 5 § 13]. In the course of time
reclining had been substituted for sitting in
the case of men, as in Greece; women and
children sat at meals, but (unlike the Greek
custom) they shared them, even when
invited guests were present, the women sit-

ting on the couch (*lectus*) of the master of the house, the children by their side or at a separate table and on stools. Masters and servants originally had their meals in common in the *ātrium*; as time went on special dining-rooms, *trīclīnia* (*see* TRICLINIUM) were built. At a banquet (*convīvium*) the very lightest dress was worn, in which it was not considered correct to appear in the street, and sandals (*sŏlĕæ*), which were taken off by a slave, brought for this purpose, before one reclined, and what was called the *synthĕsīs* (*q.v.*). Before the meal, and between courses, water was handed round for the hands. Napkins (*mappæ*) came to be used in the reign of Augustus, but only at fashionable parties. As among the Greeks, no knives and forks, but only spoons, were used; and the viands were cut up by a special slave, the *scissor*.

The dishes of which the various courses consisted were served on a tray (*rĕpŏsĭtōrĭum*) and handed round by slaves. The meal, preceded by an invocation of the gods, was regularly divided into three parts: (1) the *gustus* or *gustātĭo*, also called *prōmulsĭs*, because a drink (*mulsum*) made of must and honey was handed round with the food (boiled eggs, salads, vegetables prepared in a way to stimulate the appetite, fresh or cooked crabs, etc., and salt fish). (2) The *cena* proper. Originally (and later also among people of small means) it only consisted of a single course, afterwards of three and more, which were distinguished by the names of *prima, altĕra, tertia cena*. During this—contrary to the Greek custom—wine was drunk, though in moderate quantities, and mixed with warm or cold water to suit the taste of each guest. Then came a pause, in which all were asked to be silent while the offering was made to the Lăres, and (3) the third part of the meal, the *dessert*, was served. It consisted of pastry, cakes, fresh and preserved fruits.

Roman luxury prescribed the greatest variety in the dishes of the *cena*, both with regard to their nature and to their mode of preparation. In early times only oil, honey, salt, and vinegar, but afterwards the most varied and piquant spices of other countries, and particularly foreign fish-sauces, were employed. Pork had always been a favourite meat; fifty ways of dressing it were known. Under the Empire, when a dish was so prepared that even a *gourmand* was puzzled to tell what he was eating, it was held to be a *chef d'œuvre* of the culinary art. The art was practised by

slaves, for whom considerable prices were paid.

The later Romans were on the whole much more immoderate in eating and drinking than the Greeks; a not unusual way of making further eating possible was to take an emetic in the morning, or else after bathing, or after the meals. After the *cena*, either at the dessert or not till later in the evening, the drinking proper, or *cōmissātĭo* began. It was done *mŏrĕ Græco*, that is, according to the Greek manner: the guests were anointed and crowned with wreaths, and one was chosen by casting dice to be the master of the drinking (*măgister* or *arbĭter bĭbendi*), also called *rex* (or king), who regulated the proportion of water to wine, and the number of goblets each person was to drink. As a rule the wine was mixed with warm water, as this was considered more wholesome. Many, however, preferred the cold mixture, and drank it with ice, or else cooled it in cold water. Conversation, varied with the music of the flute and the lyre, was held by the earlier Romans to constitute the charm of dining; at a later time, intellectual pleasures gradually declined in favour more and more, and there was an ever-increasing craving for the exciting entertainments of mimes, jesters, jugglers, and female singers, dancers and flute-players, who were mostly slaves of the family. Even the Campanian custom of witnessing gladiatorial combats during meals was adopted in a few Roman houses. The development of these baneful habits was all the more deplorable in its effects, as the women and children were present at the debauches of the table.

Mĕdĕa (Gr. *Mēdeia*). The daughter of Æētēs of Colchis and of Idyia; skilled in witchcraft. For the legend of her being carried off by Jason, and how she revenged his perfidy at Corinth, *see* ARGONAUTS. From Corinth she fled to Athens, married king Ægeus, the father of Thēseus, and had a son Mēdus by him. But she was again compelled to fly with her son, as she had plotted against the life of Theseus. She came to Colchis without being recognised, and there found her father deprived of the kingship by his brother Persēs. She killed the latter, and restored Æetes to the throne. According to a later legend, Mēdus comes to Colchis to seek his mother, and is imprisoned by Perses, before whom he alleges that he is Hippŏtēs, son of Crĕŏn of Corinth. Then Mēdēa appears on a chariot drawn by serpents, and under pretence of being a priestess of Artĕmis, promises to deliver the country from the barrenness that is oppressing it, on condition the supposed son of her mortal enemy is given into her power. When this is done, she recognises her son, who with her aid kills Perses and takes possession of his grandfather's realm. The Greeks looked on Medus as the progenitor of the Medes. According to one legend, Medea became the wife of Achilles in Elysium, as did Helen according to another. At Corinth she was deemed immortal, and regarded as a benefactress of the city, which she was alleged to have delivered from a famine. Elsewhere, she was merely regarded as an ancient queen. Her seven sons and seven daughters were killed by Corinthian women at the altar of Hēra, on account of which a pestilence ravaged the town, and an oracular decree ordained that an annual expiatory offering should be made. This was observed until the destruction of the town.

Mĕdimnus. A Greek measure of capacity, six times as large as the Roman *mŏdĭŭs*, and in English about 1½ bushel. Its principal subdivisions were the *chœnix* ($\frac{1}{48}$), *xestēs* ($\frac{1}{96}$), *cŏtÿle* ($\frac{1}{192}$), *cÿăthŭs* ($\frac{1}{1152}$).

Mĕdus. Son of Ægeus and Medea (*q.v.*).

Mĕdūsa. One of the Gorgons, whose head was cut off by Perseus (*q.v.*). (*See also* GORGO.)

Mĕgæra. One of the Greek goddesses of vengeance. (*See* ERINYES.)

Mĕgălēsia. A Roman festival in honour of Rhea (*q.v.*).

Mĕgărā. Daughter of the Theban king Creon, wife of Hērăclēs (*q.v.*), afterwards married by him to Iŏlāus.

Mĕgărŏn. In many Greek temples a space divided off and sometimes subterranean, which only the priest was allowed to enter. (*See* TEMPLE.)

Mĕgasthĕnēs. A Greek historian, who stayed for a considerable time, as ambassador of king Seleucus Nīcātŏr, at the court of the Indian king Sandrăcus (B.C. 315–291), at Palibothra on the Ganges. From information about the country and the people, obtained while he occupied that position, he compiled a historical and geographical work about India, the chief treatise on that country left us by the ancients. On it are founded the accounts of Diodōrus and Arrian; beyond this only fragments are preserved. His record of the state of India at the time has been discredited; but recent investigations have to a great extent shown its trustworthiness.

Mela. *See* POMPONIUS.

Mĕlampūs. Son of Amÿthāōn (*see* ÆOLUS, 1) and of Eidŏmĕnē; brother of Bīas, the oldest Greek seer, and ancestor of the family of seers called Melampŏdĭdæ. The brothers went with their uncle Nēleus from Thessaly to Pÿlus in Messēnia, where they dwelt in the country. Melampus owed his gift of soothsaying to some serpents, which he had saved from death and reared, and who in return cleansed his ears with their tongues when he slept; on awaking he understood the voices of birds, and thus learnt what was secret. When Neleus would only give Bias his beautiful daughter Pēro on condition that he first brought him the oxen of Iphĭclus of Phÿlăcē in Thessaly, which were guarded by a watchful dog, Melampus offered to fetch the oxen for his brother, though he knew beforehand that he would be imprisoned for a year. He is caught in the act of stealing them, and kept in strict confinement. From the talk of the worms in the woodwork of the roof he gathers that the house will soon fall to pieces. He thereupon demands to be taken to another prison; this is scarcely done, when the house breaks down. When, on account of this, Phÿlăcus, father of Iphĭclus, perceives his prophetic gifts, he promises him the oxen, if by his art he will find out some way of curing his son's childlessness. Melampus offers a bull to Zeus, cuts it in pieces, and invites the birds to the meal. From these he hears that a certain vulture, that had not come, knew how it could be effected. This vulture is made to appear, and relates, that the defect in Iphiclus was the result of a sudden fright at seeing a bloody knife, with which his father had been castrating some goats; he had dug the knife into a tree, which had grown round about it; if he took some of the rust scraped off it, for ten days, he would be cured. Melampus finds the knife, cures Iphiclus, obtains the oxen, and Bias receives Pero for his wife. Afterwards he went to Argos, because, according to Homer [*Od.* xv 225–240] Neleus had committed a serious offence against him in his absence, for which he had taken revenge; while, according to the usual account, he had been asked by king Prœtus to heal his daughter, stricken with madness for acting impiously towards Dionÿsus or Hēra. He had stipulated that his reward should be a third of the kingdom for himself, another for Bias; besides which Iphĭănassa became his wife, and Lysippé that of Bias, both being daughters of Prœtus. A descendant of his son Antiphätes was Oïclēs, who was a companion of Hēraclēs in the expedition against Troy, and was slain in battle by Lāŏmĕdōn; he again was ancestor of the seer and hero Amphiaräus. Descendants of his other son Mantius were Cleitus, whom Eōs, the goddess of dawn, carried off on account of his beauty, and Pŏlўpheidēs, whom, after the death of Amphiaraus, Apollo made the best of seers. The son of Polypheides was the seer Theoclўmĕnus, who, flying from Argos on account of committing a murder, met Tēlĕmăchus at Pylus, was led by him to Ithaca, and announced to Pēnĕlŏpē the presence in Ithaca of Odysseus, and to the suitors their approaching death. The seer Polyīdus (*q.v.*) was also said to be a great-grandson of Melampus. At Argos Melampus was held to be the first priest of Dionysus, and originator of mysterious customs at festivals and at ceremonies of expiation.

Mĕlănippĭdēs. Greek dithyrambic poet. (*See* DITHYRAMBOS.)

Mĕlănippus. A Theban, who mortally wounded Tўdeus in the fight of the Seven against Thebes, and was himself slain by Amphiaräus. (*Cp.* TYDEUS.)

Mĕlanthius. *See* PHILOCLES.

Mĕlĕăgĕr (Gr. *Mĕlĕăgrŏs*). (1) Son of Œneus of Călўdōn and of Althæa, husband of Cleopatra (*see* IDAS), one of the most celebrated heroes of Greek legend. He took part in the enterprise of the Argonauts and brought about the celebrated chase of the Calydonian boar (*see* ŒNEUS), to which he invited the most renowned heroes of the time, Admētus, Amphĭăräus, Jāson, Idās, Lynceus, Castor and Pollux, Nestor, Thēseus and Pīrĭthŏus, Pēleus, Tĕlămōn, and others. Many lost their lives, till at last Meleager slew the monster. However, Artĕmis thereupon stirred up furious strife between the Calydonians and the Cŭrētĕs (who dwelt at Pleurōn) about the head and skin of the boar, the prize of victory. The Calydonians were victorious, as long as Meleager fought at their head; but when he slew the brother of his mother, she uttered a terrible curse on him, and he retired sullenly from the fray. The Curetes immediately forced the Calydonians to retreat, and were already beginning to climb the walls of Calydon, when, at the height of their distress, he yielded to the prayers of his wife, and again joined in the fight to ward off destruction from the city; but he

did not return alive, for the Erinys had accomplished the curse of his mother. According to a later legend, the Mœræ appeared to his mother on the seventh day after his birth, and announced to her that her son would have to die when a log of wood on the hearth was consumed by the flame; whereupon Althæa immediately snatched the log from the fire and concealed it in a chest. At the Calydonian Hunt Meleager fell in love with Atălantē (*q.v.*), and gave her (who had inflicted the first wound) the prize, the skin of the

* MELEAGER (BERLIN).

animal which he had killed. He slew the brothers of his mother, the sons of Thestius, when they were lying in wait for the virgin to rob her of the boar's hide. Overcome by pain at the death of her brothers, Althæa sets fire to the log, and Meleager dies a sudden death. His mother and wife hang themselves; his sisters weep so bitterly for Meleager, that Artemis for pity changes them into guinea-hens (Gr. *mĕlĕăgrĭdĕs*). Legends relate that even in the nether world Meleager retained his dauntless courage; for when Heracles descended to Hades, all the shades fled before him except Meleager and Medusa.

(2) *Greek epigrammatist.* Of Gădără in Palestine, flourished about B.C. 60. His collection of epigrams, by himself and others, entitled *Stĕphănŏs* (wreath), formed the nucleus of the Greek anthology (*q.v.*). Of his own poems there remain 128, in which amatory themes are cleverly and wittily treated.

Mĕlĕtē. See MUSES.

Mĕlĭcertēs. In Greek legend the son of Athămās and Ino, and changed, after his death by drowning, into the marine deity Palæmōn, while his mother became Leucŏthĕa. (*See* INO). His name (= *Melkart*), however, shows him to have been originally a Phœnician god. Like Ino-Leucothea, he was worshipped on all the coast of the Mediterranean, especially on that of Mĕgără and at the Isthmus of Corinth, where he was so closely connected with the cult of Poseidōn, that the Isthmian games, originally instituted in honour of this god, came to be looked upon as the funeral games of Melicertes. The Romans regarded him as a beneficent god of the sea, and identified him with *Portūnus*, the god of harbours.

Mĕlinno. Greek poetess. (*See* ERINNA.)

Melpŏmĕnē. The Muse of tragedy. For further details *see* MUSES.

Memnōn. The beautiful son of Tīthōnus and of Eōs; king of the Æthiopians. His brother Emăthīōn had ousted him from the throne, but Hērăclēs, on his expedition for obtaining the apples of the Hespĕrĭdĕs, murdered the usurper, and reinstated Memnon. After Hector's death he went to help his uncle Priam, and killed Antĭlŏchus, the son of Nestor and friend of Achilles. When the latter had slain him, Eos entreated Zeus to grant her son the boon of immortality. The Greeks originally thought that one of the two Æthiopias mentioned in Homer was the realm of Memnon, which is situated near sunrise and the dwelling-place of Eos, and hence regarded him as the builder of the royal castle at Susa. It was not till later that his kingdom was identified with the Egyptian Æthiopia, and that he was connected with the colossal statue of Amĕnōphis near Thebes. This "column of Memnon" is still standing. After its partial destruction by an earthquake in B.C. 27, the musical sound, which it gave forth when touched by the first rays of the sun, was explained as Memnon's greeting to his mother, the Goddess of Dawn. The tomb of Memnon was shown at various places. It was told of the one at Abȳdus on the Hellespont, that the companions of Memnon, who had been changed into birds (the *Mĕmnŏnĭdĕs*) on account of their excessive grief for their king, came there every year to fight and to lament at his grave. The dew-drops of the early morning were called the tears of Eos, which she shed anew every morning in sorrow for her beloved son.

Mĕnander (Gr. *Mĕnandrŏs*). (1) The chief representative of the Later Attic Comedy, born in B.C. 342, at Athens, of a distinguished and wealthy family. He received a careful education, and led a comfortable and luxurious life, partly at Athens, and partly at his estate in the Pīræūs, the harbour of Athens, enjoying the intimate friendship of his contemporary and the friend of his youth, Ĕpĭcūrus, of Thĕŏphrastus, and of Dēmētrius Phălēreus. He declined an invitation of king Ptolemy I of Egypt, so as not to have his comfort disturbed. At the height of his poetic productiveness he was drowned while bathing in the Piræus, at the age of 52. His uncle Alexis had given him some preparatory training in dramatic composition. As early as 322 he made his first appearance as an author. He wrote above a hundred pieces, and worked with the greatest facility; but he only obtained the first prize for eight comedies, in the competition with his popular rival Phĭlēmōn. The admiration accorded him by posterity was all the greater: there was only one opinion about the excellence of his work. His principal merits were remarkable inventiveness, skilful arrangement of plots, life-like painting of character, a clever and refined wit, elegant and graceful language, and a copious supply of maxims based on a profound knowledge of the world. These last were collected in regular anthologies and form the bulk of the extant fragments. Unfortunately not one of his plays has survived, although they were much read down to a late date. However, apart from about seventy-three titles, and numerous fragments (some of considerable length), we have transcripts of his comedies (in which, of course, the delicate beauties of the original are lost), in a number of Latin plays by Plautus (*Bacchĭdes, Stĭchus, Pœnŭlus*), and Terence (*Andrĭa, Eunŭchus, Hautontĭmōrūmĕnŏs, Adelphi*). Lucian also, in his *Conversations of Hĕtœræ,* and Alcĭphron in his *Letters,* have made frequent use of Menander.

(2) A Greek rhetorician, of Lăŏdĭcĕa, who probably lived at the end of the 3rd century after Christ. He is the author of two treatises *About Speeches for Display*, which add to our knowledge of the theory of the sophistic type of oratory [in Spengel's *Rhetores Græci*, iii 331–446].

Mĕnĕlāŭs. Son of Atreus, and younger brother of Agamemnon, with whom he was exiled by Thyestes, the murderer of Atreus, and fled to king Tyndărĕŏs, at Sparta, whose daughter Helen he married, and whose throne he inherited after the death of Helen's brothers, Castor and Pŏlўdeucēs (Pollux). When Paris had robbed him of his wife and of great treasures, he went with Odysseus to Troy to demand restitution, and they were hospitably received there by Antēnŏr. His just claims were refused, and his life was even in danger; he and Agamemnon accordingly called on the Greek chieftains to join in an expedition against Troy, and himself furnished sixty ships. At Troy he distinguished himself in counsel and in action, and was specially protected by Athēnē and Hēra. In the single combat with Paris he is victorious, but his opponent is rescued and carried off by Aphrŏdītē. On demanding that Helen and the treasures should be restored, he is wounded by an arrow shot by the Trojan Pandărus. He is also ready to fight Hector, and is only prevented by the entreaties of his friends. When Patroclus has fallen, he shields the dead body, at first alone, and then with the aid of Ajax, and bears it from the field of battle with Mĕrĭŏnēs. He is also one of the heroes of the wooden horse. Having recovered Helen he hastens home, but on rounding the promontory of Mălĕa he is driven to Egypt with five ships, and wanders about for eight years among the peoples of the East, where he is kindly received everywhere, and receives rich gifts. He is finally detained at the isle of Pharos by contrary winds, and with the help of the marine goddess Eidŏthĕa he artfully compels her father Prōteus to prophecy to him. He thus learns the reason of his being unwillingly detained at the island, and is also told that, as husband of the daughter of Zeus, he will not die, but enter the Elysian plains alive. After appeasing the gods in Egypt with hecatombs, he returns swiftly and prosperously to his home, where he arrives on the very day on which Orestes is burying Ægisthus and Clytæmnestra. He spent the rest of his life quietly with

Helen, in Lacedæmon. Their only daughter Hermĭŏnē was married to Nĕoptŏlĕmus, son of Achilles.

Mĕnestheus. The son of Pĕtĕus, who seized the government of Attica, while Theseus pined away in the nether world, and commanded the Athenians before Troy, where he fell. (*Cp.* DEMOPHOON, THESEUS.)

Mĕnippē. Daughter of Orīŏn, who offered to die with her sister Mĕtĭŏchē, when a pestilence was raging in Bœotia, and the oracle demanded the sacrifice of two virgins. (*See also* ORION.)

Mĕnippus. A Greek philosopher of Gădără in Syria, flourished about B.C. 250. He was originally a slave, and afterwards an adherent of the Cynic school of philosophy. His writings (now completely lost) treated of the follies of mankind, especially of philosophers, in a sarcastic tone. They were a medley of prose and verse, and became models for the satirical works of Varro, and afterwards for those of Lucian.

Mĕnœceus. (1) Grandson of Pentheus of Thebes, father of Crĕŏn and Jŏcasta.

(2) Grandson of the above, son of Creon. At the siege of Thebes by the Seven, Tīrĕsĭās prophesied that the Thebans would conquer if the wrath of Ares at the slaying of the dragon by Cadmus were appeased by the voluntary death of a descendant of the warriors that had sprung from the dragon's teeth. Menœceus, one of the last of this race, slew himself, in spite of his father's prohibition, on the castle wall, and fell down into the chasm which had once been the haunt of the dragon as guardian of the spring Dircē.

Mens. Under this name the Romans personified intelligence and prudence. After the battle at Lake Trasimene, which was lost through the carelessness of the Romans, a temple was erected to her on the Capitol. The anniversary of its foundation was celebrated on the 8th of June.

Mentŏr. (1) Son of Alcĭmus of Ithăca, friend of Odysseus who, on departing for Troy, confided to him the care of his house and the education of Tĕlĕmăchus [*Od.* ii 225]. His name has hence become a proverbial one for a wise and faithful adviser or monitor. Athēnē assumed his shape when she brought Telemachus to Pўlus [*Od.* ii 268], and when she aided Odysseus in fighting the suitors and made peace between him and their relatives [xxii 206, xxiv 446].

(2) [The most celebrated master of the toreutic art (*q.v.*) among the ancients (Pliny, *N. H.* xxxiii 154). As some of his works

were destroyed at the burning of the temple of Artĕmis at Ephesus, in B.C. 356, obviously he lived before that event, and probably flourished in the best period of Greek art, though he is never mentioned by any earlier Greek writer than Lucian (*Lexiphanes*, 7). He worked mainly in silver. The orator Crassus paid 100,000 sesterces (£1,000) for two cups chased by his hand; but, from regard to their value, refrained from using them. Varro possessed a statue wrought by him in bronze; and one Diodorus at Lilybæum, two fine cups in the style of those adorned with figures of animals by Thērĭclēs, the Corinthian potter (Cic., *Verr.* iv 38). Martial (iii 41) mentions a cup with a lifelike representation of a lizard, and often refers to him (iv 39, viii 51, ix 59, xiv 93; *cp.* Juvenal viii 104). Propertius alludes to him (i 14, 2), and supplies us with the only extant criticism of his style, implying that, while the work of Mys (*q.v.*) was remarkable for its minute execution, that of Mentor was famous for its composition and its general design (iii 7, 11).

Argumenta magis sunt Mentoris addita formæ:
At Myos exiguum flectit acanthus iter.]

[J. E. S.]

Mercenaries. Apart from a few earlier examples of the employment of mercenaries, a regular organization of such troops was formed amongst the Greeks in the course of the Peloponnesian War, especially by the Arcadians, who were compelled by the poverty of their own country to utilize their strength and courage by seeking employment outside it. It was most easily found by serving as soldiers in the continual wars between the Grecian states. When the mercenary system was at its height, Arcadians formed by far the larger portion of the mercenary forces, even as early as in the first great army of mercenaries of 13,000 men, which the younger Cyrus led against his brother Artaxerxes, king of Persia, in 400 B.C. In Greece in the 4th century the ground became more and more favourable to the growth of the mercenary body, and the citizens of the Greek states, instead of bearing arms themselves, became more and more inclined to leave their wars to be fought out by mercenaries, especially since it had become a trade to form troops of mercenaries, and to let them out wholesale for service, no matter whether to Greeks or barbarians. Even prominent men, such as Agēsĭlāŭs and Phĭlŏpœmēn, did not consider it beneath

their dignity to fight for strangers at the head of mercenaries. One of the chief recruiting places in the 4th century was Corinth, and afterwards for a time the district near the promontory of Tænărum in Lacedæmon. The generals of mercenaries were called *strătēgoi;* their captains, through whom they raised companies of different kinds of troops, known as *lŏchoi*, one hundred men in number, *lŏchăgoi*. The usual monthly pay of a common soldier was on the average a gold daric (*dareikŏs*) [=20 silver drachmæ or 13s. 4d. in intrinsic value of silver; but in intrinsic value of the gold contained in it=a little more than a guinea. (*Cp.* COINAGE, fig. 3.)] Out of this he had to maintain himself entirely, to buy his armour, and keep it in good condition. The pay of the *lochagoi* was double, and of the *strategoi* four times that amount. In later times the *strategoi*, when they entered with complete armies into the service of some power at war, seem to have generally received considerable sums at the conclusion of the contract.—The Romans also employed foreign mercenaries after the second Punic War, especially as archers and slingers, and after the time of Marius a recruited army of mercenaries (*see* LEGION) had sprung out of the earlier levied army of citizens; but the mercenary organization never took among the Romans a form similar to that among the Greeks.

Mercury (Lat. *Mercŭrius*). The Italian god of commerce, and as such identified with the Greek *Hermēs* (*q.v.*), whose descent and other qualities were accordingly transferred to him. As protector of the corn trade, especially with Sicily, which was of such great importance to Rome, he was first publicly honoured in that city by the erection of a temple near the *Circus Maxĭmus*. At the same time a guild of merchants was established, the members of which were known as *mercŭrĭăles.* At the yearly festival of the temple and the guild, May 15th, the merchants sacrificed to the god and to his mother, and at the *Porta Căpēna* sprinkled themselves and their merchandise with hallowed water. With the spread of Roman commerce the worship of Mercury extended far into the West and North.

Mĕrĕtrīcēs. *See* HETÆRÆ, at end.

Mĕrĭŏnēs. Son of Mŏlus, a half-brother of Idŏmĕneus of Crete, whom he accompanied to Troy. In Homer we read that he was there one of the bravest in the fight, and with Teucer specially distinguished in archery, an art in which the Cretans had always excelled. According to a later legend, on his return from Troy his vessel was driven to Engyion in the north of Sicily, which was supposed to be a Cretan settlement. At Gnōssus in Crete his grave was shown, and both he and Idomeneus, his friend and companion in battle, were honoured as heroes.

Mĕrŏbaudēs. A rhetorician born in Spain and distinguished as a general, and also as a Latin poet, in the first half of the 5th century after Christ. Besides a short hymn, *De Christo*, there are preserved fragments of five secular poems, the longest being part of a panegyric on the third consulate of Aëtĭus (446), with a preface in prose. They prove him to be no unskilful imitator of Claudian; in language and metre he possesses an elegance rare in his time.

Mĕrŏpē. (1) One of the Pleiads (*q.v.*), mother of Glaucus by Sīsўphus.

(2) Wife of Pŏlўbus of Corinth (also called *Pĕrĭbœa*), foster-mother of Œdĭpūs (*q.v.*).

Mĕsŏmēdēs. A Greek lyric poet of Crete, who lived about A.D. 130, and was a freedman of Hadrian. Three small poems of his have come down to us [*Anthologia Grœca*, xiv 63, xvi 323]. They are not unattractive, and the one on Nĕmĕsĭs is of peculiar interest, as its musical composition is indicated according to the ancient notation [Brunck's *Analecta*, iii 292; Bellermann, *Hymnen des Dionysius und Mesomedes*, pp. 13, 26].

Mēstra. Daughter of Ĕrўsichthōn (*q.v.*, 2). She supported her famished father by employing the power to change herself into any form she pleased, the gift of her lover Pŏseidōn. She let herself be sold in various forms, and then always returned to her father [Ovid, *Met.* viii 738–884].

Mēta. The upper column at the upper and lower end of the Roman circus, round which the competitors usually had to drive seven times. (*Cp.* Circus, Games of.)

Mĕtăgeitnĭa. An Athenian festival in honour of Apollo (*q.v.*).

Metal, Artistic Work in. See Toreutic Art.

Mĕtaulŏs (*Mĕsaulŏs*). See House (*Greek*).

Mĕtĭŏchē. See Menippe and Orion.

Mētĭs (*i.e.* "Counsel"). Daughter of Ocĕănus, first wife of Zeus, by whom she was devoured, as he feared she would bear a son mightier than himself; whereupon Athēnē (*q.v.*) sprang from the head of the god.

Mĕtœci. The name given at Athens to aliens (other than slaves) resident in Attica. When the State was most flourishing, they numbered as many as 10,000 adult men. The favourable position of Athens for commerce and the rich opportunities for carrying on trade and for selling merchandise induced both Greeks and barbarians to settle there. The Athenians besides had the reputation among the Greeks of being friendly towards foreigners. For the legal protection granted them by the State, they paid a sum of twelve *drachmœ* [8s.] annually for each man, and half as much for each independent woman; and they had to choose a patron (*prostătēs*) to conduct their dealings with the State in all public and private affairs, *e.g.* the bringing of an action. Whoever failed to do the one or the other was summoned before a lawcourt, and, if guilty, sold as a slave. They were prohibited from marrying citizens and from obtaining landed property; but they could follow any trade they pleased, on payment of a certain tax. They also had to pay the extraordinary taxes for war, and were obliged to go on military service either in the fleet or in the land-army; they might be hoplites, but not knights. At festivals it was their duty to follow the processions, carrying sunshades, pitchers, and bowls or trays (filled with honey or cakes). A decree of the people could, in return for special services, confer on them the *ĭsŏtĕleiā*, which placed them on a level with the citizens with regard to "liturgies," or public burdens, freed them from the necessity of having a patron or paying a tax for protection, and gave them the right of holding property in land and of transacting business with the people or the authorities without an intermediary; but even this privileged class did not possess the active rights of a citizen.

Mĕtōn. A Greek astronomer, of Athens, instituted in B.C. 432 the cycle of nineteen years called after him; it was intended to reconcile the lunar and the solar year: 235 lunar months of 29 or 30 days (on an average $29\frac{25}{47}$)$=19$ solar years of $365\frac{5}{15}$ days. This cycle was not adopted at Athens till much later, probably in B.C. 330. (*Cp.* Calendar.)

Metopes [*Mĕtŏpœ*, either "the intervening openings," or (Vitruv. iv 2, 4) "the spaces between the sockets" (Gr. *opai*). In Doric architecture the spaces between the triglyphs (*q.v.*) in the frieze. They were originally left open. Thus, Orestēs manages to make his way into the Tauric temple of Artemis through one of these openings (Eur., *Iph. T.* 113). They were afterwards filled with panels of wood, which were in course of time superseded by plain slabs of marble, as in the temples at Pæstum, etc. These slabs were sometimes slightly ornamented with a round shield in low relief, as in the frieze of the temple of Zeus at Olympia. More frequently they were filled with figures in relief, as in those of Sĕlīnūs (*see* SCULPTURE, fig. 1), and of the Thēsēum and the Parthĕnōn (*q.v.*). The term is also applied to similarly sculptured slabs not placed between the triglyphs, but on the wall of the *cella*, as in the temple of Zeus at Olympia. *See* OLYMPIAN GAMES, fig. 3.]

Mĕtrăgyrti. The vagrant begging priests of Rhea (*q.v.*).

Mĕtrētēs. The largest liquid measure of the Greeks, a little less than nine gallons. Its chief subdivisions were the Gr. *chous*, ($\frac{1}{12}$), *xestēs* ($\frac{1}{72}$), *cŏtÿlē* ($\frac{1}{144}$), *cÿăthŭs* ($\frac{1}{864}$).

Mezentius [or *Medientius*]. King of Cære in Etruria; he aided Turnus of Ardea against Æneas, but was killed in battle by the latter or by his son Ascănius.

Mĭdăs. An old Phrygian king, son of Gordĭās and Cÿbĕlē, in whose honour he is said to have founded a temple and instituted priests at Pessīnŭs. When the drunken Sīlēnus had lost his way and strayed into Midas' rose-gardens, the king brought him back to Dionȳsus. (According to another legend the king made him drunk by mingling wine with the spring Midas, and so caught him, that he might prophesy to him.) Dionysus granted Midas the fulfilment of his wish, that all he touched might turn to gold. But his very food and drink were changed at his touch, so that he prayed the god to take away the fatal gift. At the god's command he bathed in the Pactōlus, which ever after became rich in gold. In the musical contest between Marsȳās (or Pan) and Apollo, he decided for the former ; on which account the god gave him the ears of an ass. He concealed them beneath a high cap, so that only his barber knew about it. However, he could not keep the secret for any length of time, and at last shouted it into a hole that he had dug into the ground ; reeds grew from this hole, and whispered the secret to all the world. While this legend makes Midas himself appear as one of the Sileni belonging to the train of Dionysus (the ass being one of their attributes), the other points to him as the favourite of the divinity, whose first

priest he was deemed to be, and who showered riches upon him.

Mīlănīŏn (Gr. *Meilănīŏn*). The faithful lover of Atălantē (*q.v.*).

Mīliărĭum. The Roman milestone, a stone column, such as were set up at intervals of 1,000 (*mille*) *passūs* = 5,000 Roman feet or the military roads, partly during the last years of the Republic, and regularly since Augustus. They gave in numbers, usually preceded by M.P. (*mīlia passŭum*), the distance from the place from which the measurement was made, besides its name and that of the person who had constructed the road or erected the milestone, and of the emperor in whose reign the road had been made. A great number of these milestones, in every part of the Roman empire, has been preserved, and also the base of the central column of gilt bronze (*miliărĭum aurĕum*) erected by Augustus in the Forum near the temple of Saturn ; it was regarded as the centre of the empire. (*See* Plan of Fora, under FORUM.)

Mills (Gr. *mÿlai*, Lat. *mŏlæ*) are mentioned [twice] in Homer [*Od.* vii 104, xx 106]. The ordinary Greek tradition ascribed their invention to Dēmĕtēr. They consisted, as may be readily inferred from the specimens found in the bakers' shops at Pompeii, of two principal parts : (1) a fixed and massive conical stone (Gr. *mÿlē*, Lat. *mĕtă*), resting on a base, and furnished at the top with a strong iron pivot (fig. 2) ; and (2) a hollow double cone (Gr. *ŏnŏs*, Lat. *catillus*) in the shape of an hourglass, which, at its narrowest part, was furnished with a thick plate of iron, with holes in the centre and

(1) MILL, POMPEII.   (2) SECTION OF (1).

at four other places (fig. 1). The pivot of the lower stone passed through the central hole of this plate, and the upper stone turned round it. Into the upper cone or funnel the corn was poured and gradually fell through the holes of the plate into the space between the outer surface of the cone and the inner surface of its cap, where it was ground and fell into a channel cut round the base of the cone. Two bars of wood fastened to the middle of the upper part were used for setting it in motion; this was done either with the hands, or by means of animals.

Watermills were known in the 1st century B.C., but they were not commonly used till the 4th and 5th centuries after Christ. The public aqueducts supplied the required water. Ship-mills were invented by Belisarius when the Goths were besieging Rome in A.D. 536. The ancients had no windmills; they are an invention of the Middle Ages. There seem to have been no regular millers up to the latest classical times; the necessary amount of flour was either prepared in one's own house by slaves, or obtained from the bakers, when there was such a trade; the bakers usually were at the same time millers. Armies on the march carried small handmills with them.

Mime (*Mīmus*) really denotes a farcical mimic, a buffoon, such as used to show themselves from the earliest times in Italy and Sicily on the public places at popular entertainments, etc., and also served to while away the time during meals. It afterwards came to be applied to the farcical imitation of persons and scenes in ordinary life. The mimes of the Syracusan *Sŏphrŏn* were character-sketches in dialogue taken from the life of the people; but these were at most meant to be recited, certainly not to be acted.

In Italy, especially among the Latians and at Rome, the representation of such farcical scenes from low life on the stage was no doubt as old as the stage itself; and as great a scope was at all times given to improvisation in these as in the *Atellānæ*, from which the mimes mainly differed in not being confined to stock-characters (*see* ATELLANA). At Rome the mime was for a long time confined to fifth-rate theatres, but in B.C. 46 it appears to have ousted the *Atellānæ* as an interlude and afterpiece on the more important stages, and received at the hands of *Dĕcĭmus Lăbĕrius* and *Publĭlĭus Sўrus* a technical development on the lines of the existing kinds of drama. The native name for these national farces was *plānĭpes*, probably because the performers appeared *plānīs pĕdĭbŭs*, i.e. without the theatrical shoes used in tragedy and comedy. There were also no masks, the use of which would have of course rendered impossible the play of the features, which is such an important means of imitation. The costume worn was the *cĕntuncŭlus*, a kind of harlequin's dress, and the *rīcĭnĭum*, a peculiar little cloak. Contrary to the custom in all other dramatic performances, the female parts were really taken by women, who, like all the actors in mimes, were in very bad repute. Besides the chief actor, *archĭmīmus* or *archĭmīma*, who had to carry through the plot, there was always a second performer with a clean-shaven head, whose part is characterized by the names given him, *părăsītus* or *stŭpĭdus* (fool). The mimes were acted on the front part of the stage, which was divided from the back part by a curtain (*sĭpărĭum*). As they depicted the life of the lower classes, and as it was their chief aim to rouse the laughter of the spectators in every possible way, they were full of plebeian expressions and turns, and abounded in the most outrageous buffoonery and obscenity; cheating and adultery were the favourite subjects. In particular the dances that occurred in the mimes were remarkable for the extravagance of the grimaces and the disgusting nature of the gestures. Owing to the continually degenerating tastes of the Roman public, they and the pantomimes enjoyed the greatest popularity during the Empire, especially as here, no less than in the *Atellānæ*, a certain freedom of speech was sometimes permitted; and among dramatic representations proper they occupied the first place.

Mimĭambi. *See* IAMBIC POETRY.

Mimnermus. Of *Cŏlŏphŏn*; the creator of the erotic type of Greek elegy, an older contemporary of Solon; he flourished about B.C. 630–600. He gave his collection of love elegies the name of the beautiful fluteplayer Nanno, who on account of his advanced age would not return his love. There are only a few fragments of his poems left; their chief themes are the melancholy complaint of old age abandoned by love, the transitoriness of the life of man, and the exhortation to enjoy youth, the age of love. His language is simple and tender, and the ancients therefore called him the sweet singer [*Lĭgўastădēs*, in Solon's lines to Mimnermus, Bergk's *Poëtæ Lyrici*, Solon, fragm. 20].

Mina (Gr. *mnā;* Lat. *mĭnă*). An old Greek weight, and a sum of coined money equal to it, the sixtieth part of a talent, like which it varied in value. The weight of the *mina* (=100 *drachmæ*) was $1\frac{1}{4}$ lb., and the intrinsic value of the Attic mina of silver was £3 6s. 8d. (*Cp.* COINAGE.)

Minerva. The Italian goddess of intelligence, meditation, and inventiveness, queen of all accomplishments and arts, especially of spinning and weaving, as practised by women. She was also the patron-goddess of fullers, dyers, cobblers, carpenters, musicians, sculptors, painters, physicians, actors, poets, schoolmasters, and especially of schoolchildren. Her oldest and most important sanctuaries were at Rome on the hills of the town; on the Capitol, where she occupied the chamber on the right in the great temple common to her with Jupiter and Juno; on the Aventine, where the official meeting place of poets and actors was situated, and on the · Cælian. Her chief festival was the *Quinquātrūs* (*q.v.*). In the course of time the Greek conception gained more ground; Minerva was identified with Pallas Athēnē. This certainly happened with regard to Athene considered as the bestower of victory and booty, when Pompey erected a temple to her from the booty won in his Eastern campaigns. And Augustus must have regarded her as Athene the Counsellor when he added to his *Cūria Iūlia* a vestibule dedicated to Minerva. The Roman Minerva was represented in art in the same manner as the Greek goddess. (*See* ATHENE.)

Minervāl. The school fee among the Romans. (*See* QUINQUATRUS.)

Minōs. A mythical king of Crete, the centre of the oldest legends of that island. He is the son of Zeus and of Eurōpa; in Homer, brother of Rhădămanthys, father of Deucălĭōn and Arĭadnē, and grandfather of Idŏmĕneus. Residing at Gnōssus as the " familiar friend of Zeus," he had a " nine-yearly " rule over the flourishing island [*Od.* xix 179], an expression which later generations explained as signifying periods of nine years; at the end of which he went into a cave sacred to Zeus, in order to hold converse with his father, and to receive the laws for his island. Just as he was thought to be the framer of the famous older Cretan constitution, so he was also considered a founder of the naval supremacy of Crete before the times of Troy; Hesiod calls him the "mightiest king of all mortals," who rules with the sceptre of Zeus over most of the neighbouring peoples. Later legend gives him another brother, Sarpēdōn, and a number of children (among others Andrŏgĕōs, Glaucus, Catreus, and Phædra) by his wife Pāsĭphăē, a daughter of Hēlĭŏs and Persēĭs. When after the death of Astĕrĭōn, the husband of Europa,

he has driven away his brothers in consequence of a quarrel, he seizes the kingship of Crete, in which he is supported by Pŏseidōn, who, on his prayer that he should send him a bull for sacrifice, causes a wonderfully beautiful snow-white bull to rise from the sea. But as he, desiring to keep it for his own herd, sacrifices another, the god to punish him inspires his wife Pāsĭphăē (*q.v.*) with love for the bull. Homer [*Od.* xi 322] calls Minos the " meditator of evil "; in later times he was represented as a hard-hearted and cruel tyrant, especially on the Attic stage, because of the part he played in Attic legends. On account of the murder of his son Andrŏgĕōs (*q.v.*) at Athens, he undertook an expedition of revenge against Attica, captured Mĕgără (*see* NISUS), and compelled the Athenians to send him once in every nine years seven boys and seven girls to Crete, to be devoured by the Minotaur (*q.v.*; *see also* THESEUS). Tradition made him die in Sicily, whither he had pursued Dædălus (*q.v.*) on his flight, and where king Cŏcălus or his daughters stifled him in a hot bath. His Cretan followers interred him near Agrigentum, where his grave was shown. In Homer [*Od.* xi 568] Odysseus sees him in Hādēs with a golden sceptre in his hand, judging the shades; he does not appear in the legends as judge of the dead by the side of Æăcus and Rhădămanthys till later [Plato, *Apol.* 41 *a*, *Gorg.* 523 *e*].

Minōtaurus (i.e. *Bull of Minos*). Son of Pāsĭphăē (*q.v.*) and a bull; a monster with the head of a bull and the body of a man. Minos concealed it in the labyrinth, built near Gnōssus by Dædălus, and gave him as food the criminals, and the youths and maidens sent from Athens as a tribute, till Theseus by the help of Ariadne penetrated into the labyrinth and killed the Minotaur. It has been pointed out that he is the same as the Phœnician *Baal Moloch*, also represented with a bull's head and supplied with human sacrifices. This worship was put a stop to by Greek civilization, which may be considered with all the more reason to be represented by Theseus, as in olden days the Attic coast was perhaps actually occupied from time to time by Cretan or Phœnician settlers, who sent human sacrifices to Crete as their religious centre.

Minŭcius Fēlix (*Quintus*). The first Latin Christian author, a man of excellent education, and a distinguished lawyer at Rome. After becoming a Christian at an advanced age, he wrote in the second half of the

2nd century a dialogue entitled *Octāvius*, in which he aims at refuting the objections raised against Christianity. The work is marked by purity of diction and by acuteness and precision of argument.

Mĭnўădĕs. The daughters of Minyas, the rich king of Orchŏmĕnus and mythical ancestral hero of the race of the Minyæ; their names were *Alcăthŏĕ* (Alcĭthŏĕ), *Leucippĕ*, and *Arsippĕ*. When the worship of Dĭonўsus was introduced into Bœotia, and all the other women wandered in frenzy over the mountains in honour of the god, they alone remained at home, and profaned the festival by working at their looms, in spite of the warning of the god, who had appeared to them in the shape of a maiden. It was not till he had assumed the shapes of a bull, a lion, and a panther, had made milk and wine flow from the yarnbeams, and had changed their weft into grapes and vine-leaves, that they were terrified and drew lots who should offer a sacrifice to the god; and Leucippe, on whom the lot fell, tore her own son Hippăsus to pieces in her Bacchic fury. They then raged about on the mountains till they were transformed into bats. With this legend was connected the custom, that at the annual festival of Dionysus the priest of the god was allowed to pursue the women of the Minyan race with a drawn sword and kill them. [Ælian, *V. H.* iii 42; Plutarch, *Quœst. Gr.* 38; Ovid, *Met.* iv 1–40, 390–415.]

Mirrors. For mirrors the ancients used round or oval, also square, plates of melted and polished metal, generally of copper, mixed with tin, zinc, and other materials, often silvered and gilded. In later times

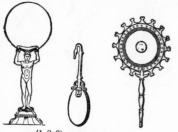

(1, 2, 3) POMPEIAN MIRRORS.
(Overbeck's *Pompeii*, p. 404, 1875.)

they were also made of massive silver. They were often provided with a decorated handle and ornamented on the back with engravings, mostly of mythological objects

(*see* cuts). The Etruscan mirrors are in this respect remarkably fine [the finest of all is represented in fig. 4]. Besides these

(4) BACK OF ETRUSCAN MIRROR.
(Berlin Museum.)

Apollo with bay tree and Satyr on left; Semele and Dionysus on right; with border of ivy-leaves.

hand-mirrors, there were also in the time of the emperors mirrors as high as a man [Seneca, *N. Q.* i 17; cp. Quintilian xi 3, § 68], which were either permanently fixed in the wall or [as in Vitruv. ix 8 § 2] let up and down like a sash.

[*Greek mirrors* were unknown to archæologists until 1867, when the first specimen was discovered at Corinth. In design they are even more beautiful than those of Etruria. They are of two kinds: (*a*) Like the Etruscan mirrors, they are generally round, consisting of a single disc with a polished convex front, to reflect the face, and a concave back, ornamented with figures traced with the engraver's burin. This variety had a handle in the form of a statuette resting on a pedestal. (*b*) Another variety, especially frequent in Greece, consists of two metallic discs, one inclosed within the other, and sometimes held together by a hinge. The cover was externally ornamented with figures in low relief, and was internally polished and silvered to reflect the face. The second disc, forming the body of the case, was decorated internally with figures engraved with a sharp point. *See* Collignon's *Greek Archæology*, fig. 136, *Leukăs* and *Cŏrinthŏs* personified, on an engraved mirror; and fig. 137, a fine relief of Ganymede and the eagle. In the British Museum we have a mirror from Corinth, representing Pan playing at the game of "Five Stones" with a Nymph attended by Erōs (Bronze Room, table-case D).]

Missio. The Roman term for the dismissal of soldiers from service, whether on account of illness (*missio causărĭa*) or of some dishonourable offence (*missio ignŏmĭnĭōsa*), or at the expiration of their period of service. The last-mentioned, *missio*

legal marriage. The imperial decree which contained a list of those dismissed, arranged according to the subdivisions of the army and with the privileges granted, was posted on a public building on the Capitol or in the Forum, and each one of those specified received an extract from this document, made out in the presence of seven wit-

* THE SACRIFICE OF MITHRAS.
(Paris, Louvre.)

hŏnesta or honourable dismissal, carried with it, under the Empire, the maintenance of the dismissed soldier. At first a fixed sum of money was given him, afterwards a parcel of land in Italy or the provinces was assigned; he also received the rights of citizenship, if he did not already possess them, and the privilege of contracting a

nesses and inscribed on a bronze *diptўchŏn* (*q.v.*). Sixty-two such military diplomas have been preserved completely or in part.

Mithrās. The Persian god of created light and of all earthly wisdom. In the course of time he became identified with the sun-god, who conquers all demons of darkness. In the time after Alexander the Great, his worship, mixed with various customs peculiar to Western Asia, was extended over all the Oriental kingdoms. In the first half of the 1st century B.C. it is said to have been introduced into the Roman provinces in the West by the Cilician pirates who were at that time masters of the Mediterranean. There are traces of his worship at Rome under Tiberius; and in the beginning of the 2nd century after Christ, under the Antonines, it became common throughout the whole Roman empire, and was kept up till the end of the 4th century. Mithras was a special favourite of the Roman armies. Being born from the rocks, he was worshipped in natural or artificial caves, such as have been found in every part of the Roman empire. He is represented as a young man in oriental dress and as an invincible hero, stabbing a bull with his dagger or standing on a bull he has thrown down. [Fine specimens of this group may be seen in the Louvre and in the British Museum and elsewhere (*see* cut.)] The cave itself was explained by the ancients to signify the world, into which the human soul must descend, that it may be purified by many trials before leaving it. Before any one was initiated in the mysteries of Mithras, it was necessary for the person to undergo a series of (it is said eighty) trials of increasing difficulty; and an undaunted, unsubdued spirit had to be maintained in fire and water, hunger and thirst, scourging, and solitude, and the aspirant was thus prepared for the initiation. It consisted of seven degrees, that of the ravens, the secret, the fighters, the lions or she-lions (for women were also received), the Persians, the sun-runners, and the fathers. Various Christian rites seem also to have been introduced into the mysteries of Mithras. Epithets like "Lord and Creator of all things," "Father and source of all life," enable us to recognise Mithras as one of the pantheistic divinities of declining heathendom.

Mitra. A kerchief which women wore round the head. *See* HAIR.

Mnēmē. *See* MUSES.

Mnēmŏsўnē. Daughter of Urănus and Gæa, and one of the Tĭtānĭdĕs, the goddess of memory, by Zeus, mother of the Muses (*q.v.*), in company with whom she was usually worshipped.

Mnēsĭclēs. A Greek architect, the builder of the *Prŏpўlœa* (*q.v.*).

Mŏdius. The principal dry measure of the Romans, equal to nearly two gallons, a sixth part of the Greek medimnus. It was divided into 16 *sextārii*, 32 *hēmīnæ*, 64 *quartārii*, 128 *ăcĕtābŭla*, 192 *cўăthi*.

Mœræ (Gr. *Moirai*). The Greek goddesses of Fate: Homer in one passage [*Il.* xxiv 209] speaks generally of the *Moira*, that spins the thread of life for men at their

* CLOTHO, ATROPOS, AND LACHESIS.
(Roman relief, in Schloss Tegel, the residence of the Humboldts, near Berlin.)

birth; in another [*ib.* 49] of several *Moirai*, and elsewhere [*Od.* vii 197] of the *Clōthēs*, or Spinners. Their relation to Zeus and other gods is no more clearly defined by Homer than by the other Greeks. At one time Fate is a power with unlimited sway over men and gods, and the will of Fate is searched out and executed by Zeus with the other gods [*Il.* xix 87; *Od.* xxii 413]; at another Zeus is called the highest ruler of destinies, or again he and the other gods can change the course of fate [*Il.* xvi 434], and even men can exceed the limits it imposes [*Il.* xx 336]. In Hesiod they are called in one passage [*Theog.* 211–7] daughters of Night and sisters of the goddesses of death (*Kērĕs*), while in another (*Theog.* 904) they are the daughters of Zeus and

Thĕmĭs and sisters of the Horæ, who give good and bad fortunes to mortals at their birth; their names are *Clōthō* (the Spinner), who spins the thread of life, *Lăchĕsĭs* (Disposer of Lots), who determines its length, and *Atrŏpŏs* (Inevitable), who cuts it off. As exerting power at the time of birth they are connected with Ilithyĭa, the goddess of birth, who was supposed to stand beside them, and was invoked together with them, these and the *Kērĕs* being the powers that decided when life should end. As at birth they determine men's destinies in life, they are also able to predict them. While on the one hand they are regarded as the impartial representatives of the government of the world, they are on the other hand sometimes conceived as cruel and jealous, because they remorselessly thwart the plans and desires of men. In art they appear as maidens of grave aspect. *Clotho* is usually represented with a spindle; *Lachesis* with a scroll, or a globe; and *Atropos* with a pair of scales or shears, or else drawing a lot (as in the cut). The Romans identified the *Moirai* with their native goddesses of fate, the *Parcæ*. These were also called *Fātă*, and were invoked, at the end of the first week of an infant's life, as *Fata Scribunda*, the goddesses that wrote down men's destiny in life.

Mœris (*Ælius*). Known as *the Atticist*. A Greek grammarian of the 2nd century after Christ. He was the author of an *Attic Lexicon*, a list, in alphabetical order, of a number of expressions and forms used by Attic writers, with the parallel expressions used in his own time.

Mŏlĭŏnĭdæ. Eurўtus and Ctĕătus, the sons of Actŏr (whence they were also called *Actŏrĭdœ*) or else of Pŏseidŏn and Mŏlĭŏne. [Homer, *Il.* xi 750, calls them by the dual and double name *Actŏrĭŏne Mŏlĭŏnĕ*.] As boys they fought against Nestŏr and the men of Pўlus. When they had grown up, they beat the army of Hĕrăclēs that threatened their uncle Augeas, but were killed by the former near Clĕŏnæ in Argolis. In Homer their sons Thalpius and Antĭmăchus are the chieftains of the Epeians before Troy. A later legend describes them as having only one body [Athenæus, ii p. 58].

Mŏmus. In Greek mythology the evil spirit of blame and mockery, according to Hesiod [*Theog.* 214] the son of Night. [According to Lucian, *Hermotimus* 20, he found fault with the man formed by Hĕphæstus for not having little doors in his breast, so

as to allow of his secret thoughts being seen. In Philostrătus (*Ep.* 21 = 37) the only faults he finds in Aphrŏdĭtē are that she is too talkative and that her sandal makes too much noise.]

Mŏnēta. See JUNO (end of article).

Money-changers. See BANKS AND BANKING.

Mŏnoptĕrŏs. An epithet descriptive of a round temple with its columns arranged in a circle and supporting a cupola. See TEMPLE (end of article).

Months. See CALENDAR.

Moon, Goddess of. Among the Greeks, *see* SELENE; among the Romans, *see* LUNA.

Mopsus. The name of two Greek seers. (1) One of the Lăpĭthæ of Œchălĭa in Thessaly, son of Ampyx and the Nymph Chlōris. He took part in the Calydonian Hunt and in the fight of the Lapithæ and the Centaurs (*see* PIRITHOUS), and afterwards accompanied the Argonauts as seer, and died of the bite of a snake in Libya, where he was worshipped as a hero, and had an oracle.

(2) Son of the Cretan seer Rhăcius and of Manto (*q.v.*), and founder, with Amphilŏchus, son of Amphĭărāus, of the celebrated oracle (*q.v.*) at Mallūs in Cilicia. Mopsus and Amphilochus killed each other in a combat for the possession of the sanctuary.

Mŏra. One of the six principal divisions of the army at Sparta, which included all Spartans and Perĭœci that were obliged to serve. It was under the command of a polemarch, and consisted of four *lŏchi*, eight *pentĕcostўĕs*, and sixteen *ĕnōmŏtĭæ*, which were under as many *lŏchăgi*, *pentĕcostĕrĕs*, and *ĕnōmŏtarchi*. These divisions were never sent on a campaign in their full strength, but only the men of particular years, specified in each case. The polemarch always took the command of the first levy.

Morpheus. The Greek god of dreams. (*See* DREAMS.)

Morsĭmus. A tragic poet (*see* PHILOCLES).

[**Mosaics.** The term *mosaic* is usually derived from a post-classical word *mūsīvum* (Gr. *mouseiŏn?*), occurring in Spartianus, *Life of Pescenninus* 6, *pictum de musivo*, and Augustine, *De Civitate Dei* xvi 8, *hominum genera musivo picta*. It is the art of arranging small cubes or *tessĕræ* of marble, coloured stone, terra cotta, glass, or some other artificial substance, so as to produce an ornamental pattern or picture, and to provide a durable form of decoration for walls and pavements. The only mosaic hitherto found in Greece Proper is that discovered in 1829, in the floor of the east portico of the temple of Zeus, at Olympia, possibly little later than the first half of the 4th century B.C. It is formed of rough round pebbles of various colours from the bed of the Alphēus, and it represents Tritons of graceful design surrounded by a tasteful border of palmettes and meandering lines (*see* Baumeister's *Denkmäler*, fig. 998).

The earliest mosaics mentioned in literature are those made for the ship of Hĭĕrŏn II, about the middle of the 3rd century, with scenes from the *Iliad*, which took 300 skilled workmen a whole year to execute (Athenæus, 206 D). To the same age themselves on the rim of the bowl. The best known copy of this is that called *The Capitoline Doves* (fig. 1), found at Hadrian's Villa near Tivoli. It is entirely composed of cubes of marble, without any admixture of coloured glass.

The art of reproducing paintings in mosaic probably originated in Egypt, and thence found its way to Italy. The largest mosaic picture of Roman workmanship is that executed for the Temple of Fortune at Præneste, restored by Sulla (Pliny, xxxvi 189). This was discovered in 1640, and is generally supposed to represent a popular *fête* on the occasion of an inundation of

(1) * THE CAPITOLINE DOVES.
(Rome, Capitoline Museum.)

belongs the only artist in mosaic whose name is recorded in literature, Sōsus of Pergămŏn, famous as the inventor of a kind of mosaic called the *ăsărŏtŏn* (the "unswept" floor), in which the floor of a room is inlaid with representations of fruits, fishes, and fragments of food that have fallen from the table (Pliny, xxxvi 184; *cp.* Statius, *Silvæ* i 3, 36). Mosaics of this type have been found not only at Pompeii, but also at Aquīlēīa and in Algiers. Acccording to Pliny, the original design by Sosus included a remarkable representation of a dove drinking and casting the shadow of its head on the water beneath, while several other doves were to be seen sunning the Nile. It probably belongs to the time of Hadrian.

Among the mosaics of Pompeii the most famous is that identified as the *Battle of Issus*, possibly a copy of the painting of the same subject by a female artist, Hĕlĕnă, "daughter of Timon the Egyptian," which was placed in the temple of Peace in the time of Vespasian (Photius, *Bibl.*, p. 482). It represents the critical moment when Alexander is charging, bare-headed, in the thick of the fray, and has just transfixed with his lance one of the leaders of the Persians; while Dărīus, with his lofty tiara and red chlămўs, is extending his right hand in an attitude of alarm and despair (figs. 2

X.A.R.BRINDAMUR. E. Schönherr. sc

(2) * BATTLE OF ISSUS.
(Mosaic from the Casa del Fauno, Pompeii; Naples Museum.)

(3) * DARIUS IN THE BATTLE OF ISSUS
(Detail of fig. 2.)

and 3). In the mosaic itself the lower border represents a river, apparently the Nile, with a crocodile, hippopotamus, ichneumon, ibis, etc., thus confirming the conjecture as to the Egyptian origin of the design.

Mosaics bearing the artist's name are seldom found. The two finest of this class are those from Pompeii inscribed with the name of Dĭoscŏrĭdēs of Sămŏs. One of these represents four masked figures playing on various instruments. The work is composed of very small pieces of glass, of the most beautiful colours and in various shades (cut in Dyer's *Pompeii*, p. 276). Another of similar construction portrays a rehearsal for a satyric drama. The ground is black, the drapery mainly white, but the robe of the flute-player is bordered with purple, the lips are a bright red, and the flutes and ornaments coloured like gold. (*See* DRAMA, fig. 2.) The finest mosaic of the early part of the 2nd century A.D. is the highly pictorial centaur-mosaic now at Berlin, found at the Villa of Hadrian (*see* Baumeister's *Denkmäler*, fig. 941). The most celebrated works of a later date include that in the *Thermæ* of Caracalla, with numerous gladiatorial figures of colossal size and ungraceful drawing (*ib.* fig. 174); and that of the Roman villa at Nennig, near Trèves. The dimensions of the latter are 50 feet by 33, and the design includes several groups of figures inclosed in a square or hexagonal framework of tesselated marble (*ib.* figs. 1001–2343). Among the mosaics in the British Museum are an Amphitrītē and Tritons, with Dĭonȳsus, Mĕlĕăger, and Atălanta, all from Halicarnassus, and of Roman times, since figures of Dido and Æneas were found in the same villa (Newton's *Travels and Discoveries*, ii 76). As mosaics still *in situ* in England may be mentioned those at Woodchester, Bignor, and Brading.[1] In the "Gallery of the Architectural Court" of the South Kensington Museum are exhibited 100 coloured plates, with copies of mosaics, collected by Dr. R. Wollaston, including a Greek mosaic of *Iphĭgĕnĭa at Aulis*, found in the Crimea, and the above-mentioned mosaic of Præneste (no. 167).

Mosaic pavements are known by different names descriptive of certain varieties of structure. (1) A *păvīmentum sectĭle* is composed of thin plates of coloured marble of various sizes, cut (*sĕcta*) into slices of

regular form and arranged in an ornamental geometrical pattern including triangles, hexagons, etc. (Vitruvius, vii 1, 3, 4; Suetonius, *Cæsar*, 46 at end). (2) The epithet *tessellātum* describes a pavement of the same general kind, but made up of regular square dies (*tessĕræ, tessellæ, tessĕrŭlæ*), forming rectangular designs (*ib.*). (3) *Vermĭcŭlātum* is applied to a design formed of small pieces of marble in various colours, arranged so as to imitate the object represented with a high degree of pictorial effect. The dies are of different shapes, so as to allow of their following the wavy contours of the outline of the object. The name is derived from the fact that the general effect of such an arrangement resembles the contortions of a cluster of worms (*vermēs*). (*Cp.* Pliny, xxxv 2: *Interraso marmore vermiculatisque ad effigies rerum crustis;* and Lucilius, quoted in Cicero's *Orator*, 149: *Quam lepide lexeis compostæ ut tesserulæ omnes—arte pavimento atque emblemate vermiculato.*) (4) The term *lĭthŏstrōtum* (Varro, *R. R.*, iii 2 § 4; 1 § 10; Pliny, xxxvi 189) was probably applied to a pavement made of small pieces of stone or marble of natural colours, and distinguished from those of coloured glass or some other artificial composition. Mosaics of glass were used to decorate ceilings (Pliny, *l.c.*).

The gilt *tesseræ* used in Christian mosaics for the background of the pictures were formed by applying to a cube of earthenware two thin plates of glass with a film of gold-leaf between them, and vitrifying the whole in a furnace. It was this discovery that led to the extensive application of mosaic for the decoration of the walls, and more particularly the apses, of Christian churches. At Rome, we have mosaics of the 4th century in the churches of S. Constantia and S. Maria Maggiore. At Ravenna, those of the lower part of the Orthodox Baptistery belong to 430 A.D.; those in the Mausoleum of Galla Placidia to 440; those in the domes of the Orthodox and Arian Baptisteries to about 553; those of San Vitale to 547; of S. Apollinare Nuovo to 549, and of the archiepiscopal palace to about the same date; and, lastly, those of S. Apollinare in Classe to about 671–677. At Milan, the mosaics of S. Lorenzo and S. Ambrogio belong to the 5th century; those of S. Parenzo in Istria to the 6th: those of S. Sophia at Constantinople were executed in the time of Justinian (527–565). At Rome, those of SS. Cosmas and Damian are ascribed to

[1] *Cp.* Morgan's *Romano-British Mosaic Pavements*, 1886.

526–530; of S. Lorenzo Outside the Walls to 577–590; of S. Agnese to 625–638; of the oratory of S. Venantius, the churches of S. Praxedes, S. Cecilia in Trastevere, and S. Maria Navicella, to the 7th century. After the 9th century the art of working in mosaic ceased for awhile in Rome and in Italy in general, to be revived at a later date in the church of S. Cyprian at Murano (1109) and the basilica of St. Mark's at Venice (in and after the 11th century), and afterwards at Rome itself. In Sicily, the mosaics of the *Cappella Palatina* in the royal palace at Palermo were finished in 1143, while those of the cathedral at Monreale were begun in 1172.

Authorities. Marquardt, *Das Privatleben der Römer*, 625–632; Blümner's *Technologie*, iii 323–343; Von Rohden on *Mosaik* in Baumeister's *Denkmäler ;* Gerspach, *La Mosaique*.] [J. E. S.]

Moschus. A Greek bucolic poet, who lived in Syracuse about B.C. 150. Four longer and four shorter poems have been handed down as his; they show the greatest elegance of expression without the truth to nature and the dramatic power of his model Theocritus.

Mŏthăcēs. *See* HELOTS.

Mūcĭus Scævŏla (*Quintus*) was born of a family in which the pontificate and great legal learning had been handed down from father to son. He was a friend of the orator Crassus and his colleague in almost all offices, was made consul in B.C. 95, and murdered by the Marians in 85. A man of great integrity and wide culture, he combined a profound knowledge of the law with remarkable eloquence. He rendered great service by being the first to reduce the legal materials accumulated in the course of time to a consistent and classified system. This he did in his lost work, *De Iūrĕ Cīvīlī*, in eighteen volumes; it formed the basis for a methodical treatment of law. Among his pupils were Cicero and the lawyer Sulpīcīus Rūfus (*q.v.*).

Mulcĭber. Epithet of Vulcan (*q.v.*).

Mullĕus. *See* CALCEUS.

Multa [wrongly spelt *mulcta*]. The Roman term for a fine, inflicted either by a magistrate for disobedience or insubordination, or at the motion of an official by the decision of the people at the *cŏmĭtĭă trĭbūta*, or prescribed in laws, wills, etc., in case any one contravened them. It originally consisted in cattle, sheep, or oxen; then, after B.C. 430, the *Lex Iūlĭa Pāpīrĭa* permitted the payment in money according to

a fixed scale (a sheep = 10 *asses*, an ox = 100 *asses*). The lowest amount of the *multa* inflicted by a magistrate in virtue of his office was a sheep; when acts of disobedience were repeated, the fine could be raised to 30 oxen (*suprēma multa*). Against heavier penalties, such, in particular, as were imposed by the tribunes of the people on account of political crimes, *e.g.* when a general had waged war unskilfully or had exceeded the limits of his power, an appeal to the *cŏmĭtĭă trĭbūtă* was granted, and they were decided by that body in the regular legal manner. The fines imposed by the people were always, and those imposed by the magistrates usually, set apart for sacred purposes ; otherwise they fell to the *ærārium*, as was the rule under the Empire. This also received a part of the penalties fixed by laws, the other was given to the plaintiff. Fines for contravention of the clauses of a will were either paid to the funds of a temple or to the community to which the testator belonged, and at Rome to the *ærarium*.

Mummĭus. A Latin writer of *Atellānæ* (*see* ATELLANA), after 90 B.C.

Mūnĭcĭpĭum. Originally the Roman term for a town the inhabitants of which, called *mūnĭcĭpēs,* only possessed part of the rights of Roman citizenship, *viz.* the private rights of *commercium* and *conūbium*, while they were excluded from the political rights, the *ius suffrāgii* and the *ius hŏnōrum*, the right to elect and to be elected to office. As Roman citizens, they did not serve (like the allies) in cohorts under a prefect, but in the legions under tribunes ; they were, however, assigned to legions distinct from the others, since they were not inscribed on the lists of the Roman tribes, and therefore could not be levied in accordance with those lists. After the dissolution of the Latin League in B.C. 338, the allied towns were put into the position of *municipia*.

At first there were two classes of *municipia*, according as they retained an independent communal constitution or not. The second class, which had no senate, magistrates, or popular assembly of its own, and was governed directly by Rome, consisted of the *præfectūræ* (*q.v.*). As the *municipia* gradually obtained the full rights of citizenship, their nature changed ; all persons were now called *municipes*, who did not belong to the town of Rome by birth, but were full Roman citizens, and hence belonged to a Roman tribe, were registered at Rome, could elect and be elected to office, and served in the Roman legions.

The *Lex Iūlia* of B.C. 90 made all the towns of Italy *municipia* with full civic rights, and every Italian country-town was now called a Roman *municipium*. Gradually the towns in the provinces received municipal rights, till finally Caracalla made all towns of the empire *municipia*. Originally one class of *municipia* had retained their own laws and their own constitution ; this arrangement underwent a change when they were received into the Roman citizenship, inasmuch as the Roman law then became binding upon them, and a regularly organized administration on the Roman model was introduced. The citizens were divided into *cūrīœ*, and at their *comitia curiata* passed all kinds of decrees, and chose officers ; most of these rights, however, passed into the hands of the local senate towards the end of the 1st century. This senate usually consisted of 100 life-members, called *dēcŭrīōnes*, and in every fifth year the vacancies were filled up from those who had held office or were qualified by their property. The highest officials were the *dŭŏ vĭri*, who were judges and presided at the assemblies of the people, especially at elections, and in the senate; the two *quinquennālēs*, chosen for a year, once in five years, and corresponding to the Roman censors ; and *quœstōrēs* and *ædīlēs*, officials with similar duties to the Roman officials of the same name. (*See* MAGISTRATUS.) Besides the *decuriones*, whose position became hereditary at the end of the Empire, there were, under the heathen emperors, a second privileged class, known as *Augustālēs*, chosen by decree of the local senate and next to that body in rank. They made up a *collēgium*, which was originally dedicated to the worship of the Julian family, and in later times seems to have also extended its functions to the worship of the other emperors. The decline of the municipal system, the prosperity of which had depended on the liberty and independence of the administration, set in at the end of the 2nd century after Christ, when the emperors began to transfer to the *municipia* the burdens of the State, and the *decuriones* gradually became mere imperial officials, who were more especially responsible for the collection of the tribute imposed.

Mural Crown. *See* CORONA.

Murcia. *See* VENUS.

Murrĭna (*vāsa*). A name given by the Romans to vessels made of an oriental mineral called *murra*, which only occurred in small plates, opaque, of dull lustre and changing colours, and very brittle. The first vessels of this kind were brought to Rome by Pompey in B.C. 61, among the spoils of king Mithridates [Pliny, *N. H.*, xxxvii 18]. In Rome enormous prices were paid for them on account of their material, which is unknown to us, but is held by many to have been a rare kind of *fluor spar* [while others identify it with *porcelain*]. Thus Nero paid for his cup with a handle, made of *murra*, the sum of a million sesterces, about £10,000 [*ib.* § 20]. *Murra*, as well as every variety of precious stone, was imitated in glass.

Mūsæus. (1) A mythical singer, seer, and priest, who occurs especially in Attic legends. He is said to have lived in pre-Homeric times, and to have been the son of Sělēnē and Orpheus or Lĭnus or Eumolpus. Numerous oracular sayings, hymns, and chants of dedication and purification were ascribed to him, which had been collected, and also interpolated, by Onŏmăcrĭtus, in the time of the Pīsistrătĭdæ. His tomb was shown at Athens on the Museum Hill, south-west of the Acropolis [Pausanias i 25 § 8].

(2) A grammarian and Greek poet, who in the beginning of the 6th century after Christ wrote a short epic of love, entitled *Hero and Leander*, which shows intense warmth of feeling, and has touches that are almost modern.

Mūsăgĕtēs, *i.e.* leader of the Muses. A title of (Apollo) the god of poets. (*See* APOLLO and MUSES.)

Mūseiŏn (Lat. *Mūsēum*). Originally a temple of the Muses, then a place dedicated to the works of the Muses. In this sense the most remarkable and most important museum of antiquity was that established at Alexandria by Ptolemy Phĭlădelphus in the first half of the 3rd century B.C. This institution contributed very largely towards the preservation and extension of Greek literature and learning. It was a spacious and magnificent edifice, supplied with everything requisite for its purpose, such as an observatory, a library, etc.; it lay near the royal palace and communicated immediately with the temple of the Muses. Noted men of erudition were there supported at the cost of the State, to enable them to devote themselves to their learned studies without interruption. They were under the supervision of principals chosen from their own body, while the priest of the Muses was at their head. Under the Roman emperors, when Egypt had become a province of the empire, it still continued, as an imperial institute and the centre of all learning, especially in mathematics and astronomy [Strabo, p. 794]. Caracalla confiscated the pensions of the learned men attached to it, and the institution itself was completely destroyed during the civil wars under Aurelian in the 3rd century.

Muses. In Greek mythology originally the Nymphs of inspiring springs, then goddesses of song in general, afterwards the representatives of the various kinds of poetry, arts, and sciences. In Homer, who now speaks of one, and now of many Muses, but

(she that extols), the Muse of *history;* with a scroll. (3) EUTERPĒ (she that gladdens), the Muse of *lyric song;* with the double flute. (4) THALIA (she that flourishes), the Muse of *comedy* and bucolic poetry; with the comic mask, the ivy wreath, and the shepherd's staff. (5) MELPŎMĒNĒ (she that sings), the Muse of *tragedy;* with tragic mask, ivy wreath, and occasionally with attributes of individual heroes, *e.g.* the club, the sword. (6) TERPSĪCHŎRĒ (she that rejoices in the dance), the Muse of *dancing;* with the lyre. (7) ERĂTŌ (the lovely one), the Muse of *erotic poetry;* with a smaller lyre. (8) PŎLYMNĬĂ or

CLIO. THALIA. ERATO. EUTERPE. POLYMNIA. CALLIOPE. TERPSICHORE. URANIA. MELPOMENE.

THE MUSES.

(Sarcophagus in the Louvre, Paris.)

without specifying their number or their names, they are considered as goddesses dwelling in Olympus, who at the meals of the gods sing sweetly to the lyre of Apollo, inspire the poet and prompt his song. Hesiod [*Theog.* 52–, 76–,] calls them the nine daughters of Zeus and Mnēmŏsȳnē, born in Pīĕrĭa, and mentions their names, to which we shall at the same time add the province and the attributes afterwards assigned to each (*see* cuts). (1) CALLĬŎPĒ (she of the fair voice), in Hesiod the noblest of all, the Muse of *epic song;* among her attributes are a wax tablet and a pencil. (2) CLĪŌ

PŎLYHYMNĬĂ (she that is rich in hymns), the Muse of serious *sacred songs;* usually represented as veiled and pensive. (9) URĂNĬA (the heavenly), the Muse of astronomy; with the celestial globe.

Three older Muses were sometimes distinguished from these. MĔLĔTĒ (Meditation), MNĒMĒ (Remembrance), AOIDĒ (Song), whose worship was said to have been introduced by the Alōīdæ, Ōtus and Ephĭaltēs, near Mount Hĕlĭcōn. Thracian settlers in the Pierian district at the foot of Olympus and of Helicon in Bœotia are usually mentioned as the original founders of this worship. At both these places were their oldest sanctuaries. According to the general belief, the favourite haunts of the Muses were certain springs, near which temples and statues had been erected in their honour : Castălĭa, at the foot of Mount Parnassus, and Agănippē and Hippŏcrēnē, on Helicon, near the towns of Ascra and Thespiæ. After the decline of Ascra, the inhabitants of Thespiæ attended to the worship of the Muses and to the arrangements for the musical contests in their honour that took place once in five years. They were also adored in many other places in Greece. Thus the Athenians offered them sacrifices in the schools, while the Spartans did so before battle. As the inspiring Nymphs of springs they were early connected with Dionysus; the god of poets, Apollo, is looked on as their leader (*Mūsăgĕtēs*), with whom they share the knowledge of past, present, and future. As beings that gladden men and gods with their song, Hesiod describes them as dwelling on Olympus along with the Chărĭtĕs and Hīmĕrŏs. They were represented in art as virgin goddesses with long garments of many folds, and frequently with a cloak besides; they were not distinguished by special attributes till comparatively later times. The Roman poets identified them with the Italian *Cămēnæ*, prophetic Nymphs of springs and goddesses of birth, who had a grove at Rome outside the *Porta Căpēna*. (*See* EGERIA.) The Greeks gave the title of Muses to their nine most distinguished poetesses : Praxilla, Mœrō, Anӯtē, Ērinna, Tĕlĕsilla, Cŏrinna, Nossis, Myrtis, and Sappho.

Museum. *See* MUSEION.

Music (Gr. *mūsĭcē*, "art of the Muses") included among the Greeks everything that belonged to a higher intellectual and artistic education. [Plato in his *Republic*, p. 136, while discussing education, says: "Can we find any better than the old-fashioned sort, gymnastic for the body and music for the soul?" and adds: "When you speak of music, do you rank literature under music or not?" "I do."] Music in the narrower sense was regarded by the Greeks not only as an agreeable amusement, but also as one of the most effective means of cultivating the feelings and the character. The great importance they attached to music is also shown by their idea that it was of divine origin; Hermēs or Apollo were said to have invented the lyre, Athēnē the simple flute, Pan the shepherd's pipe. Besides these gods and the Muses, Dionӯsus also was con-

nected with music. Numerous myths, as for instance those concerning Amphīōn and Orpheus, tell of its mighty power, and testify to the Greeks having cultivated music at a very early epoch. It was always intimately allied to poetry. Originally, epic poems were also sung to the accompaniment of the *cĭthără*, and the old heroes of poetry, such as Orpheus and Musæus, are at the same time heroes of music, just as in historical times the lyric and dramatic poets were at the same time the composers of their works. It was not until the Alexandrian times that the poet ceased to be also a musician. Owing to its connexion with poetry, music developed in the same proportion, and flourished at the same period, as lyric and dramatic poetry. Of the Greek races, the Dorians and Æolians had a special genius and capacity for music, and among both we find the first traces of its development as an art.

The actual foundation of the classical music of the Greeks is ascribed to TERPANDER (*q.v.*), of the Æolian island of Lesbos, who, in Dorian Sparta (about B.C. 675) first gave a truly artistic form to song accompanied by the *cĭthără* or *cĭthărŏdĭcē*, and especially to the citharodic *nŏmŏs* (*q.v.*). In the Peloponnesian school of the *Terpandrĭdæ*, who followed his teaching and formed a closely united guild, *citharodice* received its further artistic development. What Terpander had done for *citharodice* was done not long afterwards by CLŎNAS of Thebes or Tĕgĕa for *aulōdĭcē*, or song accompanied by the flute. The artistic flute-playing which had been elaborated by the Phrygian OLYMPUS in Asia, was introduced by Clonas into the Peloponnesus, which long remained the principal seat of all musical art. Of the two kinds of independent instrumental music, which throughout presupposes the development of vocal music and always adapts itself to this as its model, the earlier is the music on the flute, *aulētĭcē*, which was especially brought into favourable notice by SĂCĂDĂS of Argos (about B.C. 580), while the music on stringed instruments, *cĭthărĭstĭcē*, is later. Music was much promoted by the contests at the public festivals, above all, by those at the Pythian games. Its highest point of development was attained in the time of the Persian Wars, which seems to have seen the completion of the ancient system as it had been elaborated by the tradition of the schools. The lyric poets of this time, as Pindar and Sĭmŏnĭdēs, the dramatists, as

Phrўnīchus and Æschўlus, were held by the critics to be unsurpassable models. What was added in subsequent times can hardly be called a new development of the art. Athens in her golden age was the central city where professional musicians met one another,—Athens the home of Greek dramatic poetry. At this time vocal, combined with instrumental, music largely prevailed over instrumental music alone. The latter was chiefly limited to *solo* performances.

Ancient *vocal music* is distinguished in one important point from ours: throughout classical times part-singing was unknown, and there was at most a difference of octaves, and that only when men and boys sang in the same choir. Again, in classical times, the music was subordinate to the words, and was therefore necessarily much simpler than it is now. It is only in this way that we can explain the fact that an ancient audience could follow the musical representation of the often intricate language of the odes, even when the odes were sung by the whole choir. Critics regarded it as a decline of art, when, at the end of the Peloponnesian War, the music began to be the important element instead of the poetry. This change took place at first in single branches of the art, as in the solos (*mŏnōdĭæ*) in tragedy, and in the dithyrambic choruses. Thenceforward ancient music, like modern music, raised itself more and more to a free and independent position beside that of poetry.

The first place among the various kinds of music was assigned to the indigenous *cĭthărŏdĭcē*, which was connected with the first development of the musical art; and indeed stringed instruments were always more esteemed than wind instruments, in part on account of the greater technical difficulties which had to be overcome, and which led to musicians giving particular attention to them. Moreover, playing on the flute was limited to certain occasions, as its sound seemed to the ancients to arouse enthusiasm and passion [Aristotle, *Politics*, viii 3]. There is evidence that, on the one hand, the ancient theory of singing and of instrumentation (in spite of the primitive nature of the instruments) was brought to a high degree of perfection; and that, on the other hand, the public must have possessed a severely critical judgment in matters of music. The characteristic feature of ancient music is the great clearness of its form, resulting, above all, from the extreme precision of the rhythmic treatment.

[In ancient Greece there were certain kinds or forms of music, which were known by national or tribal names, Dorian, Phrygian, Lydian, Ionian, and Æolian. Of these the Dorian and Phrygian are regarded by Plato as representing the mean in respect of pitch, while the highest varieties of the Lydian (called Mixo-lydian and Syntono-lydian) are contrasted with the Ionian and with the lower variety of the Lydian (afterwards known as Hypo-lydian), the last two being described as "slack," or low in pitch (*Republic*, p. 398, and Aristotle, *Politics*, viii 5 and 7). Each of these was regarded as expressive of a particular feeling. Thus, the Dorian was deemed appropriate to earnest and warlike melodies; the Phrygian was exciting and emotional; the Mixo-lydian pathetic and plaintive. The Æolian was intermediate between the high - pitched Lydian and the low-pitched Ionian (Athenæus, p. 624 e, f, and 526. The terms Ionian and Æolian fell out of use, and the following names were generally applied to seven forms of music, beginning with the highest in pitch and ending with the lowest:—Mixo-lydian, Lydian, Phrygian, Dorian, Hypo-lydian, Hypo-phrygian, and Hypo-dorian. These seven forms were known as *harmŏnĭæ* (*harmonia* meaning literally a "fitting" or " adjustment," hence the "tuning" of a series of notes, or the formation of a "scale "). They were afterwards known as *tŏnoi*, or *trŏpoi*, the Latin *mŏdi*, and our moods or "modes." But the term "modes" is ambiguous. According to some authorities (Westphal and his followers) the ancient " modes " differed from one another as the modern major mode differs from the minor, namely in the order in which the intervals follow one another, the difference in the "modes" thus depending on the place of the semi-tones in the octave. Others suppose that the terms Dorian, Phrygian, Lydian, and the rest, were applied to different scales of the same "mode" in the modern sense of the term. Thus, Mr. D. B. Monro in his *Modes of Ancient Greek Music*, 1894, maintains that, in the earlier periods of Greek music, (1) there is no distinction between "modes" (*harmoniæ*) and "keys" (*tonoi* or *tropoi*); and (2) that the musical scales denoted by these terms were primarily distinguished by difference of *pitch* (p. 101). To the passages quoted by Mr. Monro from Plutarch (*De Musica*, cc. 6, 8, 15–17, 19), in support of the identity of the Greek "modes" and "keys," may be added Plutarch, *de* E *apud Delphos*, c. 10, where the "keys" (*tonoi*) are regarded as synonymous with the "modes" (*harmoniæ*).]

As the basis of every melodic series of sounds the ancients had the *tetrachord*, a scale of four notes, to which according to tradition the earliest music was limited. The *heptachord* consisted of two tetrachords, as the central note was at once the highest of the first and the lowest of the second tetrachord. The heptachord was certainly in use before Terpander, who is said to have given to the lyre seven strings instead of four. [Strabo, p. 618. He really increased the compass of the scale from the two conjunct tetrachords of the seven-stringed lyre to a full octave, without increasing the number of the strings. This he did by adding one more string at the upper end of the scale, and taking away the next string but one. Aristotle, *Problems*, xix 32.]

Thus arose the *octachord* or octave, and at last, after various additions, the following scale of notes was formed:

and continued to be satisfied with a system of scales ("harmonies") sung by the sole guidance of the ear. Amongst the *Canonici* were philosophers such as PHĬLŎLÄUS ARCHȲTĀS, DĔMŎCRĬTUS, PLATO, and ARIS TOTLE. LASUS of Hermione, the master of Pindar, is mentioned as the first author of a theoretical work on music. The "harmonic" ARISTOXĔNUS (*q.v.*) of Tarentum,

From the lowest *b* onwards, this scale was divided into tetrachords in such a way that the fourth note was always also regarded as the first of the following tetrachord; [the intervals between the sounds of the tetrachord were, in ascending order, semi-tone, tone, tone]. This sequence was called the *diatonic* genus. Besides this there was also the *chromatic*, the tetrachords of which were as follows, *b c ♭d e*, *e f ♭g a* [the intervals in this case were semi-tone, semi-tone, tone and a half]. Thirdly there was the *enharmonic*, the tetrachord of which [had for its intervals $\frac{1}{4}$ tone, $\frac{1}{4}$ tone, 2 tones, and accordingly] cannot be expressed in modern notation. [*See* also p. 707.]

With regard to the *musical instruments* it may be mentioned that only stringed instruments (*cp.* especially CITHARA and LYRA) and the flute (*q.v.*), which closely resembled our clarionet, were employed in music proper; and that the other instruments, such as trumpets (*see* SALPINX), Pan's pipes (*see* SYRINX), cymbals (*cymbăla*), and kettledrums (*see* TYMPANUM), were not included within its province.

In proportion to the amount of attention paid to music by the Greeks, it early became the subject of learned research and literary treatment. The philosopher PȲTHĂGŎRĀS occupied himself with musical acoustics; he succeeded in representing numerically the relations of the octave, the fifth, and the fourth. For representing the symphonic relations the Pythagorean school invented the *monochord* or *canon*, a string stretched over a sounding board and with a movable bridge, by means of which the string could be divided into different lengths; it was on this account known as the school of the *Cănŏnĭci* as opposed to the *Harmŏnĭci*, who opposed this innovation

pupil of Aristotle, was held by the ancient to be the greatest authority on music; from his numerous works was drawn the greatest part of subsequent musical literature. Of other writers on music we may mention its well-known mathematician EUCLID, and the great astronomer CLAUDIUS PTŎLĔMÆUS who perfected musical acoustics.

Among the *Romans*, a native development of music was completely wanting. They had indeed, an ancient indigenous musical instrument, the short and slender Latian flute with four holes; but their national art of flute-playing was, at an early period, thrown into the background by the Etruscan, which was practised as a profession by foreigners freedmen, and people of the lowest classes of the Roman population. Among the nine old guilds, said to have been instituted by king Numa, there was one of flute-players (*tĭbīcĭnēs*), who assisted at public sacrifices With the Greek drama, Greek dramatic music was also introduced; it was, however, limited to flute-playing (*cp.* FLUTE). Stringed instruments were not originally known at Rome, and were not frequently employed till after the second Punic War Indeed, as Greek usages and manners in general gained ground with the beginning of the 2nd century, so also did Greek music Greek dances and musical entertainment became common at the meals of aristocratic families, and the younger members of respectable households received instruction in music as in dancing. Though it was afterwards one of the subjects of higher education, it was never considered a real and effective means of training. Enter tainments like our concerts became frequent towards the end of the Republic, and formed part of the musical contests instituted by Nero, a great lover of music, in A.D. 60, on the model of the Greek contests

Domitian had an *Odēum* built on the *Campus Martius* (Field of Mars) for the musical entertainments of the *Agōn Căpĭtōlīnus*, instituted by him in A.D. 86, and celebrated at intervals from the end of the classical period.—Passages bearing on music in Roman literature have no independent value, as they are entirely drawn from Greek sources.—For Roman *military music, see* LITUUS (2) *and* TUBA.

Mūta. *See* MANIA.

Myrmĭdŏnēs. A race in Southern Thessaly, said to have originally dwelt in the island of Ægīna and to have emigrated from it with Pēleus. They fought before Troy under their chieftain Achillēs. For legends about their origin, *see* ÆACUS.

Myrmillo. *See* GLADIATORES.

Mўrōn. One of the most celebrated Greek artists, of Eleuthĕræ in Attica, an older contemporary of Phīdĭās and Pŏlўclītus, and like them a pupil of Agĕlādās. His works, chiefly in bronze, were numerous and very varied in subject, gods, heroes, and especially athletes and representations of animals, which were admired by the ancients for their lifelike truth to nature. Most famous among these were his statue of the Argive runner *Ladas;* his *Discŏbŏlus* (or Quoit - thrower, *see* cut), which we are enabled to appreciate in several copies in marble, the best being that in the Palazzo Messimi in Rome; and his

MARBLE COPY OF MYRON'S DISCOBOLUS.
(Rome, Palazzo Messimi.)

Cow on the Market-place at Athens, which received the very highest praise among the ancients, was celebrated [in 36 extant epigrams, in the *Greek Anthology,* all quoted in Overbeck's *Schriftquellen,* §§ 550–588], and may be regarded as his masterpiece. He was also the first to represent what is really a *genre* portrait, in his *Drunken Old Woman* [Pliny, *N. H.* xxxvi 32; but this is now attributed to another artist, one Socrates. Overbeck, § 2092].

Myrrha. Mother of Adōnis by her own father Cĭnўras. (*Cp.* ADONIS.)

Myrtĕa. *See* VENUS.

Myrtĭlus. Son of Hermēs, charioteer of Œnŏmāüs, whose defeat by Pĕlops was due to his treachery. When he demanded the reward that had been settled, the half of the realm of Œnomaüs, Pelops threw him into the sea near Gĕræstus in Eubœa, and that part of the Ægean was thence called the Myrtoan Sea. (*Cf.* ŒNOMAUS and PELOPS.)

[**Mўs.** A famous toreutic artist who engraved the *Battle of the Centaurs* on the inside of the shield of the Athēnē Prŏmăchŏs of Phīdias. The work was executed after a design by Parrhăsius (Pausanias, i 28 § 2), a generation after Phidias. It was Parrhasius also who designed the *Capture of Troy* for a cup embossed by Mys (Athenæus, p. 782 B). He is also mentioned in Propertius, iii 7, 12; and Martial, viii 34, 51, xiv 25.] [J. E. S.]

Mystæ. The Greek term for those who had been initiated into the mysteries of the lesser Eleusinia. (*See* ELEUSINIA.)

Mysteries. The name given by the Greeks, and later also by the Romans, to various kinds of secret worships, which rested on the belief that, besides the general modes of honouring the gods, there was another, revealed only to the select few. Such religious services formed in almost all the Greek states an important part of the established worship, and were in the hands of an important body of priests appointed by the State. If any one divulged to the uninitiated the holy ceremonies and prayers, or sometimes even the names only, by which the gods were invoked, he was publicly punished for impiety. Some mysteries were exclusively managed by special priests and assistants to the exclusion of all laymen. To others a certain class of citizens was admitted; thus the Attic *Thesmŏphŏrĭă* could only be celebrated by women living in lawful wedlock with a citizen, and themselves of pure Athenian descent and of unblemished reputation. At other mysteries people of every kind and either sex were allowed to be present, if they had carried out certain preliminary conditions (especially purification), and had then been admitted and initiated.

The usages connected with the native mysteries were similar to the ceremonies of Greek divine service; in the course of time, however, many other elements were borrowed from foreign modes of worship. They consisted usually in the recital of certain legends about the fortunes of the deity celebrated, which differed from the ordinary myths in many respects (*e.g.* the names and genealogies), and were often accompanied by a dramatic representation, with which was connected the exhibition of certain holy things, including symbols and relics. In many cases the symbols were not hidden from the public eye, but their meaning was revealed to the initiated alone. Of native mysteries those considered most holy were the *Eleusinian* mysteries of Dēmētēr; we know more about the ceremonies in this case than in any other. (*See* ELEUSINIA.) Next to these came the Samothracian mysteries of the *Cābīri* (*q.v.*), which in course of time appear to have become very similar to the Eleusinian. In these two mysteries, as indeed in all, no deeper meaning was originally attached to the legends, usages, and symbols. But, as time went on, these initiations were supposed to have a peculiar power of preserving men amid the dangers of this life by purification and expiation, of giving him a temporary blessedness, and above all of conferring a sure prospect of a state of bliss after death. [Isocrates, *Paneg.* § 28.] This change is in great part due to the influence of a sect, the *Orphĭci* (*see* ORPHEUS). Following Oriental, Egyptian, and also Pythagorean doctrines, they taught that expiation and sanctification were necessary for this and for a future life, and that these must be effected by means of the initiations and purifications which they pretended Orpheus had revealed to them. Those who enjoyed these revelations

of Orpheus constituted a religious society which gradually extended to every Greek country. Their religious services were also called mysteries, not only because the initiated alone could take part in them, but because the representations and usages connected with them had a hidden mystic meaning. It was chiefly owing to their influence that foreign mysteries were introduced into Greece, and that thus the various systems were blended together. Among foreign mysteries must be mentioned the wild and fanatic orgies of *Dionÿsus* (or *Bacchus*), *Sābāzius*, and *Cÿbĕlē*.

The first of these gained a footing in Rome and Italy under the name of *Bacchānālia*, and in 186 B.C. had to be firmly suppressed by the government on account of the excesses connected with them [Livy xxxix 8–19]; while the last-mentioned were most widely spread even in early imperial times. (*See* RHEA.) The mysteries connected with the worship of *Isis* and of *Mithras* (*q.v.*) were also held in high esteem by Greeks and Romans down to a late period. The whole system of mysteries endured to the very end of the pagan times, for the deeper meaning of its symbolism offered a certain satisfaction even to the religious requirements of the educated, which they failed to find in the empty forms of the ordinary worship. (*Cp.* ORGIES.)

N

Nænia, properly spelt **Nēnia** (*q.v.*).

Nævius (*Gnæus*). A Roman epic and dramatic poet. Born apparently in Campania, about 270 B.C., he served in the Roman army during the first Punic War; and, settling after this at Rome, he brought his first play upon the stage in 235, *i.e.* soon after the first appearance of Līvius Andronīcus. Owing to the license and recklessness with which he incessantly attacked the Roman nobles, especially the Metelli, he was thrown into prison, and though liberated thence by the tribunes of the people, was afterwards banished from Rome. He died in exile at Utĭca about 200.

His poetical account of the first Punic War (*Bellum Pœnĭcum*), written in old age in the Saturnian metre, made him the creator of the Roman national epic. The work originally formed one continuous whole, but at a later time was divided into seven books by the scholar Octāvius Lampădĭo. The fragments preserved give the

impression of its having been little more than a chronicle in verse. Indeed, even in its plan, it bears a close resemblance to the prose chronicles of the Roman annalists: for here, as there, the real subject of the poem was preceded by an account of the early history of Rome, dating from the flight of Ænēas from Troy. Nævius also made an important departure in the province of dramatic poetry by creating a national drama. Besides imitations of Greek tragedies, of which seven alone are known by name and by extant fragments, it was he who first attempted to adapt the materials of his country's history to the dramatic form handed down by the Greeks. Thus, in the *Rōmŭlus* or *Lŭpus*, he treats of the youth of Romulus and Remus; and, in the play *Clastĭdium*, of a contemporary historical event. From the number of titles of his comedies still preserved (over thirty), and from the verdict of antiquity, we may infer that his forte lay in comedy: he appears to have been no mere translator of his Greek originals, but to have handled them with considerable freedom. It was in his comedies especially that he introduced his attacks on men and events of the day.

Naiads (Gr. *Naiădĕs*). The Nymphs of rivers and springs. (*See* NYMPHS.)

Namātiānus (*Claudius Rŭtilius*). A Roman poet, by birth a Gaul and a pagan, who was *præfectus urbi* under Honorius in A.D. 416. After the sack of Rome by Alaric, he returned to his native country, ravaged at that time by the Visigoths, and described his journey home in two books, *De Rĕdĭtu suo*, of which the beginning of the first and the end of the second have perished. The poem is pure and correct in language and metrical form, and is interesting on account of its pathetic description of the misfortunes of the time.

Names. (1) The *Greeks* had no names denoting family, nothing corresponding to our surnames. Hence the name of the new-born child was left to the free choice of the parents, like the Christian name with us; the child usually received it on the seventh or tenth day after birth, the occasion being a family festival. According to the most ancient custom, the son, especially the first-born, received the name of his grandfather, sometimes that of his father, or a name derived from it(Phōcŏs—Phōcīon) or similarly compounded (Thĕŏphrastŏs— Thĕŏdōrŏs). As a rule a Greek only had one name, to which was added that of his father, to prevent confusion, *e.g.* Thūcȳdĭdēs (*scil.* the son) of Olōrus. A great many names were compounded with the names of gods (*Hĕrakleitŏs, Hĕrŏdŏtŏs, Artĕmĭdōrŏs, Diŏgĕnēs*), or derived from them (*Dĕmētrĭŏs, Apollōnĭŏs*). Frequently names of good omen for the future of the child were chosen. Sometimes a new name was afterwards substituted for the original one; so Plato was originally called Aristŏclēs, and Thĕŏphrastus Tyrtămus. Slaves were usually called after their native country, or their physical or moral peculiarities.

(2) The *Romans*, in the republican times, had their names in the following order: *prænōmen* (=our "Christian name"), *nōmen* (name of race, gentile name), *cognōmen* (surname, denoting the family). The *gentile name*, which originally (always in patrician names) had for derivative suffix *-ius* (*e.g. Iūnius, Cornēlius, Tullius*), was common to all those connected with the *gens*, men, women, clients, and freedmen. The *prænomen* was given to sons on the

third day after birth, the *dies lustrĭcus*, and was officially confirmed when the *tŏga virīlis* was assumed and the name was inscribed on the roll of citizens. The original meaning of the *prænomen*, in which there was sometimes a reference to peculiar circumstances at birth (e.g. *Lūcius* = born by day, *Mănius* = born in the morning; *Quintus*, the fifth, *Dĕcĭmus*, the tenth), came to be disregarded in the course of time, when the name was given. As a rule, the eldest son received the *prænomen* of his father. Of these there was a comparatively limited number in the noble families; some were employed only by certain *gentes*, even by certain families, as for instance *Appius* exclusively by the *Claudii*, and *Tĭbĕrius* especially by the *Nĕrōnes* who belonged to this race; while others were actually prohibited in certain families, e.g. *Marcus* in that of the *Manlii*.[1] The *prænomen* was usually written in an abbreviated form: thus, A. stands for *Aulus*, C. for *Gaius*, Gn. for *Gnæus*, D. for *Dĕcĭmus*, L. for *Lūcius*, M'. for *Mānius*, M. for *Marcus*, P. for *Publius*, Q. for *Quintus*, Ser. for *Servius*, S. or Sex. for *Sextus*, Ti. for *Tĭbĕrius*, T. for *Tītus*.

The *surname* (*cognomen*), the use of which was, in early times, not customary among the plebeians, served to denote and distinguish the different families of the same race, which often included several, patrician and plebeian. Thus the *gens Cornēlia* comprised the patrician families of the *Scĭpĭōnes, Sullæ*, etc., and the plebeian families of the *Dŏlābellæ, Lentŭli*, etc. [It is true that some patrician families had fixed *cognōmĭna* (e.g. *Nero*), but it was quite common for plebeians to take *cognomina* or to have them given; *e.g.* Cn. Pompeius *Magnus*, C. Asinius *Pollio*, and his son Asinius *Gallus*. Some plebeians never took a *cognomen*, e.g. the Antonii. But the *Tullii* are *Cĭcĕrōnes* in the last century of the Republic. *Cognomina*, whether fixed or otherwise, are generally of the nature of nicknames, or, at any rate, add a description of some personal characteristic; e.g. *Năso, Străbo, Gallus, Scrōfa, Asĭnă, Rūfus*.]

To the surname there was sometimes added a second and even a third, in later times called the *agnomen*, to indicate a lateral branch of the family, for instance the *Scĭpiones Nāsĭcæ;* or, in memory of some remarkable exploit in war (e.g. *Scĭpĭo Afrĭcānus, Asiātĭcus*, etc.), or in consequence of a popular designation (e.g. *Scĭpĭo Nāsĭca Sĕrāpio*) or of an adoption. It was the ori-

_____
[1] B.C. 384, Livy vi 20.

ginal custom for the adopted son, on passing from one *gens* to another, to add to the *prænomen, nomen*, and *cognomen* of his adoptive father the name of his own former *gens* with the termination *-ānus*. Thus the full name of the destroyer of Carthage, the son of L. Æmilius Paulus adopted by one of the Scipios, was P(ublius) Cornelius Scipio Africanus Æmilianus. After about 70 A.D. there were many irregularities in the way these names were given, the tendency being to give very many.

Women originally had only one name, the feminine form of the gentile name of their father, *e.g.* Cornelia. In later times they sometimes had a *prænomen* also, which they received on marriage. It was the feminine form of the husband's *prænomen, e.g.* Gaia. Sometimes they had both names, *e.g.* Aula Cornelia. The *prænomen* went out of use for a time during the later Republic, and it was afterwards placed after the *nomen* like a *cognomen* (e.g. *Iunia Tertia*). Under the Empire, they regularly had two names, either the *nomen* and *cognomen* of the father (*e.g.* Cæcĭlia Metella) or the *nomina* of father and mother (*e.g. Vălĕria Attia*, daughter of *Attius* and *Valeria*).

Slaves were originally designated by the prænomen of their master, e.g. *Marcĭpor = Marci puer* (slave of Marcus). Later, when the number of slaves had been greatly multiplied, it became necessary to give them names chosen at random. Freedmen regularly took the *nomen*, afterwards the *prænomen* also, of the man who freed them (or of the father of the woman who freed them), while they retained their previous name as a *cognomen ;* thus the name of the well-known freedman of Cicero was M. Tullius Tiro, and of a freedman of Livia (the wife of Augustus), M. Livius Ismărus.

Nana. *See* ATTIS.

Năŏs. The Greek term for the inner portion of a temple. (*See* TEMPLE.)

Narcissus. The beautiful son of the river-god Cēphīsus. He rejected the love of the Nymph Echō (*q.v.*), and Aphrŏdītē punished him for this by inspiring him with a passion for the reflexion of himself which he saw in the water of a fountain. He pined away in the desire for it: to see one's reflexion in the water was hence considered as a presage of death. The flower of the same name, into which he was changed, was held to be a symbol of perishableness and death, and was sacred to Hādēs, the divinity of the world below. Persĕphŏnē had just gathered

a narcissus, when she was carried off by Hades.

* NARCISSUS.

(Mural painting from Pompeii. Naples Museum.)

Nauarchus (Gr. *nauarchŏs =* commander of a ship). The Spartan term for the commander of the fleet, chosen for one year · also a general term for the captain of a ship, regularly so used in the fleets of the Roman Empire.

Naucrārĭæ. Administrative districts at Athens dating from prehistoric times; they were 48 in number, 12 from each of the old *phylæ*. Each of them was obliged to furnish two horsemen and a ship towards the army and navy. The *naucrāri*, who were at their head, seem to have formed a college or corporate body, who occupied themselves especially with all military and financial affairs, while current business was managed by the *prytăneis*, whose office was the *Prytăneiŏn*. Clīsthĕnēs raised their number to 50, 5 from each of the 10 new *phylæ*, and probably restricted in functions to the services to the State, and especially the fleet. It is likely that they were given up after the fleet had been increased by Themistocles; their place was probably taken by the *trierarchies*. (*See* LEITOURGIA.)

Naumăchĭæ. A name given by the Romans to contests between ships, represented for the amusement of the people, and commemorating naval engagements famous in history. The first representation of this kind was given by Cæsar in B.C. 46 in a basin dug out for this purpose on the *Campus Martius*, on which occasion a Tyrian and an Egyptian fleet fought against each other, each with 2,000 rowers and 1,000 marines on board. In B.C. 2, Augustus, at the dedication of the temple of Mars Ultor, had a seafight between Athenians and Persians, represented with thirty ships. The greatest of all *naumachiæ* was that of Claudius in A.D. 52; it took place on the Fucine Lake, and 19,000 men in the dress of Rhodians and Sicilians fought in two fully armed men-of-war. For similar contests the *arēna* of the amphitheatre was sometimes filled with water. The crews of the ships consisted of gladiators, prisoners, and criminals who had been condemned to death.

Nauplĭus. (1) Son of Poseidōn and Amȳmōnē (*see* DANAUS), founder of Nauplia, and a famous navigator.

(2) A king of Eubœa, husband of Clȳmĕnē. (*See* CATREUS.) After the unjust execution of his son Pălămēdēs (*q.v.*) at the siege of Troy, the Greeks refused to give him the satisfaction he demanded. Thereupon he avenged his son's death by raising deceptive fire-signals, and stranding the returning Greeks among the breakers near the cliffs of Căphārēūs in Eubœa. He thus caused the shipwreck and destruction of a large number. He is said to have finally thrown himself into the sea.

Nausĭcăa. The discreet and beautiful daughter of the Phæacian king Alcĭnŏŭs and Ārētē. She met Odysseus when he was cast ashore on the island of Schĕrĭa, and conducted him to her father's palace (Homer, *Od.* vi).

Nautŏdĭci. Commercial judges: at Athens, a judicial board, having cognisance in disputes between traders and suits against foreigners who pretended to be citizens. The former class of cases they settled themselves; the latter they prepared and brought before the Heliastic court. In Demosthenes' time they had ceased to exist, and both kinds of suits came under the jurisdiction of the *Thesmŏthĕtæ*.

Năzărĭus. A Latin panegyric writer; the author of an eulogy on the emperor Constantine, delivered 321 A.D.

Nĕarchus. A Greek writer of Crete, resident afterwards at Amphĭpŏlis. He was a friend of Alexander the Great in his youth, and administered the satrapy of Lycia for five years after the battle of Granīcus (334 B.C.). He then took part in the Indian expedition (327 B.C.) and returned, as commander of the fleet, down the Indus and along the coast of Asia, to the mouth of the Tigris.

After Alexander's death he attached himself to Antĭgŏnus. He wrote an account of his voyage, which was rich in geographical discoveries. Of this we possess, besides fragments, an abstract in Arrian's *Indĭca.* The investigations of later times have in many respects confirmed the trustworthiness of his statements concerning ancient India.

Nectar. The drink of the Greek gods (*see* AMBROSIA), which Homer describes as a red wine [*Il.* xix 38] which Hebe pours out for the immortals [*ib.* iv 3].

Nĕcȳsĭa. Feast in honour of the dead. (*See* BURIAL.)

Nĕfasti Dĭēs. *See* FASTI.

Nēleus. Son of Pŏseidōn and Tȳrō the daughter of Salmōneus, brother of Pĕlĭas. The brothers are exposed after birth by their mother, who afterwards married Crētheus of Iolcus: they are found by a herdsman and brought up by him until they grow up and are acknowledged by their mother. After Cretheus' death they quarrel about the possession of Iolcus, and Nēleus, together with Mĕlampūs and Bĭas, the sons of his half-brother Amȳthāōn, retires into exile in Messēnia, where Aphăreus, Tyro's cousin, allows them to occupy Pȳlus. By Chlōris, daughter of Amphīōn, the king of the Minyan Orchŏmĕnus (it is only a later myth that identifies him with Amphion of Thebes) he is father of twelve sons, of whom Pĕrĭclȳmĕnus and Nestōr (*q.v.*) are the most celebrated, and one daughter, the beautiful Pērō, bride of Bias (*see* MELAMPUS). On his refusing to purify Hērăclēs from the murder of Iphĭtus, Heracles invades his country and slays all his sons except Nestor, who chances to be absent from home at the time. Nestor becomes the champion and avenger of the aged Neleus when the Epeans and their king Augeas, emboldened by his misfortune, venture on acts of injustice towards him. According to one account it was Neleus who renewed the Olympian games and died at Corinth, where, it was said, he was buried at the isthmus; according to others, he was slain along with his sons by Heracles.

Nĕmĕă (the Nemean Games). One of the four Greek national festivals, which was celebrated in the valley of Nĕmĕă in the territory of the Argive town Clĕōnæ. In historic times the festival was held in honour of Zeus, who had here a temple with a sacred grove. Originally it is said to have consisted of funeral games, instituted by the Seven during their expedition against Thebes, in memory of the boy Archĕmŏrus (see SEVEN AGAINST THEBES). Hēráclēs afterwards changed it into a festival in honour of Zeus. From about 575 onwards, athletic competitions were added to the festival, after the model of those at Olympia; and, like the latter, it was only gradually that it developed into a general Hellenic celebration. It was held twice in a period of four years, once in August, every fourth year, once in winter, every second or first Olympic year. [It is more probable, however, that the so called "Winter Nemea" were only local games held in Argos, and that the panhellenic Nemea were celebrated in alternate years at the end of every first and third Olympic year, at a time corresponding to our July. The question is discussed by Unger in the *Philologus* xxxiv 50, but Droysen, in *Hermes* xiv 1, considers it still unsettled.] The management of the festival was originally possessed by the Cleonæans, but soon passed, together with the possession of the sanctuary, into the hands of the Argives. The games consisted of gymnastic, equestrian, and musical contests (for the two former, cp. OLYMPIAN GAMES); the prize was a palm-branch and a garland of fresh *sĕlīnŏn* [often rendered "parsley," but more probably identical with the "wild celery"].

Nĕmĕan Lion, The. *See* HERACLES.

Nĕmĕsiānus (*Marcus Aurēlius Olympius*), of Carthage. A Roman poet famous in his own times, belonging to the end of the 3rd century A.D. He flourished under the emperor Carus and his sons (212–284). We possess from him the first 425 lines of a fairly elegant poem on the Chase (*Cȳnĕgĕtĭcă*), and four eclogues, in which he has closely followed Calpurnius (*q.v.*, 2).

Nĕmĕsĭs. A post-Homeric personification of the moral indignation felt at all derangements of the natural equilibrium of things, whether by extraordinarily good fortune or by the arrogance usually attendant thereon. According to Hesiod she is daughter of Night, and with Aidōs, the divinity of Modesty, left the earth on the advent of the iron age. As goddess of due proportion she hates every transgression of the bounds of moderation, and restores the proper and normal order of things. As, in doing this, she punishes wanton boastfulness, she is a divinity of chastisement and vengeance. She enjoyed special honour in the Attic district of Rhamnus (where she was deemed to be the daughter of Ōcĕănus), and is often called the Rhamnusian goddess; her statue there was said to have been executed by

Phĭdias out of a block of Parian marble which the Persians had brought with them in presumptuous confidence to Marathon, to erect a trophy of victory there. She was also called *Adrasteia*, that name, appropriate only to the Phrygian Rhea-Cȳbĕlē, being interpreted as a Greek word with the meaning, "She whom none can escape." She was also worshipped at Rome, especially by victorious generals, and was represented as a meditative, thoughtful maiden with the attributes of proportion and control (a measuring-rod, bridle and yoke), of punishment (a sword and scourge) and of swiftness (wings, wheel, and chariot drawn by griffins).

Nĕmŏrensis. Epithet of Diana (*q.v.*).

Nēnia (*not* nænia). A name given by the Romans to the funeral dirge in honour of the dead, sung to the accompaniment of flutes, at first by the relatives, in later times by hired mourners (*præfĭcæ*). There was also a goddess so called, the dirge personified, who had a chapel outside the *Porta Vīmĭnālis*.

Nĕŏcŏri ("wardens," properly *sweepers of the temple*). The Greek term for certain officials subordinate to the priests, on whom devolved the cleaning and keeping in repair of the temple to which they were attached. In important temples, especially in Asia, the office of a *neocorus* was considered a distinction by which even the greatest personages felt honoured. In the imperial period of Rome, whole cities, in which temples of the emperors existed, styled themselves their *neocori*. [Ephesus is described in Acts xix 35 as the *neocorus*, or "temple-keeper," of Artemis.]

Nĕŏdāmōdeis. *See* HELOTS.

Neoplatonism. A form of later Greek philosophy, founded upon Plato. (*See* PHILOSOPHY.)

Nĕŏptŏlēmus (also called Pyrrhus; *i.e.* the fair). Son of Achilles and Dēĭdămīa. He was brought up by his grandfather Lȳcŏmēdēs in Scȳrŏs. After Achilles' death, however, he was taken by Odysseus to Troy, since, according to the prophecy of Hĕlĕnus, that town could be taken only by a descendant of Æacus. Here, like his father, he distinguished himself above all by a courage which none could withstand. He slew Eurȳpȳlus, son of Tĕlĕphus, and was one of the heroes in the Wooden Horse, where he alone remained undaunted. Later legend depicted him as fierce and cruel: at the taking of Troy he killed the aged Priam at the altar of Zeus, hurled Hector's son.

Astȳănax, down from the walls, and offered up Pŏlyxĕna upon his father's tomb. In Homer he arrives safely with much booty at Phthīa, his father's home, and weds Mĕnĕlāus' daughter Hermĭŏnē, who was promised him during the siege of Troy [*Od.* iv 5]. Later legend represents him as accompanied by Andrŏmăchē, Hector's wife, who is allotted him as part of his booty, and Helenus, and then, on the strength of a prophecy of Helenus, as going to Epirus and settling there. It was to a son of his by Lanassa, granddaughter of Hĕrăclēs, that the later kings of Epīrus traced back their descent, and accordingly styled themselves *Æăcĭdæ;* while from his son by Andrŏmăchē, Mŏlossus, the district of Molossia was said to derive its name. He afterwards went to Phthīa, to reinstate his grandfather Pēleus in his kingdom (whence he had been expelled by Acastus), and wedded Hermione. He soon, however, met his death at Delphi, whither, according to one story, he had gone with dedicatory offerings, or, according to another, to plunder the temple of Apollo in revenge for his father's death. The accounts of his death vary, some attributing it to Orestes, the earlier lover of Hermione; others to the Delphians, at the instance of the Pythian priestess; others again to a quarrel about the meat-offerings.

The scene of his death was the altar, a coincidence which was regarded as a judgment for his murder of Priam. His tomb was within the precincts of the Delphic temple, and in later times he was worshipped as a hero with annual sacrifices by the Delphians, as he was said to have vouchsafed valuable assistance against the Gauls when they threatened the sacred spot [B.C. 279, Pausanias, x 23].

Nĕphĕlē. Wife of Athămās, mother of Phrixus and Hellē. (*See* ATHAMAS.)

Nĕpŏs. *See* CORNELIUS (1).

Neptūnus. The Italian god of the sea, husband of Sălācia (the goddess of salt water), identified by the Romans with the Greek Pŏseidōn. This identification dated from 399 B.C., when a *Lectisternium* was ordained in his honour by the Sibylline books. Like Poseidon, he was worshipped as god of the sea and of equestrian accomplishments. As such he had a temple in the Circus Flaminius, whilst in the Circus Maxĭmus the old Italian god Consus had

an altar in a similar capacity. In after times Agrippa built a temple and portico to Neptune on the Field of Mars in honour of his naval victory over Sextus Pompeius and Antonius. A festival of Neptune (*Neptūnālia*), accompanied by games, was celebrated on July 23rd. The old harbour god of the Romans was Portūnus (*q.v.*). *See* POSEIDON.

Nĕreïds (Gr. *Nērĕïdĕs*). The Nymphs of the sea, daughters of Nēreus (*q.v.*) and Dōris.

Nēreus. The eldest son of Pontus and Gæa, husband of Dōris, daughter of Ōcĕănus, father of 50 (according to a later account, 200) beautiful Sea-nymphs, the Nereids. He is described as a venerable old man, of a kindly disposition towards mortals, and as dwelling in a resplendent cave in the depths of the Ægean.

NEREID, BORNE ALONG BY A TRITON.
(Naples Museum.)

Like all gods of water, he has the gift of prophecy and of transforming himself into any shape he chooses to assume. He is represented as an old man with the leaves of seaweed for hair and a sceptre or trident. His daughters are likewise benevolent beings, well disposed to mortals. They live with their father in the depths, but rise to the surface in order to amuse themselves with every kind of pastime and to assist sailors in distress. They were especially worshipped on the islands, on the coasts, and at the mouths of rivers, and were depicted in works of art as charming maidens, sometimes lightly clothed, sometimes naked, often riding on dolphins and Tritons (*see* cut). The Nereids most often mentioned in mythology are Amphitrītē and Thĕtĭs, with Gălătēă.

Nessus. A Centaur, who used to ferry travellers over the river Evēnus. On attempting to outrage Dēĭănīra, the wife of Hērăclēs, he was shot by the latter with one of his poisoned arrows. Upon this he presented Deianira with a portion of his poisoned blood, professedly to enable her to regain her husband's affections, should he prove false to her. The robe smeared with the blood proved fatal to Heracles (*q.v.*). [*Cp.* Soph., *Trachiniæ*, 558, 1141.]

Nestōr. Son of Nēleus and Chlōris, ruler of the Messenian and Triphylian Pўlus, and later also, after the extinction of the royal family there, of Messēnia; wedded to Eurўdĭcē, by whom he had seven sons and two daughters. He was the only one of twelve sons of Neleus who escaped being slain by Hērăclēs, since he was, it is said, living at the time among the Gerenians in Messenia, from whom he derives the name *Gĕrēnĭŏs*, given him in Homer. After this disaster, the king of the Epēans, Augeās, illegally keeps back a four-horsed chariot, which Neleus has sent to Elis to compete in a contest. Neleus, as yet hardly a youth, retaliates by driving off the herds of the Epeans; upon which the latter with a large army besiege the Pylian fortress of Thўrŏessa on the Eurōtās. Neleus forms one of the relieving army, serving as a foot-soldier, owing to his father's having, from regard to his youth, had the war-horses concealed from him. He slays in battle Augeas' son-in-law, and, fighting from the dead man's chariot, wins a most brilliant victory, so that the Pylians offer thanks to him among men even as they offer them to Zeus among the gods. In like manner in the war against the Arcadians, when he was the youngest of all the combatants, he killed the gigantic and much dreaded hero Ereuthălĭŏn. He also took an important part in the battle between the Centaurs and the Lăpĭthæ. In old age, when he was ruling over the third generation of his people, he was involved in the expedition against Troy, owing, as the story went, to the obligation incurred by his son Antĭlŏchus as a suitor of Helen; with Odysseus he gains the help of Achilles and Patroclus for the undertaking, and himself sails, in the company of his sons Antilochus and Thrăsўmēdēs, with 90 ships to the seat of war at Ilium. Here, according to Homer, "Neleus the horseman," in spite of his great age, takes a prominent part among the heroes in council and battle alike: the qualities which adorn him are wisdom, justice, eloquence ("from his lips flows language sweeter than honey" [*Il.* i 248]), experience in war, unwearied activity, and courage. All value and love him, none more than Agamemnon, who wishes that he had ten such counsellors: in that case, he says, Troy would soon fall [*Il.* ii 372]. He is so great a favourite with Homer that in ancient times it was conjectured that the poet was himself a native of Pylos. After the destruction of Troy he returns in safety with his son Thrăsўmēdēs to Pylos, Antilochus (*q.v.*) having for the sake of his father, who was in sore peril, sacrificed his own life in battle against Memnōn. Ten years afterwards, Tēlĕmăchus still finds him at Pylos, amidst his children, in the enjoyment of a cheerful and prosperous old age. [On the "cup of Nestor," *see* TOREUTIC ART.]

Newspapers. *See* ACTA.

Nexum. In the old Roman legal system the solemn process on entering upon a relationship of debtor and creditor under the form of *mancĭpātio* (*q.v.*). In the formula used therein the borrower gave the lender, in case of non-fulfilment of the obligation incurred, the right to seize him without more ado as his bondsman. There was no limit in respect of time to the right of the creditor over a debtor whose person thus became forfeit to him: it consisted in the fact that the creditor could keep the *nexus* in prison and make him work as a slave for him. The latter, however, continued to be a citizen; but, as long as the debt existed, was considered dishonoured, and was accordingly excluded from service in the legion and voting in the assemblies of the people. After the Lex Pœtēlĭa Păpīria of 326 B.C. had, in the interest of the plebeians, for the most part abolished personal security, the *nexum* gradually passed into a mere contract of loan.

[In Prof. Nettleship's *Lectures and Essays*, pp. 363–6, there is a note showing that the proper meaning of *nexum* is "a thing pledged (bound)," and of *nexus -i*, "a prisoner"; that the evidence for making *nexum* mean "a solemn process" is very weak; and that *nexus -ūs* is the proper word for the contract or bond between debtor and creditor. In almost all the passages where *nexum -i* is supposed to mean "a process," it might as well come from *nexus -ūs*. Cicero, however, in *Pro Cæcina* 102, has *nexa atque hereditates;* and in *De Rep.* ii 59, *propter unius libidinem omnia nexa civium liberata nectierque postea desitum.*]

Nicander (Gr. *Nĭcandrŏs*). A Greek poet born at Cŏlŏphŏn in Asia, about 150 B.C. He was an hereditary priest of Apollo, as well as a physician, and lived a great deal in Ætolia as well as later in Pergămŏn. He wrote numerous works, such as those on agriculture, of which considerable fragments are still preserved, and on mythological *mĕtămŏrphōsēs* (used by Ovid), etc. Two of his poems, written in a dull and bombastic manner, are still extant: the *Thērĭăca*, on remedies against the wounds inflicted by venomous animals; and the *Alĕxĭpharmăca*, on poisons taken in food and drink, with their antidotes.

Nicē (Gr. *Nīkē*). The Greek goddess of victory, according to Hesiod, daughter of Pallas and Styx, by whom she was brought to Zeus to assist him in his struggle with the Titans: thenceforward she remains always with Zeus on Olympus. Sculptors often represent her in connexion with divinities who grant victory: thus the Olympian Zeus and the Athēnē on the Acrŏpŏlĭs at Athens held in one hand a statue of *Nĭcē*. (*See* ZEUS, fig. 2; and, for another *Nĭcē*, cp. PÆO-NIUS.) She was generally represented as winged and with a wreath and a palm-branch. As herald of victory she also has the wand of Hermēs. This mode of representing her was adopted for the statues of the goddess specially revered by the

* WINGED VICTORY IN BRONZE.
(Cassel Museum.)

Romans under the name *Victōria*. *Vīca Pŏta* ("Victorious Issue") was an earlier designation of the same goddess. Such statues were erected chiefly on the Capitol by triumphant generals. The most famous was the statue [brought from Tarentum and therefore probably the work of a Greek artist] which Augustus dedicated to her in the *Cūria Iūlia*, in memory of his victory at Actium. When the *Curia Iulia* had been destroyed by fire in the reign of Titus and rebuilt by Domitian, the statue was placed in the new building, and was adored as the guardian goddess of the senate until Christianity became the religion of the empire.

Nĭcĭās. An Athenian painter [a son of Nĭcŏmēdēs, and a pupil of Euphrānor's pupil Antĭdŏtus]. He lived during the latter half of the 4th century B.C. as a younger contemporary of Praxĭtĕlēs. [The latter, when asked which of his works in marble he specially approved, was in the habit of answering, *those that had been touched by the hand of Nicias;* such importance did he attribute to that artist's method of tinting, or " touching up with colour," *circumlĭtĭo* (Pliny, *N. H.* xxxv 133). He painted mainly in encaustic; and] was especially distinguished by his skill in making the figures on his pictures appear to stand out of the work, by means of a proper treatment of light and shade. He was celebrated for his painting of female figures and other subjects which were favourable to the full expression of dramatic emotions, such as the Rescue of Andrŏmĕdă and the Interrogation of the Dead by Odysseus in the lower world. This latter picture he presented to the city of his birth, after Ptolemy the First had offered sixty talents (about £12,000) for it. [Pliny, *N. H.* xxxv §§ 130-133. He insisted on the importance of an artist's choosing noble themes, such as cavalry engagements and battles at sea, instead of frittering away his skill on birds and flowers (Demetrius, *De Elocutione,* 76.)]

Nicŏlāus. A Greek historian of Damascus. At the suggestion of the Jewish king Herod the Great, whose devoted friend he was, and who had recommended him to Augustus, he wrote a comprehensive history of the world down to his own times in 144 books, which is partly preserved in important fragments exhibiting an agreeable style. His panegyrical biography of Augustus has come down to us almost entire.

Nĭcŏmăchus. (1) A Greek painter, probably of Thebes, about 360 B.C. He was celebrated as an artist who could paint with equal rapidity and excellence, and was regarded as rivalling the best painters of his day. A famous painting of his was the Rape of Proserpine. [Pliny, *N. H.* xxxv 108.]

(2) Of Gĕrăsa in Arabia, a follower of the Pythagorean philosophy, about 150 A.D. He composed an introduction to Mathematics

in two books and a handbook on Harmony, of which only the first book is preserved entire, the second consisting of two fragments which cannot be said with certainty to come from Nicomachus. The first-mentioned work gives valuable information as regards the arithmetic of the Greeks in earlier times. It was translated into Latin by Boëthius.

Nigidius Figulus (*Publius*). A friend and contemporary of Cicero, next to Varro the most learned Roman of his day, born about 98 B.C. He was an adherent of Pompey, and after his defeat went into exile, where he died in 45. He had a propensity to mysticism, which led him to the Pythagorean philosophy, astrology and magic, which he actually practised. His writings On theology, natural history, and grammar were in some cases very voluminous, but owing to their obscurity and subtlety, in spite of their erudition, they met with far less notice than those of Varro.

Niobe. Daughter of Tantalus and Dïone, sister of Pelops and wife of Amphïon of Thebes. Like her father, she stood in close connexion with the gods, especially with Leto, the wife of Zeus, and fell into misfortune by her own arrogance. In maternal pride for her numerous progeny of six sons and six daughters, the ill-fated woman ventured to compare herself to Leto, who had only two children. To punish this presumption Apollo and Artemis slew with their arrows all Niobe's children, in their parents' palace. For nine days they lay in their blood without any to bury them, for Zeus had changed all the people into stone. On the tenth day the gods buried them. Niobe, who was changed to stone on the lonely hills of Sïpylus, cannot even in this form forget her sorrow. Thus runs Homer's account [*Il.* xxiv 614], in which we have the earliest reference to "a colossal relief roughly carved on the rocks" of Mount Sïpylus in Lydia, the face of which is washed by a stream in such a manner that it appears to be weeping [*cp.* Jebb on Soph., *Ant.* 831]. The accounts of later writers vary greatly in respect of the number of the daughters of Niobe and of the scene of her death. Sometimes the spot where the disaster occurs is Lydia, sometimes Thebes, where moreover the grave of Niobe's children was pointed out: the sons perish in the chase or on the race-course, while the daughters die in the royal palace at Thebes or at the burial of their brethren. This story describes Niobe as returning from Thebes to her home on Sipylus,

and as there changed into a stone by Zeus, at her own entreaty. The fate of Niobe was often in ancient times the theme both of poetry and of art. The group of the children of Niobe discovered at Rome in 1583 and now at Florence (part of which is shown in the cut) is well-known: it is probably the Roman copy of a Greek work which stood in Pliny's time in a temple of Apollo at Rome, and with regard to which it was a moot point with the ancients whether it was from the hand of Scopas or of Praxitèlès [Pliny, *N. H.* xxxvi 28. *Cp.* Stark, *Niobe und die Niobiden*, 1863].

NIOBE.
(Florence, Uffizi.)

Nisus, son of Pandïon, brother of Ægeus of Athens, king of Megara, and reputed builder of the seaport Nisæa. When Mïnos, in the course of his expedition of reprisal against Ægeus, besieged Megara, Scylla, Nisus' daughter, from love for the Cretan king, brought about her father's death by pulling out a golden or (according to another account) a purple hair on the top of his head, on which his life and the fate of the realm depended.

Minos, however, did not reward her treachery; he fastened her to the stern of his ship, and thus drowned her in the Saronic Gulf, or, according to others, left her behind him; whereupon she cast herself into the sea, and was changed either into a fish or into a bird called Ciris.

Nobility (*Nobïlïtas*). The aristocracy of office, which at Rome took the place of the patrician aristocracy of birth, after the admission of the plebeians to all the offices of state and the levelling of the distinction between patricians and plebeians consequent thereon. It comprised those patrician and plebeian families whose members had held one of the curule magistracies. These families, for the most part the most illustrious and wealthy, had the influence and money, which afforded them the necessary means to canvass for and hold an office. Thus, in spite of the theoretical equality of rights now existing, they almost completely excluded from the higher magistracies all citizens who had neither wealth nor noble relatives to support them. It was quite exceptional for a man who did not belong to the nobility to be fortunate enough to attain to them. If he did so, he was styled a *hŏmo nŏvus* (a new man, an upstart). It was one of the privileges of the nobility that they enjoyed the right to possess images of their ancestors. (*See* IMAGINES.)

Nŏmen. *See* NAME.

Nŏmenclātor. The Roman term for a slave who had the duty of reporting to his master the names of his slaves (often very numerous), of those who waited on him in the morning, of other visitors, and of those who met him when he was walking abroad. The latter duty was especially important if his master was a candidate for office, and, in order to gain votes, was anxious to canvass many of the electors in the public streets. [The word is properly written *nomencŭlātor*, as is proved by the evidence of glosses and MSS. *Cp.* Martial, x 30, 30; Suetonius, *Aug.* 19, *Calig.* 41, *Claud.* 34.]

Nŏmŏphȳlăcĕs (Guardians of the Laws). A board found in different states of Greece, which had to see to the observance of the requirements of the law, especially in the deliberative assemblies. At Athens, after the abolition of the Areopăgus as a board of supervision (about 461 B.C.) a college of seven *nomophylaces* was introduced as a check upon the senate, the public assembly, and the magistrates.

Nŏmŏs (*Greek*). (1) Originally, an ancient kind of *solo* in epic form in praise of some divinity. It was either " aulŏdic " or "cĭthărŏdic"; that is, it was sung to the accompaniment of the flute or the cĭthăra. The citharodic *nomos* was from ancient times used at the festivals of Apollo, whom the Dorians especially worshipped. It received its artistic form from Terpander (about 675 B.C.) principally by a systematic distribution into five or seven parts, of which three were the essential portions, the middle one forming the cardinal point of the whole. It formed an important element in the Delphian festival of the Pythian Apollo. On the other hand, the aulodic *nomos*, which Clŏnäs of Tĕgĕa had introduced in imitation of the *nomos* of Terpander, was early excluded from this festival. By the side of the ancient *nomoi*, in which the words were sung to an instrumental accompaniment, there arose another variety formed on the same model. In this the song was

dramatically recited to the tune of the flute or cithara, according as the nomos was "aulodic " or "citharodic." Of the former kind was the *nomos* introduced by the flute-player Săcădās of Argos (about 580) at the Pythian games, and hence called the *Pythian nomos*, a musical representation of the destruction of the dragon Pȳthō by Apollo. At a later period the province of the *nomos* was more and more extended and secularized, until it became the most important part of the musician's profession. [Plutarch, *De Musica*, cap. iii–x, pp. 1132–4.]

(2) " Law." *See* ECCLESIA

Nŏmŏthĕtæ. At Athens a commission for the examination of proposed laws. (*See* ECCLESIA, 1.)

Nōnæ. The Roman name for the 5th or 7th day of the month (*see* CALENDAR, 2).

Nōnius Marcellus. A Latin scholar, born at Thubursĭcum in Africa, who composed in the beginning of the 4th century A.D. a manual of miscellaneous information on points of lexicography, grammar, and antiquities, bearing the title of *De Compendĭōsā Doctrīnā*. It consisted originally of twenty books, one of which is lost. It is evidently founded on the works of earlier scholars, and in some parts exhibits verbal coincidences with Aulus Gellius. Though not showing the least genius or critical acumen, the work is of great importance owing to its numerous quotations from lost authors, especially of the archaic period. [*See* Prof. Nettleship's *Lectures and Essays*, pp. 277–331.]

Nonnus. A Greek poet of Pănŏpŏlis in Egypt, belonging to the 5th century A.D. As a pagan, he wrote with poetic talent, and in a spirited though highly rhetorical style, a vast epic, called the *Dĭŏnȳsĭăcă*, in forty-eight books, one of the chief sources for our knowledge of the Dionysiac cycle of legends. As a Christian, he composed a paraphrase of the Gospel of St. John in Greek hexameters.

Nŏtĭtĭa Dignĭtātum. A list of the officers of the court, and the civil and military magistrates. This official manual belongs to the end of the 4th century B.C., which is of great value for the statistics of the Roman empire at that time. It contains also the *insignia* of each magistrate represented in drawings.

Nŏvius. A writer of *Atellānæ* (*q.v.*) flourishing about 90 B.C. Like his contemporary and rival Pompŏnius, he was a master of ready speech of a coarse and droll description. Some of his witty verses are quoted by Cicero [*de Or.* ii 255, 279, 285]. Over forty titles of his works are mentioned, among them, as in the case of Pomponius, some which suggest travesties of mythological subjects; e.g., *Hercules as Auctioneer*.

Nummŭlārĭi. *See* MONEYCHANGERS.

Nummus (*coin*). A special name for the commonest coin at Rome, which generally served as the unit of reckoning, the *sestertius* (*q.v., under* COINAGE).

Nundĭnæ. The Roman term for the market day held on the last day of the week of eight days, on which countrymen rested from labour and came to Rome to buy and sell, as well as to do other business. Accordingly the Nundinæ were used for public announcements, especially concerning public assemblies and the business to be conducted in them. The actual holding of the assemblies on these days was avoided, so as not to prevent the people from attending to the business of the market. Originally too no legal business was conducted on them, and it was not till the beginning of the 3rd century B.C. that it was introduced. The Nundinæ, though not a regular feast-day, were nevertheless celebrated in private life by inviting strangers to one's table and exempting children from going to school.

Nycteus. Son of Pŏseidŏn and the Pleiad Cœlænŏ, brother of Lўcus (*q.v.*, 1) and father of Antĭŏpē (*q.v.*). After the early death of Cadmus' son Pŏlўdŏrus he administered the government of Thebes for Labdăcus, who was a minor, until he met his death in battle with Epōpeus, his daughter's husband.

Nymphs (properly "the young maidens"). Inferior divinities of Nature who dwell in groves, forests and caves, beside springs, streams and rivers; in some cases too on lonely islands, like Călypsō and Circē. The nymphs of the hills, the forests, the meadows and the springs (called in Homer daughters of Zeus, while Hesiod makes the nymphs of the hills and the forests together with the hills and the forests children of earth) appear as the benevolent spirits of these spots, and lead a life of liberty, sometimes weaving in grottoes, sometimes dancing and singing, sometimes hunting with Artĕmis or revelling with

Dionȳsus. Besides these divinities it is especially Apollo, Hermēs and Pan who are devoted to them and seek after their love; while the wanton satyrs are also continually lying in wait for them. They are well disposed towards mortals and ready to help them : they even wed with them. According to the various provinces of nature were distinguished various kinds of nymphs : nymphs of rivers and springs, the *Naiads*, to whom the Oceanids and Nereids are closely related; nymphs of the hills, *Orĕads*; nymphs of the forests and trees, *Drȳads* or *Hămadrȳads*; besides this they often received special names after certain places, hills, springs and grottoes. The Naiads, as the goddesses of the nourishing and fructifying water, were especially rich in favours, giving increase and fruitfulness to plants, herds and mortals. Hence they were also considered as the guardian goddesses of marriage, and the besprinkling of the bride with spring-water was one of the indispensable rites of the marriage ceremony. On the same principle, legendary lore represents them as nursing and bringing up the children of the gods, as for instance Zeus and Dionȳsus. Further, owing to the healing and inspiring power of many springs, they belong to the divinities of healing and prophesying, and can even drive men into a transport of prophetic and poetic inspiration. The Muses themselves are in their origin fountain-nymphs. Popular belief assigned to the nymphs in general an exceedingly long life, without actual immortality. The existence of Dryads, it was supposed, was closely bound up with the origin and decay of the tree in which they dwelt. They enjoyed divine honours from the earliest times, originally in the spots where they had power, at fountains, and in groves and grottoes. In later times shrines of their own, hence called *Nymphœa*, were built to them, even in cities. These eventually became very magnificent buildings, in which it was customary to celebrate marriages. Goats, lambs, milk, and oil were offered to them. Works of art represented them in the form of charming maidens, lightly clothed or naked, with flowers and garlands; the Naiads drawing water or carrying it in an urn.

O

Ōbē. The Spartan term for each of the 30 sub-divisions of the *phȳlæ* (*q.v.*).

Ŏbŏlus. A weight as well as a silver coin

among the Greeks = ⅙ drachma; the Attic obolus amounted in intrinsic value to 1·3*d* (*Cp.* COINAGE.) The ancients used to put this coin in the mouths of the dead, as passage-money for Charon the ferryman in the lower world.

Obsĕquens. A Latin author. (*See* LIVY, 2.)

Occŭpātĭŏ. The Roman term for the appropriation of untilled portions of the State lands, consequent upon the invitation of the State, and having for its object the cultivation of the soil. (*See further* AGER PUBLICUS.)

Ŏcĕănus. In Greek mythology, originally the ancient river of the world which flows around and bounds the earth and sea, it-self unbounded and flowing back into itself. From Oceanus arise all seas, rivers, streams, and fountains. Hērŏdŏtus is the first to oppose this view [ii 23, iv 8, 36]. To Homer, Oceanus is the beginning of all things, even of the gods : he, the original father, and his wife, *Tĕthȳs*, the original mother. With her he lives, a gentle and hospitable old man, in the farthest west away from the world and its doings. He keeps aloof even from the assemblies of the gods, although river gods and nymphs appear there. It is with the aged pair that Hēra grows up, and it is to them that she flees on the outbreak of the war with the Titans. According to Hesiod [*Theog.* 133, 337-370], Oceanus and Tēthȳs are children of Urănus and Gæa; the former the oldest of the Titans, who after the fall of Crŏnus submitted to Zeus. From him are sprung 3000 sons and as many daughters, the *Ŏcĕănĭdĕs.* The oldest of the family, which is spread over the whole earth, are Ăchĕlōüs and Styx. Oceanus was represented as a venerable old man with a long beard : on his head are bull's horns, after the usual manner of river gods; or crab's claws, as customary with gods of the sea; and he is surrounded by sea monsters.

Ŏcellus. A Greek philosopher, a follower of the Pythagorean school (*cp.* PYTHAGORAS).

Ochlocracy (mob-rule). The name among the Greeks for that form of democracy in which the citizens were admitted to the government of the State without any grada-tion of classes, or any legal provision for checking the caprice of the populace. Under such a constitution public matters fell into the hands of the lowest class of the people.

Octăĕtĕrĕs (Gr. *Okt-*). A period of eight years. (*See* CALENDAR.)

Ŏdeiŏn (Lat. *Ŏdēum*). The Greek term for a building constructed for musical per-formances on the plan of a theatre, but with far slighter proportions and provided with a roof for acoustical purposes. Hence

also the stage was not so deep, and ended in three walls which abutted with one another at obtuse angles. [The oldest Odeion in Athens was that in the ·neighbourhood of the fountain of Ennĕăcrūnus (Pausan., i 4, 1), on the Ilissus, south of the Olympĭēum. This Odeion was probably built in the time of the Pīsistrătĭdæ.]

The building which served as a pattern for all later ones of this kind was the Odeion built by Pĕrĭclēs about 445 B.C., intended at first for the musical contests at the Panathenaic games, but afterwards used by poets and musicians for rehearsals, by philosophers for discussions, and some-times even for judicial business. This building was restored after its destruction by fire (87 B.C.) by king Ariobarzănēs II, Phĭlŏpātŏr. The first at Rome was built by Domitian (about 86 A.D.); a second by Trajan. That of Hērŏdēs Attĭcus (*q.v.*) was considered the largest and most mag-nificent in ancient times : it was built soon after 160 A.D. at Athens, below the south-western cliff of the Acropolis, in honour of his deceased wife Annia Rēgilla, and ᴀ considerable part of it is still standing. It held about 8000 persons and had a roof composed of beams of cedar wood.

Ŏdysseus (the Latin equivalent is *Ulixēs ;* erroneously written *Ulysses*). King of Ĭthăcă, son of Laërtēs and Anticlēa, daughter of Autŏlȳcus. In post-Homeric legend he is called a son of Sīsȳphus, borne by Anticlea before her marriage with Laērtes. According to Homer, his name, "*the hater*," was given him by his grandfather Autolycus, because he himself had so often cherished feelings of hatred during his life [*Od.* xix 402]. His wife Pēnĕlŏpē (or Pēnĕlŏpeia), daughter of Icărius (*see* ŒBALUS), is said by later legends to have been obtained for him by her uncle Tyndărĕŏs in gratitude for counsel given by him. (*See* TYNDAREOS.) When his son Tĕlēmăchus was still an infant, Agămemnŏn and Mĕnĕläus, as Homer tells us, prevailed on him to take part in the ex-pedition against Troy. Their task was hard, as it had been predicted to him that it would be twenty years before he saw his wife and child again. Later writers relate that he was bound as one of Helen's suitors to take part in the scheme, but tried to escape his obligation by feigning madness, and among other acts yoked a horse and an ox to his plough and so ploughed a field. When however Pălămēdēs, who with Nestŏr and Menelaus was desirous of taking him to Troy, proceeded to place Telemachus in the

furrow, he betrayed himself and had to
accompany them to war. He led the men
of Ithaca and the surrounding isles to Troy
in twelve vessels. In contrast to the later
legend, which represents him as a cowardly,
deceitful and intriguing personage, he
always appears in Homer among the noblest
and most respected of the heroes, and, on
account of his good qualities, he is the declared favourite of Athēnē. He combines in
his person courage and determined pérsever-
ance with prudence, ingenuity, cunning and
eloquence. Accordingly he is employed by
preference as a negotiator and a spy. Thus,
after the disembarkation, he goes with
Menelaus into the enemy's city to demand
the surrender of Helen. Again, he is among
those who are despatched by the Greeks
to reconcile with Agamemnon the enraged
Achilles. With Dĭŏmēdēs, who delights
in his company, he captures the spy
Dŏlōn and surprises Rhēsus; with the same
hero he is said by later legend to have
stolen the Pallādium from Troy. When
Agamemnon faint-heartedly thinks of flight,
he opposes this idea with the utmost decision.
Everywhere he avails himself of the right
time and the right place, and, where courage
and cunning are needed, is ever the foremost.
After Achilles' death, in the contest with
Ajax, the son of Tĕlămōn, he receives the
hero's arms as a recognition of his services,
and by his ingenuity brings about the fall
of Troy. Shortly before it, he steals into
the city in the garb of a beggar, in order to
reconnoitre everything there; he then climbs
with the others into the wooden horse, and
contrives to control the impatient and the
timid alike until the decisive moment.

His adventures during the return from
Troy and on his arrival in his native
country form the contents of the *Odyssey*
of Homer. Immediately after the departure
Odysseus is driven to the Thracian Ismărus,
the city of the Cĭcŏnĕs, and, though he
plunders them, loses in a surprise seventy-
two of his companions. When he is now
desirous of rounding the south-east point of
the Peloponnesus, the promontory of Mălĕa,
he is caught by the storm and carried in nine
days to the coast of North Africa, on to the
land of the *Lŏtŏphăgi* (Lotus-eaters) whence
he has to drag his companions by force to
prevent their forgetting their homes for
love of the sweet lotus food. Thence the
voyage passes into the legendary world of
the Western sea, then little known to the
Greeks. Odysseus comes first to the
country of the *Cÿclŏpĕs* (*q.v.*), where, with

twelve of his comrades, he is shut up in
a cavern by Pŏlÿphēmus. The monster
has already devoured half of Odysseus'
companions before the latter intoxicates him
(fig. 1), deprives him of his one eye, and by his
cunning escapes with his comrades. From
this time the anger of Pŏseidōn, on whom
Polyphemus calls for revenge, pursues him
and keeps him far from his country. On the
island of *Æŏlus*, the Keeper of the Winds
(*q.v.*), he finds hospitable entertainment,
and receives on his departure a leathern
bag in which are inclosed all the winds
except the western. The latter would carry
him in nine days to the coast of Ithaca, but,
whilst Odysseus is taking rest, his comrades
open the bag, which they imagine to contain

(1) * ODYSSEUS OFFERING WINE TO THE CYCLOPS.
(Statuette in Vatican Museum, Rome.)

treasure, and the winds thus released carry
them back to Æolus. He orders them off
from his island, regarding them as enemies
of the gods. On coming to Tēlĕpÿlus, the
city of Lămus, king Antĭphătēs and his
Læstrÿgŏnĕs, cannibals of immense stature,
shatter eleven of their vessels, and the
twelfth is saved only by Odysseus' wari-
ness. (*See* PAINTING, fig. 5.) On the island
of Ææa the sorceress *Circē* turns part of
his crew into swine, but, with the help of
Hermēs, he compels her to restore them to
their human shape and spends a whole
year with her in pleasure and enjoyment.
When his companions urge him to return
home, Circe bids him first sail toward the
farthest west, to the entrance into the

lower world on the farther bank of Ocĕănus, and there question the shade of the seer Tīrĕsĭās concerning his return. (*See* HADES, REALM OF.) From the latter he learns that it is the malice of Poseidon that prevents his return, but that nevertheless he will now attain his object if his comrades spare the cattle of Hēlĭŏs on the island of Thrīnă̆cĭa; otherwise it will only be after a long time, deprived of all his comrades and on a foreign ship, that he will reach his home. Odysseus then returns to the isle of Circe and sets out on his homeward voyage, supplied by her with valuable directions and a favouring wind. Passing the isles of the *Sirens* (*q.v.*) and sailing through *Scylla and Chărybdis* (*q.v.*), he reaches the island of Thrīnă̆cĭa, where he is compelled to land by his comrades. They are there detained for a month by contrary winds; at length his comrades, overcome by hunger, in spite of the oath they have sworn to him, slaughter, during his absence, the finest of the cattle of Helios. Scarcely are they once more at sea, when a terrible storm breaks forth, and Zeus splits the ship in twain with a flash of lightning, as a penalty for the offence. All perish except Odysseus, who clings to the mast and keel, and is carried back by the waves to Scylla and Charybdis, and after nine days reaches the island of Ōgȳgĭa, the abode of the nymph *Că̆lypso*, daughter of Atlas. For seven years he dwells here with the nymph, who promises him immortality and eternal youth, if he will consent to remain with her and be her husband. But the yearning for his wife and home make him proof against her snares. All the day long he sits on the shore gazing through his tears across the broad sea ; fain would he catch a glimpse, were it only of the rising smoke of his home, and thereafter die. So his protectress, Athēnē, during Poseidon's absence, prevails on Zeus in an assembly of the gods to decree his return, and to send Hermēs to order Calypso to release him. Borne on a raft of his own building, he comes in eighteen days near to Schĕrĭa, the island of the Phæăcians, when Poseidon catches sight of him and shatters his raft in pieces. However, with the aid of the veil of Ino Leucŏthĕa (*q.v.*), he reaches land in safety and meets with Nausĭcăa, the king's daughter, who conducts him into the Phæacian city before her parents Alcĭnŏus (*q.v.*) and Arētē. He receives the most hospitable treatment, and is then brought loaded with presents by the Phæacians on

board one of their marvellous vessels to his country, which he reaches after twenty years' absence, while asleep. He arrives just in time to ward off the disaster that is threatening his house. After his mother Anticlēa had died of grief for her son, and the old Lāertēs had retired to his country estate in mourning, more than a hundred noble youths of Ithaca and the surrounding isles had appeared as suitors for the hand of the fair and chaste Pēnĕlŏpē, had persecuted Telemachus, who was now growing up to manhood, and were wasting the substance of the absent Odysseus. Penelope had demanded a respite from making her decision until she had finished weaving a shroud intended for her father-in-law, and every night

(2) * PENELOPE.
(*Ant. Denkm.* I 3, p. 17.)

unravelled the work of the day. In the fourth year one of her attendants betrayed the secret; she had to complete the garment, and when urged to make her decision promised to choose the man who should win in a shooting match with Odysseus' bow, hoping that none of the wooers would be able even so much as to bend it. Just before the day of trial, Odysseus lands on the island disguised by Athene as a beggar. He betakes himself to the honest swineherd *Eumœus*, one of the few retainers who have remained true to him, who receives his master, whom he fails to recognise, in a hospitable manner. To the same spot Athene brings Telemachus, who has returned in safety, in spite of the plots of the suitors. from a journey to

Nestor at Pylus and Menelaus and Helen in Sparta. Hereupon Odysseus makes himself known and, together with his son and retainer, concerts his plan of revenge. In the shape of a beggar he betakes himself to the house, where he manfully controls his anger at the arrogance of the suitors which is displayed towards himself, and his emotion on meeting Penelope. Next day the shooting match takes place. This involves shooting through the handles of twelve axes with the bow of Eurўtus (*q.v.*), which the latter's son Iphĭtus had once presented to the young Odysseus. None of the suitors can bend the bow, and so Odysseus takes hold of it, and bends it in an instant, thus achieving the master-shot. Supported by Telemachus, Eumæus, and the herdsman Phĭlœtius, and with the aiding presence of Athene, he shoots first the insolent Antĭnŏus, and then the other suitors. He next makes himself known to Penelope, who has meanwhile fallen into a deep sleep, and visits his old father. In the meantime the relatives of the murdered suitors have taken up arms, but Athene, in the form of Mentōr (*q.v.*) brings about a reconciliation. The only hint of Odysseus' end in Homer is in the prophecy of Tiresias, that in a calm old age a peaceful death will come upon him from the sea.

In later poetry Tēlĕgŏnus, the son of Odysseus by Circe, is sent forth by his mother to seek out his father. He lands at Ithaca, and plunders the island: Odysseus proceeds to meet him, is wounded by him with a poisonous sting-ray, given by Circe to her son as a spear-point, and dies a painful death, which thus comes " from the sea." On Telegonus discovering that he has killed his father, he carries the dead body home with him, together with Penelope and Telemachus, and there the latter live a life of immortality, Telemachus becoming husband of Circe, and Telegonus of Penelope. Besides Telegonus, the legend told of two sons of Odysseus by Circe, named Agrius and Lătīnus, who were said to have reigned over the Etruscans. Telegonus in particular was regarded by the Romans as the founder of Tuscŭlum [Ovid, *Fasti,* iii 92], and Præneste [Horace, *Odes* iii 29, 8]. In later times the adventures of Odysseus were transferred as a whole to the coast of Italy: the promontory of Circeii was regarded as the abode of Circe, Formiæ as the city of the Læstrygones. Near Surrentum was found the island of the Sirens; near Cape Lăcīnium that of Calypso, while near to Sicily were the isle of Æolus, Scylla,

and Charybdis, and, on the Sicilian shore, the Cyclopes. Odysseus is generally represented as a bearded man, wearing a semi-oval cap like that of a Greek sailor. (*See* fig. 1.)

Œbălus. King of Sparta, father of Hippŏcŏŏn, Tyndărĕŏs, and Icărius by the Nymph Băteia. The first of these expels his brethren from their home, but falls with all his sons in battle against Hērăclēs and ' Cēpheus of Tĕgĕa; upon this Tyndărĕŏs (*q.v.*) returns and takes possession of his father's realm. Icarius, who remains in Acarnania, becomes by Pŏlўcastē, or (according to another account) by the Naiad Pĕrĭbœa, father of Pēnĕlŏpē, the wife of Odysseus.

Œcus (*Greek*). The dining-room of a Roman dwelling-house. (*See* HOUSE.)

Œdĭpūs. Son of Lăĭus, descendant of Cadmus through his paternal grandfather Labdăcus and his great-grandfather Pŏlўdōrus. According to *Homer* [*Od.* xi 271–280], he kills his father and marries his mother Ĕpĭcastē (in later accounts Iŏcastē); the gods, however, immediately cause the misdeed to be known, and Epicaste hangs herself; Œdipus however rules on in Thebes, haunted with many sufferings by the vengeful spirit of his mother. Homer also mentions the funeral games celebrated in his honour [*Il.* xxiii 679], but does not tell of the birth of his sons and the grounds of their feud. According to the ancient *Œdĭpŏdeiă* of Cinæthōn, Œdipus after Iocaste's death marries Eurўgăneia, whence sprang his sons Etĕoclēs and Pŏlўnīcēs, and his daughters Antĭgŏnē and Ismēnē [Paus., ix 5, 11]. According to the ancient legend, Œdipus curses his sons either because Polynices had set before him at the banquet the table and goblet which Cadmus and Laius had used (which he regarded as an attempt to remind him of his transgression), or because they had inadvertently sent him the haunch-bone of a victim instead of the shoulder-bone.

In the hands of the *tragedians*, especially of Æschўlus and Sŏphŏclēs (in the *Œdipus Tyrannus*), the legend has been changed into the following form. Laius, husband of Iocaste, daughter of Mĕnœceus, and sister of Crĕŏn, has a curse resting on him in consequence of some misdeed. He is told by the oracle of Apollo that he will die by the hand of his son. When a son is born to him, he accordingly orders a slave to expose him, with his feet pierced, upon Cīthærōn. The slave consigns the child to the care of a shepherd belonging to the king of

Corinth, Pŏlўbus, and he takes it to his master. The boy, who derives the name Œdipus (Swellfoot), from his swollen feet, is adopted by the childless Polybus and his wife Pĕrĭbœa in place of offspring of their own. On reaching manhood, he is reproached during a carousal with not being the son of his presumptive parents, and betakes himself without their knowledge to Delphi, in order to find out the truth. The terrible response of the oracle, to the effect that he will slay his own father and then beget children in wedlock with his mother, causes him to avoid Corinth. At the place in Phōcĭs where the road from Delphi to Daulis leaves the road to Thebes, he is met by his real father, who is on a journey to Delphi to question the god concerning the devastation of his land by the Sphinx. As Œdipus will not move aside, a quarrel arises, and he kills his father together with his attendants, one of whom alone escapes. He proceeds to Thebes, and there frees the city from its plague by solving the Sphinx's riddle; as a reward he receives from Creon the dominion of Thebes and the late king's widow, Iocaste, for a wife; and the latter bears him four children (given by the older myth to Eurўgăneia). Years afterwards failure of crops and pestilence come upon Thebes, and the oracle promises liberation from the disaster only if the murder of Laius be requited by the banishment of the murderer. The result of Œdipus' eager endeavours to identify this person is the discovery of the horrors which he has unconsciously perpetrated. Iocaste hangs herself in despair, and Œdipus puts out his own eyes. Deposed from his throne, and imprisoned at Thebes by his sons to conceal his shame from men's eyes, or (according to another account) driven by them into banishment, whither his daughters accompany him, he pronounces against his sons a curse, to the effect that they shall divide their inheritance with each other by means of the sword, a curse which is fulfilled with awful exactness. (See SEVEN AGAINST THEBES.)

His grave was afterwards shown at the village of Ĕtĕōnus, on the borders of Attica and Bœotia, in the sanctuary of Dēmētĕr, and worship done to him as to a hero. At Athens too, in a sacred demesne of the Ĕrīnўĕs, between the Areŏpăgus and the Acrŏpŏlĭs, was a monument to Œdipus, whose bones were supposed to have been brought hither from Thebes.—Sophocles,

in his *Œdipus at Cŏlōnus*, follows another legend. He represents him as coming to the Attic deme of Colonus at the bidding of Apollo, and as finding there, in the sanctuary of the now propitiated Eumĕnĭdĕs, the longed-for peace of the grave. His bones, the place of burial of which was known to none, are a precious treasure for the country, to guard it from hostile invasions.

Œneus (*i.e.* vintner). King of Călўdon, in Ætolia, the hills of which he was the first to plant with the vine received from Dionўsus. He was son of Portheus or Porthāōn, and brother of Agrius and Mĕlăs; by Althæa, daughter of Thestius, he became the father of Tўdeus, Mĕlĕăger, and Dēĭănīra. (*See* HERACLES.) As he once forgot Artĕmis in a sacrifice, she sent the Calydonian boar, which ravaged the country, and, even after its slaughter in the famous Calydonian Hunt, occasioned the death of Meleager (*q.v.*). From the plots of his brother Melas he had been delivered by Tydeus through the murder of Melas and his sons, but after the deaths of Tydeus and Meleager, his other brother Agrius, and the sons of that brother, deprived him of his throne and cast him into prison. His grandson Dĭŏmēdēs however revenged him with the aid of Alcmæōn: to whom he had once given hospitable entertainment, and who was desirous of taking Œneus with him to Argos, after he had given over the throne of Calydon to his son-in-law Andræmōn, whose son Thŏăs, in Homer [*Il.* ii 638], leads the Ætolians to Troy. But the two sons of Agrius, who have escaped death, lie in wait for him in Arcadia, and there slay the old man. Dĭŏmēdēs carries his body to Argos, and deposits it in the city which after him was called Œnŏē. While in Homer Œneus is dead before the expedition to Troy, later mythology represents him as surviving the Trojan War, and as restored to his kingdom by Diomedes on the latter's flight from Argos.

Œnŏmäüs. Son of Ărēs and the Pleiad Stĕrŏpē, king of Pīsa in Elis, father of Hippŏdămīa. He endeavoured to prevent his daughter's marriage, either because he loved her himself, or because an oracle had predicted his death in the event of her marriage. In consequence of this he imposed upon her suitors the condition that they must contend with him in a race from Pisa to the altar of Pŏseidōn, on the Corinthian isthmus: if he overtook them with his horses, which were as swift as the winds, he transfixed them with his spear.

He had already slain thirteen (or, according to another account, eighteen) suitors in this way, when Pĕlops arrived. Pelops bribed Myrtĭlus, the charioteer of Œnomaus. Myrtilus accordingly either neglected to insert the linch-pins in the chariot-wheels or substituted waxen ones for them, and Pelops, by the help of the horses which Poseidon presented to him, succeeded in defeating Œnomaus. Œnomaus died of the fall from his chariot; according to another story, he committed suicide (cp. PELOPS).

Œnŏnē. A nymph of mount Ida, bride of Paris before he carried off Helen. In resentment at her lover's faithlessness, she refused to help him when he was mortally wounded ; and, in her remorse at her refusal, ended by hanging herself.

Officials, Official System, Magistrates. Of all the official systems established among the Greeks, that in vogue among the Athenians is the best known to us. The qualifications for public office at Athens were genuine Athenian descent, blameless life, and the full possession of civic rights. If religious duties were attached to the office, physical weakness was a disqualification. No one was allowed to hold two offices at a time, or the same office twice, or for a longer period than a year. The nomination was made in some cases by election, in others by the drawing of lots. Election took place by show of hands in the ecclēsĭa, or, on the mandate of the ecclesia, in the assemblies of the several tribes. (See CHEIROTONIA, ECCLESIA.) In election by lot [on the introduction of which see Note on p. 706] the proceeding was as follows. The Thesmŏthĕtæ presided in the temple of Thēseus. (See THESMOTHETÆ.) Two boxes or vessels were placed there, one containing white and coloured beans, and the other the names of the candidates, written on tablets. A tablet and a bean were taken out at the same time, and the candidate whose name came out with a white bean was elected. Before entering on his office (whether he had been chosen by lot or election), every official had to undergo an examination of his qualifications (dŏkĭmăsĭa). If the result was unfavourable, a substitute was appointed, either by a simultaneous casting of lots in the manner described, or (if the office was elective) by a new election. During their term of office the officials were subject to constant supervision, and were liable to suspension or deposition by the Ecclesia, through the proceeding called ĕpĭcheirŏ-

tŏnĭa (a new show of hands). On the expiration of his term, every official was bound to give an account of himself (euthȳna) The regular officials[1] had each a place of office (archeĭŏn). If the officials formed a society, as in the majority of cases, the business was (so far as joint administration was possible) distributed among the members. If the society appeared in public as a whole, one of the members presided as prȳtănĭs. (See PRYTANIS.) In the cases at law which came under their jurisdiction it was incumbent on the officials to make the necessary arrangements for the trial and to preside in court. They received no salary, but their meals were provided at the public expense, either at their residences or in the Prȳtănēum. The emblem of office was a garland of myrtle. The offence of insulting an official in the performance of his duty was punishable with ătīmĭa. (See, for details, APODECTÆ ARCHONTES, ASTYNOMI, EPIMELETÆ, COLACRETÆ, POLETÆ, STRATEGI, TAMIAS.)

There were numerous attendants on the officials (hȳpērĕtai), who received a salary and their meals at the public expense Such were the clerks (grammătĕis) and heralds (kērȳkĕs). For Sparta, see EPHORS for Rome, MAGISTRATUS, ACCENSI, LICTORS APPARITOR.

Ogȳgēs (Ogȳgus). One of the Bœotian autochthŏnĕs, or aborigines, son of Bœotus or (according to another account) of Pŏsei dŏn. He was king of the Hectēnĕs, the oldest inhabitants of Bœotia, which was visited during his reign by an inundation of Lake Cōpăĭs, named after him the Ogygiar flood.

Oïclēs. Son of Antĭphătēs, grandson o Mĕlampūs, father of Amphĭărāus. He fel as a companion of Hēráclēs in the battle against Lāŏmĕdōn of Troy.

Oil was very extensively used in ancien times. Apart from its use as an article o food and for burning in lamps, it served to anoint the body after the bath and in the pălœstra. The oil most used was tha obtained by means of olive presses from the olive tree, which seems to have been trans planted from Syria to Greece and thence to Italy. The best olive oil produced among the Greek states was that of Attica ; her the olive tree was considered a gift of the national goddess Athēnē, who by means o it had obtained the victory in her contes

---

[1] Some were only appointed to carry out special duties on special occasions ; these were called Epĭmēlētai.

with Pŏseidōn for the possession of the country. Here also the olive tree was under the special protection of the State; no one was allowed to cut down olive trees on his own plot of land, except for specified purposes, and then only a specified number. Moreover many olive trees standing on private ground were regarded as the property of the goddess of the State, and it was therefore forbidden on pain of death to cut them down. They were under the special control of the Areŏpăgus, which had them inspected from time to time by certain officials, and they were farmed out by the State [Lysias, *Or.* ix]. Part of the oil thus obtained had to be sold by the farmer to the State at a fixed price; this was only used for festive purposes, especially to be distributed in prizes to the victors in the Panathenaic contests [Pindar, *Nem.* x 35].

In Italy the olive tree, which spread thence to France and Spain, grew so well that the Italian oil, especially from the neighbourhood of the South Italian cities Vĕnăfrum and Tărentum, and that from the Sabine country, was considered the finest in the world and so met with a ready sale abroad. The best kind was considered to be oil from unripe olives, especially the first from the press [Pliny, *N. H.* xv 1–34]. The manufacture of fragrant oils and ointments, of which the ancients made a far more extensive use than ourselves, was very important. There was a very large number of preparations of this kind which were used for embrocations of the person, pomades for the hair of the head and beard, for perfuming the dress, bath-water and the like. They were prepared, some by a cold method, some by a hot, by mixing oils pressed for the most part from fruits, such as the oil of olives, nuts, and almonds, with the volatile oils derived from native or oriental vegetable substances. The most expensive kinds were brought from the East, the birthplace of this manufacture, as, for example, the much-prized *nardĭnum*, pressed from the flowers of the Indian and Arabian grass *nardus* [Pliny, *N. H.* xiii 1–25]. For preserving them vessels of stone were preferred, especially those of alabaster [*ib.* § 19]. To meet the demand, vast perfume manufactories existed everywhere in abundance.

Oīleus. King of the Locrians, father of the lesser Ajax (*q.v.*, 1).

Olēn. A mythical poet of Lўcia belonging to early Greek times, standing in connexion with the worship of Apollo in Dēlŏs and represented as having composed the first hymns for the Delians. The legend which was especially attributed to him was that of Apollo's sojourn among the Hyperboreans.

Oligarchiă ("Rule of the Few"). The name given in Greek writers to that form of constitution where a portion of the community, privileged either by reason of nobility of birth or of wealth, are exclusively, or at least in preference to others, in possession of power. The former case is an example of an absolute despotism; the latter resulted where the magistracies, though filled exclusively from the privileged classes, nevertheless depended on popular election; or where the mass of the people possessed a share in deliberation or in the drawing up of decrees, while to the privileged body was reserved the right of making proposals, convoking and presiding over the assemblies, and ratifying the decrees.

Olympiad (Gr. *Olympiăs*). A period of four years from one celebration of the Olympian games (*see* OLYMPIAN GAMES) to another. The Olympiads were counted from the victory of Cŏrœbus (776 B.C.); the last, the 283rd, ended 394 A.D., with the abolition of the Olympian games. This method of reckoning never passed into everyday life but is of importance, inasmuch as, through the historian Tīmæus, about 240 B.C., it became the one generally used by the Greek historians.

Olympian Games (Gr. *Olympiă*). The chief national festival of the Greeks, which was celebrated in honour of Zeus at Olympia, in the Peloponnesian district Pīsātĭs, belonging to the Eleans, at the point where the Clădĕŭs runs into the Alphĕŭs. The institution of this ancient festival is sometimes referred to Pisus, the mythical founder of the city Pisa, which was afterwards destroyed by the Eleans, and before whose gates lay the sanctuary of Zeus; sometimes to Pĕlops, in whose honour funeral games were held at this point on the banks of the Alpheus.

These were restored, it is said, by Hērăclēs, who instituted the regular order of the festival. This opinion did not become current until the Dorian States, established after the immigration of the Hērăclīdæ into the Peloponnesus, had been admitted to a share in the festival, which was originally frequented only by the Pisatans and their immediate neighbours. This admission dates from Lўcurgus of Sparta and Iphĭtus of Elis, who, at the direction of the Delphic oracle, restored the festival of Zeus, now fallen into oblivion, and established the

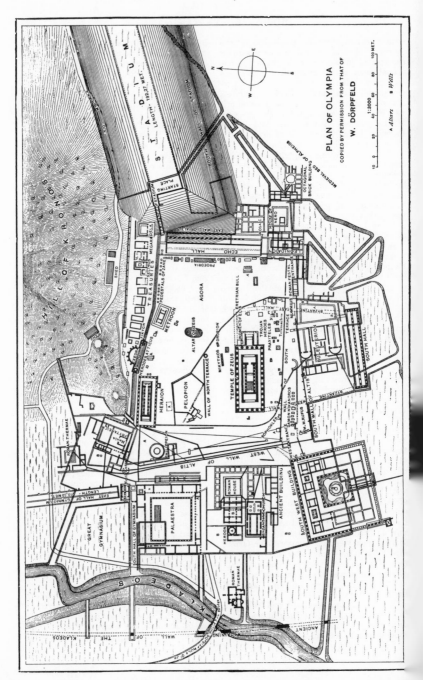

PLAN OF OLYMPIA

COPIED BY PERMISSION FROM THAT OF

W. DÖRPFELD

1:3000

A Altars   B Wells

sacred Truce of God (*see* EKECHEIRIA), which insured a safe conduct at the time of the festival for all strangers resorting thither, even through hostile territory. In course of time the membership extended itself further, over all the Hellenic states in and out of Greece; and the festival was not only visited by private individuals, but also received sacred envoys from the several states. Through all the assaults of time it lasted on, even during the Roman rule, and was not abolished until 394 A.D., under the reign of Thĕŏdŏsius.

From the time of the above-mentioned restoration by Iphitus and Lycurgus it was a quinquennial celebration; that is, it was held once in every four years, in midsummer (July to August), about the beginning or end of the Greek year. A regular and continuous list of the victors was kept from 776, when Cŏrœbus won the race in the

the temples of Zeus, Hēra (*Hēraiŏn*), the Mother of the Gods (*Mētrŏŏn*), and the holy inclosure of Pelops (*Pĕlŏpĭŏn*), besides a multitude of altars consecrated some to gods and some to heroes, and a countless host of dedicatory offerings and statues of every kind, among them, south-east of the temple of Zeus, the *Nīcē* of Pæonius (*q.v.*).

The temple of Zeus, which was begun about 572 B.C. by the Elean Libo, was not completed in its main outline until about 450. It was a Doric hypæthral building (*i.e.* it had no roof over the *cella*, or temple proper); it was also peripteral (*i.e.* it was surrounded by a single row of columns). It was built of the local conchyliferous limestone [called *pŏrŏs* by Pausanias, v 10 § 2]. In its more finished parts it was overlaid with fine stucco, giving the appearance of marble, and was also richly decorated with colour. It was 210 feet in length, 91 in

(1) EASTERN PEDIMENT OF THE TEMPLE OF ZEUS AT OLYMPIA; DESIGNED BY PÆONIUS.
(Contest between Pelops and Œnomaüs.)

(2) WESTERN PEDIMENT OF THE TEMPLE OF ZEUS AT OLYMPIA; DESIGNED BY ALCAMENES.
(Battle between the Centaurs and Lapithæ.)

stădĭum, and with this year begins the Olympiad reckoning prevalent among the historians from the time of Tīmæus. The duration of the festival was in course of time extended to at least five days.

The place where the festival was celebrated was the *Altis* (*see* Plan), a sacred precinct at the foot of the hill of Cronus (*Krŏnŏs*), 403 feet high. The precinct, which was about 750 feet long by 570 feet broad, was surrounded by a wall ascribed to Hērăclēs, having entrances at the N.W. and S.W. The centre, both by position and by religious association, was formed by the great sacrificial *altar of Zeus*, which rose on an elliptical base 128 feet in circumference to a height of 32 feet, and was composed of the ashes of the victims mingled with the water of the Alpheus. Round it were grouped the four most important sanctuaries,

breadth, and 65 in height. The outer hall had 6 columns along its breadth and 13 along its length (each 34 feet high), while the inner hall had a double row of 7 columns. The eastern pediment was occupied by a representation of the contest between Pĕlops and Œnŏmäus, with Zeus as the centre (fig. 1); the western, by one of the battle between the Centaurs and Lăpĭthæ, with Apollo as centre (fig. 2). The former was designed by the already-mentioned Pæonius; the latter, by Alcămĕnēs of Athens.

The accompanying cuts indicate the figures belonging to the two pediments, so far as their fragmentary portions were recovered in the excavations begun by the Germans in 1875. [While the outer metopes beneath these pediments had no ornament except a large plain boss on each, twelve other metopes sculptured with reliefs used to adorn the outer walls at each end of the *cella* or temple proper, six over the door of the *prŏnāŏs*, and six over that of the *ŏpisthŏdŏmŏs*. All of these have been discovered: four by the French in 1829, and eight by the Germans in 1875–9. Their subjects are the labours of Heracles. The best preserved of the series, and one of them which, as compared with the rest, is apparently the work of a mature and well-trained school of sculpture, is that representing Heracles bearing the heavens. Atlas stands by, offering to Heracles the apples of the Hespĕrĭdĕs, and on the other side one of the daughters of Atlas is touching the hero's burden with her arm, as though endeavouring to aid him in sustaining it (fig. 3).] In the chamber at the western end of the *cella* stood the greatest work of Greek art, wrought in gold and ivory by Phīdĭās (*q.v.*). Outside the sacred inclosure, though still in direct connexion with it, were, to the west, the *Gymnăsĭum*, and to the east the *Hippodrome* and the *Stădĭum*. [The *Hippodrome* has been washed away by the encroachments of the Alpheus. The *Stadium*, which was 600 Olympic feet in length, has been excavated to an extent sufficient to determine the length of the single course, between the starting-place and the goal, to be 192·27 metres = 630·81845073 English feet. The Olympic foot therefore measured ·3204 of a metre = 1·05120036 feet. The parallel grooves in the slabs of stone at each end of the *Stadium* still show the spot where the feet of the competitors in the footrace were planted at the moment immediately preceding the start. There is room for 20 at either end, separated from one another by posts at intervals of four Olympic feet from one another (fig. 4).]

The festival consisted of two parts: (1) the presentation of *offerings*, chiefly of course to Zeus, but also to the other gods and heroes, on the part of the Eleans, the sacred embassies and other visitors to the feast; and (2) the *contests*. In the first Olympiad the contest consisted of a simple match in the *Stadium* (race-course) which had a length of a trifle more than 210 yards. The runners ran in heats of four, and then the winners in each heat com-

peted together, the first in the final heat being proclaimed victor. About 724 B.C. the double course (*dĭaulŏs*) was introduced, in which the runners had to make a circuit of the goal and return to the starting-point; about 720 came the *dŏlĭchŏs* or long race,

(3) * ONE OF THE METOPES OF THE TEMPLE OF ZEUS
AT OLYMPIA.
(Reduced from Overbeck's *Gr. Plastik*, fig. 93.)

where the distance of the *stadium* had to be covered either 6, 7, 8, 12, 20, or 29 times [Scholiast on Soph., *Electra* 691]; in 708, the *pentathlŏn*, or five-fold contest, consisting of leaping, running, quoit (*diskŏs*) and spear-throwing, and wrestling (the last

(4) * THE STARTING-PLACE IN THE STADIUM AT OLYMPIA.

being also practised by itself) ; in 688, boxing. In 680 chariot-racing on the *Hippodrome* was introduced, and, though this was twice as long as the *Stadium*, it had to be traversed from eight to twelve times in both directions (at first with four horses, after 500 with mules, and after 408 with two horses). From 648 there were races, in which the horsemen, towards the end of the race, had to leap from their horses and run beside them with the bridle in their hands. With the same year began the practice of the *pancrătĭŏn* (a combination of wrestling and boxing); with 520, the race in armour, with helmet, greaves and shield, though afterwards the shield alone was carried. Competitions between heralds and trumpeters also found a place here. Originally it was only men who took part in the contests; but after 632, boys also shared in them.

The contests were open only to freemen of pure Hellenic descent, provided that no personal disgrace had in any way attached to them; but, after the Romans came into closer relationship with Greece, they were opened to them also, and indeed (as is well known) the Romans were not officially considered barbarians. Even to barbarians however, and to slaves, permission was given to view them, while it was refused to all married women [Pausanias, vi 20, § 9], or more probably all women whatsoever, except the priestess of Dēmētēr, who even received a place of honour among the spectators. Those who took part in the competitions had to take a solemn oath at the altar of Zeus to the effect that they had spent at least ten months in preparation for the games, and that they would not resort to any unfair trick in the course of their contest: this oath was taken for boy competitors by an older relative. Special practice for thirty days at Elis was also usual, but probably only for those who were coming forward for the first time. The duties of heralds and judges were discharged by the *Hellănŏdĭci*, appointed by popular election from among the Eleans themselves. Their number rose in course of time from 1 to 2, 9, 10, and 12, but after 348 it was always 10. Distinguished by purple robes, wreaths of bay-leaves, and a seat of honour opposite the *Stadium*, they kept guard over the strict observance of all the minute regulations for the contests, and in general maintained order. In these duties they were supported by a number of attendants provided with staves. Transgressions of the laws of the games, and unfairness on the part of competitors, were punished by forfeiture of the prize or by fines of money, which went to the revenue of the temple. Out of the money from penalties of this kind, a whole row of bronze images of Zeus (called *zānĕs*) was erected in front of the eleven treasure-houses along the eastern end of the northern wall of the Altis.

The games were opened with the sound of trumpets and the proclamation of heralds, the marshalling of the various competitors in the *Stadium*, accompanied by the announcement of their name and country by the herald, and the appointment by lot of the pairs of combatants. The victors in the several pairs of competitors had then apparently to contend in couples with each other until one couple alone remained, and the winner in this was declared victor. If the number of combatants had been uneven, so that one of them had remained without an opponent, he had finally to meet this rival. The contests were accompanied by the music of flutes. The name of the victor (and one, whom no adversary had come forward to meet, counted for victor), as well as his home, were proclaimed aloud by the herald, and a palm-branch presented to him by the *Hellănŏdĭci*. The actual prize he only received at the general and solemn distribution on the last day of the festival. This was originally some article of value, but, at the command of the Delphic oracle, this custom was dropped, and the victors were graced by a wreath of the leaves of the sacred wild olive, said to have been originally planted by Heracles, which had been cut with a golden knife by a boy of noble family with both parents living. After about 540 the victors also possessed the right to put up statues of themselves in the Altis.

The festival ended with a sacrifice made by the victors wearing their crowns at the six double altars of the hill of Cronus, and with a banquet in the *Prytănēum* of the Altis. Brilliant distinctions awaited the victor on his return home, for his victory was deemed to have reflected honour on his native land at large. He made his entry, clad in purple, upon a chariot drawn by four white horses, amidst the joyous shouts of all the people, and then rode amid an exultant escort to the temple of the highest god, and there deposited his wreath as a votive offering. During the ride, as also at the banquet which followed thereupon, the song of victory, often composed by the most celebrated poets, was chanted by choral bands. There was no lack of other rewards: at Athens the Olympian victor received 500 *drachmœ*, the right to a place of honour at all public games, and board in the *Prytaneum* for the rest of his life. The opportunity afforded by the assembling of so vast a crowd from all parts of Greece at Olympia was utilized, from about the middle of the 5th century before Christ, by authors, orators, poets, and artists, to make themselves known in the widest circles by the recital or exhibition of their works. When the compliment of a crown was offered by one state to another, the distinction was made generally known by being proclaimed by the heralds at the Olympian Games.

[Olympīēum (Gr. Ὀλυμπῐεῐŏn). The temple of Zeus Olympīus in the southern quarter of Athens, between the Acrŏpŏlis and the Ilissus. It was built on the site of an ancient temple of Zeus ascribed to Deu-călĭŏn. The building was begun after 535 B.C., under the tyrant Pīsistrătus, but was suspended on the expulsion of his son Hippias, B.C. 510. Its original architecture was probably Doric. The names of the architects were Antistătēs, Callæschrus, Antĭmăchĭdēs, and Pōrĭnus. It was continued in the Corinthian style under the Syrian king Antĭŏchus Epĭphănēs (B.C. 175–164), who employed for the purpose a Roman architect, Cossutius. It was completed by the Roman emperor Hadrian, probably between A.D. 125 and 130, the year of its dedication. On this occasion an oration was delivered by the famous rhetorician Pŏlĕmōn, and Olympic games instituted on the model of those at Olympia. The emperor identified himself with Zeus and assumed the title of Olympius, causing a statue of himself to be placed in the temple and claiming divine honours from the priests. The first of these priests was the celebrated Hērōdēs Ăttĭcus (q.v.). When Pausanias visited Athens about 170 A.D., the temple had been recently finished. He gives no description of the fabric, but states that the image of the god was of enormous size, only excelled by the cŏlossi of Rhodes and Rome (i 18 § 6–8). It was of gold and ivory, and on its base were reliefs representing the battle of the Athenians with the Amazons (i 17 § 2). In the precinct a great number of statues of Hadrian were erected by the cities of the Greek world; the largest of these, that erected by Athens, stood at the west end of the temple. Among the statues of earlier date was one of Isŏcrătēs. There was also a fine group consisting of some Persians upholding a bronze tripod, and also an archaic bronze statue of Zeus. Lastly, in the precinct there was a temple of Crŏnus and Rhea, the sacred inclosure of which extended down to the Ilissus.

Some of the Doric columns of the original building were carried off to Rome by Sulla

in 86 B.C. to adorn the temple of Iŭpĭter Căpĭtōlīnus. In respect to its architecture the temple must be regarded as mainly the work of the 2nd century B.C. rather than the 2nd century A.D. The building was octostyle, dipteral, and probably hypæthral. As designed by Cossutius in the former century, it must have possessed more than 100 Corinthian columns, arranged in double rows of 20 each on the north and south sides, and in triple rows of 8 each at the ends. The columns were of Pentelic marble, 56½ feet high, and 5–5½ feet in diameter. The ruins in their present condition consist of 16 columns in two groups. To the east stand 13, which are comparatively intact, and for the most part bear their architraves. About 100 feet to the west are three others, two still erect; the third was overthrown by a storm in 1852. The excavations of 1861 showed that the temple did not lie in the centre of the precinct, but considerably nearer its northern wall.

The temple of the era of Pīsistrătus is mentioned by Thūcȳdĭdēs (ii 5) as one of the old temples in the southern part of the city. In respect to its origin, as well as its vast dimensions, Aristotle (Pol. v 11) compares it to the works of the dynasty of Cypsĕlus at Corinth, the Pyramids of Egypt, and the public buildings erected by Pŏlȳcrătēs of Sămos. As a monument of tyranny it was naturally left unfinished by democratical Athens. Livy (xli 20 § 8) describes it as unum in terris in-cŏhātum pro magnĭtūdĭnĕ dĕi. In allusion to the long time during which it remained uncompleted, Lucian (Icaromen. 24) represents Zeus as getting impatient to know when the Athenians intended to finish his temple. Lastly, Vitruvius (vii præf. 15–17) mentions it as one of the four most famous examples of marble architecture.

The ruins were first identified by a Prussian archæologist, Transfeldt, in 1673–4, and independently by Stuart and Revett, whose great work on the Antiquities of Athens was published in 1762–1816. The first description pretending to any accuracy of detail was in the letter sent from Smyrna by Francis Vernon in 1676 and published in Spon's Voyage. The site has been explored in recent times by Rhuso-pulos in 1861 (Ephemeris Arch., 1862, pp 31 ff.), and Penrose (Journal of Hellenic Studies, viii 272, and Principles of Athenian Architecture, new ed.). A com-prehensive monograph on the subject by

L. Bevier is included in the *Papers of the American Classical School at Athens*, 1885, vol. i 183-222.] [J. E. S.]

Olympus. (1) A mountain situated in Thessaly, the summit of which [nearly 10,000 feet above the sea] rises from the region of the earth's atmosphere into the sky, and was, according to the earliest popular belief of the Greeks, the abode of the higher hence named Olympian) gods. Below the summit, which, according to Homer's description, is never ruffled by winds or drenched with rain, but is always radiant in cloudless splendour [*Od.* vi 42-45], comes the region of clouds, which Zeus at one time gathers together and at another dispels; it forms the boundary between the celestial region and that of the earth; and accordingly Homer elsewhere implies that the clouds are the gates of heaven, which are guarded by the Hours [*Il.* v 749]. On the highest peak Zeus has his throne, and it is there that he summons the assemblies of the gods. The abodes of the other gods were imagined to be placed on the precipices and in the ravines of the mountain. When the height of the vault of heaven came to be regarded as the abode of the gods, the name Olympus was transferred to the sky.

(2) One of the mythic poets and musicians belonging to Phrygian mythology, pupil of Marsyas. The art of flute-playing, invented by Marsyas, was supposed to have been perfected by Olympus. A Phrygian family, in which the art of flute-playing was hereditary, traced their descent from him. The Phrygian Olympus, who lived about the 7th century before Christ, invented the auletic *nŏmŏs* (*q.v.*), and brought it into esteem among the Asiatic Greeks, was said to have been descended from the mythical Olympus.

Omen. The Roman term for a favourable or unfavourable sign, especially a word spoken by chance, so far as it drew the attention of the hearers to itself and appeared to be a prognostic. An omen could be accepted or repudiated, and even taken in an arbitrary sense, except in the case of words which already had in themselves a favourable or unfavourable signification. For example, when Crassus was embarking on his unfortunate expedition against the Parthians, and a man in the harbour was selling dry figs from Caunus with the cry *Caunĕās*, which sounded like *cave ne eas*, " beware of going," this was an evil omen [Cic., *De Div.* ii 84]. On festal occasions care was taken to protect oneself from such omens ; for example, when sacrifice was being made, by

veiling the head, by commanding silence, and by music that drowned any word spoken. People were particularly careful at solemn addresses, new year greetings, and the like. On the other hand, for the sake of the good omen, it was usual to open levies and censuses by calling out those names that were of good import, such as Vălērĭus (from *vălēre*, to be strong), Salvĭus (from *salvēre*, to be well), etc. [Cic., *Pro Scauro*, 30. The word *omen* probably means a voice or utterance].

Omphălē. Daughter of Iardănus, widow of Tmōlus, and queen of Lȳdia, with whom Hērăclēs spent three years in bondage. (*See* HERACLES.)

Omphălŏs. A marble boss in the temple of Apollo at Delphi, which was regarded as the centre of the earth. (*See* DELPHIC ORACLE.)

Ŏnăger. A catapult for hurling stones. (*See further*, ARTILLERY.)

Ŏnātas. A Greek artist, the chief representative of the Æginetan school of sculpture in bronze, about 460 B.C. Besides statues of the gods, such as an *Apollo* at Pergămŏn, admired for its size and execution [Pausanias, viii 42 § 7], we hear of groups of his, rich in figures, drawn either from the heroic epoch, as for example the *ten Greek heroes* casting lots as to who should undertake the battle with Hector [*ib.* v 25 § 8]; or from contemporary history, such as the *votive offering of the Tarentines*, containing equestrian and pedestrian combatants, and consecrated at Delphi for their victory over the barbarian Peucetians [*ib.* x 13 § 10]. He also executed a group representing *Hiĕrō* of Syracuse with the chariot in which he had been victorious at Olympia [*ib.* viii 42 § 8]. [His most remarkable work was the bronze figure of the *black Dēmētēr*, in a cavern thirty stadia from Phĭgăleia in the south-east corner of Elis (*ib.* viii 42).]

Ŏnēsandrus (wrongly *Onosandrus*). A Greek philosopher, the composer of a work dedicated to Q. Verānius, consul in 49 A.D., and dealing with the Duty of a General, in which he treats the subject in philosophical commonplaces, without any practical acquaintance with it, and simply from an ethical point of view.

Ŏnēsĭcrĭtus. A Greek historian, of the island of Astȳpălæa or Ægīna. In advanced years he was a pupil of the Cynic Diŏgĕnēs, and then accompanied Alexander the Great upon his expedition. By order of Alexander he investigated, with Nĕarchus, the route by sea from India to the mouths

of the Euphrātēs and Tigris. He afterwards lived at the court of Lӯsīmăchus,
king of Thrace. During Alexander's life
he began a comprehensive history of that
personage, which fell into disrepute owing
to its exaggerations and its false accounts
of distant lands [Strabo, p. 628]. Only
scanty fragments of it are preserved.

Ŏnīrŏcrĭtĭcē (Gr. *Ŏneirŏkrītĭkē*). The art
of interpreting dreams. (*See* MANTIKE and
DREAMS.)

Ŏnīrŏs (Greek *Ŏneirŏs*). The god of
dreams (*q.v.*).

Ŏnŏmacrĭtus. An Athenian, who lived
at the court of Pīsistrătus and his sons.
At the request of Pisistratus, he prepared
an edition of the Homeric poems. He was
an industrious collector, and also a forger
of old oracles and poems. Those which go
under the name of Orpheus are regarded as,
for the most part, concocted by himself. He
was detected in forging an oracle of Mūsæus,
and banished from Athens by the Pisistra-
tīdæ; but he was afterwards reconciled to
them, and in their interest induced Xerxes,
by alleged oracular responses, to decide
upon his war with Greece [Herodotus, viii 6].

Ŏnŏsandrus. *See* ONESANDRUS.

Ŏpālia and **Ŏpĕconsīva.** Feasts of the
Roman goddess Ops (*q.v.*).

Ŏpheltēs. Son of king Lӯcurgus of Nĕmĕa.
He was killed by a serpent at the time of
the expedition of the Seven against Thebes
(*q.v.*), owing to the negligence of his nurse
Hypsīpӯlē (*q.v.*), who laid the boy on the
grass while she showed the thirsty heroes
the way to a spring of water. It was in his
memory that the Nemean games were originally celebrated, and he was worshipped
there under the name Archĕmŏrus (*q.v.*),
given him by the seer Amphĭărāus.

Ŏpisthŏdŏmus (*lit.* a back chamber). The
room which in many Greek temples adjoined
the temple chamber itself at the rear, and
which often served for the preserving of the
temple treasure, and indeed even of the
State moneys. For the latter purpose the
Athenians used the *opisthodomus* [of the
old temple of Athēnē, and afterwards (according to the ordinary view) the western
chamber] of the Parthĕnōn at Athens [Aris-
toph. *Plutus*, 1192; Dem. *Syntax.* 14;
Timocr. 136]. (*See* TEMPLE, and plan of
ACROPOLIS.)

Oppian. A Greek didactic poet, of Ana-
zarbus in Cilicia. In the second half of
the 2nd century A.D., under the emperor
Marcus Aurēlius, he composed a didactic
poem *Hălieutĭca* in five books, on the

habits of fishes and the method of capturing them. It is written in an ornate,
though often bombastic, style. He was
formerly confounded with Oppian, the
author of a didactic poem on the Chase,
consisting of four books, and entitled *Cӯnĕ-
gĕtĭca*, written in a harsh, dry style, and
in halting verse. The author of the *Cyne-
getica* lived under Caracalla about the end
of the 2nd century, and came from Apamēa
in Syria. A poem on bird-catching, *Ixeu-
tĭca*, preserved to us only in a paraphrase
by Eutĕcnĭus, was alsó wrongly ascribed
to the author of the *Hălieutĭca*.

Ops (*abundance, plenty*). The old Italian
goddess of fertility, wife of Saturn, with
whom she shared the temple on the Capitol
and the festival of the *Sāturnālĭa*, while
the *Ŏpālia* were held in her honour on the
19th December. As goddess of sowing and
reaping she had, under the name *Consīvia*,
on August 25th a special festival, the *Ŏpĕconsīva*, at which however only the Vestals
and one of the *pontĭfĭcēs* could be present.
As her abode was in the earth, her worshippers invoked her while seated and
touching the ground [Macrobius, *Saturnalia*, i 10]. Just as Saturn was identified
with Crŏnus, so Ops was afterwards identified with Rhea, and then, as mother of
Jupiter, honoured along with Jupiter himself on the Capitol.

Optātiānus. *See* PORFIRIUS.

Optĭmātēs (*lit.* "those belonging to the
best or noblest"). At Rome, in the last
century of the Republic, this title was
borne by the adherents of the "best" men
in a political sense (*i.e.* the conservatives),
working in the interests of the Senate
and the aristocracy of office (*nŏbĭlĕs, see*
NOBILITY), and in opposition to the demo-
crats (*pŏpŭlārēs*).

Oracles (Gr. *manteĭă*, "oracular responses,"
or the "seats of oracles"; *chrēstērĭă* is used
in the same senses, and also of victims
offered by those consulting an oracle). The
seats of the worship of some special divinity, where prophecies were imparted with
the sanction of the divinity, either by the
priests themselves or with their co-operation. There were a great many such places
in all Greek countries, and these may be
divided, according to the method in which
the prophecy was made known, into four
main divisions: (1) *oral* oracles, (2) oracles
by *signs*, (3) oracles by *dreams*, and (4)
oracles of the *dead*.

The most revered oracles were those of
the first class, where the divinity, almost in-

variably the sea-god Apollo, orally revealed his will through the lips of inspired prophets or prophetesses. The condition of frenzy was produced for the most part by physical influence: the breathing of earthly vapours or drinking of the water of oracular fountains. The words spoken whilst in this state were generally fashioned by the priests into a reply to the questions proposed to them. The most famous oracle of this kind was that of Delphi (*see* DELPHIC ORACLE). Beside this there existed in Greece Proper a large number of oracles of Apollo, as at Abæ in Phōcis, in different places of Bœotia, in Eubœa, and at Argos, where the priestess derived her inspiration from drinking the blood of a lamb, one being killed every month. Not less numerous were the oracles of Apollo in Asia Minor. Among these that of the Didymæan Apollo at Mīlētus traced its origin to the old family of the Branchĭdæ, the descendants of Apollo's son Branchus. Before its destruction by Xerxes, it came nearest to the reputation of the Delphian. Here it was a priestess who prophesied, seated on a wheel-shaped disc, after she had bathed the hem of her robe and her feet in a spring, and had breathed the steam arising from it. The oracle at Clărus near Cŏlŏphōn (*see* MANTO) was also very ancient. Here a priest, after simply hearing the names and the number of those consulting the oracle, drank of the water of a spring, and then gave answer in verse.

The most respected among the oracles where prophecy was given by *signs* was that of Zeus of Dōdōna (*q.v.*), mentioned as early as Homer [*Od.* xiv 327 = xix 296], where predictions were made from the rustling of the sacred oak, and at a later time from the sound of a brazen cymbal. Another mode of interpreting by signs, as practised especially at the temple of Zeus at Olympia by the Iămĭdæ, or descendants of Iămus, a son of Apollo, was that derived from the entrails of victims and the burning of the sacrifices on the altar. There were also oracles connected with the lot or dice, one especially at the temple of Hērăclēs at Būra in Achæa; and prophecies were also delivered at Delphi by means of lots, probably only at times when the Pȳthia was not giving responses. The temple of the Egyptian Ammōn, who was identified with Zeus, also gave oracles by means of signs.

Oracles given in dreams were generally connected with the temples of Asclēpius. After certain preliminary rites, sick per-

sons had to sleep in these temples; the priests interpreted their dreams, and dictated accordingly the means to be taken to insure recovery. The most famous of these oracular shrines of the healing god was the temple at Epidaurus, and next to this the temple founded thence at Pergămum in Asia Minor. Equally famous were the similar oracles of the seer Amphĭărāus at Ōrōpus, of Trŏphōnius at Lĕbădēa in Bœotia, and of the seers Mopsus and Amphĭlŏchus at Mallus in Cilicia (*q.v.*). In later times such oracles were connected with all sanctuaries of Isis and Sĕrăpis.

At *oracles of the dead* (*psȳchŏmanteia*) the souls of deceased persons were evoked in order to give the information desired. Thus in Homer [*Od.* xi] Odysseus betakes himself to the entrance of the lower world to question the spirit of the seer Tīrĕsĭas. Oracles of this kind were especially common in places where it was supposed there was an entrance to the lower world; as at the city of Cĭchȳrus in Ēpīrus (where there was an Acherusian lake as well as the rivers of Achĕrōn and Cōcȳtus, bearing the same names as those of the world below), at the promontory of Tænărum in Lăcōnia, at Hērăclēa in Pontus, and at Lake Avernus near Cūmæ in Italy. At most of them oracles were also given in dreams; but there were some in which the inquirer was in a waking condition when he conjured up the spirits whom he wished to question.

While oracles derived either from dreams or from the dead were chosen in preference by superstitious people, the most important among oral oracles and those given by means of signs had a political significance. On all serious occasions they were questioned on behalf of the State in order to ascertain the divine will: this was especially the case with the oracle of Delphi (*see* DELPHIC ORACLE). In consequence of the avarice and partisanship of the priests, as well as the increasing decline of belief in the gods, the oracles gradually fell into abeyance, to revive again everywhere under the Roman emperors, though they never regained the political importance they had once had in ancient Greece.

Such investigation of the divine will was originally quite foreign to the ROMANS. Even the mode of prophecying by means of lots (*see* SORTES), practised in isolated regions of Italy, and even in the immediate neighbourhood of Rome, as at Cære, and especially at Præneste, did not come into use, at all events for State purposes, and was generally regarded with contempt. The Romans did not consult even the Sibylline verses in order to forecast the future. On the other hand, the growth of superstition in the imperial period not only brought the native oracles into repute, but caused a general resort to foreign oracles besides. The inclination to this kind of prophecy seems never to have been more generally spread among the masses of the people than at this time. Apart from the Greek oracular deities, there were the oriental deities whose worship was nearly everywhere combined with predictions. In most of the famous sanctuaries the most various forms of prophecy were represented, and the stranger they were, the better they were liked. In the case of the oral oracles the responses in earlier times were for the most part composed in verse: on the decay of poetic productiveness, they began to take the form of prose, or of passages from the poets, the Greeks generally adopting lines of Homer or Eurïpïdēs, the Italians, lines of Vergil. The public declaration of oracles ended with the official extermination of paganism under Thĕŏdŏsĭus at the end of the 4th century.

Orchēstic. *See* DANCING.

Orchēstra. The space of the Greek theatre situated in front of the stage, in which the chorus went through its evolutions. In the Roman theatre it was absorbed in the area occupied by the audience. (*See* THEATRE.)

Orcus. In Roman mythology, a peculiar divinity of the dead, a creation of the popular beliefs. He carried men off to the lower world, and kept the dead imprisoned there. His name, like that of the Greek Hādēs, served to denote the lower world. (*Cp.* DIS PATER.)

Ōrĕads (Gr. *Ōreiădĕs*). The mountain Nymphs. (*See* NYMPHS.)

Ōreibăsĭos (Lat. *Orĭbăsĭus*) of Pergămum, physician and adviser of the emperor Julian the Apostate, after whose death (363 A.D.) he was banished by his successors Vălens and Vălentīnĭānus, and lived among the barbarians. He was afterwards recalled. He seems not to have died before the beginning of the 5th century. At the suggestion of Julian he composed, on the plan of abstracts from earlier works, a medical treatise (*Sÿnăgōgē Iătrĭkē*) in 72 books, of which some 22 are preserved, partly in the Greek original and partly in a Latin rendering. He himself prepared for his son Eustăthĭus a conspectus (*Synopsis*) of the larger work

in 9 books, only part of which has been published.

Ōrestēs. The youngest child and only son of Agamemnōn and Clytæmnēstra. In Homer [*Od.* iii 306] it is only stated that in the eighth year after the murder of his father, who was never able to see him again after his return home, he came back from Athens and took a bloody vengeance on Ægisthus and his mother. In later legend he is described as doomed to death, but saved from his father's murderers by his nurse Arsĭnŏē or his sister Electra, and brought by a trusty slave to Phănŏtē on Parnassus to king Strŏphĭus, husband of Anaxĭbĭa, the sister of Agamemnon. Here he lives in the most intimate friendship with Pÿlădēs, his protector's son, until his twentieth year, and then comes with his friend, by Apollo's direction, to Mÿcēnæ, and in concert with Electra effects the deed of vengeance. This deed is represented in Homer as one indisputably glorious and everywhere commended; but in later legend Orestes is, after his mother's murder, attacked by delusions and harassed by the Erīnÿēs. According to Æschÿlus, in his *Eumĕnĭdĕs*, the Furies do not suffer him to escape even after he is purified in the Delphian temple. Acting on the advice of Apollo, he presents himself at Athens before the court of the Areŏpăgus, which on this occasion is instituted by Athēnē for the trial of homicide. The goddesses of vengeance appear as prosecutors, Apollo as his witness and advocate, and on the trial resulting in an equality of votes, Athene with her voting pebble decides in his favour. According to Eurĭpĭdēs, in his *Iphigenĭa among the Tauri*, Orestes goes with Pylades (as in Æschylus) by Apollo's advice, to the Tauric Chersonese, in order to fetch thence the image of Artemis which had fallen from heaven in former times. The friends are captured upon landing, and according to the custom of the country, are to be sacrificed to Artemis, when the priestess, Iphĭgĕnĭa (*q.v.*), and Orestes recognise one another as sister and brother, and escape to Greece with the image of the goddess. According to the Peloponnesian myth, Orestes spent the time of his delusion in Arcadia [*Pausanias*, viii 5 § 4], and after he had on one occasion in a fit of frenzy bitten off a finger, the Eumenides appeared to him in a dream, in white robes, as a token of reconciliation. After he is cured, he places himself, by the murder of Alētēs, Ægisthus' son, in possession of his father's dominion, Mÿcēnæ, and marries his sister Electra to Pylades. Hermĭŏnē, daughter of Mĕnĕlāus, had been betrothed to himself, but during his wanderings she was carried off by Achilles' son Nĕoptŏlĕmus. After Orestes had slain the latter at Delphi, he married Hermione, and through her came into possession of Sparta. His son by this marriage was Tīsămĕnus. He died of a serpent's bite in Arcadia, and was buried at Tĕgĕa: his reputed remains were afterwards, by the direction of the oracle, brought to Sparta [*Herod.* i 67].

Orgĕŏnĕs. The Athenian term for the members of a society for the observance of a divine cult not belonging to the State religion, especially those who, without belonging to the old families (*see* GENNETÆ), nevertheless like them formed a family union originating in descent from the same ancestors, and possessed a special family worship. The adoption of the children of families belonging to such a religious society occurred, as with the Gennētæ, at the same time as their enrolment into the phratries at the feast of the Apătūria (*q.v.*).

Orgies (Gr. *orgĭa*). The ordinary Greek term for ceremonies, generally connected with the worship of a divinity, but especially secret religious customs to which only the initiated were admitted, and equivalent in meaning to "mysteries." It was customary to designate as Orgies the mysteries of the worship of Dĭonȳsus in particular. These were sometimes celebrated with wild and extravagant rites.

Orībăsĭus. *See* OREIBASIOS.

Orīōn. (1) A mythical hunter of gigantic size and strength and of great beauty. He was the son of Hȳrĭeūs of Hȳrĭa in Bœotia; or (according to another account) of Pŏseidōn, who gave him the power to walk over the sea as well as over dry land. He is sometimes represented as an earthborn being.

Many marvellous exploits were ascribed to him: for instance, the building of the huge harbour-dam of Zanclē (Messana) and the upheaving of the promontory of Pĕlōrum in Sicily [Diodorus, iv 85]. After his wife Sīdē had been cast into Hādēs by Hērā for having dared to compare herself to that goddess in beauty, he crossed the sea to Chios in order to woo Mĕrŏpē, the daughter of Œnŏpĭōn, son of Dionȳsus and Ariadnē. As he violated her in a fit of intoxication, Œnopion blinded him in his sleep and cast him out upon the seashore. He groped his way, however, to Lemnos and the smithy of Hēphæstus, set one of the latter's work-

men, Cĕdălĭōn, upon his shoulders, and bade him guide him to the place where the sun rose; and in the radiance thereof his eyesight returned. Œnopion hid himself beneath the earth to escape his vengeance. Eōs, smitten with love for Orion, carried him off to Dēlŏs (Ortȳgia), and there lived with him, until the gods in their anger caused him to be killed by Artĕmis with her arrows. According to another story, Artemis shot him in Chios or Crete, either for having challenged her to a contest with the quoit, or for having endeavoured to outrage her whilst engaged in the chase. Another legend relates that the earth, terrified by his threat that he could root out every wild creature from Crete, sent forth a scorpion, which killed him with its sting. His tomb was shown in Tănăgra. In Homer [*Od.* xi 572] Odysseus sees him in the lower world as a shade still pursuing with his club of bronze the creatures whom he slew in former times. As regards the legend of his being placed among the stars, *see* PLEIADES. The morning rising of his constellation, which was already known as early as Homer [*Il.* xviii 488] denoted the beginning of summer, his midnight rising denoted the season of the vintage, and his late rising the beginning of winter and its storms. Whilst he sinks, the Scorpion, which was likewise placed among the stars, rises above the horizon. Sirius (Gr. *Seirĭŏs*), the star of the dog-days, is described, as early as Homer [*Il.* xxii 29], as the dog of Orion. Of his daughters Mĕnippē and Mētĭŏchē, it was related that they were endowed by Aphrŏdītē with beauty and by Athēnē with skill in the art of weaving; and when, on the occasion of a pestilence ravaging Bœotia, the sacrifice of two virgins was required by the oracle, they voluntarily, to save their country, pierced their throats with their shuttles. As a reward for their voluntary sacrifice, Persĕphŏnē and Pluto changed them into comets; while a sanctuary was built in their honour at Orchŏmĕnus, and expiatory offerings were yearly paid to them.

(2) A Greek scholar born at Thebes in Egypt, who taught about the middle of the 5th century A.D. at Alexandria and Constantinople. He is the author of a somewhat important etymological lexicon, and an anthology of maxims collected from the old Greek poets.

Orīthȳīa. Daughter of Erechtheus, king of Athens, wife of Bŏrĕās, mother of Călăis and Zētēs. (*Cp.* BOREAS.)

Orosius of Spain, a presbyter in Lusitania. About 417 A.D., and at the wish of Augustine, whom he had sought out in Africa, he composed his history against the heathen (*Histŏrĭæ contra Pāgānōs*) in seven books, the first attempt at a Christian universal history, from Adam to 410 A.D. The theory of his work is, that the whole history of mankind is directed by the one God who created them, and it aims at refuting the charges brought against Christianity by showing, that it was not to Christianity and the abolition of the heathen religion that the calamities of the time were due, but that such calamities had always existed, and to a still greater degree before Christian times. His chief authority is Justin, besides whom he mainly used Livy, Tăcĭtus, Suetōnius, and Eutrŏpius. His view of the four kingdoms of the world, Babylon, Macedon, Carthage, and Rome, prevailed throughout the whole of the Middle Ages.

Orpheūs, the famous mythical poet, son of Œagrus and the Muse Callĭŏpē, who gave birth to him on the banks of the Hebrus in Thrace. Such was his power in song, that he could move trees and rocks and tame wild beasts thereby. When his wife, the Nymph Eurÿdĭcē, died of a serpent's bite (*see* ARISTÆUS), he descended into the lower world, and so moved Persĕphŏnē by the music of his song, that she permitted him to take Eurydice back with him to the upper world, on condition of his not looking round during his passage through the realm of the dead. In spite of this, his impatience led him to gaze back, and Eurydice had to return for ever to Hādēs [Vergil, *Georg.* iv 453–527]

Mythology describes him as taking part in the Argonautic expedition, and represents him as encouraging and assisting his comrades by his song on many occasions, especially while they were passing the Sirens. He was torn in pieces upon Hæmus by the Thracian Mænads, either for having opposed the celebration of their orgies, or because, after losing Eurydice, he conceived a hatred of all other women. His scattered limbs were buried by the Muses in the district of Pĭĕrĭa on Olympus; but his head and lyre, which the Mænads had cast into the Hebrus, floated down into the sea, and across it to Lesbos, the isle of poets in later days; and here they were buried at Mēthymna [Lucian, *Adv. Indoctum*, 11]. The name of Orpheus (apparently not known to Homer and Hesiod) was assumed by the mystic and religious sect of the Orphĭci, who claimed

him as their founder. They arose at some time after the 6th century B.C. In opposition to the received views concerning the gods, and especially concerning the state of the soul after death, and in close connexion with Oriental and Egyptian ideas, they taught the necessity of a purification of a soul by religious consecration and the use of the methods of expiation alleged to have been made known by Orpheus. They declared that Orpheus was the most ancient of the poets, living long before Homer, and attributed to him a number of poems of mythical

purport. Out of this apocryphal Orphic literature there have been preserved from the time of the decay of paganism : (1) an epic poem on the exploits of Orpheus during the Argonautic expedition (*Argōnautĭca*) ; (2) eighty-eight songs of consecration or hymns, prayers to various gods and dæmons, written in hexameter verse and in a bombastic style, intended to be recited at bloodless offerings of incense ; (3) an epic poem upon the magical powers of precious stones (*Lĭthĭca*).

Orsĭlŏchĭa. *See* IPHIGENIA.

Oscan Plays. *See* ATELLANA.

Oschŏphŏria. At Athens a festival in honour of Dionysus. (*See further* DIONYSIA, 1.)

Osīris. An Egyptian god, who, with his sister and wife Isis (*q.v.*), enjoyed in Egypt the most general worship of all the gods. He is the male god of the fructification of the land. From him comes every blessing and all life; he gives light and health; he causes the Nile to overflow with its fertilizing waters, and all things to continue in their established order. He is always represented in human shape and with a human head (*see* cut). His hue, as that of a god who bestows life, is green; his sacred tree is the ever-green tamarisk. The Greeks identified him with Dĭonȳsus. Originally he ruled as king over Egypt, where he introduced agriculture, morality, and the worship of the gods, until his brother Tȳphōn (Set) contrived by deceit to shut him up in a chest and put him to death by pouring in molten lead. The murderer cast the chest into the Nile, which carried it into the sea. After long search the mourning Isis found the chest on the coast of Phœnicia at Byblus, and carefully concealed it. Nevertheless Typhon discovered it in the night, and cut the corpse up into fourteen pieces, which he scattered in all directions. Isis, however, collected them again, and buried them in Philæ or Abȳdus, in Upper Egypt. When Hōrus, the son of Osiris and Isis, grew up, he took vengeance upon Typhon when, after a most obstinate struggle, he had defeated him in battle. Although Osiris lived no longer upon the earth, he was ever regarded as the source of life. In the upper world he continues to live and work by the fresh power of his youthful son Horus, and in the lower world, of which he is king, the spirits of those who are found to be just are awakened by him to new life. His hue as ruler of the lower world is black, his robes white, his symbol an eye opened wide as a sign of his restoration to the light of day.

Osiris, by his ever-renewed incarnation in the form of the black bull Apis, the symbol of generative power, assures for the Egyptians the endurance of his favour, and the consequent continuance of their

OSIRIS.

life in this world and the next. In this incarnation he is called *Osarhapi* (Osiris-Apis), the origin of the Greek Sěrāpis (*q.v.*) or Sarapis. The fortunes of Osiris were celebrated in magnificent annual festivals connected with mourning ceremonies, in which the Egyptians, as is observed by the ancients [*e.g.* Plutarch, *De Iside et Osiride*, 32, and Ælian, *De Nat. Animalium* 10, 46], lamented in Osiris the subsidence of the Nile, the cessation of the cool north wind (whose place was taken for a time by the hot wind Typhon), the decay of vegetation, and the shortening of the length of the day.

Ostium. The entrance hall in the Roman dwelling-house. (*See* HOUSE.)

Ostracism (Gr. *ostrăkismŏs* ; i.e. vote by potsherd). A mode of judgment by the people practised in various Greek states [Argos, Měgără, Mīlētus], and especially at Athens, by which persons whose presence appeared dangerous to liberty were banished for a certain period, without, however, thereby suffering any loss in reputation or property. Ostracism was introduced at Athens in 509 B.C. [it was applied (amongst others) to Thěmistŏclēs, Aristīdēs, Cīmōn, and Alcĭbĭădēs], and was last exercised in 417 against a demagogue, one Hyperbŏlus, whose insignificance made the measure ridiculous, and so produced its abolition [Thuc. viii 73; Plutarch, *Nicias* 11, *Alcibiades* 13]. Every year the question was put to the people, whether the measure appeared necessary: if they so decided (and it was only exceptionally that there was occasion for it), the citizens who possessed the franchise assembled in the market-place, and each wrote upon a sherd (*ostrăkŏn*) the name of the person whose banishment he deemed desirable. The man whose name was found upon not less than 6,000 sherds had to leave the country in ten days at latest, for ten or (later) five years. He could, however, at any time be recalled by a decree of the people; and the question, as before, was decided by not less than 6,000 votes [Aristotle, *Pol.* iii 13 § 15, 17 § 7, v 3 § 3, *Const. Athens*, 22 ; Plutarch, *Aristid.* 7. *Cp.* Grote's *History of Greece*, chap. xxxi.].

Ŏtus. One of the two Alōădæ (*q.v.*).

Ŏvātio. The Roman term for a minor form of triumph. (*See further* TRIUMPH.)

Ŏvĭdĭus Nāso (*Publius*). A Roman poet, born March 21st, 43 B.C., at Sulmo (now *Solmona*) in the country of the Pæligni, son of a wealthy Roman of an old equestrian family. He came at an early age to Rome, to be educated as a pleader, and enjoyed the tuition of the most famous rhetoricians of the time, Porcius Latro and Arellius Fuscus. It was not long before the instinct for poetry awoke in him with such power that it needed all his father's resolution to keep him to his legal studies; his oratorical exercises were simply poems in prose, as is testified by one of his fellow students, the elder Sĕnĕcă [*Controv.* ii 10, 8]. After he had visited Greece and Asia to complete his education, he entered into political life at his father's desire, and filled several subordinate offices. But he soon withdrew again from public business, partly on the ground of his health and partly from an inclination to idleness, and lived only for poetry, in the society of the poets of his day, among whom he was especially intimate with Propertius. He came into note as a poet by a tragedy called the *Mĕdĕa*, which is now lost, but is much praised by ancient literary critics, and about the same time he produced a series of amatory, and in parts extremely licentious, poems.

When little more than a mere boy, as he says himself [*Tristia*, iv 10, 69], he was given a wife by his father; but this marriage, like a second one, ended in a divorce. He derived more satisfaction, as well as the advantage of contact with the court and with men of the highest distinction, from a third marriage, with a widow of noble family and high connexions. To her influence, perhaps, should be referred the fact that he turned his attention to more important and more serious works. He had almost completed his best known work, the *Mĕtămorphōsēs*, when suddenly, in 9 A.D., he was banished for life by Augustus to Tŏmi on the Black Sea, near the mouths of the Danube. The cause for this severity on the part of the emperor is unknown; Ovid himself admits that there was a fault on his side, but only an error, not a crime [*Tristia* i 3, 37]. At all events, the matter directly affected Augustus; and as Ovid describes his eyes as the cause of his misfortune, it is conjectured that he had been an unintentional eye-witness of some offence on the part of the frivolous granddaughter of the prince, the younger Julia, and had neglected to inform the emperor of the matter. His indecent amatory poems, to which he also points as the source of the emperor's displeasure, can at most only have been used as a plausible excuse in the eyes of the public, as they had been published more than ten years before.

After a perilous voyage Ovid reached the place of his exile in the winter of 10–11 A.D.; and there, far from his wife and from his only daughter, who had inherited the poetic talent of her father, far from his friends and all intercourse with men of genius, he had to pass the last years of his life in desolation among the barbarous Gĕtæ. Even in his exile his poetic talent did not fail him. It was then that he composed his poems of lamentation, entitled the *Tristia*, and his letters from Pontus, touching proofs of his grief, though also of his failing powers. His ceaseless prayers and complaints had succeeded in softening Augustus, when the latter died. All his efforts to gain forgiveness or alleviation of his condition met with no response from Tiberius, and he was compelled to close his life, broken-hearted and in exile, 17 A.D.

His extant works are (1) Love poems (*Amōrēs*), published about 14 B.C., in five books, and again about 2 B.C. in three books. The latter edition is the one we possess; some of its forty-nine elegies depict in a very sensual way the poet's life, the centre of which is the unknown Cŏrinna. (2) Letters (*Epistŭlæ*), also called *Hĕrŏĭdĕs*, rhetorical declamations in the form of love-letters sent by heroines to their husbands or lovers, twenty-one in number; the last six of these, however, and the fourteenth, are considered spurious. (3) Methods for beautifying the face (*Mĕdĭcāmĭna Făcĭĕi*), advice to women respecting the art of the toilette; this piece has come down to us in an incomplete form. (4) The Art of Love (*Ars Amandi* or *Amātōria*), in three books, published about 2 B.C., advice to men (books 1 and 2) and women (book 3) as to the methods of contracting a love-affair and insuring its continuance, a work as frivolous as it is original and elaborate. (5) Cures for Love (*Rĕmĕdĭa Amōris*), the pendant to the previous work, and no less offensive in substance and tone. (6) The fifteen books of the Transformations (*Metamorphoses*), his only considerable work. It is composed in hexameter verse; the material is borrowed from Greek and (to a less extent) from Roman sources, being a collection of legends of transformations, very skilfully combining jest and earnest in motley alternations, and extending from chaos to the apotheosis of Cæsar. When it was completed and had received the last touches, the work was cast into the flames by Ovid in his first despair at banishment, but was afterwards rewritten from other copies

(7) A Calendar of Roman Festivals (*Fasti*), begun in the last years before his banishment, and originally in twelve books, corresponding to the number of the months. Of these only six are preserved, probably because Ovid had not quite completed them at Rome, and had not the means to do so at Tomi. It was originally intended for dedication to Augustus. After Augustus' death the poet began to revise it, with a view to its dedication to Germānĭcus; he did not, however, proceed with his revision beyond the first book. It contains in elegiac metre the most important celestial phenomena and the festivals of each month, with a description of their celebration and an account of their origin according to the Italian legends. (8) Poems of Lamentation (*Tristia*), to his family, to his friends, and to Augustus, belonging to the years 9–13 A.D., in five books; the first of these was written while he was still on his journey to Tomi. (9) Letters from Pontus (*Epistŭlæ ex Ponto*), in four books, only distinguished from the previous poems by their epistolary form. (10) *Ibis*, an imitation of the poem of the same name by Callĭmăchus, who had attacked under this name Apollōnius of Rhodes, consisting of imprecations on a faithless friend at Rome, written in the learned and obscure style of the Alexandrian

poets. (11) A short fragment of a didactic poem on the fish in the Black Sea (*Hălĭeutĭca*), written in hexameters. Besides these Ovid wrote during his exile numerous poems which have been lost, among them a eulogy of the deceased Augustus in the Getic tongue, a sufficient proof of the strength of his bent and talent for poetry. In both of these respects he is distinguished above all other Roman poets. Perhaps no one ever composed with less exertion; at the same time no one ever used so important a faculty for so trivial a purpose. His poetry is for the most part simply entertaining; in this kind of writing he proves his mastery by his readiness in language and metre, by his unwearied powers of invention, by his ever-ready wit, elegance, and charm, though, on the other hand, he is completely wanting in deep feeling and moral earnestness. By his talent Ovid (as well as Vergil) has had great influence on the further development of Roman poetry, especially with regard to metre. Many imitated his style so closely, that their poems were actually attributed to himself. Among these, besides a number of *Hĕrōĭdĕs* (see above), we have the *Nux*, the nut tree's complaint of the ill-treatment it met with, a poem in elegiac verse, which was at all events written in the time of Ovid.

P

Păcātus (*Lătīnus Drĕpănius*). A Roman rhetorician of Burdĭgăla (*Bordeaux*), a younger contemporary and friend of the poet Ausonius. We possess from his pen a panegyric on the emperor Thĕŏdŏsĭus the Great, delivered before the Senate at Rome in 389 B.C. It is distinguished beyond the other speeches of this class by a certain vigour of thought, and is also of value as an historical authority.

Păcŭvĭus (*Marcus*). The Roman tragedian, born about 220 B.C. at Brundĭsĭum, son of Ennius' sister, and pupil of the poet. He spent most of his life at Rome, where he gained his livelihood as a dramatic poet and as a painter. In his old age he returned to Brundisium, and died there, at the age of ninety, about 130 B.C. He is the first Roman dramatist who confined himself to the composing of tragedies. Titles and fragments of some thirteen of his imitations of Greek plays are preserved, as well as fragments of a *prætexta* (*q.v.*) entitled *Paulus*, whose hero was probably the victor

of Pydna, Æmĭlĭus Paulus. If this small number justifies any opinion on his poetical activity, he was far less productive than his predecessor Ennius and his successor Accius. Nevertheless, he and Accius were considered the most important tragedians of Rome. In the judgment of literary critics, who followed the traditions of the Ciceronian age, he was preferred to Accius for finish and learning, but Accius excelled him in fire and natural power [Horace, *Ep.* ii 1, 55, 56; Quintilian, x 1, 97; see Prof. Nettleship, "On Literary Criticism in Latin Antiquity," in *Journal of Philology*, xviii 263]. His style was praised for its copiousness, dignity, and stateliness, but Cicero [*Brutus*, 258] declines to give him credit for pure and genuine Latinity. Even in Cicero's time, however, the revival of his plays was often welcomed by Roman audiences.

Pæan (Gr. *Paian*, properly *Paiēōn*, the "healer," "helper"). In Homer [*Il.* v 401, 899], the physician of the Olympian gods;

then an epithet of gods who grant recovery and deliverance, especially of Apollo. The pæan, which appears in Homer [*Il.* i 473, xxii 391], was connected originally with Apollo and his sister Artĕmis. It was a solemn song for several voices, either praying for the averting of evil and for rescue, or giving thanks for help vouchsafed. The name was, however, also used in an extended sense for invocations to other gods. The pæan was struck up by generals before the battle and by armies on the march against the enemy, as well as after the victory. Similarly it was sounded when the fleet sailed out of harbour. Pæans were sung at entertainments between the meal and the carousal, and eventually also at public funerals.

Pædăgŏgus (Gr. *Paidăgōgŏs*, lit. "boy-leader"). The name among the Greeks for the slave who had the duty of looking after the son of his master whilst in boyhood, instructing him in certain rules of good manners, and attending him whenever he went out, especially to school and to the *pălœstra* and *gymnăsium*. With the Romans in earlier times it was an old slave or freedman who had a similar duty as *custos;* but after it became the custom to have even children taught to speak Greek, his place was filled by a Greek slave, who bore the Greek name and had the special duty of instructing his pupils in Greek.

Pædŏnŏmus (Gr. *Paidŏnŏmŏs*). At Sparta, the overseer of the education of the young. (*See* EDUCATION, 1.)

Pædŏtrĭbēs. In Greece, the master who imparted gymnastic instruction in the *palœstra.* (*See* EDUCATION, 1.)

Pænŭla (*Latin*). A mantle of shaggy frieze or leather, thick and dark-coloured, without sleeves, buttoned or stitched up in front, in the direction of its length. A hood (*cŭcullus*) was generally fastened on to it, and drawn over the head. It was chiefly worn by people of low rank and slaves, but also by the higher classes, and even by ladies, in bad weather, on a journey, and in the country.

Pæōnius. (1) A Greek sculptor of Mendē in Thrace. About 436 B.C. he was employed in the decoration of the temple of Zeus in Olympia. [According to Pausanias, v 10 § 6], he was the sculptor of the marble groups in the front, or eastern, pediment of the temple, representing the preparations for the chariot-race between Pĕlops and Œnŏmäus. (*See* OLYMPIAN GAMES, fig. 1.) Important portions of these have been

brought to light by the German excavations. He was also the sculptor of the figure of Nīkē, more than life-size, dedicated by the Messenians [*ib.* v 26 § 1], which has been restored to us by the same means. With the exception of the head, it is in fairly good preservation (*see* cut).

(2) *See* EUTROPIUS.

*NIKE OF PÆONIUS.
(Olympia.)
For Grüttner's restoration, see Mrs. Mitchell's *Selections from Ancient Sculpture*, pl. 14, 1.

Pägänälia. In Italy, a movable festival of the old village communities (*see* PAGUS), celebrated after the winter-sowing in January, on two days separated by an interval of a week. On this occasion a pregnant sow was sacrificed to Tellūs or to Cĕrēs, who at a later period was worshipped together with Tellus.

Pägus. In Italy, in ancient times, the *pagus* was a country district with scattered hamlets (*vīci*). The same name was given to its fortified centre, which protected the sanctuaries of the district and served as a refuge in time of war. The separate districts were members of a larger community. After cities had developed out of the places where the people of these districts assembled the *pāgi* were either completely merged in their *terrĭtōrium*, or continued to exist merely as geographical districts, without importance for administration, or as subordinate village communities. In Rome the earliest population consisted of the *montānī* the inhabitants of the seven hills of the city, and the *pāgāni*, the inhabitants of the level ground of the city. Out of the two Servius Tullius made the four city tribes. The country tribes doubtless arose similarly out of *pagi*, the names of which were in some cases transferred to them. Like the old division into *pagani* and *montani*, the old districts under the authority of *măgistri* long continued to exist for sacred purposes. They had their special guardian deities, temples, and rites, which survived even the introduction of Christianity. To the district festivals belonged especially the *Pāgānālĭa (q.v.)*, the *Ambarvālĭa (q.v.)*, at which the festal procession carefully traversed the old boundaries of the district; and, lastly, the *Termĭnālĭa (see* TERMINUS).

Painting. Among the Greeks painting developed into an independent art much later than sculpture, though it was used very early for decorative purposes. This is proved by the evidence of painted vases belonging to the ages of the most primitive civilization, and by the mural paintings discovered by Schliemann at Tīryns. The scanty notices in ancient authors respecting the first discoveries in this art connect it with historical persons, and not with mythical names, as in the case of sculpture. Thus it is said [by Pliny, *N. H.* xxxv 16] that [either Phĭlŏclēs, the Egyptian, or] Clĕanthēs of Corinth was the first to draw outline sketches; that Tĕlĕphānēs of Sĭcўōn developed them further; that Ecphantus of Corinth introduced painting in single tints (monochrome); and that Eumārus of Athens (in the second half of the 6th century) distinguished man and woman by giving the one a darker, the other a lighter colour. Cĭmōn of Clĕōnæ is mentioned as the originator of artistic drawing in profile [*cătăgrăpha, hoc est oblīquās ĭmăgĭnēs,* Pliny xxxv 56, *cp.* 90]. It is further said of him that he gave variety to the face by making it look backwards or upwards or downwards, and freedom to the limbs by duly rendering the joints; also that he was the first to represent the veins of the human body, and to make the folds of the drapery fall more naturally [*ib.* 56].

Painting did not, however, make any decided advance until the middle of the 5th century B.C. This advance was chiefly due to PŎLYGNŌTUS of Thăsŏs, who painted at Athens. Among other claims to distinction, it is attributed to him that he gave greater variety of expression to the face, which hitherto had been rigidly severe. His works, most of them large compositions rich in figures, give evidence of a lofty and

poetic conception; they appear to have been, in great part, mural paintings for decorating the interior of public buildings [Pausănĭas, x 25–31; i 15, 22 § 6]. The colours were first applied in uniform tints so as to fill in the outlines, and fresh lines and touches were then added to indicate where the limbs and muscles began, and the folds of the garments. The drawing and the combination of colours were the chief considerations; light and shade were wanting, and no attention was paid to perspective. It is doubtful whether at this early time, besides mural paintings (executed *al fresco* on carefully smoothed stucco-priming with plain water-colours), there were any pictures on panels, such as afterwards became common; but we may fairly assume it. These were painted on wooden panels *in tempera;* i.e. with colours mixed with various kinds of distemper, such as gum or size, to make them more adhesive.

In the same century the *encaustic* method of painting was discovered, though not elaborated till the following century. [The process, as described in Roman times by Vitrūvius (vii 9), was as follows: "The medium used was melted white wax (*cĕră pŭnĭcă*), mixed with oil to make it more fluid. The pot containing the wax was kept over a brazier, while the painter was at work, in order to keep the melted wax from solidifying. The stucco itself was prepared by a coating of hot wax applied with a brush, and it was polished by being rubbed with a wax candle, and finally with a clean linen cloth. After the picture was painted, the wax colours were fixed, partly melted into the stucco, and blended with the wax of the ground by the help of a charcoal brazier, which was held close to the surface of the painting, and gradually moved over its whole extent" (Middleton's *Ancient Rome in* 1888, p. 417).] The encaustic method had several advantages over painting *in tempera :* it lasted longer and was more proof against damp, while the colouring was much brighter; on the other hand, it was much more laborious and slow, which explains the fact that the majority of encaustic paintings were of small size.

While the pictures of Polygnotus certainly did not deceive by too much truth to nature, it was [his younger contemporary] the Samian ĂGĂTHARCHUS who practised scene-painting (Gr. *skĕnŏgrăphĭa*) at Athens, and thus gave an impulse to the attempt at illusory effect and the use of perspective. [He painted the scenery for a play of Æschўlus (Vitruv. vii *præf.* 10), and decorated the interior of the house of Alcĭbĭădēs (Andŏcĭdēs, *Alcib.* 17).] The Athenian APOLLŎDŌRUS (about B.C. 420) was the actual founder of an entirely new artistic style, which strove to effect illusion by means of the resources of painting. [He was the first, says Pliny, to give his pictures the appearance of reality; the first to bring the brush into just repute (*l.c.* 60).] He also led the way in the proper manage-

torial representation, rendering on a flat surface the relief and variety of nature, and the consequent attainment of the greatest possible illusion. Its principal representatives were ZEUXIS of Hērăclēa and PARRHĂSĬUS of Ephesus; TĪMANTHĒS also produced remarkable works, though not an adherent of the same school. It was opposed by the *Sicyonian* school, founded by Eupompus of Sĭcўōn, and developed by Pamphĭlus of Amphĭpŏlĭs, which aimed at greater precision of technical training, very

(1) *ACHILLES DELIVERING BRISEIS TO THE HERALDS.
(House of the Tragic Poet, Pompeii.)

ment of the fusion of colours and their due gradation in different degrees of light and shade [Pliny, *l.c.* 60]. [It was to this that he owed his title of shadow-painter (*skĭagrăphŏs:* Hēsўchĭus on *skia*).]

The *Attic* school flourished till about the end of the 5th century, when this art was for some time neglected at Athens, but made another important advance in the towns of Asia Minor, especially at Ephesus. The principal merits of this, the *Ionic* school, consist in richer and more delicate colouring, a more perfect system of pic-

careful and characteristic drawing, and a sober and effective colouring [Pliny, *l.c.* 75, 76]. PAUSĬAS, a member of this school, invented the art of foreshortening and of painting on vaulted ceilings, besides perfecting the encaustic art, which was much more favourable for purposes of illusion and picturesque effectiveness than painting *in tempera* [*ib.* 123–127]. Greek painting reached its summit in the works of APELLĒS of Cōs, in the second half of the 4th century; he knew how to combine the merits of the Ionian and the Sicyonian schools, the perfect grace of the former with the severe accuracy of the latter.

After him the most famous artist was PRŌTŎGĔNĔS of Caunŏs. The following contemporaries, some older and some younger than himself, deserve also to be mentioned: Nĭcŏmăchus and Aristīdēs of Thebes, Euphrānŏr of Corinth, Nīcīăs of Athens, the Egyptian Antĭphĭlus, Thĕŏn of Sămŏs, and Aĕtīŏn. After the age of Alexander, the art of painting was characterized by a striving after naturalism, combined with a predilection for the representation of common, every-day scenes, and of still-life. This branch of painting was also carried to great perfection, and Pīræīcus was the most celebrated for it. Among painters of the loftier style the last noteworthy artist was TĬMŎMĂCHUS of Byzantium. [For the ancient authorities on the history of Painting, *see* Overbeck's *Schrift-quellen;* comp. Brunn's *Künstler-geschichte*, and Woermann's *History of Painting*, bk. ii.]

Among the *Romans* a few solitary names of early painters are mentioned, for instance, Făbĭus Pictor and the poet Păcŭvĭus [Pliny, xxxv 19]; but nothing is known as to the value of their paintings, which

decoration [Vitruv. vii 5]. Indeed the love of display peculiar to the Romans, which had led them gradually to accumulate the principal works of the old Greek masters at Rome as ornaments for their public and private edifices, brought about an extra-

(2) * STILL-LIFE.
(Pompeii.)

ordinary development of decorative art, attested by the numerous mural paintings that have been found in Italy, chiefly at Pompeii and Herculaneum.

These paintings were mostly executed

(3) * ORPHEUS.
(*Casa di Orfeo*, Pompeii.)

served to decorate buildings. The way in which landscapes were represented by a certain S. Tadius [or Ludius (?), *ib.* 116; the best MS has *studio*] in the reign of Augustus is mentioned as a novelty. These landscapes were mainly for purposes of

al fresco on damp stucco, seldom with colours *in tempera* on the dry surface. The principal subjects represented are figures from the world of myth, such as Mænads, Centaurs, male and female, Satyrs, etc.; scenes from mythology and heroic legends, frequently copies of famous **Greek** originals [one of the best examples of which is *Achilles delivering Brīsēis to the Heralds* (*see* fig. 1)]; landscapes (fig. 5); still-life (fig. 2); animals (fig. 3); and also scenes from real life. (*See* also cuts under IPHIGENIA and VILLA.) From a technical point of view

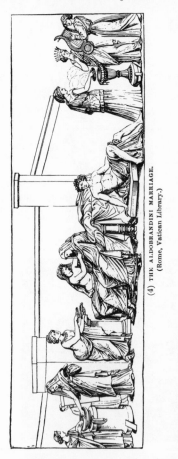

(4) THE ALDOBRANDINI MARRIAGE.
(Rome, Vatican Library.)

these works do not go beyond the limits of light decorative painting, and are especially wanting in correct perspective; but they show fine harmony, varied gradation, and delicate blending of colour, and frequently a surprising depth and sincerity of expression: qualities which must have charac-

terized the lost masterpieces of the ancient artists to a much more remarkable degree, and cannot but give us a very high idea of them. One of the finest mural paintings is that known as the *Aldobrandini Marriage* [discovered in 1606 near the Arch of Galliēnus, and] named after its first owner, Cardinal Aldobrandini, now in the Library of the Vatican at Rome. It is copied from an excellent Greek original, and represents, in the style of a relief, the preparations for a marriage (*see* fig. 4). ["It is composed," says Woermann in his *History of Painting*, i 115, "not pictorially, but yet with taste. It exhibits several individual motives of much beauty; its colouring is soft and harmonious; and it is instinct with that placid and serious charm which belongs only to the antique. In technical execution, however, the work is insignificant, and in no way rises above the ordinary handling of the Roman house-decorator in similar subjects." The Vatican Library also possesses an important series of landscapes from the *Odyssey*, found during the excavations on the Esquiline in 1848–1850. Landscapes of this kind are mentioned by Vitruvius, vii 5, among the subjects with which corridors used to be decorated in the good old times. They represent the adventure with the Læstrȳgŏnĕs (fig. 5), the story of Circē, and the visit of Odysseus to the realm of Hādēs, thus illustrating a continuous portion of the poem, *Od.* x 80–xi 600. The predominant colours are a yellowish brown and a greenish blue, and the pictures are divided from one another by pilasters of a brilliant red. They furnish interesting examples of the landscape-painting of the last days of the Republic or the first of the Empire, and, in point of importance, stand alone among all the remains of ancient painting (Woermann, *l.c.*, and *Die Odyssee-landschaften vom Esquilin*, with chromolithographs of all the six landscapes). On mosaic-painting and vase-painting, *see* MOSAICS and VASES.]

[The processes of painting are represented in several works of ancient art, *e.g.* in three mural paintings from Pompeii (Schreiber's *Bilderatlas*, viii 2, 4, and ix 3; *see* SCULPTURE, fig. 18). Even some of the implements and materials used by artists have been discovered. Thus, in 1849, at St. Médard-des-Près in the Vendée, a grave was opened, containing a female skeleton, surrounded by eighty small vessels of glass, in most of which remains of ancient pigments were still preserved. Besides these, there was a small cup of brown glass (fig. 6, *a*);

a knife of cedar-wood, with its blade reduced to rust (*b*); a small bronze box (*c*) with a movable lid and four partitions, holding materials for pigments; a mortar of alabaster, and a smaller one of bronze (*d*); also two small cylinders of amber and two brush-handles of bone. One of the glass vessels contained bits of resin; another, wax; a third, a mixture of both; a fourth, a mixture of lamp-black and wax, with

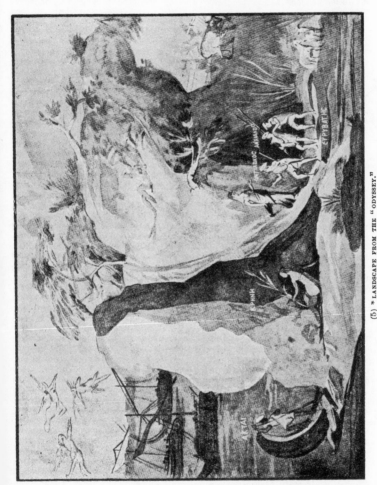

(5) * LANDSCAPE FROM THE "ODYSSEY."
The messengers of Odysseus meeting the daughter of Antiphătēs, king of the Læstrỹgŏnĕs (*Od.* x 87-110).
(Rome, Vatican Library.)

one or two elegant bronze spoons (*e*), either for removing colours from the palette, or for adding some liquid to mix them together; a small shovel, made of rock crystal, containing gold embedded in gum (*f*); and an oblong palette of basalt (*g*). There were traces of sebacic acid, possibly due to the presence of oil.

Our principal information about ancient pigments (Gr. *pharmăkă;* Lat. *mĕdĭcāmenta, pigmenta*) comes from Thĕŏphrastus (*De Lăpĭdĭbus*), Dīoscŏrĭdēs (v), Vitruvius (vii), and the elder Pliny (xxxiii and xxxv). It is observed by Cicero in the *Brutus* § 70, that only four colours were used by Pŏlȳgnōtus, Zeuxis, Tīmanthēs, and their contemporaries, as contrasted with their successors, Aëtĭŏn, Nīcŏmăchus, Prōtŏgĕnēs,

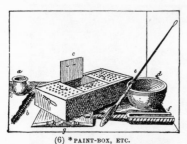

(6) *PAINT-BOX, ETC.

(First published by B. Fillon, *Description de la Villa et du Tombeau d'une Femme Artiste Gallo-romaine*, Fontenay, 1849.)

and Apellēs. Pliny (xxxv 50), who identified the colours as white (*mĕlĭnum*), yellow (*sil Attĭcum*), red (*Sĭnōpĭs Pontĭca*), and black (*ātrāmentum*), even places Aëtion, Nicomachus, Apelles, and Mĕlanthius under the same limitation. But it is hardly probable that such important colours as blue and green were dispensed with, even in the primitive art of Pŏlȳgnōtus; much less in the more advanced art of Zeuxis and his contemporaries; and least of all in that of Apelles and Protogenes. The earliest artists, however, may well have used comparatively few colours, and those of the simplest kind, the *cŏlōrēs austēri* of Pliny xxxv 30, as contrasted with the *colores flŏrĭdi*, such as vermilion, "Armenian blue," "dragon's blood," malachite green, indigo, and purple. These were characteristic of later developments of art, and were so costly that they were not paid for by the artists, but by those who gave them their commissions (*ib.* 44; Vitruv., vii 5, 8).

The pigments known to the ancients were as follows:

White. The pigment used in Greece was a "pipe-clay" called *mĕlĭnum* (Gr. *mēlĭăs*), found in veins in the island of Mēlŏs. It was not available for fresco-painting (Pliny, xxxv 49). A white earth of Eretria was employed by Nīcŏmăchus and Parrhăsius (*ib.* 38). A commoner pigment was the *crētă Sĕlĭnūsia* of Sĕlīnūs in Sicily, used for mural paintings (*ib.* 49, 194), and the *creta ānŭlāria*, made by mixing chalk with the glass composition worn in the rings of

the poor (*ib.* 48). For fresco-painting they used *părœtŏnium*, a hydrated silicate of magnesia, so called from a cliff on the African coast near Egypt (*ib.* 30), which in Rome was adulterated with *creta Cĭmōlia* (*ib.* 36). For other purposes they employed whitelead (Gr. *psimȳthĭŏn ;* Lat. *cērussa*), an artificial product, the finest sorts of which came from Rhodes, Corinth, and Sparta. It is carbonate of lead, and is still used under various names (*e.g.* ceruse). It is sold in its crude form as "Chemnitz or Vienna white," and mixed with sulphate of barium in "Dutch, Hamburg, and Venetian white."

Yellow. The pigments in use were yellow ochre and orpiment. The best kind of yellow ochre (Gr. *ōchrā ;* Lat. *sil*) was found in the mines of Laurīum. It was also found in Scȳros, Achaia, Gaul, Cappădŏcia, Cyprus, and Lȳdia. The Attic variety was first used by Pŏlȳgnōtus and Mīcōn ; it was afterwards preferred for the high lights, while the kinds from Scyros and Lydia were reserved for the shadows (*ib.* xxxiii 158–160, xxxvii 179). It is a diluted brown ochre or hydrated peroxide of iron, being composed of oxygen, water, and iron, mixed with more or less clay. Orpiment, or trisulphide of arsenic (Gr. *arsĕnĭcŏn ;* Lat. *auripigmentum*), was of two kinds : (1) of a golden yellow, from Mȳsia on the coast of the Hellespont; and (2) a duller kind, from Pontus and Cappadocia (Dioscorides v 120). It could not be used for frescoes (Pliny xxxv 49). Yellow ochre and orpiment (under the name of "king's or Chinese yellow") are still in use.

Red. One of the oldest pigments was ruddle (Gr. *miltŏs ;* Lat. *rubrĭca*). This is a red earth coloured by sesquioxide of iron. In the Homeric age it was used to ornament the bows of ships. In later times the clay from which Greek vases were made owed its brilliant hue to the ruddle of Cape Cōlĭăs on the Attic coast (Suidas, s.v. *Kōlĭădŏs kĕrămĕcs*, and Pliny, xxxv 152). The best kind came from Cappadocia, by way of Sĭnōpē (hence called *Sĭnōpĭs Pontĭcă*, *ib.* 31, 36, xxxiii 117), or through Ephesus (Strabo, p. 540). It was also found in North Africa (*cĭcercŭlum*, Pliny, xxxv 32), especially in Egypt and at Carthage; also in Spain and the Balearic Islands, and Lēmnŏs and Cĕŏs. There was a treaty forbidding the export of ruddle from Ceos except only to Athens (Hicks, *Gr. Historical Inscriptions*, p. 186). It could be artificially produced by calcining yellow ochre, a discovery due to Cȳdīas, a contemporary of Euphrānōr (Theophr., *l.c.* 53). Another mineral supplying a red, sometimes a yellow, pigment, was sandarach (Gr. *sandărăchē;* Lat. *sandărăca*), found in Paphlăgŏnĭa, probably disulphide of arsenic ("realgar"). As this mineral is poisonous, the mortality in the mines was very high. An artificial substitute, called *cerussa usta,* or *usta* alone, was therefore generally preferred. This was obtained by burning white lead, a discovery attributed to the painter Nīcīas (Pliny, xxxv 38). The result is "red lead," *i.e.* red oxide of lead. There was besides a colour compounded of equal parts of ruddle and sandarach, called *sandyx* (Pliny, xxxv 40), which is also the designation of a natural pigment of which little is known (Vergil, *Ecl.* iv 45). Of greater importance than these is cinnabar (Gr. originally *kinnăbărĭ,* afterwards *ammĭŏn;* Lat. *mĭnĭum*), found in Spain, especially at Sīsăpō (Pliny, xxxiii 121). An artificial kind was made at Ephesus from the red sand of the *agri Cilbiānī.* This discovery is assigned to Callīas (*ib.* 113). The name *cinnabari* was often erroneously given to a red resin, now called dragon's blood, and produced from the *călămus drăco,* a kind of palm growing in the Sunda Islands and elsewhere. The ancients probably imported it from the island of Socotra, as it is a product of the Somali coast on the adjacent mainland of Africa.—A *purple* pigment (Gr. *ostreĭŏn;* Lat. *ostrum, purpŭrissum*) was prepared by mixing *crētă argentărĭă* with the purple secretion of the *mūrex* (*see* PURPLE); the best kind was made at Pŭtĕŏli (Pliny xxxv 45).

Blue. The pigment used from the earliest times was called in Greek *kȳănŏs,* in Latin *cœrŭlĕum,* a blue silicate of copper, generally mixed with carbonate of lime (chalk). It is not to be confounded with the modern *cœruleum,* which is stannate of cobalt. *Kȳănŏs* was found in small quantities in copper mines, and artificial kinds were made in Scythia, Cyprus, and Egypt (Theophr., *l.c.* 51, 55). Vitruvius mentions only the artificial *cœruleum* of Alexandria and Pŭtĕŏli. The method of manufacturing it was brought from Egypt by Vestŏrius. It was prepared by heating strongly together sand, *flŏs nitri* (carbonate of soda), and filings of copper. This "Egyptian azure" was reproduced by Sir Humphry Davy, by taking fifteen parts by weight of carbonate of soda, twenty of powdered opaque flints, and three of copper filings, and heating them strongly for two

hours. The product, when pulverized, supplied a fine deep sky blue. The "Alexandrian frit" is in part a species of artificial *lapis lazuli,* the colouring matter of which is naturally inherent in a hard siliceous stone (*Phil. Trans. Royal Society,* 1815, p. 121). It was not available for fresco-painting, but could be used for painting *in tempera* (Pliny, xxxiii 162). The name *kȳănŏs* was given to a blue mineral, which is to be identified as *lapis lazuli,* a silicate of sodium, calcium, and aluminium, with a sulphur compound of sodium. This was pounded into a pigment, now known as ultramarine. *Kyanos* was also the name of the blue carbonate of copper from the copper mines of Cyprus, where *lapis lazuli* is not to be found. Artificial blue pigments were produced by colouring pulverized glass with carbonate of copper. "Armenian blue" (Gr. *Armĕnĭŏn*) is described by Pliny (xxxv 47) as made from a mineral like *chrȳsŏcolla* (malachite?) in colour, the best kinds being almost as good as *cœruleum.* It is probably a kind of ultramarine.—Indigo (*indĭcum*) was also used. The way in which it is mentioned in Vitruvius (vii 9, 6, and 10, 4) implies that it had been recently introduced. It could not be used for frescoes. Modern experiment has proved that the colouring basis of the blue found in ancient mural paintings is oxide of copper. Cobalt has also been discovered in ancient specimens of transparent blue glass.

Green. Several pigments were in use : (1) *chrȳsŏcolla* (or malachite ?, hydrated dicarbonate of copper), pounded and sifted, and mixed with alum and woad (*lūtum,* Pliny, xxxiii 87). Malachite green, sometimes called mountain, or Hungary, green, is also a modern pigment. (2) *Crētă vĭrĭdĭs,* the best kind of which came from Smyrna (Vitruv., vii 7, 4). It is a species of ochre containing silica, oxide of iron, magnesia, potash, and water; and is still used under the names of terra verte, verdetta, green earth, Verona green, green bice, or holly green. (3) Verdigris (Gr. *ĭŏs;* Lat. *œrūgo, œrūca,* Vitruv., vii 12, 1). This is an acetate of copper (sometimes crystallized), *i.e.* a compound of acetic acid and oxide of copper. Malachite green and Verona green have both been traced in ancient paintings. Verdigris has not been found ; hence it has been conjectured by Sir H. Davy, that what was originally a diacetate of copper has in the course of centuries changed into carbonate of copper (*l.c.,* p. 112). It is described as "the least durable of copper greens; light fades it in water; damp and foul air first bleach it, and then turn it black " (Standage, *Manual of Pigments*, p. 21).

Black. The pigment (Gr. *mĕlăn ;* Lat. *ătrāmentūm*) was almost always produced by combustion. Pŏlȳgnōtus and Mīcōn produced it by drying and burning the lees of wine (Gr. *trȳgĭnŏn*). Apelles was the discoverer of "ivory black" (*ĕlĕphantĭnum*, Pliny, xxxv 42). A common material was the smoke of burnt resin (our lamp-black), or burnt pine-twigs (Vitruv., vii 10, 1). Pliny (xxxv 41) also mentions a natural black pigment which is difficult to identify; it may be peat, or else oxide of iron, or oxide of manganese. The best black pigment was called *atramentum Indĭcum* (Gr. *mĕlăn Indĭkŏn*), doubtless the same as "Chinese black," which originally found its way to the West through India, and thus obtained its alternative name of "Indian ink." But it cannot be used for frescoes, and no traces of it have been found in the mural paintings of antiquity. The black in these paintings is always carbonaceous.

Some of the remains of ancient colours and paintings at Pompeii, and in the "Baths of Titus" and of Livia, and elsewhere, were analysed by Sir Humphry Davy (*l.c.*, pp. 97–124: *Some Experiments and Observations on the Colours used in Painting by the Ancients*). In an earthen vase from the "Baths of Titus" containing a variety of colours, the *reds* proved to be red oxide of lead, with two iron ochres of different tints, a dull red and a purplish red "nearly of the same tint as prussiate of copper"; all three were mixed with chalk or carbonate of lime (p. 101). The *yellows* were pure ochres mixed with carbonate of lime, and ochre mixed with red oxide of lead and carbonate of lime (p. 104). The *blues* were a kind of smalt, with carbonate of lime (p. 106). Of *greens* there were three varieties; "one, which approached to olive, was the common green earth of Verona; another, which was pale grass-green, had the character of carbonate of copper mixed with chalk; and a third, which was sea-green, was a green combination of copper mixed with blue copper frit" (p. 110). A pale, rose-coloured substance, found in the "Baths of Titus," which in its interior "had a lustre approaching to that of carmine," was found to be either of vegetable or animal origin; if the latter, it was most probably a specimen of Tyrian purple (pp. 113–15). In the *Aldobrandini Marriage* (fig. 4) the reds and yellows were all

ochres; the greens, preparations of copper; the blues, "Alexandrian frit"; the purple, a mixture of red ochre and carbonate of copper; the browns, mixtures of ochres and black; the whites were all carbonates of lime (*ib. passim*).

For further details *see* Blümner's *Technologie*, iv 457–518.]   [J. E. S.]

Pălæmōn. (1) A Greek sea-god. *See* MELICERTES.

(2) *Quintus Remmius.* A Latin grammarian of Vicetia (*Vicenza*), the son of a female slave. He acquired a learned education whilst accompanying his master's son to school, and, after he had been set free, taught at Rome in the first half of the first century after Christ, under Tiberius and Claudius, with extraordinary success [in spite of his thoroughly disreputable character]. The earlier scholars, and especially Varro, had made the older literature the centre of their linguistic studies. Palæmon, as head of a new school, devoted himself especially to Vergil, just as Greek literary criticism had concentrated itself on Homer. [He seems to have treated grammar in the practical spirit of a clever schoolmaster, and to have done his best to deride the scientific labours of Varro. His grammar (*ars*, Juvenal, vii 251) was doubtless much consulted by later grammarians. It is now lost.] The grammar that bears his name is wrongly attributed to him. [*See* Prof. Nettleship in *Journal of Philology*, xv 192.]

Pălæphătus. A Greek author who followed the Peripatetic philosophy. He composed in the 4th century B.C. a historical and allegorical explanation of Greek myths in several books. Of this work we possess only a short abstract, probably composed in the Byzantine age under the title, *On Incredible Tales*. In former times it was a favourite school book.

Pălæstra (*i.e.* wrestling school). The name given by the Greeks to the place in which the young were instructed in wrestling and boxing under the guidance of a master called a *pædŏtrĭbēs*. There were a considerable number of such schools at Athens, which had been built, some at public expense, some by private undertaking. In later times they were also connected with the *Gymnăsĭa*. (*See* GYMNASIUM and GYMNASTICS.)

Pălămēdēs. The son of Nauplius and brother of Œax, a hero of the post-Homeric cycle of Trojan legend. Odysseus envied his wisdom and ingenuity, and was bent on avenging himself on Palamedes for detecting his feigned madness. Accordingly, he is said to have conspired with Dĭŏmēdēs and drowned him whilst engaged in fishing; or (according to another account) they persuaded him to enter a well, in which treasure was said to be concealed, and then overwhelmed him with stones. According to others, Agămemnōn also hated him as head of the peace party among the Greeks. He accordingly got Odysseus and Diomedes to conceal in his tent a letter purporting to be written by Priam, as well as some money, and then accuse him as a traitor; whereupon he was stoned to death by the people. His brother Œax informed his father of the sad event by writing the news on an oar and throwing it into the sea, upon which he took a terrible vengeance on the returning Greeks (*see* NAUPLIUS, 2). Palamedes was considered by the Greeks as the inventor of the alphabet and of lighthouses; also of measures and weights, and of dice and draughts and the discus.

Pălēs. The Italian goddess of shepherds. Her festival, the *Pălīlia* or *Părīlia*, held on April 21st, was properly a herdsmen's festival to promote the fruitfulness of the flocks and to purify the sacred groves and fountains from all unintentional injury or pollution caused by the herds. It was deemed the anniversary of the founding of Rome, the former abode of shepherds. Accordingly it was celebrated at Rome, as in the villages, by the whole of the inhabitants, with the ancient rites of a shepherds' festival. It was customary to purify house, steading, and sheep with sulphur, and, as a special means of expiation, to offer incense, together with a mixture of the blood of the October horse (*see* MARS), the ashes of the unborn calf which was burned at the feast of Tellus, and bean-straw which was obtained from the Vestals. When these solemn purifications were over, the cheerful part of the festival began. Bonfires were made of straw and hay; the shepherds leaped across them thrice; cakes of millet were also offered to the goddess; and the festival was concluded by a feast in the open air. After the 2nd century of our era the festival was combined with that of *Dea Roma*, and was celebrated as her birthday with festal processions and Circensian games, which continued till the 5th century.

Pălĭci. Two spirits worshipped in the the neighbourhood of Mount Etna in Sicily, as benevolent deities and protectors of agriculture. They are sometimes described as sons of Adrānus, a native hero honoured

through the whole of Sicily; sometimes, of Hēphæstus and the Nymph Ætna; sometimes, of Zeus and Thălīa, a daughter of Hephæstus, who concealed herself in the earth from fear of Hēra's jealousy, whereupon two hot sulphur springs burst out of the ground. Beside these springs solemn oaths were taken, especially in legal proceedings, the swearer, who must have previously kept himself from all defilement, touching the brink; if the oath were false, blinding or instantaneous death followed. According to another account, a tablet inscribed with the oath was thrown into the water, and swam on the surface if the oath were true, but sank in the contrary case, while flames devoured the perjurer. The neighbouring sanctuary of the Palici served as an oracle and also as a shelter for fugitive slaves. [Diodorus Siculus, xi 89.]

Pălīlĭa. A feast among the Romans held in honour of the goddess Pălēs (*q.v.*).

A ROMAN LADY WEARING THE PALLA.
Statue of the younger Agrippĭna, wife of Claudius and mother of Nero (Naples Museum).

Palla. A Roman mantle worn by women, consisting of a square piece of cloth, which matrons wore over the *stŏla*, in the same way as the men wore the *tŏga*. They let one third fall down in front over the left shoulder, but drew the rest away over the back, and then either brought it forward over the right shoulder, or drew it under the right arm, but in either case threw the end back over the left arm or shoulder (*see* cut). The *palla* could also be drawn over the head, just like the *toga*. Other women, who were not privileged to wear the *stola*, wore the *palla* over the tunic, folded together about the body, fastened together on the shoulders with buckles, and open on the right side, or held together in the same way with buckles. It then lay double over the breast and back, but fell down in one thickness to the feet.

Pallădĭum (Gr. *pallădĭŏn*). An old carven image in the citadel at Troy, on which the prosperity of the city depended. It is said to have been three cubits high, with feet shut close together, an upraised spear in its right hand, and in its left either a distaff and spindle, or a shield. Athēnē was said to have made it as an image of Pallas, daughter of Trītōn, whom she had slain unawares while playing at wrestling. Legends differ in their account of the manner of its coming to Troy. According to one of them, Pallas gave it as a dowry to Chrȳsē, the bride of Dardănus, and he brought it to Dardania, whence Ilus carried it to Troy; according to another, Zeus caused it to fall down to Ilus (*q.v.*) from heaven. Since Troy could not be conquered so long as it possessed this image, Dĭŏmēdēs stole it with the help of Odysseus and brought it to Argos. But, according to the Attic story, it was Dēmŏphŏŏn (*q.v.*, 2) of Athens who deprived him of it. The *palladium* preserved in Rome in the temple of Vesta was traced back to Æneas, the assumption being that there had been a second image in Troy besides that stolen by Diomedes. Other Italian towns also boasted of the possession of a *palladium*.

Pallădĭus (*Rŭtilius Taurus Æmĭlĭănus*). A Latin author, in the 4th century A.D., who, by borrowing from the teaching of his predecessors and by his own experience, composed a work upon husbandry in fourteen books. Of these the first contains general precepts; books ii–xiii give the operations of agriculture in each of the successive months, while the fourteenth treats of the grafting of trees, in eighty-five elegiac couplets. His book, though written in dry and feeble language, was much used in the Middle Ages on account of its practical arrangement.

Pallas. (1) Pallas Athēnē (*see* ATHENE). (2) Son of the Titan Crīus, husband of Styx, father of Nīkē. (3) Son of Pandīon, who robbed his brother of the dominion of Athens, but was, together with his fifty gigantic sons, slain by the youthful Thēseus.

Pallĭāta. A branch of Roman comedy. (*See* COMEDY, 2.)

Pallium. The Roman name for a large Grecian cloak, which was also worn by Romans among the Greeks. It was especially the garb of the philosophers. In Rome it was also worn by courtesans.

Pallor and Păvor (*lit.* "Paleness and Fright"). The Roman personifications of terror, and companions of the war-god Mars. As early as the time of king Tullus Hostīlius sanctuaries are said to have been erected in their honour. On coins *Pallor* was represented as a boy with dishevelled hair and perturbed bearing, and *Pavor* as a man with an expression of horror and with bristling hair.

Paltŏn. The lance of the Greek cavalry. (*See* WEAPONS.) [Also a light spear used by the Persian cavalry (Xen., *Cyrop.* iv 3, 9; vi 2, 16).]

Pălŭdămentum. The short, red mantle of Roman generals, fastened on the left shoulder and worn over the armour. They assumed it on the Capitol on their departure to the war, but on their return they exchanged it for the *tŏga*, the garb of peace, before their entry into the city. Under the Empire, when the emperor was the commander-in-chief, the purple *paludamentum* became exclusively a token of imperial power. It only became the usual attire of the emperors in the 3rd century after Christ. Accordingly, after that time entrance on imperial power was termed "assuming the purple."

Pamphĭlus. A Greek painter of Amphĭpŏlis in Macedonia, who lived in the first half of the 4th century B.C., chiefly at Sĭcȳŏn, as head of the school there founded by his master Eupompus. He is the originator of the scientific teaching of art: he traced back all practice of art to scientific principles. He maintained that painting could not be brought to perfection without arithmetic and geometry. In spite of the fact that his fee for instruction was one talent (£200), the number of his pupils was considerable; the greatest among them being Apelles. Through his influence instruction in drawing was introduced among the subjects of Greek education [Pliny, *N. H.* xxxv 76. The only work of this artist now known to us by name is his picture of the *Suppliant Hēraclīdæ*, to which Aristophanes alludes in the *Plutus*, 385].

Pān (*lit.* " the pasturer ") [from the same root as the Lat. *pastor* and *pānis*]. Originally an Arcadian god of hills and woods, the protecting deity of flocks, herdsmen, and hunters; the son either of Hermēs and a daughter of Dryops, or of Zeus and the Arcadian Nymph Callisto. The ancients represented him with a puck-nose and bearded, with shaggy hair, two horns, and goat's feet. They imagined him as wandering by day through hill and dale with the Nymphs, guarding the flocks, especially the goats, and chasing wild animals [Homeric Hymn, xix]. In the heat of noonday he sleeps, and is then very sensitive to any disturbance; therefore at this time no shepherd blows his pipe [Theocr. i 16]. In the evening, sitting in front of his grotto, he plays on the *syrinx*, or Pan's pipe, which he himself invented. He is even said to have formed it from the reed into which a Nymph named *Syrinx* was changed while fleeing from his love [Ovid, *Met.* i 705]. There are many other tales of his love adventures with the Nymphs. As he excites the sudden ("panic") terror which attacks the wanderer in forest solitudes, so he was also said to have caused the panic which put to flight the Persians at Mărăthōn; and on this account a grotto in the Acrŏpŏlis of Athens was dedicated to him, and he was honoured with an annual sacrifice and torch procession [Herod., vi 105]. As a spirit of the woodland, he is also a god of prophecy, and hence there were oracles of Pan Like the similar figures of

PAN.
(Florence.)

Sīlēnus and the Satyrs, he was brought into connexion with Dīŏnȳsus, in whose train he proved himself useful on his Indian expedition by means of the terror he inspired. As one of the gods of nature, he was one of the companions of Cȳbĕlē, and by reason of his amorousness, he is associated with Aphrŏdītē. In later times, owing to a misinterpretation of his name (as though it stood for *pan*, "the universe"), he was made a symbol of the universe. His cult was chiefly confined to the country. He was either worshipped with the Nymphs in grottoes, or his image was set up under the trees, where his worshippers brought it simple offerings such as milk, honey, must, rams, or lambs. Mountains, caves, old oaks, and pine trees, and the tortoise, were sacred to him; his attributes are the *syrinx*, a shepherd's crook, a garland of pine leaves or a twig of the pine tree. The fancy of later times invented as his companions young Pans, or *Pānisci*, a species of imps of the forest, who were fabled to torment mankind by all sorts of apparitions, nightmares, and evil dreams. The Romans identified Pan with the Italian *Faunus* (*q.v.*).

Pănætius. A Greek philosopher of Rhodes, born about 180 B.C.; the most important representative of Stoicism in his time From Athens, where he had received his education, he went to Rome, about 156 B.C. Being there received into the circle of the younger Scipio and of Lælius, he was able to gain numerous adherents among the Roman nobles by his skill in softening the harshness and subtlety of the Stoic teaching, and in representing it in a refined and polished form. After Scipio's death (129) he returned to Athens, where he died, as the head of the Stoic school, about 111. Only unimportant fragments of his writings remain. The most important of them, the *Treatise on Duty*, supplied the groundwork of the *De Officiīs* of Cicero.

Pănăthēnæa (Gr. *Pănăthēnaīa*). The most ancient and most important of Athenian festivals. It was celebrated in honour of Athēnē, the patron deity of Athens. Claiming to have been founded as early as by Erichthŏnĭus, it is said to have been originally named only *Athēnæa*, and to have first received the name of *Panathenæa* at the time when Thēseus united all the inhabitants of Attica into one body. In memory of the union itself was kept the festival of the *Sўnœcĭă*, or *Sўnœcĕsĭă*, on the 16th of Hĕcătombæōn (July–August), which may be regarded as a kind of prepatory solemnity to the *Panathenœa*. There was a festival of the ordinary or *lesser Panathenœa* celebrated every year, and from the time of Pīsistrătus, the *great Panathenœa* held every fifth year, and in the third year of every Olympiad, from the 24th to the 29th of Hecatombæon. Pisistratus, in the year 566 B.C., added to the original chariot and horse races athletic contests in each of the traditional forms of competition. He, or his son Hipparchus, instituted the regulation, that the collected Homeric poems should be recited at the feast of *Rhapsōdi*. In 446 Pericles introduced musical contests, which took place on the first day of the festival, in the Odēum, which he had built. Competitions of cyclic choruses and other kinds of dances, torch races and trireme races, added to the splendour of the festival. The care and direction of all these contests were committed to ten stewards (*athlŏthĕtœ*), who were elected by the people for four years, from one great Panathenaic festival to the next. In the musical contests, the first prize was a golden crown; in the athletic, the prize was a garland of leaves from the sacred olive trees of Athene, together with large and beautiful vases filled with oil from the same trees. Many specimens of these Panathenaic vases have been found [in Italy, Sicily, Greece, and at Cȳrēnē. They have the figure of Athene on one side, and a design indicating the contest for which they are awarded on the other. Most of them belong to the 4th century B.C., 367–318; the "Burgon Vase," in the British Museum, to the 6th century. *Cp.* Pindar, *Nem.* x 35]. The tribe whose ships had been victorious received a sum of money, part of which was destined for a sacrifice to Pŏseidōn.

The culminating point of the festival was the 28th day of the month, the birthday of the goddess, when the grand procession carried through the city the costly, embroidered, saffron-coloured garment, the *peplus* (*q.v.*). This had been woven in the preceding nine months by Attic maidens and matrons, and embroidered with representations from the battle of the gods and Giants. It was carried through the city, first of all as a sail for a ship moving on wheels, and was then taken to the Acrŏpŏlis, where it adorned one of the statues of Athene Pŏliăs. The procession is represented in a vivid manner in the well-known frieze of the Parthĕnōn. It included the priests and their attendants, leading a long train of animals festally adorned for sacrifice; matrons

and maidens bearing in baskets the various sacrificial implements (*see* CANEPHORI); the most picturesque old men in festal attire, with olive branches in their hands, whence came their name, *thallŏphŏrœ*; warriors, with spear and shield, in splendid array; young men in armour; the cavalry under the command of both the *hipparchi;* the victors in the immediately preceding contests; the festal embassies of other

* PANATHENAIC AMPHORA.
Inscribed ΤΩΝ ΑΘΗΝΗΘΕΝ ΑΘΛΩΝ, "a prize from Athens."
(Millingen, *Uned. Mon.*, pl. 1.)

states, especially of the colonies; and, lastly, the aliens resident in Athens. Of these last, the men bore behind the citizens trays with sacrificial cakes, the women waterpots, and the maidens sunshades and stools for the citizens' wives; while on the freedmen was laid the duty of adorning with oak-leaves the market-places and streets through which the procession moved. The feast ended with the great festal sacrifice of a hecatomb of oxen, and with the general banqueting which accompanied it. At the yearly minor *Panathenœa*, on the 28th and 29th of Hecatombæon, contests, sacrifices, and a procession took place, but all in a more simple style. In later times the festival was removed to spring, perhaps in consequence of Roman influence, in order to make it correspond to the *Quinquātrūs* of Minerva.

[All the ancient authorities are collected by Michaelis, *Der Parthenon*, pp. 318–333.]

Pancrātĭum. The combination of boxing and wrestling in Greek gymnastics (*q.v.*).

Pandărĕōs, of Milētus, the son of Mĕrŏpus, stole from Mīnōs of Crete a living dog made of gold, the work of Hēphæstus, which was the guardian of the temple of Zeus, and gave it to Tantălus to keep it safely. When Zeus demanded the dog back, Pandareos fled with his wife Harmŏthĕa to Sicily, where both were turned into stones. For his daughter Aēdōn, *see* AËDON. Of his two other daughters (Mĕrŏpē and Clĕŏdŏra or Cămeira and Clÿtĕa), Homer [*Od.* xx 66–78] relates that they were brought up by Aphrŏdītē, after their early bereavement, and were endowed by Hera with beauty and wisdom, by Artĕmis with lofty stature, and by Athēnē with skill in handiwork; but while their foster-mother went to Olympus to implore Zeus to grant the maidens happy marriages, they were carried off by the Hărpies, and delivered to the Erīnÿĕs as servants, and thus expiated their father's guilt.

Pandīōn. (1) Son of Erichthŏnius, father of Procnē and Erechtheus (*q.v.*).

(2) Son of Cĕcrops and Mĕtĭădūsa, grandson of Erechtheus, king of Athens. Driven into exile by the sons of his brother Mētĭōn, he went to Mĕgără, where he married Pÿlĭa, the daughter of king Pÿlās, and inherited the kingdom. His sons, Ægeus, Lÿcus, Pallās, and Nīsus, regained Attica from the Mētĭŏnĭdæ, and the first three shared it among themselves, while Nisus (*q.v.*) received Megara.

Pandŏkeiŏn (*Greek*). The Greek name for a kind of private inn which harboured and entertained travellers. (*Cp.* INNS.)

Pandōra ("the all-gifted"). The woman made out of earth by Hephæstus, and endowed by the gods with perfect charm and beauty, but also with deceit, flattering speech, and cunning thought. (*See further under* PROMETHEUS.)

Pandrŏsŏs (*Greek*). Daughter of Cĕcrops of Athens, first priestess of Athēnē, honoured together with her in a sanctuary of her own, the *Pandrŏseiŏn*, on the Acrŏpŏlis of Athens. (*Cp.* CECROPS.)

Pănĕgÿrĭcŭs. The name given among the Greeks to a speech delivered before a *pănĕgÿrĭs;* that is, an assembly of the whole nation on the occasion of the celebration of a festival, such as *Pănăthēnœa* and the four great national games. This oration had reference to the feast itself, or was intended to inspire the assembled multitude with emulation, by praising the great deeds of their ancestors, and also to urge them to unanimous co-operation against their common foes. The most famous compositions of this kind which have been preserved are the *Panegyricus* and *Pănăthēnăĭcus* of Isŏcrătēs, [neither of which, however, was actually delivered in public.] In later times eulogies upon individuals were so named. This kind of composition was especially cultivated under the Roman Empire by Greeks and Romans. In Roman literature the most ancient example of this kind which remains is the eulogy of the emperor Trajan, delivered by the younger Pliny in the Senate, 100 A.D., thanking the emperor for conferring on him the consulate, a model which subsequent ages vainly endeavoured to imitate. It forms, together with eleven orations of Māmertīnus, Eumĕnĭus, Năzārĭus, Păcātus Drĕpănius, and other unknown representatives of the Gallic school of rhetoric, from the end of the 3rd and the whole of the 4th centuries A.D., the extant collection of the *Panegyrici Lătini*. Besides these, we possess similar orations by Symmăchus, Ausŏnius, and Ennŏdius. There are also a considerable number of poetical panegyrics; *e.g.* one upon Messala, composed in the year 31 B.C., and wrongly attributed to Tibullus; one by an unknown author of the Neronian time úpon Calpurnius Piso; and others by Claudian, Sīdŏnius Apollīnāris, Mĕrŏbaudes, Cŏrippus, Priscian, and Vĕnantius Fortūnātus (*q.v.*).

Pānisci. *See* PAN.

Pan's Pipe. *See* SYRINX and PAN.

Panthĕōn (properly Gr. *Pantheiŏn*, "the all-divine place"; Lat. *Panthēum*). The only ancient building in Rome whose walls and arches have been completely preserved. It is one of the greatest architectural monuments of antiquity, and is fitted, as no other building is, to show us the solidity, boldness, and splendour of Roman architecture. The original object of the temple, which, according to the inscription on the architrave of its porch, was built by Agrippa in 27 B.C., is unknown. We only know that the seven principal niches of the interior were once occupied by images of the gods. We have evidence that among them were Mars and Vĕnus, the patron deities of the Julian house, and the deified Cæsar, the principal representative of that house. In later times the term *Pantheon* was wrongly supposed to mean a temple of all the gods. This view prompted Pope

Boniface IV to dedicate the building, in 609 A.D., as a Christian church to the memory of all the martyrs, under the name of *S. Marīa ad Martȳrēs* (now *S. Maria Rotonda*, or simply *La Rotonda*). The building had already been repeatedly restored in ancient times by Domitian, Hadrian, and last of all, in 202 A.D., by

of these in front support a massive pediment, behind which rises another pediment of still higher elevation, resting against the square projection which connects the portico with the dome. The other columns divide the portico into three parallel portions, originally vaulted over. In the interior of the portico on each side of the

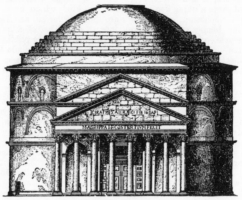

(1) THE PANTHEON, ROME.
(Front elevation.)

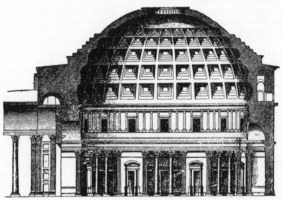

(2) THE PANTHEON, ROME.
(Longitudinal section.)

Septĭmius Sĕvērus and Caracalla. It consists of a circular structure, 142 feet 6 inches in height and inner diameter, with a portico 103 feet long formed by sixteen Corinthian columns 47 feet high. Eight

entrance are two niches, which formerly contained colossal statues of Augustus and Agrippa. The massive walls of the great rotunda, which is completely circular in form, are divided by ring-cornices into two stories, an upper and a lower. Above these springs a cupola of concrete, of vaster dimensions than any that had been attempted in previous times. The diameter of this lofty cupola corresponds to that of the vast cylindrical building on which it rests. The walls of the latter are 19 feet thick. The interior of the cupola is divided into five rows of deeply sunk panels (*lăcūnāria*) 28 in each row. At its vertex an opening about 27 feet in diameter lights the whole of the interior (*see* cuts). The gilt-bronze tiles of the roof were taken by the emperor Constans II to Constantinople in 655 A.D. The remains of the costly marble wall-linings of the interior, which dated from the last restoration, and consisted of 56 compartments, divided by 112 Corinthian columns, and covered with white marble, porphyry, serpentine, and pavonazetto, were not carried off until 1747. In 1632 the girders of gilded bronze which supported the roof of the portico were melted down by Urban VIII, to be cast into pillars for the baldacchino in St. Peter's [and into cannon for the castle of S. Angelo].

Pantŏmīmus. The representation of a dramatic subject by dancing and rhythmic gesticulation alone, as practised by the Romans. It originated in the custom of the ancient Roman drama, of only allowing an actor on the stage to make the necessary movements of dancing and gesticulation, while another actor sang the recitative to the accompaniment of the flute. This recitative was called *cantĭcum*, and was a monologue composed in rhythmical form. The illustrative dance was raised to a separate, independent branch of art by *Pÿlădēs* and *Băthyllus* under Augustus, 22 B.C. There were comic and tragic pantomimes, but the latter variety prevailed on the stage of the Empire. The subjects were chiefly taken from tragedies founded on mythological love stories, and treated so that the chief situations were included in a series of *cantica*. All of these were represented by a single *pantomimus*, the dancer, as well as the performer, being designated by that name. He thus had to represent several characters, male and female, in succession, while a chorus, accompanied by flutes and other instruments, sang the corresponding song. The pauses necessary for the change of mask and costume for each successive part were apparently filled up with the recital of music by the chorus, which served to connect the chief scenes with each other. It was only

in the latest times of the Empire that women were employed in pantomime. Pantomime, aiming at sensual charm alone, went beyond all bounds of decorum in the representation of delicate subjects. As an understanding of the subtleties of the art required a cultivated taste, pantomime was specially favoured by the higher classes, while the *mime*, with his buffoonery, was more pleasing to the multitude. On the true dramatic ballet of imperial times, *see* PYRRHIC DANCE.

Panyasis [quantity doubtful; Avienus, *Arat. Phœn.* 175, makes it *Pănÿăsis*. There was another form *Panyassis*]. A Greek poet of Hălĭcarnassus, uncle of Hērŏdŏtus. He was put to death by the tyrant Lygdämis about 454 B.C. for being the leader of the aristocratic party. He composed a poem in fourteen books entitled *Hērăclēa* (exploits of Hērăclēs), which was reckoned by later writers among the best epics. The few fragments preserved are in an elegant and graceful style.

Paper. *See* WRITING MATERIALS.

Păpīniānŭs (*Æmĭlĭus*). The most important among the Roman jurists; born about 140 A.D., a contemporary and friend of the emperor Septĭmĭus Sĕvērus, whom he accompanied on his expedition to Britain in the capacity of *præfectus prætōrĭo*. Severus, on his deathbed at York, left to him the guardianship of his sons Gĕtă and Cărăcalla; yet the latter caused Papinianus to be put to death in the next year, 212, on the day after the murder of his brother Geta. Of all his works, the thirty-seven books of *Quæstĭōnēs* (legal questions), and the nineteen books of *Responsa* (legal decisions) were considered the most important. Till the time of Justinian these formed the nucleus of that part of jurisprudence which was connected with the explanation of the original authorities on Roman law. We only possess fragments of them, in the form of numerous excerpts in the "Digest." (*See* CORPUS JURIS CIVILIS.)

Păpīrius (*Păpīrĭānum Iūs*) *See* JURISPRUDENCE.

Pappŏsīlēnus. *See* SILENUS.

Pappus. A Greek mathematician of Alexandria, who lived about the end of the 4th century A.D. We still possess his *Mathematical Collections* in eight books, consisting of extracts from numerous mathematical writings, of great importance for the history of mathematics.

Păpÿrus. *See* WRITING MATERIALS.

Părăbăsĭs. A characteristic, but not

indispensable, part of the chorus in the Old Attic comedy. About the middle of the piece, when the action of the play had been developed up to a certain point, the chorus, which had up to this time turned towards the actors on the stage, now turned to the audience. This stepping forward towards the audience is itself also termed *parabasis*. In this position they made an appeal to the public on behalf of the poet, who could thus give expression to his personal views and wishes, and offer advice, as well as explain the purport of his play, etc. This address stood wholly outside the action of the play. When the *parabasis* was complete, which was seldom the case, it consisted of seven parts, partly spoken by the leader of the chorus, partly sung by the chorus. One of these parts was called the *parabasis* in a narrower sense, and consisted chiefly of anapæstic tetrameters.

Pārāli. Lit. " the people of the coastland." (*See* SOLONIAN CONSTITUTION.)

Pārascēnium. *See* THEATRE.

Parasite (Gr. *părăsītŏs*, lit. " table companion "). Denoted originally among the Greeks the priest's assistant, who (like the priest) received his support from the offerings made to the temple, in return for certain services. These services included collecting and keeping the supplies of corn due to the temple, helping at certain sacrifices, and preparing the banquets connected with certain festivals [*Athenæus*, p. 234]. The assistants of civil officials, who (like the latter) were maintained at the expense of the State, were also called parasites in many places [*ib.* 235]. The word received quite another meaning in the middle and later Greek Comedy, where it means the hanger on, who lays himself out for playing the flatterer and buffoon, with a view to getting invited to dinner. The parasite was transferred as a standing character to the Roman imitations of Greek comedy.

Pārastăs. *See* HOUSE (*Greek*).

Parcæ. The Italian goddesses of Fate. (*Cp.* MŒRÆ.)

Pārentālĭă. The general festival in honour of deceased relatives, celebrated by the Romans from February 13th to 21st. (*See* MANES.)

Parian Chronicle (*Chrŏnĭcŏn* or *Marmor Părĭum*). A marble tablet found at Paros in 1627, now [among the Arundel Marbles in the University Galleries] at Oxford. It is written chiefly in the Attic, but partly in the Ionian dialect, and consists of ninety-three lines, some of which are no longer

complete. It originally contained a number of dates of the political, but chiefly of the religious and literary, history of the Greeks, from the Athenian king Cecrops to the Athenian archon Dĭognētus, 264 B.C.; in its present condition, however, it only goes down to 354 B.C. All the dates are given according to Attic kings and archons, and the historical authorities on which it depends must have been Attic authors. The origin and aim of the tablet are unknown. [It was first published by Selden in 1628; it has since been printed by Boeckh (*Corpus Inscr. Græc.* ii, no. 2374), who considers that the leading authority followed is Phanĭās of Ĕrĕsŏs, and also by C. Müller, *Frag. Hist.*

Pārĭlia = *Pălīlĭa* (*q.v.*).   [*Gr.*, i 535-90.]

Pāris (or *Alexandrŏs*, Gr.). The second son of Priam and Hĕcŭba. His mother having dreamt before this birth that she had brought forth a firebrand, which set all Troy in flames, Priam had the new-born babe exposed on Mount Ida by the advice of his son Æsăcus. Here a she-bear suckled the babe for five days; then a shepherd found him, and reared him with his own children. Paris won the name of *Alexandros* (" protector of men ") by his bravery as a shepherd, defending herdsmen and cattle. On Mount Ida he married Œnōnē, daughter of the river-god Cĕbrēn. He decided the strife of the goddesses Hēra, Aphrŏdītē, and Athēnē for the golden apple of Ĕrĭs (*see* PELEUS), having been appointed arbiter by Hermēs at the command of Zeus. Paris preferred the possession of the fairest woman, promised him by Aphrodite, to power and riches, or wisdom and fame, promised by Hera and Athene respectively. He therefore awarded to Aphrodite the prize of beauty, but drew upon himself and his fatherland the irreconcilable hatred of the goddesses whom he had passed over. When Priam was once celebrating funeral games in memory of his lost son, and commanded the finest bull in all the herds grazing on the mountain to be brought as a prize, Paris came to Troy as its driver. He took part in the contests and vanquished his brothers, even Hector Seized with envy, they wished to kill him but Cassandra recognised him, and he was joyfully received by his parents. In spite of the warning of the forsaken Œnone, who still loved him tenderly, Paris set out on a voyage to Sparta, at the instigation of Aphrodite. Here he carried off Helen, the wife of Mĕnēlāus, whom the goddess herself had quickly inspired with love for th handsome stranger. With her he carried away the treasures of his host, and brought her through Egypt and Phœnicia to Troy. In the war that arose from his deed, Paris showed himself, according to Homer, sometimes valiant and courageous, especially as an archer, but chiefly only at the persuasion of others; at other times cowardly and effeminate. The Trojans detested him as the cause of the disastrous war. After he had treacherously slain Achilles (q.v.), he himself was fatally wounded by an arrow of Hērăclēs, while in single combat with Phĭloctētēs. His corpse was dishonoured by Mĕnĕlāus, but yet was afterwards given to the Trojans for burial. According to another account, when he knew his death was near, he asked to be carried to Œnone. When they had parted, she had bidden him come to her, if he should ever be mortally wounded; but now, mindful of the sorrow she had endured, Œnone rejected him, and he died soon after his return to Troy. When Œnone, repenting of her cruelty, hastened with the remedy, and found him already dead, she hanged herself. In sculpture Paris is represented as a beautiful beardless youth with a Phrygian cap.

Parma. The circular leathern shield of the Roman light infantry. (*See* SHIELD.)

Parmĕnĭdēs. A Greek philosopher and poet, born of an illustrious family about 510 B.C., at Élĕa in Lower Italy. He was held in high esteem by his fellow citizens on account of his excellent legislation, to which they ascribed the prosperity and wealth of the town; and also on account of his exemplary life. A "Parmenidean life" was proverbial among the Greeks [Cebes, *tabula*, 2]. Little more is known of his biography than that he stopped at Athens on a journey in his sixty-fifth year, and there became acquainted with the youthful Socrates. He is the chief representative of the Eleatic philosophy. Like his great teacher, Xĕnŏphănēs, he also formulated his philosophical views in a didactic poem, *On Nature*, the form of which was considered inartistic [Cicero, *Acad.* ii 74]. According to the proem, which has been preserved (while we only possess fragments of the rest), the work consisted of two divisions. The first treated of the truth, the second of the world of illusion ; that is, the world of the senses and the erroneous opinions of mankind founded upon them. In his opinion truth lies in the perception that existence is, and error in

the idea that non-existence also can be. Nothing can have real existence but what is conceivable, therefore to be imagined and to be able to exist are the same thing, and there is no development; the essence of what is conceivable is incapable of development, imperishable, immutable, unbounded, and indivisible; what is various and mutable, all development, is a delusive phantom; perception is thought directed to the pure essence of being; the phenomenal world is a delusion, and the opinions formed concerning it can only be improbable.

Părŏdŏs (*Greek*). A technical term of the Greek drama, used to denote, (1) the entrance of the chorus upon the orchestra; (2) the song which they sang while entering; (3) the passage by which they entered. (*See* THEATRE.)

Parrhăsĭus. A famous Greek painter of Ephĕsus, who with Zeuxis was the chief representative of the Ionic school. He lived about 400 B.C. at Athens, where he seems to have received the citizenship. According to the accounts of ancient writers, he first introduced into painting the theory of human proportions, gave to the face delicate shades of expression, and was a master in the careful drawing of contours [Pliny, *N. H.* xxxv 67, 68]. His skill in indicating varieties of psychological expression could be appreciated in the picture representing the Athenian State or *Dēmŏs*, in which, according to ancient authors, he distinctly pourtrayed all the conflicting qualities of the Athenian national character [*ib.* 69]. Another of his pictures represented two boys, one of whom seemed to personify the pertness, and the other the simplicity, of boyhood [*ib.* 70]. His inclination to represent excited states of mind is attested by the choice of subjects like the feigned madness of Odysseus [Plutarch, *De Audiend. Poet.* 3], and the anguish of Philoctētēs in Lēmnŏs [*Anthol. Gr.* ii 348, 5]. His supposed contest with Zeuxis is well known. The grapes painted by Zeuxis deceived the birds, which flew to peck at them; while the curtain painted by Parrhasius deceived Zeuxis himself [Pliny, *ib.* 65].

Parricide (Lat. *parrīcīdium*, according to the usual, but very doubtful explanation derived from *patricidium*, "murder of a father "). A term used among the Romans for the murder of any relative with whom one is united by bonds of blood or duty, but sometimes also for treason and rebellion against one's country. In earlier times the examination in trials for homicide was conducted by two *quæstōrēs parricidii*, on whom it was also incumbent to bring the accusation before the *cŏmĭtĭa* for trial. Sulla transferred the decision in all cases of parricide to a standing tribunal (*see* QUÆSTIO PERPETUA), which had also to try cases of assassination and poisoning. The punishment for parricide was drowning in a leathern sack (*cullĕus*), into which were sewn, besides the criminal, a dog, a cock, a viper, and an ape [Cicero, *Rosc. Am.* 70; Juvenal viii 214]. The murder of relations in other degrees of relationship was punished by exile (*interdictĭō ăquæ et ignis*). See EXILĬUM.

he composed the only work of his which has survived, under the title, *Of the Sorrows of Love*. This is a collection of thirty-six prose stories of unhappy lovers, compiled from ancient poets, especially from those of the Alexandrine school. Apart from the light it throws on the Alexandrine poets, of whose works it contains fragments, it has a special interest as a precursor of the Greek novel.

Parthĕnōn (*Greek*). " The maiden's chamber," particularly a temple of Athēnē *Parthĕnŏs* (the virgin goddess), especially that on the Acropolis of Athens, distin' guished by the grandeur of its dimensions,

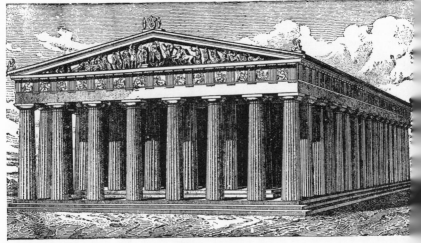

(1) THE PARTHENON.
(From the south-west, restored.)

Parthĕnĭă. A species of religious songs, sung to the accompaniment of the flute with cheerful, lively movements by choirs of maidens.

Parthĕnĭus. A Greek grammarian and poet, of Nīcæa in Bīthўnia, who was brought captive to Rome during the war with Mithrĭdātēs. After his release, he lived there till the time of Tĭbĕrĭus, esteemed as a scholar and poet, especially as a writer of elegiac poems. He was acquainted with Vergil, whom he taught Greek, and one of his poems is said to have been the model for the *Mŏrētum ;* but he was more closely connected with the elegiac poet, Cornēlius Gallus. For Gallus

the beauty of its execution, and the splendour of its artistic adornment. [There was an earlier temple of Athene immediately to the south of the Erechthĕum (*see* plan of ACROPOLIS), and the foundations of a new temple were laid after the Persian War, probably in the time of Cīmōn. This temple was never completed; on the same site there was built a temple of less length, but greater breadth, which is usually called the *Parthenon*.] It was built at the command of Pericles by the architects Ictīnus and Callĭcrătēs. It took about five years in building, and was finished in 438 B.C. (fig. 1). Its further adornment with sculptures in the pediments, and with metopes and frieze was completed under the direction of Phĭdias, who himself took part in the work. The temple, built wholly of Pentelic marble, is 65 feet high. The *stylobate*, or platform, on which the columns stand (fig. 2, *C*), is 228 feet in length, and 101 feet in breadth [=225 × 100 in Attic feet, giving 9 : 4 as the ratio of length to breadth]. Under the stylobate is the

feet high, eight at each end, and fifteen on each side. The architrave from the first was adorned with 92 metopes sculptured in high relief (*see*, for the position of the metopes, fig. 2, *G*). Shields and votive inscriptions were subsequently placed there by Alexander the Great, in 338 B.C. [Plut., *Alex.* 16]. The subjects were: on the E. the battle of the gods and giants; on the

(2) *SECTION OF NORTH-EAST PORTION OF THE PARTHENON,

shewing *A*, substructure; *B B B*, steps of crepidoma; *C*, stylobate; *D*, tympanum of eastern pediment; *E*, coffered ceiling; *F*, frieze of the cella; *G*, metopes and triglyphs; *H* is part of the range of Parnes (*Wiener Vorlegeblätter*).

crĕpĭdōma, or basis proper, formed of three steps (fig. 2, *B B B*) resting on a massive substructure, 250 feet long and 105 feet broad, and founded on the rock at the highest part of the plateau of the Acropolis (fig. 2, *C*). The temple is peripteral, its walls being entirely surrounded by a colonnade of forty-six Doric columns, about 35

S., that of the Centaurs and Lăpĭthæ (fig. 3); on the W., the victory of the Athenians over the Amazons; and on the N., the destruction of Troy. The sculptures of the eastern pediment (*D*) represented the birth of the goddess, those of the western the strife of Athēnē with Pŏseidōn for the possession of Attica. These pediments are 93 feet long, and 11 feet 4 inches high. The *cella*, or temple proper, is 194 feet long, and 69½ feet wide, with six columns at each

(3) * A METOPE FROM SOUTH OF THE PARTHENON.
(British Museum.)

end, 33 feet in height. Opposite the outermost columns at each end are *antæ*, formed by the prolongation of the side walls of the *cella* (*see* plan of ACROPOLIS). Along the top of the outer wall of the *cella* ran a continuous frieze, 524 feet in length, with representations of the Panathenaic procession

goddess, wrought in gold and ivory, the masterpiece of Phīdias (*cp.* ATHENE, near the end). The western chamber of the *cella* was fronted by a portico, and was called by the special name of the *Parthenon*. [Within this smaller chamber were kept vessels for use in the sacred processions, with various small articles of gold or silver. Modern writers have hitherto generally identified this small chamber with the *ŏpisthŏdŏmŏs* (lit. back-chamber), which was used as the treasury, or State bank, of Athens; but it is held by Dörpfeld that this term should be confined to the corresponding chamber of the early temple south of the Erechtheum.]

In the Middle Ages the temple was converted into a church, dedicated to the Virgin Mary, and then into a mosque, and remained in good preservation till 1687. In that year, during the siege of Athens by the Venetians, the building was blown up by the explosion of a powder magazine that the Turks had stored in it, and, with the exception of the two pediments, was almost completely destroyed. Most of the sculptures preserved from the pediments and metopes, and from the frieze of the temple chamber, are now among the Elgin Marbles in the British Museum.

(4) FROM THE NORTH FRIEZE OF THE PARTHENON.
(British Museum; slabs XXXV, XXXVI.)

carved in very low relief (fig. 2, *F*, and figs. 4 and 5). At the east end of the *cella*, the *prŏnăŏs*, or portico, leads into the eastern chamber, which was 100 Greek feet in length, and was therefore called the *hĕcătompĕdŏs*. It was divided longitudinally into three parts by two rows of nine columns each, and above these was a second row of columns forming an upper story. The central space was open to the sky (hypæthral). At its western end, under a protecting canopy, stood the statue of the

Parthĕnŏpæus. According to the older tradition, the beautiful son of Tălăus of Argos, and the brother of Adrastus; according to others, the son of Atălanta and Mĕlănīŏn. He was one of the *Seven against Thebes*, and was killed on the Theban wall during the storming of the city; the piece of rock that laid him low was hurled by Pĕrĭclўmĕnus. His son by the Nymph Clўmĕnē is Prŏmăchus, one of the Epĭgŏni.

Pāsĭphăē. Daughter of Hēliŏs and Persēïs, sister of Aëtēs and Circē, wife of

Mīnŏs. She was enamoured of the white bull presented by Poseidon to Minos (*q.v.*), and thereby became the mother of the monstrous Minotaur. (*See* MINOTAURUS.)

Pāsĭtĕlēs. A Greek artist of the 1st century B.C., a native of S. Italy. He was actively engaged at Rome on important works in marble, ivory, silver, and bronze, and was also an author. He originated a new school, which was not immediately connected with any of the existing tendencies of art, but was founded on a careful study of nature and the masterpieces of earlier sculptors. It aimed above all at correctness of form, combined with elegance of representation and a mastery of *technique*. [Pasiteles chased in silver a representation of the infant Roscius (Cic., *De Div.* i 79), and

among the Romans (*see* FAMILIA). *Pater patrātus*, the spokesman of the *fĕtĭālĕs* (*q.v.*). *Pătĕr mātūtīnŭs*, a special name of Janus (*q.v.*).

Pătĕră. The broad, flat dish or saucer used by the Romans for drinking and for offering libations. (*See* VESSELS.)

Pătrĭă Pŏtestas. See FAMILIA.

Patricians (*patrĭcĭī*, lit. the relatives of the *patrēs*, or heads of families of the old tribes. In the oldest times of Rome, the actual citizens who constituted the *pŏpŭlus Rōmānus*. They were divided into three tribes,—*Ramnēs, Tĭtĭēs,* and *Lŭcĕrēs,* each consisting of ten *cūrĭæ.* (*See* CURIA.) The union of these latter formed the national assembly, the *cŏmĭtĭă cūrĭātă.* (*See* COMITIA, 3.) Besides

POSEIDON.   APOLLO (*or* DIONYSUS).   PEITHO (*or* DEMETER).   APHRODITE.   EROS.

(5) * FROM THE EAST FRIEZE OF THE PARTHENON.
(Acropolis Museum, Athens; slab vi.)

executed an ivory statue of Jupiter for the temple dedicated by Metellus (Pliny, *N. H.* xxxvi 40). According to his contemporary Varro, he never executed any work without modelling it first (*ib.* xxxv 156). Among his pupils was Stĕphănus, who in his turn was the master of Mĕnĕlāus.] (*See* SCULPTURE.)

Passŭs. The pace, or double step, a Roman measure of length=5 Roman feet (*pes*) or 1·479 metres [=4 English feet 10¼ inches]. 1,000 *passūs* formed a Roman mile, 1,478·70 metres [or 1,616 yards, 2 feet, 2 inches, or about 143 yards less than an English mile. The *passus* is sometimes estimated as 1·48 metre; 1,000 *passus* being then 1,480 metres or 1,618 yards, *i.e.* 142 yards less than an English mile].

Pătĕr Fămĭlĭās. The master of a house

these there were originally only *clĭentēs*, settlers enjoying no legal rights, with the citizens for their protectors (or *patrōnĭ*). Afterwards, when a new element of the population, endowed with partial citizenship, called the *plebs* (*q.v.*), sprang up from the settlement of subjugated Latin tribes, the *patricii* stood in contrast to them as old citizens possessing full rights. Later, the plebeians received a fuller citizenship through the centurial constitution framed by Servius Tullius (*see* CENTURIA), while they gained at the same time the right of voting in the *comitia centŭrĭātă*, composed of patricians and plebeians, together with the obligation of serving in the field and paying taxes, hitherto obligatory on the patricians alone. In contrast to the plebeians, the patricians thus formed a hereditary aristocracy, with the exclusive right to hold public offices, whether civil or religious. Nothing short of a decision by the *comitia curiata* could either remove any one from the patrician body or (on rare occasions) enrol a plebeian among the patricians. The contraction of marriages between patricians and plebeians was not allowed till 445 B.C. A violent struggle arose between the two parties, after the establishment of the Republic in 510 B.C., on the subject of the admission of the plebeians to State offices. This struggle lasted till 300 B.C., and the patricians were, step by step, forced to give up their exclusive right to one office after another. First of all, they had to give up the quæstorship (409), then the consulate (367), the dictatorship (356), the censorship (351), the prætorship (338), and finally the most important priestly offices, the pontificate and the augurship (300). Only politically unimportant offices were left reserved for them, the temporal office of *interrex*, and the priestly offices of *rex sacrōrum* and the three *flāmĭnĕs māiōrēs*. The political importance which the patrician *comitia curiata* possessed, through its right to confirm the decisions of the *comitia centuriata*, was lost in 286. The *comitia trĭbūtă*, in which the *plebs* had the preponderance, thus became the most important organ of the democracy.

An aristocracy of holders of public offices was thus formed, consisting of the patricians together with the more important plebeian families. The members of such families, whether patrician or plebeian, were called *nŏbĭlēs*. The number of patrician families dwindled greatly owing to the civil wars (on their number towards the end of the Republic, *see* GENS). Cæsar and Augustus increased them by introducing plebeian families, and subsequent emperors gave the patriciate as a distinction. Under Constantine the Great, *patricius* became a personal title, which conferred a rank immediately below the consuls. The external distinctive marks of a patrician were the *tŭnĭcă lātĭclāvĭă* (*see* TUNICA) and a peculiar sort of shoe (*see* CALCEUS) adorned with an ivory crescent (*lūnŭla*).

Patrŏclus [*Pătrŏclŭs*, almost always in *Iliad*, Pătrŏclŭs once only in vocative (*Il.* xix 287)]. Son of Mĕnœtius and Sthĕnĕlē, the bosom friend of Achilles. He fell before Troy by the hand of Hector (*see* ACHILLES).

Patrŏnus. The Roman term for the protector of a single client, or of a whole community (*see* CLIENTES); the emancipator in relation to his freedman; and the judicial representative of accuser or accused. For the distinction between *patronus* and *advŏcātus, see* the latter.

Paulus. (1) *Iulius.* A Roman jurist of high repute in the beginning of the 3rd century A.D., contemporary with Papinian and Ulpian. With the former, he was legal assessor to the emperor Septĭmius Sĕvĕrus. With the latter, he was *prœfectus prœtōrĭo* under Alexander Severus, after he had been sent into exile by Hĕlĭŏgăbălus. He was most productive as a legal author, but in literary skill and finish stood far below his two contemporaries. The extracts from his numerous monographs or more comprehensive works form a sixth part of the "Digest." Besides these extracts his *Sententiœ*, a very popŭlar compendium of undisputed principles on the most frequent points of law, has been preserved in a shortened form.

(2) *See* FESTUS (1).

Pausănĭās. The Greek traveller and geographer, a native of Lydia. He explored Greece, Macedonia, Asia, and Africa; and then, in the second half of the 2nd century A.D., settled in Rome, where he composed a *Pĕrĭēgēsĭs* or Itinerary of Greece in ten books. Book i includes Attica and Mĕgărĭs; ii, Corinth with Sĭcўŏn, Phlĭūs, Argŏlis, Ægīna, and the other neighbouring islands; iii, Lăcōnĭa; iv, Messēnĭa; v, vi, Elis and Olympia; vii, Achæa; viii, Arcădia; ix, Bœōtia; x, Phōcĭs and Lŏcrĭs. The work is founded on notes, taken on the spot, from his own observation and inquiry from the natives of the country, on the subject of the religious cults and the monuments of art and architecture. Together with these there are topographical and historical notices, in working up which Pausanias took into consideration the accounts of other authors, poets as well as prose writers. Although his account is not without numerous inaccuracies, omissions, and mistakes, it is yet of inestimable value for our knowledge of ancient Greece, especially with regard to its mythology and its religious cults, but above all for the history of Greek art. The composition of his work (especially in the earlier books) shows little skill in plan, execution, or style.

Pausĭās. A Greek painter, a pupil of Pamphĭlus and a follower of the Sicyonian school. He lived about 360 B.C. at Sĭcўŏn, and invented the art of painting vaulted ceilings, and also of foreshortening; he brought encaustic painting to perfection. He painted chiefly children and flowers. One of his most famous pictures was the Flower Girl (*Stĕphănoplŏcŭs*), representing the flower-girl Glўcĕra, of whom he was enamoured in his youth [Pliny, *N. H.*, xxxv 123–127].

[Pausōn. A Greek painter whom Aristotle contrasts with Pŏlygnōtus in terms implying that the former was a caricaturist (*Poetics* 2 § 2). Elsewhere Aristotle says that young people should not look at the pictures of Pauson, but rather at those of Polygnotus or of any other "ethical" artist (*Politics* viii 5 § 7). He is sometimes identified with the Pauson who is mentioned with contempt by Aristophanes (*Ach.* 854, *Thesm.* 948, and *Plutus*, 602).]

[J. E. S.]

Păvor. *See* PALLOR.

Pax. The Roman goddess of peace (*Cp.* EIRENE.)

Pĕcŭlātus. The Roman term for misappropriation of public property, whether by officials (*e.g.* in the delivery of booty) or by private persons. Such offences, which seldom occurred in the more ancient times of the Republic, were then judged by the national tribunal. In later times they must have become more frequent, since various laws were issued against them, and a special court of justice (*see* QUÆSTIO) was appointed to try them. Besides the payment of compensation, the condemned person suffered disgrace and banishment (*interdictio ăquæ et ignis, see* EXILIUM), and, in the time of the Empire, transportation.

Pĕcūlĭum. The Romans considered the master of the house (*păter fămĭlĭăs*) the lawful owner of all the earnings of the members of the family under his control, whether bond or free (*see* FAMILIA). Whatever sum of money he gave to a grown up son or to a slave for his own use, was called the *peculium* of the latter. This gift could be revoked at pleasure, and could not be disposed of by will. Augustus first granted this right to soldiers, in the case of property won in war (*peculium castrense*), and Constantine extended it to that gained in a civil office (*peculium quăsi castrense*).

Pĕdārĭi. Those members of the Roman Senate (*q.v.*) who had occupied no office of State, and hence took a lower rank. They might only share in the voting, but did not enjoy the right of expressing individual opinions.

Pĕdĭēis. *See* SOLONIAN CONSTITUTION.

Pēgăsŭs. The winged *Steed of the Fountain*, named Pegasus, according to Hesiod [*Theog.* 281], because he was born at the springs (*pēgæ*) of Ocean. Begotten by Pŏseidōn, he sprang forth with Chrȳsāōr from the bleeding body of his mother Mĕdūsa, when her head was cut off by Perseus. [*See* SCULPTURE, fig. 1.] On his birth he soared into the air, and the spot

* PEGASUS AND BELLEROPHON.
(Rome, Spada Palace.)

where he first rested was the acropolis of Corinth. While Pegasus paused there to drink at the fountain of Peirēnē, Bellĕrŏphōn (*q.v.*) caught and tamed him, by the favour of Athēnē and Poseidon. It was on Pegasus that Bellerophon was mounted when performing his heroic exploits, including his conquest of the Chĭmæra. Afterwards, when Pegasus had thrown his rider, the steed flew upward to the immortals, to dwell in the palace of Zeus, and to bring him his thunder and lightning. By later writers, Pegasus is described as the steed of Eōs or of the Muses. On the spot where he struck Hĕlīcōn with his hoof, there gushed forth the inspiring fountain of the Muses known as *Hippŏcrēnĕ* ("the fountain of the steed"). The spring of *Hippocrene* near Trœzēn and that of Peirene on the Acrŏcŏrinthus were said to have had a similar origin. On the coins of Corinth the most common type from the earliest times is the winged Pegasus. The current representation of Pegasus as the poets' steed is a modern invention.

Peirælcus. *See* PIRÆICUS.

Peirēnē (*Greek*). The spring struck out by the winged steed Pĕgăsus on the citadel of Corinth. For another tradition of its origin, *see* SISYPHUS.

Peirĭthŏŭs (Lat. *Pīrĭthŏŭs*). Son of Dia by her husband Ixīon, or (according to another account) by Zeus; prince of the Lăpĭthæ, and friend of Thēseus. When he was celebrating, on Mount Pēlĭŏn, his marriage with Hippŏdămīa, daughter of Atrax, one of the Lapithæ, there arose the celebrated battle between the Lapithæ and the Centaurs, which ended in the defeat of the latter. The Centaurs and the most distinguished Greek heroes had been invited to the wedding; but one of the former, Eurўtīon, in drunken boldness, attempted to carry off the bride, and, following his example, the other Centaurs fell upon the women of the Lapithæ. Since Theseus and one of the Lapithæ, Cæneus (*q.v.*), rescued the bride, Peirithous assisted the former in the abduction of Helen. Accompanied by Theseus, Peirithous descended into the world below, in order to carry off Persĕphŏnē, and was compelled to pine there in everlasting chains as a punishment, while Theseus (*q.v.*) was released by Hērăclēs. Peirithous' son Polўpœtēs marched to Troy with Lĕonteus, the grandson of Cæneus, and after the fall of Troy is said to have founded with him the city of Aspendus in Pamphўlia.

Peisandrŏs (Lat. *Pisander*). A Greek epic poet of Cămīrus, in Rhodes, about 640 B.C. He wrote a *Hērăclēa* in two books, which is numbered among the better class of epic poems. He was the first to equip Hercules with the club and the lion's hide, and he probably also fixed the number of his labours at twelve. Only uninteresting fragments remain.

Peithō. In Greek mythology the personification of persuasion Like Erōs and the Graces, with whom Hesiod mentions her [*Works and Days*, 73], she usually appears in the train of Aphrŏdītē. She was, indeed, considered the daughter of the goddess, and was honoured together with her, as in Athens. She was also connected with Hermēs as the god of eloquence.

Pĕleiădĕs. Priestesses at Dōdōna (*q.v.*).

Pēleus. Son of Æacus and of Endēïs, and brother of Tĕlămōn. He was banished with his brother, on account of the murder of his step-brother Phōcus, whom he had slain with the *discus* out of envy at his strength and skill. His father banished him from Ægīna, but he was purified from his murder, and hospitably received by his uncle Eurўtīon, king of Thessalian Phthīa. Eurytion gave to Peleus his daughter Antĭgŏnē, mother of the beautiful Polўdōra, and one-third of his land as a dowry. Peleus accompanied Eurytion in the Calydonian Hunt, and killed him unawares with a javelin. Thereupon he fled from Phthia to Iolcus, where, once again, king Acastus cleansed him from the guilt of bloodshed. Because he rejected the proposals of Astў-dămeia, the wife of Acastus, she slandered him to his wife and to her husband, telling the former that Peleus was wooing her daughter Stĕrŏpē, and the latter that he wished to persuade her to infidelity. Antigone killed herself for sorrow, but Acastus planned revenge. When Peleus, wearied by the chase, had fallen asleep on Pēlĭŏn, Acastus left him alone, after hiding in a dunghill his irresistible sword, the work of Hēphæstus and the gift of the gods. When Peleus awoke and sought his sword, he was attacked by the Centaurs, and only delivered by the presence among them of Chīrōn, his maternal grandfather. With Chiron's help he recovered his sword, slew Acastus and his wife, and took possession of the throne of Iolcus. The gods decreed him the sea-goddess Thĕtĭs (*q.v.*) as his wife. With Chiron's help he overcame her resistance in a grotto by the sea, although she endeavoured to escape by changing into fire, water, beast, or fish. The marriage was celebrated in Chiron's cave on the summit of Pēlĭŏn, and the immortals appeared and gave Peleus presents: Pŏseidōn, the undying steeds Bălīus and Xanthus, and all the gods the weapons with which Achilles afterwards fought before Troy; Chiron presented him with a lance made of an ash tree on Mount Pelion. Apollo and the Muses sang of the deeds of Peleus and of his unborn son. But Ĕrĭs, or Strife, also appeared, uninvited, and threw among the goddesses a golden apple with the inscription, *For the Fairest*, thus giving the first cause for the Trojan War (*q.v.*). In this war the only offspring of this marriage, the hero Achilles, is said to have found an untimely end during his father's lifetime. According to a later tradition, unknown to Homer, Thetis forsook her husband, because his presence hindered her from making her son immortal.

Pĕlĭās. Son of Pŏseidōn and of Tȳrō, who was afterwards the wife of Crētheus. He was the brother of Nēleus, half-brother of Æsōn, Phĕrēs, and Amȳthāon, father of Acastus and Alcēstis. He deprived Æson of the dominion of Iolcus, and sent Æson's son Jāsōn to Colchis to fetch the golden fleece. He did so because the youth, now fully grown, was claiming his father's throne. In Jason's absence Pelias killed Æson, and drove his wife to suicide. In revenge, when Jason returned, his wife Mēdēa persuaded the daughters of Pelias to cut him to pieces and seethe him in a caldron, under the pretext of restoring him to youth. His son Acastus instituted in his honour funeral games which were greatly celebrated by poets and artists.

Pĕlŏpīa. Daughter of Thȳestēs, mother of Ægisthus by her own father. (*See* ÆGISTHUS and ATREUS.)

Pĕlops. Son of the Lydian or Phrygian king Tantălus and Dĭōnē, daughter of Atlas. When he was a child, his father slew him, cut him to pieces and seethed him, and set him as food before the gods. The gods did not touch the horrible meal; only Dēmētēr, absorbed in grief for her stolen daughter, ate one shoulder. By the command of Zeus, Hermēs replaced the pieces in the caldron, and Clōthō drew the boy from it in renewed beauty, while Demeter replaced the missing shoulder by one made of ivory. Hence it was that his descendants, the Pĕlŏpīdæ, bore on one shoulder a mark of dazzling whiteness. Pelops, when grown to manhood, went to Pīsa in Elis as a wooer of Hippŏdămīa, daughter of king Œnŏmäus. He won the victory, the bride, and the kingdom, by the help of the winged steeds given him by Pŏseidōn, and by the treachery of Myrtĭlus, the chariot driver of Œnomaus. When Myrtilus (or Myrsilus), a son of Hermēs, claimed the promised reward, half the kingdom, Pelops hurled him from his chariot into the sea. Through his curse and the anger of Hermes, the baneful spell was once more cast upon the house of Pelops. He returned to Pisa, and, after he

had made himself master of Olympia, he is said to have restored the games with great splendour, a service for which his memory was afterwards honoured above that of all other heroes. By another act of violence he obtained possession of Arcadia, and extended his power so widely over the peninsula that it was called after his name the *Pĕlŏponnēsus*, or "island of Pelops." By Hippŏdămīa he had six sons (*cp.* ALCATHOUS, ATREUS, PITTHEUS, THYESTES), and two daughters; and by the Nymph Axĭŏchē, a son Chrȳsippus. The latter, his father's favourite, was killed by Atreus and Thyestes, at the instigation of Hippodamia, and his dead body was cast into a well. Peleus discovered the crime, and banished the murderers from the country. Hippodamia thereupon took refuge with her sons at Mīdĕa in Argŏlis. On her death, Peleus buried her bones in the soil of Olympia.

Peltastæ. The Greek light-armed foot-soldiers, forming an arm intermediate between the heavily equipped hoplites (*q.v.*) and the sharpshooters, *gymnētæ* (*q.v.*). The name is taken from the *peltē*, a light shield of Thracian origin (*see* SHIELD). For attack they had a javelin, or *ăcontĭŏn*, and a long

PELTAST.

From a vase-painting.

(Stackelberg, *Gräber der Hellenen*, Taf. xxxviii.)

sword. These troops originated in Thrace and North Greece, and the *peltastæ* serving in the Peloponnesian War and in the armies of the younger Cyrus and Agēsĭläus belonged to those countries. Iphĭcrătēs equipped his mercenaries with this kind of armament, introducing at the same time linen doublets and, instead of greaves, what were called after him *ĭphĭcrătĭdĕs*, something between boots and leggings [Diodorus xv 44]. In the Macedonian army their place was taken by the *hȳpaspistæ*.

Pĕnātēs, with *Vesta* and *Lăr*, the household gods of the Romans; strictly the guardians of the storeroom (*pĕnus*), which in old Roman houses stood next the *ātrium;* in later times, near the back of the building (*pĕnĕtrālia*). They were two in number, and presided over the well-being of the house, their blessing being shown in the fulness of the store-room. This chamber therefore, as being sacred to them, was holy, and not to be entered except by chaste and undefiled persons. The hearth of the house was their altar, and on it were sculptured the figures of the two *Penates* beside that of the *Lar*. Often they were represented dancing and raising a drinking-horn, to symbolise a joyful and prosperous life. The offerings to them were made jointly with those to the *Lar* (*see* LARES). There were also *Penates* belonging to the State. These at first had their temple in the quarter *Vēlĭa*, where their statues stood below those of the Dĭoscūrī. Afterwards it was supposed that the original Penates, brought from Samothrace to Troy, and thence conveyed by Æneas to Lavīnium, were identical with certain symbols kept, with the *Pallădium*, in a secret part of the temple of Vesta. The Penates of the Latin League, which were at first regarded as the Trojan Penates, were enshrined in the sanctuary at Lavinium. Annual offerings were brought to them by the Roman priests, and also by consuls, prætors, and dictators on assuming or laying down office, and by generals on their departure for their provinces.

Pēnělōpē. Daughter of Icărius and the Nymph Pĕrĭbœa, the faithful wife of Odysseus (*q.v.*) and mother of Tēlĕmăchus.

Pĕnestæ. In Thessaly the descendants of the older population subdued by the Thessalians. They managed the property of the owners as serfs bound to the soil, paying a moderate tax, and being also liable to be called out for military service. But their lords could not remove them from the land nor put them to death.

Pentăcŏsĭŏmĕdimni. The first of the four classes of citizens instituted at Athens by Sŏlōn. (*See* SOLONIAN CONSTITUTION *and* EISPHORA.)

Pentathlŏn. In Greek gymnastics a contest compounded of the *five* events (running, jumping, wrestling, throwing the discus and the javelin). After each separate event the defeated stood out, till finally two contested the victory in the wrestling. (*See* GYMNASTICS.)

Pentēcontŏrus. A kind of Greek ship in which there were fifty oarsmen arranged in a single row. (*See* SHIPS.)

Pentēcostўs. In the Spartan army, a division of the *lŏchos* (*q.v.*).

Pentērēs. A quinquereme; *i.e.* the form of Greek ship in which there were five rows of oarsmen one above the other. (*See* SHIPS.)

Penthĕsĭlēa. Daughter of Arēs and Ŏtrērā, and queen of the Amazons (*q.v.*), with whom she came to Priam's aid after Hector's death. Her courage reduced the Greeks to sore straits, till she was mortally wounded by Achilles; and, even as she died, her youth and beauty filled the heart of her conqueror with love. [Quintus Smyrnæus, i.]

Pentheus. Son of Ĕchīon and Ăgāvē, the daughter of Cadmus, whom he succeeded in the sovereignty of Thebes. When Dĭonўsus came to Thebes, and the women celebrated a Bacchic festival for him on Cĭthærōn, he hastened thither to prevent it, but was taken by his own mother for a wild beast, and torn to pieces by her and the other women [Eur., *Bacchæ*]. His grandson was Mĕnœceus, the father of Crĕōn and Ĭŏcastē. *See* cut under AGĀVE.

Pĕphrēdō. One of the Grajæ (*q.v.*).

Peplus. (1) A Greek woman's garment, large, broad, hanging in folds, and usually richly embroidered. It was thrown over the rest of the clothing, and wrapped round the whole of the body. (2) In particular, the State robe of Athēnē, which was a work of art, embroidered with groups from the battle of the Giants, representations of the exploits of heroes under Athene's guidance, scenes of Attic history, and portraits of celebrated men. It was woven by the wives and maidens of Attica for the statue of Athene as goddess of the State, and presented at the Panathenaic festival.

Perdŭellĭō. The Roman term for all acts whereby an individual within the State showed himself an enemy, *perduellis*, of the established constitution. It included attempts at despotic power, usurpation or abuse of magisterial powers (*e.g.* the execution of a citizen), violation of the sanctity of the *trĭbūni plēbis*, etc. In the time of the kings, the king himself tried crimes of the kind, or handed over the decision to two deputies appointed in each instance by himself, *dŭŏ vĭri căpĭtālēs* or *perduelliōnis*, from whom an appeal lay to the people; after Servius Tullius, to the *cŏmĭtĭa centŭrĭāta*. Under the Republic *duo viri* were still appointed as presiding judges, till this gradually fell into disuse, and trials of the kind came in general to be dealt with by the popular court. In earlier times the penalty was death by hanging on a tree, by throwing from the Tarpeian Rock, or by beheading; later, banishment, and after the tribunes brought cases of *perduellio* before the *comitia tributa*, fines as well. From the latter half of the 2nd century B.C. the less important cases began to be treated as offences of *maiestas ;* and by Cæsar's Julian law, 46 B.C., all cases of *perduellio* were included under this name. (*See also* MAIESTAS.)

Pĕrĕgrīnus. The description in Roman law of all foreigners or persons other than citizens sojourning or domiciled within Roman territory. Originally *peregrini* were entirely without rights, unless they obtained a *pătrōnus*, except in cases where there was a treaty (*fœdus*) with the State

they were always excluded. (*See also* CIVITAS.)

Pergamene Sculptures. These sculptures belong to the acropolis of Pergănŏn in Asia Minor, discovered by the accomplished architect Humann in 1871, and excavated in and after 1878 under the superintendence of Humann and the distinguished archæologist Conze, with the assistance of R. Bohn and others. The work was done at the expense of the Prussian government, and the sculptures then brought to light are now in the Museum at Berlin. The first rank among

(1) BATTLE OF ZEUS AND THE GIANTS.
(Relief from Pergamon; Berlin Museum.)

to which they belonged, regulating the legal position of the subjects of the two States respectively. But the increasing intercourse between Rome and other States, and the consequent growth in the number of *peregrini* in Rome, made it necessary to grant to all foreigners a definite competency to acquire property, enter into obligations, and the like ; and for the decision of civil suits between foreigners and citizens, or of foreigners among themselves, a special *prætor (q.v.)* was appointed. From the public, private, and sacrificial law of Rome

them is occupied by the remains of the sculpture representing the fight between the gods and the snake-legged Giants, a colossal composition in high relief, which occupied a space 7 ft. 6½ ins. high, and extended over the outer surface (about 118 sq. ft. in area) of the upper part of the platform of an altar about 39 ft. high, which was probably built by king Eumĕnēs II (197–159 B.C.). Of this about half remains, whereof a third consists of more or less well-preserved slabs, and the rest of fragments large and small. They exhibit an astonishing mastery of form and *technique*, and a vivid realism that is often terrible, combined with a truly grand style, and are among the most important productions of ancient art. Only fragmentary portions of the names of the sculptors in *marble* belonging to the Pergamene school (*see* SCULPTURE) have been found. [Sŏgŏnus, Phȳrŏmăchus, Strătŏnīcus, and Antīgŏnus, mentioned in Pliny, *N. H.* xxxiv 34, were sculptors in *bronze*. The name of Mĕnĕcrătēs in the genitive case has been traced in one of the inscriptions, and has led to

has sunk to the earth. In his left hand he shakes his ægis over a second opponent, who writhes on the ground in pain. A snake-legged Giant holds out his left arm, wrapped round with the skin of a wild beast, to protect him from the onslaught of the god. By the side of Zeus, and taking part in the conflict, hovers his eagle.

The counterpart to this was presumably the group with *Athēnē* in the centre (fig. 2). The goddess appears in full armour, with the heavy round shield on her left arm ; on her head, the front portion of which is un-

(2) ATHENĒ IN THE BATTLE OF THE GIANTS.
(Relief from Pergamon; Berlin Museum.)

the conjecture that his sons Apollōnius and Tauriscus, the sculptors of the Farnese Bull, were among the artists who worked at Pergamon. The "great marble altar, 40 ft. high, with colossal figures, comprising a battle of the Giants," is mentioned in the *Lĭber Mĕmŏrĭālis* of Ampĕlĭus (*q.v.*).]

The most important parts of the work are shown in the cuts. The powerful figure of *Zeus* (fig. 1), wrapped in flowing drapery, is most impressive. With his thunderbolt of triple fork and flaming crest, he has already transfixed the thigh of a Giant, who

fortunately destroyed, is the tall Corinthian helmet; and on her breast, the ægis, carved with the greatest care. She is advancing with fierce strides towards the right, dragging along with her by the hair a young Giant with a vast pair of wings. Her sacred serpent is also fighting for her. The motive of the piece vividly reminds one of the Lăŏcŏŏn group, which is closely allied in form and expression. The group of Athene and the Giants is most effectively completed by the figure of Nīkē with outspread wings flying up to the victorious goddess, and by the mighty form of Mother Earth, with the upper portion of her body rising up from the deep. Her name (*Gē*) is written over her right shoulder. With imploring gestures she is raising to heaven her face, surrounded by her unbound locks; for they are her own children who are thus being laid low by the might of the celestial gods.

One of the most remarkable groups is that in which the triple Hĕcătē appears among the fighting Olympians. The sculptor has given her three heads (one wanting); and three pairs of arms, all of them bearing weapons (fig. 3). In other groups of combatants we find Hēlĭŏs on his four-horse chariot, with Eōs riding in front; Dĭŏnȳsus; the sea-gods with their stately following of sea-centaurs and other divinities of the

Pŏlȳbus of Corinth, and foster-mother of Œdĭpūs (*q.v.*).

Pĕrĭbŏlus. The court of a Greek temple. (*See* TEMPLES.)

Pĕrĭclȳmĕnus. (1) Son of Nēleus and Chlōrĭs, brother of Nestōr. He is the chief hero of the defence of Pȳlŏs against Hērăclēs, to whom he gave much trouble by his prowess, as well as by his power of transforming himself, like the sea-gods, into every possible shape. This power had been given him by Pŏseidōn, who was reputed to be his father. Finally he succumbed to the arrows of Heracles, and by his death sealed the doom of Pylos.

(2) A Theban, son of Pŏseidōn and Chlōris, daughter of the seer Tīrĕsĭas. In the war of the *Seven against Thebes* he

(3) HECATE, ARES, AND GIANTS.
(Relief from Pergamon; Berlin Museum.)

ocean; the goddess Cȳbĕlē, seated on a lion, etc. Beside these there have been found about thirty other slabs carved in relief, of smaller dimensions (5 ft. 2·8 ins. high), including some on the story of Tēlĕphus, the patron hero of the State of Pergămōn. These formed part of a smaller frieze, running round the inner side of an Ionic colonnade, rising above the larger frieze, on the platform, and inclosing the altar proper. The torsoes of a large number of colossal statues, mostly female, which likewise originally stood on the platform, have also been discovered. On the *Pergamene School, see* SCULPTURE.

Pergămēnum. *See* WRITING MATERIALS.

Pĕrĭactŏs (*Greek*). *See* THEATRE.

Pĕrĭbœa (also called Mĕrŏpē). Wife of

slew Parthĕnŏpæus, and was in pursuit of Amphĭărāus at the moment when the latter sank into the earth.

Pĕrĭēgētæ (lit. "those who guide strangers about," and show them what is worth notice). A term applied by the Greeks to the authors of travellers' guide-books enumerating and describing what was worthy of note, especially buildings or monuments, in the several cities or countries. This kind of literature was especially in vogue from the 3rd century B.C. onwards. Its chief representatives are *Pŏlĕmōn* of Trŏăs (about 200), whose numerous works are now unfortunately preserved in fragments only; and after him the Athenian *Hēlĭŏdōrus*, author of a great work on the Acropolis, likewise lost. Larger fragments survive of a handbook to Greece by a certain *Hērăclĭdēs*, and of the interesting work on Alexandria by *Callixĕnus* of Rhodes. The only complete work of this kind remaining is the valuable description of Greece by *Pausănĭās* (2nd century A.D.).

Pĕriœci. The name of those inhabitants of the Spartan State who, unlike the serfs or helots (*q.v.*), had kept the possession of their lands and personal liberty after the Dorian occupation, but without having the citizenship. They too, like the helots, were at least twice as numerous as the ruling Spartīātæ. Their name (lit. *dwelling around*) indicates that they lived on the plain in the neighbourhood of the chief city which was occupied by the Spartiatæ. Probably they were more or less doricised by Dorian colonists sent into their towns, whereof as many as a hundred are mentioned. They were occupied partly in cultivating their farms (which, we learn, were smaller than those of the Spartiatæ); partly in manufactures and industry, in which the ruling caste were forbidden to engage; partly in trade. Besides certain taxes, they were bound to military service, either as hoplites or as light-armed troops (as in the case of the *Scīrītæ* or inhabitants of *Scīrītis*, who formed a special body of light infantry, and were reserved for outpost duty when in camp, for advance and rearguard, and in battle for service on the left wing). After the Peloponnesian War they formed the chief strength of the army. (*See* WARFARE.) In the army they were also eligible as officers of the lower ranks; but from all civil offices they were excluded, as also from the popular assembly. They were completely subject to the orders of the Spartiatæ; and when they made themselves troublesome, they could be put to death by the ephors without trial or conviction.

Peripatetics (Gr. *pĕrĭpătētĭkoi*, lit. "persons given to walking about"). The followers of Aristotle's philosophy. They derived their name from Aristotle's habit of walking with his disciples in the shady avenues of the Athenian Gymnasium called the *Lўcēum*, while he discussed the problems of philosophy. (*See also* ARISTOTLE *and* PHILOSOPHY.)

Pĕriphētēs. Son of Hēphæstus; a monster at Ĕpĭdaurus, who slew the passers by with an iron club (whence he was called *cŏrў-nētēs* or club-bearer), till he was himself slain by the young Thēseus.

Pĕriptĕrŏs. An epithet describing a temple completely surrounded by a colonnade supporting the entablature. (*See* TEMPLES.)

Peristyle (Gr. *pĕristўlŏn*). A court surrounded by columns. (*See* HOUSE.)

Pĕrō. The shoe of the ordinary Roman citizen. (*See* CALCEUS.)

Persĕphŏnē (also *Persĕphassa;* Lat. *Prŏserpĭnă*). Daughter of Zeus and Dēmētēr. As the wife of Hādēs, she is the dread queen of the world below. Her special name in Attic cult is Cŏrē (lit. "the Maiden"). As a maiden, while plucking flowers (near Enna in Sicily, according to the story common in later times), she was carried off into the lower world by Hādēs on his car, with the consent of her father. To appease her mother's wrath, Zeus sent Hermēs to bring her back; but, since she had eaten part of a pomegranate given her by Hades (*i.e.* had already become his wife), she could only spend two-thirds of the year in the upper world with her mother. At the end of that time she had always to return to her husband, and rule as the dark goddess of death; whereas, while with her mother, she was regarded as the virgin daughter, and the helper of the goddess who presides over the fertility of the earth. Hence Persephone is emblematic of vegetable life, that comes and goes with the changing seasons. In spring, when the seeds sprout up from the ground, she rises to her mother; when the harvest is over, and the vegetation dies, and the seed is laid again in the dark grave of earth, she returns to her subterraneous kingdom. From this notion of the seed buried in the dark earth and again rising to light was developed that conception of the myth as an image of immortality which lies at the base of the Eleusinian mysteries. To express her rising and descending, her festivals were celebrated in spring and after the harvest. In spring she was worshipped at the lesser *Eleusĭnĭă* in Attica, and at her flower-festival of the *anthcsphŏrĭă*, in the Peloponnesus, but more especially in Sicily. In autumn, there was held in Attica the *great Eleusinia ;* i.e. the wedding-feast on her marriage with the god of the lower world. She was generally worshipped together with her mother; hence they were spoken of as "the two goddesses." In the Eleusinian mysteries she was also connected with Dĭonўsus, who, under the mystic name Iacchus, was regarded as her son, brother, or bridegroom. In later times she was confused with other divinities, especially Hĕcătē, as the goddess of night and of the world of spirits. She was represented either as the young and beautiful daughter of Dēmētēr, with *cornācōpĭa*, ears of corn, and a cock, the emblem of her rising in spring, or as the grim spouse of Hades, with rich adornments and the symbolic pomegranate. (*See cut,* and *cp.* DEMETER, fig. 1.)

The Roman name *Prōserpĭnă* is regarded by some as an altered form of the Greek Persephone; by others as a native name only accidentally similar to the Greek, denoting a goddess who assisted in the germination (*proserpĕrĕ*) of the seed, and, owing to the similarity of the two goddesses, transferred to Persephone after the introduction of her cult as the divinity of the lower world. (*See* HADES ; *see also* LIBITINA.)

Persēs. (1) Son of the Titan Crīus, father of Hĕcătē.

(2) Brother of Æētēs of Colchis. (*See* MEDEA.)

Perseus. Son of Zeus and Dănăē, grandson of Acrĭsĭus (*q.v.*). An oracle had declared that Danaë, the daughter of Acrisius, would give birth to a son who would kill his grandfather. Acrisius committed Perseus with his mother to the sea in a wooden box, which was carried by the waves to the isle of Sĕrīphus. Here the honest fisherman Dictys son of Magnēs (*see* ÆOLUS, 1) brought it to land with his net, and took care of mother and child. Dictys' brother Pŏlўdectēs, however, the king of the island, conceived a passion for the fair Danaë, and finding the son in the way, betrayed the young Perseus, who was now grown out of boyhood, into promising, on the occasion of a banquet, to do anything for him, even should he order the head of Mĕdūsa, and held him to his word. Encouraged and assisted by Athēnē and Hermēs, Perseus reached the Graiæ (*q.v.*), in the farthest part of Lĭbўa; and by capturing the single eye and tooth which they possessed in common, compelled them to show him the way to their sisters the Gorgons (*q.v.*). He also made them equip him for the undertaking with the winged sandals, the magic bag, and the helmet of Hādēs, which made the wearer invisible. Hermes added to these a sharp sword shaped like a sickle.

Thus provided, he flew to the Gorgons on the shores of Ocĕănus, found them asleep, and, since their glance turned the beholder to stone, with face averted smote and cut off Medusa's head, which Athene showed him in the mirror of her shield, while she guided his hand for the blow. He thrust it quickly into his bag, and flew off through the air, pursued by the other two Gorgons ; but, by virtue of his helmet, he escaped them, and came in his flight to Æthĭŏpĭa.

* PERSEPHONE, HADES, AND CERBERUS.
(Rome, Vatican.)

Here he rescued Andrŏmĕda (*q.v.*), and won her as his bride. Returning with her to Seriphus, he avenged his mother for the importunities of Pŏlўdectēs by turning the king and his friends into stone by the sight of Medusa's head ; set Dictys on the throne of the island ; gave up the presents of the Graiæ to Hermes, who restored them ; and presented the Gorgon's head to Athene, who set it in the middle of her shield or breast-plate. Then he returned with his mother and wife to Argos. But before his arrival Acrisius had gone away to Lārissa in Thessaly, and here Perseus unwittingly killed him with a *discus* at the funeral games held in honour of the king of that country. He duly buried the body of his grandfather, but, being unwilling to succeed to his inheritance, effected an exchange with Mĕgăpenthēs, his uncle Prœtus' son, took Tīryns in exchange for Argos and built Mĭdĕa and Mўcēnæ. By Andromeda he had one daughter, Gorgŏphŏnē, and six sons. The eldest, Persēs, was regarded as the ancestor of the Persians ; Alcæus, Sthĕnĕlus, and Electrўōn were the fathers respectively of Amphĭtrўōn, Eurystheus, and Alcmēnē, the mother of Hērăclēs. Perseus had a shrine (*hĕrōŏn*) on the road between Argos and Mycenæ, and was worshipped with divine honours in Seriphus and Athens.

Persius Flaccus (*Aulus*). A Roman satirist; born 34 A.D. at Vŏlăterræ, in Etruria, of a good equestrian family. Losing his father when six years old, at the age of twelve he went to Rome, and enjoyed the instructions of the most eminent teachers, more especially of one for whom he had the greatest reverence, Annæus Cornūtus, who initiated him in the Stoic philosophy, and introduced him to the acquaintance of Lucan. After the first poetic attempts of his youth, which he himself burnt, his energies were directed to satiric verse, under the influence of Lūcīlius and Horace. On his early death, in 62, the six satires which he left, after some slight revision by Cornutus, were published by his friend, the poet Cæsius Bassus. In these Persius deals with the moral corruption of his age, from the standpoint of a Stoic preacher of ethics. Both in thought and expression a tendency to echo Horace is constantly apparent. He composed slowly, and was himself conscious that he had no true poetic faculty.[1] His mode of expression is frequently difficult and involved to the verge of obscurity. The need of explanations was accordingly felt in comparatively early times; but the collection of *scholia* bearing the name of Cornutus shows hardly any traces of ancient learning.

Pervĭgĭlĭum (lit. "a night-watch"). A nocturnal festival in honour of a divinity, especially that of the *Bŏnă Dĕă*, at which originally only married women were allowed to be present. In imperial times, when the presence of men was permitted, a nocturnal festival to Vĕnŭs was also instituted. Such a festival, extending over three nights in the spring, is referred to in an anonymous poem called the *Pervĭgĭlĭum Vĕnĕrĭs*, of the 2nd or 3rd century A.D. It consists of ninety-three trochaic *septēnārĭi*, separated into unequal *strŏphæ* by the recurring refrain, *Crās ămet qui nunquam ămāvit, quique amavit cras amet.* It celebrates in a lively strain the power of Venus, particularly as displayed in springtime, lauding her as the giver of life to all, and as the ancestress and patroness of Rome.

Pĕtăsus. A flat felt hat, with a broad and round brim, usually worn among the Thessalians. The brim is often parted into four bow-shaped indentations (fig. 2). It is said to have been introduced into Greece along with the *chlămўs* as a distinguishing mark of the *ĕphēbī*. Hermēs is usually represented with the winged *petasus*. The

[1] The prologue, in which this self-criticism is expressed, is omitted by Jahn in his latest edition.

Romans wore a similar hat in the country, and when travelling; in the city it was

(1)   (2)

PETASUS.

(1) Gerhard, *Arch. Zeitung*, 1844, tav. xiv.
(2) Müller, *Denkm.* i, no. 327.

generally used only in the theatre, as a protection from the sun.

Pĕtrōnĭus Arbĭter. Author of a satiric romance, certainly of the time of Nero, and probably the Gaius Petronius whose licentiousness and congenial tastes obtained for him the high favour of Nero, at whose court he played the part of *arbĭter ēlēgantĭæ* (*maître de plaisir*), until, in 66 A.D., in consequence of the intrigues of his rivals, he committed suicide by opening his veins [Tacitus, *Ann.* xvi 18, 19]. Of his social romance, entitled *Sătŭræ*, which must originally have consisted of about twenty books, only fragments are left to us, being part of books xv and xvi. The most complete and famous is the "Banquet of Trimalchio" (*Cēna Trimalchĭōnis*). Judging from the fragments, the scene was laid under Tiberius, or possibly Augustus, in S. Italy, chiefly in an unnamed colony in Campania, partly in Crŏtōn. The work is astonishing for the truth with which both manners and men are painted. A masterly hand appears in the treatment of the dialogue, adapted as it is in every instance to the character of the speaker, now plebeian, in the mouth of Trimalchio, the freedman who has become a millionaire; now refined, in the cultivated Greek Encolpius; or again bombastic, in the case of the poet Eumolpus. All situations in life (with a preference for the filthiest), and even literature and art, come under discussion. In the prose are introduced numerous and sometimes extensive pieces of poetry, mostly intended to parody some particular style.

Peutinger Tablet (*Tăbŭla Peutingĕrĭăna*, named after its former owner, Konrad Peutinger, one of the councillors of Augsburg). A chartographic representation of the Roman world; now at Vienna. It is a copy of a map of the 3rd century A.D. (*See* also ITINERARIA.)

Pĕzĕtæri. In the Macedonian army, the free but not noble class of the population, who formed the heavy infantry (*hoplĭtæ*). (*See* WARFARE.)

Phæācĕs. A fabulous people in Homer, to whom Odysseus comes in his wanderings [*Od.* vi-viii]. They stand as near to the gods as the Giants and *Cyclōpĕs*, seeing them face to face. Originally settled in Hўpĕreia, they were compelled by the violence of their neighbours the *Cyclopes* to migrate, under their king Nausĭthŏüs, son of Pŏseidōn and Pĕrĭbœa, daughter of Eurўmĕdōn, the last king of the Giants, to the happy island of Schĕrĭa, where they built a city. On the arrival of Odysseus their ruler was Alcĭnŏüs, the wise son of Nausithoüs; his wife was Árētē, his brother's daughter, and besides many sons he was the father of the fair Nausĭcăa, Odysseus' preserver. Far from the turmoil of the world, the Phæācĕs are described as leading a life of undisturbed happiness in the enjoyment of the goods wherewith they are richly blessed; above all Alcinoüs, who had the fairest of orchards and a most beautiful palace. Their business is solely with the sea, with shipping and the provision of all that belongs to it. Their ships are of wondrous sort. Without steersman or rudder, divining of themselves the wishes and thoughts of all men, and knowing all lands, they traverse the sea swift as a bird or a thought, wrapped in mist and darkness, yet have never suffered wreck or foundering. But when the ship, that brought the sleeping Odysseus in one night to Thrace, came back, Pŏseidōn, of whose envious malice a prophecy had long ago bidden them beware, changed it to a rock in sight of harbour, and the Phæaces were in fear that the rest of the saying would come true, and mountains rise up all round their city. Though it is obvious that the Phæaces and their abodes, Hypereia and Scheria, are purely mythical, the kingdom of Alcinoüs was early identified as Corcўra (*Corfu*). He had a shrine there, and the harbour was named after him. Near the island was also shown the petrified ship. Hence the later Argonautic legends made even Jāsōn and Mēdēa touch at Corcyra on their flight from Æētēs, and, like Odysseus, find protection and help from Alcinoüs. (*See* ARGONAUTS.)

Phædra. Daughter of Mīnōs and Pāsĭphăē, wife of Thēseus, and mother of Acāmās and Dēmŏphŏōn. When her stepson Hippŏlўtus rejected her love, she compassed his death by slandering him to Theseus. Afterwards, in remorse for her guilt, she put an end to her life. (*See* HIPPOLYTUS.)

Phædrus. A Roman poetical fabulist; by birth a Macedonian of the district of Pĭērĭa, he came early to Rome as a slave, and acquired a knowledge of Roman literature while still a boy. If the traditional title of his five books of fables after Æsop is to be trusted (*Phædri, Augusti lĭberti, făbŭlæ Æsōpĭæ*), he was set free by Augustus. To Phædrus belongs the credit of introducing fable-writing into Latin poetical literature; a fact of which he was fully conscious, but which secured him neither relief from his miserable position, nor recognition on the part of the educated public; his patrons seem to have been only freedmen like himself. In fact, he even drew upon himself, by his two first published books, the illwill and persecution of the all-powerful favourite of Tĭbĕrĭus, Sējānus, who suspected in them malicious references to contemporary events. In consequence he did not publish the remaining books till after the fall of Sejanus in 31 A.D., and the death of Tiberius in 37.

The five books are preserved, though not in a complete form. Whether the further collection of thirty-two fables transcribed from a MS in the 15th century by Archbishop Nicolo Perotti (*Făbŭlæ Perottĭānæ*) [and published at Naples in 1809] are a genuine work of Phædrus, is doubtful. The matter of the fables is only to a small extent borrowed from Æsop. Some include stories from history, partly referring to the present or immediate past. In relation to the Greek originals, the material is not always skilfully used, especially in the "morals." The drawing of the characters is at first very cramped, but is afterwards more broadly treated; the language fluent, and in general correct; the metre too (iambic *sēnārĭus*), used with strictness, though wanting the purity which, in this kind of verse, became general from the time of Catullus. About the 10th century an author calling himself Rōmŭlus, drew up a prose version of Phædrus, which served as a model for the mediæval collections of fables.

Phaëthōn. Son of Hēlĭŏs (who is himself sometimes called Phäĕthōn) and the Sea-nymph Clўmĕnē, wife of Mĕrops, king of Æthĭŏpĭa. When he grew up, he demanded of his father, as a proof of his birth, the privilege of driving the chariot of the sun for a single day. He proved, however, too weak to restrain the horses, who soon ran away with him, and plunged, now close up to heaven, now right down to earth, so that both began to take fire. At last, to save the whole world from destruction, Zeus shattered the young man with his lightning, his corpse falling into the river Erĭdănus. His sisters, the Hēlĭădēs, Ægle, Phăëthūsa, and Lampĕtĭē, wept for him unceasingly, and were changed into poplars; whence it is that their tears still ooze from those trees, and are hardened by Helios into amber.

Phaininda (*Greek*). A kind of Greek game of *ball* (*q.v.*)

Phălangītæ. The soldiers of the Macedonian phalanx (*q.v.*).

Phălanx. The Greek term for the order of battle in which heavy infantry were drawn up, in an unbroken line, several ranks deep. (*See* HOPLITÆ.) The most famous phalanx was that formed by king Philip, constituting the chief strength of the Macedonian army. It was first 8, afterwards 12–16 deep. In the eight-rank formation, the lances (*sarissæ*) being eighteen feet long, those of all ranks could be presented to the enemy. They were grasped with the right hand at the butt, and, with the left, four feet from the butt end; hence the lances of the first rank projected fourteen feet, while the spear-heads of the last rank were level with, or just in front of, the men in the front rank. In the deeper formation, and after the reduction of the length of the *sarissa* to fourteen feet, only the first five ranks presented their weapons to the front; the rest held them slanting over the shoulders of their comrades in front. The name phalanx, or *taxis*, was also applied to the separate regiments of the *phălangitæ*. The line of each such phalanx was divided, from front to rear, into four *chiliarchies*, each chiliarchy into four *syntagmăta*, each syntagma into four *tetrarchies*. The importance of this formation lay in its power of resistance to hostile onset, and in the weight with which it fell, when impelled against the enemy's lines. Its weaknesses were want of mobility, the impossibility of changing front in face of the enemy, and unsuitability for close, hand to hand engagement. The Roman legions also fought in phalanx in the older times before Cămillus. Under the emperors the phalanx was used after about the 2nd century A.D., in fighting against barbaric nations.

Phălăris. The infamous tyrant of Agrigentum, notorious for his cruelty; he died 549 B.C. His name is affixed to 148 Greek letters, in which he appears as a gentle ruler, and a patron of art and poetry; but [as proved in Bentley's *Dissertation* in 1699] they are really a worthless forgery, probably by a Sophist of the 2nd century A.D.

Phălēræ. The Roman term for bosses of thin bronze or silver, or of gold-leaf impressed in relief. They were loaded at the back with pitch, and fitted to a plate of copper, being fastened to it with leather straps. They served sometimes as decorations for the harness on the head or breast of horses, sometimes as signs of military rank, worn across the whole coat of mail. [*See* cut, *under* CIPPUS.]

Phanĭăs or **Phænĭăs.** [Of Erĕsŏs in Lesbŏs, a pupil of Aristotle, and a countryman and friend of Thĕŏphrastus. He flourished about 336 B.C. He was a very prolific writer on philosophy, physics, and history. Only fragments of these works remain. He was also the author of a chronicle of his native city, entitled *The Prȳtăneis of Eresos.* This is supposed to have been one of the principal authorities followed in the *Parian Chronicle* (*q.v.*).]
[J. E. S.]

Phănŏclēs. A Greek elegiac poet of the Alexandrine period. He celebrated in erotic elegies the loves of beautiful boys. A considerable fragment remaining describes the love of Orpheus for Călăïs, the beautiful son of Bŏrĕas, and his death ensuing therefrom. The language is simple and spirited, and the versification melodious.

Phantăsus. *See* DREAMS.

Phărĕtră. The quiver. (*See* BOWS.)

Phărŏs. The lighthouse on the eastern summit of the small island of the same name in front of the harbour of Alexandria. It was a tower of white marble, built for Ptolemy Phĭlădelphus by Sŏstrătus of Cnĭdus, in 270 B.C., at a cost of 800 silver talents (£160,000), and accounted by the ancients one of the wonders of the world. It rose pyramidally in a number of decreasing stories of different forms (the lowest square, the next octagonal, the third circular). It was adorned with galleries and pillars to a considerable height.[1] It

[1] Josephus, *De Bello Judaico* v 4, says that the tower of Phasael in Jerusalem, which was 90 cubits (or about 135 feet) in height, was about the same height as the Pharos. This is much more likely to be a correct estimate than that of Edrisi, who makes it 300 cubits, each cubit being equivalent to three palms (*Climates of the World,* written in Arabic 1153, Lat. trans. 1796, p. 349), or that of Stĕphănus of Byzantium (*s.v.* Φάρος) who makes it 306 *orgȳiai,* or about 1,836 feet (These references are due to Prof. Middleton.)

was still standing, in great part, about 1300 A.D. In later times all lighthouses were called after it, and large numbers of these were built by the Romans round Italy, and on all the coasts of the empire. The tower at Ravenna approached the Alexandrian in magnificence. Light-ships were also used by the ancients.

Phāsĭs. The term in Attic law for an information against secret crimes, such as contravention of regulations relating to customs, trade, or mining, illegal occupation of common rights, felling of the olive trees sacred to Athēnē, dishonest administration of wards' estates and *sӯcŏphantĭa*. The informer received a portion of the fine as reward.

Phēgeūs. King of Psōphĭs in Arcadia, son of Alphēus, and brother of Phŏrōnēūs. After inducing his sons, Agēnŏr and Prŏnŏŭs (or Arīōn and Tĕmĕnus) to kill Alcmæon, the first husband of his daughter Arsĭnŏē or Alphĕsĭbœa (*q.v.*), he and they were all murdered by the sons of Alcmæon. (*See* ACARNAN.)

Phĕrĕcrātēs. After Crătīnus, Eupŏlis, and Aristŏphănēs, of whom he was an older contemporary, the most eminent writer of the Old Attic comedy. He was famed among the ancients for his wealth of invention and for the purity of his Attic Greek. We have the titles of fifteen of his comedies, and a few fragments of his plays.

Phĕrĕcydēs. (1) Greek philosopher, of the isle of Sӯrŏs, about 600–550 B.C.; said to have been the first writer of prose. He wrote in the Ionic dialect of the origin of the world and the gods (*cosmŏgŏnĭa* and *thĕŏgŏnĭa*). The poetic element seems to have held a predominant place in his prose. He is also said to have been the first to maintain the doctrine of the transmigration of souls, which his pupil Pӯthăgŏrās borrowed from him.

(2) *See* LOGOGRAPHI.

Phĭālē. The flat drinking-cup of the Greeks. (*See* VESSELS.)

Phĭdĭās (Gr. *Pheidĭās*). The famous Greek artist, born about 500 B.C. at Athens, pupil of Ăgĕlādās, and eminent as architect, bronze founder, sculptor, and painter. His great powers were displayed in the buildings erected under the administration of his intimate friend Pericles on the Acrŏpŏlĭs at Athens, and at Olympia, where he was commissioned to execute the statue of Zeus for the temple there.

Returning to Athens in 432, he was accused, by intriguers against Pericles, of misappropriating the gold supplied him for the drapery of Athēnē's statue in the Parthĕnōn. From this he could readily clear himself, having so contrived the drapery that it could easily be taken off and weighed [Plut., *Pericles* 31]. But being afterwards accused of impiety, on the ground that he

* Figure traditionally identified as PHIDIAS.
(Strangford Shield, British Museum.)

"Phidias was oppressed with envy by reason of the renown of his works, and chiefly because, in the battle of the Amazons, which was represented on the shield of the goddess, he had introduced a likeness of himself as a bald old man holding up a great stone with both hands."— Plut., *Pericles* 31.

had introduced portraits of himself and Pericles on the goddess' shield, he was thrown into prison, where he died of an illness in the same year (*ib.*). Among all his works, the foremost rank was taken, according to the testimony of antiquity, by the statue of Zeus at Olympia, and three statues of Athene on the Acropolis at Athens; *viz.* the statue in the Parthenon constructed, like the Zeus, of ivory and gold, and two others, Athene Prŏmăchŭs and the "Lemnian Athene," of bronze.

These works (for which *see* ATHENE *and* ZEUS) have perished; but of the marble sculptures of the Parthenon (*q.v.*), which were probably constructed from his designs, and certainly under his direction, the greater part still remains. Most of them are in the British Museum. They fully substantiate the judgment of antiquity, which looked on him as the representative of artistic perfection, as the one man who in his art combined perfect sublimity with perfect beauty. It was said of him that he alone had seen the exact image of the gods and revealed it to men. He fixed for ever the ideal types of Zeus and of Athene, the gods who, in the spiritual dignity of their attributes, are foremost of all the divinities of Greece.

Phĭdĭtĭă (Gr. *Pheidĭtĭă*). *See* SYSSITIA.

Phĭlēmōn. A Greek poet of the New Attic comedy, of Sŏli in Cilicia, or of Syracuse, born about 362 B.C. He came early to Athens, and first appeared as an author in 330. He must have enjoyed remarkable popularity, for he repeatedly won victories over his younger contemporary and rival Mĕnander, whose delicate wit was apparently less to the taste of the Athenians of the time than Philemon's smart comedy. To later times his successes over Menander were so unintelligible, that they were ascribed to the influence of malice and intrigue. Except a short sojourn in Egypt with king Ptolemy Phĭlădelphus, he passed his life at Athens. He there died, nearly a hundred years old, but with mental vigour unimpaired, in 262, according to the story, at the moment of his being crowned on the stage. Of his ninety-seven works, fifty-seven are known to us by titles and fragments, and two are preserved in the Latin version of Plautus (*Mercător* and *Trĭnummus*).

Phĭlēmōn and Baucis. An old married couple in Phrygia, famed in antiquity for their true love. When Zeus and Hermēs were wandering through the country in human form, and found no shelter with the richer inhabitants, the aged pair received them hospitably. The gods therefore, while destroying all the rest of the neighbourhood by floods in punishment for the inhospitable treatment they had met with, changed their miserable cottage into a magnificent temple. Here the two held the priestly office for the rest of their life, and finally, on their prayer that they might not be separated by death, were both at the same moment changed into trees [Ovid, *Met.* viii 611–724].

Phĭlētās. A Greek grammarian and poet, of the island of Cŏs. He lived in the second half of the 4th century, latterly as tutor to Ptolemy II (Phĭlădelphus) in Alexandria. Besides epics he composed elegies on his beloved Battis, which were highly prized at Alexandria and Rome, and were imitated by Prŏpertius [iv 1, 1]. We possess only scanty fragments of these elegies.

Phĭlippĭdēs. A Greek writer of the New Comedy, about 300 B.C.; a friend of king Lўsĭmăchus of Thrace. He is said to have died of joy at winning a dramatic prize. Of the forty-four plays attributed to him only fragments survive.

Phĭliscus. A Greek tragedian of Corcÿra, in the first half of the 3rd century B.C.; he was priest of Dĭonÿsus in Alexandria, and, as such, stood at the head of the Dionysiac guild of actors in that city. He was one of the "Pleiad" (*q.v.*) of Alexandrian tragic poets. [His portrait is preserved in a relief in the Lateran Museum. *See* cut under TRAGEDY (*Greek*).]

Phĭlistus. A Greek historian, of Syracuse,

born about 435 B.C. He encouraged the elder Dĭŏnÿsius, by advice and assistance, in securing and maintaining the position of despot in his native state; but was himself banished by Dionysius in 386, and lived a long while at Adria in Ēpīrus, busied with historical studies. Recalled by Dionysius the younger, he counteracted the salutary influence of Dĭōn and Plato at that tyrant's court, and brought about the banishment of both. As commander of the fleet against Dion and the revolted Syracusans, he lost a naval battle, and in consequence either committed suicide or was cruelly murdered by the angry populace (356). He left an historical work, begun in his exile, called *Sĭcĕlĭca*, a history of Sicily in thirteen books. Books i–vii dealt with the events of the earliest times to the capture of Agrĭgentum by the Carthaginians in 406; viii–xi, with the rule of the elder Dionysius; xii and xiii, with that of the younger. The last portion, which remained incomplete owing to his death, was finished by his countryman Athānās. Only unimportant fragments of this have survived. According to the judgment of the ancients, he imitated Thucydides somewhat unsuccessfully, and betrayed in his work the one-sided attitude natural to his political views [Plutarch, *Dion* 36; Dionysius Halic., *Ad Cn. Pompeium*, 5].

Phĭlo (Gr. *Phĭlōn*). (1) [*The sculptor;* the son of Antĭpăter. He flourished in the time of Alexander the Great. Among his works was the statue of Hēphæstĭōn, and that of Zeus Ourĭōs, at the entrance of the Bospŏrus (Cic., *Verr.* II iv 129). The dedicatory verses inscribed on the pedestal of the latter are now in the British Museum (quoted on p. 40 of Dem., *Adv. Leptinem*, ed. Sandys). Pliny (xxxiv 91) mentions him as one of the sculptors who made *athlētas et armātos et vēnātōrēs sacrĭfĭcantēsquĕ*.]

(2) [*The Athenian architect* who built for Dēmētrĭus Phălēreus, about 318 B.C., the portico to the great temple at Eleusis. It had 12 Doric columns in front, and its dimensions were 183 feet by 37½ feet (see plan on p. 211). Under the administration of Lўcurgus, he constructed an *armāmentārĭum* or arsenal at Zĕa in the Peiræus, containing tackle, etc., for 400 ships (Pliny, *N. H.* vii 125). It was destroyed by Sulla (Plutarch, *Sulla* 14), but apparently rebuilt, since it is described by Vălērĭus Maxĭmus (viii 12, 2) as still existing (*cp.* Cic., *De Or.* i 62, and Strabo, p. 395 D). An inscription published in *Hermes*, 1882, p. 351, and in

the *Corpus Inscriptionum Atticarum*, ii, no. 1054, contains the contract for the work, with full details of its structure and fittings.]

(3) *Of Byzantium ;* a celebrated mechanician. He wrote, in the 2nd century B.C., a work on mechanics, of which only one book, on the construction of engines of war, and portions of two others, on siege-warfare, are extant.

(4) [*Philo of Larissa*, an Academic philosopher, a pupil of Clītŏmăchus. He came to Rome in 88 B.C., being one of a number of eminent Greeks who fled from Athens on the approach of its siege during the Mithridatic war. He was a man of versatile genius and a perfect master of the theory and practice of oratory. Cicero had scarcely heard him before all his inclination for Epicureanism was swept from his mind, and he surrendered himself wholly to the brilliant Academic (*Brutus* § 306; cp. *De Nat. Deor.* i §§ 17, 113; *Tusc. Disp.* ii §§ 9, 26). One of his works, twice mentioned, though not by any definite title (*Acad.* i 13, ii 11), supplied Cicero with his historic account of the New Academy (Cicero's *Academica*, ed. Reid, pp. 2, 52).]

(5) *The Jew.* Born of a priestly family at Alexandria, about 25 B.C., he carefully studied the different branches of Greek culture, and, in particular, acquired a knowledge of the Platonic philosophy, while in no way abandoning the study of the Scriptures or the creed of his nation. In 39 A.D. he went to Rome as an emissary to the emperor Călĭgŭla in the interest of his fellow countrymen, whose religious feelings were offended by a decree ordering them to place the statue of the deified emperor in their synagogues. This embassy, which led to no result, is described by him in a work which is still extant, though in an incomplete form.

Philo is the chief representative of the Graeco-Judaic philosophy. He wrote numerous Greek works in a style modelled on that of Plato. These are remarkable for moral earnestness, passionate enthusiasm, and vigour of thought. They include allegorical expositions of portions of the Scriptures, as well as works of ethical, historical, or political purport. Several of his works only survive in Armenian versions. His philosophy, especially his theology, is an endeavour to reconcile Platonism with Judaism.

(6) [*Philo Byblius*, or Herennius Byblius. - A Roman grammarian, born at Byblus in Phoenicia. His life extended from about

the time of Nero to that of Hadrian. A considerable fragment of his "translation" of the ancient Phoenician writer Sanchūnīăthōn is preserved in the first book of the *Præpărātĭō Evangĕlĭca* of Eusĕbĭus.]

Phĭlŏchŏrus. A Greek historian, living at Athens between 306 and 260. As an upholder of national liberty he was among the bitterest opponents of Dēmētrĭus Pŏlĭorcētēs and of his son Antĭgŏnus Gŏnătās, who put him to death after the conquest of Athens. Of his works, the *Atthis* was a history of Athens from the earliest times to 262 B.C., in seventeen books. It was highly esteemed and often quoted for its wealth of facts and thoroughness of investigation, especially as regards chronology. We still possess a considerable number of fragments.

Phĭlŏclēs. A Greek tragedian, son of Æschўlus' sister. He wrote a hundred plays in the manner of Æschylus, and won the prize against Sophocles' *Œdĭpūs Tўrannus.* Only scanty fragments of his plays remain. The drama was also cultivated by his sons Morsĭmus and Mĕlanthius, by Morsimus' son Astўdămās (about 399 B.C.), and again by the sons of the latter, Astydamas and Philocles.

Phĭloctētēs. The son of Pœas, king of the Mālians in Œta. He inherited the bow and arrows of Hērăclēs (*q.v.*). He was leader of seven ships in the expedition against Troy; but, on the way out, was bitten by a snake at Lēmnŏs, or the small island of Chrysē near Lemnos, and, on account of the intolerable stench caused by the wound, was abandoned at Lemnos on the advice of Odysseus. Here in his sickness he dragged out a miserable life till the tenth year of the war. Then, however, on account of Hĕlĕnus' prophecy that Troy could only be conquered by the arrows of Heracles, Odysseus and Dĭŏmēdēs went to fetch him, and he was healed by Măchāōn. After he had slain Paris, Troy was conquered. He was one of the heroes who came safe home again. [The story of Philoctetes was dramatized by Æschylus and Euripides (B.C. 431), as well as by Sophocles (409). It is also the theme of numerous monuments of ancient art. See Jebb's introduction to Soph. *Phil.*, p. xxxvii.]

Phĭlŏdēmus. A Greek philosopher of the Epicurean school, of Gădăra in Palestine. He was a contemporary of Cicero, who praises his learning, and also his taste as a poet [*De Finĭbus* ii 119; *in Pisonem*, 68, 70]. We have thirty-four epigrams by him, chiefly on amatory and indelicate subjects:

and considerable fragments of a number of prose writings (on music, rhetoric, syllogisms, vices and virtues, piety, anger, etc.), which have come to light among the Herculanean *păpy̆rī*.

Phĭlŏlāus. A Greek philosopher, a pupil of Py̆thăgŏrās (*q.v.*). He was the first to commit to writing the doctrines of the Pythagorean school. He wrote in Doric Greek. Only a few fragments of his writings remain.

Phĭlŏmēlă. *See* PROCNE.

Philosophy. (I) GREEK PHILOSOPHY. The first beginnings of philosophy in Greece came from the Ionians of Asia; and it is in agreement with the character of that people, naturally inclined to the phenomenal or sensualist view, that what the *Ionian* philosophers sought was the material principle of things, and the mode of their origin and disappearance. THĂLĒS of Mīlētus (about 640 B.C.) is reputed the father of Greek philosophy. He declared Water to be the basis of all things. Next came ANAXĬMANDER of Miletus (about 611-547), the first *writer* on philosophy; he assumed as first principle an undefined substance without qualities, out of which the primary antitheses, hot and cold, moist and dry, became differentiated. His countryman and younger contemporary, ANAXĬMĒNĒS, took for his principle Air; conceiving it as modified, by thickening and thinning, into fire, wind, clouds, water, and earth. HĒRACLITUS of Ephesus (about 535-475) assumed as the principle of substance ætherial Fire. From fire all things originate, and return to it again by a never-resting process of development. All things therefore are in a perpetual flux. Philosophy was first brought into connexion with practical life by PY̆THĂGŎRĀS of Sămŏs (about 582-504), from whom it received its name ("the love of wisdom"). Regarding the world as a perfect harmony, dependent on number, he aimed at inducing mankind likewise to lead a harmonious life. His doctrine was adopted and extended by a large following, especially in lower Italy. That country was also the home of the Eleatic doctrine of The One, called after the town of Ēlĕa, the headquarters of the school. It was founded by XĔNŎPHĂNĒS of Cŏlŏphŏn (born about 570), the father of pantheism, who declared God to be the eternal unity, permeating the universe, and governing it by his thought. His great disciple PARMĔNĬDĒS of Ēlĕa (born about 511) affirmed the one unchanging existence to be alone true and capable of being conceived;

and multitude and change to be an appearance without reality. This doctrine was maintained dialectically by his younger countryman ZĒNŌ in a polemic against the vulgar opinion, which sees in things multitude, becoming, and change. EMPĔDŎCLĒS of Agrĭgentum (born 492) appears to have been partly in agreement with the Eleatic school, partly in opposition to it: on the one hand, maintaining the unchangeable nature of substance; while, on the other, he supposes a plurality of such substances—to wit, the four elements, earth, water, air, and fire. Of these the world is built up, by the agency of two ideal principles as motive forces; *viz.* love as the cause of union, hate as the cause of separation.

ANAXĂGŎRĀS of Clazŏmĕnæ (born about 500) also maintained the existence of an ordering principle as well as a material substance, and while regarding the latter as an infinite multitude of imperishable primary elements, qualitatively distinguished, conceived divine reason as ordering them. He referred all generation and disappearance to mixture and resolution respectively. To him belongs the credit of first establishing philosophy at Athens, in which city it reached its highest development, and continued to have its home for 1,000 years without intermission. The first explicitly materialistic system was formed by DĔMŎCRĬTUS of Abdēra (born about 460). This was the doctrine of Atoms,—small primary bodies infinite in number, indivisible and imperishable, qualitatively similar, but distinguished by their shapes. Falling eternally through the infinite void, they collide and unite, thus generating existence, and forming objects which differ in accordance with the varieties, in number, size, shape, and arrangement, of the atoms which compose them.

The efforts of all these earlier philosophers had been directed somewhat exclusively to the investigation of the ultimate basis and essential nature of the external world. Hence their conceptions of human knowledge, arising out of their theories as to the constitution of things, had been no less various. The Eleatics, for example, had been compelled to deny the existence of any objective truth, since to the world of sense, with its multitude and change, they allowed only a phenomenal existence. This inconsistency led to the position taken up by the class of persons known as SOPHISTS (*q.v.*), that all thought rests solely on the apprehensions of the senses and on subjective impression, and that therefore we have no other standard of action than utility for the individual.

A new period of philosophy opens with the Athenian SŌCRĂTĔS (469–399). Like the Sophists, he rejected entirely the physical speculations in which his predecessors had indulged, and made the subjective thoughts and opinions of men his starting point; but whereas it was the thoughts and opinions of the individual that the Sophists took for the standard, Socrates endeavoured to extract from the common intelligence of mankind an objective rule of practical life. For this purpose he employed the two forms of philosophical inquiry of which he is the inventor, induction and definition. Such a standard he saw in knowledge, by which term he understood the cognition in thought of the true concept of an object, and identified it with Virtue; that is to say, such action as proceeds from clear cognition of the concept appropriate to the circumstances. Thus, although Socrates did not himself succeed in establishing a genuine ethical principle, he is nevertheless the founder of ethics, as he is also of dialectic, the method of the highest speculative thought. Of Socrates' numerous disciples many either added nothing to his doctrine, or developed it in a one-sided manner, by confining themselves exclusively either to dialectic or to ethics. Thus while the Athenian XĔNŎPHŎN contented himself, in a series of writings, with exhibiting the portrait of his master to the best of his comprehension, and added nothing original, the Megarian school, founded by EUCLĪDĔS of Mĕgără, devoted themselves almost entirely to dialectic investigation; whereas ethics preponderated both with the Cynics and Cyrenaics, although the position taken up by these two schools was in direct antithesis. For ANTISTHĔNĔS of Athens, the founder of the Cynics, conceived the highest good to be the virtue which spurns every enjoyment; while ARISTIPPUS of Cўrēnē, the founder of the Cyrenaics, considered pleasure to be the sole end in life, and regarded virtue as a good only in so far as it contributed to pleasure.

Both aspects of the genius of Socrates were first united in PLATO of Athens (428–348), who also combined with them all the principles established by earlier philosophers, in so far as they had been legitimate, and developed the whole of this material into the unity of a comprehensive system. The groundwork of Plato's scheme, though nowhere expressly stated by him, is the threefold division of philosophy into dialectic, ethics, and physics; its central point is the theory of ideas. This theory is a combination of the Eleatic doctrine of the One with Heraclitus' theory of a perpetual flux and with the Socratic method of concepts. The multitude of objects of sense, being involved in perpetual change, are thereby deprived of all genuine existence. The only true being in them is founded upon the ideas, the eternal, unchangeable (independent of all that is accidental, and therefore) perfect types, of which the particular objects of sense are imperfect copies. The number of the ideas is defined by the number of universal concepts which can be derived from the particular objects of sense. The highest idea is that of the Good, which is the ultimate basis of the rest, and the first cause of being and knowledge. Apprehensions derived from the impressions of sense can never give us the knowledge of true being; i.e. of the ideas. It can only be obtained by the soul's activity within itself, apart from the troubles and disturbances of sense; that is to say, by the exercise of reason. Dialectic, as the instrument in this process, leading us to knowledge of the ideas, and finally of the highest idea of the Good, is the first of sciences, scĭentĭa scĭentĭārum. In physics, Plato adhered (though not without original modifications) to the views of the Pythagoreans, making Nature a harmonic unity in multiplicity. His ethics are founded throughout on the Socratic; with him too virtue is knowledge, the cognition of the supreme idea of the Good. And since in this cognition the three parts of the soul, cognitive, spirited, and appetitive, all have their share, we get the three virtues, Wisdom, Courage, and Temperance or Continence. The bond which unites the other virtues is the virtue of Justice, by which each several part of the soul is confined to the performance of its proper function. The school founded by Plato, called the Academy, from the name of the grove of the Attic hero Acădēmus, where he used to deliver his lectures, continued for long after. In regard to the main tendencies of its members, it was divided into the three periods of the Old, Middle, and New Academy. The chief personages in the first of these were SPEUSIPPUS (son of Plato's sister), who succeeded him as the head of the school (till 339), and XĔNŎCRĂTĔS of Chalcēdōn (till

314). Both of them sought to fuse Pythagorean speculations on number with Plato's theory of ideas. The two other Academies were still further removed from the specific doctrines of Plato (*see below*).

The most important among Plato's disciples is ARISTOTLE of Stagïra (384–322), who shares with his master the title of the greatest philosopher of antiquity. But whereas Plato had sought to elucidate and explain things from the suprasensual standpoint of the ideas, his pupil preferred to start from the facts given us by experience. Philosophy to him meant science, and its aim was the recognition of the "wherefore" in all things. Hence he endeavours to attain to the ultimate grounds of things by induction; that is to say, by *a posteriori* conclusions from a number of facts to a universal. In the series of works collected under the name of *Orgănŏn*, Aristotle sets forth, almost in a final form, the laws by which the human understanding effects conclusions from the particular to the knowledge of the universal. Like Plato, he recognises the true being of things in their concepts, but denies any separate existence of the concept apart from the particular objects of sense. They are as inseparable as matter and form. In this antithesis, matter and form, Aristotle sees the fundamental principles of being. Matter is the basis of all that exists; it comprises the potentiality of everything, but of itself is not actually anything. A determinate thing only comes into being when the potentiality in matter is converted into actuality. This is effected by form, the idea existent not as one outside the many, but as one in the many, the completion of the potentiality latent in the matter. Although it has no existence apart from the particulars, yet, in rank and estimation, form stands first; it is of its own nature the most knowable, the only true object of knowledge. For matter without any form cannot exist, but the essential definitions of a common form, in which are included the particular objects, may be separated from matter. Form and matter are relative terms, and the lower form constitutes the matter of a higher (*e.g.* body, soul, reason). This series culminates in pure, immaterial form, the Deity, the origin of all motion, and therefore of the generation of actual form out of potential matter. All motion takes place in space and time; for space is the potentiality, time the measure of the motion. Living beings are those which have in them a moving principle, or soul. In plants, the function of soul is nutrition (including reproduction); in animals, nutrition and sensation; in men, nutrition, sensation, and intellectual activity. The perfect form of the human soul is reason separated from all connexion with the body, hence fulfilling its activity without the help of any corporeal organ, and so imperishable. By reason the apprehensions, which are formed in the soul by external sense-impressions, and may be true or false, are converted into knowledge. For reason alone can attain to truth either in cognition or action. Impulse towards the good is a part of human nature, and on this is founded virtue; for Aristotle does not, with Plato, regard virtue as knowledge pure and simple, but as founded on nature, habit, and reason. Of the particular virtues (of which there are as many as there are contingencies in life), each is the apprehension, by means of reason, of the proper mean between two extremes which are *not* virtues; *e.g.* courage is the mean between cowardice and foolhardiness. The end of human activity, or the highest good, is happiness, or perfect and reasonable activity in a perfect life. To this, however, external goods are more or less necessary conditions.

The followers of Aristotle, known as *Peripatetics* (THEŎPHRASTUS of Lesbos, EUDĒMUS of Rhodes, STRĀTŌ of Lampsăcus, etc.), to a great extent abandoned metaphysical speculation, some in favour of natural science, others of a more popular treatment of ethics, introducing many changes into the Aristotelian doctrine in a naturalistic direction. A return to the views of the founder first appears among the later Peripatetics, who did good service as expositors of Aristotle's works. The tendency of the Peripatetic school to make philosophy the exclusive property of the learned class, thereby depriving it of its power to benefit a wider circle, soon produced a reaction; and philosophers returned to the practical standpoint of Socratic ethics. The speculations of the learned were only admitted in philosophy where immediately serviceable for ethics. The chief consideration was how to popularise doctrines, and to provide the individual, in a time of general confusion and dissolution, with a fixed moral basis for practical life. Such were the aims of *Stoicism*, founded at Athens about 310 by ZĒNŌ of Cittĭum, and brought to fuller systematic form by his successors as heads of the school, CLĒANTHĒS of Assŏs and especially CHRŸSIPPUS of Sŏli died about 206). Their doctrines contained little that was new, seeking rather to give a practical application to the dogmas which they took ready-made from previous systems. With them philosophy is the science of the principles on which the moral life ought to be founded. The only allowable endeavour is towards the attainment of knowledge of things human and divine, in order to regulate life thereby. The method to lead men to true knowledge is provided by logic; physics embraces the doctrines as to the nature and organization of the universe; while ethics draws from them its conclusions for practical life. All knowledge originates in the real impressions of things on the senses, which the soul, being at birth a *tăbŭlă răsă*, receives in the form of presentations. These presentations, when confirmed by repeated experience, are syllogistically developed by the understanding into concepts. The test of their truth is the convincing or persuasive force with which they impress themselves upon the soul. In physics the foundation of the Stoic doctrine was the dogma that all true being is corporeal. Within the corporeal they recognised two principles, matter and force, *i.e.* the material, and the deity permeating and informing it. Ultimately, however, the two are identical. There is nothing in the world with any independent existence: all is bound together by an unalterable chain of causation. The concord of human action with the law of nature, of the human will with the divine will, or life according to nature, is Virtue, the chief good and highest end in life. It is essentially one, the particular or cardinal virtues of Plato being only different aspects of it; it is completely sufficient for happiness, and incapable of any differences of degree. All good actions are absolutely equal in merit, and so are all bad actions. All that lies between virtue and vice is neither good nor bad; at most, it is distinguished as preferable, undesirable, or absolutely indifferent. Virtue is fully possessed only by the wise man, who is no way inferior in worth to Zeus; he is lord over his own life, and may end it by his own free choice. In general, the prominent characteristic of Stoic philosophy is moral heroism, often verging on asceticism.

The same goal which was aimed at in Stoicism was also approached, from a diametrically opposite position, in the system founded about the same time by ÉPĬCŬRUS, of the deme Gargēttus in Attica (342–268), who brought it to completion himself.

Epicureanism, like Stoicism, is connected with previous systems. Like Stoicism, it is also practical in its ends, proposing to find in reason and knowledge the secret of a happy life, and admitting abstruse learning only where it serves the ends of practical wisdom. Hence logic (called by Epicurus *cănŏnĭcŏn*, or the doctrine of canons of truth) is made entirely subservient to physics, physics to ethics. The standards of knowledge and canons of truth in theoretical matters are the impressions of the senses, which are true and indisputable, together with the presentations formed from such impressions, and opinions extending beyond those impressions, in so far as they are supported or not contradicted by the evidence of the senses. In practical questions the feelings of pleasure and pain are the tests. Epicurus' physics, in which he follows in essentials the materialistic system of Dēmŏcrĭtus, are intended to refer all phenomena to a natural cause, in order that a knowledge of nature may set men free from the bondage of disquieting superstitions. In ethics he followed within certain limits the Cyrenaic doctrine, conceiving the highest good to be happiness, and happiness to be found in pleasure, to which the natural impulses of every being are directed. But the aim is not with him, as it is with the Cyrenaics, the pleasure of the moment, but the enduring condition of pleasure, which, in its essence, is freedom from the greatest of evils, pain. Pleasures and pains are, however, distinguished not merely in degree, but in kind. The renunciation of a pleasure or endurance of a pain is often a means to a greater pleasure; and since pleasures of sense are subordinate to the pleasures of the soul, the undisturbed peace of the soul is a higher good than the freedom of the body from pain. Virtue is desirable not for itself, but for the sake of pleasure of soul, which it secures by freeing men from trouble and fear and moderating their passions and appetites. The cardinal virtue is wisdom, which is shown by true insight in calculating the consequences of our actions as regards pleasure or pain.

The practical tendency of Stoicism and Epicureanism, seen in the search for happiness, is also apparent in the *Scepticism* founded by PYRRHO of Elis (about 365–275). Pyrrho disputes the possibility of attaining truth by sensuous apprehension, reason, or the two combined, and thence infers the necessity of total suspension of judgment on things. Thus can we attain release from all bondage to theories, a condition which is followed, like a shadow, by that imperturbable state of mind which is the foundation of true happiness. Pyrrho's doctrine was followed by the *Middle* and *New Academies* (*see above*), represented by ARCĔSĬLĀUS of Pitănē (316–241) and CARNĔĀDĔS of Cўrēnē (214–129) respectively, in their attacks on the Stoics, for asserting a criterion of truth in our knowledge; although they considered that what they were maintaining was a genuine tenet of Socrates and Plato. The latest Academics, such as ANTĬŎCHUS of Ascălŏn (about 80 B.C.), fused with Platonism certain Peripatetic and many Stoic dogmas, thus making way for *Eclecticism*, to which all later antiquity tended after Greek philosophy had spread itself over the Roman world. After the Christian era Pythagoreanism, in a resuscitated form, again takes its place among the more important systems; but the pre-eminence belongs to Platonism, which is notably represented in the works of PLUTARCH of Chærŏnēa and the physician GALEN, while Scepticism is maintained by another physician, SEXTUS EMPĪRĬCUS.

The closing period of Greek philosophy is marked in the 3rd century A.D. by the establishment in Rome, under PLŌTĪNUS of Lўcŏpŏlis in Egypt (205–270), of *Neoplatonism*, a scientific philosophy of religion, in which the doctrine of Plato is fused with the most important elements in the Aristotelian and Stoic systems and with Oriental speculations. At the summit of existences stands the One or the Good, as the source of all things. It generates from itself, as if from the reflexion of its own being, reason, wherein is contained the infinite store of ideas. Soul, the copy of the reason, is generated by and contained in it, as reason is in the One, and, by informing matter in itself nonexistent, constitutes bodies whose existence is contained in soul. Nature therefore is a whole, endowed with life and soul. Soul, being chained to matter, longs to escape from the bondage of the body and return to its original source. In virtue and philosophic thought it has the power to ɤlevate itself above the reason into a state ᴎf ecstasy, where it can behold, or ascend ɑp to, that one good primary Being whom reason cannot know. To attain this union with the Good, or God, is the true function of man, to whom the external world should be absolutely indifferent. Plotinus' most important disciple, the Syrian PORPHẏRĬUS, contented himself with popularising his master's doctrine. But the school of IAMBLĬCHUS, a disciple of Porphyrius, effected a change in the position of Neoplatonism, which now took up the cause of polytheism against Christianity, and adopted for this purpose every conceivable form of superstition, especially those of the East. Foiled in the attempt to resuscitate the old beliefs, its supporters then turned with fresh ardour to scientific work, and especially to the study of Plato and Aristotle, in the interpretation of whose works they rendered great services. The last home of philosophy was at Athens, where PRŎCLUS (411–485), sought to reduce to a kind of system the whole mass of philosophic tradition, till in 529 A.D. the teaching of philosophy at Athens was forbidden by Justinian.

(II) ROMAN PHILOSOPHY is throughout founded on the Greek. Interest in the subject was first excited at Rome in 155 B.C. by an Athenian embassy, consisting of the Academic Carnĕădēs, the Stoic Dĭŏgĕnēs, and the Peripatetic Crĭtŏlāus. Of more permanent influence was the work of the Stoic Pănætius, the friend of the younger Scipio and of Lælius; but a thorough study of Greek philosophy was first introduced in the time of CICERO and VARRO. In a number of works they endeavoured to make it accessible even to those of their countrymen who were outside the learned circles. Cicero chiefly took it up in a spirit of Eclecticism; but among his contemporaries Epicureanism is represented in the poetical treatise of LUCRĒTIUS on the nature of things, and Pythagoreanism by NIGĬDIUS FĬGŬLUS. In imperial times Epicureanism and Stoicism were most popular, especially the latter, as represented by the writings of SĔNĔCĂ, CORNŪTUS, and the emperor MARCUS AURĒLIUS; while Eclectic Platonism was taken up by APŬLĔIUS of Madaura. One of the latest philosophical writers of antiquity is BŎĒTHIUS, whose writings were the chief source of information as to Greek philosophy during the first centuries of the Middle Ages. [The original authorities on ancient philosophy are collected in Ritter and Preller's *Historia Philosophiæ Græcæ et Romanæ ex Fontium Locis contexta*.]

Phĭlostrătus. (1) *Flavius Philostratus the elder*, a Greek Sophist, of Lēmnŏs, son of a celebrated Sophist of the same name. He taught first in Athens, then at Rome till the middle of the 3rd century A.D. By order of his great patroness Jūlia Domna, the learned wife of the emperor Septĭmĭus Sĕvērus, he wrote (*a*) the romantic *Life of Apollŏnĭus of*

Tўăna. Besides this we have by him (*b*) a work entitled *Hērŏīcus*, consisting of mythical histories of the heroes of the Trojan War in the form of a dialogue, designed to call back to life the expiring popular religion. (*c*) *Lives of the Sophists*, in two books, the first dealing with twenty-six philosophers, the second with thirty-three rhetoricians of earlier as well as later times, a work important for the history of Greek culture, especially during the imperial age. (*d*) Seventy-three letters, partly amatory in subject. (*e*) A fragment of a work intended to revive interest in the old *Gymnastic.* Lastly (*f*), the *Imāgĭnēs* in two books, being descriptions of sixty-six paintings on all possible subjects. Of these it is doubtful whether, as he pretends, they really belonged to a gallery at Naples [a statement accepted by Brunn, *Künstlergeschichte,* ii 178; *Jahrb. f. Philol. Supplementband* 4, 179 pp., and 1871]; or whether their subjects were invented by himself [as maintained by Friederichs, *Die Philostratischen Bilder,* 1860; and Matz, *De Philostratorum in Describendis Imaginibus Fide,* 1867]. Like all his writings, this work is skilful and pleasing in its manner, and the interest of its topic makes it particularly attractive. It is not so much designed to incite to the study of works of art, as to exhibit the art of painting in a totally new field; and herein he is followed both by his grandson and namesake, and by Callistrătus (*q.v.*).

(2) *Philostratus the younger,* son of the daughter of (1), of Lēmnŏs. He lived chiefly at Athens, and died at Lemnos, 264 A.D. Following his grandfather's lead, he devoted himself to the rhetorical description of paintings; but fell considerably behind his model both in invention and descriptive power, as is proved by the sixteen extant *Imāgĭnēs,* the first book of a larger collection.

Philoxĕnus. A famous Greek dithyrambic poet, of Cўthēră. He came as a prisoner of war into the possession of the Athenian musician Mĕlănippĭdēs, by whom he was educated and set free. He lived long at Syracuse, at the court of the tyrant Dĭŏnўsĭus I, who threw him into the stone-quarries for outspoken criticism on his bad poems. On his escape from Sicily he revenged himself on the tyrant, who was short-sighted or perhaps blind of one eye, by witty raillery in the most famous of his twenty-four dithyrambs, the *Cyclops,* which describes the love of the one-eyed Pŏlўphēmus for the beautiful Nymph Gălătēa. He died 380 B.C. at

Ephesus, after visiting various places in Greece, Italy, and Asia Minor for the public performance of his compositions. These were celebrated among the ancients for originality of expression and rich variety of melody. We have only some considerable fragments of a lyric poem entitled *The Banquet,* in which the burlesque subject affords a comic contrast to the dignified Doric rhythm.

Phīneus. (1) Son of Bēlus, and brother of Cēpheus. He contested against Perseus the possession of Andrŏmĕda (*q.v.*), who had previously been his betrothed. He was turned into stone by Perseus by means of the head of Mĕdūsa.

(2) Son of Agēnōr, reigning at Salmўdēssus in Thrace; he possessed the gift of prophecy. He put away his first wife Clĕŏpatra, daughter of Bŏrĕās and Ōrīthўīa, who had borne him two sons, and married Idæa, daughter of Dardănus. She induced him by slanders to destroy the sight of the sons whom he had by his first wife. For this Zeus punished him, giving him the choice of death or blindness. He chose never more to see the sun, whereat Hēlĭŏs, enraged by the slight, sent the Harpies, who stole or defiled his food, so that he suffered perpetual hunger. From this plague he was not delivered till the landing of the Argonauts, when Călăĭs and Zētēs, the brothers of his first wife, drove off the Harpies from him for ever. In gratitude, Phīneus, by virtue of his prophetic powers, instructed the Argonauts as to the rest of their route. His brothers-in-law sent the wicked step-mother back to her home, freed their sister and her sons from the dungeon in which they were pining, and set the sons, who recovered their sight, on their father's throne.

Phlĕgĕthōn. *See* PYRIPHLEGETHON.

Phlĕgŏn. A Greek writer, of Trallēs in Caria, freedman of the emperor Hadrian. He wrote in the first half of the 2nd century A.D. a work entitled *Pĕrĭ Thaumăsĭōn* ("On Wonderful Events"). It is a tasteless composition, but instructive as to the superstitions of antiquity. Also a dry catalogue of persons who attained a great age (*De Macrŏbĭīs*). Of his great chronological work, a catalogue of victors at the Olympian games in 229 Olympiads (B.C. 776 to A.D. 137) only fragments remain.

Phlĕgra (Phlegræan fields). The scene of the fight between the gods and the giants. (*See* GIGANTES.)

Phlĕgўās. Son of Ărēs and Chrўsē, father

of Ixīon and Cŏrōnĭs; king of the powerful robber-tribe Phlĕgўæ in the neighbourhood of the Bœotian Orchŏmĕnus. To revenge his daughter (see ASCLEPIUS), he set fire to the temple of Apollo at Delphi, and was killed with all his people either by the arrows of the god or by the bolt of Zeus. He had also to atone for his sin in the underworld.

Phŏbĕtŏr. A dream-god. (See DREAMS.)

Phōcus. Son of Æăcus and the Nymph Psămăthē; slain by his half-brothers Tĕlă-mōn and Pēleus, who were therefore sent into banishment by Æacus.

Phŏcўlĭdēs. A gnomic poet of Mīlētus, born about 540 B.C. He wrote in hexameters and in elegiac metre. Of his terse and pointed maxims, we have a few remaining. An admonitory poem in 230 hexameters, bearing his name, is the work of an Alexandrine Jewish Christian, who took most of his material from the Old Testament.

Phœbē. A special name of Artĕmis as moon-goddess. (See SELENE.)

Phœbus. A special name for Apollo (q.v.).

Phœnix. Son of Amyntŏr and Hippŏ-dămīa. Being banished by his father out of envy, he fled to Pēleus, and was entrusted by him with the education of his son Achilles (q.v.), whom he accompanied to Troy.

Phōlus. A Centaur, inhabiting Mount Phŏlŏē in Arcadia. When Hērāclēs visited him on his expedition against the Ērўman-thian boar, he opened in his guest's honour a cask of wine belonging to the Centaurs in common, presented by Dĭonȳsus. Allured by the strong scent of the wine, the Centaurs rushed up to the cave armed with trunks of trees and masses of rock, and fell upon Heracles. He drove them from the cave with firebrands, and slew some with his poisoned arrows. The rest took to flight (see CHIRON). The hospitable Pholus also met his death, having let fall on his foot an arrow, which he took from the body of one of the fallen, the wound proving rapidly fatal.

Phorbās. Son of Lăpĭthēs, honoured as a hero by the Rhodians, for having come at the bidding of the oracle to free their island from a plague of serpents. He was placed among the stars as the constellation Ŏphĭūchus (snake-holder). Another legend made him come from Thessaly to Elis, where he assisted king Alectŏr against Pĕlops, and as a reward received in marriage the king's sister Hyrmīnē, the mother of Augeās and Actŏr (see MŏLĭŏNĭDÆ). Being a mighty boxer, he challenged in his

pride the gods themselves, but Apollo overcame and slew him.

Phorcўs. A Greek sea-god, son of Pontus and Gæa, brother of Nēreus and Thaumās and of Eurўbĭa and Cētō, by whom he begat the Graiæ, the Gorgons, and the dragon Lādōn, who guarded the apples of Hes-pĕrĭdĕs. He is also called the father of the Nymph Thŏōsa, mother of the Hesperides, Sirens, and Scylla.

Phorminx. A Greek stringed instrument. (See CITHARA.)

Phormĭs, or **Phormŏs.** A Greek poet, writer of Dorian comedy. (See COMEDY.)

Phŏrōnēūs. Son of Inăchus and the Ocean-nymph Mĕlĭa, founder of the state of Argos. The origin of all culture, civil order, and religious rites in the Peloponnesus was ascribed to him. In particular, he was reputed as the originator of the worship of Hēra at Argos, and, like Prŏmētheus else-where, as the man who first brought fire from heaven down to earth. Hence he was regarded as a national hero, and offerings were laid on his tomb. His daughter Nĭŏbē was said to be the first mortal whom Zeus honoured with his love.

Phōtĭus. A Greek scholar of the Byzantine period, Patriarch of Constantinople A.D. 857-867 and 871-886; died 891. Besides playing a prominent part in the ecclesiastical controversies of his time, he was conspicuous for his wide reading of ancient literature. Apart from theological writings, he left two works which are of great service to the student of antiquity. The one, the Bibliŏthēca, is an account of 280 works, some of which are now lost, some only imperfectly preserved, which he read on his embassy to Assyria, with short notices and criticisms of matter and style, and in some cases more or less complete abstracts; the other a Lexicon or alphabetical glossary, of special value in connexion with the Greek orators and historians.

Phrātrĭā (lit. brotherhood). Denoted among the Greeks the subdivision of a phȳlē (q.v.) embracing a number of families. In Attica the four old Ionic phȳlæ contained three phratriæ in each, twelve in all; and each phratria comprehended thirty families (see GENNETÆ). When the old phȳlæ were suppressed by Clīsthĕnēs, the phratriæ remained in existence as religious associations for the observance of the ancient forms of worship, which did not admit of being suppressed. They had, however, no political importance, except that the sons (by birth or adoption) of a citizen had to be enrolled in the register of *phrătŏrĕs*, or members of the *phratria* of their natural or adoptive father. This was done by the *phratriarchi* (presidents) at the chief festival of the *phratriæ*, the Apăturia (*q.v.*). Newly married husbands also introduced their wives into the *phratria*. Each *phratria* had a separate place of worship (*phrātriŏn*), with the altars of its deities. Zeus and Athēnē were common to all, but each *phratria* worshipped other special deities of its own.

Phrixus. Son of Athămās and Nĕphĕlē, threatened with death as a sacrifice through the malice of his stepmother Inō, escaped with his sister Hellē on a ram with golden fleece, sent him by Zeus, Hermēs, or Nephele. Helle was drowned on the way in the sea which bears her name, the Hellespont; but Phrixus arrived safely in Colchis, where he sacrificed the ram to Zeus as the "aider of flight" (*Zeus Phyxĭŏs*), and presented the golden fleece to king Acētēs. Acetes hung it on an oak in the grove of Arēs, and gave Phrixus his daughter Chalcĭŏpē to wife. Phrixus sent his sons Cȳtissŏrus and Argus home. The former saved his grandfather Athămās from being sacrificed; the latter built the ship *Argo*, which was named after him. (*See* ATHAMAS and ARGONAUTS.)

Phrȳnĭchus. (1) A Greek tragic poet, of Athens, an older contemporary of Æschylus. He won his first victory as early as 511 B.C. He rendered a great service to the development of the drama by introducing an actor distinct from the leader of the chorus, and so laying the foundation for the dialogue. But the dialogue was still quite subordinate to the lyrics of the chorus. In this department he won extraordinary celebrity by the grace and melody of his verses, which continued to be sung at Athens long after. Besides mythical subjects, he dealt with events of contemporary history, *e.g.* the conquest of Mīlētus by the Persians. At the representation of that event the audience burst into tears, and the poet was fined 1,000 drachmæ for recalling the disasters of his country, all further performance of the piece being prohibited [Herod., vi 21]. Again, in his *Phœnissœ* (so named after the chorus of Sidonian women) he dealt with the battle of Sălămīs. This play, which was put on the stage by Thĕmistŏclēs in 478, was the model of Æschylus' *Persæ*. Phrynichus, like Æschylus, is said to have died in Sicily. We only possess the titles of nine of his plays and a few fragments.

(2) A Greek poet of Athens; one of the less important writers of the Old Attic Comedy, and a frequent butt of the other comic poets. In B.C. 405, however, his *Muses* took the second prize after Aristophanes' *Frogs*. We have only short fragments of about ten of his plays.

(3) A Greek Sophist, who lived in the second half of the 3rd century A.D. in Bithynia; author of a *Selection of Attic Verbs and Nouns*, compiled with great strictness in the exclusion of all but the best Attic forms. We have also notable excerpts from a work of his in thirty-seven books, dedicated to the emperor Commŏdus, and entitled the *Sophistic Armoury* (*Părasceuē*). It was founded on the most comprehensive learning, and designed to supply the orator with everything necessary for good and pure expression. The arrangement is alphabetical, and it includes examples from the best authors, the different styles being carefully distinguished.

Phȳlarchus. (1) A Greek historian, born probably at Naucrătĭs in Egypt about 210 B.C., lived long at Sĭcȳon, afterwards in Athens; author of a great historical work in 28 books, dealing with the fifty years from the invasion of the Peloponnesus by Pyrrhus to the death of Clĕŏmĕnēs, king of Sparta (272–221). His enthusiastic admiration of that monarch appears to be the cause of the severe judgment passed on Phylarchus by Pŏlȳbĭus [ii 56], who represents the prejudiced Achæan view. His style was lively and attractive, but unduly sensational. His work was much used by Trogus Pompeius and by Plutarch [in his lives of Clĕŏmĕnēs and Arātus]. Only a few fragments remain.

(2) The Athenian term for (*a*) the president of a *phȳlē* (*q.v.*); (*b*) one of the ten subordinate officers commanding the citizen cavalry. (*See* HIPPEIS.)

Phȳlē. The Greek term for a division of a nation, connected together by (supposed) descent from a common ancestor of the stock. Thus the population of Attica, even before Solon, was divided into four *phylæ*, tracing their origin from four legendary sons of Ion, and called *Gĕlĕontĕs, Hoplētĕs, Ægĭcŏrēs*, and *Argădēs*. Probably the division was local, the names referring to the peculiarity or main occupation of the members of each division; for *Hopletes* appears to mean warriors, *Ægicores*, goatherds, and *Argades*, agriculturalists. The meaning of *Geleontes* (or *Teleontes*), however, is quite uncertain. Each *phyle* was presided over by a *phȳlŏbăsĭleus* (king of the *phyle*) and divided into three *phrātrĭæ* (brotherhoods, *see* PHRATRIA), each *phratria* being subdivided into thirty families. Each family contained about thirty households, and was named after a supposed common progenitor, in whose honour the households celebrated a common cult. Similarly the *phratrĭæ* and *phylæ* were united by the worship of special protecting deities. These old Ionic *phylæ* were suppressed by Clīsthĕnēs, who divided the people into ten entirely different *phylæ*, named after ancient heroes (*Erechthēĭs*, *Ægēĭs*, *Pandīŏnĭs*, *Lĕŏntĭs*, *Acămantĭs*, *Œnēĭs*, *Cĕcrŏpĭs*, *Hippŏthōntĭs*, *Aiantĭs*, *Antĭŏchĭs*). They were subdivided into fifty *naucrărĭæ* and one hundred *demi* (*q.v.*).

In 307 B.C., in honour of Dēmētrius Pŏlĭorcētēs and his father Antĭgŏnus, the *phylæ* were increased by two, called *Dēmētrĭăs* and *Antĭgŏnĭs*, which names were afterwards changed, in honour of Ptolemy Phĭlădelphus of Egypt and Attălus I of Pergămŏn, into *Ptŏlĕmāĭs* and *Attălĭs*. In later times, another, *Adrĭānĭs*, was added in honour of the emperor Hadrian. Besides priests for the cult of their eponymous hero, the *phylæ* had presidents, called *phўlarchĭ*, and treasurers (*tămĭæ*). The assemblies were always held in Athens, and were concerned, not only with the special affairs of the *phyle*, but also with State business, especially the notification of the persons liable to State burdens (*See* LEITOURGIA.) The ten *phylæ* of Clisthenes served also as a foundation for the organization of the army. The forces were raised when required from the muster-roll of the *phylæ*, and divided accordingly into ten battalions, which were themselves also called *phylæ*.

The Dorian stock was generally divided into three *phylæ*: *Hyllēĭs*, *Dўmānēs*, and *Pamphўlĭ*, purporting to be named after Hyllus, son of Hērăclēs, and Dymān and Pamphўlus, sons of king Ægĭmĭus. When families not of Dorian origin formed part of the forces of the State, they constituted an additional *phyle*. In the purely Dorian state of Sparta the three *phylæ* were divided into thirty *ōbæ*, answering to the families at Athens.

Phyllis. Daughter of the Thracian king Sīthōn. From despair at the delay of her betrothed Dēmŏphŏōn (*q.v.*, 2) in coming to wed her, she put an end to her life, and was changed into an almond tree. [Ovid, *Heroides*, 2.]

Physicians. The GREEKS traced the origin of the healing art to a deified son of

the healing god Apollo and a pupil of the sage centaur Chīron; viz. *Asclēpius*, whose sons Pŏdălīrĭus and Māchāŏn, in Homeric poetry, act before Troy both as warriors and as surgeons. The temples of Asclepius, distinguished for their healthy situation on headlands and lofty hills, in the midst of groves and near medicinal springs, were much resorted to as *sānătŏrĭa*, especially those at Ĕpĭdauros, Cnĭdus, and Cōs, and were for centuries the chief seats of the gradual development of leechcraft. The priests, who styled themselves *Asclēpĭădæ*, *i.e.* descendants of Asclepius, made use of memoranda on the treatment of patients, contained partly in the votive tablets which these hung up in the temple, and partly in the temple chronicles. Thus in course of time they collected a varied stock of experimental maxims, which were handed down from father to son. Some of the Asclepiadæ practised their art singly, as travelling physicians, but were bound by oath to teach it to Asclepiadæ alone. At the same time there were not wanting physicians who, standing outside of that close corporation, practised medicine independently as a means of living; but they were less highly regarded than the Asclepiadæ, and never achieved a higher standing till the healing art had burst its narrow limits and had expanded into a free science. This was brought about mainly by the influence of philosophy, which, beginning with Pŷthăgŏrās, himself a proficient in the art, and continuing chiefly under Empĕdŏclēs and Dēmŏcrĭtus, drew medicine within the range of her researches. Into literature the healing art was introduced by HIPPOCRĂTĒS, an Asclēpiad of Cōs, born about 460 B.C., who combined the hereditary wisdom of his race with the spirit of speculative philosophy.

Besides physicians who were paid for their trouble by their respective patients, we find as early as the 6th century, at Athens chiefly, but in other places too, public physicians appointed and remunerated by the State. Some went to their patients' houses, others had rooms where they were consulted by their patients. They often kept assistants, both free and slaves; and they manufactured their own medicines. The style of living adopted by many physicians points to respectable incomes: Dēmŏcēdēs, a public physician at Athens in the 6th century, had a salary of 100 minæ (about £333). At Alexandria, thanks to the munificence of the Ptolemies, medicine made considerable progress, chiefly through ĔRĂSISTRĂTUS and HĔRŎPHĬLUS, the two men who knew most about human anatomy. A pupil of the latter, PHĬLĪNUS of Cōs (about 250), in opposition to the *Dogmatic* school set up by the sons of Hippocrates and dominated by philosophic theories, founded an *Empirical* school, which relied solely on tradition and on individual experience.

In 219 B.C., when a member of that school, the Peloponnesian ARCHĂGĂTHUS, set up a surgery in a booth (*tăberna*) assigned him by the Senate, and was admitted to the citizenship, the Greek art of healing gained a footing among the ROMANS. Yet the physician practising for pay did not enjoy the same consideration as in Greece; Roman citizens fought shy of a profession which, respectable as it might be, was left almost entirely in the hands of foreigners, freedmen, and slaves. Romans of rank usually kept a freedman or slave as family doctor, *lĭbertus* (or *servus*) *mĕdĭcus.* A considerable part was played at Rome by Cicero's friend ASCLĒPĬĂDĒS of Prūsa, whose system, mainly directed to practical skill, received its theoretic justification from the school of *Mĕthŏdĭci* founded by THĔMĬSŌN of Lāŏdĭcēa (about 63 B.C.). When Cæsar had granted the citizenship to foreign physicians as well as teachers, not only did the former flock in large numbers to Rome from Greece, Egypt, and the East, but many natives adopted the medical profession, as CELSUS in the reign of TĬbĕrĭus, whose treatise, *De Mĕdĭcīnā,* must be regarded as the chief contribution made to the science by the Romans. To the physicians at Rome, of whose receipts a notion may be formed from the statement that a certain Stertĭnĭus had an income of £6,500 from his town practice, Augustus granted immunity from all public duties, a privilege afterwards extended to the provinces.

As soon as the Empire was fully established, physicians with a fixed salary began to be appointed at the court, in the army, for the gladiators, and in the service of various communities. Antōnīnus Pius, in the 2nd century A.D., arranged, for the province of Asia in the first instance, that physicians should be appointed by the town authorities, five in small towns, seven in those of moderate size, and ten in capitals; they were to be remunerated by the town, exempt from all burdens, and free to carry on a private practice besides. There was no real supervision of physicians on the part of the State, and the various schools

and nationalities were at perfect liberty to practise.

Under the Empire the art began to divide into separate branches, and in large towns, especially Rome, the several specialties had their representatives. Thus, in addition to doctors for internal cures, the *medici* proper, there were surgeons (*chīrurgi* or *vulnĕrărĭi*), oculists, dentists, aurists; physicians male or female, for diseases of women; also for ruptures, fistula, etc.; further *ĭătrŏlīptœ*, probably at first mere assistants who rubbed in the embrocations, etc., afterwards a species of doctors. The physicians at Rome, as in Greece, supplied their own medicines, and turned them to profit by crying up the dearest drugs, of which they kept the secret, as the best. The medicines were provided with a label setting forth the name of the remedy and that of its inventor, the complaints it was good for and directions for use. We get a fair notion of these labels from the dies used by Roman oculists to mark the names of their eye-salve on the boxes in which they were sold; a good many of these have been preserved. [C. I. Grotefend, *Die Stampe der röm. Augenärzte;* there are several in the British Museum, together with two very small inscribed vases such as were used to contain the eye-salves.] The chief authority for the *mătĕrĭa mĕdĭca* of those times is the work of DĬOSCŎRĬDĒS of the 1st century A.D. About the same time the school of *Methodici,* whose principal representative was SŌRĀNUS (about 110), was confronted by a *New Dogmatic* school, otherwise called the *Pneumatic* school, founded by the Cilician ATHĒNÆUS. To the *Eclectic* school, founded towards the end of the 1st century by AGĂTHĪNUS of Sparta, belongs more especially the Cappadocian writer ARĒTÆUS. The most renowned of the later physicians is GALEN (*Gălēnŏs*) in the 2nd century, who in his numerous writings embraced the whole range of the medical knowledge of antiquity. Medicine made no further progress in ancient times. Of the encyclopædic works of OREIBĀSIUS and AĒTĬUS (at the end of the 4th century and beginning of the 6th), the value lies in their extracts from older writings. Among the Romans SCRĪBŌNIUS LARGUS (in the middle of the 1st century) and SĔRĒNUS SAMMŌNĬCUS (at the beginning of the 3rd) wrote on Remedies, the latter in verse. We have, lastly, to mention CÆLĬUS AURĒLIĀNUS, the translator of works by Soranus (in the 5th century), and VĔGĒTIUS, the author of a detailed book on veterinary science (in the 4th century).

Phỹtǎlus. A hero of Eleusis; he received from Dēmētēr the fig tree, as a reward for hospitable entertainment [Pausanias, i 37, § 2]. His descendants, the *Phỹtǎlĭdœ*, by ancient custom, performed the purification for blood-shedding in Attica, according to the legend, because they had absolved Thēseus under similar circumstances [Plutarch, *Thes.* 12, 22]. (*See* THESEUS.)

Pīcumnus. An old Italian god of agriculture, credited with the invention of the use of manure. He was said to be the husband of Pōmōna. His brother *Pīlumnus* was honoured by bakers as the inventor of the pestle (*pīlum*) for crushing corn; and the two together were protecting deities to women in child-bed and to new-born infants. Hence, in the country, festal couches were set for them in the *ātrĭum* when children were safely brought to birth. According to another ancient view, there were three divinities protecting mother and child, who prevented the mischievous intrusion of Silvānus into the house. These powers (representing the triumph of civilization over the wild forest life) were impersonated by three men, who went round the house in the night, and knocked on the threshold of the front and back doors, first with a hatchet and then with a pestle, and lastly swept them with a broom. The names of these deities were *Intercĭdōna*, god of the hewing of timbers, *Pīlumnus*, of the crushing of corn into meal by the pestle, and *Dēverra*, of the sweeping together of grain [Varro, quoted by Augustine, *De Civitate Dei*, vi 9]. Picumnus, as appears in the name, is identical with Pīcus (*q.v.*).

Pīcus. An Italian god of agriculture, and especially of manure, hence called son of Stercŭtus ("the dunger," *i.e.* Saturn). He also appears as a forest-god with prophetic powers, and as father of Faunus [Vergil, *Æn.* vii 48]. In Latin legend he plays a prominent part as a warlike hero, the earliest king of Latium, of great wealth, who was finally changed into a woodpecker, *picus* (*ib.* 187-190). [According to Ovid, *Met.* xiv 320-396] this was because he spurned the love of Circē and was faithful to the beautiful Nymph Cänens. Probably Picus was originally the woodpecker, the symbol of Mars as giver of fertility and warlike prowess, and from this symbol there was developed a separate deity.

Piĕtās. The Roman goddess of domestic affection. In Rome she had a special temple,

vowed at the battle of Thermŏpȳlæ in 191 B.C. by Acīlĭus Glābrĭō, and consecrated by his son in 181. The popular legend was, that it was erected as a memorial to a daughter, who had supported with the milk from her breast the life of her mother (or father) when condemned to death by starvation [Valerius Max., v 4 § 7]. On coins the goddess appears as a matron strewing incense on an altar; her symbol is the stork.

Pigments. *See* PAINTING (p. 447).

Pigrēs. A Greek poet, author of the *Bǎtrǎchŏmȳŏmǎchĭa*. (*See* HOMER, *ad fin.*)

Pīlentum (*Latin*). A sort of spring-cart, used chiefly by women. (*See* CHARIOTS.)

Pillĕus (Gr. *pīlŏs*); [less correctly spelt *pĭleus.*] A round felt cap with little or no brim, lying close to the temples. It was the mark of fishermen, sailors, and artisans; hence Castor and Pollux, Odysseus, Chărōn, Hēphæstus, and Dædǎlus are represented with it. The upper classes wore it only

(1)   (2)   (3)

PILLEUS.

(1) Panofka, *Bilder antiken Lebens*, viii 5.
(2) Do., xiv 3.
(3) Müller's *Denkmäler*, I xlvii 215a.

in the country or when travelling; but it was worn in Rome by the whole people at the *Sǎturnālĭa*, and by freedmen as a sign of their new position. It was placed on the head of slaves when sold, as a sign that the vender undertook no responsibility. (*See* cuts, and *cp.* ODYSSEUS, fig. 1, and coin under BRUTUS.)

Pīlum. The javelin of the Roman legionaries (about six feet long), which was hurled at the enemy's ranks at the beginning of the engagement, before proceeding to the use of the sword. It consisted of a wooden shaft three feet long, easily grasped in the hand, and an iron head of the same length, culminating in a barbed point, and provided with a socket to which the shaft was attached by iron rivets. Mǎrĭus had the heads constructed of soft weak iron, the point only being steeled. In this way, if the point stuck in the shield of an enemy, the iron was bent by the weight of the shaft, rendering the weapon useless and difficult to draw out, while it made the shield unmanageable so long as it remained in it [Plutarch, *Marius*, 25]. When well thrown, the pilum would penetrate both shield and armour. (*See* cut.)

Pilumnus. One of the three deities conceived by the Italian tribes to protect women in childbed, and their offspring, from the mischief of the forest god Silvānus. (*See* PICUMNUS.)

Pindar (Gr. *Pindărŏs*). The greatest of the Greek lyric poets, born about 522 B.C. at Cȳnoscĕphălæ, near Thebes; son of the flute-player Daïphantus, of the ancient and noble family of the Ægīdæ. His instruction in music, begun by his father, was continued by the musician and dithyrambic poet Lasus of Hermĭŏnē and the two Bœotian poetesses Myrtis and Cŏrinna. He subsequently enjoyed the instructions of the eminent musicians Agăthŏclēs and Apollŏdŏrus at Athens. He lived chiefly at Thebes, but was renowned and honoured far and wide, among free communities as well as by tyrants and monarchs, not only for his skill in his art, but also for his profound piety. As a special favourite of Apollo, he was given a seat in the temple at Delphi, and was regularly invited to the divine banquet called the *Thĕoxĕnĭa*. When he was condemned to a fine by his fellow citizens for glorifying the hostile city of Athens, the Athenians recouped him and accorded him the honour of *prŏxĕnĭa*, and afterwards erected a bronze statue in his honour. He was on the most intimate terms with Amyntās of Macedon, the Aleuădæ in Thessaly and Arcĕsĭlăŭs of Cȳrēnē, but more especially with Thērŏn of Agrĭgentum and with Hĭĕrŏn of Syracuse, at whose court he lived 476–472. He died a peaceful death 422, aged eighty, in the theatre at Argos. It is well known that, in the destruction of Thebes, Alexander the Great spared Pindar's house and descendants alone [Dion Chrysostom, *Or.* ii, p. 25 M; *cp.* Milton's third English sonnet].

As a poet, Pindar was remarkably prolific.

PILUM.
(In the Museum at Mainz, restored.)

His works, divided by the Alexandrian scholars into seventeen books, included *hymns*, *pœans*, *dithyrambs*, *prŏsŏdĭa*, *parthĕnĭa*, *encŏmĭa*, *scŏlĭa*, *thrēnĭ*, and *ĕpĭnīcĭa* [*cp.* Horace, *Odes* iv 2]. Of most of his poetry we have only fragments, but the four books of *ĕpĭnīcĭă* are nearly complete. These were songs celebrating the victors in the great national games, and sung by a chorus, sometimes at the scene of the victory, sometimes at the feast on the victor's return home. They contain fourteen Olympian, twelve Pythian, eleven Nemean, and eight Isthmian odes. Pindar's poetry is characterized by magnificence and sublimity of thought, expression, and metrical form. It is permeated by deep and warm religious sentiments resting on the popular creed, still unimpugned by sophistic teaching, and only ennobled by the impress of the poet's personality. He does not celebrate the victors by particular description; he takes his main ideas from the circumstances of the victor's home or personal position, or from the nature of the contest, and works them into a plot always artistic, though often obscured by the interlacing of the strands of thought and by the myths which are interwoven in appropriate detail. Harmony in thought, expression, and metre make the shortest and longest of his poems equally complete in themselves as works of art. Pindar's poetic language is the Ionic Homeric dialect, intermingled with Æolic and especially with Doric forms.

By some mistake his name (*Pindărus Thēbānus*) became attached to an abstract of Homer's Iliad written in Latin hexameters for the use of schools in the 1st century A.D., and much used in the Middle Ages.

Piræïcus. A Greek painter, probably of the time after Alexander the Great. He was the chief representative of what is called *rhŏpŏgrăphĭa* ("painting of petty subjects, such as still-life"). He painted *genre* pictures in the Dutch style (barbers' and cobblers' shops), and subjects in still-life, of small size, but of proportionately careful execution. [Propertius, iii 9, 12 : *Pirĕïcus parvă vindĭcat arte lŏcum*. In Pliny, *N. H.* xxxv 112, the manuscript reading is *rhўpărŏgrăphŏs* ("rag and tatter painter "), defended in Brunn's *Künstlergeschichte*, ii 260, against Welcker's usually accepted emendation *rhŏpŏgrăphŏs*, "toy-painter," "painter of small and trivial subjects," from *rhŏpŏs*, "petty wares," "odds and ends." The word *rhŏpŏgrăphĭa* is actu-

ally found in Cicero, *Ad Atticum* xv 16*b*,
and its opposite, *mĕgălŏgrăphĭa*, in Vitruvius, vii 4 § 4.]

Piscīna (fish-pond). A pool or basin of
water in Roman bath-rooms. (*See* BATHS.)

Pistor. The Roman baker. (*See* BAKERS
AND BAKING.)

Pĭthœgĭa. The first day of the festival
of the *Anthestēria*. (*See* DIONYSIA.)

Pĭthŏs (*Greek*). A Greek wine-jar of
earthenware, with a wide mouth and a
close-fitting lid. (*See* VESSELS.)

Pittheus. King of Trœzēn, father of
Æthra, the mother of Thēseus (*q.v.*).

Pĭtyŏcamptēs (*Greek*, " pine-bender "), a
name applied to the robber Sĭnĭs (*q.v.*).

Plănĭpes. *See* MIME.

Plato (Gr. *Plătōn*), who shares with
Aristotle the first place among the philosophers of antiquity, was born at Athens
428 B.C. (according to the story, on the 21st
of May, the birthday of Apollo). His father,
Aristōn, traced his descent from king Codrus;
his mother, Pĕrictĭōnē, belonged to the same
family as Sŏlōn. Originally called after
his grandfather Aristŏclēs, he afterwards

obtained the name of Plato (said to have been
given by Sōcrătēs) either from the breadth
of his shoulders or from the ample flow of
his speech. His youth falls in the time
of the Peloponnesian War, when Athens,
though already entering on the decline of
its political greatness, was still distinguished
by the greatest activity in all intellectual
paths. He had an education befitting his
rank and including, according to Athenian
custom, both gymnastic and musical culture; but from the first he consistently held
aloof from public life, in spite of the numerous advantages which his birth and connexions would have insured him in such
a career. Crĭtĭas, for instance, who was
afterwards the leader of the Thirty, was
his mother's cousin. After at first devoting

himself to poetical studies, and himself composing poetry, he soon took up philosophy.
In this subject he is said to have received
the instructions of Crătўlus, a follower of
Hēraclītus. At the age of twenty he entered
the circle of Socrates' disciples, and soon
took a prominent position among them. In
399, after Socrates' death (at which he was
prevented by illness from being present),
he went to Mĕgără, to his old fellow disciple
Euclīdēs, and thence is said to have travelled
to Cўrēnē and Egypt. He certainly spent
some time in Magna Græcia with the
Pythagoreans, Archўtās of Tărentum and
Tīmæus of Locri, and thence visited Syracuse on the invitation of the elder Dionў-
sius. His strong independence, however,
and his intimate friendship with Dionysius'
brother-in-law, the noble Dion, soon drew
upon him the mistrust of the tyrant. The
story relates that he was sold as a slave
into Ægīna by order of Dionysius, and
ransomed by a friend. Returning to Athens
about 388, he established in a garden near
the Academy (a gymnasium so named after
the hero Acădēmus), in the north-west part
of the city, a philosophical school, over
which he presided for forty years. Here
he lived unmarried, taking no part in the
affairs of State, but devoting his energies
exclusively to the pursuit of knowledge,
interrupted only by two journeys to Sicily.
The first of these he undertook in 367, on
the accession of the younger Dionysius, in
order, in conjunction with Dion, to win the
young ruler to the cause of philosophy and
induce him to convert the tyranny into a
constitutionally organized monarchy. This
attempt completely failed; and the only
result was the banishment of Dion. His
second journey was in 362. His object was
to reconcile Dionysius with Dion, but in this
he was equally unsuccessful; in fact, his own
life was in danger, and he was only saved
by the intercession of Archytas of Tarentum.
However, the accounts of these last two
journeys are little to be depended upon.

Besides the narrower circle of his immediate pupils—among whom the most celebrated are Aristotle, Speusippus, his sister's
son, and Xĕnŏcrătēs,—the Academy was also
frequented by a large number of educated
men, and even women. It is said that
Plato's advice in political matters was asked,
not only by statesmen at home, but even
by foreign States. His teaching was given
partly in the shape of informal conversation,
partly in consecutive and systematic lectures on philosophical subjects. Even to

his old age his activity was unwearied ; and he was carried off by an easy death (it is said, while actually engaged in composition), in the eighty-first year of his life (348). He was buried in the neighbourhood of the Academy, where his tomb still existed in the 2nd century A.D. His plot of land remained nearly a thousand years in the possession of the Platonic school.

As works of Plato, thirty-six writings in fifty-six books (the thirteen letters being reckoned as one), have been handed down to us. These were divided by Thräsyllus, a Neo-Pythagorean of the time of Tĭbĕrĭus, into nine tetralogies, as follows : (1) *Euthy̆phro*, *Apology of Socrates*, *Crĭto*, *Phædo*. (2) *Crăty̆lus*, *Thĕætētus*, *Sŏphistēs*, *Pŏlĭtĭcus*. (3) *Parmĕnĭdēs*, *Phĭlēbus*, *Sympŏsĭum*, *Phædrus*. (4) *Alcĭbĭădēs I and II*, *Hipparchus*, *Antĕrastæ*. (5) *Thĕāgēs*, *Charmĭdēs*, *Lăchēs*, *Ly̆sĭs*. (6) *Euthy̆dēmus*, *Prōtăgŏrās*, *Gorgĭās*, *Mĕnō*. (7) *Hippĭās I and II*, *Iŏn*, *Mĕnexĕnus*. (8) *Clĭtŏphō*, *Republic* (ten books), *Tĭmæus*, *Crĭtĭas*. (9) *Mĭnōs*, *Laws* (twelve books), *Epĭnŏmis*, *Letters*. Besides these, eight other writings bear his name ; but these were marked as spurious even in ancient times. Of the genuine writings of Plato none have been lost, owing to the fact that the study of them was kept up without a break through all the intervening centuries ; but a number of the above-mentioned are of more or less doubtful authenticity, though there is not in all cases sufficient evidence to prove their spuriousness. Besides the *Letters* and the *Epinomis* (an appendix to the *Laws* composed by Plato's pupil, Philippus of Opūs), the writings of the fourth tetralogy as well as the *Theages*, the *Minos*, and the *Clitopho*, are reckoned as undoubtedly spurious. Of questionable genuineness also is a series of epigrams which has been handed down under Plato's name.

Many attempts have been made to arrange the Platonic writings in the order of time, but unanimity on the subject has never been attained. An old, though disputed, tradition reckons the *Phædrus* as the first, while the *Laws*, which is said to have been published by the aforesaid Philippus after the author's death, are generally acknowledged to be the last ; the *Republic* also belongs, at any rate, to the later writings.

The writings of Plato are among the greatest productions, not only of Greek literature, but of the literature of the world. They are equally admirable in matter and in form, combining, as they do, fulness and depth of thought with the highest mastery of style, while at the same time they are penetrated by the noblest spirit. The form is throughout that of dialogue ; and in the dialogues Plato himself never appears as a speaker, but he makes his master, Socrates, the interpreter of his views. The dramatic setting and execution, the delineation of the characters, the language, perfectly adjusted to the personality of the speakers and to the circumstances supposed, — now faithfully reproducing the simple manner of expression usual in conversation, now giving clear expression to the thought with all the incision of dialectics, now rising to poetic elevation,—all show the most consummate art and make it doubtful, whether in Plato we should rather admire the artist and the poet, or the philosopher. On his teaching and his school, *see* PHILOSOPHY.

Plaustrum. A wagon. (*See* CHARIOTS.)

Plautus (*Tĭtus Maccĭus*). The greatest of the Roman comic poets, born 254 B.C. at Sarsĭna in Umbria, of humble extraction. Having earned some money by finding employment at Rome among workmen engaged by persons who gave theatrical representations, he set up a business outside the city ; but in this undertaking he lost his property. Returning to Rome, he fell into such poverty that he was obliged to take service with a miller, and earn wages by turning a handmill. It was here that he began to write comedies in verse, and in later times three pieces were still known, which he was said to have composed while thus employed. He continued actively writing to an extreme old age, and died in 184 B.C.

His productivity must have been altogether extraordinary, even if a considerable portion of the 130 pieces which were known by the ancients under his name, were not really his work ; for not only were the pieces of a certain Plautus reckoned as his, on account of the similarity of name, but numerous comedies by forgotten poets, who worked in his style, were generally ascribed to him as the most popular of poets. Not only was he a favourite with the public and long remained so (even in Cicero's time pieces by him were put upon the stage), but he also early attracted the interest of scholars, to whom he offered a rich material for study in the departments of philology, criticism, and the history of literature. Special and peculiar attention was paid to him by Varro, who composed several works about him and established the claims of 21 comedies as undisputedly genuine. Of these

"Varronian plays" we still possess 20 more or less complete, and of the last, the *Vīdŭlārĭă*, considerable fragments. These extant plays (in addition to which there are a number of fragments of lost plays), are the oldest complete monuments of Roman literature. They have not come down to us quite in their original form, but bear manifold traces of having undergone revision on the occasion of representations after the poet's death, especially in the latter half of the 2nd century B.C. This is particularly the case with the prologues, which are prefixed to most of the pieces.

The plays have been handed down in the following order: *Amphĭtrŭō*, *Asĭnāria* (comedy of asses), *Aulŭlāria* (comedy of a pot), *Captīvi* (the prisoners), *Curcŭlio*, *Cāsĭna*, *Cistellāria* (comedy of a chest), *Epĭdĭcus*, *Bacchĭdes*, *Mostellāria* (comedy of ghosts), *Mĕnœchmi*, *Mīles glŏrĭōsus* (the braggart), *Mercātor* (trader), *Pseudŏlus*, *Pœnŭlus* (the Carthaginian),*Persa* (the Persian), *Rŭdens* (the cable), *Stĭchus*, *Trĭnummus* (the three coins), *Trŭcŭlentus* (the grumbler), *Vĭdŭlāria* (Comedy of a trunk). The titles refer sometimes to characters, sometimes to the action of the piece. If several of them are comparatively weak in plot and character-drawing, still not a few belong to the first rank. Such are the *Aulularia*, *Menœchmi* (the former the model of Molière's *Avare*, the latter of Shakespeare's *Comedy of Errors*), *Captivi*, *Bacchides*, *Mostellaria*, *Miles gloriosus*, *Pseudolus*, *Rudens*, and *Trinummus*. The *Amphitruo* is remarkable as an instance of comic treatment of a mythical subject. The *Miles* is one of the oldest pieces; the *Stichus* was brought out in 200, the *Pseudolus* in 192, the *Trinummus* about 190; the *Truculentus* also dates from the extreme old age of the poet. Though Plautus followed Greek models, such as Phĭlēmōn, Dĭphĭlus, and Mĕnander, he did not simply translate his originals, but worked them up with great freedom and nationalised them by additions of his own. He is a master in the use of language, metre, and material, and possesses an inexhaustible and pungent, if often coarse, wit. That he understood how to handle serious and moral subjects is proved by the *Captivi* and *Trinummus*. He must be reckoned among the greatest geniuses of his nation.—The name of the *Aulularia* of Plautus was once erroneously given to a play with the alternative title of the *Quĕrŏlus*, a wretched production of the 4th century A.D.

Plĕbiscītum. The Roman name for a decree of the *cŏmĭtĭa trĭbūta*. For more see COMITIA (3).

Plēbs. A part of the population of Rome, which derived its origin mainly from the conquered Latins settled on Roman territory by the kings Tullus Hostīlius and Ancus Martius. At first these possessed only the passive rights of citizenship, being excluded from all its privileges as well as from service in war, and forming a community sharply separated from the old citizens, the patricians. In particular, they did not possess the right of concluding valid marriages with patricians, although they were otherwise equal in matters of private law. When, by the constitution of Servius Tullius, they were compelled to serve in war and to pay war-taxes, they obtained the right of voting with the patricians in the *cŏmĭtĭa centŭrĭāta*. After the establishment of the Republic in 510 B.C., the plebeians began the struggle with the patricians, who were then in sole possession of the secular and priestly offices. The aim of the plebeians was to secure complete equality of rights, answering to their equality of duties. An important engine in this struggle was the tribunate of the people (*see* TRIBUNI PLEBIS) established in 491, as well as the *comitia trĭbūta*. (*See* COMITIA, 3.) The plebeians had the chief weight in that assembly, and after 448 it was invested with the right of passing decrees binding on the whole people. Among their first acquisitions was the right of entering into valid marriages with the patricians (445 B.C.). One after another, the plebeians gained admittance to the most important offices of State and the priesthoods, down to the year 300, so that only insignificant offices remained reserved for the patricians (*q.v.*). When the struggle of the orders was thus settled, the opposition between patricians and plebeians lost its practical importance. The two orders were completely blended together, and the place of the aristocracy of birth was taken by the aristocracy of office, the members of which were called *nŏbĭlēs*. From this time the name *plebs* passed to the lower ranks of the people, as contrasted with this "nobility."

Plēctrum. *See* LYRE.

Plēĭădēs or **Plēĭădĕs** (*Greek*). The seven daughters of Atlas and the Ocean-nymph Plēĭŏnē, born on the Arcadian mountain Cyllēnē, sisters of the Hȳădĕs. The eldest and most beautiful, *Maia*, became the mother of Hermēs by Zeus; *Electra* and *Tăўgĕtē*, of Dardănus and Lăcĕdæmōn by the same; *Alcўŏnē*, of Hўrῐeus by Pŏseidŏn; *Cĕlænō*, of Lўcus and Nycteus by the same; *Stĕrŏpē* or *Astĕrŏpē*, of Œnŏmăus by Arēs; *Mĕrŏpē* (*i.e.* the mortal), of Glaucus by Sīsўphus. Out of grief, either for the fate of Atlas or for the death of their sisters, they killed themselves and were placed among the constellations. According to another legend, they were pursued for five years by the Giant hunter Ōrīon (*q.v.*), until Zeus turned the distressed Nymphs and their pursuer into neighbouring stars. As the constellation of the seven stars, they made known by their rising (in the middle of May) the approach of harvest, and by their setting (at the end of October) the time for the new sowing. Their rising and setting were also looked upon as the sign of the opening and closing of the sailing season. One of the seven stars is invisible; this was explained to be Merope, who hid herself out of shame at her marriage with a mortal. The constellation of the Pleiades seems also to have been compared to a flight of doves (Gr. *pĕleiădĕs*). Hence the Pleiades were supposed to be meant in the story told by Homer of the ambrosia brought to Zeus by the doves, one of which is always lost at the *Planctæ* rocks, but is regularly replaced by a new one [*Od.* xii 62]. Among the Romans, the constellation was called *Vergĭlῐæ*, the stars of spring.

Plēῐăs ("a group of seven stars"). The name given by the Alexandrine critics to a group of seven tragic poets, who wrote at Alexandria under Ptolemy Phῐlădelphus in the first half of the 3rd century B.C. Their names were: Alexander Ætōlus, Phῐliscus, Sōsῐthĕus, Hŏmērus, Æantῐdēs, Sōsῐphănēs, and Lўcŏphrŏn.

Plēmŏchŏē. Literally, "an earthen vessel for water"; hence the name *plēmŏchŏæ* given to the last day of the Eleusinian festival, when this kind of vessel was used for pouring out water. (*See* ELEUSINIA.)

Plĕthrŏn. (1) A measure of length among the Greeks = ⅙ of a stadium = 100 Greek feet = little more than 101 English feet, or 33 yds. 2 ft. (2) A unit of square measure, the square of 100 Greek feet, or 10,000 Greek square feet; *i.e.* an area of the extent of 10,226·2656 square feet, or about 1136·24 square yards, *i.e.* about two perches less than a rood (or quarter of an acre).

Pliny. (1) *The elder, Gaius Plīnius Sĕcundus.* A Roman representative of encyclopædic learning, born 23 A.D., at Nŏvum

Cōmum (*Como*), in Upper Italy. Although throughout his life he was almost uninterruptedly occupied in the service of the State, yet at the same time he carried on the most widely extended scientific studies. To these he most laboriously devoted all his leisure hours, and thus gained for himself the reputation of the most learned man of his age. Under Claudius he served as commander of a troop of cavalry (*præfectus ălæ*) in Germany; under Vespasian, with whom he was in the highest favour, he held several times the office of imperial governor in the provinces, and superintended the imperial finances in Italy. Finally, under Tῐtus, he was in command of the fleet stationed at Mῐsēnum, when in 79, at the celebrated eruption of Vesuvius, his zeal for research led him to his death. For a detailed account of this event, as well as of his literary labours, we have to thank his nephew, the younger Pliny [*Ep.* iii 5; vi 16]. Besides writings upon military, grammatical, rhetorical, and biographical subjects, he composed two greater historical works: a history of the Germanic wars in twenty books, and a history of his own time in thirty-one books. His last work was the Natural History (*Nātūrālis Histŏria*), in thirty-seven books, which has been preserved to us. This was dedicated to Titus, and was published in 77; but he was indefatigably engaged in amplifying it up to the time of his death. This Encyclopædia is compiled from 20,000 notices, which he had extracted from about 2,000 writings by 474 authors. Book i gives a list of contents and the names of the authors used. ii is on astronomy and physics. iii–vi, a general sketch of geography and ethnography, mainly a list of names. vii–xix, natural history proper (vii, anthropology; viii–xi, zoology of land and water animals, birds, and insects; xii–xix, botany). xx–xxxii, the pharmacology of the vegetable kingdom (xx–xxvii) and of the animal kingdom (xxviii–xxxii). xxxiii–xxxvii, mineralogy and the use of minerals in medicine and in painting, sculpture, and the engraving of gems, besides valuable notices upon the history of art. A kind of comparative geography forms the conclusion.

Considering the extent and varied character of the undertaking, the haste with which the work was done, the defective technical knowledge and small critical ability of the author, it cannot be surprising that it includes a large number of mistakes and misunderstandings, and that its contents are of very unequal value, details that are strange and wonderful, rather than really important, having often unduly attracted the writer's attention. Nevertheless, the work is a mine of inestimable value in the information it gives us respecting the science and art of the ancient world; and it is also a splendid monument of human industry. Even the unevenness of the style is explained by the mosaic-like character of the work. At one time it is dry and bald in expression; at another, rhetorically coloured and impassioned, especially in the carefully elaborated introductions to the several books. On account of its bulk, the work was in early times epitomized for more convenient use. An epitome of the geographical part of Pliny's Encyclopædia, belonging to the time of Hadrian, and enlarged by additions from Pompōnius Mela, and other authors, forms the foundation of the works of Sōlīnus and Martīānus Căpella. Similarly the *Mĕdĭcīna Plinii* is an epitome prepared in the 4th century for the use of travellers.

(2) *The younger, Gaius Plīnius Cæcĭlius Sĕcundus*, nephew and adopted son of the elder Pliny, born 62 A.D. at Nŏvum Cōmum. After the early death of his father Cæcilius, he was carefully brought up by his mother Plinia, and by his adoptive father. He was trained in rhetoric under Quintilian, and began his public career as an advocate in the nineteenth year of his age. After serving in Syria as military tribune, he devoted himself under Domitian to the service of the State, and became the emperor's *quæstor*, and also a tribune of the people and *prætor* (93). Under Trajan, he held the consulship in 100, and about 112 governed the province of Bīthȳnia as imperial legate. He died about 114, very widely respected on account of his mild and benevolent character, his exemplary private life, his ability as an orator, his refined taste, and his services to letters. He was distinguished by the favour of the emperor, and was in friendly intercourse with the most celebrated men of his time, and the representatives of literature. Among his friends appear Quintilian [*Ep.* ii 14 § 9], Sīlius Itălĭcus [iii 7], Martial [iii 21], Suetōnius [i 8; iii 8; v 10; ix 34], and above all Tăcĭtus [i 6, 20; iv 13; vi 6, 16, 20; vii 20, 33; viii 7; ix 10, 14], to whom he was bound by the most genuine mutual attraction.

Of his poems and forensic speeches, which he published himself, nothing has been preserved, with the exception of a panegyric addressed to Trajan, which he pronounced in the Senate in 100 A.D. in order to thank the emperor for the consulship conferred upon him. This he afterwards published in a revised form. It is composed in an affected and artificial style, and is full of the most exaggerated pieces of flattery addressed to the emperor; it served as a pattern for the later panegyrists. Besides this, we possess a collection of letters in nine books, dating from the years 97–108, edited by himself. To this collection there is added a tenth book, consisting of the official correspondence between him and Trajan, belonging chiefly to the time of his Bithynian governorship, published, we may presume, after his death. [The best known letters in this book are that on the punishment of the Christians, No. 97, and the emperor's reply, No. 98.] His letters, in which he happily imitates Cicero, give a clear picture of his own personality, his studies, and his intercourse with his friends, as well as of the public, social, and literary life of his time, and are therefore valuable as authorities for the history of the same.

Plōstellum Pœnĭcum. A threshing-machine used by the Romans. (*See* THRESHING.)

Plōtīnus. A Greek philosopher, born 205 A.D., at Lȳcŏpŏlĭs in Egypt. In the 28th year of his life he applied himself to philosophy, and attended the lectures of the most celebrated men of that time in Alexandria. But none of these was able to satisfy him, until in Ammōnius Saccas, the founder of Neo-Platonism, he discovered the teacher whom he had sought. With him he stayed for eleven years; then, in 243, he joined the expedition of the emperor Gordian against the Persians, in order to learn the Persian philosophy. In this object he failed, owing to the unsuccessful issue of the undertaking; he was even obliged to flee for his life to Antioch. In 244 he went to Rome, where he worked till 269 with great success, and gained the emperor Gallĭēnus himself and his wife Sălōnīna as converts to his teaching, so that he even dared to conceive the idea of founding an ideal city in Campania, with the approval and support of the emperor: this city was to be called *Plătŏnŏpŏlĭs*, and its inhabitants were to live according to the laws of Plato. Gallienus was not disinclined to enter into the plan; however, it was wrecked by the opposition of the imperial counsellors.

Plotinus died in 270, on the estate of a friend in Campania. With the 50th year of his age he had begun to reduce his teaching to a written form: the fifty-four treatises, which have been preserved to us, were published after his death by his pupil and biographer Porphyry, who revised their style and arranged them in order; they were published in six *Ennĕads* (sets of nine books). Plotinus was the first to give a systematic development to the Neo-Platonic doctrine, or, at least, the first to put it forth in writing, not indeed with the charm of the Platonic dialogues, still less with their dialectic force, but nevertheless with depth of thought and in pithy, though at times careless and incorrect, language. It is true that there appears even in him a mystical tendency, especially in his doctrine of the ecstatic elevation of the soul to the divine being, to which he himself (according to the testimony of Porphyry) attained on four occasions; but he is still completely free from the phantastic and superstitious character of the later Neo-Platonism.

Plough (Gr. *ărŏtrŏn;* Lat. *ărātrum*). This well-known agricultural implement, according to the story generally current in

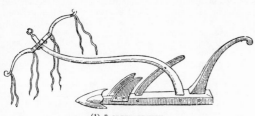

(1) * GREEK PLOUGH.

(Relief on the pedestal of a statue of Demeter, found in Magnesia; Ginzrot, *Wagen und Fahrwerke der Alten*, p. 34.)

Greece, was an invention of Dēmētēr, the goddess of agriculture, who taught its use to Triptŏlĕmus (*q.v.*). Originally it was constructed of a strong, hook-shaped piece of timber, whereof the longer end (Gr. *histŏbŏĕus;* Lat. *būris*) served at once as plough-tail and pole, while the other acted as sharebeam (Gr. *ĕlȳmă;* Lat. *dentālĕ*). This was fitted in front with the share (Gr. *hȳnis;* Lat. *vŏmer*), and behind with the upright plough-tail (Gr. *ĕchĕtlĕ;* Lat. *stīvă*). At the end of the pole was affixed the yoke, in which the oxen or mules by which it was to be drawn were harnessed (*see* cuts). Besides the natural hook-shaped

plough, we have, as early as Hesiod (8th century B.C.), a notice of the artificially constructed instrument, in which the main parts, the pole, the share-beam, and the plough-stock (*gȳĕs*) connecting them, were of different sorts of wood [*Works and Days*, 425–434]. Roman ploughs had also two earth-boards (*aurēs*), which served to smooth the furrow [Vergil, *Georgic* i 172].

(2) ITALIAN PLOUGH AND PLOUGHMAN.

(From an ancient bronze, found at Arezzo; Micali, *Monumenti per servire alla Storia d. ant. Popoli Ital.*, pl. 114.)

The *plaustraratrum* (wagon-plough) used in Upper Italy was a different kind. In this the plough-stock rested on two low wheels, the pole being let into the axle. [In Pliny, *N. H.* xviii 172, the MSS have *plaumorati*, altered by Hardouin into *plaustraratri*. Neither word is found elsewhere.]

Plutarch. A Greek writer of biographies and miscellaneous works, who was born at Chærŏnēa in Bœotia, about 50 A.D. He came of a distinguished and wealthy family, and enjoyed a careful education. His philosophical training he received at Athens, especially in the school of the Peripatetic Ammōnius [of Lamptræ in Attica, who is identified with Ammonius] the Egyptian. After this he made several journeys and stayed a considerable time in Rome, where he gave public lectures on philosophy, was in friendly intercourse with persons of distinction, and conducted the education of the future emperor Hadrian. From Trajan he received consular rank, and by Hadrian he was in his old age named *prŏcūrātor* of Greece. He died about 120 in his native town, in which he held the office of *archŏn* and of priest of the Pythian Apollo.

His fame as an author is founded principally upon his *Parallel Lives*. These he probably prepared in Rome under the reign of Trajan, but completed and published late in life at Chæronea. The biographies are divided into connected pairs, each pair placing a Greek and a Roman in juxtaposition, and generally ending with a comparative view of the two; of these we still possess forty-six: *Thēseus* and *Rōmŭlus*, *Lўcurgus* and *Nŭma*, *Sŏlōn* and *Vălĕrius Publĭcŏla*, *Thĕmĭstŏclēs* and *Cămĭllus*, *Pĕrĭclēs* and *Făbius Maxĭmus*, *Alcĭbĭădēs* and *Cŏrĭŏlānus*, *Tĭmŏlĕōn* and *Æmĭlius Paulus*, *Pĕlŏpĭdās* and *Marcellus*, *Aristīdēs* and *the elder Cătо*, *Phĭlŏpœmēn* and *Flāmĭnīnus*, *Pyrrhus* and *Mărius*, *Lўsander* and *Sulla*, *Cĭmōn* and *Lŭcullus*, *Nĭcĭās* and *Crassus*, *Eumĕnēs* and *Sertōrius*, *Agēsĭlăŭs* and *Pompēĭus*, *Alexander* and *Cæsar*, *Phōcĭōn* and *the younger Cătо*, *Agis* and *Clĕŏmĕnēs* and *the two Gracchi*, *Dēmosthĕnēs* and *Cicero*, *Dēmētrius Pŏlĭorcētēs* and *Antōnius*, *Dĭōn* and *Brutus*. To these are added the four specially elaborated lives of *Artaxerxēs Mnēmōn*, *Arātus*, *Galba*, and *Otho;* a number of other biographies are lost.

Plutarch's object was, not to write history, but out of more or less important single traits to form distinct sketches of character. The sketches show indeed a certain uniformity, inasmuch as Plutarch has a propensity to pourtray the persons represented either as models of virtue in general, or as slaves of some passion in particular; but the lives are throughout attractive, owing to the liveliness and warmth of the portraiture, the moral earnestness with which they are penetrated, and the enthusiasm which they display for everything noble and great. For these reasons they have always had a wide circle of readers. More than this, their historical value is not to be meanly estimated, in spite of the lack of criticism in the use of the authorities and the manifold inaccuracies and mistakes, which, in the Roman lives, were in part the result of a defective knowledge of the Latin language. There are a large number of valuable pieces of information in which they fill up numerous gaps in the historical narratives that have been handed down to us. Besides this work, eighty-three writings of various kinds (some of them only fragments and epitomes of larger treatises) are preserved under the name of Plutarch. These are improperly classed together under the title *Mŏrālia* (ethical writings); for this designation is only applicable to a part of them. The form of these works is as diverse as their tenour and scope : some are treatises and reports of discourses; a large number is composed in the form of Platonic or Aristotelian dialogues ; others again are learned collections and notices put together without any special plan of arrangement. A considerable portion of them are of disputable authenticity or have been proved to be spurious. About half are of philosophical and ethical tenour, and have for the most part a popular and practical tendency, some of them being of great value for the history of philosophy, such as the work on the opinions of the philosophers (*De Plăcĭtīs Phĭlŏsŏphŏrum*) in five books. Others' belong to the domain of religion and worship, such as the works *on Isis and Osiris*, *on the Oracles of the Pythian Priestess*, and *on the Decay of the Oracles ;* others to that of the natural sciences, while others again are treatises on history and antiquities, or on the history of literature, such as the Greek and Roman Questions, and the Lives of the Ten Orators. [This last is undoubtedly spurious.] One of most instructive and entertaining of all his works is the *Table-talk* (*Quæstĭōnes Convĭvĭāles*) in nine books, which deal *inter alia* with a series of questions of history, archæology, mythology, and physics. But even with these works his literary productiveness was not exhausted ; for, besides these, twenty-four lost writings are known to us by their titles and by fragments. In his language he aims at attaining the pure Attic style, without, however, being able altogether to avoid the deviations from that standard which were generally prevalent in his time.

Plŭtĕus. (1) A pent-house or mantlet used by the Romans in sieges. (For more *see* SIEGE.) [(2) The backboard of a bed, or the raised end of a couch. (3) A dwarf wall or parapet. (4) A bookshelf, bookcase, or desk.]

Plūtō (Gr. *Plūtōn*). In Greek mythology, the prince of the underworld = Hādēs (*q.v.*).

Plūtus. The Greek personification of riches; born in Crete as the son of Dēmētēr and her beloved Iăsīōn or Iăsĭus, whom Zeus out of jealousy killed with lightning. He was supposed to have been blinded by Zeus, because he distributes his gifts without choice. In Thebes and Athens he was represented as a child on the arm of Tўchē and of Eirēnē (*q.v.*, with cut).

Plyntērĭa. A festival at Athens in honour of Athēnē, goddess of the city. (For more *see* CALLYNTERIA.)

Pnyx. A place at Athens (no longer to

be identified with certainty), in which the assemblies of the people were held.

Pŏdălīrĭus. Son of Asclēpius and Ēpĭŏnē. Like his brother Măchāon (*q.v.*), leech to the Greeks before Troy, and a brave warrior besides.

Pŏdarcēs. (1) The name of Priam (*q.v.*) in his youth.

(2) Brother of Prōtĕsĭlāus (*q.v.*), and after his death commander of his troops.

Pŏdargē (" the swift-footed "). One of the Harpies (*q.v.*).

Pœās. King of the Malians at the foot of Œta. He set light to the pyre of Hēráclēs, in return for which the hero gave him his bow and his poisoned arrows. His son was Phĭloctētēs (*q.v.*).

Pŏlĕmarch. (1) The third among the Athenian archons (*q.v.*). (2) Among the Spartans this was originally the designation of a high officer, who, without any specific command, was employed by the king for special duties. In later times it denoted the commander of a *mŏra* (*q.v.*).

Pŏlĕmōn. The name of several Greek authors:

(1) *The Pĕrĭēgētēs*, the most celebrated of that class of writers (*see* PERIEGETES). Born in the district of Trōås, he afterwards settled at Athens, where he was presented with the citizenship, about 200 B.C. He there worked up the material which he had collected from inscriptions, dedications, and public monuments of all kinds, into a number of works (*inter alia*, on Athens, and on the holy road from Athens to Eleusis), which in succeeding times were much quoted and highly valued as a mine of archæological facts, and of important points connected with the history of art. The fragments which are preserved enable us to recognise him as a well-read author.

(2) *Antōnĭus Polemon*, the *Sophist*, or rhetorician; a native of Lāŏdĭcēa, who lived in the first half of the 2nd century A.D. and presided over a flourishing school of rhetoric in Smyrna. He was much esteemed by his contemporaries and in high favour with the emperors Trajan, Hadrian, and Antōnīnus Pius. Towards the end of his life he was a martyr to the gout, and accordingly put an end to his life in his 56th year, by causing himself to be buried alive in the tomb of his ancestors at Laodicea. His fame was founded principally on the pithiness and adroitness of his improvisations. There are preserved two declamations by him, artificial variations upon the same theme [funeral orations in honour of Cȳnæ-

gīrus and Callĭmăchus, the generals who fell at Marathon].

Pōlētæ. A financial board at Athenᵤ, composed of ten members chosen yearly from the tribes by lot. Their chief duties were the leasing of the public taxes and the selling of confiscated goods. [Aristotle, *On the Constitution of Athens*, 47.]

Pŏlĭās (or *Pŏlĭūchus*, " protectress of the city "). A special name of Athēnē (*q.v.*) in many Greek cities, but particularly at Athens.

Pollux. (1) *See* DIOSCURI.

(2) *Jūlĭus Pollux.* A Greek rhetorician, a native of Naucrătis in Egypt, in the latter half of the 2nd century A.D., tutor of the emperor Commŏdus, from whom he received an appointment as a public teacher in Athens. His contemporaries, such as Lucian, ridiculed him for his small capacity. [Lucian is supposed to have attacked him in his *Rhētŏrum Prœceptor*, his *Lexĭphănēs*, and his *De Saltātĭŏne*, chap. 33.] We possess from his hand a dictionary in ten books dedicated to his pupil. This is arranged, not in the order of the alphabet, but according to subjects. In spite of all its confusion, and its want of critical acumen, it throws much light on the language, literature, and antiquities of Greece.

Pŏlȳænus. A Greek writer, born in Macedonia, lived in the middle of the 2nd century A.D., as a rhetorician and advocate at Rome, under Marcus Aurēlius and Lūcius Vērus. When the latter was setting out for the war against the Parthians in 162, Polyænus, being prevented by his age from taking part in the campaign, addressed to him a collection of military stratagems compiled from old writers, under the title *Strătēgĭcă*, or *Strătēgēmătă*, in eight books. In spite of many serious errors, this laborious and copious collection is not without value for purposes of historical research.

Pŏlȳbĭus. One of the most important Greek historians, born about 204 B.C. at Mĕgălŏpŏlĭs; the son of Lȳcortăs, general of the Achæan League in 185-4 and after 183. Through his father, and his father's friend Phĭlŏpœmēn, he early acquired a deep insight into military and political affairs, and was afterwards entrusted with high federal offices, such as the commandership of the cavalry, the highest position next to the federal generalship. In this capacity he directed his efforts towards maintaining the independence of the Achæan League. As chief representative of the policy of neutrality during the war of the Romans against Perseus of Macedonia, he attracted the suspicion of the Romans, and was one of the 1,000 noble Achæans who in 166 were transported to Rome as hostages, and detained there for seventeen years. In Rome, by virtue of his high culture, he was admitted to the most distinguished houses, in particular to that of Æmilĭus Paulus, the conqueror in the Macedonian War, who entrusted him with the education of his sons, Făbius and the younger Scipio. He was on terms of the most cordial friendship with the latter, whose counsellor he became. Through Scipio's intercession in 150, Polybius obtained leave to return to his home with those of the Achæans who still survived. But, in the very next year, he went with his friend to Africa, and was present at the capture of Carthage, 146 B.C. After the destruction of Corinth in the same year, he returned to his native land, and made use of his credit with the Romans to lighten, as far as he could, the lot of his unfortunate countrymen. When Greece was converted into a Roman province, he was entrusted with the difficult task of organizing the new form of government in the Greek towns, and in this office gained for himself the highest recognition both from the conquerors and from the conquered, the latter rewarding his services by setting up statues to him, and by other marks of honour. [Polybius, *Epitome*, xl 10; Pausanias, viii 9, 30, 37, 44, 48. The pedestal of such a statue has been discovered at Olympia.] The succeeding years he seems to have spent in Rome, engaged on the completion of his historical work, and occasionally undertaking long journeys through the Mediterranean countries in the interests of his history, more particularly with a view to obtaining actual ocular knowledge of historical sites. After the death of his patron, he returned to Greece, and died in 122, at the age of eighty-two, in consequence of a fall from his horse.

During his long sojourn in Rome, his study of the history and constitution of Rome, as well as his personal experiences, inspired him with the conviction, that the Roman people owed the magnificent development of their power, not to fortune, but to their own fitness, and to the excellence of their political and military institutions, as compared with those of other States, and that therefore their rapid rise to world-wide dominion had been in some measure an historical necessity. In order to enlighten his countrymen on this point, and thereby to supply them with a certain consolation for their fate, he composed his Universal History of the period between 220 and 146 B.C., in forty books. Of these the first two are in the form of an Introduction, and give a compendium of events in Italy, Africa, and Greece, from the destruction of Rome by the Gauls to the first Punic War, thus recording the rise of the Roman supremacy. The first main division (books iii–xxx) contained in synchronistic arrangement the occurrences from 220 to 168; that is, of the time in which Rome was founding its world-wide dominion through the Hannibalic, Macedonian, Syrian, and Spanish wars. The second (books xxxi–xl) described the maintenance and consolidation of this dominion against the attempts to overthrow it in the years 168–146. Of this work only books i–v have been preserved in a complete form; of the rest we possess merely fragments and epitomes. This is especially to be regretted in those parts in which Polybius narrates events which came within his own experience. He is the first representative of that particular type of historical composition, which does not merely recount the several facts and phenomena in chronological order, but goes back to the causes of events, and sets forth their results. His work rests upon a knowledge of the art of war and of politics, such as few ancient historians possessed; upon a careful examination of tradition, conducted with keen criticism; partly also upon what he had himself seen, and upon the communications of eye-witnesses and actors in the events. It sets forth the course of occurrences with clearness, penetration, sound judgment, and love of truth, and, among the circumstances affecting the result, lays especial stress on the geographical conditions. It belongs therefore to the greatest productions of ancient historical writing, though, in respect to language and style, it does not attain the standard of Attic prose. The language is often wanting in purity, and the style stiff and inharmonious.

Pŏlўbus. King of Corinth, foster-father of Œdĭpūs (*q.v.*).

Polychromy. The ancient practice of colouring pieces of sculpture, as well as certain portions of the exterior and interior of buildings. (*See* SCULPTURE, at end.)

Pŏlўclītus (Lat.; Gr. *Pŏlўcleitŏs*). Next to his somewhat older contemporary Phīdĭās, the most admired sculptor of antiquity. He was a native of Argos, and, like Phidias, a pupil of Agĕlādas. His name marks an epoch in the development of Greek art, owing to his having laid down rules of universal application with regard to the proportions of the human body in its mean standard of height, age, etc. In close accordance with these rules he fashioned a typical figure, the *Dŏrўphŏrus*, a powerful youth with a spear in his hand: this figure was called the *Cănŏn*, and for a long time served as a "standard" for succeeding artists [Pliny, *N. H.* xxxiv 55]. The rules which he practically applied in the *Canon* he also set forth theoretically in a written work [Galen, in Overbeck's *Schriftquellen*, §§ 958, 959]. It is also said of him that, when he made statues in an attitude of rest, instead of dividing the weight of the body equally between the two feet, according to the custom which had hitherto prevailed, he introduced the practice of causing them to rest upon *one* foot, with the other foot lightly raised, whereby the impression of graceful ease and calm repose was for the first time fully produced [Pliny, *l.c.* 56]. Except the celebrated chryselephantine colossal statue of Hèra (*q.v.*), which he made for the temple of

* THE FARNESE DIADUMENUS.
(British Museum.)

the goddess at Argos [Pausanias, ii 17 § 4], when it was rebuilt after a fire in 423 B.C., he produced statues in bronze alone, and almost exclusively of men in the prime of youth, such as the *Doryphorus* already mentioned; the *Dĭădūmĕnus*, a youth of softer lineaments, who is tying a band round his head [Pliny, *l.c.* 55; Lucian, *Philopseudes,* 18]; and an *Amazon,* which was preferred even to that of Phidias [Pliny, *l.c.* 53]. These statues may still be identified in copies of a later time (*see* cut, and compare cut under AMAZONS). He also worked as an architect. The theatre at Epidaurus (of which considerable remains still exist), and the circular structure called the *Thŏlŏs,* and the temple of Asclēpius [Pausanias, ii 27; *cp.* plan in Baedeker's *Greece,* p. 241], are now generally assigned to the younger Polyclitus.

[*Polyclitus the Younger* was a pupil of the Argive sculptor Naucўdēs. Among his works was a statue of the athlete *Agēnŏr* (Pausanias, vi 6 § 2), and of *Zeus Phĭlĭŏs* at Mĕgălŏpŏlĭs, in which the god was represented with some of the attributes of Dīonȳsus (*ib.* viii 31 § 4). The statues of *Zeus Meilĭchĭŏs* at Argos (*ib.* ii 20 § 1), and those of *Apollo, Lētō and Artĕmis* on Mount Lўcōnē near Argos (*ib.* 24 § 5), may possibly be assigned to the elder Polyclitus (Overbeck, *Schriftquellen,* §§ 941–3).] [J. E. S.]

Pŏlўdectēs. Son of Magnēs, king of the island of Sĕrīphus; attempted to compel Dănăē to marry him, but was turned into a stone by her son Perseus (*q.v.*) by the sight of the head of Mĕdūsa.

Pŏlўdeucēs (Lat. *Pollux*). *See* DIOSCURI.

Pŏlўdōrus. (1) *Son of Cadmus* and Harmŏnĭa, father of Labdăcus, and great-grandfather of Œdĭpūs.

(2) Youngest *son of Priam* and of Lăŏthŏē, his father's favourite son. He was killed while yet a boy by Achilles. The tragedians make him the son of Priam and Hĕcŭba, who, before the fall of Troy, committed him with many treasures to the care of their guest-friend, the Thracian king Pŏlўmēstŏr (or Polymnēstŏr). After the capture of Troy Polymestor puts the boy to death, in order to get possession of the gold, and throws the body into the sea. The waves cast it up on the Trojan shore, and here Hecuba finds it, just as Pŏlyxĕnă is on the point of being sacrificed. Out of revenge she, with the help of the captive Trojan women, kills the two children of the murderer, and blinds Polymestor himself. According to another version, Ilĭŏnē, Priam's daughter and Polymestor's wife, brings up the brother, who has been committed to her charge, as her own son, while she gives up her child Dēïphĭlus (or Dēïpўlus) instead of Polydorus. The Greeks, who wish to exterminate the race of Priam, win over Polymestor by promising him the hand of Electra and a large present of money in

return for the murder of Polydorus. Polymestor then murders his own son, and is blinded and killed by Ilione.

(3) A *Greek sculptor*, of the school of Rhodes, author (in conjunction with Agēsander and Athēnŏdōrus) of the celebrated group of Lāŏcŏōn (*q.v.*).

Pŏlygnōtus. The celebrated Greek painter of the island of Thāsŏs. He worked chiefly in Athens, whither he had been invited by Cĭmōn about 460 B.C., and where he received the citizenship. His most celebrated paintings were the *Capture of Troy* and the *Descent of Odysseus into Hades*, in the hall erected by the Cnidians at Delphi. We possess a description of them in considerable detail by Pausanias [x 25-31]. Other celebrated paintings by him (though several of his contemporaries were associated with him in their execution) were to be seen in the Stŏa Pœcīlē, the *Capture of Troy* and the *Battle of Marathon* [*ib.* 15], and in the temples of the Dioscūri [*ib.* 18 § 1], and of Thēseus at Athens. Though his works were only tinted outlines traced upon a coloured background, without shading and without any perspective, and sketched, as it were, in simple relief, all on the same plane, still his clear, rhythmical composition, the delicacy of his drawing, the impressiveness of his contours, and the nobility of his figures were highly celebrated [Overbeck's *Schriftquellen*, 1067-1079].

Pŏlyhymnĭa (or *Pŏlymnĭa*). The Muse of serious songs of adoration. (*See* MUSES.)

Pŏlyīdus. Son of Cœrănus, grandson of Abās, great-grandson of Mĕlampūs, father of Euchēnōr, Astȳcrătĭa, and Manto; like his ancestor, a celebrated seer, who flourished, according to different accounts, either at Corinth or Argos or Mĕgăra. To his son he prophesied his death before Troy; and the son of Mīnōs, Glaucus (*q.v.*, 2), he raised from the dead. At Megara he cleansed Alcăthŏŭs from the murder of his son Callĭpŏlĭs, and erected the temple of Dionȳsus.

Pŏlymēstōr. A Thracian king. He murdered Pŏlydōrus, the son of Priam, who had been entrusted to his protection, and was blinded by Hĕcŭba and the captive Trojan women. (*Cp.* POLYDORUS.)

Pŏlymnĭa. See POLYHYMNIA.

Pŏlynīcēs (Gr. *Pŏlŭneikēs*). Son of Œdĭpūs and Iŏcastē, was driven out of Thebes by his brother Etĕŏclēs (*see* ŒDIPUS), and fled to Adrastus (*q.v.*) of Argos, who gave him his daughter Argīa in marriage, and brought about the expedition of the *Seven against*

Thebes in order to restore him. He fell in single combat with Eteocles. His body, which had been thrown to the birds, was buried by his sister Antĭgŏnē (*q.v.*). His son was Thersander (*q.v.*).

Pŏlyphēmus. Son of Pŏseidōn and the Nymph Thŏōsa; the one-eyed Cyclops, who held Odysseus prisoner in his cave and ate several of the companions, until the hero made him drunk and blinded him. Later legends made him the lover of the beautiful Nymph Gălătĕă.

Pŏlyptȳchŏn. *See* DIPTYCHON.

Pŏlȳtĕchnus. *See* AËDON.

Pŏlyxĕna. Daughter of Priam and Hĕcŭbă, the betrothed of Achilles, who, at his wedding with her in the temple of the Thymbræan Apollo, was killed by Paris. After the fall of Troy the shade of Achilles demanded the expiation of his death with her blood, and she was sacrificed on his funeral pyre.

Pŏmērium. A name given by the Romans to the space, originally along the city-wall within and without, which was left vacant and reckoned holy. This space was marked off by stones, and in respect to the auspices formed the limit between city and country. [*See* Livy, i 44, and Cicero, *De Natura Deorum* ii 11, ed. J. B. Mayor.]

The old Pomerium remained unchanged until the time of Sulla; after him it was again extended by Cæsar, Augustus, Claudius, Nero, Vespasian and Titus, Hadrian, and probably also Trajan and Aurelian. An extension of the Pomerium was only admissible on the ground of an extension of the legal boundaries of the Empire. [Tacitus, *Ann.* xii 23.]

Pŏmōna. The Latin goddess of fruit trees, who in Rome had a flamen of her own (*Pŏmōnālis*). Like Vertumnus, who was regarded as her husband, she was particularly honoured in the country. Art represents her as a fair damsel, with fruits in her bosom, and the pruning-knife in her hand.

Pompēĭus Trogus. A contemporary of Livy, author of the first Roman general history. He was of Gaulish origin; his grandfather received the Roman citizenship from Pompeius in the Sertorian War, and his father served under Cæsar, and discharged at the same time the offices of a secretary, an ambassador, and a keeper of the seals. His extensive work in 44 books was drawn from Greek sources, and was entitled *Histŏriæ Philippĭcæ*, because the history of the various peoples was grouped round the

Macedonian empire founded by Philip; it began with Ninus, and reached down to his own time. With the historical narrative there were interwoven interesting descriptions relating to geography, ethnography, and natural science ; and indeed he is said to have also composed zoological and botanical works. Of the histories we now possess only lists of the contents of the several books (called the *prŏlŏgi*) and the epitome of Justin. (*See* JUSTINUS.)

Pompōnius. (1) *Lūcius Pompōnius Bŏnōniensis*, i.e. of Bŏnōnia (*Bologna*), flourished about 90 B.C. He was the first to raise the hitherto improvised popular plays called *Atellānæ* (*q.v.*) to a species of art by the introduction of written composition in the metrical forms and technical rules of the Greeks. He is particularly praised for richness of fancy, liveliness in plays upon words, and readiness in the use of rustic and farcical language. [Velleius Pat., ii 9 § 6 ; Macrobius, *Saturnalia* vi 9 § 4 ; Seneca, *Controv.* vii 18 § 9.] About 70 titles of plays by him are mentioned, a productiveness explained by the small compass of the *Atellanæ* as being after-pieces. Some titles point to travesties of mythological subjects, such as the *Supposititious Agamemnon* and the *Award of the Armour* (of Achilles).

(2) *Tĭtus Pompōnius Attĭcus.* *See* ATTICUS.

(3) *Lūcius Pompōnius Sĕcundus.* The most important tragedian of the time of the Empire, probably the last who wrote for the stage. He lived under Tĭbĕrĭus and was a partisan of Sējānus, after whose fall (31 A.D.) he had to submit to be kept in custody by his brother for six years, until Călĭgŭla gave him his freedom. In 44 he was consul; in 50 he fought with success against the Chatti, and received triumphal honours from Claudius. His poetical productions are highly spoken of by Tacitus [*Ann.* xii 28] and Quintilian [x 1 § 98]. We possess only very scanty remains of his tragedies.

(4) *Pompōnius Mela.* A native of Tingentera in Spain. He composed a description of the world in three books (*De Chŏrŏgrăphĭā*), the earliest work of this kind which we possess, and the only special work on the subject, which Roman literature has to show. According to a notice in the book [iii 49], it was written either in 40 A.D., when Călĭgŭlă triumphed over the Britons, or in 44, when Claudius did the same. The author's information does not rest upon personal inspection, but it is drawn from good, though mostly antiquated, Greek sources. Writing in a brief and concise style, he describes in the form of a coasting-voyage, with North Africa for its starting-point, the various countries of the then known world in geographical order, until he comes back by way of Western Africa to the point from which he set out. His language bears the rhetorical character of his time.

(5) *Sextus Pompōnius.* A distinguished jurist of the first half of the 2nd century A.D. He composed, among other works, a history of law and jurisprudence down to the time of Hadrian, which is frequently quoted in the Digest.

(6) *Pompōnius Porphýrĭō.* Roman grammarian, who lived in the first half of the 2nd century A.D., and composed a commentary on Horace, a fragmentary abridgment of which is still preserved.

Pontĭfex. A member of the highest priestly college in Rome, to which belonged the superintendence over all sacred observances, whether performed by the State or by private persons. The meaning of the name is uncertain; the interpretation which follows most obviously from the form of the word, that of " bridge-builder," referred in particular to the sacred bridge on piles (*pons sublĭcĭus*) over the Tiber, is open to many objections.[1] The foundation of the college is ascribed to Numa; at first it probably consisted of six patrician members, with the addition of the king, whose place, after the abolition of the Monarchy, was transferred to the *pontifex maxĭmus* (high-pontiff); from 300 B.C. it was composed of nine members (4 patrician and 5 plebeian), from the time of Sulla of fifteen (7 patrician and 8 plebeian); Cæsar added another member; and the emperors also raised the number at their pleasure. The office was for life, as was also that of the president. While, in the time of the Monarchy, the pontiffs were probably named by the king, under the Republic the college for a long time filled up its own numbers by co-optation, and also appointed the high-pontiff from among its members. From somewhere about 250 B.C. the election of the latter took place in the *cŏmĭtĭa* of the tribes under the presidency of a pontiff, and, from 103 B.C., the

---

[1] Professor Nettleship argues in support of it in his *Lectures and Essays*, p. 27. If the Italian immigration came overland, the office of bridge-builder would be of great importance. It is apparently connected with river-worship.

other members were also elected in the *comitia* out of a fixed number of candidates presented by the college. Under the Empire a preliminary election was held by the Senate, and merely confirmed by the *comitia*.

Besides the pontiffs proper, there were also included in the college the *rex sacrorum*, the three higher flamens and the three *pontĭfĭcēs mĭnōrēs*, who assisted the pontiffs in transactions relating to sacrifices and in their official business, besides sharing in the deliberations and the banquets of the whole college : these ranked according to length of service. In the earlier time an advanced age, with freedom from secular offices, was necessary for eligibility to the pontificate ; the high-pontiff, among other restrictions, was not allowed to leave Italy, was obliged to have a wife without reproach, and might not enter upon a second marriage or see a dead body, much less touch one. As regards his position, he was, as spiritual successor of the king, the sole holder and exerciser of the pontifical power ; and his official dwelling was in the king's house, the *rēgia* of Numa adjoining the *Fŏrum*, the seat of the oldest State worship. The college existed by his side only as a deliberative and executive body of personal assistants. He appointed to the most important priestly offices of the State, those of *flāmen*, of vestal, and of *rex sacrōrum ;* he made public the authoritative decisions of the college. In matters which came within the limits of his official action, he had the right of taking auspices, of holding assemblies of the people, and of publishing edicts. He also exercised a certain jurisdiction over the persons subject to his high-priestly power, especially the flamens and Vestals, over whom his authority was that of an actual father. Owing to the great importance of the office, the emperors from the time of Augustus undertook it themselves, and retained it, even in Christian times, until the year 382. As regards the functions of the college, besides performing a number of special sacrifices in the service of the household gods, they exercised (as already mentioned) a superintendence over the whole domain of the religious services recognised by the State, public and private. In all doubts which arose concerning the religious obligations of the State towards the gods, or concerning the form of any religious offices which were to be undertaken, their opinion was asked by the Senate and by the other secular bodies, who were obliged unhesitatingly to follow it.

In the various religious transactions, expiatory offerings, vows, dedications, consecrations, solemn appropriations, undertaken on behalf of the State, their assistance was invited by the official bodies, in order that they might provide for the correct performance, especially by dictating the prayers.

The knowledge of the various rites was handed down by the *libri pontĭfĭcĭi*, which were preserved in the official dwelling of the high-pontiff and kept secret. These included the forms of prayer, the rules of ritual for the performance of ceremonial observances, the *acta pontĭfĭcum*, i.e. the records relating to the official actions of the college, and the *commentārĭi pontĭficum*, i.e. the collection of opinions delivered, to which they were as a rule obliged to have recourse when giving new ones.

An important and indeed universal influence was exercised by the pontiffs, not only on religious, but also on civic life, by means of the regulation of the calendar, which was assigned to them as possessing technical knowledge of the subject ; and by means of their superintendence over the observance of the holidays. Owing to the character of the Roman reckoning of the year, it was necessary from time to time to intercalate certain days, with a view to bringing the calendar into agreement with the actual seasons to which the festivals were originally attached ; and special technical knowledge was needed, in order to be sure on what day the festivals fell. This technical knowledge was kept secret by the pontiffs as being a means of power. It was for the month actually current that they gave information to the people as to the distribution of the days, the festivals falling within the month, and the lawful and unlawful days (*fasti* and *nĕfasti, q.v.*) for civil and legal transactions. In 304 B.C. the calendar of the months was made public by Gnæus Flāvius ; but the pontiffs still retained the right of regulating the year by intercalations, and thereby the power of furthering or hindering the aims of parties and individuals by arbitrary insertion of intercalary months. This they kept until the final regulation of the year introduced by Cæsar as high-pontiff in 46 B.C. Closely connected with the superintendence of the calendar was the keeping of the lists of the yearly magistrates, especially of the consuls, since it was by their names that the years were dated, as well as the keeping of the yearly chronicle. (*See* ANNALS.)

As experts in the law of ritual, the pontiffs

had the superintendence over many transactions of private life, so far as ceremonial questions were connected with them, such as the conclusion of marriages, adoption by means of arrogation, and burial. Even upon the civil law they had originally great influence, inasmuch as they alone were in traditional possession of the solemn legal *formŭlæ*, known as the *lēgis actĭōnēs*, which were necessary for every legal transaction, including the settlement of legal business and the forms for bringing lawsuits. They even gave legal opinions, which obtained recognition in the courts as customary law, by the side of the written law, and grew into a second authoritative source of Roman law. Until the establishment of the prætorship (366 B.C.), a member of the college was appointed every year to impart information to private persons concerning the legal forms connected with the formulating of plaints and other legal business. The *legis actiones* were made public for the first time by the above-mentioned Flavius at the same time as the calendar. (*See* JURISPRUDENCE.)

Pontius. A special name of the sea-god Glaucus (*q.v.*).

Pontus. The sea, son of Gæa, and, by her again, father of Nēreus, Thaumās, Phorcȳs, Cētō, and Eurȳbĭa.

Pŏpīnæ. Roman cook-shops. (*See* INNS.)

Poplĭfŭgia. The festival of the flight of the people. (*See* CAPROTINA.)

Porfīrius Optātĭānus (*Publĭlĭus*). A Latin poet, who composed, about 330 A.D., a series of short poems in praise of Constantine, constructed in a highly artificial manner. [All the lines in each poem contain exactly the same number of letters.] By this composition he obtained his recall from banishment and won the favour of the emperor. The commendatory letter of Constantine, as well as the thanks of the poet, have come down to us with the poem.

Porphȳrĭōn. (1) One of the Giants. (*See* GIGANTES.)

(2) *See* POMPONIUS (6).

Porphyry (Greek, *Porphȳrĭŏs*). A Greek scholar and philosopher; in the latter capacity a votary of Neoplatonism. He was born 233 A.D. at Bătănæa in Syria, and received his education at Tyre, and afterwards studied grammar, rhetoric, and philosophy at Athens with Longīnus, who instead of his Syrian name *Malchus* (" king "), gave him the Greek name *Porphȳrĭŏs* (" clad in royal purple "). The fame of the Neoplatonist Plōtīnus drew him in 263 to Rome, where,

after some initial opposition, he for six years enthusiastically devoted himself to the study of the Neoplatonic philosophy. Being attacked by a dangerous melancholy, the result of overwork, he went, on the advice of Plotinus, to Sicily, whence after five years he returned to Rome, strengthened in mind and body. Here, until his death (304), he taught philosophy in the spirit of Plotinus, especially by bringing the teaching of his master within the reach of general knowledge by his clear and attractive exposition. His most important scholar was Iamblĭchus. A man of varied culture, Porphyry was particularly prolific as an author in the domain of philosophy, grammar, rhetoric, arithmetic, geometry, and music; however, most of his works, including the most important, are lost, among them a treatise against the Christians in fifteen books, which was publicly burned under Thĕŏdŏsius II (435). We have to lament the loss of his history of Greek philosophy before Plato in four books, of which we now possess only the (certainly uncritical) *Life of Pȳthăgŏrās*, and that not complete. Besides this there are preserved a *Life of Plotinus; a Compendium of the System of Plotinus*, in the form of aphorisms; a work on abstaining from animal food (*De Abstĭnentĭā*) in four books, from the Pythagorean point of view, valuable for its fulness of information on philosophy, and on the religions, forms of ritual, and customs of various peoples; an *Introduction to the Categories of Aristotle*, and a commentary on the same, in the form of questions and answers; a compendium of his own practical philosophy in the form of a *Letter to Marcella*, a widow without property, and with seven children, whom Plotinus married in his old age on account of her enthusiasm for philosophy; *Scholia on Homer*, discussions on a number of Homeric questions, an allegorical interpretation of the Homeric story of the grotto of the Nymphs in the Odyssey; and a *Commentary on the Harmonics of Ptolemy*.

Porrīma. *See* CARMENTA.

Portĭcus. The Roman name for a colonnade. (*See* STOA.)

Portland Vase. *See* GEMS, at end.

Portōrĭum. The custom levied by the Romans upon imports and exports; it was introduced as early as the time of the kings, and was generally leased to *publĭcāni* (*q.v.*). In 60 B.C. it was abolished for Italy, but was re-introduced by Cæsar for foreign goods, and after that time always continued to exist. Free and allied cities were, in earlier times, allowed to levy the customs for their own territory, but from these Romans were to be exempt. Under the emperors customs were levied not only at the frontier of the Empire, but also at the frontiers of the several provinces or of combinations of provinces united in one excise-district. Besides this the percentage levied on the purchasing price of articles was different in different districts. The export of many articles was forbidden, especially of corn, oil, wine, salt, iron, and gold.

Portūnus. The Roman god of harbours.[1] Like Janus, the god of coming in and going out, he was represented with a key, and was perhaps only a personification of one attribute of Janus. He had a special *flamen* in Rome (*Portūnālis*), and at the harbour on the Tiber he had a temple, where a festival, the *Portunalia*, was held in his honour every year on August 17th. In later times he was identified with the Greek Pălæmōn.

Pŏseidippus. One of the most eminent poets of the New Comedy, a native of Cassandrēa in Macedonia. He began to exhibit for the first time in the third year after the death of Mĕnander, or in B.C. 289. Of his pieces, as many as forty are mentioned by name, but only fragments of them are preserved. It was probably in imitation of one of these that the *Mĕnæchmi* of Plautus was written.

Pŏseidōn. The Greek god of the sea and of everything liquid, son of Crŏnus and Rhĕa; a younger brother of Zeus, according to Homer; an elder brother, according to Hesiod. At the distribution of the world the rule over the sea and all its gods and creatures fell to him, as the rule over the sky fell to Zeus, and that over the underworld to Plūto. His wife is Amphitrītē, his son Trītōn, his daughter Benthĕsĭkȳmē. As described by Homer [*Il.* xiii 21], he has his dwelling in the depth of the sea in a golden palace near Ægæ, according to the usual acceptation on the north coast of the Peloponnesus, where lay also his other place of worship mentioned by Homer, Hĕlĭcē [*Il.* viii 203], afterwards overthrown by an earthquake. On leaving his palace, he is clad in a golden robe and wields in his hand a golden whip, while he stands in a chariot drawn by swift-footed steeds with hoofs of bronze and manes of gold, with the monsters of the deep bounding and frisking around him, as he drives over the sea, which joy-

fully opens before his advance. As Zeus bears the lightning, so Poseidon bears the mighty trident, with which he stirs up the sea, cleaves rocks, and makes fountains and horses spring forth from them. Another symbol of the stormy flood is the bull, for which reason men offered sacrifice to Poseidon with dark-coloured bulls, while on the other hand, the dolphin is a symbol of the peaceful and calm sea. For, while he sends storm and shipwreck, he is also a beneficent god, who sends favourable winds. Every occupation on or by the sea, navigation, trade, fishing, is subject to his power; he also it is who grants victory by sea. Seafaring peoples traced their origin to him. But, as the sea was thought of as supporting the earth and as pressing into its hidden clefts and hollows, so Poseidon was worshipped from one point of view as "the supporter of the earth" (*gaiĕŏchŏs*), from the other as "the shaker of the earth" (*ennŏsĭgaiŏs, ĕnŏsichthōn*), who makes the earth quake beneath the blows of his trident. As such he was worshipped in districts which were a prey to earthquakes, as in Sparta, or in those which could show traces of great convulsions, as in Thessaly, where he was said to have opened up the Vale of Tempē, and formed the outlet of the Pēnēŭs into the sea by shattering the wall of rock which inclosed the valley. In the interior Poseidon was often worshipped as the creator of waters, especially of springs and the blessing brought by them; so particularly in Argŏlis and Arcadia, where, as being the fertilizing god, he was even regarded as the lover of Dēmētēr and father of Persĕphŏnē. In the course of time, under the predominance of the conception of Poseidon as god of the sea, his worship in such inland places fell into the background, and was displaced by that of other deities. Hence arose the legends of his contests with other gods for particular countries, as with Athēnē for Athens and Trœzēn, and with Hēra for Argŏlis, and of exchanges, as that of Delphi for the island of Călaurīa, which belonged to Apollo. He was also regarded as the creator and tamer of the horse: sometimes he was said to have brought it out of a rock by a blow, sometimes the earth was said to have been impregnated by him, and so given it birth; accordingly he was frequently worshipped as an equestrian god (*hippĭŏs*). Thus in the Attic deme of Cŏlōnus he was worshipped together with Athene, who was said to have invented the bridle. He was also specially worshipped at the equestrian games at the

---

[1] Perhaps originally the god of house and home, *portus* in its old sense of the entrance to a house (*cp.* Prof. Nettleship's *Essays*, p. 26).

Isthmus. Owing to the great diffusion of his worship through all the Greek races of the mother-country, as well as of the colonies, he plays a chief part in Greek legend, appearing as early as the Trojan story, in which he stands on the side of the Greeks in irreconcilable wrath against Troy, on account of the deception practised on him by Lāŏmĕdŏn. Similarly Odysseus cannot be protected from his rage on account of the blinding of his son Pŏlўphēmus, except by the unanimous will of the other gods. The unruly wildness of the sea, which is reflected in his character, appears also frequently in his sons, such as Orīŏn, Pŏlўphēmus, Cycnus, Antæus, Būsīris, Amўcus, Cercўŏn, and others. But he was also deemed to be the

COLOSSAL STATUE OF POSEIDON.
(Rome, Lateran Museum.)

ancestor of numerous noble families, especially of the Ionian race, which from old times worshipped him as a national god, and from their home on the north coast of the Peloponnesus carried his worship over with them to Asia. Here, in his chief sanctuary, on the promontory of Mўcălē, the Ionians celebrated their national festival, the Paniōnia. From the Ionian race and its representative, Thēseus, arose also the national festival of Poseidon observed by all Greece at the Corinthian Isthmus, where the Isthmian

games were celebrated in alternate years. The Greeks, after their victory over the Persians, set up a bronze colossus more than 10½ feet high in honour of the Isthmian god [Herod., ix 81].

The horse, the dolphin, and the pine tree were deemed sacred to Poseidon; it was with wreaths of pine that the victors in the Isthmian games were crowned. He was worshipped with human sacrifices, but more generally with sacrifices of horses and bulls, especially black ones; these were not unfrequently hurled alive into rivers. Besides horse-races, bull-fights were held in his honour. His temples were usually to be found on promontories, isthmuses, and tongues of land. His usual *attributes* were the trident and the dolphin, and also the tunny-fish. He was represented as a powerful, kingly man, like Zeus, but without his exalted calm, more compact in figure, and with thicker and curlier hair on his head. He is draped sometimes in a long robe, sometimes with a light scarf, which allows his powerful frame to be more fully displayed (*see* cut). Colossal statues of him often stood by harbours and on promontories. With Poseidon the Romans identified their sea-god *Neptūnus* (*q.v.*).

Pŏseidōnius. A Greek philosopher; a native of Apămēa, in Syria, born about 135 B.C., from his later place of residence generally called the Rhodian. He was the most distinguished pupil of the Stoic Pănætius, whose instruction he enjoyed at Athens, and the most scientific and most learned among the later Stoics. After an extended scientific journey in western Europe, he accepted the direction of the Stoic school at Rhodes, where he took part in public affairs with such success that his fellow citizens made him *prўtănis*, and in 86 sent him as envoy to Rome. From this time he remained in continual friendly intercourse with Romans of distinction, especially Cicero and Pompeius [Cic., *Ad Att.* ii 1 § 2, *Tusc. Disp.* ii 61]. He died at the age of 84. His literary labours were very extensive. Besides numerous philosophical treatises, he composed mathematical and astronomical writings, and a great historical and geographical work in 52 books as a continuation of Pŏlўbius. [He is frequently quoted by Strabo, *e.g.* pp. 147, 182, 215, 269, 757.] The substance of the *Tactics* of his pupil Asclēpĭŏdŏtus seems to have been derived from his discourses. [*See* Cicero, *De Natura Deorum,* ed. J. B. Mayor, II, p. xvi ff.]

Possessĭō. The Roman term for the *de facto* possession of an article without actual proprietary right (*dŏmĭnĭum*). The name was given in particular to those lands, properly belonging to the State, which were taken into cultivation by what was called *occŭpātio.* For more *see* AGER PUBLICUS.

Postal Service. Under the Roman Empire a postal service proper was first formed in the time of Augustus. This, however, was not intended for the use of the public, but served only for the conveyance of magistrates and of government despatches ; just as the great network of roads, with which the Romans covered the whole empire, was laid down, not for the purposes of traffic, but in the first instance for the transport of the armies and of the materials of war. Under the Republic the correspondence of officials was carried as a rule by special messengers ; the conveyance of the officials themselves was laid upon the provincials, who were bound to provide relays of horses and supplies. Augustus instituted a State post (*cursus publĭcus*) with a military organization, which conveyed the official despatches from station to station by means of couriers. For the conveyance of the magistrates stations were instituted, with changes of horses (*mūtātĭōnēs*) and with night-quarters (*mansĭōnēs*). Private persons were allowed to use the State posts only by special permission on the part of the governors, afterwards of the emperor, and upon definite orders given [*diplōmăta :* Pliny, *Ep.* x, the last two letters]. The cost of the posting-houses was made a charge upon the several localities, though occasionally the emperors undertook the provision of draught-animals and carriages. Besides the horse they rode, the couriers had a spare horse to carry the letter bags. Passengers were conveyed in carriages called *rēdæ,* drawn by horses and mules ; while goods were forwarded on vans, which were drawn by oxen. Besides this, vessels were stationed at various points on the rivers to carry letters, passengers, and goods, just as there was postal communication over sea, especially from Ostia, the port of Rome, outwards, to the islands and chief ports of the Mediterranean.

Postvorta. *See* CARMENTA.

Pŏthŏs. The Greek personification of amorous longing, an attendant of Erōs (*q.v.*).

Pottery. The simplest, and at the same time one of the oldest, branches of the primeval art of working in clay is the manufacture of bricks and tiles, the invention of which (at Athens) was ascribed by the Greeks to the mythical personages Eurўălus and Hŷperbĭus [Pliny, *H. N.* vii 194]. So far as bricks were used at all, their use was generally confined to private buildings ; and Greeks and Romans for ages employed only unbaked or sun-dried bricks. Bricks baked in the kiln came into use at a later date. The first to employ them extensively were the Romans, probably at the period when the population of the city rendered it necessary to build houses of several stories, which demanded a more solid material. In imperial times such bricks were the common material for private and public buildings. The walls were built of them, and then overlaid with stucco or marble. Building with baked bricks extended from Rome into Greece, and, generally speaking, wherever the Romans carried their arms, they introduced their exceptional aptitude for making excellent bricks. Bricks which presented flat surfaces, tọ be used for walls or pavements, were made of the most various dimensions, but were for the most part thinner than ours. Besides these, there were also rounded bricks for building dwarf columns, and for the construction of circular walls. For roofs flat tiles were chiefly used (Lat. *tĕgŭlă*), which were provided with a raised rim on both of their longer sides, and were so formed that the upper fitted into the lower. Concave tiles also were used (Lat. *imbrex*) of the form of a half cylinder, which covered the adjoining edges of the flat tiles. The lowest row was commonly finished off with ornamental moulding. From the same material as bricks were also made pipes for conveying water, for sewers, and for warm air ; the section in the first two cases was round, in the last, square.

Pottery in its proper sense, the manufacture of utensils, is very old. The potter's wheel was known even before Homer's time [*Il.* xviii 600]. Its invention was variously ascribed to the Corinthian Hŷperbĭus [Pliny vii 198] and to the Athenian Talus, nephew of Dædălus. Corinth and Athens, where the neighbouring promontory of Cōlĭăs furnished an inexhaustible supply of fine potter's clay, were, in fact, the headquarters of the manufacture of Greek pottery. Next came Ægīna, Sămŏs, Lacedæmon, and other places in Greece itself, which always remained the principal seat of this manufacture, especially in the form of vases of painted clay. These were exported in large numbers to the countries on the Mediterranean and Black Seas. The high estimation in which Greek, and especially Attic, pottery was held is proved by the numerous vases which have been discovered in tombs, chiefly in Italy. Moreover they represent almost every period. The excellence of the workmanship lies in the material, which is very fine, and prepared with the utmost care; also in the execution and in the baking. Its thinness, as well as the hardness of its sides, even in vessels of large dimensions, astonishes experts in such matters. The shapes are mostly produced by the potter's wheel, but also by hand in the case of vessels too large to be conveniently placed on the wheel; for example, the largest wine-jars. [The prehistoric pottery from Mўcēnæ, the Troad, and other Hellenic sites, was also made by hand.] Whereas small vessels were made of a single piece, in the case of large ones, the body, handles, feet, and neck, were fashioned separately, and then united. They were first dried in the sun, then twice baked, before and after the painting. The colours are no less admirable than the workmanship. The clay shows a beautiful bright reddish yellow, which is produced by the addition of colouring matter, and is also further intensified by a thin coating of glaze. The black colour, which often verges upon green, and is of a brilliant lustre, is then applied. Either (1) the design stands out black against the bright background, or (2) the figures appear in red on a black ground, the former being the earlier method. Other colours, especially white or dark-red, were applied after the black glaze had been burnt into the clay by the second baking, and served as a less lasting adornment. In later times yellow, green, blue, brown, and gold were also used.

[In the case of vases with *black* figures, the vase was first turned on the wheel, and, in order to give it a surface of deeper red, clay finely ground and mixed with water to the consistency of cream, technically known as "slip," was applied by a brush or otherwise while it was still revolving. The outline of the design was next roughly sketched, either with a point or in light-red ochre with a brush. The vase was then dried in the sun, and again put on the wheel, and the glaze, finely powdered and mixed with water, was applied to it with a brush as it revolved. The vase was then in some cases fired for the first time in the kiln in order to provide a smooth, almost non-absorbent surface for the use of the painter. The painter then put on the black enamel figures and ornaments with a brush. After the firing of the enamel, the details were drawn in by *incised lines*, cutting through the enamel down to the clay body of the vase. In vases with *red* figures instead of the *figures* being painted in black, the *ground* is covered with black enamel and the figures left, showing the glazed red "slip" which covers the whole vase. This method produced a great artistic advance in the beauty of the figures, the details and inner lines of which could be executed with freedom and ease by brush-marked lines, instead of by the laborious process of cutting incised lines through the very hard black enamel (Prof. Middleton on "Pottery" in *Encyc. Brit.* xix 608, 609).]

Lastly, the form deserves all praise. The vases of the best period present the most tasteful elegance of form, that is at once fine and strong, and the most delicate proportion of the various parts to each other and to the whole, without interfering with their practical utility (*see* cuts under VASES and VESSELS). It was not until the times when taste had begun to degenerate that the fashion was introduced of giving to clay ware, by means of moulds, all kinds of grotesque forms of men and beasts, and of furnishing them with plastic (as well as painted) ornamentation.

[The *technique* of ancient pottery is illustrated by figs. 1 and 2. The first repre-

(1) * A GREEK POTTER. (Gem from Millin, *Peint.* ii, vignette.)

(2) * A GREEK POTTER. (Gem from Millin, *Peint.* i, vignette.)

sents a youth seated in front of an oven, from the top of which he takes with two sticks a small, two-handled vase which has been newly glazed. The second shows the potter giving the last polish to a finished vase, while two other vessels are standing to dry on an oven, the door of which is closed (Guhl and Koner's *Life of the Greeks and Romans*, p. 141, Eng. ed.). Among the votive tablets in the Louvre there are two from Corinth. The first of these represents an early Greek type of kiln, which is domed over, and has a space for the fuel on one side, and a door in the side of the upper chamber, through which the pottery could be put in and withdrawn. The second shows a potter applying painted bands while the vessel revolves on the wheel (Prof. Middleton, *l.c.*, figs. 3 and 20). *See* also VASES.]

The ROMANS, with whom, as early as the time of the second king, Nŭma, a guild (*collēgium*) of potters existed, neither had vessels of painted clay amongst their household goods, nor did they employ it for the ornamentation of their graves. In earlier times at least, they used only coarse and entirely unornamented ware. They imported artistically executed vases from their neighbours, the Etruscans. In the last hundred years of the Republic, as well as in the first hundred years after Christ, the chief place for the manufacture of the red crockery generally used in households was Arrētium (*Arezzo*) [Pliny, xxxv 160; Martial, i 54, 6, xiv 98; Dennis, *Etruria*, ii 335]. The ware of this place was distinguished by a coral-red colour, and was generally furnished with glaze and delicate reliefs; in fact, ornamentation in relief was widely employed in later Roman pottery. Very much valued was the domestic ware, called *vāsa Sămǐa*, which was an imitation of the earlier pottery brought from the island of Samos. It was formed of fine, red-coloured clay, baked very hard, of thin make, and very delicate workmanship. It was glazed and generally adorned with reliefs, and served especially for the table use of respectable people who could not afford silver.

While this fine ware was made by hand, the manufacture of ordinary pottery as well as of bricks and pipes, especially under the Empire, formed an important industry among capitalists, who, on finding good clay on their estates, built potteries and tileworks, and either worked them on their own account through slaves or had them carried on by lessees. The emperor himself, after the time of Tiberius, and the members of the imperial family, especially the females, pursued a similar trade, as is shown by the trade-mark which, according to Roman custom, was borne by clay manufactures.

The production of *large* statues of clay, apart from the purpose of modelling, belongs amongst the Greeks to the early times. It continued much longer amongst the Italians, especially amongst the Etruscans, who furnished the temple at Rome

with clay images of the gods before the victorious campaigns in the East brought marble and bronze productions of Greek art to Rome. On the other hand, throughout the whole of antiquity, the manufacture of *small* clay figures of very various kinds, for the decoration of dwellings and graves, and for playthings for children, etc., was most extensively practised. They were generally made in moulds, and after baking were decorated with a coating of colour. The

(3) TANAGRA FIGURINE.

excellence which Greek art attained in this department, as in others, is shown by the "figurines" discovered at Tănăgra in and after 1874, specimens of which are given in figs. 3, 4. Very important too was the manufacture of clay reliefs, partly with figured representation and partly with arabesque patterns, for the embellishment of columns, windows, cornices, and also of tombstones and sarcophagi. [*See* Dumont and Chaplain, *Céramiques*, 1888; Kekulé, *Thonfiguren aus Tanagra*, 1878, *Die antiken Terracotten*, 1880, and *Die Terracotten von Sicilien*, 1884; Heuzey, *Catalogue des figurines antiques de terre cuite du Musée du Louvre*, 1882, *id.* 60 plates, 1883; and the popular work by Pottier, *Les Statuettes de Terre Cuite dans l'Antiquité*, 1890.]

(4) BARBER IN TERRA-COTTA.
From Tanagra (*Arch. Zeit.* 1874, taf. 14).

Præcinctĭŏnēs. *See* THEATRE.

Præcō. The Latin term for a public crier, such as those who were employed in private life, especially at auctions. Their profession was eminently lucrative, but was not considered at all respectable. Similarly those employed by the State ranked as the most insignificant of its paid servants (*see* APPARITOR). Their duties were to summon the meetings of the people and the Senate, to command silence, to proclaim aloud the proposals under consideration, to announce the result of the individual votes, and also the final result; in legal proceedings, to cite the parties to the case, their counsel, and witnesses, to announce the close of the proceedings, and the jury's dismissal; to invite the people to funeral feasts and to games, and to assist at public auctions and other sales, etc., etc. Consuls, prætors, and censors had three decuries of such attendants; quæstors, and probably also tribunes and ædiles, one. They also attended on extraordinary magistrates and on governors of provinces.

Præfectūra. An Italian township possessing no jurisdiction of its own, but having a prefect to administer justice (*præfectus iūre dicundo*) sent to it every year, generally on the nomination of the *prætor*

urbānus. When all Italian towns received full citizen rights, 90 B.C., these towns among the rest became *mūnĭcĭpĭa* (*see* MUNICIPIUM), and retained the old name merely as a tradition.

Præfectus (one set over others, a superior). The title given by the Romans to officials of many kinds, who were all however appointed, not elected. Thus, under the Republic, *præfecti iūre dĭcundo* was the name of those who were appointed by the prætor to administer justice in those Italian communities which were called *præfectūræ* (*q.v.*); even later these townships retained the name for the judges elected by themselves. In the republican armies the six Roman officers appointed by the consuls to command the contingents sent by the Italian allies to the consular armies were called *præfecti sŏcĭum* (officers in command of the allies), while their cohorts were led by native *præfecti cŏhortĭum.* In the times of the Empire these titles were borne by the commanders of the auxiliary cohorts, while the officers of the cavalry divisions were *præfecti ĕquĭtum.* Military engineering was under the direction of a *præfectus fabrum* (pioneers); the several fleets of the Empire under a *præfectus classis* (*see* SHIPS). *Præfectus castrōrum* (camp-commander) was the name, under the Empire, of the commander in the permanent camps of the legions, usually a centurion who had completed his term of service. His chief functions were, in time of peace, to superintend garrison-service (*i.e.* to distribute the watches and other duties); in war, the arrangement and supervision of the camp, the transportation of the baggage, and the construction of roads, bridges, and entrenchments. This title of *præfectus* was also given to the knight who commanded the legions stationed in Egypt; while an imperial governor, called *præfectus Ægypti*, administered that country, which was treated as an imperial domain, and outside the general provincial administration. At a later time each legion had upon its staff of officers its own commander of the camp, styled *præfectus lĕgĭōnĭs*, to whom in 3 A.D. even the command of the legion was transferred. *Præfectus vĭgĭlum* was the commander of the cohorts organized by Augustus to make Rome secure by night.

A very high and influential office under the Empire was that of the *præfectus prætōrio*, the commander of the imperial guard (*see* PRÆTORIANI). Originally a purely military office, it acquired in process of time an ever-increasing importance. It had attached to it the control of affairs in the emperor's absence, criminal jurisdiction over Italians outside Rome, and the like. Sometimes ambitious men contrived to employ this position to obtain for themselves the real power in the State, and raised whom they pleased to the imperial throne, sometimes ascending it themselves. After the prætorians were disbanded by Constantine in 324, the four who were then *præfecti prætorio* were made governors of the four *præfecturæ* into which that emperor divided his dominions. Another important office under the Empire was that of the *præfectus urbi* (city prefect). Such an office had existed in the time of the kings and in the early years of the Republic, to supply the place of the king or the consuls when absent. When the latter came to be represented by the prætors, it was only during the *fĕrĭæ Lătīnæ* (at which festival all magistrates were present) that a *præfectus urbi Lătīnārum* was appointed. Augustus revived it in its old form. On several occasions he appointed a *præfectus urbi* during his absence from the city. The city prefecture first became a standing office for the maintenance of public order in Rome after Tiberius. Subsequently the *præfectus urbi* (whose authority extended a hundred miles from Rome, and who had three city cohorts to assist him) exercised, together with the police authority enforced at an earlier period by the ædiles, a correlated criminal jurisdiction, which in course of time expanded so much that the city prefecture became the highest criminal authority at Rome. After the transfer of the seat of empire to Byzantium, the *præfectus urbi* united in himself the military, administrative, and judicial powers in what was once the capital, and was now formed into a separate district for purposes of administration. One of the most important offices under the Empire was that of the *præfectus annōnæ* (corn-supply, *see* ANNONA), whose duty it was to provide Rome with the necessary corn, and whose countless subalterns were distributed over the whole Empire. For the *præfectus ærārii* (State chest) *see* ÆRARIUM.

Prætexta or **prætextata** (sc. *făbŭlă*). A class of Roman tragedies, which found its materials, not in the Greek myths, but, in the absence of native legendary heroes, in ancient and contemporary Roman history. The name was derived from the fact that the heroes wore the national dress, the

tŏgă prætexta, the official garb, edged with purple, of the Roman magistrates. *Nævius* introduced them, and, following his example, the chief representatives of tragic art under the Republic, *Ennius, Păcŭvius,* and *Accius,* composed, in addition to tragedies imitated from Greek originals, independent plays of this kind, which were however cast in the form they had borrowed from the Greeks. We also hear of some plays of this class written by poets of imperial times. The solitary example preserved to us is the tragedy of *Octāvia,* wrongly ascribed to Seneca (*q.v.*), which perhaps may date from 1 A.D. (*Cp.* TOGATA.)

Prætor. Originally a title of the Roman consuls, but afterwards used to denote that magistrate to whom the administration of justice in Rome was transferred when the consulship, to which this power had hitherto been attached, was thrown open to the commons in 366 B.C. At first reserved for the patricians, it became a plebeian office as early as 337. The prætor was elected in the *cŏmĭtĭa centŭrĭāta,* with one of the consuls presiding, on the same day and with the same auspices as the consuls, who entered on their office simultaneously with him. On account of the increase in legal business, a second prætor was appointed in 242, to whom was transferred the hearing of cases between citizens and foreigners (*inter cīvēs et pĕrĕgrīnos*), and between foreigners (*inter peregrinos*), while the other decided between citizens. The latter, who ranked first, was called *prætor urbānus* (city prætor) ; the former, *prætor inter peregrinos,* and (after the time of Vespasian) *prætor pĕrĕgrīnus.*

The prætors had their respective departments determined by lot after their election. While the *prætor peregrinus* might have a military command also entrusted to him, the city prætor, on account of the importance of his office, might not be absent from Rome, strictly speaking, for longer than ten days. He represented his absent colleague, and also the consuls in their absence, presiding, as the highest magistrate present, at the public games, watching over the safety of Rome, summoning the *comitia centuriata,* holding the military levies, and the like. As early as 227 the number was further increased by two. To these was entrusted the administration of Sicily and Sardinia. Two others were added in 197 to administer the two provinces of Spain. In 149, on the establishment of the *quæstĭōnēs perpĕtŭæ* (*q.v.*), a standing criminal court for certain stated offenders, the rule was introduced that the entire body of prætors should stay in Rome during their year of office; the prætors *urbanus* and *inter peregrinos* having jurisdiction in civil cases, as hitherto, while the others presided in the *quæstiones*, and had to instruct the jurors as to the case before the court, and to carry out the sentence passed. After the completion of their year of office, they all proceeded as *proprætors* or *proconsuls* to the prætorian provinces assigned them by lot. In consequence of the multiplication of the *quæstiones* and of the provinces, the number of prætors was raised by Sulla to eight, by Cæsar to ten, fourteen, and sixteen. Under the Empire the prætorship lost its former importance, the civil jurisdiction of the *prætor urbanus* and *peregrinus* being in part transferred to the *præfectus urbi* and *præfectus prætōrĭō*, while the criminal jurisdiction of the others ceased with the gradual decay of the *quæstiones*, and the prætors only retained particular departments of their judicial power and general administration. Their most important function was the management of the games, some of which had already, in republican times, been assigned to the *prætor urbanus*. When their year's office had expired, they went as *proconsuls* to the senatorial provinces. Their election was transferred to the Senate by Tiberius. Under the Republic, the statutory age for the office was forty; under the Empire, thirty. The prætor's *insignia* were the *toga prætexta*, the *sella cŭrūlis*, and, in the provinces, six lictors; in Rome, probably two. Like the consul, he had the honour of a triumph open to him.

Prætōrĭāni. The bodyguard of the Roman emperor. Even in the armies of the Republic there was a separate corps, the *cŏhors prætōrĭa*, to guard the general, and protect the headquarters. The organization of a bodyguard for the emperor, one of whose permanent powers was the chief military command, was among the first administrative measures of Augustus. The supreme command was generally held by two *præfecti prætōrĭō* in the emperor's name. The guard consisted of nine, and at a later time, of ten *cohortēs prætoriæ*, each composed of ten centuries of infantry, and ten squadrons of cavalry (*turmæ*), and commanded by a *trĭbūnus* (*see* TRIBUNI MILITUM). They had higher rank and pay than the legions, and a shorter time of service (sixteen years instead of twenty). While the

other cohorts were stationed at various places in Italy, where the emperors were in the habit of staying, there were quartered in Rome, to keep watch in the emperor's palace, three cohorts, which at first were billeted on separate parts of the city, until under Tiberius they were placed in a fortified camp (*castra prætoria*) to the north-east of the city, outside the *agger*. By being thus united, they gained such importance, that they were able to raise an emperor to the throne, and to overthrow him. To break down their influence, and to make them simply a picked corps, Septĭmĭus Sĕvērus, towards the end of the second century, brought legions to Italy, and made a regulation that the guard, which had hitherto been recruited exclusively from Italy and a few Romanised provinces, should have its ranks filled up from deserving legionary soldiers, and should serve for a longer time. To be thus transferred to the guard was considered a promotion. The guard was broken up by Constantine the Great.

Prætōrĭum. The headquarters in the Roman camp; a wide space, on which stood the general's tent, the altar of the camp, the *augŭrāle*, and the *trĭbūnāl* (*see* CASTRA). In the provinces this name was given to the official residence of the governor.

Prævārĭcātĭō (*lit.* "deviation from the straight path"). The Latin term for the improper conduct of a case on the part of a prosecutor in favour of the defendant, or on the part of a *patrōnus* to the detriment of his client. The penalty was forfeiture of the right to prosecute, and to act as an advocate. If the acquittal of the defendant was demonstrably due to *prævaricatio*, the case might be undertaken anew by a second prosecutor.

Prandĭum. The second morning meal of the Romans. (*See* MEALS.)

Prātĭnās. [The quantity of the second syllable is uncertain, probably *long*. Fick, *Gr. Personen-namen*, p. xxxv, deriving it from *prătŏs*, Doric for *prōtŏs*, makes it a collateral form for *prōtīnŏs = prōtĭŏnŏs*.] A Greek dramatist, of Phlīus, who lived about 496 B.C. at Athens. He was a contemporary and rival of Æschȳlus, and is believed to have invented the satyric drama. At any rate, he was a very prolific writer in this department of literature. He also wrote tragedies, dithyrambs, and *hўporchēmăta*, of which we possess a fairly long and highly original fragment [preserved by Athenæus, xiv 617]. His son Aristĭās was also a dramatic poet.

Praxilla. Of Sĭcўŏn; a Greek poetess, about 450 B.C., composed hymns and dithyrambs, but was especially famous for her *scŏlĭă*. We only possess insignificant fragments of her poems.

Praxĭtĕlēs. One of the most famous Greek sculptors, born at Athens about 390 [probably the son of Cēphīsŏdŏtŭs, the sculptor of the statue of *Eirēnē* (*q.v.*) *with the Infant Plūtŭs*]. He and his somewhat older contemporary, Scŏpās, were at the head of the later Attic school. He chiefly worked in marble, but at the same time occasionally used bronze. His recorded works exhibit every age and sex in the greatest variety of the divine and human form. Still he paid most attention to youthful figures, which gave him the opportunity of displaying all the charm of sensuous grace in soft and delicate contours.

THE *HERMES* OF PRAXITELES.
(Olympia.)

Among his most celebrated works the naked *Aphrŏdītē*, of Cnĭdus, stands first, according to the enthusiastic descriptions of the ancients, a masterpiece of the most entrancing beauty [*e.g.* Pliny, *N. H.* xxxvii §§ 20, 21; *cp.* APHRODITE, fig. 2]. Not less famous were his representations of *Erōs*, among which the marble statue at Thespiæ was esteemed most highly [*ib.*, § 22; *cp.* EROS]; his *Apollo Saurŏctŏnŏs*

(lizard-slayer) in bronze [*ib.*, xxxiv § 70]; and a youthful *Satyr* in Athens [Pausanias, i 20 § 1]. As to the group of Nĭŏbē's children, preserved at Rome in Pliny's time, it was disputed even among the ancients whether it was the work of Praxiteles or, as is more probable, of Scopas [*N. H.* xxxvi § 28; *cp.* NIOBE]. Of all these, only later copies have been preserved. An important original work by him [mentioned by Pausanias, v 17 § 3] was unearthed in 1877 by the German excavators at Olympia, *Hermēs with the Child Dĭonŷsus in his Arms*, which was set up in the *cella* of the temple of Hēra. The arms and legs are partly mutilated, but otherwise it is in an excellent state of preservation. (*See* cut.)

His sons, Cēphīsŏdŏtus the younger, and Tīmarchĭdēs, were masters of some importance.

Priam (Gr. *Prĭămŏs;* Lat. *Prĭămus*). Son of Lăŏmĕdōn and Strŷmō, brother of Tīthōnus and Hēsĭŏnē, the last king of Troy. Originally his name was Pŏdārcēs (the swift-footed); the name Priamus, which is interpreted to mean "ransomed," is supposed to have been given to him after the first sacking of Troy by Hērăclēs. Heracles allowed Hesione to select one of the prisoners, and when she decided in favour of her sole surviving brother, she was permitted to ransom him with her veil. Legends represented him as rich alike in treasures and in children. He had fifty sons and fifty daughters by different wives; by his second wife, Hĕcŭbă (Gr. *Hĕkăbē*) alone, nineteen sons; among them Hectōr, Părĭs, Dēĭphŏbus, Hĕlĕnus, Pŏlŷdōrus, Trŏïlus; by his first, Arisbē, Æsăcus. Among his daughters were Crĕüsa, the wife of Æneas, Cassandra, and Pŏlyxĕna. In his young days he was a mighty warrior, as in the conflict with the Amazons; but at the outbreak of the Trojan War, he was so old and feeble that he took no part in the combat, and only twice left the city to conclude the compact for the duel between Paris and Mĕnĕlāus, and to beg the dead body of Hector from Achilles. He met his death in the sack of the city by the hand of Neoptolemus, at his family altar, whither he had fled with Hecuba and his daughter.

Prĭăpeïa. A collection of some eighty elegant but indecent Latin poems in various metres on the subject of Prĭāpus. Judging from their execution, they may be referred to the time of Augustus, and may probably be traced to the circle of

Messāla, who, like other distinguished men of that age, occupied himself with trivial amusements of this kind.

Prĭăpus. According to the usual account, son of Dīonȳsus and Aphrŏdītē, a god of the fruitfulness of the field and of the herds. Horticulture, vine-growing, goat and sheep-breeding, bee-keeping, and even fishing, were supposed to be under his protection. The original seat of his worship lay in the towns of Asia Minor, situated on the Hellespont, especially Lampsăcus. From here it afterwards spread over Greece and Italy. His statues were usually placed in gardens, generally in the form of rude *hermæ* cut out of wood, stained with vermilion, with a club and sickle and a phallic symbol of the creative and fructifying powers of nature. The sacrifices offered to him included asses, as well as the first-fruits of the garden and the field.

Priests. (1) *Greek.* The ministers of a particular sanctuary, charged with the duty of attending to the service of the god of the place. Their duty was to offer appropriate sacrifices and perform other holy offices at the appointed time and manner, and also to assist and instruct worshippers, as to the rites they were to observe. They had to slay the victim, to select the parts for offering, and to lay them on the altar, to utter the accompanying prayers, and the like. In sacred functions which were performed elsewhere (as by the father at the family altar, and by certain State officers, *e.g.* by the first three archons at Athens, the kings at Sparta), their assistance was not required, although it was often invited.

The general name *hĭĕreus* represents the priest in his character of an offerer of sacrifice and a minister of sacred rites. In the different cults, however, the priests often took the most various names, and with reference to individual cults had peculiar functions. The priesthoods were filled partly by right of inheritance from within certain families (as some of them were in almost all Greek states; but especially at Athens); partly by election or by a kind of appointment combining election and lot. A general qualification was legitimate descent from citizens, an irreproachable character, and freedom from bodily defects. (The worship of Artĕmis at Ephesus required the priests to be eunuchs, but it is to be observed that this was not a Greek worship.) Many priesthoods were only filled by men, others by women only; in many temples there were priests and priestesses together; but upon

the whole it was a rule, though not without exceptions, that the priests of gods were men, of goddesses, women. In regard to the necessary age, again, the regulations were very various; many priesthoods could only be filled by quite young persons. Virginity and celibacy were required for certain priesthoods, *e.g.* for those of the virgin goddesses Athēnē and Artemis. A rule existed in many places, that a woman more than once married was disqualified for the priesthood. At any rate, ritual prescribed chastity for a certain time before undertaking any priestly duty. Here and there, too, the priests were forbidden to taste certain kinds of food. The office was held for very various periods, one year, several years, a life-time. The priests generally wore long hair and white vestments; many of them were clothed in saffron-coloured robes, as (among others) the priests of Dīonȳsus. The priestly ornaments included garlands from the leaves of various trees, always according to the character of the god, and wreaths or fillets of many kinds. The priestly staff is often mentioned. The priests often had an official residence within the temple inclosure.

They derived their maintenance partly from the revenue of the temple property, partly from their share of the sacrifices, the skins of the animals sacrificed, and other dues of the same kind, and sometimes from actual offertories. Among their privileges, besides their inviolability, were freedom from military service, and a seat of honour at assemblies of the people and at the theatre. In many places dates were reckoned from the time when the priest of the chief divinity entered on office, *e.g.*, in Argos from the priestess of Hēra's first year of ministry [Thucydides, ii 2 § 1]. Besides the priests there were many kinds of temple-servants, for the preservation of the sacred buildings, the administration of their revenues, and the performance of the various rites. (*Cp.* CERYX, HIERODULI, HIEROPŒI, NEOCORI, PARASITE.)

(2) *Roman.* At Rome, the State religion was under the management of a number of priesthoods, which, by the order of the State, performed the regularly prescribed sacred rites or those specially decreed by the State on their recommendation. In the time of the kings the superintendence of the entire ritual belonged to the kings, among whom Nŭma, as the founder of an organized worship of the gods, holds a

prominent place. The most important priesthoods which originated in the time of the kings were the *Flāmĭnēs*, the *Augŭrēs*, the *Vestālēs*, the *Sālĭi*, the *Fĕtĭālēs*, the *Pontĭfĭcēs*, the *Lŭperci*, the *Fratrēs Arvālēs*, and the *Cŭrĭōnēs*. Besides these, in course of time there arose the *Rex Sacrōrum* to offer certain sacrifices originally offered by the king, the custodians of the Sibylline oracles, the *Ĕpŭlōnēs* to discharge a part of the pontifical duties, the priests of the new cults gradually introduced, and lastly the priests of the deified emperors, *e.g.* the *Sŏdālēs Augustālēs*. A number of State cults were handed over to individual clans (*gentes*) and associations. (*See* SODALITAS.)

After the establishment of the Republic, a distinguished position was attained by the college of the *pontĭfĭcēs*, who, like the king in earlier times, superintended the entire ritual. They were the technical advisers of the Senate on any new questions that arose in regard to it. Next to them in importance were the augurs and the custodians of the Sibylline oracles. These priesthoods, together with that of the *epulones*, were styled the four great colleges (*quattŭor summa collēgĭa*), and an equal honour was afterwards given to that of the *sodales Augustales*.

The appointment of the priests, for whom the same qualifications were required as among the Greeks, proceeded in various ways, by nomination, co-optation, and election. They entered on office by inauguration, an act in which the chief pontiff, acting through the augurs, inquired of the god concerned whether the new priest was acceptable to him. His reception into the college was accompanied by a banquet given by the new priest, which became proverbial for its luxury. When officially engaged all State priests (apart from their peculiar *insignia*) wore the *prætexta*, the purple-edged robe of Roman magistrates. They also enjoyed the distinction of a seat of honour at festivals and games, and exemption from military service, from the duties of citizens, and from taxation. The great priesthoods were posts of honour, and, like the political offices, were without remuneration. On the other hand, some priests and priestesses (*e.g.* the Vestal Virgins and the augurs), besides the use of the sacred or public lands belonging to their temples, received a regular annual salary. The cost of the establishment was defrayed from several sources. The priests

had under their management a fund which was maintained from landed property and current receipts (including fees for admission to the temple and for the offering of the sacrifice). They also had a claim to certain parts of the victim, and other perquisites ; besides this, they all, especially the *curiones* (*see* CURIA), and those associations to which State cults were entrusted, received the necessary money from the public chest. The cost of repairing the temples and of all sacrifices and festivals especially ordered by the State was defrayed from the same source. Similarly the State provided the priests either with public slaves or with free and salaried servants, to wait upon them. (For a particular kind of priests' assistants, *see* CAMILLI.) All State temples did not have particular priests assigned them ; temples without priests of their own were under the superintendence of a sacristan (*ædĭtŭus*) ; and it was usually only once in the year that sacrifice was offered at the great festival of such temples by a State priest specially appointed for the purpose. No priest could be called to account by any civil magistrate except the censor. The *pontifex maxĭmus* had the power of punishing the other priests. The position of a priest of a cult not recognised by the State, but merely tolerated, was naturally different. With regard to their maintenance, they were themselves, like the sanctuaries they superintended, supported by the contributions of the votaries of their own cult.

Primĭpĭlus. *See* CENTURIONES

Princeps. The Latin word for "a chief," "a leader," "the foremost person." Thus, in the Roman constitution, *princeps Sĕnātūs* is the senator who was placed first on the roll of the Senate drawn up by the censors. When the Senate was voting, if no consuls-designate were present, he was asked for his opinion by the presiding magistrate before any one else. Just as under the Republic the leading men in the State were called *princĭpēs*, Augustus, the founder of the Monarchy, took with general consent the title of *princeps*. This was quite in harmony with the old constitution, and at the same time recognised his equality with the other citizens. For the same reason his successor, Tiberius, set special store on the title of *princeps*. As the monarchical power became consolidated, and the old republican ideas disappeared, the consciousness of the original meaning of the title disappeared with them. *Princeps* came to be equivalent to *impĕrātor;* but it never became an official title like *Imperator, Cœsar, Augustus.* Like the Senate, the knights had a *princeps,* the *princeps iŭventūtis* (the youth). This title was borne by the knight whose name appeared first in the censor's list of that body. By way of compliment to the knights, Augustus caused his grandsons, Gaius and Lucius Cæsar, to be styled *principes iuventutis.* Ever after, the emperor's youthful sons were regularly entitled *principes iuventutis* until their entrance on a magistracy. At the time of Rome's complete decay this title was not unfrequently borne by those associated with the emperors in the government. On the meaning of *principes* in military language, *see* LEGION.

Priscian (*Prisciānus*). (1) A Latin grammarian of Cæsărĕa in Mauritania; who lived, at the beginning of the 6th century A.D., as a teacher of the Latin language in Constantinople. He there compiled, in addition to a number of smaller grammatical works, his *Institūtiōnēs Grammăticœ* in 18 books, the fullest and completest systematic Latin grammar which has come down to us. This work, which is of great importance owing to its ample quotations from ancient literature, was for a long time, in the Middle Ages, the school book in ordinary use, and formed the foundation for the earlier treatises on Latin Grammar in modern times. We also possess an insipid panegyrical poem written by Priscian on the emperor Anastăsius, and a translation of the Cosmography of the geographer Diŏnỹsius, in hexameter verse.

(2) A physician who lived in the 5th century, named *Thĕŏdōrus Prisciānus,* has left us a *Mĕdĭcīna Prœsentănĕa* (a book of rapid curatives) in five books.

Prŏbŏlē (*Greek*). A motion for a judicial prosecution. In Attic legal procedure it was a particular kind of public indictment. In the first assembly of every prytany, on the archon's inquiring whether the people were satisfied with the conduct of the magistrates, any citizen might accuse a magistrate of official misconduct. If the assembly considered there was foundation for the charge, the magistrate was temporarily suspended or even absolutely deposed from his office, and a judicial prosecution was instituted. Even against a private citizen, especially for doing an injury to magistrates, or to sacred persons or things, for interrupting a festival, embezzling public money, or instituting a vexatious prosecution, a complaint could be brought before the people in order to see whether they considered the case suitable for a judicial trial. [The most celebrated example of this procedure is the case of Demosthenes against Meidīās for assaulting him in the discharge of public functions at the *Diŏnỹsĭa.*] However, this neither bound the man who laid the plaint to bring forward an actual indictment, nor the jury to follow in the formal trial the preliminary verdict of the people, although it would always influence them.

Prŏbus (*Marcus Vălĕrius*). A famous Roman scholar and critic, born at Bērỹtus in Syria. He flourished in the second half of the 1st century A.D. He devoted almost all attention to the archaic and classical literature of Rome, which had been previously neglected, and to the critical revision of the most important Roman poets, as Lucrētius, Vergil, and Horace, after the manner of the Alexandrine scholars. Some of his criticisms on Vergil may possibly be preserved to us in a commentary to the *Eclogues* and *Georgics,* which bears his name. From a commentary, or criticism, on Persius we have his biography of that poet; and from his work *De Nŏtīs* we have an extract containing the abbreviations used for legal terms. Other grammatical writings bearing his name are the work of a grammarian of the 4th century.

Prŏclus. The most important representative of the later Neo-Platonic school, born 412 A.D. at Byzantium. He received his first instruction at Xanthus in Lycia, and betook himself to Alexandria to complete his education. There he attached himself chiefly to Hērōn the mathematician, and to the Aristotelian Olympĭŏdōrus. Before the age of twenty, he removed to Athens to attend the lectures of the most celebrated Platonists of the time, Sỹrĭānus and Plūtarchus. On the death of the latter he became head of the Platonic school until his own death in 485. His disciples were very numerous; and his learning and zeal for the education of the young, combined with his beneficence, his virtuous and strictly ascetic life, and his steadfastness in the faith of his fathers, gained him the enthusiastic devotion of his followers. We possess an account of his life, full of admiration for his character, by his pupil and successor, Mărīnus. The efforts of Proclus were directed to the support of paganism in its struggle with the now victorious Christianity, by reducing to a system all the philosophic and religious traditions of antiquity. His literary activity was very great, and extended over almost every department of knowledge; but Platonic philosophy was the centre of the whole. His philosophical works, now extant, are a commentary on a few dialogues of Plato (mainly on the *Timæus*), also his chief work on the theology of Plato, as well as a summary of the theology of Plōtīnus, with writings treating several branches of philosophy from his own point of view. Some of his minor works have only reached us in a Latin translation. As specimens of his mathematical and astronomical works, we have a commentary on the first book of Euclid, a sketch of the astronomical teaching of Hipparchus, Ptolemy, and others, a slight treatise on the heavens, etc. One of his grammatical writings survives in his commentary on Hesiod's *Works and Days*. Lastly, we have two epigrams by him, and six hymns. It is doubtful whether the *Grammatical Chrestomathy*, extracts from which, preserved by Phōtius, are the only source of our knowledge of the Greek cyclic poets, was really written by him, and not rather by a grammarian of the same name in the 2nd century A.D.

Prŏcnē. A daughter of the Athenian king Pandīŏn and Zeuxippē, sister of Phĭlŏmēlă. She was given in marriage by her father to the Thracian prince Tēreus, in Daulĭs near Parnassus, in return for assistance given him in war. Tereus became by her the father of Itўs. Pretending that his wife Procne was dead, Tereus fetched her sister Philomela from Athens, and ravished her on the way. He then cut out her tongue that she might be unable to inform against him, and concealed her in a grove on Parnassus; but the unfortunate girl contrived to inform her sister of what had happened by a robe into which she ingeniously wove the story of her fate. Taking the opportunity of a feast of Dĭonўsus in Parnassus, Procne went in quest of her sister, and agreed with her on a bloody revenge. They slew the boy Itys, and served him up to his father to eat. When Tereus learnt the outrage, and was on the point of slaying the sisters, the gods changed him into a hoopoe or hawk, Procne into a nightingale, and Philomela into a swallow, or (according to another version) Procne into a swallow, and Philomela into a nightingale. (*See* AËDON.)

Prŏconsul (=*prō consŭlĕ*, "deputy-consul"). The name at Rome for the officer to whom the consular power was entrusted for a specified district outside the city. The regular method of appointing the proconsul was to prolong the official power of the retiring consul (*prōrŏgātio impĕrĭi*) on the conclusion of his year of office. In exceptional cases, however, others were appointed proconsuls, generally those who had already held the office of consul. This was especially done to increase the number of generals in command. The proconsuls were appointed for a definite or indefinite period; as a rule for a year, reckoned from the day on which they entered their province. This period might be prolonged by a new prorogation. In any case the proconsul continued in office till the appearance of his successor. With the growth of the provinces, the consuls as well as the prætors were employed to administer them, as proconsuls, on the expiry of their office. After Sulla this became the rule; indeed, the Senate decided which provinces were to be consular and which prætorian. The regulation, in 53 B.C., that past consuls should not govern a province till five years after their consulship broke down the immediate connexion between the consulship and succession to a province, and the proconsuls thereby became in a more distinctive sense governors of provinces. After Augustus the title was given to governors of senatorial provinces, whether they had held the consulship before or not. As soon as the proconsul had been invested with his official power (*imperium*), he had to leave Rome forthwith, for there his *imperium* became extinct. Like the consuls, he had twelve lictors with bundles of rods and axes, whom he was bound to dismiss on re-entering Rome. In the province he combined military and judicial power over the subject peoples and the Roman citizens alike—only that in the case of the latter, on a capital charge, he had to allow them an appeal to Rome. To administer justice, he travelled in the winter from town to town. In the case of war he might order out the Roman citizens as well as the provincials. His power was absolutely unlimited, so that he might be guilty of the greatest oppression and extortion, and was only liable to prosecution for these offences on the expiry of his office. He might advance a claim for a triumph, or an *ŏvātio* (*q.v.*), for military services. When the senatorial provinces came generally to have no army, under the Empire, the duties of the proconsuls became limited to administration, political and judicial.

Prŏcŏpĭus. A Greek historian of Cæsărēa in Palestine, a rhetorician and advocate by profession. In and after 526 A.D. he attended the general Bĕlĭsărĭus as private secretary and adviser in nearly all his campaigns. He was afterwards made a senator, and in 562, when prefect of Constantinople, was deposed from his office by a conspiracy, and shortly afterwards died suddenly, more than seventy years old. He has left us a history of his own times down to 554 in eight books, dealing especially with the wars of. Justinian against the Persians, Vandals, and East Goths; a panegyric on the buildings of Justinian; and the *Anecdŏta*, or secret history, supplementing the first-mentioned work. It discloses the scandals of the court of the day, and, on account of its contents, was not published until after the death of the author. His information is partly derived from the oral testimony of others, but he prefers to record his own experiences. This, and his fresh treatment of his subject, together with his pure and, on the whole, simple style, make him one of the most eminent authors of his age.

Prŏcris. Daughter of Erechtheus, and wife of Cĕphălus (*q.v.*).

Prŏcrustēs. *See* DAMASTES.

Prŏcŭlŭs (*Semprōnius*). A Roman jurist, founder of the school called after him the *Prŏcŭlĭāni*. (*See* ANTISTIUS LABEO and JURISPRUDENCE.)

Prŏcūrātor, under the Roman Republic, meant the fully accredited agent of a private citizen. Under the Empire, the title was given to those who, as household officers of the emperor, were considered administrators of the imperial purse. The fiscal administration of the imperial provinces was in the hands of a *procurator* of equestrian rank, under whom were freedmen of the emperor's, bearing the same title, and attending to particular departments of the administration. In the senatorial provinces, also, there was an imperial *procurator*, independent of the governor, to manage the domains and to collect the revenues belonging to the *fiscus*. Further, there were particular provinces which, before they were administered as actual provinces, were governed as domains by an administrator appointed by the emperor and personally responsible to him. He likewise was styled *procurator*, and in general had a position similar to that of the other governors. Such a *procurator*

was Pontius Pilate in Judæa, which for a long time was under a *procurator*. The imperial chief treasury was administered by a *procurator a rătĭŏnĭbŭs*, also called *procurator fisci*, at first an imperial freedman, but after the 2nd century a knight. To administer the imperial privy purse, into which flowed the revenues from the crown lands and the private fortune of the emperor, there were special procurators.

Prŏdĭcus. A Greek Sophist of Cĕōs, contemporary with Sŏcrătēs. He repeatedly visited Athens as an ambassador from his native country. The applause which his speeches gained there induced him to come forward as a rhetorician. In his lectures on literary style he laid chief stress on the right use of words and the accurate discrimination between synonyms, and thereby paved the way for the dialectic discussions of Socrates. None of his lectures have come down to us in their original form. We have the substance only of his celebrated fable of the *Choice of Hērăclēs* [preserved by Xenophon, *Memorabilia*, ii §§ 21–34].

Prŏdĭgĭum. The Latin term for an unnatural or, at any rate, unusual and inexplicable phenomenon, which was always treated as requiring expiation (*prŏcūrātĭo*). This was only done on behalf of the State, if the phenomenon had been observed on ground belonging to the State. The Senate, acting on the advice of the pontiffs, ordained either particular sacrifices, to specified deities, or a nine days' sacrifice, or a public intercession, and left the execution of the ordinance to the consuls. If a *prodigium* caused so much alarm that the usual means of expiation seemed insufficient, the Senate had recourse to the Sibylline books, or the Etruscan *hăruspĭcēs*. (*See* HARUSPEX.) For the *prodigium* of a thunderbolt, *see* PUTEAL.

Prŏdrŏmi. Greek skirmishers. (*See* HIPPEIS.)

Prŏĕdrĭa. The right of occupying the front row of seats next the *orchēstra*, at the dramatic performances in the Greek theatre. This distinction was enjoyed by the priests, the chief magistrates, distinguished citizens, the descendants of those who had fallen in battle for their country, and members of foreign states whom it was desired to honour, especially ambassadors. The term also denotes the presidency at the Council (*see* BOULE), and in the assemblies of the people. [In the 5th century B.C. the *prўtănēs*, under their *ĕpistătēs*, presided over the Council and the assemblies of the people; in the 4th, the *prŏĕdrī* were instituted. The latter were appointed on each occasion from nine of the tribes, and the presidential duties were transferred to them and their *epistates* (a member of the tenth tribe). See Aristotle, *Constitution of Athens*, 44, pp. 163-4, ed. Sandys.]

Prœtus. Son of Abās of Argos, and twin brother of Acrīsīus. Expelled from his home by his brother, he fled to the king of the Lycians, Iŏbătēs, who gave him in marriage his daughter Anteia (in the tragedians, Stĕnŏbœa), and compelled Acrisius to resign in his favour the sovereignty of Tīryns. Here the Cyclōpēs built him a town of impregnable strength. His daughters were punished with madness either for their opposition to the worship of Dīonȳsus or (according to another account) for their disrespect for Hēra. This madness spread to the other women of the land, and was only cured by the interposition of Mĕlămpūs (*q.v.*). His son Mĕgăpenthēs exchanged with Perseus the rule of Tiryns for that of Argos. (*Cp.* BELLEROPHON.)

Prōlĕtārĭi. The name in the Roman centuriate system (*see* CENTURIA) of those citizens who were placed in the lowest of the five property-classes, and who were exempt from military service and tribute. They took their name from the fact that they only benefited the State by their children (*prōlēs*). Another name for them is *căpĭtĕ censi*, i.e. those who were classed in the list of citizens at the census solely in regard to their status as citizens (*căput*). Afterwards, the richer among them were taken to serve in the wars : these were then called *proletarii;* and those without any property at all, *capite censi.* In and after the time of Mărius, when the levy of troops was no longer founded on the census, the Roman armies were recruited by preference from the last class.

Prŏmăchus (fighter in the front rank, protector). (1) An epithet of Athēnē (*q.v.*).

(2) Son of Parthĕnŏpæus and the Nymph Clȳmĕnē, one of the Ĕpīgŏni (*q.v.*).

Prŏmēthēĭă. *See* PROMETHEUS.

Prŏmētheus (the man of forethought). Son of the Titan Iăpĕtŭs and the Ocean-nymph Clȳmĕnē, brother of Atlas, Mĕnœtius, and Ĕpīmētheus, father of Deucălĭōn (*q.v.*). The most ancient account of him, as given by Hesiod [*Theog.* 521-616] is as follows. When the gods, after their conquest of the Titans, were negotiating with mankind about the honour to be paid them, Prome-

theus was charged with the duty of dividing a victim offered in sacrifice to the gods. He endeavoured to impose upon Zeus by dividing it in such a way as cleverly to conceal the half which consisted of flesh and the edible vitals under the skin of the animal, and to lay thereon the worst part, the stomach, while he heaped the bones together and covered them with fat.

Zeus divined the stratagem, but, out of enmity towards man, purposely chose the worse portion and avenged himself by refusing mortals the use of fire. Thereupon Prometheus stole it from Olympus and brought it to men in a hollow reed. As a set off to this great blessing, Zeus resolved to send them an equally great evil. He caused Hēphæstus to make of clay a beautiful woman named *Pandōra,* that is, the all-gifted ; for the gods presented her with all manner of charms and adornments, coupled however with lies, flattering words, and a crafty mind. Hermēs brought her, with a jar as her dowry, in which every evil was shut up, to the brother of Prometheus, named Epimetheus (*i.e.* the man of afterthought, for he never thought of what he did until it had brought him into trouble). In spite of his brother's warning not to receive any present from Zeus, he was ensnared by her charms and took her to wife. Pandora opened the jar, and out flew all manner of evils, troubles, and diseases, before unknown to man, and spread over all the earth. Only delusive Hope remained in the jar, since, before she could escape, Pandora put the lid on the jar again [*Works and Days,* 54-105]. But Prometheus met with his punishment. Zeus bound him in adamantine fetters to a pillar with an eagle to consume in the day-time his liver, which grew again in the night. At last Hērăclēs, with the consent of Zeus, who desired to increase his son's renown, killed the eagle, and set the son of Iăpĕtus free. According to this account, the guile of Prometheus, and his opposition to the will of Zeus, brought on man far more evil than good.

Æschȳlus, on the other hand, taking the view suggested by the Attic cult of Prometheus, in which the fire-bringing god was honoured as the founder of human civilization, gave the myth an entirely different form in his trilogy of *Prometheus the Firebearer, Prometheus Bound,* and *Prometheus Released.* In these Prometheus is still of course the opponent of Zeus, but, at the same time, he is represented as full of the most devoted love for the human race.

Æschylus makes him son of Thĕmĭs, by whom he is put in possession of all the secrets of the future. In the war with the Titans, his advice assisted Zeus to victory. But when the god, after the partition of the world, resolved on destroying the rude human race, and to create other beings in their stead, Prometheus alone concerned himself with the fate of wretched mortals, and saved them from destruction. He brought them the fire he had stolen from Hephæstus at Lēmnŏs, the fire that was to become the source of all discoveries and of mastery over nature; and raised them to a higher civilization by his inventive skill and by the arts which he taught mankind. For this he was punished by being chained on a rock beside the sea in the wilds of Scythia. Ōcĕănus advised him to bend beneath the might of Zeus; but he consoled himself with the knowledge that, if the god begat a son by a certain goddess known to himself alone (*Thĕtĭs*), that son would dethrone his father. When no menaces could tear from him the secret, Zeus hurled him with a thunderbolt into Tartărus together with the rock to which he was chained. From this abode he first emerged into the light of day a long time after, to be fastened on Mount Caucăsus and torn by the eagle until another immortal voluntarily entered Hādĕs for him. At last Heracles, on his journey to the Hespĕrĭdĕs, shot the eagle; the centaur Chīrōn (*q.v.*), suffering from his incurable wound, gladly renounced his immortality; and, after Prometheus had revealed the name of the goddess, he was set free. But, as a sign of his punishment, he ever after bore on his finger an iron ring and on his head a willow crown. He returned to Olympus, and once more became adviser and prophet of the gods. Legends related that he moulded men and animals of clay, and either animated these himself with the heavenly fire or induced Zeus or Athēnē to do so [Ovid, *Met.*, i 81; Horace, *Odes*, i 16, 13]. In Athens Prometheus shared with Hēphæstus a common altar in the Academy, in the sacred precinct of Athēnē, and was honoured with a torch race in a yearly festival called the *Prŏmēthēĭă.*

Prŏnāŏs (*Greek*). In a Greek temple, the entrance hall to the temple proper, or *nāŏs*. (*See* TEMPLE.)

Prŏpertius (*Sextus*). A Roman elegiac poet born at Asĭsĭum (*Assisi*), in Umbria. [Prop. v 1, 121–6 and 65–6; i 22, 9. The date of his birth is uncertain. He was

somewhat older than Ovid, and was probably born about 50 B.C.] He lost his parents at an early age; and, through the general confiscation of land in 42, was deprived of the greater part of his paternal estate. Still, he possessed enough to live a careless poet's life at Rome, whither he had proceeded soon after coming of age [about 34 B.C.]. He there associated with his patron Mæcēnās and with brother poets such as Vergil and Ovid. To complete his studies he afterwards went to Athens. When he was still quite young, the poet's spirit woke within him, and expanded through his attachment to the beautiful and witty Hostia. Under the name *Cynthia,* she henceforth was the subject of his love-poems. For five years [B.C. 28–23] this attachment lasted, though often disturbed by the jealousy of the sensitive poet and the capriciousness of his mistress. When it had come to an end, and even after Cynthia's death (probably before B.C. 18), the poet could not forget his old passion. He himself died young. He often expresses forebodings of an early death; there is no indication in his poems that any of them were written later than 16 B.C. They have come down to us in four books, but some scholars are of opinion that the poet himself had divided them into five, and that the original second and third books have been united, perhaps through the oversight of friends at the publication of the last. Propertius himself seems to have only published the first. In the first four books amatory poems preponderate. The fifth book, the confused order of which may well be referred to the poet's untimely death, deals mainly with subjects taken from Roman legends and history, in the same way as Ovid subsequently treated them in the *Fasti.*

Propertius possesses a poetical genius with which his talent is unable to keep pace. Endowed with a nature susceptible of passion as deep as it was strong, as ardent as it was easily evoked, and possessed of a rich fancy, he strives to express the fulness of his thoughts and feelings in a manner modelled closely on that of his Greek masters; and yet in his struggle with linguistic and metrical form, he fails to attain the agreeable in every instance. His expression is often peculiarly harsh and difficult, and his meaning is frequently obscured by far-fetched allusions to unfamiliar legends, or actual transcripts of them. Herein he follows the example of his models, the Alexandrine poets, Callĭmăchus and Phĭlētas. Nevertheless he is a great poet, and none of his countrymen [except Catullus] have depicted the fire of passion so truly and so vividly as he.

Prŏprætor (*prō prætōrĕ*). The name among the Romans of a past prætor who, on the expiration of his office, proceeded to administer (generally for a year) the prætorian province assigned him by lot at the beginning of his office. Occasionally this title was also borne by those who, without having been prætors immediately before, were invested with prætorian

celebrated was that built at the west end of the Acrŏpŏlĭs (*see* plan of ACROPOLIS). This was built of Pentĕlic marble between 437 and 432 B.C., under the auspices of Pericles, at a cost of 2,012 talents (about £402,400). The architect was Mnēsĭclēs. The main building, a quadrangle of large dimensions, inclosed by walls to the right and left, and open in the direction of the city and the Acropolis, was transversely divided by a wall into two porticoes, that in front being about twice the depth of that behind. The dividing wall had five openings, the widest in the middle, and two smaller on each

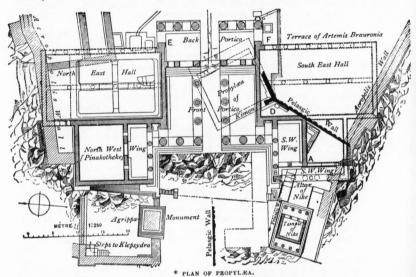

* PLAN OF PROPYLÆA.
The dotted portions were projected only.
(Miss Harrison's *Mythology, etc., of Athens*, p. 352, after Dörpfeld, *Mittheilungen*, 1885).

powers; in particular, by the quæstors left behind by the governors in the provinces. Apart from the fact that the proprætor had only six lictors, he had essentially the same position in the province as the proconsul (*q.v.*). Under the Empire this title was also given to the governors of the imperial provinces, as distinguished from the proconsuls, the governors of the senatorial provinces.

Prŏpўlæă (*Greek*). A temple-like porch leading into a temple inclosure. [Thus there were *propylæa* to the temple of Athēnē at Sūnīum, and of Dēmētēr at Eleusis (*see* plan of ELEUSIS)]. The most

side. The deeper portico in front of this dividing wall was faced by six Doric columns with the spaces between them corresponding in breadth to the five openings in the dividing wall, the space in the centre being nearly 18 feet, the two on each side about 12 and 11 feet. The portico beyond the division was similarly faced by six Doric columns. The columns of the outer portico were 29 feet high, those of the inner somewhat less, but the ground on which they stand is 6½ feet higher, so that the pediment of the inner portico was nearly 5 feet higher than that of the outer portico. Two rows of three slender Ionic columns, about

33 feet high, stood on either side of the road that rises towards the middle entrance. These divided the deep outer portico into three colonnades spanned by slender beams of marble with a coffered ceiling decorated with gilt palmetto ornaments on a blue ground. Four steps led from outside to the two side colonnades of the outer portico; and from the farther end of the latter five marble steps rose to the side doors of the division between the porticoes. A considerable part of the columns is still standing. To the main building were attached two side-wings, still in fairly good preservation, not so high, but, like the main building, furnished with columned chambers. The larger of these, the north-west wing (now generally called the *Pinăcŏthēca*), contained a collection of pictures. [The south-west wing is much smaller, and does not correspond to that on the north-west. The architect, as suggested by Dr. Dörpfeld, was probably compelled to modify his original plan because it would have intruded on the sacred precincts of Athēnē Nīkē. A projected south-east hall was similarly given up because of the precincts of Artĕmis Braurōnia; and a corresponding north-east hall was not carried out, owing to the outbreak of the Peloponnesian War (*cp.* plan).] For the room in the Greek house called *prŏpўlaiŏn, see* HOUSE.

Prŏrŏgātĭō. The Roman term for the extension either of a man's year of office (*prorogatio măgistrātūs*), or of a supreme command (*prorogatio impĕrii*), or of a provincial administration (*prorogatio provinciæ*).

Prŏscēnĭum. *See* THEATRE.

Prŏserpĭna. *See* PERSEPHONE.

Prŏsŏdĭum. A kind of song generally sung to the accompaniment of the flute at festal processions to the temple or the altar, chiefly in the worship of Apollo. It had a rhythm corresponding to the measure of the march.

Prostăs. *See* HOUSE (*Greek*).

Prostŷlŏs (*Greek*). Literally, "with columns in front," an epithet of a temple (*năŏs*) with the columns in front of its portico standing completely free from the front wall of the temple itself. (*See* TEMPLE, fig. 2.)

Prŏtăgōnistēs. In the Greek drama, the actor who played the leading part.

Prŏtăgŏrās. A Greek Sophist of Abdēra, born about 480 B.C. He passed some forty years in travelling through the different towns of Greece as a teacher, but stayed

chiefly at Athens. There he was highly honoured on account of his learning, especially by Pĕrĭclēs, until he was expelled for atheistical statements in a treatise *On the Gods*, and his works were publicly burnt. He died at the age of 70. His teaching was chiefly directed to the exposition of grammar and rhetoric. In his philosophical views he followed Hēraclītus, transferring the teaching of the latter, on the eternal flux of matter to human knowledge, which, as he thought, was merely a subjective and relative, not an objective and absolute truth. This is the point of his celebrated proposition, "Man is the measure of all things : of those which are, that they are ; of those which are not, that they are not" [Plato, *Theætetus*, 152 ; Diogenes Laertius, ix 51.]

Prŏtĕsĭlāŭs. Son of Īphĭclus, king of Phŷlăcē, in Thessaly. He was the first to leap on to the soil of Troy at the landing of the Greeks, although he knew that the first who set foot on Trojan ground must die. He was forthwith killed by Hector. His men were then led by his younger brother, Pŏdarcēs. His wife, Lăŏdămeiă, daughter of Acastus, obtained from the gods the boon that Protesilaus, to whom she had only been married for one day, might return to earth for three hours. When he died again, she joined him in death. According to another legend, she had a wax image of him made, to which she paid divine honours ; and, when her father burnt it on a funeral pile, she threw herself on the flames in despair, and died.

Prŏteus. According to Homer [*Od.* iv 354–569] an old man of the sea, a subject of Pŏseidōn, who tended the seals which are the flocks of Amphitrītē. Like all marine deities, he possessed the gift of prophecy and the power of assuming any shape he pleased. He used to sleep at mid-day on the island of Phărŏs, near Egypt. When Mĕnĕlāus, on his return from Troy, was detained by contrary winds on the island, he surprised Proteus, by the advice of his daughter Idŏthĕa, and, in spite of all his transformations, held him fast until he told him the means for returning home. According to later legends [Herodotus, ii 112, 118 ; Euripides, *Helen*], Proteus was a son of Poseidon, and was an Egyptian king living on the island of Pharos, to whom Hermēs conducted Helen when she was carried off by Paris, while only a phantom followed Paris to Troy. Menelaus, as he returned from Troy, received his wife again from him.

Prŏthў̆rŏn. *See* HOUSE (*Greek*).

Prŏtŏgĕnēs. A celebrated Greek painter of Caunus in Caria, who lived for the most part at Rhodes, in the time of Alexander the Great and his first successors. He died 300 B.C. His poverty seems to have prevented him from attending the school of any of the celebrated masters of his age, for no one is named as his instructor. He long remained poor until the unselfish admiration which his contemporary and brother painter Apellēs showed for his works raised him in riper years to great celebrity. His works, owing to the excessive care he bestowed on them, were few in number; but their perfect execution led to their being ranked by the unanimous voice of antiquity among the highest productions of art. His most celebrated works were a *Resting Satyr*, and also a painting representing the Rhodian hero *Iālў̆sus*. On the latter he spent seven or, according to others, as many as eleven years. To insure its permanence he covered it with four distinct coats of paint, so that when the upper coating perished the lower might takes its place [Pliny, *N. H.*, xxxv 101–105].

Prŏvincia. A Roman term implying, (1) a sphere of duty, especially that assigned to a consul or prætor, within which he exercised his *impĕrĭum.*

(2) A territory acquired by the Romans outside the limits of Italy, subject to the payment of taxes and administered by a governor. Under the Republic, the organization of a conquered land as a province was managed by the conquering general, with the advice of a commission of ten senators, who were nominated by the Senate and received their instructions from that body. The previous administration was altered as little as possible, so far as it was not in conflict with the interests of Rome. The *lex provinciæ* thus established fixed for the future the form of government. The first provinces were Sicily (from 241 B.C.) and Sardinia with Corsica (from 231). Their number rose under the Republic to fifteen, *i.e.* (besides the two already mentioned), the two provinces of Spain (*Ultĕrĭor* and *Cĭtĕrĭor*), Illў̆ria, Măcĕdŏnĭa, Achāïa, Asia Minor, the two Gauls (*Transalpīna* and *Cĭsalpīna*), Bīthў̆nĭa, Cў̆rēnē and Crete, Cĭlĭcĭa, Sў̆ria. Their governors were either proprætors (at first prætors) or proconsuls. The Senate decided which provinces were to be consular, which prætorian; and the consuls and prætors had their respective provinces assigned to them by lot. In the

case of the consuls this was done immediately after their election; in the case of the prætors, after their actual accession to office. When their year's office was completed, they proceeded as proconsuls and proprætors to their provinces, and stayed there a year until they were relieved by their successors, unless, as frequently happened, it proved necessary to prolong their *imperium.*

It was towards the end of the Republic (52 B.C.), that it became a rule that no consul or prætor should be allowed to be governor of a province until five years after he had ceased to hold his office. The Senate also settled for every governor his supply of money, troops, ships, and subordinates. These last included one or more *lēgāti*, a *quæstor*, and a numerous staff. In the governor's hands was concentrated the entire administrative power over the province. He commanded the garrison troops, he had the right of raising a levy of Roman citizens and provincials alike, and of making requisitions to obtain the means for war. He also possessed jurisdiction in criminal and civil cases, in the former, with power of life and death, except that Roman citizens had the right of appeal (*prŏvŏcātĭo*). While it was carefully prescribed how much the governors could require from the provincials for the support of their person and attendants, their powers made it possible for them to enrich themselves by all manner of extortion, and this became the rule to a most extraordinary extent. Against such oppression the provincials had no protection, so long as the governor's office lasted. It was only on its termination that they could in earlier times lay a complaint before the Senate, which seldom led to anything; while, after 149 B.C., they had open to them the procedure of bringing a charge of extortion, which was attended with great difficulty and expense. (*See* REPETUNDARUM CRIMEN.) These extortions were repeated anew year after year, together with the exorbitant demands of the tax-collectors (*see* PUBLICANI); and the governors, when invoked against them, in spite of their authority, rarely ventured to interpose, from fear of the equestrian plutocracy. The result was, that, at the end of the Republic, the provinces were in absolute poverty. A real improvement in their condition was brought about by the regulations enforced under the Empire, when some provinces attained a high pitch of prosperity.

In 27 B.C. Augustus divided the then existing provinces into *imperial* and *senatorial*. He entrusted ten, in a state of complete tranquillity, to the Senate; *viz.* Africa, Asia Minor, Achaia, Illÿria or Dalmătia, Macedonia, Sicily, Crete with Cÿrēnē, Bĭthÿnia, Sardinia, and South Spain. He took into his own hands the twelve which still required military occupation. These were: North Spain, Lūsĭtānia, the four provinces of Gaul (*Narbŏnensis, Lugdŭnensis* or *Celtĭca, Aquĭtānia,* and *Belgĭca*), Upper and Lower Germany, Syria, Cilicia, Cyprus, and Egypt. Changes were made in this partition later on; but the provinces acquired after 27 B.C. fell to the emperor. For the senatorial provinces the governors were appointed on the whole in the ancient manner, *i.e.* by the lot, and for one year; but with this difference, that five, and afterwards ten to thirteen, years had to elapse after the consulship or prætorship before past consuls or past prætors proceeded to their provinces. The former received the provinces which were from the very first called consular, *viz.* Asia and Africa, the latter the others, which were prætorian; but both sets of governors alike were styled *proconsuls,* and were attended by the same retinue as heretofore. The imperial provinces, which became three times as numerous by the time of Trajan, were governed by the emperor himself through deputies whose continuance in office depended on the will of the emperor who appointed them. These deputies, according to the importance of the province, were either of consular or prætorian rank, *lēgāti Augusti pro prœtōre* (*see* LEGATI), or *prōcūrātōrēs* (*q.v.*). Egypt alone, which was governed as an imperial domain, was under a *prœfectus* (*q.v.*). The financial administration of the senatorial provinces was managed by quæstors; that of the imperial, by procurators, who also collected in the senatorial provinces the revenues directly due to the emperor. Augustus established a fixed stipend for all officers outside Rome, and thus afforded a real relief to the oppressed provincials. Considerable alleviation was also secured for them by the limitation to the employment of State tax-collectors. The same result was promoted by the longer continuance of the administration in the imperial provinces, and the greater facilities granted for bringing an indictment, by means of a regular procedure before the Senate. Moreover the emperor, after the proconsular power over all pro-

vinces had been conferred on Augustus, 23 B.C., ranked as the highest authority over all the governors, and heard complaints as well as appeals.

Prŏvŏcātĭō. The Roman term for the appeal from the verdict of the magistrate to the decision of the people.

Under the kings the court of appeal was the *cŏmĭtĭa cūrĭăta;* after Servius Tullius, the *comitia centŭrĭăta.* While, under the arbitrary rule of the kings, the right of appeal was allowed, on the establishment of the Republic, in 509 B.C., this was imposed on the consuls as a duty, and was repeatedly enjoined by special enactments in all cases where it was a question of life and death, or of corporal punishment. The appeal was only valid within the city, and the *pŏmērĭum,* but not in the camp. Moreover, no one could appeal against the dictator. When afterwards (454 B.C.), besides the consuls, the tribunes and ædiles acquired the right of imposing a fine (*multa, q.v.*), a maximum limit was fixed for it, and if that was exceeded, there was an appeal to the *comitia trĭbūta.*

As this appeal was expected in all legitimate cases, trials of this kind were held immediately before the *comitia* concerned with such appeals; and after the verdict had been pronounced by the magistrate presiding, it was either confirmed or reversed by the votes of the people. About 195 B.C. the right of appeal was extended over the whole of Italy and the provinces. After permanent courts for certain offences had been established, the *quæstĭōnēs perpĕtŭœ* (*see* QUÆSTIO), the jurisdiction of the people, and with it the appeal thereto, became more and more limited. For the *provocatio* under the Empire, *see* APPELLATIO.

Proxĕnus (State-friend). The Greek term for the representative of a State who was appointed, from the citizens of another State, to attend to the interests of its citizens there resident, as often as they needed legal protection and assistance. In the interests of foreigners, many States appointed such representatives from among their own citizens. Their position may be compared with that of our consuls. The *proxenus* received many distinctions and honours from the State which he represented. To be nominated *proxenus* was in some cases only an honorary distinction, which the State conferred on such foreigners as resided in it as aliens (*see* METŒCI), and were therefore unable to do any service abroad for the citizens of the State in which they resided. This distinction insured many privileges, such as freedom from taxation and from public burdens which otherwise fell on the resident aliens, and, in general, exemption from tolls and taxes; also the right to acquire property in land, free admission to the Senate and to the assemblies of the people, etc. [*See* Monceaux, *Les Proxénies Grecques*, 1886.]

Prūdentĭus Clēmens (*Aurēlĭus*). The most important among the Christian Latin poets, born 348 A.D., of a respectable family in Spain. After a rhetorical and legal education, he first practised as an advocate, discharged the duties of a civil and criminal judge in Spain, held a high military appointment at court, and in later years retired to a monastery, where he devoted himself to writing sacred poems, and died about 410 A.D. He published a collection of his sacred poems in 405 A.D. They are composed with rhetorical skill, in epic and lyric metres (in the latter of which Horace in his model); and they include subjects of the most varied kind : Hymns for daily prayer (*Căthēmĕrĭnōn lĭber*); a martyrology (*Pĕrĭ Stĕphănōn*); a conflict between the virtues and the vices for the soul of man, etc.

Prȳtăneiă. The term in Athenian law for a sum of money paid by both parties at the commencement of a private suit, to defray the expense of the action. In actions for sums between 100 and 1,000 *drachmœ* it was three *drachmœ;* for larger sums, thirty. The defeated party had to refund this sum to the successful litigant. (*See* JUDICIAL PROCEDURE, I.)

Prȳtăneiă (*Greek*). [(1) Any public office held by rotation for given periods; *e.g.* in Herodotus, vi 110, the chief command for the day, held by each of the ten generals in turn. (2) The period of thirty-five or thirty-six days, *i.e.* about one-tenth of the year, during which each of the ten *phȳlœ* presided in turn over the Council and *ecclēsĭa*. The order was determined by lot. The presiding tribe was represented by its *ĕpistătēs*, who was appointed by lot to preside for the day, and could not hold this office more than once in each year (Aristotle, *On Constitution of Athens*, 44).]

Prȳtăneis (sing. *prȳtănĭs*, "a president"). The name in various Greek free States for the highest officials. In many States, especially in early times, one, two, or five *prytaneis* ruled with almost kingly power. At Athens *prytanis* was the name for the member of a body of officials who presided over that body when it had any public business to transact. This title was also given to the presidents of the *naucrārĭœ* (*q.v.*), and Council [who, with their *ĕpistătēs* at their head, presided over the Council and *ecclēsĭa* during the 5th century B.C. In the 4th century the presidential duties were transferred to the *prŏĕdrī* and their *epistates*. (*See* Aristotle, *Constitution of Athens*, 44, pp. 163–4, ed. Sandys.)]

Prȳtănēum (Gr., *prŭtăneiŏn*). In many Greek towns, a public building consecrated to Hestĭa (*q.v.*), and containing the State hearth. At Athens, it was here that the State offered hospitable entertainment as a public compliment to foreign ambassadors, to Athenian envoys on their return from the successful discharge of their mission, also to citizens who had done good service to the State, especially to distinguished generals, and victors in the great Panhellenic games, and sometimes even to their descendants. In the case of those who were Athenian citizens, this privilege was usually granted for life.

Psămăthē. A daughter of a king of Argos, mother of Lĭnus (*q.v.*) by Apollo.

Psēphisma. The Greek, and especially the Athenian, term for a resolution of the people arrived at by voting. (*See* ECCLESIA, 1.)

Pseudŏdiptĕrŏs ("falsely dipteral"). An epithet describing a temple which is surrounded on all four sides by only a single row of columns, placed at intervals which correspond to the position of the outer row of columns in a dipteral temple. (*See* TEMPLES, fig. 6.)

Pseudŏpĕriptĕrŏs ("falsely peripteral"). An epithet of a temple in which the side columns were "engaged" in the wall of the *cella*, instead of standing out at a distance from it. (*See* TEMPLES.)

Psȳchē. In Greek mythology, the personification of the human soul as the being beloved by Ĕrōs (*Amor*). She is represented as a butterfly, or as a young maiden with butterfly's wings, sometimes as pursued by Eros in various ways, or revenging herself on him, or united with him in the tenderest love. Apŭlēĭus (*q.v.*), in his tale of the *Golden Ass* [*Met.* iv 28–vi 24], has availed himself of this representation. He makes them the hero and heroine of an old popular tradition, in which a loving couple, after a sorrowful separation, are restored to one another for ever. The love-god causes the charming Psyche, the youngest of the three daughters of a king, to be carried off by Zĕphy̆rus to a secluded spot, where he visits her at night alone, without being seen or recognised by her. Persuaded by her sisters, she transgresses his command, and wishes to see him, when the god immediately, vanishes. Amid innumerable troubles and appalling trials she seeks her lover, till at length, purified by the sufferings she has endured, she finds him again, and is united to him for ever. In the myth, as told by Apuleius, her daughter is called *Vŏluptas.*

Psy̆chŏmanteiŏn. A Greek term for an oracle of the dead. (*See* ORACLES.)

Psy̆chŏpompŏs. The guider of souls, another name for Hermēs.

Ptărĕlāus. King of the Tăphii and Tēlĕbŏæ in Acarnānia. He was killed by his daughter Cŏmæthō, who pulled out the golden hair, on the possession of which depended the immortality accorded him by Pŏseidōn. (*See* AMPHITRYON.)

Ptŏlĕmæus. (1) *Ptolemy I*, called *Sōtēr* (" saviour " or " preserver "), son of Lagus, born 366 B.C.; general of Alexander the Great, after whose death (323) he received Egypt as his province. He took the royal title in 306. In the last years of his rule he founded the famous Museum and the great Library of Alexandria, and attracted thither all the foremost poets and scholars of the time. He died in 283. While he was on the throne, he wrote a history of Alexander the Great, which was noteworthy for its accuracy, more especially in military detail, and for its avoidance of exaggeration. Among the works on Alexander it took the first place. Only comparatively short fragments of it have been preserved. Next to Aristŏbūlus, he is the principal authority for Arrian's *Anăbăsis.*

(2) *Claudĭus Ptolemæus.* A famous Greek mathematician, astronomer, and geographer. He came from Ptŏlĕmăïs Hermeiou [ruins at modern *Menschie*] in Upper Egypt, and lived and worked in the 2nd century A.D. The most important of his writings which have been preserved are:

(*a*) *Gĕŏgrăphĭcē Hy̆phēgēsĭs* (" instructions for the drawing of maps "), a geographical work in eight books, the first of which contains the principles of mathematical geography and the drawing of maps, and the calculation of the longitudes and latitudes of places in the then known world; ii–vii contain tables of names of places in the maps described, arranged according to degrees and their subdivisions; viii contains an astronomical table of climates. This work is one of the chief sources of our knowledge of ancient geography.

(*b*) His principal astronomical and mathematical work, in thirteen books, is called the *Great Syntaxis of Astronomy,* also known as the *Almagest* (from the Arabian translation, *Tabrir al Magesthi,* through which it first became known to the Western world). This gives (with corrections) a summary of the researches of the earlier astronomers, and describes the Ptolemaic system of the universe, with the earth as a fixed centre, the system which was not superseded till the time of Copernicus (1473–1543).

(*c*) The *Harmonics,* in three books; next to that of Aristoxĕnus the most important work on ancient music. Of his remaining works we may mention the *Canon of Kings,* a fragment of his chronological tables, calculating in Egyptian years the duration of the reign of fifty-five kings: twenty Babylonians after Nabonassar (747 B.C.), ten Persians, thirteen Ptolemies, and the Roman emperors down to Antōnīnus Pĭus.

Publĭcāni. The Romans gave this name to those who did business with the State by becoming contractors for public buildings and for supplies, and to farmers of public lands, especially those who farmed the public taxes (*vectīgālĭa*) for a certain time, on payment of a fixed sum. In Rome, as indeed throughout the ancient world (*cp.* TELONÆ), the collection of taxes was made, not by paid officials, but by farmers of taxes, who belonged to the equestrian order, as the senators were excluded from such business. The farmers of taxes, by the immense profits which they made, became a politically powerful class of capitalists. As the various taxes in the different provinces were let out as a whole by the censors, joint-stock companies were formed, *sŏcĭĕtātēs publĭcānōrum,* whose members received a proportionate return for their invested capital. One member, the *manceps,* made a tender at the public auction, concluded the contract with the censors, and gave the necessary security. The duration of the contract was a *lustrum,* i.e. the period between one censorship and another, in imperial times always five years; it began on the 15th of March.

The general superintendence was given to a *magister societatis* in Rome, who vacated office every year; the management of details was in the hands of numerous officials.

According to the amount of the taxes farmed, the *publicani* received special

names. The highest class, *dĕcŭmānī*, were
the farmers of the *dĕcŭmă*, the tenth part
of the produce of the agricultural lands
which had been taken from the old possessors. The *pĕcŭārii* or *scriptŭrārii*, were
the farmers of the *scriptŭra*, the tax levied
for the use of the State pastures. The
conductōrēs portŏrĭōrum were the farmers
of the *portŏria*, the import and export dues,
etc. In order to make the greatest possible
gain, the *publicani* were guilty of the most
grievous oppression of the provincials, whose
only hope of relief lay in the governor, who
was rarely able to help them for fear of
these influential societies. Under the Empire the position of the provincials was
improved; for the emperor, as the governor-
in-chief of all the provinces, heard the final
appeal in the case of any grievances. In
imperial times, the *decumani* ceased to
exist, and the letting out of taxes was entrusted to the official boards specially concerned with them.

Publilius Sўrus (*i.e.* "the Syrian"). A
Roman writer of mimes (*see* MIME), a younger contemporary and rival of Lăbĕrius; he
flourished about 43 B.C. Probably born at
Antioch in Syria, he came to Rome in early
youth as a slave. On account of his wit he
was liberated by his master, and received
a careful education. As a writer of mimes
and as an improviser, he was exceedingly
popular, and, after the death of Laberius,
held sole sway on the stage. His mimes
contained, in addition to the farcical humour
of this sort of writing, a great number of
short, witty sayings. These were so much
admired that they were excerpted at an early
date, and used in schools, while the pieces
themselves were soon forgotten.

In the Middle Ages these sayings were
popular under the name of Sĕnĕcă. We
have an alphabetical collection of nearly two
hundred of these apophthegms, bearing the
title, *Publilii Syri Mimi Sententiœ* [*e.g.*
"Necesse est multos timeat, quem multi
timent"; "Beneficium accipere, libertatem
est vendere"; and (the motto of the
Edinburgh Review) "Iudex damnatur cum
nocens absolvitur"].

Pŭdīcĭtĭă. The Roman goddess of
modesty and chastity. She was at first worshipped in a chapel in Rome exclusively by
the patrician matrons. When, in 296 B.C.,
the patrician Vergīnia was excluded from this
worship by her marriage with the plebeian
consul Vŏlumnius, she erected in her own
house a chapel to the goddess, so that the
plebeian matrons might worship there.

Afterwards this cult died out with the
decay of morals. In imperial times altars
were erected to Pudicitia in honour of the
empresses. The goddess was represented
as a draped matron, concealing her right
hand in her garment.

Pulpĭtum. The stage of the Roman
theatre. (*See* THEATRE.)

Purpŭră. The finest and most costly
dye of the ancients, a discovery of the
Phœnicians; already known to the Greeks
in the Homeric age. [This may be inferred
from the frequent epithet *porphўrĕŏs* applied to robes, rugs, etc.] It was also
known to the Romans in the time of their
kings. It was obtained from two kinds
of shells in the Mediterranean Sea: (1)
from the trumpet-shell (Gr. *kērψx*; Lat.
būcĭnum, mūrex) [=*buccĭnĭum lăpillus*];
(2) from the true purple-shell (Gr. *por-
phўra*; Lat. *purpŭra, pĕlăgĭa*)·[=*murex
brandaris* or *trĭbŭlus*]. These shells
respectively contained in a diminutive
bladder a small quantity of (1) scarlet
coloured, (2) black and red coloured juice.
The juice collected from a number of these
shells was placed in salt [in the proportion
of about one pint of salt to every seventy-
five pounds avoirdupois of juice], and heated
in metal vessels by the introduction of warm
vapours; then the raw material, wool and
silk, was dyed in it. The best and dearest
purple was always the Phœnician, especially
that of Tyre, although it was prepared by
other inhabitants of the Mediterranean.
As the colour of the *bucinum* was not lasting, it was not used by itself, but only in
combination with the true *purpura* for
producing certain varieties of purple dye.
By mixing *bucinum* with black *pĕlăgĭum*,
the juice of the true purple-shell, the
fashionable violet, called the "amethyst"
purple was produced; and, by a double process of dyeing, first in half-boiled *pelagium*,
and then in *bucinum*, Tyrian purple was
produced. This had the colour of clotted
blood, and when looked at straight appeared black, when held to the light it
glowed with colour. A pound of violet
wool cost in Cæsar's time 100 *dĕnārii*
(£4 7s.), Tyrian purple wool above 1,000
denarii (£43 10s.). By mixing *pelagium*
with other matter, water, urine, and orchilla,
the bright purple dyes, heliotrope-blue,
mauve-blue, and violet-yellow, were obtained. Other colours were produced by
the combination of the different methods of
dyeing; first dyeing the material with
violet colour, purple dye, and scarlet (pro-

duced by *kermes* [from the *coccus ĭlĭcis*]; then by using the Tyrian method, they obtained the *tўrĭanthĭnum*, the Tyrian shell-purple, and the variety called the *hysgĭnum* [from Gr. *hysgē* = a variety of *prĭnŏs*, or *quercus coccĭfĕra*. (Pliny, *N. H.* ix 124–141.) For further details, see Blümner's *Technologie*, i 224–240].

Purple robes were used at an early date by the Greeks as a mark of dignity. Even the Athenian archons wore purple mantles officially. In Rome at one time broad, at another narrow, stripes of purple on the *tŏga* and tunic served as marks of distinction for senators, magistrates, and members of the equestrian order. The robes of the general were dyed in purple (*see* PALUDA-MENTUM); so also was the gold-embroidered mantle worn by one who celebrated a triumph. For a long time home-purple was used; Tyrian purple was not introduced till the middle of the 1st century B.C., and from that time it became a luxury. In spite of repeated attempts to check by imperial decrees the use of real purple among private individuals, robes trimmed with purple, or altogether dyed with it, became more and more used. Only a complete robe of *blatta*, the finest kind of purple, of which there were five varieties, was reserved as an imperial privilege, and any private persons who wore it were punished as being guilty of high treason. [*Codex Theodosianus* iv 40, I: *purpŭra quæ blatta vel oxўblatta vel hўăcinthĭnă dicitur.*] From the 2nd century A.D. the emperors took part in this lucrative industry, and from the end of the 4th century A.D. the manufacture of the *blatta* became an imperial monopoly.

Pŭtĕāl. The Latin term for a circular stone inclosure, consisting of a dwarf wall, surrounding either (1) the mouth of a well, or (2) a spot struck by lightning. Italian superstition demanded that every flash of lightning which struck and was buried in the earth should have, as it were, a grave and a propitiatory offering, as in the case of a human being. According to the place where the flash fell, this offering was made, either by the State or by private individuals, in the earlier times according to the directions of the *pontĭfĭcēs*, at a later date after consultation with the Etruscan *hăruspĭcēs*. The earth which was touched by the divine fire was carefully collected [Lucan i 606], and inclosed in a coffin constructed out of four side-pieces and without any bottom (this was

the burying of the lightning). Then round the coffin a shaft, consisting of four walls and open at the top, was built up to the surface of the ground. A place which had thus been consecrated by the offering which the *haruspices* made of a sheep two years old (*bĭdens*) was specially called a *bĭdentăl*, and was not allowed to be desecrated. According to the pontifical rite introduced by Numa, the propitiatory offering consisted of onions, hair, and sardels. If a human being had been struck by lightning, his body was not burnt, but buried on the spot [Pliny, *N. H.* ii 145]. Such a spot was called a *bidental*, and a propitiatory offering was made on his behalf [Festus, p. 27; Nonius, pp. 53, 26].

[The *puteal*, with bay wreaths, lyres, and a pair of pincers, may be seen on coins of the *gens Scrĭbōnia* (*see* cut). The ancient *puteal* in the Forum, near the *Arcus Fābĭānus*, was repaired by Scribonius Libo, whence it was called the *Puteal Lĭbōnis* or *Puteal Scrĭbonĭānum*. In its neighbourhood he erected a tribunal for the prætor, which led to its becoming the resort of litigants, money-lenders, etc. (Hor., *Sat.* ii 6, 35, *Ep.* i 19, 8; Cic., *Pro Sestio* 18).]

* PUTEAL.
(On a denarius of L. Scribonius Libo.)

Pŭtĕus. The fountain in a Roman house. (*See* HOUSE.)

Pўănĕpsĭă. A festival celebrated at Athens on the seventh day of *Pўănĕpsĭŏn*, the end of October, in honour of the departing god of summer, Apollo. The festival received its name from the cooked beans which were offered to the god as firstfruits of autumn. Another firstfruit offering of this festival was the *Eirĕsĭōnē*, a branch of olive or bay, bound with purple and white wool, and hung about with all sorts of autumn fruits, pastry, and small vessels full of honey, wine, and oil. This branch was borne by a boy whose parents were both alive; a song, which bore the same name *Eiresione*, was sung, while he was escorted by a procession to the temple of the god, where the wreath was deposited as a votive offering. Other branches were hung at the doors of the houses. In later times this festival was also kept as a mark of gratitude for the safe return of Thēseus from Crete, which was supposed to have taken place on this day; and the cooking of the beans was regarded as commemorating the cooking of the scanty remains of the provisions of his ships. [In the ancient calendar of the Attic festivals built into the wall of the metropolitan church at Athens, the festival of the *Pyanepsia* is represented by a youth carrying the *Eiresione*. See cut in Miss Harrison's *Mythology, etc., of Athens*, p. 168; *ib.* cxxxv.] Besides Apollo, the *Hōræ* were worshipped at the *Pyanepsia* with offerings and invocations, as the goddesses of the blessings of the year.

Pygmălĭŏn. (1) In Greek mythology a king of Cyprus, who became so enamoured of the statue of a maiden which he himself was carving in ivory that he implored Aphrŏdītē to endue it with life. When the goddess granted his prayer, he married the maiden, and she bore to him a son named Păphŏs [Ovid, *Met.* x 243].

(2) *See* DIDO.

Pygmē. Boxing. (*See* GYMNASTICS.)

Pȳlădēs. Son of Strŏphĭus, king of Phănŏtē, near Parnassus, and of Anaxĭbĭă, a sister of Agămemnŏn ; famous on account of his faithful friendship with Orestes (*q.v.*). He was the husband of Electra.

Pȳlăgŏræ. See AMPHICTYONS.

Pȳrămus and Thisbē. Two Babylonian lovers, the children of hostile neighbours. As their parents declined to sanction their marriage, they could only converse with one another through a crevice in a wall common to both houses. On one occasion they had agreed to meet at night at a mulberry tree near the city. Thisbe arrived there first, but, while fleeing from a lion, stained with the blood of his prey, she dropped her veil ; this the beast tore and befouled with blood. Pyramus, finding the veil, killed himself in despair at the supposed death of his beloved. When Thisbe, returning from her flight, found his corpse, she also killed herself with his sword. The fruit of the mulberry tree was coloured by their blood, and has ever since borne the same hue [Ovid, *Met.* iv 55].

Pȳrĭphlĕgĕthŏn. A river of the nether world. (*See* HADES, REALM OF.)

Pyrrha. Daughter of Ĕpĭmĕtheus, wife of Deucălĭŏn, with whom she alone escaped the flood which bears his name. (*See* DEUCALION.)

Pyrrhic Dance (Gr. *Pyrrĭchē*). A mimic war-dance among the Greeks, representing attack and defence in battle. It originated with the Dorians in Crete, who traced it back to the Cūrētēs, and in Sparta, where it was traced to the Dĭoscūri. In Sparta, where boys of five years old were trained for it, it formed a chief part of the festival

of the *Gymnŏpædĭa.* The war-dance performed at Athens at the Panathenaic festival celebrated Athēnē as the victor over the Giants.

In the Roman imperial times the Pyrrhic dance was a kind of dramatic ballet, which was performed by dancers, male and female, and represented (like the Roman pantomime) mythological subjects, taken frequently from the legend of Dĭonȳsus, such as the march of the god against the Indians, the doom of Pentheus, but also from other sources, such as the judgment of Păris and the fate of Īcărus. For these performances the emperors frequently brought to Rome from Asia, the home of this dance, boys and girls of noble birth ; but there were also dancers, male and female, who were brought up to it as a regular trade. At times the Pyrrhic dance was performed in the amphitheatre by criminals especially trained for this purpose.

Pyrrhŏn. A Greek philosopher of Elis, who flourished about 365–275 B.C. ; the founder of Scepticism. (*See* PHILOSOPHY.)

Pȳthăgŏrăs. (1) *The Greek philosopher;* born on the island of Sămŏs about 580 B.C., son of Mnēsarchus. He is said to have been the first man who called himself a "philosopher," or lover of wisdom. The certain facts about his life are extraordinarily few, since in the course of time his life became obscured by a web of legend and tradition, as is shown by the biographies of the Neoplatonists Iamblĭchŭs and Porphȳrius.

As the story goes, he was a disciple of Phĕrĕcȳdēs of Sȳrŏs, and spent a large part of his earlier life on journeys, during which he studied the civilization and the mystic lore of the East, and especially the wisdom of the Egyptians. When, on his return to Samos, he found his country under the yoke of the tyrant Pŏlȳcrătēs, he migrated to Lower Italy, and settled in 529 at Crŏtŏn. Here, in order to bring about a political and social regeneration of the Lower Italian towns, which had been ruined by the strife of parties, he founded a society, whose members were pledged to a pure and devout life, to the closest friendship with each other, to united action in upholding morals and chastity, as well as order and harmony in the common weal. The aristocratic tendency of this society caused a rising of the popular party in Crŏton, in which Pythagoras, with 300 of his adherents is supposed to have perished ; according to other accounts, he marched with a few followers to Mĕtăpontum, where he died soon afterwards (504). Pythagoras has left nothing of his teaching in a written form. The *Golden Sayings* which bear his name are certainly not genuine, though they may have originated at an early date. They consist of seventy-one maxims written in hexameters, with little to commend them as poetry.

It follows then that there is as much uncertainty about the system of Pythagoras as about his life, for it is impossible to ascertain which of the precepts of the Pythagorean school are due to himself, and which are later additions by his disciples. We can only ascribe to him with certainty the doctrine (1) of the transmigration of souls, and (2) of number as the principle of the harmony of the universe and of moral life; and, further, certain religious and moral precepts. The first disciple of Pythagoras who described his philosophical system in writing was *Philolāus*, either of Croton or Tārentum, a contemporary of Socrātes (about 430 B.C.). Of this document, which was written in the Doric dialect, we possess only a few fragments. *Archȳtās* of Tarentum was another important follower of this school. He was a friend of Plato, and was distinguished as a general, statesman, and mathematician. He flourished about 400–365, but the fragments which bear his name are not genuine. The same may be said of the writings attributed to *Ŏcellus Lūcānus* and to *Tīmœus* of Locri, *Concerning the Nature of the Universe* and *Concerning the Soul*, and of the seven letters of *Thĕānō*, the supposed wife of Pythagoras, *Concerning the Education of Children, Jealousy, The Management of the Household*, etc.

(2) A *Greek sculptor* of Rhēgium in Lower Italy, who flourished in the second half of the 5th century B.C. He devoted himself exclusively to working in bronze. His favourite subjects were statues of heroes and of the victors in athletic games. Striving after an exact imitation of nature, he is said to have been the first to express the sinews and veins. He also rendered the hair of the head more carefully than his predecessors, and, in the pose of his statues, paid special attention to symmetry and rhythm. [Pliny, *N. H.* xxxiv 59, vii

152; Pausanias, vi 4 § 3, 6 § 1, 6 § 4, 7 § 10, 18 § 1.]

Pȳthĭa. (1) The prophetess of Apollo at Delphi. (*See* DELPHIC ORACLE.)

(2) *The Pythian games.* Next to the Olympic games, the most important of the four Greek national festivals. From 586 B.C. they were held on the Crissæan plain below Delphi. They took place once in four years, in the third year of each Olympiad, in the Delphic month Būcătius (the middle of August). Before this time (586 B.C.) there used to take place at Delphi itself, once in eight years, a great festival in honour of Apollo, in which the minstrels vied with one another in singing, to the accompaniment of the *cĭthăra*, a pæan in praise of the god, under the direction of the Delphic priests. After the first Sacred War, when the Crissæan plain became the property of the priesthood, the Amphictȳons introduced festivals once in four years, at which gymnastic contests and foot-races took place, as well as the customary musical contest. This contest also was further developed. Besides minstrels who sang with the *cithara*, players on the flute, and singers to accompaniment of the flute, took part in it (the last-named, however, for a short time only). The gymnastic and athletic contests, which were nearly the same as those held at Olympia, yielded in significance to the musical ceremonies, and of these the Pythian *nŏmŏs* was the most important. It was a composition for the flute, worked out on a prescribed scheme, and celebrating the battle of Apollo with the dragon Pȳthōn, and his triumph. At first the prize for the victor was of some substantial value, but at the second festival it took the form of a wreath from the sacred bay tree in the Vale of Tempē. The victor also received, as in the other contests, a palm-branch. The judges were chosen by the Amphictyons. The Pythian, like the Olympic games, were probably not discontinued till about 394 A.D.

Pȳthōn. A monstrous serpent produced by Gæa, which haunted the caves of Parnassus. It was slain by Apollo with his first arrows. (*See* APOLLO and DELPHIC ORACLE.)

Q

Quadrans (= *tĕruncĭus*). A Roman copper coin, a quarter of an *as* = 3 *uncĭæ*. (*See* COINAGE, 2.) The *quadrans* was the usual

price paid for a bath. [It was equivalent to about half a farthing.]

Quadrīga (*Latin*). A chariot drawn by

four horses, used in battle and in athletic games. (*See* CIRCUS, GAMES OF.) The cut

QUADRIGA.
(Syracusan *decadrachma*.)

represents a *quadriga* with weapons as the prize of victory.

Quadrīgārius. A Roman annalist. (*See* ANNALISTS.)

Quæsitor. The Roman title of the president of an extraordinary or ordinary criminal court (*quæstĭō extraordĭnārĭa* or *perpĕtŭa*). According to Sulla's rules of procedure, six prætors chosen for criminal cases presided, and, when this number was not sufficient, additional judges, *iŭdĭcēs quæstĭōnis*, were provided.

Quæstĭō. The Roman term for a court of inquiry, either *extraordĭnārĭa*, an extraordinary commission appointed by the senate or people for special criminal cases, or *perpĕtŭa*, an ordinary criminal court for certain defined offences. The first court of this kind was held B.C. 149 to try a case of extortion.

In course of time, by the laws of *Gaius Gracchus* and of *Sulla*, the number of these tribunals was increased. In Cicero's time there were eight ordinary courts to try cases of extortion, high treason (*māiestās*), embezzlement(*pĕcŭlātus*), unlawful canvassing for an office (*ambĭtus*), violence (*vīs*), assassination, poisoning, and forgery. Every *quæstio* had a president (*see* QUÆSITOR), either one of the prætors chosen by lot, or when the number of these was not sufficient, a *iŭdex quæstĭōnis*, in addition to a certain number of sworn judges. (*See* JUDEX.)

It was open to any one except to women, infants, and those who were *infāmēs*, to begin a criminal prosecution, even if he himself had not been the party injured. There was no public prosecutor; but the State, by means of pecuniary rewards and conferring of dignities, encouraged the prosecution of criminals. If, however, the accused party was found innocent, it was open to him to prosecute his accuser for chicanery. (*See* CALUMNIA.) The case was begun by the *postŭlātĭo*, a request, with a statement of the crime and name of the accused, for permission to prosecute, made to the prætor at an open sitting in the market-place. If several persons offered themselves as accusers, the choice was made by *dīvīnātĭo* (*q.v.*, 2). But, besides the principal accuser, others were allowed, who signed the indictment, and were therefore called *subscriptōrēs*. When permission had been obtained, there followed the *nōmĭnis dēlātĭo*, the handing in of the indictment; the *rĕceptĭo* and *inscrĭptĭo*, the reception and entry of the same in the official list by the prætor; the *interrŏgātĭo*, the examination (also by the prætor) of the accused, who was now *rĕus* (*q.v.*). Unless he pleaded guilty, or clearly proved his innocence, the *dĭēi dictĭo*, or date of hearing the case, was fixed, at the earliest in ten days, in special cases not till 100 days later. It was the duty of the complainant to collect in the meantime the necessary evidence and witnesses, and for this purpose he received an official authorization. At the sitting of the court, which was held publicly, by the sworn judges (*cognĭtĭo*), after the judges and parties had been cited, the accuser delivered his accusation in a continuous speech, the *subscriptores* followed him, then the accused and his *pătrōni*. The duration of these speeches (*actĭōnēs*) was at first unlimited, but afterwards, to correct the abuse of this privilege, a water-clock was introduced, which limited the time of each speaker; the time allowed for the defence was about a third greater than that for the accusation. Then followed the proof (*prŏbātĭo*) of the case. For this documents, circumstantial evidence, and declarations of witnesses were used. Next, unless the case was adjourned for the production of further proof (*amplĭātĭo*), or for a new trial on the third day (*compĕrendĭnātĭo*), the votes of the judges on the question of guilt or innocence were taken. The voting was usually in secret. The judges received from the president wooden tablets covered with wax, on the one side inscribed with a C (*condemno*, I condemn), on the other with an A (*absolvo*, I acquit). They erased one of these letters and threw the tablets into an urn. [In cases where they were unable to decide respecting the guilt or innocence of the accused, they could signify the same by writing on the tablet the letters N. L., *non lĭquĕt*.]

The result of the voting was then formally

proclaimed by the president; and if a fine was inflicted, the amount (*lītīs æstīmātīo*) was then decided by the president and the sworn judges. A man once acquitted could not be re-tried for the same offence unless his acquittal had been procured by collusion (*see* PRÆVARICATIO) of the accuser. There was no way of altering the verdict of the sworn judges; and the punishment was exacted immediately after the sentence had been given. If it was one of degradation (*infāmia*), or exile (*interdictio āquæ et ignis*, *see* EXILIUM, 2), the man so punished could be reinstated in the rights he had forfeited (*restītūtīo in intěgrum*). This was done by a decree of the people; in later times, by the emperor's pardon. These courts of sworn judges lasted till the beginning of the 3rd century A.D.

Quæstors (*quæstor* from *quæsitor*, the investigator, searcher). The Latin term originally given to two officials chosen by the king; they had to track any one suspected of a capital offence. In the time of the Republic they performed the same office for the consuls, by whom they were chosen every year. When the administration of justice in criminal cases came into the hands of the *cŏmītīa centŭrīāta*, the quæstors received, in addition to their old privilege of pleading by the mandate of the consuls, which they lost later, the management of the State treasury (*ærārium*) in the temple of Saturn. They became recognised officials when they were elected at the *comitia trĭbūta* under the presidency of the consuls (probably about 447 B.C.). The quæstors had no regular badges of office. In 421 their number was doubled, and the plebeians were granted the right of appointing to the office of quæstor, though they did not exercise it till twelve years later. The four quæstors shared their duties, so that two of them acted as masters of the treasury (*quæstōrēs ærārii*) and remained in the city (hence their name *quæstōres urbāni*), while the other two accompanied the consuls on campaigns, in order to administer the military chest.

It was part of the duty of the two former to collect the regular revenues of State (taxes and custom-dues) and the extraordinary revenues (fines, levies for war, and money produced by the sale of booty); further, to make payments, which might not be made to the consuls except by special permission of the Senate; to control the accounts of income and expenditure, which were managed under their responsibility by a special class of officials (*scrībæ*); to make arrangements

for public burials, for the erecting of monuments, for the entertainment of foreign ambassadors, etc., at the expense of the treasury. Further, they preserved at their place of business—the temple of Saturn—the military standards, also the laws, the decrees of the Senate, and the *plēbiscīta*, and kept a register of the swearing in of the officials, which took place there.

After the subjection of Italy, four more quæstors were appointed, in 267 B.C. They were stationed in different parts of Italy, at first at Ostia and Arīmīnum, probably to supervise the building of fleets. Sulla increased their number to twenty, ten of whom were appointed, in the place of the previous two, to accompany the proconsuls and proprætors to the provinces, two to help the consul who remained in the city, and two to help the other two original quæstors at their work in the city. The quæstors employed in the provinces (Sicily alone had two of these, stationed at Syracuse and Lĭlÿbæum respectively) were principally occupied with finance; they managed the provincial treasury, and defrayed out of it the expenses of the army, the governor, and his retinue; any surplus they had to pay in to the State treasury at Rome, and to furnish an exact statement of accounts. The governor might appoint them his deputies, and if he died they assumed the command; in both of these cases they acted *pro prætōre*, i.e. as proprætors (*q.v.*). Cæsar raised their number to forty, in order to be able to reward a greater number of his adherents; for the office gave admittance to the Senate, and the position of quæstor was looked upon as the first step in the official career. The age defined by law was from twenty-seven to thirty years. When the beginning of the magisterial year was fixed for January 1st, the quæstors assumed office on December 5th, on which day the quæstors in the *ærarium* decided by lot what the work of each should be.

Even under the Empire, when the normal number of quæstors was increased to twenty and the age reduced to twenty-five, the office of quæstor remained the first step to higher positions in the State. But the power of the quæstors grew more limited as the management of the treasury was entrusted to special *præfecti ærarii*, so that the city quæstors had only charge of the archives, to which the supervision of the paving of streets was added. After the division of the provinces between the emperor and the Senate, quæstors were only employed in the senatorial provinces, and were not abolished till the constitution of the provinces in general was altered by Diocletian. Four quæstors were told off for service to the consuls. The two *quæstores princĭpĭs*, or *Augusti*, were a new creation : they were officers assigned to the emperors, if the latter were not consuls, in which case they would already be entitled to two quæstors. As secretaries to the emperor, they had to read his decrees to the Senate at its sittings. From these quæstors was developed, in the time of Constantine, the *quæstor sacri pălātĭi*, the chancellor of the Empire.

Quattŭorvĭri. The Roman term for an official body consisting of four men. (*See* VIGINTISEXVIRI.)

Quindĕcimvĭri. The Roman term for an official body consisting of fifteen men, especially that appointed for the inspection of the Sibylline books. (*See* SIBYLLÆ.)

Quinquātrŭs. A festival celebrated at Rome on the 19th of March, in honour of Mars and (in a greater degree) of Mĭnerva, whose temple had been founded on this day on the Aventine. An incorrect explanation of the name *quinquatrus*, which means the fifth day after the ides, led to the festival in honour of Minerva being afterwards prolonged to five days. It was celebrated by all whose employment was under the protection of the goddess, such as teachers and their pupils. The latter obtained a holiday during the festival, and began a new course of study when it was over. The former received at this time their yearly stipend—the *mĭnervăl*. The festival of Minerva was also celebrated by women and children (in their capacity of spinners and weavers), by artisans and artists of every kind, and by poets and painters. The first day of the festival was celebrated with sacrifices by the State in honour of the founding of the temple. On the following days the gladiators performed, and there were social gatherings in the houses. On June 13 the minor *quinquatrus* took place. This festival lasted three days. It was celebrated by the guild of the flute-players, an important and numerous body at Rome. They honoured the goddess as their special patroness by meeting at her temple, by masked processions through the city, and by a banquet in the temple of Jupiter of the Capitol.

Quinquennālēs. The officials chosen every five years in the Italian municipalities (*see*

MUNICIPIUM), corresponding to the Roman censors.

Quinquĕrēmēs. Roman ships (*q.v.*) with five banks of oars.

Quintilian (*Marcus Făbĭus Quintĭlĭānus*). The celebrated Roman rhetorician, born about 35 A.D. at Călăgurris in Spain. After he had received his training as an orator at Rome, he went home about 59 A.D., but returned again to Rome in 68 A.D. in the train of Galba. He there began to practise as an advocate, and also gave instruction in rhetoric. In this latter capacity he achieved such fame that he was able to open a school of rhetoric in the reign of Vespasian, and received payment from the State. After twenty years' work he retired from his public duties in A.D. 90, and after some time devoted himself to the education of the grandchildren of Dŏmĭtilla, Domitian's sister, for which he was rewarded by the emperor with the rank of consul. Though materially prosperous, his happiness was disturbed by the loss of his young wife and his two sons. [He died between 97 and 100 A.D.]

Of his works on rhetoric, composed in his later years, we possess the one that is most important, that on the training of an orator (*De Instĭtūtĭōnĕ Orātŏrĭā*) in twelve books. This he wrote in two years; but it was not until after repeated revision that he published it, just before the death of Domitian in 96. He dedicated it to his friend, the orator Victōrĭus Marcellus, that he might use it for the education of his son Gĕtă. This work gives a complete course of instruction in rhetoric, including all that is necessary for training in practical elocution, from the preliminary education of boyhood and earliest youth to the time of appearance in public. It describes a perfect orator, who, according to Quintilian, should be not only skilful in rhetoric, but also of good moral character, and concludes with practical advice. Especially interesting is the first book, which gives the principles of training and instruction, and the tenth book, for its criticisms on the Greek and Latin prose authors and poets recommended to the orator for special study. [Many of these criticisms, however, are not original.] Quintilian's special model, and his main authority, is Cicero, whose classical style, as opposed to the debased style of his own time, he imitates successfully in his work. A collection of school exercises (*dēclāmātĭōnēs*) which bears his name is probably not by him, but by one of his pupils. [The most recent editor, however (Constantine Ritter, 1884), regards the great bulk of them as genuine.]

Quintus Smyrnæus. A Greek epic poet of Smyrna. Towards the end of the 4th century A.D., he composed a bald imitation of Homer, entitled the *Posthŏmērĭcă*, in fourteen books, a continuation of the *Iliad* after the manner of the cyclic epic writers from the death of Hector to the shipwreck of the Achæans on their journey home.

Quirīnus. The Sabine name of Mars, as the god who brandished the lance (from Sabine *curis*=Latin *quiris*, the lance). The Sabines worshipped him under this name as the father of the founder of their old capital, *Cŭrēs*, just as the Romans honoured Mars as the father of Rōmŭlus. When the Sabines migrated to Rome, they took the cult and the name of the god of their race to their new abode on the Quirinal hill. In this way Quirinus, though identical with Mars, had a distinct and separate worship on the slope of the Quirinal. He possessed a temple with priests (*see* FLĀMEN and SĂLII) and a special festival. When, in the course of time, their connexion was forgotten, Quirinus was identified with the deified Romulus, the son of Mars. For Janus Quirinus *see* JANUS.

Quirītēs (derivation uncertain). The name of the oldest inhabitants of Rome, the Latin *Ramnēs* and the Sabine *Tĭtĭēs* taken together. Afterwards it became the name of the Roman people (*pŏpŭlus Rōmānus Quirītĭum* or *populus Romanus Quirites*) in home affairs, while *Romani* was used in connexion with foreign affairs. *Quirites* was also used to indicate peaceable citizens, or civilians, as opposed to soldiers (*mīlĭtēs*) [Tac. *Ann.* i 42; Suet. *Jul.* 70; Lucan v 358].

R

Races. *See* CHARIOTS; CIRCUS, GAMES OF; HIPPODROME. For footraces, *see* GYMNASTICS.

Ræda (or *rēda*, wrongly spelt *rhēda*). The Roman travelling-carriage with four wheels. (*Cp.* CHARIOTS, 2.)

Ramnēs. One of the three old patrician tribes at Rome. (*See* PATRICIANS.)

Rĕcĭtātĭōnēs. At Rome books were sometimes read aloud before their publication. This custom was introduced in the time of Augustus by Asīnĭus Pollĭō. At first these readings took place only before friends specially invited; afterwards they were publicly announced, and were held before great assemblies, either in the theatre or at the public baths or in the Forum, admission being open to all. Introduced, in the first instance, with a view to obtaining the criticisms of the audience, to help the author in his final revision of his work, they soon became of such importance that they determined the success of the work so recited. At the same time second-rate talent was often blinded to its imperfections by the exaggerated applause of a clique. In the time of the younger Pliny these recitations were so much in fashion that [in the April of a particular year] hardly a day passed without one. [*Ep.* i 13 § 1. *Cp.* iii 7 § 5; 18 § 4; v 17 § 4; vii 7; Juvenal, i 3; iii 9; vii 70, with Mayor's note.] They seem to have continued till the 6th century A.D.

Rĕcognĭtĭō of the Roman knights, *see* EQUITES.

Rĕcŭpĕrātōrēs. The Roman term for a sworn committee, or board, of three to five members, convened by the prætor. Such a board had to adjudicate at Rome and in the provinces in money cases (more especially on claims for compensation and damages). At first only cases between Romans and foreigners were heard in this way, and were settled within ten days. Afterwards a board of this kind decided on all legal points which had to be settled promptly.

Rĕgĭfŭgĭum. A Roman festival celebrated on Feb. 24th, to commemorate the expulsion of the kings. At this festival the *rex sacrōrum* offered sacrifice on the *cŏmĭtĭum*, and then hastily fled. (*See* REX SACRORUM.) [Probably in this case, as in many others, the sacrifice was originally regarded as a *crime*. The fact that the Sälii were present is recorded by Festus (*s.v.* Regifugium). Possibly their presence had the same significance as the ceremony of leaping, etc., performed by them in March, presumably with a view to driving evil demons away from the city (*Classical Review*, v 51 *b*).]

Rĕlēgātĭō. Banishment from Rome, in imperial times a milder form of exile (*see*

DEPORTATIO, which did not affect the rights as a citizen of a man sentenced to it.

Religion. (I) The gods of the Greeks were originally personifications of the powers of nature, limited in their activity to that province of nature from the phenomena of which they are derived. As these phenomena were regarded as acts or sufferings of the gods in question, a cycle of myths was thus developed. In the minds of the people, the special significance of these myths necessarily vanished in proportion as the original connexion of the gods with the phenomena of nature receded to the background, while greater prominence was given to the conception of the gods as personal beings holding sway, primarily in their own province of nature, and then beyond those limits, and no longer exclusively in connexion with the powers of nature. In the oldest records of the intellectual life of Greece—the Homeric poems—this transition has already been carried out. The Homeric deities are exclusively occupied with the governing of mortals, whose whole life is represented as being under their influence; while traces of the old connexion with the phenomena of nature are rarely found, and the old myths had long since become unintelligible tales, in which the actions of the gods appeared unreasonable and immoral, since their meaning was no longer clear. In regard to religion, as in other matters, the Homeric poems are of the utmost importance; for if in historical times a certain uniformity prevails in the representation of the deities, this may be traced in no small degree to the influence of Homer and of other poets (especially Hesiod) who were under his influence, and who gave distinct form to the vague representations of an earlier time. Nevertheless this uniformity only existed in a general way, in detail there was the greatest confusion, for the Greeks never attained to a uniform religious system and to fixed religious dogma. They possessed only a contradictory and ambiguous mythology. The only thing which was comparatively established, was the traditional worship; but in this there was great diversity of place and time.

The common belief was, that the gods were superhuman, though they were like mortals in form and in the ordinary necessities of life (food, drink, sleep); that they had power over nature and human beings; that all good and evil came from them; that their favour could be obtained by behaviour which was pleasing to them, and lost by that which displeased them. Among the Greek gods there was no representative of evil, neither in popular belief was there one of absolute perfection and holiness; and the deities were represented as ceing subject to moral weakness and deviation from right —a belief which was fostered by the traditional mythology. The gods possessed immortality, but did not exist from the beginning of all things.

In the opinion of the Greeks, the ruling race of gods, the Olympians—so called from their abode, Olympus—were the third race of gods. The first ruler was *Urănus* (Heaven), who, by his mother *Gœa* (Earth), who bore him spontaneously, himself became the father of the Titans. He was expelled by his son *Crŏnus*, whose daughters, by his sister *Rhĕa*, were *Hestĭa*, *Dĕmĕtēr*, and *Hēra*, and his sons, *Hādĕs* (Pluto), *Pŏseidōn*, and *Zeus*. He was himself expelled by his last-named son. When Zeus, by the aid of his brothers and sisters, had overcome the Titans, who rebelled against the new order of things, he divided the world with his brothers. The earth and Olympus remained common property; Hādĕs obtained the nether world; Pŏseidōn, the sea; Zeus, the heavens; and, as being the strongest and wisest, he also had authority over all the other gods, who worked his will, received from him their offices and spheres of action, and served him as helpers in the government of the universe. According to this division of province, the gods are divided into the divinities of *heaven* and *earth* and *sea*.

As in all religions founded on nature, so with the Greeks, the gods of heaven take the first place. They are specially called *Olympians ;* and, in contrast to the gods of the earth and sea, are called the gods above, or the upper gods. The principal deities after Zeus are *Hērā*, *Athēnē*, *Apollo*, *Artĕmis*, *Aphrŏdītē*, *Hēphœstus*, *Arēs*, *Hermēs*, and *Hestia*. Round them are grouped a number of minor deities, who either escort and serve the upper gods (as, for instance, *Thĕmĭs*, and the *Hōrœ*, the *Graces*, the *Muses*, *Erōs*, *Nīkē*, *Īrĭs*, *Hēbē*, *Ganymede*), or else represent distinct phenomena of the heavens, as *Hēlĭŏs* (the sun), *Sĕlēnē* (the moon), *Eōs* (the dawn); or execute special services in the heaven-ordained government of the universe, as the goddess of birth, *Eileithyia*, the healing god, *Asclē-pius*, and the goddesses of destiny (*Mœrœ*, *Nĕmĕsis*, *Tŷchē*). The gods of the sea, besides *Poseidon* and his spouse *Amphi-*

trītē and his son *Trītōn*, are *Ŏcĕănus* and
his offspring, *Nēreus* and the *Nereids*, *Prōteus*, *Ino* (*Leucŏthĕa*), *Mĕlĭcertēs* (*Pălæmōn*),
Glaucus (*Pontius*). The gods of the earth
are *Gœa* herself, *Rhĕa* (*Cȳbĕlē*), *Dĭonȳsus*,
Prĭăpus, *Pān*, the *Nymphs* and *Satyrs*,
Dēmētēr and her daughter *Persĕphŏnē*,
with her spouse *Hādēs* (*Pluto*). The last
two are the rulers of the nether world, to
which *Hĕcătē* and the *Ĕrīnyĕs* also belong.

The number of beings regarded as deities
was never clearly defined. From the earliest times in Greece we find deities worshipped in one place, who were not known
in another. But some of these, as Dionysus
and Pan, became common property in course
of time; and, the more lasting and more
extensive the intercourse became with other
peoples, more especially in the colonies, the
introduction of foreign deities became
greater. Some of these were identified with
the gods already worshipped, while others
preserved their original attributes, subject,
of course, to modifications, to suit the spirit
of the Greeks. This aptitude for natura-
lising foreign religions declined more and
more as Greece ceased to flourish. On the
other hand, some original deities lost their
independence, and were merged into others,
such as Helios and Apollo, Selene and
Artemis. In the popular belief of the post-
Homeric time, another numerous class of
superhuman beings sprang up, which were
regarded as being between gods and men,
the *demons* (Gr. *Daimŏnĕs*) and *Heroes* (*q.v.*).

As to their nature and their number, there
was less uniformity than in the case of the
real gods. The Heroes had only local importance. Even in the case of the gods universally worshipped, it was by no means
all (not even the most important) that had
a place everywhere in the public worship.
In the case of certain gods, their worship
was only exceptional; and those gods who
by order of the State were worshipped in
any particular place did not necessarily enjoy
for ever the position to which they were
entitled. Even Zeus, who was universally
regarded as the highest of the gods, and
figured in the cult of most of the different
States was not himself worshipped as supreme; but those gods who had always had
the first place in the cult of the respective
States, took precedence over him, and these
were not always divinities of pre-eminent
importance. In Athens, Pallas Athēnē was
worshipped as the principal deity, Hera in
Argos; among the Dorians, especially at
Delphi, Apollo; among the Ionians, Posei-

don; at Rhodes, Helios; at Naxos, Dionysus; at Thespiæ, Eros, at Orchŏmĕnus, the
Chărĭtĕs (or Graces). Even in the case of
the same deities, the local customs often
differed considerably, in respect of the
names that were given to them, their attributes, and the form of worship. These
differences were due, partly to local causes
and local opinions, partly to foreign influence; and were occasionally so considerable, that doubts arose whether different
deities were not really represented under
the same name, as, for instance, Aphrodite.

The deities were supposed to be specially
gratified by the careful observance of the
traditional ritual. This continued to be
carried on according to ancient custom, so
that the details of these ancient cults were
often curious, and their connexion with the
religious ideas on which they rested was
often unintelligible. However, with the
development of morality the view began
to prevail, that the observance of duties
towards the State and fellow men was also
favoured by the gods as guardians of the
providential order of the world; but, in the
eyes of the multitude, the principal meaning of *eusĕbeĭă* (piety) was the performance
of the ordained worship of the gods. Again,
the care of the State was confined to the
outward forms of religion, and to the maintenance of the traditional legal ritual.
Alterations in this ritual, and the introduction of new cults, were only made by
authority of the legislative power, usually
after an oracle had been consulted to determine the divine will. Besides the worship
of the deities recognised by the State,
private objects of devotion were found
everywhere. For instance, in the case of
foreign deities, at Athens, where there were
many strangers, either passing through or
permanently resident, foreign religions
were tolerated, so long as they did not
endanger the traditional worship or excite
public disturbance by their outward ritual.
Many such cults were naturalised in this
way, and became, in course of time, part
of the State religion. Conquest, again, contributed largely towards the introduction of
novelties; for the acquisition of new territory involved that of the religious rites held
therein. And, lastly, old religions, which
had been looked upon as supremely holy,
even if they were not absolutely superseded
in the course of time, became less important
in comparison with others of later origin.

Shrines, and the statues of the gods preserved in them, were the central points of

the worship of the different deities. As long as the gods were not represented as having human form, stones, especially those fallen from heaven, or blocks of wood, were the objects of worship. By various stages of progress the gods were at length represented by actual images. At first they were made of wood, then of stone and metal. Clay, and even wax, were generally used for private objects of devotion. Though the real purpose of these symbols and images was to represent the divinity to the worshippers by means of a visible sign, nevertheless, in the popular belief, it was generally presumed that the divinity was actively present in them. Accordingly, the welfare of the State was often supposed to be bound up with the possession of certain symbols and images of the gods.

The decline of the Greek religion began with the decline of the State after the Peloponnesian War. Although the philosophers had already directed their assault against the belief of the people, which, with its anthropomorphism and its inconsistency, exposed itself in many ways to the attacks of the critical spirit, yet the faith of the multitude in the old gods remained unshaken, for it had long attributed the deliverance from the perils of the Persian Wars to their mighty and merciful influence. But after the Peloponnesian War the notions of the philosophers gained ground among the people, and undermined the old belief, without, however, supplying any alternative to the religious feeling, which could no longer be satisfied with the outward forms of worship which still survived. With unbelief superstition came in, which was fostered (especially after the Macedonian epoch) by the foreign and barbarous cults, and the degenerate forms of mysticism which were imported from Asia and Egypt.

(II) The Italian tribes, from which the Roman people sprang, had a common origin with the Greeks, and a common foundation of religious ideas; but on Italian soil these religious ideas received an essentially different direction. Like the Greeks, the Italians regarded the deities as persons, separated as to sex, and united in couples; but, while the imaginative Greeks saw in their gods ideal forms full of individual life, the more sober mind of the Italian tribes, especially of the Romans, got no further than the abstract. Holding to the fundamental idea, they worshipped in the gods the abstract powers of nature, under whose influence man believed himself to be at

every moment. The original Italian gods were grave and venerable, and, in a certain sense, more moral than those of the Greeks; but they lacked plastic form and poetic beauty. Accordingly, it is only with certain reservations that we can speak of a Roman mythology, in a sense corresponding to that of the Greeks. The Romans lacked an Olympus and a Hādēs, and knew nothing of stories about the race and relationship and the love-affairs of their deities. In this abstract nature of the Roman gods, it is intelligible that the Romans, during the first 200 years from the foundation of Rome, possessed no images of their gods, but represented them by symbols; e.g. Jupiter by a flint-stone, Mars by a spear, Vesta by fire, which, even in later times, remained the symbol of the goddess. In the earliest Roman religion the deities of two Italian races, the Latins and the Sabines, were united, Rome having been originally peopled by the union of these tribes. The most important gods were the god of light and the god of all beginning, Iānus; the god of heaven, Iupiter, the greatest protector of the nation, with whom was joined the feminine element in Iūnō, just as Iāna (Diana) was connected with Janus; Mars, originally the protector of agriculture, the ancestral god of the Latin race; Quirīnus, originally the corresponding god of the Sabines; and Vesta, the goddess of the hearth of the State. Besides these principal deities, others were worshipped as patrons of the farmers and shepherds. Their activity extended over the earth, the fields, and the woods; they blessed the fruits of the field and garden, and gave prosperity to the cattle. Such were Tellūs, Cērēs, Sāturnus and Ops, Liber and Libĕra, Faunus, Silvānus, Flōra, Vertumnus, Pōmōna. The gods of the sea, however, who had such an important position in the Grecian mythology, had not nearly the same importance in Roman ideas as the gods of heaven and earth; for in the earliest times the sea was little regarded by the Romans. Another object of religious worship was the gods of the house and family, the Lărēs and Pĕnātēs. But, besides these, there was an unlimited number of divine beings; for the Romans assumed that there were divine representatives of every inanimate or animate object, of every action and every event. Not only did every human being possess a special protector (GENIUS, q.v.), but a number of deities watched over his development from conception to birth, and his further growth, mentally and bodily. (*See* INDIGITAMENTA.)

·Again, there were manifold protecting gods for the different events of life, as *Tūtānus* and *Tūtūlīna*, who were invoked in times of trouble; *Orbōna*, invoked by childless couples; and *Fĕbris*, the goddess of fever. There were also separate gods for separate employments, and for the places where they were carried on. In this way the different institutions and phases of agriculture possessed special deities (as *Rōbīgus* and *Rōbīgo*, protectors of the crops against blight). So also with the different branches of cattle-breeding (*Būbŏna*, goddess of the breeding of horned cattle; *Ĕpŏna*, goddess of the breeding of horses; *Pălēs*, of the breeding of sheep). Similarly with the separate parts of a house: *Forcŭlus*, god of the door; *Cardĕa*, goddess of the hinge; *Līmentīnus* and *Līmentīna*, deities of the threshold. To these divine beings fresh ones were continually added, as the inclination of the Romans to recognise and trace divine influence in every single event led to the establishment of new cults after every new revelation of divine power. In this way the introduction of bronze coinage led to a *dĕus Æscŭlānus*, and later, that of silver coinage to a *deus Argentīnus.* Historical events gave an impulse to the personification of intellectual and moral qualities, such as *Concordia*, *Hŏnōs*, *Virtūs*, *Mens*, etc. The same principle which recognised that there were some gods unknown, ·or, at any rate, not worshipped at Rome, led to the tolerance of private performance of foreign cults. Hence also it came about that the gods of conquered countries found a place in the Roman State religion, and occasionally were even introduced into the actual worship of Rome. In the latter case, however, the home deities preserved their rights in so far as the shrines of the newly imported deities were outside the limits of what was called the *Pŏmērium* (*q.v.*).

The religion of the Romans was gradually but completely altered by the influence of that of the Greeks. This influence made itself felt as early as the time of the latest kings. Shrines of the gods were first introduced under the elder Tarquin, and under the last Tarquin three supreme gods of the State were established: Jupiter, the representative of supreme power; Juno, of supreme womanhood; Minerva, of supreme wisdom. These three deities received, as a token of their inseparability, a common temple on the Capitol, and were therefore called the Capitoline gods. This Greek influence was firmly established at the end of the time of the kings by the Sibylline books, which originated among the Greeks of Asia Minor. (*See* SIBYLLINE BOOKS.) By means of these a number of Greek and Asiatic gods were in course of time introduced into the Roman cult, partly as new deities, such as Apollo, Cўbĕlē (*Magna Māter*), Æscŭlāpius; partly under the names of native gods, with whom they were often identified in a very superficial way, as Dēmētēr with Cĕrēs, Dīonȳsus with Līber, Persĕphŏnē with Lībĕră, Aphrŏdītē with Vĕnus; and with them were introduced many innovations in the old established worship of the gods, especially the *Lectisternium* (*q.v.*). When, after the second Punic War, Greek ideas irresistibly made their way in Rome, it became more and more common to identify the gods of Rome with those of Greece; and thus the original significance of many Roman deities was either obscured or even entirely lost. Divinities highly venerated of old were put into the background, and those of less importance came to be regarded as supreme, owing to their supposed analogy to Greek gods. In this way the following twelve were established by analogy to the Greek form of religion: *Iupĭter* (Zeus), *Iūno* (Hēra), *Neptūnus* (Poseidon), *Mĭnerva* (Athēnē), *Mars* (Arēs), *Vĕnus* (Aphrodite), *Apollo*, *Dĭāna* (Artĕmis), *Vulcānus* (Hēphæstus), *Vesta* (Hestĭa), *Mercŭrĭus* (Hermēs), and *Cĕrēs* (Demeter).

The Roman religion was from the beginning an affair of State. Religious, as well as political, institutions emanated from the kings, who, as high priests, organized the worship by law and laid the foundation of a law of ritual. The second king, Nŭma, was regarded as the real founder of the Roman cult, and of the priesthood charged with the carrying out of the same. After the kings had been abolished, religion was still controlled by the State, and the priests (*q.v.*) continued to be State officials, who were empowered by the State, on the one hand, to superintend the performance of the different cults, and, on the other (and this was the more important office), to give judgment in all matters of religion. They thus exercised considerable influence. Under the Republic, the royal prerogative of formulating decrees in all matters of religion was transferred to the Senate. As the Roman State in early times was exclusively composed of patricians, the public religion was originally their exclusive property; the plebs were not allowed to participate in that religion, and were only allowed to worship the Roman gods in private. Therefore, in the long struggle, in which the plebs, with their ever-increasing power, endeavoured to secure their rights (a struggle that ended in 300 B.C.), it was a question of religion as well as of politics. As regards the worship of the gods, according to Roman ideas, a pure and moral life was pleasing to them and gained their favour. This was, however, conditional on the exact performance of the outward ritual which the system of religion ordained for their cult. It consisted in a very prolonged ceremonial, performed according to the strictest injunctions and with painful minuteness of detail. This ceremonial was performed in public and private life, so that no community lacked its special shrines and sacrifices (see SACRA), and nothing of any importance was undertaken without religious sanction, which involved in particular the discovery of the divine will by means of certain signs (see AUSPICIA). The forms of outward worship were retained long after the decay of belief in the gods had set in. This decay was caused by the preponderance of the Greek element, and the contemporary introduction of Greek enlightenment; and it soon spread to the forms of worship. During the greater part of the republican period, the priests allowed religion to take a secondary place to politics, and, either from indifference or ignorance, neglected their official duties.

Under the Empire, when even the deification of deceased emperors was introduced (see APOTHEOSIS), an attempt was made to give an artificial life to the ancient forms of worship; but religious feeling could not be rekindled by forms which had long lost their meaning. When this feeling revived, it preferred, as in Greece, to find refuge in strange Oriental rites, especially those of Mithrās and of Īsis and Sĕrāpis, which, by means of their mysteries and their expiatory ceremonies, offered a certain degree of satisfaction, though, at the same time, they led the way to every conceivable kind of superstition.

The suppression of paganism began in the 4th century, from the time when Constantine decided in favour of Christianity, in 324 A.D. It commenced in the eastern half of the Roman empire, while in the western half, and at Rome in particular, the Roman form of worship remained essentially undisturbed until the reign of Thĕŏ-

dŏsĭus the Great (379–395), the resolute exterminator of paganism. In 394 the Olympic games were held for the last time; in Rome the endowment of all public forms of worship out of the funds of the State was withdrawn, the priests were driven from the temples, and the temples closed. Nevertheless certain heathen customs long survived, such as the auguries of the consuls and some few festivals that admitted of being celebrated without offering sacrifice or entering a temple. Thus the Lŭpercālĭa were not abolished until 494, when they were transformed into a Christian festival.

Rēlĭgĭōsĭ Dĭēs ("critical days", "days of scruple or restraint"). Certain special days were so called among the Romans which, owing to religious scruples, were deemed unsuitable for particular undertakings, especially for beginning them. On such days only what was absolutely necessary was done. So far as they are unsuited for sacred, political, legal, or military undertakings, they belong to the dies nĕfasti. (See FASTI.) As regards private affairs, these days were of different kinds. Some were of ill omen for journeys, others for weddings. In the latter case the day previous was also avoided, so that the first day of married life should not be a day of unhappy omen. Among such days were those consecrated to the dead and to the gods of the nether world, as the Părentālĭa and the Fĕrālĭa, and days when the mundus, i.e. the world below, stood open (see MANES); the Lĕmŭria (see LARVÆ); also days sacred to Vesta, days on which the Sălĭi passed through the city, or those which were deemed unlucky owing to their historical associations (ātrī dĭēs, "black days"), such as the anniversary of the battle on the Allia (July 18th); also all days immediately after the calends, nones, and ides, on account of the repeated defeats and disasters experienced by the Romans on those days.

Rĕnuntĭātĭo. The Roman term for the solemn and formal announcement of the names of the magistrates elected at the cŏmĭtĭa by the votes of the people. The announcement was made by the returning officer who presided at the election, and was necessary to give validity to the election.

Rĕpĕtundārum Crīmen (from repetundæ pĕcūnĭæ, "money which is ordered to be restored"). The name given by the Romans to the charge brought against officials for extorting money from Roman subjects or allies. Such charges were at first brought before the Senate, which heard the case itself, or else passed it on to a commission, or, again, caused it to be brought before the *cŏmĭtĭa* by the tribunes. At last, in 149 B.C., a standing court of justice (*see* QUÆSTIO *perpetua*), in fact, the first in Rome, was instituted by the *Lex Calpurnia*, containing more precise definitions of acts liable to punishment, with forms of legal procedure, and determining the amount of the penalty. The increasing inclination of the officials to use the administration of the provinces as means of enriching themselves at the expense of the provincials led to repeated legislation with a view to increasing the penalty. The last law on the subject was Cæsar's *Lex Iūlia*, which was the basis of the procedure in such cases under the Empire. During that period, in consequence of the improved condition of provincial government, extortion on the part of officials became much rarer. Such extortion was generally punished by having to pay four times the amount extorted. It was also attended with a certain degree of disgrace (*infămia*), even if a still more severe punishment were not added for other offences committed at the same time and (as usual) included in the indictment (*e.g.* the offence of *læsa māiestās*).

Restĭtūtĭō (reinstating). A term applied by the Romans to cancelling a legal decision, especially to the restoration of rights of citizenship forfeited by condemnation in a criminal court. Under the Republic this restoration could be legally obtained only by a vote of the people. Under the Empire, the emperor alone possessed the privilege of granting it.

Rētĭārĭus. *See* GLADIATORES.

Rĕus. The term used by the Romans for the person accused, especially in a criminal trial. In such a case custom required the accused to appear in public in the garb of mourning, with beard and hair in an unkempt condition, in neglected attire, and stripped of every sign of rank. The mere accusation involved some suspense of legal rights, preventing the *reus* from standing for any office and from exercising the functions of a judge. The higher officials were exempt from criminal accusation while in office and when engaged in the discharge of public business. Lastly, lawsuits between two persons connected by ties of family or office, such as parents and children, patrons and clients, were regarded as inadmissible.

Rex Sacrōrum (or *Rex Sacrĭfĭcŭlus*), the "king of sacrifice." The name given by the Romans to a priest who, after the abolition of the royal power, had to perform certain religious rites connected with the name of king. He resembles the *archŏn băsĭleus* of the Athenian constitution. He was always a patrician, was elected for life by the *pontĭfex maxĭmus* with the assistance of the whole pontifical college (of which he became a member), and was inaugurated by the augurs. Although he was externally of high rank and, like the *pontifex maximus*, had an official residence in the *Rēgia*, the royal castle of Nŭma, and took the chair at the feasts and other festivities of the *pontĭfĭcēs*, yet in his religious authority he ranked below the *pontifex maximus*, and was not allowed to hold any public office, or even to address the people in public. His wife (like the wives of the flamens) participated in the priesthood. Our information as to the details of the office is imperfect. Before the knowledge of the calendar became public property, it was the duty of the *rex sacrorum* to summon the people to the Capitol on the calends and nones of each month, and to announce the festivals for the month. On the calends he and the *rēgīna* sacrificed, and at the same time invoked Janus. Of the other sacrifices known to us we may mention the *rēgĭfŭgium* on Feb. 24th, when the *rex sacrōrum* sacrificed at the *cŏmĭtĭum*, and then fled in haste. This has been erroneously explained as a commemoration of the flight of Tarquĭnius Sŭperbus, the last of the Roman kings; but it is much more probably one of the customs handed down from the time of the kings themselves, and perhaps connected with the purificatory sacrifice from which the month of February derived its name. At the end of the Republic the office, owing to the political disability attaching to the holder, proved unattractive, and was sometimes left unfilled: but under Augustus it appears to have been restored to fresh dignity, and in imperial times it continued to exist, at any rate, as late as the 3rd century.

Rhădămanthўs (Lat. *Rhădămanthus*). Son of Zeus and Eurōpa, brother of Mīnōs. He was praised by all men for his wisdom, piety, and justice. Being driven out of Crete by his brother, he is described as having fled to the Asiatic islands, where he made his memory immortal by the wisdom of his laws. Thence he is said to have removed to Ōcălĕa in Bœotia, to have wedded Alcmēnē, after the death of Amphĭtrўōn, and to have instructed her son Hĕrăclēs in

virtue and wisdom. In Homer [*Od.* iv 564]
he is described as dwelling in the Elysian
fields. Here Alcmene, after her decease,
is said to have been wedded to him anew.
Later legend made him the judge of the
dead in the under-world, together with
Æacus and Minos.

Rhapsodist (Gr. *rhapsōdŏs*). The Greek
term originally designated the man who
adapted the words to the epic song, *i.c.* the
epic poet himself, who in the earlier time
recited his own poetry. Afterwards the
term specially denoted one who made the
poems of others a subject of recitation.

At first such rhapsodists were generally
poets themselves; but, with the gradual
dying out of epic poetry, they came to hold
the same position as was afterwards held
by the actors, professionally declaiming the
lays of the epic poets. Epic verses were
originally sung to musical accompaniment,
but after the time of Terpander, as lyric
poetry became more independently cultivated, the accompaniment of stringed instruments fell into disuse; and then gradually,
instead of a song-like recitation, a simple
declamation, in which the rhapsodist held a
branch of bay in his hand, came to be generally adopted. This had happened even before
the time of Plato and Aristotle [*see* especially Plato's *Ion*]. As in earlier times the
singers moved from place to place, in order
to get a hearing at the courts of princes or
before festive gatherings, so the rhapsodists
also led an unsettled and wandering life. In
Athens [Lycurgus, *Leocr.* § 102] and many
other towns [as at Sĭcȳōn, before the time
of the tyrant Clīsthĕnēs (Herod., v 67)],
public recitations of the Homeric poems were
appointed, at which the rhapsodists competed
with one another for definite prizes, and thus
found opportunity to display their art. It
is true that other epic poems, and even the
iambic poetry of Archĭlŏchus and Sĭmōnĭdēs
of Amorgus, were also recited by rhapsodists;
still at all times the labours of such reciters
continued to be devoted in the first place to
Homeric poetry [Pindar, *Nem.* ii 2; Plato,
Ion 530 D, *Rep.* 599 E, *Phædr.* 252 B].
Hence they were also called *Hŏmĕrĭdæ*
and *Hŏmĕristæ* [Aristotle in *Athenæus*, 620
B]. It was to the older rhapsodists that
the Homeric poems primarily owed their
wide diffusion among the Greeks. In the
course of time the high esteem in which the
rhapsodists originally stood began to decline,
because many practised their art as a matter
of business, and in a purely mechanical
fashion. Still their employment survived

long beyond the classical time, and not only
did the public competitions continue to
exist, but it was also the custom to introduce rhapsodists at banquets and on other
occasions.

Rhĕa. Daughter of Urănus and Gæa,
wife of her brother, the Titan Crŏnus,
by whom she gave birth to the Olympian
gods, Zeus, Hādēs, Pŏseidōn, Hēra, Hestia,
Dēmētēr. For this reason she was generally
called the *Mother of the gods*. One of her
oldest places of worship was Crete, where
in a cave, near the town of Lyctus or else
on mounts Dircē or Ida, she was said to
have given birth to Zeus, and to have hidden
him from the wiles of Cronus. The task of
watching and nursing the newborn child
she had entrusted to her devoted servants
the *Cūrĕtĕs*, earth-born demons, armed with
weapons of bronze, who drowned the cry of
the child by the noise which they made by
beating their spears against their shields.
The name of Curetes was accordingly given
to the priests of the Cretan Rhea and of the
Idæan Zeus, who executed noisy war-dances
at the festivals of those gods. In early
times the Cretan Rhea was identified with
the Asiatic *Cȳbĕlē* or *Cȳbĕbē,* "the Great
Mother," a goddess of the powers of nature
and the arts of cultivation, who was worshipped upon mountains in Mysia, Lydia,
and Phrygia.

In the former character she was a symbol
of the procreative power of nature; in
the latter, she originated the cultivation
of the vine and agriculture, together with
all other forms of social progress and civilization, which depend upon these. Thus
she was regarded as the founder of towns
and cities, and therefore it is that art represents her as crowned with a diadem of
towers.

The true home of this religion was the
Phrygian Pessīnūs, on the river Sangārius,
in the district afterwards known as Galatia,
where the goddess was called *Agdistis*
[Strabo, p. 567] or *Angdistis*, from a holy
rock named Agdus upon Mount Dindȳmus
above the town. Upon this mountain, after
which the goddess derived her name of
Dindȳmĕnē, stood her earliest sanctuary,
as well as her oldest effigy (a stone that had
fallen from heaven), and the grave of her
beloved Attis (*q.v.*). Her priests, the emasculated *Galli*, here enjoyed almost royal
honour. In Lydia she was worshipped,
principally on Mount Tmōlus, as the mother
of Zeus and the foster-mother of Dĭonȳsus.
There was also a temple of Cybele at Sardis.

Her mythical train was formed by the *Cŏrўbantĕs*, answering to the Curetes of the Cretan Rhea; these were said to accompany her over the wooded hills, with lighted torches and with wild dances, amid the resounding music of flutes and horns and drums and cymbals. After these the priests of Cybele were also called Corybantes, and the festivals of the goddess were celebrated with similar orgies, in the frenzy of which the participators wounded each other or, like Attis, mutilated themselves. Besides these there were begging priests, called *Mĕtrăgyrtæ* and *Cўbēbi*, who roamed from place to place, as inspired servants and prophets of the Great Mother. On the Hellespont and on the Propontis, Rhea-Cybele was likewise the chief goddess; in particular in the Troad, where she was worshipped upon Mount Ida as the *Idæan Mother*, and where the *Idæan Dactўli (q.v.)* formed her train. From Asia this religion advanced into Greece. After the Persian Wars it reached Athens, where in the *Mĕtrōum*, the temple of the Great Mother, which was used as a State record-office, there stood the ideal image of the goddess fashioned by Phīdĭās [Pausanias, i 3 § 5]. The worship of Cybele did not, however, obtain public recognition here, any more than in the rest of Greece, on account of its orgiastic excesses and the offensive habits of its begging priests. It was cultivated only by particular associations and by the lower ranks of the people.

In *Rome* the worship of the Great Mother (*Magna Māter*) was introduced for political reasons in 204 B.C., at the command of a Sibylline oracle, and for the purpose of driving Hannibal out of Italy. An embassy was sent to fetch the holy stone from Pessīnūs; a festival was founded in honour of the goddess, to be held on April 4–9 (the *Mĕgălēsia*, from the Greek *mĕgălē mĕtĕr = magna mater*); and in 217 a temple on the Palatine was dedicated to her. The service was performed by a Phrygian priest, a Phrygian priestess, and a number of *Galli* (emasculated priests of Cybele), who were allowed to pass in procession through the city in accordance with their native rites. Roman citizens were forbidden to participate in this service, though the prætor on the Palatine, and private persons among the patricians, celebrated the feast by entertaining one another, the new cult being attached to that of Maia or Ops. The worship of Cybele gained by degrees an ever-wider extension, so that under the early Empire

a fresh festival was instituted, from March 15–27, with the observance of mourning, followed by the most extravagant joy. In this festival associations of women and men and the religious board of the *Quindĕcimvĭri (q.v.)* took part. In the first half of the 2nd century A.D. the *Taurŏbŏlĭa* and *Crĭŏbŏlĭa* were added. In these ceremonies the person concerned went through a form of baptism with the blood of bulls and rams

* CYBELE.

From an Athenian *ex-voto* relief (Berlin).

killed in sacrifice, with the object of cleansing him from pollutions and bringing about a new birth. The oak and pine were sacred to Rhea-Cybele (*see* ATTIS), as also the lion. She was supposed to traverse the mountains riding on a lion, or in a chariot drawn by lions. In art she was usually represented enthroned between lions, with the mural crown on her head and a small drum in her hand.

Rhēa Silvia. Daughter of the Alban king Nŭma. Her uncle Ămūlius, who had driven his brother from the throne, made her a Vestal Virgin, so that none of her descendants might take vengeance for this violent deed. When, however, she bore to Mars the twins Rŏmŭlus and Rĕmus, and was thrown for this into the Tiber, Tĭbĕrīnus (*q.v.*), the god of the river, made her his wife. According to an older tradition, the mother of the founders of Rome was Ilia, daughter of Æneäs (*q.v.*) and Lavīnia.

Rhēda. *See* RÆDA.

Rhēsus. Son of Eïŏnēus, or Strȳmōn, and one of the Muses, king of the Thracians. He came to help Priam, but, in the very night after his arrival before Troy, was surprised by Dïŏmēdēs and Odysseus, and slain by the former, together with twelve of his companions, while Odysseus took away his swift horses of glistening whiteness. It had been prophesied that, if these fed on Trojan fodder, or drank of the Xanthus before Troy, the town could not be taken.

Rhetoric. Among the *Greeks*, *rhĕtŏrĭkē* comprised the practical as well as the theoretical art of speaking, and *rhĕtōr* denoted an orator no less than a teacher of oratory. Among the *Romans*, it denoted only the latter, the actual speaker being called *ōrātor*. The first men, who reduced oratory to a system capable of being taught, appeared among the Sicilian Greeks, who, according to the testimony of the ancients, were distinguished for the keenness of their understanding and their love of disputation [Cicero, *Brutus* 46]. The Syracusan CŎRAX (*circ.* 500 B.C.) is said to have been the first who elaborated systematic rules for forensic speeches, and laid them down in writing in a manual on the art of rhetoric (*technē*). His pupil TĬSĬĀS (born *circ.* 480), and after him the Leontine GORGĬĀS, further cultivated the art, and from about 427 carried it to Greece itself, and in particular to Athens. In the judicial proceedings and the assemblies of the people, the practice of oratory had long been familiar at Athens, though it had not been reduced to technical rules, and oratory had had a conspicuous representative in PERICLES. At Athens the theory of oratory was further cultivated by the SOPHISTS (Gr. *Sŏphistai*, "men who professed knowledge or wisdom"). Their instruction in style and rhetoric was enjoyed by numerous Athenians, who desired by the aid of study and practice to attain to expertness in speaking.

The first Athenian, who, besides imparting instruction in the new art, applied it practically to speaking in the assemblies of the people and before courts, and who published speeches as patterns for study, was ANTĬPHŎN (died B.C. 411), the earliest of the "Ten Attic Orators." In his extant speeches the oratorical art is shown still in its beginnings. These, with the speeches interwoven in the historical work of his great pupil Thūcȳdĭdēs, give an idea of the crude and harsh style of the technical oratory of the time; while the speeches of ANDŎCĬDĒS (died about 399), the second of the Ten Orators, display a style that is still uninfluenced by the rhetorical teaching of the age. The first really classical orator is LȲSĬĀS (died about 360), who, while in possession of all the technical rules of the time, handles with perfect mastery the common language of every-day life. ISŎCRĂTĒS (436–338) is reckoned as the father of artistic oratory properly so called ; he is a master in the careful choice of words, in the rounding off and rhythmical formation of periods, in the apt employment of figures of speech, and in everything which lends charm to language. By his mastery of style he has exercised the most far-reaching influence upon the oratorical diction of all succeeding time. Of the three kinds of speeches which were distinguished by the ancients, *political* (or *deliberative*), *forensic*, and *show-speeches* (or *declamations*), he specially cultivated the last. Among his numerous pupils is ISÆUS (about 400–350), who in his general method of oratory closely follows Lysias, though he shows a more matured skill in the controversial use of oratorical resources. The highest point was attained by his pupil DĒMOSTHĔNĒS, the greatest orator of antiquity (384–322); next to him comes his political opponent ÆSCHĬNĒS (389–314). The number of the Ten Orators is completed by their contemporaries HȲPĔRĬDĒS, LȲCURGUS, and DĪNARCHUS. In the last of these the beginning of the decline of oratorical art is already clearly apparent.

To the time of Demosthenes belongs the oldest manual of rhetoric which has been preserved to us, that of ANAXĬMĔNĒS of Lampsăcus. This is founded on the practice of oratory, and, being intended for immediate practical use, shows no trace of any philosophical groundwork or philosophical research. Greek rhetoric owes to ARISTOTLE its proper reduction into a scientific system. In contrast to Isocrates, who aims at perfection of form and style, Aristotle, in his *Rhetoric*, lays special stress on subject-matter, and mainly devotes himself to setting forth the means of producing conviction. When Athens had lost her liberty, practical oratory was more and more reduced to silence; the productions of the last orators, such as DĒMĒTRIUS of

Phălērum, were only a feeble echo of the past. Demetrius is said to have been the first to give to oratorical expression a tendency towards an elegant luxuriance. He was also the first to introduce the custom of making speeches upon imaginary subjects by way of practice for deliberative and forensic speaking.

In later times the home of oratory was transferred to the free Hellenic or hellenized communities of the coasts and islands of Asia Minor, especially Rhodes. On the soil of Asia a new style was developed, called the Asiatic. Its originator is said to have been HĒGĒSĬĂS of Magnēsia near Mount Sīpўlus. He flourished in the latter half of the 3rd century. In avowed opposition to the method of Demosthenes, who spoke in artistically formed periods, Hegesias not only went back to the simpler constructions of Lysias, but even endeavoured to outvie the latter in simplicity, breaking up all that he had to say into short sentences, and carefully avoiding periods of any length [Cic., *Orator* 226]. On the other hand, he sought to give a certain vividness to his speeches by an elaborately arranged order of words, and by a far-fetched and often turgid phraseology. This was the prevailing fashion until the middle of the 1st century B.C. Even in Rome it had numerous followers, especially Hortensius, until by the influence of Cicero it was so utterly crushed out, that Hegesias was soon forgotten, even among the Greeks. A peculiar kind of oratory prevailed in Rhodes, where a closer approach was again made to the Attic models, and particularly to the representatives of the simple style, such as Hyperidēs. Conspicuous orators of this school were APOL-LŌNIUS and MŎLŌN, both of Alăbanda in Caria, in the first half of the 1st century B.C. [These two orators are expressly distinguished from one another by Strabo, p. 655; they are confounded even by Quintilian, who erroneously speaks of Apollonius Molon, iii 1, 16; xii 6, 7.]

The theory of oratory remained until about the end of the 2nd century B.C. exclusively in the hands of the philosophers, and was little regarded by the Asiatic orators. After that time the orators and practical teachers of the art again applied themselves with eagerness to theoretical studies; the theorists adopted an eclectical method, seeking to combine the philosophical and more scientific proceeding of Aristotle with that of Isocrates, which addressed itself rather to

the turns of phrase and the outward forms of oratory. The most noteworthy system was introduced by HERMĀGŎRĂS of Tĕmnŏs (about 120 B.C.), whose writings, which are no longer extant, supplied the chief foundation for the theoretical studies of the Romans at the beginning of the 1st century B.C. The system of rhetoric elaborated by him was afterwards further worked out and improved in detail. In the time of the Empire the rhetorical schools in general flourished, and we possess an extensive rhetorical literature of that age reaching as far as the 5th century A.D. It includes the works of authors who mainly treated of the literary and æsthetic side of rhetoric, especially those of DĬŎNŸSIUS of Hălĭcarnassus, the champion of Atticism and of refined taste, and the unknown author of the able treatise *On the Sublime* (*see* LONGĪNUS); also those of technical writers, such as HERMŎGĔNĒS, the most noteworthy representative of the scholastic rhetoric of the age, APSĪNĒS, MĔNANDER, THĔŌN, APHTHŎNĬUS, and others. On the revival of Greek oratory, after the end of the 1st century, and particularly in the 2nd century, *see* SOPHISTS.

(II) *Roman.* As among the Athenians, so also among the *Romans*, the institutions of the State early gave occasion for the practice of political and forensic oratory. Until the end of the 3rd century B.C., this oratory was wholly spontaneous. The speech of the aged APPIUS CLAUDIUS CÆCUS, delivered in 280 against the peace with Pyrrhus, and afterwards published, was long preserved as the earliest written monument of Roman oratory. Numerous political speeches were published by the well-known MARCUS PORCIUS CĂTO, the most noteworthy orator during the first half of the 2nd century. After the second Punic War, in spite of all the opposition of a Cato and of those who thought with him, Greek culture forced its way irresistibly into Rome, and the Romans became eager to conform to the Greek theory of oratory also. SERVĬUS SULPĬCĬUS GALBA (*circ.* 144 B.C.) is spoken of as the first man who composed his speeches in accordance with the rules of Greek art, and not long afterwards the younger GRACCHUS (died 121) proved himself a consummate orator through the combination of natural gifts and art. Even at this time the publication of orations after delivery was a general custom, and men were already to be met with who actually wrote speeches for others. At the beginning of the 1st century B.C., the most noteworthy orators were Marcus Antōnius and Lūcius Lĭcĭnius Crassus.

Rhetorical instruction was originally imparted by Greeks. In the first decade of the 1st century the freedman Plōtius Gallus came forward as a teacher of rhetoric, and other Latin teachers followed him. These found a large number of hearers, but the censors interfered to stop the practice, as an innovation on the custom of their forefathers. It is true that this attempt to oppose the current, which had already set in, was in vain. Still it was only by freedmen that rhetorical instruction in Latin was given until the time of Augustus, when the Roman knight Blandus was the first free-born man who came forward as a public teacher of rhetoric. Even the Latin rhetoricians derived their theory exclusively from Greek sources, especially from Hermăgŏrăs, to whose influence the two earliest extant rhetorical writings of the Roman school are to be referred ; these are the work of Cornĭfĭcius, and the youthful production of Cicero, the De Inventĭōnĕ. Cicero, the greatest orator of Rome, and the only orator of the Republic of whom any complete speeches are extant, composed in his later years several other valuable writings upon rhetorical subjects, founded on his practice as an orator ; viz. the De Orātōre, the Brūtus, and the Orātor. Besides Cicero, the last age of the Republic possessed a series of other conspicuous orators, such as Hortensius, Cælius, Brutus, and, above all, Cæsar. A few more representatives of the oratory of the Republic survived to the time of Augustus. The most important of these is Asĭnĭus Pollio. But, with the old constitution, the occasions and materials for oratory also disappeared under the Monarchy, and the hindrances and limitations to its public exercise increased in the same proportion. Practice was gradually superseded by theory, orators by rhetoricians, speeches by declamations. The exercises of the rhetorical schools, which now became one of the chief centres of intellectual life, paid almost exclusive attention to the form, and dealt with imaginary subjects of political and forensic oratory, called suasōrĭæ and controversĭæ, which were as far as possible removed from the practice of life. A vivid picture of these exercises is preserved by the reminiscences of the rhetorician Sĕnĕca, the father of the well-known philosopher. The manner of speaking contracted in the schools was adopted on the few occasions on which practical oratory could still be exercised, and these occasĭons were accordingly turned into exhibitions of theatrical declamation. It was in vain that men like Quintilian, in his work on the training of an orator (Instĭtūtĭŏ Orātŏrĭa), and Tăcĭtus, in his Dialogue on Orators, pointed to the true classical patterns, and combated the fashion of their time, from which even they were not entirely free. Like these, the younger Pliny belongs to the end of the 1st century a.d. ; his Panegyric, addressed to Trajan, the only monument of Roman oratory after Cicero preserved in a complete form, became the model for the later panegyrists. In the 2nd century a.d., Fronto, and the school named after him, sought to revive the old Roman spirit by a tasteless imitation of archaic expressions and forms of speech. The same style is practised, though with more ability, by the African Apŭlēĭus. After the end of the 3rd century, the oratorical art had its chief seat in the towns of Gaul, especially in Trèves (Trĕvĭri) and Bordeaux (Burdĭgălă). Here a style of oratory was matured which possessed a certain smoothness and copiousness in words, but showed great lack of ideas. Upon the representatives of this style, the " Panegyrists," see Panegyricus.

Rhĭānus. A Greek poet and grammarian, a native of Bēnē in Crete, in the latter half of the 3rd century b.c. In his youth he was a slave and the overseer of a pălæstra ; in his later life he wrote, in the learned manner of the Alexandrines, besides epigrams, a number of epics. Of these the most famous was the Messēnĭăca, celebrating in six books the second Messenian War and its mythical hero Aristŏmĕnēs. Besides an epic fragment, we still possess eleven of his epigrams.

Rhinthŏn. A Greek comic poet, son of a potter of Tărentum, who lived about 300 b.c., and invented a style of composition of his own, which was much diffused in Magna Græcia, and is said to have been imitated even by the Romans. It was called the Hĭlărŏtrăgœdĭa, i.e. cheerful tragedy. It was a travesty of tragic myths by the intermixture of comic scenes. The scanty fragments of the thirty-eight plays of Rhianus do not give us any adequate idea of this kind of composition.

Rhœcus. A Greek artist of Sămŏs, about 500 b.c., inventor of brass-founding, and architect of the celebrated temple of Hēra in his native island [Herod., iii 60]. (See Architecture and Sculpture.)

Rhyt̆ŏn. A kind of drinking-horn. (*See* VESSELS.)

Rĭcĭnĭum. A covering for the head worn by the Roman women (*See* CLOTHING.)

Rings. Among the Greeks and Romans these were worn originally only as signet-rings on the fourth finger of the left hand. Among the Romans of the olden time, as among the Spartans, they were exclusively of iron. Then golden rings came in as distinguishing marks of senators and magistrates, and afterwards also of knights. It was only in the course of the imperial age that the golden signet-ring lost its original meaning, and became finally a sign of free birth, or of the privileges thereto attached. Extravagant sums were paid for ornamental rings, the value of which consisted partly in the stone itself, partly in the art displayed in the stone-cutting. Among the Greeks this kind of luxury arose at an early time; among the Romans it began only in the last years of the Republic, while it considerably increased under the Empire. Men, as well as women, used sometimes to wear rings on all their fingers.

RINGS.

Roads. The earliest levelled roads in Greece were the "sacred ways." These led to the most important religious centres, where national festivals were celebrated, such festivals also serving the purpose of public markets or fairs. In general, the Greeks set a high value on excellent and well-levelled roads, which made travelling easy. But, in the best days of Greece, only unpaved roads were known, paved roads being of comparatively late origin.

The grandest work in ancient road-making was that done by the Romans, who, mainly for military purposes, connected Rome with her newly acquired provinces by means of high-roads. They laid out their roads as far as possible in straight lines. The nature of the ground is almost entirely disregarded; where mountains intervened they were broken through, and interposing streams and valleys were spanned with bridges and viaducts.

The first Roman high-road, which, even in its present condition, is worthy of admiration, was the *Vĭă Appĭă*, so called after the censor Appius Claudius, who constructed it. It was made in B.C. 312 to join Rome to Căpŭa, and was afterwards continued as far as Brundĭsĭum. This "queen of roads," as it is called [by Statius, *Silvæ* ii 2, 12, *Appia longarum teritur regina viarum*], was a stone causeway, constructed, according to the nature of the country, with an embankment either beneath or beside it, and was of such a width that two broad wagons

(1) * VIA APPIA, NEAR ARICCIA.
(Canina, *Arch. Rom.*, tav. 183.)

could easily pass each other. [Fig. 1 shows part of this road below the village of *Ariccia*, where it runs for a considerable distance on an embankment faced with freestone, and with massive balustrades and seats on both sides, as well as vaulted openings in the basement to serve as outlets for the mountain streams.] The surface was paved with polygonal blocks of hard stone, generally basalt, fitted closely together, and so laid down that the centre of the road was at a higher level than the sides, to allow

(2) * PAVEMENT OF VIA APPIA.
(Piranesi, *Antichità di Roma*, iii 7.)

the rain-water to run off. [Fig. 2 shows the construction of the pavement.] According to a subsequent method, the

Roman roads first received a foundation of rubble or *breccia*, on which rested a layer of flat stones 8 inches thick; above this was an equally thick layer of stones set in lime, which was covered by another layer of rubble about 3 inches deep; above the rubble was laid down the pavement proper, consisting of either hard stone (*silex*) or else irregular blocks of basaltic lava.

In the time of the emperor Hadrian, the cost of constructing such a road amounted to £900 per Roman mile (about 1·5 kilom. =about ⅘ English mile). From the end of the 2nd century B.C. posts set up at distances of 1,000 paces from each other served to measure distances. (*See* MILIARIUM.)

The making and maintenance of the roads in Italy were provided for at the expense of the *ærārĭum*, or State-treasury. During the republican age the roads were under the supervision of the censors. From the time of Augustus they were under imperial officials entitled *cūrātōrēs vĭārum*. In the provinces, in general, the cost of the military roads, and indeed of all public works, was defrayed out of the provincial taxes. In the imperial provinces soldiers were also frequently employed in constructing roads. In a few cases toll was levied by special imperial permission.

Rŏbīgus, the male, **Rŏbīgo**, the female deity among the Romans who protected the corn from blight (*robigo*). On April 25th a festival called the *Rŏbīgālĭa*, supposed to have been instituted by Nŭma, was held in their honour in their grove, distant nearly five miles from Rome. The citizens marched to the spot in white festal attire, under the conduct of the *flāmen Quĭrīnālĭs*, *Robigus* having at first apparently represented only a particular function of Mars (or Quĭrīnus), as protector of the arable land. After a prayer, accompanied by offerings of incense and wine, for the preservation of the ripening seed, the *flamen* offered sacrifice with the entrails of a young sorrel dog and a sheep. Certain races were also held.

Rōma (*Dĕa Rōma*). The personification of the world-ruling city, first worshipped as a goddess by some cities of Asia Minor in the 2nd century B.C. She was represented under the image of a Tŷchē (*q.v.*), with the mural crown on her head and with all the attributes of prosperity and power. Under Augustus her cult in the Hellenic cities was united partly with that of Augustus, partly with that of the deified Cæsar, *Dīvus*

Iūlius. In Rome she was always represented in military shape, sometimes like a Mĭnerva, sometimes like an Amazon. On the obverse of silver coins she appears with a winged helmet (*see* cuts).

HEAD OF ROMA.

Between the old Forum and the Colosseum Hadrian erected a handsome double temple in honour of Roma and of Vĕnus, as ancestress of the Roman people. This was consecrated on April 21st, the day of the foundation of Rome and the festival of the *Părīlia*. (*See* PALES.) It was afterwards called the *templum urbis*. The ruins still remain. For the site, *see* plan of the Roman Fora under FORUM; for a restoration of the interior, *see* ARCHITECTURE, fig. 13.

Romance. Romantic narratives, especially of imaginary adventures of travel, appear among the *Greeks* with particular frequency after the time of Alexander the Great, owing to Greece having then been brought into contact with the East (*see* EUHEMERUS); but these are known to us only by their titles and by fragments. Such ethnographical fables form, moreover, the oldest element in the romance respecting Alexander which is preserved under the name of CALLISTHĔNĒS. By earlier writers love-stories are only incidentally introduced, although in the form of popular local legends they were disseminated in all the districts of Greece. From the time of Antĭmăchus they were adopted with particular predilection as themes for poetic treatment by the elegiac poets, especially in the Alexandrine age. There is extant a prose compilation of such legends collected from historians and poets by the poet PARTHĔNIUS in the time of Augustus.

The earliest example of prose narratives of the amatory type is the "Milesian Tales" (*Mīlēsĭăca*) of ARISTĪDĒS of Mīlētus (about 100 B.C.), which are regarded as forerunners of the later love-romances. Even in the earliest example of such a romance which is known to us (at least as to its general contents), the *Wonders beyond Thūlē* of Antonius DĬŏGĔNĒS (probably in the 1st century A.D.), there appears that combination of fantastic adventures of travel with a tale of love which is common to all the later romances, almost without exception. This branch of literature came to maturity in the age of the later Sophists, who, among their other literary exercises, wrote amatory compositions in the form of narratives and letters. We possess works of this kind by PHĬLOSTRĀTUS, ALCĬPHRŎN, and his imitator ARISTÆNĔTUS. One of the oldest of the romances which spring from this time is that of the Syrian IAMBLĬCHUS (in the 2nd century), entitled *Băbÿlŏnĭăcă*. This is extant only in an epitome. The romances of XĔNŎPHŎN of Ephesus, HĒLĬŎDŌRUS of Emĕsa, LONGUS, ACHILLES TATIUS of Alexandria, and CHĂRĬTŎN of Ephesus are extant in a complete form. Among these that of Heliodorus is distinguished for its artistic and skilful plot, and the pastoral romance of Longus for its poetical merit. The treatment of these romances is to a considerable extent sketched out in accordance with a fixed pattern, and consists of a simple multiplication of successive adventures. Two lovers are separated by untoward chances, generally robbers by land and sea; and it is only after manifold trials and wonderful experiences in slavery and in strange lands that they are finally once more united. In the pourtrayal of love they deliberately endeavour to catch the spirit of the Alexandrine elegy; the language is the artificial and affected language of the sophistic age. Such "dramas," as the later writers call them, were also frequently composed in the Byzantine period; *e.g.* by EUSTĂTHĬUS.

Among the *Romans* the earliest work of the kind was the translation of the *Milesiaca* of Aristides by Sĭsenna (about 70 B.C.); for this reason the Roman epithet for a romance is *Milesia*. The most important and the only original production is the satirical romance of manners of PĔTRŌNIUS (middle of the 1st century A.D.). This work, which is unfortunately preserved only in fragments, is of a kind which has no parallel in Greek literature. The *Mĕtămorphōsēs* of APŬLĔIUS, which are likewise of the highest value for the history of manners at the time (2nd century), and are interesting on account of the novel-like narratives inserted in them, are derived from a Greek model. Besides these works, this form of composition is still represented in extant Latin literature by the translation of the Alexander-romance of the pseudo-Callisthenes by Iūlius VĂLĔRIUS (about 200).

Similarly, the writings of the pretended DĬCTYS and DĂRĒS (4th and 5th centuries), which are examples of the literature of forgery relating to the destruction of Troy, are probably to be referred to Greek sources. Lastly, there is the wonderful history of APOLLŌNIUS of Tyre, a revised version of a Greek romance (6th century), which was much read in the Middle Ages.

Rŏrārĭi. The name given in the old Roman legion to the citizens of the lowest property-class, who were armed only with a dart and a sling. These had to open the fighting in the capacity of skirmishers, and, when the close combat began, to withdraw behind the line. In later times their place was taken by the *vēlĭtēs* (*q.v.*).

Rostra (properly the ships' prows, from *rostrum*, the iron-bound prow, *lit.* "beak," of a ship). The orators' platform in the Forum at Rome, so called because it was embellished with the bronze prows of the ships of the Latin fleet captured at Antium in 338 B.C. [Livy, viii 14]. Besides these it was also decorated with other monuments of the greatness of Rome, such as the Laws of the Twelve Tables, the *cŏlumna rostrāta* of Dŭĭlĭus, and numerous statues of men of mark. Originally it stood between the part of the Forum called the *Cŏmĭtĭum* and the Forum proper, opposite the *Cūria* [no. 18*a* in Plan *s.v.* FORUM]; but in 44 B.C. Cæsar moved it to the north end of the Forum under the Capitol [no. 6 in same Plan; *cp.* Cic., *Phil.* ix 2], and here built up part of it by the employment of the old materials. It was not completed until after his death, by Antōnius. This new platform, which was afterwards repeatedly restored, appears by the existing remains to have consisted of an erection 11 feet higher than the pavement of the Forum, about 78 feet in length, and 33 feet in depth [*Cp.* Middleton's *Remains of Ancient Rome*, 244, 246.] The front was decorated with two rows of ships' prows. The way up to the platform was at the back. This platform also was used down to the latest times of the Empire as a place for setting up honorary statues. [The *Rostra Iūlia*, so called to distinguish it from the other *rostra*, was the projecting *pŏdium* of the *hērŏŏn of Julius Cæsar*, built by Augustus, (no. 21 in plan). Affixed to this were the prows of the vessels captured at Actium: Dion Cassius, li 19 (Middleton, *l.c.*, pp. 252–8).]

Rŭdis. The wooden foil of the gladiators. (*See* GLADIATORES.)

Rūmĭna and **Rūmĭnus** [der. *rūmis* or

rūma, " a teat "]. Ancient Italian pastoral deities, who protected the suckling cattle and received offerings of milk. In Rome their sanctuary stood at the foot of the Palatine Hill, in the neighbourhood of the Lŭpercāl; in the same place was the Ruminal fig tree (probably a primitive emblem of the nurturing goddess) [the *Rūmīnă fīcus* of Ovid, *Fasti* ii 412], under which Rōmŭlus and Rĕmus were said to have been suckled by the wolf.

Rŭtīlius Lŭpus (*Lucius*). A Roman rhe-torician who composed in the time of Tiberius (14–37 A.D.) a work upon the figures of speech, abridged from a Greek treatise by the younger Gorgias. Of this work two books (*Schēmătă Lexĕōs*) have been preserved. The value of the work consists in its translations of striking passages quoted as examples, mainly from the lost speeches of the Greek orators. It was used by the anonymous author of a later *Carmen de Fĭgūris et Schēmătĭbus* in 186 hexameters.

Rŭtīlius Namātĭānus. *See* NAMATIANUS.

S

Sabāzius. A Thracian and Phrygian deity, whom the Greeks usually identified with Dīonȳsus [Diodorus, iv 4], and some-times also with Zeus. His orgiastic worship was very closely connected with that of the Phrygian Mother of the Gods, Rhea-Cȳbĕlē, and of Attis. Along with this it was intro-duced into Athens in the 5th century B.C. [Aristophanes, *Vespœ* 9, *Lysistr.* 388; De-mosthenes, *De Cor.* § 260]. In later times it was widely spread in Rome and Italy, especially in the latter days of paganism. Like many of the oriental deities, he repre-sented the flourishing life of nature, which sinks in death, always to rise again. As an emblem of the yearly renovation of nature, the symbol specially appropriated to him was the snake. Accordingly, at the celebration of his mysteries, a golden snake was passed under the clothes and drawn over the bosom of the initiated. [Clement of Alexandria, *Protrept.*, p. 6. In the *Characters* of Theophrastus, when the *superstitious man* " sees a serpent in his house, if it be the red snake, he will invoke Sabazius " (xxviii, ed. Jebb).]

Săbīnus (*Măsŭrĭus*). One of the most celebrated Roman jurists, a pupil of Atēīus Căpĭto in the time of Tiberius, and founder of the school of jurists called after him that of the *Săbīnĭāni.* (*See* ATEIUS CAPITO and JURISPRUDENCE.)

Săcellum. The Latin name for a small sanctuary, which was a mere altar, or an inclosed uncovered place with an altar, or a little temple with either an altar or an image for purposes of worship. In Rome the greater part of these sanctuaries were among the oldest and holiest places of worship.

Săcerdōs (*Mănĭus Plŏtĭus*). A Latin gram-marian, perhaps of the end of the 3rd cen-tury A.D.; wrote in Rome an *ars grammatica* in three books. The third treats of metre.

Sacra. The Latin term for all trans-actions relating to the worship of the gods, especially sacrifice and prayer. They are either *sacra prīvāta* or *publĭca.* The former were undertaken on behalf of the individual by himself, on behalf of the family by the *păter fămĭlĭās,* or on behalf of the *gens* by the whole body of the *gentīles.* The centre of the domestic service of the gods is formed by the worship of the Pĕnātēs and Lărēs. In particular cases recourse was also had to certain specified deities. Besides this, private *sacra* were attached to particular families ; these passed to the heir with the succession and became a burden on him. Hence an inheritance without *sacra* (*hērēdĭtās sĭnĕ sacris*) proverbially signi-fied an unimpaired piece of good fortune [Plautus, *Capt.* 775, *Trin.* 483]. As the family had *sacra,* so also had the *gens* (*q.v.*), which had arisen out of the family by expansion. These were performed by a sacrificial priest (*flāmen*) appointed from among the *gentīles,* the celebration taking place in his own house or in a special *săcellum* in the presence of the assembled *gentīles.* The *sacra publica* were under-taken *pro pŏpŭlo* collectively, (1) by the *cūrĭœ, pāgi,* or *vīci,* into which the com-munity was divided, whence such sacrifices were called *sacra pŏpŭlāria ;* or (2) by the individual *gentes* and societies (*see* SODA-LITAS), to which the superintendence of a particular cult had been committed by the State ; or (3) by the magistrates and priests of the Roman State. The *sacra* of the *gentes* were with few exceptions performed in public, though the multitude present remained silent spectators ; only in a few cases they took part in the procession to the place of worship or in the sacrificial feast.

Sacrāmentum. The Roman term for the

military oath of allegiance, originally the preliminary engagement entered upon with the general by newly enlisted troops [Cic., *Off.* i 11 § 36 ; Livy, xxii 38 § 2]. The oath was taken first by the legates and tribunes. These officers then administered it to the soldiers in the following manner : one soldier in each legion recited the formula of the oath, and the rest were called up by name, and, coming forward one by one, swore to the same oath with the words *ĭdem in me*, i.e. "The same (holds good) for me." The oath remained in force only till the next campaign, and whenever there was a new general a new oath was taken. After the introduction of the twenty years' service by Mărĭus (about 100 B.C.) the men raised for service took the oath, not one by one, but all together and for the whole time of service, in the name of the State, afterwards in that of the emperor.

Sacramentum in the oldest and most general form of civil lawsuit, named after it *lēgĭs actĭŏ per sacramentum*, is a deposit made beforehand by the parties in the suit. It was originally five sheep or five oxen, according to the value of the object in dispute, afterwards a sum of money at the rate of ten *assēs* for each sheep and one hundred for each ox. The deposit was given back to the successful party, while that of the loser was originally applied to religious purposes ; afterwards it went to the *ærārium*, or public treasury.

Sacrārium. The domestic chapel. (*See* HOUSE, Roman.)

Sacrifices, among the ancients, formed the chief part of every religious act. According to the kind of sacrifice offered, they were divided into (*a*) bloodless offerings and (*b*) blood offerings. (*a*) The former consisted in firstfruits, viands, and cakes of various shape and make, which were some of them burned and some of them laid on the altars and sacrificial tables (*see* figs. 1 and 2) and removed after a time, libations of wine, milk, water with honey or milk, and frankincense, for which in early times native products (wood and the berries of cedars, junipers, and bay trees, etc.) were used. Asiatic spices, such as incense and myrrh, scarcely came into use before the seventh century in Greece or until towards the end of the Republic at Rome.

(*b*) For *blood-offerings* cattle, goats, sheep, and swine were used by preference. Other animals were only employed in special cults. Thus horses were offered in certain Greek regions to Pŏseidōn and Hēlĭŏs, and at

Rome on the occasion of the October feast to Mars; dogs to Hēcătē and Rŏbīgus, asses

(1) * SACRIFICIAL TABLE
(with terminal bust of Priapus, and implements of sacrifice)
AND SACRED TREE OF DIONYSUS
(with *thyrsus* and *tympanum*).
Mural painting from Pompeii (Boetticher's *Baumcultus*, fig. 12).

(2) * SACRIFICIAL TABLE WITH OFFERINGS.
(Terra-cotta relief from Pompeii.)

to Prĭāpus, cocks to Asclēpius, and geese to Īsĭs. Sheep and cattle, it appears, could be offered to any gods among the Greeks. As regards swine and goats, the regulations varied according to the different regions. Swine were sacrificed especially to Dēmētēr and Dïonȳsus, goats to the last named divinity and to Apollo and Artĕmis as well as Aphrŏdītē, while they were excluded from the service of Athēnē, and it was only at Sparta that they were presented to Hērā. At Epĭdaurus they might not be sacrificed to Asclepius, though elsewhere this was done without scruple. [Part of the spoils of the chase—such as the antlers or fell of the stag, or the head and feet of the boar or the bear—was offered to Artĕmis Agrŏtĕrā (*see* fig. 3).]

As regards the sex and colour of the victims, the Romans agreed in general with the Greeks in following the rule of sacrificing male creatures to gods, female to goddesses, and those of dark hue to the infernal powers. At Rome, however, there were special regulations respecting the victims appropriate to the different divinities. Thus the appropriate offering for Jupiter was a young steer of a white colour, or at least with a white spot on its forehead; for Mars, in the case of expiatory sacrifices, two bucks or a steer; the latter also for Neptune and Apollo; for Vulcan, a red calf and a boar; for Līber and Mercury, a he-goat; for Juno, Mĭnerva, and Diana, a heifer; for Juno, as Lucina, an ewe lamb or (as also for Cĕrēs and the Bŏna Dĕa) a sow; for Tellūs, a pregnant, and for Proserpine a barren, heifer; and so on.

The regulations as regards the condition of the victims were not the same everywhere in Greece. Still in general with them, as invariably with the Romans, the rule held good, that only beasts which were without blemish, and had not yet been used for labour, should be employed. Similarly, there were definite rules, which were, however, not the same everywhere, concerning the age of the victims. Thus, by Athenian law, lambs could not be offered at all before their first shearing, and sheep only when they had borne lambs. The Romans distinguished victims by their ages as *lactantēs*, sucklings, and *māiōrēs*, full grown. The sacrifice of sucklings was subject to certain limitations: young pigs had to be five days old, lambs seven, and calves thirty. Animals were reckoned *maiores* if they were *bĭdentēs;* i.e. if their upper and lower rows of teeth were complete. There were exact require-

ments for all cases as regards their sex and condition, and to transgress these was an offence that demanded expiation. If the victims could not be obtained as the regulations required, the pontifical law allowed their place to be taken by a representation in wax or dough, or by a different animal in substitution for the sort

(3) * OFFERING TO ARTEMIS AGROTERA.
(From a sarcophagus in the Louvre.)

required. In many cults different creatures were combined for sacrifice: *e.g.* a bull, a sheep, and a pig (*cp.* SUOVETAURILIA), or a pig, a buck, and a ram, and the like. In State sacrifices, victims were sometimes sacrificed in great numbers; *e.g.* at the Athenian festival in commemoration of the victory at Marathon, 500 goats were slain. (*Cp.* HECATOMBE.) Human sacrifices as a means of expiation were not unknown to the earliest Greek and Roman worship, and continued in certain cases (*e.g.* at the feast of the Lycæan Zeus and of Jupiter Lătĭāris) until the imperial period; however, where they continued to exist, criminals who were in any case doomed to death were selected, and in many places opportunity was further given them for escape.

In general, it was considered that purity in soul and body was an indispensable requirement for a sacrifice that was to be acceptable to a divinity. Accordingly the offerer washed at least his hands and feet, and appeared in clean (for the most part, white) robes. One who had incurred blood-guiltiness could not offer sacrifice at all; he who had polluted himself by touching anything unclean, particularly a corpse, needed special purification by fumigation. Precautions were also taken to insure the withdrawal of all persons who might be otherwise unpleasing to the divinity; from many sacrifices women were excluded, from others men, from many slaves and freedmen. At Rome, in early times, all plebeians were excluded by the patricians.

The victims were generally decked out with ribbons and wreaths, and sometimes the cattle had their horns gilded. If the creature voluntarily followed to the altar or even bowed its head, this was considered as a favourable sign; it was an unfavourable sign if it offered resistance or tried to escape. In that case, with the Romans, the object of the sacrifice was deemed to be frustrated. Among the *Greeks* those who took part in the sacrifice wore wreaths; a firebrand from the altar was dipped in water, and with the water thus consecrated they sprinkled themselves and the altar. They then strewed the head of the victim with baked barley-grains, and cast some hairs cut from its head into the sacrificial fire. After those present had been called upon to observe a devout silence, and avoid everything that might mar the solemnity of the occasion, the gods were invited, amidst the sound of flutes or hymns sung to the lyre and dancing, to accept the sacrifice propitiously. The hands of the worshippers were raised, or extended, or pointed downwards, according as the prayer was made to a god of heaven, of the sea, or of the lower world respectively. The victim was then felled to the ground with a mace or a hatchet, and its throat cut with the sacrificial knife. During this operation the animal's head was held up, if the sacrifice belonged to the upper gods, and bowed down if it belonged to those of the lower world or the dead. The blood caught from it was, in the former case, poured round the altar, in the latter, into a ditch. In the case just mentioned the sacrifice was entirely burned (and this was also the rule with animals which were not edible), and the ashes were poured into the ditch. In sacrifices to the gods of the upper world, only certain portions were burned to the gods, such as thigh-bones or chine-bones cut off the victim, some of the entrails, or some pieces of flesh with a layer of fat, rolled round the whole, together with libations of wine and oil, frankincense, and sacrificial cakes. The remainder, after removing the god's portion, as it was called, for the priests engaged in the sacrifice, was either roasted at once for the sacrificial banquet and so consumed, or taken home. Festal sacrifices at the public expense were often combined with a public meal. Sacrifice was made to the gods of the upper air

in the morning; to those of the lower world in the evening.

Among the *Romans*, as among the Greeks, reverent silence prevailed during the sacrificial operations; in case a careless word should become an evil omen, and to prevent any disturbance by external surroundings, a flute-player played and the offerer of the sacrifice himself veiled his head during the rite. The prayer, formulated by the *pontĭfĭcĕs*, and unintelligible to the priests themselves from its archaic language, was repeated by the votary after the priest, who read it from a written form, as any deviation from the exact words made the whole sacrifice of no avail. As a rule, the worshipper turned his face to the east, or, if the ceremony took place before the temple, to the image of the divinity, grasping the altar with his hands; and, when the prayer was ended, laid his hands on his l'ps, and turned himself from left to right (in many cults from right to left), or, again, walked round the altar and then seated himself. Then the victim, selected as being without blemish, was consecrated, the priest sprinkling salted grains of dried and pounded spelt (*mŏlă salsa*) and pouring wine from a cup upon its head, and also in certain sacrifices cutting some of the hairs off its head, and finally making a stroke with his knife along the back of the creature, from its head to its tail. Cattle were killed with the mace, calves with the hammer, small animals with the knife, by the priest's attendants appointed for the purpose, to whom also the dissection of the victims was assigned. If the inspectors of sacrifice (*see* HARUSPEX) declared that the entrails (*exta*), cut out with the knife, were not normal, this was a sign that the offering was not pleasing to the divinity; and if it was a male animal which had been previously slaughtered, a female was now killed. If the entrails again proved unfavourable, the sacrifice was regarded as of no avail. On the other hand, in the case of prodigies, sacrifices were offered until favourable signs appeared. In other sin-offerings there was no inspection of entrails. Sin-offerings were either entirely burned or given to the priests. Otherwise the flesh was eaten by the offerers, and only the entrails, which were roasted on spits, or boiled, were offered up, together with particular portions of the meat, in the proper way, and placed in a dish upon the altar, after being sprinkled with *mola salsa* and wine. The slaughter of the victim took place in the morning, whilst the *exta* were offered at evening, the intervening time being taken up by the process of preparation.

Sæcŭlārēs Lŭdī (properly *Lŭdī Tĕrentīnī* or *Tărentīnī*). The " Secular Games " arose from some gentile sacrifices of the Valerian family, which were offered to the gods beneath the earth at the *Terentum* (or *Tarentum*), a spot in the Campus Martius where a volcanic fire smouldered. The first celebration of the *Ludi Terentini* of which there is actual evidence took place 249 B.C., by the direction of the Sibylline books, in honour of Dīs and Proserpine. Owing to the vow then made, to repeat them at the beginning of every *sæcŭlum*, or period of one hundred years, they were called the " Secular Games." Like all cults prescribed by the Sibylline books, they are of non-Roman origin, being, in fact, borrowed from the Etruscans, who at the conclusion of a mean period of 100 years, reckoned according to the longest human life in a generation, used to present an expiatory offering on behalf of the new generation to the gods beneath the earth. The games seem to have been next held, not in 149, but in 146; the one following was omitted on account of the Civil Wars, and the games were not held again until the time of Augustus, in 17 B.C. [It was for this occasion that Horace wrote his *Carmen Sæcŭlāre*.] The date was fixed by a reckoning different from that hitherto followed, by taking 110 years as the normal standard of the *sæculum*. In later times sometimes the new reckoning was adopted, sometimes the old ; as early as Claudius we have a return to the old, and in 47 A.D. that emperor celebrated with secular games the 800th year of Rome. Similarly the years 900 and 1000 of the city were celebrated. The ritual order of the games, which Augustus only altered by the introduction of Apollo, Diana, and Lātōna among the deities worshipped, was as follows : At the beginning of the season of harvest, heralds invited the people to the festival, which none had ever seen, nor would see again ; and the commission of fifteen, which was charged with the due celebration of all festivals enjoined by the Sibylline books, distributed the means of expiation, consisting of torches, sulphur, and pitch, to all free persons on the Capitol and in the Palatine temple of Apollo. At the same time in the temple of the Capitoline Jupiter, in that of the Palatine Apollo, and in that of Diana on the Aventine, wheat, barley, and beans were handed to the people for an offering of firstfruits. At the feast

proper, which lasted three days and three nights, the emperor upon the first night sacrificed to the Parcæ three rams, which were completely burnt up, upon three altars at the *Terentum*. This was accompanied by the burning of torches and the chanting of a hymn. At the same place, and on the same or the following day, a black hog and a young pig were offered to Tellus, and dark-coloured victims to Dis and Proserpine. On the first day white bulls were sacrificed to Jupiter, and a white cow to Juno on the Capitol, after which scenic games were held in honour of Apollo. On the second day the matrons prayed to Juno on the Capitol ; on the third, a sacrifice of white oxen took place in the Palatine temple of Apollo, while twenty-seven boys and the same number of maidens sang the *carmen sæculare* in Greek and in Latin.

Săgitta. Arrow. (*See* BOWS.)

Săgittārĭī. The bowmen in the Roman armies. These were generally raised by levy or furnished by the allies. The Cretan, Balearic, and Asiatic bowmen were specially celebrated.

Săgum. The military cloak of the Roman soldiers, which consisted of a four-cornered piece of cloth worn over the armour and fastened upon the shoulder by a clasp. It was a symbol of war, as the *tŏga* was the symbol of peace.

Sălācĭa. A Roman goddess of the salt water. She was identified with the Greek Amphitrītē, and regarded as the wife of Neptune.

Sălārĭum. A Roman term signifying properly the allowance of salt which the governor furnished for the magistrates and officers who formed his retinue ; then the gratification in money which took the place of the salt. Under the Empire it was the pay of the imperial magistrates, as well as of the physicians and professors in the service of the State.

Sălĭī (" dancers "). An old Italian college of priests of Mars ; said to have been introduced at Rome by Nŭma and doubled by Tullus Hostīlius. The earlier college was called the *Salii Pălātīni*, and the later the *Salii Agōnālēs* or *Collīni*. The former derived their name from their *cŭrĭa* on the Palatine Hill ; the latter, from the Colline Gate, near which stood their sanctuary on the Quirinal. Both colleges consisted of twelve life-members of patrician family, and recruited their numbers from young men, whose parents were required to be still living ; at their head was a *măgister*, a *præsul* (leader in the dance), and a *vātēs* (leader in the song). The cult of the *Palatinę Salii* had to do with Mars, that of the *Colline* with Quīrīnus; but the chief connexion of both was with the holy shields, *ancīlia*. (*See* ANCILE with cut.) The chief business of the Salii fell in March, the beginning of the campaigning season. On March 1st they began a procession through the city, each of them dressed in an embroidered tunic, a bronze breastplate, and a peaked helmet, girt about with a sword, with one of the holy shields on the left arm, and in the right hand a staff, while trumpeters walked in front of them. At all the altars and temples they made a halt, and, under the conduct of the two leaders, danced the war-dance in three measures, from which they take their name of Salii or "dancers," accompanying it by singing certain lays, beating their shields meanwhile with the staves. Every day the procession came to an end at certain appointed stations, where the shields were kept over the night in special houses, and the Salii themselves partook of a meal proverbial for its magnificence [Horace, *Odes* i 37, 2]. Until March 24th the *ancilia* were in motion; within this time some special festivities, were also held, in which the Salii took part. On March 11th there was a chariot-race in honour of Mars (*Equīrĭa*) and a sacrificial feast in honour of the supposed fabricator of the shields, Māmūrĭus Veturius: on the 19th was the ceremony of the cleansing of the shields, and on the 23rd the cleansing of the holy trumpets (*tŭbæ*) of the priests, called the *tŭbĭlustrĭum*. The days on which the *ancilia* were in motion were accounted solemn (*rēlĭgĭōsi*), and on these days men avoided marching out to war, offering battle, and concluding a marriage. In October, the close of the campaigning season, the *ancilia* were once more brought out, in order to be cleansed in the Campus Martius. The lays of the Salii, called *axāmenta*, were referred to Numa, and were written in the archaic Saturnian verse, and in such primitive language, that they were scarcely intelligible even to the priests themselves, and as early as the beginning of the 1st century B.C. were the object of learned interpretation. [Quintilian i 6 § 40. Two or three connected bits of these lays have come down to us (Allen's *Remnants of Early Latin*, p. 74). The most intelligible is the following, in a rude Saturnian measure:

|| *Cumé tonds, Leucésie,* | *præ tet tremónti,* ||
Quom tibei cúnei | *déxtumúm tonáront;* ||

i.e. *Cum tŏnas, Lucetie* (thou god of light), *præ te trĕmunt, cum tĭbĭ cŭnĕī* (bolts of lightning) *a dextrā tŏnŭĕrunt.*] Besides Mars, other deities, such as Janus, Jupiter, and Minerva, were invoked in them; the invocation of Mamurius Veturius formed the close [Ovid, *Fasti*, iii 260 ff.]. After the time of Augustus the names of individual emperors were also inserted in the lays

Sallustius Crispus (*Gaius*). The celebrated Roman historian, born 86 B.C., of a plebeian family, at Amīternum, in the land of the Sabines. After a youth spent in excesses, in 52, he made, as tribune of the people, a most violent attack on Cicero, the defender of Milo and the senatorial party. By the censors of the year 50 he was turned out of the Senate, ostensibly for immorality, but really on political grounds, because he was a partisan of Cæsar. By the latter he was made quæstor in 49, and thereby reinstated in his senatorial rank. An expedition to Illyria, the conduct of which had been committed to him by Cæsar, after the battle of Pharsālus, miscarried. He was more successful in 47 as proprætor in Africa, where Cæsar committed to him the province of Numidia, with the title of *proconsul*. Here he was guilty of such extortions, that it was only by the favour of Cæsar that he escaped a condemnation. The treasures thus acquired enabled him to lay out the magnificent gardens known by his name on the Quirinal, and to devote his life entirely to learned pursuits, as, in consequence of the murder of Cæsar, he had withdrawn from all political activity. His two earliest productions, on the Catilinarian Conspiracy (the *Bellum Cătĭlīnæ*) and on the Jugurthine War (*Bellum Iŭgurthīnum*) are preserved complete. Of his most important work, the five books of *Histŏrĭæ*, only four speeches, two letters, and a series of fragments have come down to us. His work, after a survey of the earlier times, contained a short description of the civil war between Mārĭus and Sulla, and then a detailed history from 78 to 67. The other writings ascribed to him—two letters to Cæsar about the reorganization of the State (*Epistŭlæ ad Cæsărem de Rēpublĭcā*) and a *Declāmātĭō in Cĭcĕrōnem*—are rhetorical fabrications of a later time.

Sallust is undoubtedly the first artistic historian among the Romans. He deals not with the mere narration of events, but also with the explanation of their inner meaning. His model is Thucydides, whom he strives to imitate, not only in his love of truth and his impartiality, but also in the general plan of his works, especially in the interweaving of speeches in order to characterize situations and persons, as well as in his phraseology, which is often brief and compressed even to obscurity. To literary form he paid more attention than was given by any Roman historian before him. In his language he purposely diverged from the ordinary language of the time, especially by closely imitating the style of the elder Cato. This mannerism of style, as well as the inconsistency between his earlier life and the censorious moral rigour displayed in his writings, drew upon him severe criticism, even among his contemporaries. Nevertheless his works have always had a high reputation.

Salmōneūs. Son of Æŏlus, husband of Alcĭdĭcē, and father of Ty̆rō (*see* NELEUS). He founded Salmōnē in Elis, whither he had migrated from Thessaly. He usurped the name and the sacrifices of Zeus. He even imitated thunder and lightning by trailing dried skins and caldrons behind his chariot and flinging torches into the air. For this reason Zeus slew him with the lightning, and destroyed his town together with its inhabitants. His second wife, Sĭdērō, had ill-treated her step-daughter Tyro, and was therefore slain by Tyro's sons, Pĕlĭās and Nēlēŭs, at the altar of Hēra, where she had taken refuge.

Salpinx. The Greek name for the long trumpet, like the Roman *tŭba*, with which the signals were given in the army. It was also employed in religious ceremonies. (*See* cut.)

SALPINX.

Sălŭs. The personification of health and prosperity among the Romans. As goddess of health, she was identified with the Greek Hy̆gʹĭeĭă (*q.v.*), the daughter of Asclēpius, and represented in the same way. As the deity representing the welfare of the Roman people (*Sălus Pŭblĭca Pŏpŭli*

Rōmāni) she had from the year 302 B.C. a temple on the Quirinal. Under the Empire, she was also worshipped as guardian goddess of the emperors (*Salus Augusta*). Prayers were frequently made to her by the priestly colleges and the political bodies, especially at the beginning of the year, in times of sickness, and on the birthdays of the emperors. As her counterpart among the Sabines, we have the goddess *Strēnĭa*. (*See* STRENÆ.)

Sălūtātĭō. The morning greeting which Romans of rank were in the habit of receiving from clients, friends, and admirers in the *ātrĭum* during the first two hours of the day; for this purpose the callers gathered in the vestibule even before sunrise. [Martial, iv 8: *prĭma sălūtantēs atque altĕra contĭnet hora;* Pliny, *Ep.* iii 12, *officia antēlūcāna.*]

Sambūca (Gr. *sambȳkē*). A triangular, stringed instrument resembling a harp, having a piercing tone. When played, its pointed end stood downwards.

Samnis. *See* GLADIATORES.

Sancus. Usually called *Sēmo Sancus* (*see* SEMONES). A genius worshipped by the Sabines, Umbrians, and Romans, representing holiness and good faith in human life. In Rome, he was principally worshipped under the name *Dĕus Fĭdĭus* (from *fĭdēs,* "faith") as god of oaths, god of the public laws of hospitality and of nations, also of international intercourse and of the safety of the roads, which were placed under his protection. An oath in his name could be taken only under the open sky; therefore even his temple had a hole in the roof, and, when an oath by him was taken at home, the man swearing went into the uncovered court. On account of many points of resemblance he was identified with Hercules. He had a temple on the Quirinal (the foundation of which was celebrated June 5), and another on the island in the Tiber [Ovid, *Fasti*, vi 213–218].

Sandălĭum. A Greek covering for the foot, principally worn by women, consisting of a thick sole of wood, cork, or leather, with a strap carried over the foot in front of the socket of the great toe, passed between this and the second toe, and tied to the other bands fastened to the edge of the sole before and behind. The back was supported by strap-work, which was often very neatly intertwined above the ankles. (*See* cuts.)

Soles of the more simple kind were bound underneath the foot by a strap running crosswise over the instep, or by two straps fastened to the side-edges and tied together in a knot or by a clasp. Soles were also worn, which were provided with a close-fitting piece of leather at the heel and with a piece of leather, sometimes narrow, sometimes broad, at the sides. These last were so laced together by straps round the ankles, that the toes and the flat of the foot remained uncovered. (*Cp.* SOLEA.)

SANDALS OF VARIOUS KINDS.

(1) & (5) *Museo Pio-Clement.* iv tav. viii, xiv. (3) *Museo Borbonico,* **x**, liii.
(2) Winckelmann, *Opere,* tav. lii. (4) Clarac, *Musée,* v 848, no. 2139.

Sapphō. The greatest poetess of antiquity, born at Mȳtĭlēnē or Erĕsus in Lesbŏs, lived between 630 and 570 B.C., being a younger contemporary of Alcæus (*see* cut). She was married to a rich man of Andrŏs, and had a daughter named Claïs. About 596 she was obliged to flee from Lesbos, probably in consequence of political disturbances, and to remain some time in Sicily. In

* SAPPHO AND ALCÆUS.

"*Dark-haired, pure, and sweetly smiling Sappho,*
Fain would I say something, save that shame prevents me."
—ALCÆUS, fragm. 55, Bergk.

(Terra-cotta relief from Melos, British Museum.)

her later years she was again living in Lesbos, in the society of young girls with an inspiration for poetry. (*See* ERINNA.) Although, according to the principles expressed in her own poems, and according to trustworthy testimonies of antiquity, she was a woman of pure and strict life, yet later scandal unwarrantably put an immoral interpretation on this society. Equally unfounded is the legend emanating from the Attic comedians, that she threw herself from the Leucadian rock into the sea out of despair at the rejection of her love by a handsome seaman named Phāŏn {fragm. of Menander's *Leucadia*}.

Her poems were divided by the Alexandrine scholars into nine books according to their metres; and besides the purely lyric songs, among which the *Epĭthălămĭa*, or wedding-lays, were particularly celebrated, they included elegies and epigrams. Two of her odes, with a number of short fragments, are still extant. Her odes were for the most part composed in the metre named after her the *sapphic strŏphē* (or stanza), which was so much used by Horace. They are among the tenderest and most charming productions in the whole range of extant Greek literature, and afford some perception of the points of excellence ascribed to Sappho by antiquity: sincerity and depth of feeling, delicacy of rhythm, and grace and melodiousness of language.

Sărāpĭs. *See* SERAPIS.

Sarcŏphăgus. Properly *lĭthŏs sarcŏphăgŏs,* a kind of stone (alum-slate) found near Assŏs, in the district of Trŏăs in Asia Minor; so called because it had the peculiar property, that all corpses laid in it were completely consumed in forty days, with the exception of the teeth. [*Cp.* Pliny, *N. H.* ii 211.] Usually coffins were only inlaid with it in order to hasten decomposition. Then the name is given generally to any stone-coffin, such as those which were customary among Greeks and Romans, among the latter particularly after the 2nd century A.D. (*Cp.* SCULPTURE, and for a

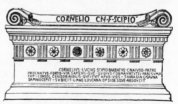

SARCOPHAGUS OF L. CORNELIUS SCIPIO BARBATUS.
(Rome, Vatican Museum.)

specimen *see* MUSES.) The cut represents the sarcophagus of L. Cornēlius Scipio Barbātus, consul 298 B.C., great-grandfather of the elder Scipio Africanus, of the 3rd century B.C. It is made of common stone, and is the only example remaining from the old Roman time.

Sărissa. The thrusting-lance of the Macedonian hoplites (*see* PHALANX) and light cavalry, which in the time of Philip and Alexander was 18 feet long, afterwards 14 ; from this lance the light cavalry were called *sărissŏphŏri* (sarissa-bearers).

Sarpēdōn. According to Homer, son of Zeus and Lăŏdămīa and grandson of Bel-lĕrŏphōn ; like his cousin Glaucus (*q.v.*, 4), a prince of the Lycians and ally of Priam. At the storming of the Greek camp he, in company with Glaucus, was the first upon the enemy's wall ; on his falling by the hand of Patroclus, a fearful battle arose over his body, until Apollo, by the command of Zeus, rescued the disfigured corpse from the Greeks, and, after washing it and anoint-ing it with ambrosia, had it carried through the air to Lycia by the twin brothers Sleep and Death [Homer, xvi 419–683]. Later writers describe him as a son of Zeus and Eurōpa, and brother of Mīnōs ; driven out by the latter, he won for him-self a lordship in Lycia, and lived there by the favour of Zeus for three generations.

Satire (Lat. *sătira*, older form *sătūra*). The word properly denotes a medley of heterogeneous things, and in particular a kind of dramatical farce, which consisted of a mixture of speech, song, music, and dancing. (*See* FESCENNINI.)

Before the rise of an artistic type of Roman drama, these farces were performed on festive occasions by itinerant minstrels, the representation taking place upon the public stage erected at Rome in 390 B.C. After the introduction of the Greek drama by Līvĭus Andrŏnīcus, 240 B.C., the *sătūrœ* sank to the position of after-pieces (*exŏdĭa*) which were improvised by masked Roman youths after the conclusion of the performance proper ; in this shape they lasted until they were entirely supplanted by the *Atellānœ*. As an artistic composi-tion the *satura* is wholly undramatical, and designates in the first instance a col-lection of miscellaneous pieces of poetry of heterogeneous contents and metres ; in this form it seems to have been first introduced into literature by ENNIUS. A definite impress, fixing its character for all future time, was given to the *satura* in the 2nd century B.C. by LŪCĪLĬUS, who made it essentially what we now under-stand by satire, and is therefore designated

by Horace [*Sat.* ii 1, 62] as the inventor of this branch of literature. Even his satires, as may be gathered from the fragments that survive, were of a very miscellaneous char-acter, as regards matter and as regards form. All possible aspects of the life of the time were made the objects of a discus-sion, which might be serious, jocular, or censorious, as occasion required. It was composed in the form sometimes of an essay, sometimes of a letter, sometimes of a dia-logue, and in the conversational style in vogue at the time. In his earlier poems he made use of various metres, afterwards almost exclusively of the hexameter. The significant example of Lucilius invited emu-lation all the more, because the prosaic and didactic element in satire was in the most thorough accordance with the Roman char-acter and poetical capacities. Accordingly a number of imitators are mentioned reaching down to the end of the Republic, though, in the judgment of Horace, their endeavour to attain the level of their model was a vain one [*Sat.* i 10, 47]. A revival and develop-ment answering to the more refined taste of the time was given to the Lucilian *satura* by Horace, who, however, confined himself to social and literary life, and used the hexameter alone. In the latter respect his example was followed by PERSIUS and JUVENAL ; but these treated the contrast between the ideal and the actual, which provokes the satire, not with the humour of Horace, but with bitterness and severity.

An ancient (or pre-Lucilian) style of *satura* was revived towards the end of the Republic by the "most learned of the Romans," Tĕrentius VARRO, with his *Menippean Satires*, in which, following the example of the Cynic Mĕnippus of Gădăra, he treated serious subjects in humorous fashion and in a mixed form of prose and poetry. This mixed form was also adopted in the time of Nero by PĔTRŎNIUS in his satirical romance of manners, and by SĔNĔCĂ in his satire on Claudius, as well as in later times by the emperor JULIAN in his *Cœsărĕs*, written in Greek.

The satire is a thoroughly Roman species of poetry [Quintilian, x 1 § 93: *Satura quidem tota nostra est*] ; for though there is much in the poetry of the Greeks which, in regard to subject-matter, corresponds in some degree to the satire, still they were never able to produce a literature of this kind stamped with a definite character of its own, and described by a distinctive name.

Sătūra. See SATIRE.

Sāturnālĭa. A Roman festival in honour of Saturnus (*q.v.*).

Sāturnus ("the sower"). An ancient Italian god of seedtime and harvest, with a sickle as symbol; husband of Ops, father of Pīcus. In later times he was identified with the Greek Krŏnŏs, who, thrust out by Zeus, came across the sea to Latium, was received by Jānus, settled as king on the Capitoline Hill (as it was called in after times), brought agriculture and its blessings to the people, and subsequently disappeared. His reign was regarded as the golden age of Italy. At the foot of the Capitoline Hill a temple, built by the last Tarquin on the site of a very ancient altar, was dedicated to him and to his wife Ops. Under this temple was the Roman treasury (*œrārium Saturni;* No. 4 in plan, *s.v.* FŏRUM). Except during his festival, his statue was, throughout the year, wound round the feet with woollen fillets. People offered sacrifices to him with uncovered head, according to the Greek rites. His own festival, the *Sāturnālĭa,* took place on December 17, and consisted of sacrifices in the open air in front of the temple and also of an outdoor banquet, at which the senators and knights appeared, after laying aside the *tŏga* for a loosely fitting gown called *synthĕsĭs.* After the feasting, they separated with the cry, "*Io Saturnalia!*" The festival was also celebrated in private society; schools had holidays, law-courts were closed, all work was stopped, war was deferred, and no punishment of criminals took place for seven days from December 17 to 23. During that time there were all kinds of fantastic amusements. The festival was symbolical of a return to the golden age. People gave presents to one another, in particular wax tapers (*cērĕi*) and dolls (*sĭgillārĭa*). They also entertained one another, and amused themselves with social games; in particular, they gambled for nuts—the symbol of fruitfulness. Every freedom was given to slaves, and they were first entertained at the banquet and served by their masters, in remembrance that under the rule of Saturnus there had been no differences in social rank.

Satyric Drama. One of the three varieties of the Attic drama. Its origin may be traced back to Prātīnās of Phlīūs (about 500 B.C.). It is probable that, after settling in Athens, he adapted the old dithyramb with its chorus of Satyrs, which was customary in his native place, to the form of tragedy which had been recently invented in Athens. This new kind of drama met with so much approval, and was so much developed by Pratinas himself, as well as by his son Aristĕās, by Chœrĭlus, by Æschўlus, and the dramatists who succeeded him, that it became the custom to act a satyric drama after a set of three tragedies. The seriousness of the preceding plays was thus relieved, while the chorus of Satyrs and Sīlēni, the companions of Dĭonўsus, served to indicate the original connexion between that divinity and the drama. The material for a satyric drama, like that for a tragedy, was taken from an epic or legendary story, and the action, which took place under an open sky, in a lonely wood, the haunt of the Satyrs, had generally an element of tragedy; but the characteristic solemnity and stateliness of tragedy was somewhat diminished, without in any way impairing the splendour of the tragic costume and the dignity of the heroes introduced. The amusing effect of the play did not depend so much on the action itself, as was the case in comedy, but rather on the relation of the chorus to that action. That relation was in keeping with the wanton, saucy, and insolent, and at the same time cowardly, nature of the Satyrs. The number of persons in the chorus is not known, probably there were either twelve or fifteen, as in tragedy. In accordance with the popular notions about the Satyrs, their costume consisted of the skin of a goat, deer, or panther, thrown over the naked body, and besides this a hideous mask and bristling hair. The dance of the chorus in the satyric drama was called *sĭcinnĭs,* and consisted of a fantastic kind of skipping and jumping. The only satyric play now extant is the *Cyclops* of Eurīpĭdēs. The Romans did not imitate this kind of drama in their literature, although, like the Greeks, they used to have merry after-pieces following their serious plays. (*See* EXODIUM.)

Satyrs. In Greek mythology, spirits of the woodland, in the train of Dĭonўsus, with puck noses, bristling hair, goat-like ears, and short tails. They are depicted as wanton, cunning, and cowardly creatures, and always fond of wine and women. They dwell in woods and on mountains, where they hunt, and tend cattle, dance and frolic with the Nymphs (for whom they lie in ambush), make music with pipe and flute, and revel with Dĭonўsus. Their own special dance is called *sĭcinnĭs.* They were considered as foes to mankind, because they played people all kinds of roguish pranks, and frightened them by impish tricks. The hare, as a wanton, cowardly, and amorous

(1) * COPY OF THE SATYR (OR FAUN) OF PRAXITELES.
(Rome, Capitoline Museum.)

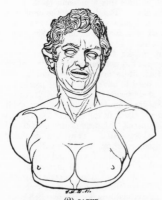

(2) SATYR.
(*Fauno colla macchia*, Munich, Glyptothek, No. 99.)

creature of the woodland, was their appropriate symbol.

In art and poetry they gained a higher significance, owing to the festivals of Dionysus. (*See* SATYRIC DRAMA.) In early art they are represented for the most part as bearded and old, and often very indecorous. As time went on, they were represented as ever younger and more graceful, and with an expression of amiable roguishness (*see* cuts). [The artist who led the way in this transformation was Praxĭtĕlēs. The statue of the Satyr which Pausanias (i 20 § 1) saw at Athens, in the Street of Tripods, is generally supposed to be the original from which the statue in the Capitoline Museum and many others of the same type are derived. "In the *Satyr of Praxiteles* all that is coarse and ugly in form, all that is mean or revolting in expression, is purged away by the fire of genius. Of external marks of his lower nature nothing is left but *the pointed ears and the arrangement of the hair over the forehead*, which is a reminiscence of the budding horns of the goat" (Perry's *Greek and Roman Sculpture*, p. 437). (*See* fig. 1.)

(3) YOUTHFUL SATYR WITH THE INFANT DIONYSUS.
(Naples, Museum.)

The Satyr represented in fig. 2 was regarded by Winckelmann as, in point of execution, one of the most beautiful works of ancient art.] (*Cp.* SILENUS.)

Sauroctŏnŏs ("lizard slayer"). A special name of Apollo (*q.v.*).

Scēnē (Lat. *scæna*). The stage. (*See* THEATRE.)

Scepticism. A philosophical school founded by Pyrrho of Elis (about B.C. 365–275), which refused to acknowledge that truth was obtainable by the perception of the senses and the cognisance of the mind. In literature it is chiefly represented by the physician Sextus Empīrĭcus. (*Cp.* PHILOSOPHY.)

Schĕrĭā. The mythical island of the Phæacians (*see* PHÆACES), identified with the historic Corcȳra.

Schools. *See* EDUCATION.

Scīrītæ. A body of light infantry in the Spartan army, consisting of the *pĕrĭœci* (*q.v.*) of the district Scirītis.

Scīrōn. A robber who lived on the boundary between Mĕgără and Attĭca, and compelled the travellers, whose goods he had seized, to wash his feet, only in order to kick them into the sea, where an immense tortoise devoured their dead bodies. He was slain by the youthful Thēseus (*q.v.*).

Scīrŏphŏrĭă. An Athenian festival celebrated on the 12th of the month *Scĭrŏphŏrĭōn* (June–July), called after it. It was in honour of Athēnē, who was worshipped under the name of Scīrăs near Scīrōn, a spot on the "holy way" leading from Athens to Eleusis. It had its name from the large white sunshade (*scĭrŏn*) beneath which the priestess of Athene (the patron goddess of the city), the priest of Erechtheus, and the priest of Hēlĭŏs went to Sciron to sacrifice. The sunshade was a symbol of heavenly protection against the rays of the sun, which began to burn more intensely during the month of the festival. This protection was invoked with special reason, for the dry limestone rock was thinly covered by a meagre surface of soil in the neighbourhood of Athens, and particularly near Sciron itself. In this, as in other festivals of invocation, there were also expiatory offerings; and hence they carried in the procession the hide of a ram that had been sacrificed to Zeus as the mild and gracious deity (*meilĭchĭŏs*).

Scŏlĭă. Short lyrical poems, usually consisting of a single *strŏphē*, which were intended to be sung after dinner over the wine. The ancients ascribed their invention to Terpander, and they received their first development among the Lesbians, and were written by such masters of song as Alcæus, Sappho, Praxilla, Tīmŏcrĕōn, Sīmŏnĭdēs, and Pindar. The last mentioned, however, gave them a more artistic form, with several strophes, in accordance with the rules of Dorian lyric verse. This class of poetry found a congenial home in the brilliant and lively city of Athens, where, to the very end of the Peloponnesian War, it was the regular custom at banquets, after all had joined in the *pœān*, to pass round a lyre with a twig of myrtle, and to request all guests who had the requisite skill to sing such a song on the spur of the moment. To judge from the specimens that have been preserved, their contents were extremely varied: invocations of the gods, gnomic sayings, frequently with allusions

to common proverbs and fables, and the praises of the blessings and pleasures of life. The most famous *scŏlĭŏn* was that of a certain Callistrătus on Harmŏdĭus and Aristŏgītōn, who had killed the tyrant Hipparchus, son of Pīsistrătus. It consists of four strophes, but the last three are only variations of the first.

Scŏpās (of Părŏs). One of the most celebrated Greek sculptors. With Praxĭtĕlēs, he stood at the head of the later Attic school, in the first half and towards the middle of the 4th century. He was also an architect, and in his younger days superintended the reconstruction of the temple of Athēnē at Tĕgĕa, which had been burnt down in 394 B.C. The groups in the two pediments, representing the chase of the Calydonian boar and the combat of Achilles and Tēlĕphus, were executed by his hand, or at any rate under his direction. [Pausanias viii 45 §§ 4–7. The exact site of this temple was ascertained in 1879, and fragments of the sculptures in the pediments were discovered during the excavations. They include the heads of two youthful heroes, and the mutilated head of the Calydonian boar.] In conjunction with other artists he executed in 350 the designs on the sepulchre of Mausōlus. (*See* MAUSOLEUM.) His most important work, a group with numerous figures, representing Achilles being conducted to the island of Leucē, and including Pŏseidōn, Thĕtĭs, Achilles, and Tritons and Nereids riding on sea monsters, afterwards ornamented the temple of Neptune near the Circus Flāmĭnĭus in Rome [Pliny, *N. H.* xxxvi 26]. In Pliny's time [xxxvi 28] there was doubt as to whether the group of Niobids (*see* NIOBE) in the Roman temple of Apollo Sŏsĭānus was the work of Scopas or of Praxiteles. The number of single statues, especially of gods and demigods, by his hand, which were known to the ancients, was very great. Among these was the Apollo placed by Augustus in the temple on the Palatine, clothed in a long robe, with a crown of bay-leaves on his head, sweeping the chords of his lyre [Pliny, xxxvi 25; Propertius, ii 31, ll. 5, 16]; the colossal seated figure of Arēs in the temple built by Brutus Gallæcus near the Circus Flaminius [Pliny, § 26]; the nude statue of Aphrŏdītē in the same temple [*ib.*]; and the frenzied Mænad [*Anthologia Græca* i 74, 75; iii 57, 3]. The influence of some of these works has been traced in copies and imitations that are still extant. [Thus, the *Mœnad* is supposed to have supplied the type for such representations as that exemplified in the gem of Agāvē (*q.v.*) with the head of Pentheus.]

Scorpĭō. A kind of engine for projectiles, in earlier times identical with the catapult, and in later times with the *ŏnăger.* (*See* ARTILLERY.)

Scrībæ (writers). The highest class among the inferior paid officials at Rome (*see* APPARITOR). They did not perform ordinary writers' services, which were usually assigned to slaves, but occupied the position of clerks, registrars, accountants, and secretaries. Of special importance were the *scribæ quæstŏrĭi* attached to the *trĭbūni ærārĭi.* They formed three commissions of ten members each, and kept the accounts of the treasury. Two of their number were also attached to each provincial quæstor as accountants. The *scribæ* also of the different ædiles and tribunes appear to have formed a commission of ten members, while those taken from among them by the consuls, prætors, and censors seem to have been employed only during their term of office. The *pontĭfĭcēs* also had their *scrībæ.*

Scrībōnius Largus. A Roman physician who accompanied the emperor Claudius to Britain in 43 A.D. Between that year and 48 he compiled a treatise on medicine (*Compŏsĭtĭōnēs Mĕdĭcāmentōrum*), which we possess in a somewhat imperfect form. It contains 271 prescriptions, arranged according to the parts of the body, from the head downwards.

Scrīptōrēs Histŏrĭæ Augustæ. The name given to the six authors of biographies of the Roman emperors, united at an uncertain date into a single collection. The biographies extend from Hadrian to Numerian, 117–284 A.D. (with the exception of the years 244–253). Of the six biographers, *Ælĭānus Spartĭānus, Volcātĭus Gallĭcānus,* and *Trĕbellĭus Pollĭō* wrote under Diocletian; *Flāvĭus Vŏpiscus Sўrācūsius, Ælius Lamprĭdius,* and *Julius Cāpĭtŏlīnus* under Constantius Chlōrus and Constantine the Great. The biographies are merely dry compilations from the lost writings (1) of Mărĭus Maxĭmus (who at the beginning of the 3rd century, under Alexander Sĕvērus, continued the work of Suetōnĭus by writing the lives of the emperors from Nerva to Ēlăgăbălus) ; and (2) of his contemporary Jūnius Cordus, who wrote biographies of the less famous emperors. In spite of their deficiencies in style and spirit, they are of value as authorities for history.

Sculpōnĕa. The wooden shoe of the Roman peasants and slaves.

Sculpture. The origin of painting as an art in Greece is connected with definite historical personages. That of sculpture is lost in the mists of legend. It was regarded as an art imparted to men by the gods; for such is the thought expressed in the assertion that the earliest statues fell from heaven. The first artist spoken of by name, DÆDĂLUS, who is mentioned as early as Homer, is merely a personification of the most ancient variety of art, that which was employed solely in the construction of wooden images of the gods. This is clearly proved by his name (= "the cunning artificer "). To him were attributed a series of inventions certainly separated far from each other in respect of time and place, and embracing important steps in the development of wood-carving and in the representation of the human form. Thus he is said to have invented the saw, the axe, the plummet, the gimlet, and glue [Pliny, *N. H.* vii 198], to have been the first to open the eyes in the statues of the gods, to separate the legs, and to give freer motion to the arms, which had before hung close to the body [Diodōrus iv 76]. After him the early school of sculptors at Athens, his reputed native city, is sometimes called the school of Dædalus [Pausanias v 25 § 13]. During a long residence in Crete he is said to have instructed the Cretans in making wooden images (*xŏănă*) of the gods [*ib.* viii 53 § 8].

The invention of modelling figures in clay, from which sculpture in bronze originated, is assigned to the Sicyonian potter BŪTĀDĒS at Corinth [Pliny, xxxv 151]. The art of working in metals must have been known early in Greece, as appears from the Homeric poems [esp. *Il.* xviii 468–608, "the shield of Achilles "]. An important step in this direction was due to GLAUCUS of Chios, who in the 7th century B.C. invented the soldering of iron [Herodotus, i 25 ; Pausanias, x 16 § 1], and the softening and hardening of metal by fire and water [Plutarch, *De Defectu Orac.* 47]. The discovery of bronze-founding is attributed to RHŒCUS and THĔŎDŌRUS of Sămŏs about 580 [Pausanias, viii 14 § 8]. The high antiquity of Greek sculpture in stone may be inferred from a work of the very earliest period of Greek civilization, the powerful relief of two upright lions over the gate of the castle at Mycēnæ. (*See* ARCHITECTURE, fig. 2.)

Sculpture in marble, as well as in gold

and ivory, was much advanced by two famous "pupils of Dædalus," DĪPŒNUS and SCYLLIS of Crete, who were working

ATHENE. PERSEUS. PEGASUS. MEDUSA.

(1) * PERSEUS CUTTING OFF THE HEAD OF MEDUSA.
Metope from Selinus (Museum, Palermo).

in **Argos** and Sĭcўōn about 550 B.C. [Pliny,

(3) * THE HARPY MONUMENT AT XANTHUS.

xxxvi §§ 9, 14; Pausanias, ii 15 § 1, 22 § 5], and founded an influential school of art in the Peloponnesus. [This school included Hēgўlus and Thĕoclēs (Pausanias, vi 19 § 8, 17 § 2); Dontas and Dŏrўcleidās (*ib.*, vi 19 § 12, v 17 § 1); Clĕarchus of Rhēgium (iii 17 § 6); Tectæus and Angĕlīōn (ii 32 § 5, ix 35 § 3).] Among their works are recorded not only statues of gods, but also of heroes, often united in large groups. Some conception of the artistic productions of this period may be formed from scattered monuments still extant, originating in different parts of the Greek world; *e.g.* the rude and more primitive

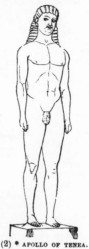

(2) * APOLLO OF TENEA.
(Munich, Glyptothek.)

metopes of Sĕlīnūs in Sicily (fig. 1); the statues of Apollo from the island of Thērā and from Tĕnĕā, near Corinth (fig. 2); the reliefs on the Harpy Monument from the acropolis of Xanthus in Lycia (figs. 3 and 4), etc. These works, in spite of their archaic stiffness, show an effort after individual and natural expression, though the position of the foot in striding, with the sole completely touching the ground, and the unemotional and stony smile on the mask-like face, are common to all. Even after Greek sculpture had mastered the representation of the human body, not

(4) * RELIEF FROM THE HARPY MONUMENT.
(British Museum.)

only at rest, but also in the most violent movement, it still continued unable to overcome the lifeless rigidity of facial expression. This is seen in the Trojan battle-scenes (date about 480) on the Æginetan pediments. Here the figures are represented in every variety of position in the fight, and depicted, not indeed with any ideality, but with perfect mastery even to the smallest detail; whereas the faces are entirely destitute of any expression appropriate to their situation. (*See* fig. 5, and the *West Pediment* under ÆGINETAN SCULPTURES.) The athletic forms in which the Æginetan heroes are represented indicate another important extension of the sphere of artistic representation. From about 544 B.C. it had become usual to erect statues of the victors in the athletic contests, Olympia especially abounding in these. [Ol. 59; Pausanias, vi 18 § 7; the statues there mentioned are of wood.] By this innovation the art was freed from the narrow limits to which it had been confined by the traditions of religion, and led on to a truer imitation of nature. In this department the school of Ægina was specially active, attaining its highest perfection in the bronze statuary of GLAUCĬAS, CALLŎN, and above all ŎNĀTĀS (500–460).

(6) **MARBLE COPY OF MYRON'S** *DISCOBOLUS.*
(Rome, Palazzo Massimi.)

Sculpture in bronze flourished simultaneously in the Peloponnesus at SĬCȲŎN under CĂNĂCHUS [for a supposed copy of his Apollo *see* CANACHUS] and his brother ARISTŎCLĔS, the founder of a school which lasted long after, and at Argos under ĂGĔLĀDĀS, the teacher of Phīdĭās, Mȳrŏn, and Pŏlȳclītus. The transition to the period of the finest art is represented by CĂLĂMIS of Athens, PȲTHĂGŎRĀS of Rhēgium, and especially MȲRŎN, another Athenian, in whom the art attained the highest truth to nature, with perfect freedom in the representation

(5) * **THE DYING HERO OF THE EASTERN PEDIMENT OF THE**
TEMPLE OF ATHENE, ÆGINA.
(Munich, Glyptothek.)

of the human body, and was thus prepared for the development of ideal forms.

This last step was taken at Athens, in the time of Pericles, by PHIDĬĀS. In his creations, particularly in his statues of the gods, whether in bronze or in ivory and gold, he succeeded in combining perfect beauty of form with the most profound ideality, fixing for ever the ideal type for Zeus and Athēnē, the two deities who were pre-eminently characterized by intellectual dignity. (*See* ATHENE, ZEUS, and PARTHENON, figs. 4 and 5.) For one of his heroic subjects *see* fig. 7.

Of the pupils of Phidias the two who worked most nearly in the same spirit were AGŎRĂCRĬTUS and ALCĂMĒNĔS, the author of the sculpture of the western pediment of the temple of Zeus at Olympia, part of which still remains. The perfection of Attic art at this time can be realized when we consider that, with all their beauty of execution, the extant marble sculptures of the Parthĕnōn, Thēsēum, Erechthĕum, and the temple of " Wingless Victory" must be regarded as mere productions of the ordinary workshop [as compared with the lost masterpieces of Phidias]. The school of Phidias had rivals in the naturalistic school which followed Myron, including his son LȲCĬUS and CRĒSĬLĀS of Cȳdōnĭa. [For a supposed copy of his *Pericles, see* CRESILAS.] Independent of both schools stood PÆŎNIUS of Mendē, whose *Victory,* as well as part of his sculptures on the east pediment of the temple of Zeus at Olympia, are still extant [*see* PÆONIUS and OLYMPIAN

GAMES (fig. 1)]; and CALLĬMĂCHUS, the "inventor" of the Corinthian order of architecture [Vitruvius, iv 1 § 10] and of the ap-

contemporary PŎLȲCLITUS, whose colossal gold and ivory statue of the Argive Hēra directly challenged comparison with the

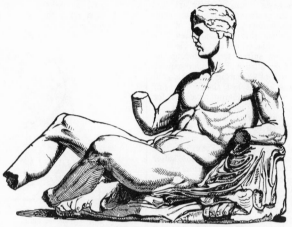

(7) * THESEUS.
From the west pediment of the Parthenon; also identified as either an Athenian river-god (*Ilissus* or *Cephisus*) or *Olympus.*
(British Museum.)

plication of the auger to working in marble [Pausanias, i 26 § 6]. Another school of

(8) * FARNESE DIADUMENUS OF POLYCLITUS.
(British Museum.)

sculpture in opposition to that of Athens was founded at Argos by Phidias' younger

works of Phidias in its materials, its ideality, and its artistic form, and established the ideal type of that goddess. He mainly devoted himself, however, to work in bronze, the department in which Argos had long been pre-eminent; and made it his aim to exhibit the perfection of beauty in the youthful form (fig. 8). He also established a *cānŏn* or scheme of the normal proportions of the body. Of his pupils the chief was *Naucȳdēs* of Argos.

As in the first period of Greek sculpture, represented by Myron, Phidias, and Polyclitus, the schools of Athens and Argos held the first rank beyond dispute, so it was also in the second period, which embraces the 4th century down to the death of Alexandei the Great. Athens, moreover, during this period remained true to the traditions of Phidias, and still occupied itself mainly with the ideal forms of gods and heroes, though in a spirit essentially altered. The more powerful emotions, the more deeply stirred passions, of the period after the Peloponnesian War were not without their influence on art. The sculptors of the time abandoned the representation of the dignified divinities of the earlier school, and turned to the forms of those deities whose nature gave room for softer or more emotional expression, especially Aphrŏdītē and Dĭŏnȳsus and the circle of gods and dæmons who surrounded them. The highest aim of their art was to pourtray the profound pathos of the soul, to give expression to the play of the emotions. With this is connected the preference of this school for marble over bronze, as more suited for rendering the softer and finer shades of form or expression. The art of executing work in gold and ivory was almost lost, the resources of the States no longer sufficing, as a rule, for this purpose. The most eminent of the New Attic school weɾᵌ Scŏpās of Părŏs and Praxĭtĕlēs of Athens. Scopas, also famous as an architect, was a master of the most elevated pathos. Praxiteles was no less masterly in regard to the softer graces in female or youthful forms, and in the representation of sweet moods of dreamy reverie. In his statues of Aphrodite at Cnĭdus and Erŏs at Thespiæ he established ideal types for those divinities. The Hermes with the infant Dionysus, found at Olympia, remains as a memorial of his art

(9) THE *HERMES WITH THE INFANT DIONYSUS* OF PRAXITELES.
(Olympia.)

(fig. 9). Of the productions of this school (in which the names of Bryæus, Lĕŏchărēs, and Tĭmŏthĕus, who was joined with Scopas in his work on the Mausŏlēum at

Halicarnassus, ought also to be mentioned) an opinion may be formed from the spirited reliefs on the choragic monument of Lȳsĭcrătēs (*q.v.*) at Athens. We have also extant, in a copy, the Niobid group (*see*

(10) NIOBE.
(Florence, Uffizi.)

Niobe), concerning the original of which it was much disputed, even in ancient times, whether the author were Scopas or Praxiteles [Pliny, xxxvi 28]. In contrast to the ideal aims of Attic art, the Sicyonian school still remained true to its early naturalistic tendencies and to the art of sculpture in bronze, of which Argos had so long been the home. At the head of the school stood one of the most influential and prolific artists of antiquity, Lȳsippus of Sĭcȳŏn. His efforts were directed to represent beauty and powerful development in the human body (fig. 11). Hence Hērăclēs, as the impersonation of human physical strength, was pourtrayed by him oftener, and with more success, than any other deity, and his type fully established. Lysippus was most prolific as a portrait sculptor, a branch of art which had been much advanced in the invention by his brother Lȳsistrătus of the method of taking plaster casts of the features [Pliny, xxxv 153].

After Alexander the Great the practice of the art, which had thus developed to perfect mastery of *technique*, began to deteriorate with the general decay of the countries of Greece proper, and to give place to the flourishing artistic schools of Asia Minor and the neighbouring islands. The characteristic of this period is the rise of a method of treatment which strives after effect. Instead of the *naïveté* of earlier times we get a certain deliberate calculation of a theatrical type, a tendency to make the exhibition of technical skill an

(11) THE *APOXYOMENOS* OF LYSIPPUS.
(Marble Copy, Vatican.)

end in itself. The most productive school was that of *Rhodes*, at the head of which stood a pupil of Lysippus, CHĂRĒS of Lindus, who designed the famous Cŏlossus of Rhodes, the largest statue of ancient times. Two well known extant works in marble proceeded from this school, the group of *Lăŏcŏŏn* (*q.v.*) and his sons, by AGĒSANDER, ATHĒNŎDŌRUS, and PŎLȲDŌRUS, found at Rome in 1506, now one of the chief treasures of the Vatican Museum, and the *Farnese Bull* at Naples. This last group, by APOLLŌNIUS and TAURISCUS of Trallēs, represents the revenge of Zēthus and Amphīōn on Dircē (*see* cut under DIRCE), and is the largest extant antique work which consists of a single block of marble. Both these are admirable in skill and *technique*, embodying with the greatest vividness the wild passions of a moment of horror; but the theatrical effect and the exhibition of technical skill are unduly exaggerated. [To the Rhodian school is conjecturally assigned the fine group representing Mĕnĕlāus bearing the body of Patroclus, several imperfect copies of which are still extant (fig. 12). It is sometimes, however, regarded as one of the later products of the same school as the group of Niobe, and assigned to

the early part of the 3rd century B.C. (Friederichs - Wolters, *Gipsabgüsse*, no. 1397.) The *Pasquino* at Rome is probably the original of the copy in the Vatican and of both of those in Florence.]

The second in rank of the schools of this period was that at *Pergămŏn*, where the sculptors Isŏgŏnus, Phȳrŏmăchus, Strătŏnīcus, and Antĭgŏnus celebrated in a series of bronze statues the victories of the kings Eumĕnēs I (263–241) and Attălus I (241–197) over the Gauls. There are still extant, at Venice, Rome, and Naples, single figures from a magnificent offering of Attalus, which stood on the Acropolis at Athens, and consisted of groups of figures illustrating the conflict between the gods and the Giants, the battle of the Athenians and Amazons, the fight at Marathon, and the destruction of the Gauls by Attalus. Other masterpieces of the school are the work popularly called the *Dying Gladiator*, now identified as a Gallic warrior, who has just stabbed himself after a defeat (fig.

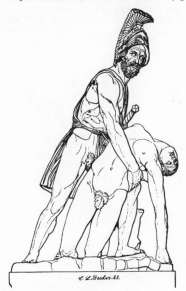

(12) * MENELAUS BEARING THE BODY OF PATROCLUS.

13), and the group in the Villa Ludovisi, called *Pœtus and Arria*, which really represents a Gaul killing his wife and himself. But the most brilliant proof of

their powers is furnished by the reliefs of
the battle of the Giants from the acropolis
at Pergamon. This work—brought to light
by Humann in 1878, and now at Berlin

To Greek art in *Egypt* belong the types
of Isis and Harpŏcrătēs, and the fine reclining figure of the river-god Nilus, with
sixteen charming boys playing round him.

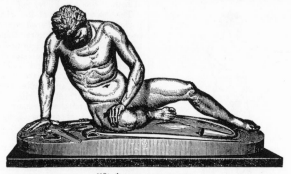

(13) * THE DYING GAUL.
(Rome, Capitoline Museum.)

—is among the most important artistic
products of antiquity. (*See* PERGAMENE
SCULPTURES.) To this period may also
be referred with certainty the original of
the celebrated *Belvedere Apollo*, which

The artistic activity of the kingdom of
the Sĕleucĭdæ in *Syria* is represented by
Eutўchĭdēs, a pupil of Lysippus, and his
famous *Tўchē*, a work in bronze representing the presiding destiny of the city

(14) APOLLO BELVEDERE.
(Rome, Vatican.)

(15) * TYCHE OF ANTIOCH.
Marble statuette (Rome, Vatican).

probably had reference to the rescue of
the temple of Delphi from the Gallic army
in B.C. 280, which was supposed to be the
work of the god (fig. 14).

of Antioch on the Orontēs [Pausanias, vi 2
§ 6; *see* fig. 15].

After the subjugation of Greece by the

Romans in the middle of the 2nd century, Rome became the headquarters of Greek artists, whose work, though without novelty in invention, had many excellences, especially in perfect mastery of *technique*. Of the artists of the 1st century B.C. and the early imperial times the following are worthy of mention: APOLLŌNIUS of Athens (*Belvedere torso of Hercules* at Rome), GLŸCŌN (*Farnese Hercules* at Naples, *see* cut, *art.* HERACLES), and CLĒŎMĒNĒS (*Venus de' Medici* at Florence), though the works of all these are more or less free reproductions of the creations of earlier masters; also AGĀSĪĀS of Ephesus, sculptor of the *Borghese Gladiator* in the Louvre at Paris, a very fine work in the spirit of the Pergamene school (*see* cut under AGASIAS).

In the same period PĀSĪTĔLĒS, an Italian Greek of great versatility, attempted a regeneration of art on the basis of careful study of nature and of earlier productions. This movement in favour of an academic eclecticism was continued by Pasiteles' pupil, STĔPHĂNUS, who has left us a youthful figure (*Villa Albani*), and Stephanus' pupil MĔNĔLĀUS, the artist of the fine

(16) * ORESTES AND ELECTRA.
(Rome, Villa Ludovisi.)

group called *Orestes and Electra* (fig. 16). There was a revival of Greek art in the first half of the 2nd century A.D. under Hadrian, when a new ideal type of youthful beauty was created in the numerous

representations of the imperial favourite Antĭnŏus (*see* cut under ANTINOUS).

The artistic work of the *Romans* before the introduction of Greek culture was under *Etruscan* influence. The art of that people was chiefly displayed in pottery and the closely connected craft of bronze-founding, which they developed with great technical skill and for which they had a special predilection. They not only filled their towns with quantities of bronze statues, Volsĭnĭi alone containing about 2,000 at the time of its conquest by the Romans in 265 B.C. [Pliny, xxxiv 34], but provided Rome also for a long time with works of the kind. Judging from the extant monuments, such as the *Mars of Todi* at the Vatican, the *Boy with a Goose under his Arm* at Leyden, and the *Robed Statue of Aulus Mĕtellus* at Florence, the character of their art seems wanting in freedom of treatment and in genuine inspiration. After the conquest of Greece, Greek art took the place of Etruscan at Rome; and, thanks to the continually increasing love of magnificence among the Romans, which was not content with the adornment of public buildings and squares, but sought artistic decoration for private dwellings, a brisk activity in art was developed, whereof numberless extant works give evidence. Beside the Greek influence, to which we owe many copies of the masterpieces of Greek art gradually accumulated in Rome, a peculiarly Roman art arose. This was especially active in *portrait sculpture*.

Portrait statues were divided, according as they were in civil or military costume, into tŏgātæ and lŏrĭcātæ or thŏrācātæ (lŏrīca=thŏrax, a coat of mail). To these were added in later times the so-called *Achillēæ*, idealized in costume and pose [Pliny, xxxiv §§ 8, 118]. It was customary to depict emperors in the form of Jupiter or other gods, and their wives with the attributes of Juno or Venus. Of the innumerable monuments of this description special mention is due to the statue of Augustus in the Vatican (fig. 17); the marble equestrian statues of Balbus and his son at Naples (found at Herculaneum); the bronze equestrian statue of M. Aurēlius on the square of the Capitol at Rome; the seated statues of Agrippina the elder in the Capitoline Museum, and the younger at Naples.

Hand in hand with portrait sculpture went the art of *historical reliefs*. In ac-

cordance with the realistic spirit of Rome,
as opposed to the Greek custom of idea-
lizing persons and events, this department
strove to secure the greatest possible

(17) * PORTRAIT STATUE OF AUGUSTUS.
Found in 1863.
(Rome, Vatican.)

accuracy and truth. The most important
works of the kind are the reliefs on the
Arch of Titus (*see* cut under TRIUMPH);
those on the Arch of Constantine, taken
from the Arch of Trajan (*see* cut under
TRIUMPHAL ARCHES); and those on the
columns of Trajan and M. Aurelius (*see*
cut under ARCHITECTURE, ORDERS OF, p.
58 *b*). Roman historical sculpture is seen
already on its decline in the reliefs of the
Arch of Septīmĭus Sĕvērus (203 A.D.), and
the decline is complete in those of the
Arch of Constantine. A subordinate branch
of relief sculpture was employed on the
sarcŏphăgi common from the 2nd century
A.D. The subjects of these reliefs are rarely
taken from events in the man's actual life,
they are most usually scenes from legends
of Greek gods or heroes, often after compositions of an earlier period, and accordingly showing a Greek character in their
treatment. (*See* cut under MUSES.)

Materials. White marble was the
material chiefly employed: in the earlier
times of Greek art, the local kinds, in
Attica particularly the Pentelic, which is
"fine in grain and of a pure white"
(Middleton's *Rome in* 1888, pp. 11, 12).

From the 4th century on that of Părŏs
was preferred. [This is a very beautiful
marble, though of a strongly crystalline
grain; it is slightly translucent.] It was
used in Roman times in preference to the
similar marble of Luna (*Carrara*), a "marble
of many qualities, from the purest white
and a fine sparkling grain like loaf sugar,
to the coarser sorts disfigured with bluish-
gray streaks." (*ib*). It was sometimes
used for columns in Rome. The marble
of Hymettus "appears to have been the
first foreign marble introduced into Rome.
It resembles the inferior kind of Luna
marble, being rather coarse in grain and
frequently stained with gray striations"
(*ib.*). Coloured marble first became popular under the emperors; *e.g.* black for
Egyptian subjects (statues of Isis), red for
Dĭŏnȳsus, Satyrs, and others in his train.
To the same period belongs the use of
striped and spotted kinds of marble,
coloured alabaster, porphyry, and granite.
Different colours of stone were also combined (*e.g.* drapery of black marble or
porphyry).

A noteworthy peculiarity of ancient
sculpture, as also of architecture, is the
habit of embellishing all kinds of marble
work by the application of colours (*Polychromy*), which is known from references
in ancient writers. [Plato, *Rep.* 420 C,
speaks of "painting statues." Plutarch,
De Gloria Athen. 348 F, mentions "dyers"
of statues side by side with gilders and
encaustic painters. Lastly, Pliny, xxxv
133, states that Praxiteles owned he was
much indebted to the *circumlĭtĭŏ*, or touching up, of his works by the painter Nĭcĭās.]
It is also attested by traces still present
on many works. [Thus the straps of the
sandal of the *Hermes* of Praxĭtĕlēs still
show traces of red and gold; and the
statues at Pompeii, especially those of late
date, are in many cases coloured, especially
certain parts of the drapery. The accompanying cut (fig. 18) introduces us into the
studio of an artist engaged in embellishing with paint a terminal statue of Hermes.
The original sketch in colours lies on the
ground, and she is pausing to examine her
work, which is also watched with interest
by two bystanders. (*Cp.* Treu, *Sollen
wir unsre Statuen bemalen?* Berlin, 1884.)
Wood and pottery were always painted. [It
is sometimes supposed that] even sculptures intended for the adornment of buildings, *e.g.* metopes and friezes, not only
had painted backgrounds (generally blue or

red), but were themselves richly adorned with colouring. [It is also held that] originally, even the bare parts of stone figures were painted; afterwards a coating of wax was thought enough [Vitruvius, vii 9]. In particular statues, many artists coloured only the characteristic parts, fringes of garments, sandals, armour, weapons, snoods or head wrappings, and of the parts of the body the lips, eyes, hair, beard, and nipples. Probably the cheeks, too, received a light reddish tinge; but all was done with discretion. The colours chiefly used were red, blue, and yellow, or gilding. The employment of different materials for the extremities, and for the drapery, also produced the effect of colouring. Similarly metal-sculpture secured variety of colour by the application of gold, silver, and copper to the bronze. The sparkle of the eyes was often represented by inlaid precious stones or enamel. Particular parts in marble statues, such as attributes, weapons, implements, were also made of metal. [There are examples of this in the pediments of Ægīna and in the frieze of the Parthĕnōn. Under the Empire metal was sometimes used for the drapery. Thus the Braschi Antĭnŏus in the Vatican was formerly draped in bronze.]—On ancient *stone-cutting*, see GEMS; on *terracottas*, see POTTERY; on working in *metal*, see TOREUTIC ART.

Scŭtum. The large wooden shield of the Roman legionaries. (*See* SHIELD.)

Scȳlax. Of Cărȳanda in Caria. He undertook, at the command of the Persian king Darius Hystaspis, about 510 B.C., a voyage to explore the coast of Asia from the Indus to the Red Sea, and composed a report of his voyage, which is now lost. His name is erroneously attached to a description, composed before the middle of the 4th century B.C., and preserved only in a corrupt and incomplete form, of a voyage from the northern Pillar of Hercules along the European coast of the Mediterranean, through the Hellespont and Bospŏrus, round the shores of the Euxine, then along the Asiatic and African coast of the Mediterranean to the southern Pillar of Hercules, and out beyond it to the island of Cernē.

Scylla. (1) In Homer, daughter of Crătæïs; a terrible monster of the sea, with a loud bark like that of a young dog, twelve shapeless feet, and six long necks, each of them bearing a horrid head with three rows

of teeth closely set. Her lower half lies in a dark cavern, which is in the middle of a rock, smooth of surface, not to be climbed, and rising up into the clouds; while with her heads she fishes for dolphins, sea-dogs, and the larger animals of the sea. If a ship come too near to her, with each of her six heads she snatches up a man of the crew, as from the ship of Ŏdysseus. Oppo-

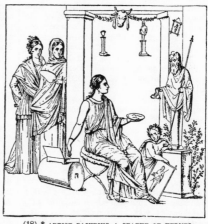

(18) * ARTIST PAINTING A STATUE OF HERMES.
(Mural painting from Pompeii; Naples Museum.)

site her, a bow-shot off, is a lower rock with a wild fig tree on it, and under it the whirlpool of Chărybdis, which three times in the day sucks in the sea and discharges it again in a terrible whirlpool, against which even the help of Pŏseidōn is unavailing. Whoever tries to avoid one of the two evils falls a prey to the other [Homer, *Od.* xi 85–110]. In later times Scylla and Charybdis, the position of which is left uncertain by Homer, were supposed to be placed in the Strait of Messina, Scylla being identified with a projecting rock on the Italian side. She was also made a daughter of Phorcys and of Hĕcătē Crătæïs. When Hērăclēs, as he is passing by, is robbed by her of one of Gērȳon's oxen, he slays her in her cavern; but her father burns her corpse, and thus recalls her to life. According to another myth, she was originally a beautiful princess or sea Nymph, loved now by Zeus, now by Poseidon or Glaucus or Trītōn, until she was changed by the jealousy of her rivals, Hēra, Amphitrītē, or Circē, into a monster, imagined as a maiden above, but as ending below in the body of a fish, begirt with hideous dogs.

(2) Daughter of Nīsus (*q.v.*).

Scyllis. A Greek sculptor, from Crete, who worked about the middle of the 6th century B.C. in Argos and Sĭcўŏn, and who, with his countryman Dĭpœnus, founded an influential school of art in the Peloponnesus [Pliny, *N. H.* xxxvi 9, 14; Pausanias, ii 15 § 1, 22 § 5]. (*See* SCULPTURE.)

Scymnus. A Greek geographer, from Chios, author of a lost description of the earth. There has been wrongly attributed to him a fragment of a description of the earth composed in iambic *sēnārĭ*, describing the coast of Europe from the Pillars of Hercules to Apollōnĭa in Pontus. The unknown author lived in Bīthўnĭa, and dedicated his work, which is composed from good sources, but in a somewhat pedantic tone, to king Nĭcŏmēdēs, probably Nicomedes III (91–76 B.C.).

Scўphus (Gr. *skўphŏs*). A bowl-shaped cup. (*See* VESSELS.)

Scўtălē. A staff, used especially in Sparta by the ephors for their secret despatches to officials, particularly to commanders, in foreign countries. A narrow strip of white leather was wound about a round staff so that the edges came exactly together; it was then written on crosswise, and sent to its destination after being unrolled again. What had been written could only be read when the strip was again wound round an exactly similar staff, such as was given to every official when going abroad on public service.

Scythians (Gr. *Skŭthai*). A corps of archers amongst the Athenians, formed of State slaves, who performed the duties of police and were also employed in war. (*See further* SLAVES, I, *at end.*)

Seats. *See* CHAIRS.

Secretary. *See* GRAMMATEUS and SCRIBÆ.

Secular Games. *See* SÆCULARES LUDI.

Sĕcūtor. *See* GLADIATORES.

Sĕdŭlius (*Cælius*). A Christian poet of the second half of the 5th century; he died young. At first he wrote secular poetry, but afterwards composed a poem in five books on the miracles of Christ (*Carmen Paschălĕ*), a simple narrative following the gospels, in many points imitating Vergil. This was followed by a prose version (*Opus Paschale*), laboured and bombastic in style; also by an elaborate comparison of the Old and New Testaments in fifty-five couplets, and a hymn to Christ in twenty-three quatrains of iambic dimeters, remarkable for the partial employment of rhyme as a musical element. The verses commence with the successive letters of the alphabet. [Portions of this hymn have always been in use in the Church of Rome. We quote the first two stanzas:

> *A solis ortus cardine*
> *ad usque terræ limitem,*
> *Christum canamus Principem,*
> *ortum Maria Virgine.*
>
> *Beatus Auctor sæculi*
> *servile corpus induit;*
> *ut carne carnem liberans*
> *ne perderet quos condidit.*]

Seer. *See* MANTIKE.

Seisachtheia (lit. "shaking off of burdens"). The term used for the removal of the burden of debt effected by Solon. All debts were cancelled, and the securing of debts upon the person of the debtor was made illegal. [Aristotle's *Constitution of Athens*, 6.] (*See* SOLONIAN CONSTITUTION.)

Sĕlēnē. The Greek goddess of the moon, daughter of the Titan Hўpĕrīŏn and Theia, sister of Hēlĭŏs and Eŏs. She was

PHOSPHORUS. OCEANUS. HESPERUS.

✻ SELENE.

(Roman altar in the Louvre, Paris.)

described as a beautiful woman with long wings and golden diadem, from which she shed a mild light [Homeric Hymn xxxii 7], riding in a car drawn by two white horses or mules or cows. The horns of the latter symbolised the crescent moon. In later times she was identified with Artĕmis (or else with Hĕcătē and Persĕphŏnē), as was Hēlĭŏs with Phœbus Apollo, and therefore was herself called *Phœbē*. After this she was also regarded as a huntress and archer, recognisable by her crescent as the goddess of the moon. She was worshipped on the days of the new and full moon. She bore to Zeus a daughter Pandīa, worshipped at Athens with her father at the festival of Pandīa [Dem., *Or.* 21 § 9]. On her love for Endȳmĭŏn, *see* ENDYMION.

Sella. A seat. On its use as a *chair* and a *litter*, *see* those articles.

Sella Cŭrūlis. The Latin term for the chair of office belonging to the curule magistrates (consuls, prætors, curule ædiles, dictator, *măgister ĕquĭtum*, and *flāmen Dĭālis*), and also to the emperors. It was of ivory, without a back, and with curved legs, like those of a camp-stool, so arranged that it could be folded up. The seat was of plaited leather straps. The curule magistrates sat on this seat while engaged in all official business, and also took it with them in war.

Selli. *See* DODONA.

Sĕmĕlē. Daughter of Cadmus and Harmŏnĭa, beloved of Zeus. Hēra, jealous of her, took the form of her nurse Bĕrŏē, and induced her to obtain of Zeus a solemn promise to fulfil her wish, and then to request him to show himself to her in all his divine splendour. When Zeus appeared amid thunder and lightning, Semele was consumed by the flames, and, dying, gave birth to a six months' child, Dĭonȳsus, whom Zeus saved from the fire and hid in his thigh till the due time of birth. Her son, on being made a god, raised her up from the world below, and set her in the heavens under the name of *Thȳŏnē*. *See* DIONYSUS; and for Dionysus and Semele *see* MIRRORS.

Sĕmentīvæ Fērĭæ. A festival of seed-time, celebrated in honour of Tellūs (*q.v.*).

Semnæ. A name of the Erīnȳĕs (*q.v.*).

Sĕmōnēs. The Latin name for certain supernatural beings. They appear to have been, like the *Lărēs*, a kind of *Gĕnĭĭ*, or demigods, and guardian deities of the State. [The word has often been connected with *se-*, to sow (cp. *sē-mĕn*); and would thus mean "sowers."] On *Semones* and *Semo Sancus*, *see* SANCUS.

Semprŏnius Asellĭŏ. A Roman annalist. (*See* ANNALISTS.)

Senate (*sĕnātŭs*, from *sĕnex*, an old man). The Roman State council, consisting in the earliest times of one hundred members, but before the expulsion of the Tarquins increased to three hundred, which for a long time remained its normal number. Originally none but patricians (*patrēs*) were eligible for membership; but (if tradition may be trusted) in the time of the last kings, plebeians, especially those of equestrian rank, were admitted, and on this account the senators were called by the collective title of *patres* (*et*) *conscripti*.

Under the Republic the plebeians were eligible for membership from the outset, though they only acquired by degrees the right to wear the distinguishing dress. The election of senators (*lectio senatūs*) rested during the regal period as a rule with the king and the *cūrĭæ;* during the Republic, at first with the consuls, afterwards with the censors, who also had power to expel unworthy members; otherwise, the office was held for life. Admission to the Senate could be claimed by the curule magistrates, who, after laying down their office, possessed the right of expressing their opinion in the Senate (*iŭs sententĭæ dīcendæ*) until the next census, at which the censors could only pass them over on stating special grounds for so doing. Next to these were considered the claims of the plebeian ædiles, the tribunes, and the quæstors, who lost this right with the expiration of their office, and the most wealthy class of citizens, the knights, who, however, if they had not yet been elected to any office, took a lower rank under the name of *pĕdārĭī*, and were only entitled to express their assent to the opinion of others. When the quæstors also were regularly added to the Senate, the minimum age legally qualifying for membership was fixed at twenty-eight years. In course of time a legal claim to admission was gained by the tribunes and plebeian ædiles, and finally also by the quæstors, through the enactment of Sulla, who increased the Senate by the number of three hundred knights elected by the people, and conferred on the quæstors, now increased to twenty, the right of admission to the Senate immediately after the expiration of their office. Cæsar raised the number of senators to 900, and under the triumvirs it even rose beyond 1,000. Augustus, however, limited it to 600, fixed the senatorial age at twenty-five, and enacted as a necessary qualification the possession of property worth at least one million sesterces (£10,000). Under the Empire a yearly list of the senators was published by the emperor. Prominent Italians and provincials gradually obtained admission, though at a later time only on condition of investing a certain part of their property in land in Italy. The first rank among the senators was taken by those who had held a curule magistracy, the last by those who had never filled any office at all. The title of *princeps senatūs* was bestowed on the member set by the censors at the head of the list, usually an ex-censor, and always, it would appear, a patrician. His only privilege was that he was the first to be asked by the presiding officer to declare his opinion. From Augustus onwards the emperor for the time being was *princeps senatus* [though the title of *princeps* was independent of this position].

The distinguishing dress of members of the Senate was the *tŭnĭca lātĭclāvia*, an under-garment with a broad purple stripe, and a peculiar kind of shoe (*see* CALCEUS). Among various other privileges enjoyed by senators was the right to a front seat in the theatre and at the games. Besides the senators themselves, their wives and children had several special privileges and distinctions, particularly under the Empire.

The right of summoning the Senate (*vŏcātĭō*) was in early times held by the king; at the beginning of the Republic, only by the consuls and the extraordinary magistrates, such as *interrex*, *dictātor*, and *măgister ĕquĭtum;* later, by the tribunes of the people and the prætors also; later still, only with the consent or at the command of the consuls ; but, under the Empire, this restriction was removed. The emperor also had power to summon the Senate. It was convened by the voice of a herald or by the issue of a public placard; but, under the Empire, when (after the time of Augustus) meetings were regularly held on the Kalends and Ides, such notice was only given in the case of extraordinary meetings. Every senator was bound to attend, or to give reason for his absence, under penalty of a fine. Under the Empire, senators of more than sixty years of age were excused from compulsory attendance. When important business was before the Senate, no senator was allowed to go to a distance from Rome; special leave had to be obtained for a sojourn out of Italy. There

was no number fixed as the *quorum* necessary for passing a resolution. Augustus attempted to enforce the presence of two-thirds of the members, but without success. Under the later Empire seventy, and finally only fifty, formed a *quorum*. Meetings of the Senate were not subject to the distinction between *dĭēs fasti* and *nĕfasti*. (*See* FASTI.) As a rule, they could be held on any day on which the presiding magistrates were not otherwise engaged. No valid resolution could be passed before sun-rise or after sun-set. The meetings always had to be held in some place consecrated by the augurs, called a *templum*. Originally the meeting-place was the *Vulcānāl*, a place consecrated to Vulcan, above the *cŏmĭtĭum* in the Forum; later, after the time of Tullus Hostīlĭus, it was the *Cūrĭa* (*q.v.*). Meetings were also held, at the choice of the magistrates that summoned them, in other consecrated places as well, in particular, the temples of the gods ; they were held outside the city, in the temple of Apollo and Bellōna on the *Campus Martius*, when business was to be conducted with magistrates who were still in possession of the military command, and consequently were not allowed to enter the city, or with foreign ambassadors whom it was not wished to admit within the walls.

Meetings were usually held with open doors. Admission without special leave was allowed to magistrates' servants, and, until the second Punic War, and later also after Augustus, to senators' sons over twelve years of age. The senators sat on benches, the officials summoning the meeting on a raised platform, the consuls and prætors on their *sella cŭrūlis*, and the tribunes on their special benches. Before opening the assembly the official summoning it had to sacrifice a victim and take the auspices in his own house. Augustus introduced the custom of the senators offering prayer one by one at the altar of the god in whose temple the meeting took place. In the *Curia Iūlia* [16 in plan under FORUM] there were an altar and statue of Victory set up for this purpose. Business was opened by the summoning official, who brought before the meeting the matter to be discussed. This was called *rĕlātĭō*. When the business of the meeting had been duly settled, it was open to the other magistrates present to bring forward fresh matters for discussion. At regular meetings under the Empire, the consuls had precedence in bringing forward business, unless it was claimed by the emperor, who could also, at an extraordinary meeting, take precedence of the magistrate who convoked it. The emperor usually caused his address to be read for him in the form of a speech by the *quæstor principis*. At an audience of ambassadors, their speeches were heard before the business was laid before the meeting. After this followed the "questioning" (*rŏgātŏ*) of the senators, called on one after another by name in order of their rank and seniority. Towards the end of the Republic and under the Empire, after the consular elections the consuls-designate came first. If the emperor himself was presiding, he called first on the consuls then in office. The senators so called upon either stood up in their place and delivered their opinions in a speech, in which they were able (as sometimes happened) to touch on other matters than the one in hand; or, without rising, declared their assent to some opinion already delivered. After the different opinions had been delivered, they were collected together by the president and arranged for voting on. The voting took place by *discessio*, or separation into groups, the supporters of the various views taking up their position together. A bare majority decided the question. If there was any doubt, the numbers were counted.

After the division the president dismissed the Senate, in order, with the aid of a committee of senators, to draw up the resolution of the Senate (*senatūs consultum*) on the lines of the minutes of the meeting, unless an objection to it was raised by any of the officials present. The resolution was headed with the names of the consuls, followed by the date and place of meeting, the names of the proposers and of the members of the committee for drawing up the resolution; last of all followed the resolution itself, drawn up in certain fixed forms. The resolutions of the Senate were communicated to those concerned by word of mouth or by writing. Those that related to the nation were published by the magistrates at the popular assembly, or by means of wooden (or in special cases bronze) tablets publicly displayed. Of resolutions affecting international relations two copies on bronze were prepared, one of which was hung up in the temple of *Fĭdēs* at Rome, the other in a temple of the other nation concerned. Resolutions of the Senate were preserved in early times in the office of the plebeian ædiles, later in the *Ærārĭum*, the office of the quæstors.

Under the Monarchy the power of the Senate was very limited. Its most important privilege was the power of appointing an *interrex* after the death of a king for the purpose of carrying on business and nominating a new king. During the Republic it soon extended its influence, as it had to be consulted, and its advice followed, by the magistrates on all important measures of administration. At length the whole government of the State came practically into its hands, and the magistrates were only the instruments for carrying out its will. Its predominance found expression in its taking the first place in the well-known formula, *senatus pŏpŭlusque Rŏmānus*, especially as this was employed even in cases where the Senate acted without the co-operation of the people. In the time of the Gracchi the power of the Senate suffered a deadly blow, which it had to a great extent brought upon itself. In particular, it became customary to affix to resolutions of the people a stipulation that within a few days the Senate should swear allegiance to them. The last century B.C. saw the complete downfall of the Senate's authority. Augustus attempted to raise it by every means at his disposal. But in spite of important privileges conferred upon it, the Senate only possessed the semblance of power in opposition to the military force of the emperor. Afterwards it sank to a mere shadow, when, from the time of Hadrian onwards, a special imperial council, the *consĭlĭum princĭpĭs*, was instituted to deal with matters of paramount importance.

The principal duties of the Senate consisted in (1) the supervision of religion, which it retained even under the Empire. This included the maintenance of the State religion, the introduction of foreign worships, arranging for the consultation of the Sibylline books, the establishment of new festivals, games, festivals for prayer and thanksgiving, etc. (2) The supervision of the whole of the State property and finances, and control of expenditure (*e.g.* the colonization and allotment of State lands, the revenues for building and the maintenance of public gardens, for the army, for games, etc.). Under the Empire the Senate had also the nominal control of the State treasury, until this was amalgamated with the imperial *fiscus.* (3) In reference to foreign affairs, the Senate had considerable influence over the declaration of war, the nomination of commanders, the decisions for the levy of troops and war taxes, the provinces, rewards (such as triumphs and others), and the conclusion of peace and the ratification of treaties. Furthermore, the Senate had supreme power in all matters of diplomacy, as it appointed ambassadors, received and gave audience to foreign ambassadors, and conferred such tokens of honour as the titles of confederates and friends of the Roman people. Over the subjects of the Roman people it exercised an almost sovereign authority, particularly in reference to the assigning of provinces. Under the Empire, it retained control of the senatorial provinces alone. It was still sometimes consulted about concluding peace and ratifying treatises, and about business with foreign allies, and also had the right of conferring such honours as those of apotheosis, or of statues and triumphs. On the other hand, its influence over military matters could no longer continue side by side with the military power of the emperor. (4) In legislation it exercised considerable influence during the Republic, as it prepared legislative proposals to be brought before the people by the magistrates, and had the right of annulling laws passed by the people in the event of their being defective in point of form. Its resolutions also, by virtue of a kind of prescription, had considerable statutory authority. Under the Empire, when the legislative power of the people was entirely abolished, they had authority completely equal to that of the laws themselves. They were, however, merely formal ratifications of the will of the emperor, who in every year exacted from the Senate on January 1st an oath of allegiance to his independent enactments. On the accession of a new emperor the Senate conferred on him the imperial power by an enactment termed *lex rēgĭa;* this, however, was a mere formality. (5) During the republican age, the Senate possessed no judicial power of its own (apart from the fact that, until the time of the Gracchi, the judges all belonged to the senatorial order); but the magistrate only acted as adviser to the judges in criminal jurisdiction, *i.e.* in cases of treason and perjury on the part of allies and subjects, and in serious cases of poisoning and murder such as endangered the public peace. Under the Empire, the Senate possessed formal jurisdiction in cases of breach of contract, disturbance in Italy, malpractices in office and extortion of provincial governors, and especially all cases of high treason and offences of senators. From the 2nd century onward all this juris-

diction passed over to the imperial courts. (6) During the Republic, the elections were only indirectly under the influence of the Senate, by means of the presiding officials, and also owing to their right of annulling elections on the score of mistakes in form, and, lastly, by having the appointment of the days for the elections. Under the Empire, it gained from Tiberius the right of proposing all the magistrates with the exception of the consuls; this right, however, was rendered insignificant by the fact that the candidates were recommended by the emperor. The right also of nominating the emperor, which it claimed when the occupant of the throne was removed by violence, was, owing to the practical power of the army, as illusory as its pretended right of deposition.

Sĕnātŭs Consultum. *See* SENATE.

Sĕnĕcă. (1) *Annæus, the rhetorician;* born of an equestrian family, at Cordŭba (*Cordova*) in Spain, towards the end of the Republic. In the time of Augustus he studied at Rome, where he lived in intimacy with the most famous rhetoricians and orators, and died at a very great age, probably not till after the death of Tiberius (37 A.D.). [He was the father of Seneca the philosopher, and (by his son Mela) grandfather of Lucan the poet.] According to the testimony of Seneca the philosopher, he was a man of pristine virtue and severity, much devoted to the maintenance of ancestral customs [Seneca, *Ad Helviam Matrem* 17, 3: *patris mei antīquus rĭgor; māiōrum· consuctūdĭnī dēdĭtus*]. As a stylist he was a great admirer of Cicero. In his old age, relying simply on his marvellous memory, he composed at his son's desire a collection of declamations for the use of schools of rhetoric, modelled on the treatment of the subjects by the most famous rhetoricians of his youth. It bears the title, *Orātōrum et Rhētŏrum Sententiæ Dīvīsiōnēs Cŏlōrēs,* one book containing seven themes called *suasōriæ,* and ten books, thirty-five *controversiæ.* Of these we now possess only books i, ii, vii, ix, x, and the greater part of the introductions to books iii and iv, besides an abstract of the whole, belonging to the 4th or 5th century. The contents give a vivid picture of the work of the schools of rhetoric in the time of Augustus and Tiberius, and are an important authority for the history of Roman rhetoric.

(2) *Lucius Annæus, the philosopher,* son of (1), born at Cordŭba, about 5 B.C.

In early youth he came to Rome, where, besides studying rhetoric, he devoted himself particularly to philosophy. While still young he entered active life as an orator, and in the service of the government. In 1 A.D. he was banished to Corsica by Claudius, at the instigation of Messalīna, on the ostensible charge of being a participator and an accomplice in the debaucheries of Julia, the daughter of Germānĭcus. Not till eight years later did Claudius recall him at the request of Agrippīna the younger, the emperor's niece and wife, and appoint him tutor to the youthful Nero, Agrippina's son by a former husband. After the young prince had ascended the throne in 54 A.D., Seneca still remained in the circle of those most closely attached to him, especially during the first five years of the reign, and exercised a beneficial influence over his former pupil, who manifested his thanks by making him valuable presents, and conferring upon him the consulship for 57. In 62 the intrigues of his opponents caused him to withdraw completely from the court and from public life. The conspiracy of Piso in 65 finally afforded Nero the early desired pretext for removing him. As the mode of his death was left to himself, he had his veins opened, and as death did not ensue with sufficient rapidity, he finally had himself put in a vapour-bath. During his lifetime he had often been reproached for finding more pleasure than a philosopher should in the good things of life. How little value he really set upon them was shown by the readiness with which he parted from them and the composure with which he met his end.

Next to Cicero, he is the most famous philosophical writer of Rome, and one of the most gifted and original of Roman authors in general. As a philosopher, he was essentially a follower of the Stoics; but he directed his attention less to abstract speculation than to practical wisdom, which undoubtedly, as in his own instance, verges closely on mere prudence in the conduct of life. His writings are in a popular style, but they are characterized by copious knowledge and wide acquaintance with the human heart, and are remarkable for their richness in aphorisms that are at once profound in thought and terse in expression. The moral tone of his writings caused Christian tradition to represent him as a friend of the Apostle Paul, and even to invent a correspondence between them.

[Cp. Lightfoot's Philippians, 1868, pp. 260–331.] In versatility of genius, ease of production, and elegance of form, Seneca may be compared with Ovid. In style he accommodated himself completely to the taste of the times, which strained after rhetorical effect, though he fully recognised its degeneracy.

Among his numerous prose writings are the following: (1) three letters of condolence (De Consōlātĭōnĕ)–-to his mother Helvia, to Pŏlўbĭus (the favourite of Claudius), and to Marcia (the daughter of Crĕmūtĭus Cordus. The two first were composed in Corsica. (2) A series of discourses on philosophy and morals, the most important being those on Mercy (De Clēmentĭă), in two books, addressed to Nero; on Anger (De Irā), in three books; on Giving and Receiving Favours (De Bĕnĕfĭcĭĭs), in seven books. (3) A collection in twenty books of 124 letters to his young friend Lūcīlĭus, mostly on questions of philosophy. (4) Investigations in Natural Science (Quæstĭōnĕs Nātūrālĕs) in seven books, dedicated to the same Lucilius, the the first and only text-book on physics in Roman literature. In addition to these he wrote a biting satire on the death of the emperor Claudius (Lūdus de Morte Claudii) entitled the Pumpkinification (Apŏcŏlŏcyntōsĭs), instead of deification (ăpŏthĕōsĭs), in which prose and verse are mingled after the manner of Varro's Menippean Satires.

We have express testimony that Seneca was also a poet [Tacitus, Ann., xix 52]. Besides certain epigrams, the following tragedies are ascribed to him: Hercŭlēs Fŭrens, Thўestēs, Phædra, Œdĭpūs, Trōădĕs, Mēdēa, Agamemnōn, Hercŭlēs Œtæus, three fragments upon the Theban myth united under the title of Thēbăĭs or Phœnissæ, and the fābŭla prætextāta (q.v.) entitled Octāvĭa. These are the only tragedies in all Roman literature that have come down to us. It may be taken as proved, that the last of these dramas, which treats of the tragic end of Octavia, the daughter of Claudius and wife of Nero, and in which Seneca himself appears, cannot be attributed to him, but belongs to a later date, though there are no decisive reasons for doubting the genuineness of the remainder. Their matter and form are borrowed from the Greek; [but their general character probably resembles that of the tragedies written in the Augustan age by Pollio and by Vărĭus, rather than that of the ancient dramatists, such as Ennius and Pācŭvius]. In their pointed expression they exhibit the same talent for style as his prose works, the same copiousness, philosophical bent, and rhetorical manner (the last frequently carried beyond the limits of taste). They seem to have been designed more as declamatory exercises than for actual performance on the stage.

Septĕrĭŏn. A festival celebrated every nine years at Delphi, in memory of the slaying of the serpent Pȳthōn by Apollo. [Plutarch, *Quæstiones Gr.* 12 (where some texts have *Steptĕrĭŏn*), and *Def. Orac.* 15.]

Septĭmĭus (*Lūcĭus*). The translator into Latin of the spurious work of Dictys (*q.v.*, 2) on the Trojan War.

Sĕrāpĭs (or *Sarapis*, Egyptian *Asarhapi* = *Osiris-Apis*). The Egyptian god Osīris (*q.v.*), in the character of god of the lower world; his corresponding incarnation as god of the upper world was the bull Apis. His worship was first independently developed in the time of the Ptolemies in

BUST OF SERAPIS.
(Rome, Vatican.)

Alexandria, the most beautiful ornament of which city was the magnificent temple of Serapis, the *Sĕrāpĕĭŏn.* By the elimination of foreign elements, the conception of the god was so widely extended as to include the Egyptian Osiris, the Greek Plŭto, the Greek god of healing, Asclēpius, and Zeus-Iupiter (*see* below). This new worship (together with the cult of Isis) rapidly spread from Egypt over the Asiatic coast, the Greek islands, and Greece itself, and found a firm footing even in Rome and Italy, in spite of repeated interference on the part of the State. Under the Empire [particularly in the time of Hadrian] it extended throughout the Roman world.

Serapis was especially worshipped as a god of healing, and with his temples were connected dream-oracles that were much resorted to. He was represented, like Pluto, with an animal by his side, having the head of a dog, lion, or wolf, and a serpent coiled round its body. As Zeus-Serapis he is to be seen in the colossal bust in the Vatican (*see* cut), with a *mŏdĭus*, or cornmeasure, the symbol of the lower world, upon his head.

Sĕrēnus Sammōnĭcus. A Roman physician and author who lived in the time of Sĕvērus and Caracalla. The latter caused him to be put to death in 212 A.D. To him, or more probably to his son Quintus Serenus, the instructor of the second Gordiānus, must be attributed a didactic poem on medicine (*De Mĕdĭcīnā Præceptā*) in 1,115 well-written hexameters, a collection of domestic prescriptions much used in the Middle Ages. It mostly follows Pliny.

Sēria. A cask used by the Romans. (*See* VESSELS.)

Servĭus Hŏnōrātus (*Mārĭus*). A Roman grammarian, who lived towards the end of the 4th century A.D. He taught grammar and rhetoric at Rome, and composed (besides a commentary on the grammar of Dōnātus, and some short treatises on grammar) a commentary on Vergil remarkable for its copious historical, mythological, and antiquarian notes [most of which are probably derived from the writings of much earlier scholars]. It has not, however, reached us in its original form.

Sestertius (contracted from *sēmis tertius, i.e.* $2\frac{1}{2}$, expressed by the Roman symbol usually printed HS., *i.e.* II + S(*emis*), two units and a half). A coin, during the Republic of silver, under the Empire of copper, or more usually brass = $\frac{1}{4}$ *dēnārĭus*, originally $2\frac{1}{2}$ *assēs* (whence the name), later [*i.e.* after 217 B.C.] six *asses*. It was then worth 2·1*d.* Under the early Empire it was worth about 2·4*d.* After 209 B.C., when the Romans instituted a silver coinage, the copper *as* was suddenly reduced to 4 oz., and the *sestertius* ($2\frac{1}{2}$ × 4 oz.) became equivalent to one old *as* of 10 oz., instead of the original pound of 12 oz. It long continued to be used as the ordinary monetary unit. During the Republic and the first 300 years of the Empire, amounts were reckoned in sesterces. Owing to the common use of *milia sestertium* (for *milia sestertiorum*), it became customary to treat *sestertium* as a neuter singular, and to omit *milia*. *Sestertium* thus denotes a sum of 1,000 sesterces = (at 2·1d. per sesterce) £8 15s. A million sesterces (£8,750) was called originally *dĕcĭēs centēna* (lit. ten times one hundred thousand) *sestertium*, which was shortened to *decies sestertium*. 100,000 sesterces had thus become a customary unit for reckoning large sums of money. (*Cp.* COINAGE.)

Set. An Egyptian god. (*See* OSIRIS and TYPHON.)

Seven against Thebes, The. Œdĭpūs, king of Thebes, had pronounced a curse upon his sons Etĕŏclēs and Pŏlўnīcēs, that they should die at one another's hand. In order to make the fulfilment of the curse impossible, by separating himself from his brother, Polynices left Thebes while his father was still alive, and at Argos married Argeia, the daughter of Adrastus (*q.v.*). On the death of his father he was recalled, and offered by Eteocles, who was the elder of the two,[1] the choice between the kingdom and the treasures of Œdipus; but, on account of a quarrel that arose over the division, he departed a second time, and induced his father-in-law to undertake a war against his native city. According to another legend, the brothers deprived their father of the kingdom, and agreed to rule alternately, and to quit the city for a year at a time. Polynices, as the younger, first went into voluntary banishment: but when, after the expiration of a year, Eteocles denied him his right, and drove him out by violence, he fled to Argos, where Adrastus made him his son-in-law, and undertook to restore him with an armed force. *Adrastus* was the leader of the army; besides *Polynices* and *Tўdeus* of Călўdōn, the other son-in-law of the king, there also took part in the expedition the king's brothers *Hippŏmĕdōn* and *Parthĕnŏpœus* (*q.v.*), *Căpăneus*, a descendant of Prœtus, and *Amphĭărāus* (*q.v.*), the latter against his will, and foreseeing his own death. The Atrīdæ were invited to join in the

[1] This is the common tradition, followed by Euripides (*Phœn.* 71). Sophocles, however, exceptionally makes Polynices the elder brother (*Œd. Col.* 375, 1294, 1422).

expedition, but were withheld by evil omens from Zeus. When the Seven reached Nĕmĕā on their march, a fresh warning befell them. Hypsĭpўlē, the nurse of Ŏphcltēs, the son of king Lўcurgus, laid her charge down on the grass in order to lead the thirsty warriors to a spring, during her absence the child was killed by a snake. They gave him solemn burial, and instituted the Nemean games in his honour; but Amphiaraüs interpreted the occurrence as an omen of his own fate, and accordingly gave the boy the name of Archĕmŏrŏs (*i.e.* leader to death). When they arrived at the river Asōpus in Bœotia, they sent Tydeus (*q.v.*) to Thebes, in the hope of coming to terms. He was refused a hearing, and the Thebans laid an ambush for him on his return. The Seven now advanced to the walls of the city, and posted themselves with their troops one at each of its seven gates. Against them were posted seven chosen Thebans (among them Mĕlănippus and Pĕrĭclўmĕnus). Mĕnœceus (*q.v.*) devoted himself to death to insure the victory for the Thebans. In the battle at the sanctuary of the Ismenian Apollo they were driven right back to their gates; the giant Capaneus had already climbed the wall by a scaling ladder, and was presumptuously boasting that even the lightning of Zeus should not drive him back, when the flaming bolt of the god smote him down, and dashed him to atoms. The beautiful Parthenopæus also fell, with his skull shattered by a rock that was hurled at him. Adrastus desisted from the assault, and the armies, which had suffered severely, agreed that the originators of the quarrel, Eteocles and Polynices, should fight out their difference in single combat. Both brothers fell, and a fresh battle arose over their bodies. In this, all of the assailants met their death, except Adrastus, who was saved by the speed of his black-maned charger. According to the older legends, his eloquence persuaded the Thebans to give the fallen due burial. When the bodies of the hostile brothers were placed on the pyre, the flames, which were meant to destroy them together, parted into two portions. According to the version of the story invented by the Attic tragedians, the Thebans refused to bury their foes, but at the prayer of Adrastus were compelled to do so by Theseus; according to another version, he conquered the Thebans and buried the dead bodies at Eleusis in Attica (Æschylus, *Septem contra Thēbas*). For the burial of Polynices, *see* ANTIGONE; further *see* EPIGONI.

Seven Wise Men, The. Under this name were included in antiquity seven men of the period from 620-550 B.C., distinguished for practical wisdom, who conducted the affairs of their country as rulers, lawgivers, and councillors. They were reputed to be the authors of certain brief maxims in common use, which were variously assigned among them; the names also of the seven were differently given. Those usually mentioned are: CLEŌBŪLUS, tyrant of Lindus in Rhodes ("Moderation is the chief good"); PĒRĬANDER, tyrant of Corinth, 668-584 ("Forethought in all things"); PITTĂCUS of Mĭtўlēnē, born about 650, deliverer and *æsymnētēs* of his native city ("Know thine opportunity"); BĬAS of Priēnē in Caria, about 570 B.C. ("Too many workers spoil the work"); THĂLĒS of Mĭlētus, 639-536 ("Suretyship brings ruin"); CHĬLŌN of Sparta ("Know thyself"); SŎLŌN of Athens ("Nothing too much," *i.e.* observe moderation).

Sĕvĕrus, Arch of. *See* TRIUMPHAL ARCHES.

Sextius Niger (*Quintus*). Lived during the last years of the Republic and under Augustus. He was the founder of a philosophical system, which aimed at the improvement of morals on the principles of the Stoics and Pythagoreans. Like his son, who bore the same name, he wrote in Greek. He is the author of a collection of Greek maxims of a monotheistic and ascetic character, a Christianized Latin translation of which, written in the second half of the 4th century by the presbyter Rūfīnus, is still extant.

Sextus Empĭrĭcus (so called because he belonged to the empirical school of medicine). A Grecian philosopher, a follower of the Sceptical school, who lived at the beginning of the 3rd century A.D. He is the author of three works on philosophy, (1) the *Pyrrhonistic Sketches* in three books, an abridgment of the Sceptical philosophy of Pyrrho; (2) an attack on the dogmatists (the followers of the other schools of philosophy) in five books; (3) an attack on the mathematicians (the followers of positive sciences—grammar, with all the historical sciences, rhetoric, arithmetic, geometry, astrology, and music) in six books. These works are remarkable for their learning and acuteness, as well as for simplicity and clearness of style. They form a valuable contribution to our knowledge of the general philosophical literature of Greece, and the Sceptical philosophy in particular.

Shield. The most important weapon of defence among the peoples of antiquity. The *Greeks* had two principal forms of shield in use, with broad flat rims, and the

GREEK SHIELDS.
(Guhl and Koner, figs. 269, 270.)

curved surface of the shield rising above them: (1) the *long* shield of oval shape that covered the wearer from mouth to ankles, suspended by a belt passing [round the neck and] the left shoulder, with a handle for the left hand. A variation of this form is the Bœotian shield (figs. 3, 4), the two sides of which have in the middle a semicircular or oval indentation. (2) The *round* shield, covering the wearer from the chin to the knee, also called the Doric shield; this had one loop, through which the left arm was inserted, and one which was held by the left hand (figs. 5 and 6). The shield of the Macedonian phalanx was round, but small enough to be easily handled, and with only one loop for the arm. Both forms were in use from ancient times; at a later date the Argolic shield seems to have predominated, though the long shield that was planted on the ground in a pitched battle remained a peculiarity of Spartan warfare until the 3rd century B.C. In Homer [*Il.* vii 245, xviii 481, xx 274-281] shields are made of skins placed one over another, with one plate of metal above; in later times the material appears to have been generally bronze, but also wood, leather, and wickerwork. The *pelta* is of Thracian origin; it was the defensive weapon of the light-armed peltasts, made of leather without a rim, and with a level surface, of small size and weight, and of various forms (square, round, and crescent-shaped, as in fig. 8).

Shields sometimes bore devices in painting or metal-work (figs. 1, 2); besides those chosen by the fancy of the individual, devices indicating different nations came

(8) SOLDIER WITH PELTA.
(Va-e-painting; Stackelberg's *Gräber der Hellenen*, Taf. xxxviii.)

into general use after the Persian War. Many Grecian races, *e.g.* the Lacedemonians, displayed the first letters of their name. The Athenian token was an owl, the Theban a club or a sphinx.

The shields most in use among the Romans were (1) the large oblong *scūtum*, bent in the form of a segment of a cylinder, covering the whole of the wearer; this was constructed of boards, covered with leather, and bound at the top and bottom with iron; it was always carried by the legionaries. (2) The circular leathern *parma*, carried by the light infantry. (3) The *cětra*, borrowed from the Spaniards; it resembled the *parma*, and was carried by the light auxiliary cohorts. The different divisions of the force were distinguished by devices painted on their shields.

Ship. The difference between the long, narrow ship of war and the short, broad merchant-vessel was much more pronounced in antiquity than in modern times, and existed as early as the time of Homer [*Od.* ▼ 250, ix 323]. The former type, however, was not yet devoted to fighting by sea, but to the transport of troops, who also served as rowers. The merchant ships were generally worked as *sailing* vessels, and were only propelled by oars in case of need, so that they required a very small crew. On the other hand, the ships of war depended for propulsion on a strong crew of rowers, who sat in a line on both sides of the vessel. A vessel with one bank of oars (*mŏnērēs*) was specially described according to the total number of the rowers; *e.g.* a pentēcontŏrŏs was a vessel with fifty rowers (*see* fig. 1). For a long time the main strength of Greek fleets consisted in such vessels. Afterwards *dĭērēs* (Lat. *bĭrēmĭs*), with two and (during the last ten years before the Persian Wars) *trĭērēis*

(*trĭrēmēs*), with three banks of oars on either side, came into use. The latter were most generally employed until the end of the Peloponnesian War. Next came the *tětrēreis* (*quadrĭrēmēs*), introduced from Carthage. In 399 B.C. the elder Dionysius of Syracuse built *pentēreis* (*quinquĕrēmēs*) and *hexē-reis;* Alexander the Great *heptēreis*, *octēreis*, *ennēreis*, and *děcēreis*. In the wars of the successors of Alexander, a further advance was made to ships with fifteen and sixteen banks of oars, and (later still) thirty and forty banks. The most practically useful form of war-vessel was the *pentēres*, which was especially used in the Punic wars.

The rowers sat close together, with their faces toward the stern of the vessel; those in the highest row were called *thrānĭtœ*, those in the middle *zeugĭtœ*, and the lowest *thălāmĭtœ ;* but the question of the exact arrangement of their seats, and of the oars, is not yet made out with sufficient clearness. [Fig. 2, from an ancient monument, shows the *thranĭtœ* and their oars; the rest of the rowers have their oars alone visible.] Figs. 3 and 4 are conjectural sketches, indicating the way in which the crew of a trireme was probably arranged. The number of rowers in an ancient trireme was 170, that of a Roman quinquereme in the Punic wars, 300; it is recorded that an octoreme of Lȳsĭmăchus carried a crew of 1,600. The oars were very long, and the time was kept by means of the music of the flute, or solely by a stroke set by a boat-swain (Gr. *kĕleustēs ;* Lat. *hortātor, pau-sārius*) with a hammer or staff, or by his voice. The vessels were steered in ancient times by means of one or two large paddles at the side of the stern. The rigging of a ship of war was extremely peculiar. The mast, which was not very high, and carried a square sail attached to a yard, was lowered during an engagement, when a small fore-mast with a similar sail was used in its

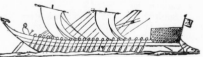

(1) PENTECONTOROS.
(Millingen, *Vases Grecs de Sir John Coghill*, pl. lii.)

stead. Only merchantmen appear to have carried three sails. The war vessels of antiquity were in length seven or eight times their breadth, and drew almost 3 ft.

of water. In order to attain the highest possible speed with manual propulsion, and to be easily drawn overland (a process frequently resorted to), they were lightly built, with rather flat bottoms, and very shallow. They were on this account not

water, was a horizontal beak (Gr. embŏlŏs ; Lat. rostrum), usually with three spikes one over another, capped with iron; this formed the chief weapon of ancient naval warfare. We learn that it first came into use in 556 B.C. The captain of a larger

(2) * MARBLE BAS-RELIEF OF AN ATHENIAN TRIREME.
(Found on the Acropolis about 1852, probably from a monument of victory in a trireme race;
Annali d. Instituto, 1861, tav. d' adg. M 2.)

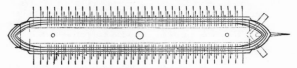

(3) PLAN OF A TRIREME.
(Designed by Graser, De Veterum re Navali.)

particularly seaworthy in stormy weather ; whereas merchant vessels, owing to their heavier build and greater depth, were much more sea-worthy. A stay made of two strong beams or a cable stretched between the two ends of the vessel (hўpŏzōma) was usually employed to strengthen the hull lengthways. The bows and stern which were built alike, were alone covered with half-decks, while the middle of the vessel was at first open, and even in later times completely decked vessels were not so general as with us. Merchant-vessels, however, had a regular full-deck. The deck sometimes carried wooden turrets, usually two, fore and aft. Most ships of war had an eye painted or carved on the bows. At the bows, on a level with the

(4) ROWERS IN PROFILE (ib.).

ship of war was called a trĭērarchŏs (com-mander of a trireme); the chief officer was the helmsman (Gr. kўbernētēs; Lat. gŭber-nātor); the second officer (Gr. prōreūs, prōrātēs; Lat. prōrēta) was stationed on the bows. The total crew of an Athenian trireme, including the rowers, numbered about 200 men, of whom about twenty were sailors, and only ten to eighteen marines. This small number is explained by the fact that among the Greeks a sea-fight consisted chiefly in clever manœuvring, with the ob-ject of disabling the enemy's vessels by breaking their oars or of forcing them to run aground.

When the Romans had established a fleet, during the first Punic War, they introduced the tactics of land-battles into their naval warfare, by carrying on their ships an increased number of land-soldiers (on their quinquērēmēs 120), who were posted on the bows, and attempted to lay hold of the enemy's vessels with grap-pling-irons and boarding-bridges, and to overpower their crews in hand to hand encounter. In the battle of Actium (31 B.C.) the lightly built *triremes* of Octavian, which were named *līburnæ*, after the Liburnians of Dalmatia, from whom this shape was borrowed, were matched with distinguished success against the eight, nine, and ten-banked vessels of Antonius. Under the Empire the fleets were, as a general rule, no longer intended for great naval battles, but for the safeguard of the seas and coasts, for the convoy of transports and for purposes of administration. The consequence was that vessels of excessive height were continually becoming rarer, and *triremes*, and especially *liburnæ*, were almost exclusively employed. In later times the name *liburna* came to denote simply a ship of war. Augustus organized a Mediterranean fleet with two headquarters, Mīsēnum in the Tyrrhenian Sea and Rǎvenna in the Adriatic. These two fleets were called *classēs prœtōrǐæ*, because, like the *cǒhortēs prœtoriæ*, they were under the immediate command of the emperor. Other stations for the fleets were afterwards established in all parts of the sea, and the great rivers and inland seas of the empire. Their commanders were called *prœfecti*, and were nominated by the emperor, as a rule, from among the military officers of equestrian rank. On the crews of the navy, *see* CLASSIARII.

Besides regular men of war, the navies also contained various ships of the line to act as spies and carry despatches (Gr. *kělēs* and *lembǒs ;* Lat. *cělox* and *lembus*), or to convoy transport vessels, light cutters (*ǎcǎtǒs, ǎcǎtǐǒn*), privateers (*mўǒpǎrǒ*), etc. Fire-ships were used as early as 414 B.C. by the Syracusans against the Athenians.

Of merchantmen there existed in antiquity various kinds and sizes. In the time of the Empire the art of shipbuilding was developed with extraordinary success at the great trading city of Alexandria, where ships were built of great seaworthiness, remarkable sailing powers, and immense tonnage. [See Torr's *Ancient Ships*, 1894.]

Shoe. *See* CALCEUS.

Sǐbyllæ [in the singular, Lat. *sǐbylla ;* Gr. *sǐbulla*, from Doric *siǒ-bolla = theou-boulē*, " the will of God "]. The name given in antiquity to inspired prophetesses of some deity, in particular Apollo. They were usually regarded as young maidens dwelling in lonely caves or by inspiring springs, who were possessed with a spirit of divination, and gave forth prophetic utterances while under the influence of enthusiastic frenzy. They were described sometimes as priestesses of Apollo, sometimes as his favourite wives or daughters. We have no certain information as to their number, names, country, or date. Though Plato [*Phœdrus*, 294 B] knew of only one, others mention two, three, four [the *Erythrœan*, the *Samian*, the *Egyptian*, and the *Sardian*], and even ten or twelve : [the *Babylonian*, the *Libyan*, the (elder and younger) *Delphian*, the *Cimmerian*, the (elder and younger) *Erythrœan*, the *Samian*, the *Cumœan*, the *Hellespontine*, the *Phrygian*, and the *Tiburtine*]. In the earliest times they are mentioned as dwelling in the neighbourhood of the Trojan Ida in Asia Minor, later at Ěrўthræ in Ionia, in Samǒs, at Delphi, and at Cūmæ in Italy. The most famous was the *Erythrœan Sibyl*, Hěrǒphǐlē, who is usually considered identical with the *Cumœan*, as she is represented as journeying by manifold wanderings from her home to Cumæ. Here she is said to have lived for many generations in the crypts beneath the temple of Apollo, where she had even prophesied to Æneās. In later times the designation of Sibyl was also given to the prophetic Nymph *Albŭněa* near Tibur [Lactantius, i 6 § 12].

The *Sibylline books*, so often met with in Roman history, had their origin in a collection of oracular utterances in Greek hexameters, composed in the time of Sǒlǒn and Cўrus at Gergis on Mount Ida, and ascribed to the Hellespontic Sibyl, buried in the temple of Apollo at Gergis. This collection was brought by way of Erythræ to Cumæ, and finally, in the time of the last king, to Rome. According to the legend, the Cumæan Sibyl offered to Tarquǐnius Sŭperbus nine books of prophecy ; and as the king declined to purchase them, owing to the exorbitant price she demanded, burnt all but three of them, which the king purchased for the original price, and had them preserved in a vault beneath the Capitoline temple of Jupiter. When they were destroyed in the burning of the Capitol in 83 B.C., the Senate sent envoys to make a collection of similar oracular sayings distributed over various places, in particular Īlǐum, Erythræ, and Samos. This new collection was deposited in the restored temple, together with similar sayings of native origin ; *e.g.* those of the Sibyl at Tǐbur, of the brothers Marcius, and others. From the Capitol they were transferred by Augustus as *pontǐfex*, in 12 B.C., to the temple of

Apollo on the Palatine, after they had been examined and copied; here they remained until about 405 A.D. They are said to have been burnt by Stĭlĭcho. The use of these oracles was from the outset reserved for the State, and they were not consulted for the foretelling of future events, but on the occasion of remarkable calamities, such as pestilence, earthquake, and as a means of expiating portents. It was only the rites of expiation prescribed by the Sibylline books that were communicated to the public, and not the oracles themselves. As these books recognised the gods worshipped, and the rites observed, in the neighbourhood of Troy, they were the principal cause of the introduction of a series of foreign deities and religious rites into the Roman State worship, of the amalgamation of national deities with the corresponding deities of Greece, and a general modification of the Roman religion after the Greek type.

Tarquinius is said to have entrusted the care of the books to a special college of two men of patrician rank. After 367 B.C. their number was increased to ten, half patrician and half plebeians; and in the 1st century B.C., probably in the time of Sulla, five more were added. These officials were entitled respectively *dŭumvĭrī, dĕcemvĭri,* and *quindecimviri sacrīs făcĭundīs.* They were usually ex-consuls or ex-prætors. They held office for life, and were exempt from all other public duties. They had the responsibility of keeping the books in safety and secrecy, of consulting them at the order of the Senate, of interpreting the utterances they found therein, and of causing the measures thus enjoined to be carried out; in particular, they had the superintendence of the worship of Apollo, the *Magna Māter,* and Cĕrēs, which had been introduced by the Sibylline books.

These Sibylline books have no connexion with a collection of *Sibylline Oracles* in twelve books, written in Greek hexameters, which have come down to us. The latter contain a medley of pretended prophecies by various authors and of very various dates, from the middle of the 2nd century B.C. to the 5th century A.D. They were composed partly by Alexandrine Jews, partly by Christians, in the interests of their respective religions; and in part they refer to events of the later Empire.

Sĭcinnĭs. The wild choral dance of the Greek *satyric drama (q.v.). See* also CHORUS.

Sĭdē. The wife of Ŏrīŏn *(q.v.);* she was thrown into Hādēs by Hērā for venturing to compare herself with her in point of beauty.

Sĭdōnĭus Ăpollĭnārĭs *(Gaius Sollius).* A Roman author, born about 430 A.D. at Lugdūnum (Lyons). He belonged to one of the most prominent Christian families in Gaul. He married the daughter of the future emperor Avītus. Under Anthĕmĭus, in 467 he was *præfectus urbi* at Rome, and in 472 he became bishop of Clermont, in Auvergne, and in that capacity headed the resistance against the Western Goths. He died in 483. He was distinguished among his contemporaries for learning and culture, and for a knowledge of ancient literature which was rare in that age. Of his works we possess twenty-four poems, among which are three panegyrics on the emperors Avitus, Majorian, and Anthemius, and two *ĕpĭthă-lămĭa,* which are somewhat clever in form; they are, however, as bombastic and as destitute of thought and taste as his nine books of *Letters,* modelled on those of Pliny and Symmăchus. His writings are nevertheless not without value, owing to the light they throw on the history and the general circumstances of his time.

Sieges. If an immediate attack by filling up the trenches, beating in the gates, and scaling the walls failed or promised to be useless, the siege was carried on partly by blockade, partly by attack in form. In the first case the besiegers were content with surrounding the town with an inner and outer wall. The latter was intended as a protection against attack on the part

(1) BATTERING RAM (*ARIES*).

of a relieving force. The besiegers then waited till the besieged were forced to capitulate. In other cases they attempted to make a breach in the wall with a battering ram (fig. 1); to undermine the wall, and so overthrow it; to make a way under by mines into the city; or to raise a mound level with the wall, and so get to the top. The process of undermining the walls was carried on by soldiers, who tore up the foundations with the aid of various mining tools. This was done under the protection of the *testūdō,* a wooden erection in the form of a slanting desk. This was carried by hand or wheeled close up to the wall with its open front towards it. Like all machines of the kind, it was provided on the top and sides with wet skins or cushions as a protection against fire thrown down upon it. *Chĕlŏnē* (Gr.) or *testudo* (Lat.) was the general name for all kinds of sheds of the sort. The name was, *e.g.*, given to the penthouse of shields formed by the soldiers during the storming of a hostile fortification (fig. 2). The second and following ranks held their shields in a slanting position over their heads; the first rank and the men in the wings held them straight up in front of them. In case of mining, properly so called, the mining-hut (*muscŭlus*) was employed: a long and narrow structure, pushed up in the same way on wheels close under the walls. A shed or penthouse, 22–26 feet in length and breadth, with a slanting roof extending to the ground, served to give protection to the workmen employed in levelling the ground, and filling up the trenches for the approach of the engines. The mound (Lat. *agger ;* Gr. *chōmă*) was

(2) TESTUDO.

From the Column of Antoninus (Bellori, *Col. Antonin.*, tav. 36).

directed straight from the surrounding wall to the most suitable part of the besieged fortifications. It rose by a gradual ascent to the top of the latter. It was made of earth and fascines, held together at the side by wooden scaffolding or stone walls. The soldiers who worked at it were protected by *plŭtĕi*, semicircular coverings of wickerwork, moving forward on three wheels, or by *vīnĕæ*. These were light scaffolding, 10 ft. broad and double as long, with a flat or double roof of boards or wickerwork, and covered with the same on three sides. Partly upon the mound, partly on one side of it, were erected these wooden

movable towers (Lat. *turrēs ambŭlātŏriæ ;* Gr. *hÿpŏtrŏchoi*), which were brought up on wheels or rollers to the walls. Their height depended on that of the wall and on their position on the level or on the mound ; the average was 88–196 ft., containing from ten to twenty stories. These towers generally served as batteries, the upper stages being armed with artillery. Besides this, archers and slingers would be posted on the outer galleries of the different stories, which were protected by breastworks. Sappers would be lodged in the lower stories. On the level of the wall bridges (*sambūcæ*) were provided. A crane (*tollēnŏ*) was used ·to hoist single soldiers to the top of the wall. This was a machine like the bucket of a well, fitted at the end with a basket or box.

The besieged, in their turn, had various contrivances against these weapons of attack. Two-pronged forks to turn over the scaling ladders, cranes with large tongs to seize the soldiers in their ascent and drop them into the town. The various kinds of *testudo* were met by throwing down great masses of stone, pouring down molten lead, pitch, or other combustibles, or by the use of burning arrows or other missiles of the same kind. The mound they endeavoured to neutralise by setting it on fire or undermining it ; in the latter case the tower would sink as soon as it came upon the proper place. Against the towers they tried fire, artillery discharged from the walls, or the erection of counter-towers. If a breach was threatened, a second or minor wall was erected to meet it out of the material of the neighbouring houses. The most important siege engines were invented by the Greeks, from whom they came to the Romans. (*See* ARTILLERY.)

Signum. The Roman name for a military standard, usually consisting of a badge (*insigne*) on a staff, carried by legions, maniples, and cohorts, as distinct from the *vexillum* (*q.v.*). The latter was a square flag fastened on a cross-bar (*see* fig. 2, *a*), carried by the cavalry and allied infantry detachments. In the time of the manipular arrangement (*see* LEGION), each maniple had its peculiar *insigne*, the eagle (the sign of the first *mănĭpŭlus*), the wolf, the Minotaur, the horse, or the boar. After Mărĭus had made the eagle (*q.v.*) the standard representing the *signum* of the whole legion, the forms of other animals were no longer employed. Instead of them the maniples had a spear with an outstretched hand upon the point (fig. 2, c, d, h, i). Afterwards the *signa* were also furnished with

(1) * FUNERAL MONUMENT (*CIPPUS*) OF THE STANDARD-BEARER (*SIGNIFER*) PINTAIUS. (Bonn Museum).

a *vexillum* (fig. 2, b) and with various ornaments on the pole, in particular round

cohorts, probably as early as the time of Cæsar, had particular *signa ;* after Trajan they borrowed from the Parthians the *drăcō.* This was the image of a large dragon fixed upon a lance, with gaping jaws of silver, and with the rest of its body formed of coloured silk. When the wind blew down the open jaws, the body was inflated. [Vegetius, *De Re Militari* ii 13; Ammianus Marcellinus, xvi 10 § 7. This last is to be seen on monuments among the standards of foreign nations (k, m), who also had a standard resembling a mediæval banner (l).] On the march and in an attack with close columns, the *signa* were carried in the first line; in a pitched battle, behind the front rank.

Sīlēnus (Gr. *Seilēnŏs*). A primitive deity in the legends of Asia Minor. He is a divinity of the woodland and the fountains, whom people tried to catch in order to make him prophesy and sing to them. Thus king Mīdās of Phrygia got him into his power by mixing wine with a spring from which he used to drink, and made him instruct him in all kinds of wisdom. Afterwards, as a son of Hermēs and a Nymph, or of Pan, and as the oldest of all the Satyrs, he was added to the train of Dīonȳsus, and was regarded as his teacher and trainer and his constant companion. He is said to have prompted the god to invent the cultivation of the vine and the keeping of bees. He is described as a little old man, potbellied, with bald head and snub nose, his whole body very hairy; never without his

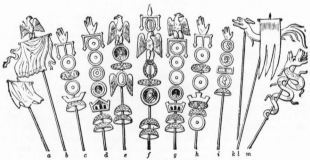

a, c, d, g, h, i, Bellorius, *Col. Antonin.*; b, c, f, De Rubeis, *Arcus Constant.*; k, l, De Rubeis, *Arcus Severi*; m, *Museo Borbonico*, iii tav. lviii.
(2) STANDARDS FROM VARIOUS MONUMENTS.
(Guhl and Koner, fig. 524.)

plates, often with representations of gods, emperors, and generals (e, f, g). The

skin of wine, always drunk, and hence usually riding on an ass, and led and supported by the other Satyrs; or, again, as tending and educating the child Bacchus, as he is represented in the celebrated group in the Louvre at Paris. A similar group in the Vatican at Rome is reproduced in the accompanying cut. Figures of him standing

SILENUS AND THE INFANT DIONYSUS.
(Rome, Vatican.)

or reclining were used, especially at Athens, as caskets for keeping within them precious pieces of carved work [Plato, *Symp.* 215, A, B]. There were also *Sileni* which were regarded in Asia as the inventors of the native music on the flute and the *syrinx* (*see* MARSYAS); their father was *Pappo-silenus*, who was represented as completely covered with hair and bestial in form.

Sīlĭus Ĭtălĭcus (*Gaius*). A Roman poet, born A.D. 25, probably at Ĭtālĭca [near *Seville*], in Spain. After having been consul in 68, and proconsul in Asia, he retired from public life, and went to his estates in the south of Italy, to spend the rest of his life in learned studies and in the composition of poetry. He paid almost divine honours to the memory of his

favourite poet Vergil, whom he selected as his model [Martial, xi 48, 49; vii 63], but whom he rarely equalled. He died in 102 by starving himself to death [Pliny, *Ep.* iii 7; vii 63]. We possess a poem of his on the second Punic War in seventeen books (*Pūnĭca*); it is founded on careful historical studies, but is far from brilliant, and, in spite of all its ornamental details, contains little that is truly poetic. He appears to have been soon forgotten. [Quintilian's silence in his enumeration of the epic poets of Rome has been rightly ascribed to the fact that the poet was still alive, and had not yet published his poem. The poet's younger and abler contemporary Stātīus, in *Silvæ* iv 7, 14, alludes to Silius' *Punica* i 233.]

Silli. A peculiar kind of Greek lampoons in an epic form, such as Xĕnŏphănēs of Cŏlŏphŏn was the first to level against poets and philosophers. The principal representative of this class was Tīmōn of Phlĭūs. (*See* TIMON.)

Silvānus. An old Italian divinity, related to Faunus. Originally he was a god of woods and of plantations of trees in fields and gardens; subsequently he was regarded as protector of the fields and gardens themselves, as well as of the cattle that grazed in the meadows, and especially those in or near the woods. He was at the same time guardian of the boundaries between meadows. The Italian country people therefore honoured him with worship under three different aspects: (1) as *dŏmes-tĭcus*, protector of the house and all that belongs to it; (2) as *agrestis*, to whose care the shepherd and his flock were recommended; (3) as *ŏrĭentālis*, he that watches over the boundaries. In this last capacity he used to have a grove dedicated to him on the boundary of different estates. At the harvest festivals, farmers, vinedressers, and those who had plantations of trees, offered him, on rustic altars, corn, grapes, and fruits, and also pigs and rams. Like Faunus, he was afterwards identified with *Pan ;* and to him, as to Pan, the sudden terror caused by the solitude of a wood was ascribed. It was also believed that there were numerous *Silvāni.*

Silver Shields, Bearers of. A corps of guards in the army of Alexander the Great. (*See* ARGYRASPIDES.)

Sīmōnĭdēs. (1) *Of Amorgŏs.* A Greek iambic poet. He was born in the island of Sămŏs, from which he led a colony to the island of Amorgŏs; he lived about the

middle of the 7th century B.C., as a younger
contemporary of Archĭlŏchus, from whom
he is distinguished by the fact that his
writing is less personal, and contains more
general reflexions on the constant characteristics of human nature. He did not
direct his attacks against single persons,
but against whole classes. Thus, in an
extant fragment of 118 lines, a derisive
poem on women, he gives a general description of female characters, deriving the
various bad qualities in women from the
characteristic qualities of the animals from
which he makes them out to be descended.

(2) *Of Cĕōs.* One of the most celebrated
and many-sided of the lyric poets of Greece.
Born about B.C. 556 at Iŭlis in Ceos, he
went at an early age to Greece proper,
where he occupied a high position at Athens
under the Pisistratid Hipparchus, and
after his death in 514 in Thessaly, at the
courts of the Scŏpădæ and Aleuădæ. His
fame was highest at the time of the Persian
Wars, the heroes and battles of which he
celebrated in epigrams, elegies, and melic
poems. He was a friend of the most remarkable men of his time; for instance, with
Thĕmistŏclēs and Pausănĭas. He is said to
have won fifty-six victories in poetic contests; thus after the battle of Marathon
(490) he defeated the most famous poets, including Æschўlus, in an elegy on the men
who had fallen in the conflict. He passed
the last ten years of his life with the tyrant
Hĭĕro of Syracuse, and died in Sicily, at an
advanced age, in 468 B.C. He was a polished
and excellently educated man of the world,
with great knowledge of it, and on this
he drew cleverly for his poems. He was
blamed for courting the favour of the
wealthy and the powerful, and he was reputed to have been the first who accepted
payment for his poems; but even if he really
did frequently write poetry to order, and
for considerable sums of money, yet, with
admirable tact, he knew how to keep every
appearance of mercenary work far from his
creations. To rare fertility of production
he added extraordinary poetic gifts, that
enabled him to produce remarkable, and
indeed perfect, work in the most varied
branches of lyric poetry, from the terse
simplicity of the epigram to the elaborate
structure of an antistrophic composition.
His most celebrated works were his epigrams, of which many have been preserved,
his elegies, and his dirges, which were
preferred even to those of Pindar. As may
be seen from the fragments of his elegies

and choice poems, he sought less to enchant
by the grandeur of his ideas, like Pindar,
than to touch by the sincerity of his sentiment; and accordingly his carefully chosen
language shows great smoothness, softness,
and grace, and correspondingly melodious
rhythms. Besides his other remarkable
talents, he possessed a very powerful
memory; he was on this account held to be
the inventor of a method of improving the
memory known as the mnemonic art. [This
is recorded in the *Parian Chronicle; cp.*
Quintilian xi 2 § 11.]

Simplĭcĭus. A Peripatetic philosopher of
the 6th century after Christ, and a native
of Cĭlĭcĭa. When Justinian in 529 closed
the school of philosophy in which he taught
at Athens, he and six other philosophers
emigrated to the court of the Persian king
Chosrŏēs. When he made peace with
Justinian in 533, and obtained from him
leave for the philosophers to return un-
molested, Simplicius went to Alexandria,
where he died in 549. We still possess
some excellent commentaries of his on
several writings of Aristotle (*Categories,
Physics, De Cælo, De Anĭmā*), and on the
Encheirĭdĭŏn of Epĭctētus.

Sĭnis, or **Sinnis.** Son of Pŏseidōn or
(according to another account) son of Pŏlў-
pēmōn; a robber who haunted the Isthmus
of Corinth, and was called the pine-bender
(*Pĭtўŏcamptēs*), because he tore travellers
to pieces by bending down pines and then
suddenly letting them go. He was killed
by the youthful Theseus.

Sĭnōn. A kinsman of Odysseus, who, on
the apparent departure of the Greeks from
Troy, volunteered to stay behind, and persuaded the Trojans to place the wooden
horse within their citadel. (*Cp.* TROJAN
WAR.)

Sĭpărĭum. The smaller curtain on the
Roman stage, about half way between the
front and the back. [It was drawn up
between the scenes.] (*See* THEATRE.)

Sirens (Gr. *Seirēnĕs*). The virgin
daughters of Phorcys, according to later
legend of Ăchĕlŏūs and one of the Muses.
In Homer there are two, in later writers
three, called Lĭgeῖa, Leukŏsĭa, and *Par-
thĕnŏpē,* or *Aglăŏphēmē, Molpē,* and
Thelxĭĕpeῖa. Homer describes them as
dwelling between Circe's isle and Scylla,
on an island, where they sit in a flowery
meadow, surrounded by the mouldering
bones of men, and with their sweet song
allure and infatuate those that sail by.
Whoever listens to their song and draws

near them never again beholds wife and child. They know everything that happens on earth. When Odysseus sailed past, he had stopped up the ears of his companions with wax, while he had made them bind him to the mast, that he might hear their song without danger[*Od.* xii 41–54, 153–200]. Orpheus protected the Argonauts from their spell by his own singing [Apollonius Rhodius, iv 903]. As they were only to live till some one had sailed past unmoved by their song, they cast themselves into the sea, on account either of Odysseus or of Orpheus, and were changed to sunken rocks. When the adventures of Odysseus came to be localised on the Italian and Sicilian

A SIREN.
Paris, Louvre.)

shore, the seat of the Sirens was transferred to the neighbourhood of Naples and Sorrento, to the three rocky and uninhabited islets called the *Sīrēnūsæ* [the *Sīrēnum scŏpŭli* of Vergil, *Æn.* v 864; *cp.* Statius, *Silvæ* ii 2, 1], or to Capri, or to the Sicilian promontory of Pĕlōrum. There they were said to have settled, after vainly searching the whole earth for the lost Persĕphŏnē, their former playmate in the meadows by the Achelöüs; and later legend also assigned this as the time when they in part assumed a winged shape. They were represented as great birds with the heads of women, or with the upper part of the body like that of a woman, with the legs of birds, and with

or without wings (*see* cut). At a later period they were sometimes regarded as retaining their original character of fair and cruel tempters and deceivers. But they are more generally represented as singers of the dirge for the dead, and they were hence frequently placed as an ornament on tombs; or as symbols of the magic of beauty, eloquence, and song, on which account their sculptured forms were seen on the funeral monuments of fair women and girls, and, of orators and poets: for instance, on those of Isŏcrătēs and Sophocles. [Such a Siren may be seen, beating her breast and tearing her hair, above the *stēlē* of Aristīon in the Street of Tombs at Athens. The National Museum at Athens contains several examples of stone Sirens, not as reliefs, but as separate figures "in the round"; and a funeral monument of this type may be noticed on a vase in the British Museum (*Cat.* C. 29), where the Siren is standing on a pillar and playing the lyre. *Cp.* Eurīpĭdēs, *Hel.* 169; *Anthologia Palatina* vii 710 and 481; with Miss Harrison's *Myths of the Odyssey*, pp. 146–182, and *Mythology and Monuments of Athens*, pp. 582–5.]

Sīrius (Gr. *Seirĭŏs ;* lit. "the scorcher"). The dog-star, representing among the constellations the dog of Orīon (*q.v.*).

Sīsenna. A Roman historian. (*See* ANNALISTS.)

Sīstrum. A kind of rattle, used in the worship of Īsĭs, and borrowed, at the same time with it, from the Egyptians. It consisted of a thin oval band of metal, fastened to a handle, and crossed by a number of little metal rods, bent at either end, and loosely inserted in the band. (*See* cut under ISIS.)

Sīsўphus (*i.e.* "the crafty"). The son of Æŏlus, brother of Ăthămās, husband of the Pleiad Mĕrŏpē. His son is Glaucus, the father of Bellĕrŏphōn. He is regarded as the builder of Ĕphўra (afterwards Corinth) and as originator of the Isthmian Games. In legends he appears as extremely cunning and crafty; in Homer he is called the "slyest of all men" [*Il.* vi 153]. The reason why he is punished in the other world, where he is forced for ever to keep on rolling a block of stone to the top of a steep hill, only to see it roll again to the valley, and to start the toilsome task again [*Od.* xi 593], is not mentioned by Homer; and later legends vary on this point. According to the account which gives the best idea of his cunning, Sisyphus discloses to the river-god Āsōpus, in search of his daughter Ægina (see ÆACUS), how she had been carried off by Zeus; but this information was not given until Asopus has satisfied the condition laid down by Sisyphus, by creating the spring Peirēnē, which ever after supplied the citadel and town of Corinth [Pausanias ii 5 § 1]. Zeus desires to kill Sisyphus as a punishment for revealing the facts, and sends Death to him; but Sisyphus fetters Death in strong chains, and no one dies, till at last Arēs sets him free and hands Sisyphus over to him. But he commands his wife not to inter him, and succeeds in persuading Plūtō and Persĕphŏnē to let him return for awhile to the upper world in order to punish her want of love. Having no desire to return to Hades, he forgets his promise, and eventually Hermēs has to come and fetch him. In the post-Homeric legends Odysseus, on account of his cunning, is made the son of Sisyphus and Anticleia [Sophocles, *Ajax* 190, *Phil.* 417; Eur., *Iph. at Aulis*, 524].

Sītŏphȳlăcĕs. At Athens, a board, originally consisting of ten members, five in the city itself and five in the Peiræus, which superintended the corn trade, and prevented prices becoming exorbitant. [In the time of Aristotle (*Constitution of Athens*, 51) there were twenty in the city, and fifteen in the Peiræus.] (*See* COMMERCE.)

Slaves. (I) Among the *Greeks*, besides a class of serfs like the *Pĕnestœ* of Thessaly and the *Helots* of Sparta, who had come to this condition through being conquered in war, we find, even in Homeric times, actual slaves, not differing to a very great extent from the free. They seem to have been possessed in large numbers only by princes and chieftains, who either obtained them as booty on expeditions, or bought them from such robbers of men as the Phœnicians. In historic times we find the institution of slavery very much developed, so that there is scarcely a State in which even poorer citizens do not own a male or female slave to do the rough work unworthy of a free man. In Attica, when the State was in its most flourishing condition, there were 360,000 slaves, about four times the number of free men. The Greeks justified slavery by alleging that there were certain barbarians who had been intended by nature to serve. As a matter of fact, the slaves were for the most part barbarians. In exceptional cases Greeks also were captured in war; and were thus reduced to permanent slavery; but as a rule they were exchanged or freed on paying a ransom. The countries of Asia Minor, Thrace, and the northern regions comprehended under the name of Scythia sent the greatest numbers to the *slave-markets*, of which the most important were at Dēlŏs, Chĭŏs, and Byzantium. Athens also had a slave-market, especially used by citizens who wished to expose slaves for sale that they wanted to get rid of. Most of the slaves in Attica were such as had been born from female slaves. The wealthy sometimes possessed several hundreds of them, of whom naturally only a part would be kept in the house. Some of the remainder worked on the farms in the country, while others served on the merchantmen as rowers or sailors; [others in the mines at Laurīum]; others again, either singly, or in numbers in a manufactory and under a superintendent, were engaged in some trade on their master's account. The owners also sometimes let out slaves to others. The *domestic slaves* were employed in every conceivable kind of occupation in the house, and were also entrusted with the education of the boys, whom they had to accompany everywhere, especially to the school and to the *pălœstra*; such slaves were called *pœdăgōgi*. Indeed, as a rule, even the commonest Greek, if he could possibly manage it, never went out unescorted by a slave; while, if he was rich, a number of slaves followed him.

Their treatment differed according to the character and the pecuniary position of the owner, and also depended on their own good qualities and usefulness. In general, the Athenians were noted for being more humane towards their slaves than the rest of the Greeks. There were laws also that referred to them, and protected them against excessive caprice and harshness. But they had no legal rights; they could neither bring a charge, nor appear as witnesses. It was only when they were put on the rack that their evidence had any weight attached to it. But the master could not kill a slave unless the latter had been condemned in a law-court; otherwise, he had to pay a penalty to some divinity. If cruelly treated, a slave could seek protection, usually in the temple of Thēseus, and claim to be sold to another master. In case of maltreatment by a stranger, the master could bring a legal action, and obtain heavy damages. Slaves had no particular dress prescribed for them by law; but they were not allowed to let their hair grow long. They were not prohibited from entering temples and sanctuaries or from taking part in public religious festivals; but they were excluded from the use of the gymnasia and from the assemblies of the people. Manumissions were not rare, especially those made by a clause in the owner's will, or if a slave bought his freedom with the savings made by permission of his master; sometimes manumission was a reward for giving information about grave crimes, or for distinguished service in war; for slaves were not unfrequently employed in military service, especially in the fleet as rowers and sailors, or as marines. For the position of the liberated slaves, see FREEDMEN. At Athens there was also a special class of *public slaves*. Chief among them were those called *Sc̄ythæ* or archers, at first 300, then 600, and finally even 1,200; the name *Speusīniī* was also given them from a certain Speusīnus, who is said to have established this institution [Pollux, viii 132, and *Etymologicum Magnum*]. They served as police, and their office was at first on the market-place, and afterwards on the Areōpăgus. They were further employed for military purposes, like the similar corps, also consisting of public slaves, of 200 mounted archers (*hippŏtoxŏtæ*). The lower servants of the State officials, such as criers, scribes, beadles, gaol-keepers, hangmen, were mostly (the last mentioned always) public slaves, and so were the workmen at the mint. Their position was one of much greater freedom than that of the private slaves, and did not differ greatly from that of the *mĕtœci*.

(II) The *Romans*, like the Greeks, possessed slaves from the earliest times; but their number was at first trifling, on account of the small households of the old Romans, and their simple manner of life. But great estates gradually became frequent, and slaves were used by preference for agricultural work, because they were not subject to levy for military service. Luxury became more general, and a number of wants, previously unknown, were created by it; and in process of time the custom of employing slaves for industrial purposes was borrowed from the Greeks. All this caused a continual increase in the number of slaves, until in some cases they were collected in several thousands. Some of these were born in the house, and were called *vernæ*; they were regarded as particularly faithful and trustworthy, and enjoyed certain liberties accordingly. The remainder were for the most part acquired among the spoils of war, or were introduced from other countries where slaves were kept. Those taken in war were sold by the quæstor either on

the spot immediately or at the nearest market-place, or, according to the technical terms, either *sub hastā* (under the lance) or *sub corōnā* (under the wreath, which was placed on the head of captives in war to show that they were for sale). For this purpose *slave-dealers*, whose profitable trade was regarded with contempt, were always represented in the train of Roman armies. They also bought slaves in great numbers at the principal slave-marts, as at Rome and Dēlŏs. At Rome the ædiles superintended this kind of business, on which the government levied a tax for import and a further tax on the sale. The slave was placed on a platform, with his feet whitened with chalk or gypsum, if he had just come across the sea, and with a label round his neck, showing his home, age, abilities, and bodily defects, if any, the vendor being responsible for the correctness of these statements; if he would not bind himself in any such way, this was shown by placing a cap (*pillĕŭs*) on the slave's head. Slaves distinguished for their beauty, their skill, or their literary or musical accomplishments, were not exhibited publicly, but in special places, and to such as were able to pay the prices for them, which frequently ran very high. Those born in the house were also sold by private agreement, without being exposed. There were slaves of every nationality, and on this depended in general the names by which they were called and the work which was assigned them. The *fămĭlĭa* (a designation including all the slaves, or *fămŭli*, belonging to the same master) was generally divided into that of the country (*familia rustĭca*) and that of the town (*familia urbāna*).

The work done by the slaves was of the most varied character, and the great diversity of their occupations is partly explained by the fact that almost every kind of work required a special slave, and it was considered not consistent with good breeding, and a sign of poverty, if the same slave was entrusted with several different duties. Thus there were in the country special slaves for the various branches of agriculture, horticulture, and the tending of cattle, the cultivation of olives and vines, the keeping of bees and of poultry, and for the preserves and fishponds. These slaves were under the supervision of the *vīlĭcus* (farm-bailiff) or *actor* (steward), who had to render the accounts to the master or his representative.

The number of *town-slaves* was not due to

actual requirements, but depended on the luxurious fashions which became more and more prevalent in the last two centuries of the Republic. In older times the house and everything belonging to it was in charge of the *ædĭtŭus* (majordomo, steward), who managed all household affairs, received and spent money, negotiated sales and purchases, and disposed of the stores. When the extension of the household made it necessary to keep a special person to control the expenditure, the steward's functions were limited to seeing that the house and furniture were properly cleaned and in a good state. Besides him there were subordinate servants for the various dwellings, the spare rooms for visitors, the shrine of the household gods, the images of the ancestors, the various kinds of furniture, the art collections, and the wardrobe; and there was also a porter (*iānĭtor* or *ostĭārĭus*) who, according to an old custom, was chained like a dog. [Suetonius, *De Rhet.* 3; Columella, 1 pr. § 10; Ovid, *Amōrēs* i 6, 1.]

The kitchen was in charge of a special *chef*, an even more expensive slave than the *vĭlĭcus;* and under him were a host of assistants, wood-carriers, market-men, pastry-cooks, etc. The service at table also necessitated a numerous attendance of dressers, servers, carvers, fore-tasters, cup-bearers, table-clearers, and others, who similarly were under a special foreman, the *trĭclĭnĭarcha*, who saw to the general arrangements and to the lighting. The master and mistress of the house were served by special valets (*cŭbĭcŭlārĭi*), who also had to announce visitors, and pages and chambermaids and special servants for the bath and the toilette. It was considered of especial importance that, when the master or mistress of the house left it on foot or in a litter, the slaves following them should be numerous and richly attired. Some slaves went before their master (*anteambŭlōnēs*), especially the *nomenclātor*, who informed his master of the names of the persons they met; others followed (*pĕdĭsĕqui*); others again were told off for attending their master with torches and lanterns on leaving parties in the evening. The litter of each member of the family was carried by from six to eight *lectĭcārĭi*, particularly strong men, and by preference Cappadocians. For travelling across country there was always a large escort, consisting of crowds of equerries, outriders, grooms, etc. . The most important position among the servants was occupied by those whom the master himself chose to

assist him in his business or his recreations; as for instance those who attended to money matters and to the supervision of the slaves, secretaries, physicians, readers at meals or during the bath or before going to sleep, literary men, librarians, and transcribers of books. For other kinds of recreation there were also slaves who had received a musical training, *pantŏmĭmi*, fools, and jesters.

The various classes of slaves had each its special foreman, with a substitute whom he either received from his master, or bought with his savings. These formed the class of the *ordĭnārĭi*, who enjoyed the special confidence of their master; this class included such servants as looked after the food, clothing, and medical attendance of the slaves, the maintenance and watching of the various buildings, the accounts of the household (*cellārĭus*), and the expenses of the master (*dispensātor*). Young slaves were trained for the various requirements of the household; according to their abilities, they were taught some trade or art, or had practice given them either in keeping accounts or in learned studies. Under the Empire, those who were destined to be pages received their education in special *pædăgōgĭa* or establishments, kept not only by the emperor, but also by private citizens. As in Greece, trained slaves were established in some trade by themselves, or let out on hire; such was the case even with slaves who were artists or men of learning. Even posts of independence, such as the administration of an estate in the country, or of a bank, or the command of a ship, were entrusted to slaves, who received a share in the profits, or paid interest on the capital invested, or a fixed sum of money when the capital was their own. For the slaves were allowed to acquire a private fortune (*pĕcūlĭum*) from what they saved on their allowances and from the regular profits of their service. The masters regarded this arrangement with favour, especially as it represented a kind of caution money in case any damage was done.

The Roman slave was, in the eyes of the law, a mere chattel, and hence absolutely without any rights and completely exposed to the caprice of his master. The latter could compel him to do the meanest and most shameful things, could torture or kill him, or cast him out when he was old or weakly; and as this treatment was legally permitted, it was carried out in practice when occasion offered. Special cruelty was experienced by the country-slaves, who worked in chains in the greater part of Italy, and were kept in a guarded work-house (*ergastŭlum*) at night; some of them were branded, or had one half of their heads shaven. It was therefore a severe punishment for a town-slave to be sent into the country. The usual mode of killing slaves was crucifixion, which was put down by the Christian emperors. If a slave dared to wreak vengeance on his master, every slave who was under the same roof at the time was put to death with him. This cruelty of treatment, which grew continually in the last centuries of the Republic, brought on repeated and terrible *insurrections of the slaves*. Under the Empire they received some legal protection; in its very beginning, the master's right to condemn his slaves to fight with wild beasts was taken away from him and transferred to a regular judge: the prefect of the city at Rome, and the procurator in the provinces. These officials were also empowered, by Antōnīnus Pius, to receive the complaints of slaves about cruel treatment, and to sell the slaves to another master, in case their complaints were found to rest on truth. Hadrian deprived the owners of the right of killing and torturing slaves at their pleasure, or of selling them to keepers of gladiatorial schools or to procurers; and, finally, Constantine placed the intentional killing of a slave on a level with murder. A kind of married relation between slaves, called *contŭbernĭum*, was permitted at an early time. Under the Empire, it became a rule to regard it as lasting and indissoluble, and even to celebrate the marriage of slaves by wedding festivities. Having no legal rights, the slave could not give evidence in a law court, and, as in Greece, only what he said when under torture was deemed worthy of credit. The Roman, like the Athenian, government had *public slaves* (*servi publĭci*), who, on the whole, had the same legal position as the private slaves. They lived in public buildings assigned to them by the censors, and received from the public chest a yearly sum to pay for their board (*cĭbārĭa*). They were partly employed as custodians of temples and public buildings (*œdĭtŭi*), partly as servants to the various priesthoods and to those magistrates who had duties relating to the police, namely, the censors and ædiles (who under Augustus had under their control a *familia* of 600 *servi publici* for the prevention of fires), the overseers of the water supply, and of the prisons, and those who had to

see capital sentences carried out. The slaves of the latter included the hangman (*carnĭfex*) who was entrusted with the special duty of executing slaves, and who had to live outside the Esquiline Gate. (*See also* FREEDMEN.)

Sleep (Gr. *Hypnŏs*; Lat. *Somnus*). The son of Night and twin-brother of Death (*q.v.*) [*Il.* xiv 231; xvi 672]. With his brother Death, according to Hesiod, he dwells in the eternal darkness of the farthest West [*Theog.* 759]. Thence he sweeps over land and sea, bringing sleep to men and gods, since he has power over all alike, and could lull to sleep even Zeus himself. On the chest of Cypsĕlus at Olympia, both brothers were depicted as boys sleeping in the arms of their mother, Death being painted in black and Sleep in white [Pausanias, v 18 § 1]. Sleep was represented in art in very various forms and situations, and frequently with the wings of an eagle or a butterfly on his forehead, and a poppy-stalk and a horn, from which he dropped slumber upon those whom he lulls to rest. The earlier conception made Dreams the sisters of Sleep, but in later times the dream-god figures as his son. Hermēs was also a god of sleep.

Sling (Gr. *sphendŏnē*; Lat. *funda*). A weapon for hurling missiles, consisting of a thong, broad in the middle and growing narrower towards the ends. The missile was either a round stone of the size of a hen's egg, a ball of baked clay, or a leaden bolt cast in the shape of an acorn. It was placed in the broad part of the thong, and the slinger (Gr. *sphendŏnētēs*; Lat. *fundĭtor*), holding the thong by both ends in in one hand, swung it several times round his head, and discharged the ball at the mark by means of letting go one end of the thong. The most famous slingers of antiquity were the inhabitants of the Balearic Isles; they carried three slings, made of plaited rushes, hair, and the sinews of wild beasts, for long,

SLINGER.
(Trajan's Column, Rome.)

short, and intermediate shots respectively. Various leaden slingbolts, bearing marks or characteristic inscriptions, have been preserved. Under the Empire there came into use the sling-staff (Lat. *fustĭbălus*), a staff four feet in length, to the end of which a leathern sling was fastened. One thong of this reached to the other end of the staff, and was together with this held fast by the *fustībālātor*, who swung the staff several times round his head, and suddenly let go the longer thong, thus throwing a larger missile with much greater force than was possible with a simple sling.

Soccus. A loose slipper, or light, low shoe, fitting either foot, which the Romans adopted from the Greeks. It was the characteristic of comedy, as the *cŏthurnus* was of tragedy [Horace, *A. P.* 80 (of the iambic metre): "Hunc *socci* cēpērĕ pĕdem, grandesque *cothurni*"].

Sŏcii. Among the Romans, the *socii*, as distinguished in constitutional law from Roman subjects, were the allies who, while their independence was recognised, stood in a more or less dependent relation to the Roman State. Under the Republic, up to the time when the right of citizenship was conferred on all the free inhabitants of Italy (89 B.C.), the Latins, and the Italian communities on the same footing with them, enjoyed a privileged position amongst the other allies. In the military organization of the Roman Republic the contingents which they furnished were called *socii*, in contradistinction to the legions and the non-Italian auxiliaries. (*See* AUXILIA, and *cp.* LEGION.) *Socii nāvālēs* are the crews, furnished by the allied towns, of the ships of war.

Sōcrătēs. Of Athens; born 469 B.C., son of the sculptor Sōphrŏniscus and the midwife Phænărĕtē. He pursued for a time his father's art, but soon gave it up, holding it to be his proper task in life to labour at the moral and intellectual improvement of himself and his friends. His indifference to external necessities enabled him to bear his poverty with the same equanimity which he preserved in dealing with the quarrelsome temper of his wife Xanthippē. He took no part in affairs of State, yet did not withdraw from the performance of his duties as a citizen in war and peace. He did not give formal instruction, but sought by means of dialectical discourse, in which any one might join without payment, to lead on the young people who used to collect around him to think and act in accordance with reason. Different as are the representations of him given by his pupils Xĕnŏphōn and Plato, yet they agree in this, that he was a character of absolute moral purity, whose clear peace of mind

was troubled by no passion, in whom reason at all times asserted its supremacy over sensuality, and whom no considerations could move from the declaration of his convictions. He preserved this unshaken fidelity to his convictions, not only in earlier passages of his life, but also at the time when a capital charge was brought against him, of being out of accord with the religion of the State, of introducing new gods (an accusation founded upon his belief in the *dæmōn*, an inward voice, which used to warn him from evil and urge him towards good), and of corrupting youth. Although it would have been an easy thing for him to have escaped the sentence of death, he did not hesitate for a moment in giving expression to his conviction in the most open manner, and for that conviction was put to death by being compelled to drink a draught of hemlock. (*See* also PHILOSOPHY and PLATO, with cut.)

Sŏdālītās. [The word properly means an association or club, and was especially applied to the] religious brotherhoods among the Romans. By order of the State, they attended to the cult of some particular object of worship by jointly celebrating certain sacrifices and feasts, especially on the anniversary of the foundation of that cult.

The members, called *sŏdālēs*, stood in a legally recognised position of mutual obligation, which did not allow any one of them to appear against another as a prosecutor in a criminal case, or to become *patrōnus* of the prosecutor of a *sodalis*, or to officiate as judge upon a *sodalis*. Such a brotherhood were the *Sodales Augustālēs*, appointed A.D. 14 by the Senate for the cult of the deified Augustus, a college of 21, and afterwards of 28, members of senatorial rank, which also took upon itself the cult of Claudius after his deification, and bore, after that, the official title *Sodales Augustales Claudiālēs*. Besides these there were the *Sodales Flāviales Tǐtiales* for the cult of Vespasian and Titus, the *Hadriānales* for that of Hadrian, *Antōnīnǐāni* for that of Antoninus Pius and of the successively deified emperors. (*Cp.* COLLEGIUM.)

[The secular clubs, *sŏdālǐtātēs*, or *collēgǐa sŏdālǐcǐa*, were, in the later Republican age, much turned to account for political objects, and their organization used for purposes of bribery. *See* Cicero's speech *Pro Plancio.* It was very common for young Romans to belong to an ordinary *sodalitas.* Both Horace and Ovid were members of one.]

Sōl. The Italian sun-god, identified with the Greek Hēlĭŏs (*q.v.*).

Sōlārĭum. A sundial (*see* GNOMON); also the flat roof of the Roman dwelling-house (*see* HOUSE, 2).

Soldiers. *Greek, see* WARFARE. *Roman, see* LEGION. For the game of "soldiers" (*lūdus latruncŭlōrum*), see GAMES.

Sŏlĕa. The shoe usually worn by Romans when at home. Outside the house they wore it only when going out to dinner. During the meal itself it was taken off. It was a strong sole of wood, cork, or leather, which was fastened on the foot by two straps. One of these passed between the great toe and the second toe, and was connected by a buckle or otherwise with a strap running lengthwise over the instep. The second strap went round the ankle. (*See* cuts to SANDALIUM.)

Sŏlĭdus. A Roman gold coin, introduced by the emperor Constantine about 312 A.D., which remained in use until the downfall of the Byzantine empire; its weight was $\frac{1}{72}$ lb., its value 12s. $8\frac{1}{2}d$. (*See further under* COINAGE.)

Solīnus (*Gaius Iūlĭus*). A Roman writer who composed, probably in the second half of the 3rd century A.D., a collection of *Mĕmŏrābĭlĭa* (*Collectānĕa Rērum Mĕmŏrābĭlĭum*, better known by its later title *Pŏlўhĭstōr*). The most important portion (the geographical) is an abstract of a treatise on geography compiled from Pliny's Natural History.

Sŏlĭum. *See* BATHS and CHAIRS.

Sŏlōn. Of Athens, son of Exēcestĭdēs, born about 640 B.C., died 559, the famous Athenian lawgiver. (*See* below on the SOLONIAN CONSTITUTION.) He is one of the "Seven Wise Men." He also holds a high position amongst the lyric, and especially amongst the elegiac, poets of Greece. The noble patriotism and kindly wisdom which marked the whole of his life found expression in his poems, which were in part connected with the political condition of his own city, and were also intended to teach universal principles of humanity in an appropriate poetical form. His elegies are said to have amounted to 5,000 lines in all. Among his political elegies may be mentioned that on Sălămĭs, by which, in his earlier years, he roused his fellow citizens to reconquer that island when it had been taken from them by the Megarians; also his *Exhortations to the Athenians.* To his

ethical elegies belong the *Exhortations to Himself.* Of the last two poems in particular we possess extensive fragments [in which the elegiac measure is raised to a new dignity by being made the vehicle of ethical teaching. One of the finest fragments owes its preservation to its being quoted by Demosthenes, *De Falsā Lēgātĭōne*, § 255]. There are also some fragments of minor poems in iambics and trochaics as well as a *skŏlĭŏn*. [In Aristotle's *Constitution of Athens*, 5, 12, we have several quotations from Solon's poems, including about twenty lines which are otherwise unknown.]

Solonian Constitution. At the time of Solon the Athenian State was almost falling to pieces in consequence of dissensions between the parties into which the population was divided. Of these the *Dĭacrĭi*, the inhabitants of the northern mountainous region of Attica, the poorest and most oppressed section of the population, demanded that the privileges of the nobility, which had till then obtained, should be utterly set aside. Another party, prepared to be contented by moderate concessions, was composed of the *Părăli*, the inhabitants of the stretch of coast called Părălĭa. The third was formed by the nobles, called *Pĕdĭeis* or *Pĕdĭăci*, because their property lay for the most part in the *pĕdĭŏn*, the level and most fruitful part of the country. Solon, who enjoyed the confidence of all parties on account of his tried insight and sound judgment, was chosen archon by a compromise, with full power to put an end to the difficulties, and to restore peace by means of legislation. One of the primary measures of Solon was the *Seisachtheia* (disburdening ordinance). This gave an immediate relief by cancelling all debts, public and private. At the same time he made it illegal for the future to secure debts upon the person of the debtor [Aristotle, *Constitution of Athens*, 6].

He also altered the standard of coinage [and of weights and measures, by introducing the Euboic standard in place of the Pheidonian or Æginetan, *ib.* 10]. 100 new drachmæ were thus made to contain the same amount of silver as 73 old drachmæ.

He further instituted a timocracy (*q.v.*), by which the exclusive rights which the nobles had till then possessed were set aside, and those who did not belong to the nobility received a share in the rights of citizens, according to a scale determined by their property and their corresponding services to the State. For this purpose he divided the population into four classes, founded on the possession of land. (1) *Pentăcŏsĭŏmĕdimni*, who had at least 500 *medimni* (750 bushels) of corn or *mĕtrētœ* of wine or oil as yearly income. (2) *Hippēīs*, or knights, with at least 300 *medimni*. (3) *Zeugītœ* (possessors of a yoke of oxen), with at least 150 *medimni*. (4) *Thētĕs* (workers for wages), with less than 150 *medimni* of yearly income. Solon's legislation only granted to the first three of these four classes a vote in the election of responsible officers, and only to the first class the power of election to the highest offices; as, for instance, that of archon. The fourth class was excluded from all official positions, but possessed the right of voting in the general public assemblies which chose officials and passed laws. They had also the right of taking part in the trials by jury which Solon had instituted. The first three classes were bound to serve as hoplites; the cavalry was raised out of the first two, while the fourth class was only employed as light-armed troops or on the fleet, and apparently for pay. The others served without pay. The holders of office in the State were also unpaid. Solon established as the chief *consultative* body the Council of the Four Hundred (*see* BOULE), in which only the first three classes took part, and as chief *administrative* body the Areopagus (*q.v.*) which was to be filled up by those who had been archons. Besides this, he promulgated a code of laws embracing the whole of public and private life, the salutary effects of which lasted long after the end of his constitution.

[According to Aristotle's *Constitution of Athens*, 4, a Council of 401 members was part of Drăcōn's constitution (about 621 B.C.). The members were selected by lot from the whole body of citizens. Solon (who was archon in 594) reduced the Council to 400, one hundred from each of the four tribes; and extended in some particulars the powers already possessed by the Areopagus (*ib.* 8).]

Somnus. The Roman god of sleep (*q.v.*).

Sophists (Gr. *sŏphistai*). Properly a name given by the Greeks to all those who professed knowledge, or a particular knowledge or a particular art. Hence the Seven Wise Men are often thus called; but the name was especially applied to the educated men of ready speech, who, from about the year 450 B.C., used to travel through Greece from place to place, and imparted what they knew for money. They have the merit of having popularized the interest in knowledge which had up to that time been confined within narrow circles, and especially of having contributed to the formation of eloquence. For they were the first to make style an object of study, and to institute serious investigations into the art of rhetorical expression. Their teaching was chiefly intended to give their pupils versatility in the use of speech, and thus to fit them for taking part in public life. As the subject of their discourses, they chose by preference questions of public interest to persons of general education. The expression, however, always remained the important thing, while positive knowledge fell more and more into the background. Some of them even started from the position, that virtue and knowledge were only subjective notions. *Prōtăgŏrās* of Abdēra, who appeared about 445 B.C., is named as the first Sophist; after him the most important is *Gorgĭās* of Lĕontīni; *Prŏdĭcus* of Cĕōs and *Hippĭās* of Elis are contemporaries of the other two. Wherever they appeared, especially in Athens, they were received with the greatest enthusiasm, and many flocked to hear them. Even such men as Pericles, Euripides, and Socrates sought their society; and Socrates owed to them much that was suggestive in his own pursuit of practical philosophy, though, on the other hand, he persistently attacked the principles underlying their public teaching. These principles became further exaggerated under their successors, who did not think they needed even knowledge of fact to talk as they pleased about everything. Accordingly the skill of the Sophist degenerated into mere technicalities and complete absence of reason, and became absolutely contemptible. [*See* Grote's *History of Greece*, chap. lxvii, and Dr. H. Sidgwick's essay in the *Journal of Philology*, iv 288.]

With the revival of Greek eloquence, from about the beginning of the 2nd century A.D., the name of Sophist attained a new distinction. At that time the name was given to the professional orators, who appeared in public with great pomp and delivered declamations either prepared beforehand or improvised on the spot. Like the earlier Sophists, they went generally from place to place, and were overwhelmed with applause and with marks of distinction by their contemporaries, including even the Roman emperors. *Dion Chrysos-*

tom, *Hĕrōdēs Attĭcus, Aristīdēs, Lucian*, and *Phĭlostrātus* the elder, belong to the flourishing period of this second school of Sophists, a period which extends over the whole of the 2nd century. They appear afresh about the middle of the 4th century, devoting their philosophic culture to the zealous but unavailing defence of paganism. Among them was the emperor *Julian* and his contemporaries *Lĭbănĭus, Hĭmĕrĭus*, and *Thĕmistius. Sўnĕsĭus* may be considered as the last Sophist of importance.

Sŏphŏclēs. One of the three great Greek tragedians, son of Sŏphillus, the wealthy owner of a manufactory of armour, was born probably in 495 B.C. in the deme Cŏlōnus near Athens. He received a careful education in music, gymnastics, and dancing, and as a boy of fifteen was chosen to lead the pæan sung by the chorus of boys after the victory of Sălămīs. He afterwards showed his musical skill in public, when he represented the blind singer Thămȳrĭs in his drama of the same name, and played the cīthără with such success that he was painted as Thamyris with the cithara in the Stŏă Poicīlē. Again, in the play called the *Nausĭcăă*, he won for himself general admiration in acting the part of the princess of that name, by the dexterity and grace with which he struck the ball [Athenæus, p. 20 E]. In all things his external appearance and demeanour was the reflex of his lofty mind. At his very first appearance as a tragic poet in 468, when 27 years old, he gained a victory over Æschўlus, who was thirty years older, and from that time to extreme old age he kept the first place in tragedy. Unlike Æschylus and Euripides, he never accepted the invitations of foreign princes. Though possessing no special inclination or fitness for political affairs, as his friend, the poet Ĭŏn of Chĭŏs, declares, he yet took his part in public life. Thus, in 440 B.C. he was one of the ten generals who, with Pericles, were in command of the fleet sent against Sămŏs. Owing to his practical skill he was also employed in negotiations with the allies of Chios and Samos. During the Peloponnesian War he was again one of the generals, together with Nĭcĭăs. In 435, as *Hellēnŏtămĭăs*, he was at the head of the management of the treasure of the allies, which was kept on the Acrŏpŏlĭs; and, when the question arose in 413, of giving to the State an oligarchical constitution, he was on the commission of preliminary investigation. He also filled a priestly office.

The charm and the refinement of his character seem to have won him many friends. Among them was the historian Hĕrŏdŏtus, who much resembled him. He was also deemed by antiquity as a man specially beloved by the gods, especially by Asclēpius, whose priest he probably was, and who was said to have granted him

* SOPHOCLES.
(Rome, Lateran Museum.)

health and vigour of mind to extreme old age. By the Athenian Nĭcostrătē he had a son, *Ĭŏphōn*, who won some repute as a tragic poet, and by Thĕŏrĭs of Sĭcўōn another son, *Ariston*, father of the *Sophocles* who gained fame for himself by tragedies of his own, and afterwards by the production of his grandfather's dramas. There was a story that a quarrel arose between Sophocles and his son Iophon, on account of his preference for this grandson, and that, when summoned by Iophon before the court as weak in mind and unable to manage his affairs, he obtained his own absolute acquittal by reading the chorus on his native place in the *Œdīpūs Cŏlōnēus* [Plutarch, *Moralia*, p. 775 B]. But this appears to be a legend founded on a misunderstood pleasantry of a comic poet. The tales of his death, which happened in 405, are also mythical. According to one account, he was choked by a grape; according to others, he died either when publicly reciting the *Antīgŏnē*, or from excessive joy at some dramatic victory. The only fact unanimously attested by his contemporaries is, that his death was as dignified as his life. A singular story is connected even with his funeral. We are told that Dĭonȳsus, by repeated apparitions in dreams, prompted the general of the Spartans, who were then investing Athens, to grant a truce for the burial of the poet in the family grave outside the city. On his tomb stood a Siren as a symbol of the charm of poetry. After his death the Athenians worshipped him as a hero and offered an annual sacrifice in his memory. In later times, on the proposal of the orator Lȳcurgus, a bronze statue was erected to him, together with Æschylus and Euripides, in the theatre, and of his dramas, as of theirs, an authorized and standard copy was made, in order to protect them against arbitrary alterations.

Sophocles was a very prolific poet. The number of .his pieces is given as between 123 and 130, of which above 100 are known to us by their titles and by fragments. But only seven have been preserved complete : The *Trāchīnīœ* (so named from the chorus, and treating of the death of Hērăclēs), the *Ajax*, the *Phĭloctētēs*, the *Electra*, the *Œdīpūs Tȳrannus*, the *Œdipus at Colonus*, and the *Antīgŏnē*. The last-mentioned play was produced in the spring of 440 ; the *Phĭloctetes* in 410; the *Œdipus at Colonus* was not put on the stage until 401, after his death, by his grandson Sophocles. Besides tragedies, Sophocles composed pæans, elegies, epigrams, and a work in prose on the chorus. With his tragedies he gained the first prize more than twenty times, and still more often the second, but never the third. Even in his lifetime, and indeed through the whole of antiquity, he was held to be the most perfect of tragedians ; one of the ancient writers calls him the " pupil of Homer "

[*Vita Anon., ad fin.*]. If Æschylus is the creator of Greek tragedy, it was Sophocles who brought it to perfection. He extended the dramatic action (1) by the introduction of a third actor, while in his last pieces he even added a fourth ; and (2) by a due subordination of the chorus, to which, however, he gave a more artistic development, while he increased its numbers from twelve to fifteen persons. He also perfected the costumes and decoration. Rejecting the plan of Æschylus, by which one story was carried through three successive plays, he made every tragedy into a complete work of art, with a separate and complete action, the motives for every detail being most skilfully devised. His art was especially shewn in the way in which the action is developed from the character of the *dramatis personœ*. Sophocles' great mastery of his art appears, above all, in the clearness with which he portrays his characters, which are developed with a scrupulous attention to details, and in which he does not content himself, like Æschylus, with mere outlines, nor, as Euripides often 'did, with copies from common life. His heroes, too, are ideal figures, like those of Æschylus. While they lack the superhuman loftiness of the earlier poet's creations, they have a certain ideal truth of their own. Sophocles succeeding in doing what was impossible for Æschylus and Euripides with their peculiar temperaments, in expressing the nobility of the female character, in its gentleness as well as in its heroic courage. In contrast to Euripides, Sophocles, like Æschylus, is profoundly religious; and the attitude which he adopts towards the popular religion is marked by an instinctive reverence. The grace peculiar to Sophocles' nature makes itself felt even in his language, the charm of which was universally praised by the ancients. With his noble simplicity he takes in this respect also a middle place between the weightiness and boldness of the language of Æschylus, and the smoothness and rhetorical embellishment which distinguish that of Euripides.

Sŏphrŏn. Of Syracuse. A Greek writer of mimes, an elder contemporary of Euripides. He composed in the Dorian dialect prose dialogues, partly serious, partly comic, which faithfully represented scenes of actual life, mostly in the lower classes, interspersed with numerous proverbs and colloquial forms of speech. In spite of their prose form, Sophron's mimes were regarded as poems by the ancients. In Athens they are said to have become known through Plato, who thought very highly of them, and made use of them for the dramatic form of his dialogues [Quintilian, i 10 § 17; Diogenes Laertius iii 13]. After his death it is said that they were found under his pillow, together with the comedies of Aristophanes. In the Alexandrine age, Theocrītus took them for a pattern in his *Idylls* [especially in the *Adōnĭāzūsæ*, *Id.* 15]. The Greek grammarians also paid particular attention to them on account of the popular idioms they contained. The fragments preserved are so scanty, that they give no notion of the contents and form of the pieces; in any case they cannot have been intended for public representation. Sophron's son, Xĕnarchus, who lived during the reign of Dĭŏnỹsĭus I, also wrote mimes.

Sŏphrŏnistæ. Officers amongst the Greeks who looked after the moral behaviour of the youth in the gymnasia (*q.v.*). [Aristotle, *Constitution of Athens*, 42.]

Sōrānus. A Greek physician from Ephesus, who lived in the first half of the 2nd century A.D., under Trajan and Hadrian. His writings are now represented by a work of considerable extent on the diseases of women, and a surgical treatise on fractures. The writings of Cælius Aurēliānus (*q.v.*) on *Acute and Chronic Diseases* are translated from him.

Sortēs (properly "lots"). Small tablets used for augury in different parts of Italy, especially in the temple of Fortūna at Præneste [Cicero, *De Divin.* ii 41 § 86]. They were of oak or bronze, with some saying engraved upon them, and were shuffled and drawn by a boy. Seventeen such sayings (four in the original bronze, and the rest copies) are still preserved. They are known as the *sortes Prænestīnæ*, but they appear to have really belonged to the oracle of Gērȳŏn at Pătăvĭum (*Padua*).

The same name was given (1) to passages of some book used to foretell events, the method being to open the book at random, for which purpose Christians used the Bible; or (2) to lines of poetry, especially of Vergil, written on leaves, and drawn at haphazard. [*Sortes Vergĭlĭānæ* are mentioned in Spartiānus, *Hadrian* 2, and alluded to in Lamprĭdĭus, *Alex. Severus* 14.—In the cut given under Mœræ, Lăchĕsis is holding three *sortes.*]

Sōsĭgĕnēs. A Greek mathematician from Egypt, who assisted Cæsar in the correction of the Roman calendar in 46 B.C. (*Cp.* CALENDAR.)

Sōsĭphănēs. Of Syracuse; a Greek tragedian of the Alexandrine *Plēĭăs* (*q.v.*), who lived about 300 B.C. Of his plays only a few lines have been preserved.

Sōsĭthĕus. Of Alexandria in the Troad; a Greek tragedian, one of the Alexandrine *Plēĭăs* (*q.v.*). He lived in the first half of the 3rd century B.C., in Athens and in Alexandria in Egypt. In an epigram of the Greek Anthology [vii 707] he is celebrated as the restorer of the satyric drama. We still possess an interesting fragment of his satyric plays, the *Daphnis* [twenty-one lines in Nauck's *Tragicorum Gr. Fragm.*, p. 822, ed. 1889].

Sōspĭta ("the *saving* goddess"). Epithet of several Roman goddesses (*e.g.* of Juno).

Sōsus. A celebrated artist in mosaic, who was working apparently at the time of the Attălĭdæ in Pergămŏn. It was there that he executed his famous work, "The Unswept House" (*ăsărōtŏs oikŏs*), so called because remnants of food, and all that is usually swept away, were represented strewn about in the most artistic way upon the floor. "Much to be admired in this work [says Pliny, xxxvi 184] is a dove drinking, and darkening the water by the shadow of its head; while other doves are sunning and pluming themselves on the rim of the vessel." This is copied in the mosaic [found in Hadrian's Villa at Tivoli, and now] in the Capitoline Museum at Rome. (*See* MOSAICS, fig. 1.)

Sōtădēs. A Greek poet from Mărōneia in Thrace, who lived at Alexandria under Ptolemy Phĭlădelphus about 276 B.C. He is said to have been drowned in the sea in a leaden chest for some sarcastic remark about the marriage of the king with his own sister Arsĭnŏē. He composed in Ionic dialect and in a peculiar metre named after him (*Sōtădēŭs* or *Sōtădĭcŭs versus*), poems called *cĭnædi*, malicious satires partly on indelicate subjects, which were intended for recitation accompanied by a mimic dance, and also travesties of mythological subjects, such as the Iliad of Homer. He found numerous imitators.

Sōtēr ("*saviour*"). An epithet of several Greek gods (*e.g.* of Zeus), [and also of several kings, *e.g.* Ptolemy I, king of Egypt].

Spartī (Gr. *Spartoi*, "the men sown"). The men in full armour who sprang up from the teeth of the dragon of Ārĕs when sown by Cadmus. On their birth they immediately fought with one another, till only five remained. The survivors helped

Cadmus to found Thebes, and were the ancestors of the Theban nobility.

Spartiānus. A Roman historian. (*See* SCRIPTORES HISTORIÆ AUGUSTÆ.)

Spartiātæ. In Sparta the ruling class of those who had the full rights of citizens, as distinguished from the subject *Pĕrĭœci* and *Helots* (*q.v.*). They were the descendants of the Dorians, who had formerly conquered the land under the leadership of Aristŏdēmus. As to the manner in which they were divided, *see* PHYLÆ. Their number is said never to have exceeded 10,000, and, as they were utterly opposed to the admission of foreign elements, it was constantly decreasing. At the time of the Persian wars it still amounted to 8,000, about 320 B.C. to little more than 1,000.

They were called *hŏmoioi* (men sharing equal rights), with reference to the equality established amongst them by the legislation of Lȳcurgus, (1) in their education (*q.v.*), which was exclusively directed towards fitting them for service in war; (2) in their way of living, especially in the meals which they had in common (*see* SYSSITIA); (3) in their property; (4) and in their political rights.

To every family of *Spartiatæ* an equal portion of land was assigned by Lycurgus, with a number of helots who had settled upon it, who had to cultivate the property and deliver the produce to its possessor. The *Spartiatæ* themselves were not allowed to engage in a handicraft, or in trade, or in agriculture; their whole life had to be devoted to the service of the State, and therefore they had their abode in Sparta itself. The allotted land and the helots were accounted State property, and the possessors had no kind of right to dispose of them. Families which were dying out were preserved by adopting sons of families related to them, and similarly heiresses were married to men without inheritance of their own. If a family consisted of several male members, then the eldest was considered as head of the family, and had to support his brothers. The original equality of property came to an end, partly through the extinction of many families and the transference of their lot of ground, partly by the silent abrogation of the old law, which did not allow the *Spartiatæ* to possess silver or gold, but chiefly after the law of Epĭtădēus, by which the free disposal of land was allowed, if not by sale, at least by gift during lifetime and by will. But the principle of aristo-

cratic equality long continued in form; and only those who did not fulfil the conditions attached to the equality of rights, or who did not obey the injunctions of Lycurgus as to the education of the young, and as to the life of adult citizens, or who did not contribute to the common meals, suffered a diminution of their political rights. This involved exclusion from the government and administration of the State, as well as from the right of electing or being elected to office; but the punishment affected the individual only, and did not descend to his children, nor did it touch his position in personal law.

Spēs. The Roman personification of hope, especially of hope for a good harvest, and (in later times) for the blessing of children. There were several temples to *Spes* in Rome. She was represented as a youthful figure, moving along lightly in a long robe, which was raised a little in her left hand, while her right bore a bud, either closed or just about to open. In the course of time she came to be usually considered as a goddess of the future, invoked at births and marriages, and on similar occasions.

Sphæristērium (Gr. *sphairistērĭŏn*). A court for the game of ball in the *gymnasia* and *thermæ*. *Sphæristĭcē* was the name of the art of playing at ball (*q.v.*).

Sphendŏnē. A fastening for the hair of the Greek women. (*See* HAIR.)

Sphinx ("the throttler"). A monster borrowed from Egyptian religion and symbolism, originally represented with the body of a winged lion and the breast and head of a maiden, and subsequently in still more wonderful forms (as a maiden with the breast,

EGYPTIAN SPHINX.

feet, and claws of a lion, the tail of a serpent, and the wings of a bird; or as a lion in front and a human being behind, with vulture's claws and eagle's wings). According to

Hesiod, Sphinx was the daughter of the Chĭmæra and Orthrus; according to others, of Echidna and Tўphon. Hēra (or, according to others, Ārēs or Dīonўsus) in anger at the crimes of Laïus, sent her to Thebes from Ethiopia. She took up her abode on a rock near the city and gave every passer by the well-known riddle: "What walks on four legs in the morning, on two at noon, and on three in the evening?" She flung from the rock all who could not answer it. When Œdĭpūs explained the riddle rightly as referring to man in the successive stages of infancy, the prime of life, and old age, she flung herself down from the rock.

Spinning. See WEAVING.

Spŏlĭă. The Roman term for the arms taken from an enemy defeated in single combat, and also for those portions of the captured armour which were promised by the general to soldiers who distinguished themselves. They were hung up in a temple with a dedicatory inscription [Vergil, *Æn.* iii 288] or in the vestibule of the house, where they remained, even if the house passed into other hands. *Spolia ŏpīmă* were the arms taken from the hostile general by a Roman leader commanding under his own auspices, and were consecrated to Jūpĭter Fĕretrius on the Capitol. This is said to have been first done by Rōmŭlus, who is the traditional founder of the sanctuary of Feretrius [Livy, i 10 § 6]. They were legitimately won on only two subsequent occasions [by Aulus Cornēlĭus Cossus from the king of Veii, and by M. Claudius Marcellus from the king of the Gæsātæ, Plutarch, *Marcellus* 8].

Stădĭum (Gr. *stădĭŏn*). The course for foot-races amongst the Greeks; the usual length of it was 600 Greek feet, a measure which Hēráclēs, according to the myth, had appointed for the course at Olympia. (*See* OLYMPIAN GAMES, fig. 4.) Subsequently this became the standard unit for measuring distances. On both of the longer sides of the course were natural or artificial elevations with terraced seats for the spectators. At one end there was generally a semicircular space especially intended for wrestling, and this was the place for the umpires. Near this was the pillar which marked the goal.

The starting-point was also [sometimes] indicated by a pillar at the other end, which was originally straight, and in later times curved like the end near the goal. For the different kind of races, *see* GYMNASTICS.

Stăsīnus. A Greek epic poet. (*See* EPOS.)

Stătă Māter. An Italian goddess who gave protection in cases of fires and conflagrations. (*See* VULCAN.) [Cicero, *De Legĭbus* ii 28; she is sometimes identified with *Vesta.*]

Stătēr (lit. "a standard" coin). (1) The principal gold coin of Greece. The Attic *stater* of gold, a gold piece of two gold *drachmæ* = twenty silver *drachmæ,* = 13*s.* 4*d.,* in intrinsic value of silver. To the same standard of currency belonged the Macedonian gold *stater* first struck by Philip II and Alexander the Great. (2) The silver *stater* is a term applied in later times to the Athenian tetradrachm, of four

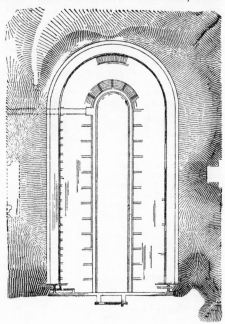

silver *drachmæ* (= 2*s.* 8*d.* in intrinsic value). (*See* COINAGE.)

Stătĭus. (1) *See* CÆCILIUS.

(2) *Publius Păpĭnĭus Statius.* A Roman poet, born at Naples about 45 A.D. His father, who afterwards settled in Rome, and was busy there as a teacher, was himself a poet, and the son owed his training to him. Early in life he gained the approval of his contemporaries by his poetic talent, especially in improvisation, and several times won the victory in poetic competitions. Yet he remained all his life dependent on the favour of Domitian and of the great men of Rome, whose goodwill he sought to propitiate by the most servile flatteries. In later life he went back to Naples, where he died about 96. Two epic poems of his are preserved, both dedicated to Domitian, (1) the *Thēbăĭs* in twelve books, published after twelve years' labour in 92, on the struggle of the sons of Œdĭpūs for Thebes, perhaps in imitation of the poem of the same name by Antĭmăchus; and (2) the two first books of an incomplete *Achillēĭs.* We also have his *Silvæ,* a collection of occasional poems, mostly in hexameters, but partly in lyrical verse. Statius is distinguished among his contemporaries by skill and imagination, but suffers from the tendency of the time to make great display of learning and rhetorical ornament. His poems were much read both in antiquity and in the Middle Ages.

Stēlē (*Greek*). An upright tablet or slab of stone. At Athens such tablets were set up in a public place, especially on the Acrŏpŏlis. Laws, decrees, treaties, etc., as well as sentences of punishment against defaulters were engraved upon them, and thus made publicly known. The use of *stelæ* for funeral monuments was common in all Greek countries. In earlier times they are narrow and thin slabs of stone, slightly tapering towards the top, which is crowned either with *anthĕmĭă* (decorations of flowers and leaves, *see* cut), or with a small triangular pediment ornamented with rosettes. The shorter but broader *stele,* crowned with a pediment, is later than the other kind. Many such *stelæ* resemble small shrines or chapels [Perry's *Greek*

GREEK STELE.

Sculpture, fig. 121]. Besides the inscription referring to the dead, they often bear representations of them in relief, as in the famous monument to Dexĭlĕōs, B.C. 390, near the Dĭpўlum at Athens. [For a *stele,* more than a century earlier, with a warrior in low relief, *see* HOPLITES.]

Stentōr. One of the Greeks before Troy, who could shout as loudly as fifty men together [*Il.* v 785]. He is said to have been a Thracian or Arcadian, and to have found his death in a contest of shouting with Hermēs.

Stĕphănŏs (*Greek*). The garland (*see* CORONA), also a metal band for the forehead, like a diadem. (*See* HAIR, MODE OF WEARING.)

Stĕphănus. (1) [A sculptor of the archaistic school of Pāsĭtĕlēs (a contemporary of Pompey). His name appears on a well-known statue of a nude youth in the *Villa Albani,* which is repeated with very slight alteration in a male statue forming part of a group was the Naples Museum. Among his pupils was the sculptor Mĕnĕlāus. (*See* SCULPTURE, fig. 16.)]   [J. E. S.]

(2) *Of Byzantium.* Author of a comprehensive geographical work, about 500 A.D., originally consisting of more than fifty books in the form of a lexicon, compiled out of more than 100 authors, which also contained notices of myths, history, etc., with constant indication of authorities. Besides fragments of the original, we possess only a meagre epitome by a grammarian named Hermŏlāus; but even in this mutilated form it is of great value.

Stĕrŏpē. One of the Pleiads, mother of Œnŏmăüs, by Ares.

Stĕrŏpēs. One of the Cŷclōpēs (*q.v.*).

Stēsĭchŏrus. The most famous representative of the earlier Dorian lyrical poetry, at Hĭmĕrā in Sicily, about 630 B.C. Originally called *Tĭsĭăs,* he received the name of Stesichorus ("marshal of choruses"), possibly from his office of directing the choruses and superintending their practice. It is related that he was struck blind for a lampoon on Helen, as the cause of the Trojan War, but received his eyesight again when he composed a lyrical poem recanting the first, and called *pălĭnōdĭă* [Plato, *Phædr.* 243A]. He died, aged eighty-five, at Catăna, where he had a tomb in front of the gate named after him. The choral ode had been divided by Alcman into *strŏphē* and *antĭstrŏphē.* Stesichorus is said to have completed its form by adding the *ĕpŏdŏs* (epode), which was sung by the chorus as they remained stationary after the completion of the two preceding movements. He is regarded as the founder of the loftier style of lyric poetry. His festal songs, afterwards divided into twenty-six books, were chiefly on mythological themes, especially the myths of Thebes and Troy, in simple metrical forms closely allied to epic verse, and in an epic dialect which contains a few Doric idioms. His splendid power of expression received the highest praise from the ancients; he was called the Homer of lyric poets [cp. Quintilian x 1 § 62], and it used to be said that Homer's soul had passed into him [*Anthologia Palatina* vii 75]. We only possess fragments of his poetry.

Sthĕnĕlus. (1) Son of Perseus and Andrŏmĕdă, and father of Eurystheus. (*Cp.* AMPHITRYON.)

(2) Son of Căpăneus and Euadnē (*q.v.*). He took part in the expedition of the Epĭgŏni against Thebes and in the Trojan War, where he fought as the brave comrade and charioteer of Dĭŏmēdēs.

Sthĕnō. One of the Gorgons (*q.v.*).

Sthĕnŏbœa. *See* ANTEIA.

Stĭlus [wrongly spelt *stylus*]. An iron instrument, pointed at one end and flat at the other, for writing on tablets covered with a thin coating of wax. (*See* WRITING MATERIALS.)

Stipendium. The Roman military pay. Originally the tribe had to contribute the necessary means to provide for its contingent. It was only at the beginning of the war against Veii in 404 B.C. that payment of a sum by the State was introduced. This was given to the soldiers, either before or after the campaign, as compensation for the costs of their living during its continuance. When this had gradually become a regular payment, it became customary in making it to deduct everything which the State provided for the army in the way of clothing, arms, and food; but under the Empire maintenance was given free. In the time of Pŏlўbĭus the pay of legionaries was 120 *dēnării* (£4 4s.); of centurions twice, and of knights three times that amount. Cæsar increased it to 225 *denarii* (£7 17s.) for a legionary, Domitian to 300 (£10 10s.). The prætorians received under Tiberius 720 *denarii* (£25 5s.).

Stipendium is also the name of the fixed normal tax imposed on conquered provinces, which might consist of money, or produce, or both. During the Republic, when a country was conquered, this was usually fixed according to the amount of the existing taxes, and the country divided into fiscal districts, and the officials of the chief places in each compelled to pay in the portion which fell to them. Under Augustus the taxes were for the first time fixed upon the basis of a measurement of the ground occupied, and of a computation of property (*census*). The *stipendium* was either a ground-tax (*trĭbūtum sŏlĭ*), or a personal tax (*tributum căpĭtĭs*), which was partly a poll-tax, partly a property-tax, partly a tax on the trade carried on by the individual. In exceptional cases special taxes were also imposed. Those bound to pay the *stipendium* were called *stĭpendĭārĭi*.

Stŏā. The Greek term for a colonnade, such as those built outside or inside temples, around dwelling-houses, gymnasia, and market-places. They were also set up separately as ornaments of the streets and open places. The simplest form is that of a roofed colonnade, with a wall on one side, which was often decorated with paintings. Thus in the market-place at Athens the *stoa pœcĭlē* (the Painted Colonnade) was decorated with Pŏlygnōtus' representations of the destruction of Troy, the fight of the Athenians with the Amazons, and the battles of Mărăthōn and Œnŏē. The *stŏa băsĭleĭŏs*, also in the market-place, in which the *archōn băsĭleus* sat as judge, was probably divided longitudinally into three parts by two rows of columns, and was the pattern for the Roman *băsĭlĭcă* (*q.v.*).—Zēno of Cĭtĭum taught in the *stoa pœcile*, and his adherents accordingly obtained the name of *Stoics.*

Among the Romans similar colonnades attached to other buildings, or built out in the open, were called *portĭcūs*. They were named from the neighbouring edifices (e.g. *porticus Concordĭœ*, close to the temple of Concord); from their builders (e.g. *porticus Pompēĭa*); also from the pictures set up in them (e.g. *porticus Argŏnautārum*); and from the business chiefly carried on in them, as *porticus Argentārĭa*, the hall of the money-changers. These halls were the chief places for public intercourse among the Greeks and Romans.

Stŏbæus (*Iŏannēs*). Of Stŏbi in Macedonia. About 500 A.D. he composed, for the education of his son Septĭmĭus, a philosophical anthology in four books, from the extracts which he had made in the course of his extensive reading from more than 500 Greek poets and prose writers. It is of great value, as it includes numerous fragments of works now lost, and is particularly rich in quotations from the works of the Greek dramatists.

The collection, which originally seems to have formed one whole work, has been separated into two distinct portions in the course of time: (1) The "physical, dialectical, and ethical eclogues" (or selections) in two books (imperfect at the beginning and end); and (2) the *Flŏrĭlĕgĭum*, also in two books, on ethical and political subjects, the sections of which are in great part so arranged that each virtue is treated in connexion with its opposite vice.

Stoics. The adherents of a school of philosophy (*Stoicism*), founded by Zēnō of Cĭtĭum about 310 A.D. They derived their name from the Painted Stŏä (*see* STOA) in Athens, in which Zeno lectured. For further details, *see* PHILOSOPHY.

Stŏla. The outer garment worn by Roman matrons above the *tŭnĭca intĭma* or chemise. It was longer than the body, slit open at the top on either side and fastened together by clasps, while below it was provided with a border (*instĭtă*) woven on to it, and was gathered up below the breast by a girdle so as to form broad falling folds (*rūgæ*). It had either no sleeves or half-sleeves, according as the under tunic had or had not half-sleeves. For the garb of women unmarried or in disgrace, *see* TOGA. Under the Empire the *stola* fell gradually out of use. After the 4th century A.D. there appears in its stead the *dalmătĭca*, worn by men and women, a kind of tunic with sleeves.

Strabo (Gr. *Străbōn*). The Greek geographer. He was born of a good family at Amăseia in Pontus about 63 B.C. After the conclusion of his education in philosophy he devoted himself to historical and geographical studies, and undertook long journeys in Asia Minor, also in Egypt up to the boundaries of Ethiopia, and in parts of Greece and Italy, paying several visits to Rome. He composed a great historic work in forty-seven books, which from the fifth book onwards formed a continuation of Pŏlўbĭus down to his own time; but of this only a few fragments remain.

His *Gĕŏgrăphĭcă*, however, we possess complete in seventeen books, with the exception of a few gaps in the seventh book. This was finished about A.D. 23. It is the principal geographical work that has come down to us from ancient times. It consists of descriptions of countries and peoples, and is specially valuable on account of the extent and importance of the historical and topographical matter it contains, partly derived from personal observation, but chiefly drawn from the best authorities, particularly from Ĕrătosthĕnēs. The first two books contain (1) a criticism, not always just, of the more ancient geographers from the time of Homer; and (2) the mathematical part of physical geography, the weakest portion of the work; books iii–x describe Europe (iii Spain, iv Gaul, Britain, Ireland, and the Alps, v and vi Italy, vii the north and east of Europe to the Danube, viii–x Greece); xi–xvi Asia; xvii Africa. Strabo gives detailed accounts of manners and customs, history and constitutions, whereas, in topography, he generally gives only what is of most importance. His style is clear and attractive. Notwithstanding a great extension of geographical knowledge, the work was not superseded by any later one, and indeed even in the Middle Ages was still used in selections as a school-book in Constantinople. [See Tozer's *Selections*,1893.]

Strătēgus (*Greek*). A general. Among the *Lacedæmonians*, it was a special designation of leaders of those armies which were not commanded by the kings. They were appointed by the public assembly, or by the ephors commissioned thereby. At Athens, there was annually elected, by show of hands (*chēĭrŏtŏnĭă*) in the public assembly, a board of *Ten Generals*, who had the superintendence of all military affairs. Only those were elected to this high and influential office who were lawfully married, and who possessed landed property in Attica. In earlier times they superintended operations both by land and sea, and assumed the actual command in turn on successive days, while they held a council of war in common. In later times no more were sent to the seat of war than were deemed sufficient for the purpose; and, from the time when the Athenians carried on their wars mainly by means of mercenaries, soldiers of experience, who did not belong to the board, were not unfrequently entrusted with the command, and were called *strategi* during the continuance of the war. Those *strategi* who remained at home, besides seeing that the country was protected against hostile invasion, had the control of the war-taxes and the *trĭērarchĭă*, the selection and equipment of the troops and the jurisdiction affecting all the law-suits connected with the war-taxes and trierarchy, as well as all the military offences which had not been punished by the general at the seat of war.

Their chamber of office was called the *strătēgĭŏn*, and here they dined together at the expense of the State. [The office of *strătēgŏs* was not created by Clīsthĕnēs, but was at least as old as the time of Drăcōn (Aristotle, *Constitution of Athens*, 4). In the 4th century we find the *strategi* no longer elected from each of the ten *phȳlæ*, but from the whole body of citizens without distinction of *phȳlē* (*ib.* 61).]

The highest officer of the Ætolian and the Achæan league, who was not only a commander of the federal army, but also president of the council and assemblies of the league, also bore the title of *strategus*.

Strēnæ. Gifts which it was customary for the Romans to make at the new year with accompanying good wishes. The word is connected with the name of a Sabine tutelary goddess, *Strenia*, who corresponds to the Roman *Sălūs*, and from whose precinct beside the *Vĭa Sacra* at Rome consecrated branches were carried up to the Capitoline at the new year. The *strenæ* consisted of branches of bay and of palm, sweetmeats made of honey, and figs or dates, as a good omen that the year might bring only joy and happiness [Ovid, *Fasti*, i 185–190]. The fruits were gilded [Martial viii 33, 11] as they are now in Germany; and the word, as well as the custom, survives in the French *étrennes*. Pieces of money, especially the ancient *ăs*, with the image of Jānus, who was specially honoured on this day, were also sent as presents, as well as small lamps of terracotta or bronze stamped with a motto and with minute representations of the usual gifts. Clients in particular were in the habit of complimenting their patrons with such presents; and, during and after the time of Augustus, the emperors benefited considerably by this custom, which lasted till the fifth century, although abolished several times by special edict [Suetonius, *Oct.* 57 and 91, *Calig.* 42].

Stringed Instruments. *See* CITHARA, LYRA, SAMBUCA.

Stylus. (*See* STILUS.)

Stymphălĭdĕs (*the Stymphalian birds*). According to the Greek legend these birds infested the lake Stymphălus in Arcadia. They had brazen claws, beaks, and wings, and were able to discharge their own feathers like arrows. Their destruction formed one of the labours of Hērăclēs (*q.v.*).

Styx. The eldest daughter of Ōcĕănus and Tēthȳs, by Pallas, son of the Titan Crīus. She became the mother of Zēlus (zeal), Nīkē (victory), Krătŏs (power), and

Bĭa (strength). She was the first of all the immortals who hastened with all her offspring to help Zeus against the Titans. In return for this Zeus retained her children with him in Olympus, and Styx herself became the goddess by whom the most solemn oaths were sworn. She is the Nymph of the mighty river of the same name (the tenth part of the water of Oceanus) which flows in the nether world. She dwells in the distant west, on the borders of the night, in a house supported by silver columns and overshadowed by lofty mountains. When one of the gods had to take an oath by Styx, Iris fetched some of her sacred water in a golden cup: whoever swore falsely thereby was punished by having to lie speechless and breathless for a year, and by banishment for nine years from the council of the gods [Hesiod, *Theog.* 775–806].

Sublĭgācŭlum. The linen bandage worn by the Roman gymnasts whilst performing their exercises. It was passed round the waist and between the legs.

Suetōnius Tranquillus (*Gaius*). The Roman historian, born about 75 A.D. He lived during the time of Trajan as an advocate and teacher of rhetoric in Rome, in close intimacy with the younger Pliny, to whose influence he owed many favours. Under Hadrian he was appointed private secretary to the emperor; but in 121 he fell into disgrace, and appears thenceforth to have devoted his life to learned studies and to varied research. He died about the middle of the 2nd century. Like Varro, he collected notes on all kinds of subjects, history, literature, antiquities, philology, physical sciences, and worked them up in numerous writings (some of them apparently in Greek). Amongst these an encyclopædic work called *Prāta*, in at least ten books, occupied a prominent position; and just as he himself frequently quoted Varro, so he in his turn was frequently quoted by later writers. Apart from titles and fragments the following works of his are still intact: (1) The lives of the first twelve emperors (*De Vĭtā Cæsărum*) in eight books books i–vi treating of one emperor each, from Cæsar to Nero; vii, of Galba, Otho, Vitellius; viii, of Vespasian. Titus, and Domitian. This work contains an abundance of more or less important facts about the public and private life of the emperors, grouped in a systematic manner, and expressed in clear and simple language. (2) Of his literary and historical work, *De*

Vĭrīs Illustrĭbus, which apparently included the Roman poets, orators, historians, grammarians, and rhetoricians down to the time of Domitian, we possess the lives of Terence and of Horace, and a fragment of that of Lucan, besides extracts made by the grammarian Dĭŏmēdēs and by St. Jerome from the book *De Pŏētīs*. From the book *De Histŏrĭcis*, we have a fragment of the biography of the elder Pliny, and the greater part of the chapter *De Grammătĭcis et Rhĕtŏrĭbus*. In the beginning of the 3rd century, under the reign of Alexander Severus, his work on the *Lives of the Cæsars* was continued by Mărĭus Maxĭmus, who treated of the emperors from Nerva to Ēlăgăbălus.

Suffectus. A magistrate elected in place of one who vacated office before the end of the year for which he was elected. The substitute continued in office for the rest of the year. (*Cp.* CONSULES.)

Sŭĭdās.[1] A Greek lexicographer who lived about 970 A.D., and compiled, from the lexicographical, grammatical, and explanatory works of his predecessors, a lexicon which contains explanations of words, and accounts, mainly biographical, of earlier writers. The work is put together hastily, and without skill or discrimination. It is also marred by numerous mistakes. Nevertheless it is very valuable, owing to the wealth of information on literary history contained in it, much of this not being found elsewhere.

Sulla. *See* ANNALISTS.

Sulpĭcĭa. Several Roman poetesses bear this name. For the first, *see* TIBULLUS. A second, who is mentioned by Martial about the time of Domitian, wrote amatory poems which are lost. A poem in seventy hexameters and entitled a Satire, being a complaint to the Muse for the expulsion of the philosophers from Rome by Domitian (89 and 93 A.D.), is written in her name; but this puerile performance is of a later date, her name having been wrongly attached to it.

Sulpĭcĭus. (1) *Servĭus Sulpĭcĭus Rūfus.* A Roman jurist, born about 105 B.C., prætor in 65, and consul in 51. He supported Cæsar in the civil war, and was appointed by him proconsul of Achaia in 46; he died in 43 on the journey to Mŭtĭna as ambassador of the Senate to Antōnius [Cicero, *Phil.* ix]. After he had abandoned his rivalry with his contemporary Cicero in the field of oratory, he applied himself to jurisprudence, and contributed to its systematic

development by numerous writings [*cp.* Cicero, *Pro Murēnā*, § § 15–30, and *De Legibus* i 17].

(2) *Gaius Sulpĭcius Apollĭnāris*, of Carthage. A distinguished grammarian of the 2nd century A.D., and teacher of Aulus Gellius (*q.v.*). His extant writings consist of metrical summaries of the comedies of Terence and of the Æneid of Virgil.

(3) *Sulpicius Sĕvērus*, of Aquĭtānĭa, gave up a brilliant career as advocate and orator, to devote himself to the Christian priesthood and an ascetic life, and wrote, between 400 and 405 A.D., a short history of the Old Testament and the Christian Church in two volumes, entitled *Chrŏnĭcă*. It is a work executed on the model of Sallust and Tacitus, and displays great industry and stylistic finish.

Summānus. An ancient Etruscan deity of the nocturnal heavens, to whom was ascribed thunder by night; as that by day was ascribed to Jūpĭter. He had a chapel on the Capitol, and his image in terra cotta stood on the pediment of the great temple. Besides this he had a temple near the Circus Maxĭmus, where on the 20th of June an annual sacrifice was offered to him. His true significance became in later times so obscure that his name was falsely explained as meaning the highest of the Mānēs (*summus Mānium*) and equivalent to *Dīs pater*, or the Greek Pluto.

Sun God. *See* HELIOS and APOLLO.

Sun-dial. *See* GNOMON.

Sŭŏvĕtaurīlĭa. A Roman sacrifice, consisting of a boar (*sūs*), a ram (*ŏvis*), and a bullock (*taurus*), which was offered in nearly all cases of lustration (*cp.* cut under TRIUMPH). For female deities the female animal, and on certain occasions young animals, were selected.

Supplĭcātĭōnēs. The Roman fast days, or days of humiliation, celebrated originally in times of great distress, after the Sibylline books had been duly consulted. The whole population, both of the towns and surrounding country, free-born and emancipated men, women, and children, took part in the solemnity. The whole ceremony had a Greek rather than a Roman colour. From the temple of Apollo, priests and laymen, crowned with wreaths of bay, marched in procession to the sound of singing and the notes of the lyre, visiting all the holy places, especially those where *lectisternĭa* (*q.v.*) were held. According to the rite introduced from the oriental Greeks of Asia Minor, the Romans touched

[1 Gr. Souidas. Ordinarily, but erroneously, pronounced as two syllables, as in Pope's *Dunciad*, iv 28. "For Attic phrase in Plato let them seek; I poach in Suidas for unlicensed Greek."]

with their faces the threshold of the sanctuaries, prostrated themselves before the statues of the gods, clasping their knees and kissing their hands and feet. While the prayers were being said, incense and wine were offered, the prayers being rehearsed by the members of the *collĕgĭum* entrusted with the care of the Sibylline books (*see* SIBYLLÆ), and the performance of the holy rites prescribed by them. On such days the temples ordinarily closed to the public, or only accessible under certain restrictions, were (so far as practicable) thrown open to all. The thanksgivings decreed by the Senate after great victories were celebrated in a similar manner. These originally lasted only one day, but in the course of time were lengthened, until, at the end of the Republic, they sometimes extended over forty or fifty days, and were often united with a public feasting of the people.

Sŭsărĭōn. The originator of the Attic comedy. (*See* COMEDY, 1.)

Sword. The ordinary sword of the Greeks (*xĭphŏs*, figs. 2 and 5), had a straight two-edged blade 16 to 18 inches long, and 2 to 2½ inches broad; the handle, which was often made in one piece with the blade,

(1) Scabbard (Gerhard, *Auserles. Vasenbilder,* Taf. cci).
(2) Sword (do.).
(3) Sword (Millingen, *Peintures des Vases,* pl. v).
(4) *Machaira* in sheath (*ib.* pl. lvii).
(5) Sword (*Monumenti dell' Inst.,* 1856, tav. x).

GREEK SWORDS AND SCABBARDS.
(Guhl and Koner, fig. 277.)

was 4 to 5 inches long, and without a bend, but with a cross or shell-shaped guard. The scabbard was of metal or leather mounted with metal, and frequently covered the hilt as well as the blade (*see* fig. 1). It hung by a belt thrown over the shoulder, usually on the left side, on a level with the hip. At the beginning of the 4th century B.C., a sword of nearly double this length was introduced by Īphĭcrătēs for the light infantry called peltasts. A sword slightly curved on one side from the hilt upwards, and only sharpened on this side, was the *măchaira* (figs. 3 and 4). This was the shape of the Spartan sword (*xўēlē*), which was peculiarly short. For the Roman sword, *see* GLADIUS.

Sycophant (Gr. *sŭkŏphantēs*), originally signified, according to the popular derivation, one who brought into notice cases of the prohibited export of figs from Attica. The term was afterwards applied to a professional informer and accuser. There were many such persons, who carried on a lucrative business in Athens at the time of the decay of the democracy, in spite of the fact that the authors of false accusations were punished most severely.

Symbŏlă. The Greek term for treaties between two states, determining the procedure in the event of lawsuits taking place between their respective subjects. A common provision of these contracts was that a party who lost his cause, when tried by the laws of the foreign state, could appeal to those of his own; and similarly the party who had been worsted in his own state was allowed to appeal to the law in his opponent's state. Such treaties were made chiefly to facilitate commercial communications between different states.

Symmăchus (*Quintus Aurēlĭus*). A Roman orator and writer of letters, who lived in the latter part of the 4th century A.D. He was of noble birth, and was prefect of Rome in 384 under Thĕŏdŏsius the Great, and afterwards consul in 391. Although he fearlessly adhered to the decaying paganism, and even moved the restoration of the altar of Victoria in the council-chamber of the Senate in an address to the emperor, he was nevertheless respected by his Christian opponents for the purity of his life, and for his great learning. The fragments of his *Orations* consist of three not entirely complete panegyrics on Valentinian I and his son Gratian, written in his youth, and larger fragments of six senatorial orations. We possess a collection of his *Letters* arranged apparently by his own son, who also was a statesman of mark. It is divided into ten books on the same plan as those of Pliny, and containing in the last book the official correspondence (*rĕlātĭōnēs*) of father and son with the emperor. This is the most valuable part of a collection which is not unimportant as affording much information about the author's life and times.

Symmŏrĭă. A *co-partnership*, or *company.* (1) A term used at Athens to denote a company formed to raise the property tax instituted in the year 428 B.C., to defray war expenses. (*See* EISPHORA.) Each of the ten *phȳlœ* appointed 120 of its wealthier citizens, and these were divided into two *symmoriœ* of sixty members each, so that the number of members in the twenty *symmoriœ* amounted to 1,200 (called *symmŏrītœ*). Out of each of the twenty *symmoriœ*, fifteen of the wealthier citizens were chosen, making 300 in all, whose duty it was to pay the taxes in advance on behalf of the rest. This sum had to be refunded to them by the rest in conjunction with the poorer taxable citizens, who were likewise apportioned off to various *symmoriœ*, but without becoming actual members of them, and were drawn upon by the real *symmoritœ* to an extent proportional to their means. (2) After 358, this method was applied to the duty of equipping the war vessels, known as the *trĭĕrarchĭā*. (*See* LEITOURGIA.) Each of the twenty *symmoriœ* had a certain number of ships assigned to it, the real *symmoritœ* (not including the poorer citizens) divided the expense among themselves, and a varying number (at the most sixteen), of the richest had to raise the money advanced for a ship. To manage its affairs, each *symmoria* had its superintendents, curators, and assessors. The magisterial control was in both cases in the hands of the *strătēgi*, being connected with the military supplies. Though, by this arrangement, the raising of taxes and fitting out of the ships were accelerated, yet it was open to abuse if the *symmoritœ* unduly burdened the poor by an unjust distribution. In the disputes which thus arose, the decision rested with the *strategi*. If any one thought that another ought to have been taxed instead of himself, he could avail himself of *antĭdŏsĭs* (*q.v.*) Even the *mĕtœci*, who (like the citizens) had to pay war taxes, were divided into *symmoriœ*. [Aristotle, *Constitution of Athens*, 61, describes one of the *strategi* as individually responsible for superintending the *symmoriœ* for building triremes.]

Symplēgădĕs. In Greek mythology two cliffs or floating islands near the entrance of the Black Sea, which crushed all vessels that tried to pass between them. The Argonauts, with the help of Hēra (or Athēnē), were the first to succeed in sailing through; after this the rocks became immovably fixed. (*Cp.* ARGONAUTS.)

Sympŏsĭum. A Greek drinking-party. *Sympŏsĭarchus*, the master of the revels. (*See* MEALS.)

Sympŏsĭus (*Cœlĭus Firmĭānus*). A Roman poet who lived at the end of the 4th and beginning of the 5th century A.D.; author of a collection of 100 riddles in verse, each written in three fairly correct hexameters.

Sȳnēgŏri. The Athenian term for advocates chosen by the people. In the pleadings (*see* ECCLESIA, 1, *a*) which took place, when any alteration was made in the laws, they had to defend the hitherto existing laws. In State trials it was their duty to conduct the cause on behalf of the people or to speak in support of the actual prosecutor.

Sȳnĕsĭus. A Greek philosopher, born 378 A.D. at Cȳrēnē, of distinguished parentage. He studied the Neo-Platonic philosophy in Alexandria under Hȳpătĭa, and was her most famous and most devoted pupil. He afterwards became a Christian, and was made bishop of Ptŏlĕmāïs in 410. He died about 430. The zeal and faithfulness with which he discharged his office and the tenacity with which he held to his philosophical convictions, which he endeavoured to reconcile with his Christian faith, are shown by his writings. These consist of several speeches and dissertations, amongst which that entitled *Diōn* is particularly interesting, as showing how he came to be a philosopher, while his *Praise of Baldness* is distinguished for its wit and genius. They also comprise a collection of 160 letters, which present us with a faithful picture of his character and work; in later times they were regarded as models of epistolary style. Lastly, they include ten hymns in iambic verse, which, although avowedly Christian, are at the same time inspired throughout by Neo-Platonic ideas.

Sȳnœcĭă. The Greek name for a lodging house which held several families.

Sȳnœcĭă (or *Sȳnœcĕsĭă*, both *neuter plural*). The eve of the Athenian festival of the Pănăthēnæa (*q.v.*).

Synthĕsĭs. A comfortable, brightly coloured garment usually worn by the Romans at meal-times, and only in public during the *Sāturnālĭa*.

Syria Dĕa. A deity of generation and fecundity worshipped in Syrian Hĭĕrăpŏlĭs under the name *Atargătis*, whom the later Greeks and the Romans simply called the Syrian goddess. From the time of the sovereignty of the Seleucĭdæ, when the ancient paganism was highly honoured in Hierapolis, the worship of this goddess spread among the Greeks, and from them found its way to Rome (where she had a temple in the days of the Empire) and to other parts of Italy, and still farther west. The old idea of her attributes had so widened in the course of time that she shared those of Jūno, Vĕnus, Rhĕa, Cȳbĕlē, Mĭnerva, Dĭăna, the Parcæ, and other goddesses. She is represented on Roman monuments, seated on a throne between two lions. Her priests were generally eunuchs. They were in the habit of making excursions into Greece and Italy to extend the worship of the goddess by means of ecstatic dances and prophecies, and to collect pious alms for her sanctuary.

Syrinx. An Arcadian Nymph, daughter of the river-god Lādōn; she was changed by her sisters into a reed in her flight from the enamoured Pan. Pan cut this reed into seven (or nine) pieces, and joined them together with wax in gradually decreasing lengths, to form the instrument called a *syrinx* or "Pan's pipe." This was chiefly used by herdsmen and shepherds, and is one of the attributes found in pictorial representations of Pan.

Syssĭtĭă (*neut. pl.*). The common meals taken in public among the Dorians in Sparta and Crete, and confined to men and youths only. In *Sparta*, all the *Spartĭātæ*, or citizens over twenty years of age, were obliged to attend these meals, which were there called *pheidĭtĭă*. No one was allowed to absent himself except for some satisfactory reason. The table was provided for by fixed monthly contributions of barley, wine, cheese, figs, and money to buy meat; the State only paid for the maintenance of the two kings, each of whom received a double portion. The places where the *syssitia* were held were called tents, and the guests were divided into messes of about fifteen members, vacancies in which were filled up by ballot, unanimous consent being indispensable for election. The messmates were called tent-companions, as they actually were in time of war. The table-companions of the two kings, who had a common table, were those who formed their escorts in the field. Accordingly, the generals of divisions in the army had the control of the *syssitia*. The principal dish was the well-known black broth (meat cooked in blood, seasoned with vinegar and salt), of which each person received only a certain amount, together with barley bread and wine, as much as they liked. This was followed by a course of cheese, olives, and figs. Besides this, the table-companions were allowed (and indeed were sometimes required as a penalty for small offences) to give a second course, consisting of wheaten bread, or venison caught by themselves in the chase; no one was allowed to obtain this by purchase. In Crete the people always sat down while eating, and in Sparta this was originally the custom; but after a short time they were in the habit of reclining on wooden benches.

In *Crete* there was a public fund for the *syssitia*. This absorbed one-half of the State revenue, and every citizen contributed to it a tithe of the produce of his land, as well as an annual sum of money for each slave. This fund not only bore the expense of the meals of the men and boys above a certain age, but also paid a sum sufficient to defray the expenses incurred by the women, children, and slaves in dining at home. These companies, which dined in common, were here called *hĕtærĭæ*. The boys, who sat near their fathers on the ground, only received meat to the extent of one-half the portion of an adult. The youths dined together and had to wait upon their elders; they had also to be content with an amount of wine which was measured out to them from a large bowl of mixed wine, whilst the older men could replenish their cups as they pleased. Here, as in Sparta, there were penalties for intemperance. After the repast some time was spent in conversation on politics and other subjects, principally for the instruction of the youths.

T

Tăbellārĭus. A letter-carrier or courier. (*See* LETTERS.)

Tăberna. (1) a shop (*see* HOUSE); (2) a tavern (*see* INNS).

Table (Gr. *trăpĕză*; Lat. *mensa*). Tables served in ancient times only for the support of vessels necessary for meals; not (as with us) for writing and reading as well.

As the couches on which people reclined at meal-times were not high, the tables were mostly lower than ours. Some were quadrangular and had four legs (fig. 1); this was for a long time the only form customary among the Romans. Others had circular or oval tops, and rested either on one leg or (more frequently) on three, to which the shape of animals' feet was given by preference (figs. 2, 3).

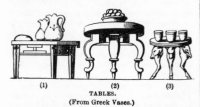

(1)　　　　(2)　　　　(3)
TABLES.
(From Greek Vases.)

The Greeks set a high value on the artistic adornment of their tables; but the Roman love of display expended more money on these articles of furniture than on any other. The feet were wrought in the finest metal, ivory, or stone work. The construction of the top of the table was a matter of special luxury. It was composed either of the nobler metals, rare kinds of stone, or costly varieties of wood. Especially costly were the *mŏnŏpŏdĭă* or *orbēs*, tables resting on one leg, with the wooden top cut out of a single log in the whole of its diameter. The most expensive and most sought-after wood was that of the *citrus*, an evergreen growing in the Atlas Mountains (which has been identified with the cypress, or juniper). The price of these *mensæ citrĕæ*, which were generally supported by one ivory leg, varied according to the dimensions of the diameter, which were sometimes as much as four feet, and also according to the beauty of the grain, which was brought out by polish. The prices named for single specimens of such tables ranged from £5,438 to £15,226 [Pliny, *N. H.*, xiii 92, 96, 102]. On account of the costliness of this kind of wood, the tops were sometimes made of some common material, especially maple, and covered over with a veneer of *citrus*.

The small *ăbăcus* served as a sideboard. Its square top, which was generally furnished with a raised rim, rested on one support (*trăpezŏphŏrŏn*) which was made of marble, bronze, or silver, and lent itself readily to sculptural treatment. Another kind of ornamental table was the *delphĭca*, in the form of a Greek tripod with a round top. Tables were also included in the ordinary furniture of a temple, especially such as stood directly in front of the statue of the god, and on which were laid the offerings not intended to be burnt. (*See* SACRIFICES, figs. 1, 2.)

Tablīnum. A room in a Roman dwelling-house. (*See* HOUSE.)

Tăcĭtus (*Cornēlĭus*). The celebrated Roman historian, born about the year 54 A.D., apparently of an equestrian family. Nothing is known of his birthplace, and it is only a conjecture that he was born at Intĕramna (*Terni*). In his rhetorical education he came under the immediate influence of the most distinguished orators of the time, Marcus Aper and Jūlĭus Sĕcundus, and he made his first appearance as an advocate at an early age. In 77 he married the daughter of the consul of that year, Julius Agrĭcŏla, shortly before the latter's departure for Britain [Tac., *Agr.* 9]. In 78–79 he held the quæstorship under Vespasian; in 80–81 he was ædile or tribune under Titus, and in 88 under Domitian. In 90 he left Rome with his wife on some official commission, and had not returned in 93, when his father-in-law died [*ib.* at end]. In 97, under Nerva, he was *consul suffectus*. He appears for the last time in active public life in 100, when, with his friend the younger Pliny, he appeared on the side of the prosecution in an important law-suit [Pliny, *Ep.* ii 12 § 2]. The date of his death is unknown, but he probably survived the accession of Hadrian in 117.

His writings are: (1) A dialogue on the decline of eloquence (*Dĭălŏgus de Ōrātŏrĭbŭs*), one of his earliest works, written apparently [under the influence of Quintilian] in the early part of the reign of Domitian, and originating in a close study of Cicero's rhetorical writings. It is one of the ablest works of the imperial age, and in language and style is so different from his later works that its genuineness has frequently been disputed. (2) The life of his father-in-law Agricola (*De Vītā et Mōrĭbŭs Iūlĭi Agrĭcŏlæ*), published at the beginning of Trajan's reign, and written in dutiful commemoration of the deceased; it is in the manner of Sallust, from whom Tacitus to a large extent borrowed his style. (3) The "Germānia" (*De Sĭtū, Morĭbus, ac Pŏpŭlīs Germanĭæ*), written soon after his *Agricola*; a description of the Germany of that time, which is founded on careful research, and is especially important as the source of all our knowledge of the ancient history of Germany. (4) A history of his own times, from Galba to the death of Domitian (69–96), under the title *Histŏrĭæ*, in fourteen books, of which books i–iv and the first half of v, covering not quite two years (69–70), have alone been preserved. (5) The history of the Julian house, in sixteen books, published between 115 and 117, beginning with the death of Augustus. (Hence the original title *Ab Excessu divi Augusti ;* the usual title, *Annālēs*, rests on no authority.) Books i–iv are still complete ; the latter part of the fifth and the beginning of the sixth is missing (the reign of Tiberius A.D. 14–37); while the second half of the eleventh, the whole of books xii–xiv and the first half of xv (the reign of Claudius from the year 47 and the history of Nero as far as 68) are still extant.

The two principal works of Tacitus thus give us a complete history of the emperors from Tiberius to Domitian. He was probably prevented by his death from completing his design by writing an account of the reign of Augustus, from the battle of Actium, and also including the reigns of Nerva and Trajan. In both works the chronological arrangement of the materials is predominant ; they are founded on the most searching and comprehensive study of the historical authorities, and are marked by a thoroughly critical spirit. Tacitus is always extremely careful to ascertain and to record the truth ; he is never satisfied with a mere narrative of events, but seeks to elicit their causes from the facts themselves. He is an adept in fathoming the hidden thoughts and motives of human agents. His method of treatment is, in external appearance, entirely objective ; but an undercurrent of sympathy, now sad, now cheerful, with the events related, is everywhere betraying itself. He is avowedly and resolutely impartial, and his judgment is eminently fair. It is only severe when he is dealing with wrongs done to the State, and to the moral laws of the universe. Thoroughly convinced of the value of virtue, he hates vice, which he seeks to terrify by exposing it to the ignominy of after ages. With all his admiration for the greatness of republican Rome, he is a stanch imperialist, being convinced of the necessity of the Empire for the stability of the State. In contrast with the bright elegance and richness of expression characteristic of his earliest work, as he advances in his literary activity his style becomes more sombre and pathetic, in accordance with the gloomy and tragic events which he has to describe. He becomes increasingly fond of rhetorical colouring, and avoids the ordinary diction of prose, while seeking to attain sublimity and novelty of style, less by archaisms than by an approximation to poetical expression. His grave and serious purpose finds its counterpart in his efforts to express himself with a terseness and precision which is often peculiarly pointed and epigrammatic. It is in the *Annals* that this last trait displays itself in its most characteristic form, and on the most extensive scale.

Tāgēs. The son of a Gĕnĭus and grandson of Jūpĭter, said to be a boy with the wisdom of an old man, who, at Tarquīnĭi, in Etruria, suddenly rose out of a freshly ploughed field. He taught the chiefs (*lŭcŭmōnēs*) of the twelve Etruscan tribes, who were summoned by the ploughman Tarchōn, how to interpret the sacrifices, together with the lore of thunder and lightning and other kinds of divination which in later times were practised by the *hăruspĭcēs* (*q.v.*). Having done this, he disappeared again as suddenly as he had appeared. The lore of Tages was at first transmitted orally from generation to generation in the chief families, but was afterwards handed down in a comprehensive literature [Cicero, *De Div.* ii 50, 51 ; Ovid, *Met.* xv 558 ff ; Lucan, i 637].

Tāgŏs. The federal commander who was elected by the States composing the Thessalian federation. He was only elected when occasion required, usually in case of war. He was chosen from the most distinguished of the nobility, generally from the Aleuădæ. It was his duty to levy soldiers from the States belonging to the federation, to be their commander, and to fix the amount of tribute to be paid by each member of the league.

Tălassĭo (*Tălassius, Tălassus*). The Roman god of marriage, corresponding to the Greek Hўmĕnæus. He was one of the unknown gods, and was only invoked by the appellation *Talasse* in the refrain to the *ĕpĭthălămĭa* sung when the bride was brought home. A later account makes him one of those who, with Rōmŭlus, were principally concerned in the rape of the Sabine women, and hence explains the proverbial use of his name at all marriages [Livy, i 9 § 12].

Tălaüs. Great-grandson of Crĕtheus, son of Bĭās and Pērō, father of Adrastus, Parthĕnŏpæus, Mēcisteus, and Ĕrĭphȳlē. He was one of the Argonauts, and was killed by Mĕlampūs. (*See* ADRASTUS.)

Talent (Gr. *tălantŏn*, Lat. *tălentum ;* lit. "the balance," and "the thing weighed"). The Greek term for (1) the highest measure of weight; (2) the designation of a sum of money consisting of a number of coins originally equal to it in legal weight and value. It was divided into 60 *mĭnæ* or 6,000 *drachmæ*. Among the different talents in use in Greece the most widely spread was the Attic, of which $\frac{1}{6000}$th part (*drachma*) weighed 57½ lbs. [The intrinsic value of the metal contained in this sum of money was about £200.] (*See* COINAGE.)

Tălōs. (1) A brazen giant in Crete whom Hēphæstus had given to Mīnōs. This giant guarded the island. He went round the island three times a day and scared away those who approached it by throwing stones at them ; or, if they landed, he sprang into the fire with them and pressed them to his glowing bosom till they were burnt to death. A vein of blood ran from his head to his foot, where it was closed by a nail. When the Argonauts came to Crete, Mēdēa caused the nail to fall out by means of a magic song. According to another account, Pœās, the father of Phĭloctētēs, shot it out with his bow, whereupon Talos bled to death.

(2) Nephew of Dædălus. His ingenuity and skill excited the envy of Dædalus, who threw him headlong from the Acropolis at Athens. (*See* DÆDALUS.)

Tămĭăs. A treasurer ; a title borne by several officials in Athens. (1) The most important of these was the treasurer (*ĕpĭmĕlētēs*) of the revenue, elected by show of hands every four years. He received from the *ăpŏdĕctæ* (general collectors) all the money which was to be disbursed for public expenses, and he paid away into the treasuries of the several authorities what was necessary for purposes of administration in their respective departments. He also provided the funds voted by the people for extraordinary purposes. (2) The same name was also borne by the ten treasurers of the goddess Athēnē, who had the care of the treasure of the goddess which was kept in the inner chamber of the Parthĕnōn, besides the State treasure which (according to the ordinary account) was kept in the same place. They were elected annually by lot, one from each of the *phȳlæ*. (3) Similarly, we have a board of ten regularly constituted treasurers to the rest of the gods. Their duty was to manage the sacred

treasures, which in earlier times were kept in the separate temples, but in 418 B.C. were transferred to the Parthenon. [(4) Under the title of *tamias tōn strătĭōtĭkōn*, we read of a financial officer of the war department. He was probably appointed after the Peloponnesian War in place of the *hellēnŏtămĭæ* (*q.v.*). Besides his duties in connexion with the war department, he had a share in the management of the Panathenaic festival (Aristotle, *Constitution of Athens*, 49).]

Tantălus. A wealthy king of Sīpȳlus in Phrygia (or Lydia), son of Zeus and Plūtō, father of Pĕlops and Nĭŏbē, grandfather of Atreus and Thȳestēs. As the favourite of the gods, he was allowed to take part in their deliberations and to share their meals ; but his good fortune making him overbearing, he insulted them and was thrown into Tartărus. The traditions differ as to the nature of his misdemeanour. According to one, he publicly revealed the secret decrees of Zeus ; another relates, that he purloined nectar and ambrosia from the table of the gods to distribute to his friends ; a third, that having invited the gods to a repast, he set before them the flesh of his son Pelops, whom he had cut to pieces and boiled, in order to test their omniscience ; while, according to a fourth, he perjured himself in order to retain possession of the golden dog stolen for him from the temple of Zeus by Pandărĕōs (*q.v.*). Homer [*Od.* xi 590] describes him as suffering in the world below from unappeased hunger and thirst, being at the same time immersed in water to the chin, whilst the finest fruits hang before his eyes. Whenever he opens his mouth to enjoy the repast, the water dries up and the fruits vanish into the air. According to Pindar [*Isth.* i 7 (8), 21], he himself is suspended in the air, while above his head hangs a huge rock, which is ever threatening to fall and crush him. (*See cut under* HADES, REALM OF.) Euripides combined both legends.

Tăraxippus. A demon who caused horses to shy. (*See* HIPPODROME.)

Tartărus. According to the earliest Greek views, a dark abyss, which lay as far below the surface of the earth as the earth is from the heavens. Above Tartarus were the foundations of the earth and sea. It was surrounded by an iron wall with iron gates set up by Pŏseidōn, and by a trebly thick layer of night, and it served as the prison of the dethroned Crŏnus, and of the conquered Titans who were guarded by the *hĕcăton-*

cheirĕs, the hundred-armed sons of Urănus. In later times its signification altered, and it came to mean the lower regions as the place of damnation, in which the wicked who had been condemned by the judges of the world below suffered endless torments. (*See* HADES, REALM OF.) As a person, Tartarus is the son of Æthēr and Gē; and, by his mother, he is the father of Tўphoēūs.

Tauriscus. A Greek artist of Trallēs, belonging to the school of Rhodes. He and his fellow countryman Apollōnius were the sculptors of the celebrated group of Dircē. (*See* cut on p. 195.)

Taxes. In Athens, as in the free states of Greece generally, the citizens were freed from every personal tax; only for their slaves they had to pay the *trĭŏbŏlŏn*, a yearly poll-tax of three obols (4*d.*) for each. On the other hand, among the residents who were not citizens, the *mĕtœci* (*q.v.*) paid a yearly protection tax of twelve drachmæ (8*s.*) for each independent man, and six *drachmœ* for every woman who managed her own house, and the freedmen paid the *trĭŏbŏlŏn* in addition. Besides this, all tradesmen who were not citizens had to pay a trade tax. (For extraordinary taxes on property *see* EISPHORA ; for the more or less costly public services undertaken by wealthy citizens, *see* LEITOURGIA.) As indirect taxes may be mentioned: (1) the tax of 1 per cent. on the selling price paid at the sale of a piece of land. (2) The market tax, which was paid, partly at the gates, partly at the place of sale, by strangers and *mĕtœci* for the wares offered for sale in retail dealing ; different articles were charged at different rates. (3) The tax on imports and exports, which was 2 per cent. on all imported or exported goods without distinction of kind. The State did not levy its dues and taxes itself, but caused them to be let out to individuals or companies by special officials, called the *Pŏlētœ* (*q.v.*). (*See* TĒLŌNÆ.)

As at Athens, so under the *Roman Republic*, there was no direct taxation for citizens, except the property tax raised in extraordinary cases. (*See* TRIBUTUM.) The Roman citizen paid indirect taxes in the harbour tax (*see* PORTŌRIUM), and the tax introduced after 357 B.C. on the manumission of slaves at the rate of 5 per cent. of the value of the slave set free (*vīcēsĭma mănŭmissĭōnis*). Both taxes were let by the State to *publĭcāni* (*q.v.*). Rome did not receive from her allies in Italy either direct or indirect taxes, apart from the obligations as to supplying soldiers and

ships imposed on them by the alliance. After the right of citizenship was granted to them in 89 B.C. they were placed on the same footing as the citizens with respect to indirect taxes. But the provinces had to pay all the more to Rome, partly by direct, partly by indirect taxation. Yet, especially with regard to the former, there was no similarity of treatment, but every province had its own form of taxation, which, as a rule, was assimilated to the system existing in it at the time of its conquest. Some provinces paid a fixed yearly sum (*see* STIPENDIUM), which was raised by communal districts through the chief towns of each district, while others paid a certain quota of the varying produce of the cultivated land in the province (*see* DĒCŬMA), which was farmed out to *publicani*. The provinces felt indirect taxation chiefly through the harbour tax, and indeed every province seems to have formed a separate fiscal district. Under the *Empire* it was only the indirect taxes that were at first made higher for the citizens, as Augustus added to the taxes on harbours and manumission the *centēsĭma rērum vēnālĭum*, 1 per cent. on the price of articles sold at auctions; the *quinta et vicesima mancipiorum*, or 4 per cent. on the price of every slave bought, and the *vicesima hērēdĭtātum et lēgātōrum*, of 5 per cent. on all inheritances above 100,000 sesterces, which did not fall to the nearest blood-relations, and on all legacies. The freedom of the citizens from direct taxation continued unimpaired, and when Caracalla, in 212 A.D., had granted to all free subjects of the Empire the right of citizenship, Italy, at least, maintained its freedom from taxation, until Diocletian (in 284) removed the last distinctions between the inhabitants of Italy and of other parts of the Empire, and introduced into Italy the same taxation as obtained in the provinces. It had in course of time been reduced to a more uniform system, on the basis of a general census of the Empire. The chief tax was the land tax (*tributum sŏli*), the total sum of which was promulgated every year by the emperor for the whole Empire, and divided amongst the provinces according to the number of taxable units (*iŭgă* or *căpĭtă*) which each province was set down as containing in the periodically revised registers. Connected with this tax in money were contributions in kind to the imperial stores for the army and the officials, who had a claim to them. The male and fem le population of the country not possessing land paid after a certain age (20-25 years) a poll tax (*tributum căpĭtis*), the amount of which was fixed by imperial ordinance, and for women was about half the sum imposed on men. Citizens resident in towns, and not possessing land, paid a tax partly on their property, partly, as far as they happened to be engaged in a trade, on their working capital and on the trade itself. The taxes apportioned to each town with its districts were raised by tax collectors (*exactŏrēs*), but the *dĕcŭriŏnēs*, or members of the municipal senates (*see* MUNICIPIUM), were responsible for the amount and had to advance it themselves.

Taxiarchus. The Greek term for a commander of a *taxis*, which contained a variable number of men. In Athens the ten commanders of the ten *taxeis* were so called. They were elected annually by show of hands, one for each tribe. They also had to look after the levying and distribution of recruits, and they were thus concerned in the drawing up of the register of those citizens who were liable to serve. On the Macedonian *taxis*, see PHALANX.

Tă̄ygĕtē. One of the Pleiădĕs (*q v.*).

Tĕcmēssă. Daughter of the Phrygian king Teuthrās, mother of Eurȳsăcēs by Ajax son of Tĕlămōn. (*See* AIAS, 2.)

Teirĕsĭăs (Lat. *Tīrĕsĭăs*). The famous blind soothsayer of Thebes, son of Euērēs and Chărīclō, and a descendant of the Spartan Udæus. The cause of his blindness has been variously stated. According to one tradition, the gods took his sight away when he was seven years old, because he revealed to men things which they ought not to have known. According to another, he became blind when, on his seeing Athēnē in the bath, she splashed water into his eyes. When invoked by his mother, the goddess could not restore his sight, but endued him with a knowledge of the language of birds, and presented him with a staff, by means of which he could walk like a man with perfect vision. According to a third account, he was blinded by Hēra, because in a dispute between her and Zeus he decided against her, and Zeus compensated him by granting him the gift of prophecy and a life seven (or nine) times as long as that of other men. He is also said to have been changed into a woman for a short time. He plays an important part in the story of Œdĭpūs and the wars against Thebes. In the wars of the *Seven against Thebes* he declared that the Thebans would be victori-

ous if Crĕōn's son Mĕnœceus were to sacrifice himself. In the war of the *Epĭgŏni* he advised the Thebans to enter into negotiations for peace, and to avail themselves of the opportunity thus afforded to take to flight. During the flight, or else at the conquest of Thebes by the Epigoni, he was made a prisoner, and with his daughter Manto (*q.v.*), who also possessed the gift of prophecy, was consecrated to the service of the Delphian Apollo. He died at the well Tilphŏssa, near Hăliartus, where his grave was pointed out, while he was also honoured by a cenotaph in Thebes. Homer [*Od.* xi 90–151] represents him as carrying his golden staff as soothsayer even in the world below, when Odysseus consults him as to his way home; and of all the shades, he alone, by favour of Persĕphŏnē, possesses unimpaired memory and intellect [*Od.* x 495]. He had an oracle at Orchŏmĕnus in Bœotia, which is said to have ceased to give responses after a plague.

Tĕlămōn. Son of Æăcus and Endĕïs, and brother of Pēleus. Having assisted Peleus in murdering their half-brother Phŏcus, he was expelled from Ægīna by his father, and was received by Cenchreus of Sălămīs, whose daughter Glaucē became his wife; and, on the death of Cenchreus, Telamon became king of Salamis. By his second wife Pĕrībœa, daughter of Alcăthŏüs, he became father of Ajax. He was one of the heroes who joined in the Calydonian Hunt, and also one of the Argonauts. He further took part in the expedition of his friend Hērăclēs against the Amazons and against Lăŏmĕdōn of Troy. At the conquest of Troy he was the first to scale the walls, and that he did at the very spot where it was built by his father. As his share in the spoil, Heracles gave him the king's daughter Hēsĭŏnē, by whom he became the father of Teucer (*q.v.*, 2).

Telchĭnēs. A primeval people sprung from the sea, and living on the island of Rhodes. They are said to have been the earliest workers in metal, and to have made images of the gods, together with the sickle of Crŏnus and the trident of Pŏseidōn. Poseidon is said to have been entrusted to them by Rhĕa to be brought up, just as Zeus was to the Cŭrĕtēs of Crete. They were also represented as envious sorcerers and dæmons, who were enemies of both gods and men. They were therefore killed by Apollo or, according to another account, destroyed by Zeus in an inundation. According to a third account, this inundation led to their leaving the island, and dispersing themselves over Lycia, Cyprus, Crete, and Greece.

Tĕlĕcleidēs. A Greek poet of the old comedy, and a violent opponent of Pericles [Plutarch, *Per.* 3, 16]. He is said to have written only six pieces, of which a few fragments are still extant.

Tĕlĕgŏnus. Son of Odysseus and Circē. At his mother's command he set out to find his father. Landing on the coast of Ĭthăcă, he began to plunder the fields, and Odysseus came out armed against him. Telegonus did not recognise his father, and mortally wounded him with the spine of a sting-ray which Circe had given him to serve as the barb of his lance. When he learned that the wounded man was his father, he took the body home with him, accompanied by Tĕlĕmăchus and Pĕnĕlŏpē, and subsequently married the latter. He was supposed to be the founder of Tusculum [Horace, *Od.* iii 29, 8] and Præneste, near Rome. [Plutarch, *Parall. Min.* 41, and Propertius, ii 32, 4. The legend of Telegonus was the theme of the *Tĕlĕgŏnēa*, by the cyclic poet Eugammō, of Cўrēnē. The strange manner in which Odysseus met his end is mentioned in Oppian, *Halieutica* ii 497.]

Tĕlĕmăchus. Son of Odysseus (*q.v.*) and Pĕnĕlŏpē.

Tĕlĕphus. Son of Hērăclēs and Augē, the daughter of Alĕŭs of Tĕgĕa and priestess of Athēnē. She concealed the child in the temple of the virgin goddess, and the country in consequence suffered a blight. By consulting an oracle, Aleus discovered the cause of the blight, and gave his daughter to Nauplius to drown her in the sea; but he exposed the infant on Mount Parthĕnĭŏn, where he was suckled by a hind and brought up by shepherds. Auge was given by Nauplius to Teuthrās, king of Mўsia, who made her his wife. When Telephus grew up, he consulted the oracle of Delphi to learn who his parents were, and was ordered to go into Asia to Teuthrās. Teuthras welcomed his wife's son, and married him to his daughter Argĭŏpē, and at his death appointed Telephus his successor. The Greeks, on their way to Troy, landed on the coast of Mysia and began to plunder it, thinking they had reached Troy. Telephus opposed them bravely, and killed Thersander, son of Pŏlўnīcēs; but, being forced by Achilles to fly, Dĭŏnўsus in his wrath caused him to stumble over a vine, and Achilles wounded him in the thigh with

his lance. As the wound did not heal, and he was told by the oracle that it could only be healed by him who had inflicted it, Telephus disguised himself as a beggar, and went to Argos, whither the Greeks had been driven back by a storm. Under the advice of Clўtæmnēstra he carried off Agamemnōn's infant son, whom he stole from his cradle, and took refuge on the house altar, threatening to kill the child unless Agamemnon compelled Achilles to cure his wound. This had the desired effect, and Achilles healed the wound with the rust, or with the splinters, of the lance which had inflicted it. Being designated by the oracle as the guide to Troy, he showed the Greeks the way, but refused to take part in the war, because his wife, Astўŏchē, was a sister of Priam. His son *Eurўpўlus* rendered the Trojans the last aid they received before the fall of their town. This he did at the prompting of his mother, whom Priam had bribed by means of a golden vine wrought by Hēphæstus, and given by Zeus to Trōs in compensation for carrying off Ganymede. Eurypylus was killed by Nĕoptŏlĕmus after having performed many brave exploits. In the Mysian town of Pergămōn, and especially by the kings of the house of Attălus, Telephus was revered as a national hero.

Tĕlĕsilla. Of Argos. A lyric poetess, who flourished about the year 508 B.C. After a defeat of the Argives, she is said to have placed herself at the head of a band of Argive women, and to have repelled an attack of the Spartan king Clĕŏmĕnēs. The figure of a woman in front of the temple of Aphrŏdītē at Argos, with books lying at her feet, while she herself is looking at a helmet, as though about to put it on, was said to represent Telesilla [Pausanias, ii 20 § 7]. She is said to have become a poetess because, on consulting an oracle respecting her health, she received as answer that she would receive health from the Muses. Scarcely anything remains of her poems, which consisted of hymns to Apollo and Artĕmis.

Tĕlĕsphŏrus (*i.e.* he who brings to an end). In Greek mythology, a boy who was regarded as the genius of health. (*See* ASCLEPIUS [and esp. *Journal of Hellenic Studies*, iii 283–297].)

Tellūmō. *See* TELLUS.

Tellūs. The Italian deity of mother-earth, often called *tellus māter*. She was invoked during earthquakes (her temple in Rome having been dedicated in 268 B.C. in consequence of an earthquake in the time of war). She was also invoked in solemn oaths as the common grave of all things, together with the Mānēs and with Jūpĭter, the god of heaven. Like the Greek Dēmētēr, she was also the goddess of marriage, but was most revered in conjunction with Cĕrēs as goddess of fruitfulness. Thus in her honour were held the festival of the sowing (*fĕrĭæ sēmentīvæ*), celebrated in January at the end of the winter seed time, fixed by the *pontĭfex* to be held on two consecutive market days. The *pāgānālĭa* were celebrated at the same time in the country, when a pregnant sow was sacrificed to Tellus and Ceres. Besides these, there was the feast of *fordicīdĭa* or *hordicīdĭa*, at which cows in calf (*fordæ*) were sacrificed to her. This was held on the 15th of April to insure plenty during the year, and was celebrated under the management of the *pontĭfĭcēs* and the Vestal Virgins, partly on the Capitol in the thirty *cūrĭæ*, and partly outside the town. The ashes of the unborn calves were kept by the Vestal Virgins till the feast of the *Părīlĭa* (*see* PALES), when they were used for the purpose of purification. Besides the female deity, a god *Tellūmō* was also worshipped.

Tĕlōnæ (Gr. *tĕlōnai*, lit. "buyers of the taxes"). Among the Athenians, these were the farmers of the taxes and imposts, which were not collected by State officers, but were sold at certain times by auction to the highest bidder. Smaller taxes were taken up by single persons who collected the money themselves. For larger taxes demanding a large capital, companies were often formed, represented by one person called the *tĕlōnarchēs*, who concluded the contract with the State. Sureties had also to be produced on this occasion. Such companies employed subordinate officers to collect the taxes. The payments were made by the farmers at certain periods at the senate-house, or *bouleutĕrĭŏn*, and one payment was usually made in advance when the contract was made. In default of payment, the farmer became *ătīmŏs*, and in certain circumstances might be imprisoned. If the debt was not paid by the expiration of the 9th *prŷtăneiă*, it was doubled, and the property of the debtor and his sureties confiscated. The *ătīmĭă* descended to the children until the debt was paid. On the other hand, the farmer was protected by the State against fraud by severe laws. He was also exempt from military service, so that he might not be hindered in performing his duties. For the similar institution among the Romans, *see* PUBLICANI.

Temples. In ancient times temples were regarded as the dwelling-places of the gods to whom they were dedicated. They might contain an image or not, but the latter case was exceptional. As they were not houses of prayer intended for the devotion of a numerous community, they were usually of very limited extent. There were, however, temples of considerable size, among which was that of Artĕmis in Ephesus, 438 feet long by 226 broad; that of Hēra in Sămŏs; that begun by Pīsistrătus and finished by Hadrian, and dedicated to Zeus Olympĭus in Athens (*see* OLYMPIEUM); and the temple of Zeus of Agrĭgentum, which was never quite completed. All of these were almost as large as the first-mentioned. Only temples like that at Eleusis, in which the celebration of mysteries took place, were intended to accommodate a larger number of people. The great sacrifices and banquets shared by all the people were celebrated in the court of the temple (Gr. *pĕrĭbŏlŏs*), which included the altars for sacrifice, and was itself surrounded by a wall with only one place of entrance. It was a feature common to all temples that they were not built directly on the surface of the ground, but were raised on a sub-structure which was mounted by means of an uneven number of steps, so that people were able as a good omen to put their right foot on the first and last step.

The usual shape of Greek temples was an oblong about twice as long as wide, at the front and back of which was a pediment or gable-roof (Gr. *ăĕtŏs* or *ăĕtōmă*; Lat. *fastīgĭum*). Round temples with dome-shaped roofs were quite the exception. The principal part of the temple was the chamber containing the image of the god. This stood on a pedestal, which was often placed in a small niche, and usually stood facing the east, opposite folding-doors which always opened outwards. Before the image stood an altar used for unbloody sacrifices. This chamber, called in Greek *năŏs*, and in Latin *cella*, generally received its light through the door alone, but sometimes there was also an opening in the roof. There were also temples designated *hypæthral* (from *hўpaithrŏs*, "in the open air"); [1] in these there was no roof to the middle chamber

---

[1] [Vitruvius, iii 1 § 22. The Attic form is *hўpaithrĭŏs*.]

of the *cella*, which was separated from the lateral portions by one or more rows of pillars on each side.

Generally each temple belonged to only one god; but sometimes a temple was regarded as the dwelling-place of several deities, either those who were worshipped in groups, as the Muses, or those who were supposed to stand in close alliance or other relationship to each other, such as the twins Apollo and Artemis; and Apollo, as leader of the Muses, together with the Muses themselves. Frequently only one god had an image and altar in the chief *cella*, while others were worshipped in adjoining chapels. Lastly, there were double temples, with two *cellæ* built in opposite directions. (*See* ARCHITECTURE, fig. 13.) Many temples had, besides the *cella*, a kind of "holy of holies" (*ădўtŏn* or *mĕgărŏn*) which was only entered by the priests, and only by them at certain times, and which was sometimes under the ground. Usually an open porch or vestibule (*prŏnāŏs*), with pillars in front, stood before the *cella*, and in it were exposed the dedicatory offerings. There was often also an inner chamber behind the image (*ŏpisthŏdŏmŏs*) which served for various purposes, the valuables and money belonging to the temple being often kept there. It was surrounded by a wall, and the door was well secured by locks.

The various kinds of temples are usually distinguished according to the number and arrangement of the pillars. Thus: (1) A temple *in antīs* (fig. 1) is one in which the *pronaos* (sometimes also the *opisthodomos*) was formed by the prolongation of the side walls of the temple (Lat. *antæ ;* Gr. *părastădĕs*) and by two columns placed between the terminal pilasters of the *antæ*.

(1) TEMPLE IN ANTIS.   (2) PROSTYLOS.

(2) *Prŏstўlŏs*, with the columns in front (fig. 2), is an epithet descriptive of a temple, the front of whose *pronaos* was formed in all its breadth by a row of columns quite separate from the walls, and with the columns at the extremities standing in front of the *antæ*.

(3) *Amphiprŏstўlŏs* (fig. 3) describes a

temple with the columns arranged as in (2) at the back as well as in the front.

(3) AMPHIPROSTYLOS.

(4) *Pĕriptĕrŏs* (fig. 4) describes a temple surrounded on all sides by a colonnade supporting the architrave. This is the type

(4) PERIPTEROS.

most frequently employed by the Greeks. (*See* PARTHENON, cuts 1 and 2.)

(5) *Pseudŏpĕriptĕrŏs* ("false *peripteros*") is an epithet of a temple in which the architrave appears to be carried by pilasters or by "engaged" columns in the walls of the cella. This form is seldom used by the Greeks, but often by the Romans.

(6) *Diptĕrŏs* (fig. 5) describes a temple surrounded by two ranges of columns.

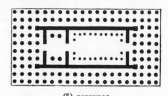

(5) DIPTEROS.

(7) *Pseudŏdiptĕrŏs* ("false *dĭptĕrŏs*," fig. 6). A temple surrounded with only a single

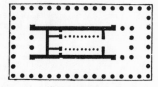

(6) PSEUDODIPTEROS.

range of columns, but at such a distance

that they correspond in position to the exterior range of the dipteral temple.

According to the number of columns in front, which must always be an even number, since the entrance was in the middle, it is usual to distinguish temples as *tetra-, hexa-, octa-, dĕcă-,* or *dōdĕcă-stȳlŏs* (with 4, 6, 8, 10, or 12 columns). The number of columns along each side was usually one more than twice the number along the front, but this was not the invariable rule. For the *architrave* and for the columns of the different *orders, see* pp. 57, 58. The *frieze* resting on the architrave, and (in the Doric order) the *metopes* in particular (*q.v.*), as well as the two pediments (Gr. *tympănă*), were decorated with sculptures, and these sculptures, as well as the walls of the temple often had a more life-like and more varied appearance given to them by appropriate colouring. The coping of the roof, as well as the angles of the pediment, were ornamented by *acrŏtērĭă*, which consisted of statues, vases, or *anthĕmĭa* (groups of flowers and leaves; *cp.* cut to ÆGINETAN SCULPTURES).

In the plan of their temples the ROMANS originally followed the Etruscans (*cp.* TEMPLUM, below). The ground-plan of the Etruscan temple was nearly a square, the ratio of the depth to frontage being 6:5. Half of the space was taken up by the cella, and the rest by the columns. The architrave was of wood, and without any special frieze. The great temple with three *cellæ* on the Roman Capitol was built in the Etruscan style, the middle and largest *cella* being sacred to Jupiter, and the smaller ones on either side to Minerva and Juno. (*Cp.* JUPITER.) Under Greek influence the different forms of the Greek temple began to be imitated at Rome, the most prevalent type being that described as *prostylos*, which lent itself most easily to the requirements of a *templum* in the strict sense of the term. An important alteration in the Greek form of temple was brought about by the introduction of vaulted arches or groined ceilings, which were seldom used by the Greeks, and never on a large scale, but were brought to great perfection by the Romans. They took the form of a cylindrical vaulting in the case of a quadrangular *cella*, and a dome in the case of the round temples, which were frequent with the Romans. The two principal forms of the latter are (1) the *mŏnoptĕrŏs*, which consisted of a single circle of columns standing on a platform mounted by steps and supporting the columns which bore a dome on a circular architrave. (2) The *pĕriptĕrŏs*, with the same arrangement of columns, but with a circular *cella* in the middle which was covered by a dome rising from the surrounding colonnade. In a third variety, of which we have an example in the *Panthĕŏn* (*q.v.*), the circular body of the building is not surrounded by columns externally, but only provided on one side with an advanced portico.

Templum. The Roman term for a space marked out by the augurs (*see* AUGURES) according to a certain fixed procedure. Its ground-plan was a square or rectangle, having its four sides turned to the different points of the compass; its front however, according to strict Roman custom, faced towards the west, so that any one entering the temple had his face turned towards the east. It was not until later that the front was frequently made to face the east. The building erected on this space, and corresponding to it in plan, did not become a *fānum*, or sanctuary of the gods, until it had been consecrated by the *pontĭfĭcēs*. (*See* DEDICATIO.)

As, however, there were *fana* which were not *templa*, e.g. all circular buildings, so there were *templa* which were not *fana*. Of this sort were the places where public affairs were transacted, such as the *rostra* in the Forum, the places where the *cŏmĭtĭa* met or the Senate assembled, and even the city of Rome itself. The sanctuaries of the gods were designed as *templa* if they were intended to serve for meetings of the Senate, and if the form of worship prescribed for such sanctuaries were appropriate to the definition of a *templum*.

Tennēs (or *Tĕnēs*), son of Cycnus (*q.v.*, 2). He (with his sister Hēmĭthĕä) was thrown by his father in a chest into the sea, in consequence of the slanderous accusations brought against him by his stepmother. He was borne, however, by the waves to the island of Tĕnĕdŏs (so named from him), where he became king. He was afterwards reconciled to his father, and fell, with him, by the hand of Achilles, when the father and son, as allies of the Trojans, were opposing the landing of the Greeks on the shores of Asia.

Tensa. The chariot used for processions, or for the gods at the Circensian games. (*See* CHARIOTS.)

Tĕpĭdārium. A tepid bath-room. (*See* BATHS.)

Těrěbra. A military engine for boring into the walls of a besieged town. (*See* ARIES.)

Těrentiānus Maurus. A Latin grammarian, born in Maurĭtānĭa. At the close of the 3rd century B.C. he wrote a didactic poem on prosody and metre, composed in the most varied forms of verse *(De Littĕrīs, Syllăbīs, Metrīs)*. The estimation in which he was held by later grammarians is proved by their frequent quotations from him.

Těrentīnī Lūdī. *See* SÆCULARES LUDI.

Těrentĭus. (1) *Publĭus Těrentĭus Āfĕr* (or the African). A celebrated Roman comic poet. He was born in Carthage about 185 B.C., and came to Rome as a slave in the possession of the senator Terentius Lūcānus, who, on account of his promising talents and handsome person, gave him a good education and set him free. As early as 166, on the recommendation of the consul Cæcĭlĭus Stātĭus, he produced his first play, the *Maiden of Andrŏs (Andrĭa)*, which met with great success. He succeeded in winning the favour and friendship of the most distinguished men, such as the younger Scipio and Lælius. He was less successful with his next piece, *The Mother-in-Law (Hĕcўra)*, which came out in the following year, and was without doubt his feeblest production. It was only on its third representation in 166 that it met with any success. Meanwhile, in 163, two years after the first production of the *Hecyra*, he ventured to appear before the public with a new piece, *The Self-Tormentor (Hautontĭmŏrūmĕnŏs)*. This was followed in 161 by the *Eunūchus*, which was very warmly received, and by the *Phormĭo*. In 160, after bringing out another play, *The Brothers (Adelphi)*, he went to Greece, where he died 159 B.C.

Terence, like the other poets who wrote *palliātæ (see* COMEDY, 2), borrowed from the older Greek poets, especially from Mĕnander (only the *Hecyra* and *Phormio* being taken from Apollŏdōrus). This he did however with a certain freedom ; and sometimes by fusing together similar Greek compositions, and borrowing appropriate scenes from other poets, he managed to expand the simple plot of the Greek original. Evidently of a refined mind, he had no taste for the lively realism of a Plautus. On the contrary, he aimed at artistic correctness of plot, delicate delineation of character, and elegance of form. He had nothing of the vivacity, force, and wit of Plautus, and fell far behind Menander in freshness and vigour, for which reason Cæsar pertinently called him Menander's half [*o dīmĭdĭātĕ Menander*, quoted by Suetonius in his life of Terence].

In his style, although a foreigner, he caught the refined tone of Roman society so successfully as to cause his detractors to maintain that he had been assisted in his compositions by his noble patrons, a reproach from which he does not entirely exonerate himself in the prologue to the *Adelphi*. His works do not appear to have maintained their reputation on the stage with the public at large for any length of time after his death. They have, nevertheless, remained for all time the favourite literature of cultivated readers. Ancient critics also made them a subject of study, and wrote many commentaries on them. We still possess the important commentary by Ælĭus Dōnātus, belonging to the middle of the 4th century A.D., as well as the less valuable one by Eugrăphĭus of the 10th century, when Terence was (as for some time previously) a favourite text-book. These have come down to us besides the *didascălĭæ (q.v.)* to the several pieces, and the metrical arguments by Sulpĭcĭus Apollĭnāris.

(2) *Publĭus Terentĭus Varro Ătăcĭnus.* A Roman poet, born 82 B.C. by the river Atax in Gallia Narbōnensis; he died before 36 B.C. According to an ancient authority, he only began to study Greek literature in his 35th year. Accordingly his satires on the model of Lūcīlĭus, and his epic poem on Cæsar's war with the Sĕquāni *(Bellum Sĕquănĭcum)* must belong to his earlier years. He afterwards followed the fashion of imitating the Alexandrian School, which was just coming into vogue, and composed, besides elegies and didactic poems after Greek models, his epic poem, entitled the *Argōnautæ*, in four books, a free imitation of the *Argōnautĭca* by Apollōnĭus Rhŏdĭus. This masterpiece, which has been much praised by later poets, and of which (as of his poems in general) only scattered fragments remain, appears to have been the most remarkable production in the domain of narrative epic poetry between the time of Ennius and that of Vergil.

(3) *Marcus Terentĭus Varro Rĕātĭnus* (i.e. a native of Rĕătĕ in the Sabine territory). The most learned of the Romans; born 116 B.C. of an ancient senatorial family. He devoted himself to study at an early age, under the direction chiefly of the learned antiquarian and philologist Ælĭus Stĭlo, without however withdrawing from public life either

in time of peace or war. He held the public offices of tribune, curule ædile, and prætor. In 67 he was lieutenant to Pompey in the war against the pirates; in 49 he again held a command under Pompey in the province of Spain beyond the Ibērus, but was taken prisoner by Cæsar after the capitulation of Ilerda. Although he afterwards rejoined Pompey, Cæsar received him into favour, and he returned to Rome in 46 B.C., where he is said to have had the superintendence of the great library which Cæsar destined for the public use. In spite of his abstaining henceforward from taking any active part in public affairs, he was proscribed by Antony in 43, and only narrowly escaped with his life. Pardoned by Octavianus, he lived till the year 27, full of vigour and literary activity to the last.

Varro's learning comprised all the provinces of literature known at that time, and in productivity he was equalled by no Romans, and only a few Greeks. According to his own statement, he had composed 490 books before his 78th year; the total number of his works, either in prose or verse, theoretical or practical, exceeded 70, in more than 600 books. Of these, the three books on agriculture (*Rērum Rustĭcārum Libri*), written in the form of a dialogue in his 80th year, in which he treats the subject exhaustively, drawing from his own experience as well as from more ancient sources, are the only ones that have been completely preserved. Further, of the original 25 books on the Latin language (*De Linguā Lătĭnā*) dedicated to Cæsar, in which he systematically treats, under the head of etymology, inflexions and syntax, only books v–x exist, in a mutilated condition. This work was followed by a number of other grammatical writings. It is only through a series of extant titles of his works that we know of his literary and historical studies, which were especially directed to dramatic poetry, and in particular to the comedies of Plautus, as well as of his researches into the history and antiquities of his own nation. His principal work, of which much use has been made by later writers, the *Antīquĭtātēs Rērum Hūmānārum et Dīvīnārum*, in 41 books. This was the most important of his writings on these subjects, as it gave a complete account of the political and religious life of the Romans from the earliest times. The 15 books, entitled *Ĭmāgĭnēs* or *Hebdŏmădēs*, published about B.C. 39, contained 700 portraits of celebrated Greeks and Romans,

in sets of seven in each group, with epigrams written beneath them. His nine *Discĭplīnārum Libri* gave an encyclopædia of the arts pertaining to general culture (grammar, dialectics, rhetoric, geometry, arithmetic, astronomy, music, architecture, medicine). His 76 *Libri Lŏgistŏrĭci* included shorter popular treatises of a historical and philosophical nature, described by titles appropriate to their contents, borrowed from the names of well-known persons (e.g. *Sīsenna de Histŏrĭā*). Among Varro's numerous and varied poetical works we will only mention, as the most original, the 150 books of Menippean Satires (*Sătŭræ Mĕnippēæ*), which were completed before 45 B.C., a species of composition which he introduced into Roman literature in imitation of the Cynic Mĕnippus of Gădără. In these Satires, written alternately in prose and different kinds of verse, he treats of philosophical questions, especially those relating to morality, science, etc., chiefly with the view of exposing the failings of the age. Only a number of titles and fragments of this work have been preserved.

(4) *Quintus Terentius Scaurus.* The most renowned Latin scholar and critic of the time of Hadrian (117–138 A.D.), commentator on Plautus and Vergil, and author of treatises on Latin grammar and poetry. A small work, *De Orthŏgrăphĭā*, of some value for the history of the Latin language, bears his name [but is probably not written by this Scaurus].

Tēreūs. King of Daulis, husband of Prŏcnē (*q.v.*).

Tergĭversātĭō. The Roman term for the dereliction of duty involved in a legal prosecution being dropped by the prosecutor. Under Nero this offence was punished by fines and disgrace (*infămĭa*).

Termĭnus. The Roman god of bounds, under whose special protection were the stones (*termini*) which marked boundaries. The regulations respecting these stones and the religious customs and institutions connected with them went back to the time of king Nŭma. At the setting of such a stone every one living near the boundary assembled; and in their presence the hole prepared for the reception of the stone was watered with the blood of a sacrificial animal; incense, field-produce, honey, and wine were sprinkled over it, and a victim sacrificed. The stone, anointed and decked with garlands and ribbons, was then placed upon the smouldering bones and pressed into the earth. Whoever pulled up the stone was cursed, together with his draught-cattle, and any one might kill him with impunity and without being defiled by his blood. In later times the punishment of fines was instituted instead.

The festival of the *Termĭnālĭa* was celebrated in Rome and in the country on the 23rd of February. The neighbours on either side of any boundary gathered round the landmark, with their wives, children, and servants; and crowned it, each on his own side, with garlands, and offered cakes and bloodless sacrifices. In later times, however, a lamb, or sucking pig, was sometimes slain, and the stone sprinkled with the blood. Lastly, the whole neighbourhood joined in a general feast: A lamb was also sacrificed in the grove of Terminus, which was six Roman miles from Rome, near the ancient border of the town of Laurentum. On the Capitol there was a stone dedicated to *Terminus*, which had originally stood in the open air, but when the temple of Jupiter was founded by the last king, Tarquĭnĭus Sŭperbus, it was inclosed within the building, as the augurs would not allow it to be removed.

Terpander (Gr. *Terpandrŏs*). A Greek poet and musician, a native of Antissa in Lesbŏs. He is the true founder of Greek classical music, and also of lyric poetry, both Æolian and Dorian. He was the first to clothe in artistic form the kind of choral song, called *nŏmŏs*, used at the festivals of Apollo; he also introduced other important innovations into music. He is sometimes erroneously described as having added three strings to the original lyre of four strings [Strabo, p. 618]; but it is more probable that the lyre of seven strings was already in existence in his own time [Aristotle, *Probl.*, xix 32]. The principal scene of his labours was Sparta, whither he had been summoned by order of the Delphic oracle to quell a disturbance amongst the people. It was at Sparta that he reduced to order the music of the Dorians. It was here too that he won the prize at the musical competition at the Carnēĭă. Between 672 and 648 B.C. he carried off the prize four times in succession at the Pythian games in Delphi. Only a few verses of his own poems are extant.

Terpsĭchŏrē. The Muse of dancing. (*See* MUSES.)

Tertullĭānus (*Quintus Septĭmĭus Flōrens*). One of the most important of the Latin Fathers. He was born at Carthage of pagan parents about 160 A.D., and died about 230. After receiving a careful education in rhetoric and jurisprudence (and probably practising as a lawyer), he embraced Christianity, and became a presbyter in his native town. After defending Christianity against paganism, he joined the ascetic and fanatic sect of the Montanists, and became their champion against the Church. His writings reflect with faithfulness his general ability; his rhetorical training and legal subtlety; his rugged, combative, and passionate character; and his lively and often impetuous imagination. They are written in the colloquial language of his time, which had many points of close contact with that spoken by the lower classes. His literary activity, which extended over a considerable length of time, was at its height in the reigns of Sĕvērus and Caracalla. His *Apŏlŏgĭă*, written about 198, holds the foremost place amongst his works. It is one of his earliest writings, and was addressed to the provincial governors of the Roman empire, in defence of Christianity, during a time of bitter persecution.

Tessĕra (*Latin*). (1) A die (*see* DICE). Also (2) a ticket of admission to the theatre (*q.v.*, II).

Testūdō (Lat.; Gr. *chĕlōnē*, "*tortoise-shell*"). The general designation for different kinds of sheds for the protection of soldiers engaged in a siege. (*See* cut 2 under SIEGES.)

Tēthўs, wife of Ocĕănus (*q.v.*).

Tetradrachmŏn. A Greek silver coin equivalent to four *drachmæ* (*see* COINAGE).

Tĕtrălŏgĭă. The Athenian term given to the group of four plays which the poets produced in rivalry with each other at the dramatic contests held at the feast of Dĭonŷsus. After the introduction of the satyric drama, this, or a drama of a comparatively cheerful character (such as the *Alcestis* of Euripides), formed the fourth piece of three tragedies or of a trilogy. By a tetralogy is more particularly meant such a group of four dramas as had belonged to the same cycle of myths, and had thus formed a connected whole. Of such a kind were the tetralogies of Æschylus. It is doubtful, however, whether he found this type of connected tetralogy already in use, or was the first to introduce it. Sophocles abolished the connexion between the several pieces, and Euripides followed his example. A complete tetralogy is not extant, although a trilogy exists in the *Oresteia* of Æschylus, consisting of the tragedies *Agămemnōn, Chŏephŏrœ,* and *Eumĕnĭdĕs ;* the satyric play appended to it was the *Prōteus.*

Tetrarch (Gr. *tĕtrarchēs*). Properly the ruler of one of the four parts of a district divided into four governments. Also the title of a petty prince, like the rulers in those provinces of Asia which were allowed by Rome to retain a certain independence.

Teucer (Gr. *Teukrŏs*). (1) A son of Scă- mander and the Nymph Idæa; the most ancient king of Troy, from whom the people were called Teucri. According to another legend, he, with Scamander, was driven by famine from Crete, and found refuge with Dardănus; while another version of the story describes Dardanus as having been received by Teucer.

(2) A son of Tĕlămōn of Sălămīs (thus named from his descent from Hēsĭŏnē, the Teucrian king's daughter); half-brother of Ajax. He was the best archer amongst the Greeks before Troy. On his return from the war, accused by his father of par- ticipation in his brother's murder, and banished from the country, he sought a new home in Cyprus, by the advice of Apollo, where Bēlus of Sidon, in return for assis- tance rendered him in war, made over to him the government, and he founded the town of Salamis. After his father's death, it is said that he returned to his native town of Salamis, but was driven away by his nephew and went to Spain.

Thălămus. The Greek term for a com- modious room in a house, and especially the nuptial chamber. (*See* HOUSE.)

Thălĭă (Gr. *Thăleiă*). (1) One of the Graces. (*See* CHARITES.)

(2) The Muse of dancing and pastoral poetry. (*See* MUSES.)

Thallō. Goddess of flowers, who presided over spring. (*See* HORÆ.)

Thămўrĭs. A Thracian bard, mentioned by Homer [*Il.* ii 595], son of Phĭlammōn and the Nymph Argĭŏpē. He boasted that he could rival the Muses, and was therefore deprived by them of sight and voice, and the power of playing the lute. According to later legends, he expiated his arrogance by being punished in Hādēs.

Thănătŏs. The Greek personification of death. (*See* DEATH.)

Thargēlĭă. The principal feast of Apollo in Athens, held on the seventh day of *Thar- gelĭŏn* (May–June), the birthday of the god. Originally it was connected with the ripen- ing of the field produce. A procession was formed, and the first fruits of the year were offered to Apollo, together with Artĕmis and the Hōræ. It was at the same time an expiatory feast, at which a peculiar propi- tiatory sacrifice was offered, which was to purify the State from all guilt, and avert the wrath of the god, lest he should exer- cise his avenging and destroying power in burning up the harvest with parching heat, and in visiting the people with pesti- lence. Two persons, condemned to death, a man and a woman, as representatives of the male and female population, were led about with a garland of figs round their necks to the sound of flutes and singing, and scourged with seaweed and with the branches of a fig tree. They were then sacrificed at a certain spot on the sea- shore, their bodies burned, and the ashes cast into the sea. In later times they seem to have been contented with throwing the expiatory victims from a height into the sea, catching them as they fell, and banish- ing them from the country. Besides these sacrifices, festal processions and choral contests between men and boys took place. At the same time the great feast of Apollo was probably held at Dēlŏs, to which the Athenians sent a sacred embassy in the ancient ship in which Theseus is said to have sailed to Crete, and which was always kept in repair.

Thaumās. Son of Pontus and Gæa, hus- band of Electra, one of the Ocĕănĭdĕs, and father of the Harpies and Irĭs.

Thĕānō. The pretended wife of Pytha- goras the philosopher. Seven extant letters on jealousy, on the education of children, the management of a household, etc., are attributed to her.

Theatre.

(I) *The Greek Theatre.*

The Greek theatre was originally in- tended for the performance of dithyrambic choruses at the feast of Dĭonўsus. (*See* DITHYRAMBOS.) From the first it consisted of two principal parts : (*a*) the circular dancing-place, *orchēstră,* with the altar (*thўmĕlē*) of the god in the centre; and (*b*) the place for the spectators, or the *thĕātrŏn* proper. The *theatron* was in the form of a segment of a circle, greater than a semi-circle, with the seats rising above one another in concentric tiers (*see* fig. 1). The seats were almost always cut in the slope of a hill. [There are ex- ceptions to this rule at Mĕgălŏpŏlĭs and Mantĭneia, where there is an artificial substructure.] When the dithyrambic choruses had developed into the drama, a structure called the *skēnē* (Lat. *scœna*) was added, with a stage for dramatic representations. It was erected on the side of the *orchestra* away from the spectators, and at such a height and distance as to allow of

having " built " the theatre.] The remains of this theatre have been exposed to view since the excavations of 1862. [Further excavations in the direction of the stage buildings were made in 1877 and 1886.] [1]

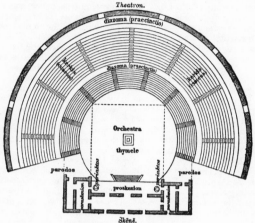

(1) PLAN OF A GREEK THEATRE.

the stage being in full view from every part of the theatre.

The first stone theatre was that built at Athens, the home of the Greek drama; and the theatres in every part of the Hellenic world were constructed on the same general principles. It is said that at a performance about 496 B.C., when Æschўlus, Prātīnās, and Chœrīlus were competitors, the wooden scaffolding on which the spectators were standing broke down; and that it was accordingly resolved to construct a theatre of stone instead [Suidas, *s.v.* Pratinas]. The building was near the east end of the southern slope of the Acrŏpŏlīs; and in its construction partial use was made of the rock against which it rested. It was not, however, completed until between 340 and 330 B.C., when Athens was under the financial administration of Lycurgus. [*Cp.* inscription in *Corp. Inscr. Att.* ii 176, or Hicks, *Manual of Greek Historical Inscriptions*, No. 128; Pseudo-Plutarch, *Lives of the Ten Orators*, p. 841 *c*; Pausanias, i 29 § 16. All these authorities speak of Lycurgus as having "completed" the theatre. It is Hўpĕrīdēs alone (*Fragm.* 139 Sauppe), who, in a speech on behalf of the children of Lycurgus, rhetorically describes him as

[1] [In connexion with these last excavations a theory was started by Dr. Dörpfeld, of the German School of Archæology at Athens. According to his view, (1) the sacred precinct called the *Lēnaĭon* contained in the 5th century B.C. no permanent building for dramatic purposes, but only two temples, the older dating from the time of Pisistrătus, and close to it a circular orchestra, seventy-eight feet in diameter. Andŏcĭdēs, *De Mysteriis*, § 38, speaks of certain conspirators descending "from the *Ŏdĕum* into the *orchēstra*," not the *theatron;* and in Aristophanes the word *theatron* is applied to the *auditorium* alone. (2) The first permanent building was completed by Lycurgus in 330 B.C., and consisted of a stone wall sixty-five feet seven inches long, with two wings rising like towers on either side. Behind the wall was an oblong room for the actors, and in front of the wall to the north there was a new *orchestra*. Rows of seats were constructed at the same time; but at present there was no raised stage. (3) At some later date there was built a permanent *proscĕnium* of stone, ten or twelve feet high. (4) Under Claudius (the "Nero" of the inscription on the *hўposcĕnium*) the orchestra received its pavement of marble, and about this time the stage was raised. (5) In the 3rd century A.D., one Phædrus, whose name appears on the inscription on the *hўposcĕnium*, erected a new stage in front of the older one. To this period, in other words to Romish times, belongs also the continuous stone balustrade separating the *auditorium* from the *orchestra*.

On the other hand, it has been observed (1) that B.C. 330 is a very late date for the Athenians to have erected their earliest stone theatre. (2) The

With the spread of dramatic representations stone theatres were built in every part of the Hellenic world; and, shortly after the time of Alexander the Great, they were practically universal. It has been estimated that the theatre at Athens had room for 27,500 persons [*Zeitschrift für bildende Kunst*, xiii p. 202]. Plato is only using round numbers when he speaks of a play of Agăthōn having been witnessed by 30,000 spectators [*Symp.* 175 E]. Among other large theatres may be mentioned, in Greece, those of Megalopolis, Sparta, and Epidaurus; in Sicily, that of Syracuse; in Asia Minor, those of Ephesus and Mīlētus. There were also large theatres in Crete. [Among other theatres of Greek origin, remains of which are still in existence, are the following: in *Greece*, at the Peiræus, at Thŏrĭcus, Ōrōpus, Sĭcўōn, Argos, Mantineia, Rhiniassa and Dramyssus in Epīrus, and in Mēlŏs and Dēlŏs. In *Sicily*, at Acræ, Tyndāris, Taurŏmĕnĭōn, and Sēgesta (fig. 3). In *Asia Minor*, at Aspendus, Pergē, and Sidē in Pamphylia; Myra, Pătără, and Talmissus in Lycia; Iassŏs in Caria; Assŏs and Pergămōn in Mysia; and Hĭĕrăpŏlĭs and Aizāni in Phrygia.]

It is estimated that in the theatre at Athens the space assigned to each spectator was about thirteen inches in breadth; the depth of the seat was sufficient to allow room behind for the feet of the spectator sitting immediately above. To facilitate access to the various parts of the *audītōrium*, the

erection of a wooden structure, including a vast number of seats, twice a year, or the keeping of such structure in repair, would have been a troublesome task. (3) The evidence from literature in favour of wooden seats is inconclusive. Aristophanes (*Thesm.* 395) and Crătīnus (*Fragm. Incert.* 51) speak of *ikrĭă* or "benches"; but this may be only a survival of the older term when it was no longer strictly accurate. (4) The evidence already quoted as to Lycurgus is on the whole in favour of his having *completed* a structure that was already partially finished. (5) The retaining wall supporting the rows of stone seats on either side is built with enormous blocks of conglomerate, hidden by a thin wall of the finest *pŏrŏs* limestone. It is this conglomerate which is understood to be one of the grounds on which Dr. Dörpfeld assigns a late date to the structure. But (as observed by Professor Middleton in corroboration of a paper read by Prof. Jebb to the above effect) the pointing of the blocks is all "drafted" masonry, and all the joints are marked with a shallow groove, and the whole face dressed with a very broad chisel parted into fourteen teeth just as in the walls of Cĭmōn. For this reason Prof. Middleton holds that the *auditorium* belongs to the middle of the 5th century, while the permanent stage buildings may be assigned to the time of Lycurgus. *Adhuc sub iudice lis est.*]

parallel tiers of seats were separated by one or more broad passages running from end to end, and horizontally dividing the tiers into several zones; these passages were called *diazōmătă* (Lat. *præcinctiōnēs*). The seats were also divided vertically by stairs radiating from below, and intersecting the *diazomata* at right angles. The wedge-like blocks thus formed were called *kerkĭdĕs* (Lat. *cŭnĕi*). The number of the stairs varies according to the size of the theatre. In the theatre at Athens there are fourteen, giving access to thirteen blocks of seats. [The audience were probably arranged according to their respective tribes, and the number of the tribes was raised in later times from ten to twelve or thirteen.] In the Greek theatre the normal number of the stairs was even; in the Roman it was usually uneven. They either ascend straight throughout the whole building, or are differently arranged in the several zones of seats. [Thus, in the theatre at Epidaurus, designed by Pŏlўclītus the younger, there are twelve *kerkides* in the lower zone, and twenty-two in the upper; only eleven flights of stairs ascending straight from the lowest to the highest part of the *auditorium*.]

In the Athenian theatre, the front row of seats, which was the nearest to the *orchestra*, consisted of sixty-seven marble stalls; forty-five of these were reserved for priests and other ministers of religion, and the rest for the officials of the State. The central seat in this row was reserved for the priest of Dionysus. The right of occupying a reserved seat in one of the front rows was called *prŏĕdrĭă* [Aristophanes, *Eq.* 575, 702, 1405]; and it was in this part of the theatre that seats were provided for public benefactors, for the *strătēgi*, for the orphans of those who had fallen in war [Æschines, *Ctes.* 174], and for ambassadors from foreign states [Demosthenes, *De Cor.* 28]. The judges of the dramatic competitions sat together in a body, and would naturally have some of the best places assigned to them. Behind the front row were placed a number of inferior priests and priestesses. It is not known how the rest of the spectators were arranged, but it is probable that the members of each tribe sat in the same part of the theatre. The tickets of admission discovered in Attica are of two kinds: (*a*) ordinary leaden tokens about the size of either a florin or (more frequently) a sixpenny-bit, with Dionysus or a mask on the obverse, and the name or number of a tribe on the reverse; (*b*) counters of bone or ivory, about the size of half-a-crown, with a head on one side, and on the other a Greek or Roman numeral—never higher than xv (fig. 2). The latter were for the use of persons enjoying the right of *proedria*, and belong to the Roman period (Benndorf's *Beiträge*, p. 36 ff; Baumeister's *Denkmäler*, figs. 1833-5). The price of a ticket was two obols (about 3*d*.); and, in the case of poorer citizens, this payment was made out of the *theoric fund*.

(2) * IVORY TICKET.
With head of Crönus.
(Gonzenbach Collection, Smyrna.)

Women were generally present at the performance of tragedies; but from that of comedies those of the higher classes usually stayed away. In the 5th century, the women sat in a separate part of the theatre (Aristophanes, *Pax* 964); at the back, according to Pollux (ix. 44); and with the resident aliens behind them..Boys were admitted (Plato, *Laws*, 658 C); slaves probably not. The provision against sun and rain customary in the Roman theatre was unknown to the ancient Greeks. [Those who could afford it brought cushions and carpets to sit on (Æschines, *Ctes.* 76; *Fals. Leg.* 111). By command of the oracle at Delphi, all the spectators wore wreaths of bay leaves in honour of Dionysus (Demosthenes, *Meid.* 52).]

The *orchestra* was considerably below the level of the stage. [In the theatre at Epidaurus, the stage is almost exactly twelve feet high; in that of Megalopolis, excavated in 1890, the height is about six feet.] The chorus entered the orchestra by means of passages (*părŏdoi*) on either side of the stage. These also gave access to the audience, who came in by the *orchestra*, and thence mounted the flights of steps leading to the seats assigned them. The *orchestra* was connected with the stage by means of steps, by which the chorus ascended on the rare occasions when the action of the play involved their presence on the stage [*e.g.* Sophocles, *Œd. Col.* 856-7; Aristophanes, *Eq.* 490-4; cp,

Acharn. 324-7, *Av.* 353-400. But, as a general rule, the chorus remained in the *orchestra*, at a lower level than the stage].

Strictly speaking, it was only the decorated wall at the back of the stage that was called the *skēnē* (lit. "booth"). The same name was, however, given to the stage-buildings, and (far more frequently) to the stage on which the actors performed. The more distinctive designation for the stage is *proscēnium* (Gr. *prŏskēnĭŏn*, "the space in front of the *skēnē*, or booth"), or *lŏgeiŏn* ("the speaking-place").[1] It is also called *ŏkrĭbās*

[1] [The ordinary view that the actors occupied a narrow raised stage behind the *orchestra* was first attacked by Höpken, *De Theatro Attico sæculi a. Chr. quinti* (Bonn, 1884), who is supported by Dr. Dörpfeld. It is true that the stage-buildings excavated at Epidaurus are twelve feet higher than the *orchestra*, but these buildings are regarded by Dr. Dörpfeld as the background of the actors' stage, partly because there are no steps leading down to the orchestra. On the other hand, (1) Vitruvius, v 7, tells us that the Greek stage was from ten to twelve feet high, but narrower than the Roman. (2) The theatre of Epidaurus may possibly have been provided with wooden steps; Dr. Dörpfeld himself (*Berlin Philol. Wochenschrift*, 1890, p. 1434) sees no objection to ascribing its *proscenium* to the 3rd or 2nd century B.C. The height of this stage, twelve feet, corresponds to that given by Vitruvius as characteristic of the Greek theatre. (3) Several passages of Aristophanes imply that the actors were on a higher level than the chorus (*Eq.* 149, c. schol.; *Vesp.* 1341, 1514; *Av.* 175-8, 268). (4) The use of steps to connect the *orchestra* with the stage is attested by a writer in the earlier part of the 3rd century B.C., Athenæus, the author of a work on engines of war, *Mech.*, p. 29 (ed. Wescher), who compares certain ladders used in sieges to those "placed in theatres against the *proscenia* for the actors" (*cp.* Pollux iv 127). (5) Such steps may be seen on vases of Southern Italy, beginning with the 3rd century, representing comic scenes (*e g.* Baumeister, figs. 902 and 1828 = British Mus. F 101; Schreiber's *Bilderatlas*, I, v 11, 13; Heydemann in *Jahrb. des Deutsch. Archäol. Inst.* 1886, p. 260). (6) The use of *ἐπὶ τῆς σκηνῆς*, "upon the *skēnē*," in Aristotle's *Poetics*, implies something raised above the level of the ground (*Classical Review*, v 97). (7) In the summer of 1893 an inscription was found in the theatre at Delos identifying the *proscēnium* with the *logeion*. The theatres at Magnesia and Tralles have also been excavated. At Tralles there is a double flight of steps leading up from the *orchestra* to the front of the *proscenium*, ten or twelve feet high. In spite of the steps, the *proscenium* is explained by Dr. Dörpfeld as merely a background for the actors in the *orchestra*. At Magnesia he accepts it as a true stage ten feet in height, but he ascribes it to Roman times (*Mittheilungen*, xviii 410; xix 86; *Journ. Hellenic Studies*, 1894, p. 230). The evidence from the theatre at Megalopolis may be regarded as inconclusive (*Class. Rev.* v 284, and *Excavations at Megalopolis*, 1892, p. 91). Cp. *Am. Journ. of Philol.* xiv 68, 198, 273.]

[Plato, *Symp.* 194 B] or *bēma* [Plutarch, *Phocion* 34, and inscription on the *hyposcēnium* of the theatre at Athens]. On either side of the *proscenium* were wings, called *parascēnia*, which, together with the space behind the real *skēnē*, served as dressing-rooms for the actors, and store-rooms for the costumes and machinery. The name of *hyposcēnium* was given to the hollow space beneath the floor of the stage, and also to the lower wall adorned with pillars and statues facing the *orchestra*. A flight of steps leading out upon the stage from underneath was occasionally used for bringing ghosts and spectres upon the stage. They were called " Charon's steps " [Pollux, iv 132].

The scenery was very simple. Like many other things connected with the stage, it is said to have been first introduced by

to the right of the audience represented views in the immediate neighbourhood of the city where the scene of the action is laid. The *periaktos* to the left represented a more distant country. In correspondence with this, the entrance to the right of the audience was reserved for actors coming from the immediate neighbourhood; while that to the left was for those who came from a distance [Pollux, iv 126; Vitruvius, v 6; Servius on Vergil, *Georg.* iii 24]. In connexion with the action of the play, accessories, such as altars, statues, and tombs, were introduced when necessary. There is no direct evidence for a drop curtain in the Greek theatre.

Machinery of various kinds was used to imitate thunder and lightning. For the former, casks filled with pebbles were sent rolling down bronze surfaces [Pollux, iv

(3) THE THEATRE AT SEGESTA.
(As restored by Strack.)

Æschylus [Vitruvius, vii *præf.* 11]; but we have better authority for ascribing its introduction to Sophocles [Aristotle, *Poet.* iv 16]. The first painter of stage scenery (*skēnŏgrăphĭa*) is said to have been Agătharchus [Vitruvius *l.c.*]. The principal decoration consisted of a light and movable screen placed in front of the wall at the back of the stage. On this screen was painted the scene of the play. In tragedy, it was usually the front of a king's palace, with three doors. The interior of a house was never represented by means of painted scenery, but only by means of the mechanical device call the *ekkỹklēma*. Towards the foreground of the stage, on each side, there was a revolving stand of three side-scenes, called a *pĕrĭaktŏs*,—a contrivance which allowed of the scenery at either or both ends of the stage being changed without changing the background. The *periaktos*

130]. There were also contrivances for making persons appear or disappear in the air [*ib.* 132]. But of these we know hardly anything except the names by which they were designated. In order to make the actor's voice more audible at a distance, vessels of bronze of different tones were sometimes suspended in niches in various parts of the *auditorium* [Vitruv. i 1,9; v 5. Niches of this kind have been observed in the remains of the theatre at Aizāni in Phrygia, at Gĕrăsă in the *Dĕcăpŏlis*, and in Crete.] Theatres were frequently used for public purposes unconnected with the drama. At Athens the custom of using the theatre for assemblies of the people prevailed from the middle of the 3rd century B.C.

Fig. 3 represents the theatre of Sĕgesta in Sicily [situated near the crest of a hill. The lower part of the *auditorium* is in nearly perfect preservation. The structure is Greek, but the stage-buildings were altered in Roman times].

[For further details, see A. Müller, *Die Griechischen Bühnenalterthümer*, 1886; or A. E. Haigh, *The Attic Theatre*, 1889.]

(II) *The Roman Theatre.*

In Rome, where dramatic representations, in the strict sense of the term, were not given until 240 B.C., a wooden stage was erected in the Circus for each performance, and taken down again. The place for the spectators was a space surrounded by a wooden barrier, within which the public stood and looked on in a promiscuous mass. It was not until 194 B.C. that a place was set apart for the senators nearest to the stage, but without any fixed seats; those who wanted to sit had to bring their own chairs; sometimes, by order of the Senate, sitting was forbidden. In 154 B.C. an attempt was made to build a permanent theatre with fixed seats; but it had to be pulled down by order of the Senate. In 145 B.C., on the conquest of Greece, theatres provided with seats after the Greek model were erected; these, however, were only of wood, and served for one representation alone. Such was the splendid theatre built in 58 B.C. by the ædile Æmĭlĭus Scaurus, containing, among other decorations, 3,000 bronze statues, and provided with 80,000 seats. The first stone theatre was built by Pompey in 55 B.C., a second one by Cornēlĭus Balbus, 13 B.C., and in the same year, the one dedicated by Augustus to his nephew Marcellus, and called by his name, the ruins of which still exist (fig. 4). The first of these contained 17,500, the second 11,510, and the third 20,000 seats. Besides these, there were no other stone theatres in Rome; wooden theatres continued to be erected under the Empire.

The Roman theatre differed from the Greek. In the first place, the *auditorium* (*căvĕa*), which was divided in the same way as in the Greek by horizontal passages and by stairs (only into an uneven number of divisions), formed a semicircle only, with the front wall of the stage-building as its diameter, whilst in the Greek it was larger than a semicircle. Again, a covered colonnade ran round the highest story of the Roman theatre, the roof of which was of the same height as the highest part of the stage. The orchestra, moreover, which was enclosed by the *cavea*, contained places for spectators; these were, at first, reserved exclusively for the senators; foreign ambassadors whom it was wished to honour were afterwards admitted to them. The most distinguished places were the two balconies over the entrances to the orchestra, on the right and left side of the stage; in one of these sat the giver of the entertainment and the emperor, in the other the empress and the Vestal Virgins. Places of dignity were also assigned to magistrates and priests, probably on the *pŏdĭum*, or the space in front of the lowest row of seats, where there was room for a few rows of chairs. The first fourteen rows of the ordinary seats were, after 68 B.C., appropriated to the *ĕquĭtēs ;* after them came the general body of citizens, who were probably

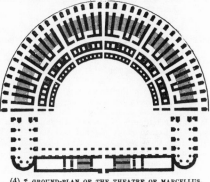

(4) * GROUND-PLAN OF THE THEATRE OF MARCELLUS.

arranged in the order of their tribes ; in the upper part of the *căvĕa* were the women, who sat apart, in accordance with a decree of Augustus (they had formerly sat with the men); the lowest classes were relegated

(5) * BONE TICKET, POMPEII.

(Denoting row 12, in the block named after Æschylus; Overbeck, *Pompeii*, p. 150, ed. 1875.)

to the highest tiers. Even children were admitted, only slaves being excluded. Admission was free, as was the case with all entertainments intended for the people.

The tickets of admission (*tessĕræ*) did not indicate any particular seat, but only the block of seats and the row in which it would be found. An awning could be drawn over the whole *auditorium ;* it was suspended on masts which were made fast to the external wall of the theatre. In order to cool the atmosphere, and prevent disagreeable odours, fragrant liquids (especially water scented with saffron), were shot into the air, and fell in fine spray over the *cavea.*

The façade of the stage-building, the *scæna,* consisted generally of three stories, and was richly decorated with architecture and sculpture. The stage itself (*pulpĭtum*) was raised five feet at the most above the orchestra, in order that the spectators might easily overlook every part of it. It was considerably longer and wider than the Greek stage, as in the Roman theatre there were nearly as many actors as parts, and the Romans were very fond of splendid stage-processions. There were two altars on the stage, one dedicated to Lĭber in remembrance of the Dionysian origin of the drama, the other to the god in whose honour the play was held.

With regard to the scenery, which certainly cannot have been introduced before 99 B.C., and the scene-shifting, for which elaborate machinery of various kinds existed, the Roman stage did not essentially differ from the Greek, except that it had a curtain. This, called *aulœum,* was lowered at the beginning of the play, instead of being drawn up as with us, and it was not raised again until the end: there was also a smaller curtain, *sĭpărĭum,* which served as a drop-scene. A portico was often built behind the stage to afford shelter to the spectators in bad weather.

Thĕmis. One of the Tītānĭdĕs; daughter of Urănus and Gæa, and Jupiter's second wife after Mētis ; mother of the Hōræ and Mœræ (Lat. *Parcæ*). She is the goddess who, with Jupiter, presides over law and order. She also reigns with him in Olympus as his trusted assessor and no longer as his wife ; she represents divine justice in all its relations to man. The rights of hospitality are especially under her protection ; hence she is protector of the oppressed, and honoured in many towns as the saving goddess (*Sōteira*). She also had the power of foretelling the future, and for this reason the Delphic oracle was in her possession for some time before it came into that of Apollo. She was especially honoured in Athens, Delphi, Thebes, Olympia, and Trœzēn. In works of art, she is represented as a woman of commanding and awe-inspiring presence, holding a pair of scales and a *cornucopia,* the symbol of the blessings of order.

Thĕmistius. A Greek rhetorician of Paphlagonia, who lived in the second half of the 4th century A.D., as teacher of philosophy and oratory at Constantinople. He was much honoured by his contemporaries for his noble disposition and his learning and eloquence, which gained for him the name of *Euphrādēs,* or eloquent speaker. He was honoured with various marks of distinction by the emperors. Constantius made him a senator ; Julian described him as the first philosopher of his age ; Theodosius selected him as tutor to his son Arcadius, and in 384 nominated him to the prefecture. He died about 388. Thirty-four of his speeches have been preserved, one of them in a Latin translation only. They are partly philosophical and political, but principally eulogistic orations, either in compliment to or in memory of various emperors, composed in a clear, pleasant style, and valuable for the information they contain respecting contemporary history. Besides these, we possess four paraphrases by him of parts of Aristotle.

Thĕmistō. The third wife of Athămās (*q.v.*), who married her under the impression that his wife Ino was dead. When he heard, however, that Ino was living as a votary of Dīonўsus, in the ravines of Parnassus, he secretly sent for her. Themisto, on hearing this, determined, in revenge, to kill Ino's children, and ordered a slave, who had lately come to the house, to dress her children in white and Ino's in black, so that she might be able to distinguish them in the night. But the slave, who was Ino herself, suspecting the evil intention, exchanged the clothes. Themisto, in consequence, killed her own children, and, on becoming aware of her mistake, slew herself also.

Thĕmistŏgĕnēs. Of Syracuse, supposed (on inadequate grounds) to be the author of the *Anăbăsĭs,* which has come down to us under the name of Xĕnŏphōn (*q.v.*).

Thĕŏclўmĕnus. Son of the soothsayer Pŏlўphīdēs, grandson of Mĕlampūs. When a fugitive from Argos, for a murder which he had committed, he met with Tĕlĕmăchus in Pўlus, who succoured him and brought him to Ĭthăcă. By means of his inherited gift of prophecy, he here made known to Pĕnĕlŏpĕ the presence of Odysseus in the island, and warned the suitors of their fate.

Thĕŏcrĭtus. The founder and principal representative of Greek bucolic poetry, born about 325 B.C. in Syracuse, or (according to another account) in the island of Cōs, pupil of the poet Phĭlētäs and friend of the poet Arätus. He lived alternately in Alexandria, at the court of Ptolemy II (*Phĭlădelphus*), and in Sicily with Hĭĕrō, where he was much esteemed for his poetical skill and refinement. He died about 267. Besides a number of epigrams, thirty-two poems, some of considerable length, known as *idylls*, have come down to us. Some of these are probably spurious. Those that are undoubtedly genuine are of great poetical merit. They include the true bucolic idylls, descriptive of the life of shepherds and herdsmen, and also the *genre* pictures of every-day life and of the mythical age, together with hymns and eulogistic poems to his princely patrons, an *ĕpĭthălămĭum* in honour of Helen, and some pieces in lyrical form. His poems of ordinary life are especially remarkable for their minutely faithful and dramatic descriptions. Most of his idylls are written in a largely modified epic language, with a skilful admixture of the forms of the Doric dialect spoken in Sicily, which still further enhanced their popular character. Two of the lyrical poems [xxviii, xxix] are composed in the Æolic dialect.

Thĕŏdectēs. Of Phăsēlĭs, in Lycia, a Greek rhetorician and tragic poet. He carried off the prize eight times, and in 351 B.C. his tragedy of *Mausōlus* was victorious in the tragic contest instituted by queen Artĕmĭsĭa in honour of her deceased husband Mausolus. In the rhetorical contest, held at the same time, he was defeated by Thĕŏpompus. Only unimportant fragments of his fifty tragedies are extant.

Thĕŏdōrus. (1) Of Sămŏs, son of Rhœcus. In conjunction with his father, he erected the labyrinth of Lēmnŏs [Pliny, *N. H.* xxxvi 90], and advised the laying down of a layer of charcoal as part of the foundation of the temple of Artĕmis, at Ephesus [Diogenes Laertius ii 103]. He is said to have lived for a long time in Egypt, where he and his brother Tēlĕclēs learnt the Egyptian canon of proportion for the human figure [Diodōrus, i 98]. He was considered by the Greeks as one of the inventors of casting in bronze [Pausanias, viii 14 § 8]. He wrote a work on the temple of Hēra at Samos, which was begun by his father [Herodotus, iii 60 ; Vitruvius, vii, pref. 12].

(2) Son of Telecles, and nephew of (1). He flourished in the time of Crœsus and Pŏlўcrătēs, whose ring he made [Herodotus, i 51, iii 41]. [J. E. S.]

Thĕognĭs. A Greek elegiac poet, born about 540 B.C., of a rich and noble family in Mĕgără. He lived at a time when bitter feuds had broken out in his native town between the nobles and the other citizens. On the fall of his party, having espoused the cause of the aristocracy, he was despoiled of his fortune and driven into exile. It was not until many years later that he was able to return to the home for which he yearned, and he was probably still alive at the time of the Persian Wars. From the remains of his elegies, which are mostly addressed in a hortatory form to the noble youth Cycnus, it may be seen that they were closely connected with the political fortunes of the poet. They exhibit the pride and rancour of the aristocrat, in whose eyes all his own party are " good " and " noble," as contrasted with the adherents of the popular party, who are denounced as " base " and " cowardly." The loss of the great bulk of his poems was due to their containing an extraordinary abundance of proverbs, which were at an early date extracted from his writings, to serve (especially at Athens) as precepts for the conduct of youth. Under his name we still possess a dreary collection of all kinds of proverbial couplets and precepts, which are strung together without coherence or plan, being connected by means of merely casual catchwords, and including adventitious elements, such as sayings of Tyrtæus, Mimnermus, Sŏlŏn, and others.

Thĕŏn. (1) *Of Sămŏs.* A Greek *painter* who flourished in the second half of the 4th century B.C. His pictures were celebrated for their powerful effect on the imagination, which caused those who looked at them to forget that they were only counterfeits of reality. The picture of a young hoplite charging the enemy was especially celebrated for this effect of illusion [Ælian, *Var. Hist.* ii 44].

(2) *Of Smyrna.* A *Platonist* living in the first half of the 2nd century A.D. He was the author of a work of great value in connexion with ancient Greek arithmetic : on the principles of mathematics, music, and astronomy required for the study of Plato.

(3) *Of Alexandria.* One of the last members of the Alexandrian *Museum*, born about 365 A.D. He is the author of a commentary on Euclid and on the astronomical tables of Ptŏlĕmæus.

(4) *Ælius.* A rhetorician of Alexandria. He wrote, in the 5th century A.D., a book on rhetoric, to which were appended exercises on style, called *prŏgymnasmătă*, deserving of much commendation both for their conciseness and lucidity of exposition, and for their criticisms on the style of the Attic orators.

Thĕŏphrastus. A Greek philosopher, born 371 B.C. at Ĕrĕsus, in Lesbŏs. At Athens, he was at first the pupil of Plato, and then of Aristotle, who, on account of his fascinating powers of language, is said to have given him the name of Theophrastus ("divine speaker"), instead of his original name Tyrtămus. Appointed by Aristotle guardian of his son and heir to his library, and designated by him as his successor in the leadership of the Peripatetic school, he continued at its head, and pursued, in an independent spirit, the philosophy of his master. After long enjoying the highest esteem, he died in the eighty-fifth year of his age, in 287.

Like Aristotle, he succeeded in combining with his philosophical studies (of which only the fragment of a work on *metaphysics* has been preserved), various investigations in natural science, especially in *botany*, of which science he may be said to be the founder, just as Aristotle is considered to be the originator of zoology. Of his botanical works we still possess a *Natural History of Plants*, in ten books, and six books of the eight *On the Origin* (or physiology) *of Plants*. A small pamphlet, containing an outline of *mineralogy*, has also been preserved, together with other scientific works. His *Characters* are probably an abridgment of a larger work. They consist of thirty sections, descriptions of various types of character, and are remarkable for the knowledge of life and keenness of observation which they display, and for the intuitive skill and vivacity of expression with which they are written.

Thĕŏpompus. (1) A Greek *poet* of the Old Comedy, a younger contemporary of Aristophanes; he is known to have been engaged in composition as late as about 370 B.C. Only fragments remain of his twenty-four dramas, which prepared the way for the transition to the Middle Comedy.

(2) A Greek *historian*, born at Chĭŏs about 380 B.C. He left home, probably about 361, with his father, who was banished by the democratic party on account of his predilection for the Spartans, and, having been trained in oratory by Isŏcrătēs, spoke with great success in all the larger towns of Greece. He distinguished himself so greatly in the rhetorical contest instituted (351) by queen Artĕmĭsĭa, wife of Mausŏlus, in honour of her deceased husband, that he obtained a brilliant victory over all competitors. He afterwards travelled, with the object of acquiring material for his historical works. The favour shown him by Alexander the Great induced him to return to Chios at the age of forty-five; but on the death of his patron he found himself again obliged to flee from his opponents, whose hatred he had incurred by his vehement adoption of the sentiments of the aristocracy. He took refuge with king Ptolemy I at Alexandria about 305. Here he did not, however, meet with a favourable reception, and was compelled to withdraw, as his life was in danger. Of his subsequent fate nothing is known.

Besides numerous orations, he composed two large histories, founded on the most careful and minute research: (*a*) *Hĕllĕnĭcă*, in twelve books, a continuation of Thucydides, covering the period from 411–394; and (*b*) *Phĭlippĭcă*, in fifty-eight books, treating of the life and times of Philip of Macedon. Of these works only fragments remain. The charge of malignity, which was brought against him by the ancients, seems to have originated in the reckless manner in which, on the testimony of Dĭonȳsius of Halicarnassus [*Ep. ad Cn. Pompeium*], he exposed the pettiness and baseness of the politics of those times, especially those of the Macedonian party. There seems to be better foundation for the charge brought against him of being too fond of digressions; for when, in later times, the digressions in the *Philippica* were omitted, the work was thereby reduced to sixteen books.

Thĕŏrĭæ (Gr. *thĕŏrĭai*). The Greek name for the sacred embassies, which were sent by individual States to the great national festivals, as well as to those of friendly States; for instance, that sent by the Athenians to the festival of Apollo at Dēlŏs. A number of important men were appointed to this office, the principal of whom was known as the *archĭthĕŏrŏs*. Part of the cost, which was considerable, was borne by the State and part by the *architheoros*, on whom, as also on his companions (*synthĕōri*), devolved the honourable and patriotic duty of appearing with the utmost splendour. In Athens the *architheoria* was one of the *lǐturgǐæ* undertaken by the wealthier citizens. (*See* LEITOURGIA.) The members of the sacred embassy were treated as honoured guests by the State to which they were deputed.

Thĕōrǐcŏn ("theatre-money"). A distribution of two obols (about 3*d.*) a head, granted from the time of Pericles to the poorer Athenian citizens, from the common warchest (*see* HELLENOTAMIÆ), to enable them to attend the representations at the theatre, two obols being the entrance fee levied by the lessees of the theatre. By degrees this grant was distributed to citizens who laid claim to it in the case of other entertainments. It was abolished towards the end of the Peloponnesian War, but again introduced after the restoration of the democracy; and a special fund, to which, by a decree of the people, the whole surplus of the revenue was to be devoted, was set apart for this purpose, under a special board, who had even for a time the management of the finances of the State. Demosthenes first succeeded, shortly before the battle of Chærŏnēa (338 B.C.), in putting an end to this system, which so severely taxed the resources of the State in time of war.

Thĕoxĕnǐa ("entertainments given to the gods"). A festival celebrated in many parts of Greece in honour, not only of the principal local divinity, but of many others who were considered as his guests. Such was the feast held at Delphi in honour of Apollo in the month hence called *Thĕoxĕnǐŏs* (August). Of the manner of its celebration nothing is known. Distinguished men, such as Pindar and his descendants, were also invited to the sacrificial feast. Elsewhere other gods appeared as hosts at the feast, as the Dǐoscūri, the patrons of hospitality, in Părŏs and Agrǐgentum.

Thērǐtās ("the savage one"). A name given at Sparta to Arēs (*q.v.*).

Thermæ. The name given by the Romans to the public buildings, founded in and after the time of Agrippa, which combined, with *warm baths*, the arrangements of a Greek *gymnasium*. These included open and covered colonnades for conversation, instruction, and different exercises, especially the game of ball. The most extensive and splendid establishments of the sort were to be found in Rome, and are still to be seen, though, for the greater part, in ruins. Of the existing remains the most important are those of the *Thermæ of Caracalla.* (*Cp.* ARCHITECTURE, fig. 14, p. 56; and *see* BATHS.)

Thersander (Gr. *Thersandrŏs*). Son of Pŏlȳnīcēs and Argeia, husband of Dēmōnassa the daughter of Amphǐārāus, and king of Thebes after the taking of that city by the Epǐgŏni (*q.v.*). According to post-Homeric traditions he took part in the expedition against Troy, but was killed on first landing by Tēlĕphus. In Vergil ["Thessandrus," *Æn.* ii 261], on the other hand, he is one of the heroes of the wooden horse. His son and successor was Tīsămĕnus. His grandson, Autĕsīōn, at the bidding of the oracle, went over to the Dorians who had settled in Lacedæmon; and his greatgrandson Thērās founded a colony in the island of Callistē, which from that time was called Thērā. It was from him that Thērōn, the tyrant of Agrǐgentum in Sicily, traced his descent.

Thersītēs. The most ill-favoured of the Greeks assembled before Troy, and also a man of evil tongue. He was severely chastised by Odysseus [*Il.* ii 212–277] for speaking evil of Agamemnon. According to later tradition, Achilles slew him with a blow of his fist for stabbing in the eye the Amazon Penthĕsǐlĕă, whom he had himself laid low, and also for falsely accusing Achilles [Quintus Smyrnæus, i 768–823].

Thēsaurus. The Greek term for a room in which all kinds of objects, provisions, jewels, etc., were stored; hence a "treasury" or "treasure house." In ordinary life the underground store-chambers, circular vaulted rooms with an opening above, similar to our cellars, were thus named. The same name was given to treasurehouses which each State maintained within the precincts of Panhellenic sanctuaries, as repositories for their offerings to the gods. Such were those at Olympia and Delphi. The subterranean tombs, shaped like beehives, and of a construction dating from remote Greek antiquity, which have been found in various places, have been wrongly described as "treasure houses." The most celebrated of these are the so called *thesaurus* of Atreus at Mȳcēnæ (*see* ARCHITECTURE, fig. 3), and that of Mǐnȳās at Orchŏmĕnus (*see* TROPHONIUS). The latter is only partly, the former wholly preserved. The ground-plan of these structures is circular, and consists of one enclosed room with a domed roof, constructed of horizontal layers of massive stone blocks, projecting one over the other. This circular chamber was used probably for services in honour of the dead. The actual resting-place of the body was a square room adjoining. The large room at Mycenæ is fifty feet in diameter, and about the same in height. It consists of thirteen courses, the uppermost of which was only a single stone. It was decorated with hundreds of bronze plates, the holes for the nails being still visible.

Thēsēus. The Hērāclēs of Ionian-Attic fable; son of Æthra and the Athenian king Ægeus or, according to another story, Pŏseidōn. Ægeus, having consulted the oracle at Delphi, in consequence of both his marriages proving childless, and having received an obscure reply, applied to the wise Pittheus of Trœzēn, who gave him his daughter Æthra in marriage. On his return to Athens he laid his sword and shoes under a rock, and charged Æthra, as soon as his son was able to lift it, to send him with these tokens to Athens. When Theseus, who had been educated by his grandfather, had attained the age of sixteen, and had dedicated his forelocks to the Delian or Delphic Apollo, his mother conducted him to the stone; he lifted it with ease, and set out to go to his father at Athens, bearing the sword and shoes. On the way he had a series of adventures with various monsters, from which he emerged victorious. At Ēpĭdaurus he vanquished Pĕrĭphētēs (q.v.); on the Isthmus of Corinth, Sĭnĭs (q.v.); at Crommўŏn, not far from Mĕgără, the wild sow Phæa (i.e. "the gray one"); on the borders of Megara and Attica, the robber Scīrōn (q.v.). In Eleusis he overcame and slew Cercўŏn (q.v.). Farther on he rid the land of the monster Dămastēs (q.v.). He then proceeded on his way to Ægeus at Athens, being purified of bloodshed by the Phўtălĭdæ (see PHYTALUS) on reaching the Cēphissus. His father had meanwhile married Mēdēa, who had fled to him from Corinth, and who recognised Theseus as the son of the house, and persuaded Ægeus to poison the stranger during a meal. The father, however, recognised his son in time, by means of the sword which Theseus used to cut up his meat, and Medea disappeared through the air with Medus, her son by Ægeus. When Pallas, who had deprived his brother of the throne, heard of what had happened, he and his fifty gigantic sons hastened to Athens; but they were all slain by the young hero, who

was warned in time by the herald. Lĕōs. After this he seized the bull of Marathon (see HERACLES), which had devastated the country, and sacrificed it to Apollo Delphīnius at Athens. When the time drew near for the third payment of the tribute of seven youths and seven maidens, exacted by Mīnōs (q.v.) for the Mīnōtaur, he volunteered to accompany them, and to deliver his country from this horrible tribute by slaying the monster. Through Aphrŏdītē's favour he gained the love of Arĭadnē, the daughter of Minos, who gave him a thread that she had received from Dædălus, by means of which he was able to find his way into the Labyrinth to the Minotaur, and emerge again in safety after having slain the monster. Ariadne allowed him to carry her away on his return home with the rescued youths and maidens. But in the island of Dia (see ARIADNE) he forsook her, either from faithlessness or (according to another account) at the special command of the gods. In his joy at his success, he forgot the signal agreed upon with Ægeus, that if he succeeded in his enterprise a white sail should be hoisted in place of the black one, and he was thus the cause of his father's death. (See ÆGEUS.)

As king of Athens, he justified his right to the significant name of "founder," by inducing the independent Attic communities to recognise Athens as the capital and centre of the whole country; and in this manner he became the founder of the Attic State. To commemorate this event he is said to have instituted the feast of the union of the tribes (Synoikĭa or Mĕtoikĭa), and to have caused the Athēnæa, a festival instituted by Erichthŏnius, to be celebrated by all Attica, under the name of Pănăthenæa (the festival of united Athens). In the same way the institution of the Isthmian games is attributed to him in commemoration of his victory over Sinis. He is also said to have taken part in the Argonautic expedition and in the Calydonian Hunt, as well as in the expedition undertaken by Heracles against the Amazons. In reward for the bravery which he displayed on this occasion, Antĭŏpē, the sister of the queen of the Amazons, was bestowed upon him; she became the mother of Hippŏlўtus. According to another tradition, he and his friend Pīrĭthŏüs, king of the Lăpĭthæ, carried her away, and, to avenge the deed, the Amazons invaded Attica. (See ANTIOPE, 2.) After Antiope's death he married Phædra, the daughter of Minos, sister of Ariadne, and mother of Ăcămās and Dēmŏphŏōn. On her death by her own hand (*see* HIPPOLYTUS), he carried off Helen, with the help of Pirithous, to his stronghold Aphidnæ. He, in his turn, assisted Pirithous in his battle with the Centaurs, and even descended into the world below to help his friend to carry away Persĕphŏnē. They were punished severely for this sacrilegious attempt, as they were fastened to a rock, on which they were compelled to sit for ever.

Theseus, however, was after some time delivered by Heracles, when the latter was fetching Cerbĕrus, and returned with him to the light of day. There he found everything changed. The Dīoscūri had in the meantime taken and destroyed his town of Aphidnæ, had freed Helen, and had carried away captive his own mother. Mĕnesthēus, son of Pĕtĕōs, had usurped the government of the country. Theseus thereupon took his sons Acamas and Demophoön to Elĕphēnōr, king of the Abantĕs, and went himself to the island of Scȳrŏs, where the king, Lȳcŏmēdēs, treacherously threw him from a rock into the sea.

He was worshipped as a hero at Athens; yet it was not until after the Persian War that the reverence paid him assumed a more important form, when he is said to have been seen at the battle of Marathon in full armour at the head of his country-men. Bones, supposed to be his, were brought by Cĭmōn from Scyros to Athens, at the bidding of the Delphic oracle, in 476 B.C., and a splendid temple, which served as an asylum especially for slaves, and in which public officials were chosen by lot, was erected over the spot where they were buried. The building commonly called the Thēsēum (Gr. *Thĕseiŏn*) is a peripteral hexastyle temple *in antīs*, surrounded by thirty-four most beautiful Doric columns; six on each of the narrow, and eleven on each of the long sides, the whole of Pentelic marble. (*See* ARCHITECTURE, fig. 6.) The festival of the *Thēseiă*, if not actually instituted at that time, was held afterwards with great splendour, with contests and feasting, on the eighth day of the month *Pȳănepsiŏn* (October–November), and the eighth of each month was dedicated to him, as it was to his divine father, Poseidon. Representations of his heroic deeds, especially his combats with the Amazons and Centaurs, served in par-

ticular as decorations of public buildings. Poetry, dramatic poetry especially, and art rivalled each other in doing him honour. He is generally represented in works of art as a powerful, beardless youth (*cp.* SCULP-TURE, fig. 7), but of a slighter build than his prototype Heracles, whose club and lion's skin are assigned him in later representations, instead of the sword with which he is armed in earlier times.

Thesmŏphŏrĭă. A festival to Dēmētēr, as the foundress of agriculture and of the civic rite of marriage, celebrated in many parts of Greece, but especially at Athens. It was held at Athens from the 9th to 13th of Pȳănepsiŏn, the beginning of November, and only by married women of genuine Attic birth and of blameless reputation. Two of the wealthiest and most distinguished women were chosen out of every district to preside over the festivals; their duty was to perform the sacred functions in the name of the others, and to prepare the festal meal for the women of their own district. Even the priestess who had the chief conduct of the whole festival had to be a married woman. On the first day of the feast the women went in procession, amid wanton jests and gibes, to the *deme* of Hălīmūs, on the promontory of Cōlĭās, where nightly celebrations were held in the temple of Dēmētēr and her daughter Cŏrē. After their return in the early morning of the third day, a festival lasting for three days was held in Athens. No sacrifices were offered on the last day but one, which was spent amid fasting and mourning. On the last day, on which Demeter was invoked under the name of *Kallĭgĕneiă* (or goddess of fair children), a feast was held amid mimic dances and games, which probably referred to the mythical stories of the goddess and her daughter.

Thesmŏthĕtæ. The six junior archons at Athens, on whom devolved, specially, the administration of certain branches of the law. For further details, *see* ARCHON.

Thespis. Of Ĭcărĭă; the founder of Greek *tragedy* (*q.v.*).

Thestĭus. Son of Arēs and Dēmŏnĭcē; king of Ætolia, father of Althæa and Lēda (*q.v.*).

Thētĕs. The lowest of the four property-classes instituted by Solon. (*See* SOLONIAN CONSTITUTION and EISPHŎRA.)

Thĕtĭs. Daughter of Nēreus and Dōrĭs, wife of Pēleus, and mother of Achilles. On many occasions she proved herself of assistance to the gods. When Zeus was threatened by Hēra, Athēnē, and Pŏseidōn, she called Brĭāreus (or Ægæōn) to his aid. When Hēphæstus was cast out of heaven by Zeus, she took him and hid him for nine years. Again, when Dĭonȳsus was fleeing before Lȳcurgus, she afforded him protection in the sea. Brought up by Hēra, she was wooed by Zeus and Poseidon. But when Thĕmis foretold that Thetis would bear a son who would be greater than his father, she was married against her will to a mortal, Peleus (q.v.). This marriage was the source of the greatest sorrow to her. Her attempt to make her only son Achilles immortal was frustrated by her husband, and caused an estrangement between them, and she was fated to see her glorious and godlike son cut off in the prime of life.

Thĭǎsus. The Greek designation of a society which had selected some god for its patron, and held sacrifices, festal processions, and banquets at stated times in his honour. Frequently the members of such societies, which took their name either from their divine patron or else from the days of festal celebration, pursued other common ends, sometimes of business, sometimes of social life. The name *thiasus* was specially applied to the festivals in honour of Dĭonȳsus, and, in the representations of poetry and art, to the mythical retinue of the god, which consisted of Sīlēni, Satyrs, Nymphs, Mænads, etc.

Thisbē. *See* PYRAMUS.

Thŏlus. A term applied by the Greeks to any round building with a conical roof or cupola. At Athens it indicated the Rotunda used for the official head-quarters of the *Prȳtănēs* (*see* BOULE), who also dined here at the public expense. It was situated near the Senate-house (*boūleutēriŏn*). [Aristotle, *Constitution of Athens*, 43.]

Thŏrāx. The Greek term for a *cuirass*, either of metal (usually bronze) or of leather. The *metal cuirass* consisted of two separate pieces, one covering the chest and stomach, and the other the back, attached to one another by means of clasps or buckles. They terminated with a curved edge just above the hip, and at this part were often covered with a leathern belt (*zōstēr*), fastened with buckles, to bind both pieces more firmly together. Another belt (*mitra*), lined with leather, was worn under the armour and above the *chĭtōn*. This was fitted with a plate of metal growing broader towards the middle, and serving to protect the belly. In later times the front plate of the cuirass

was extended downwards, so as to cover the belly as far as the navel. As an additional protection to the belly and the upper part of the legs, there was on the inner side of the lower edge of the cuirass a series of short strips of leather or felt, covered with plates of metal, often in several layers. They resembled a kilt, and were called *ptĕrȳgĕs* (lit. "feathers"). Smaller strips of the same kind were worn under the arms to protect the arm-pits.

THORAX.
(From Greek Vases.)

The *leather cuirass* (*spŏlǎs*) was a kind of shirt reaching over the navel and hips, and fringed with flexible strips along its lower edge. It was open either in front or on one side (usually the left), and was there fastened together by means of clasps or buckles. It was also provided with an upright piece protecting the neck, and with two shoulder-straps. It was frequently covered, either completely, or only under the arms, with metal, especially in the form of scales.

Linen cuirasses are also mentioned, even in ancient times. These were probably either thickly quilted or strongly woven corselets. (*See* cuts, and *cp.* cut under HOPLITES.)

Thrēnŏs. The Greek term for a dirge sung by a chorus to the accompaniment of flutes, either at the burial, or at the funeral feast.

Threshing. The Greeks and Romans practised in early times the same method of separating the corn from the ear as other ancient nations. A threshing-floor, carefully prepared for the purpose, was constructed in the open air, and the corn trodden out by oxen, mules, or horses, driven round in a circle. Sometimes it was beaten out with sticks. The Romans sometimes used machines. One of these was the *trĭbŭlum*, a board or beam with a sharp edge of stone or iron underneath, loaded with weights on the top and drawn by oxen, which were driven by a man sitting on the handle. Another was the *plostellum Pœnĭcum*, borrowed from the Carthaginians. This consisted of several rollers or cylinders fitted with iron spikes.

the pupil of the rhetoricians Antĭphŏn and Gorgĭãs, and of the philosopher Anaxăgŏrãs. The earliest trustworthy notice we have of him belongs to the year 421 B.C., when we find him at the head of an Athenian fleet stationed at the island of Thăsŏs at the time when the Spartan Brăsĭdãs was besieging Amphĭpŏlĭs in Thrace. He was summoned to the help of the besieged, but, on his arrival, found the place already in the hands of the enemy, and had to content

* BUST OF THUCYDIDES.
(Holkham Hall, Norfolk.)

Thrĭnăcĭã. A mythical island, on which the herds of the Sun-god grazed [*Od.* xi 107, xii 127, xix 275; afterwards identified with Sicily, *Trinacria*]. (*Cp.* HELIOS and ODYSSEUS.)

Thūcўdĭdēs. The celebrated Greek historian, son of Ŏlŏrus, an Athenian, probably descended from the Thracian prince Olorus, whose daughter Hēgēsippē was the wife of Miltĭădēs and mother of Cĭmōn. He was born about 471 B.C., and is said to have been

himself with garrisoning the neighbouring town of Ēïōn, and securing it against Brasidas. On account of his delay in coming, he was put on his trial for treason, and banished. For twenty years he remained away from Athens. Part of this time he spent in Thrace, where he owned valuable gold-mines opposite Thasos, and part in the Peloponnesus. He probably lived for some time in Sicily. In 404, when the exiles were recalled to Athens, he returned to his native town, but only to be murdered either at Athens or in Thrace, a few years later (not later than 395 B.C.).

At the very beginning of the Peloponnesian War Thucydides foresaw, as he himself says, that the struggle would surpass all earlier wars in magnitude and importance, and accordingly at once resolved to write its history, and began his preparations for his narrative without delay. His banishment afforded him the opportunity of calmly observing the course of events, of making inquiries from both parties, and ascertaining the truth with the greatest accuracy. At all events, at this time he was already beginning the composition of certain parts of his work. He proceeded to elaborate the whole directly after his return from banishment, but had only reached the twenty-first year of the war (411), when death prevented the completion of his task.

The existing history was published by another hand, and was continued by Xĕnŏphōn as well as by Thĕŏpompus. Its general plan is simple and artless in the highest degree. After a critical examination of early Greek history and an exposition of the internal and external causes of the war, the history follows the succession of events, with a strict division of each year into summer and winter. This arrangement, while it supplies us with the chronological sequence of events in an accurate form, sometimes prevents our obtaining a general view of the whole, and leads to facts which are intimately connected with one another becoming separated by the course of the narrative.

The matter falls into three great divisions: (1) the Archidamian war down to the peace of Nĭcĭas, 421 B.C. (books i–v 24); (2) the interval of disquiet, together with the great Sicilian expedition, down to 413 (v 25–vii); (3) the Decelēan war, of which the first two years alone are included in the eighth book. The first four books alone are marked by even and uniform execution. Next to this part in excellence comes the history of the Sicilian expedition (vi and vii). Far inferior to the rest of the work are books v and viii. The latter presents us with only a sketchy collection of historical materials.

In writing the history of the Peloponnesian War, his aim (as he himself states at the beginning of his work) was to produce a possession for all time, and not only a showy declamation for the listeners of the moment. This object he has attained, since he founds his work on the most careful investigation of facts, carried out with most conscientious criticism. Endued with the most penetrating insight, he searches into the connexion and causes of events. His narrative is characterized with an unswerving love of truth, calmness, and impartiality of judgment, without the incidental digressions with which the history of Herodotus is interwoven, and is marked by an abstinence from all personal reflexions. The speeches, which are inserted in accordance with the universal custom of ancient historians, are in no author so far from being mere displays of rhetorical skill. In no history are they distinguished by such depth of philosophy and richness of thought as in that of Thucydides, who uses them exclusively with the object of unfolding the motives of actions and expounding the sentiments of the speakers.

He displays a marvellous skill in lucid description, as in the harrowing account of the plague of Athens; equally striking is his vivid portraiture of the characters of distinguished personages.

In accordance with his personal character, his style is grave and elevated. It does not exhibit the easy flow and charming grace of a Lўsĭas, Isŏcrătēs, Xenophon, or Plato. On the contrary, it is often harsh and rugged, interspersed with archaic and poetical phrases, and is concise to the verge of obscurity and unintelligibility. This is especially the case in the speeches, which, with their fulness of thought and their effort to express as much as possible in the fewest words, are among the most difficult portions of Greek literature.

Thўestēs. Son of Pĕlops, brother of Atreus (q.v.).

Thўĭădēs. Women who celebrated wild orgies in honour of Dĭonўsus.

Thўmĕlē. The altar of Dĭonўsus which stood in the centre of the orchestra in the Greek theatre (q.v.).

Thўōnē. The name of the deified Sĕmĕlē (q.v., and cp. Dionysus).

Thўōnēus. Another name of Dĭonўsus (q.v.).

Thyrsus. A staff carried by Dĭonўsus and his attendants, and wreathed with ivy and vine-leaves, terminating at the top in a pine-cone. (See cut, and cp. Dionysus, fig. 3.)

SATYR WITH THYRSUS.
(Cameo in Naples Museum.)

Tĭbĕrīnus. The god of the river Tiber; according to tradition, an old king of the country, who is said to have been drowned while swimming across the river Albŭlă, which thenceforth was named Tiber (*Tĭbĕrĭs*) after him. The Roman legends represented him as raising the mother of Rŏmŭlus and Rĕmus, Rhēa Silvĭa, who had been thrown into the Tiber, to the position of his consort and of goddess of the stream. As the river was of great importance to Rome, the river-god was highly honoured, and was invoked by the *pontĭfĭcēs* and augurs in their prayers for the welfare of the State. His shrine was on the island of the Tiber, where offerings were made to him on Dec. 8th. On June 7th fishermen celebrated special games in his honour (*lūdi piscātōrĭi*) on the opposite bank of the Tiber. Under the name of *Volturnus*, i.e. "the rolling stream," or " river " generally, he appears to have had a flāmen (*Volturnālis*) and a feast, the *Volturnālĭa*, on Aug. 27th. Of extant representations of the god the finest is a colossal figure in the Louvre, representing him in a reclining posture, as a victor crowned with bay, holding in one hand a rudder, and in the other a *cornūcōpĭa*, with the she-wolf and Romulus and Remus by his side.

Tībĭa. *See* FLUTE.

Tĭbullus (*Albĭus*). A Roman elegiac poet, born about 55 B.C., of a wealthy and ancient equestrian family, which had lost a considerable part of its property in the Civil Wars. However, he still owned an estate at Pĕdum, between Tĭbur and Prænestĕ, and was able to lead a comfortable life. He obtained the favour of Messāla Corvīnus, whom he accompanied on his Aquitanian campaign in 31 B.C. Messala's invitation to accompany him to Asia he at first declined, being captivated by love for *Dēlĭa*, a freed-woman whose proper name was Plānia. Afterwards, when he had determined to make the journey, he fell ill, and was compelled to remain behind at Corcȳra. He returned to Rome, and there received the sad tidings that Delia was faithless to him, and had given her affections to a rich suitor. The poems which refer to his relations with Delia are contained in the first book of his elegies. The second book has as its subject his mistress *Nĕmĕsis*, who likewise embittered his love by her faithlessness. According to an epigram by a contemporary poet, he died soon after Vergil, in the year 19 B.C. or early in 18.

Four books of elegies have come down to us under his name, but of these only the first two can be assigned to him with certainty. The whole of the third book is the work of a feeble imitator, who represents himself as called Lygdămus, and as born in the year 43. It treats of the love-passages between the poet and his mistress *Nĕæra*. Of the fourteen poems of the fourth book, the first, a panegyric in 211 hexameters, on Messala, composed during Messala's consulship in 31, is so poor a production that it cannot be assigned to Tibullus ; especially as he already enjoyed the full favour of Messala, which is solicited by the author of the poem. Moreover, poems 8-12, short love-letters of a maiden to a lover named Cĕrinthus, possibly Tiberius' friend Cornūtus, are from the pen of a poetess, Sulpĭcĭa, probably the granddaughter of the famous jurist, Servĭus Sulpĭcĭus. There is no ground for not attributing the remaining poems to Tibullus. The spurious works owe their preservation among those of Tibullus to the fact that they are the production of the circle of Messala; and were published with the genuine works as part of the literary remains either of Messala or of Tibullus, who himself, at the very most, published the first book only during his lifetime.

Among the ancients, Tibullus was considered the first master of elegiac composition. The two themes of his poetry are love and country life. Within this narrow range the poet moves with considerable grace and truthfulness of feeling, expressing his homely thoughts in correspondingly homely and natural language, without any of the obscure erudition characteristic of Propertius, but also without that poet's versatility and artistic skill.

Tīmæus. (1) A Greek *philosopher*, an adherent of the Pythagorean school ; the alleged author of works on the nature of the world and the soul of the universe. (*See* PYTHAGORAS.)

(2) A Greek *historian* born in 352 B.C. at Taurŏmĕnĭum, in Sicily, where his father, Andrŏmăchus, established in 358 the remnant of the Naxians after the destruction of their town by Dĭŏnȳsius I in 403. He was instructed by Phĭliscus of Mīlētus, one of the pupils of Isŏcrătēs. As a member of one of the noblest and wealthiest families of Sicily, he was banished by the tyrant Agăthŏclēs in 310, and went to Athens, where he lived for fifty years, occupied in the composition of

his history. Late in life he returned to his home, and died there in 256 B.C. at the age of ninety-six. He composed a *History of Sicily* from the earliest times down to 264 B.C., in sixty-eight books, and a work *On the Campaigns of Pyrrhus:* only fragments of these compositions have come down to us. He himself experienced in nearly every quarter the same hostile criticism which his predecessor's works received at his own hands, especially from Pŏlўbĭus [xii 1-16,] who pronounces him wholly incapacitated for writing history on account of his lack of critical acumen, his malignity, his partiality, and his tendency to superstition. He was the first among Greek authors who regularly adopted the reckoning by Olympiads as the basis of all chronological statements.

(3) A *Sophist*, probably born 3 A.D. He compiled a Platonic dictionary, a part of which is still extant.

Tīmanthēs. A Greek painter, from the island of Cythnus, flourished about 400 B.C.; celebrated by the ancients for his genius no less than for his art. The most admired of his works was his painting of the *Sacrifice of Iphĭgĕnĭa*, in which the expression of the different degrees of sympathetic grief and mourning was brought out in a masterly manner. The face of Agämemnōn was hidden in a mantle; a striking way of representing the father's untold anguish. [Cicero, *Orator* 74; Pliny, *H. N.* xxxv 73; Quintilian, ii 13 § 12; Valerius Maximus, viii 11 § 6. The same device is adopted in the mural painting from Pompeii reproduced under IPHIGENIA.]

Tīmēmă (*Gr.*, "valuation," "assessment"). (1) The value at which an Athenian citizen's property was rated for taxation. *Cp.* Lat. *census.* (*See* SOLONIAN CONSTITUTION and EISPHORA).

(2) In legal language, a fine. Cp. *lītĭs æstĭmātĭō.* (*See* JUDICIAL PROCEDURE.)

Timocracy (Gr. *tĭmŏkrătĭă*, government according to property-tax or valuation of property). The name given among the Greeks to that form of government in which, while the citizens were equal in other respects, their share in the government was regulated by a certain gradation corresponding to the amount of their property. Thus those whose property entailed the greater expenditure in public services possessed proportionately greater privileges. The *Solonian constitution* (*q. v.*) was founded on this principle.

Tīmŏcrĕōn. A Greek lyric poet, of Iālў-

sus in Rhodes, who flourished about 480 B.C. He was a renowned athlete, and a friend of Thĕmistŏclēs. Suspected of treasonable intrigues with the Persians, he was banished from his home; and, not obtaining his recall by aid of Themistocles, he attacked him, as well as his rival Sĭmōnĭdēs, the friend of Thĕmistŏclēs, with scurrilous lampoons in the form of Æolian and Dorian lyrics. He also composed *scŏlĭa.* Of his writings only a few fragments have come down to us, which show him to be a man of ability and of vehement passion. [Plutarch, *Themistocles,* 21.]

Tīmŏmăchus. Of Byzantium. The last Greek artist of note; he probably flourished in the 3rd century B.C. Amongst his most celebrated pictures were his *Ajax aroused from his Madness* and his (unfinished) *Mēdēa.* The latter was represented in the act of deliberating whether she is to slay her children. For these paintings Cæsar afterwards paid the sum of eighteen talents. Of his *Medea* we have several copies, as in two of the mural paintings of Herculaneum and Pompeii [Baumeister's *Denkmäler,* No. 948 and 155. Pliny, *N. H.* xxxv §§ 26, 136, 145 ; vii 126].

Tīmōn. A Greek philosopher and poet, of Phlīūs, who flourished about 250 B.C. He composed three books of *Silloi* (*q.v.*), in which, in the form of a parody of the epic poetry of Homer, he wittily ridiculed the dogmatic philosophers from the Sceptic point of view. As the chief representative of this style of writing he was styled simply the *Sillographer.* We only possess fragments of his works.

Tīmōthĕus. A Greek dithyrambic poet. (*See* DITHYRAMBOS.)

Tīrō (*Marcus Tullĭus*). The learned freedman and friend of the orator Cicero. He wrote the life of his master, whom he long survived, edited his speeches and letters, and collected his witty sayings. Besides this he composed grammatical and encyclopædical works. He is especially famous as the inventor of Roman shorthand writing, and his name is assigned to a large collection of stenographical symbols (*nŏtæ Tirōnĭānæ*). He lived to the age of 100.

Tīrōcĭnĭum ("a recruit's term of service"; from *tīro*, a "recruit"). The Roman term for the interval between the assumption of the *tŏgă vĭrīlĭs* (in the 16th or 17th year) which marked the beginning of independence and of liability to compulsory military service, and the entrance on a military career or official activity in general. Under the Republic this time was fixed at a year. It was looked upon as the last stage of education, and in this a youth qualified himself either in the army for service in war or in the Forum for a political life.

In the latter instance the young man was handed over to the care of a man of proved experience in public affairs, whom he attended in the Forum and in the lawcourts. In the former case he followed in the train (*cŏhors*) of a general, where, without performing the service of a common soldier, he fitted himself for the position of an officer.

Tĭsĭphŏnē. One of the Greek Furies. (*See* ERINYES.)

Tītān. Another name of the sun-god. (*See* HELIOS.)

Tītans. The children of Urănus and Gæa, six sons and six daughters: *Ōcĕănus* and *Tēthўs, Hўpĕrīōn* and *Theia* (parents of Hēlĭŏs, Sĕlēnē, Eōs), *Cœus* and *Phœbē* (parents of Lētō and Astĕrĭa), *Crŏnus* and *Rhĕa* (parents of the Olympian deities), *Crīus* (father by Eurўbia of Astræus, Pallas, and Persēs), *Iăpĕtus* (father of Atlas, Mĕnœtius, Prŏmētheus, and Epĭmētheus, by the Ocean-nymph Clўmĕnē), *Thĕmĭs* (mother of the Hours and Fates), and *Mnēmŏsўnē* (mother of the Muses). Like the parents, the children and grandchildren bear the name of Titan. Incited to rebellion by their mother Gæa, they overthrew Uranus (*q.v.*) and established as sovereign their youngest brother Cronus. He was dethroned in turn by his son Zeus, whereupon the best of the Titans and the majority of their number declared for the new ruler, and under the new order retained their old positions, with the addition of new prerogatives. The rest, namely, the family of Iapetus, carried on from Mount Othrys a long and fierce struggle with the Olympian gods, who fought from Mount Olympus. Finally, by help of their own kindred, the Hĕcătonchēĭrēs and the Cyclōpĕs, whom by Hēra's counsel Zeus had set free from their prison, they were conquered and hurled down into Tartărus, where the Hecatoncheires were set to guard them. A later legend represents the Titans as reconciled with Zeus and released from Tartarus, and assigns them a place with Cronus in the Islands of the Blest.

Tīthōnus. Son of Lăŏmĕdōn of Troy, brother of Priam, carried off by Eōs on account of his beauty. She obtained for him from Zeus the gift of immortality, but forgot at the same time to ask for eternal youth. When he afterwards became completely wrinkled and bent by age, and was powerless to move without assistance, and merely chirped like a cicada, she shut him up in a solitary chamber. According to another version, Eos changed him into a cicada. His sons were Emăthĭōn and Memnōn (*q.v.*).

Tĭtĭēs. One of the three ancient patrician tribes at Rome. (*See* PATRICIANS.)

Tĭtĭnĭus. A Roman comic poet, the earliest representative of the *fābŭla tŏgāta.* (*See* COMEDY.) He flourished about 150 B.C. Owing to his skill in portraying character, he was ranked next to Terence. Of his comedies we only possess fifteen titles and three fragments of a popular character.

Tĭtўus. Son of Gæa, a giant in Eubœa, who offered violence to Lētō, and in consequence was killed by the arrows of her children Apollo and Artĕmis., He paid the penalty of this outrage in the lower world, where he lay stretched over nine acres of ground, while two vultures perpetually gnawed at his liver (the liver being supposed to be the seat of the passions).

Tŏga. The distinctive garb of the Roman citizen when appearing in public (*see* cut). Its use was forbidden to exiles and to foreigners; it was indispensable on all official occasions, even in imperial times, when more convenient garments had been adopted for ordinary use. It consisted of a white woollen cloth of semicircular cut, about five yards long by four wide, a certain portion of which was pressed by the fuller into long narrow plaits. This cloth was doubled lengthways, not down the centre, but so that one fold was deeper than the other. It was next thrown over the left shoulder in such a manner that the end in front reached to the ground, and the part behind was about twice a man's height in length. This end was then brought round under the right arm, and again thrown over the left shoulder so as to cover the whole of the right side from the arm-pit to the calf. The broad folds in which it hung over were thus gathered together on the left shoulder. The part which crossed the breast diagonally was known as the *sĭnus*, or bosom. It was deep enough to serve as a pocket for the reception of small articles.

In earlier times the Romans wore the *toga* even in warfare, although one of considerably less width. It was worn on such occasions in a peculiar mode called the *cinctus Gābīnus* (or girding in the Gabian manner, after the town Gabii). In this, the end which, in the other mode, was thrown over the left shoulder, was drawn tightly round the body, so that in itself it formed a girdle, leaving both arms free and

ROMAN CLAD IN THE TOGA.

preventing the garment from falling off. This garb was subsequently retained only for certain ceremonial rites, as at the founding of towns, at the *ambarvālia*, during incantations, at the opening of the temple of Janus, and at sacrificial observances of diverse kinds. After the *săgum* had been introduced as a military garment, the *toga* served as the exclusive garb and symbol of peace. Women also in olden times used to wear the *toga*: afterwards this was only the case with prostitutes; and disgraced wives were forbidden to wear the *stŏla*, the matron's dress of honour. The colour of the *toga*, as worn by men (*toga vĭrīlĭs*), was white: a dark-coloured *toga* (brown or

black, *toga pulla* or *sordĭda*) was only worn by the lower classes, or in time of mourning, or by accused persons. A purple stripe woven in the garment was the distinctive mark of the curule magistrates and censors, of the State priests (but only when performing their functions), and afterwards of the emperors. This, which was called the *toga prætexta*, was also worn by boys until they attained manhood, and by girls until marriage. The *toga picta* was a robe adorned with golden stars; it was worn by a general on his triumph, by the magistrate who was giving public games, in imperial times by consuls on entering office, and by the emperor on festal occasions. On the *toga candĭda*, see CANDIDATUS. The foot-gear appropriate to the *toga* was the *calcĕus* (*q.v.*).

Tŏgāta. [The general term for a play with an Italian plot and surroundings, including *prætextātæ* (tragedies) and *tabernāriæ* (comedies). *See* Diomedes, p. 489, Keil, who makes it clear that the term *togata* is not confined to comedy, and that Horace, *De Arte Poetica* 288, is wrong in distinguishing *togata* from *prætexta*, as comedy from tragedy.] (*See* COMEDY, 2, and PRÆTEXTA.)　　　　　[H. N.]

Toilet. *See* HAIR, MODES OF DRESSING; and CLOTHING.

Tŏllēnŏ. A Roman siege-engine. (*See* SIEGES.)

Torch-race (Gr. *Lampădēdrŏmĭa*). The torch-race was a contest held at night, especially at Athens, at the Pănăthēnæa and the festivals of Hēphæstus, Prŏmētheus, Pan, and the Thracian moon-goddess called Bendis [Plato, *Rep.* 328 A]. In this contest young men ran, with torches in their hands, from the altar of Prometheus in the Acădēmĭa (where the torches were lighted) to the city; and whoever reached the goal with his torch alight was the winner. Other

* RIDER CARRYING A TORCH. .
(Silver coin of Tarentum; Luynes, Choix de Méd. Gr., pl. 3, 1.)

young men without torches ran after the torch-bearers; and the latter, if overtaken, had to hand over their torches to the former. To do this without letting the torches go out, required great skill [Pausanias, i 30 § 2]. In the time of Socrates the torch-bearers sometimes rode on horseback [Plato, above quoted]. The contest was attended with considerable cost, as the scene of the race had to be illuminated ; and at Athens the duty of providing for it was one of the public services incumbent on the wealthier citizens. (*See* LEITOURGIA.) [The torch-race is sometimes represented on vases, *e.g.* in Gerhard's *Ant. Bildw.*Taf. 63, 1, copied in Baumeister's *Denkmäler*, fig. 563. A rider carrying a torch may be seen in the accompanying cut.]

[**Toreutic Art** (Gr. *tŏreutĭkē*, sc. *technē*). The art of embossing metal, or working it in ornamental relief or intaglio (Pliny, *N. H.* xxxiv 54, 56 ; xxxv 77). The Greek verb *tŏreuein* means " to work in relief or *repoussé*," and also " to chase " in metal ; *tŏreutŏs* is an epithet of cups that are " chased " or "worked in relief " ; *tŏreiă* is used of a " carving in relief " ; the artist is called a *tŏreutēs ;* and his characteristic tool the *torēus* (Lat. *cœlum*). The corresponding Latin term is *cœlătūra*, which, as defined by Quintilian (ii 21 § 9), *auro, argento, œre, ferro ŏpĕră effĭcit ;* while *scalptūra ĕtĭam lignum, ĕbur, marmor, vitrum, gemmas complectĭtur*. While sculpture in bronze is primarily concerned with designing the work of art which has to be cast in the mould, the toreutic art has to do with the elaboration and finish of the metallic form when it is already cast. In the case of large works in bronze, the task of the *toreutes* is simply to remove slight flaws and to add a few finishing touches ; in that of smaller works, his art becomes of paramount importance. The term *toreutes* is virtually confined to artists who produce for ordinary use articles in metal, which owe their value as works of art solely to the adornment bestowed upon them.

In the best times of Greek art, the favourite metal for this purpose was silver ; but gold and bronze and even iron were also used. The art was often applied to the embellishment of armour, especially shields; and even chariots were sometimes ornamented with embossed silver (Pliny, xxxiii 140, *carrūcæ argento cœlătæ*). Articles of plate, especially large silver platters, were occasionally adorned with ferns or ivy-leaves (*lancēs fĭlĭcătæ, pătĕræ hĕdĕră-cĭæ*); and goblets were decorated with mythological subjects in relief (*ănăglypta*), such as figures in gold riveted on vessels

of silver, or in silver on bronze. These figures were either in high or low relief (*emblēmătă*, or *crustæ*). The art was also put into requisition for ornamenting furniture, for embossing plates of gold, and for making wreaths of that metal.

In the Homeric age, copper, gold, silver, iron, tin, and lead were in use in different degrees. Copper, especially when mixed with tin to form bronze, was the ordinary material for armour and for all kinds of utensils ; gold is named in connexion with articles of furniture, armour, and jewellery, but is generally described as imported from abroad ; silver is less frequently mentioned. Iron was rare, in comparison with copper ; but was used for implements of agriculture as well as for armour and tools. A block of iron is given as a prize at the funeral games in honour of Patroclus (*Il.* xxiii 826). Copper being the commonest metal, a worker in any kind of metal is called in Homer a coppersmith (*chalkeus*); thus, in *Od.* iii 425, it is applied to one who in the same context is described as a goldsmith (*chrȳsŏchŏŏs, ib.* 432). The hammer and anvil sufficed for the manufacture of armour and the simpler varieties of household utensils. The process of beating out the metal and fashioning it with the hammer was called *ĕlaunein* (*Il.* vii 223, xii 295); and a derivative of this verb, *sphȳrēlătŏs,* " wrought with the hammer," was after-wards used as an epithet of statues made of plates beaten out with the hammer, as opposed to those of cast metal (Herodotus, vii 69). It was in fact applied to all kinds of products of hammering, and to work in *repoussé*, large or small. The same process was used in making plates of metal to cover tripods and candelabra, as well as shields, scabbards, chariots, and also images of the gods. In such cases the plate of beaten metal was applied to a core of wood by what was termed *empaistĭkē technē* (Athenæus, 488 B). The chair of Pēnĕlŏpē is thus covered with ivory and silver (*Od.* xix 56), and the bed of Odysseus, with ivory, silver, and gold (xxiii 200). The cuirass of Agămemnōn (*Il.* xi 24 ff.) has twenty-one alternate stripes of various kinds of inlaid metal, both before and behind, the metals mentioned being gold and tin and *kȳănŏs*, which is now iden-tified as an imitation of *lapis lazuli* stained blue with carbonate of copper. The golden belt of Hēraclēs is adorned with figures of bears, boars, and lions, and battle-scenes, in relief (*Od.* xi 609). The brooch of Odysseus represents a stag attacked by a dog (*Od.* xix 226). The cup of Nestor is pierced with rivets of gold, has four handles with two golden doves to each handle, and two supports running from the base of the cup to the lower part of the bowl, designed to strengthen the central stem (*Il.* xi 632, with Dr. Leaf's note). The structure of this singular cup was the theme of learned disquisitions in ancient times (Athenæus, 489); it has now been made intelligible by the early cups discovered at Mўcēnæ and Cære (Helbig, *Das Homerische Epos aus den Denkmälern erläutert*, p. 272). In the cup from Mycenæ (Schliemann's *Mycenæ*, fig. 346; Schuchhardt, *Schliemann's Excavations*, fig. 240), we see the supports continued into the handles above them, and even two doves as ornaments on the top of the handles. Elsewhere in Homer a *lĕbēs* (in *Il.* xxiii 885, *Od.* iii 440), and a *crātēr* (in *Od.* xxiv 275), are described as "adorned with flowers," *i.e.* with the lotus-flowers and rosettes characteristic of archaic decoration (Schliemann, *Mycenæ*, fig. 344). The shield of Achilles, as wrought by Hēphæstus, is an elaborate work, including numerous figures distributed over separate compartments and inlaid in various kinds of metal. The metal facing has apparently a bronze ground, inlaid with gold, silver, and *kўănŏs;* and the designs may be best regarded as resembling the peculiar combination of Egyptian and Assyrian styles which was introduced into Europe by the Phœnicians (*Il.* xviii 478–607, ed. Leaf; cp. Helbig, *l.c.*, chap. xxxi, and Murray's *Greek Sculpture*, chap. iii).

In the Homeric age the articles in metal which were most highly prized are generally described as imported from abroad. Thus the silver *crater* given as a prize at the funeral games of Patroclus is the work of Sidonian craftsmen (*Il.* xxiii 743). It is the king of the Sidonians who sends a *crater* to Menelaus (*Od.* iv 616; *Il.* xxiii 741). The tripods and basket of Helen are said to have been brought by Mĕnĕlāus from Egypt (*Od.* iv 126). The cuirass, as well as the chariot, of Agamemnon, are described as a present from the king of Cyprus (*Il.* xi 24).

According to Greek mythology, the first blacksmiths were the *Idæan Dactўli* (*q.v.*); the first goldsmiths, the *Telchīnes* (*q.v.*). The legends about the latter imply that the forms and processes of the art were transmitted to Greece from the East. They are described as dwelling in turn in Crete, Rhodes, Cyprus, Cŏs, Lycia, and in various cities of Greece, especially at Sīcўŏn, which, according to Pliny (xxxvi 4), was long the home of all kinds of manufacture in metals. Working in metal was afterwards much advanced by two important inventions, (1) that of casting in moulds, attributed to a Samian artist Rhœcus, son of Phīlĕās, and his son Thĕŏdōrus; and (2) that of soldering, ascribed to Glaucus of Chīŏs (Pausanias, x 16 § 1), who was also famed for his skill in hardening and softening iron (Plutarch, *De Def. Orac.* 47).

The toreutic art is described by Pliny as having been founded by Phīdīās (xxxiv 54) and brought to perfection by Pŏlўclītus (56). For the former, it is sufficient to refer to the chryselephantine statue of Zeus at Olympia, and that of Athēnē in the Parthĕnŏn. Among other sculptors who were also *tōreutæ* may be mentioned Călămĭs, Mўrŏn, Euphrānŏr, Bŏēthus, Strătŏnīcus, Aristŏn, Eunīcus, Hĕcătæus, Pŏsīdŏnīus, Pāsĭtĕlĕs, and Zēnŏdōrus. The artists who excelled in the chasing of silver (*argento cœlando*) are enumerated by Pliny (xxxiii 154–157), who observes that no one had attained renown by the chasing of gold. The first named is *Mentŏr*, the most celebrated of all, and with him *Acrăgās, Boēthus* (Cicero, *Verr.* 2 iv 32, *hydriam Boēthi mănu factam præclāro ŏpĕrĕ et grandi pondĕrĕ*), and *Mys* (*q.v.*). The last of these executed in bronze, from the designs of Parrhăsius, the battle of the Centaurs and Lăpĭthæ which adorned the shield of the Athēnē Prŏmăchŏs of Phidias (Pausanias, i 28, 2). Pliny's second group includes *Călămĭs* and Antīpăter, who is probably mentioned by mistake for *Dĭŏdōrus* (*Anthologia Græca* i 106, 16). His third group consists of *Strătŏnīcus* and *Tauriscus*, both of Cyzīcus; *Aristŏn* and *Eunīcus* of Mўtĭlēnē; and lastly *Hĕcătæus*. In the next we have *Pāsĭtĕlēs* (in the time of Pompey); also *Pŏsīdŏnīus* of Ephesus, with *Hĕdystrăchĭdēs, Zōpўrus,* and *Pўthĕās.* After these, he adds, there was an artist named *Teucer*, famous as a *crustārĭus,* a worker of plaques in low relief. Thereupon, he continues, art fell into abeyance, and only works ascribed to the old masters were of any account, even when the design had been almost worn out by use. The age of imitations and forgeries followed. The work of Calamis was skilfully copied by *Zēnŏdōrus* (Pliny, xxxiv 47), the sculptor of the colossal bronze statue of Nero (*ib.* 45).

In the above list Pliny is probably following the order of fame rather than that sibly to the age of the Dïădŏchi. To the same age may be ascribed Pytheas and two

(1) * CYLIX, WITH SCENES FROM A FOUNDRY.
(Berlin Museum.)

of time. Stratonicus, Ariston, Eunicus, and Posidonius, all belong to Asia, and pos- artists remarkable for their skill in the most minute and delicate kinds of work,

Callĭcrătēs of Lacedæmon and *Myrmēcĭdēs* of Athens, who inscribed an elegiac couplet in letters of gold on a grain of sesame, and carved a *quadrĭga* of ivory which a fly could cover with its wings (Ælian, *Var. Hist.* i 17; Cicero, *Acad.* ii 120; Pliny, vii 85, xxxvi 43).

Some of the technical processes of working in metal can be illustrated from the remains of ancient art. Thus on a *cўlix* in Berlin (fig. 1) exhibiting scenes from a foundry, we have (1) two workmen, one attending to the fire in a furnace, the other resting on a hammer, and a boy blowing the bellows ; on the wall hang two hammers and a saw, and a number of metal plaques with heads and figures in relief; (2) a workman putting together a bronze statue, the head of which lies apart on the ground ; (3) two workmen scraping the excrescences off a statue of a warrior by means of a hooked instrument resembling a strigil. The first of the above scenes is closely similar to the design on a vase in the British Museum (B 458) representing the forge of Hephæstus at Lēmnŏs. Again, a mural painting from Pompeii shows us one of the attendants of Hephæstus seated at his work ; in his right hand he holds a hammer, and in his left a sharp graving-tool (Gr. *toreus;* Lat. *cœlum*), with which he is tracing the ornament on the helmet of Achilles (fig. 2). According to the ornament required, tools were used of different kinds, with the extremity blunt, round, or square; as well as punches for *repoussé* work.

Among the extant specimens of the art a foremost place in point of time must be given to those discovered by Schliemann at Hissarlik in the Troad, especially the bracelets, ear-rings, diadems, and discs of gold, figured in *Ilios*, and in Schuchhardt, *Schliemann's Excavations* (figs. 35, 54, 56–58). Those of a more advanced type, found at Mycenæ in and after 1874, include plaques and golden studs in *repoussé*, bowls and diadems; also sepulchral masks of gold, imitating the human countenance and placed on the faces of the dead ; arms and other objects in gold, copper, and bronze. The blade of a short, two-edged sword (Schliemann's *Mycenæ*, fig. 446), when set free from the incrustations on its surface,

revealed a spirited representation of a hunt with five armed men pursuing three lions. The bronze ground is covered with dark enamel, the lions and the limbs of the huntsmen are inlaid with gold of different hues; their clothing and their shields with silver, and other details with black (fig. 3). Still more interesting in respect to artistic design are the two prehistoric gold cups found in 1889 at *Vaphio,* the ancient Phărĭs near Amўclæ, adorned with remarkable reliefs representing men hunting wild bulls (*Ephem. Arch.* 1889, pl. 7–10; *Gazette des Beaux Arts,* 1890, pp. 428 and 434).

(2) * THE MAKING OF THE ARMOUR OF ACHILLES.
(Mural painting, Pompeii; Helbig, Taf. 17.)

We must also mention the *small bronzes* which abound in museums of ancient art. These may be divided into (*a*) *Greek bronzes of archaic style,* such as those of the 6th century B.C. discovered at Dōdōna (*e.g.* the flute-player, fig. 4). Many such bronzes are votive; *e.g.* the Naxian statuette in the Berlin Museum, inscribed as "dedicated by Deinăgŏrăs to Apollo the Far-darter," and the Apollo dedicated by Pŏlycrătēs, probably an Argive of that name, now in the Museum at St. Petersburg. (*b*) *Bronzes of later style,* such as those of Pompeii and Herculaneum, preserved in large numbers in the Naples Museum. Earlier Italo-Greek statuettes are rare; *e.g.* the bronze from Tărentum representing a general in the act of addressing his troops (Collignon, *Gr. Arch.*, fig.

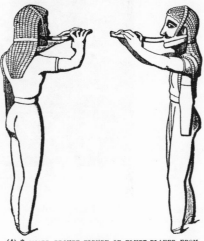

(8) * ENAMELLED SWORD-BLADE FROM MYCENÆ.
(Milchhöfer, *Die Anfänge der Kunst im Griechenland*, p. 116.)

134). Among *objects for ornament* we have numerous bronze reliefs in *repoussé* work, which are often perforated with holes for the purpose of attaching them to some other material, whether to strips of leather or articles of furniture. Some of the finest

of them are pieces of armour, such as the cheek-guard of a helmet with the combat between Pollux and Lynceus found at Dodona (Collignon, fig. 135), and the *Bronzes of Sīrīs*, two shoulder-pieces of Greek armour found in Southern Italy and now in the British Museum (Second Bronze Room, table-case D; Baumeister's *Denkmäler*, fig. 2204–5). In the same museum is the *Castellani cista*, a cylindrical casket in wood, covered with bands of silver fixed with rivets, and representing lions and winged animals, with lotuses and palmettes of an oriental character (fig. 5). Another group of examples includes the *Greek and*

(4) * SMALL BRONZE FIGURE OF FLUTE-PLAYER FROM DODONA.
(Carapanos, pl. 10.)

Etruscan Mirrors, with their metal backs or cases ornamented with figures traced by the engraver's burin (fig. 6); and the *cistæ Prænestīnæ* (of the 3rd century B.C.). The finest of these is the *Ficoroni cista*, in the Museo Kircheriano at Rome, with figures in outline representing a scene from the Argonautic expedition and with the archaic inscription, *Novios Plautios med Romai fecid* (Daremberg and Saglio, fig. 1544). There are several others in the First Bronze Room of the British Museum, one with the *Judgment of Paris*, another with *Bellĕrŏphŏn and Sthĕnŏbœa*.

Among *silver vases* of various ages may be mentioned the archaic *pătĕra* of Amăthūs in Cyprus, with concentric bands of besieging warriors and winged sphinxes showing the influence of Assyrian and Egyptian art (Cesnola's *Cyprus*, p. 277; Daremberg, fig. 927); the Munich vase, with representations of captive Trojans, in low relief; the magnificent *amphŏra* of the 4th century B.C., found at Nicopol in South Russia in the tomb of a Scythian king with a frieze in high relief running round the upper part, representing Scythians tam-

cup, found at the ancient Antium, and sometimes supposed to be copied from a Greek original by Zōpy̆rus (*ib.*, fig. 976); the *paterœ* of Hildesheim (*q.v.*), about the time of Augustus; that of Rennes, of the 3rd century A.D., in the Paris *Cabinet des Antiques* (*ib.* 972); and the vases from Bernay in the same collection. Further, in the British Museum we have a number of embossed and chased caskets, vases, or

(5) * THE CASTELLANI CISTA.
(British Museum.)

ing and tending their horses, while the body of the vase is covered with ornaments

(6) ETRUSCAN MIRROR.
(Berlin Museum.)

in *repoussé*, including large birds and flowers (Daremberg, fig. 975); the Corsini

ornaments, found at Rome in 1793, and ascribed to the end of the 5th century A.D. As a late Roman specimen of *ŏpus interrāsĭlĕ*, or open work in which part of the silver is cut away on the same general principle as in fig. 5, we have a *canthărus* of dark red glass mounted in silver gilt, found near Tiflis in 1871, and now in the Museum of the Hermitage, St. Petersburg (fig. 7).

One of the richest collections of *Greek jewellery*, that of the Hermitage Museum, comes from the ancient Pantĭcăpæum (*Kertch*). The Vatican and the Louvre contain remarkable specimens of Etrusco-Greek jewels, mainly found at Vulci and Cære. Modern ingenuity has at present failed to recover the secret of the process of " granulation " employed in many of these jewels, a kind of decoration in which the surface of the gold leaf is covered with minute and almost invisible globules of gold (*see* frontispiece to Martha's *L'Art Etrusque*). The *Antiquarium* of Munich possesses a votive crown of gold, superbly executed, with

sprays of oak-leaves and fes-
toons of flowers with winged
figures among them (fig. 8).
Lastly, in the British Museum
we have specimens of Phœ-
nician art, ascribed to the
8th century B.C., in the gold
jewellery from Cămīrus in
Rhodes. In the same museum
"the Melos necklace, and
the sceptre from the tomb at
Tarentum, are admirable
specimens of that fine combination of filagree and
vitreous enamels which
characterizes the Greek goldsmith's art in the middle
of the 4th century B.C., and
the bracelet and ear-rings
from Capua, ornamented with
lions' heads, are still more
precious, as examples of
repoussé work in its perfection" (Newton's *Essays*,
p. 393).

Authorities. Brunn, *Gr.
Künstler*, ii 397–412; Marquardt, *Das Privatleben der
Römer*, pp. 669–718[2]; Saglio,
article on *Cœlatura* in Daremberg and Saglio's *Dict. des
Antiquités;* and Blümner's
Technologie, vol. iv, pp. 228–
413. *Cp.* the short sketch
in the last chapter of Collignon's *Manual of Greek
Archæology*.]   [J. E. S.]

Tormentă. The heavy
Roman engines of war. (*See*
ARTILLERY.)

Tower of the Winds. An
interesting example of the
later Attic architecture, still
standing in Athens. It was
built by Andrŏnīcus Cyr-
rhestēs [Vitruvius, i 6 § 4]
about the middle of the 1st
century B.C., and it served
at once as the public clock
and weather-cock of Athens.
It is an octagonal tower
of marble, with prominent
porches, each supported by
two simple Corinthian
columns, on the north-east
and north-west. On the
south it has a kind of turret,
to contain the cistern for the
water-clock. The eight sides

(7) * GLASS CUP WITH OPEN REPOUSSÉ WORK IN SILVER.
(St. Petersburg, *Hermitage Museum.*)

(8) * GOLDEN CROWN, FROM ARMENTO.
(Munich, *Antiquarium.*)

correspond to the directions from which
the eight winds blow. The figures of these
are represented in beautiful reliefs on the
frieze, and beneath them on the marble
walls are engraved the lines of the sundial.
The culminating point of the sloping roof was
once surmounted by a bronze Triton, placed
on a Corinthian capital, so as to revolve
and point with his staff to the figure of

TOWER OF THE WINDS (or, *Hŏrŏlŏgĭum of
Andronicus Cyrrhestes*), ATHENS.

the wind which was blowing at the time
(*see* cut).

Trăbĕa. The purple-striped cloak worn
by Roman *augurs* and Roman *ĕquĭtēs* (*q.v.*).

Tragedy. (I) Tragedy in GREECE originated in the lyric dithyramb; *i.e.* in the
song of a chorus at the rites held in honour
of Dīŏnȳsus. This song, in accordance with
the cult of the god, expressed at one time
exuberant joy, at another deep sorrow. The
cult of Dionysus is also indicated by the
very name of tragedy, signifying goat-song;
i.e. (according to the usual explanation) the
hymn sung by the chorus in their dance
round the altar at the sacrifice of the goat,
which was dedicated to Dionysus. Others
derive the name from the fact that, to represent Satyrs, the chorus were clad in goat-
skins, and hence resembled goats. These
choral songs seem to have received a certain
dramatic form as early as the time of *Arīŏn*,
to whom the dithyramb owes its artistic
development. The true drama, including
tragic and satyric plays, was evolved subsequently in Athens.

Tradition ascribes the origin of tragedy
to a contemporary of Sŏlōn named *Thespis*,
of Icărĭa, which was a chief seat of the cult
of Dionysus. The date assigned to this is
540 B.C. Thespis was at the same time poet,
leader of the chorus, and actor. According
to the testimony of the ancients, his pieces
consisted of a prologue, a series of choral
songs, standing in close connexion with the
action, and dramatic recitations introduced
between the choruses. These recitations
were delivered by the leader of the chorus,
and were partly in the form of monologues,
partly in that of short dialogues with the
chorus, whereby the action of the play was
advanced. The reciter was enabled to
appear in different *rôles* by the aid of
linen or wooden masks. These also are said
to have been contrived by the poet himself.
The invention of Thespis, whose own pieces
soon lapsed into oblivion, won the favour
of Pīsistrătus and the approval of the
Athenian public. Tragedy thus became a
substantial element in the Attic festival of
Dionysus. Thespis' immediate followers
were *Chœrĭlus*, *Prătīnās* (the inventor of
the satyric drama), his son *Aristĭās*, and
Phrȳnĭchus. Phrynichus especially did
good service towards the development of
tragedy by introducing an actor apart from
the leader of the chorus, and so preparing
the way for true dialogue. He further
improved the chorus, which still, however,
occupied a disproportionate space in comparison with the action of the play.

Tragedy was really brought into being
by *Æschȳlus*, when he added a second actor
(called the *deutĕrăgōnistēs*) to the first, or
prōtagonistes, and in this way rendered
dialogue possible. He further subordinated
the choruses to the dialogue.

Sŏphŏclēs, in whom tragedy reaches its
culminating point, added to Æschylus' two
actors a third, or *trĭtagonistes;* and Æschylus
accepted the innovation in his later plays.
Thenceforward three actors were regularly
granted by lot to each poet, at the public
expense. Only rarely, and in exceptional
cases, was a fourth employed. Sophocles
also raised the number of the chorus from
twelve to fifteen. The only other important
innovation due to him was, that he gave
up the internal connexion, preserved by
Æschylus, among the several plays of a
tetralogy which were presented in competition by the tragic poets at the festival
of Dionysus. (*See* TETRALOGIA.)

The third great master of tragedy is
Eurīpĭdēs, in whom, however, we already

observe a decline in many respects from the severe standard of his predecessor. During and after the age of these masters of the art, from whom alone have complete dramas come down to us, many other tragic poets were actively employed, whose works are known to us by name alone, or are only preserved in fragments.

It is remarkable that, in the case of the great tragic writers, the cultivation of the Muse of tragedy seems to have been hereditary among their descendants, and among those of Æschylus in particular, for many generations. His son Euphŏriŏn, his nephew Phĭlŏclēs, his grand-nephews Morsĭmus and Mĕlanthius, his grandson Astȳdămăs, and his great-grandsons Astydamas and Philocles, were poets of more or less note. In the family of Sophocles may be mentioned his son Iŏphŏn and his grandson Sophocles; and in that of Euripides, his son or nephew of the same name.

Among the tragic poets of the 3rd century, Iŏn, Achæus, Aristarchus, and Nĕŏphrŏn were accounted the most eminent. Agăḫhŏn may also be included as the first who ventured to treat a subject of his own invention, whereas hitherto mythical history, especially that of Homer and the cyclic poets, or; in rare instances, authentic history, had furnished the materials of the play. After the Peloponnesian War tragedy shared the general and ever-increasing decline of political and religious vitality. In the 4th century, besides the descendants of Æschylus, we must mention Thĕŏdectēs, Aphăreus, and Chærēmŏn, who partly wrote for readers only.

The number of tragedies produced at Athens is marvellous. According to the not altogether trustworthy records of the number of plays written by each poet, they amounted to 1,400. The works of the foremost poets were represented over and over again, especially in the theatres of Asia Minor, under the successors of Alexander. During the first half of the 3rd century Ptolemy Phĭlădelphus built a great theatre in Alexandria, where he established competitions in exact imitation of those at Athens. This gave a new impetus to tragic poetry, and seven poets became conspicuous, who were known as the Alexandrine *Plĕĭăs*, Alexander Ætŏlus, Philiscus (*see* cut), Sōsĭthĕus, Hŏmērus, Æantĭdēs, Sōsĭphănēs, and Lȳcŏphrŏn. The taste of the Alexandrine critics deemed them worthy to occupy a place beside the five great tragic poets of Athens, Æschylus, Sophocles, Euripides, Ion, and Achæus.

Inasmuch as tragedy developed itself out of the chorus at the Dionysiac festivals, so, in spite of all the limitations which were introduced as a result of the evolution of the true drama, the chorus itself was always retained. Hence Greek tragedy consisted of two elements : the one truly dramatic, the prevailing metre of which was the iambic

* PHILISCUS TRAGŒDIARUM SCRIPTOR MEDITANS (PHILISCUS IN MEDITATION)
(Relief in Lateran Museum, Rome.)

trĭmĕter ; the other consisting of song and dance (*see* CHORUS) in the numerous varieties of Dorian lyric poetry. The dramatic portion was generally made up of the following parts : the *prŏlŏyŏs,* from the beginning to the first entry of the chorus; the *epeisŏdĭŏn,* the division between each choral song and the next; and the *exŏdŏs,* or concluding portion which followed the last chorus. The first important choral part was called the *părŏdŏs ;* and the song following an *epeisŏdion,* a *stăsĭmŏn.* There were further songs of lamentation by the chorus and actors together, which were called *kommoi.* A *solo* was sometimes sung by the actor alone ; this became especially common in the later tragedies.

(II) ROMAN TRAGEDY was founded entirely on that of the Greeks. In early times there existed crude dramatic productions (*see* SATIRE), which provided an opening for the translation from the Greek dramas brought on the stage by *Līvius Andrŏnīcus.* He was a Greek by birth, but was brought to Rome as a captive about 200 B.C. It is to him that Roman tragedy owes its origin. His dramas and those of his successors were more or less free versions of Greek originals. Even the tragedies, or historical plays, drawn from national Roman materials, called *făbŭlæ prætextæ* or *prætextătæ* (*see* PRÆTEXTA), the first writer of which was his immediate successor *Nævius* (about 235 B.C.), were entirely modelled on the Greek. The most noteworthy representatives of tragedy under the Republic were *Ennius* (B.C. 239-170), *Păcŭvius* (220-130), and *Accius* (170-104), besides whom only a few other poets produced any works about this time. It is true that the scanty fragments we possess of these dramas admit of no positive judgment as to their merit, but there is no doubt that they rank far below the original creations of the Greeks. It may also be clearly inferred from the fragments, that declamation and pathos formed a characteristic attribute of Roman tragedy, which was intensified by a studied archaism of expression. Moreover, the titles of their plays that have come down to us show that preference was given to subjects relating to the Trojan epic cycle; this is to be explained by the Trojan origin claimed by the Romans. Next to this the most popular were the myths of the Pĕlŏpĭdæ, of the Theban cycle, and of the Argonauts. Euripides was the favourite model ; after him Sophocles: rarely Æschylus. Roman tragedy, like Greek, was made up of spoken dialogue

in iambic trimeters and musical portions called *cantĭca* (*q.v.*). On the chorus in Roman tragedy *see* CHORUS (near the end).

In the time of Augustus the representatives of tragedy were Asĭnius Pollĭo, Vărĭus, and Ovid; under Tiberius, Pompōnius Sĕcundus; under Nero and Vespasian, Cūrĭātius Māternus, of whose works scarcely a line has been preserved. The only tragedies of Roman antiquity which we possess are those of the philosopher *Sĕnĕcă,* which show great mastery of form and a fertile imagination, but suffer from an intolerable excess of rhetorical declamation. It is doubtful whether they were intended for the stage at all, and not rather for public recitation and for private reading.

Trajan's Column. *See* ARCHITECTURE, ORDERS OF.

Transvectĭō. The festal parade of the Roman knights. (*See* EQUITES.)

Trăpezĭtæ. *See* BANKS AND BANKING.

Trăpezŏphŏrŏn. *See* TABLE.

Treasury. *See* ÆRARIUM.

Trĕbellius Pollĭo. A Roman historian. (*See* SCRIPTORES HISTORIÆ AUGUSTÆ.)

Trēsvĭri or **Triumvĭri.** The Roman term for a college or board of three men. For the *triumviri căpĭtālēs, mŏnētālēs, nocturni, see* VIGINTISEXVIRI.

Trĭārĭi. *See* LEGION.

Trĭbŏn. A garment worn in Doric states by men and *ĕphēbi,* generally in a double fold over the *chĭtōn.* It was considerably shorter than the *hĭmătĭŏn* (*q.v.*). At Athens also there was a tendency to imitate Spartan simplicity, especially amongst the philosophers, among whom this garment was worn chiefly by the Cynics.

Trĭbōnĭānus. A celebrated Roman jurist of Sĭdē in Pamphylia, who was at first an advocate, and afterwards held a high official position under Justinian, and, in conjunction with the most distinguished lawyers of his time, made a code of Roman law. (*See* CORPUS IURIS CIVILIS.)

Trĭbŭlum. The Roman threshing machine. (*See* THRESHING.)

Trĭbūnāl. The Roman term for a platform of wood or stone (in the camp, generally of turf), on which magisterial personages sat in their chair of office (*see* SELLA CURULIS) when discharging their public duties ; *e.g.* the consuls, when presiding at the *cŏmĭtĭa,* and the prætors when sitting in judgment. In Roman theatres this name was given to the two places of honour immediately to the right and left of the stage, the one for the person who gave the play and for the emperor, the other for the Vestal Virgins and the empress.

Trĭbūni Ærārii (from *œs* = *stĭpendĭum*, "pay") The name given amongst the Romans in earlier times to the wealthy members of the several tribes, who were entrusted with the levying of the war-tax (*see* TRIBUTUM) and the distribution of pay to the soldiers from the proceeds of it. What position they held after the payment of the troops was handed over to the quæstors is not clear, from want of information on the subject. In the 1st century B.C. they appear as a distinct class, from which, during the years 70–46 B.C., the third *dĕcŭrĭa* of judges was appointed to represent the plebeians, the other two consisting of senators and knights.

Trĭbūni Mīlĭtum (military tribunes). The superior officers of the Roman legions, six in number, two of whom always held the command for two months on alternate days. They were appointed before the levy took place, as they themselves had to be in office at that time. Originally they were nominated by the consuls; afterwards partly by them and partly by the people, inasmuch as the people elected twenty-four out of the number of candidates in the *cŏmĭtĭa trĭbūta* for the four legions which were levied regularly every year, while the consuls retained the appointment for the remaining legions. They were not as a rule taken from veteran centurions, but for the greater part from young men of senatorial or equestrian rank, who had served their first campaign in the train or on the staff of a general, and then began their political career with this office. As a mark of distinction, all of them wore the gold ring of the equestrian order. They also wore a narrow or broad purple stripe on their *tŏga*, according as they were of equestrian or senatorial rank respectively. In the time of the Empire, they always led the legion on the march and in battle. They did not, however, as under the Republic, rank immediately below the commanders-in-chief, but under the *lēgātŭs lĕgĭōnĭs*, the commander of the legion and its auxiliary troops.

Trĭbūni Plēbĭs (tribunes of the commons). The name given among the Romans to the official representatives granted to the plebeians in 494 B.C., as a protection against the oppression of patricians and the consuls. At first they were two in number, then five, and (after 457) ten. Only free-born plebeians were eligible for the office, which

was annual. The election took place at first in the *cŏmĭtĭa cūrĭāta*, but after 471 in the *comitia trĭbūta*, under the presidency of any tribune who happened to be in office at the time. At first they were only magistrates of the *plebs*, and were without any *insignia* of office, or even lictors, instead of whom they had several attendants (*vĭātōrēs*). This continued even after they were fully recognised as public officials. On the other hand, they possessed the privilege guaranteed to them by the *plebs* under solemn oath, on the institution of their office, of being "sacrosanct" and inviolable; and, under the protection of this right, they extended their originally limited powers by judicious encroachments.

Their earliest right, which was at first exercised in favour of the *plebs*, but soon on behalf of all citizens, was that of protection (*auxĭlĭum*), which they could use against all magistrates with the exception of the dictator. This enabled them to prevent the execution of official orders by a simple veto (*intercessĭo*). In face of any opposition they were authorized to have recourse to compulsory measures such as arrest, fines, or imprisonment. Their power only extended over Rome and its immediate neighbourhood, and was further restricted by the right of veto, which they could exercise against one another. For the protection of the individual they only interposed when their aid was asked. For this purpose their house stood open day and night to any who sought their assistance, and they themselves could never be absent from the city a whole day, except during the *fērĭœ Lătīnœ*, when all business was suspended. Without appeal they could interpose in any measure which affected the whole *plebs*, such as the levying of troops and the raising of the war-tax (*trĭbūtum*). This right of intercession, which originally was confined to the *auxilium*, and which could never be exercised except by the tribune in person, and simultaneously with the proceeding that was to be prohibited, was in course of time gradually extended, until finally the veto of the tribunes enabled them to suspend almost all official proceedings; administrative measures, transactions with the Senate, and meetings of the people for the purpose of legislation and election, etc. They had the right of calling meetings of the *plebs* for the discussion of affairs relating to that body. From the time that the authority of these meetings extended over all State business, and their decrees (called *plēbiscīta*), were considered binding on the whole people, this right enabled the tribunes to propose changes in private or public law. It is true that, for carrying out their proposals, they were dependent on the sanction of the Senate; but, as they were safe from the risk of prosecution, they sometimes assumed, in case of need, an authority superior to that body. Originally they had no official relations with the Senate, but afterwards, by virtue of their inviolability, they obtained the right of sitting on their benches (*subsellia*) at the open door of the senate-house, so as to be present at the deliberations, and in case of need to interfere by virtue of their *auxilium*. Soon, however, they even obtained a seat in the Senate, and a general right of veto; until finally they acquired the right of summoning a meeting of the Senate, and of making proposals. At the same time they acquired the privilege of entrance into the Senate at the first census after the expiration of their office.

The office of tribune, really the highest in the State, was employed by demagogues in the later days of the Republic in the interests of a party and to the injury of the commonwealth. By Sulla, in 80 B.C., its power was cut down to the very narrowest limits, chiefly by the regulation that, after the tribunate, no one was eligible for a curule office. However, as soon as 50 B.C. there came a complete reaction and a return to the old state of things, which finally entailed total anarchy, and, as a natural consequence, the sole rule of Cæsar and Augustus. In 48 B.C. Cæsar, to secure his position, assumed the tribunician power, at first without limit of time, and afterwards without limit of extent; and in 36 Augustus followed his example. From that time the tribunate became the pivot of the imperial power. Nevertheless, until beyond the time of Constantine, tribunes to the number of ten continued to exist. They were elected by the Senate, and as a rule from among the senators, but were in complete dependence on the will of the emperor. In order to find candidates for the office, which was now but little sought after, Augustus made the candidature in the case of the plebeians for the prætorship dependent on having held the tribunate. The office was also thrown open to sons of freedmen.

Trĭbūnus Cĕlĕrum. The designation, under the Roman Empire, of the commander of the cavalry, nominated by the emperor for the time being.

Trĭbŭs. Originally the name of each of the three classes of Roman patricians (*Ramnes, Tĭtĭēs,* and *Lŭcĕrēs*), who were divided into ten *cūrĭæ* (*q.v.*). In direct contrast with this was the classification made by king Servius, whereby Roman citizens, together with the whole territory of Rome, were divided into four city (*tribūs urbānæ*) and twenty-six country tribes (*tribus rustĭcæ*). These were geographical divisions, according to which the census was taken, troops levied, and the war tax imposed and collected. From time to time the number was diminished; but it increased again until 241 B.C., when it was raised to thirty-five (four city and thirty-one country tribes), and this number remained fixed for the future, even under the Empire. The new citizens admitted after 241 were distributed amongst the existing tribes. This was the case with all the Italian communities, which in 89 B.C., by the extension of the citizenship to all dwellers in Italy, were included in the tribes. Every citizen (with the exception of those called *ærārĭi, q.v.*) belonged to some special tribe, to which he himself or his ancestors had been assigned, even when he no longer had his home there. Accordingly, in the official designation of a free citizen, the name of his tribe was added to his family names. Originally the country tribes were on an equality with those of the city, but subsequently they were deemed superior, on the ground that they consisted of owners of property in land, whilst the chief part of the city tribes was made up of merchants, workmen, and the proletariate, who possessed no landed property, and amongst whom freedmen were included.

The tribes attained political importance on the establishment of the *cŏmĭtĭa trĭbūta* (*q.v.*), in which those present voted as individuals, and not as members of property-classes, as in the *comitia centŭrĭāta*. The *comitia trĭbuta* thus had a democratic character. The importance of the tribes was further increased on the reform of the *comitia centuriata* (*q.v.*), since each of the thirty-five tribes was thereby divided into five property-classes, each consisting of two *centurĭæ, sĕnĭōrēs* and *iŭnĭōrēs*. Under the Empire they lost all political importance; the country-tribes were used merely as geographical subdivisions, while the lists of the whole number of the thirty-five tribes were treated as a register for the distribution of the State doles of corn. Thus the tribes sank at last into corporate groups of pauperized citizens.

Trĭbūta Cŏmĭtĭa. *See* COMITIA (3).

Trĭbūtum. Originally an extraordinary means of revenue among the Romans, levied on the burgesses in the proportion of 1–3 per thousand in times of war, when the means of the State treasury were of themselves not sufficient, and more especially after 406 B.C., when the State first took over the payment of the soldiers' wages. When the war was over, the money was generally repaid from contributions or from the booty. Subsequent to the conquest of Macedonia, 167 B.C., the income of the State from the provinces was so considerable, that the burgesses, although not legally exempt, ceased any longer to be subject to this payment. The strictly regulated taxes of the provinces also went by the same name, *tribūtum sŏli*, the ground-tax, and *tribūtum căpĭtis*, the personal tax. (*See* STIPENDIUM.) Italy, up to his time exempt, was also made liable to these taxes by Diocletian, towards the end of the 3rd century A.D. (*Cp.* TAXES.)

Trīclīnium. The Roman dining-table of four sides, with three low couches (*lecti*)

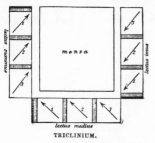

TRICLINIUM.

placed round it so as to leave the fourth side free for the servants (*see* plan). The *lecti*, arranged for three persons each, were broad, cushioned places, lower towards the outside and sloping upwards with a side-support; on each of the three places was a pillow, on which the diners, as they lay at table, supported themselves with their left arm, their feet being towards the outside. The allotment of the nine places was made in accordance with strict rules of etiquette. The middle couch, *lectus mĕdĭus*, and the one on its left, *lectus summus* (the highest), were appointed for the guests, the former for the most dis-

tinguished guests; that on its right, *lectus īmus* (the lowest), was for the host, his wife, and a child or a freedman. On the *lectus summus* and *imus*, the place of honour (*lŏcus summus*) was on the left side, on which was the support of the couch, and consequently the most convenient seat. The place appointed for the chief person of the company, the *locus consŭlāris*, was, however, on the *lectus medius*, and not on the left, but on the right and unsupported side, next that of the host, who took the first place of the *lectus imus*.

For the tables of costly citrus-wood with round tops, and similar tables, which were introduced towards the end of the Republic, a peculiar crescent-shaped couch was used. This was called *sigma* from its shape **C**, one of the forms of the Greek letter bearing that name. It was also called *stĭbădĭum*, and as a rule was suitable only for five persons. On the *sigma* the places of honour were the corner-seats, the first place being that on the "right wing" (*in dextro cornu*), the second that on the left (*in sĭnistro cornu*); the remaining seats were named from this onward, so that the last was on the left side of the first.

The dining-room itself was also called *triclinium*, even when it contained several dining-tables. Romans of distinction in later times had several such rooms for different times of the year; in the winter they dined in the interior of the house by lamplight, in summer in an arbour attached to the house or in the upper story.

Trĭērarch (Gr. *trĭērarchēs;* Lat. *trĭērarcha*). Originally the commander of a trireme; afterwards of any large war-ship.

Trĭērarchĭa. The superintendence of the equipment of a war-ship; one of the public burdens imposed on Athenian citizens. (*See* LEITOURGIA.)

Trĭērēs. A Greek ship with three banks of oars. (*See* SHIPS.)

Triglyphs ("three channels"). A name given in the Doric frieze to surfaces which, projecting over every column and between every two columns, are ornamented with three parallel channels, two complete ones in the middle and two halves at the corners. Between the triglyphs are the metopes (*q.v.*). (*Cp.* ARCHITECTURE, ORDERS OF; and PARTHENON, fig. 2.)

Trĭgōn. A kind of game with a *ball*. (*See* BALL, GAMES OF).

Trilogy (Gr. *trĭlŏgĭă*). A set of three tragedies which, together with a satyric drama, formed a tetralogy (*q.v.*). The several tragedies were generally, but not always, connected with each other in subject. The only surviving example is the *Oresteiă* of Æschylus, consisting of the *Agămemnōn*, *Chŏēphŏræ*, and *Eumēnĭdĕs*.

Triphĭŏdŏrus. *See* TRYPHIODORUS.

Triptŏlĕmus. Son of Eleusis (or of Cĕlĕus, *see* DEMOPHOON) a favourite of Dēmētĕr, who sent him about the world on a car drawn by serpents to extend the cultivation of grain, and with it agriculture. On his return to Attica, Celeus of Eleusis made an attempt upon his life, but, at the bidding of Demeter, was obliged to give up the country to him. He founded the town of Eleusis, and, as first priest of Demeter, instituted the services there held in her honour, as well as the *Thesmŏphŏrĭă* (*q.v.*). In various parts of Greece, as well as in Italy and Sicily, he was honoured as the founder and promoter of husbandry, but especially in Eleusis, where, as the local hero, he had a temple dedicated to him, and a spot called the threshing-floor of Triptolemus on the Rharian plain. The Argive legend connected him with its local genealogies, and told how, while seeking Io in Tarsus and Antioch, he founded Greek settlements and instituted the cultivation of corn. In the Attic legend of Eleusis, he is also represented as a judge of the dead. (*See* DEMETER, fig. 1, and VASES, fig. 12.)

Triptychŏn. *See* DIPTYCHON.

Trireme (Lat. *trĭrē-mĭs*). A Roman ship with three banks of oars. (*See* SHIP.)

Tritagonist (Gr. *trĭtăgōnistēs*). The third actor in the Greek drama, who played in the least important parts.

Trītŏgĕneiă. A special surname of Athēnē

Trītōn. Son of Pŏseidōn and Amphītrītē. He is described as living with them in a golden palace in the depths of the sea. The mythical lake *Trītōnĭs*, near the Mediterranean coast of Libya, was regarded as his peculiar abode, especially in the story of the Argonauts. He was represented as a man in his upper parts, terminating in a dolphin's tail; his special attribute is a twisted sea-shell, on which he blows, now

(1) TRITON.
(Rome, Vatican.)

violently, now gently, to raise or calm the billows. In the course of time there grew up the notion of a large number of Tritons, all represented as beings of double form and sometimes with the fore-feet of a horse as well as a human body and a fish's tail (called *Centauro-tritons* or *Ichthyŏ-tauri*).

(2) CENTAURO-TRITON AND NEREID.
(Naples Museum.)

They were, however, always regarded as attendants on the other sea-gods while riding or driving over the waves; and they were represented accordingly in works of art (*see* cuts).

Triumph. The Roman festal procession at the head of a victorious host through the city to the Capitol, the highest distinction which could be accorded to a victorious commander. Only the regular holder of the highest command (*impĕrĭum*), a dictator, consul, or prætor, was entitled to this honour, and that too even when the decisive victory had not been fought under his immediate direction. It was also essential that the victory should be an important one gained in a regular war; *i.e.* not against citizens or rebellious slaves. Permission to celebrate a triumph was granted, with the necessary expenses, by the Senate. Up to the day of the triumph, the general was obliged to remain before the city, because his command expired at the moment he entered it. Accordingly it was outside the city, generally in the temple of Bellōna, that the Senate assembled to receive his report.

conquered country, models of the captured fortresses, ships, etc., either carried on men's shoulders or placed in chariots; then the crowns of honour dedicated to the triumphant generc¹ by the towns of the province, originally of bay leaves, later of gold. Then the white bulls intended for sacrifice on the Capitol, with gilded horns, decorated with ribands and garlands, and accompanied by youths and boys in holiday attire, carrying gold and silver chalices. Then followed in chains the distinguished captives who had been spared for the triumph, and whose fate it was, when the triumphal car reached the slope of the Capitol, to be dragged off to prison, there almost invariably to meet with immediate execution. Behind these followed the lictors of the general in purple tunics, with their

(1) TRIUMPHAL PROCESSION.

Relief from the Arch of Titus, representing the spoils from the temple at Jerusalem, including the seven-branched candlestick, the table for shewbread, and the golden trumpets.)

On the day of the triumph, the procession, starting from the *Campus Martius*, proceeded through the *Porta Triumphālis* into the *Circus Flāmĭnĭus ;* then, after entering the city through the *Porta Carmentālis*, it marched on into the *Circus Maxĭmus*, and thence to the *Via Sacra*, and up this across the Forum to the Capitol (*see* plan under FORUM). The streets were adorned with garlands, the temples opened, and, as the procession passed by, the spectators greeted it with the acclamation, *Io trĭumphĕ !* The procession was headed by the State officials and the Senate. Then followed trumpeters, and after them the captured spoils (*see* fig. 1); next came painted representations of the

fascēs wreathed in bay leaves; then a body of musicians playing on the lyre, and priests with censers; and lastly the triumphal car, gilded, and garlanded with bay leaves, and drawn by four white horses, which were also wreathed with garlands. On it stood the general; in earlier times his body was dyed with vermilion [Pliny, *N. H.* xxxiii 111]. His head was wreathed with bay, and he wore the garb of the Capitoline Jupiter, furnished him from the treasury of the Capitoline temple; *viz.* a purple tunic embroidered with golden palm-shoots (*tŭnĭcă palmātă*), a toga decorated with golden stars on a purple ground (*tŏgă pictă*), gilded shoes, and an ivory sceptre in his left hand, with an eagle on the top; in his right hand he carried a branch of bay. Over his head a public slave, standing behind him, held the golden crown of Jupiter, and, while the people shouted acclamations, called to him, "Look behind you, and remember you are mortal." [Tertullian, *Apol.* 33.] He also guarded himself against envy and the evil eye by an amulet which he wore either on his person or tied to the car. With him on the car, and sometimes on the horses, sat his youngest children, while his grown up sons rode behind with his lieutenants and officers. The soldiers brought up the rear, all wearing decorations, and shouting *Io triumphe!* In accordance with ancient custom, they also alternately sang songs in praise of their general, and uttered ribald jests at his expense. On arriving at the temple of Capitoline Jupiter, the general, as a token of his victory, placed on the lap of the god the bay leaves wreathed around the *fasces*, together with his own branch of bay, or (in later times) a palm-branch, the *fasces*, and his laurel-shoot. He then offered the sacrifice of thanksgiving (*cp.* fig. 2).

(2) SACRIFICE OF TRAJAN.
(Bas-relief from Arch of Constantine.)

The festival, originally limited to one day, gradually extended itself to several. It concluded with a banquet to the State officials and the Senate, and sometimes also with an entertainment for the soldiers and people. If the permission to celebrate the ordinary triumph were refused to a general, he could undertake one on his own account to the temple of Jūpĭter Lătĭāris on the Alban Hill. If the conqueror had not fought under his own auspices, or if his exploits did not appear to merit the highest form of triumph, he was allowed to hold one of an inferior kind called an *ŏvātĭō.*

In this the conqueror entered the town either on foot (as in earlier times) or on horseback, clad in the *toga prætexta*, and with a wreath of myrtle on his brow. Under the Empire, only the emperors triumphed, because the generals commanded as their lieutenants (*lēgāti Augusti*), under the auspices of the emperors, and not under their own. Victorious generals were then obliged to content themselves with the *ornāmenta trĭumphālĭā ;* i.e. the right of appearing on holiday occasions in the insignia of triumph, the *tunica palmata*, or *toga picta*, and wreath of bay leaves. After Trajan's time, even this kind of military distinction ceased, as all consuls were permitted to wear the triumphal decorations during festal processions.

Triumphal Arches. A type of monumental architecture peculiar to the Romans. They were erected as memorials in honour of victorious generals, and (in later times) in honour of individual emperors. In architectural design they united the Roman arch with the Greek column. In Rome (not to mention the remains of the Arch of Drusus) there are still extant, (1) the arch which the Senate and people erected after the death of TITUS, in memory of the conquest of Judæa (70 A.D.). This consists of two massive piers of Pentelic marble inclosed by pilasters and joined together by a vaulted arch, and of a lofty entablature, on which the dedication is inscribed. On the inner jambs of the arch are two fine reliefs, representing (i) the emperor on the triumphal car, and (ii) a group of soldiers bearing the spoils of the Jewish War. (*See* TRIUMPH, fig 1.) (2) The Arch of SEPTIMIUS SĔVĔRUS, with three entrances. This is of remarkable dimensions, but the decoration, though far richer, is overcharged; it was erected by the people in 203 A.D. in honour of the emperor after his victories over the Parthians. (3) The Arch of CONSTANTINE, also with three entrances. This was built after 311 A.D. (*see* cut), by using certain portions (*viz.* the reliefs on both the fronts and on the inner sides of the middle arch) of one of the triumphal arches of Trajan, which was destroyed for this purpose. Among those not in Rome must be mentioned that at Orange in the south of France. Arches of honour were also erected for other services. Such are that of Augustus at Ārīmĭnum (*Rimini*) on the occasion of the completion of the road leading to that place from Rome; that of Trajan at *Ancŏna*, on the restoration of the harbour. In Rome itself, between the site of the *Vēlābrum* and the *Fŏrum Bŏărĭum*, there is a richly decorated, but coarsely sculptured, gateway with a flat lintel, bearing an inscription recording its erection (in A.D. 204) in honour of Septimius Severus and other members of the imperial house by the silversmiths or bankers (*argentārĭī*) and other merchants of the *Forum Boarium*. The arch of the Sergii at *Pola* in Istria is a family memorial.

Trĭumvĭri. *See* TRESVIRI.

Trogus. *See* POMPEIUS TROGUS.

Troiæ Lūdus. *Cp.* CIRCUS, p. 139.

Trŏĭlus. A younger son of Priam and Hĕcŭbă, who was slain by Achilles. According to the later legend, Achilles lay in wait for the boy when he was exercising his horse near a well in front of the city, and slew him as he fled to the temple of Thymbræan Apollo, just by the altar of the god, at the very spot where he himself was destined afterwards to meet his fate. According to another account, Troilus ventured to meet Achilles in open conflict, but was dragged to death by his own horses. (*See* VASES, fig. 10.)

Trojan War. The story of the Trojan War, like the story of the Argonauts, underwent, in the course of time, many changes and amplifications. The kernel of the story is contained in the two epic poems of Homer: the *Iliad* and the *Odyssey*. The incidents, either narrated or briefly touched upon in these, were elaborated or developed by the post-Homeric poets, partly by connecting them with other popular traditions, and partly by the addition of further details of their own in ŋtion. While in Homer it is simply the rape of Helen which is the occasion of the war, a later legend traced its origin to the marriage of Pēleus and Thĕtĭs, when Ērĭs threw down among the assembled gods the golden apple inscribed *For the fairest.* The quarrel that ensued between Hēra, Athēnē, and Aphrŏdītē for the prize of beauty was decided by Părĭs in favour of Aphrodite, who in return secured him the possession of Helen, while Hera and Athene became, from that time onward, the implacable enemies of the whole Trojan race.

According to Homer, after Helen had been carried off by Paris, Mĕnĕlāŭs and Agămemnōn visited all the Greek chieftains in turn, and prevailed on them to take part in the expedition which they were preparing to avenge the wrong. According to the later account, the majority of

TRIUMPHAL ARCH OF CONSTANTINE, ROME.
(Adorned with reliefs from the Arch of Trajan.)

the chieftains were already bound to follow the expedition by an oath, which they had sworn to Tyndărĕōs. Agamemnon was chosen commander-in-chief; next to him the most prominent Greek heroes are his brother Menelaus, Achilles and Patroclus, the two Ajaxes, Teucer, Nestŏr and his son Antĭlŏchus, Odysseus, Diomēdēs, Idŏmĕneus, and Philoctētēs, who, however, at the very outset of the expedition had to be left behind, and does not appear on the scene of action until just before the fall of Troy. Later epics add the name of Pălămēdēs.

The entire host of 100,000 men and 1,186 ships assembled in the harbour of Aulis. Here, while they were sacrificing under a plane tree, a snake darted out from under the altar and ascended the tree, and there, after devouring a brood of eight young sparrows and the mother-bird herself, was turned into stone. This omen Calchăs, the seer of the host, interpreted to mean that the war would last nine years, and terminate in the tenth with the destruction of Troy [*Iliad* ii 299–332]. Agamemnon had already received an oracle from the Delphian god that Troy would fall when the best of the Greeks quarrelled. In Homer the crossing to Troy follows immediately; but in the later story the Greeks at first land by mistake in Mysia, in the country of Tēlĕphus (*q.v.*), and being dispersed by a storm and driven back to Greece, assemble afresh at Aulis, whence they are only permitted to set out after the sacrifice of *Iphĭgĕnīa* (an incident entirely unknown to Homer). On the Greek side the first to fall is *Prōtĕsĭlāŭs*, who is the first to land. The disembarkation cannot take place until Achilles has slain the mighty *Cycnus* (*q.v.*, 2). After pitching their camp, Odysseus and Menelaus proceed as ambassadors to Troy, to demand the surrender of Helen. But this proposal, in spite of the inclination of Helen herself and the admonition of the Trojan *Antēnŏr*, falls to the ground, owing to the opposition of Paris, and war is declared. The number of the Trojans, whose chief hero is *Hectŏr*, scarcely amounts to the tenth part of that of the besiegers; and although they possess the aid of countless brave allies, such as *Æneās*, *Sarpēdōn*, and *Glaucus*, in their fear of Achilles they dare not risk a general engagement. On the other hand, the Achæans can do nothing against the well-fortified and defended town, and see themselves confined to laying ambuscades and devastating the surrounding country, and compelled by lack of provisions to have resource to foraging expeditions in the neighbourhood, undertaken by sea and by land under the generalship of Achilles. At length the decisive tenth year arrives. The Homeric *Iliad* narrates the events of this year, confining itself to the space of fifty-one days.

Chrȳsēs, priest of Apollo, comes in priestly garb into the camp of the Greeks to ransom his daughter Chrȳsēïs from Agamemnon. He is rudely repulsed, and Apollo consequently visits the Greeks with a plague. In an assembly of the Greeks summoned by Achilles, Calchas declares the only means of appeasing the god to be the surrender of the girl without ransom. Agamemnon assents to the general wish; but, by way of compensation, takes from Achilles, whom he considers to be the instigator of the whole plot, his favourite slave Brīsēïs. Achilles withdraws in a rage to his tent, and implores his mother Thĕtis to obtain from Zeus a promise that the Greeks should meet with disaster in fighting the Trojans until Agamemnon should give her son complete satisfaction [*Il.* i]. The Trojans immediately take the open field, and Agamemnon is induced by a promise of victory, conveyed in a dream from Zeus, to appoint the following day for a battle [ii]. The hosts are already standing opposed to one another, prepared

for fight, when they agree to a treaty that the conflict for Helen and the plundered treasures be decided by a duel between Paris and Menelaus. Paris is overcome in the duel, and is only rescued from death by the intervention of Aphrodite [iii]. When Agamemnon presses for the fulfilment of the treaty, the Trojan Pandărus breaks the peace by shooting an arrow at Menelaus, and the first open engagement in the war begins [iv], in which, under the protection of Athene, Diomede performs miracles of bravery and wounds even Aphrodite and Arēs [v]. Diomede and the Lycian Glaucus are on the point of fighting, when they recognise one another as hereditary guest-friends. Hector goes from the battle to Troy, and the day ends with an indecisive duel between Hector and Ajax son of Telamon. In the armistice ensuing both sides bury their dead, and the Greeks, acting on the advice of Nestor, surround the camp with a wall and trench [vii]. When the fighting begins afresh, Zeus forbids the gods to take part in it, and ordains that the battle shall terminate with the discomfiture of the Greeks [viii]. On the following night Agamemnon already begins to meditate flight, but Nestor advises reconciliation with Achilles. The efforts of the ambassadors are, however, fruitless [ix]. Hereupon Odysseus and Diomede go out to reconnoitre, capture Dŏlōn, a Trojan spy, and surprise Rhēsus (*q.v.*), king of the Thracians, the newly arrived ally of the enemy [x]. On the succeeding day Agamemnon's bravery drives the Trojans back to the walls of the town; but he himself, Diomede, Odysseus, and other heroes leave the battle wounded, and the Greeks retire behind the camp walls [xi], to attack which the Trojans set out in five detachments. The opposition of the Greeks is brave; but Hector breaks the rough gate with a rock, and the stream of enemies pours itself unimpeded into the camp [xii]. Once more the Greek heroes who are still capable of taking part in the fight, especially the two Ajaxes and Idŏmĕneus, succeed with the help of Pŏseidōn in repelling the Trojans, while Telamonian Ajax dashes Hector to the ground with a stone; but the latter soon reappears on the battlefield with fresh strength granted him by Apollo at the command of Zeus [xiii]. Poseidon is obliged to leave the Greeks to their fate; they retire again to the ships, which Ajax in vain defends [xv]. The foremost ship is already burning, when Achilles gives way to the entreaties of his friend Patroclus, and sends him, clad in his own armour, with the Myrmidons to the help of the distressed Greeks. Supposing it to be Achilles himself, the Trojans in terror flee from the camp before Patroclus, who pursues them to the town, and lays low vast numbers of the enemy, including the brave Sarpedon, whose corpse is only rescued from the Greeks after a severe fight. At last Patroclus himself is slain by Hector with the help of Apollo [xvi]; Achilles' arms are lost, and even the corpse is with difficulty saved [xvii]. And now Achilles repents of his anger, reconciles himself to Agamemnon, and on the following day, furnished with new and splendid armour by Hēphæstus at the request of Thetis [xviii], avenges the death of his friend on countless Trojans and finally on Hector himself [xxii]. With the burial of Patroclus and the funeral games established in his honour [xxiii], the restoration of Hector's corpse to Priam, and the burial of Hector, for which Achilles allows an armistice of eleven days [xxiv], the *Iliad* concludes.

Immediately after the death of Hector the later legends bring the Amazons to the help of the Trojans, and their queen *Penthĕsĭlēa* is slain by Achilles. Then appears *Memnōn*, who is also mentioned by Homer; at the head of his Æthiopians he slays Antĭlŏchus son of Nestor, and is himself slain by Achilles. And now comes the fulfilment of the oracle given to Agamemnon at Delphi; for at a sacrificial banquet a violent quarrel arises between Achilles and Odysseus, the latter declaring craft and not valour to be the only means of capturing Troy. Soon after, in an attempt to force a way into the hostile town through the Scæan gate, or, according to later legend, at the marriage of Priam's daughter Pŏlyxĕnă in the temple of Thymbræan Apollo, Achilles falls slain by the arrow of Paris, directed by the god. After his burial, Thetis offers the arms of her son as a prize for the bravest of the Greek heroes, and they are adjudged to Odysseus. Thereupon his competitor, the Telamonian Ajax, slays himself. For these losses, however, the Greeks find some compensation. Acting on the admonition of *Hĕlĕnus*, son of Priam, who had been captured by Odysseus, that Troy could not be conquered without the arrows of Hērăclēs and the presence of a descendant of Æăcus, they fetch to the camp *Phĭloctētēs*, the heir of Heracles, who had been abandoned on Lēmnŏs, and *Nĕoptŏlĕmus*, the young son

of Achilles, who had been brought up on Scȳrŏs. The latter, a worthy son of his father, slays the last ally of the Trojans, Eurȳpȳlus, the brave son of Tēlĕphus; and Philoctetes, with one of the arrows of Heracles, kills Paris. Even when the last condition of the capture of Troy, *viz.* the removal of the *Pallădĭum* from the temple of Athene on the citadel, has been successfully fulfilled by Diomede and Odysseus, the town can only be taken by treachery. On the advice of Athene, *Ĕpeius*, son of Pănŏpeus, builds a gigantic wooden horse, in the belly of which the bravest Greek warriors conceal themselves under the direction of Odysseus, while the rest of the Greeks burn the camp and embark on board ship, only, however, to anchor behind Tĕnĕdŏs. The Trojans, streaming out of the town, find the horse, and are in doubt what to do with it. According to the later legend, they are deceived by the treacherous Sĭnōn, a kinsman of Odysseus, who has of his own free will remained behind. He pretends that he has escaped from the death by sacrifice to which he had been doomed by the malice of Odysseus, and that the horse has been erected to expiate the robbery of the *Palladium;* to destroy it would be fatal to Troy, but should it be set on the citadel, Asia would conquer Europe. The fate of *Lăŏcŏŏn* (*q.v.*) removes the last doubt from the minds of the Trojans; the city gate being too small, they break down a portion of the wall, and draw the horse up to the citadel as a dedicatory offering for Athene. While they are giving themselves up to transports of joy, Sinon in the night opens the door of the horse. The heroes descend, and light the flames that give to the Greek fleet the preconcerted signal for its return. Thus Troy is captured; all the inhabitants are either slain or carried into slavery, and the city is destroyed. The only survivors of the royal house are Hĕlĕnus, Cassandra, and Hector's wife Andrŏmāchē, besides Ænēās (*q.v.*; for the fate of the rest *see* DEIPHOBUS, HECUBA, POLYDORUS, 2, POLYXENA, PRIAM, TROILUS). After Troy has been destroyed and plundered, Agamemnon and Menelaus, contrary to custom, call the drunken Greeks to an assembly in the evening. A division ensues, half siding with Menelaus in a desire to return home at once; while Agamemnon and the other half wish first to appease by sacrifice the deity of Athene, who has been offended by the outrage of the Locrian Ajax (*see* AIAS, 1). The army consequently sets out on its journey in two parts. Only Nestor, Diomede, Neoptolemus, Philoctetes, and Idŏmĕneus reach home in safety; while Menelaus and Odysseus have first to undergo wanderings for many a long year. Death overtakes the Locrian Ajax on the sea, and Agamemnon immediately after his arrival home.

Trŏpæum (Gr. *trŏpaiŏn*). The Greek term for a monument of victory, composed of the arms captured as booty, and set up on the spot where the conquered enemy had turned to flight. Representations of the stump of a tree with cross-pieces and armour or weapons suspended from them, are often to be seen on coins (*see* cut). The Romans borrowed the custom from the Greeks, but generally erected as memorials of victory permanent monuments, with representations of the war carved in relief, and with trophies of arms suspended over the undecorated portions.

TROPHY.
(Bœotian coin.)

Trŏphŏnius and Agămēdēs. Sons of Ergīnus of Orchŏmĕnus, legendary heroes of architecture. Many important buildings were attributed to them, among others the temple of Apollo at Delphi [Homeric Hymn to Apollo, 118; Strabo, p. 421; Pausanias x 5 § 13], that of Pŏseidōn at Mantĭneia [Paus. viii 10 § 2], the *thălămŏs* of Alcmēnē in Thebes [*ib.* ix 11 § 1], the treasuries of Augeās in Elis [*Scholia* to Aristophanes, *Nubes* 508], and Hўrĭēus in Bœotian Hyria [Paus. ix 37 § 4]. In the last named they inserted one stone so cleverly that it could be easily removed from the outside and the treasure stolen by night. But on one occasion, when Agamedes was caught in the trap laid by Hyrieus to discover the thief, Trophonius, to save himself from being betrayed as his brother's accomplice, cut off the head of Agamedes. Being pursued however by the king, he was swallowed up in the earth at Lĕbădēa, and by the command of Apollo a cult and an oracle were dedicated to him as Zeus Trophonius.

The oracle was situated in a subterranean chamber, into which, after various preparatory rites, including the nocturnal sacrifice of a ram and the invocation of Agamedes, the inquirers descended, to receive, under circumstances of a mysterious nature, a variety of revelations, which were afterwards taken down from their lips and duly interpreted. The descent into the cave, and the sights which there met the eye, were so awe-inspiring, that the popular belief was that no one who visited the cave ever smiled again [Athenæus, 614 A; *cp.* Aristophanes, *Nubes* 508]; and it was proverbially said of persons of grave and serious aspect, that they had been in the cave of Trophonius.

According to another story, the brothers, after the completion of the Delphic temple, asked Apollo for a reward, and he promised they should have on the seventh day the best thing that could be given to man; and on that day they both died a peaceful death [Cicero, *Tusc. Disp.* i 114; Plutarch, *Consolatio ad Apollonium* 14].

Trōs. Son of Erichthŏnius, father of Ilus founder of Troy, and of Assărăcus and Gănўmēdēs. (*Cp.* DARDANUS.)

Trŭa (*trulla*). A kind of ladle. (*See* VESSELS.)

Trўphĭŏdōrus. A Greek epic writer of Egypt, who composed at the beginning of the 6th century B.C. a *Conquest of Ilium* in 691 hexameters, a very indifferent poem.

Tŭba. The Latin name for a straight wind-instrument of deep, clangorous sound, which was used at sacrifices, games, and

TUBA.

funerals, and in war among the infantry to give the signal for attack and retreat, and was blown by the *tŭbĭcĕn* (*see* cut). (*Cp.* LITUUS, 2.)

Tŭbĭlustrĭum. A festival in honour of Mars. (*See* SALII.)

Tullĭus. *See* CICERO and TIRO.

Tŭnĭcă (*Latin*). A garment for men and women worn next the person. With men it was a loose shirt of woollen stuff, consisting of pieces sewn together at the sides, and having either no sleeves or only short ones reaching half way down the arm. Longer sleeves were considered effeminate, and first came into general use in the 3rd and 4th centuries A.D. Ordinarily the *tunica* was girded up over the hip, and reached to the knees only. It was considered unbecoming to allow it to appear beneath the lower part of the *tŏgă*. It was worn by the Roman at home and at work, and also by slaves and strangers. Senators and patricians were distinguished by a *tunica* with a broad purple stripe (*lātus clāvus*, hence *tunica lātĭclāvĭa*) extending from the neck to the under seam; the knights by a narrow one (*angustus clavus*, hence *tunica angusticlavia*). The purple *tunica*, adorned with golden palm-branches (*tunica palmāta*), was, with the *toga picta* (*see* TOGA), the dress of a general on the occasion of a *triumph* (*q.v.*). It very early became the custom to wear beneath the tunic proper a *tunica intĕrĭor*, which was of wool. Linen shirts did not come into use until the 4th century A.D. Women also wore a double tunic, an under one consisting of a garment fitting closely to the body and reaching over the knee, and over this the *stŏla* (*q.v.*).

Turma. A sub-division of the Roman cavalry. The 300 knights originally belonging to each legion were divided into 10 *turmæ* of 30 men: each of these had 3 *dĕcŭrĭŏnēs*, the first of whom commanded the whole *turma*, and 3 *optĭŏnēs* (adjutants). The divisions of allied cavalry called *ālæ* (*see* ALA), each consisting of 300 men, contained 5 *turmæ* of 60 men each. Under the Empire the independent divisions of cavalry of 500 or 1,000 men, which were also called *alæ*, consisted of 16 or 24 *turmæ*. The cavalry divisions of 120 horsemen in a cohort of 500 strong, which formed the unit in many cohorts, and of 240 horsemen in a cohort of 1,000 strong, were divided into 6 and 10 *turmæ* respectively. (*See* COHORS.)

Turnus. Son of Daunus and Vĕnīlĭa, brother of Jūturna (*q.v.*), king of the Rutulians at Ardĕa. He was induced by Amāta, the sister of his mother, and wife of Lătīnus, to make war upon Æneas for his bride Lavīnĭa, who had already been betrothed to himself. After many hard fights he was slain in single combat by his rival.

Turpĭlĭus (*Sextus*). A Roman writer of comedies, a younger contemporary of Terence. He died at Sinuessa in 103 B.C. We only possess some of the titles and a few fragments of his plays. He was the last important writer of the *fābŭla pallĭāta* (*q.v.*).

Tūtēla. The office of guardian among the ROMANS. It affected not only minors, but also widows and grown up daughters up to the time of their marriage, with the exception of the Vestals. In the case of *impūbĕrēs* or *pūpilli*, ordinary minors, the guardian (*tūtor*) managed their property

until the time of their majority, which with girls began at twelve, with boys at fourteen. At this age the guardianship determined, and girls became, like widows, possessed of independent power over their property, but still remained so far under guardianship, that they were unable to take legal proceedings without the consent of their guardians.

Three kinds of *tūtōrēs* have been distinguished: (1) *tutor testāmentārĭus*, who was named in the will. By a provision in the will women were sometimes allowed the choice of their guardian, who was then called *tutor optīvus* ("chosen guardian"), to distinguish him from the *tutor dātīvus* (or "specified guardian"). If no guardian was named in the will, or the guardian named declined the office, or subsequently resigned it, the next of kin stepped in as (2) *tutor lēgĭtĭmus*. In the case of a widow, this was the son, if of age, or the husband's brother, and so on. In the case of a daughter, the brother, if of age, the uncle on the father's side, and so on. Among the patricians, if there were no kinsmen, the *gentĭlēs* undertook the duties. (3) If there were neither a *tutor testamentarius* nor a *tutor legitimus*, then the prætor appointed a *tutor Atĭlĭānus*, so called because the *lex Atĭlĭa* (about 188 B.C.) had introduced this kind of guardian. Under the Empire these guardians were named by the consuls, from the time of Marcus Aurēlius by a regular *prætor tūtēlāris*. Women having three children were exempted from all guardianship by Augustus. Then Claudius abolished guardianship on the part of the *agnātĭ* in the case of all women. Diocletian extended this abolition to the case of minors. After the time of Diocletian, guardianship over women fell into disuse, and afterwards women were themselves allowed to act as guardians. A guardian found guilty of betraying his trust was punished by *infāmĭa* (*q.v.*). (*Cp.* CURA.)

Among the ATHENIANS the guardian (*ĕpĭtrŏpŏs*), if not named by the father in the will, was generally appointed by the archon from the nearest relations. The archon was also the proper authority in suits relating to guardianship, which, during the minority of the ward, could be brought forward in the form of a public prosecution; and, after the ward had attained his majority, in that of a private lawsuit.

Tūtor. A guardian. (*See* TUTELA.)

Tūtŭlus. A kind of Roman *head-dress*, formed by plaiting the hair high above the forehead. It was characteristic of the flamen and his wife. (*See* HAIR, MODES OF DRESSING.)

Twelve Tables (*Dŭŏdĕcim Tăbŭlæ*). The laws of the Twelve Tables represent the first attempt made by the decemvirs, 451–450 B.C., to reduce to a regular code the older unwritten and imperfectly formulated laws of custom—criminal, civil, and religious (*iūs publĭcum, prīvātum, sacrum*)—which had up to that time prevailed in Rome. To this end improvements were adopted which were suggested by the constitutions and laws of other nations. The code thus formed was the source of the whole system of Roman jurisprudence, and, so far as civil law was concerned, survived until the latest times. The importance ascribed to the Twelve Tables by the Romans is clear from their forming a principal part of the education of Roman boys; even in the boyhood of Cicero they were still learnt by heart in the schools of Rome. As in course of time many passages became obscure, through changes in the language and in the state of the laws, various commentaries were added to them, some as early as 204 B.C., by Ælĭus Cătus (*see* JURISPRUDENCE); some as late as the 2nd century A.D., by Gaius. The laws were written on twelve tablets of bronze, but it is doubtful whether the originals survived the capture of Rome by the Gauls in 390 B.C. It was probably copies of these that were still standing in the Roman Forum in the 2nd century after Christ. Only detached fragments, occasionally quoted in other writings, have survived to modern times, yet these give a clear idea of the succinct style in which the laws were written. [The standard critical edition is by R. Schoell, 1866, followed in the main in Wordsworth's *Fragments and Specimens of Early Latin*, Bruns' *Fontes Iuris Rōmāni*, and F. D. Allen's *Remnants of Early Latin*, 1880, §§ 174–207.]

Týchē. In Greek mythology, originally the goddess of chance; only occasionally mentioned in the older poets. In the course of time she came to be extensively worshipped as a goddess of prosperity, who had cities under her special protection. With the general decay of belief in the gods she became one of the mightiest and most commonly named of all supernatural powers. She is generally represented with a *cornucopia* as the bestower of blessing, with a rudder as the pilot of destiny, and with wings, wheel, and ball, as emblems of her variability. [For the personified

Tyche of Antioch on the Orontes, *see* SCULPTURE, fig. 15.]

Tȳdeūs. Son of Œneus of Călȳdōn and Pĕrĭbœa; father of Dĭŏmēdēs. Being obliged to fly from his home, owing to the murder of his paternal uncle Mĕlās, and of his sons, he took refuge with Adrastus (*q.v.*) at Argos, and married his daughter Dēīpȳlē. Though small of stature, he possessed a bold spirit and great strength, together with the special favour of Athēnē. As one of the *Seven against Thebes*, he was sent to Thebes before the commencement of hostilities in the hope of coming to terms with the Theban chiefs. He found them banqueting with their king Etĕŏclēs. On their refusal to listen to him, he called them out to combat, and defeated them one after the other. On his return, the Thebans, in revenge, laid an ambuscade, consisting of fifty youths, under two leaders; but with the help of Athēnē he slew them all, and only suffered one of the leaders, Mæŏn, son of Hæmōn, to escape. In the disastrous conflict under the walls of Thebes, he was fatally wounded by the Theban Mĕlănippus, when Athene, with the permission of Zeus, appeared to grant him life and immortality. Then his old antagonist, Amphĭārāus, laid before him the head of Melanippus, whom he had just slain; and Tȳdeus, in savage fury, cleft open his skull and sucked out the brain of his enemy. Outraged by this horrible deed, the goddess recoiled from his presence and delivered him over to death. The corpse was buried by Mæon out of gratitude for having been spared by Tydeus.

Tympănŏn (*Greek*). A hand-drum, used more especially at the noisy revels of Dĭŏnȳsus and Cȳbĕlē, a broad rim of wood or metal covered with skin (*see* cut); sometimes also set round with a concave and semicircular sound-board.

TYMPANON.

Tyndărĕŏs. Son of king Œbălus of Sparta, brother of Icărĭus and Hippŏcŏōn. Expelled by the latter, he took refuge in Ætolia, with king Thestius, who gave him his daughter Lēda to wife. She became the mother of Helen, Clȳtæmnēstra, and Castor and Pollux. (*See* LEDA.) Hēráclēs restored him to the throne of Sparta. When Helen was wooed by the noblest chieftains of Greece, Tyndareos, acting on the advice of Odysseus, made the assembled suitors swear to protect the husband whom Helen should choose against every act of injustice. By this oath they subsequently found themselves bound to the expedition against Troy. As he had on one occasion forgotten to sacrifice to Aphrŏdītē, she turned his daughters into adulteresses. On the death of his sons he surrendered to his son-in-law, Mĕnĕlāus, the throne of Sparta, where he was buried, and his tomb pointed out to travellers.

Tyndărĭdæ. [A patronymic formed from Tyndărĕs.] The children of Tyndărĕōs, especially the Dīoscūri (*q.v.*).

Typhŏēus (*Tȳphōn*). According to Hesiod [*Theog.* 869], the youngest son of Gæa by Tartărus; a giant of enormous strength, with one hundred snake-heads, eyes darting fire, and various voices, which sometimes sounded like the voice of the gods, sometimes like the lowing of a bull or the roaring of a lion, or like the howl of a dog, and sometimes like a shrill whistle. He was the symbol of the fire and smoke in the interior of the earth, and of their destructive forces. Hence he was also the father of devastating hurricanes. By Echidna he was the father of the dogs Orthŏs and Cĕrbĕrus, and the Lernæan hydra [the Chĭmæra, the lion of Nĕmĕă, the eagle of Prŏmĕtheus, and the dragon of the Hespĕrĭdĕs]. He contended with Zeus for the throne of the lower world, but after some severe fighting was hurled to the ground by lightning, and thrown into Tartărus. In Homer he lies beneath the earth, in the land of the Arĭmi [*Il.* ii 783], and Zeus assails that region with his thunderbolts. According to another account Ætna was hurled upon him, and out of it he sends forth streams of flame [Æschylus, *Prometheus* 370, *Septem contra Thebas* 493]. He was afterwards identified with the Egyptian god *Set*, the god of the *sirocco*, of death, of blight, of the eclipse of sun and moon, and of the barren sea, the author of all evil, and the murderer of his brother Ŏsīrĭs (*q.v.*).

Tyrant (Gr. *tȳrannŏs*). The word *tyrannus* originally meant no more than a ruler, and carried no association of blame, but was used subsequently in the special sense of a ruler who exercises unconstitutional, irresponsible, and absolute power. Such tyrannies arose most commonly in the 7th and 6th centuries B.C., in oligarchical states; *i.e.* in states governed in the interests of their party by an aristocratical minority. Men of courage and ability, not unfrequently themselves members of the aristocracy, availed themselves of the discontent of the people in order to win popularity, and then with their help overthrew the existing authority, and possessed themselves of the government. For this purpose many used the official powers constitutionally delegated to them. The tyrants exercised their authority mostly in their own interests; and, when they did not misuse it, the people on the whole fared better under the new rule than under the old, while it also served to remove existing anomalies, and to make room for fresh developments. Many of the tyrants of this time have earned a high reputation for themselves, partly by the extension of their power abroad, and partly by the impetus they gave to trade, and commerce, and architecture, and by the encouragement of art. Nevertheless, the dynasties of tyrants in this period were seldom of long duration. They generally formed the transition from aristocratic oligarchies to democracies. Under this last form of constitution it was less the actual instances of misconduct on the part of tyrants, than dislike to monarchs in general, that led men to associate with the name of a tyrant the idea of a cruel and arbitrary ruler. When the democracies had reached their furthest limit, tyrannies were developed from them, as in earlier days they had been developed from oligarchies; but unlike those of earlier days, this development was not progress, but only a general dissolution and deterioration. Such tyrannies, so far from working any good for the State, served merely to promote the pleasures and interests of irresponsible rulers and their ministers. [*Cp.* Aristotle, *Politics*, iv 10; v, chaps. 5, 6, 12.]

Tȳrō. Daughter of Salmōneus, by Pŏseidōn; mother of Nēleus (*q.v.*) and of Pĕlĭās, and, by Crētheus, mother of Æsōn.

Tyrtæus. A celebrated Greek elegiac poet of the 7th century B.C., son of Archembrŏtus, born either at Athens or at Aphidna in Attica. He transplanted the Ionian elegy to Dorian Sparta. According to the ordinary story, the Spartans, being hard pressed in the second Messenian War, on the advice of the Delphic oracle, asked the Athenians for a general, and they sent them the lame Tyrtæus. By the power of his poetry, he healed the divisions among the Spartans, and roused them to such bravery that they won the victory. His poems stood in high esteem at Sparta, and served as a means of education for the youth. In the field they were read at evening after supper. Besides fragments of an elegy entitled *Eunŏmia* (*lawfulness*), by means of which he put an end to the divisions subsisting among the Spartans, and an anapæstic *March*, we possess three complete specimens of his war songs, called *Hypŏthēkai*, or *exhortations*, in which he encourages young men to take to heart the duty and honour of courage. Their themes are singularly simple and pathetic, and they are among the most beautiful remains of ancient poetry.

Tzetzēs (*Iōannēs*). A Greek grammarian and poet of the second half of the 12th century A.D. He lived in Constantinople, and though for his time he may be called learned, he was a most conceited and superficial personage, as is amply proved by his numerous writings. Besides commentaries on Homer, Hesiod, Aristŏphănēs, Lўcŏphrōn,

and other writers, which are valuable for the authorities quoted in them, he composed, in 1,665 wretched hexameters, an epic poem entitled *Ilĭăca*, containing the legend of Troy from the birth of Paris till the opening of the *Iliad*, the incidents of the *Iliad* in detail, and the further course of the war up to the return of the Greeks. Besides this he wrote a *book of histories* of 12,661 "political verses." These are commonly but wrongly called *chiliads*, from an arbitrary division of the work into books of 1,000 lines each. He is also the author of a collection of stories partly mythical, partly historical, worthless in themselves, but valuable as including numerous items of information which would otherwise have been unknown to us.

U

Ulixēs. *See* ODYSSEUS.

Ulpiānus (*Dŏmĭtĭus*). Next to Păpīnĭānus the most celebrated among Roman jurists. He was born at Tyre about 170 A.D. He began his career in Rome under Septĭmĭus Sĕvērus as assessor of Papinianus; and, under Elăgăbălus and Alexander Sĕvērus, whose preceptor and guardian he had been, filled the office of a *præfectus prætŏrĭŏ*. During his tenure of this office he was murdered (228) before the eyes of the emperor by the prætorians, whom he had exasperated by the strictness of his discipline. His two chief works, on the prætorian law, *Ad Edictum*, in 83 books, and on the civil law (*Ad Săbīnum*) in 51 books, were held in high esteem, and formed the foundation of the Pandects of Justinian's *Corpus Iūris*. Of this portion the extracts from his writings form a full third. Besides these excerpts we have a small part of his *Rēgŭlārum Līber Singŭlāris* and of his *Institutions*.

Ulyssēs. *See* ODYSSEUS.

Umbrācŭlum (*umbella*). A sun-shade. (*See* CLOTHING.)

Urănia. (1) Epithet of Aphrŏdītē (*q.v.*).
(2) The Muse of astronomy (*see* MUSES).
(3) A Greek game at ball (*q.v.*).

Urănus (lit. heaven). Son and husband of Gæa, the Earth, who bore to him the Titans, the Cyclōpēs, and Hēcătoncheirēs. He did not allow the children born to him to see the light, but concealed them in the depths of the earth. Enraged at this, Gæa stirred up her children against him, and Crŏnus, the youngest of the Titans, unmanned him with the sickle which his mother had given to him. From the blood that fell upon the earth were born the Ērīnўēs and the Giants. The member which was cut off fell into the sea, and out of the foam produced around it there came into being the goddess called Aphrŏdītē (hence called *Aphrŏgĕneiă*, i.e. foam-born).

Urna. A Roman water-vessel. (*See* VESSELS.)

V

Vălĕrius. (1) *Vălĕrius Antĭăs*, a Roman annalist. (*See* ANNALISTS.)
(2) *Maxĭmus*, a Roman historian. Of his life we know only that he accompanied the proconsul Sextus Pompeius to Asia in 27 A.D. On his return he composed, between 29 and 32 A.D., a collection of historical anecdotes in nine books, *Factōrum et Dictōrum Mĕmŏrābĭlĭum Libri*, which he dedicated to the emperor Tiberius. The

book consists of an uncritical collection of extracts taken mostly from Livy and Cicero, but also from Sallust and Pompeius Trogus. These are divided into domestic and foreign instances under different headings, mostly descriptive of moral qualities. The style is bad, and full of declamatory bombast; the character of the compiler reveals itself in abject flattery of Tiberius. Nevertheless, owing to the convenient selection of anecdotes which the book offered to orators and authors, it was much quoted in the succeeding generations down to the Middle Ages. It has come down to us with two epitomes, drawn up in late Roman times, by *Iūlĭus Părĭs* and *Iānŭārĭus Nĕpōtĭānus.* The short dissertation, *De Prænōmĭnĭbus,* appended to the work, has nothing to do with Valerius himself. It is an epitome drawn up by the above-mentioned Paris from the first portion of a work on Roman names by an unknown writer, who quotes old authorities on the subject, especially Varro.

(3) *Gaius Valerius Flaccus Balbus Sētīnus.* A Latin writer of epic verse, born at Sētia, who flourished under Vespasian and Titus, and died before 90 A.D. We have an unfinished epic by him on the expedition of the Argonauts (*Argōnautĭca*) in 8 books, which was begun about the time of the destruction of Jerusalem (70), and was dedicated to Vespasian. The poem is a free paraphrase of the work of Apollōnĭus Rhŏdĭus, with touches borrowed from other poets. It is written in language which, though careful and tastefully chosen, is sometimes difficult and obscure, and over-laden with rhetorical adornment. [Cf. Summers, *A Study of the Argonautica of Valerius Flaccus,* 1894.]

(4) *Iūlĭus Vălĕrĭus.* Of Africa, who lived about the end of the 3rd century A.D., and wrote a Latin translation of the Pseudo-Callisthēnēs. (*See* CALLISTHENES.)

Vărĭus Rūfus (*Lūcĭus*). A celebrated Roman poet. His poetical career began in the later days of the Republic. Like his younger friend Vergil, he was much honoured and appreciated by Augustus and Mæcēnās, to whom he also introduced his friend Horace. Vergil, at his death, in 19 B.C., left him and Plōtius Tucca his literary remains, and Augustus entrusted to them the revision and publication. He died before the year 12 B.C. At the opening of the Augustan era he was the most conspicuous of the Latin epic poets; but he obtained his greatest reputation by his tragedy *Thўestēs,* which, with the *Mēdēa* of Ovid, was considered the greatest effort of Roman literature in this department. The work was brought out at the games held in honour of the victory at Actium 29 B.C., and was rewarded by Augustus with a *honorarium* of a million sesterces (£8,750). Of this, as of his epic poems (on the death of Cæsar and panegyric on Augustus), only a few verses survive.

Varro. *See* TERENTIUS (2) and (3).

[**Vases,** of Greek origin, may be classified under four heads, with several subdivisions in each : (I) *archaic* vases, (II) those with *black* figures, (III) those with *red* figures, and (IV) those of the *decadence.*

(I) *Archaic Vases.*

(1) Among the oldest are those found in the island of *Thērā,* the modern Santorin, one of the most southerly of the Cyclădēs. They were found buried beneath the *débris* of a volcanic eruption which took place in pre-historic times, and they have been ascribed, for geological reasons, to as early a date as the 18th or 20th century B.C. The colour of their ornamentation, which is extremely simple, is usually a dull brown on a gray ground. Among the commoner designs are plants artlessly copied from nature, *e.g.* white lilies on a reddish-brown ground. A rarer specimen exhibits a series of animals resembling black stags running round the vase, with broad bands of red beneath them (Baumeister's *Denkmäler,* figs. 2050–2056).

(2) At a time when Phœnician influence was predominant in the Ægean, a later variety of archaic vases was produced in several of the *Cyclades* and in other islands of the Mediterranean, especially in Mēlŏs, Thera, Rhodes, and Cyprus. They are probably not later than the 12th or 13th century B.C. Those of Thera are later than the group already mentioned, being found above the volcanic *débris.* These vases are usually large jars with a dull gray ground, decorated with bands and curves and zigzags of a dull brown colour (Collignon, *L'Archéologie Grecque,* fig. 105).

(3) Hand-made pottery of early date and primitive decoration has been found in some of the northern islands of the Ægean, in the Cyclades, and especially at Hissarlik in the Troad. Vases of the same class have been found in Cyprus (British Museum, Vase Room I, Cases 1–4).

(4) Another early class is that usually called *Mўcēnæ ware,* from the fact that attention was first drawn to it through the excavations at Mycenæ. It is largely represented among the southern islands of the Ægean, and in parts of the mainland of Greece. In the earliest type the patterns are in a dull colour on a dull ground ; but this is succeeded by a ware of great brilliancy (*ib.* Cases 5–13).

(5) Vases with *geometrical ornamentation* have been found in many parts of Greece, especially in Mycenæ and Ægīna, as well as in Attica. Among the most important

specimens are those discovered at Athens in the neighbourhood of the *Dĭpўlŏn* gate, from which this class of vases derives its ordinary name. The designs are executed in reddish brown, sometimes on the verge of black, on a reddish ground. They include meanders, chevrons, rosettes, together with oblique lines and concentric circles, often traced with considerable care; also animals, such as horses, stags, and birds, as well as human beings. The latter are arranged in zones, and drawn in a very rude and primitive manner, being merely rough silhouettes with slender waists, and with the thighs and chest disproportionately developed.

group, being nearly contemporary with the earlier specimens of "Corinthian vases" (Conze, *Melische Thongefässe;* Baumeister, figs. 240, 2086).

(7) *Corinthian vases* is the usual designation of a variety of archaic vases first found in the district of Corinth, but since discovered in other parts of the Hellenic world, and even in Etruria, especially at Cære (Dennis, *Etruria*, i 282). The decoration is distinctly oriental. It includes rosettes borrowed from Assyrian art, as well as fantastic monsters, birds with human heads, flying creatures with wings curved backward, and other symbols that

(1) * DIPYLON VASE.
(Mon. d. Inst. ix 40, 1.)

Among the scenes represented are warriors riding in chariots, figures marching in procession, and funeral ceremonies (fig. 1). There is no trace of oriental influence.

(6) Certain vases of *Mĕlŏs*, ascribed to the 7th or 8th century B.C., form a small group with clear indications of an oriental character. Besides straight lines, that may be regarded as survivals from the earlier geometric style, they display zones of wild animals of an oriental type, and decorative subjects (such as chĭmæras confronting one another) derived from Asia. Meanwhile, the figures of divinities have assumed shapes approximating to the Hellenic type. These vases form a transition to the next

were intelligible to oriental nations, but had no special significance to the Greeks. It is characteristic of this group of vases that the figures are now arranged in *continuous friezes*. The ground is a yellowish white, and the design is sometimes dull, sometimes bright in colour, and is not unfrequently a deep black, touched with purple or red. This group may be divided into : (*a*) Vases with zones of *animals*, such as lions, goats, tigers, and antelopes, either facing one another (as in the two confronted lions in the British Museum Vase, A 1), or marching in file, with their dark bodies relieved with touches of red, and with the muscular details indicated with the dry point; the field is interspersed with rosettes (see figs. 2 and 3). (*b*) Vases with designs representing *human figures*, with mythological themes set amid zones of animals, and other varieties of oriental decoration. (*c*) Vases with *mythological* subjects bearing *inscriptions* in Corinthian characters ascribed to the earlier half of the 7th century B.C. The most remarkable specimen of this kind is the *Dodwell pyxis*,[1] now in

(2) * ARCHAIC GREEK VASES.
(Birch, *Ancient Pottery*, figs. 126, 127; the vase to the extreme left is in the British Museum.)

(3) * CORINTHIAN VASE, FROM VULCI.
Height, 8½ inches; greatest diameter, 11¼ inches.
(Museum of Geology, Jermyn Street, C 30.)

the Pinakothek at Munich, with its body decorated with rows of oriental animals in black and red, and its lid adorned with a scene from the Calydonian Hunt, in which Agămemnŏn and other heroes are distinguished by their names (Baumeister, fig. 2046). It is on such vases that we find the earliest signatures of the names of their artists; *viz.*, Chărēs on a *pyxis* resembling that just mentioned, and Tīmōnĭdās on an elegantly shaped and carefully painted vase at Athens, representing Achilles lying in wait for Trŏīlus (Baumeister, fig. 2100). At Athens the introduction of the "Corin-

thian" style of vase has been ascribed to the middle of the 7th century B.C. The transition is represented in a group of vases called *Phălerŏn ware*, first found on the road between Athens and the port of Phaleron (British Museum, *ib.* Cases 20, 21).

(8) The pottery of *Rhodes* (Baumeister, figs. 2083–5) reached its highest development about the time of the later Dipylon vases (*ib.* fig. 2072). The most celebrated specimen of Rhodian ware is the *pĭnax* or platter in the British Museum representing a combat between Mĕnĕlāus and Hectōr over the wounded Euphorbus, with their names inscribed in archaic letters ascribed to the end of the 7th century. This is probably the earliest known vase bearing a Greek inscription. The design has some dramatic interest, though the painting (which is in brown and red ochres on a red ground) is but rudely executed (fig. 4) Platters of the same type have been found at Naucrătĭs in Egypt.

(II) *Vases with black figures.*

These were in vogue from about 540–460 B.C., not to mention later times, down to the 4th century, when they were reproduced in imitation of earlier work. They are painted in glossy *black* enamel on a *red*, slightly glazed, clay ground, or (less frequently) on a cream-white ground. The hands, arms, and faces of female figures are painted white (fig. 5), while red is used to define clearly all kinds of details, such as hair, crests of helmets, variegated patterns or borders in a garment. The faces are almost always in profile, and yet the eyes are shown front-wise—a method of treatment which survived even among vases of the next period. The countenance is destitute of expression, and uniform in type; and the figures stand out as silhouettes against the light. The designs are usually mythological, and mainly Dionysiac. Among many other subjects we have scenes from the Trojan war, the labours of Hēraclēs, and the legends of Attica, especially that of Thēseus. Some of the principal subdivisions are the following:

(1) Vases with *cream-white ground*. Of the few specimens of this kind the most remarkable is the *cȳlix*[1] of Arcĕsĭlās, king of Cȳrēnē, in which the king is to be seen superintending the weighing out of a number of bales of *silphium*, the most valuable product of the country (Aristophanes, *Plutus*

---

[1] A *pyxis* is a perfume-box, with a rounded body, and a lid surmounted by a knob.

[1] A *cylix* is a flat, shallow, and very wide saucer, with two side handles and a tall stem or foot.

925). All the figures, which are painted in black touched up with red, and even the scales, which are similarly treated, have their names painted beside them (fig. 6).

(2) Vases in the style of (the potter) *Ergŏtīmus* and (the painter) *Clītĭas*. The names of these artists are preserved on the François vase found at *Chiusi* (Clūsĭum), and now in the Florence Museum,— a magnificent *crātēr*,[1] with its body decorated with three zones of figures, and with

two other zones running round the neck. The main subject is a procession of deities driving to the marriage of Pēleus and Thĕtĭs in a procession of seven *quadrĭgæ* (of the type represented in the cut to article CHARIOT). The other subjects are the funeral of Patroclus, Achilles pursuing Trŏïlus, the battle of the Lăpĭthæ and Centaurs, the Calydonian Hunt, Theseus and Ariadnē, etc. All these compositions are marked by a rare beauty, and evince a keen artistic feeling and a singular fertility of imagination. There are no less than 115

(4) * RHODIAN PINAX.
(British Museum, Vase Room I, Table-Case D; A 2C8.)

[1] A *crater* is a large vase for mixing wine with water.

explanatory inscriptions. The vase is ascribed to 550–500 B.C. (fig. 7).

(3) Vases of the style of *Nīcosthĕnēs*.
These are characterized by greater firmness
of design, and, above all, by a peculiar palmetto ornament on the neck of the vase—a
very graceful combination of lotus flowers,
with interlacing knots (Baumeister, fig.
2195). Nicosthenes is the most productive
vase-painter known to us ; but his designs
have generally little more than an ornamental
value. Black-figured vases signed by this
artist (68 in all, including 48 *amphŏrœ* and

forms are designed with great energy and
with an evident desire to emphasize their
anatomical structure. All trace of oriental
ornamentation has vanished. Among the
artists in this group are Amāsĭs (British
Museum, B 188 and 426 ; Miss Harrison,
in *Magazine of Art*, 1885, p. 503; *Mythology,
etc., of Athens*, p. xxvii); Tlēsōn (represented by 36 cylices, 22 with figures, and
the rest without); and Hermŏgĕnēs (17
cylĭcĕs, 10 with figures and the rest without, one of the former being in the Fitz-
william Museum, Cambridge).

(5) * BLACK-FIGURED HYDRIA, FROM VULCI.
Height, 22 inches ; diameter of shoulder, 13 inches.
(Museum of Geology, Jermyn Street ; C 31.)

13 *cylĭces*) have been mainly found at Vulci,
and Cervetri (the ancient Cære); and single
specimens at Chiusi, Girgenti, and Athens
(*Journ. Hellenic Studies*, 1885, pl. xliv;
and Klein's *Meistersignaturen*, p. 51). A
crater by this artist may be seen in the
British Museum (B 273, a Battle of the
Giants).

(4) Vases of the *severe* style. In these
the surface of the black figures is seldom
touched up with any other colour, but the
details of the limbs and drapery are indicated by incisions with a dry point. The

(5) *Panathenaic amphŏrœ*. These were
presented as prizes to the victors in the
Panathenaic games. They are in the form
of an *amphora*, with a lid at the top, and
were filled with oil from the sacred olive
trees of Attica (Pindar, *Nem.* x 35; Aristotle, *Constitution of Athens*, 80). The
obverse has an armed figure of Athēnē, with
helmet, shield, and lance, and, on either
side, a column surmounted by an owl, a
cock, a small vase, or a figure. In the
field are usually two inscriptions running
down the columns, indicating (*a*) the purpose

of the vase, and (b) the archon of the year (fig. 8). The reverse shows the nature of the contest for which the prize was given. These vases have been found in Italy (at Cære), in the district of Cyrene (including one signed by Cittus, belonging to the 4th century, and now in the British Museum B 639), and in other parts of the Hellenic world. One, bearing the name of Sīcělus, was found at Tărentum, and is assigned to the 5th century. Until lately only a single

in Room IV. The latter belong to the 4th century.) Numerous fragments of such vases have been noticed on the Acropolis, near the temple of Aïhene Pŏlïäs, to whom they had doubtless been dedicated. In this class of vases the black figures are no conclusive proof of antiquity. When this style had been long superseded, the archaic type of Athene, in black and white, and with incised lines on a red ground, was kept up for many years, as is proved by the dates

(6) * CYLIX OF ARCESILAS, FROM VULCI.

(Paris, *Bibliothèque Nationale;* copied in colours as frontispiece to Birch's *Pottery,* ed. 2; and in Duruy's *Histoire des Grecs,* i 702.)

example had been found at Athens itself. This is the "Burgon amphora" in the British Museum (Vase Room, II, B 1; on pedestal 4, between Cases H and I). Athēnē is in black, with the flesh coloured white, and with the inscription and the touches in the drapery in crimson. On the other side is a charioteer driving a *bīga.* The vase is ascribed to the 6th century. (In the same room there are fourteen other Panathenaic vases, and ten

of the archons inscribed upon them, ranging from 336 to 313 B.C. (Many of these vases are reproduced in colours in *Monumenti dell' Inst. Arch.* x; and single vases in Birch's *Ancient Pottery,* p. 430; and Duruy, *Hist. des Grecs,* i 762.)

Transition.—Before vases with *black* figures were superseded by those with *red,* some artists worked in both styles. Sometimes, indeed, both may be seen on the same vase. Thus, on an amphora in the

(7) * THE FRANÇOIS VASE, FROM CHIUSI.
(Florence Museum.)

British Museum, (B 254) we have, on the obverse, Ajax and Achilles, beside the altar of Athene, engaged in a game resembling draughts; they are painted in *black* with chocolate-red touches, and with minute details, such as the drapery over their armour "executed in incised lines of extreme fineness and gem-like treatment" (Prof. Middleton, *Encyclopædia Britannica*, xix, p. 612). On the reverse we have, in *red* figures on a black ground, Hēráclēs strangling the Nemean lion in the presence of Athene. Similarly on two cups, in the same museum, we have red figures on a black ground outside, with black figures on a red ground inside. Elsewhere, an amphora, signed by Andŏcīdēs, shows the simultaneous employment of both styles (*Bull. dell' Inst. Arch.*, 1845). Other artists of the transition, whose remaining works exhibit both styles on the same vase (always a *cylix*), are Hischȳlus, Nīcosthĕnēs, Pamphæus, Chĕlis, Epictētus, and Epīlȳcus. Apart from vases in both styles combined, the first three artists, with Andocides, are represented by black-figured and also by red-figured vases; the last

(8) * PANATHENAIC AMPHORA.
(Millingen, *Uned. Mon.*, pl. i.)

three, by red-figured vases alone (Klein, *Meistersignaturen*, p. 7).

(III) *Vases with Red Figures* (fig. 9).

Fragments of red-figured vases have been found under the *débris* of the old temples on the Acropolis, burnt by the Persians in 480 B.C. Thus the most ancient vases in this style belong to the same date as some of the black-figured vases. Those with red figures probably continued until the early part of the 2nd century B.C. This class is by far the most numerous, and it also includes the finest specimens. It is generally characterized by the disappearance of all traces of conventional and traditional treatment. The number of figures is fewer, the execution simpler and more refined, and

the artist of the celebrated *cylix* at Berlin with Achilles tending the wounded Patroclus in its centre, and the twelve gods on its outer surface (Baumeister, fig. 2398). Another is CHACHRȲLĬŎN, who is known by about sixteen vases, with compositions of an elegant design, marked by an archaic severity, but already showing signs of a greater freedom and elasticity of style. Among his works is a *cylix*, now in Florence, in the centre of which is a winged Ērōs floating over the sea, and on the outside six of the exploits of Thēseus (Miss Harrison's *Mythology, etc., of Athens*, p. cxii); also a *cylix* in the British Museum, with Theseus and Ariadne, as well as Theseus and Antĭŏpē (*ib.* pp..cxxii., cxxxix). A similar vase, now in Munich, with the

(9) * RED-FIGURED GREEK VASES OF THE BEST PERIOD.

the draperies and other details treated with an exquisite purity of taste. In the earlier specimens the drawing is strongly sculpturesque; the forms noble and massive, treated with breadth and simplicity, and kept strictly to one plane. The following are the main sub-divisions :

(1) The *severe* style. The compositions are somewhat stiff and ungraceful ; the expression of the face recalls the earlier style; but art is obviously on the point of bursting its trammels and asserting its freedom. The hair and beard are arranged with care, and the folds of the drapery fall straight to the ground. The date of these vases is about 500 B.C. Among the artists of this period, SŌSĬĀS excels in the execution of detail, treated with a rare energy. He is

conflict of Hēräclēs and Gērȳŏneus, in the presence of Athene and Iŏlāus, is the joint work of Chachrylion and his younger contemporary EUPHRŎNĬUS. Euphronius is the artist of a fine *cylix* with the adventures of Theseus, now in the Louvre (*ib.*, pp. cxiii. and 148; Baumeister, fig. 1877); of one in the British Museum (822 = E 28, Vase Room III, Case D), with Heracles and Eurystheus; of another, now at Perugia, representing Achilles slaying Trŏïlus (fig. 10) ; and lastly, of one at Berlin, with a polychrome design on a white ground for its central subject, Achilles and Dĭŏmēdēs. He is also the artist of a *psyktēr* (or winecooler) at St. Petersburg, with women reclining and playing the game of the *cottăbus*; and of a *crätēr*, now in the Louvre, with the wrestling of Heracles and Antæus. Almost all his extant works were found either at Vulci or Cære, and most of them are figured in the *Wiener Vorlegeblätter* v (*see also* Klein's *Euphronios*, ed. 2).

xxxv). Another is no less instructive as to the literary and musical education of Athenian youth (fig. 11); and, lastly, one in the British Museum (852 = E 48) gives us a graphic picture of a *symposium*

(10) * CYLIX SIGNED BY EUPHRONIUS: ACHILLES SLAYING TROILUS.
(Perugia.)

Among other masters of this time was Dūris, one of whose 21 extant *cylices* represents the exploits of Theseus (Baumeister, fig. 1873), while others are of special interest for their details of ancient armour (*e.g.*, *ib.*, fig. 220; Schreiber's *Bilderatlas*,

(*Wiener Vorlegeblätter*, vi 10; Schreiber's *Bilderatlas*, lxxvii 9). Another artist, Hīĕrōn, is still represented by 16 *cylices* and 3 *cŏtŭli* ; one of the *cotuli*, now in the British Museum (Vase-room III, case E, E 137), shows us Triptŏlĕmus starting on his journey in his winged car, in the presence of Persĕphŏnē, Dēmētēr, and the personification of Eleusis (fig. 12); one of the *cylices* now in the Berlin Museum, has

Paris, an *Iliŭpersis* (Louvre), a Comus scene (Würzburg), and Satyrs and Sĭleni (British Museum, E 77).

(2) In vases of a *more graceful* style we

(11) * CYLIX SIGNED BY DURIS.

Above the central subject (a youth adjusting his sandàl) runs the inscription, Δορις εγραφσεν (i.e. Δοῦρις ἔγραψεν). The inscriptions on the exterior stand for: μοῖσά μοι ἀμφὶ Σκάμανδρὸν εὔρροον ἄρχομ᾽ ἀείδειν, and Ἱπποδάμας καλός.

(Berlin Museum, 2285.)

the Mænads dancing in the presence of an archaic image of Dionysus (*ib.*, p. 287). Lastly, the artist BRYGŎS is represented by 8 *cylices*, including among their subjects a Triptolemus (Frankfurt), a Judgment of

find that forms of rude strength have given place to those of youthful grace, and stiff attitudes have yielded to others that are charming in their simplicity and their truth to nature; while the folds of the drapery float softly about the limbs. Among the best examples are the fine *amphoræ* from Nola in the Naples Museum ; *e.g.*, that representing the Last Night of Museum, with the battle of the Athenians and Amazons. Though found at Cumæ, it has all the characteristics of the Attic style, and has nothing in common with the Italo-

(12) * COTYLUS, OR CUP, SIGNED BY HIERON
(British Museum, Vase Room III, Case E ; E 137 ; *cp.* Miss Harrison's *Mythology and Monuments of Athens*, pp. l, lxv, ci.)

Troy (Baumeister, fig. 795 ; Birch, figs. 138, 139), as well as the beautiful *stamnŏs*[1] with the dancing Mænads in the same collection (fig. 13 ; *cp.* DIONYSUS, fig. 3).

On vases of the 4th century, the subjects are less exclusively mythological than before, and the artist's fancy delights in playing with scenes of daily life. We have an instance of this in a *cylix* of Vulci, where the swallow is welcomed as the herald of spring (Baumeister, fig. 2128).

(3) The *Attic style of perfect elegance* is exemplified in vases sometimes of small dimensions, in the shape of a *pyxis*, an *œnŏchŏ ̈e*, or an *ărўballus*.[2] They are readily recognised by the beautiful black ground, and by the garlands of pointed myrtle leaves that frequently decorate them, but above all by the extreme delicacy of their pictorial designs. One of the most interesting is an *aryballus* in the Naples

Greek products of the same period (Heydemann, No. 239). Another is an *aryballus* found at Æxōnē, representing the train of

(13) * MÆNADS.
(From *stamnos* in Naples Museum; Panofka, *Dionysos und Thyaden*, pl. i 2 ; Euripides, *Bacchæ*, ed. Sandys, pp. xxxii and cxxiv.)

Dionysus; the gracefulness of the attitudes, the expression of the faces, and the exquisite delicacy of the design, make it a masterpiece (Collignon, *Arch. Gr.*, fig. 115). Scenes of daily life are also to be noticed, such as ladies engaged on their toilet or calling on their friends. The skill of the

[1] A large jar for holding wine or oil, with two small, ear-shaped handles. (*See* VESSELS, fig. 1, no. 18.)

[2] The *œnochoë* is a small wine jug (*see* VESSELS, fig. 1, nos. 26-30); the *aryballus*, a globular vase, shaped like a pouch (*ib.*, no. 36).

artist is lavished even on small vases which were little more than playthings for children, and are covered with designs representing the games of childhood.

(4) *Vases of larger dimensions*, in the shape of a *hydria*, a *calpis*, a *cĕlĕbĕ*, a *crātĕr*, or an *amphora*, with characteristic differences in their subjects. The *amphora* often exhibits a betrothal, or a wedding procession, with the bride and a number of maidens bringing presents of vases, or caskets of jewels. The *pĕlĭkē* and *hydria* frequently show us scenes of ordinary life, interiors with ladies either at their toilet, or else at their work surrounded by pet birds. The *crater* and *canthărus* are usually reserved for Dionysiac subjects.[1]

(5) Vases with *gilded* ornaments, or with *reliefs* touched up with gold. From the 4th century onwards it became common to gild certain parts of the costume, such as bracelets, earrings, beads in necklaces, as well as berries in garlands of bay or myrtle. On small vases of the Attic style gilding is often applied with discretion, while on larger vases it is used to excess. The brilliancy of the painting is, at the same time, often enhanced by touches of bright colour, and tints of red, green, white, blue, and violet are applied to the draperies. One of the most beautiful vases of this type is the *pelike* founded at Camīrus, now in the British Museum. The scene is Pēleus carrying off Thĕtĭs (Vase Room III, E 451). The *peplŏs*, which is falling to the ground from the white form of the goddess, is of a sea-green with a white border ; she herself and her attendant Nymphs are richly adorned with gold, while the field of the design is filled with figures floating gracefully in the air (*Encycl. Brit.* xix pl. v).

(6) Similarly we have an Athenian red-figured *lĕcȳthus*, found at Marion in Cyprus, representing the death of the Sphinx at the hand of Œdĭpūs in the presence of Athene, Æneās, Apollo, and the Dĭoscūri, with accessories of white colour and gilding on the forms of the Sphinx and Athene. It is ascribed to 370 B.C. (*Journ. Hellenic Studies*, viii 320, pl. 81).

[1] The *hydria* is a large water vase (*see* fig. 5 and VESSELS, fig. 1, no. 17) ; the *calpis*, a modification of the *hydria*, with a rounder body, a shorter neck, and with cylindrical handles (*ib.*, no. 16) ; the *celebe*, a *crater* with columnar handles (no. 24) ; the *amphora* is a large oval vase with two handles (nos. 20–23) ; the *pelike*, an amphora with rather large handles, and a body broader below than above (no. 19) ; and the *cantharus*, a wine-cup with two long ears (no. 12).

(7) The *white lĕcȳthi of Attica.* The neck and foot of the *lecythus*[2] are covered with a very brilliant black varnish, while the body has a white ground with figures carelessly but skilfully drawn in reddish-brown outline and coarsely filled in with colours. Such *lecythi* are only found in tombs in the neighbourhood of Athens. Aristophanes, in a play belonging to 392 B.C., speaks of " those who paint *lecythi* for the dead " (*Eccl.* 996). Their manufacture probably extended over the 4th and 3rd centuries B.C., and especially over B.C. 350–300. We learn from works of art that they were used at the laying out (*prŏthĕsĭs*) of the dead body. Among the subjects most commonly represented oι them are (1) the laying out of the body, (2) lamentations at the tomb, (3) funeral offerings (fig. 14), (4) Charon and the ferry-boat (Miss Harrison, *l.c.*, p. 586) ; more rarely, we have the deposition of the body treated with consummate grace (Collignon, fig. 119). One of the specimens in the British Museum shows

(14) * FUNERAL OFFERINGS ON ATHENIAN LECYTHUS.
(Stackelberg, *Gräber der Hellenen*, Taf. xlv.)

Electra at the tomb of Agamemnon (Birch, p. 395 ; Vase Room, III, case F). As a different type of vase with polychrome painting on a white ground, we have a fine *cylix* from a Rhodian tomb, now in the British Museum, representing Aphrodite seated on the back of a flying swan (Vase Room III D 52). It has been well remarked that " for delicacy of touch and refined beauty of drawing this painting is quite unrivalled. The exquisite loveliness of Aphrodite's head and the pure grace of her profile, show a combination of mechanical skill united to imaginative power and realiza-

[2] A vase of tall cylindrical shape, with a long, narrow neck (*see* VESSELS, fig. 1, no. 33).

tion of the most perfect and ideal beauty" (Prof. Middleton in *Encycl. Brit.*, xix, p. 613, with plate v; *cp.* Baumeister, fig. 938).

In place of paintings we sometimes find figures in relief applied as a kind of frieze to the body of the vase. The most beautiful examples show a combination of relief, polychromy, and gilding. Such is the famous vase found at Cumæ and now at St. Petersburg; the groundwork of which is covered with a brilliant black, and is vertically fluted. It has two friezes with figures in relief, the upper representing Triptolemus and the Eleusinian goddesses; the lower, lions, dogs, panthers, and griffins (Baumeister, fig. 520).

and Northern Italy, but abound in Sicily and in Southern Italy, especially at Ruvo, Armento, and Sant' Agata di Goti. The best among them range from *after* B.C. 404, perhaps from B.C. 300 to nearly 200. After this the style of the paintings became extremely coarse, and about 100 B.C. painted vases ceased to be made.

The *technical processes* followed in the manufacture of vases have in part been treated under POTTERY. Fig. 16 exhibits the design on a vase in which some of the details of ornamentation are represented in actual course of being carried out. In the centre stands Athene, the patron-goddess of all kinds of handicraft, with a crown in her

b

a   *d*   *e*   *c*

(15) * THREE LARGE VASES OF THE DECADENCE, WITH TWO SMALLER VASES.

(a) An *amphora*, known as the Poniatowski vase, found in a tomb at Bari in Apulia, and,now in the Vatican Museum, representing the myth of Triptolemus (Lenormant and De Witte, *Élites Céramographiques*, III, lxiii). (b) A *crater*, found at Sant' Agata de' Goti, now in the Louvre, closely resembling the one by Asteas, Naples, 3226; Cadmus slaying the dragon. (c) A *candelabrum amphora*, with an open building and figures grouped in two rows. (d) A *prochous* with a female head. (e) A *carchesium* (Dubois Maisonneuve, *Introd. à l'Etude des Vases Ant.*, pl. vii. ii, lxvii, xxxvii).

IV. *Vases of the Decadence.*

The red colour of the figures is now paler, the glaze often of a dull, leaden hue; the ornaments are numerous and large in proportion to the subjects (fig. 15 a, b, c). The figures are no longer few and detached, but grouped in masses on the large vases, and the composition is not statuesque, but essentially pictorial. White opaque colour is freely introduced for the flesh of the females and children, and even for that of the males; as art declines, it almost supersedes red.

Such vases are rarely found in Greece

hand to reward the successful craftsman. On either side of her a winged Nīkē is placing a wreath on the head of one of those engaged in painting the decorations of the vases. The shapes represented are, beginning from the left, *amphŏra, canthărus, prŏchŏus* (in *cantharus*), *crātēr, amphora*, and above the last, on the extreme right, a small *cantharus* and an *œnŏchŏē*.

Uses. Nearly all the 20,000 vases already discovered were found in tombs. The earliest recorded discovery of such vases was on the occasion of the rebuilding of Corinth, B.C. 46, when the tombs of the city destroyed a century before were rifled of their contents, which became known in Rome as *nĕkrŏkŏrinthĭă* (Strabo, 382). Vases were doubtless originally made for the use of the living; but in process of time it became customary to place the more ornamental varieties in the sepulchres of the dead, and the custom led to the manufacture of ornamental vases for this special purpose (fig.17). An exception to the rule is furnished by the Greek city of Naucrătis, founded in the Delta of Egypt, apparently in the 7th century B.C., where a large number of fragments of pottery have been found in heaps near the ruins of the temples of Apollo and Aphrodite. Many of the fragments bear incised inscriptions recording the dedication of the vases to those deities (*British Museum Guide*, 1890, p. 188). The vases in everyday use, as opposed to those found in tombs, were much plainer: those represented in vase-paintings are almost always coloured black, without any paintings. Among the more interesting exceptions is a beautiful *pyxis*, or perfume-box, in the British Museum (Vase Room III, E 770), representing a lady's toilet, with several painted vases set about the room as ornaments, and filled, like *jardinières*, with flowers or olive-branches (*Encyc. Brit.*, **xix**, p. 614, fig. 31; *cp.* Birch, *l.c.*, p. 354).

The *subjects* are mainly mythological, but are also frequently taken from real life, and include religious rites, athletic contests, dances and marriages, funerals, and scenes from the drama. Among the few historical subjects are Crœsus on his funeral pyre (Duruy, *Hist. des Grecs*, i 680), Arcĕsĭlās of Cyrene (fig. 6), and Darius

preparing to invade Greece (a large vase in the Naples Museum).

For a long time almost all the vases discovered were found in Etruria and in South

(16) * INTERIOR OF A VASE MANUFACTORY.

(*Hydria* from the *Museo Campfí*, Ruvo; *Annal. d. Instituto*, 1876; *tav. d'agg.* D E.)

Italy and Sicily. Most of those discovered in Etruria, although popularly known as Etruscan vases, are really of Greek manufacture. The finest of those found in Italy were unearthed mainly at Capua, Nola, and Vulci, no less than 3,000 of various kinds having been recovered, in 1829, at Vulci alone. More recently an increasing number

(17) * A CHILD'S COFFIN, WITH VASES.
(Stackelberg, *Gräber der Hellenen*, Taf. vii.)

of fine vases has been found near Athens and Corinth, in the islands of the Ægean, on the western shores of Asia Minor, and in the region of Cyrene.

The principal public *collections* are those in the British Museum, the Louvre, and the Paris *Bibliothèque;* also in the museums of Berlin, Munich, Vienna, Florence, Rome (especially the *Museo Gregoriano*), Naples, Athens, and St. Petersburg.

Literature. A popular summary of the subject is included in Collignon's *Manuel d'Archéologie Grecque*, pp. 253–312, which has been mainly followed in the above article, with additional details from Birch's *Ancient Pottery*, from Prof. Middleton's article on "Pottery" in the *Encyclopædia Britannica*, from Von Rohden's *Vasenkunde* in Baumeister's *Denkmäler*, and other sources. Among further aids to the study of vase-paintings may be mentioned the illustrations edited by Millin and Millingen (republished in part by Reinach, 1890), Inghirami, Gerhard, Lenormant and De Witte, and Benndorf, Dumont and Chaplain; the second editions of Klein's *Euphronios*, 1886, and *Meistersignaturen*, 1887, and the same writer's *Lieblingsinschriften*, 1890; Hartwig's *Meisterschalen;* also Lau and Brunn, *Die griechischen Vasen*, 1877, and the forty large plates of Genick and Furtwängler's *Gr. Keramik*, 1883; lastly, Rayet and Collignon's *Histoire de la Céramique Grecque*, 1888, and *Designs from Greek Vases in the British Museum*, 1894.

On the *manufacture* of Vases, *see* POTTERY; on their *shapes, see* VESSELS.]

[J. E. S.]

Vectigālia. The Roman term originally denoting only the revenues flowing into the State chest from the State domains, and for the most part collected by contract. (*See* PUBLICANI.) The domains consisted of cultivated grounds, the rent of which was paid in money or kind; of pastures and meadows, for the use of which a payment (*scriptūra*) was made; of forests, from which revenue was derived mainly by the letting of pitch huts; of lakes and rivers let for fishing; and of mines and salt-works. With a view to protecting the citizens from exorbitant prices, the sale of salt had already been made a State monopoly in the earliest years of the Republic, and it remained such till late into the times of the Empire. In letting salt mines the price of the salt was fixed in the contract, as was also the case with many articles produced from mines. The term *vectīgal* also includes the rent paid for buildings, shops, booths and baths erected on public sites; the payment for the use of bridges and roads, of public water-ways, and sewers in cases where private properties drained into them; export and import tolls (*see* PORTORIUM), as well as all other indirect taxes. Such was the tax which was introduced into Rome in 357 B.C., and under the emperors was levied throughout the whole empire, the *vīcēsīma lībertātīs* or *mănumissīōnīs;* a tax of 5 per cent. paid on every manumitted slave, either by himself or his master. To these were added under Augustus the *centēsīma rērum vēnālium*, a tax of 1 per cent. on all articles sold at auctions; the *quinta et vicesima mancīpīōrum*, a tax of 4 per cent. on every slave sold; and the *vicesima hērēdītātum et lēgātōrum*, a tax of 5 per cent. on all inheritances over 100,000 sesterces (£875), and on all legacies not falling to the next of kin. This impost, with the increase of celibacy and the custom of leaving complimentary legacies to the whole circle of one's friends, proved exceedingly productive, and, though originally limited to Roman citizens, was, with the franchise, extended by Caracalla to all the inhabitants of the Empire, and at the same time raised to 10 per cent.

Vēdĭŏvis. *See* VEIOVIS.

Vĕgĕtĭus. (1) *Flāvius Vĕgĕtius Rĕnātus.* A Roman writer on military affairs, who, under a commission from Thĕŏdŏsĭus I, composed, between 384 and 395 A.D., a work in four books on military affairs (*Epĭtŏmē Rĕi Mĭlĭtārĭs*) consisting of extracts from earlier writers on this subject (especially Căto, Celsus, and Frontīnus). He raises no claim to personal knowledge or to stylistic merits, but only to a recognition of his industry. Although it is on the whole an arid and uncritical compilation, the book is valuable for the light it throws on the Roman military system.

(2) *Publius Vegetius.* A writer of a somewhat later date than (1), who composed an extensive work on veterinary science (especially on the treatment of horses and mules, and hence entitled *Mūlŏmĕdĭcīnă*).

Vēiŏvĭs (also *Vēdiŏvĭs*). An old Italian deity whose peculiar attributes were early forgotten. At Rome he had a famous shrine in the depression between the two peaks of the Capitoline Hill, the Capitol and the Arx. There lay his *ăsȳlum* and afterwards his temple, between two sacred groves. His statue, by the side of which stood a goat as a symbol, had a youthful, beardless head, and carried a bundle of arrows in its right hand; it was therefore supposed that he was the same as the Greek Apollo. Others saw in him a youthful Jupiter; while at a later date he was identified with Dīs, the god of the world below. He was probably a god of expiation, and hence at the same time the protector of runaway criminals. The goat, which was sacrificed to him annually on the 7th of March, appears elsewhere in the Roman cult as an expiatory sacrifice.

Vēlĭtēs ("skirmishers"). The name given in the old Roman legion to the 1,200 citizens of the lowest class in the census, who were distributed among the sixty centuries; they differed from the other soldiers in having lighter armour. (*See* LEGION.) When Marius introduced a uniform type of armour throughout all the ranks, this distinction disappeared.

Vēlĭus Longus. A Latin grammarian of the first half of the 2nd century A.D.; the composer of a work, *De Orthŏgrăphĭā*, which is still extant.

Vellēĭus Pătercŭlus (*Marcus*). A Roman historian born about 19 B.C. He entered the army early, and from 4 A.D., partly as an officer in the cavalry, and partly as a legate, he accompanied Tiberius for eight years on all his campaigns into Germany, Pannonia, and Dalmatia. In 15 A.D. he held the prætorship, for which he was warmly recommended by Augustus and Tiberius. In 29-30 A.D. he composed in a few months a short sketch of Roman history in two books (*Histŏrĭæ Rōmānæ libri duo*) which he dedicated to his patron Vinicius, one of the consuls for the year 30. The work has come down to us in a very confused and fragmentary condition. Only a few chapters remain of the first book, which ends with the destruction of Carthage. Whether considered as a historian or as a stylist, he is a dilettante. He had no special call to be a historian, and was destitute of any more than ordinary knowledge or appropriate preparation, although not devoid of imagination and genius. His *brochure* was composed with extreme haste, and merely consists of a number of items of information hurriedly put together. Hence its superficial execution and its numerous mistakes. After the manner of annalists, his work becomes more diffuse the nearer he approaches his own time. It ends with a panegyric on the imperial house, and especially on Tiberius, inflated with fulsome flatteries and high-sounding phraseology. According to him, the fortune of Rome, which had declined after the destruction of Carthage, and had been rising again from the time of Augustus, had reached its culminating point under Tiberius. He may be identified as the inventor of the courtly style of writing history. He does not linger long over facts, but prefers to dwell on the portrayal of the various characters that present themselves in the course of the history. His language is sometimes careless and commonplace, sometimes ornate and affected, with all manner of poetical expressions. His fancy for composing striking sentences and his undue predilection for antithesis have an unfortunate effect on his style.

Venantius Fortūnātus (*Hŏnōrĭus Clēmens*). A Latin poet, born about 535 A.D. at Tarvīsĭum (*Treviso*) in North Italy. After a learned education in Ravenna, he proceeded, about 560, to Gaul, where he became an ecclesiastic at Poitiers, and died as bishop about 600. Among his works, we possess an epic poem on St. Martin, as well as a collection of 300 poems in eleven books, of very various kinds, including panegyrics, epigrams, letters, elegies, hymns; and hence called *Miscellānĕa.* These poems, which are mostly elegiac, are not unsuccessful in form, and are of great value for the history of the time. One of the most interesting is the companion piece to the *Mŏsella* of Ausŏnius, the description of a journey by the Moselle and Rhine from Metz to Andernach (*De Nāvĭgĭō sŭō*).

Vēnātĭōnēs. The contests of beasts with one another, or of men with beasts, that formed part of the shows of which the Romans were passionately fond. They were first introduced at the games of Marcus

Fulvius Nōbĭlĭor, 116 B.C. Those who took part in these contests were called *bestĭārĭī.* They were either criminals and prisoners of war, who were poorly armed or completely unarmed, pitted against wild beasts which had previously been made furious by hunger, branding, and goading; or else hired men who, like gladiators, were trained in special schools and fully armed. Even in the last century of the Republic, and still more under the Empire, incredible expenses were incurred in the collection of the rarest animals from the remotest quarters of the globe, and in the other arrangements for their baiting. Thus Pompey provided a show of 500 lions, 18 elephants, and 410 other African animals; and Calĭgŭla caused 400 bears and the same number of animals from Africa to tear each other to pieces. Occasionally at these combats with wild beasts the man condemned to death was attired in an appropriate costume, so as to represent a sanguinary scene from mythology or history, as, for example, Orpheus being torn to pieces by bears. Down to the end of the Republic these shows took place in the Circus, and the greater exhibitions were held there even after that time, until the amphitheatres became the usual places of performance; and indeed, when they were combined with the gladiatorial exhibitions, they took place in the early morning before them. [The repugnance of some of the more cultivated Romans for these exhibitions is shown in a letter of Cicero's, *Ad Fam.* vii 1 § 3.] They were continued down to the 6th century.

Among the Greeks, especially the Athenians, cock-fights and quail-fights were very popular. At Athens cock-fights were held once a year in the theatres at the public expense. The training of fighting cocks was conducted with great care. Certain places, such as Tănăgra in Bœotia, Rhodes, and Dēlŏs, had the reputation of producing the largest and strongest. To whet their eagerness for the combat, they were previously fed with garlic. Their legs were armed with brass spurs, and they were set opposite to each other on tables furnished with raised edges. Bets, often to an enormous amount, were laid on the fights by the gamesters, as well as by the spectators.

Vĕnŭs. Originally a Latin goddess of spring, presiding over flower-gardens and vines, and as such worshipped by gardeners, husbandmen, florists, and vine-dressers. At Lavĭnĭum there was an ancient sanctuary dedicated to her by the Latins; on the other hand, in Rome, she had in olden times no State worship, at least under this name. Her earliest Roman name appears to have been *Murcĭa,* which was interpreted later on as *Myrtĕa,* goddess of myrtles. How she came to be identified with the Greek love-goddess Aphrŏdītē is not clear. The oldest historical mention of her worship in this character is in 217 B.C., when, by the order of the Sibylline books, after the disaster at Lake Trasimene, a temple dedicated to the Venus of Mount Eryx in Sicily, an ancient and well known place for the worship of Aphrŏdite Urănĭa, was built on the Capitol.

Besides the various forms of worship which she enjoyed, corresponding to the Greek cult of Aphrodite, Venus had a special significance as *Gĕnĕtrix,* or mother of the Roman people through her son Æněās. She was especially worshipped as mother of the race of the Jūlii, which claimed descent from her grandson Iūlus, the son of Æneas. It was on this account that Cæsar, in the Forum built by him in 46 B.C., erected a magnificent temple in her honour as *Gĕnĕtrix,* in which games were annually held for eleven days. To her, as mother of the whole Roman race, as well as to Roma, the personification of Rome, Hadrian dedicated a splendid double temple, completed 135 A.D., the ruins of which can still be seen in the neighbourhood of the Coliseum. In later times this was called *templum urbis.* (*See* ARCHITECTÚRE, fig. 13.)

The 1st of April was sacred to Venus as the day on which she was worshipped by the Roman matrons, together with *Fortūna Vĭrīlĭs,* the goddess of prosperity in the intercourse of men and women, and also with Concordia, as *Verticordĭa,* the goddess who turns the hearts of women to chastity and modesty. Other holidays were kept to her in the same month as goddess of prostitution. (*See also* VENUS LIBITINA. On the types of Venus in works of art, *cp.* APHRODITE.)

Vergil [Lat. *Publius Vergĭlĭus Mărō;* not *Virgilius.* The spelling *Vergilius* is attested, not only by the best manuscripts, but by inscriptions]. The famous Roman poet, born 15th October, 70 B.C. at Andēs, a village near Mantua, on the Mincius, where his father possessed a small estate. After receiving his early education at Crĕmōna and (after assuming in 55 B.C. the toga of manhood) at Milan, he proceeded in 53 to Rome, where he devoted himself to rhetorical, philosophical, and physical studies. Prevented by weakness of health and bashfulness of manner from looking forward to any success as a pleader or in the service of the State, he returned home, and in the quiet of the country devoted himself to the study of the Greek poets. His meeting with the refined and poetically gifted Asīnīus Pollīō, who in 43 took command of Transpadane Gaul as lieutenant of Antony, appears to have given him his first impetus to poetic composition. His earliest publication, his ten *Eclogues*, which were written in the years 43-37, were afterwards collected under the title of *Būcŏlĭca* ("Pastoral Poems"). These are imitations of the idyls of Theocritus; they are, however, less natural, the pictures of country and shepherd life being interspersed throughout with references to contemporary events, to his own fortunes, and to important persons such as Octavianus, Pollio, and Cornēlĭus Gallus, to whom the poet wished either to commend himself or to show his gratitude by his complimentary allusions. He had on several occasions been compelled by the force of circumstances to appeal to the protection and help of influential men. For instance, at the distribution of land to the veterans in 41 B.C. his own estate was appropriated, and it was only the advocacy of Pollio and of Cornelius Gallus which enabled him to recover it. In the following year, when Pollio was obliged to give place to Alfēnus Vārus, his property was again threatened; but by the influence of Mæcēnās, to whom Pollio had recommended him, amends were made him by the presentation of another estate. His fame as a poet was established by the *Eclogues*. Henceforward, by the liberality of noble friends, especially Octavīānus and Mæcenas, whom he won not merely by his art, but, like all with whom he came into contact, by his modesty and good nature, he was enabled to devote himself to his studies without fear of interruption. He lived in turns in Rome (where he possessed a house), or on his estate at Nola, or in Naples, where he mainly resided, owing to his weak health.

Here, in 30 B.C. he completed the didactic poem in four books begun seven years previously, entitled the *Georgics* (*Gĕōrgĭcă*, on agriculture), which he dedicated to Mæcenas. In this, the first Latin poem of this kind, we have a masterpiece of Latin poetry. The author treats of Roman husbandry under its four chief branches, tillage (book i), horticulture (ii), the breeding of cattle (iii), the keeping

of bees (iv); and handles a prosaic theme with thorough knowledge and consummate art, together with a loving enthusiasm and a fine sympathy for nature. [The work was founded mainly on the poems of Hesiod and Ārātus, but also gives evidence of familiarity with writers on agriculture, as well as of independent agricultural knowledge.]

Immediately after finishing the *Georgics* he began the epic poem of the *Æneid*, which he had already promised to Octavianus. Its appearance was looked forward to by all educated Rome with extraordinary anticipation. After eleven years of unremitting labour (for to him composition in general was a laborious task) he was ready with a rough draft of the whole, and determined on a journey to Greece and Asia, intending to spend three years there in polishing his work and afterwards to devote himself entirely to philosophy. At Athens he met Octavianus (who had received in B.C. 27 the title of Augustus). The latter induced him to return home with him: Vergil consented, but fell ill, apparently from a sunstroke, at Megara. On the sea voyage his condition grew worse, and soon after landing he died at Brundīsĭum, 21st September, 19 B.C. His remains were buried at Naples.

It was the poet's original intention that, in the event of his dying before his work was completed, the twelve books of the *Æneid* should be consigned to the flames. In the end, however, he bequeathed it to his friends and companions in art Vārĭus Rūfus and Plōtius Tucca, on condition that they should not publish any part of it. But, by the command of Augustus, they gave it to the world, after submitting the work to a careful revision, and only removing what was superfluous, while refraining from all additions of their own.

In spite of its incomplete form, the work was enthusiastically welcomed on its first appearance, which had excited the highest anticipations, as a national epic of equal worth with the poems of Homer. This approval was due to its national purpose, the poetic glorification of the origin of the Roman people in the adventures of Æneas, the founder of the Romans through his descendant Rōmŭlus, and in particular the ancestor of the imperial house of the Julii through his son Ascănius, or Iulus. In view of its purpose, little notice was taken of the weak points in the poem, which can only in part be excused by the fact that it lacks the author's finishing touches. We may, indeed, admire the art which the poet has shown in moulding together the vast mass of material collected with so much effort from the poetic and prose writings of Greeks and Romans, the excellences of the language and of the metrical form, and the beauty of many individual portions; but it cannot be denied that in artistic completeness and originality the *Æneid* falls far below the *Georgics*. In particular, the endeavour to pourtray a real hero was beyond the capacity of the gentle, almost womanly, character of the poet; Æneas is a true hero neither in endurance nor in action. Further, the endeavour to rival Homer is mainly limited to imitation. This is apparent not only in countless single instances, but also in the plot of the whole poem. Vergil obviously wished to unite the excellences of the *Odyssey* and *Iliad* in one work by describing in the first six books the wanderings of Æneas, and in the last six his conflicts for the throne of Latium.

In spite of many faults, which were noticed even in ancient times, Vergil has remained the most widely read, the most admired, and the most popular poet of his nation, and no other writer has exercised such an influence on the subsequent development of the Roman literature and language. This remark applies to prose as well as poetry. As was the case with the poems of Homer among the Greeks, Vergil's works, and especially the *Æneid* as a national epic, were used down to the latest times for school teaching and as a basis of school grammar. They were imitated by authors, particularly by epic and didactic poets. In later times single verses and parts of verses (*see* CENTO) were used to compose new poems of the most varying contents; and finally the most famous scholars made them the object of their studies both in verbal and in general interpretation. Some relics of their labours are preserved in the different collections of *scholia*, especially in that comprehensive commentary on his collected poems which bears the name of *Servius Honoratus*. Of smaller value are the commentaries of the pseudo-Probus on the *Bucolics* and *Georgics*, and of Tiberius Donatus on the *Æneid*.

The name of Vergil was also borne in ancient times by a number of poems, which passed as the works of his youth, but can hardly any of them have been his compositions: (1) the *Catalecta* [or more correctly *Catalepton*], fourteen small poems in iambic and elegiac metre. (2) *Culex* ("the midge"), supposed to have been written by Vergil in his sixteenth year, a most insipid poem. (3) The *Ciris*, the story of the transformation of Scylla, the daughter of the Megarian king, into the bird Ciris (*see* NISUS), obviously composed by an imitator of Vergil and Catullus. (4) The *Diræ*, two bucolic poems: (*a*) the *Diræ* properly so called, imprecations on account of the loss of an estate consequent on the proscription of A.D. 41; and (*b*) the *Lydia*, a lament for a lost love, both of which have as little claim to be the writings of Vergil as of the grammarian Valerius Cato, to whom also they have been ascribed. (5) The *Moretum*, so called from the salad which the peasant Simylus prepares in the early morning for the day's repast, a character sketch as diverting and lifelike as (6) a poem deriving its title from the *Copa*, or hostess, who dances and sings before her inn, inviting the passers by to enter. This last poem is in elegiac metre. [Vergil's life was written by Suetonius from earlier memoirs and *memoranda. See* Prof. Nettleship's *Ancient Lives of Vergil,* Clarendon Press, 1879.]

Verrius Flaccus (*Marcus*). A Roman freedman, "who obtained renown chiefly by his method of teaching. To exercise the wits of his pupils, says Suetonius, he used to pit against each other those of the same age, give them a subject to write upon, and reward the winner with a prize, generally in the shape of a fine or rare copy of some ancient author" (Prof. Nettleship's *Essays,* p. 203). He educated the grandsons of Augustus and died under Tiberius. He devoted himself to literary and antiquarian studies resembling those of the learned Varro. Thus, he wrote books *De Ortho-graphia* and *Rerum Memoria Dignarum ;* but his most important work was entitled *De Verborum Significatu.* This may claim to be the first Latin lexicon ever written. It was arranged alphabetically; it gave interpretations of obsolete words, and explained the meaning of the oldest institutions of the State, including its religious customs, etc. We only possess fragments of an abridgment made by Festus (*q.v.*), and a further abridgment of the latter, dedicated to Charlemagne, by Paulus. A calendar of Roman festivals drawn up by him was set up in marble at Præneste, near Rome; of this there are some fragments still preserved containing the months of January to April inclusive and December.

These fragments are known as the *Fasti Prœ-nestīnī* [*Corpus Inscr. Lat.* i, p. 311]. [In the library of Trinity College, Cambridge, there is a slab of stone bearing the name VERRIVS FLACCVS, probably the lexicographer's epitaph. *See* also Prof. Nettleship's *Lectures and Essays*, pp. 201–247.]

Vēr Sacrum (*a sacred spring*). A dedication practised by the Italian tribes, whereby, in times of severe hardship, all the products of the succeeding spring, *i.e.* the months of March and April, were consecrated to the gods. All the fruits and cattle were actually offered up in sacrifice; while the children that were then born, as soon as they were grown up, were driven out of the country as forfeited to heaven, and required to seek a new home. Whole generations in this way left their country, those of the Sabine stock being led by the animals sacred to Mars—a bull, a woodpecker, or a wolf. In Rome, whose origin is traced back by many to a *ver sacrum*, the *pontĭfĭcēs* superintended the vow and its fulfilment. The *ver sacrum* was vowed for the last time in the second Punic War. [B.C. 217, Livy xxii 10; but the vow was not fulfilled until twenty-one years afterwards, B.C. 195 and 194, *ib.* xxxiii 44 and xxxiv 44].

Vertumnus ("the turner," "changer"). An Italian god of fruits, who presided over the changing year, especially over the fruits of the earth, whether in orchards or in gardens. Hence he was generally represented as a gardener and a cultivator of the soil, with fruits in his lap and a pruning knife in his hand, and was honoured by the country folk with the produce of their orchards, etc. In the belief of the people, he possessed the faculty of changing himself into all possible shapes, and they related how by one of his transformations he won Pōmōna for his wife. In Rome his statue of bronze stood in the Tuscan quarter, where a considerable trade went on; he was on

* VERTUMNUS.

this account regarded as the protector of business and exchange. Sacrifice was offered to him in his chapel on the Aventine on August 13th. [Propertius, iv 2.]

Vessels. An immense number of vessels for different purposes is mentioned by the ancients. It is impossible within the present limits to speak of more than a certain number of the most important. In ordinary life much use was made of pottery, which was sometimes ornamented with paintings. (*See* POTTERY and VASES.) Next to clay, bronze was the favourite material. The precious metals, marble, and other stones, such as porphyry, travertine, alabaster, and onyx, were also used, and the vessels made of these and of bronze were often adorned with carved work. On the employment of glass for this purpose, *see* GLASS. (*Cp.* also MURRINA.) It can hardly be said that wood was much in use. Vessels intended to hold wine, oil, salt meat, salt fish, olives, corn, and the like, were generally of clay. The largest of them was the *pĭthŏs* (Gr.) or *dōlĭum* (Lat.), a butt in the form of a gourd, used for storing oil and wine. This vessel, which was lined with pitch, was often so large that a man could easily get inside it. It was one of these butts in which Dĭŏgĕnēs made his abode. They were generally let into the floor of the cellar, and counted as immovable furniture. The Greek *bĭkŏs* and the Roman *sēria* were smaller vats of the same kind, used for storing salt-meats, figs, corn, etc. For purposes of sale and of use, the wine and oil were passed from the *dolium* into the *amphŏra* (Gr. *amphŏreus*), and the *cădus* (Gr. *kădŏs*). These were vessels with two handles, and a slim body pointed at the foot. They were either buried up to the middle in the ground, or set up slanting against the wall (fig. 1, nos. 20–23; fig. 2 *a*, *b*). The *cadi* were specially used by the Romans for the storage of Greek wines. Wine and oil were also, especially in the country, put into leather bags (Gr. *askŏs*; Lat. *ūter*), as is the case now in the East and in the south of Europe. The bag was made by sewing a number of skins together, and was tapped by untying one of the legs. For drawing and holding water they used the *hydria*, or *kalpis* (Lat. *urna*), carried on the head or shoulders. This was a vessel with a short neck and large body, often with three handles, two smaller ones for carrying, and one behind for drawing and pouring out (fig. 1, nos. 16, 17). The *lăgȳnŏs* (Lat. *lăgōna* or *lăgœna*) was a wine-jar It had a narrow neck, rather a wide mouth, and a handle (fig. 1, no. 34). It was hung up as a sign in front of wine shops, and was put before the guests at table. The *lēkȳthŏs* or *ampulla* was used for oil (fig. 1, no. 33); the *ălābastrŏn* or *alabaston* (fig. 1, no. 35) for fragrant ointments. This vessel was named from the material of which it was usually made. Both the *lekythos* and *alabastron* had narrow necks, so that the liquid ran out in drops. The *alabastron* was round at

spoons were used (*trūa, trulla,* fig. 3), as well as various sorts of cups (*cÿăthus,* fig. 1, nos. 10, 13–15). These resembled our tea and coffee cups, but had a much higher handle, rising far above the rim, and contained a definite measure. Drinking-vessels were made in the form of bowls, beakers, and horns. To the first class belonged the flat *phĭălē,* or saucer without handle or base, corresponding to the Roman *pătĕră* generally used in sacrifices (fig. 1, nos. 1, 2); the *kymbĭŏn,* a long deep vessel

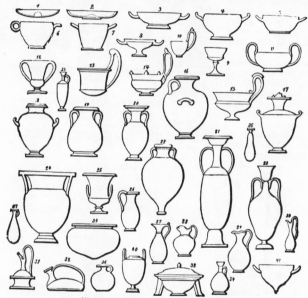

(1) * VARIOUS SHAPES OF GREEK VASES.
(Jahn's *Vasensammlung in der Pinakothek zu München,* Taf. i, ii.)

1, 2, *phĭălē.* 3, *cÿlix.* 4–7, *scÿphus.* 8, *cÿlix.* 9, *holmŏs.* 10, *cÿăthus.* 11, *carchēsĭŏn.* 12, *canthărŏs.* 13–15, *cÿăthus.* 16, *kalpis.* 17, *hydria.* 18, *stamnŏs.* 19, *pēlĭkē.* 20–23, *amphŏra.* 24, *cĕlēbē.* 25, *crātēr.* 26–30, *œnŏchŏē.* 32, *askŏs.* 33, *lēkȳthŏs.* 34, *lagœna.* 35, *ălābastrŏn.* 36, *drÿballŏs.* 37, *bombȳlios.* 38, 39, name unknown. 40, *lĕkănē.* 41, *cylix.*

the foot, and therefore required a stand to support it.

The general term *krātēr* (Lat. *crātēra* or *crēterra*) was used to denote the vessels in which wine was mixed with water at mealtimes (fig. 1, no. 25; *cp.* HILDESHEIM, THE TREASURE OF). They were moderately large, with wide necks and bodies, and two handles. Sometimes they had a pedestal, sometimes they were pointed or round beneath, in which case they required a support (*hÿpŏkrātērĭŏn*). For ladling and pouring out the wine,

without handles, so called from its likeness to a boat; and the *kÿlix* (Lat. *cǎlix*) with handle and base (fig. 1, nos. 3 and 8). Among the beakers may be mentioned the *skÿphŏs* (Lat. *scÿphŭs*) attributed to Hēräclēs (fig. 1, nos. 4–7). This was a large cup originally of wood, and used by shepherds, sometimes with a round, sometimes with a flat bottom. Another was the *kanthărŏs* (*canthărŭs*) peculiar to Dĭŏnÿsus (fig. 1, no. 12), with a high base and projecting handles. The *karchēsĭŏn* (*carchēsium,* fig. 1, no. 11) was tall, slightly contracted at its sides, and with slender handles reaching from the rim to the foot [Macrobius, *Sātūrnālia* v 21]: the *kĭbōrĭŏn* (*cĭbōrĭum*) resembled the husks of the Egyptian bean. The class of drinking horns included the *rhўtŏn* (fig. 4), with its mouth shaped like the head of an animal.

As may be seen from the names, the Romans borrowed most of their drinking vessels from the Greeks. They were generally fitted with silver; and, during the imperial times often ornamented with finely cut gems.

It is unnecessary to enumerate the various vessels used for washing, cooking, and eating, the characteristics of which were not strikingly different from our own. But we may observe that for domestic purposes of all kinds the ancients used basket work of canes, rushes, straw, and

used for holding the wool used in weaving and embroidery: the low *kănĕŏn*, or basket

(2) * VESSELS OF GLASS OR TERRA-COTTA FROM POMPEII.
(Overbeck's *Pompeii*, p. 402, fig. 249, ed. 3=fig. 250, ed. 4.)

a and *b*, *amphŏra*. *c*, two glass *lagœna* in terra-cotta *incŭtĕga*. *d*, *e*, *f*, wine-glasses. *g*, wine-strainer. *h*, glass funnel, *infundĭbŭlum*. *i*, cup and saucer. *k*, oil-flask. *l*, small flask. *m*, cup. *n*, wine-taster. *o*, jug. *p*, gourd-shaped bottle. *q*, vessel with pointed base. *r*, strainer. *s*, small vase for unguents. *t*, strainer.

of round or oval shape (fig. 5, *c*), for bread and fruit. The Athenian maidens carried *kănĕă* on their heads at the Panathenaic procession. (*See* CANEPHORI.) For baskets of other shapes, see fig. 5, *d*, *e*, *f*.

(3) BRONZE LADLES (*trŭa*).
(From Pompeii.)

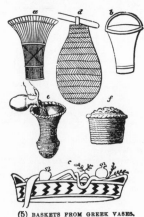

(5) BASKETS FROM GREEK VASES.
(Guhl and Koner, fig. 203.)

(4) GREEK DRINKING-HORNS (*rhўtŏn*).
(Panofka, *Griechische Trinkhörner*.)

leaves, especially palm leaves. The *kălăthŏs*, made in the form of a lily (fig. 5, *a* and *b*), was

Vesta. The Italian, particularly the Latin, goddess of the hearth and of its fire, corresponding in her name, as well as in her nature, to the Greek HESTIA (*q.v.*) Like Vesta, besides her special cult on the hearth of every home, she was also worshipped by the State. This worship was introduced by Nŭma from Lavīnium, whither Ænēās had brought the *Pĕnātēs* and the sacred fire from Troy. Hence it was that Roman consuls and dictators, on taking up and laying down their office, sacrificed in the temple of Vesta at Lavinium. It was customary in Italy as in Greece for the colonies to kindle the fire of their own Vesta at the hearth of the mother city.

The ancient round *temple of Vesta*, which served as the central point of the city, was built by Numa. In its neighbourhood was the so called *ātrĭum of Vesta*, the abode of the virgin priestesses of the goddess, the Vestals [excavated in 1883-4; Middleton's *Remains of Ancient Rome*, i 307–329]. Here the goddess was worshipped not in the form of a statue, but under the symbol of the eternal fire, which it was the chief duty of the Vestals to keep alight. On every 1st March it was renewed. If it went out of itself, a great national disaster was held to have occurred, and the guilty Vestal was scourged by the pontifex. The fire could only be rekindled by a burning glass, or by the primitive method of friction by boring a piece of wood from a fruit tree. Corresponding to the *lărēs* and *pĕnātēs* of the domestic hearth, there were, according to later usage, the *penates* of the State in the temple of Vesta; and similarly, on the temple-hearth, a sacrifice was offered daily, consisting of the plainest form of food in a simple vessel of clay. The daily purifications could only be made with flowing water, which the Vestals carried in pitchers upon their heads from the fountain of Ĕgĕrĭa, or of the Muses. By day every one had the right of admission to all the temple, save only that part in which the *pallādĭum* and other mystic relics were kept, where the Vestals alone had the right to enter. It was only by night that men were excluded.

As goddess of the sacred fire of the hearth in every house and for the city in general, Vesta was also the goddess of every sacrificial fire. Hence she was worshipped with Jānus at every religious service, Janus being invoked at the opening, Vesta at the close. Her own festival, the *Vestālĭa*, was kept on July 9th. The matrons of the town walked barefooted in procession to her temple, to implore the blessing of

the goddess for their households, and to offer sacrifice to her in rude dishes, in remembrance of the time when the hearth served generally for the baking of bread. The millers and bakers also kept holiday. The mills were crowned, and the asses employed in them had garlands and loaves suspended about their necks. The worship of Vesta survived to the last days of paganism, and was abolished by Gratian in 382 A.D. Although there was no image of the goddess in the actual temples, her statues were not uncommon at Rome in later times. Like the Greek Hestia, she was represented sometimes as standing, sometimes as sitting, completely clothed and veiled, with chalice torch, sceptre, and palladium. For cut, *see* HESTIA.

Vestals (*virgĭnēs vestālēs*, Vestal Virgins). The priestesses of Vesta. At Rome their number was at first four, but had already been increased to six during the last years of the kings. Every girl possessing the necessary qualification was liable to be called on to undertake the duty, and no exemption was granted, except upon very strict conditions. The office was confined to girls of not less than six and not more than ten years of age, without personal blemish, of free, respectable families, whose parents were still alive and resident in Italy. The choice was made by lot out of a number of twenty, nominated by the pontifex. The virgin appointed to the priestly office immediately quitted her father's authority and entered that of the goddess. After her inauguration by the pontifex, she was taken into the *ātrĭum* of Vesta, her future place of abode, was duly attired, and shorn of her hair. The time of service was by law thirty years, ten of which were set apart for learning, ten for performing and ten for teaching the duties. At the end of this time leave was granted to the Vestals to lay aside their priesthood, return into private life, and marry. They seldom took advantage of this permission. They were under the control of the pontifex, who, in the name of the goddess, exercised over them paternal authority. He administered corporal chastisement if they neglected their duties, more particularly if they allowed the sacred fire to go out; and, if any one of them violated her vow of chastity, he had her carried on a bier to the *campus scĕlĕrātus* (the field of transgression), near the Colline Gate, beaten with rods and immured alive. Her seducer was scourged to death. No man was allowed to enter their apartments. Their service consisted in maintaining and keeping pure the eternal fire in the temple of Vesta, watching the sacred shrines, performing the sacrifices, offering the daily and, when necessary, the special prayers for the welfare of the nation, and taking part in the feasts of Vesta, Tellūs, and Bŏnă Dĕă. They were dressed entirely in white, with a coronet-shaped head-band (*infŭla*), and ornamented with ribands (*vittæ*) suspended from it, and at a sacrifice covered with a white veil [called the *suffībŭlum*. This was a sort of hood made of a piece of white woollen cloth with a purple border, rectangular in form. It was folded over the head and fastened in front below the throat by a *fĭbŭla* (Festus, p. 340, ed.

* A VESTAL VIRGIN.

(Portrait statue of one of the chief Vestals, of the time of Trajan or Hadrian, showing the sacred vestment called the *suffibulum*.)

(Müller, quoted in Middleton's *Rome*, i 320)]. The chief part in the sacrifices was taken by the eldest, the *virgo vestalis maxĭma*.

The Vestal Virgins enjoyed various distinctions and privileges. When they went out, they were accompanied by a lictor, to whom even the consul gave place; at public games they had a place of honour; they were under a guardian, and were free to dispose of their property; they gave evidence without the customary oath; they were, on account of their incorruptible character, entrusted with important wills and public treaties; death was the penalty for injuring their person; those whom they escorted were thereby protected from any assault. To meet them by chance saved the criminal who was being led away to punishment; and to them, as to men of distinguished

merit, was assigned the honour of burial in the Forum.

Vestĭbŭlum. An entrance-court before a Roman house. (*See* HOUSE.)

Vĕtĕrāni. [A Latin word properly meaning old soldiers.] During the later Republican period and under the Empire the term was applied to those who at the end of their time of service retired from the legion. They were kept with the army under the standard, under which they were taken to the military colonies appointed for them, and again served there for an indefinite period. (*Cp.* VEXILLARII.)

Vexillārii. Roman veterans who, at the end of their period of service, retired from the legion, but were kept together under a standard (*vexillum*) up to the time of their final dismissal. They formed, by the side of the legion, a select corps like the *ēvŏcāti* of earlier times. They were exempt from ordinary service, and only bound to take part in actual fighting. [They may be briefly described as the oldest class of *vĕtĕrāni*, and the last to be summoned to take the field.]

Vexillum. The Latin name for a four-cornered flag, attached to a cross-pole, and carried by the *vexillārĭus*. (*See* SIGNUM, fig. *a*.) Every squadron (*turma*), and probably every detachment of a body of troops which formed a separate command, had a red, white, or purple *vexillum* of this kind, and hence were themselves called a *vexillum*, or sometimes a *vexillātĭo*. The latter word, however, from the end of the 3rd century A.D., signifies a squadron of cavalry. At Rome a red flag was displayed on the Capitol during the deliberations of the *cŏmĭtĭa centŭrĭăta*, and was in time of war planted as the signal for battle on the general's tent or the admiral's ship. *Vexilla* served also as marks of distinction for the higher officers.

Vĭa Appĭa. *See* ROADS.

Vĭātor ("messenger"). A subordinate official (*see* APPARITOR), employed by the Roman magistrates for sending a message or a summons, or for executing an arrest. The consuls and prætors had probably three *dĕcŭrĭæ* of *vĭātŏrēs*; the tribunes had a special *decuria*, as also had the *quæstōrēs ærārĭi*, and the officers who took their place under the Empire, *viz.* the *præfecti ærarii*; also the ædiles, the *trēsvĭrī căpĭtālēs*, and the *quattŭorviri vĭĭs purgandīs*. They also appear in connexion with provincial governors and sacerdotal bodies.

Victor. *See* AURELIUS.

Victōria. The Roman goddess of victory. (*See* NICE.)

Victōrīnus (*Gaius Mărĭus*). A Latin rhetorician, born in Africa, who, about the middle of the 4th century A.D. taught at Rome, where St. Jerome enjoyed his instruction. In his old age he became a convert to Christianity, and served its cause by his writings. Besides numerous theological works, he is the author of a comprehensive treatise mainly on metres, called *Ars Grammătĭcă*, in four books. His name is also given to some other grammatical writings, as well as some poems on biblical subjects; but it is doubtful whether they are from his hand. A commentary on Cicero's work *De Inventĭōnĕ*, which used to be ascribed to him, was more probably composed by one Făbius Marius Victorinus.

Vicus. A Latin word originally meaning a house, and afterwards a collection of houses. In a town, *vicus* was a street or section of the town; in the country, a rural community composed of farms lying close together, with temples and altars of its own, a common chest and annually elected overseers (*măgistri*, or *œdĭlēs*), to whom was assigned the care of the cult, buildings, and local police. The religious centre of the separate townships or *vici* was the *compĭtum* (crossway), with the chapel of the *lărēs compĭtālēs* erected there, in whose honour was annually held the festival of the *Compĭtālĭa*. Augustus divided Rome into fourteen districts and 265 *vici*, and ordained that four magistrates should be chosen annually from every *vicus*, partly to superintend the cult of the *lares*, partly to perform the official duties of citizens. This arrangement survived with a few changes till the decline of the Empire.

Vĭgĭlēs (" watchmen "). An organized military body of seven cohorts, each of 1,000 men, appointed by Augustus to superintend the firemen and night-police of Rome. (*See* COHORS.)

Vĭgĭlĭæ (" night-watch "). The name given at Rome to the four divisions of the night (generally from 6 p.m. to 6 a.m.) and to the night-guards of four men each, who relieved one another every watch. In camp the beginning of the night-watch was signalled by a blast blown before the general's tent (*prœtōrĭum*) by all the buglers; and further, at the end of every night-watch, the duration of which was reckoned by the water-clock, a bugler gave the signal for the relief.

Vĭgintīsexvĭri (twenty-six men). The collective name given at Rome to twenty-six officers of lower rank (*măgistrātūs mĭnōrēs*). They were divided into six different offices, and were originally nominated by the higher officers to be their assistants, but were subsequently chosen by the people at the *cŏmĭtĭa trĭbūta*, and it was by this appointment that they first became magistrates proper. The term included (1) *Iūdĭces dĕcemvĭri* (ten-men judges), or *decemviri (st)lītĭbus iūdĭcandīs* (ten-men for the decision of disputed suits), originally named by the tribunes to inquire into those civil suits in which their assistance had been invoked in certain appeals from the decision of the consuls. Afterwards the decision of such cases was left to them by the consuls from the very commencement. In time their relations with the tribunes grew less close, and they became judicial magistrates, who were probably chosen in the *comitia tributa*, under the presidency of the *prætor urbānus*. Of their functions in detail, little more is known from the time of the Republic than that they decided actions for freedom, and that they made the arrangements for the trials heard before the court of the *centumviri*. This latter duty then lost in the last days of the Republic, but it was restored to them by Augustus. (2) *Quattuorvĭri iūrī dīcundo* (four men for pronouncing judgment), whose duty it was to pronounce judgment at law in the ten towns of Campania, like the *præfecti iuri dicundo*, who were nominated by the prætor in the other municipalities; they survived only till the time of Augustus. (3) *Trĕsvĭri nocturni* (three men for night-service), originally servants of the consuls, who were responsible for the peace and safety of Rome by night, especially in respect of danger by fire. When to this duty was added that of investigating criminal charges, they became regular magistrates under the title *tresviri căpĭtālēs*. In this capacity they had to track out escaped criminals, to examine prisoners under the authorization of the higher magistrates, to inspect the public prisons, and to superintend the carrying out of capital sentences and of corporal punishments. Hence prison-warders and executioners were placed under them. Under the Empire it was also their duty to burn offensive books.[1] (4) *Tresviri mŏnĕtālēs* (three men for the mint), who

---

[1] [*See* Fausset on Cicero, *Pro Cluentio* 60.]

had, under the Republic, the superintendence of the coinage of gold and silver,
under the Empire that of the copper currency only. (5) *Quattuorviri viis in urbe
purgandīs* (four men for cleansing the
streets in the city). And (6) *Duoviri viis
extra urbem purgandis* (two for cleansing

under - magistrates became *vigintiviri*
(twenty men). These were chosen from
the knights, and the office of the viginti-
virate served as the preliminary step to the
quæstorship.

Vīlĭcus. The Latin term for the steward
of an estate. (*See* VILLA and SLAVES.)

(1) * VILLA MARINA.
(Mural painting from Pompeii; Gell and Gandy's *Pompeiana*, pl. 60.)

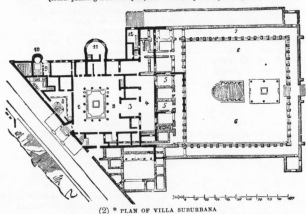

(2) * PLAN OF VILLA SUBURBANA
of M. Arvius Dĭŏmēdēs (Donaldson's *Pompeii*, ii 1).

1, door. 2, *pĕristȳlĭum.* 3, *tablĭnum.* 4, gallery. 5, *œcus.* 6, court. 7, *cryptŏportĭcus.*
8, triangular court with cold bath. 9, *tĕpĭdărĭum.* 10, *călĭdărĭum.* 11, bedroom. 12, staircase
leading to lower story.

the streets outside the city), who were
under the direction of the ædiles. Under
Augustus the *duoviri* last named disappeared as well as the *quattuorviri iuri
dicundo*, and the collective name for the

Villa. A Latin word signifying a
property in the country, consisting of a
block of buildings for habitation and for
domestic purposes. With the decline of
agriculture and with the growing preference

in favour of country-houses, there arose the distinction between *villa rustĭca* and *villa urbāna*. The former served for agricultural purposes; the latter, so called because built in the town style of architecture, only for pleasure. Many villas were designed only for one of the two objects, others were built for both. The *villa rustica* included apartments for the *vīlĭcus*, or steward (a trustworthy slave or freedman, who had to superintend money-matters), the book-keeper (*actor*), and the slaves, stalls, and store-rooms. In the erection of the *villa urbana*, efforts were made to unite the charm of beautiful landscape with the greatest comfort and convenience, and to procure advantages which a house in the town hemmed in on all sides by other houses could not always afford. It contained separate rooms and colonnades for summer and winter, the former facing the north, the latter the south; baths, rooms set apart for physical exercises, library, and art collections. Outside were parks, preserves, fish-ponds, aviaries, etc. Towards the end of the Republic, and still more under the Empire, luxury in such establishments reached its highest point. [In Pliny's *Letters*, v 6, we have an elaborate description of his Tuscan *villa ;* and, in ii 17, a minute account of his *villa* at Laurentum, on the coast of Latium. The accompanying cuts give a view of a *villa mărīna* (fig. 1) and a ground-plan of a *villa suburbāna* (fig. 2)].

Vĭnālĭa. A wine festival kept by the Romans in honour of Jupiter twice every year: (1) on April 23rd (*Vinalia prĭōra*), when the wine of the previous year was broached, and a libation from it poured on the sod; and (2) on August 19th (*Vinalia rustĭca*, the country festival of wine), when sacrifice was made for the ripening grapes. With both festivals was associated the worship of Venus, who, as goddess of gardens, had vineyards also under her protection.

Vĭnĕa. A shed used by besieging armies to protect themselves against the missiles of the enemy. (*See* SIEGES.)

Virbĭus. An Italian god, identified with Hippŏlўtus, who was raised to life by Asclēpĭus, and worshipped together with Diana as presiding genius of the wood and the chase. (*Cp.* DIANA and HIPPOLYTUS.)

Virgĭlĭus. *See* VERGIL.

Virtūs. The Roman personification of bravery in war. (*See* HONOS.)

Vīs. The Roman legal term for acts of violence. In earlier times offences of

this kind were included under the head of *perdŭellĭō* (*q.v.*) and high treason (*see* MAIESTAS). A special offence termed *vis*, including disturbances of the peace, violent attacks upon the magistrates and the Senate, and the illegal use of weapons, was first taken cognisance of by the law of Plautius, 89 B.C., and a special standing court established to deal with it. (*See* QUÆSTIO.) The penalty was proscription (*interdictĭō ăquæ et ignis*). Afterwards more serious cases of *vis*, which had meanwhile become subject to civil process, came to be considered as criminal offences, and were punished with confiscation of the third part of one's property and disqualification for public offices. Under the Empire the penalties were increased to death or exile.

Vitrūvĭus Pollĭō (*Marcus*). A military engineer who flourished in the time of Julius Cæsar and Augustus. In his old age Octavia, the sister of Augustus, procured him a pension. The leisure thus acquired he employed in composing a work on architecture in ten books (*De Archĭtectūrā*), drawn from Greek sources and from his own experience. This work, the only one of the kind which has come down to us from ancient times, was composed between 16–14 B.C. and dedicated to Augustus. The first seven books treat of architecture proper (i, architecture in general; ii, building-materials; iii, temple-building; iv, orders of architecture; v, public buildings; vi, private buildings in town and in the country; vii, ornamentation of buildings); book viii, of water and waterways; ix, of the construction of water-clocks; x, of machines. Although the author is proud of his accomplishments, they do not include a capacity for giving his subject a scientific treatment. His method of expression is not seldom obscure and unintelligible; sometimes it is artificial and distorted; sometimes vulgar. An anonymous excerpt from the work is still preserved under the title *De Dīversīs Fabrĭcīs Archĭtectŏnĭcæ*.

Volcānus (better than **Vulcanus**). The Italian god of fire and of the art of forging and smelting; corresponding to, and identified with, the Greek Hēphæstus. As god of the forge, he also bears the name *Mulcĭber*, the softener or smelter of metal. As a beneficent god of nature, who ripens the fruit by his warmth, he is the husband of the Italian goddess of spring, *Maia* or *Maiesta*, who shared the sacrifices offered by his priest, the *flāmen Volcānālis*, after he had become identified with Hephæstus.

Venus, who is identified with Aphrŏdītē, was regarded as his wife. Among his shrines in Rome the most noteworthy is that called *Volcānāl*, a level space raised above the surface of the Cŏmĭtĭum, and serving as the hearth of the spot where the citizens' assemblies were held. His chief festival, the *Volcānālia*, was kept on August 23rd, when certain fish were thrown into the fire on the hearth, and races were held in the Circus Flămĭnĭus. Sacrifices were offered to him as god of metal-working on May 23rd, the day appointed for a cleansing of the trumpets used in worship (*tŭbĭlustrium*). As lord of fire he was also the god of conflagrations; hence his temples were built outside the city, while his temple in Rome was situated in the Campus Martius. Juturna (*q.v.*) and *Stata Māter*, who causes fires to cease, were worshipped with him as goddesses who protect from fires, and a public sacrifice was offered to them and him at the festival of the *Volcanalia*. (*Cp.* HEPHÆSTUS.)

Volturnus. *See* TIBERINUS.

Vŏpiscus. A Roman historian. (*See* SCRIPTORES HISTORIÆ AUGUSTÆ.)

Vōta. Religious vows were extraordinarily common among the Romans both in public and private life. Public vows (*vota publĭca*) were sometimes extraordinary, sometimes ordinary. As regards the former, a religious vow was uttered in times of need, in the name of the State, to the effect that, if the gods averted the danger, and caused the prosperity of the State to remain unimpaired for the next five or ten years, a special thank-offering would be paid them, consisting of presents of cattle, large sacrifices, banquets (*lectisternia*), a tithe of the booty, a temple, games, etc. In older times a *vĕr sacrum* (*q.v.*) was also promised. These vows were drawn up in writing under the direction of the *pontĭfĭcēs*, recited by the *pontifex maxĭmus*, and privately rehearsed after him by a consul or prætor. The *pontifex* then put away the document in the presence of witnesses, for purposes of reference when the vow was executed. Ordinary vows for the good of the State were offered on the Capitol by the higher officials on entering office (the consuls on January 1st) and on leaving for their province. This was called the *vōtōrum nuncŭpātio*. After 30 B.C. a special *votum* was offered up for the welfare of the emperor and his family, on January 3rd. Down to the 7th century A.D., both in Rome and throughout the Empire, this day, which was itself called *votum*, was kept as a holiday by all bodies both civil and religious.

Under the Empire vows were regularly made for longer periods of time (five, ten, fifteen, twenty years, *vota quinquennālĭa*, *dĕcennalia*, *quindĕcennalia*, *vīcennalia*). Besides these there were extraordinary *vota* for the return and safety of the emperor, the *accouchement* of the empress, the birthday and accession day of the emperor, and the like. Private vows (*vota prīvāta*) were made on the most varied occasions. They might be solemnly offered in a temple, or made suddenly in times of momentary peril. In the former case a sealed writing containing the vow was fastened to the knees of the god's image, and then taken by the priest of the temple into his keeping, to be opened at the proper time. In the latter case, if the prayer was fulfilled, the vow had to be most scrupulously executed. The offering was generally accompanied by a votive tablet, which was placed on the walls of the temple, and contained an inscription or a relief or a picture relating to the vow. Thus shipwrecked mariners offered painted representations of the wreck in the temples of Neptune or Isis [Horace, *Odes* i 5, 13–16; Persius, i 90].

Vulcānus. *See* VOLCANUS.

Vulcātĭus Gallĭcānus. A Roman historian. (*See* SCRIPTORES HISTORIÆ AUGUSTÆ.)

W

War Dance. *See* PYRRHIC DANCE.

Warfare. (1) *Greek.* The distinctively warlike people among the Greeks were the *Spartans*, whose whole life from early youth to advanced age was spent in the continual practice of martial exercises. Even the meals shared in common by all Spartans who had attained the full rights of citizens, were arranged with reference to military service. (*See* SYSSITIA.) Owing to constant practice in military exercises of every possible kind, the Spartan army possessed a dexterity in the handling of weapons, and a tactical education, which, combined with their lofty sentiment of military honour, for a long period ensured their supremacy over the other Greek races. The duty of service, which began with· the twentieth year, and admitted of no exceptions, did not terminate until capacity for service came to an end; but with his sixtieth year the soldier became exempt from foreign service. Originally the heavy-armed infantry, or hoplites, consisted solely of Spartans; but even at the time of the Persian Wars, side by side with the Spartans, whose troops in their larger divisions were termed lŏchoi, the pĕrĭœci also served as soldiers, but in separate divisions. The helots who accompanied the army served as personal attendants to the hoplites (see HȲPASPĬSTÆ), and as light-armed troops in battle. A picked corps of the hoplites, specially employed as a royal body-guard, were those known as hippeis (horsemen) composed of 300 Spartans under thirty years of age, who were selected by the three hippagrĕtœ, and commanded by them. A peculiar corps of lighter infantry was formed from the Scīrītæ (the inhabitants of the district of Scīrītis), who were specially employed on the out-post service of the camp; they were used as scouts on the march, and in battle had their position assigned them on the left wing. The Spartans also kept up a fleet, in which the helots were employed as marines and oarsmen; in cases of great emergency they were transformed into heavy-armed soldiers and served in the army, after which they received their freedom. (See NEODAMODEIS.) From the end of the 5th century B.C. the Lacedæmonian army was divided into six mŏrœ, each commanded by a polemarch. Owing to their steadily decreasing numbers the Spartans only formed the nucleus of the battalions, which were brought up to their full complement by the addition of perĭœci. The officers, however, were exclusively Spartans, and the place of honour was always reserved for that body. In military expeditions the perĭœci, nĕŏdămōdēis, allies, and mercenaries, while the Spartans acted only as officers (see XENAGOS) and members of the royal staff. On the cavalry, which only played a subordinate part among the Spartans, see HIPPEIS. The ephors had the command of the veterans in time of war. In the earlier times the kings divided the supreme authority; but after 512 B.C. one alone commanded, unless the circumstances of the case required more than one general. The fleet was commanded by nauarchoi.

Among the Athenians the citizens of the first three classes were alone eligible as hoplites, and they were chosen, according to Solon's law, from the pentăcŏsĭŏmĕdimni, hippeis, and zeugĭtœ ; the fourth class, the thētĕs, were freed from service, and were only exceptionally employed at sea, but sometimes as light-armed troops on land. They were very rarely heavily armed, and were always remunerated at the expense of the State. The age of military service extended from the eighteenth to the sixtieth year; there were thus forty-two classes of age, and every man was mustered in a certain list (kătălŏgŏs) under the name of the archōn ĕpōnȳmus under whom he had first attained the age of service.[1] The first two of these classes were only employed (as pĕrĭpŏloi) to patrol the frontiers. Foreign service began in the twentieth year. From these classes, which were on each occasion called out by a special vote of the people, only so many as were absolutely necessary were taken out of each of the ten phȳlœ or tribes. The members of the Council, and probably all other officials, were exempt from service. The men who were levied were enrolled, according to their phylœ, in ten battalions, taxeis (see TAXIARCHUS), which are sometimes called phȳlœ, while their subdivisions are called lŏchoi. On the occasion of a levy the troops were sometimes equipped by the aid of the aliens resident in Attica (see METŒCI), and also, in the days of the earlier Attic confederation, by means of the contingents contributed by the allies. It was the hoplites who were benefited by this equipment. From the time of Pericles, and during the Peloponnesian War, the cavalry received pay and maintenance money, usually amounting in all to 4 obols (5½d.) a day. The State also allowed pay and maintenance for the horseman's personal attendant. On the Athenian cavalry, which was more important than the Lacedæmonian, see HIPPEIS. As to the fleet,

[1] [This is the view of Schömann, Antiquities of Greece, Eng. trans., p. 423; but in Aristotle's Constitution of Athens 53, a distinction is drawn between the archōn of the year in which service began and the ĕpōnȳmus, who was one of the forty-two eponymoi tōn hēlikiōn (the ages of military service). Who these eponymoi were is uncertain; possibly (as suggested by Mr. Kenyon) they were forty-two heroes of the legendary history of Athens. In any case they must not be confounded either with the eponymous heroes who gave their names to the ten tribes instituted by Clīsthĕnēs, or with the archōn eponymus, who gave his name to the year in which he was chief archon.]

on which Athens mainly relied in time of war, the Council (*see* BOULE) had to see that a certain number of vessels of war were built annually. The supervision of the ships in the docks (*nĕōrĭa*) was exercised by a special board, the ten *ĕpĭmĕlētœ* of the *neoria*. It was their duty to consign the vessels, with the equipments allowed by the State, to the trierarchs (*see* LEITOURGIA), wealthy citizens who undertook to complete the equipment of the vessels, to provide sailors and oarsmen, and to take the command over them; while the marines, the *ĕpĭbătai*, were under their own commanders. The *strătēgoi* (*q.v.*) held the chief command over the fleet as well as over the land forces.

In most of the other Greek states the hoplites, consisting of wealthy citizens, formed the main strength of the army, and generally helped to turn the scale in engagements in which the light-armed troops and the cavalry played a subordinate part. They fought in the *phălanx* (*q.v.*), in closely serried lines eight deep. The pick of the troops were stationed on the right wing as the post of honour, to advance to meet the foe amid the singing of the *pœān*. When at a distance of about 200 yards, at the signal of a trumpet, they raised the battle-cry (*ălălă*) and charged either at a run or at quick march. It was only the Spartans who slowly advanced at an even pace and to the sound of flutes. Requesting permission to bury the dead was the formal admission of defeat. The enduring token of victory was a trophy composed of the armour captured from the defeated side. It was usual to join battle on ground which was suitable for the *phalanx*. The Peloponnesian War was the means of introducing many innovations, including the formation of a regular force of light infantry, called *peltastœ* (*q.v.*). Still more decisive in the transformation of the general system of Greek warfare was the famous retreat of the Ten Thousand, the first important mercenary army among the Greeks which tried to make the phalanx of hoplites suit the ground better, and to utilize at the same time the light infantry, or peltasts, and the *gymnētĕs* (spearmen, bowmen, and slingers). Iphĭcrătĕs, the first distinguished general of mercenary troops, introduced a lighter equipment by substituting a small *pelta* for the heavy shield, adopting a longer sword and spear, lighter shoes, and a linen corslet.

In the course of the 4th century B.C. the army composed of civilians gave way more and more to the mercenary army, which, by its intimate knowledge of the use of its weapons gained an immense advantage in actual war. (*See* MERCENARIES.) An important novelty was oblique battle-order, the discovery of Epămīnŏndăs. In this the great mass and strength of the hoplites was drawn up in considerable depth on one of the two wings, without any expansion of the front. The hoplites could thus make a vigorous attack on the centre of the enemy's wing, whilst the true centre and other wing of the assailants was held in reserve, with a view to advancing later to crush the enemy.

The *Macedonian* method of warfare, invented by king Philip II and his son Alexander, was founded on the Greek military organization adapted to Macedonian requirements. For this purpose that organization was duly developed, and the different parts of the army, the infantry and cavalry, light and heavy-armed troops, military levies, allies and mercenary troops, were blended together into a far freer and more effective system than the Greeks ever attained in their art of war. In point of numbers the strongest component part of the Macedonian army, as elsewhere, was the heavy and light infantry. The former consisted of the *pezĕtœroi*, a body of Macedonians of free but not noble origin, corresponding to the Greek hoplites, but not so heavily armed. Like the hoplites, they fought in a *phalanx*, but this was generally deeper than theirs, being eight and afterwards sixteen men deep. They fell into six *taxeis*, corresponding to the number of the districts of Macedonia, each of which was represented by one *taxis*. (*See* further under PHALANX.) The *hўpaspistœ* (*q.v.*) were the equivalent of the Hellenic peltasts, and were a standing corps of 3,000 men. Besides these there were strong contingents of other kinds of light infantry, especially spearmen and archers. While in the Greek armies the number of the cavalry had always been small, they formed nearly one-sixth of the whole army which Alexander took with him on his Asiatic expedition, and consisted of an equal number of heavy and light cavalry. (*See* further under HIPPEIS.) The central point in the great battles of Alexander was the *phalanx*; on the right of this were placed the *hypaspistœ*, the heavy and light Macedonian cavalry, the spearmen, and archers; on the left, the Thracian peltasts, the Hellenic contingent of cavalry, together with the Thessalian cavalry, and light troops and horsemen and archers. The two wings were reckoned from the centre of the phalanx; the right being generally reserved for the attack, and led by the king. The light troops began the attack, which was followed up by the heavily armed Macedonian cavalry supported by the *hypaspistæ*. The heavy infantry came up in detachments to keep the line unbroken, and formed an oblique battle-array. Thus the main attack was made by the heavy cavalry, and no longer by the phalanx, as with the Greeks. The phalanx formed instead a solid centre of the whole array, which it was impossible for the enemy to break through, and which, in the event of its making the attack, was perfectly irresistible. Under the *Dĭădŏchi*, or successors of Alexander, the phalanx of heavy infantry formed the centre of the battle array, but less with a view to its taking part in the attack than to lengthen out the formation and give it a solid basis. The battle was decided by the wings, which were composed of cavalry, one wing being destined for the attack, while the other remained on the defensive. The light infantry, and the elephants (*q.v.*) used by the *Diadochi* in war, were incidentally brought to bear as occasion required, more especially to cover the preparatory movements of the cavalry on the attacking wing.

In the course of the 3rd century B.C. the cavalry declined in numbers and importance; and the heavy-armed infantry, which was now armed with the long *sarissa* even in Greece itself, became increasingly effective. The phalanx was used independently for purposes of attack, and this attack was generally decisive. During this century, large standing armies of mercenary troops became common. In Greece proper, the only army of importance at this time was that of the Achæan League, after its reorganization by Phĭlŏpœmēn. Greek warfare succumbed in the struggle with the Romans, mainly because the limitations attaching to the tactics of the phalanx were ill-suited to a hand to hand engagement. (*See* LEGION; and *cp.* CASTRA, DILECTUS, SACRAMENTUM, and STIPENDIUM. *See* also SIEGES and SHIP.)

War Gods. (1) *Greek. See* ARES and ENYO (1).

(2) *Roman. See* MARS and BELLONA (1).

War Tribunes. *See* TRIBUNI MILITUM.

Watchmen. *See* VIGILES and VIGILIÆ.

Water-clock. *See* CLEPSYDRA.

Weapons. The weapons of attack and defence employed by the GREEKS of historic times are essentially the same as those with which the Homeric heroes appear equipped in an earlier age. The changes gradually introduced, especially after the Persian Wars, tended to make the armour lighter and to give greater power of movement to the combatants. For defensive armour they used a *helmet* (*q.v.*); a *cuirass* (*see* THORAX); a *girdle* (*zōma*) of leather or felt, covering the lower part of the body, and reaching down to the middle of the thighs. Sometimes this consisted of narrow strips called *ptĕrўgĕs* (wings) arranged either in single or double rows, and covered with metal. Sometimes it was a complete coat plated with bands of metal. The *greaves* (*knēmĭs*) covered the front part of the legs from the ankles to just above the knee, and consisting of flexible metal plates or leather fastened behind with buckles. The weapons of defence were completed by the *shield* (*q.v.*).

For offensive weapons they had, beside the *sword* (*q.v.*), the *lance* (*dŏrŭ*), five to seven feet long. This was of iron, sometimes broader, sometimes narrower, and sometimes hooked and with an iron joint on the butt end which served to fix the spear more easily in the ground, or could be used as an offensive weapon when the regular head was broken off. The cavalry used a shorter lance (*paltŏn*) for hurling as well as thrusting; this was much shorter than the Macedonian *sarissa* (*q.v.*). The other weapons of attack were *javelins* (*ăkontĭŏn*) of different sizes, the longer kinds of which were hurled by means of a thong (*see* GYMNASTICS, fig 1), bows and arrows (*see* BOWS), and *slings* (*q.v.*). On the equipment of the different kinds of troops, *see* GYMNETÆ, HIPPEIS, HOPLITES, PELTASTÆ.

Among the ROMANS the full equipment of defensive armour similarly consisted of *helmet* (*q.v.*), *cuirass* (*see* LORICA), *greaves* (*ocrĕa*), and *shield* (*q.v.*). With regard to the greaves, it must be noted that in later times the infantry wore them only on the right foot, which was unprotected by the shield.

Besides the *sword* (*q.v.*), the horse and foot of the legion alike used, as an offensive weapon, the *lance* (*see* HASTA). It was only the light-armed troops that fought with *javelins* and *slings*. Then the *pīlum* (*q.v.*) was introduced first for a part and finally for the whole of the legion. This was the missile which the Romans hurled at the commencement of an engagement, before coming to close quarters with their swords. For fuller details on the changes that took place in the Roman arms *see* LEGION. *Bows* were not a national Roman weapon, and were only used by their allies. On the engines of war, *see* ARTILLERY.

Weaving was practised among Greeks and Romans from the earliest times. They regarded Athēnē and Mĭnerva respectively as the inventress of spinning and weaving, together with the distaff and spindle. The weaving of wool was more especially pursued, because the original (and down to late times the ordinary) dress of Greeks and Romans was of that material. From the earliest date working in wool formed part of the household duties of women, who either wove with their own hands the greater part of the clothing necessary for ordinary use, or superintended its manufacture by their slaves. Apart from the coarse fabric used by the lower classes and slaves, the only articles made by tradespeople were costly woven stuffs, such as coverlets, carpets, curtains, etc., the manufacture of which demanded greater practice and more complicated processes.

In spinning, the woman held the distaff (Gr. *ēlăkătē;* Lat. *cŏlus*) wrapped about

WOMAN SPINNING.
(Vase-painting.)

with carded wool in her left hand or under the left arm, or fixed it in her girdle. With the right she drew out and twisted the fibres, and attached them to the spindle (Gr. *atraktŏs*; Lat. *fūsus*). The latter was caused to revolve rapidly, and its rotation was made more rapid and steady by means of a small wheel called the whorl (*vortĭcellum*), fitted to its lower extremity. When the spindle was full, what was wound

was taken off and placed in the spinning basket (*kălăthŏs*).

For weaving, the oldest looms were upright with a vertically inserted warp, through which the weaver had to draw the woof by passing backwards and forwards across the loom. After the introduction of the improved horizontal loom (supposed to be an invention of the Egyptians), at which the weaver worked sitting, the old-fashioned looms were retained in Italy only for weaving flax and for making what was called the *tŭnĭca recta*. According to a long-established custom, the boy put this on when receiving the *tŏga* of manhood; and the bride also assumed it on the evening before her wedding. As a rule only plain stuffs were woven in lengths, and only those of one colour were in general use; but patterns were also worn. The ancients were also inventors of the peculiar art of weaving in colours, the *technique* of which the Greeks had very early borrowed from the Orientals, since the Homeric women are well acquainted with it [*Il.* xiv 178; xxii 440]. They were no less skilled in weaving in gold, which also came from the East. The principal place for silk-weaving was, till the time of Pliny [*N. H.* xi 77], the Greek island of Cōs, where the fine, transparent Coan fabrics were made from the cocoons imported thither. Silk-stuffs imported by various means from China were also taken to pieces, coloured, and then worked up with linen yarn, cotton-wool, or sheep's wool to half-silk stuffs, called *sērĭcæ vestēs*. Stuffs entirely of silk first came into use in the 3rd century A.D.

Wills. (1) Amongst the ATHENIANS, a testator was not allowed, in default of legitimate heirs, to bequeath his property to one not of his own family. (*See* GENNĒTÆ.) It was Solon who first legislated for the removal of this restriction, which custom, however, continued to maintain. Solon, however, granted free testamentary powers only in those cases where there were no legitimate sons. If there were any such sons, a will could only be made in favour of other persons in the event of the sons dying before their majority. If a father had daughters only, he could make a will in favour of other persons only on condition that they married his daughters. Children, born out of wedlock, who had not been legitimized, were only allowed to have a legacy bequeathed them, which was not to exceed 1,000 drachmæ (£33) in amount. Besides persons under age or of unsound mind, those who held an official post, and had not yet rendered an account of their administration, were considered incapable of making a will. The will, when drawn up, was sealed in the presence of witnesses and deposited with a responsible person in order that it might be opened, also in presence of witnesses, immediately on the death of the testator, in case he might have given any special directions for his funeral.

(2) Amongst the ROMANS the most ancient form of will is the *testāmentum cŏmĭtĭīs călātīs*, called thus, because it was drawn up in the patrician *comitia calata* (*q.v.*) at which the pontifex was present. Besides this form, of which only patricians could avail themselves, one which plebeians could use was introduced in the time of the kings, the *testamentum in procinctū*. This consisted in a verbal declaration made by a soldier, who was a citizen, in the presence of three or four of his comrades, while the general was taking the auspices before joining battle. Both these forms were superseded by the *testamentum per æs et libram* or *per fămĭlĭæ mancĭpātĭŏnem*, called *mancipatio* (*q.v.*), on account of the proceedings observed on the occasion. By means of a feigned sale the testator handed over his fortune (*familia*) to a feigned purchaser (*famĭlĭæ emptor fīdūcĭārĭus*) in the presence of six witnesses, on condition that he divided it among those nominated as the testator's heirs on his death. This process was simplified in later times, although, for the sake of form, the *famĭlĭæ emptor* was retained; but a single person was appointed heir, and charged with the duty of paying the individual legacies. If the testamentary disposition was delivered in writing, as was regularly the case, the witnesses sealed the will, and each one signed his name near the seal. The deed was deposited with a friend or in a temple, or with the Vestal Virgins, and, after it had been opened in due course, a copy was made and the original placed in the public archives.

The form of the *prætorian* will was still simpler. It was sealed before the prætor in the presence of seven witnesses. In the time of the emperors, soldiers enjoyed the privilege of making wills in any form they pleased, which were perfectly valid if the soldier died in the service or within the first year of leaving it. The *testamentum per æs et libram* was abolished in 439 A.D. by Theodosius II, and the form of the prætorian will was changed to the simple one of the Justinian law, by which a man could legally register his will. The right of making a will (*iūs testamenti factĭōnis*) was only possessed by independent Roman citizens and Vestal Virgins, and only those women besides who, by the death of the person in authority over them, had come into the possession of legal rights (*sŭī iūrĭs*), though only with the approval of their guardians. (*See* TUTOR.) Sons who were under parental control were granted the privilege under Augustus as a reward for their services in the field (*pĕcūlĭum castrensĕ*). Under Constantine it was granted as a reward to persons holding a civil office.

Slaves and those who were not Romans (*pĕrĕgrīni*) had not the right of making a will, yet the former might be testamentary heirs, if they received their freedom at the same time, and the latter might receive a bequest in trust. In order to prevent the accumulation of property in the hands of women, the *Lex Vŏcōnĭa* (169 B.C,) forbade women being appointed heirs [in cases where the testator's property exceeded £1,000], but permitted them to receive a legacy that did not exceed half the amount of the inheritance. In the interest of blood relations the *Lex Falcĭdia* (40 B.C.) established that only three-quarters of the heritage should be distributed in legacies, and that at least one-quarter should fall to the share of the natural heir. Augustus ordained that unmarried (*cœlĭbĕs*) and childless (*orbi*) persons should only inherit from relations within six degrees. The former in particular were to be deprived of the whole of their bequests, unless they married within a hundred days; the latter were only to receive half; he also laid a tax of five per cent. on testamentary property. Not to be mentioned in the will was tantamount to being excluded from the inheritance; it was however the custom to mention disinherited children especially by name, and to add the reason for their being disinherited. All those were considered the principal heirs (*hĕrēdĕs*), who received shares that could be expressed in terms of a recognised fraction of the *as*, which was divided into twelve *unciæ*. The sole heir was called *heres ex asse ;* the co-heirs, on the other hand, were designated according to the share of their inheritance; for instance, *heres ex triente*, heir to a third part. (*See also* INHERITANCE.)

Winds were regarded by Greeks and Romans alike as divine beings. In Homer, who only mentions the four chief winds, *Bŏrĕās* (North), *Zĕphўrus* (West), *Eurus*

(East), and *Nŏtus* (South), they are, according to one account [*Od.* x 1–75], committed by Zeus to the charge of Æŏlus (*q.v.*, 2). But elsewhere they appear as independent personalities, who, dwelling in Thrace [*Il.* ix 5, of Boreas and Zephyrus], display their activity at the command of Zeus and other gods, and are invoked by men with prayers and sacrifices [*Il.* xxiii 195]. Hesiod [*Theog.* 378] calls these winds children of Astræus and Eōs, and distinguishes them as beneficent beings from the destructive winds, the children of Typhoëus [*Theog.* 869]. Some particular myths speak only of Boreas and Zephyrus (*q.v.*), from whom, on account of their swiftness, famous horses were supposed to be descended. Thus [in *Il.* xvi 150] the horses of Achilles are called the children of Zephyrus and Pŏdargē, one of the Harpies (*see* HARPYIÆ.). The latter, in accordance with their original nature, are also deities of the wind, or rather of the storm. In historical times the cult of the winds in general, or that of Boreas or Zephyrus in particular, flourished at special places in Greece. In Italy also they were held in much veneration, particularly the fructifying wind Făvŏnius, which corresponded to Zephyrus. In Rome the tempests (*tempestātēs*) had a sanctuary of their own with regular sacrifices at the *Porta Cāpēna*, which was founded in 259 B.C., in consequence of a vow made for the preservation of a Roman fleet in a storm at sea. Roman generals when embarking usually offered prayers to the winds and storms, as well as to the other gods, and cast offerings and bloody sacrifices into the waves to propitiate them. To the beneficent winds white animals were offered, and those of a dark colour to the malignant equinoctial and winter storms. The victims were generally rams and lambs.

In works of art the winds are usually represented with winged head and shoulders, open mouth, and inflated cheeks. The most noteworthy monument, from an artistic point of view, is the *Tower of the Winds* (*q.v.*) still standing in excellent preservation at Athens, on which eight winds are represented (*Boreas*, N.; *Kaikĭas*, N.E.; *Apēliōtēs*, E.; *Eurus*, S.E.; *Notus*, S.; *Lips*, S.W.; *Zephyrus*, W.; *Argēstēs* or *Scīrōn*, N.W.).

Wine. From the very earliest times wine was the daily beverage of the Greeks, and was made in every Greek country. The best was produced on the coasts and islands of the Ægean, such as Thăsŏs, Rhodes, Cyprus, and, above all, Chĭŏs and Lesbŏs.

The cultivation of the vine was common in Lower Italy befŏre its colonization by the Greeks, and the Romans had vineyards in very early times. Wine was however long regarded as an article of luxury, and was limited in its use. The regular production of wine (the method of which was importĕd from Greece, together with the finer varieties of vines) first came in with the decline of the cultivation of cereals. The home-grown wines were of little esteem, as compared with the Greek, and especially the highly prized island wines, until the 1st century B.C. After this date the careful treatment of a number of Italian, and more particularly of Campanian brands (such as the Falernian, Cæcŭban, and Massic), procured for them the reputation of being the first wines of the world. They formed an important article of export, not merely to the collective provinces of the Roman empire, Greece herself not excepted, but also beyond the Roman frontier. It was to the advantage of Italy that, in the western provinces, down to the 3rd century A.D., the cultivation of the vine was subject to certain limitations. No new vineyards could be added to those already existing, and the Italian vines could not be introduced, although Gaul produced many varieties of wine. Under the Empire wine was the main article of produce and of trade in Italy, Greece, and Asia, and the wine merchants of Rome, who had, from the commencement of the 2nd century, formed two corporations, one for the eastern and another for the western trade, held an important position. In the 1st century there were already eighty famous brands in the Roman trade. Of this number Italy supplied two-thirds.

The vine was grown partly on poles or espaliers, partly on trees, especially on elms, which, if the ground between were still used for agriculture, were planted at a distance of 40, sometimes of 20, feet apart. The grapes intended for manufacture into wine were trodden with naked feet and then brought under the press. The must was then immediately poured into large pitched earthenware jars (Gr. *pĭthŏs*, Lat. *dōlĭum ;* *see* VESSELS). These were placed under ground in a wine-cellar, facing the north to keep them cool, and kept uncovered for a year in order to ferment thoroughly. The inferior wines which were of no great age were drunk immediately from the jar [*de dolio*

haurīre ; Cicero, *Brutus* 228]. The better
kinds, which were meant for preservation,
were poured into *amphŏræ.* These were
closed with stone stoppers, sealed with pitch,
clay, or gypsum, marked with a brand, furnished with a label giving their year and
measure (*tessĕra* or *nŏta*), and placed in the
ăpŏthēcă. This was a room in the upper
story, built by preference over the bath-room
in order to catch the smoke from the furnace,
and thus to make the wine more mellow.

One method of improving the wine which
was used in the East and in Greece was to
keep the wine in goat-skins, because the
leather tended to cause evaporation of the
water. In Italy the wine-skins appear to
have been only used in transport. To produce flavour, strength, and bouquet, various
means were employed, such as adding gypsum, clay, chalk, marble, resin, pitch, and
even sea water, the last being especially in
use in Greece and Asia Minor. Bad wines
were improved by being mixed with fine
brands and good lees; adulteration was
extremely common. The number of artificial wines was very large; *e.g.* honey
wine, raisin wine, and boiled must (the
beverage of the common people and slaves),
a poor drink prepared by pouring water on
the remains of the pressed grapes.

The place of our liqueurs was taken by
flavoured wines, of which more than fifty
kinds are mentioned. These were simply
extracted from herbs, flowers, or sweet smell-
ing woods (thyme, myrtle, sweet rush,
rose, hearts-ease, pine-cones and pine-wood,
cypress, etc.), or mixed with oils, such as
nard or myrrh. There were also wines made
from fruits such as apples, pomegranates,
pears, dates, figs, or mulberries. In respect
of colour three sorts of wine were distinguished: the black or dark red (*cŏlor
sanguĭnĕus* and *nĭger*) which was considered the strongest; the white (*albus*),
which was thought thin and weak; and the
brown or amber-coloured (*fulvus*), which
was considered particularly serviceable for
promoting digestion. As in its ordinary
treatment the wine often retained much
sediment, it had to be made clear before
it was drunk. This was done either with
yolk of eggs or by straining the wine
through a cloth or sieve, which was filled
with snow to make it cool. Greeks and
Romans alike generally drank their wine
mixed with water. (*Cp.* MEALS.)

Wine-god. *See* DIONYSUS (Liber).

Wisdom, Goddess of. *See* ATHENE and
MINERVA.

Wonders of the World. Seven ancient
buildings or works of art, distinguished
either for size or splendour: *viz.* (1) the
Egyptian pyramids; (2) the hanging gardens of Sĕmīrămĭs at Babylon; (3) the
temple of Artĕmis, at Ephesus; (4) the
statue of Zeus (*q.v.*) by Phīdīās, at Olympia;
(5) the Mausōlēum (*q.v.*) at Hălĭcarnassus;
(6) the Cŏlossus of Rhodes (*see* CHARES, 2);
and (7) the lighthouse on the island of
Phărŏs, off Alexandria in Egypt.

Writing Materials. From an early date
the Greeks employed in the production of
books a paper prepared from the Egyptian
păpŷrus plant. This was probably manufactured as follows: as many strips as
possible of equal size were cut out of the
cellular tissue of the stalk; these were
laid side by side, and crossed by a second
layer. The layers were firmly fastened
together by being damped with size and
pressed. The breadth of the scroll depended on the height of the stalk, while its
length could be extended at pleasure. After
the time of Augustus, the preparation of
the papyrus by a process of bleaching was
brought to such perfection that the best
Egyptian kind took only the third place.
Under the Empire eight different kinds
were distinguished, the two best of which
were called the *charta Augusta* (only used
for letters), and the *charta Līvĭa ;* these
were 10½ inches broad. The worst kind
was only used for packing. As a rule the
papyrus-rolls of moderate length were
written only on one side, and the writing
was divided into columns. [Pliny, *N. H.*
xiii 68–83]. For the binding of the
papyrus-rolls, *see* BOOKS.

The use of skins for the purposes of writing was at least as old as that of papyrus.
The finer method of preparing them was,
however, first discovered during the first
half of the 2nd century B.C. at Pergămum,
whence the name *charta Pergămēna,*
"parchment." But as late as the 1st
century A.D. papyrus was more generally
employed, probably on account of its
greater cheapness; and it was not till the
4th century that parchment came into more
general use, as being more durable, and
admitting of being written upon on both
sides.

The pen was a split reed (*călămus*), the
best being supplied by Egypt and Cnĭdus
in Caria.

The ink (*ătrāmentum*) employed was a
preparation resembling Indian ink, made
of soot and gum, or of the juice of the

cuttle-fish. Both of these could be erased with a sponge, whereas ink made of oxide together in the form of a book. (*See* DIPTYCHON.) The writing materials most

INK-STAND WITH REED PEN, ROLL WITH *CORNUA* AND PARCHMENT LABEL, STILUS, WAX TABLET, AND ACCOUNT BOOK.
(Mural Painting from Pompeii; *Museo Borbonico* i 12, 2.)

of iron and gallnuts, which appears to have been introduced later, and to have been the only kind capable of being used for parchment, left more or less clear traces behind, even if rubbed out with pumice-stone. In ordinary life people used for letters, notices, and despatches, as also in schools, wooden tablets (*tăbellœ*) with a raised rim, within which was spread a thin layer of wax. On this the characters were scratched with the point of a metal or ivory instrument called a *stĭlus ;* they could be effaced with the other end of the instrument, which was bent or flattened out like a paper-folder. Two or more such tablets could be fastened

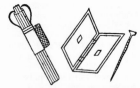

BUNDLE OF REED-PENS, WAX TABLET, AND STILUS.
(Sepulchral relief from Perret, *Catacombes de Rome*, lxxiii 6.)

commonly employed among the Greeks and Romans are shown in our cuts.

X

Xanthus. A Greek historian. (*See* LOGOGRAPHI.)

Xĕnāgŏs. The Spartan commander of the several contingents in the Peloponnesian League [Thucydides ii 75 ; Xenophon, *Hell.* iv 2 § 19].

Xĕnarchus. *See* SOPHRON.

Xĕnóphănēs. A Greek philosopher and poet, born about 570 B.C. at Cŏlŏphŏn in Asia Minor. At the age of 25, after the conquest of his native city by the Persians, he was expelled from his home, and thenceforth led an unsettled and wandering life, in the course of which he recited his own poems as rhapsodies. Accordingly, he lived from time to time at the court of the Pīsistrătĭdæ at Athens, and at that of Hĭĕrōn at Syracuse, and for a longer period at Zanclē and Cătăna in Sicily. His later years he apparently spent at Élĕa (Lat.*Vĕlĭa*) in South Italy, a colony of the Phōcæans, in the founding of which he took part. In one fragment he describes himself as an old man of 92 ; according to another account, he lived to be more than 100. He is the founder of the Eleatic philosophy and of pantheism, inasmuch as he combated the anthropomorphic view of the gods dominant in Homer and Hesiod, and in the popular belief in general. He asserted the doctrine of a one all-ruling divinity, who, as true existence, opposed to appearance or nonexistence, as the One and the All, the Whole, undivided, unmoved, and eternal, underlies the universe and is identical with it. He resembles man neither in form nor understanding; being all eye, all ear, all intellect, by the power of his mind and without extraneous effort he sways and governs all things.

Apart from two elegiac poems, we possess only fragments of the writings of Xenophanes : *viz.* part of the didactic poem, *Concerning Nature*, his principal work, which he himself recited ; part of an epic poem on the founding of Colophon and

Elea; and fragments of the *Silloi*, or satires in which he attacked the opposing views of poets and philosophers.

Xĕnŏphŏn. (1) *The historian*, son of the Athenian Gryllus, born about 431 B.C. He was one of the most trusted disciples of Socrates. On the invitation of his friend, the Theban Gryllus, he betook himself in 401 to Sardis, in order to make the acquaintance of the younger Cȳrus, and attached himself without any definite military rank to the Greek mercenaries, who formed the most important part of the force led by that Persian prince against his brother, king Artaxerxēs. When Cyrus had fallen in the battle of Cunaxa in Babylonia, and the Greek commanders had soon after been treacherously murdered by the Persians, he undertook, together with the Spartan Chīrīsŏphus, the leadership of the despairing forces of the Greeks, and effected the memorable retreat of the Ten Thousand from the heart of Mesopotamia through the high tablelands of Armenia to the coast of the Black Sea, and thence to Byzantium, in a manner as masterly as that in which he has himself described it. After he had helped the Thracian prince Seuthēs to recover his paternal kingdom, he led the remainder of the army to join the Spartan commander Thimbrōn, who was at war with the Persian satraps of Asia Minor. Banished on this account from Athens, he remained in the Spartan service, accompanied king Agēsĭlāus in his campaigns in Asia, then returned with him to Greece, and took part in the war against the Bœotians and Athenians, and in the battle of Cŏrōnēa in 394.

In gratitude for his services, the Spartans, at the conclusion of the war, gave him a country seat near Scillus, on the land which they had wrested from the Eleans, not far from Olympia. He employed himself in agriculture, hunting, and the breeding of horses, and composed· some of his extant writings. When the Eleans, after the battle of Leuctra in 371, again took possession of Scillus, Xenophon was expelled. He then settled at Corinth, where he remained after the repeal of his sentence of banishment from Athens. In the battle of Mantĭnēa in 362 his sons Dĭŏdōrus and Gryllus fought in the Athenian army, and the former died a heroic death. Xenophon ended his life some time after the year 355, being more than eighty years of age.

The principal works of Xenophon are; (1) the *Anăbăsĭs*, in seven books, a description, as already mentioned, of the campaign of Cyrus, and the retreat of the Ten Thousand, composed about twenty years after the events narrated, but founded on memoranda made at the time, as may be inferred from the minuteness and precision of its details. From the fact that Xenophon is always spoken of in the third person, it has been conjectured, without sufficient reason, that the writer was really the Syracusan Thĕmistŏgĕnēs, whom Xenophon incidentally mentions as the composer of a history of the Retreat to the Sea. (2) The *Hellĕnĭca*, in seven books. The first two are a continuation of the history of Thucydides from 411 to the end of the Peloponnesian War; and the third is an account of the reign of the Thirty Tyrants, their overthrow, and the restoration by Thrăsȳbūlus of the democratic constitution at Athens. These are written in the form of annals. The remaining books, in which events related to each other are grouped together, give the rest of the history of Greece down to the battle of Mantĭnēa in 362. (3) The *Cȳropædĭa* (Gr. *Kūrou paideia*), in eight books, containing the story of the education and life of Cyrus, resting on a historical foundation of facts thrown into an idealized form. It is, in fact, a political and philosophical romance, showing how, according to Socratic principles, one who is to be a ruler must be brought up, and how he must act when on the throne. (4) The *Apŏmnĕmŏneumăta*, generally called by the Latin title, *Mĕmŏrăbĭlĭa* (Memoirs), in four books. These are reminiscences of Socrates, and are a simple and faithful delineation of his work and teaching, composed after 393 B.C. with the object of defending Socrates against the charge of impiety towards the gods, and of corrupting the youth. It seems probable that the work as preserved is an abridgment only. Shorter writings, handed down under the name of Xenophon, but the genuineness of which is partly suspected, are (5) the *Agēsĭlāus*, a panegyric on Agesilaus II, king of Sparta, written soon after the king's death (361). (6) The *Apology of Socrates.* (7) The *Sympŏsĭum* (banquet), an extremely interesting description of a banquet, at which Socrates sets forth his views on beauty and love. This was the model of similar narratives by later writers, especially of the *Symposium* of Plato. (8) The *Œcŏnŏmĭcus* (on domestic economy), the most considerable of the smaller works, and a continuation in some measure of the *Memorabilia*. It is a discourse of Socrates on the management of a household, especially on husbandry. (9) *Hĭĕrōn*, a dialogue between the poet Sĭmō-nīdēs and Hieron, tyrant of Syracuse, on the burden of responsibility that weighs on the possessor of royal power, and on the happiness caused by wisely administering it. (10) *Dē Rēpublĭcā Lăcĕdæmŏnĭōrum* (On the Spartan Constitution), a glorifi-cation of Sparta written soon after the battle of Cŏrōnēa (394). (11) *De Vectī-gālĭbus* (On the Revenues), composed after the conclusion of the Social War, and there-fore, if genuine, in the last years of Xeno-phon's life, containing suggestions to the Athenians for the improvement of their revenue, without oppressing the allies. (12) *Hipparchĭcus* (Directions for an Athenian Commander of Cavalry in War and Peace), apparently written shortly before the battle of Mantĭnēa in 362. (13) *De Rē Equestri* (On the Management of the Horse), written for his youthful friends, with a consider-able degree of completeness, and much practical knowledge of the subject. (14) The *Cӯnēgĕtĭcus* (On the Chase); judging by its lively, spirited tone, one of his earliest works. A number of letters are ascribed to him, which are undoubtedly spurious. The same must be said of the *De Republica Atheniensium* (On the Athenian Constitution), which was apparently com-posed before B.C. 424 by an Athenian of oligarchical views.

His style, like the man himself, is plain and simple, at times even insipid; it was exceedingly admired by the ancients on account of its natural charm. His Greek is certainly not the purest Attic; but, apparently on account of his long sojourn abroad, is frequently mixed with poetical and dialectical words and forms. The *Cyropædia*, the *Œconomicus*, and the *Symposium* are the most carefully elabo-rated of his writings. His practical and unimaginative nature shows itself also in the style of his historical and philosophical books. In the latter he appears throughout as a moralist, with no talent for speculation. The former are entirely destitute of any grand leading idea, or any insight into the underlying connexion of events. They deal for the most part with what has a practical interest only. His preference for the Spartan character, which entirely controls his representation of the contem-porary history of Greece in the *Hellenica*, is also characteristic of the man.

(2) *A Greek romance-writer of Ephesus*, who composed towards the end of the 2nd century A.D. his *Ephesian Stories*, in five books, which in a light and simple style describe the adventures of a young couple named Atheia and Abrŏcŏmēs. It has frequently served as a model for later romance-writers, especially for Chărĭtōn, and apparently also for Hēlĭŏdōrus.

Xĭphŏs. The straight, two-edged sword of the Greeks. (*See* SWORD.)

Xūthus. Brother of Æŏlus (*q.v.*, 1), and husband of Crĕūsa, the daughter of Erech-theus; adoptive father of Īōn (*q.v.*).

Xÿĕlē. The short, slightly curved, one-edged sword of the Spartans. (*See* SWORD.)

Z

Zagrĕūs. A name of Dĭonӯsus (*q.v.*).

Zēno (Gr. *Zēnōn*). (1) *Of Elĕa ;* born about 485 B.C., a disciple of the philoso-pher Parmĕnĭdēs, whose doctrine he sought to prove by indirect arguments. (*Cp.* PHILOSOPHY). Of his writings only iso-lated fragments are preserved.

(2) *Of Cittium* in Cyprus. He came in 390 B.C. as a merchant to Athens, and there, through the study of the writings of the Socratic philosophers, was led to devote himself to philosophy. At first he attached himself to the Cynic philosopher Crătēs, whose doctrine was, however, too unscientific to give him permanent satisfac-tion ; he then studied under the Megarian Stilpo, and the Academics Xĕnŏcrătēs and Pŏlĕmōn, and founded about 310 a school of

philosophy of his own, which received the name of Stoic from the *Stŏa Pœcĭlē*, where he held his discourses. After fifty-eight years devoted to the teaching of philosophy, he died at an advanced age, held in the highest honour by the Athenians. Of his numerous writings we possess only a few meagre fragments. His doctrine received its complete development from his fol-lowers Clĕanthēs and Chrӯsippus. (*See* PHILOSOPHY.)

Zēnŏbĭus. A Greek Sophist of Antioch, who lived at Rome as teacher of rhetoric in the first half of the 2nd century B.C., and availing himself of the works of earlier writers, made a collection of proverbs, still extant in an abridged form.

Zēnŏdŏtus. The first considerable philological critic of the Alexandrian school. He came from Ephesus, and lived in the first half of the 3rd century B.C. at Alexandria as tutor to the sons of Ptolemy Philadelphus, and superintendent of the library founded by that king. He undertook the first critical edition of the Homeric poems, and thus laid the foundation for the works of Aristophanes of Byzantium, his most celebrated pupil, and of Aristarchus.

Zephyrus. The West Wind, son of Astræus and Eōs, the messenger of spring, and the lover of the flower-goddess Chlōris, who bore to him Carpus, the god of fruit. Spurned by the beautiful Hyacinthus (*q.v.*), he caused his death, by blowing the quoit of his rival Apollo against his head. The Romans identified him with *Fāvŏnĭus*, the breeze of springtide. In art he is represented as partly unclothed, and carrying flowers in the folds of his robe.

Zētēs. Son of Bŏrĕās and Orīthўīa, and brother of Călăïs (*q.v.*).

Zēthus. Son of Antĭŏpē (*q.v.*, 1) and of Zeus, brother of Amphīōn and husband of Aëdōn. (*Cp.* AËDON and AMPHION.)

Zeugītæ. The third of the propertyclasses into which the citizens of Athens were distributed by Sŏlōn. (*See* SOLONIAN CONSTITUTION and EISPHORA.)

Zeūs. The greatest god in the Greek mythology; according to the common legend the eldest son of Cronus (Krŏnŏs) and Rhĕa, hence called Crŏnīdēs. According to a myth indigenous to Crete, he was the youngest son, and Rhea, in dread of Cronus, who had swallowed all his previous children, bore him secretly in a cave of the island, where he was suckled by the goat *Amalthĕa* (*q.v.*), while the Cūrētĕs (*q.v.*) drowned the cries of the child by the clash of their weapons; but Rhea outwitted Cronus by giving him a stone to swallow instead. When he was grown up, Zeus married Mētĭs (*q.v.*), who, by means of a charm, compelled Cronus to disgorge the children he had swallowed. When, with the help of his brothers and sisters, Pŏseidōn, Hādēs, Hestĭa, Dēmētēr, and Hērā, he had overthrown Cronus and the Titans, the world was divided into three parts, Zeus obtaining heaven, Poseidon the sea, and Hades the lower world; the earth and Olympus being appointed for the common possession of all the three. But the king of the gods is Zeus, whose power, as Homer says, is greater than that of all the other gods together.

Next to him, but in a subordinate position, stands, as queen of the gods, his sister and consort Hera, the mother of Arēs, Hēphæstus, and Hēbē, who was regarded as pre-eminently his rightful wife. Not incompatible with this however was the idea that the marriage with Hera was the earliest of a series of marriages with other goddesses: first, according to Hesiod, with Metis, whom he swallowed, in order to bring forth Athēnē from his own head; then with Thĕmĭs, the mother of the Hours and the Fates; afterwards with Eurўnŏmē, the mother of the Graces; Demeter, the mother of Persĕphŏnē; Mnēmŏsўnē, the mother of the Muses; and Lētō, the mother of Apollo and Artĕmĭs. The fact that still later, in Dōdōna, Diōnē, the mother of Aphrŏdītē, was also honoured as the wife of Zeus, shows the origin of the legend. Originally different wives of Zeus were recognised in the different local cults. When the legend of the marriage with Hera had become the predominant one, an attempt was made to harmonize the different versions of the story by the supposition of successive marriages. In the same way the loves of Zeus with half-divine, halfmortal women, of whom Alcmēnē, the mother of Hērăclēs, was said to be the last, were originally rural legends, which derived the descent of indigenous divinities, like Hermēs and Diŏnўsus, or of heroes and noble families, from the highest god; and not until they had become the common property of the whole Greek people, which was practically the case as early as the time of Homer, could the love affairs of the greatest of the gods become the theme of those mythical stories which are so repugnant to modern taste.

The very name of Zeus (Sanskrit, *dyaus*, the bright sky) identifies him as the god of the sky and its phenomena. As such he was everywhere worshipped on the highest mountains, on whose summits he was considered to be enthroned. Of all places the Thessalian mountain Olympus (*q.v.*, 1), even in the earliest ages, met with the most general recognition as the abode of Zeus and of the gods who were associated with him. From Zeus come all changes in the sky or the winds; he is the gatherer of the clouds, which dispense the fertilizing rain, while he is also the thunderer, and the hurler of the irresistible lightning. As by the shaking of his *ægĭs* (*q.v.*) he causes sudden storm and tempest to break forth, so he calms the elements again, brightens the sky, and sends forth favouring winds. The changes of the seasons also proceed from him as the father of the Hours.

As the supreme lord of heaven, he was worshipped under the name of Olympian Zeus in many parts of Greece, but especially in Olympia, where the Olympian games (*q.v.*) were celebrated in his honour. The cult of Zeus at the ancient seat of the oracle at Dodona recognised his character as dispenser of the fertilizing dew. Among the numerous mountain-cults in the Peloponnesus, the oldest and most original was that of the Lycæan Zeus, on Mount Lycæus in Arcadia, where human beings were actually sacrificed to him in propitiation. (*See* LYCÆA.) In Attica, again, many festivals refer to the god as a personification of the powers of nature. Various rites of purification and expiation were observed in his honour as the god of wrath (Gr. *Maimaktēs*), in the month Mæmactērīon (Nov.–Dec.) at the beginning of the winter storms; while towards the end of winter he was worshipped as the gracious god (Gr. *Meilĭchĭŏs*) at the festival of the *Dĭăsĭă* (*q.v.*). Among the islands, Rhodes and Crete were the principal seats of the worship of the sky-god; not only his birth, but also his death was there celebrated, and even his grave was shown, in accordance with the widely spread notion that the annual death of Nature in winter was the death of the god. In Asia, the summit of Mount Ida in the Troad was especially and beyond all other places sacred to Zeus.

As he presides over the gods and the whole of nature, so also is he the ruler of men, who all stand in need of his help, and to whom, according to Homer, he weighs out their destinies on golden scales [*Il.* viii 69, xxii 209], and distributes good and evil out of the two jars which stand in his palace, filled the one with good and the other with evil gifts [xxiv 527]. But his natural attributes are goodness and love; hence Homer calls him "the father of gods and men." He gives to all things a good beginning and a good end: he is the saviour in all distress: to Zeus the saviour (Gr. *sōtēr*) it was customary to drink the third cup at a meal, and in Athens to sacrifice on the last day of the year. From him comes everything good, noble, and strong, and also bodily vigour and valour, which were exhibited in his honour, particularly at the Olympian and Nemean games. He is also the giver of victory; indeed the goddess of victory (*see* NICE), and her brothers and sister, Force, Might, and Strife (Gr. *Bĭă*,

Krătŏs, Zēlŏs), are his constant companions. From him, as ruler of the world, proceed those universal laws which regulate the course of all things, and he knows and sees everything, the future as well as the past. Hence all revelation comes in the first instance from him. At times he himself announces to mortals his hidden counsels by manifold signs, thunder and lightning and other portents in the sky, by birds, especially the eagle, which was sacred to him, by prophetic voices (*see* MANTIKE), and special oracles. (*See* DODONA and AMMON.) At times he makes use of other deities for this purpose, chiefly of his son Apollo, through whose mouth he speaks at Delphi in particular. Thus the course of the world is ordained by him; he is the author and preserver of all order in the life of men. In conjunction with Thĕmĭs, Dĭkē, and Nĕmĕsĭs, he watches over justice and truth, the foundations of human society; in particular he is the special god who guards the sanctity of the oath; he is also the avenger of perjury, the keeper of boundaries and of property, the defender of the laws of hospitality and the rights of the suppliant. But nevertheless to him who has offended against the laws of human life, Zeus, as the supreme god of atonement, offers the power of expiating his guilt by rites of purification. As he presides over the family and community of the gods, so also he is the chief patron of the family and of all communal life. In the former relation he was especially worshipped in all branches of the family as protector of house and home (Gr. *herkeiŏs*), and defender of the domestic hearth (*ĕphestĭŏs*): in the latter, as the shield of the State, *e.g.* in Athens at the *Dĭipōlĭă* (*q.v.*); as director of the popular assembly and of the council; as the god of covenants; as the source of kingship, whose symbol, the sceptre, was traced back to him. From him also proceed both national and personal freedom; hence a sanctuary was dedicated at Athens by freedmen to Zeus the Liberator (*ĕleuthĕrĭŏs*); and after the battle of Platæa a thanksgiving festival, *Eleuthĕrĭă*, was instituted by the allied Greeks, which was still celebrated by the Platæans in Roman times, and attended by deputies from the other states. Zeus is to the Greeks—as Jupiter (*q.v.*), who in his principal characteristics exactly corresponds to him, is to the Romans,—the essence of all divine power. No deity received such wide-spread worship; all the others were, in the popular belief, subordinated to him.

at a greater or less distance. The active operations of most of the gods appear only as an outcome of his being, particularly those of his children, among whom the

(1) BUST OF ZEUS.
Found at *Otricoli* (Rome, Vatican.)

nearest to him are Athēnē and Apollo, his favourites, who often seem to be joined with their father in the highest union.

The eagle and the oak were sacred to Zeus; the eagle, together with the sceptre

forth in the spectator the feeling that no earthly dwelling would be adequate for such a divinity. The bearded head was ornamented with a wreath of olive leaves, the victor's prize at Olympia. The upper part of the body, made of ivory, was naked, the lower part was wrapped in a golden mantle falling from the hips to the feet, which, adorned with golden sandals, rested on a footstool. Beside this lay golden lions. The right hand bore the goddess of victory, the left the sceptre, surmounted by an eagle. Like the base, and the whole space around, the seat of the throne was decorated with various works of art. It was supported by figures of the goddess of victory; and on the back of the throne, which rose above the head of the god, were represented the hovering forms of the Hours and the Graces [Pausanias, v 11; Strabo, p. 353]. This statue was the model for most of the later representatives of Zeus. Among those that are extant the well-known bust of Zeus (fig. 1) found at Otricoli (the ancient *Ocrĭcŭlum* in Umbria) and now in the Vatican Museum, is supposed (as well as some others) to be an imitation of the great work of Phidias. In the most direct relation to the latter stand the figures of Zeus on the coins of Elis (fig. 2). Among the standing statues of Zeus the most famous

(2) THE OLYMPIAN ZEUS.
(Coins of Elis of the time of Hadrian, from the collections in Paris and Florence respectively.)

and the lightning, is also one of his customary attributes. The most famous statue of Zeus in antiquity was that executed by Phīdīas in gold and ivory for the temple at Olympia. It represented the enthroned Olympian god, with a divine expression of the highest dignity, and at the same time with the benevolent mildness of the deity who graciously listens to prayer. The figure of the seated god was about forty feet high; and since the base was as high as twelve feet, the statue almost touched with its crown the roof of the temple, so as to call

was the bronze *cŏlossus*, forty cubits (or sixty feet) high, by Lȳsippus at Tărentum [Pliny, *N. H.* xxxiv 40].

Zeuxis. A celebrated Greek painter of the Ionic school, a contemporary of Parrhăsĭus; he was a native of Hērăclēa in South Italy, and lived till about 400 B.C. at different places in Greece, at last, as it appears, settling in Ephesus. According to the accounts of his works which have been preserved, in contrast to the great mural painter, Pŏlygnōtus, he specially devoted himself to painting on panels. He endea-

voured above all things to make his subjects attractive by investing them with
the charm of novelty and grace. He also
has the merit of having further improved
the distribution of light and shade, introduced by his elder comtemporaries. Specially celebrated was his picture of Helen,
painted for the temple of Hērā on the Laci-
nian promontory [Cicero, *De Invent.* ii 1 § 1].
He aimed at the highest degree of illusion.
As is well known, he is said to have painted
grapes so naturally that the birds flew to
peck at them [Pliny, *N. H.* xxxv 61–66].
(*Cp.* PARRHASIUS.)

Zōnārās (*Iōannēs*). A Greek historian,
who lived at Constantinople as chief of the
imperial bodyguard and first private secretary to the emperor under Alexius I, Com-
nēnus. He next became a monk, and composed a history of the world down to 1118
A.D., divided into eighteen books. Its value
consists in its exact quotations from lost
works of earlier writers, especially from

those of Dio Cassius, referring to the
Empire. The history of his own time he
recorded as an eye-witness.

Zōsīmus. A Greek historian who lived
as a high officer of State at Constantinople
in the second half of the 5th century A.D.,
and composed a work, distinguished for its
intelligent and liberal views, on the fall of
the Roman Empire. It is in six books : i,
giving a sketch of the time from Augustus
to Diocletian ; ii–iv, a fuller account of
events down to the division of the Empire
by Thĕŏdŏsius the Great ; v and vi treat
in greater detail of the period from 395–410;
the conclusion of book vi is probably wanting, as Zosimus had the intention of continuing the history up to his own time. He
attributes the fall of the Empire in part
to the overthrow of heathenism and the
introduction of Christianity, with which, of
course, he was not acquainted in its purest
form, but only in the degenerate state into
which it had sunk in the 4th century.

NOTE ON ELECTION TO THE OFFICE OF ARCHON (p. 59).

THE introduction of the lot in the appointment of administrative offices has in modern
times been generally ascribed to Cleisthĕnēs. Thus E. Curtius in his *History of Greece*
(i, p. 478, Ward) observes : "To the opinion that at all events it belongs to his period and
is connected with his reforms I firmly adhere, though many voices have been raised
in favour of the view of Grote, according to which the election of public officers by
lot was not introduced until the time of Pericles." But it has been shown by Fustel
de Coulanges (*La Cité Antique*, p. 213) that the lot, being a religious institution, must be
of great antiquity. According to Aristotle's *Constitution of Athens* (c. 8), it was enacted
by Solon that the nine archons should be appointed by lot out of 40 candidates selected
by the tribes. From this and other passages in the same treatise it has been inferred
that election to the office of archon went through the following stages : "(1) Prior to
Draco, the archons were nominated by the Areopagus ; (2) under the Draconian constitution [about 621 B.C.] they were elected by the ecclesia ; (3) under the Solonian constitution
[about 594 B.C.], so far as it was not disturbed by internal troubles and revolutions, they
were chosen by lot from 40 candidates selected by the four tribes ; (4) under the constitution of Cleisthĕnēs [508 B.C.] they were directly elected by the people in the ecclesia ;
(5) after 487 B.C. they were appointed by lot from 100 [or, less probably, 500] candidates
selected by the ten tribes ; (6) at some later period (c. 8) the process of the lot was
adopted also in the preliminary selection by the tribes." (*See* also Mr. J. W. Headlam's
Election by Lot at Athens, 1891, especially pp. 79, 88, 183.) It was in 457 B.C. (*ib.* 26)
that the *zeugītœ* first became eligible for the office. The duties of the archons are
enumerated in Aristotle's *Constitution of Athens*, chaps. 56–61.

ON GREEK MUSICAL NOTATION, AND ON EXTANT SPECIMENS OF GREEK MUSIC (p. 408).

The ancient Greeks employed a *notation* of their own. They possessed altogether 67 symbols, and each of these appears in two forms, one for singing and the other for the instruments. The instrumental notes were usually placed below the corresponding notes for singing, or just after them. For the vocal notes the twenty-four letters of the common later Ionic alphabet were used, and for instrumental notation 15 symbols from an old Greek alphabet, without change for the two octaves of the diatonic scale, corresponding to the white notes of the modern keyboard; but these letters were modified by accent or other alteration to represent the enharmonic and chromatic scales. These notes only indicate height and depth of sound; the duration of each note is shown in singing by the length of each syllable, above which the note was placed like an accent; but for independent instrumental music five different degrees of length were distinguished, and they were designated above the notes themselves.

[We now have about eight specimens of ancient music :—(1) the beginning of the first Pythian Ode of Pindar, published in the seventeenth century by Kircher, *Musurgia*, i 541, and reprinted in Boeckh's Pindar, *De Metris Pindari*, iii 12, but generally regarded as destitute of authority ; (2) a hymn to Callĭŏpē, and (3) a hymn to Apollo, both composed by one Dĭŏnȳsius (*q.v.*, 4); (4) a hymn to Nĕmĕsĭs, ascribed to Mĕsŏmēdēs (*q.v.*); (5) some short instrumental passages or exercises ; (6) an inscription found at Tralles in 1883, giving a musical setting of four short gnomic sentences ; (7) a papyrus fragment of the music of a chorus of Euripides, *Orestes*, 338–344; (8) fourteen fragments found at Delphi in 1893, two of them containing a large part of a hymn to Apollo, composed after the repulse of the Gauls from Delphi in 279 B.C. (first published in *Bulletin de correspondance hellénique*, xvii 569–610). (2), (3) and (4) were published in 1582, and may be seen in Bellermann's *Hymnen des Dionysius u. Mesomedes*, 1840, and in Chappell's *History of Music*, 1874. (5) may be found in Bellermann's *Anonymus*, pp. 94–96. (6), (7) and (8) are printed and discussed in Monro's *Modes of Ancient Greek Music*, pp. 87–94, 130–141. The Hymn to Apollo (8) appears to be composed in a mode practically identical with the modern minor.]

GENERAL INDEX.

INDEX TO ILLUSTRATIONS.[1]

[1] For those cuts only which appear under a different heading from their own title.

Biographical Notes

Dr. Oskar Seyffert was a distinguished Latin scholar in Berlin and one of the editors of *Berliner Philologische Wochenschrift*. The first edition of the English translation of *Dictionary of Classical Antiquities* appeared in 1891.

Henry Nettleship, M.A., was a Fellow of Corpus Christi College and Corpus Professor of Latin Literature at the University of Oxford.

Dr. J. E. Sandys was a Fellow and Tutor of St. John's College and Public Orator at the University of Cambridge.